Hemmings
COLLECTOR CAR
ALMANAC

15th EDITION

1932 Auburn Boattail Roadster
©Dave Looper

Publisher & Editor-in-Chief – *Terry Ehrich*
Vice President – *Perez Ehrich*
Editor – *Richard Lentinello*
Managing Editor – *Mary Pat Glover*
Editorial Assistant – *Mary Brott*
Listings Preparation – *Nancy Bianco*
Technical Assistance – *Mary McGuinness*
Wholesale Marketing – *Kathy Ryder*
Assistant Manager of Circulation/Marketing – *Marian Savage*

Customer Service – *Carol Dewey, Amy Hansen, Lisa Knapp, Kelly Kwasniak, Merri Moore, Amy Pearson, Sharon Sigot*
Advertising Sales Manager – *Lesley McFadden*
Advertising Sales – *Tim McCart, Brian McCoskey, Laurie Mulhern, Randy Shannon, Jeff Yager*
Art & Production Manager – *Edward Heys*
Art & Production Staff – *Tammy Bredbenner, Tom Comerro, Beverly Douglass, Anita Finney, Karen Gaboury, Adelaide Jaquith, Linda Knapp, Peg Mulligan, Rob Randall, Abby Shapiro, Nancy Stearns, Peg Stevens, Bonnie Stratton, Jane Tudor, Laurie Weaver, Carol Wigger*

FRONT COVER PHOTOGRAPHS
Foreground picture: 1956 Chrysler Imperial *by Don Spiro*
Background pictures left to right: 1970 Mercury Cougar Eliminator *by Robert Gross,*
1929 Du Pont Model G Merrimac Speedster *by Roy D. Query,* 1932 Ford Hi Boy *by Harley Koopman*

BACK COVER PHOTOGRAPHS
Clockwise from top left: 1962 Studebaker Gran Turismo Hawk *by David Gooley,*
1967 Austin Mini Cooper S *by David Gooley,* 1938 Chevrolet Master Deluxe *by Harley Koopman,*
1931 Ford Model A Station Wagon *by Don Spiro,* 1930 Cadillac V-16 Coupe *by Roy D. Query*

WHOLESALE INFORMATION:
Dealers, vendors, newsstands:
Wholesale copies for resale, contact:
Kathy Ryder, *Hemmings Collector-Car Almanac,* PO Box 945, Bennington, Vermont 05201
or phone 1-800-227-4373, Extension 552

A publication from Hemmings Motor News, ©2001
PO Box 256, Bennington, Vermont 05201 • 1-800-227-4373
www.hemmings.com
Published and printed in the U.S.A.

ISBN 0-917808-74-6
ISSN: 0363-4639
LCCN: 76-649715

Hemmings COLLECTOR-CAR ALMANAC™

is brought to the collector-car hobby by:

Hemmings Motor News™

"The bible" of the collector-car hobby since 1954. Your ticket to the hobby!
(see full listing on page 572)

Special Interest Autos
SIA
Cars That Matter™

The hobby's most authoritative and informative glossy magazine.
(see full listing on page 573)

Hemmings Rods & Performance™

Dedicated to today's Street Rod, Racing, Muscle and Performance Markets.
(see full listing on page 572)

Dear Reader,

Welcome to the *Almanac*'s family!

Our **Collector-Car Almanac** is the world's most complete directory to the old auto hobby. Here are over 3,500 listings for clubs, dealers, vendors, salvage yards, services, and individuals serving the hobbyist. And there's much more, including the most complete listing of old car museums you'll find anywhere.

This edition of the *Almanac* also contains 84 listings for Legislative Watch Organizations. These groups were formed to take on the vital chore of protecting the interests of the collector car hobby/industry. From what threats should we be protected? So-called "Clunker Bills" and related governmental actions that threaten to reduce or eliminate the supply of old cars & parts, and legislation or regulation that would impose additional costs or restrictions on our enjoyment of old cars. Become involved! These important listings begin on page 559.

To old hands, this *Almanac*'s excellence is no surprise – it's an offshoot of *Hemmings Motor News* and *Special Interest Autos*, two of the most respected publications in the hobby.

Hemmings Motor News is known as "the bible" of the collector-car hobby. *"HMN"* has been published monthly since 1954, and now serves nearly 500,000 readers (paid circulation over 245,000 monthly, average 2 readers per copy). We also serve tens of thousands of advertisers worldwide. *Hemmings Motor News* is literally The World's Largest Collector-Car Hobby Publication.

HMN is about 98% advertising of collector cars for sale and related items down to the most obscure and hard-to-find parts, literature, services, tools, supplies, and more. During 2000, *HMN* averaged over 700 pages per month! That's a fat package for the annual subscription price of just $28.95.

www.hemmings.com – *Hemmings Motor News* online is the world's largest "E-Community center" for antique, vintage, and special-interest cars and trucks, parts, services, car show dates and info, car clubs, automobilia collectibles, and more! Our searchable database makes it easy to locate, buy or sell, by make, model, year and location. Plus, you can visit Car Club Central, kick tires in Dealers' Showrooms nationwide, convene your own virtual Online Car Show, E-mail a friend, or shop our Motor Mall for the latest in die-cast collectibles and other automobilia. It's easy, it's fun, it's FREE!

Visit www.hemmings.com to see why we're the fastest growing E-Community center for the collector car and truck hobby.

Thirty years ago, when finned Cadillacs, porthole T-birds, side-curtained MGs, and Ram Air GTOs were just used cars (selling for less than a years' insurance premium on a new car today) *Special Interest Autos* became the hobby's authoritative source of in-depth collector car information.

Special Interest Autos is the world's only automobile magazine specializing in present–day road tests of vintage cars, trucks, and other uncommon and unique collector vehicles you won't discover elsewhere. From Brass Era beauties to computer controlled muscle machines of the eighties, each issue features driveReports on at least four collector cars, tracing developmental histories and including complete driving impressions of restored or fine original examples of the cars – information which helps you choose which collector car will suit you and informs you all about the collector cars you and your friends already own.

SIA's exclusive comparisonReports face off two, three or four collector cars of similar vintage & price against each other – and we pull no punches! You'll also find valuable insights to the hobby via such new columns as *Sleepers, Market Driven, Value Timeline* and *Motor Books* – the kind of information, facts & figures, and stunning photography, you'll enjoy reading.

Just $19.95 buys a one-year subscription (six issues) of *Special Interest Autos* mailed directly to your home. So come along and cruise with us in style as we explore the collector car hobby of the 21st century.

Hemmings Rods & Performance – the hobby's most informative performance car magazine devoted to street rods, custom cars, hot rods, muscle cars, and all sorts of exciting high-performance street machines. Inside you'll discover informative technical articles and in-depth car features detailing exacting how the cars were built. Best of all, each issue is jamb-packed with thousands of classified ads offering performance cars and parts for sale, as well as the industry's most complete directory of aftermarket manufacturers, suppliers and specialists. From mechanical and electrical parts to body kits, billet wheels and chrome accessories, each issue is a powerhouse of who's who in the world of street rodding and performance cars and trucks. If it's go-fast and look-good parts you want, as well as vintage speed parts for that old flathead, you'll find them all in *Hemmings Rods & Performance* magazine. Published six-times a year, you can test drive a sample copy for just $3.95, or visit the Hemmings tent at a car show or swap meet near you.

Hemmings Bookshelf offers a wide & carefully selected list of old car books to aid, educate, and entertain the restorer and enthusiast. Titles offered cover how-to topics, value & investment guides, interchange manuals, marque histories, and more – everything from old farm tractors to '60s and '70s muscle cars, from low-bucks hobby cars to Ferraris & Duesenbergs. We ship promptly, and we refund promptly if you're not satisfied. See our monthly ads in *HMN*.

We welcome visitors to our Bennington, Vermont offices, and at our Hemmings Motor News Sunoco Filling Station & Store at 216 Main Street (Vermont Route 9) in downtown Bennington, and we're always glad to hear from readers through the mail.

Your "feedback" and opinions are critical to us, because our long-established goal is to make all our publications useful, comprehensive, and a good value for the dollar! Please help us know how we're doing by writing us at PO Box 256, Bennington, Vermont 05201, or by calling us at 1-800-CAR-HERE. Thank you!

Sincerely yours,
Terry Ehrich

Publisher & Editor-in-Chief

P.S. Check out our web site at www.hemmings.com

How To Pick
A Restoration Shop

By Richard A. Lentinello

Clean, organized facilities are a clear indication that the shop will produce a quality end product, as shown by the tidy conditions surrounding these two Duesenbergs undergoing body-off restorations at Al Prueitt & Sons in Glen Rock, Pennsylvania.

Restoring old cars, regardless of make or model, is a very expensive proposition. It is also an extremely time-consuming process that requires a considerable amount of skilled labor. It's a big investment, eclipsed only by a homeowner's mortgage and a child's college education.

Before engaging in a restoration, considerable thought must be given to the end product: what you want it to be and how you will use it. Are you looking for a 100-point, concours-perfect automobile or a really nice street restoration? Whichever you choose, you must decide how you want your vehicle restored before your search for a restorer begins. There are many different kinds of shops, each with a different level of work quality.

Ideally we would all like to restore our beloved cars ourselves, but few of us have the necessary skills, tools, facilities and time. This is why most people commission shops to either carry out an entire restoration or perform several of the more specialized tasks involved that are beyond the scope of even the more experienced enthusiast. Your financial resources will dictate whether you can carry out a full mechanical rebuild at the same time as a complete body/chassis rebuild.

Let us assume that you are looking for a shop to perform a complete ground-up restoration to show quality. It is important to choose a shop that provides clear and accurate communication with its clients and is aware of the many unique problems involved in such a venture. By doing so you will avoid conflict later on, or at least keep it to a minimum.

To ascertain which restoration facilities offer the best service and quality, you should visit at least three or four different shops during working hours. This will give you a good idea of how a restoration shop operates and the skill level of its work force. Soon you'll be able to separate the good from the bad.

Rule number one when looking for a restorer: Never, ever, go to a local garage or body shop, even if they advertise a restoration service. They simply do not have the skill or knowledge necessary for such a job. They only know tune-ups and collision work. They haven't the faintest idea about the intricacies of a true restoration, especially if they try to assure you that there is nothing magical about it. Always keep in mind that restoration firms are not body shops and body shops are not restoration firms. They are two distinctly different types of businesses.

Like any business that relies solely on a skilled work force to produce a finished product (as opposed to a manufacturer or retailer), a restoration business is very difficult to run due to the extensive use of hand labor, which always limits the cash flow. By understanding the numerous problems that a shop proprietor has to deal with, you will be able to comprehend why he has to perform certain tasks, charge for each of those tasks accordingly and expect you to make payments promptly.

To get the best job for your money, it is important to deal with a shop that specializes in your particular car make and/or model. No one knows everything there is to know about a particular vehicle and its parts, nor can they successfully solve all its inherent problems in a timely manner. If they've never worked on your type of vehicle before, your car or truck may be the experimental vehicle they are looking to learn on.

Dealing with non-specialists will result in higher restoration costs because they take longer to do things due to their unfamiliarity with the car. When you are being charged by the hour, every minute counts. Also, the end result will likely not be of the same quality, nor will the car be restored to the correct specifications.

To obtain the services of a quality restoration facility, see "Restoration Shops" in Section Two. There are more than 18 pages of listings to meet all your restoration needs, from complete body-off show quality restorations to partial driver restorations. Make an appointment to visit a few of the shops listed that are located near you to see if their work meets with your approval.

When you think you have found the proper facility to restore your car, don't be afraid to ask the shop owner questions about his experience and the techniques he uses. If he is honest and his business has a good reputation, he will gladly answer all your questions. Ask him about his background and how long he has been in the restoration business. Ask about his employees and their individual experience in the field. Take the time to inspect the workshop, and take a detailed look at the work being performed on the cars under restoration.

The ideal restoration facility will have all the necessary tools and equipment needed to carry out its work in the most efficient manner with the best results. Besides standard hand tools, a bead blast cabinet, lathe, half-ton press, metal brake, and a full complement of both gas and MIG welding equipment are essential items that every good shop should have. A self-contained spray booth is another crucial item. Not only will the paint-work be of a higher quality, but it also makes the work place safer for the employees and lessens the damaging effects of toxic paint fumes on our environment.

It is also important for you to inspect a couple of vehicles that the restorer has completed. Ask for at least three references from former customers. Call them and ask about their dealings with the shop. By knowing as much about the restorer as possible, you will know what to expect, which will let you negotiate the contract accordingly.

Because no two cars are alike and no two cars are in the same condition when their restorations begin, it would be unjust for you to compare your estimate with that of another vehicle. Because each restoration is unique, a program must be outlined that is tailored to the specific requirements of the car and its owner.

It is often very difficult for the shop owner to provide an estimate that will hold true throughout the length of the restoration process. Because the restorer doesn't have X-ray eyesight, he simply cannot judge the amount of rust and body repair that might

be required without disassembling the entire vehicle and inspecting every component. And because they cannot foresee every single problem, most restorers have a clause in their contracts that states an additional charge will be incurred if extra work is required.

Specialized restorers who have extensive experience with a particular model car or truck already know exactly how many hours of labor it will take them to strip and paint that vehicle, restore its frame and rebuild the suspension. This will allow them to charge a flat rate for each job because the work really doesn't vary much from car to car, no matter if it's a 1967 Camaro or a 1969 Camaro. However, if extra repair work is necessary to the body or frame due to a car's below-average condition, then the customer will be charged for the additional work.

Most of the big-dollar restoration shops that specialize in highly collectible cars, such as Bugattis, Ferraris and Packards, bill their clients on a time-plus-material basis due to their ability to pay for a true, perfect, 100-point restoration. Being charged an hourly rate is the most expensive way to pay for a restoration. But if you want the absolute highest

Some shops are more specialized than others, especially those that have coachbuilding abilities. This hand-made Ferrari Testa Rossa body, and its egg crate grille, are outstanding examples of the panel beater's craft.

quality possible there is no alternative, particularly from the restorer's perspective, since he will have to put in endless hours of labor until every single aspect of the car is perfect.

Be very skeptical of the shop that will restore your vehicle for a price that seems too good to be true. Once they have your car apart, if the work is much more extensive that they anticipated (and it usually is), you can be sure they will cut corners in places you won't notice. This can lead to a dangerous situation if they decide not to replace fatigued brake lines or a weak suspension support bracket.

After both parties have agreed to terms, you must provide a deposit so the restorer can begin working. This not only shows your genuine intention, but it lets the shop start ordering the parts and supplies they will need during the next few weeks. The better-run shops will invoice you on either a weekly, biweekly or monthly basis, depending on what you have agreed to. Each invoice statement should include detailed labor descriptions, a listing of all purchased parts and a brief outline of the progress that is being made. Invoices will also vary in amount depending on how much time was put in and which parts were bought during that period.

Most restoration shops usually require a substantial deposit before work begins. This varies among shops, but it can be as much as half the total estimate. Since most people are a little wary of leaving such a large sum of money, finding a restorer who is understanding and flexible is almost as important as finding one who is qualified in the first place.

If you have any questions regarding the shop's invoices, inquire at once. If the restorer can not justify his expenses, order him to stop all work immediately and iron out the problem before the charges get out of hand. If all charges are realistic, pay your bill promptly. Should you fail to pay your bills in a timely manner, the shop has the right to stop work and your project will get pushed aside, only to lose its spot in line when you decide to pay what is owed. Up-to-date accounts always receive top priority.

Assuming the cost of a continuous restoration is beyond your means, you should set a budget with the shop owner prior to the start of the project. The restorer will then work against advanced installments until all the money is used up. Should you take more than thirty days to furnish additional money, a nominal monthly fee for storage and interest charges may be incurred. This is only fair, as space costs money.

One often-overlooked item is insurance. Although the law states that all shops must be insured, you really don't know how much coverage they carry. It is therefore wise, especially if your vehicle is rare and highly valuable, to carry full coverage on the car while it's being restored at the shop and while it is being transported.

It is also important for you to take photographs of the entire restoration. This documentation will be extremely valuable when you need to substantiate your claimed ground-up restoration should you decide to sell the vehicle at a later date or to make an insurance claim. Detailed photos showing the car before and during the rebuild are most important. The "before" photos will greatly assist the restorer later should any doubts arise about how to install a piece of trim or reassemble a particular component correctly. The photos showing the work in progress will prove how extensive the rebuild really was.

The photos will also provide documentation on the parts status. Prior to delivering the vehicle to the restorer's workshop, you should inventory each and every part and note if it is good, broken or missing. Take note of the condition of all the glass, including all scratches and chips. This will help avoid misunderstandings between you and the restorer later on.

Since restoration is a labor-intensive craft, most cars and trucks will take more than a year to restore.

The vehicle with a solid, rust-free body will take less time, of course, but it all depends on whether you want perfection or if you can tolerate minor flaws. The final fitting of the windshield, bolting on the bumpers and installing all the delicate chrome trim pieces are painstaking procedures that take a lot of time. One slip of the screwdriver and your new paint is ruined. It is also impossible to avoid delays waiting for parts that may be on back order. Searching for a rare part that is missing or not available as a reproduction will also contribute to delays. Parts are expensive and they add up rather quickly, so don't forget to include them in your budget.

When your vehicle is complete, it should be handed over to you after the restorer has given it an extensive road test to see if everything performs as it should. There should be no problems at all. The car must be satisfying to drive and provide the same level of responsiveness that it did when it was new. Only then will you know if the restoration was a success. Remember, a fine restoration is substantially more than just cosmetics.

In conclusion, whatever estimate you're given for the work, add a minimum contingency of 25 percent. This way when the time comes to pay the bills, you won't be surprised. During the restoration, keep in touch with the shop and try to visit as often as possible.

Be friendly to the people who are rebuilding your car and let them know how much you appreciate their work. Make sure everything you want is in writing and shoot as many photographs of the restoration as possible. You should also get some sort of a warranty on mechanicals and body and paint. It's usually 10,000 miles and one year, respectively.

And before you take your "new" vehicle out on the road, get it appraised by a professional, then have it properly insured. There are more than one hundred appraisers throughout the country listed in Section Two who will appraise your vehicle professionally. Then insure it for what the restoration cost, not its stated value. This way all your restoration expenses will be covered should anything unfortunate happen; there are more than a dozen insurance companies listed in Section Two that specialize in collector cars, trucks, motorcycles and street rods. They/ will gladly put together a liability package to meet your specific needs.

Good luck and happy motoring.

CONTENTS

Section One – Specialists by Make or Model *(2,340 listings)*

Organized alphabetically by make or model, this section includes all vendors, dealers and suppliers concerned with the following specific vehicles 13

Abarth 13	Edsel 72	Morgan 139
AC 13	Essex 72	Morris 139
Alfa Romeo 13	Ferrari 73	Nash 140
Alvis 14	Fiat 75	NSU 141
AMC 15	Ford 1903-1931 75	Oldsmobile 141
American Austin/Bantam 16	Ford 1932-1953 79	Opel 143
Amphicar 16	Ford 1954-up 86	Packard 144
Anglia 17	Mustang 95	Peugeot 146
Aston Martin 17	Thunderbird 100	Pierce-Arrow 146
Auburn 18	Franklin 105	Plymouth 146
Audi 18	GMC 105	Pontiac 148
Austin 18	Graham 106	Porsche 152
Austin-Healey 19	Harley-Davidson 107	Renault 154
Avanti 21	Hispano-Suiza 108	Rolls-Royce/Bentley 155
BMW 21	Honda 108	Rover/Land Rover 158
Bricklin 23	Hudson 108	Saab 159
Bugatti 24	Hupmobile 109	Stanley 159
Buick/McLaughlin 24	Indian 109	Stearns-Knight 160
Cadillac/LaSalle 27	Jaguar 109	Studebaker 160
Checker 33	Jensen 116	Stutz 161
Chevrolet 33	Kaiser Frazer 116	Sunbeam 161
Chevelle/Camaro 50	Lagonda 117	Talbot-Lago 162
Corvair 54	Lamborghini 117	Terraplane 162
Corvette 55	Lancia 117	Toyota 162
Chrysler 62	Lincoln 118	Triumph 162
Citroen 65	Locomobile 120	TVR 165
Cobra 65	Lotus 120	Vanden Plas 165
Cooper 66	Marmon 121	Volkswagen 165
Crosley 66	Maserati 121	Volvo 166
Cushman 67	Mercedes-Benz 122	Wills Sainte Claire 167
Daimler 67	Mercer 127	Willys 167
Davis 67	Mercury 127	Zimmer 168
DeLorean 68	Merkur 129	
DeSoto 68	Metropolitan 129	
DeTomaso/Pantera 68	MG 130	
Dodge 69	Moon 134	
Duesenberg 72	Mopar 134	

Tourguide – A state-by-state index to Section One vendors 169

Section Two – Generalists *(3,792 listings)*

Organized alphabetically by subject, this section lists businesses offering specific types of parts or services for a range of automotive marques 173

accessories 173	brokers 221	decals 253
air conditioning 180	camshafts 222	differentials 254
anti-theft 181	car & parts locators 223	driveshafts 254
apparel 182	car care products 225	electrical systems 254
appraisals 183	car covers 229	engine parts 258
artwork 191	car dealers 230	engine rebuilding 263
auctions & shows 195	carburetors 235	exhaust systems 267
automobilia 199	carpets 237	fans 270
babbitting 208	castings 238	fiberglass parts 270
batteries 208	chassis parts 239	filters 271
bearings 209	cleaning products 242	financing 271
bicycles 209	clutches 242	fire engines 271
body parts 210	coachbuilders & designers 242	fuel system parts 272
bodywork 215	comprehensive parts 243	gaskets 273
brakes 217	consultants 249	glass 274
brass cars/parts 221	custom cars 251	grille emblem badges 276

(Section Two continued)

hardware	276
heaters	278
hubcaps	278
ignition parts	279
instruments	281
insulation	284
insurance	284
interiors & interior parts	285
kit cars & replicars	293
leather restoration	294
license plates	295
lighting equipment	296
limousine rentals	297
literature dealers	297
locks & keys	303
lubricants	304
machine work	304
manufacturing	306
military vehicles	308
models & toys	309
motorcycles	314
novelties	317

painting	319
paints	320
petroliana	321
photography	323
plaques	324
plastic parts	324
plating & polishing	325
racing	329
radiator emblems & mascots	332
radiators	333
radios	335
restoration aids	337
restoration shops	342
rubber parts	360
rust removal & stripping	363
rustproofing	365
service shops	365
sheetmetal	369
special services	372
steering columns	376
steering wheels	376
storage	377

storage care products	379
street rods	380
striping	387
suspension parts	388
tires	392
tools	394
tops	397
trailers	399
transmissions	401
transport	404
trucks & tractors	408
trunks	412
upholstery	412
videos	415
water pumps	416
wheels & wheelcovers	416
windshield wipers	418
wiring harnesses	419
woodgraining	420
woodwork	421

Tourguide – A state-by-state index to Section Two vendors 425

Section Three – Clubs *(3,372 listings)*

A comprehensive listing of clubs and organizations, divided into **sub-sections** for Multi-Marque Clubs, Marque Clubs, Registries, Specialty Clubs, Legislative Organizations and State or Local Clubs.
....431

Multi-Marque Clubs	431
Marque Clubs	459
Abarth	459
AC	459
Alfa Romeo	459
Allard	459
Alvis	459
AMC	459
American Austin/Bantam	460
Amphicar	461
AMX	461
Austin-Healey	461
Austin	462
Auto Union	462
Avanti	462
Berkeley	462
Bitter	463
BMW	463
Brough	463
Bugatti	463
Buick	463
Cadillac	464
Checker	465
Chevrolet	465
Chevelle/Camaro	467
Corvair	468
Corvette	471
Chrysler	478
Citroën	478
Cooper	478
Crosley	478
Cushman	478
Daewoo	479
DAF	479
Daimler	479
Datsun	479
Davis	479
Delahaye	479
DeLorean	479

DeSoto	479
DeTomaso/Pantera	480
Diamont T	480
Divco	480
DKW	480
Dodge	480
Dual Ghia	480
Edsel	481
English Ford	481
Eshelman	481
Excaliber	481
Ferrari	481
Fiat	482
Ford	482
Mustang	502
Thunderbird	508
GEO	511
Glasspar	511
GM	511
Gotfredson	512
Graham Brothers.	512
Harley-Davidson	512
Heinkel Trojan	512
Hillman	512
Hispano Suiza	512
Hudson	512
Hupmobile	514
Indian	514
International Harvester	514
ISO/Bizzarini	514
Jaguar	514
Jewett	514
Kaiser Frazer	515
King	515
King Midget	515
Kissel	515
Knox	515
Lamborghini	515
Lancia	515

Lincoln	515
Lotus	516
Marmon	516
Maserati	516
Mazda	516
Mercedes-Benz	516
Mercury	517
Metz	517
MG	517
Mopar	519
Morgan	523
Nash	523
NSU	524
Nyberg	524
Oakland	524
Oldsmobile	524
Opel	525
Packard	526
Patriot	527
Peerless	527
Pierce-Arrow	527
Plymouth	527
Pontiac	528
Porsche	531
Renault	532
Reo	532
Riley	532
Rolls-Royce	532
Rover	532
Saab	532
Sabra	532
Saxon	533
Shay	533
Simca	533
Squire	533
Stevens-Duryea	533
Studebaker	533
Stutz	533
Subaru	533

Sunbeam..........................533
Tatra...............................534
Toyota.............................534
Triumph...........................534
Tucker.............................536
TVR.................................536
Vanden Plas....................537
Volkswagen.....................537
Volvo...............................537
Willys..............................538
Zimmer...........................538
Registries..........................539
AMX................................539
Austin.............................539
Brabham.........................539
Bristol.............................539
Buick..............................539
Chalmers........................539

Clenet.............................539
Delage............................539
De Vaux..........................540
Dodge............................540
English Ford....................540
Erskine...........................540
Fiat.................................540
Ford................................540
Mustang..........................540
Honda.............................540
Inter-State......................540
Jordan............................541
Kaiser.............................541
Kellison...........................541
Manx..............................541
Mercury..........................541
Monteverdi......................541
Morris.............................541

Muntz.............................541
Packard..........................541
Paige..............................541
Pontiac...........................542
Rootes............................542
Scripps-Booth.................542
Stephens........................542
Sunbeam........................542
Velie...............................542
Vespa.............................542
Victoria...........................542
Willys..............................542
Zimmerman.....................542
Specialty Clubs................542
State or Local Clubs.........550
Legislative Watch Organizations..559

Section Four – Publications & Information Sources *(181 listings)*

Organized alphabetically, this section is a listing of publishers, archivists and libraries which are sources of information for the old-auto hobby 563

information sources...................563
books & publications 567

periodicals..............................571
newsletters.............................574

research & reference libraries ...575

Section Five – Salvage Yards *(67 listings)*

Organized alphabetically by state, this section lists salvage yards which offer collectible cars and parts...577

Section Six – Museums *(315 listings)*

Organized alphabetically by state, this section lists private and public museums or showrooms with vintage cars in their collections 583

Section Seven – Useful Lists and Compilations

Classic Cars, 1925-1948 — Classic Car Club of America 607
Certified Milestone Cars, 1945-1972 610
U.S. Vehicle Makes, Past to Present 613

Index to this Almanac

An alphabetical index to every listing in the almanac...629

Index to Display Advertisers

An alphabetical index to every display advertiser in the almanac................................664

Section One
Specialists by Make & Model

2,340 listings

Section One provides a comprehensive roster of specialists in one or a limited number of particular car makes. Marques are presented alphabetically, and vendors offering parts, supplies, literature, services or cars appear alphabetically under every marque in which they specialize. Certain extremely popular models, such as Corvette and Thunderbird, are presented as separate categories following the appropriate main marque category.

The taglines in the right-hand box of each listing offer a quick guide to the primary services or products offered by each marque specialist.

Vendors who specialize in several marques will have an abbreviated listing under each pertinent marque category with a cross reference to the vendor's full listing. This full listing appears under the category of that vendor's most significant concentration.

Hobbyists seeking services or products appropriate to a variety of car marques should also consult Section Two, which lists vendors by general product or service categories.

Highway One Classic Automobiles and Highwayone.com
1035 California Dr
Burlingame, CA 94010
650-342-7340; FAX: 650-343-0150
E-mail: djboscacci@msn.com

classic automobiles

Open Monday-Friday 9 am to 6 pm, Saturday by appointment. Buying, selling and marketing of classic automobiles. Web site: www.highwayone.com

Museo Abarth
1111 Via Bayless
Marietta, GA 30066-2770
770-928-1446

museum

See full listing in **Section Six** under **Georgia**

C Obert & Co
2131-D Delaware Ave
Santa Cruz, CA 95060-5706
800-500-3428 orders
831-423-0218; FAX: 831-459-8128
E-mail: fiatplus@aol.com

**parts
repairs**

See full listing in **Section One** under **Fiat**

Cobra Restorers Ltd
3099 Carter Dr
Kennesaw, GA 30144
770-427-0020; FAX: 770-427-8658

**parts
restoration
service**

See full listing in **Section One** under **Cobra**

EVA Sports Cars
RR 1
Vankleek Hill, ON Canada K0B 1R0
613-678-3377; FAX: 613-678-6110

kit cars

See full listing in **Section Two** under **kit cars & replicars**

Finish Line
3593 SW 173rd Terr
Miramar, FL 33029
954-436-9101; FAX: 954-436-9102
E-mail: e.alibrandi@att.net

**parts
supplies**

See full listing in **Section One** under **Cobra**

JWF Restorations Inc
11955 SW Faircrest St
Portland, OR 97225-4615
503-643-3225; FAX: 503-646-4009

restoration

AC restoration specialist. 40 years' experience. Partial to full restorations done to street or concours standards.

Ragtops & Roadsters
203 S 4th St
Perkasie, PA 18944
215-257-1202; FAX: 215-257-2688
E-mail: info@ragtops.com

**British automobiles
engine rebuilding
vintage race prep
restoration/service**

Open shop only. Monday-Friday 9 am to 5 pm, evenings and Saturday by appointment. Minor repairs to full concours restorations of all British and special interest automobiles. Vintage race car prep and restoration. The more unusual the car, the more we enjoy it. Mechanical, engine rebuilds, interior trimming, body and paint refinishing, fabrication. Web site: www.ragtops.com

Alfa Heaven Inc
2698 Nolan Rd
Aniwa, WI 54408-9667
715-449-2141

parts

Mail order only. Monday-Friday 8 am to 5 pm, Saturday by appointment only. Specializing in new and used parts, performance parts, fiberglass repro parts for 1975 thru current models Alfa Romeo. Museum houses mostly Alfa Romeo, but also has one Maserati, a Ferrari and a Lancia. We also have the prototype Giulietta Spider and specialize in first of Series Alfas. Specializing in 1970s Japanese motorcycle parts. Web site: www.alfaheaven.com

Alfas Unlimited Inc	engine rebuilding
89 Greenwoods Rd W, Rt 44	parts
Norfolk, CT 06058	restoration
860-542-5351; FAX: 860-542-5993	service
E-mail: alfasun@esslink.com	

Repair and restoration shop and mail order parts. Monday-Saturday 10 am to 6 pm. Authorized Alfa Romeo dealer. Vintage Alfa restorations for racing or street. Also repair shop for modern Alfas. Complete restorations including body, paint, engine and any other mechanical components. Twenty years' experience in Alfas. Many new, NOS and used parts for sale as well as vintage and modern Alfas for sale, for race or street. Member VSCCA, SVRA, AROC.

Algar	parts
1234 Lancaster Ave	
Rosemont, PA 19010	
800-441-9824, 610-527-1100	
FAX: 610-525-0575	
E-mail: algarferrari.com	

See full listing in **Section One** under **Ferrari**

Centerline Products	cars
Box 1466, 4715 N Broadway	parts
Boulder, CO 80306	
303-447-0239; FAX: 303-447-0257	

Mail order only. Monday-Friday 9:30 am to 5:30 pm. Specializes in Alfa Romeo parts, new and used, and used Alfa cars. Deals in all models, Giulietta, Giulia thru 164. Web site: www.centerlinealfa.com

Concours Cars of Colorado Ltd	accessories
2414 W Cucharras St	parts
Colorado Springs, CO 80904	service
719-473-6288; FAX: 719-473-9206	

See full listing in **Section One** under **BMW**

Grand Prix Classics Inc	racing cars
7456 La Jolla Blvd	sports cars
La Jolla, CA 92037	
858-459-3500; FAX: 858-459-3512	
E-mail: info@grandprixclassics.com	

See full listing in **Section Two** under **racing**

Mac's Euro Motorcars & Transport	Alfa Romeos
1520 Burr Oak Rd	parts
Homewood, IL 60430	transport
708-799-3469	

Alfa Romeo cars and parts for sale, trade and wanted, 1954-1974. Giulietta, Giulia cars, Series 750-101-105-115, all models. I also do auto transport for Alfa Romeos and all other makes of cars, trucks, motorcycles, tractors and parts.

Orion Motors European Parts Inc	parts
10722 Jones Rd	
Houston, TX 77065	
800-736-6410, 281-894-1982	
FAX: 281-849-1997	
E-mail: orion-yugo@yugoparts.com	

Mail order and retail store. All parts for Alfa Romeo, Fiat, Yugo. Direct importer of parts from country of origin and other sources. Web site: yugoparts.com

Rayce Inc	parts
3637 NE 2nd St	
Gainesville, FL 32609	
800-426-2221, 352-335-8900	
FAX: 352-335-8930	

Parts for Alfa Romeo, Fiat, Peugeot, Saab, Volvo, Yugo only, (1968-1996). Web site: www.rayce.com

Replicarz	books
166 Spruce St	kits
Rutland, VT 05701	models
802-747-7151	videos
E-mail: replicarz@aol.com	

See full listing in **Section Two** under **racing**

Garry Roberts & Co	cars
922 Sunset Dr	parts
Costa Mesa, CA 92627	service
949-650-2690; FAX: 949-650-2730	
E-mail: garryroberts@fea.net	

See full listing in **Section One** under **Ferrari**

Rosso Bianco Sportscar Museum	museum
Obernauer Str 125	
D-63743	
Aschaffenburg Germany	
06021 21358; FAX: 06021 20636	

See full listing in **Section Six** under **Germany**

Doug Schellinger	automobilia
13717 W Green Meadow Dr	books
New Berlin, WI 53151	sales literature
414-328-1907	toys
E-mail: dsac@execpc.com	

See full listing in **Section One** under **Fiat**

Voss Motors Inc	service manuals
4850 37th Ave S	
Seattle, WA 98118	
888-380-9277 toll free; 206-721-3077	
E-mail: vossmotors@books4cars.com	

See full listing in **Section Two** under **literature dealers**

Wolf Steel	Alfa Romeo body
1 Ballerina	parts
Frelighsburg, QC Canada J0J 1C0	
450-298-5078; FAX: 450-298-5088	
E-mail: allen@alfaparts.net	

See full listing in **Section One** under **Jaguar**

Sandringham House Museum & Grounds	museum
Sandringham	
Nr King's Lynn	
Norfolk PE356EN England	
01553-772675; FAX: 01485-541571	

See full listing in **Section Six** under **England**

A-1 Shock Absorber Co
Shockfinders Division
365 Warren Ave, PO Box 2028
Silverthorne, CO 80498
800-344-1966, 970-389-3193 cell
FAX: 970-513-8283

| shocks-all types |
| coil springs |
| Koni shocks |
| leaf springs |
| steering gears |

See our ad on the last page

All American Rambler
11661 Martens River Cir #M
Fountain Valley, CA 92708
714-662-7200
E-mail: rambler411@aol.com

| cars |
| manuals |
| memorabilia |
| parts/tech info |

Mail order and open shop. Monday-Friday 9 am to 5 pm, Saturday by appointment only. Specializes in parts for 1958-1963 Rambler Americans. Also tech service manuals for all Ramblers, tail lenses for most Ramblers. Buy, sell, trade. If we don't have it, we will help you find it. Bob (Mr Rambler) Pendleton. Web site: http://members.aol.com/rambler411/private/rambler.html

American Performance Products
675 S Industry Rd
Cocoa, FL 32926
321-632-8299; FAX: 321-632-5119
E-mail: amc@oldcarparts.com

parts

Mail order and open shop. Monday 9:30 am to 8:30 pm, Tuesday-Friday 9:30 am to 5:30 pm. Specializing in American Motors Corp vehicle parts for all AMC including AMX, Javelin, Spirit, Gremlin, Hornet and Jeep, performance and stock. Secure online catalog. Web site: www.oldcarparts.com

AMX Enterprises Ltd
7963 Depew St
Arvada, CO 80003-2527
303-428-8760

information source

Larry Mitchell, owner. AMC performance and handling expert. Engine building & supplying of reproduction and some new parts.

Blaser's Auto, Nash, Rambler, AMC
3200 48th Ave
Moline, IL 61265-6453
309-764-3571; FAX: 309-764-1155
E-mail: blazauto@sprynet.com

NOS parts

Mail order and open shop. Monday-Friday 9 am to 5 pm CST. We specialize in new old stock Nash, Rambler and AMC parts for most 1949-1987 models. We offer one of the largest inventories of new parts for these fine automobiles. Featuring quality service manuals and parts books. We offer quality windshield gaskets as well as select rear window gaskets for 1963-1969. With 57 years of experience in sales and service of these vehicles makes us an excellent choice for your one stop shopping. We do not offer a catalog but your one call does it all. Fast worldwide shipping plus we accept all major credit cards and COD for your purchases.

Dom Corey Upholstery &
Antique Auto
1 Arsene Way
Fairhaven Business Park
Fairhaven, MA 02719
508-997-6555

| carpets/seats |
| conv tops/dash |
| covers |
| door panels |
| headliners |
| upholstery |

See full listing in **Section Two** under **interiors & interior parts**

For Ramblers Only
2324 SE 34th Ave
Portland, OR 97214
503-232-0497
E-mail: ramblers@teleport.com

| accessories |
| parts |

Mail order and open shop. Weekdays 10 am to 2 pm and weekends 10 am to 6 pm. Specializing in parts and accessories, NOS and used, for 1958-1969 Rambler and AMC. Carpets and trunk mats for Ramblers only. Windshield gaskets for most Ramblers. Wiper motors and fuel pumps.

Galvin's Rambler Parts
7252-R Stockton Blvd
Sacramento, CA 95823
916-424-4202; FAX: 916-424-4240

parts

Mail order. Specializing in new and used parts, including reproduction items and literature for 1958-1988 Ramblers and AMCs. No Jeep or Metropolitan. Web site: www.ramblerparts.com

Gear Vendors Inc
1717 N Magnolia Ave
El Cajon, CA 92020
619-562-0060; FAX: 619-562-1186
E-mail: info@gearvendors.com

| overdrive |
| transmissions |

See full listing in **Section Two** under **transmissions**

Jeepsamerica
367 Washington St
Weymouth, MA 02189
781-331-4333; FAX: 781-331-6947
E-mail: mconsiglio1@yahoo.com

| parts |
| service |

See full listing in **Section One** under **Chrysler**

Kennedy American Inc
7100 State Rt 142 SE
West Jefferson, OH 43162
614-879-7283

parts

Mail order and open shop. Monday-Friday 9 am to 6 pm. New, select used and reproduction parts for American Motors, Rambler, AMX, Javelin and Jeep vehicles from 1950s to present.

Kip Motor Company Inc
2127 Crown Rd
Dallas, TX 75229
972-243-0440; FAX: 972-243-2387
E-mail: kipmotor@aol.com

| literature |
| parts |
| restoration |

See full listing in **Section One** under **Austin**

Mike's Auto Parts
Box 358
Ridgeland, MS 39158
601-856-7214

| NOS Mopar |
| NOS GM |
| NOS Ford |
| parts for all makes |

See full listing in **Section One** under **Chrysler**

Section One – Marque Specialists

South Texas AMC
30115 Hwy 281 N, Ste 126
Bulverde, TX 78163
830-980-3165
E-mail: akjamc@juno.com

> parts
> **restoration**

Mail order and open shop. Monday-Saturday 8 am to 5 pm. Specializing in new, NOS, reproduction and used parts, restoration, engine building, cars and projects for AMC cars. Specialist in AMX, Javelin and performance models but will do any car. Web site: www.southtexasamc.bigstep.com

Eddie Stakes' Planet Houston AMX
1902 Wycliffe
Houston, TX 77043
713-464-8825
E-mail: eddiestakes@
planethoustonamx.com

> parts
> **parts locator**

Mail order only. Phone hours Monday-Friday 11 am to 1 pm CST. Specializing in 1968-1974 AMX and Javelin used, reproduction and NOS parts since 1983. Buy, sell, trade. I buy single parts, entire collections, also AMC literature, toys, promos, models, films, etc. The web's largest AMC vendors' list and over 1,000+ free leads on AMCs for sale on my web site. Current catalog ($7) lists parts, paint, trim, VIN codes, national AMC clubs and chapters, markets, production, more; proud sponsor/ founder AMC Southwest West Regional every summer. Web site: www.planethoustonamx.com

Stencils & Stripes Unlimited Inc
1108 S Crescent Ave #21
Park Ridge, IL 60068
847-692-6893; FAX: 847-692-6895

> NOS decals
> **stripe kits**

See full listing in **Section Two** under **decals**

Treasure Chest Sales
413 Montgomery
Jackson, MI 49202
517-787-1475

> parts

See full listing in **Section One** under **Nash**

Pat Walsh Restorations
Box Q
Wakefield, MA 01880
781-246-3266; FAX: 781-224-3311
E-mail: pwalshrest@aol.com

> literature
> **rubber parts**

See full listing in **Section Two** under **rubber parts**

Webb's Classic Auto Parts
5084 W State Rd 114
Huntington, IN 46750
219-344-1714; FAX: 219-344-1754

> NOS parts
> **reproduction parts**
> **service manuals**
> **used parts**

Mail order and open shop. Monday-Friday 9 am to 5 pm, weekends by appointment. Specializing in NOS, used and repro parts for Rambler and AMC from 1950 and newer. Large line of AMX/Javelin parts. Large selection of technical service manuals and parts books for Nash, Hudson, Rambler, AMC, Jeep and 1983-up Renault. Many aftermarket parts available for AMC and other makes. Send SASE with your needs. Discover, Visa, MC and AmEx accepted. Web site: www.webbsclassic.com

Wenner's
5449 Tannery Rd
Schnecksville, PA 18078
610-799-5419; FAX: 610-799-6107
E-mail: amcpartsloon@aol.com

> NOS parts

Evenings and weekends. Large inventory of AMC, Rambler and Nash parts. Specializing in NOS plus some used and aftermarket parts available.

Wymer Classic AMC
Mark & George Wymer
340 N Justice St
Fremont, OH 43420
419-332-4291, 419-334-6945 after 5 pm

> NOS/used parts
> **owner's manuals**
> **repairs**
> **service manuals**

Mail order and open shop. Monday-Friday 8 am to 5 pm EST. An American Motors dealership from 1958-1982. Repairs all AMC and Nash cars. Still has a large supply of NOS and used parts from our AMC, Rambler, salvage yard from 1958-1982 and all the specialty tools to repair the cars. Selection of technical service manuals, service literature, specification books and owner's manuals from 1955-1982 for Nash, Hudson, Rambler, AMC, Jeep, Renault, Metropolitan. Can do repair work on Packard cars. Have some Packard literature and memorabilia.

Golden Mile Sales Inc
J DeAngelo
2439 S Bradford St
Allentown, PA 18103-5821
PH/FAX: 610-791-4497, 24 hours
E-mail: abguy@enter.net

> NORS parts
> **NOS parts**
> **sheetmetal**

1930-1940 American Austin/Bantam vehicles, NOS, NORS parts, sheetmetal. Buy, sell, trade. All services. World's largest active source. SASE appreciated. Visit Fall Hershey Chocolate Annex, spaces C4W19-22. MasterCard, Visa.

Heinze Enterprise
7914 E Kimsey Ln
Scottsdale, AZ 85257
480-946-5814

> instrument
> **restoration**

Mail order and open shop. Free list of items for sale for American Austin, Bantam and Crosley. Also instrument restoration and refacing. Reproducer of vintage auto parts. Mechanical temperature gauge rebuilding. Send SASE for listing.

Gordon Imports Inc
14330 Iseli Rd
Santa Fe Springs, CA 90670-5296
562-802-1608, 714-523-3512
FAX: 562-404-1904

> parts

Mail order and business open Monday-Friday 8 am to 5:30 pm. Call for weekend hours, special appointments available. Amphicar parts for all years of Amphicars.

Anglia Obsolete 1311 York Dr Vista, CA 92084 760-630-3136; FAX: 760-630-2953 E-mail: dean@angliaobsolete.com	parts

Mail order only. New, used, reproduction parts for English Fords, 1939-1959, 8 hp and 10 hp cars and commercial vehicles. Models include: 7W, 7Y, Anglia, Prefect, Popular, Thames, E93A Series, 100E Models and some 105E Series. Web site: www.angliaobsolete.com

Kip Motor Company Inc 2127 Crown Rd Dallas, TX 75229 972-243-0440; FAX: 972-243-2387 E-mail: kipmotor@aol.com	literature parts restoration

See full listing in **Section One** under **Austin**

Dick Ames Stainless Steel Exhaust 4850 Fallcrest Cir Sarasota, FL 34233 941-923-8321; FAX: 941-923-9434 E-mail: dickamesfl@aol.com	exhaust systems

See full listing in **Section One** under **Jaguar**

Jerry Bensinger 1197 Trails Edge Dr Hubbard, OH 44425-3353 330-759-5224; FAX: 330-759-5225 E-mail: jbenzr@aol.com	car dealer

See full listing in **Section Two** under **car dealers**

Betws-Y-Coed Motor Museum Betws-Y-Coed Conwy Valley Gwynedd LL24 0AH England 01690710760	museum

See full listing in **Section Six** under **England**

British Luxury Automotive Parts 257 Niagara St Toronto ON Canada M6J 2L7 416-693-8400; FAX: 416-694-3202 Cell: 416-820-4323	new & used parts

See full listing in **Section One** under **Jaguar**

British Wire Wheel 444 Airport Blvd, #114 Watsonville, CA 95077 800-732-9866, 831-763-4200 FAX: 831-763-1780	hubs tires wire wheels

See full listing in **Section One** under **Austin-Healey**

Classic Auto Restoration 15445 Ventura Blvd #60 Sherman Oaks, CA 91413 818-905-6267; FAX: 818-906-1249 E-mail: rollsroyce1@earthlink.net	acquisitions restoration sales

See full listing in **Section One** under **Rolls-Royce/Bentley**

Charles S Crail Automobiles 36A Calle Cesar Chavez Santa Barbara, CA 93103 805-568-1934; FAX: 805-568-1533 E-mail: crailauto@aol.com	auto sales

See full listing in **Section One** under **Rolls-Royce/Bentley**

Chris Davis The Old Vicarage 49 Yates Hay Rd, Malvern Link Worcestershire, WR14 1LH England PH/FAX: 01684-560410	bronzes

See full listing in **Section Two** under **artwork**

Drummond Coach and Paint 531 Raleigh Ave El Cajon, CA 92020 619-579-7229; FAX: 619-579-2128	painting restoration

See full listing in **Section One** under **Ferrari**

The Fine Car Store 1105 Moana Dr San Diego, CA 92107 619-223-7766; FAX: 619-223-6838	car dealer

See full listing in **Section One** under **Ferrari**

Kensington Motor Group Inc PO Box 2277 Sag Harbor, NY 11963 516-537-1868; FAX: 516-537-2641 E-mail: kenmotor@aol.com	consignment sales

See full listing in **Section One** under **Mercedes-Benz**

Lake Oswego Restorations 19621 S Hazelhurst Ln West Linn, OR 97068 PH/FAX: 503-636-7503	restoration sales

Sales and restoration for 1950s and 1960s Aston Martins, XK Jaguars and other European sports cars.

Rolls-Royce of Beverly Hills 11401 West Pico Blvd Los Angeles, CA 90064 800-321-9792, 310-477-4262 FAX: 310-473-7498 E-mail: smrr64@aol.com	parts

See full listing in **Section One** under **Rolls-Royce/Bentley**

Royal Coach Works Ltd 2146 Lunceford Ln Lilburn, GA 30047 PH/FAX: 770-736-3960 E-mail: royalrow@cs.com	appraisals

See full listing in **Section Two** under **appraisals**

Steelwings
229 Railroad Dr
Ivyland, PA 18974
215-322-7420 parts/service
PH/FAX: 215-322-5517 sales

parts
sales
service

Mail order and open shop. Monday-Friday 8 am to 5 pm, open most weekends (call to confirm). Specializing in Aston Martin Lagonda. Prewar-current. Large selection of cars for sale. Advice on sales or service freely given. Web site: www.steelwings.com

AUBURN

Firewall Insulators & Quiet Ride Solutions
6465 Pacific Ave, Ste 249
Stockton, CA 95207
209-477-4840; FAX: 209-477-0918
E-mail: timcox@quietride.com

air plenums
auto insulation
firewall insulators
gloveboxes
sound deadening

See full listing in **Section Two** under **upholstery**

Interesting Parts Inc
Paul TerHorst
27526 N Owens Rd
Mundelein, IL 60060-9608
PH/FAX: 847-949-1030
847-558-9732 cell
E-mail: pterhorst@interaccess.com

automobilia

See full listing in **Section Two** under **comprehensive parts**

NATMUS Roadside Market
1000 Gordon M Buehrig Pl
Auburn, IN 46706
PH/FAX: 219-925-9100
E-mail: natmus@ctlnet.com

automobilia

See full listing in **Section Two** under **automobilia**

John's Car Corner
Rt 5, PO Box 85
Westminster, VT 05158
802-722-3180; FAX: 802-722-3181

body/mech parts
car dealer
repairs/restoration

See full listing in **Section One** under **Volkswagen**

Neuspeed
3300 Corte Manpaso
Camarillo, CA 93012
805-388-7171; FAX: 805-388-0030

parts

Mail order and open shop. Monday-Friday 8 am to 5 pm PST. Specializing in Audi A4 and A6, Volkswagen (watercooled only) 1975-up and Honda Civic, Accord, Acura. Web site: www.neuspeed.com

BritBooks
PO Box 321
Otego, NY 13825
PH/FAX: 607-988-7956
E-mail: britbooks@britbooks.com

books

See full listing in **Section Four** under **books & publications**

British Triumph & Metropolitan
9957 Frederick Rd
Ellicott City, MD 21042-3647
410-750-2352 evenings
E-mail: pete_groh@yahoo.com

British Leyland
original British
keys
WASO
Wilmot Breeden

See full listing in **Section One** under **Metropolitan**

Downton
91 Eastgate St
N Elmham
Norfolk NR20 5HE England
+44 1362 667122; FAX: +44 1362 667133
E-mail: downton@compaqnet.co.uk

minis
rebuilding

Specializing in Austin and Morris Mini. We specializing in rebuilding and converting the finest Minis to customer order. We offer unique upgrades exclusive to Downton, walnut, leather, sports suspension and tuned engines up to 107 bhp. Contact in the US: PH: 732-310-8553; FAX: 732-863-1331, New Jersey. Web site: www.downton.com or www.njminis.com

Don Flye
5 Doe Valley Rd
Petersham, MA 01366
978-724-3318

parts

See full listing in **Section One** under **Austin-Healey**

Jaguar Car Keys
9957 Frederick Rd
Ellicott City, MD 21042-3647
410-750-2352
E-mail: petegroh@yahoo.com

original British
keys

See full listing in **Section One** under **Jaguar**

Kip Motor Company Inc
2127 Crown Rd
Dallas, TX 75229
972-243-0440; FAX: 972-243-2387
E-mail: kipmotor@aol.com

literature
parts
restoration

Mail order and open shop. Monday-Friday 9 am to 6 pm, Saturday 9 am to 12 noon. Parts, service, restoration, manuals and literature, etc, for British orphans: Austin, Berkeley, English Ford, Hillman, Humber, Metropolitan, Morris, Riley, Sunbeam-Talbot, Singer, Triumph Herald, Vauxhall, Vanden Plas, etc. Free catalogs. Complete restoration shop. Web site: www.kipmotor.com

Mini Store
PO Box 7973
Van Nuys, CA 91409-7973
PH/FAX: 818-893-1421
E-mail: minicoopers@socal.rr.com

cars
repairs
restorations

Open by appointment only. Specializing in restored Minis, restorations of Minis and complete mechanical repairs. Also bench labor available for Austin, Morris Mini, Cooper and Cooper S cars.

Patton Orphan Spares | parts
52 Nicole Pl
West Babylon, NY 11704
516-669-2598

See full listing in **Section One** under **Renault**

The Presidential Cars Museum | museum
Chateau de Montjalin
Sauvigny le Bois 89200 France
(333) 863-44642
FAX: (333) 863-16683
E-mail: odelafon@aol.com

See full listing in **Section Six** under **France**

Seven Enterprises Ltd | accessories parts
802 Bluecrab Rd, Ste 100
Newport News, VA 23606
800-992-7007; FAX: 800-296-3327
E-mail: seven@7ent.com

Mail order and open shop. Monday-Friday 10 am to 6 pm. Parts and accessories for Mini Cooper and MGB. Competition parts also for Mini-Mini Coopers 1959-present, MGB 1962-1980. Web site: www.7ent.com

West of England Transport Collection | museum
15, Land Park
Chulmleigh Devon EX18 7BH England
01769 580811

See full listing in **Section Six** under **England**

1 CAAT Limited Co | restoration
1324 E Harper Ave
Maryville, TN 37804
865-983-7180
E-mail: jhenriks@icx.net

See full listing in **Section Two** under **restoration shops**

American-Foreign Auto Electric Inc | parts rebuilding
103 Main St
Souderton, PA 18964
215-723-4877

See full listing in **Section Two** under **electrical systems**

Apple Hydraulics Inc | brake rebuilding shock rebuilding
1610 Middle Rd
Calverton, NY 11933-1419
800-882-7753, 631-369-9515
FAX: 631-369-9516
E-mail: info@applehydraulics.com

See full listing in **Section Two** under **suspension parts**

Automotive Artistry | restoration
679 W Streetboro St
Hudson, OH 44236
330-650-1503
E-mail: dale@cmh.net

See full listing in **Section One** under **Triumph**

British Auto Shoppe | parts service
1909 5th Ave
Moline, IL 61265
309-764-9513; FAX: 309-764-9576

See full listing in **Section One** under **MG**

British Car Keys | keys
Rt 144 Box 9957
Ellicott City, MD 21042-3647
410-750-2352
E-mail: britishcarkeys@hotmail.com

Mail order only. Specializing in original Wilmot Breeden keys for British cars. Keys have letters and numbers on side of key. For early British cars, Jaguar, MG, Triumph, Austin, 1949-1969. Web site: http://britishcarkeys.com

British Car Specialists | parts repairs restoration
2060 N Wilson Way
Stockton, CA 95205
209-948-8767; FAX: 209-948-1030
E-mail: healeydoc@aol.com

Specializing in service, repairs, parts, restorations for British cars, MG, Jaguar, Austin-Healey, Triumph, Rover. Web site: www.britishcarspecialists.com

British Miles | accessories literature parts restoration
9278 Old E Tyburn Rd
Morrisville, PA 19067
215-736-9300; FAX: 215-736-3089

See full listing in **Section One** under **MG**

British Parts NW | parts
4105 SE Lafayette Hwy
Dayton, OR 97114
503-864-2001; FAX: 503-864-2081
E-mail: bpnw@onlinemac.com

See full listing in **Section One** under **Triumph**

British Racing Green | new parts rebuilt parts used parts
30 Aleph Dr
Newark, DE 19702
302-368-1117; FAX: 302-368-5910
E-mail: info@brgparts.com

See full listing in **Section One** under **MG**

British Restorations | car dealer restoration
4455 Paul St
Philadelphia, PA 19124
215-533-6696

See full listing in **Section One** under **Jaguar**

British Sportscars & Classics | conversion kits engines transmissions
4225 Aurora N
Seattle, WA 98103-7307
206-634-3990

See full listing in **Section One** under **Jaguars**

British Wire Wheel | hubs tires wire wheels
444 Airport Blvd, #114
Watsonville, CA 95077
800-732-9866, 831-763-4200
FAX: 831-763-1780

Mail order and open shop. Monday-Friday 8 am to 5 pm. 25 years in the business serving British car owners. We sell and service Dayton and Dunlop wire wheels, hubs, adapters, knock-offs, conversions and related wheel care items for all wire wheeled cars. Tires too, both radial and bias-ply in many top brands: Avon, Dunlop, Michelin, Vredestein, plus others. Worldwide shipping of properly mounted and balanced tire and wheel assemblies, ready to put on your car. Web site: www.britishwirewheel.com

| **Donovan Motorcar Service Inc**
4 Holmes Rd
Lenox, MA 01240
413-499-6000; FAX: 413-499-6699
E-mail: donmtcar@aol.com | race prep
restoration
service |

See full listing in **Section One** under **Jaguar**

| **Doug's British Car Parts**
2487 E Colorado Blvd
Pasadena, CA 91107
818-793-2494; FAX: 818-793-4339
E-mail: dougsbritish@msn.com | accessories
parts |

See full listing in **Section One** under **Jaguar**

| **Doug's British Car Parts**
606 Pub St
Galloway, OH 43119
614-878-6373; FAX: 614-688-3077
E-mail: braden.13@osu.edu | accessories
parts |

See full listing in **Section One** under **Triumph**

| **English Auto**
501 Mt Ephraim Rd
Searsport, ME 04974
207-548-2946; FAX: 207-548-6470
E-mail: eauto@mint.net | restoration |

Specializing in restoration of British and classic cars. Web site: www.englishautousa.com

| **Don Flye**
5 Doe Valley Rd
Petersham, MA 01366
978-724-3318 | parts |

Mail order and open shop by appointment only. Specializing in British used parts for Austin-Healey 100-6 thru BJ8, Austin America, MG TD, A, Midget and B, Triumph TR3-TR6.

| **Fourintune Garage Inc**
W63 N147 Washington Ave
Cedarburg, WI 53012
262-375-0876; FAX: 262-675-2874 | restoration |

Open shop, Monday-Friday, 9 am to 5 pm CST. Specializes in Austin-Healey restoration. We can locate and restore to your specifications.

| **Harbor Auto Restoration**
315 SW 15th Ave
Pompano Beach, FL 33069
954-785-7887; FAX: 954-785-7388
E-mail: harbor@harbor-auto.com | restoration |

See full listing in **Section Two** under **restoration shops**

| **Healey Lane**
5920 Jones Ave
Riverside, CA 92505
800-411-HEALEY (4325)
FAX: 909-689-4934
E-mail: healeylane@aol.com | parts
restoration
service |

Austin-Healey restoration, parts, service, sales for all years and models made 1953-1967.

| **Healey Surgeons Inc**
7211 Carroll Ave
Takoma Park, MD 20912
301-270-8811; FAX: 301-270-8812 | parts
restoration |

Mail order and open shop. Monday-Friday 9:30 am to 5 pm. Parts and restoration for Austin-Healey 100-4, 100-6, 3000, 1953-1967.

| **Heritage Upholstery and Trim**
250 H St, PMB 3000
Blaine, WA 98231
604-990-0346; FAX: 604-990-9988 | interior kits
trim
upholstery |

Classic British car upholstery and trim using original materials, Connolly Leather, Wilton Wool. Interior kits to a very high standard. Concours show quality. Web site: www.heritagetrim.com

| **International Restoration Specialist Inc**
PO Box 1303
Mt Airy, NC 27030
336-789-1548 | parts
restoration
sales |

See full listing in **Section Two** under **restoration shops**

| **Lake Oswego Restorations**
19621 S Hazelhurst Ln
West Linn, OR 97068
PH/FAX: 503-636-7503 | restoration
sales |

See full listing in **Section One** under **Aston Martin**

| **Mini Motors Classic Coachworks**
2775 Cherry Ave NE
Salem, OR 97303
503-362-3187; FAX: 503-375-9609
E-mail: urbanbugeye@cs.com | parts
restoration
sales
service |

Mail order and open shop. Monday-Friday 8 am to 5:30 pm, evening/weekend appointments available. Typically 15-20 restorations ongoing. Services: body fabrication, paint, interior, mechanical service, parts and sales, custom parts casting and manufacturing. In business for 21 years, specializing in British cars and other collectibles. Ask about our 5-speed transmission conversion for Sprite/Midgets and factory replica hardtops for Austin-Healey Mk I Sprites.

| **Motorhead Ltd**
2811-B Old Lee Hwy
Fairfax, VA 22031
800-527-3140; FAX: 703-573-3195 | parts
repairs |

Parts, repairs and restoration of British sports cars. Please ask for parts catalogs on MGB, Sprite, Midget, Spitfire, TR6, TR250, TR7, TR8. Web site: www.motorheadltd.com

| **Omni Specialties**
10418 Lorain Ave
Cleveland, OH 44111
888-819-6464 (MGMG)
216-251-2269; FAX: 216-251-6083 | parts
restoration
service |

See full listing in **Section One** under **MG**

| **Ragtops & Roadsters**
203 S 4th St
Perkasie, PA 18944
215-257-1202; FAX: 215-257-2688
E-mail: info@ragtops.com | bodywork/painting
British automobiles
engine rebuilding
vintage race prep |

See full listing in **Section One** under **AC**

| **Rogers Motors**
34 Codeyville Rd, PO Box 603
Shutesbury, MA 01072
413-259-1722
E-mail: jollyrogersmo@hotmail.com | used parts |

See full listing in **Section One** under **Jaguar**

| **Smooth Line**
2562 Riddle Run Rd
Tarentum, PA 15084
724-274-6002; FAX: 724-274-6121 | body panels
removable hardtops |

See full listing in **Section Two** under **tops**

Sports Car Haven
2-33 Flowerfield Industrial Pk
St James, NY 11780
631-862-8058
E-mail: sch94@aol.com

new & used parts
race prep
restoration
service

See full listing in **Section One** under **Triumph**

Sports Car Haven
3414 Bloom Rd, Rt 11
Danville, PA 17821
570-275-5705

parts
restoration
service

See full listing in **Section Two** under **restoration shops**

Sports Car Rentals & Sales
PO Box 265
Batesville, VA 22924
804-823-4442
E-mail: info@sportscarrentals.com

car rentals

See full listing in **Section Two** under **special services**

Sports Car Services
2450 Westminster W Rd
Westminster, VT 05158
802-387-4540

parts
service

See full listing in **Section One** under **MG**

Triple C Motor Accessories
1900 Orange St
York, PA 17404
717-854-4081; FAX: 717-854-6706
E-mail: sales@triple-c.com

accessories
models

See full listing in **Section One** under **MG**

Van Nuys M-B
14422 Oxnard St
Van Nuys, CA 91403
818-988-5455

parts
restoration
sales
service

See full listing in **Section One** under **Mercedes-Benz**

Victoria British Ltd
Box 14991
Lenexa, KS 66285-4991
800-255-0088, 913-599-3299

accessories
parts

See full listing in **Section One** under **MG**

Von's Austin-Healey Restorations
10270 Barberville Rd
Fort Mill, SC 29715
803-548-4590; FAX: 803-548-4816
E-mail: vons@vnet.net

parts
repairs
restoration

Mail order and open shop. Monday-Thursday 7 am to 6 pm. Specializing in Austin-Healey restoration, repair and service. We also do mail-in repair service and parts sales. Although Austin-Healey is our specialty, we do restore all British cars. Web site: www.vonsaustinhealey.com

---

White Post Restorations
One Old Car Dr, PO Drawer D
White Post, VA 22663
540-837-1140; FAX: 540-837-2368
E-mail: info@whitepost.com

brakes
restoration

See full listing in **Section Two** under **brakes**

Avanti Auto Service
Rt 322, 67 Conchester Hwy
Glen Mills, PA 19342-1506
610-558-9999

repair
restoration

See full listing in **Section Two** under **restoration shops**

Nostalgic Motor Cars
47400 Avante Dr
Wixom, MI 48393
248-349-4884, 800-AVANTI-1
800-AVANTI-X; FAX: 248-349-0000

car dealer
parts

Mail order and open shop. Avanti dealer, cars and parts. World's largest manufacturer and supplier of 1963-1985 Avanti parts.

Penn Auto Sales Co
3131 Draper Drive, Unit G
Fairfax, VA 22031
PH/FAX: 703-278-9299
E-mail: rogrpenn@netscape.net

car dealer
parts
service

Mail order and shop open by appointment only. Avanti sales. All years. Avanti factory franchised dealer since 1970. Parts and service, 1963-1991. Also will provide information on restoration and parts.

Southwest Avanti Sales & Service
7110 N Red Ledge Dr, Ste #147A
Phoenix, AZ 85253
480-948-7853; FAX: 240-525-0518
E-mail: wfsf602@aol.com

parts
repairs
sales

Mail order and open shop. Monday-Saturday 8 am to 6 pm. Complete Avanti store. Sales, repairs, parts, restorations of all Avantis, 1963-1991.

Volunteer Studebaker
228 Marquiss Cir
Clinton, TN 37716
615-457-3002; FAX: 775-514-1386
E-mail: studebaker_joe@msn.com

parts
parts locator

See full listing in **Section One** under **Studebaker**

2002 AD
11066 Tuxford St
Sun Valley, CA 91352
800-420-0223; FAX: 818-768-2697
E-mail: bmwsales@2002ad.com

cars
parts
restoration

Mail order and open shop. Monday-Friday 8 am to 5 pm, Saturday 8 am to 2 pm PST. Specializing in parts, restoration, car sales, auto repair for BMW classic cars, 1950s, 1960s, 1970s, 1980s. Web site: www.2002ad.com

Asom Electric
1204 McClellan Dr
Los Angeles, CA 90025
310-820-4457; FAX: 310-820-5908

electrical systems
rebuilding

See full listing in **Section Two** under **electrical systems**

The Auto Doctor Inc
23125 Telegraph Rd
Southfield, MI 48034
248-355-1505; FAX: 248-355-3460

mechanical parts
service repairs

Mail order and open shop. Monday-Friday 7 am to 6 pm, Saturday 9 am to 3 pm. Mechanical parts and service repairs for BMW, Jaguar, Saab, Audi, VW, Porsche, Mercedes and Range Rover.

Autosport Inc
2110 W Vernal Pk
Bloomington, IN 47404
812-334-1700; FAX: 812-334-1712

restoration

See full listing in **Section One** under **MG**

Bavarian Autosport
275 Constitution Ave
Portsmouth, NH 03801
800-535-2002; FAX: 800-507-2002

accessories
parts

Telephone orders Monday-Thursday 8 am to 9 pm, Friday 8 am to 7 pm, Saturday 9 am to 4 pm; catalog showroom open Monday-Friday 9 am to 5:30 pm, Saturday 9 am to 4 pm. When your BMW mechanic says he can't get it, chances are we can. Our 3-story warehouse contains thousands of parts and accessories for 1600, 2002, 2800, 3.0, Bavaria and all others. Same day shipping of in-stock items. FedEx 3-day Express Service is standard. Free 116-page color catalog. Web site: www.bavauto.com

Bavarian Quality Parts
A Silvermine Classics Inc Company
2205 Rt 82
LaGrangeville, NY 12540
800-782-7199; FAX: 845-223-5394
E-mail: sales@bavarianquality.com

parts

Mail order and web only. I specialize in outstanding customer service and a huge inventory with the most part numbers in the business for Series 1600-2002, Bavarian and CS, 3-5-6-7 and 8 Series, Z Series classic BMWs. Parts are easy to find in our unique sectioned catalog. Order on-line or call for your free catalog. Web site: www.bavarianquality.com

BCP Sport & Classic Co
10525 Airline Dr
Houston, TX 77037
281-448-4739; FAX: 281-448-0189

parts
service

See full listing in **Section One** under **MG**

Bentley Publishers
1734 Massachusetts Ave
Cambridge, MA 02138-1804
800-423-4595; FAX: 617-876-9235
E-mail: sales@rb.com

books
manuals

See full listing in **Section Four** under **books & publications**

Bimmer Magazine
42 Digital Dr #5
Novato, CA 94949
415-382-0580; FAX: 415-382-0587

magazine

See full listing in **Section Four** under **periodicals**

BMW Group
Petuelring 130
Munchen 80788
Bavaria Germany
089-382-23307
FAX: 089-382-43601
E-mail: bmw.tradition@bmw.de

museum

See full listing in **Section Six** under **Bavaria**

Bud's Parts for Classic Mercedes-Benz
9130 Hwy 5
Douglasville, GA 30134
800-942-8444; FAX: 770-942-8400

parts
restoration
service

See full listing in **Section One** under **Mercedes-Benz**

Concours Cars of Colorado Ltd
2414 W Cucharras St
Colorado Springs, CO 80904
719-473-6288; FAX: 719-473-9206

accessories
parts
service

Concours Cars, established in 1978. Provides professional service, parts, select accessories and performance tuning on European automobiles. We service all European cars from Britain, Italy, Germany, Sweden and France. We are a Bosch authorized service center and all our technicians are ASE Master techs.

CSi
1100 S Raymond Ave, Ste H
Fullerton, CA 92831
714-879-7955; FAX: 714-879-7310
E-mail: csila@compuserve.com

parts

Mail order and open shop. Monday-Friday 9 am to 7 pm. Specializing in new and used parts, performance upgrades and accessories for all BMWs and all Japanese marques, of all years. Web site: www.partsbytel.com

Foreign Motors West
253 N Main St
Natick, MA 01760
508-655-5350; FAX: 508-651-0178

car sales

See full listing in **Section One** under **Rolls-Royce/Bentley**

Griot's Garage
3500-A 20th St E
Tacoma, WA 98424
800-345-5789; FAX: 888-252-2252
E-mail: info@griotsgarage.com

car care products
paint
tools

See full listing in **Section Two** under **tools**

Hjeltness Restoration Inc
630 Alpine Way
Escondido, CA 92029
760-746-9966; FAX: 760-746-7738

restoration
service

See full listing in **Section Two** under **restoration shops**

International Automobile Archives
Kai Jacobsen
Wiesenweg 3b
85757 Karlsfeld Germany
011-49-8131-93158
FAX: 011-49-8131-505973
E-mail: doubledseven@t-online.de

sales literature

See full listing in **Section Two** under **literature dealers**

JAM Engineering Corp
PO Box 2570
Monterey, CA 93942
800-JAM-CORP, 831-372-1787
E-mail: jam@jameng.com

carburetors

See full listing in **Section Two** under **carburetors**

Maximillian Importing Co Inc   parts
PO Box 749
Parkton, MD 21120
800-950-2002; FAX: 410-357-0298
E-mail: max2002cs@aol.com

Mail order. New, used and reproduction parts for classic BMW models from 1928-present. Specialist in the 2002, 3.0 CS, Bavaria models, as well as seemingly unique/hard to find parts. Web site: www.partsforbmws.com

Thomas Montanari Automotive Artist   illustrations paintings prints
51 Lamb-Hope Rd
Hopewell, NJ 08525
609-466-7753; FAX: 609-466-7939
E-mail: tmontanari@aol.com

See full listing in **Section Two** under **artwork**

Palo Alto Speedometer   instruments
718 Emerson St
Palo Alto, CA 94301
650-323-0243; FAX: 650-323-4632
E-mail: pacspeedo@pacbell.net

See full listing in **Section One** under **Mercedes-Benz**

Peninsula Imports   accessories parts trim
3749 Harlem Rd
Buffalo, NY 14215
800-999-1209; FAX: 905-847-3021
E-mail: imports@ican.net

Mail order and open shop. Monday-Friday 8 am to 5:30 pm, Saturday 8 am to 2 pm. We specialize in distribution of hard parts, accessories and trim, including starters, alternators, European lighting, Weber carburetors, ignition, fuel system, exhaust, gaskets, filters, radiators, rubber parts, steering wheels, suspension, tops, bras, car covers, transmissions, engines, cams, pistons, bearings, brakes, clutch and hydraulic parts, carpet kits, interior panels, body panels, glass, etc. For Audi, BMW, Mercedes, VW, Porsche, Saab, Volvo, MG, Triumph, Jaguar, Alfa Romeo, Fiat, Ferrari, Lamborghini, Maserati, Honda, Mazda, Hyundai, Toyota, Mitsubishi, Nissan, etc. Web site: www.peninsulaimports.com

John T Poulin   car dealer parts restoration service
Auto Sales/Star Service Center
5th Ave & 111th St
North Troy, NY 12182
518-235-8610

See full listing in **Section Two** under **car dealers**

Rocky Mountain Motorworks Inc   accessories parts
1003 Tamarac Pkwy
Woodland Park, CO 80863
800-258-1996; FAX: 800-544-1084
E-mail: sales@motorworks.com

See full listing in **Section One** under **Volkswagen**

Vintage Auto Parts   car dealer new/used parts
PO Box 323
Temple, PA 19560-0323
610-939-9593

Mail order or by special appointment. 10 am to 12 noon, 5 pm to 7 pm answering machine. Specializing in BMW 300, 600 and 700, Crosley, Corvair, Citicar (EV), Fiat 500 and 600, Honda 600 and Civic, 1950 Jeepster, Metro, NSU, Panhard, Subaru 360, VW II, III, IV and 181 and LeCar. Also Zundapp cycle and NSU. Special interest cars and new and used parts cars, $250-up. Thousands of new parts for Subaru 360 cars. SASE for info. 100 vehicles, restore or parts, no list. Plan on selling out by end of 2001, including lot, available offers over $75,000.

Vintage Sales   sales
Paul Padget
7641 Reinhold Dr
Cincinnati, OH 45237
513-821-2143

See full listing in **Section One** under **Mercedes-Benz**

White Post Restorations   brakes restoration
One Old Car Dr, PO Drawer D
White Post, VA 22663
540-837-1140; FAX: 540-837-2368
E-mail: info@whitepost.com

See full listing in **Section Two** under **brakes**

Bricklin

Bob's Brickyard Inc   parts
1030 N Hickory Ridge Tr
Milford, MI 48380
248-685-9508; FAX: 248-685-8662
E-mail: bobsbrick@aol.com

Mail order parts and total restoration. Specialize in Bricklin parts and service. Free parts list.

Bricklin Literature   collectibles literature
3116 Welsh Rd
Philadelphia, PA 19136-1810
888-392-4832, Ext 215-338-6142
E-mail: bricklin.literature@excite.com

Mail order only. Carry a variety of collectible items such as literature, books, toys, magazines, video, music, and other unique items related to the Canadian made Bricklin automobile made during 1974-1976. Please send a SASE for a complete listing of items available. All items guaranteed for satisfaction. Web site: http://bricklinliterature.econgo.com/

Conte's Corvettes & Classics   leasing parts sales service
851 W Wheat Rd
Vineland, NJ 08360
856-692-0087; FAX: 856-692-1009
E-mail: corvettes@contes.com

See full listing in **Section One** under **Corvette**

The Gullwing Garage Ltd   appraisals literature parts service
Bricklin SVI Specialists
5 Cimorelli Dr
New Windsor, NY 12553-6201
845-561-0019 anytime

Telephone calls accepted until 10 pm, 7 days a week. Parts service, appraisals, pre-purchase assistance literature for Bricklin SVI, 1974-1976. Over 7,000 original genuine Bricklin parts (1974-1976) with access to thousands more. Aftermarket items such as: consoles, carpet sets, seat covers, fiberglass panels, air scoops, ground affects, gas shocks, antennas, radios, wheels, s/s exhaust pipes. Specializing in air door systems, headlight systems and door glass track system repairs. Prompt, personal, friendly service. Will travel to repair your Bricklin.

Betws-Y-Coed Motor Museum Betws-Y-Coed Conwy Valley Gwynedd LL24 0AH England 01690710760	museum

See full listing in **Section Six** under **England**

Blackhawk Collection 1092 Eagles Nest Pl Danville, CA 94506-3600 925-736-3444; FAX: 925-736-4375 E-mail: info@blackhawkcollection.com	acquisitions sales

See full listing in **Section One** under **Duesenberg**

Charles S Crail Automobiles 36A Calle Cesar Chavez Santa Barbara, CA 93103 805-568-1934; FAX: 805-568-1533 E-mail: crailauto@aol.com	auto sales

See full listing in **Section One** under **Rolls-Royce/Bentley**

Dragone Classic Motorcars 1797 Main St Bridgeport, CT 06604 203-335-4643; FAX: 203-335-9798	car dealer

See full listing in **Section Two** under **car dealers**

Guild of Automotive Restorers 44 Bridge St, PO Box 1150 Bradford, ON Canada L3Z 2B5 905-775-0499; FAX: 905-775-0944 E-mail: cars@guildclassiccars.com	restoration sales service

See full listing in **Section Two** under **restoration shops**

LMARR Disk Ltd PO Box 910 Glen Ellen, CA 95442-0910 707-938-9347; FAX: 707-938-3020 E-mail: lmarr@attglobal.net	wheel discs

See full listing in **Section One** under **Rolls-Royce/Bentley**

Northern Motorsport Ltd PO Box 1028, Rt 5 Wilder, VT 05088 802-296-2099; FAX: 802-295-6599 E-mail: bugatti46@aol.com	repair restoration sales service

See full listing in **Section Two** under **restoration shops**

Viking Worldwise Inc 190 Doe Run Rd Manheim, PA 17545 866-CJACKETS; FAX: 717-664-5556 E-mail: gkurien@dejazz.com	leather jackets

See full listing in **Section Two** under **apparel**

12 Volt Stuff, Radio & **Speedometer Repair Co** 10625-A Trade Rd Richmond, VA 23236 804-423-1055, 888-487-3500 toll free FAX: 804-423-1059 E-mail: ecs@12voltstuff.com	radios

See full listing in **Section Two** under **radios**

12 Volt Stuff, Radio & **Speedometer Repair Co** 10625-A Trade Rd Richmond, VA 23236 804-423-1055, 888-487-3500 toll free FAX: 804-423-1059 E-mail: ecs@12voltstuff.com	radios

See full listing in **Section Two** under **instruments**

A-1 Shock Absorber Co Shockfinders Division 365 Warren Ave, PO Box 2028 Silverthorne, CO 80498 800-344-1966, 970-389-3193 cell FAX: 970-513-8283	shocks-all types coil springs Koni shocks leaf springs steering gears

See our ad on the last page

Apple Hydraulics Inc 1610 Middle Rd Calverton, NY 11933-1419 800-882-7753, 631-369-9515 FAX: 631-369-9516 E-mail: info@applehydraulics.com	brake rebuilding shock rebuilding

See full listing in **Section Two** under **suspension parts**

Art's Antique & Classic Auto Services 1985 E 5th St #16 Tempe, AZ 85281 480-966-1195	restoration

Open Monday-Friday 9 am to 5 pm, Saturday 10 am to 3 pm.
Restoration of Buick cars, 1950s and 1960s. Also other GM cars.

Auto Hardware Specialties 3123 McKinley Ave Sheldon, IA 51201 712-324-2091; FAX: 712-324-2480 E-mail: rweber@rconnect.com	hardware fasteners

See full listing in **Section One** under **Chevrolet**

Be Happy Automatic **Transmission Parts** 414 Stivers Rd Hillsboro, OH 45133 937-442-6133; FAX: 937-442-5016	trans rebuild kits

See full listing in **Section Two** under **transmissions**

Bicknell Engine Company 7055 Dayton Rd Enon, OH 45323 937-864-5224	parts repair restoration

Mail order and open shop. Evenings and weekends only. Repair
service for antique, classic and special interest cars. Specializing

in Buicks and independent make cars from the 1920s-1950s. Services include: engine rebuilding, transmission rebuilding (manual and automatic), any mechanical or electrical work. Buick parts, mostly used, some NOS. Appraisal service.

Bob's Automobilia
Box 2119
Atascadero, CA 93423
805-434-2963; FAX: 805-434-2626
E-mail: bobsbuick@thegrid.net

accessories
parts

Mail order only. 1920-56 Buick parts, accessories, manuals, hubcaps, hood ornaments, floor mats. Electrical, rubber, trunk lenses. Catalog available.

Boyer's Restorations
Skip Boyer
1348 Carlisle Pike
Hanover, PA 17331
717-632-0670
E-mail: boyersrestorations@blazenet.net

parts
repairs
restorations

Mail order and open shop by appointment only. Exclusively Buick parts, new and used as well as reproductions, servicing primarily 1937-1974. Manifolds and machine turned dashes a specialty, as well as interior plastic parts, 1937-1950. 1940-1942 Buick dash restorations and partial restorations and repairs for 1937-1974. Web site: http://boyers.i.am

Buick Bonery
6970 Stamper Way
Sacramento, CA 95828
916-381-5271; FAX: 916-381-0702
E-mail: buickbonery@webtv.net

parts

Mail order and open shop. Monday-Friday before 9 am and after 12 noon PST. Specializing in Buick new, used and repro parts. Full scope stainless restoration for any make. 150+ parts Buicks, 1936-1975. Restored and better Buicks warehoused.

The Buick Nut-Joe Krepps
2486 Pacer Ln S
Cocoa, FL 32926-2606
PH/FAX: 321-636-8777
E-mail: buicknut@palmnet.net

repro parts

Mail order. Reproductions 1929-1931. Runningboard moldings and end caps, wood and wire wheel hubcaps. 1929-1935 high speed differential gears 3.5:1 ratio. 1937, 1938, 1940 grille emblems. 1940-1947 dash instrument plastics. 1971-1975 fiberglass convertible parade boots for GM B-body cars.

Buick Specialists
1311 S Central Ave #G
Kent, WA 98032
253-852-0584; FAX: 253-854-7520

parts

Mail order and open shop. Specialists in 1946-1979 Buicks. New, used and NOS parts for all models.

Chevrolet Parts Obsolete
PO Box 70027
Riverside, CA 92513-0027
909-340-2979; FAX: 909-279-4013
E-mail: cpo@att.net

accessories
parts

See full listing in **Section One** under **Chevrolet**

Classic Buicks Inc
4632 Riverside Dr
Chino, CA 91710-3926
909-591-0283; FAX: 909-627-6094

custom parts
high-performance
parts
literature

Mail order and open shop. Monday-Friday 9 am to 4 pm PST. Specializing in parts and literature for 1946-1975 Buicks. Our specialty is quality USA made engine and high-performance, rubber and weatherstrips, brake, chassis, carpets and restoration parts. Complete online catalog. Web site: www.classicbuicks.com

Classic Car Works Ltd
3050 Upper Bethany Rd
Jasper, GA 30143
770-735-3945

restoration

See full listing in **Section Two** under **restoration shops**

JA Cooley Museum
4233 Park Blvd
San Diego, CA 92103
619-296-3112

museum

See full listing in **Section Six** under **California**

Coopers Vintage Auto Parts
3087 N California St
Burbank, CA 91504
818-567-4140; FAX: 818-567-4101

parts

See full listing in **Section One** under **Cadillac/LaSalle**

D&J GTO Parts
Dan Gregory
11283 Main St
Stoutsville, OH 43154
740-474-4614; FAX: 740-474-2314
E-mail: djgto@hotmail.com

parts

See full listing in **Section One** under **Pontiac**

Durabuilt Automotive Hydraulics
808 Meadows Ave
Canon City, CO 81212
PH/FAX: 719-275-1126

hose assemblies
pumps, top cylinders
valves
window cylinders

See full listing in **Section Two** under **tops**

Egge Machine Company Inc
11707 Slauson Ave
Santa Fe Springs, CA 90670-2217
800-866-3443, 562-945-3419
FAX: 562-693-1635
E-mail: info@egge.com

bearings
gaskets
pistons/rings
timing components
valvetrain

See full listing in **Section Two** under **engine parts**

Elliott's Car Radio
313 Linfield Rd
Parkerford, PA 19457
610-495-6360; FAX: 610-495-7723
E-mail: elliottradio@aol.com

radio repairs
speaker kits

See full listing in **Section Two** under **radios**

Firewall Insulators & Quiet Ride Solutions
6465 Pacific Ave, Ste 249
Stockton, CA 95207
209-477-4840; FAX: 209-477-0918
E-mail: timcox@quietride.com

air plenums
auto insulation
firewall insulators
gloveboxes
sound deadening

See full listing in **Section Two** under **upholstery**

GM Obsolete
909 W Magnolia St
Phoenix, AZ 85007
602-253-8081; FAX: 602-253-8411
E-mail: info@gmobsolete.com

parts

Mail order and open shop. Monday-Friday 8 am to 6 pm, Saturday 9 am to 2 pm. Specializing in Buick, Oldsmobile and Cadillac parts, 1950-1990. Web site: www.gmobsolete.com

Green Valentine Inc | car dealer / woodies
5055 Covington Way
Memphis, TN 38134
901-373-5555; FAX: 901-373-5568

See full listing in **Section Two** under **car dealers**

Hamel's Automotive Inc | restorations
3306 Pleasant Ridge Rd
Wingdale, NY 12594
845-832-9454
E-mail: startnagan@aol.com

See full listing in **Section Two** under **restoration shops**

Hampton Coach | fabrics / interior kits / top kits
6 Chestnut St, PO Box 6
Amesbury, MA 01913
888-388-8726, 978-388-8047
FAX: 978-388-1113
E-mail: lbb-hc@greenet.net

See full listing in **Section One** under **Chevrolet**

Harbor Auto Restoration | restoration
315 SW 15th Ave
Pompano Beach, FL 33069
954-785-7887; FAX: 954-785-7388
E-mail: harbor@harbor-auto.com

See full listing in **Section Two** under **restoration shops**

Harnesses Unlimited | wiring harnesses / wiring supplies
PO Box 435
Wayne, PA 19087
610-688-3998

See full listing in **Section Two** under **electrical systems**

Integrity Machine | brake masters / clutch masters / wheel cylinders
383 Pipe Stave Hollow Rd
Mount Sinai, NY 11766
888-446-9670; FAX: 516-476-9675

See full listing in **Section Two** under **brakes**

J & C's Parts | parts
7127 Ward Rd
North Tonawanda, NY 14120
716-693-4090; FAX: 716-695-7144

We offer new and used 1953-1976 Buick stock and high-performance engine parts and services to include engine, carburetor, and distributor rebuilding. Also new and used restoration parts are available for 1965-1976 Buicks. We offer distributors and carburetors for 1953-1974 GM, Chrysler and Ford cars to include popular and hard-to-find numbers. Electronic ignition conversion service and kits available. ROA, GSCA, BCA member.

JECC Inc | chassis parts / gaskets / transmissions
PO Box 616
West Paterson, NJ 07424
973-890-9682; FAX: 973-812-2724

Mail order only. Specializing in torque ball seal kits, transmission gaskets and seal kits for Buicks 1934-1960. Revulcanizing torque balls for 1939 Buicks. U-joint seal kits for Chevys 1929-1954. Packard flywheel ring gears (new), 1937-1953.

Lares Manufacturing | power steering / equipment
805 S Cleveland
Cambridge, MN 55008
800-334-5749; FAX: 763-754-2853
E-mail: sales@larescorp.com

See full listing in **Section One** under **Ford 1954-up**

Lloyd's Literature | literature
PO Box 491
Newbury, OH 44065
800-292-2665, 440-338-1527
FAX: 440-338-2222
E-mail: lloydslit@aol.com

See full listing in **Section Two** under **literature dealers**

M & H Electric Fabricators Inc | wiring harnesses
13537 Alondra Blvd
Santa Fe Springs, CA 90670
562-926-9552; FAX: 562-926-9572
E-mail: sales@wiringharness.com

See full listing in **Section Two** under **electrical systems**

Normans' Classic Auto Radio | custom sales
8475 68th Way
Pinellas Park, FL 33781
727-546-1788

See full listing in **Section Two** under **radios**

Opel GT Source | parts / service / technical info
18211 Zeni Ln
Tuolumne, CA 95379
209-928-1110; FAX: 209-928-3298
E-mail: opelgts@opelgtsource.com

See full listing in **Section One** under **Opel**

Opels Unlimited | parts / service
1310 Tamarind Ave
Rialto, CA 92376
562-690-1051, 909-355-OPEL (6735)
FAX: 562-690-3352
E-mail: opelsunl@opelsunl.com

See full listing in **Section One** under **Opel**

Dennis Portka | horns / knock-off wheels
4326 Beetow Dr
Hamburg, NY 14075
716-649-0921

See full listing in **Section One** under **Corvette**

Replica Plastics | fiberglass parts
260 S Oates St, Box 1147
Dothan, AL 36302
800-873-5871; FAX: 334-792-1175
E-mail: stone@ala.net

See full listing in **Section Two** under **fiberglass parts**

Rodman's Auto Wood Restoration | wood kits
Box 86 Wheeler St
Hanna, IN 46340
219-797-3775

See full listing in **Section One** under **Chevrolet**

Harry Samuel | carpet / fabrics / interiors / upholstery covers
65 Wisner St
Pontiac, MI 48342-1066
248-335-1900
E-mail: samuelinteriors@aol.com

See full listing in **Section Two** under **interiors & interior parts**

E J Serafin | manuals
Valley Rd
Matinecock, NY 11560

See full listing in **Section One** under **Cadillac/LaSalle**

Tags Backeast
PO Box 581
Plainville, CT 06062
860-747-2942
E-mail: dataplt@snet.net

data plates
trim tags
cowl tags

See full listing in **Section Two** under **special services**

Tom's Classic Parts
5207 Sundew Terr
Tobyhanna, PA 18466
PH/FAX: 570-894-1459

parts

See full listing in **Section One** under **Chevrolet**

White Post Restorations
One Old Car Dr, PO Drawer D
White Post, VA 22663
540-837-1140; FAX: 540-837-2368
E-mail: info@whitepost.com

brakes
restoration

See full listing in **Section Two** under **brakes**

White Post Restorations
One Old Car Dr, PO Drawer D
White Post, VA 22663
540-837-1140; FAX: 540-837-2368
E-mail: info@whitepost.com

restoration

See full listing in **Section Two** under **restoration shops**

**12 Volt Stuff, Radio &
Speedometer Repair Co**
10625-A Trade Rd
Richmond, VA 23236
804-423-1055, 888-487-3500 toll free
FAX: 804-423-1059
E-mail: ecs@12voltstuff.com

radios

See full listing in **Section Two** under **radios**

**12 Volt Stuff, Radio &
Speedometer Repair Co**
10625-A Trade Rd
Richmond, VA 23236
804-423-1055, 888-487-3500 toll free
FAX: 804-423-1059
E-mail: ecs@12voltstuff.com

radios

See full listing in **Section Two** under **instruments**

A-1 Shock Absorber Co
Shockfinders Division
365 Warren Ave, PO Box 2028
Silverthorne, CO 80498
800-344-1966, 970-389-3193 cell
FAX: 970-513-8283

shocks-all types
coil springs
Koni shocks
leaf springs
steering gears

See our ad on the last page

**AAAC-Antique Automobile
Appraisal & Consulting**
PO Box 700153
Plymouth, MI 48170
PH/FAX: 734-453-7644
E-mail: aaac@ameritech.net

appraisals
Cadillac parts
consulting

Mail order and open shop by appointment. Cadillac parts from 1953-1970 including some NOS. Specializing in 1957-1960.

Appraisal and consulting service by appointment for antique, custom and special interest vehicles. Detailed and comprehensive reports with photographs. Appraisals accepted by major insurance companies. Also service for sellers, buyers, divorce, estate settlement, loans and charitable contributions. Over twenty years in the old car hobby.

**Aabar's Cadillac & Lincoln
Salvage & Parts**
9700 NE 23rd St
Oklahoma City, OK 73141
405-769-3318; FAX: 405-769-9542
E-mail: aabar@ilinkusa.net

parts

Open Monday-Friday 9 am to 5:30 pm, some Saturdays 9 am to 12 pm. Mainly used parts but some NOS and NORS. 600 Cadillac cars standing, 1939-1994, and 300 Lincoln cars standing, 1941-1994, plus many parts off. Satisfaction guaranteed. Credit cards accepted. Free advice anytime. If you write, send SASE or no negative answers.

Dennis Akerman
19 Gulf Rd, Box 107
Sanbornton, NH 03269
800-487-3903; FAX: 603-286-2761
E-mail: dennis@caddyparts.com

literature
parts

Open shop by appointment. New and used Cadillac parts and literature, 1937-1976. Call, e-mail or fax your requirements. Visa/MC. Fast, courteous service. Ship worldwide. Web site: www.caddyparts.com

Antique & Classic Automobiles
Royce A Emerson
Carlisle St, Ext D
Hanover, PA 17331
717-637-8344, 717-632-9182

car dealer

See full listing in **Section Two** under **car dealers**

Apple Hydraulics Inc
1610 Middle Rd
Calverton, NY 11933-1419
800-882-7753, 631-369-9515
FAX: 631-369-9516
E-mail: info@applehydraulics.com

brake rebuilding
shock rebuilding

See full listing in **Section Two** under **suspension parts**

Archive Replacement Parts
211 Cinnaminson Ave
Palmyra, NJ 08065
609-786-0247

parts

Mail order only. Stainless steel water outlet replacements for 1936-1948 flathead V8 Cadillac/LaSalle.

Art's Antique & Classic Auto Services
1985 E 5th St #16
Tempe, AZ 85281
480-966-1195

restoration

See full listing in **Section One** under **Buick/McLaughlin**

Auto Hardware Specialties
3123 McKinley Ave
Sheldon, IA 51201
712-324-2091; FAX: 712-324-2480
E-mail: rweber@rconnect.com

hardware fasteners

See full listing in **Section One** under **Chevrolet**

C E Babcock	1941, 1942, 1946,
619 Waterside Way	**1947 Cadillac parts**
Sarasota, FL 34242	
941-349-4990; FAX: 941-349-5751	

Accommodating 1941-1947 Cadillac parts (all models): NOS, gently used and remanufactured parts (specialist). 45 years hobbyist accumulation (over 10,000 items) available. Exclusive exact reproduction of 8 pc floorboards, body braces, trunk floors, inner splash guards, stainless and chrome trim parts, battery boxes, rocker panels, special rocker clip, horn parts, large or small, I will assist you or advise. This is not a junkyard. Most parts have been on dry shelves for several years.

Be Happy Automatic	**trans rebuild kits**
Transmission Parts	
414 Stivers Rd	
Hillsboro, OH 45133	
937-442-6133; FAX: 937-442-5016	

See full listing in **Section Two** under **transmissions**

Binder's Auto Restoration and	**salvage yard**
Salvage	
PO Box 1144, 1 Mile Maud Rd	
Palmer, AK 99645	
907-745-4670; FAX: 907-745-5510	

See full listing in **Section Five** under **Alaska**

Caddy Central	**cars**
11117 Tippett Rd	**locating service**
Clinton, MD 20735	**parts**
301-234-0135; FAX: 301-234-0140	
E-mail: cadlocator@juno.com	

One stop shopping for Cadillacs, 1956-1970. Huge selection of bumpers and body parts in dry storage. Specializing in consoli-

dation of orders for cheaper overseas delivery. Honest and reliable. Locating service also available.

Caddytown™/Pawl Engineering Co	**memorabilia**
4960 Arrowhead	**parts**
PO Box 240105	**toys**
West Bloomfield, MI 48324	
PH/FAX: 248-682-2007	
E-mail: pawl@earthlink.net	

Mail order only. Specializing in Cadillac memorabilia, parts, toys, specialties, especially 1973 Cadillac Eldorado Indy pace car, decals, registry, authenticity. All years of special built Cadillacs, limos, celebrity cars.

Cadillac International	**chrome**
32 Kinney St	**interiors**
Piermont, NY 10968	**moldings**
845-365-8290; FAX: 845-398-0085	**sheetmetal**
E-mail: cadintl@aol.com	

Mail order and open shop by appointment only. Specializing in Cadillac parts and restoration services for 1940s-1990s. Rust-free sheetmetal, moldings, chrome, interiors, rubber repro parts, rebuilt power brake units, new floor pans, bumpers, fuel tanks, mechanical, etc. Web site: www.cadillacinternational.com

Cadillac King	**parts**
9840 San Fernando Rd	**restoration**
Pacoima, CA 91331	
818-890-0621; FAX: 818-890-3117	
E-mail: eldorado@gte.net	

Mail order and open shop. Monday-Saturday 8 am to 5 pm. Specializing in Cadillac parts and restoration, 1950 till present, including Allante.
See our ad on this page

Cadillac Motor Books	**books**
PO Box 7	
Temple City, CA 91780	
626-445-1618	
E-mail: cadbooks@pacbell.net	

Mail order only. Publishers of *Cadillacs of the Forties*, *Guide to Cadillac 1950-1959*, *Cadillacs of the Sixties*, plus other Cadillac/LaSalle hardcover books. Also reprints of rare sales catalogs from the classic era. Send for complete list and information.

Cadillac Parts & Cars Limited	**car dealer**
46 Hardy	**literature**
Sparks, NV 89431	**parts**
775-826-8363	

Mail order and open shop. Any day by appointment, 8 am to 8 pm. Offers new and good used and reproduction 1938-1980 Cadillac parts, manuals, literature and collector cars for sale. Presently have 8,000 square foot facility for parts and maintain 15-20 collector car inventory of extra clean, low mileage cars.

California Collectors' Classics (CCC)	**parts**
PO Box 9262	**restoration**
San Bernardino, CA 92427	
626-527-7354	

Mail order and open shop. Specializing in restoration, parts, rebuilding of most major components for Cadillac, Lincoln and Thunderbird 1961-1985. Parts, restoration and service by appointment. Mail order sales, locating and inspection for buyer and seller of cars for sale.

Cars II	**parts**
6747 Warren Sharon Rd	
Brookfield, OH 44403	
330-448-2074; FAX: 330-448-1908	

Open shop. Monday-Friday 8 am to 6 pm. Specializes in parts for 1957-1960 Cadillac Eldorados, 1956-1962 Corvettes, 1966-1967 Olds 442.

Ed Cholakian Enterprises Inc	museum
dba All Cadillacs of the 40s and 50s	parts
12811 Foothill Blvd	
Sylmar, CA 91342	
800-808-1147, 818-361-1147	
FAX: 818-361-9738	

Mail order and open shop. Monday-Friday 8 am to 4:30 pm, weekends by appointment. Specializing in parts and service for all Cadillacs, 1940-1958. Museum open year round, Monday-Friday 8 am to 4:30 pm. 60 Cadillacs from 1940-1958 on display. Many of the cars have been used in movies or on the Discovery Channel and TNN.

See our ad on this page

Convertible Service	convertible parts
5126-HA Walnut Grove Ave	manufacture &
San Gabriel, CA 91776	service
800-333-1140, 626-285-2255	top mechanism
FAX: 626-285-9004	

See full listing in **Section Two** under **tops**

JA Cooley Museum	museum
4233 Park Blvd	
San Diego, CA 92103	
619-296-3112	

See full listing in **Section Six** under **California**

Coopers Vintage Auto Parts	parts
3087 N California St	
Burbank, CA 91504	
818-567-4140; FAX: 818-567-4101	

Mail order and open shop. Monday-Friday 8:30 am to 5:30 pm, Saturday 9 am to 4 pm. Large inventory of new and used parts for GM cars. Full stock of weatherstripping, mechanical, brake, suspension, trim, manuals, carpet sets, etc.

The Copper Cooling Works	radiators
2455 N 2550 E	
Layton, UT 84040	
801-544-9939	

See full listing in **Section Two** under **radiators**

Frank Corrente's Cadillac Corner Inc	car dealer
7614 Sunset Blvd	
Hollywood, CA 90046	
323-850-1881; FAX: 323-850-1884	
E-mail: corrente@ix.netcom.com	

Auto dealer specializing in classic Cadillacs from all over the world, including Zimmers, Excaliburs, Clenets, Rolls-Royces. We ship worldwide, fully insured, for 39 years. Web site: www.corrente-cadillac.com

CR Plastics Inc	bumper filler parts
2790 NE 7th Ave	
Pompano Beach, FL 33064	
800-551-3155	

Specializing in bumper filler parts, also known as extensions, for Cadillac 1977-1992, front and rear for Coupe deVille, Sedan deVille, Fleetwood, rear wheel drive. Cadillac Eldorado 1974-1985 front and rear. Cadillac Seville 1976-1985 front and rear. Buick Regal 2-dr 1981-1987 front and rear. We manufacture them and sell them. ABS plastic, lacquer primed, complete satisfaction guaranteed. The price war continues. Web site: www.crplastics.com – coming soon!

Tom Crook Classic Cars	car dealer
27611 42nd Ave S	
Auburn, WA 98001	
253-941-3454	

See full listing in **Section Two** under **car dealers**

Dash Specialists	interiors
1910 Redbud Ln	
Medford, OR 97504	
541-776-0040	

Mail order only. Rebuilding dash pads, door panels that are molded, armrests, consoles for all makes and models of automobiles from 1956-present. Both foreign and domestic. 25 years' experience.

Driving Passion Ltd USA	cars
Marc Tuwiner	parts
7132 Chilton Ct	salvage yard
Clarksville, MD 21029	
PH/FAX: 301-596-9078	
E-mail: lm7132@aol.com	

Mail order and open shop. Open Monday-Saturday 7 am to 6 pm. Specializing in 1959 and 1960 Cadillacs, parts, cars and locating services. Tons of trim and stainless. Rare Eldorados and convertibles, parts, glass, interior parts. Also 1953 Eldorados.

Durabuilt Automotive Hydraulics	hose assemblies
808 Meadows Ave	pumps, top cylinders
Canon City, CO 81212	valves
PH/FAX: 719-275-1126	window cylinders

See full listing in **Section Two** under **tops**

David R Edgerton, Coachworks	restoration
9215 St Rt 13	woodworking
Camden, NY 13316-4933	
315-245-3113	
E-mail: derods@excite.com	

See full listing in **Section Two** under **restoration shops**

Elliott's Car Radio | radio repairs
313 Linfield Rd | speaker kits
Parkerford, PA 19457
610-495-6360; FAX: 610-495-7723
E-mail: elliottradio@aol.com

See full listing in **Section Two** under **radios**

Faxon Auto Literature | literature
3901 Carter Ave | manuals
Riverside, CA 92501
800-458-2734; FAX: 909-786-4166

See full listing in **Section Two** under **literature dealers**

FEN Enterprises of New York Inc | parts
PO Box 1559, 1090 Rt 376 | restoration
Wappingers Falls, NY 12590
845-462-5959, 845-462-5094
FAX: 845-462-8450
E-mail: fenenterprises@aol.com

Suppliers of the finest in restoration parts and products. Combined with a full in-house restoration shop, our firm has the insight needed to help you get the correct parts for your restoration. Our full service restoration shop has upholstery, mechanical, body and paint, chrome and stainless. Customers receive the same quality parts that are used on our national award-winning restorations. Also have an in-house appraisal service for classic cars and will travel to inspect the vehicle. Frank R Nicodemus is our licensed and bonded appraiser. Web site: www.fenenterprises.com

See our ad on this page

Firewall Insulators & Quiet Ride Solutions | air plenums
6465 Pacific Ave, Ste 249 | auto insulation
Stockton, CA 95207 | firewall insulators
209-477-4840; FAX: 209-477-0918 | gloveboxes
E-mail: timcox@quietride.com | sound deadening

See full listing in **Section Two** under **upholstery**

GM Obsolete | parts
909 W Magnolia St
Phoenix, AZ 85007
602-253-8081; FAX: 602-253-8411
E-mail: info@gmobsolete.com

See full listing in **Section One** under **Buick/McLaughlin**

Hampton Coach | fabrics
6 Chestnut St, PO Box 6 | interior kits
Amesbury, MA 01913 | top kits
888-388-8726, 978-388-8047
FAX: 978-388-1113
E-mail: lbb-hc@greenet.net

See full listing in **Section One** under **Chevrolet**

Hand's Elderly Auto Care | repair
2000 Galveston St | restoration
Grand Prairie, TX 75051
PH/FAX: 972-642-4288

See full listing in **Section Two** under **restoration shops**

Harbor Auto Restoration | restoration
315 SW 15th Ave
Pompano Beach, FL 33069
954-785-7887; FAX: 954-785-7388
E-mail: harbor@harbor-auto.com

See full listing in **Section Two** under **restoration shops**

Justin Hartley | reprinted literature
17 Fox Meadow Ln
West Hartford, CT 06107-1216
860-523-0056, 860-604-9950 cell
FAX: 860-233-8840
E-mail: cadillacbooks@home.com

Mail order only. Cadillac and LaSalle shop manuals, parts books, service bulletins, owner`s manuals, body manuals, data books. 1902-1995. Republished full-size with care, pride and love. Prompt delivery. Recommended by Cadillac club judges and restoration shops. Money-back guarantee. Electronic improvement of pictures. Layflat binding. Started in 1912. References in 50 states and worldwide. MC, Visa, AmEx.

Holcombe Cadillac Parts 2933 Century Ln Bensalem, PA 19020 215-245-4560; FAX: 215-633-9916 E-mail: holcars@aol.com	parts

Mail order and open shop. Monday-Friday 9 am to 5:30 pm. Specializing in Cadillac parts, NOS, used and reproduction for 1949-1983 Cadillacs, all models. NOS parts a specialty, with over 11,000 part numbers stocked. We carry a full line of used body and trim parts. We also carry an extensive inventory of rubber weatherstripping, air conditioning, brake and general mechanical and electrical parts as well as body fillers.

Honest John's Caddy Corner 2271 FM 407 W, PO Box 741 Justin, TX 76247 888-592-2339 toll-free, 940-648-3330 FAX: 940-648-9135 E-mail: honestjohn@website	parts restoration service

Mail order and open shop. Monday-Friday 9 am to 5 pm. Parts, sales, service and restoration for 1941-1991 Cadillacs. Rebuilding and fabrication also. Online parts catalog. Accept MasterCard, Visa, Discover and American Express. Web site: www.honestjohn.com

Jacks Wholesale Division 250 N Robertson Blvd, Ste 405 Beverly Hills, CA 90211-1793 310-839-9417; FAX: 310-839-1046	limousines

See full listing in **Section One** under **Lincoln**

Jesser's Classic Keys 26 West St, Dept HVA Akron, OH 44303-2344 330-376-8181; FAX: 330-384-9129	automobilia keys

See full listing in **Section Two** under **locks & keys**

Lares Manufacturing 805 S Cleveland Cambridge, MN 55008 800-334-5749; FAX: 763-754-2853 E-mail: sales@larescorp.com	power steering equipment

See full listing in **Section One** under **Ford 1954-up**

Mahoning Auto PO Box 244 North Jackson, OH 44451 330-538-3246; FAX: 330-544-0242	chrome interiors motors

Mail order and open shop. Saturdays 9 am to 11 am and by appointment. Cadillac autos and parts for 1938-1978. Chrome, dashes, interiors, skirts, motors and more. Located near I-80 and I-76 in northeastern Ohio. Web site: www.mahoningauto.com

Mastermind Inc 32155 Joshua Dr Wildomar, CA 92595 PH/FAX: 909-674-0509 E-mail: mike@mastermindinc.net	new/used parts restoration

Mail/catalog orders and open shop. Please call for appointment. Specialize in restoration and repro parts for 1957-1960 Cadillac Eldorado Broughams. Also other 1950s and 1960s Cadillac parts and restoration, stainless molding repair, loads of new and used parts, misc services, expert air suspension rebuilding. Major emphasis and specialization in Eldorado series cars. Many unique parts and services unavailable elsewhere. Quality is our major concern. Web site: www.mastermindinc.net

Maximum Torque Specialties PO Box 925 Delavan, WI 53115 262-740-1118; FAX: 262-740-1161 E-mail: mts@elknet.net	high-perf parts restoration parts

Specializing in high-performance and restoration parts for 1968-1976 Cadillac 472-500 cid engines. Complete rebuilt engines in stock. Visit our new store: 112 S 3rd St, Delavan, WI. Web site: www.500cid.com

Mid-Jersey Motorama Inc 1301 Asbury Ave, PO Box 1395 Asbury Park, NJ 07712 PH/FAX: 732-775-9885 beeper: 732-840-6111 E-mail: sjz1@msn.com	car dealer

Open by appointment. Specializing in Mercedes, Cadillac, Land Rover, Rolls-Royce, Jaguar, Lincoln. Our 21st year in business.

OEM Glass Inc Rt 9 E, PO Box 362 Bloomington, IL 61702 800-283-2122, 309-662-2122 FAX: 309-663-7474	auto glass

See full listing in **Section Two** under **glass**

Ohio Limo and Coach Sales PO Box 681 Bellefontaine, OH 43311 937-592-3746; FAX: 937-593-3299 E-mail: ohiolimo@ohiolimo.com	car dealer

See full listing in **Section Two** under **car dealers**

Old Air Products 4615 Martin St Ft Worth, TX 76119 817-531-2665; FAX: 817-531-3257 E-mail: sales@oldairproducts.com	air conditioning

See full listing in **Section One** under **Corvette**

ORF Corp Phil Bray 8858 Ferry Rd Grosse Ile, MI 48138 734-676-5520; FAX: 734-676-9438 E-mail: carolbray@yahoo.com	rear end gears

See full listing in **Section One** under **Packard**

The Parts Place 217 Paul St Elburn, IL 60119 630-365-1800; FAX: 630-365-1900 E-mail: sales@thepartsplaceinc.com	parts

See full listing in **Section One** under **Chevrolet**

Garth B Peterson W 2619 Rockwell Ave Spokane, WA 99205 509-325-3823 anytime	accessories/chrome glass/grilles/parts radios/sheetmetal steering wheels

See full listing in **Section Two** under **comprehensive parts**

Piru Cads 402 Via Fustero Rd, Box 227 Piru, CA 93040 805-521-1741	cars parts restoration

Mail order and open shop. Monday-Saturday 10 am to 6 pm. Cadillac and LaSalle restoration 1937-1970, 1980-1992 parts, heavy in 1938-1953. Sales also, project cars, plus restored.

Dennis Portka 4326 Beetow Dr Hamburg, NY 14075 716-649-0921	**horns** **knock-off wheels**

See full listing in **Section One** under **Corvette**

Precision Rubber Box 324 Didsbury, AB Canada T0M 0W0 403-335-9590; FAX: 403-335-9637 E-mail: pat@runningboardmats.com	**rubber parts**

See full listing in **Section Two** under **rubber parts**

The Presidential Cars Museum Chateau de Montjalin Sauvigny le Bois 89200 France (333) 863-44642 FAX: (333) 863-16683 E-mail: odelafon@aol.com	**museum**

See full listing in **Section Six** under **France**

Sam Quinn Cadillac Parts Box 837 Estacada, OR 97023 503-637-3852	**parts**

Mail order only. Parts supplier for Cadillac/LaSalle, 1937-1977. NOS, rebuilt water pumps 1937-1977, fuel pumps, fender skirts, oil pumps 1949-1962. Motor mounts 1954-1964. Transmission mounts 1949-up. Ignition parts. Body parts. Locator service. V8 1937-1948 Cadillac fuel pumps; 1982 Cadillac Fleetwood Brougham, no engine, super car, for parts or whole car.

Replica Plastics 260 S Oates St, Box 1147 Dothan, AL 36302 800-873-5871; FAX: 334-792-1175 E-mail: stone@ala.net	**fiberglass parts**

See full listing in **Section Two** under **fiberglass parts**

Robert's Custom Metal 24 Lark Industrial Pkwy #D Smithfield, RI 02828 401-949-2361	**metal fabrication** **welding** **woodwork**

See full listing in **Section Two** under **sheetmetal**

Tom Rohner's Allante Store 17327 Via Del Campo San Diego, CA 92127 858-674-5779 E-mail: tom_rohner@compuserve.com	**parts**

Mail order only. Specializing in all parts for Cadillac Allantes only for 1987-1993. I have ten parts cars and 2 mini warehouses full of new and used parts. We have everything for Allantes.

Sea Yachts Inc 2029 N Ocean Blvd #410 Fort Lauderdale, FL 33304 PH/FAX: 954-561-8389 E-mail: seayachts@aol.com	**parts**

Mail order only. Collects 1954-1958 Cadillacs only as a hobby. Extra parts for sale.

E J Serafin Valley Rd Matinecock, NY 11560	**manuals**

Mail order only. Exact reproductions of owner's and shop manuals for 1930, 1931, 1934, 1935, 1936, 1940, 1941, 1947, 1949, 1957, 1959, 1961 Cadillacs and 1937 Buick. Send SASE for prices and shipping.

Dick Shappy Classic Cars 26 Katherine Ct Warwick, RI 02889 401-521-5333; FAX: 401-421-9480 E-mail: dshap@home.com	**parts**

Cadillacs 1930-1933 parts. Specializing in V16 but have parts also for 8 and 12-cylinder cars.

Showroom Auto Sales 960 S Bascom Ave San Jose, CA 95128 408-279-0944; FAX: 408-279-0918	**car dealer**

See full listing in **Section One** under **Mercedes-Benz**

Robert H Snyder PO Drawer 821 Yonkers, NY 10702 914-476-8500 FAX: 914-476-8573, 24 hours E-mail: cohascodpc@earthlink.net	**literature** **parts**

Mail order only. 1941-1949 Cadillac Fleetwood Series 75, 76 and 86 only. Free catalog available of revolving inventory of original parts only, principally small trim, garnish, fittings and miscellany. No heavy mechanical parts. Literature and collectibles of every description. All want lists invited. Web site: www.cohascodpc.com

Michael A Stahl PO Box 18036 Huntsville, AL 35804 205-882-6457 E-mail: stahlcon@aol.com	**parts**

Mail order only. Specializing in emblem cover repair kits for 1976-1996 Cadillac. Repair of sliding Cadillac crest mounted on trunk of car.

TA Motor AB Torpslingan 21 Lulea S 97347 Sweden +46-920-18888; FAX: +46-920-18821	**accessories** **parts**

Mail order and open shop. Monday-Thursday 8 am to 5 pm. Specializing in parts and accessories for Cadillacs 1941-1970.

Tags Backeast PO Box 581 Plainville, CT 06062 860-747-2942 E-mail: dataplt@snet.net	**data plates** **trim tags** **cowl tags**

See full listing in **Section Two** under **special services**

U S Oldies & Classics Vunt 3 Holsbeek 3220 Belgium 3216446611; FAX: 3216446520	**car dealer**

See full listing in **Section Two** under **car dealers**

White Post Restorations One Old Car Dr, PO Drawer D White Post, VA 22663 540-837-1140; FAX: 540-837-2368 E-mail: info@whitepost.com	**brakes** **restoration**

See full listing in **Section Two** under **brakes**

White Post Restorations One Old Car Dr, PO Drawer D White Post, VA 22663 540-837-1140; FAX: 540-837-2368 E-mail: info@whitepost.com	**restoration**

See full listing in **Section Two** under **restoration shops**

WiperWorks PO Box 57 Sewanee, TN 37375 PH/FAX: 931-598-9573	restoration

See full listing in **Section One** under **Chevrolet**

CHECKER

A-1 Shock Absorber Co Shockfinders Division 365 Warren Ave, PO Box 2028 Silverthorne, CO 80498 800-344-1966, 970-389-3193 cell FAX: 970-513-8283	shocks-all types coil springs Koni shocks leaf springs steering gears

See our ad on the last page

Blackheart Enterprises Ltd 305-12 Knickerbocker Ave Bohemia, NY 11716 516-935-6249; FAX: 516-752-1484	parts restoration

Checker taxi and Marathon parts. Thousands in stock. NOS, used and many reproduction parts only available from us. Sales and service of Checker cars and complete restoration services. Web site: www.blackheart.net

Checker Parts 9331 Johnell Rd Chatsworth, CA 91311 818-999-1485; FAX: 715-415-1916 E-mail: joe@checkerparts.com	parts restoration

Specializing in parts, restorations, movie rentals and Checkers for 1922-1982 Checkers, all models. Largest supplier of Checker parts. Web site: www.checkerparts.com

Danchuk Mfg 3201 S Standard Ave Santa Ana, CA 92705 714-751-1957; FAX: 714-850-1957 E-mail: info@danchuk.com	accessories parts restoration

See full listing in **Section One** under **Chevrolet**

Turnpike Checker Erich Lachmann Jr 495 Rt 17M North St Middletown, NY 10940-4526 845-343-4322, 5 pm-5:30 pm EST FAX: 845-343-2224, 8 am-5 pm EST	parts repairs

Mail order only. Specializing in parts and repairs for 1960-1982 Checker taxi cabs and Marathons. The last factory authorized Checker cab dealer. Front end parts, reproduction rocker panels, taxi decals, taillight lenses, vent shades.

CHEVROLET

4-Speeds by Darrell PO Box 110, 3 Water St Vermilion, IL 61955 217-275-3743; FAX: 217-275-3515	transmissions

See full listing in **Section Two** under **transmissions**

60 Chev Sam 2912 Wright Rd Hamptonville, NC 27020 336-468-1745	parts

Mail order and open shop. Open 6 days a week, 12 am to 9 pm. 1959-1960 parts, all NC good parts, 348 engine parts, rebuild differential 1955-1964.

600 Racing Inc 5245 NC Hwy 49 S Harrisburg, NC 28075 704-455-3896; FAX: 704-455-3820	5/8 scale replicas

See full listing in **Section Two** under **racing**

A & M SoffSeal Inc 104 May Dr Harrison, OH 45030 800-426-0902 513-367-0028 service/info FAX: 513-367-5506 E-mail: soffseal@soffseal.com	rubber parts weatherstripping

See full listing in **Section Two** under **rubber parts**

A-1 Shock Absorber Co Shockfinders Division 365 Warren Ave, PO Box 2028 Silverthorne, CO 80498 800-344-1966, 970-389-3193 cell FAX: 970-513-8283	shocks-all types coil springs Koni shocks leaf springs steering gears

See our ad on the last page

A-1 Street Rods 631 E Las Vegas St Colorado Springs, CO 80903 719-632-4920, 719-577-4588 FAX: 719-634-6577	parts

See full listing in **Section Two** under **street rods**

Accessoryland Truckin' Supplies 10723 Rt 61 S Dubuque, IA 52003 319-556-5482; FAX: 319-556-9087 E-mail: unityspotlights@aol.com or chevygmcparts@aol.com	accessories foglights/spotlights mounting brackets parts

Mail order and open shop by appointment. Specializing in 1941-1959 GMC and Chevy truck parts. NOS, reproduction and good used (parts for other years available). Parts and project vehicles. Catalog available. Another specialty, Unity spotlights, foglights, mounting bracket kits and repair parts for most vehicles 1930s-present, with many obsolete parts available. We also have nostalgic accessories such as Blue Dots, headlight visors, aftermarket hood ornaments, curb feelers, plus many more. Serving your parts needs since 1976.

Adler's Antique Autos Inc 801 NY Rt 43 Stephentown, NY 12168 518-733-5749 E-mail: advdesign1@aol.com	auto preservation Chevrolet knowledge parts repair restoration

See full listing in **Section Two** under **restoration shops**

Adler's Antique Autos Inc 801 NY Rt 43 Stephentown, NY 12168 518-733-5749 E-mail: advdesign1@aol.com	salvage yards

See full listing in **Section Five** under **New York**

Air Flow Research 10490 Ilex Ave Pacoima, CA 91331 818-890-0616; FAX: 818-890-0490	cylinder heads

Mail order only. Manufacturer of aftermarket small block Chevy, small block Ford and big block Chevy aluminum cylinder heads for all V8s from 1950-present.

AKH Wheels 1207 N A St Ellensburg, WA 98926-2522 509-962-3390 E-mail: akhwheel@eburg.com	Rallye wheels styled steel wheels vintage aluminum

See full listing in **Section Two** under **wheels & wheelcovers**

All Chevy/Canadian Impala 404 Allwood Rd Parksville, BC Canada V9P 1C4 250-248-8666; FAX: 888-248-1958 E-mail: canimp@nanaimo.ark.com	parts

Mail order and open shop. Specializing in reproduction parts for full-size 1955-1970 Chevy! Impala specialists. Emblems, weatherstrips, interiors, literature, reproduction body parts. Books and manuals.

American Classic Truck Parts PO Box 409 Aubrey, TX 76227 940-365-9786; FAX: 940-365-3419 E-mail: americanclassic@airmail.net	parts

Business hours are 9 am to 5:30 pm CST. Need truck parts? New or used for your Chevy or GMC 1936-1987? Visit the best web site there is at: www.americanclassic.com. We have over 6,000 pictures to help you choose your parts. Order online or by fax, phone or mail. If you need a printed, non-illustrated catalog, call or e-mail us with your information. Catalogs are free within the USA (please specify the year of truck as we have several catalogs).

See our ad on this page

Antique Auto Fasteners Guy (Chuck) Close 811 Oceanhill Dr Huntington Beach, CA 92648 714-969-9161, 562-696-3307 E-mail: redjc1@earthlink.net	fasteners hardware hose clamps molding clips

See full listing in **Section Two** under **hardware**

Antique Radio Doctor Barry Dalton 196 Kilborn Dr Grants Pass, OR 97526 541-474-2524 E-mail: radiodoc@rvi.net	radio repairs

See full listing in **Section Two** under **radios**

Apple Hydraulics Inc 1610 Middle Rd Calverton, NY 11933-1419 800-882-7753, 631-369-9515 FAX: 631-369-9516 E-mail: info@applehydraulics.com	brake rebuilding shock rebuilding

See full listing in **Section Two** under **suspension parts**

Arelli Alloy Wheels 164 W Jefferson Blvd Buena Park, CA 90620 323-733-0403; FAX: 323-733-0423 E-mail: sales@arelli.com	custom wheels

See full listing in **Section Two** under **wheels & wheelcovers**

ARS Automotive Research Services Division of Auto Search International 1702 W Camelback #301 Phoenix, AZ 85015 602-230-7111; FAX: 602-230-7282	appraisals research

See full listing in **Section Two** under **appraisals**

Aussieutes/Old Tin PO Box 26 Wendouree Victoria 3355 Australia 03 5336 FORD; FAX: 03 5339 9900 E-mail: dave@aussieutes.com	salvage yard

See full listing in **Section Five** under **Australia**

Authentic Automotive — power steering
529 Buttercup Tr
Mesquite, TX 75149
972-289-6373; FAX: 972-289-4303
E-mail: authauto@airmail.net

Mail order only. Monday-Friday 9 am to 5 pm CST. Power steering parts and complete power steering kits for 1955-1964 Chevys. Also ps component restoration and new reproduction parts that pertain to ps. Wholesale and retail. Free brochure, state year. American Express, MasterCard, Visa, Discover. Web site: www.chevyps.com

Auto Body Specialties Inc — accessories / body parts
Rt 66
Middlefield, CT 06455
888-277-1960 toll free orders only
860-346-4989; FAX: 860-346-4987

See full listing in **Section Two** under **body parts**

Auto Hardware Specialties — hardware fasteners
3123 McKinley Ave
Sheldon, IA 51201
712-324-2091; FAX: 712-324-2480
E-mail: rweber@rconnect.com

Mail order only. Specializing in original type hardware for 1929-1941 GM cars, including: screws, nuts, bolts, molding clips, hinge pins, tube nuts, anchor nuts, step bolts, hose clamps, gas caps and related items. Illustrated catalog, $2.

B & W Antique Auto Parts Inc — accessories / parts
150 W Axton Rd, Unit 2
Bellingham, WA 98226
360-398-9820; FAX: 360-398-9431
E-mail: bwautoparts@bwautoparts.com

See full listing in **Section One** under **Ford 1932-1953**

Baldwin/Chevy — parts
987 Steele Blvd
Baldwin, NY 11510
516-223-8888
E-mail: fbotte@aol.com

Mail order and open shop every day. Specializing in brakes, sheetmetal, suspension, radiators, glass, radios, wire harnesses, new, used and custom for 1955, 1956, 1957 and many other 1958-1972 Chevrolet cars, trucks, Camaro, Chevelle, Nova, Monte Carlo, Firebird and Impala. Web site: www.chevychevy.com

Bentley Publishers — books / manuals
1734 Massachusetts Ave
Cambridge, MA 02138-1804
800-423-4595; FAX: 617-876-9235
E-mail: sales@rb.com

See full listing in **Section Four** under **books & publications**

Bill's Speed Shop — body parts
13951 Millersburg Rd
Navarre, OH 44662
330-832-9403; FAX: 330-832-2098

Mail order and open shop. We are one of the foremost suppliers of obsolete and current body repair panels. Our main interest is obsolete panels from 1949-up. Also in stock, a few NOS fenders and quarters.

Bob's Radio & TV Service — radios
238 Ocean View
Pismo Beach, CA 93449
805-773-8200

See full listing in **Section Two** under **radios**

Bow Tie Chevy Association — parts
PO Box 607824
Orlando, FL 32860
407-880-1956; FAX: 407-886-7571
E-mail: info@lategreatchevy.com

Mail order and open shop. Monday-Friday 8 am to 5 pm EST. Sell parts for 1955-1972 Chevys. Web site: www.lategreatchevy.com

Bow Tie Reproductions — parts
8370 Avon Belden Rd
North Ridgeville, OH 44039
PH: 440-327-4800; FAX: 440-327-9599
E-mail: bowtie2932@aol.com

Reproduction parts for 1929-1932 Chevrolets. Quality die-formed steel fenders, aprons, runningboards, gas tank covers, radiator shells, hood doors, taillight arms, rocker panels, patch panels, decklids, stainless steel cowl bands, bumpers, headlight bars, pads, clamps, grille inserts. Over 400 different items.

Brothers Truck Parts — accessories / parts
801 Parkridge Ave
Corona, CA 92880
800-687-6672; FAX: 909-808-9788
E-mail: sales@brotherstrucks.com

See full listing in **Section Two** under **trucks & tractors**

Bumper Boyz LLC — bumper repairs / reconditioning / sandblasting
2435 E 54th St
Los Angeles, CA 90058
800-995-1703, 323-587-8976
FAX: 323-587-2013

Mail order and open shop. 7 am to 6 pm PST. Specializing in reconditioning all makes and models. GM, Ford, Chrysler. Also foreign bumpers. We repair, sandblast and triple plate bumpers. We carry accessories, bumper guards, fender wing tips plus grilles, exchange or outright. We ship nationwide also overseas. Web site: www.bumperboyz.com

Burrell's Service Inc — parts
PO Box 456
Keego Harbor, MI 48320
248-682-2390; FAX: 248-682-2376
E-mail: craigdj@oeonline.com

Mail order only. Specializing in service and parts information for 1976-1981 Chevy and Ford vans with the Vemco VX4 4-wd conversion.

Butch's Trim — molding / polishing / trim restoration
W-224 S-8445 Industrial Ave
Big Bend, WI 53103
262-662-9910
E-mail: blun61@yahoo.com

Mail order and open shop. Monday-Saturday 9 am to 4 pm. Restoration of aluminum trim, body side moldings, headlamp bezels, grilles. Dents and scratches removed. Polishing and anodizing. Stocking NOS and used for 1958-1967 Chevy.

C & P Chevy Parts — parts / restoration / supplies
50 Schoolhouse Rd, PO Box 348VA
Kulpsville, PA 19443
215-721-4300, 800-235-2475
FAX: 215-721-4539

Mail order and open shop. Monday-Friday 9 am to 5 pm. Parts and restoration supplies for 1955-1957 Chevrolets and 1955-1959 Chevrolet trucks. Visit our web site: www.1chevy.com

Section One – Marque Specialists

| Cal West Auto Air & Radiators Inc
24309 Creekside Rd #119
Valencia, CA 91355
800-535-2034; FAX: 661-254-6120
E-mail: mike@calwest-radiators.com | a/c units/condensers
fan shrouds
gas tanks
heaters/radiators
radios/wheels |

See full listing in **Section Two** under **radiators**

| Camaro Specialties
112 Elm St
East Aurora, NY 14052
716-652-7086; FAX: 716-652-2279
E-mail: camarospecial@wzrd.com | parts
restoration |

See full listing in **Section One** under **Chevelle/Camaro**

| Jim Carter's Antique Truck Parts
1508 E Alton
Independence, MO 64055
800-336-1913; FAX: 800-262-3749
E-mail: jimcartertruckparts@
worldnet.att.net | truck parts |

We specialize in quality parts for the 1934-1972 Chevrolet and GMC truck. Our trained, experienced crew knows older GM trucks and what you need in their restoration. We are one of the leaders in this fast growing truck restoration field. Let us help you make your truck just the way you want it to be. Catalogs,$5, includes a $7.50 coupon good towards your first order. Web site: www.oldchevytrucks.com

| John Chambers Vintage Chevrolet
PO Box 35068, Dept VAA
Phoenix, AZ 85069
602-934-CHEV | parts |

Mail order and open shop by appointment, customer pick-up by appointment. 1955, 1956 and 1957 Chevrolet parts: chrome parts, lenses, wiring harnesses, weatherstripping, sheet metal, interiors, mechanical items, rubber parts. Large selection of rust-free used parts from the Southwest.

| Chernock Enterprises
PO Box 134, Airport Rd
Hazleton, PA 18201
570-455-1752; FAX: 570-455-7585
E-mail: jim@chernock.com | trailers |

See full listing in **Section Two** under **trailers**

| Chevs of the 40's
2027 B St, Dept Z
Washougal, WA 98671
800-999-CHEV (2438)
FAX: 360-835-7988 | parts |

The world's most complete supplier of 1937-1954 Chevrolet car and truck parts. Shop online at our web site: www.chevsofthe40s.com

See our ad on this page

| Chevi Shop Custom Casting
338 Main Ave, Box 75
Milledgeville, IL 61051
815-225-7565; FAX: 815-225-7616
E-mail: synka@cin.net | custom castings
parts |

Retail sales of 1933-1957 Chevrolet parts. Manufacturer of custom castings in zinc aluminum alloy using spin casting and investment casting techniques. Some iron and aluminum castings (sandcastings) also done. Will custom cast for dealer or individual, one part or many, with painting or plating available also. No 1941-1954 parts and no sheetmetal. Catalog, $2. Free quotes on parts.

| Chevrolet Parts Obsolete
PO Box 70027
Riverside, CA 92513-0027
909-340-2979; FAX: 909-279-4013
E-mail: cpo@att.net | accessories
parts |

Mail order only. Carry over 50,000 NOS General Motors parts and accessories, 1965-1985. We also purchase discontinued and obsolete GM parts. When calling, please provide part numbers if possible.

| Chevy Duty Pickup Parts
1 Chevy Duty Dr
Kansas City, MO 64150
816-741-8029; FAX: 816-741-5255
E-mail: orders@chevyduty.com | pickup parts |

Mail order and retail parts store. Monday-Friday 9 am to 5:30 pm, Saturday 9 am to 12 noon. Specializes in parts and restoration supplies for 1947-1987 Chevy and GMC pickups. We have 5 fully illustrated catalogs, complete with descriptions and prices for you to order from. Web site: www.chevyduty.com

See our ad on page 37

| Chevyland Parts & Accessories
3667 Recycle Rd #8
Rancho Cordova, CA 95742
916-638-3906; FAX: 916-638-0302
E-mail: 327@chevylandparts.com | accessories
parts
restoration |

See full listing in **Section One** under **Chevelle/Camaro**

Cheyenne Pickup Parts Box 959 Noble, OK 73068 405-872-3399; FAX: 405-872-0385 E-mail: sales@cheyennepickup.com	body panels bumpers carpet weatherstripping

Specializing in new and reproduction parts for 1960-1987 Chevrolet full-size pickups and 1969-1991 Chevrolet full-size Blazers, including interior, exterior, chrome moldings, body panels, carpet, bumpers, weatherstripping, etc. Web site: www.cheyennepickup.com

Classic Auto Air Mfg Co 2020 W Kennedy Blvd Tampa, FL 33606 813-251-2356, 813-251-4994 FAX: 813-254-7419	air conditioning heating parts

See full listing in **Section One** under **Mustang**

Classic Auto Restoration Service Inc 381 National Dr Rockwall, TX 75032-6556 972-722-9663	restoration

Open Monday-Friday 8 am to 5 pm CST. Specializes in Chevrolet 1955-1972 cars and pickups. Also Ford and Mustang 1958-1968.

Classic Chevrolet Parts Inc 8723 S I-35 Oklahoma City, OK 73149 405-631-4400; FAX: 405-631-5999 E-mail: info@classicchevroletparts.com	parts

Specializing in a full product line of Chevrolet parts for 1955-1957 car, 1932-1980 Chevrolet pickup, 1964-1972 Chevelle and 1967-1981 Camaro. Web site: www.classicchevroletparts.com

Classic Chevy International PO Box 607188 Orlando, FL 32860-7188 800-456-1957, 407-299-1957 FAX: 407-299-3341 E-mail: info@classicchevy.com	modified parts monthly magazine repro parts tech help used parts

Mail order and open shop. Monday-Friday 8 am to 8 pm, Saturday 9 am to 6 pm EST. Specializing in reproduction, modified, high performance and used parts for 1955-1972 full size Chevys. Member-driven club provides a national voice uniting car clubs and enthusiasts worldwide. Members recieve monthly magazine, tech help, 4 national conventions per year, special pricing and much more. Web site: www.classicchevy.com

Classic Industries Inc Chevy/GMC Truck Parts and Accessories Catalog 17832 Gothard St Huntington Beach, CA 92647 800-854-1280 parts/info FAX: 800-300-3081 E-mail: info@classicindustries.com	accessories parts

Our parts and accessories catalog, Chevy/GMC Truck, covering all years from 1948-present. You'll find the finest quality restoraton products and late model truck accessories. Call our 24-hour toll-free catalog hotline at 888-GM-CATALOG to be placed on our advance mailing list to receive free, the industry's newest and most comprehensive parts catalog from the undisputed leader in the industry, Classic Industries. Web site: www.classicindustries.com

Classic Industries Inc Impala/Full-size Chevrolet Parts and Accessories Catalog 17832 Gothard St Huntington Beach, CA 92647 800-854-1280 parts/info FAX: 800-300-3081 E-mail: info@classicindustries.com	accessories parts

Largest selection of Impala and full-size Chevy parts and accessories ever assembled in one catalog. Over 400 full color pages of the finest quality restoration products and late model Impala SS accessories. Only $5, refundable on first order. Call our 24-hour toll-free catalog hotline at 888-GM-CATALOG and receive the industry's newest and most comprehensive parts catalog from the undisputed leader in the industry, Classic Industries. Web site: www.classicindustries.com

Classic Industries Inc Nova/Chevy II Parts and Accessories Catalog 17832 Gothard St Huntington Beach, CA 92647 800-854-1280 parts/info FAX: 800-300-3081 toll free E-mail: info@classicindustries.com	accessories parts

Largest selection of Chevy II/Nova parts and accessories ever assembled in one catalog. Nearly 400 full color pages of the finest quality restoration products and accessories. Only $5, refunded on first order. Call our 24-hour toll-free catalog hotline, 888-GM-CATALOG, and receive the industry's most comprehensive parts catalog from the undisputed leader in the industry, Classic Industries. Web site: www.classicindustries.com

Classic Performance Products 8341 Artesia Blvd, Unit C Buena Park, CA 90621 800-522-5004; FAX: 714-522-2500 E-mail: info@classicperform.com	brakes steering suspension

Specializing in steering, brakes and suspension for Chevrolet and Ford cars and trucks. Web site: www.classicperform.com

Classic Wood Mfg 1006 N Raleigh St Greensboro, NC 27405 336-691-1344; FAX: 336-273-3074	wood kits wood replacement

See full listing in **Section Two** under **woodwork**

Clester's Auto Rubber Seals Inc PO Box 1113 Salisbury, NC 28145 800-457-8223, 704-637-9979 FAX: 704-636-7390	molded rubber parts weatherstripping

See full listing in **Section Two** under **rubber parts**

Cliff's Classic Chevrolet Parts Co 619 SE 212nd Ave Portland, OR 97233 503-667-4329; FAX 503-669-4268 E-mail: clifchev@aol.com	parts

Mail order and open shop. Monday-Friday 9 am to 5:30 pm, Saturday 9 am to 1 pm. Specializing in 1955-1957 Chevrolet passenger car and 1955 2nd Series, 1959 Chevrolet truck parts, new and used. Many rebuilding/restoration services for same. Web site: www.cliffsclassicchevrolet.com

The Clockworks 1745 Meta Lake Ln Eagle River, WI 54521 800-398-3040; FAX: 715-479-5759 E-mail: clockwks@nnex.net	clock service

See full listing in **Section Two** under **instruments**

| **Coach Builders Muscle Car Parts & Services**
PO Box 128
Baltimore, MD 21087-0128
410-426-5567 | interiors
parts
rust remover |

NOS and reproduction body panels, interiors, convertible and vinyl tops, rechromed bumpers, weatherstripping, Oxisolv rust remover and metal conditioner for 1955-1957 Chevy, Chevelle, Camaro, Impala, Nova, Monte Carlo, GTO, LeMans, Firebird, 442, Cutlass, Charger, Skylark, GS, Roadrunner, GTX, Cuda, Dart. Pre-purchase inspection service (don't buy the wrong car). Specializing in the past for the future.

| **Conte's Corvettes & Classics**
851 W Wheat Rd
Vineland, NJ 08360
856-692-0087; FAX: 856-692-1009
E-mail: contes@cybernet.net | leasing
parts
sales
service |

See full listing in **Section One** under **Corvette**

| **Convertible Service**
5126-HA Walnut Grove Ave
San Gabriel, CA 91776
800-333-1140, 626-285-2255
FAX: 626-285-9004 | convertible parts
manufacture/
service
top mechanism |

See full listing in **Section Two** under **tops**

| **Coopers Vintage Auto Parts**
3087 N California St
Burbank, CA 91504
818-567-4140; FAX: 818-567-4101 | parts |

See full listing in **Section One** under **Cadillac/LaSalle**

| **CPX-RTS Auto Parts**
7552 W Appleton Ave
Milwaukee, WI 53216
414-463-2277; FAX: 414-463-2098 | parts |

Mail order and showroom sales. Monday-Friday 9 am to 6 pm, Saturday-Sunday and holidays 9 am to 1 pm. Our 26th year as THE major discounter of 1955-1975 Chevrolet, Camaro, Chevelle, Nova, Monte Carlo, El Camino parts and accessories, new, used and reproduction. "Why pay more?"

| **Creative Connections Inc**
3407 Hwy 120
Duluth, GA 30096
770-476-7322; FAX: 770-476-7028
E-mail: sales@logolites.com | brake lights
logo lights
turn signals |

See full listing in **Section One** under **Ford 1903-1931**

| **D&J GTO Parts**
Dan Gregory
11283 Main St
Stoutsville, OH 43154
740-474-4614; FAX: 740-474-2314
E-mail: djgto@hotmail.com | parts |

See full listing in **Section One** under **Pontiac**

| **Danchuk Mfg**
3201 S Standard Ave
Santa Ana, CA 92705
714-751-1957; FAX: 714-850-1957
E-mail: info@danchuk.com | accessories
parts
restoration |

Monday-Friday 7 am to 4 pm, Saturday 8 am to 3 pm. World's largest manufacturer of 1955-1957 Chevrolet restoration parts. Also carry 1964-1972 Chevelle and El Camino. Call for a catalog, visit our web site or visit our Santa Ana, CA showroom. Web site: www.danchuk.com

See our ad on page 39

| **Dave's Auto Machine & Parts**
Rt 16
Ischua, NY 14743
716-557-2402 | accessories
machine work
parts |

Mail order and open shop. Open Monday-Friday 9 am to 5 pm EST. Sometimes closed Friday if at swap meet, please call ahead. Phone hours 10 to 7 EST. Specializing in Chevrolet 1955-1972, all models car and truck parts, NOS, used only. Specializing in hp big and small block dated engine parts and accessories, including carbs, manifolds, trans, etc. Southwestern body parts car, truck, license plates car, commercial, motorcycle, pairs, singles. Machine shop service available.

| **Desert Muscle Cars**
2853 N Stone Ave
Tucson, AZ 85705
520-882-3010; FAX: 520-628-9332 | parts |

See full listing in **Section One** under **Chevelle/Camaro**

| **Dixie Truck Works**
10495 Hwy 73 E
Mount Pleasant, NC 28124
704-436-2407 | parts |

Mail order and open shop. Monday-Friday 1 pm to 7 pm, Saturday 9 am to 1 pm. 38-page catalog lists truck parts for 1942-1982 Chevrolet and GMC trucks. Our complete line of new parts includes rubber parts, bed parts, sheetmetal, chrome moldings, bumpers, grilles, emblems and many other parts. Catalogs are $3. Web site: www.dixietruckworks.com

| **Mike Drago Chevy Parts**
141 E St Joseph St
Easton, PA 18042
PH/FAX: 610-252-5701
E-mail: dragomdcp@aol.com | Chevrolet parts |

Mail order and open shop. Monday-Saturday 8 am to 5 pm. Specialize in classic Chevrolet parts for 1955-1957. We stock a full line of the finest quality reproduction parts available. New old stock as well as good used is available. Show quality chrome plating is also offered. Catalog is available, $4, refundable on first order. Web site: http://members.aol.com/dragomdcp

| **Dynamic Racing Transmissions LLC**
104-5 Enterprise Dr, Unit 1
North Branford, CT 06471
203-315-0138; FAX: 203-315-0352
E-mail: mightymitejr@aol.com | automatic
transmissions |

See full listing in **Section Two** under **transmissions**

| **East Coast Chevy Inc**
Ol '55 Chevy Parts
4154A Skyron Dr
Doylestown, PA 18938
215-348-5568; FAX: 215-348-0560 | custom work
parts
restoration |

Mail order and open shop. Monday-Friday 9 am to 5 pm, 1 Saturday per month 9 am to 12 pm (call first for Saturday). Complete inventory new, used and reproduction parts (1955-1957 our specialty). Also restoration services for 1955-1957 Chevrolets. Now stocking 1958-1970. Personal service, parts restoration and custom work. Web site: www.eastcoastchevy.com

| **East West Auto Parts Inc**
4605 Dawson Rd
Tulsa, OK 74115
800-447-2886; FAX: 918-832-7900 | European import
parts
GM parts |

See full listing in **Section Five** under **Oklahoma**

EC Parts | parts
PO Box 2459
Citrus Heights, CA 95611
916-722-2676; FAX: 916-722-4127
E-mail: rick@ecparts.net

Mail order only. Specializing in new, used and reproduction restoration parts and supplies for 1959-1987 El Camino, 1964-1983 Chevelle/Malibu, 1970-1988 Monte Carlo. Web site: www.ecparts.net

Elliott's Car Radio | radio repairs, speaker kits
313 Linfield Rd
Parkerford, PA 19457
610-495-6360; FAX: 610-495-7723
E-mail: elliottradio@aol.com

See full listing in **Section Two** under **radios**

Engineering & Mfg Services | sheetmetal
Box 24362
Cleveland, OH 44124
216-541-4585

See full listing in **Section One** under **Ford 1932-1953**

David J Entler Restorations | woodwork
10903 N Main St Ext
Glen Rock, PA 17327-8373
717-235-2112

See full listing in **Section Two** under **woodwork**

Faxon Auto Literature | literature, manuals
3901 Carter Ave
Riverside, CA 92501
800-458-2734; FAX: 909-786-4166

See full listing in **Section Two** under **literature dealers**

Fifth Avenue Antique Auto Parts | cooling systems, electrical systems, fuel systems
415 Court St
Clay Center, KS 67432
785-632-3450; FAX: 785-632-6154
E-mail: fifthave@oz-online.net

See full listing in **Section Two** under **electrical systems**

Fifties Forever | Chevrolet specialist
206 Division Ave
Garfield, NJ 07026
PH/FAX: 973-478-1306
E-mail: fiftiesforever@webtv.net

Mail order and showroom. Monday-Friday 9 am to 6 pm, Saturday 9 am to 1 pm. Complete inventory of new, used and NOS parts for 1955-1957 Chevrolets. Also many hard to find items for 1956-1967 Corvettes. Discounted prices, monthly specials, volume discounts.

John Filiss | appraisals
45 Kingston Ave
Port Jervis, NY 12771
845-856-2942
E-mail: john@filiss.com

See full listing in **Section Two** under **appraisals**

The Filling Station | literature, parts
990 S Second St
Lebanon, OR 97355-3227
800-841-6622 orders
541-258-2114; FAX: 541-258-6968
E-mail: fssales@fillingstation.com

Mail order and open shop. Monday-Saturday 9 am to 5 pm; closed Sunday. Chevrolet and GMC quality reproduction parts

for: 1916-1964 passenger cars and 1918-1972 trucks. Rubber products including: windshield, vent window, door and trunk seals. Chrome items including: mirrors and arms, hood and grille ornaments, door and window handles. Shop manuals, owner's manuals, sales and restoration literature. Brakes, suspensions and much more. Web site: www.fillingstation.com

Firewall Insulators & Quiet Ride Solutions | air plenums, auto insulation, firewall insulators, gloveboxes, sound deadening
6465 Pacific Ave, Ste 249
Stockton, CA 95207
209-477-4840; FAX: 209-477-0918
E-mail: timcox@quietride.com

See full listing in **Section Two** under **upholstery**

Ron Francis' Wire Works | fuel injection, harnesses, wiring accessories, wiring kits
167 Keystone Rd
Chester, PA 19013
800-292-1940 orders; 610-485-1937
E-mail: rfwwx@aol.com

See full listing in **Section Two** under **wiring harnesses**

George Frechette | brake cylinder sleeving
14 Cedar Dr
Granby, MA 01033
800-528-5235

See full listing in **Section Two** under **brakes**

Fred's Truck Parts | parts
4811 S Palant
Tucson, AZ 85735
520-883-7151
E-mail: fredstruckparts@aol.com

Specializing in 1947-1959 Chevy and GMC reproduction parts. Used available for 1955-1959.

The Garden of Speedin | books
4645 Q Ruffner St
San Diego, CA 92111
800-MOTORHEAD
FAX: 858-467-0777
E-mail: cars@gardenofspeed.com

See full listing in **Section Four** under **information sources**

Gardner Exhaust Systems | exhaust systems
7 Cedar Ln
Rhinebeck, NY 12572
845-876-8117; FAX: 845-871-1750
E-mail: gexhaust@aol.com

See full listing in **Section Two** under **exhaust systems**

Garton's Auto | bicycle sales lit, Ford NOS parts, sales literature
401 N 5th St (at 5th & Vine)
Millville, NJ 08332-3129
PH: 856-825-3618

See full listing in **Section One** under **Ford 1932-1953**

Gear Vendors Inc | overdrive transmissions
1717 N Magnolia Ave
El Cajon, CA 92020
619-562-0060; FAX: 619-562-1186
E-mail: info@gearvendors.com

See full listing in **Section Two** under **transmissions**

Gilbert's Early Chevy Pickup Parts | parts
470 West Rd 1 N
Chino Valley, AZ 86323
PH/FAX: 520-636-5337
E-mail: gilb@goodnet.com

Mail order only. Specializing in 1947-1966 Chevrolet and GMC trucks. Web site: www.goodnet.com/~gilb

Gold Eagle Classics
5990 SW 185th Ave Bldg H
Aloha, OR 97007
503-642-2005; FAX: 503-642-0808
E-mail: gldeagle@europa.com

accessories
parts

See full listing in **Section One** under **Chevelle/Camaro**

Golden State Parts
3493 Arrowhead Dr
Carson City, NV 89706
800-235-5717; FAX: 888-723-2495

parts

Specializing in parts for Chevrolet and GMC trucks from 1947-1987. Web site: www.golden-state-parts.com

Goodmark Industries Inc
625 E Old Norcross Rd
Lawrenceville, GA 30045
770-339-8557; FAX: 770-339-7562

sheetmetal
trim

See full listing in **Section Two** under **sheetmetal**

Great Lakes Auto "N" Truck Restoration
PO Box 251
Mayville, MI 48744
989-683-2614

parts

Specializing in 1955-1959 Chevy and GMC trucks and parts, Chevrolet Cameo trucks, NOS, used, reproduction, Cameo, Stepside, Fleetside.

Greg's Automotive
Box 1712
Santa Ynez, CA 93460
PH/FAX: 805-688-5675
E-mail: 9pm@silcom.com

accessories
books
literature

Specializing in books, literature, apparel and accessories for Chevrolet and Ford cars and trucks. Web site: www.gregsonline.com

Guldstrand Engineering Inc
912 Chestnut St
Burbank, CA 91506
818-558-1499; FAX: 818-558-1449
E-mail: gss@guldstrand.com

parts

See full listing in **Section One** under **Corvette**

Hagerty Classic Insurance
PO Box 87
Traverse City, MI 49685
800-922-4050; FAX: 616-941-8227

insurance

See full listing in **Section Two** under **insurance**

Hampton Coach
6 Chestnut St, PO Box 6
Amesbury, MA 01913
888-388-8726, 978-388-8047
FAX: 978-388-1113
E-mail: lbb-hc@greenet.net

fabrics
interior kits
top kits

Antique auto interior kits, top kits and fabrics for over 400 models of Chevrolet 1916-1954, Buick 1927-1955, Pontiac/Oakland 1930-1952, Cadillac/LaSalle 1937-1948, Oldsmobile 1931-1952 and Plymouth 1939-1941. Free literature with fabric samples and prices. Free parts and accessories catalog. Worldwide reputation for quality and service. Web site: www.hamptoncoach.com

Hand's Elderly Auto Care
2000 Galveston St
Grand Prairie, TX 75051
PH/FAX: 972-642-4288

repair
restoration

See full listing in **Section Two** under **restoration shops**

Hank's Custom Stepside Beds
12693 Clay Station Rd
Herald, CA 95638
209-748-2193; FAX: 209-748-2976
E-mail: truckbeds@softcom.net

pickup beds

See full listing in **Section Two** under **trucks & tractors**

Harmon's Incorporated
Hwy 27 N, PO Box 100
Geneva, IN 46740
219-368-7221; FAX: 219-368-9396
E-mail: harmons@harmons.com

interiors
parts

Celebrating our 28th year of bringing our customers the best service, largest variety, guaranteed quality and the fairest prices on Chevrolet restoration parts. Our 2001 catalogs total over 20,000 parts for 1955-1972 Chevrolet, 1962-1972 Nova, 1964-1972 Chevelle, 1970-1977 Monte Carlo, 1967-1980 Camaro and 1947-1980 truck. Also a wide assortment of accessories including books, paints, decals, etc. Simply call, e-mail or write to above address to order our $5 catalog and receive a 5% discount coupon. On-line store at our web site: www.harmons.com

Hawthorne's Happy Motoring
Box 1332
Coaldale AB Canada T1M 1N2
PH/FAX: 403-345-2101

appraisals
parts

See full listing in **Section Two** under **appraisals**

Heavy Chevy Truck Parts
PO Box 650, 17445 Heavy Chevy Rd
Siloam Springs, AR 72761
501-524-9575
FAX: 501-524-4873 or 800-317-2277
E-mail: heavychevy@heavychevy.com

parts

Mail order and open shop. Tuesday-Friday 7:30 am to 5:30 pm, Saturday 8 to noon. Complete line of parts for 1947-1972 Chevrolet and GMC pickups. Call for your free catalog. Web site: www.heavychevy.com

Hidden Valley Auto Parts
21046 N Rio Bravo
Maricopa, AZ 85239
602-252-2122, 602-252-6137
520-568-2945; FAX: 602-258-0951
E-mail: hvap@aol.com

parts

Mail order and open shop. Monday-Friday 8 am to 5 pm, Saturday 9 am to 3 pm. Specializing in classic, antique auto and truck parts, 1940s-1980s, American and foreign. Web site: www.membersaol.com/hvap/hvap.htm

Bruce Horkey's Wood & Parts
46284 440th St
Windom, MN 56101
507-831-5625; FAX: 507-831-0280
E-mail: woodandparts@yahoo.com

pickup parts

See full listing in **Section Two** under **trucks & tractors**

William Hulbert Jr
PO Box 151, 13683 Rt 11
Adams Center, NY 13606
315-583-5765
E-mail: radio_29chevy@yahoo.com

radios

See full listing in **Section Two** under **radios**

Hyde Products Inc
PO Box 870321
New Orleans, LA 70187-0321
504-649-4041
E-mail: hydeprod@bellsouth.net

hood holders

Mail order only. Manufacturing hood holders (props) for 1937 thru 1948 Fords, 1940 thru 1948 Chevrolets, 1940-1941 Ford pickups, 1947 thru 1954 Chevy pickups. All bolt-on. Web site: www.hydeprod.com

| **Impala Bob's Inc**
4753 E Falcon Dr, Dept HCCA15
Mesa, AZ 85215
800-IMPALAS orders
480-924-4800 retail store
480-981-1600 office
FAX: 800-716-6237, 480-981-1675
E-mail: info@impalas.com | **dash pads**
emblems
interior kits
mechanical parts
OEM tires
restoration parts
rubber parts
wiring harnesses |

Impala Bob's has everything for the classic Chevrolet restorer. We specialize in 1949-1976 Chevrolet cars including Chevelle and 1947-1972 Chevrolet/GMC truck. We offer a full line of restoration parts including moldings, emblems, trim, lenses, interior kits, dash pads, convertible parts, weatherstrips, rubber parts, body repair panels, rechromed bumpers, wiring harnesses, radiators, mechanical parts, stereos, OEM tires and batteries, engine decals, books and more. All of our catalogs are free. Mention code HCCA15. Visit our retail store on Falcon Field Airport. Web site: www.impalas.com

| **Inline Tube**
33783 Groesbeck Hwy
Fraser, MI 48026
800-385-9452 order, 810-294-4093 tech
FAX: 810-294-7349
E-mail: kryta@aol.com | **brake cables/clips**
brake/fuel lines
choke tubes
engine lines
flex hoses/valves
vacuum lines |

See full listing in **Section Two** under **brakes**

| **Instrument Services Inc**
11765 Main St
Roscoe, IL 61073
800-558-2674; FAX: 815-623-9180 | **clocks**
gauges
instruments |

See full listing in **Section Two** under **instruments**

| **Integrity Machine**
383 Pipe Stave Hollow Rd
Mount Sinai, NY 11766
888-446-9670; FAX: 516-476-9675 | **brake masters**
clutch masters
wheel cylinders |

See full listing in **Section Two** under **brakes**

| **J & K Old Chevy Stuff**
Ship Pond Rd
Plymouth, MA 02360
508-224-7616
kblaze58@aol.com | **car dealer**
parts
sheetmetal |

Mail order and open shop. Monday-Sunday 8 am to 7 pm. Sells used rot-free Chevy sheetmetal for 1955-1969 Chevys including Novas and Chevelles. Also sells used miscellaneous items for 1955-1957 and Chevy II Novas. Also buys and sells 1955-1969 Chevy cars.

| **J&M Auto Parts**
PO Box 778, Dept H
Pelham, NH 03076
603-635-3866 | **NOS parts**
repro parts |

Mail order and open shop. Shop open by appointment only. NOS and reproduction parts for 1955-79 Chevrolets, including Impalas, Chevelles, Camaros, Novas and Monte Carlos.

| **JECC Inc**
PO Box 616
West Paterson, NJ 07424
973-890-9682; FAX: 973-812-2724 | **chassis parts**
gaskets
transmissions |

See full listing in **Section One** under **Buick/McLaughlin**

| **Jersey Late Greats Inc**
PO Box 1294
Hightstown, NJ 08520
609-448-0526 | **documentation**
service
restoration details |

Maintains extensive database of original 1958-1964 Chevrolets. The only source to have completely decoded the Fisher Body cowl tags from 15 different assembly plants. Documentation service provides when, where and with what options a car was built. Also can provide restoration details which differ between plants and date of production. Before purchasing a high option car, you may want to know its originality. Cost of service: $20. Web site: www.jerseylategreats.com

| **Jesser's Classic Keys**
26 West St, Dept HVA
Akron, OH 44303-2344
330-376-8181; FAX: 330-384-9129 | **automobilia**
keys |

See full listing in **Section Two** under **locks & keys**

| **JR's Antique Auto**
21382 E Barbara Blvd
Claremore, OK 74017
918-342-4398 | **chrome parts**
interiors |

1916-1948 Chevy cars, parts and muscle cars. 1964-1972 Chevy cars, parts, interiors, motors.

| **JR's Chevy Parts**
478 Moe Rd
Clifton Park, NY 12065
518-383-5512; FAX: 518-383-2426
E-mail: jrschev@aol.com | **parts** |

Mail order only. We specialize in selling parts for 1965-1979 full-size Chevys: Impalas, Caprices, Super Sports, Bel Airs and Biscaynes. We have thousands of parts for these models, NOS and repro. Please visit our Web site: www.jrschevyparts.com

| **Kessler's Antique Cars & Body Shop**
1616 E Main St
Olney, IL 62450
618-393-4346 | **parts** |

Mail order and open shop. Monday-Friday 8 am to 5 pm. 1928-1948 Chevrolet reproduction parts. Some NOS parts. Please call before you come, we travel a lot to swap meets and we're not always there.

| **Late Great Chevrolet Association**
Robert Snowden
PO Box 607824
Orlando, FL 32860
407-886-1963; FAX: 407-886-7571
E-mail: info@lategreatchevy.com | **magazine** |

See full listing in **Section Four** under **periodicals**

| **Lee's Classic Chevy Sales**
314A Main St
Glenbeulah, WI 53023
920-526-3411 | **accessories**
literature
parts |

Mail order and open shop. Wednesday-Saturday 9 am to 4 pm. We have operated this business in the same location for 24 years. We take great pride in selling only quality parts that are guaranteed correct with customers all over the world. Parts, accessories and literature for 1955-1956-1957 Chevrolets (all models).

| **LES Auto Parts**
PO Box 81
Dayton, NJ 08810
732-329-6128; FAX: 732-329-1036 | **parts** |

Mail order and open shop. Monday-Saturday 8 am to 5 pm. Specializing in NOS GM parts for Chevrolet Impala, Chevelle, Nova, Camaro, all Pontiacs and Olds and Buick. All car parts 1950-1985.

Lloyd's Literature	literature
PO Box 491	
Newbury, OH 44065	
800-292-2665, 440-338-1527	
FAX: 440-338-2222	
E-mail: lloydslit@aol.com	

See full listing in **Section Two** under **literature dealers**

LMC Truck	accessories
PO Box 14991	parts
Lenexa, KS 66285	
800-222-5664; FAX: 913-599-0323	

Mail order catalog. Monday-Friday 7 am to 9 pm, Saturday-Sunday 9 am to 5 pm. Restore or repair your 1/2 or 3/4 ton Chevy truck 1947-1987. Our easy to read, fully illustrated free catalogs, fast service and an on-line computer order system make ordering easy. Large supply of parts and accessories include bed kits, body, interior, heating and cooling, suspension, brakes, electrical and much more. Web site: www.lmctruck.com

Lord Byron Inc	fender covers
420 Sackett Point Rd	
North Haven, CT 06473	
203-287-9881; FAX: 203-288-9456	

See full listing in **Section Two** under **car covers**

Lutty's Chevy Warehouse	reproduction parts
RD 2, 2385 Saxonburg Blvd	
Cheswick, PA 15024	
724-265-2988; FAX: 724-265-4773	
E-mail: luttys@nauticom.net	

Mail order and open shop. Monday-Wednesday 9 am to 7 pm, Thursday-Friday 9 am to 5 pm, Saturday 9 am to 2 pm EST. Specializing in reproduction parts to restore your Chevrolet

LUTTY'S CHEVY WAREHOUSE

We supply restoration parts for your Chevrolet. Do you need weatherstrip, emblems, moldings, interior, carpet or sheetmetal, new or used? We have all this in stock! '55-'56-'57, '58-'70 Impala, '62-'79 Nova, '64-'77 Chevelle & Monte Carlo, '67-'81 Camaro, '47-'72 Truck.

VISA/MC/Discover Accepted

▲ *CATALOGS $3 EACH* ▲

RD 2, 2385 Saxonburg Blvd
Cheswick, PA 15024
724-265-2988, FAX: 724-265-4773

1955-1968; Chevelle 1964-1977, including Monte Carlo; Nova 1962-1979; Camaro 1967-1981 and Chevy truck 1947-1972. Catalogs available by mail or downloadable from web site: www.luttyschevy.com

See our ad on this page

Mack Products	parts
PO Box 856	pickup beds
Moberly, MO 65270	
660-263-7444	
E-mail: jhummel@mackhils.com	

See full listing in **Section One** under **Ford 1932-1953**

Majestic Truck Parts	parts
17726 Dickerson	
Dallas, TX 75252	
972-248-6245; FAX: 972-380-8913	
E-mail: majestictrk@juno.com	

Specializing in top quality parts, NOS, reproduction, used and rare for 1947-1972 Chevy/GMC half to one ton trucks. We have a few good project trucks. Our tall red and white trailer visits Dallas/Fort Worth Metroplex meets. Visit north Dallas anytime by appointment; phone, e-mail or fax; we ship. We carry most of your needs, some of your wants and a few of your dreams. The most friendly, helpful people in truckin'.

MAR-K Quality Parts	bed parts
6625 W Wilshire Blvd	customizing parts
Oklahoma City, OK 73132	trim parts
405-721-7945; FAX: 405-721-8906	
E-mail: info@mar-k.com	

See full listing in **Section Two** under **trucks & tractors**

Marcovicci-Wenz Engineering Inc	Cosworth engines
33 Comac Loop	
Ronkonkoma, NY 11779	
631-467-9040; FAX: 631-467-9041	
E-mail: mwerace@compuserve.com	

See full listing in **Section Two** under **racing**

Master Power Brakes	brake products
110 Crosslake Park Rd	conversion kits
Mooresville, NC 28117	
704-664-8866; FAX: 704-664-8862	

See full listing in **Section One** under **Chevelle/Camaro**

Mecham Design, Performance	parts
12637 N 66th Dr	
Glendale, AZ 85304	
623-486-3155	
E-mail: demecham@uswest.net	

Mail order and open shop. Monday-Friday 8 am to 5 pm MST. Specializing in 1997-2001 Pontiac Firebird and Grand Prix, 1998-2001 Chevrolet Camaro, 1997-2001 Corvette and 1999-2001 trucks. Complete numbered series vehicles and parts graphics available for 1977-1979 macho T/As, 1982-1985 MSE Trans Ams, etc.

Charlie Merrill	broker
1041 Kenyon Rd	car dealer
Twin Falls, ID 83301	car locator
208-736-0949	

See full listing in **Section Two** under **brokers**

Merv's Classic Chevy Parts	parts
1330 Washington Ave	
Iowa Falls, IA 50126	
641-648-3168; PH/FAX: 641-648-9675	

Mail order and open shop. Specializing in reproduction, NOS and used parts for 1955-1957 Chevy automobiles.

Midwest Restoration Parts   parts
1736 E Oakton
Des Plaines, IL 60018
847-297-5090; FAX: 847-297-5097
E-mail: info@midwestrestoparts.com

Mail order and open shop. Monday-Friday 9 am to 6 pm, Saturday 9 am to 1 pm. Specializing in upholstery, lenses, weatherstrip, emblems, exterior and interior trim, sheetmetal, wheel parts for 1967-1981 Camaro, 1964-1972 Chevelle, 1955-1957 Chevy, 1958-1972 Impala, 1962-1974 Nova and 1970-1972 Monte Carlo. Web site: www.midwestrestoparts.com

Mike's Chevy Parts   restoration
7716 Deering Ave   supplies
Canoga Park, CA 91304
818-346-0070; FAX: 818-713-0715
E-mail: mikeschevyparts@aol.com

Mail order and open shop. Monday-Friday 8 am to 5 pm, Saturday 9 am to 12 pm. Specializing in new, used and reproduction parts for 1955-1970 Chevrolets, 1964-1972 Chevelles and El Caminos, 1962-1974 Novas. Complete frame straightening and front end repair. Antique auto parts and supplies.

Mike Moran   information
1349 Cleveland Rd
Glendale, CA 91202
E-mail: mikemoran24@hotmail.com

Mail order only. Technical information on Vegas, including Cosworth, also Mobil Gas economy runs, gasoline economy devices and unusual engines. SASE required.

Moroso Motorsports Park   race track
PO Box 31907
Palm Beach Gardens, FL 33420
561-622-1400; FAX: 561-626-2053
E-mail: mail@
morosomotorsportspark.com

See full listing in **Section Two** under **racing**

Mr G's Enterprises   fasteners
5613 Elliott Reeder Rd   screw kits
Fort Worth, TX 76117
817-831-3501; FAX: 817-831-0638
E-mail: mrgs@mrgusa.com

See full listing in **Section One** under **Mopar**

The National Corvette Museum   museum
350 Corvette Dr
Bowling Green, KY 42101-9134
800-53-Vette; FAX: 270-781-5286
E-mail: bobbiejo@corvettemuseum.com

See full listing in **Section Six** under **Kentucky**

Dave Newell's Chevrobilia   literature
PO Box 588   memorabilia
Orinda, CA 94563
510-223-4725

Mail order only. Original literature (sales, service, parts), showroom memorabilia, photos, films, models, jewelry, posters, etc for all Chevy cars and trucks, for all years. Impala, Chevelle, Nova, Camaro, Corvair and Corvette. Please send $5 for latest catalog of my constantly changing inventory.

Niagara CHT Productions Inc   swap meets
PO Box 112
Akron, NY 14001
716-542-2585

See full listing in **Section Two** under **auctions & shows**

Charles Noe   broker
64-1/2 Greenwood Ave   parts/auto purchases
Bethel, CT 06801   parts/auto sales
PH/FAX: 203-748-4222
E-mail: mdchas@aol.com

See full listing in **Section Two** under **brokers**

Normans' Classic Auto Radio   salvage yard
8475 68th Way
Pinellas Park, FL 33781
727-546-1788

See full listing in **Section Two** under **radios**

North Yale Auto Parts   salvage yard
Rt 1, Box 707
Sperry, OK 74073
800-256-6927 (NYAP), 918-288-7218
E-mail: nyap@ionet.net

See full listing in **Section Five** under **Oklahoma**

NOS Reproductions   parts
22425 Jefferies Rd, RR 3
Komoka ON Canada N0L 1R0
519-471-2740; FAX: 519-471-7675
E-mail: info@nosreproductions.com

See full listing in **Section One** under **Mopar**

Nova Parts   NOS parts
PO Box 985   reproduction parts
Mount Washington, KY 40047   used parts
502-239-8487; FAX: 502-231-1397

Mail order and open shop. Monday-Thursday 2-8 pm, Friday 12-5 pm, Saturday 9-2 pm. Specializing in NOS, used and reproduction for 1962-1979 Novas. Largest inventory in the US. Web site: www.chevy2only.com

Oak Bows   top bows
122 Ramsey Ave
Chambersburg, PA 17201
717-264-2602

See full listing in **Section Two** under **woodwork**

Obsolete Chevrolet Parts Co   engine parts
PO Box 68   radiators
Nashville, GA 31639-0068   rubber parts
800-248-8785; FAX: 229-686-3056   transmissions
E-mail: obschevy@surfsouth.com

We accept orders by telephone, fax, mail or you can shop online. Monday-Friday 8 am to 5:30 pm, Saturday 8:30 am to 12:30 pm. NOS and reproduction inventory of mechanical, electrical, weatherstripping, sheetmetal, trim parts, truck bed parts, interior kits and parts, air conditioning systems, radios and disc brake kits. We offer parts from 1929 to 1970s for Chevy car, truck, Chevelle, El Camino, Monte Carlo, Camaro and Chevy II. Catalogs are $3 each, specify vehicle. Web site: www.obschevy.com
See our ad on page 46

OEM Paints Inc   custom aerosol
PO Box 461736   colors
Escondido, CA 92046-1736
760-747-2100

See full listing in **Section Two** under **paints**

Old Air Products   air conditioning
4615 Martin St
Ft Worth, TX 76119
817-531-2665; FAX: 817-531-3257
E-mail: sales@oldairproducts.com

See full listing in **Section One** under **Corvette**

| The Old Car Centre
3-20075 92A Ave
Langley, BC Canada V1M 3A4
604-888-4412, 604-888-4055
FAX: 604-888-7455
E-mail: oldcarcentre@look.ca | parts |

See full listing in **Section One** under **Ford 1903-1931**

| Old Car Parts
7525 SE Powell
Portland, OR 97206
800-886-7277, 503-771-9416
FAX: 503-771-1981
E-mail: gsnovak@europa.com | parts |

Mail order and open shop. Monday-Friday 9 am to 5 pm. Specializing in GM parts for Chevrolet cars and pickups 1936-1969.

| The Old Carb Doctor
1127 Drucilla Church Rd
Nebo, NC 28761
800-945-CARB (2272)
828-659-1428 | carburetors
fuel pumps |

See full listing in **Section Two** under **carburetors**

| Old Chevy Parts Store
formally known as Palm Springs
Obsolete Automotive
120 N Pacific A-8
San Marcos, CA 92069
760-752-1479; FAX: 760-752-1528
E-mail: info@oldchevypartsstore.com | parts |

Mail order and open shop. Tuesday-Friday 7 am to 5 pm, Saturday 8 am to 4 pm. Manufacture of 1955/1957 passenger car fan shrouds, new, reproduction parts for 1955/1957 pass cars, 1958/1972 Impalas. Established in 1983. Catalogs, $4 each in US

and $8 out of country, free with purchase. Please state which model you are working on. Web site: www.oldchevypartsstore.com

| Old Coach Works Restoration Inc
1206 Badger St
Yorkville, IL 60560-1701
630-553-0414; FAX: 630-553-1053
E-mail: oldcoachworks@msn.com | appraisals
restoration |

See full listing in **Section Two** under **restoration shops**

| Old Dominion Mustang/Camaro
509 S Washington Hwy, Rt 1
Ashland, VA 23005
804-798-3348; FAX: 804-798-5105 | parts |

See full listing in **Section One** under **Mustang**

| Old GMC Trucks.Com
Robert English
PO Box 675
Franklin, MA 02038-0675
508-520-3900; FAX: 508-520-7861
E-mail: oldcarkook@aol.com | literature
parts |

See full listing in **Section One** under **GMC**

| Old Gold Retold Inc
Florida Swap Meets
6250 Tennessee Ave
New Port Richey, FL 34653
800-438-8559; FAX: 727-846-8922
E-mail: swapmet@gte.net | auction
car show
swap meet |

See full listing in **Section Two** under **auctions & shows**

| Oldenbetter Restorations Inc
22530 Hwy 49, PO Box 1000
Saucier, MS 39574-1000
228-831-2650
E-mail: oldenbeter@yahoo.com | repairs
restorations |

Mail order and open shop. Monday-Friday 7 am to 5 pm. Classic automobile restoration, British and American. In-house sheetmetal, rust repair, paint, mechanical and electrical.

| Only Yesterday Classic Autos Inc
24 Valley Rd
Port Washington, NY 11050
516-767-3477; FAX: 516-767-8964 | cars |

Classic and special interest autos from the 1930s-1960s. We specialize in Chevys, Corvettes, Fords and Pontiacs. We are authorized dealers for Shelby American Inc. in San Diego, California, selling the 4000 and 7000 Series Shelby Cobras. Tell us your interest and we will help you locate what you are looking for. Web site: www.oldautos.com

| P-Ayr Products
719 Delaware St
Leavenworth, KS 66048
913-651-5543; FAX: 913-651-2084
E-mail: sales@payr.com | replicas |

Specializing in light weight automotive engines, transmissions and motorcycle engine replicas for Chevrolet, Ford and Chrysler. Web site: www.payr.com

| The Paddock® Inc
PO Box 30, 221 W Main
Knightstown, IN 46148
800-428-4319; FAX: 800-286-4040
E-mail: paddock@paddockparts.com | accessories
parts |

Mail order and open shop. Monday-Friday 8 am to 7 pm, Saturday 9 am to 4 pm, Sunday 12 pm to 4 pm. The original supplier of muscle car parts. Specializing in interior, accessories, sheetmetal, suspension, engine, brake parts and much more for

1964-2000 Mustang, 1967-2000 Camaro, 1962-1974 Dodge/ Plymouth, 1964-1977 Chevelle, 1970-1988 Monte Carlo, 1962-1979 Nova, 1964-1974 GTO, 1958-1976 Impala, 1964-1977 Cutlass, 1967-2000 Firebird, 1955-1957 Chevy, 1947-1988 Chevy/GMC truck and 1953-2000 Corvette. Three convenient locations. Web site: www.paddockparts.com

Paragon Reproductions Inc	**Corvette repro**
8040 S Jennings Rd	**parts**
Swartz Creek, MI 48473	
800-882-4688; FAX: 810-655-6667	
E-mail: sales@corvette-paragon.com	

See full listing in **Section One** under **Corvette**

M Parker Autoworks Inc	**battery cables**
150 Heller Pl #17W, Dept HCCA02	**harnesses**
Bellmawr, NJ 08031	
856-933-0801; FAX: 856-933-0805	
E-mail: info@factoryfit.com	

See full listing in **Section Two** under **electrical systems**

The Parts Place	**parts**
217 Paul St	
Elburn, IL 60119	
630-365-1800; FAX: 630-365-1900	
E-mail: sales@thepartsplaceinc.com	

Classic car parts for General Motors vehicles. Specializing in new, used, reproduction and discontinued parts for 1960-1980. Web site: www.thepartsinc.com

Parts Unlimited Inc	**interiors**
Cliff Carr	**weatherstrips**
12101 Westport Rd	
Louisville, KY 40245-1789	
800-342-0610, 502-425-3766	
FAX: 502-425-7910, 502-232-9784	
E-mail: contactpui@aol.com	

Since 1977 we have strived to manufacture the highest quality interior components at the fairest possible price. Our products include seat covers, door panels, headliners, sunvisors, top-boots, weatherstrips, package trays/insulation, trunk dividers, armrest bases/pads, etc. All products are made in the USA. Call 800-342-0610 for the dealer nearest you. Web site: www.pui.com

Peninsula Restoration Parts	**parts**
4526 Viewmont Ave	
Victoria, BC Canada V8L 4L9	
250-727-2678; FAX: 250-727-2693	
E-mail: info@peninsularestoration.com	

Mail order and open shop. Monday-Friday 8:30 am to 5 pm, 1st and 3rd Saturday 9:30 am to 12:30 pm. Specializing in sheetmetal, interiors, weatherstrips, all accessories, OEM, repro and used parts for Chevrolet Camaro, Chevelle, Nova, GTO, Impala, Cutlass and Chevy/GMC trucks, Ford trucks, Mustang. Web site: www.peninsularestoration.com

Performance Chevy	**engine parts**
2995 W Whitton	**restoration**
Phoenix, AZ 85017	
800-203-6621; FAX: 602-254-1094	

See full listing in **Section One** under **Corvette**

Garth B Peterson	**accessories/chrome**
W 2619 Rockwell Ave	**glass/grilles/parts**
Spokane, WA 99205	**radios/sheetmetal**
509-325-3823 anytime	**steering wheels**

See full listing in **Section Two** under **comprehensive parts**

Pick-ups Northwest	**parts**
9911 Airport Way	**trim**
Snohomish, WA 98296	
360-568-9166; FAX: 360-568-1233	

Mail order and open shop. Monday-Friday 9 am to 5:30 pm, Saturday 9 am to 3 pm. Specializing in weatherstrip, interior, chrome trim, pickup box parts and wood kits for 1932-1972 Chevy and 1932-1973 Ford pickup trucks. Restoration or street rod parts. Web site: www.pickupsnw.com

Pilkington Glass Search	**glass parts**
1975 Galaxie St	
Columbus, OH 43207	
800-848-1351; FAX: 614-443-0709	

See full listing in **Section Two** under **glass**

John E Pirkle	**electrical parts**
3706 Merion Dr	
Augusta, GA 30907	
706-860-9047; FAX: 706-860-2723	
E-mail: pirklesr@aol.com	

See full listing in **Section One** under **Corvette**

Jack Podell Fuel Injection Spec	**fuel system parts**
106 Wakewa Ave	**fuel system**
South Bend, IN 46617	**rebuilding**
219-232-6430; FAX: 219-234-8632	
E-mail: podellsfi@aol.com	

See full listing in **Section One** under **Corvette**

Dennis Portka	**horns**
4326 Beetow Dr	**knock-off wheels**
Hamburg, NY 14075	
716-649-0921	

See full listing in **Section One** under **Corvette**

Power Brake Booster Exchange Inc	**brake boosters**
4533 SE Division St	
Portland, OR 97206	
503-238-8882	

See full listing in **Section Two** under **brakes**

Power Brake Systems	**brake repair**
c/o Jerry Cinotti	
431 S Sierra Way	
San Bernadino, CA 92408	
909-884-6980; FAX: 909-884-7872	

See full listing in **Section Two** under **brakes**

Power Brake X-Change Inc	**parts**
336 Lamont Pl	
Pittsburgh, PA 15232	
800-580-5729, 412-441-5729	
FAX: 412-441-9333	

See full listing in **Section Two** under **brakes**

PRO Antique Auto Parts	**parts**
50 King Spring Rd	
Windsor Locks, CT 06096	
860-623-8275	

Mail order and open shop. Monday-Friday 9 am to 5 pm. Exclusive distributor of numerous reproduction parts for 1923-1964 Chevrolets. Catalog, $3.

Prototype Research & Dev Ltd — *fiberglass bodies*
David Carlaw
230 Albert Ln
Campbellford, ON Canada K0L 1L0
705-653-4525; FAX: 705-653-4800
E-mail: davidcarlaw@hotmail.com

Specializing in 1955-1957 Chevrolet body manufacturing and sales. Exact original design Chevrolet Bel Air convertible and hardtop fiberglass bodies and parts. Replicated to accept all original moldings and interiors or full custom on a new B-bodied Chevrolet chassis.

R & R Fiberglass & Specialties — *body parts*
4850 Wilson Dr NW
Cleveland, TN 37312
423-476-2270; FAX: 423-473-9442
E-mail: rrfiberglass@aol.com

See full listing in **Section Two** under **fiberglass parts**

Red Bird Racing — *parts*
6640 Valley St
Coeur d'Alene, ID 83815
208-762-5305

Mail order only. Specializing in 1937-1954 Chevy chassis update parts. Bolt on Saginaw steering adapters, dropped spindles, Teflon button rear spring kits, front and rear tube shock mounting kits. Chevy 6-cyl split manifolds, 216-235-261 alternator brackets. GMC and Chevy 6-cyl to Turbo 350-400 kits. Inline and flathead V8 speed parts, Fenton headers. Distributor for all Offenhauser products.

Reproduction Parts Marketing — *parts, restoration, service*
1920 Alberta Ave
Saskatoon, SK Canada S7K 1R9
306-652-6668; FAX: 306-652-1123

Mail order and open shop. Monday-Saturday 8 am to 6 pm. Canada's largest stocking GM, Ford and Mopar dealer. All parts are guaranteed to be the finest available and our prices are the lowest. Also handling complete restorations. Parts, service, tech advice, appraisals, locator service.

Restoration Specialties — *interiors, restoration*
John Sarena
124 North F St
Lompoc, CA 93436
805-736-2627
E-mail: showtimechevys@msn.com

Open shop only. Monday-Friday 8 am to 5 pm PST. Partial to 1955-1957 Chevrolets, and one of the authors of the *CCCI Restoration and Judging Guidelines Manual*. Shares the love of all special interest cars of the 1940-1960s and worked with Moss Motors for nine years in designing all of the interior kits. Takes great pride in craftsmanship and it shows in finished interiors. Dealer for CARS reproduction interiors. Specializing in interior restoration, partial restoration for GM cars.

Rick's First Generation Camaro Parts & Accessories — *accessories, parts*
420 Athena Dr
Athens, GA 30601
800-359-7717; FAX: 877-548-8581
E-mail: firstgen@negia.net

See full listing in **Section One** under **Chevelle/Camaro**

Roberts Motor Parts — *parts*
17 Prospect St
West Newbury, MA 01985
978-363-5407; FAX: 978-363-2026
E-mail: sales@robertsmotorparts.com

See full listing in **Section One** under **Chrysler**

Leon J Rocco — *accessories, parts*
4125 Loring St
Butler, PA 16001
724-482-4387 after 6 pm

See full listing in **Section One** under **Chevelle/Camaro**

Rock Valley Antique Auto Parts — *gas tanks*
Box 352, Rt 72 and Rothwell Rd
Stillman Valley, IL 61084
815-645-2271; FAX: 815-645-2740

See full listing in **Section One** under **Ford 1932-1953**

Rodman's Auto Wood Restoration — *wood kits*
Box 86 Wheeler St
Hanna, IN 46340
219-797-3775

Specializing in wood kits for Chevrolets. Also custom woodwork and installation.

Ross' Automotive Machine Co Inc — *racing engines, rebuilding*
1763 N Main St
Niles, OH 44446
330-544-4466

See full listing in **Section Two** under **engine rebuilding**

Route 66 Corvette Show — *car show*
2419 A W Jefferson
Joliet, IL 60435
815-722-8388; FAX: 815-733-8389
E-mail: acs@corvetteshow.com

See full listing in **Section Two** under **auctions & shows**

Chuck Scharf Enterprises — *parts*
1019 N Minnesota St
New Ulm, MN 56073
507-354-4501

Mail order only. Specializing in 348/409 equipped 1958-1965 full size Chevrolets. We offer a full line of engine rebuild parts, 20 different engine rebuild kits, 348/409 pistons, standard, +.030, +.040, +.060. One call does it all, same day shipping. Visa, MasterCard, COD orders welcome. Free rebuild catalog.

Scotts Super Trucks — *parts*
1972 Hwy 592 W
Penhold, AB Canada T0M 1R0
403-886-5572; FAX: 403-886-5577
E-mail: info@scottssupertrucks.com

Mail order and open shop. Tuesday-Saturday 10 am to 5 pm MST. Specialize in 1967-1972 GMC/Chev trucks, but also carry a full line of new and used parts from 1934-1966 original and custom parts. Everything to restore your classic truck. Also many project trucks for sale, 1935-1972. Web site: www.scottssupertrucks.com

Sherman & Associates Inc — *body panels, body parts, fenders/floors, quarter panels*
61166 Van Dyke Rd
Washington, MI 48094
810-677-6800; FAX: 810-677-6801

See full listing in **Section Two** under **body parts**

Shiftworks — *shifters*
PO Box 25351
Rochester, NY 14625
PH/FAX: 716-383-0574

See full listing in **Section One** under **Chevelle/Camaro**

Solow Suspension | suspension parts
7731 NE 33rd Dr
Portland, OR 97211
503-288-5951; FAX: 503-288-5991
E-mail: dropshop99@hevanet.com

Specializing in 1960-1972 Chevrolet pickups, Blazers, Suburbans, 1/2 ton, 3/4 ton and 1 ton lowering and performance suspension packages. Established 1978. 23 years of quality craftsmanship. Web site: www.charleysdropshop.com

Bob Sottile's Hobby Car | car dealer
Auto Sales Inc | restoration
RD 2 Box 210B, Rt 164
Martinsburg, PA 16662
814-793-4282

See full listing in **Section One** under **Corvette**

Sound Move Inc | radios
217 S Main St
Elkhart, IN 46516
800-901-0222, 219-294-5100
FAX: 219-293-4902

Mail order and open shop. Monday-Friday 9 am to 5 pm, Saturday 9 am to 12 pm. Specializing in AM-FM radios and audio systems that install into original factory location with no modifications. For classic cars and trucks, 1940-1989. Web site: www.soundmove.com

Stencils & Stripes Unlimited Inc | NOS decals
1108 S Crescent Ave #21 | stripe kits
Park Ridge, IL 60068
847-692-6893; FAX: 847-692-6895

See full listing in **Section Two** under **decals**

Stoudt Auto Sales | parts
1350 Carbon St | sales
Reading, PA 19601 | service
800-523-8485 USA parts dept | Corvette parts
800-482-3033 USA sales dept
610-374-4856, parts info
FAX: 610-372-7283
E-mail: stoudtauto@cs.com

See full listing in **Section One** under **Corvette**

Street-Wise Performance | differentials
Richie Mulligan | new/used parts
Box 105 Creek Rd | overhaul kits
Tranquility, NJ 07879 | transmissions
973-786-7500; FAX: 973-786-7861
E-mail: street-wise@usa.net

See full listing in **Section Two** under **transmissions**

Tags Backeast | data plates
PO Box 581 | trim tags
Plainville, CT 06062 | cowl tags
860-747-2942
E-mail: dataplt@snet.net

See full listing in **Section Two** under **special services**

Bill Thomsen | salvage yard
1118 Wooded Acres Ln
Moneta, VA 24121
540-297-1200

See full listing in **Section Five** under **Virginia**

Tom's Classic Parts | parts
5207 Sundew Terr
Tobyhanna, PA 18466
PH/FAX: 570-894-1459

Mail order and pick up. Call for hours. Genuine Chevrolet parts for your Bel Air, Biscayne, Caprice, Impala, Monte Carlo, Nova

and others 1960-present. We have NOS and quality used parts available. Experienced staff to help in your search for parts. MasterCard, Visa, AmEx. Web site: www.pennautoparts.com

Tom's Obsolete Chevy Parts | parts
14 Delta Dr
Pawtucket, RI 02860
401-723-7580; FAX: 401-724-7568

Mail order and auto swap meets. New and reproduction 1955-1972 Chevrolet parts. Nova, Impala, Chevelle, Camaro. Showroom hours, 1 to 9 pm weekdays, 1 to 5 pm Saturdays.

Torque Tech Performance Exhaust | exhaust systems
1826 Woodland Dr
Valdosta, GA 31601
800-408-0016
E-mail: torque@surfsourth.com

See full listing in **Section Two** under **exhaust systems**

Tri-Five Classics | chrome plating
5000 NC Hwy 150 E | parts
Browns Summit, NC 27214 | restoration
336-656-1957; FAX: 336-656-7657
E-mail: info@tri-fiveclassics.com

Mail order and open shop. Specializing in new, used and reproduction parts, chrome plating, POR-15 dealer for 1955-1956-1957 Chevrolets (all models). Also do restorations. Web site: www.trifiveclassics.bigslep.com/

Trim Parts Inc | trim items
5161 Wolfpen Pleasant Hill
Milford, OH 45150
513-831-1472; FAX: 513-248-3402
E-mail: sales@trimparts.com

Mail order and open shop. Monday-Friday 8 am to 5 pm. Classic GM restoration, reproduction emblems, lenses, scripts and other trim items for classic GM cars and trucks. 1955-1957 Chevy, 1958-1972 full-size, 1967-1985 Camaro, 1953-1982 Corvette, 1964-1972 Chevelle, 1967-1969 Firebird, 1962-1972 Nova, 1964-1972 El Camino, 1970-1972 Monte Carlo, GTO, Corvair. Web site: www.trimparts.com

The Truck Shop | parts
104 W Marion Ave, PO Box 5035
Nashville, GA 31639
800-245-0556 orders
info: 229-686-3833, 229-686-3396
FAX: 229-686-3531

Mail order and open shop. Monday-Friday 8 am to 5 pm. Chevrolet and GMC truck parts. NOS and reproduction 1927-1987. Bed components, weatherstrips, glass channel, hubcaps, handles and controls, headliners, interior parts, emblems and moldings, manuals, mirrors, patch panels, lights, suspension, carpets, mats and much more. Catalog, $5. Web site: www.thetruckshopga.com

The V8 Store | accessories
3010 NE 49th St | parts
Vancouver, WA 98663 | service
360-693-7468
360-694-7853 nights
FAX: 360-693-0982

See full listing in **Section Two** under **custom cars**

Tom Vagnini | used parts
58 Anthony Rd, RR 3
Pittsfield, MA 01201
413-698-2526

See full listing in **Section One** under **Packard**

Varco Inc
8200 S Anderson Rd
Oklahoma City, OK 73150
405-732-1637

fitted luggage
trunks

See full listing in **Section One** under **Ford 1903-1931**

Vette Vues Magazine
PO Box 741596
Orange City, FL 32774
386-775-8454; FAX: 386-775-3042
E-mail: comments@vettevues.com

magazine

See full listing in **Section Four** under **periodicals**

Vintage Auto Parts Inc
24300 Hwy 9
Woodinville, WA 98072
800-426-5911, 425-486-0777
FAX: 425-486-0778
E-mail: erics@vapinc.com

cars
parts

See full listing in **Section Two** under **comprehensive parts**

**Vintage Ford & Chevrolet Parts
of Arizona Inc**
So-Cal Speed Shop
3427 E McDowell Rd
Phoenix, AZ 85008-3845
800-732-0076, 602-275-7990
FAX: 602-267-8439
E-mail: vintageparts@sprintmail.com

parts

See full listing in **Section One** under **Ford 1954-up**

Vintage Gas, Ltd
E-mail: info@vintagegas.com

artwork

See full listing in **Section Two** under **artwork**

Volunteer State Chevy Parts LLC
2414 Hwy 41 S, PO Box 10
Greenbrier, TN 37073
615-643-4583; FAX: 615-643-5100

accessories
parts

Mail order and open shop. Monday-Friday (Saturday?) 8 am to 6 pm CST. Specializing in obsolete parts and accessories from 1949-1972 passenger cars and trucks, includes Chevelle, Chevy II, Camaro, with special emphasis on 1955-1967 Impalas, etc.

Waldron's Antique Exhaust Inc
25872 M-86, PO Box C
Nottawa, MI 49075
616-467-7185; FAX: 616-467-9041

exhaust systems

See full listing in **Section Two** under **exhaust systems**

Wales Antique Chevy Truck Parts
143 Center
Carleton, MI 48117
734-654-8836

parts

Specializing in 1936-1972 Chevrolet trucks. Windshield, cab, door and hood rubber. Seals, weatherstrip, headlights, parking lights, taillights. Parts, brackets, outside and inside handles. Bed wood, tailgates, front and side panels. Wear strips, angles, repair panels. Books, manuals. Engine and mechanical parts, fiberglass fenders and runningboards. Hubcaps, trim rings, runningboard step plates. Also rebuilds door hinges, refaces and rebuilds gauges. Chrome work and cutting of clear and tinted glass. Used parts for 1947-1955 Chevrolet trucks. Send (2) 33¢ stamps for free catalog, state year of truck.

Wheel Vintiques Inc
5468 E Lamona Ave
Fresno, CA 93727
209-251-6957; FAX: 209-251-1620

hubcaps
wheels

Mail order only. Wheel Vintiques is a manufacturer of nostalgia, classic and OEM steel wheels and Rallyes. Also many types of classic wires. Web site: www.wheelvintiques.com

White Post Restorations
One Old Car Dr, PO Drawer D
White Post, VA 22663
540-837-1140; FAX: 540-837-2368
E-mail: info@whitepost.com

brakes
restoration

See full listing in **Section Two** under **brakes**

White Post Restorations
One Old Car Dr, PO Drawer D
White Post, VA 22663
540-837-1140; FAX: 540-837-2368
E-mail: info@whitepost.com

restoration

See full listing in **Section Two** under **restoration shops**

Willow Grove Auto Top
43 N York Rd
Willow Grove, PA 19090
215-659-3276

interiors
tops
upholstery

See full listing in **Section Two** under **interiors & interior parts**

WiperWorks
PO Box 57
Sewanee, TN 37375
PH/FAX: 931-598-9573

restoration

Mail order only. Specializing in restoration of wiper motors for 1955-1980.

The Woodie Works
245 VT Rt 7A
Arlington, VT 05250
PH/FAX: 802-375-9305
E-mail: dkwoodie@vermontel.net

woodworking

See full listing in **Section Two** under **woodwork**

Year One Inc
PO Box 129
Tucker, GA 30085
800-YEAR-ONE (932-7663)
770-493-6568 Atlanta & overseas
FAX: 800-680-6806
E-mail: info@yearone.com

parts

See full listing in **Section Two** under **comprehensive parts**

CHEVELLE camaro

4-Speeds by Darrell
3 Water St, PO Box 110
Vermilion, IL 61955
217-275-3743; FAX: 217-275-3515

transmissions

See full listing in **Section Two** under **transmissions**

| **All Chevy/Canadian Impala**
404 Allwood Rd
Parksville, BC Canada V9P 1C4
250-248-8666; FAX: 888-248-1958
E-mail: canimp@nanaimo.ark.com | parts |

See full listing in **Section One** under **Chevrolet**

| **AMK Products Inc**
800 Airport Rd
Winchester, VA 22602
540-662-7820; FAX: 540-662-7821 | parts |

See full listing in **Section One** under **Ford 1954-up**

| **ARS Automotive Research Services**
Division of Auto Search International
1702 W Camelback #301
Phoenix, AZ 85015
602-230-7111; FAX: 602-230-7282 | appraisals
research |

See full listing in **Section Two** under **appraisals**

| **Auto Custom Carpet Inc**
1429 Noble St, PO Box 1350
Anniston, AL 36201
800-633-2358, 256-236-1118
FAX: 800-516-8274 | carpets
floor mats |

See full listing in **Section Two** under **carpets**

| **Camaro Specialties**
112 Elm St
East Aurora, NY 14052
716-652-7086; FAX: 716-652-2279
E-mail: camarospecial@wzrd.com | parts
restoration |

Specializing in 1966-1972 GM muscle cars. Offer new, used, reproduction and southern parts. Now booking restorations for 1967-1969 Camaros or Firebirds. Catalogs available for Camaro, Firebird and Chevelle. Web site: www.camaros.com

| **Chevelle World Inc**
PO Box 926
Noble, OK 73068
405-872-0379; FAX: 405-872-0385 | parts |

Mail order only. Specializing in original and reproduction body parts, interior, exterior, weatherstrip, patch repair, etc, for 1967-1972 Chevelle and El Camino. Full line Chevelle World catalog for $4.

| **Chevyland Parts & Accessories**
3667 Recycle Rd #8
Rancho Cordova, CA 95742
916-638-3906; FAX: 916-638-0302
E-mail: 327@chevylandparts.com | accessories
parts
restoration |

Mail order and open shop. Monday-Friday 9 am to 6 pm and Saturday 10 am to 3 pm. Specializing in restoration parts and accessories for Camaro, Chevelle, El Camino, Nova and 1967-1972 Chevrolet pickup trucks. Web site: www.chevylandparts.com

| **Classic Chevrolet Parts Inc**
8723 S I-35
Oklahoma City, OK 73149
405-631-4400; FAX: 405-631-5999
E-mail: info@classicchevroletparts.com | parts |

See full listing in **Section One** under **Chevrolet**

| **Classic Coachworks**
735 Frenchtown Rd
Milford, NJ 08848
908-996-3400; FAX: 908-996-0204
E-mail: info@classiccoachworks.net | bodywork
painting
restoration |

See full listing in **Section Two** under **restoration shops**

| **Classic Industries Inc**
Camaro Parts and Accessories Catalog
17832 Gothard St
Huntington Beach, CA 92647
800-854-1280 parts/info
FAX: 800-300-3081 toll free
E-mail: info@classicindustries.com | accessories
parts |

Largest selection of Camaro parts and accessories ever assembled in one catalog. Over 580 full color pages of the finest quality restoration products and late model accessories. Only $5, refunded on first order. Call our 24-hour toll-free catalog hotline, 888-GM-CATALOG and receive the industry's most comprehensive parts catalog from the undisputed leader in the industry, Classic Industries. Web site: www.classicindustries.com

| **Classic Performance Products**
8341 Artesia Blvd, Unit C
Buena Park, CA 90621
800-522-5004; FAX: 714-522-2500
E-mail: info@classicperform.com | brakes
steering
suspension |

See full listing in **Section One** under **Chevrolet**

| **Coach Builders Muscle Car**
Parts & Services
PO Box 128
Baltimore, MD 21087-0128
410-426-5567 | interiors
parts
rust remover |

See full listing in **Section One** under **Chevrolet**

| **Competitive Automotive Inc**
2095 W Shore Rd (Rt 117)
Warwick, RI 02889
401-739-6262, 401-739-6288
FAX: 401-739-1497 | parts
restoration |

Mail order and showroom. Monday-Friday, 11 am to 8 pm. GM restoration supplies. Specializing in complete line of 1967-1981 Camaro and Firebird restoration supplies and parts. New, used, reproduction and obscure parts including body panels, trim, mechanical, suspensions, wiring, interior and upholstery, weatherstripping, lenses, convertibles, windows, literature, decals, fasteners, switches, bumpers, braces, grilles, manuals, emblems, headliners, etc. Also handle all GM muscle cars in 1960s and 1970s.

| **Conte's Corvettes & Classics**
851 W Wheat Rd
Vineland, NJ 08360
856-692-0087; FAX: 856-692-1009
E-mail: contes@cybernet.net | leasing
parts
sales
service |

See full listing in **Section One** under **Corvette**

| **Desert Muscle Cars**
2853 N Stone Ave
Tucson, AZ 85705
520-882-3010; FAX: 520-628-9332 | parts |

Mail order and open shop. Weekdays 9 am to 5:30 pm, Saturday 9 am to 3 pm. Specializing in restoration supplies and parts for 1955-1970 Chevrolets, 1967-1981 Camaro, 1964-1972 Chevelle, 1947-1972 Chevrolet trucks, 1964-1973 Mustangs. Deals in weatherstripping, interiors, emblems, moldings, decals, books, etc.

| **EC Parts**
PO Box 2459
Citrus Heights, CA 95611
916-722-2676; FAX: 916-722-4127
E-mail: rick@ecparts.net | parts |

See full listing in **Section One** under **Chevrolet**

The El Camino Store
57 B Depot Rd
Goleta, CA 93117
805-681-8164; FAX: 805-681-8166
E-mail: ec@elcaminostore.com

parts

Walk-in and phone orders. Monday-Friday 8 am to 5:30 pm. Sell parts for all the Chevrolet and GMC El Caminos ever made from 1959-1987. Carry an extensive inventory of weatherstripping, emblems, chrome, trim, decals, interior parts. Also manufacture our own parts and are a GM Restoration parts licensee.

ETC/Every Thing Cars
8727 Clarinda
Pico Rivera, CA 90660
562-949-6981

paint
repairs
restoration
welding

See full listing in **Section One** under **Mopar**

Firewall Insulators & Quiet Ride Solutions
6465 Pacific Ave, Ste 249
Stockton, CA 95207
209-477-4840; FAX: 209-477-0918
E-mail: timcox@quietride.com

air plenums
auto insulation
firewall insulators
gloveboxes
sound deadening

See full listing in **Section Two** under **upholstery**

Gardner Exhaust Systems
7 Cedar Ln
Rhinebeck, NY 12572
845-876-8117; FAX: 845-871-1750
E-mail: gexhaust@aol.com

exhaust systems

See full listing in **Section Two** under **exhaust systems**

Gold Eagle Classics
5990 SW 185th Ave, Bldg H
Aloha, OR 97007
503-642-2005; FAX: 503-642-0808
E-mail: gldeagle@europa.com

accessories
parts

Mail order and open shop. Monday-Friday 9 am to 6 pm, Saturday 11 am to 3 pm PST. New and reproduction classic GM auto parts and accessories for 1964-1987 Chevelle and El Camino, 1967-1981 Camaro, 1962-1972 Nova, 1960-1972 Impala. Web site: www.europa.com/~gldeagle

Greg's Automotive
Box 1712
Santa Ynez, CA 93460
PH/FAX: 805-688-5675
E-mail: 9pm@silcom.com

accessories
books
literature

See full listing in **Section One** under **Chevrolet**

J & K Old Chevy Stuff
Ship Pond Rd
Plymouth, MA 02360
508-224-7616
kblaze58@aol.com

car dealer
parts
sheetmetal

See full listing in **Section One** under **Chevrolet**

J&M Auto Parts
10 Spaulding Hill Rd
Pelham, NH 03076
603-635-3866

NOS parts
repro parts

See full listing in **Section One** under **Chevrolet**

JR's Antique Auto
21382 E Barbara Blvd
Claremore, OK 74017
918-342-4398

chrome parts
interiors

See full listing in **Section One** under **Chevrolet**

The Last Precinct Police Museum
15677 Hwy 62 W
Eureka Springs, AR 72632
501-253-4948; FAX: 501-253-4949

museum

See full listing in **Section Six** under **Arkansas**

Lectric Limited Inc
7322 S Archer Road
Justice, IL 60458
708-563-0400; FAX: 708-563-0416

parts

See full listing in **Section One** under **Corvette**

LES Auto Parts
PO Box 81
Dayton, NJ 08810
732-329-6128; FAX: 732-329-1036

parts

See full listing in **Section One** under **Chevrolet**

Lutty's Chevy Warehouse
RD 2, 2385 Saxonburg Blvd
Cheswick, PA 15024
724-265-2988; FAX: 724-265-4773
E-mail: luttys@nauticom.net

reproduction parts

See full listing in **Section One** under **Chevrolet**

Master Power Brakes
110 Crosslake Park Rd
Mooresville, NC 28117
704-664-8866; FAX: 704-664-8862

brake products
conversion kits

Manufacturer of power boosters and power disc brake conversion kits. Kits available for Fords, Pontiacs, GM cars and trucks. Stainless steel sleeving of 4-piston calipers and master cylinders. Web site: www.mpbrakes.com

Mecham Design, Performance
12637 N 66th Dr
Glendale, AZ 85304
623-486-3155
E-mail: demecham@uswest.net

parts

See full listing in **Section One** under **Chevrolet**

Midwest Restoration Parts
1736 E Oakton
Des Plaines, IL 60018
847-297-5090; FAX: 847-297-5097
E-mail: info@midwestrestoparts.com

parts

See full listing in **Section One** under **Chevrolet**

Muscle Express
135 Hibiscus St
Jupiter, FL 33458
800-323-3043 order line
561-744-3043 tech line

parts

Molded carpet, weatherstrip and interior kits, body panels plus more reproduction, used, NOS parts. Restorations, installations. Many discontinued parts, full quarter panels, fenders, tach and gauges, consoles, shifters, bucket seats. UPS daily. Credit cards.

National Parts Depot
900 SW 38th Ave
Ocala, FL 34474
800-874-7595; FAX: 352-861-8706

accessories
parts

See full listing in **Section One** under **Mustang**

Next Generation Restoration Performance by Year One — parts
PO Box 2023
Tucker, GA 30084
800-921-9214; FAX: 800-680-6806
E-mail: info@nextgenparts.com

The next generation of muscle cars needs the Next Generation catalog. Next Generation Restoration and Performance by Year One specializes in the finest available performance and restoration parts and accessories for 1982 to present Camaro and Firebird and 1979 to present Mustang. Call today for free catalog. Web site: www.nextgenparts.com

OEM Glass — auto glass
Rt 9 E, PO Box 362
Bloomington, IL 61702
800-283-2122, 309-662-2122
FAX: 309-663-7474

See full listing in **Section Two** under **glass**

Old Dominion Mustang/Camaro — parts
509 S Washington Hwy, Rt 1
Ashland, VA 23005
804-798-3348; FAX: 804-798-5105

See full listing in **Section One** under **Mustang**

Peninsula Restoration Parts — parts
4526 Viewmont Ave
Victoria, BC Canada V8L 4L9
250-727-2678; FAX: 250-727-2693
E-mail: info@peninsularestoration.com

See full listing in **Section One** under **Chevrolet**

Performance Chevy — engine parts, restoration
2995 W Whitton
Phoenix, AZ 85017
800-203-6621; FAX: 602-254-1094

See full listing in **Section One** under **Corvette**

Phoenix Graphix Inc — decals, stripe kits
5861 S Kyrene Rd #10
Tempe, AZ 85283
800-941-4550

See full listing in **Section Two** under **decals**

John E Pirkle — electrical parts
3706 Merion Dr
Augusta, GA 30907
706-860-9047; FAX: 706-860-2723
E-mail: pirklesr@aol.com

See full listing in **Section One** under **Corvette**

Rick's First Generation Camaro Parts & Accessories — accessories, parts
420 Athena Dr
Athens, GA 30601
800-359-7717; FAX: 877-548-8581
E-mail: firstgen@negia.net

Mail order and open shop. Monday-Friday 9 am to 5 pm, Saturday 10 am to 2 pm. Restoration parts, new GM NOS and used parts for 1967-1969 Camaro. Same day shipping. All credit cards, COD welcome. 24 hour order line. Fully illustrated catalog with over 3,000 parts photos. 1967-1969, it's all we do! Web site: www.firstgen.com

Leon J Rocco — accessories, parts
4125 Loring St
Butler, PA 16001
724-482-4387 after 6 pm

Mail order only. Specializing in accessories and new, used and NOS parts for 1950s, 1960s, 1970s Chevrolet, Camaro, Chevelle, Nova, Corvair, El Camino. Lights, lenses, bezels, emblems, mirrors, radios, dash knobs, switches, steering wheels, glass triangle Optikleen bottles, door and window handles, bumper jacks, misc.

Shiftworks — shifters
PO Box 25351
Rochester, NY 14625
PH/FAX: 716-383-0574

Mail order only. Shifter conversion kits for TH and overdrive automatic transmissions for 1964-1972 Chevelle, 1967-1981 Camaro, 1964-1972 Impala, 1965-1972 Nova, 1968-1981 Corvette, 1967-1981 Firebird, 1967-1972 Cutlass. Web site: www.shiftworks.com

Steve's Camaros — parts
1197 San Mateo Ave
San Bruno, CA 94066
650-873-1890; FAX: 650-873-3670

Mail order and open shop. Monday-Friday 8 am to 5 pm, Saturday 10 am to 3 pm. Specializing in 1967-1969 Camaro parts, new, reproduction; 1970-1981 new and reproduction parts. 1967-1969 Pontiac Firebird parts in stock. 1964-1972 Chevelle and El Camino Parts.

Steve's Antiques/POR-15 — bicycles, POR-15 distributor
Steve Verhoeven
5609 S 4300 W
Hooper, UT 84315
888-817-6715 toll-free, 801-985-4835
E-mail: steve@stevesantiques.com

See full listing in **Section Two** under **rustproofing**

Street-Wise Performance — differentials, new/used parts, overhaul kits, transmissions
Richie Mulligan
Box 105 Creek Rd
Tranquility, NJ 07879
973-786-7500; FAX: 973-786-7861
E-mail: street-wise@usa.net

See full listing in **Section Two** under **transmissions**

Tags Backeast — data plates, trim tags, cowl tags
PO Box 581
Plainville, CT 06062
860-747-2942
E-mail: dataplt@snet.net

See full listing in **Section Two** under **special services**

Tamraz's Parts Discount Warehouse — carpeting, upholstery, weatherstripping
10022 S Bode Rd
Plainfield, IL 60544
630-904-4500; FAX: 630-904-2329

Specializing in restoration parts. We sell everything to restore your 1964 and newer Chevelle, Cutlass, GTO, Skylark and 1967 and newer Camaro and Firebird. From bumper to bumper, road to roof. We carry seat upholstery, door panels, sheetmetal, emblems, carpet, weatherstripping, convertible tops and convertible top parts, plus much more.

Tom's Obsolete Chevy Parts — parts
14 Delta Dr
Pawtucket, RI 02860
401-723-7580; FAX: 401-724-7568

See full listing in **Section One** under **Chevrolet**

True Connections — parts
3848 Pierce St
Riverside, CA 92503
909-688-6040; FAX: 909-688-6939
E-mail: trueconnect@earthlink.net

Mail order and open shop. Monday-Thursday 9 am to 5:30 pm, Friday 9 am to 5 pm, Saturday 9 am to 2 pm. Specializing in

1964-1972 Chevelle, El Camino and Monte Carlo parts. NOS, reproduction and used parts. American made brake and suspension parts. Recondition dashes, gauges and consoles. Web site: www.true-connections.com

Volunteer State Chevy Parts LLC 2414 Hwy 41 S, PO Box 10 Greenbrier, TN 37073 615-643-4583; FAX: 615-643-5100	accessories parts

See full listing in **Section One** under **Chevrolet**

Wheel Vintiques Inc 5468 E Lamona Ave Fresno, CA 93727 209-251-6957; FAX: 209-251-1620	hubcaps wheels

See full listing in **Section One** under **Chevrolet**

White Post Restorations One Old Car Dr, PO Drawer D White Post, VA 22663 540-837-1140; FAX: 540-837-2368 E-mail: info@whitepost.com	brakes restoration

See full listing in **Section Two** under **brakes**

Worldwide Camaro Association PO Box 607188 Orlando, FL 32860-7188 800-456-1957, 407-299-1957 FAX: 407-299-3341 E-mail: info@worldwidecamaro.com	modified parts monthly magazine repro parts tech help used parts

Mail order and open shop. Monday-Friday 8 am to 8 pm, Saturday 9 am to 6 pm EST. Specializing in reproduction, modified, high performance and used parts for all generations of Camaros. Member-driven club provides a national voice uniting car clubs and enthusiasts worldwide. Members recieve monthly magazine, tech help, 4 national conventions per year, special pricing and much more. Web site: www.worldwidecamaro.com

David Casimir Philpa-Augustyn 626-584-6957	cars/parts for sale literature for sale

Mail order only.

Clark's Corvair Parts Inc Rt 2, #400 Mohawk Tr Shelburne Falls, MA 01370 413-625-9776; FAX: 413-625-8498 E-mail: clarks@corvair.com	accessories interiors literature parts sheetmetal

Mail order only. Monday-Friday 8:30 am to 5 pm. Largest Corvair parts supplier in the world with over 27 years of supplying NOS and repro parts, upholstery, carpets, door panels, sheetmetal and accessories for Corvair. Technical assistance by mail or phone. Over 625-page illustrated catalog listing over 14,000 different NOS, used, high-performance and Corvair to VW adapter parts, $6. Request our free 24-page catalog of 1963-1965 Buick Riviera upholstery and interior items. Also weatherstrips and rubber parts. Web site: www.corvair.com
See our ad on this page

Corvair Ranch Inc 1079 Bon-Ox Rd Gettysburg, PA 17325 717-624-2805; FAX: 717-624-1196	auto sales parts restoration service

Mail order and open shop. Monday-Saturday 8 am to 6 pm. Strictly 1960-1969 Corvair only parts, service and restoration facility dedicated to the Corvair auto and truck. Parts inventory includes much NOS and repro in many buildings plus a 375 car salvage yard. Also many complete and restorable projects. Visa, MC, Discover, AmEx. UPS daily.

Corvair Underground PO Box 339 Dundee, OR 97115 800-825-8247, 503-434-1648 FAX: 503-434-1626	parts

Specializes in Corvair parts, new, reproduced, rebuilt and used. Largest western supplier of Corvair parts. 300 page mail order catalog for only $6. Free newsletter available. All major credit cards accepted. Celebrating 27 years in 2001! Web site: www.corvairunderground.com

Bill Cotrofeld Automotive Inc US Rt 7, Box 235 East Arlington, VT 05252 802-375-6782	rebuilding service repair service restoration

Corvair repair and restoration shop. Monday-Friday 10 am to 6 pm. Call for Saturday or Sunday hours. Corvair restorations, repairs and rebuilding services. Call for brochure. "America's oldest Corvair shop."

Larry's Corvair Parts 14919 S Crenshaw Blvd Gardena, CA 90249 310-970-9233; FAX: 310-970-9851 E-mail: kbro@earthlink.net	parts service

Specializing in Corvair parts, service, etc, for 1960-1969. Web site: www.larryscorvair.com

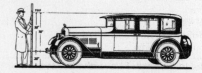

Maplewood Motors 138 Ogunquit Rd Cape Neddick, ME 03902 207-361-1340	**restoration**

Mail order and open shop. Open by appointment only. Chevrolet Corvair. Over 40 years in the auto business. Complete mechanical restoration in-house and bodyshop at other location.

Dave Newell's Chevrobilia PO Box 588 Orinda, CA 94563 510-223-4725	**literature** **memorabilia**

See full listing in **Section One** under **Chevrolet**

Silicone Wire Systems 3462 Kirkwood Dr San Jose, CA 95117-1549 E-mail: sethracer@aol.com	**ignition wire sets**

Mail order only. Manufactures ignition wire sets for all Corvairs, street and race. 8mm wire is used with special snap-in seals and silicone plug boots. Custom wire sets available. Nine colors available.

The Source Inc 13975 Mira Montana Del Mar, CA 92014-3113 858-259-1520 (machine) Voice mail & FAX: 858-259-3843 E-mail: source@adnc.com	**accessories** **parts**

Manufacturer +2,500 Corvair parts, kits, accessories, +100 in development. GM, NOS, Replacement, Ultra series. +30 years experience & engineering staff. Staff hours: Monday-Friday 12 noon to 8 pm. Telephone, voice mail, fax, e-mail: 24 hours-daily. Catalog available for $24.95 + s&h, refundable. MasterCard, Visa, Discover, AmEx.

12 Volt Stuff, Radio & **Speedometer Repair Co** 10625-A Trade Rd Richmond, VA 23236 804-423-1055, 888-487-3500 toll free FAX: 804-423-1059 E-mail: ecs@12voltstuff.com	**radios**

See full listing in **Section Two** under **radios**

12 Volt Stuff, Radio & **Speedometer Repair Co** 10625-A Trade Rd Richmond, VA 23236 804-423-1055, 888-487-3500 toll free FAX: 804-423-1059 E-mail: ecs@12voltstuff.com	**radios**

See full listing in **Section Two** under **instruments**

4-Speeds by Darrell 3 Water St, PO Box 110 Vermilion, IL 61955 217-275-3743; FAX: 217-275-3515	**transmissions**

See full listing in **Section Two** under **transmissions**

The Antique Auto Shop 603 Lytle Ave Elsmere, KY 41018 859-342-8363; FAX: 859-342-9076 E-mail: antaut@aol.com	**brake lines** **brake parts** **weatherstripping**

See full listing in **Section Two** under **brakes**

Antique Cars, Parts & Trains 200 E Broad St Millville, NJ 08332 856-825-0200	**car dealer** **literature** **parts** **trains**

Open shop. Monday-Saturday 9 am to 5 pm. Features Corvettes. Car dealer, parts, automotive literature and trains for sale. 35 miles west of Atlantic City.

Applegate and Applegate Box 129 Mount Gretna, PA 17064-0129	**owner's manuals** **sales literature**

Mail order only. Mail order during the year with participation at Carlisle Corvette show. Original Corvette sales literature and owner's manuals from 1960 to present. Reproduction aftermarket tune-up charts from 1959-1972. Reproduction factory-issued black and white 8x10 photographs from 1953-1985. Orders accepted and shipped by US Mail. Wholesale and retail sales.

ARS Automotive Research Services Division of Auto Search International 1702 W Camelback #301 Phoenix, AZ 85015 602-230-7111; FAX: 602-230-7282	**appraisals** **research**

See full listing in **Section Two** under **appraisals**

Auto Advisors 14 Dudley Rd Billerica, MA 01821 978-667-0075	**appraisals**

See full listing in **Section Two** under **appraisals**

Auto Etc Neon PO Box 531992 Harlingen, TX 78553 PH/FAX: 956-425-7487	**signs** **time pieces**

Mail order only. Nostalgic neon trademark signs and time pieces and licensed gifts for Chevrolet/Corvette & C-5 Corvette owners' and enthusiasts' home, garage, showroom and business display.

Auto Quest Investment Cars Inc 710 W 7th St, PO Box 22 Tifton, GA 31793 912-382-4750; FAX: 912-382-4752 E-mail: info@auto-quest.com	**car dealer**

See full listing in **Section Two** under **car dealers**

Automotive Artistry 679 W Streetboro St Hudson, OH 44236 330-650-1503 E-mail: dale@cmh.net	**restoration**

See full listing in **Section One** under **Triumph**

Automotive Design Center Inc 14135 S Harrison Posen, IL 60469 708-385-8222	**chassis** **frames**

Specializing in round tube chassis and frames for 1953-1962 Chevrolet Corvettes or 1942-1948 Fords. Customer can purchase frame or chassis, or Auto Design will install.

Avanti Auto Service Rt 322, 67 Conchester Hwy Glen Mills, PA 19342-1506 610-558-9999	**repair** **restoration**

See full listing in **Section Two** under **restoration shops**

B & B Cylinder Head Inc	**cylinder heads**
320 Washington St	
West Warwick, RI 02893	
401-828-4900; FAX: 401-381-0010	
E-mail: bbcyl@choiceone.net	

See full listing in **Section Two** under **engine parts**

JJ Best & Co	**financing**
737 Main St, PO Box 10	
Chatham, MA 02633	
800-USA-1965; FAX: 508-945-6006	

See full listing in **Section Two** under **financing**

Bloomington Gold® Corvettes USA	**Corvette show**
PO Box 457	
Marengo, IL 60152	
815-568-1960; FAX: 815-568-8650	
E-mail: bginfo@bloomingtongold.com	

Promotion of annual Corvette show. The granddaddy of Corvette shows, 1999 is the 27th year. The Bloomington Gold certification judging is the standard for Corvettes the world over. Held annually in Bloomington, IL. Web site: www.bloomingtongold.com

Blue Ribbon Products	**parts**
4965 Old House Trail NE	
Atlanta, GA 30342	
404-843-8414; FAX: 404-252-0688	
E-mail: wdgohr@bellsouth.net	

Mail order. Monday-Friday 9 am to 6 pm, Saturday 9 am to noon. New and reproduction parts for 1956-1967 Corvettes. Thousands of parts in stock including weatherstrip, under hood, exterior, interior and chassis parts. Many discontinued 1956-1962 parts available. Visa and MasterCard accepted. Web site: www.blueribbonproducts.com

Bud's Chevrolets, Corvettes, ZR1s	**cars**
PO Box 128, 1415 Commerce Dr	**parts**
St Marys, OH 45885	**service**
800-688-2837; FAX: 419-394-4781	

Corvettes, new and used. Over 100 in stock! Also parts and service. Authorized Chevrolet dealership.

Cal West Auto Air & Radiators Inc	**a/c units/condensers**
24309 Creekside Rd #119	**fan shrouds**
Valencia, CA 91355	**gas tanks**
800-535-2034; FAX: 661-254-6120	**heaters/radiators**
E-mail: mike@calwest-radiators.com	**radios/wheels**

See full listing in **Section Two** under **radiators**

Cars II	**parts**
6747 Warren Sharon Rd	
Brookfield, OH 44403	
330-448-2074; FAX: 330-448-1908	

See full listing in **Section One** under **Cadillac/LaSalle**

Chevyland Parts & Accessories	**accessories**
3667 Recycle Rd #8	**parts**
Rancho Cordova, CA 95742	**restoration**
916-638-3906; FAX: 916-638-0302	
E-mail: 327@chevylandparts.com	

See full listing in **Section One** under **Chevelle/Camaro**

Chicago Corvette Supply	**parts**
7322 S Archer Rd	
Justice, IL 60458	
708-458-2500; FAX: 708-458-2662	

Mail order and open showroom. Monday-Friday 9 am to 6 pm, Saturday 8 am to 2 pm. Specialize in new, reproduction and

remanufactured 1953-1982 Corvette parts, accessories and books. Also maintain one of the largest inventories of discontinued NOS (new old stock) parts in the nation. Call for our newest catalog.

Classics 'n More Inc	**repairs**
939 N Prince St	**restoration**
Lancaster, PA 17603	
717-392-0599; FAX 717-392-2371	

See full listing in **Section Two** under **restoration shops**

Conte's Corvettes & Classics	**leasing**
851 W Wheat Rd	**parts**
Vineland, NJ 08360	**sales**
856-692-0087; FAX: 856-692-1009	**service**
E-mail: corvettes@contes.com	

Open Monday, Wednesday, Friday 8 am to 5 pm; Tuesday & Thursday 8 am to 6 pm and Saturday 9 am to 2 pm. Serving the Corvette enthusiast since 1974. We offer pre-owned Corvette sales with 30 or more in stock. Expert repair service and a complete parts department with thousands of used, new and NOS parts in stock. See our web site at: www.contes.com

Robert W Cook Corvette Art	**appraisals**
8047 Moss Meadows Dr	**artwork**
Dallas, TX 75231	
214-349-6232; FAX: 214-692-7286	
E-mail: prelim@cs.com	

See full listing in **Section Two** under **artwork**

Corvette & High-Performance	**accessories**
Division of Classic & High-	**parts**
Performance Inc	
2840 Black Lake Blvd SW #D	
Olympia, WA 98512	
360-754-7890	

Mail order and open shop. Tuesday-Saturday 9 am to 5:30 pm. Specializing in new and reproduction parts for Corvettes, Camaros, Chevelles and other GM classic cars and trucks. Corvette mechanical service. UPS daily. Major credit cards accepted. Established 1984.

Corvette America	**accessories**
Rt 322, PO Box 427	**interiors**
Boalsburg, PA 16827	**parts**
800-458-3475; foreign: 814-364-2141	
FAX: 814-364-9615, 24 hours	
E-mail: vettebox@corvetteamerica.com	

Own a 1953 or 2001 Corvette? How about any year in between? If so, you must visit www.corvetteamerica.com and see the world's finest and most complete line of parts, interiors, fiberglass, accessories and gifts, over 22,900 items! Browse the complete inventory and order online. While you're there, be sure to request the free 384-page master catalog or call toll free.

Corvette Central	**accessories**
13550 Three Oaks Rd, Dept HM	**parts**
Sawyer, MI 49125	
616-426-3342; FAX: 616-426-4108	
E-mail: mail@corvettecentral.com	

Mail order. Monday-Thursday 8:30 am to 8 pm, Friday 8:30 am to 5:30 pm, Saturday 9 am to 1 pm. 1953-current model Corvette parts and accessories. Five parts catalogs available: 1953-1962, 1963-1967, 1968-1982, 1984-1996, 1997-current model. Catalogs are full of color photos and illustrations. The accessory only catalog is full of neat stuff for you and your Corvette. Restore, accessorize or maintain your Corvette with America's leader in Corvette parts and accessories. Web site: www.corvettecentral.com

Corvette Cosmetics
31 Willow Grove Rd
Shamong, NJ 08088
609-268-2288; FAX: 609-268-7770

new parts
used parts

Mail order and open shop. Monday-Friday 9 am to 5 pm. 1963-1982 new and used parts for Corvettes.

Corvette Enterprise Brokerage
The Power Broker-Mike Kitain
52 Van Houten Ave
Passaic Park, NJ 07055-5512
973-472-7021

appraisals
broker
car locator
investment
planning

Cars shown Monday-Saturday by appointment only. Corvette brokerage offering investment grade classics and new models. SASE for free catalog. Consultations and appraisals. Quality Corvettes always wanted. Look for our comprehensive value guides in fine automotive publications. Over two decades of providing America's best Vettes.

Corvette Pacifica
Division of EC Products
PO Box 2360
Atascadero, CA 93423
800-488-7671, 805-466-9261 int'l
FAX: 805-466-4782

accessories
parts

Mail order and open shop. Monday-Friday 7:30 am to 5 pm PST. Carries over 10,000 parts and accessories for 1953-1997 Corvettes. Web site: www.corvettepacifica.com

Corvette Rubber Company
H-10640 W Cadillac Rd
Cadillac, MI 49601
888-216-9412 toll-free
616-779-2888; FAX: 616-779-9833

rubber products
weatherstripping

Mail order and open shop. Monday-Friday 10 am to 5 pm. Specializing in weatherstrip and rubber products for 1953-1996 Corvettes. Web site: www.corvette-rubber.com

Corvette Service
11629 Vanowen St
North Hollywood, CA 91605
818-765-9117

race prep
repairs

Open shop only. Monday-Friday 8 am to 5 pm. Specializing in all mechanical repairs on all year Corvettes. Restoration and race car preparation. Fuel injection specialist.

Corvette Specialties of MD Inc
1912 Liberty Rd
Eldersburg, MD 21784
410-795-3180; FAX: 410-795-3247

parts
restoration
service

Mail order and open shop. Monday-Friday 9 am to 5:30 pm. Since 1977, a major supplier of new, used and reproduction parts, specializing in 1956-1967. We also offer a restoration service for clocks, gauges, instrument clusters, headlight and wiper motors. Mechanical service and restoration work is also offered at our facility. Tune-ups to frame-off restorations. We service all years.

Corvette World
RD 9, Box 770, Dept H
Greensburg, PA 15601
724-837-8600; FAX: 724-837-4420
E-mail: cvworld@sgi.net

accessories
parts

Mail order and open shop. Monday-Friday 9 am to 5 pm, Saturday 9 am to 12 pm. This family owned company has been serving Corvette owners for over 25 years. We handle a complete line of parts and accessories for 1953-1982 Corvettes, so you can go from start to finish all at one place. Our 216 page catalog is fully illustrated and contains over 10,000 GM reproduction and used parts. Call for a free copy of our catalog today. Web site: www.corvettedept.com

County Corvette
315 Westtown Rd
West Chester, PA 19382
610-696-7888; FAX: 610-696-9114

restoration
sales
service

Open shop only. Monday-Friday 8:30 am to 5:30 pm, Saturday 10 am to 2 pm. State of the art restoration, service and sales for Corvettes. Web site: www.countycorvette.com

D&M Corvette Specialists Ltd
1804 Ogden Ave
Downers Grove, IL 60515
630-968-0031; FAX: 630-968-0465
E-mail: sales@dmcorvette.com

car dealer
parts
restoration
sales
service

Mail order and open shop. Monday-Thursday 8 am to 8 pm, Friday 8 am to 6 pm, Saturday 10 am to 6 pm. Specializing in sales, service, parts and restoration for Corvettes 1953-present. 40 car indoor showroom, quality classics and low mileage late models. Full service, restoration and parts department. Web site: www.dmcorvette.com

Davies Corvette
7141 US Hwy 19
New Port Richey, FL 34653
800-236-2383, 727-842-8000
FAX: 727-846-8216
E-mail: davies@corvetteparts.com

accessories
parts

Corvette parts and accessories, all years (used and new). "Making Corvettes the best they can be since 1953." Web site: www.corvetteparts.com

**Dean's Corvette Wiper
Transmission Service**
Dean Andrew Rehse
16367 Martincoit Rd
Poway, CA 92064
858-451-1933; FAX: 858-451-1999
E-mail: 53-62vetteparts@home.com

wiper trans service

Specializing in 1953-1962 Corvettes. Rebuild your broken wiper transmissions. We can restring your broken cables, replace broken parts. Price varies. This is a division of Mary Jo Rohner's Corvette Parts Collection, 1953-1962. Web site: www.earlycorvetteparts.com

**Russ Dentico's Sales & Auto
Appraisal Consulting**
PO Box 566
Trenton, MI 48183
734-675-3306; FAX: 734-675-8908

appraisals

See full listing in **Section Two** under **appraisals**

DeWitts Reproductions
11672 Hyne Rd
Brighton, MI 48114
810-220-0181; FAX: 810-220-0182
E-mail: dewitts@ismi.net

radiators

Mail order only. Specializing in Corvette aluminum radiators and rear storage compartments for Corvettes from 1955 through 1996. Web site: www.dewitts.com

Diecast & More
11709 Oakland Dr
Schoolcraft, MI 49087
616-679-4002
E-mail: lstrong639@aol.com

die cast models
toys

See full listing in **Section Two** under **models & toys**

DiSchiavi Enterprises Inc
1248 Yardville Allentown Rd
Allentown, NJ 08501
609-259-0787

restoration

See full listing in **Section Two** under **restoration shops**

Dobbins Restoration Publishing	literature
16 E Montgomery Ave	parts
Hatboro, PA 19040	restoration
215-443-0779	

Mail order and open shop. Corvette service and restoration, parts and literature. Corvette appraisals.

Dr Vette	brakes
14364 SW 139th Ct	fuel system parts
Miami, FL 33186	repairs
800-262-9595; FAX: 305-253-3641	

Dr Vette has expanded his practice to include treatments for Corvette patients suffering from hardening of power steering components, tired lifeless power boosters, suspension depression, congestive master cylinder failure & clogged proportioning valves. His practice of 15 years continues to specialize in curing fuel & brake illnesses from line rustitis to reconstructive caliper surgery. For Dr Vette's catalog of prescribed cures in these critical areas, call 800-262-9595; do it today, feel better tomorrow.

EC Products Design Inc	accessories
PO Box 2360	parts
Atascadero, CA 93423	
800-488-5209; FAX: 805-466-4782	
805-466-4703 international	

Mail order and open shop. Monday-Friday 7:30 am-5 pm PST. Serves all auto businesses throughout the world that deal in Corvette parts. Business license required, wholesale only. Specializing in parts and accessories for 1953-1997 Corvettes. Web site: www.everythingcorvette.com

Eckler's Quality Parts & Accessories for Corvettes	accessories
5140 S Washington Ave	parts
Titusville, FL 32780	
800-327-4868; FAX: 407-383-2059	
E-mail: ecklers@ecklers.net	

Specializing in parts and accessories for 1953-2001 Corvettes. One 350+ page color catalog for 1953-2001 models, featuring enhancement accessories of every description, plus restoration items including fiberglass body panels, interiors, chassis parts, fuel systems, electrical items, glass, engine parts, exhaust systems in addition to a complete line of gift and apparel items. Web site: www.ecklers.com

Elmer's Auto Parts Inc	parts
137 Donovan St	
Webster, NY 14580	
716-872-4402; FAX: 716-872-2519	

Mail order and open shop. Monday-Saturday 9 am to 5 pm. Auto parts and salvage Corvette parts, 1953-present. Corvette rebuildable wrecks.

Fifties Forever	Chevrolet specialist
206 Division Ave	
Garfield, NJ 07026	
PH/FAX: 973-478-1306	
E-mail: fiftiesforever@webtv.net	

See full listing in **Section One** under **Chevrolet**

Firewall Insulators & Quiet Ride Solutions	air plenums
6465 Pacific Ave, Ste 249	auto insulation
Stockton, CA 95207	firewall insulators
209-477-4840; FAX: 209-477-0918	gloveboxes
E-mail: timcox@quietride.com	sound deadening

See full listing in **Section Two** under **upholstery**

Grossmueller's Classic Corvette	NOS parts
55 Sitgreaves St	used parts
Phillipsburg, NJ 08865	
908-213-8832; FAX: 908-213-7088	
E-mail: wfg@gccorvettes.com	

Specializing in 1953-1962 and 1968-1982 Corvette parts. We constantly have several cars of each year available for parts. We also manufacture many parts for the 1953-1955 cars, including carb linkage, gaskets, accelerator linkage as well as bumper brackets, splash shields and frame brackets for the 1953-1962 cars. Restoration services for all gauges, heater/defroster switches and steering columns are also available. Web site: www.gccorvettes.com

Guldstrand Engineering Inc	parts
912 Chestnut St	
Burbank, CA 91506	
818-558-1499; FAX: 818-558-1449	
E-mail: gss@guldstrand.com	

Mail order and open shop. Monday-Friday 8 am to 5 pm. The original designers for Corvette suspension and modifications. The 46-page suspension and preparation manual is full of street to racing components, applications for 1953-2001 Corvette and GM A and G-bodies. Web site: www.guldstrand.com

Gulf Coast Corvette	parts
5940 N Sam Houston Pkwy E #319	
Humble, TX 77396	
800-546-2111 order line	
281-441-2111 info line	
FAX: 281-441-3057	

Mail order and open shop. Monday-Friday 9 am to 6 pm, Saturday 9 am to 12 pm CST. Specializing in Corvette parts of all kinds. New, NOS, used and reproductions.

Hi-Tech Software	CD encyclopedia
2 Cooks Farm Rd	
Montville, NJ 07045	
PH/FAX: 973-402-9710	
E-mail: harry@htsoftware.com	

Specializing in computer CD-ROM software automobile encyclopedias. Corvette, Mustang, Camaro and others. Web site: www.htsoftware.com

Hubbard Classic Car Appraisals	appraisals
1908 Belle Terr	
Bakersfield, CA 93304-4352	
661-397-7786	
E-mail: lynnhubbard@msn.com	

See full listing in **Section Two** under **appraisals**

Instrument Services Inc	clocks
11765 Main St	gauges
Roscoe, IL 61073	instruments
800-558-2674; FAX: 815-623-9180	

See full listing in **Section Two** under **instruments**

JR's Antique Auto	chrome parts
21382 E Barbara Blvd	interiors
Claremore, OK 74017	
918-342-4398	

See full listing in **Section One** under **Chevrolet**

Lectric Limited Inc	parts
7322 S Archer Road	
Justice, IL 60458	
708-563-0400; FAX: 708-563-0416	

Specializing in wire harnesses, battery cables, spark plug wire sets, switches and T3 headlight bulbs for all GM cars. Our particular specialty is Corvette.

Long Island Corvette Supply Inc 1445 Strong Ave Copiague, NY 11726-3227 631-225-3000; FAX: 631-225-5030 E-mail: info@licorvette.com	parts

Mail order. Monday-Friday 9 am to 5 pm. Specializing in parts for 1963-1967 Corvettes. The largest and best stocked manufacturer and distributor of 1963-1967 Corvette parts. Send $3 for the biggest and best 1963-1967 Corvette parts catalog. Web site: www.licorvette.com

Marcel's Corvette Shop Inc 1000 Waterford Rd Mechanicville, NY 12118 518-664-7344; FAX: 518-664-2908 E-mail: marcel@marcelscorvette.com	sales service parts

Mail order and open shop. Monday-Friday 8 am to 5 pm, Saturday 9 am to 12 pm EST. Specializing in Corvette parts, service and sales from 1956-2001. Web site: www.marcelscorvette.com

Master Power Brakes 110 Crosslake Park Rd Mooresville, NC 28117 704-664-8866; FAX: 704-664-8862	brake products conversion kits

See full listing in **Section One** under **Chevelle/Camaro**

Mecham Design, Performance 12637 N 66th Dr Glendale, AZ 85304 623-486-3155 E-mail: demecham@uswest.net	parts

See full listing in **Section One** under **Chevrolet**

Michigan Corvette Recyclers 11995 US 223, PO Box 98 Riga, MI 49276 800-533-4650; FAX: 517-486-4124 E-mail: mcr@cass.net	Corvette parts new/used parts salvage

Mail order and open shop. Monday, Wednesday-Friday 9 am to 4:30 pm, Tuesday 9 am to 6 pm, Saturday by appointment only. Corvette only salvage yard, 1968-present. Dismantling over 200 Corvettes. Sell hard to find parts and damaged cars. Web site: www.michigancorvette.com

Mid America Direct PO Box 1368 Effingham, IL 62401 217-347-5591; FAX: 217-347-2952	accessories parts

Mail order only. Corvette, Porsche and VW Beetle parts and accessories within the following catalogs, respectively: *Mid America Designs*, *Tweeks* and *The Real Source*. Web site: www.madirect.com

Milestone Motorcars Mark Tyra 3317 Nevel Meade Dr Prospect, KY 40059 502-228-5945; FAX: 502-228-1856 E-mail: coolcars@ milestonemotorcars.com	die cast cars

See full listing in **Section Two** under **models & toys**

Morrison Motor Co Inc 1170 Old Charlotte Rd Concord, NC 28025 704-782-7716; FAX: 704-788-9514 E-mail: morrisonmotors@unet.net	car dealer

Open shop only. Monday-Friday 8:30 to 5:30, Saturday 8:30 am to 1 pm. Auto sales, specializing in Corvettes, all years, collector cars, muscle cars and late model used cars. We've been in business full time since 1970. Web site: www.morrisonmotorco.com

Muskegon Brake 848 E Broadway Muskegon, MI 49444 231-733-0874; FAX: 231-733-0635	brakes springs suspensions

See full listing in **Section Two** under **brakes**

The National Corvette Museum 350 Corvette Dr Bowling Green, KY 42101-9134 800-53-Vette; FAX: 270-781-5286 E-mail: bobbiejo@corvettemuseum.com	museum

See full listing in **Section Six** under **Kentucky**

Old Air Products 4615 Martin St Ft Worth, TX 76119 817-531-2665; FAX: 817-531-3257 E-mail: sales@oldairproducts.com	air conditioning

Mail order and open shop. Monday-Friday 8:30 am to 5 pm. Specializing in custom air conditioning systems and replacement parts for air conditioning and heating for Corvette, 1955-1957 Chevy trucks and cars, 1972 and back Chevrolet trucks, Ford trucks and cars. Web site: www.oldairproducts.com

Paragon Models & Art 3570 North Rd North Fort Myers, FL 33917 941-567-0047; FAX: 941-567-1344 E-mail: info@myhotrod.com	artwork models

See full listing in **Section Two** under **automobilia**

Paragon Reproductions Inc 8040 S Jennings Rd Swartz Creek, MI 48473 800-882-4688; FAX: 810-655-6667 E-mail: sales@corvette-paragon.com	Corvette repro parts

Finest quality 1953-82 Corvette parts in the industry. Online ordering is available on our web site, so enjoy the freedom of 24-7 shopping! We also offer a large inventory of NOS and used original parts to meet your specific demands. Receive 5% off your first order with purchase of catalog. Web site: www.corvette-paragon.com

Performance Chevy 2995 W Whitton Phoenix, AZ 85017 800-203-6621; FAX: 602-254-1094	engine parts restoration

Mail order and open shop. Monday-Friday 7 am to 3:30 pm. Specializing in Chevy 1955-1997 V8 engine parts and restoration for engines for 1955-1972.

JT Piper's Auto Specialties Inc PO Box 140 Vermilion, IL 61955 800-637-6111, 217-275-3742 FAX: 217-275-3515 E-mail: parts@pipersauto.com	parts

We have one of the largest inventories of used Corvette parts in the world. Used parts for 1954-1986 Corvettes are our specialty, however, we stock a full line of new GM, NOS, discontinued GM and reproduction Corvette parts for the 1954-1986 models. All pricing is done over the phone. So just pick up the phone and give us a call for all your 1954-1986 Corvette parts needs. Web site: www.pipersauto.com

John E Pirkle 3706 Merion Dr Augusta, GA 30907 706-860-9047; FAX: 706-860-2723 E-mail: pirklesr@aol.com	electrical parts

Specializing in starters, alternators, generators, V regulators, relays for Corvette, Chevrolet and GM cars. Web site: www.johnpirkle.com

| Jack Podell Fuel Injection Spec
106 Wakewa Ave
South Bend, IN 46617
219-232-6430; FAX: 219-234-8632
E-mail: podellsfi@aol.com | fuel system parts
fuel system
rebuilding |

Mail order and open shop. Daily 7 am to 7 pm. Specializing in the rebuilding and restoration of 1957-1965 Corvette Rochester fuel injection units with over 30 years of satisfied customers worldwide! Units bought, sold, taken in on trade. Massive parts inventory available including steel reproduction air cleaners, restored FI units in stock. Now available, genuine Tetraethyl lead. Boost 93 octane to 99.5 leaded for pennies a gallon. Call us first for all your FI needs. Catalog upon request.

| Dennis Portka
4326 Beetow Dr
Hamburg, NY 14075
716-649-0921 | horns
knock-off wheels |

Mail order only. Two separate businesses. Specializing in rebuilding and sales of GM horns for Corvette and GM cars, 1955-present. Restoration of Corvette aluminum knock-off wheels, enlarged mounting holes remachined to factory specs. Also knock-off wheel wrenches available.

| Hugo Prado Limited Edition
Corvette Art Prints
PO Box 18437
Chicago, IL 60618-0437
PH/FAX: 773-681-7770
E-mail: vetteart@aol.com | fine art prints |

Specializes in Limited Edition fine art prints of classic Corvettes and Camaros. 1957 Sebring Corvette, 1960 Roman red Corvette convertible, 1963 tuxedo black Corvette Z06, 1965 tuxedo black Corvette, 1966 rally red Corvette, 1967 marina blue Corvette, 1968 tuxedo black Corvette, 1969 Daytona yellow Corvette, 1967 Camaro SS/RS Indy pace car, 1970 Mulsanne-blue Corvette, 1971 Steel Cities gray Corvette, 1990 bright red ZR-1, 40th Anniversary Corvette, 1972 Ontario orange Corvette, 1997 torch red C5 Corvette. Web site: www.hugoprado.com

| Proteam Corvette Sales Inc
PO Box 606
Napoleon, OH 43545-0606
888-592-5086, 419-592-5086
FAX: 419-592-4242
E-mail: proteam@proteam-corvette.com | car collection
car dealer |

Corvettes 1954-1996, over 150 in stock, one location. Mostly 1972 and older. Free catalog. Dealers welcomed, worldwide transportation. Visit our web site for complete comprehensive list of Corvettes for sale: www.proteam-corvette.com

| RARE Corvettes
Joe Calcagno
Box 1080
Soquel, CA 95073
831-475-4442; FAX: 831-475-1115 | cars
parts |

Mail order. Specializing in Corvettes, 1956-1962. Complete cars, project cars, Survivors, drivers, show cars. Parts: new reproduced, used original, NOS, replacement. Technical advice and appraisals. NCRS and Bloomington judge, author, historian. Assisting people with accurate and honest information.

| RC Corvette Parts Inc
3656 Foothill Blvd
La Crescenta, CA 91214
PH/FAX: 818-541-9710 | accessories
Parts |

Specializing in Corvette parts for 1963-1967 Corvettes plus accessories. NOS parts and hard-to-find accessories that are no longer available. Manufacture 1963-1967 gas pedals with correct margins and backside ribs. Only American-made supplier.

| Repro Parts Mfg
PO Box 3690
San Jose, CA 95156
408-923-2491 | parts |

Mail order only. Specializing in reproduction and original used parts (body and mechanical) for 1953-1957 Corvettes. Web site: www.corvetteparts53to62.com

| Rik's Unlimited Corvette Parts
3758 Hwy 18 S
Morganton, NC 28655
828-433-6506; FAX: 828-437-7166
E-mail: riksvet@riksvet.com | accessories
parts |

Quality parts and accessories for 1963-1982 Corvettes: emblems, weatherstrips, interiors, brakes, moldings, suspension, bumpers and much more. Our parts catalog is packed full of illustrations and listings to help find the part you need. Call or write for catalog (cost $2). Web site: www.riksvet.com

| Rogers Corvette Center
8675 N Orlando Ave
Maitland, FL 32751
407-628-8300; FAX: 407-628-8388
E-mail: sales@rogerscorvette.com | car dealer |

Open Monday-Friday 9 am to 6 pm, Saturday 9 am to 4 pm. Quality, original, low mileage Corvettes of every year.

| Mary Jo Rohner's 1953-1962
Corvette Parts
16367 Martincoit Rd
Poway, CA 92064
858-451-1933; FAX: 858-451-1999
E-mail: classicvette@home.com | parts |

Mail order only. Specialize in new, used and reproduction Corvette parts from 1953-1962. Many rare and hard-to-find parts. Prices lower than the rest and the quality is the best! Rebuild wiper motors, defroster switches, master cylinders, clocks, full line of used parts including hardtop parts. Web site: www.earlycorvetteparts.com

| Route 66 Corvette Show
2419 A W Jefferson
Joliet, IL 60435
815-722-8388; FAX: 815-733-8389
E-mail: acs@corvetteshow.com | car show |

See full listing in **Section Two** under **auctions & shows**

| Royals' Garage
16-24 Calhoun St
Torrington, CT 06790
860-489-4500 | NOS parts
used parts |

Est 1977. Glenn and John Royals, owners. Specializing in Corvette sales, repairs, parts sales, many Corvette franchises (interiors, wheels, chroming, radiators, etc). Also general repair facility, repair any auto or truck, equipment, any year, make or model.

| Bob Sottile's Hobby Car
Auto Sales Inc
RD 2 Box 210B, Rt 164
Martinsburg, PA 16662
814-793-4282 | car dealer
restoration |

Mail order and open shop. Monday-Friday 9:30 am to 8:30 pm, Saturday 9 am to 5 pm. Buy, sell, repair and restore Corvettes. All are clean and original. Have a combined 30 years of Corvette sales, repair and restoration experience with parts too. We also do muscle cars and street rods.

| Ssnake-Oyl Products Inc
114 N Glenwood Blvd
Tyler, TX 75702
800-284-7777; FAX: 903-526-4501 | carpet underlay
firewall insulation
seat belt
restoration |

See full listing in **Section Two** under **interiors & interior parts**

Section One – Marque Specialists

Still Cruisin' Corvettes
5759 Benford Dr
Haymarket, VA 20169
703-754-1960; FAX: 703-754-1222
E-mail: chuckberge@starpower.net

appraisals
repairs
restoration

Open shop only. Monday-Friday 8 am to 5 pm, Saturday 8 am to 12 noon. Specializing in restoration or repair of Corvettes 1953-1972 and consultant for pre-purchase. Certified appraiser of all collectible cars. Expert witness for court cases. Web site: www.stillcruisincorvettes.com

Stoudt Auto Sales
1350 Carbon St
Reading, PA 19601
800-523-8485 USA parts dept
800-482-3033 USA sales dept
610-374-4856, parts info
FAX: 610-372-7283
E-mail: stoudtauto@cs.com

car dealer
parts
Corvette parts

Mail order and open shop. Monday-Thursday 9 am to 6 pm, Friday 9 am to 5 pm, Saturday 9 am to 3 pm. Sales dept Monday-Thursday 9 am to 8 pm, Friday 9 am to 5 pm, Saturday 9 am to 3 pm. Huge selection of new, used and repro parts for all years. Over 6,500 parts in stock. 35 Corvettes in stock. Same location for 43 years. Catalog. Web site: www.stoudtcorvettes.com

Street-Wise Performance
Richie Mulligan
Box 105 Creek Rd
Tranquility, NJ 07879
973-786-7500; FAX: 973-786-7861
E-mail: street-wise@usa.net

differentials
new/used parts
overhaul kits
transmissions

See full listing in **Section Two** under **differentials**

Tags Backeast
PO Box 581
Plainville, CT 06062
860-747-2942
E-mail: dataplt@snet.net

data plates
trim tags
cowl tags

See full listing in **Section Two** under **special services**

Lars Tidblom Automobil
Vegagatan 5-7
Sundbyberg 17231 Sweden
+46-8-293292
E-mail: lt.automobil@swipnet.se

parts
restoration
service

Mail order and open shop. Monday-Friday 7:30 am to 5 pm. Service, restoration to original, trimmings, parts and used parts for Chevrolet Corvette 1953-1999. GM, AC Delco, Ecklers, Corvette Central, Paragon, Zip Products, EC Products, Mid America Vette brakes and products, Lingenfelter and more.

Trim Parts Inc
5161 Wolfpen Pleasant Hill
Milford, OH 45150
513-831-1472; FAX: 513-248-3402
E-mail: sales@trimparts.com

trim items

See full listing in **Section One** under **Chevrolet**

U S Oldies & Classics
Vunt 3
Holsbeek 3220 Belgium
3216446611; FAX: 3216446520

car dealer

See full listing in **Section Two** under **car dealers**

USAopoly Inc
565 Westlake St
Encinitas, CA 92024
760-634-5910; FAX: 760-634-5923
E-mail: christian@usaopoly.com

Monopoly® game

See full listing in **Section Two** under **models & toys**

Vette Dreams Inc
1004 Peconic Ave
West Babylon, NY 11704
631-661-4613; FAX: 631-661-4623

restorations

Specializing in Corvette restorations for 1953-1972.

Vette Vues Magazine
PO Box 741596
Orange City, FL 32774
386-775-8454; FAX: 386-775-3042
E-mail: comments@vettevues.com

magazine

See full listing in **Section Four** under **periodicals**

Virginia Vettes Parts & Sales
105 Lindrick St
Williamsburg, VA 23188
757-229-0011
FAX: 757-565-1629, 24 hours
E-mail: www.info@virginiavettes.com

interiors
parts

Mail order and open shop. Saturday 7:30 am to 5 pm. Shop location: 5662 Mooretown Road, Williamsburg, VA 23188. Serve the collector and hobbyist with OEM, reproduction and good used parts. Corvette interiors, carpet, weatherstrip, special fasteners, seat covers and door panels are all made to original specifications. Free catalog showing available parts. Web site: www.virginiavettes.com

Walneck's Inc
7923 Janes Ave
Woodridge, IL 60517
630-985-4995; FAX: 630-985-2750

motorcycles
murals
posters

See full listing in **Section Two** under **artwork**

White Post Restorations
One Old Car Dr, PO Drawer D
White Post, VA 22663
540-837-1140; FAX: 540-837-2368
E-mail: info@whitepost.com

brakes
restoration

See full listing in **Section Two** under **brakes**

**Wild Bill's Corvette &
Hi-Performance Center Inc**
446 Dedham St
Wrentham, MA 02093
508-384-7373; FAX: 508-384-9366
E-mail: wildbillscorvette@
worldnet.att.net

parts
rebuilding
service

Mail order and open shop. Monday-Friday 9 am to 6 pm. Specializing in service, parts, consultation, major rebuilding and overhaul for Chevrolet Corvettes 1953-present. With 20 years' experience concentrating on 1963-1982. Member of NCRS.

WiperWorks
PO Box 57
Sewanee, TN 37375
PH/FAX: 931-598-9573

restoration

See full listing in **Section One** under **Chevrolet**

James Wood
1102 E Jefferson St
Mishawaka, IN 46545
219-256-0239; FAX: 219-254-2722
E-mail: jimwood67@hotmail.com

appraisals

See full listing in **Section Two** under **appraisals**

A & M SoffSeal Inc
104 May Dr
Harrison, OH 45030
800-426-0902; FAX: 513-367-5506
513-367-0028 service/info
E-mail: soffseal@soffseal.com

| rubber parts |
| weatherstripping |

See full listing in **Section Two** under **rubber parts**

A-1 Shock Absorber Co
Shockfinders Division
365 Warren Ave, PO Box 2028
Silverthorne, CO 80498
800-344-1966, 970-389-3193 cell
FAX: 970-513-8283

| shocks-all types |
| coil springs |
| Koni shocks |
| leaf springs |
| steering gears |

See our ad on the last page

American Dream Machines
711 Bowman Mill Rd
Strasburg, VA 22657-2808
PH/FAX: 540-465-9613
E-mail: mopar4me@shentel.net

parts

Mail order only. Used parts for 1960s and 1970s Chrysler A, B and E-bodies.

American Restoration Services
373 Glen Eagles Way
Simi Valley, CA 93065
PH/FAX: 805-583-5189

| paints |
| transmission oil |

Mail order only. Specializing in 10W, non-detergent transmission oil and correct color paints for 1930-1950s Chryslers.

Antique DeSoto-Plymouth
4206 Burnett Dr
Murrysville, PA 15668
724-733-1818 eves; FAX: 724-733-9884
E-mail: parts4u@aol.com

Mopar parts

See full listing in **Section One** under **Mopar**

Apple Hydraulics Inc
1610 Middle Rd
Calverton, NY 11933-1419
800-882-7753, 631-369-9515
FAX: 631-369-9516
E-mail: info@applehydraulics.com

| brake rebuilding |
| shock rebuilding |

See full listing in **Section Two** under **suspension parts**

Atlas Obsolete Chrysler Parts
10621 Bloomfield St, Unit 32
Los Alamitos, CA 90720
PH/FAX: 562-594-5560
E-mail: atlaschrys@aol.com

parts

See full listing in **Section One** under **Mopar**

Aussieutes/Old Tin
PO Box 26
Wendouree Victoria 3355 Australia
03 5336 FORD; FAX: 03 5339 9900
E-mail: dave@aussieutes.com

salvage yard

See full listing in **Section Five** under **Australia**

Bastian Automotive Restoration
4170 Finch Ave
Fairfield, OH 45014
PH/FAX: 513-738-4268

| appraisals |
| restoration |

See full listing in **Section Two** under **restoration shops**

Andy Bernbaum Auto Parts
315 Franklin St
Newton, MA 02458
617-244-1118

parts

See full listing in **Section One** under **Mopar**

Brewer's Performance Inc
2580 S St Rt 48
Ludlow Falls, OH 45339-9773
937-698-4259; FAX: 937-698-7109

parts

See full listing in **Section One** under **Mopar**

Classic Auto Air Mfg Co
2020 W Kennedy Blvd
Tampa, FL 33606
813-251-2356, 813-251-4994
FAX: 813-254-7419

| air conditioning |
| heating |
| parts |

See full listing in **Section One** under **Mustang**

Collector's Auto Supply
PO Box 1541
Peachland, BC Canada V0H 1X9
888-772-7848, 250-767-1974
FAX: 250-767-3340
E-mail: car@telus.net

parts

See full listing in **Section Two** under **comprehensive parts**

**Dodge City Vintage Dodge
Vehicles & Parts**
18584 Hwy 108, PO Box 1687
Jamestown, CA 95327
209-984-5858; FAX: 209-984-3285
E-mail: mike@dodgecityvintage.com

| parts |
| restoration |
| research |
| vehicles |

See full listing in **Section One** under **Dodge**

Egge Machine Company Inc
11707 Slauson Ave
Santa Fe Springs, CA 90670-2217
800-866-3443, 562-945-3419
FAX: 562-693-1635
E-mail: info@egge.com

| bearings |
| gaskets |
| pistons/rings |
| timing components |
| valvetrain |

See full listing in **Section Two** under **engine parts**

**Firewall Insulators & Quiet Ride
Solutions**
6465 Pacific Ave, Ste 249
Stockton, CA 95207
209-477-4840; FAX: 209-477-0918
E-mail: timcox@quietride.com

| air plenums |
| auto insulation |
| firewall insulators |
| gloveboxes |
| sound deadening |

See full listing in **Section Two** under **upholstery**

Jay M Fisher
Acken Dr 4-B
Clark, NJ 07066
732-388-6442

| mascots |
| sidemount mirrors |
| windwing brackets |

See full listing in **Section Two** under **accessories**

Glazier Pattern & Coachworks
3720 Loramie-Washington Rd
Houston, OH 45333
937-492-7355; FAX: 937-492-9987
E-mail: s.glazier.fam@juno.com

coachwork
interior woodwork
restoration of wood
bodied cars

Mail order and open shop by appointment only. Complete new wood for all years Chrysler Town & Country; complete restorations. Structural and concours quality interior woodwork for coachbuilt classics. Rebuild, restore or remanufacture damaged or missing parts. Specialize in Rolls-Royces, Bentleys, Chrysler T&C, etc. Award winning complete restorations.

Goodmark Industries Inc
625 E Old Norcross Rd
Lawrenceville, GA 30045
770-339-8557; FAX: 770-339-7562

sheetmetal
trim

See full listing in **Section Two** under **sheetmetal**

Green Valentine Inc
5055 Covington Way
Memphis, TN 38134
901-373-5555; FAX: 901-373-5568

car dealer
woodies

See full listing in **Section Two** under **car dealers**

Hagerty Classic Insurance
PO Box 87
Traverse City, MI 49685
800-922-4050; FAX: 616-941-8227

insurance

See full listing in **Section Two** under **insurance**

Mike Hershenfeld
PO Box 1301
Bellmore, NY 11710
PH/FAX: 516-781-PART (7278)
E-mail: mikesmopar@juno.com

parts

See full listing in **Section One** under **Mopar**

Hidden Valley Auto Parts
21046 N Rio Bravo
Maricopa, AZ 85239
602-252-2122, 602-252-6137
520-568-2945; FAX: 602-258-0951
E-mail: hvap@aol.com

parts

See full listing in **Section One** under **Chevrolet**

Hot Heads Research & Racing Inc
276 Walker's Hollow Tr
Lowgap, NC 27024
336-352-4866; FAX: 336-352-3892
E-mail: info@hothemiheads.com

parts

Mail order only. Monday-Friday 9 am to 6 pm. Early Hemi engine parts, adaptors and complete engine rebuild service for 1951-1958 Chrysler, 1952-1957 DeSoto and 1953-1957 Dodge Hemi engines. Web sites: www.powerplayhemi.com and www.hothemiheads.com

Imperial Motors
PO Box 496
Campobello, SC 29322
864-895-3474; FAX: 864-895-1248

parts

Mail order only. Chrysler, Plymouth, Dodge parts only. Chrysler parts 1955-1982. Chrysler, Plymouth, Dodge, Imperial, DeSoto, Barracuda parts. Parting out complete running cars. Rust-free sheetmetal. 30 acres of cars and parts. Visa, MasterCard, American Express, Discover. Web site: www.chryslerparts.com

International Towing & Recovery Museum
401 Broad St
Chattanooga, TN 37402
PH/FAX: 423-267-3132

museum

See full listing in **Section Six** under **Tennessee**

Jeepsamerica
367 Washington St
Weymouth, MA 02189
781-331-4333; FAX: 781-331-6947
E-mail: mconsiglio1@yahoo.com

parts
service

Open shop and internet. Monday-Saturday 8 am to 5 pm. Specializing in replacement parts and service for Jeep and all SUVs for 1940s to present.

Jeff Johnson Motorsports
PO Box 14327
Columbus, OH 43214
614-268-1181; FAX: 614-268-1141

literature

See full listing in **Section One** under **Mopar**

Kramer Automotive Specialties
PO Box 5
Herman, PA 16039
724-285-5566; FAX: 724-285-8898
E-mail: kramerauto@aol.com

body parts
interiors
sheetmetal

See full listing in **Section One** under **Mopar**

L & L Antique Auto Trim
403 Spruce, Box 177
Pierce City, MO 65723
417-476-2871

runningboard
moldings

See full listing in **Section Two** under **special services**

Layson's Restorations Inc
26164 126th Ave SE
Kent, WA 98031
253-630-4088; FAX: 253-630-4065
E-mail: laysons@foxinternet.net

parts

See full listing in **Section One** under **Mopar**

Legendary Auto Interiors Ltd
121 W Shore Blvd
Newark, NY 14513
800-363-8804
FAX: 800-SEAT-UPH (732-8874)
E-mail: sales@
legendaryautointeriors.com

soft trim

Specialists in the manufacturing of authentic reproduction seat upholstery, door panels, molded seat foam, vinyl tops and more for 1957-1979 Chrysler, Plymouth and Dodge cars, Dodge trucks, 1968-1974 AMC Javelin and AMX and 1964-1972 Buick Skylark, GS and GSX and custom vintage vinyl floor mats for General Motors muscle cars 1953-1996. Complete interior trim line including molded carpets, headliners, convertible tops, boots, and well liners, NOS interior items, etc. Catalog $5 US. Web site: www.legendaryautointeriors.com

Mike's Auto Parts
Box 358
Ridgeland, MS 39158
601-856-7214

NOS Mopar
NOS GM
NOS Ford
parts for all makes

Mail order. Specializing in NOS for Chrysler, Dodge, DeSoto, Plymouth, AMC/Jeep, Nash, Hudson, Willys and GM. Also specializing in bearings, universal joints, engine parts, brake parts, ignition parts, starter drives, spark plugs, 6-volt bulbs, tubular shocks, belts, water pumps, fuel pumps, king pin sets, transmission gears, clutches and windshield wipers for all makes cars and trucks. Also collectible wall calendars and memorabilia

Clayton T Nelson   NOS parts
Box 259
Warrenville, IL 60555
630-369-6589

See full listing in **Section One** under **Oldsmobile**

North Yale Auto Parts   salvage yard
Rt 1, Box 707
Sperry, OK 74073
800-256-6927 (NYAP), 918-288-7218
E-mail: nyap@ionet.net

See full listing in **Section Five** under **Oklahoma**

Obsolete Chrysler NOS Parts   literature
4206 Burnett Dr   parts
Murrysville, PA 15668
724-733-1818 eves; FAX: 724-733-9884
E-mail: parts4u@aol.com

Mail order and open shop. Saturdays 8 am to 5 pm. New old
stock Chrysler products, parts. Specializing in chrome trim,
medallions, fenders and bumpers, 1930s-1960s. Lots of literature also. Dodge and Plymouth NOS parts for 1938-1958.
Satisfaction guaranteed. Web site: www.oldmoparparts.com

Obsolete Parts of Iowa   NOS parts
PO Box 233
Earlville, IA 52041
E-mail: finsrus@mwci.net

See full listing in **Section One** under **Mopar**

OEM Paints Inc   custom aerosol
PO Box 461736   colors
Escondido, CA 92046-1736
760-747-2100

See full listing in **Section Two** under **paints**

Older Car Restoration   repro parts
Martin Lum, Owner   restoration
304 S Main St, Box 428
Mont Alto, PA 17237
717-749-3383, 717-352-7701
E-mail: marty@oldercar.com

See full listing in **Section Two** under **restoration shops**

P-Ayr Products   replicas
719 Delaware St
Leavenworth, KS 66048
913-651-5543; FAX: 913-651-2084
E-mail: sales@payr.com

See full listing in **Section One** under **Chevrolet**

Performance Analysis Co   climate control
1345 Oak Ridge Tpke, Ste 258   cruise control
Oak Ridge, TN 37830
PH/FAX: 865-482-9175
E-mail: george_murphy@
compuserve.com

See full listing in **Section One** under **Mercedes-Benz**

Power Brake X-Change Inc   parts
336 Lamont Pl
Pittsburgh, PA 15232
800-580-5729, 412-441-5729
FAX: 412-441-9333

See full listing in **Section Two** under **brakes**

Quality Tire Barn Inc   tires
255 Twinsburg Rd
Northfield, OH 44067
330-467-1284;
FAX: 330-467-1289 (call first)
E-mail: donquist@aol.com

See full listing in **Section Two** under **tires**

Restorations By Julius   restoration
10101-1/2 Canoga Ave
Chatsworth, CA 91311
818-882-2825; FAX: 818-882-2855
E-mail: julius@restorationsbyjulius.com

See full listing in **Section One** under **Plymouth**

Roberts Motor Parts   parts
17 Prospect St
West Newbury, MA 01985
978-363-5407; FAX: 978-363-2026
E-mail: sales@robertsmotorparts.com

Specializing in Chrysler product cars 1928-1972 and trucks
1928-1980. Rubber and weatherstrips, mechanical parts, interior
and bed parts for trucks. Web site: www.robertsmotorparts.com

Don Rook   parts
184 Raspberry Ln
Mena, AR 71953
501-394-7555; FAX: 501-394-7618
E-mail: kmrook@voltage.net

Mail order and open shop. Open anytime at home. Specializes in
parts for Chryslers and Packards of the 1940s, 1950s and
1960s, mostly Chrysler 300s 1955-1971 and specifically 1965
and 1966. Also many Packard parts from 1941-1956, trim and
chrome. No heavy and internal mechanical items. Trim and
detail pieces only. Some windshields.

Sherman & Associates Inc   body panels
61166 Van Dyke Rd   body parts
Washington, MI 48094   fenders/floors
810-677-6800; FAX: 810-677-6801   quarter panels

See full listing in **Section Two** under **body parts**

Paul Slater Auto Parts   parts
9496 85th St N
Stillwater, MN 55082
651-429-4235

See full listing in **Section One** under **Dodge**

Tags Backeast   data plates
PO Box 581   trim tags
Plainville, CT 06062   cowl tags
860-747-2942
E-mail: dataplt@snet.net

See full listing in **Section Two** under **special services**

Totally Auto Inc   parts
337 Philmont Ave   restoration
Feasterville, PA 19053   service
215-322-2277; FAX: 215-322-4755
E-mail: totalyauto@aol.com

See full listing in **Section One** under **Mopar**

Trim Parts Inc   trim items
5161 Wolfpen Pleasant Hill
Milford, OH 45150
513-831-1472; FAX: 513-248-3402
E-mail: sales@trimparts.com

See full listing in **Section One** under **Chevrolet**

U S Oldies & Classics	car dealer
Vunt 3	
Holsbeek 3220 Belgium	
3216446611; FAX: 3216446520	

See full listing in **Section Two** under **car dealers**

Varco Inc	fitted luggage
8200 S Anderson Rd	trunks
Oklahoma City, OK 73150	
405-732-1637	

See full listing in **Section One** under **Ford 1903-1931**

Vintage Woodworks	upholstery
PO Box 49	woodwork
Iola, WI 54945	
715-445-3791	

See full listing in **Section Two** under **woodwork**

Weimann's Literature & Collectables	literature
16 Cottage Rd	
Harwinton, CT 06791	
860-485-0300	
FAX: 860-485-1705, 24 hours	
E-mail: weimann@snet.net	

See full listing in **Section One** under **Plymouth**

Wheel Vintiques Inc	hubcaps
5468 E Lamona Ave	wheels
Fresno, CA 93727	
209-251-6957; FAX: 209-251-1620	

See full listing in **Section One** under **Chevrolet**

White Post Restorations	brakes
One Old Car Dr, PO Drawer D	restoration
White Post, VA 22663	
540-837-1140; FAX: 540-837-2368	
E-mail: info@whitepost.com	

See full listing in **Section Two** under **brakes**

White Post Restorations	restoration
One Old Car Dr, PO Drawer D	
White Post, VA 22663	
540-837-1140; FAX: 540-837-2368	
E-mail: info@whitepost.com	

See full listing in **Section Two** under **restoration shops**

Willow Grove Auto Top	interiors
43 N York Rd	tops
Willow Grove, PA 19090	upholstery
215-659-3276	

See full listing in **Section Two** under **interiors & interior parts**

CITROËN⌃

David Allen, Citroen Specialist	appraisals
HC4, Box 330, Rt 605	brokerage
Mustoe, VA 24465	consultation
540-468-1500; FAX: 540-468-1501	locating
E-mail: dallen@ntelos.net	

Specializing in brokerage, locating, appraisal, import, export, shipping and consultation for all marque of Citroen automobiles,

exclusively. 2CV specialist, all other models only exceptional, rare, collector; no parts.

The Presidential Cars Museum	museum
Chateau de Montjalin	
Sauvigny le Bois 89200 France	
(333) 863-44642	
FAX: (333) 863-16683	
E-mail: odelafon@aol.com	

See full listing in **Section Six** under **France**

Tony D Branda Performance	accessories
Shelby and Mustang Parts	decals
1434 E Pleasant Valley Blvd	emblems
Altoona, PA 16602	sheetmetal
814-942-1869; FAX: 814-944-0801	wheels
E-mail: cobranda@aol.com	

See full listing in **Section One** under **Mustang**

CJ Pony Parts Inc	parts
7481 Allentown Blvd	
Harrisburg, PA 17112	
800-888-6473, 717-657-9252	
FAX: 888-888-6573, 717-657-9254	
E-mail: creed@redrose.net	

See full listing in **Section One** under **Mustang**

Cobra Restorers Ltd	parts
3099 Carter Dr	restoration
Kennesaw, GA 30144	service
770-427-0020; FAX: 770-427-8658	

Mail order and open shop. Monday-Friday 9 am to 6 pm. Largest supplier of parts for Cobra roadsters (replica and original). Restoration and builder of ERA Cobras. Manufactures many parts. Catalog, $5. Web site: www.cobrarestorers.com

EVA Sports Cars	kit cars
RR 1	
Vankleek Hill, ON Canada K0B 1R0	
613-678-3377; FAX: 613-678-6110	

See full listing in **Section Two** under **kit cars & replicars**

Finish Line	parts
3593 SW 173rd Terr	supplies
Miramar, FL 33029	
954-436-9101; FAX: 954-436-9102	
E-mail: e.alibrandi@att.net	

Specializing in OEM parts and supplies for Shelby Cobras, OE and reproductions. Parts and supplies for British Leyland Group cars. Also run three registries for Mustangs of various years. Web site: www.cobraaccessories.com

JWF Restorations Inc | restoration
11955 SW Faircrest St
Portland, OR 97225-4615
503-643-3225; FAX: 503-646-4009

See full listing in **Section One** under **AC**

Loyal Ford Mercury Inc | performance parts
2310 Calumet Dr
New Holstein, WI 53061
920-898-4248; FAX: 920-898-9705
E-mail: loyal@loyalfordmercury.com

See full listing in **Section One** under **Mustang**

Milestone Motorcars | die cast cars
Mark Tyra
3317 Nevel Meade Dr
Prospect, KY 40059
502-228-5945; FAX: 502-228-1856
E-mail: coolcars@
milestonemotorcars.com

See full listing in **Section Two** under **models & toys**

Operations Plus | accessories parts
PO Box 26347
Santa Ana, CA 92799
PH/FAX: 714-962-2776
E-mail: aquacel@earthlink.net

Distributor for Unique Motor Cars. Supplier of numerous Cobra parts and accessories: body, interior, seats, windshield, lighting, mirrors, hardware, fasteners, steering wheels, seats, wheels, oil pans, coolers and adapters, knock-off hammers, vinyl graphics and memorabilia. Web site: www.cobracountry.com/opsplus

Private Garage LC | consultant
8949 SE Bridge Rd, PMB 302
Hobe Sound, FL 33455
561-545-7277; FAX: 561-546-7884

See full listing in **Section One** under **Ferrari**

XKs Unlimited | instruments parts restorations
850 Fiero Ln
San Luis Obispo, CA 93401
800-444-5247; FAX: 805-544-1664
E-mail: xksunltd@aol.com

See full listing in **Section One** under **Jaguar**

1 CAAT Limited Co | restoration
1324 E Harper Ave
Maryville, TN 37804
865-983-7180
E-mail: jhenriks@icx.net

See full listing in **Section Two** under **restoration shops**

Mini Store | cars repairs restorations
PO Box 7973
Van Nuys, CA 91409-7973
PH/FAX: 818-893-1421
E-mail: minicoopers@socal.rr.com

See full listing in **Section One** under **Austin**

J K Howell | parts
455 N Grace St
Lombard, IL 60148
630-495-1949

Mail order only. Full line of new, used, original and reproduction Cord parts and manuals. Catalog available to owners or restorers.

NATMUS Roadside Market | automobilia
1000 Gordon M Buehrig Pl
Auburn, IN 46706
PH/FAX: 219-925-9100
E-mail: natmus@ctlnet.com

See full listing in **Section Two** under **automobilia**

Edwards Crosley Parts | parts
PO Box 632
Mansfield, OH 44901
419-589-5767

Mail order and open shop. Evenings and weekends. Call before visiting. Shop address: 988 Reed Rd, Mansfield, OH 44903.

Firewall Insulators & Quiet Ride Solutions | air plenums auto insulation firewall insulators gloveboxes sound deadening
6465 Pacific Ave, Ste 249
Stockton, CA 95207
209-477-4840; FAX: 209-477-0918
E-mail: timcox@quietride.com

See full listing in **Section Two** under **upholstery**

Heinze Enterprise | instrument restoration
7914 E Kimsey Ln
Scottsdale, AZ 85257
480-946-5814

See full listing in **Section One** under **American Austin/Bantam**

Service Motors | car dealer parts
8111 St Rd 16 E, PO Box 116
Twelve Mile, IN 46988
219-664-3313

Phone hours: 9 am to 5 pm daily. Crosley parts bought, sold and traded. Complete cars for sale. Parts shipped via UPS, COD. We accept Visa, MasterCard and Discover.

Cushman

| Dennis Carpenter Cushman Reproductions
PO Box 26398
Charlotte, NC 28221-6398
704-782-1237; FAX: 704-786-8180
E-mail: info@dennis-carpenter.com | accessories
parts |

Mail order and over the counter sales. Monday-Friday 8 am to 5 pm. Manufacture and sell obsolete Cushman motor scooter parts, including body and engine parts, accessories and much more. We also buy and sell all makes of vintage motorbikes and motor scooters. Send $4 for catalog. Web site: www.dennis-carpenter.com

| Arthur W Aseltine
18215 Challenge Cut-Off Rd
Forbestown, CA 95941
530-675-2773; FAX: 530-675-9134
E-mail: awa@lostsierra.net | parts
research
restoration |

See full listing in **Section One** under **Stearns-Knight**

| Sandringham House Museum & Grounds
Sandringham
Nr King's Lynn
Norfolk PE356EN England
01553-772675; FAX: 01485-541571 | museum |

See full listing in **Section Six** under **England**

| Texas Viper Hotline
5405 Montclair
Colleyville, TX 76034
817-267-1299; FAX: 972-721-3900
E-mail: dab1213@msn.com | Prowlers
Vipers |

See full listing in **Section One** under **Dodge**

| Barry Thorne
PO Box 246
Dorking
Surrey RH5 5FU England
0044-306-711789;
FAX: 0044-306-710083 | manuals
parts |

Mail order and open shop. Anytime, any day. For 1959-1964 Daimler SP 250s and SP 251s (lhd). Also Daimler 2-1/2 V8 and V8 250. All inquiries answered. Free advice. Worldwide shipping.

DATSUN

| Banzai Motorworks
8039-B Penn Randall Pl
Upper Marlboro, MD 20772
PH/FAX: 301-420-4200
E-mail: zspert@olg.com | parts
pre-purchase
insp/consultation
repairs/restoration
service |

Mail order and open shop. Monday-Friday 8:30 am to 6 pm. The East Coast's premier Z car restoration shop. From 1970-1996, from oil changes to restorations. We do it all. Banzai Motorworks is the leading supplier of reproduction parts to the Z car hobby. We were also the major reproduction parts supplier to Nissan's 240Z restoration program. Owner Michael McGinnis has more than 31 years' experience servicing Datsuns. We know Z cars. Web site: www.zzxdatsun.com

| Stan Chernoff
1215 Greenwood Ave
Torrance, CA 90503
310-320-4554; FAX: 310-328-7867
E-mail: az589@lafn.org | mechanical parts
restoration parts
technical info
trim parts |

Mail order only. Specializing in restoration, mechanical and trim parts and technical information for 1963-1970 Datsun roadsters, Models SP(L) 310, SP(L) 311 and SR(L) 311.

| CSi
1100 S Raymond Ave, Ste H
Fullerton, CA 92831
714-879-7955; FAX: 714-879-7310
E-mail: csila@compuserve.com | parts |

See full listing in **Section One** under **BMW**

| John's Cars Inc
800 Jaguar Ln
Dallas, TX 75226
888-281-1529 parts orders only;
214-426-4100; FAX: 214-426-3116 | conversion retrofits
parts
restoration
service |

See full listing in **Section One** under **Jaguar**

| Motorsport Auto
1139 W Collins Ave
Orange, CA 92667
800-633-6331, 714-639-2620
FAX: 714-639-7460
E-mail: motorsport@worldnet.att.net | parts |

Mail order and open shop. Monday-Friday 8 am to 5 pm, Saturday 10 am to 2 pm. Parts and accessories for Datsun 240Z, 260Z, 280Z, 280ZX; Nissan 300ZX. Full line of restoration items for all Z-cars. 144 page catalog now available. Web site: www.zcarparts.com

| The Davis Registry
4073 Ruby
Ypsilanti, MI 48197-9317
734-434-5581
E-mail: kfnut@umich.edu | periodical
quarterly bulletin |

Serves as a worldwide clearinghouse for information regarding history, technical background, upkeep, restoration, preservation, current events, prices and any other aspect of the aluminum-bodied three-wheeled Davis automobile built by the Davis Motorcar Co, 4055 Woodley Ave, Van Nuys, CA, from 1947 to 1949. Sells authentic Davis literature, T-shirts, videos. Sample copy $2 postpaid. Quarterly publication. Subscription: $8/year. Checks payable to Tom Wilson. Web site: www.suarezweb.com/davis/davismen.htm

DE LOREAN MOTOR COMPANY

DeLorean Literature	collectibles
3116 Welsh Rd	literature
Philadelphia, PA 19136-1810	
215-338-6142; PH/FAX: 888-392-	
4832 ext 291-291-1979 (* for fax)	
E-mail: delorean.literature@excite.com	

Mail order only. Carry a variety of collectible items such as literature, books, toys, magazines, video and other unique items related to the DeLorean automobile made during 1981-1982. Please send a SASE for a complete listing of items available. All items guaranteed for satisfaction. Web store: http://delorean.literature.econgo.com/

DeLorean One	bodywork
20229 Nordhoff St	parts
Chatsworth, CA 91311	service
818-341-1796; FAX: 818-998-6381	

Mail order and open shop. Monday-Friday 8 am to 6 pm. Specialize in DeLorean parts, service, bodywork, electrical, suspension and sales for all DeLorean automobiles, 1981-1983.

French Stuff	accessories
PO Box 39772	engine rebuilding
Glendale, CA 90039-0772	parts
818-244-2498; FAX: 818-500-7628	transaxle
E-mail: frenchap@gte.net	rebuilding

See full listing in **Section One** under **Renault**

Michael A Stahl	parts
PO Box 18036	
Huntsville, AL 35804	
205-882-6457	
E-mail: stahlcon@aol.com	

See full listing in **Section One** under **Cadillac/LaSalle**

DE SOTO

A-1 Shock Absorber Co	shocks-all types
Shockfinders Division	coil springs
365 Warren Ave, PO Box 2028	Koni shocks
Silverthorne, CO 80498	leaf springs
800-344-1966, 970-389-3193 cell	steering gears
FAX: 970-513-8283	

See our ad on the last page

Antique DeSoto-Plymouth	Mopar parts
4206 Burnett Dr	
Murrysville, PA 15668	
724-733-1818 eves; FAX: 724-733-9884	
E-mail: parts4u@aol.com	

See full listing in **Section One** under **Mopar**

Atlas Obsolete Chrysler Parts	parts
10621 Bloomfield St, Unit 32	
Los Alamitos, CA 90720	
PH/FAX: 562-594-5560	
E-mail: atlaschrys@aol.com	

See full listing in **Section One** under **Mopar**

Hot Heads Research & Racing Inc	parts
276 Walker's Hollow Tr	
Lowgap, NC 27024	
336-352-4866; FAX: 336-352-3892	
E-mail: info@hothemiheads.com	

See full listing in **Section One** under **Chrysler**

Older Car Restoration	repro parts
Martin Lum, Owner	restoration
304 S Main St, Box 428	
Mont Alto, PA 17237	
7717-749-3383, 717-352-7701	
E-mail: marty@oldercar.com	

See full listing in **Section Two** under **restoration shops**

Plymouth, Dodge, Chrysler,	NOS parts for
DeSoto Parts	DeSoto
4206 Burnett Dr	
Murrysville, PA 15668	
724-733-1818 eves; FAX: 724-733-9884	
E-mail: parts4u@aol.com	

Mail order only. Large supply of Mopar parts. Strong in DeSoto and Plymouth. Mostly NOS. DeSoto, Plymouth chrome for 1938-1965. Send SASE with want list for reply. Satisfaction guaranteed. Web site: www.obsoletecarparts.com

Roberts Motor Parts	parts
17 Prospect St	
West Newbury, MA 01985	
978-363-5407; FAX: 978-363-2026	
E-mail: sales@robertsmotorparts.com	

See full listing in **Section One** under **Chrysler**

Weimann's Literature & Collectables	literature
16 Cottage Rd	
Harwinton, CT 06791	
860-485-0300	
FAX: 860-485-1705, 24 hours	
E-mail: weimann@snet.net	

See full listing in **Section One** under **Plymouth**

DeTomaso PANTERA

Avanti Auto Service	repair
Rt 322, 67 Conchester Hwy	restoration
Glen Mills, PA 19342-1506	
610-558-9999	

See full listing in **Section Two** under **restoration shops**

Collectors Choice LTD	parts
6400 Springfield-Lodi Rd	race preparation
Dane, WI 53529	restoration
608-849-9878; FAX: 608-849-9879	service
E-mail: collectorschoice1@prodigy.net	

Mail order and open shop. Monday-Friday 8 am to 5 pm. DeTomaso and Dodge Viper parts distributors. Specializing in

DeTomaso Panteras, AC Cobras, GT-40 Fords, Shelbys, Ferraris, Jaguars, Rolls-Royces and Vipers.

DeTomaso Registry Bill Van Ess 6780 Kitson NE Rockford, MI 49341 616-874-1004; FAX: 616-363-2870 E-mail: billvaness@juno.com	**book**

Mail order only. A registry of all the production models from DeTomaso Automobili SpA Modena. Includes all models of the Pantera, Mangusta, Vallelunga, Longchamp and Deauville. 256 pages, includes pictures and history of each model with production figures and running production changes. Current and past owners and history on the remaining cars, etc. $21 postpaid US; $25 postpaid Europe.

Hall Pantera 15337 Garfield Ave Paramount, CA 90723 562-867-3319, 562-531-2629 FAX: 562-630-8156 E-mail: hallpantera@msn.com	**parts**

Open shop. Tuesday-Friday 10 am to 5 pm PST. Specializing in DeTomaso parts, Pantera, Mangusta and Vallelunga parts. Ford SVO dealer. Web site: www.hallpantera.com

Pantera Parts Connection 645 National Ave Mountain View, CA 94043 800-DETOMAS, 650-968-2291 FAX: 650-968-2218 E-mail: larrys@panteraparts.com	**parts**

Mail order and open shop. Monday-Friday 8 am to 5 pm PST. Specializing in DeTomaso Pantera for 1971-1974. Web site: www.panteraparts.com

Pantera Parts Connection 300 Edison Way Reno, NV 89502 775-856-7011, 800-DETOMASO (338-6627) FAX: 775-856-7010 E-mail: larrys@panteraparts.com	**parts**

Mail order or online parts. Your source for genuine DeTomaso Pantera factory parts and aftermarket parts and accessories. In-house service and manufacturing and remanufacturing. Web site: www.panteraparts.com

Pantera Performance Center 1856 N Park St Castle Rock, CO 80104 303-660-9897; FAX: 303-660-9159	**parts** **restoration** **service**

Mail order and open shop. Monday-Friday 9 am to 5 pm, evenings/weekends by appointment only. Specialize in parts, service and restoration for DeTomaso Pantera.

PI Motorsports Inc 1040 N Batavia Ste G Orange, CA 92867 714-744-1398; FAX: 714-744-1397 pantera@pim.net	**parts** **restoration** **sales**

Specializing in DeTomaso automobiles for sale, parts, restoration and automobilia for 1971-1996 Panteras, Mangusta, Longchamp and Deauville DeTomaso race cars. Web site: www.pim.net

600 Racing Inc 5245 NC Hwy 49 S Harrisburg, NC 28075 704-455-3896; FAX: 704-455-3820	**5/8 scale replicas**

See full listing in **Section Two** under **racing**

A-1 Shock Absorber Co Shockfinders Division 365 Warren Ave, PO Box 2028 Silverthorne, CO 80498 800-344-1966, 970-389-3193 cell FAX: 970-513-8283	**shocks-all types** **coil springs** **Koni shocks** **leaf springs** **steering gears**

See our ad on the last page

Atlas Obsolete Chrysler Parts 10621 Bloomfield St, Unit 32 Los Alamitos, CA 90720 PH/FAX: 562-594-5560 E-mail: atlaschrys@aol.com	**parts**

See full listing in **Section One** under **Mopar**

Auto Body Specialties Inc Rt 66 Middlefield, CT 06455 888-277-1960 toll free orders only 860-346-4989; FAX: 860-346-4987	**accessories** **body parts**

See full listing in **Section Two** under **body parts**

Andy Bernbaum Auto Parts 315 Franklin St Newton, MA 02458 617-244-1118	**parts**

See full listing in **Section One** under **Mopar**

Bill's Speed Shop 13951 Millersburg Rd Navarre, OH 44662 330-832-9403; FAX: 330-832-2098	**body parts**

See full listing in **Section One** under **Chevrolet**

The Brassworks 289 Prado Rd San Luis Obispo, CA 93401 800-342-6759; FAX: 805-544-5615 E-mail: brassworks@thegrid.net	**radiators**

See full listing in **Section Two** under **radiators**

Brewer's Performance Inc 2580 S St Rt 48 Ludlow Falls, OH 45339-9773 937-698-4259; FAX: 937-698-7109	**parts**

See full listing in **Section One** under **Mopar**

Collector's Auto Supply PO Box 1541 Peachland, BC Canada V0H 1X9 888-772-7848, 250-767-1974 FAX: 250-767-3340 E-mail: car@telus.net	**parts**

See full listing in **Section Two** under **comprehensive parts**

Collectors Choice LTD 6400 Springfield-Lodi Rd Dane, WI 53529 608-849-9878; FAX: 608-849-9879 E-mail: collectorschoice1@prodigy.net	**parts** **race preparation** **restoration** **service**

See full listing in **Section One** under **DeTomaso/Pantera**

Dodge City Vintage Dodge **Vehicles & Parts** 18584 Hwy 108, PO Box 1687 Jamestown, CA 95327 209-984-5858; FAX: 209-984-3285 E-mail: mike@dodgecityvintage.com	**parts** **restoration** **research** **vehicles**

Mail order and open shop. Monday-Friday 9 am to 6 pm. Specializing in parts, reproduction, new, used. Vehicles, restorations, research and reference for Dodge, Dodge trucks, Chrysler and Plymouth, predominately 1933-1935.

Dynatech Engineering PO Box 1446 Alta Loma, CA 91701-8446 805-492-6134 E-mail: dynatechengineering@ yahoo.com	**motor mounts**

See full listing in **Section Two** under **engine parts**

Egge Machine Company Inc 11707 Slauson Ave Santa Fe Springs, CA 90670-2217 800-866-3443, 562-945-3419 FAX: 562-693-1635 E-mail: info@egge.com	**bearings** **gaskets** **pistons/rings** **timing components** **valvetrain**

See full listing in **Section Two** under **engine parts**

Firewall Insulators & Quiet Ride **Solutions** 6465 Pacific Ave, Ste 249 Stockton, CA 95207 209-477-4840; FAX: 209-477-0918 E-mail: timcox@quietride.com	**air plenums** **auto insulation** **firewall insulators** **gloveboxes** **sound deadening**

See full listing in **Section Two** under **upholstery**

Mike Hershenfeld PO Box 1301 Bellmore, NY 11710 PH/FAX: 516-781-PART (7278) E-mail: mikesmopar@juno.com	**parts**

See full listing in **Section One** under **Mopar**

Wayne Hood 228 Revell Rd Grenada, MS 38901 601-227-8426	**NORS parts** **NOS parts**

Mail order and open shop. Monday-Saturday 8 am to 6 pm. NOS, NORS parts for cars and trucks, 1930s-1960s. Specialize in fair prices and quick service. Have mostly mechanical parts and some lenses for all makes, 1930s-1960s.

Bruce Horkey's Wood & Parts 46284 440th St Windom, MN 56101 507-831-5625; FAX: 507-831-0280 E-mail: woodandparts@yahoo.com	**pickup parts**

See full listing in **Section Two** under **trucks & tractors**

Hot Heads Research & Racing Inc 276 Walker's Hollow Tr Lowgap, NC 27024 336-352-4866; FAX: 336-352-3892 E-mail: info@hothemiheads.com	**parts**

See full listing in **Section One** under **Chrysler**

Imperial Motors PO Box 496 Campobello, SC 29322 864-895-3474; FAX: 864-895-1248	**parts**

See full listing in **Section One** under **Chrysler**

Jeff Johnson Motorsports PO Box 14327 Columbus, OH 43214 614-268-1181; FAX: 614-268-1141	**literature**

See full listing in **Section One** under **Mopar**

Kramer Automotive Specialties PO Box 5 Herman, PA 16039 724-285-5566; FAX: 724-285-8898 E-mail: kramerauto@aol.com	**body parts** **interiors** **sheetmetal**

See full listing in **Section One** under **Mopar**

Layson's Restorations Inc 26164 126th Ave SE Kent, WA 98031 253-630-4088; FAX: 253-630-4065 E-mail: laysons@foxinternet.net	**parts**

See full listing in **Section One** under **Mopar**

Mack Products PO Box 856 Moberly, MO 65270 660-263-7444 E-mail: jhummel@mackhils.com	**parts** **pickup beds**

See full listing in **Section One** under **Ford 1932-1953**

Jim Mallars 5931 Glen St Stockton, CA 95207 209-477-1702 (8 to 10 am, 5 to 7 pm)	**parts**

Mail order and open shop by appointment only. For 1915-1928 Dodge Brothers 4-cylinder vehicles. New and used parts.

MAR-K Quality Parts 6625 W Wilshire Blvd Oklahoma City, OK 73132 405-721-7945; FAX: 405-721-8906 E-mail: info@mar-k.com	**bed parts** **customizing parts** **trim parts**

See full listing in **Section Two** under **trucks & tractors**

Clayton T Nelson Box 259 Warrenville, IL 60555 630-369-6589	**NOS parts**

See full listing in **Section One** under **Oldsmobile**

NOS Reproductions 22425 Jefferies Rd, RR 3 Komoka ON Canada N0L 1R0 519-471-2740; FAX: 519-471-7675 E-mail: info@nosreproductions.com	**parts**

See full listing in **Section One** under **Mopar**

Obsolete Chrysler NOS Parts 4206 Burnett Dr Murrysville, PA 15668 724-733-1818 eves; FAX: 724-733-9884 E-mail: parts4u@aol.com	**literature** **parts**

See full listing in **Section One** under **Chrysler**

Obsolete Parts of Iowa   NOS parts
PO Box 233
Earlville, IA 52041
E-mail: finsrus@mwci.net

See full listing in **Section One** under **Mopar**

Older Car Restoration   repro parts
Martin Lum, Owner   restoration
304 S Main St, Box 428
Mont Alto, PA 17237
717-749-3383, 717-352-7701
E-mail: marty@oldercar.com

See full listing in **Section Two** under **restoration shops**

Plymouth, Dodge, Chrysler,   NOS parts for
DeSoto Parts   DeSoto
4206 Burnett Dr
Murrysville, PA 15668
724-733-1818 eves
FAX: 724-733-9884
E-mail: parts4u@aol.com

See full listing in **Section One** under **DeSoto**

Precision Coachworks   parts
19 Winsor Rd   pickup beds
Billerica, MA 01821
978-663-7573
E-mail: precoach@mediaone.net

See full listing in **Section One** under **Ford 1932-1953**

Restorations By Julius   restoration
10101-1/2 Canoga Ave
Chatsworth, CA 91311
818-882-2825; FAX: 818-882-2855
E-mail: julius@restorationsbyjulius.com

See full listing in **Section One** under **Plymouth**

S&P Creations   books
971 Colleen Dr   data analysis
Newport News, VA 23608   information
757-875-5270
E-mail: theadventurer@worldnett.att.net

Mail order and open shop. Monday-Saturday 9 am to 6 pm. Specializing in 1972 thru 1980 Dodge truck restoration information, books, data analysis, appraisal and support for 1976 True Spirit, 1976-1979 Warlock and 1978-1979 Lil' Red Express truck. Web site: http://home.att.net/~theadventurer

Sherman & Associates Inc   body panels
61166 Van Dyke Rd   body parts
Washington, MI 48094   fenders/floors
810-677-6800; FAX: 810-677-6801   quarter panels

See full listing in **Section Two** under **body parts**

Paul Slater Auto Parts   parts
9496 85th St N
Stillwater, MN 55082
651-429-4235

Mail order and open shop by appointment only. Phone hours are 9 am to 9 pm CST. Specializing in 1966-1974 performance Dodge and Plymouth parts (Roadrunner, GTX, Coronet, Super Bee, Charger, Barracuda, Challenger, Dart, Duster, Demon and some others). Excellent quality used my specialty, but also some NOS parts. More items in every week. Call or write me (send SASE) with your needs. Sorry, no list or catalog. I also buy NOS and quality used parts. Serving the hobby since 1983.

Tags Backeast   data plates
PO Box 581   trim tags
Plainville, CT 06062   cowl tags
860-747-2942
E-mail: dataplt@snet.net

See full listing in **Section Two** under **special services**

Texas Viper Hotline   Prowlers
5405 Montclair   Vipers
Colleyville, TX 76034
817-267-1299; FAX: 972-721-3900
E-mail: dab1213@msn.com

Specializing in Dodge Vipers and Plymouth Prowlers. Web site: www.viperhotline.com

Totally Auto Inc   parts
337 Philmont Ave   restoration
Feasterville, PA 19053   service
215-322-2277; FAX: 215-322-4755
E-mail: totalyauto@aol.com

See full listing in **Section One** under **Mopar**

Vintage Power Wagons Inc   parts
302 S 7th St   trucks
Fairfield, IA 52556
515-472-4665; FAX: 515-472-4824

Mail order and open shop. Monday-Friday 8:30 am to 5 pm. Specializing in 1939-1970 Dodge Power Wagons, 4-wd trucks and parts.

Weimann's Literature & Collectables   literature
16 Cottage Rd
Harwinton, CT 06791
860-485-0300
FAX: 860-485-1705, 24 hours
E-mail: weimann@snet.net

See full listing in **Section One** under **Plymouth**

White Post Restorations   brakes
One Old Car Dr, PO Drawer D   restoration
White Post, VA 22663
540-837-1140; FAX: 540-837-2368
E-mail: info@whitepost.com

See full listing in **Section Two** under **brakes**

White Post Restorations   restoration
One Old Car Dr, PO Drawer D
White Post, VA 22663
540-837-1140; FAX: 540-837-2368
E-mail: info@whitepost.com

See full listing in **Section Two** under **restoration shops**

Wittenborn's Auto Service Inc   Mopar
133 Woodside Ave   Dodge
Briarcliff Manor, NY 10510-1717   Plymouth
914-941-2744; FAX: 914-769-1327

See full listing in **Section One** under **Mopar**

Year One Inc   parts
PO Box 129
Tucker, GA 30085
800-YEAR-ONE (932-7663)
770-493-6568 Atlanta & overseas
FAX: 800-680-6806
E-mail: info@yearone.com

See full listing in **Section Two** under **comprehensive parts**

Blackhawk Collection
1092 Eagles Nest Pl
Danville, CA 94506
925-736-3444; FAX: 925-736-4375
E-mail: info@blackhawkcollection.com

| acquisitions |
| sales |

Specializing in sales and aquisitions as well as exposition sale events for pre and post-war American and European classics, custom-bodied and one-of-a-kind automobiles. Web site: www.blackhawkcollection.com

Leo Gephart Inc
7360 E Acoma Dr, Ste 14
Scottsdale, AZ 85260
480-948-2286; FAX: 480-948-2390
E-mail: gephartclassics@earthlink.net

vintage cars

See full listing in **Section Two** under **car dealers**

Libbey's Classic Car Restoration Center
137 N Quinsigamond Ave
Shrewsbury, MA 01545
PH/FAX: 508-792-1560

| bodywork |
| restoration |
| service |

See full listing in **Section Two** under **restoration shops**

Northeast Classic Car Museum
NYS Rt 23, 24 Rexford St
Norwich, NY 13815
607-334-AUTO (2886)
FAX: 607-336-6745
E-mail: info@classiccarmuseum.org

museum

See full listing in **Section Six** under **New York**

ORF Corp
Phil Bray
8858 Ferry Rd
Grosse Ile, MI 48138
734-676-5520; FAX: 734-676-9438
E-mail: carolbray@yahoo.com

rear end gears

See full listing in **Section One** under **Packard**

A-1 Shock Absorber Co
Shockfinders Division
365 Warren Ave, PO Box 2028
Silverthorne, CO 80498
800-344-1966, 970-389-3193 cell
FAX: 970-513-8283

| shocks-all types |
| coil springs |
| Koni shocks |
| leaf springs |
| steering gears |

See our ad on the last page

Dennis Carpenter Ford Reproductions
PO Box 26398
Charlotte, NC 28221
704-786-8139; FAX: 704-786-8180

parts

See full listing in **Section One** under **Ford 1954-up**

Edsel Associates
2912 Hunter St
Fort Worth, TX 76112
817-451-2708
E-mail: theparts@flash.net

| brake |
| sheetmetal |
| steering |
| suspension |

Mail, e-mail, telephone orders and open shop. 1958-1960 Edsel parts, new suspension, brake, engine parts, ignition, water/fuel pumps. New and used sheetmetal, interior and exterior trim. SASE for partial list. Keep America beautiful, restore your Edsel.

Firewall Insulators & Quiet Ride Solutions
6465 Pacific Ave, Ste 249
Stockton, CA 95207
209-477-4840; FAX: 209-477-0918
E-mail: timcox@quietride.com

| air plenums |
| auto insulation |
| firewall insulators |
| gloveboxes |
| sound deadening |

See full listing in **Section Two** under **upholstery**

Mac's Antique Auto Parts
1051 Lincoln Ave, PO Box 238
Lockport, NY 14095-0238
800-777-0948 US and Canada
716-433-1500 local and foreign
FAX: 716-433-1172
E-mail: mailmacs@aol.com

| literature |
| parts |
| restoration |
| supplies |

See full listing in **Section One** under **Ford 1903-1931**

Thunderbolt Traders Inc
6900 N Dixie Dr
Dayton, OH 45414-3297
513-890-3344; FAX: 513-890-9403
E-mail: tbolt@erinet.com

battery cables

Specializing in battery cables for Edsels 1958, 1959 and 1960. Distributor of personal communication devices and selected classic and custom auto parts. Web site: www.thunderbolttradersinc.com

Creative Connections Inc
3407 Hwy 120
Duluth, GA 30096
770-476-7322; FAX: 770-476-7028
E-mail: sales@logolites.com

| brake lights |
| logo lights |
| turn signals |

See full listing in **Section One** under **Ford 1903-1931**

Firewall Insulators & Quiet Ride Solutions
6465 Pacific Ave, Ste 249
Stockton, CA 95207
209-477-4840; FAX: 209-477-0918
E-mail: timcox@quietride.com

| air plenums |
| auto insulation |
| firewall insulators |
| gloveboxes |
| sound deadening |

See full listing in **Section Two** under **upholstery**

Ferrari

Algar — parts
1234 Lancaster Ave
Rosemont, PA 19010
800-441-9824, 610-527-1100
FAX: 610-525-0575
E-mail: algarferrari.com

Specializing in parts for Ferrari and Alfa Romeo.

Apple Hydraulics Inc — brake rebuilding / shock rebuilding
1610 Middle Rd
Calverton, NY 11933-1419
800-882-7753, 631-369-9515
FAX: 631-369-9516
E-mail: info@applehydraulics.com

See full listing in **Section Two** under **suspension parts**

Bassett's Jaguar — parts / restoration / service / upholstery
53 Stilson Rd, PO Box 245
Wyoming, RI 02898
401-539-3010; FAX: 401-539-7861
E-mail: jagwillie@ids.net

See full listing in **Section One** under **Jaguar**

Jerry Bensinger — car dealer
1197 Trails Edge Dr
Hubbard, OH 44425-3353
330-759-5224; FAX: 330-759-5225
E-mail: jbenzr@aol.com

See full listing in **Section Two** under **car dealers**

Francois Bruere — artwork
8 Avenue Olivier Heuze
LeMans 72000 France
(33) 02-4377-1877
FAX: (33) 02-4324-2038
E-mail: francois.bruere@orpheograff.com

See full listing in **Section Two** under **artwork**

Collectors Choice LTD — parts / race preparation / restoration / service
6400 Springfield-Lodi Rd
Dane, WI 53529
608-849-9878; FAX: 608-849-9879
E-mail: collectorschoice1@prodigy.net

See full listing in **Section One** under **DeTomaso/Pantera**

Drummond Coach and Paint — painting / restoration
531 Raleigh Ave
El Cajon, CA 92020
619-579-7229; FAX: 619-579-2128

Specializing in Ferrari painting and restoration of paint, interior and chrome for pre-1974 Daytonas, 275 GTB 2 and 4 cam, 365, BB, BB512, California Spyders, PF Series II, Lussos, also other exotics.

Exoticars USA — machine work / paint/bodywork / restoration/service / welding/fabrication
6 Washington St
Frenchtown, NJ 08825
908-996-4889
E-mail: exoticars@erols.com

Ferrari, Maserati and Lamborghini. Cars located and inspected worldwide. Expert service and restoration, including paint and bodywork, engine rebuilding, interiors, electrical work, engine compartment detailing, motor-vac service and fabrication of parts and pieces. Basket case to First Place is our specialty.
Web site: http://exoticars-usa.com

The Fine Car Store — car dealer
1105 Moana Dr
San Diego, CA 92107
619-223-7766; FAX: 619-223-6838

Sale of antique, classic, special interest, collectible, sports, hot rods and vintage race cars. Specializing in collectible Ferrari, Jaguar and Aston Martin automobiles.

Forza Magazine — magazine
42 Digital Dr #5
Novato, CA 94949
415-382-0580; FAX: 415-382-0587

See full listing in **Section Four** under **periodicals**

Highway One Classic Automobiles and Highwayone.com — classic automobiles
1035 California Dr
Burlingame, CA 94010
650-342-7340; FAX: 650-343-0150
E-mail: djboscacci@msn.com

See full listing in **Section One** under **Abarth**

International Automobile Archives — sales literature
Kai Jacobsen
Wiesenweg 3b
85757 Karlsfeld Germany
011-49-8131-93158
FAX: 011-49-8131-505973
E-mail: doubledseven@t-online.de

See full listing in **Section Two** under **literature dealers**

International Restoration Specialist Inc — parts / restoration / sales
PO Box 1303
Mt Airy, NC 27030
336-789-1548

See full listing in **Section Two** under **restoration shops**

Kensington Motor Group Inc — consignment sales
PO Box 2277
Sag Harbor, NY 11963
516-537-1868; FAX: 516-537-2641
E-mail: kenmotor@aol.com

See full listing in **Section One** under **Mercedes-Benz**

The Klemantaski Collection — books / photography
65 High Ridge Rd, Ste 219
Stamford, CT 06905
PH/FAX: 203-968-2970
E-mail: klemcoll@aol.com

See full listing in **Section Two** under **photography**

London Stainless Steel Exhaust Centre — exhaust systems
249-253 Queenstown Rd
London, SW8 3NP England
0114420-7622-2120
FAX: 0114420-7627-0991
E-mail: info@quicksilverexhausts.com

See full listing in **Section Two** under **exhaust systems**

Marcovicci-Wenz Engineering Inc — Cosworth engines
33 Comac Loop
Ronkonkoma, NY 11779
631-467-9040; FAX: 631-467-9041
E-mail: mwerace@compuserve.com

See full listing in **Section Two** under **racing**

Thomas Montanari
Automotive Artist
51 Lamb-Hope Rd
Hopewell, NJ 08525
609-466-7753; FAX: 609-466-7939
E-mail: tmontanari@aol.com

illustrations
paintings
prints

See full listing in **Section Two** under **artwork**

Motorcar Gallery Inc
715 N Federal Hwy
Fort Lauderdale, FL 33304
954-522-9900; FAX: 954-522-9966
E-mail: motorcargallery@aol.com

car dealer

We are sellers and buyers of European classic and exotic automobiles. We specialize in limited production marques like Ferrari, Maserati, Lamborghini, Iso, Rolls-Royce, Pegaso, Monteverdi, AC, Talbot-Lago, Facel Vega, Mercedes 300S, 300SL, BMW M-1, 507, etc. We stock 40-50 high quality examples. Contact us for current inventory list. Trades welcome. Worldwide transportation available.

Motorcars International
528 N Prince Ln
Springfield, MO 65802
417-831-9999; FAX: 417-831-8080
E-mail: sales@motorcars-intl.com

accessories
sales
service
tools

Monday-Friday 8 am to 6 pm, Saturday 9 am to 3 pm. The authorized Lamborghini center. Sales, service, accessories. Pre-owned car sales of Ferrari, Porsche, Mercedes, BMW, Jaguar, Lotus, Rolls-Royce and Bentley. National locating service. Custom financing programs. Over 20 years delivering the experience of fine motoring with recognized excellence. Cash buyers for your car. Enclosed nationwide delivery. Factory authorized service and parts. Concours salon services. Aftermarket accessories specializing in custom fit car covers, floor mats and car care products. Web site: www.motorcars-intl.com

Mr Sport Car Inc
719 W 6th St
Papillion, NE 68046
402-592-7559

service

See full listing in **Section One** under **Jaguar**

Partsource
32 Harden Ave
Camden, ME 04843
207-236-9791; FAX: 207-236-6323

parts

Mail order only. Parts importer/distributor. Ferrari parts specialist, 1949-1998. 25 years' experience. Exclusively Ferrari, all models. Web site: www.partsourcenet.com

Peninsula Imports
3749 Harlem Rd
Buffalo, NY 14215
800-999-1209; FAX: 905-847-3021
E-mail: imports@ican.net

accessories
parts
trim

See full listing in **Section One** under **BMW**

Pilkington Glass Search
1975 Galaxie St
Columbus, OH 43207
800-848-1351; FAX: 614-443-0709

glass parts

See full listing in **Section Two** under **glass**

Private Garage LC
8949 SE Bridge Rd, PMB 302
Hobe Sound, FL 33455
561-545-7277; FAX: 561-546-7884

consultant

By appointment only. Specializes in investment quality Ferrari, Cobra, Mercedes-Benz and vintage racing cars. For serious collectors.

Proper Motor Cars Inc
1811 11th Ave N
St Petersburg, FL 33713-5794
727-821-8883; FAX: 727-821-0273
E-mail: propermotorcarsinc@
email.msn.com

parts
restoration
service

See full listing in **Section One** under **Rolls-Royce/Bentley**

Replicarz
166 Spruce St
Rutland, VT 05701
802-747-7151
E-mail: replicarz@aol.com

books
kits
models
videos

See full listing in **Section Two** under **racing**

Garry Roberts & Co
922 Sunset Dr
Costa Mesa, CA 92627
949-650-2690; FAX: 949-650-2730
E-mail: garryroberts@fea.net

cars
parts
service

Specializing in pre-owned Ferrari, sales, service, restorations for Ferrari. Web site: www.garryrobertsco.com

Rosso Bianco Sportscar Museum
Obernauer Str 125
D-63743
Aschaffenburg Germany
06021 21358; FAX: 06021 20636

museum

See full listing in **Section Six** under **Germany**

Showroom Auto Sales
960 S Bascom Ave
San Jose, CA 95128
408-279-0944; FAX: 408-279-0918

car dealer

See full listing in **Section One** under **Mercedes-Benz**

Spyder Enterprises Inc
RFD 1682
Laurel Hollow, NY 11791-9644
516-367-1616; FAX: 516-367-3260
E-mail: singer356@aol.com

accessories
artwork
automobilia
books

See full listing in **Section Two** under **automobilia**

Thoroughbred Motors
3935 N US 301
Sarasota, FL 34234
941-359-2277; FAX: 941-359-2128
E-mail: vintagejags@mindspring.com

car dealer
parts

See full listing in **Section One** under **Jaguar**

Tillack & Co Ltd
630 Mary Ann Dr
Redondo Beach, CA 90278
310-318-8760; FAX: 310-376-3392
E-mail: race@tillackco.com

parts
restoration

See full listing in **Section Two** under **restoration shops**

Viking Worldwise Inc
190 Doe Run Rd
Manheim, PA 17545
866-CJACKETS; FAX: 717-664-5556
E-mail: gkurien@dejazz.com

leather jackets

See full listing in **Section Two** under **apparel**

Brady Ward-Scale Autoworks
313 Bridge St #4
Manchester, NH 03104-5045
PH/FAX: 603-623-5925

models

See full listing in **Section Two** under **models & toys**

White Post Restorations
One Old Car Dr, PO Drawer D
White Post, VA 22663
540-837-1140; FAX: 540-837-2368
E-mail: info@whitepost.com

brakes
restoration

See full listing in **Section Two** under **brakes**

Auto Italia
3350 Woolsey Rd
Windsor, CA 95492
707-528-4825; FAX: 707-569-8717
E-mail: lenny@auto-italia

parts

Mail order only. New, used and reconditioned parts for Fiats, 1968-1988; Lancia Betas; Maserati Bi-Turbo. Used parts for Fiat Spiders and Maserati Bi-Turbos a specialty.

Bayless Inc
1111 Via Bayless
Marietta, GA 30066-2770
770-928-1446; FAX: 770-928-1342
800-241-1446 order line (US & Canada)
E-mail: baylessfiat@mindspring.com

accessories
parts

Mail order only. Monday-Friday 9 am to 5:30 pm. Lancia Beta Series 1975-1982 and Yugo 1985-1991. Distributors of Magneti Marelli electrical components and Alquati performance parts. Expanded 136 page catalog, $4 ($10 International). Worldwide shipping since 1971. Web site: www.baylessfiat.com

Blint Equipment Inc
2204 E Lincolnway
LaPorte, IN 46350
219-362-7021

parts
tractor rebuilding

See full listing in **Section One** under **Ford 1954-up**

Caribou Imports Inc
26804 Vista Terr
Lake Forest, CA 92630
949-770-3136; FAX: 949-770-0815
E-mail: cariboulh@aol.com

parts

Mail order and open shop. Monday-Friday 9:30 am to 5 pm. Supplies parts worldwide for Fiat and Lancia automobiles. Over 22,000 parts are available for immediate shipment. We reproduce parts that the factories have discontinued. For Fiat Spiders in particular, we are known as "The Spider Restoration Headquarters." Web site: www.caribou.cc

Fiat Auto Service
18440 Hart St, Unit J
Reseda, CA 91335
818-345-4458; FAX: 818-345-6213
E-mail: fiatsteve@aol.com

parts
repair
restoration

Specialize in new and used parts. Also full repair and restoration for Fiats, all makes and models, 1960-on.

Linearossa International Inc
3931 SW 47th Ave
Ft Lauderdale, FL 33314
954-327-9888; FAX: 954-791-6555

parts

Mail order and open shop. Monday-Friday 9 am to 5 pm. Specializing in Fiat parts, all years for 500, 600, 850, X1/9, 124 models. The only US factory distributor for OEM Fiat parts. New! Full line of Alfa Romeo 105 parts, 1966-1992 Spider/GT/GTV to 1974. Web site: www.linearossausa.com

Motormetrics
6369 Houston Rd
Macon, GA 31216
912-785-0275
E-mail: fzampa@mail.maconstate.edu

used parts

See full listing in **Section One** under **Triumph**

Museo Abarth
1111 Via Bayless
Marietta, GA 30066-2770
770-928-1446

museum

See full listing in **Section Six** under **Georgia**

C Obert & Co
2131-D Delaware Ave
Santa Cruz, CA 95060-5706
800-500-3428 orders
831-423-0218; FAX: 831-459-8128
E-mail: fiatplus@aol.com

parts
repairs

Mail order and open shop. Monday-Friday 8:30 am to 5:30 pm. Specializes in parts and repairs for Fiat, Lancia, Abarth, and Yugo. Authorized Fiat/Lancia parts center. Imports parts as necessary from Europe. Hard-to-find Fiat parts from 1955-present. Write or call for free newsletter. Web site: http://we.got.net/~fiatplus

Orion Motors European Parts Inc
10722 Jones Rd
Houston, TX 77065
800-736-6410, 281-894-1982
FAX: 281-849-1997
E-mail: orion-yugo@yugoparts.com

parts

See full listing in **Section One** under **Alfa Romeo**

Rayce Inc
3637 NE 2nd St
Gainesville, FL 32609
800-426-2221, 352-335-8900
FAX: 352-335-8930

parts

See full listing in **Section One** under **Alfa Romeo**

Doug Schellinger
13717 W Green Meadow Dr
New Berlin, WI 53151
414-328-1907
E-mail: dsac@execpc.com

automobilia
books
sales literature
toys

Mail order only. Sales literature, books, toys and automobilia for Fiat, Lancia and Alfa Romeo; also literature and memorabilia for all types of racing and high-performance.

A/Altered Hot Rod Parts
PO Box 851
Emporia, KS 66801
620-343-1796

body parts

Specializing in bodies, fenders, etc, for 1928-1931 Model A Fords, 1930 & 1931 three-window coupe body, 1928 & 1929 Vicky body, custom bobbed rear fenders, rear splash pans, roll pans, etc, also 1928-1932 chassis.

| Antique Auto Parts et al
9103 E Garvey Ave
Rosemead, CA 91770-0458
626-288-2121; FAX: 626-288-3311 | accessories
parts |

Mail order only. Phone hours Monday-Friday 9 am to 5 pm. Parts and accessories for Ford cars and trucks. SASE required for parts information.

| Antique Automotive Engineering Inc
3560 Chestnut Pl
Denver, CO 80216
303-296-7332, 800-846-7332
E-mail: ed@antiqueautoengr.com | babbitt service
engine restoration |

Open Monday-Friday 8 am to 4:30 pm; weekends by appointment. Babbitt pouring, align boring and complete engine restoration, balanced Model A Ford engines, counterbalanced crankshafts, drilled cranks for full pressure oil systems, cut-down flywheels with V8 clutches & pressure plates; hot rod Model Bs & V8s; high compression heads. New: 660 brass thrust washer. Web site: www.antiqueautoengr.com

| Apple Hydraulics Inc
1610 Middle Rd
Calverton, NY 11933-1419
800-882-7753, 631-369-9515
FAX: 631-369-9516
E-mail: info@applehydraulics.com | brake rebuilding
shock rebuilding |

See full listing in **Section Two** under **suspension parts**

| Atwell-Wilson Motor Museum
Downside Stockley Ln
Calne
Wiltshire SN110NF England
PH/FAX: 01249-813119 | museum |

See full listing in **Section Six** under **England**

| Auto Restorations
8150 S CR 1250 N
Albany, IN 47320
800-955-3139 | transmission
conversion kits |

Transmission conversion kits for Model A Fords, 1929-1931.

| Battlefield Antique
5054 S Broadview
Battlefield, MO 65619
417-882-7923
E-mail: battlefielda@aol.com | parts |

Mail order and open shop. Monday-Friday 8 am to 5 pm, weekends by appointment only. Specializing in Model A Ford new and used parts for 1928-1931.

| Bill's Model Acres Ford Farm
RD 1, Box 283, 8th St Rd
Watsontown, PA 17777
570-538-3200 | parts
restorations |

Mail order and open shop; Monday-Friday 8 am to 5 pm, evenings and weekends by appointment. Complete inventory of reproduction, rebuilt and huge inventory of used mechanical, sheetmetal and bodies for Model As. Also, reproduction and used parts and cars from 1932-1972. Bob Drake retailer. Complete or partial restoration services, mechanical and bodywork. Spin painting of spoke wheels our specialty. Reasonable shop rates. Buy, sell or trade parts and cars. ASE certified master technician. MARC and MAFCA member since 1965.

| Bob's Antique Auto Parts Inc
PO Box 2523
Rockford, IL 61132
815-633-7244; FAX: 815-654-0761 | parts |

Mail order and open shop. Monday-Friday 9 am to 4:30 pm, Saturday 9 am to 12 pm. Specializes in Model T Ford parts,

1903-1927. Quality T parts only. Known as the Model T specialists. Retail catalog upon request. Dealer inquiries invited.

| Bryant's Antique Auto Parts
851 Western Ave
Hampden, ME 04444
207-862-4019 | appraisals
chassis/engine parts
sheetmetal
wiring harnesses |

Mail order and open shop. Monday-Friday 9 am to 5 pm, Saturday by appointment. Established in 1971. Appraisal within 100 mile area in Maine. Quality Model A and T parts. Call for catalog information.

| Car-Line Manufacturing &
Distribution Inc
1250 Gulf St, PO Box 1192
Beaumont, TX 77701
409-833-9757; FAX: 409-835-2468
E-mail: car-line@car-line.net | chassis parts
engine parts
sheetmetal |

See full listing in **Section Two** under **sheetmetal**

| Cass County Historical Society
1351 W Main Ave, PO Box 719
West Fargo, ND 58078
701-282-2822; FAX: 701-282-7606
E-mail: info@bonanzaville.com | museum |

See full listing in **Section Six** under **North Dakota**

| Classic Wood Mfg
1006 N Raleigh St
Greensboro, NC 27405
336-691-1344; FAX: 336-273-3074 | wood kits
wood replacement |

See full listing in **Section Two** under **woodwork**

| Classtique Upholstery & Top Co
PO Box 278 HK
Isanti, MN 55040
763-444-4025; FAX: 763-444-9980 | top kits
upholstery kits |

Mail order and open shop. Specializing in 1914-1931 Ford interior upholstery kits, top kits, etc. Original materials, guaranteed show quality workmanship. Free samples and ordering information, advise year and body style, standard or deluxe. Established 1959.

| Creative Connections Inc
3407 Hwy 120
Duluth, GA 30096
770-476-7322; FAX: 770-476-7028
E-mail: sales@logolites.com | brake lights
logo lights
turn signals |

Specializing in logo lights, LED third brake lights and turn signals for 1928-1931 Model A Fords plus various other vintage cars and trucks. Web site: www.logolites.com

| Chuck & Judy Cubel
PO Box 278
Superior, AZ 85273
520-689-2734
FAX: 520-689-5815, 24 hours
E-mail: cubel@theriver.com | wood parts |

Call Monday-Friday 9 am to 9 pm. We've been making our oak and ash hardwood Ford parts since 1963, for the Standard Ford bodies. State year, complete body style, your name and mailing address to receive free catalog. Download your own info at: www.fordwood.com

| Mike Dennis, Nebraska Mail Order
1845 S 48th St
Lincoln, NE 68506
402-489-3036; FAX: 402-489-1148 | parts
Trippe mounting
brackets/hardware |

See full listing in **Section One** under **Ford 1932-1953**

S D Dennis | rebabbitting
708 Pineview Dr
Valdosta, GA 31602
912-242-3084

Rebabbitting service Ford As, Bs, and Cs.

Early Ford Parts | literature
2948 Summer Ave | parts
Memphis, TN 38112
901-323-2179; FAX: 901-323-2195

See full listing in **Section One** under **Ford 1932-1953**

Firewall Insulators & Quiet Ride | air plenums
Solutions | auto insulation
6465 Pacific Ave, Ste 249 | firewall insulators
Stockton, CA 95207 | gloveboxes
209-477-4840; FAX: 209-477-0918 | sound deadening
E-mail: timcox@quietride.com

See full listing in **Section Two** under **upholstery**

Ford Obsolete | chassis parts
9107-13 Garvey Ave | engine parts
Rosemead, CA 91770
626-288-2121

Mail order and open shop. Monday-Friday 11 am to 5 pm, Saturday 9 am to 3 pm. Full line of new and used chassis and engine parts for trucks and Model As, T and V8 Ford. SASE required for information.

Ford Parts Specialists | parts
Div of Joblot Automotive Inc
98-11 211th St
Queens Village, NY 11429
718-468-8585; FAX: 718-468-8686

Mail order and open shop. Monday-Friday 8:30 am to 4:30 pm. Over 12,000 different new and rebuilt parts. Specializing in the Ford family of cars and trucks 1928-1969. Engine, brake, transmission and clutch, front and rear end, a full line of rubber, electrical, wiring and ignition. Established in 1956. Three catalogs available: 1928-1948 cars and trucks, 1948/1969 F-1/100 thru F-6/600 trucks, 1949/1969 Ford family of cars. Visa, MC and COD, phone or fax orders accepted. Dealer inquiries invited.

Freeman's Garage | parts
29 Ford Rd | restoration
Norton, MA 02766 | sales
508-285-6500; FAX: 508-285-6566 | service

Mail order and open shop. Tuesday-Friday 10 am to 6 pm, Saturdays, evenings, other times by chance or appointment. Sales, service, parts for 1928-1931 Model A and AA Fords. Same location since 1957.

Fun Projects Inc | electrical parts
PMB 164, 2460 W Main St - D | mechanical parts
St Charles, IL 60175
630-584-1471
E-mail: piewagon@funprojects.com

See full listing in **Section Two** under **electrical systems**

Gaslight Auto Parts Inc | accessories
PO Box 291 | parts
Urbana, OH 43078
937-652-2145; FAX: 937-652-2147

Mail order and open shop. Monday-Friday 8:30 am to 5 pm. 38th year in business. Antique Ford parts, accessories and sheetmetal for Model A, T and early V8.

Good Old Days Garage Inc | engine building
2341 Farley Pl | Firestone tires
Birmingham, AL 35226 | parts
205-822-4569; FAX: 205-823-1944 | service

Mail order and open shop. Monday-Saturday 8:30 am to 10 pm. Parts and service for Model As. Marlar-built engines and T/A/B engine rebuilding a specialty. Uses KR Wilson tools as the Ford repair shops used. Appointment necessary to watch your block poured and align bored. Have completed 808 A and T engines at this time. Shipped to Germany, England, Australia, Quita Equidore and Santiago, Chile. My 33rd year. Honesty and reasonable prices always. A full service Model A shop. Come visit.

Bill Gratkowski | woodgraining
515 N Petroleum St
Titusville, PA 16354
814-827-1782 days or eves
E-mail: billgrains@csonline.net

See full listing in **Section Two** under **woodgraining**

Hancock's Engine Rebuilders | engine rebuilding
and Balancing Service
2885 Cherokee Rd
Athens, GA 30605
706-543-7726; FAX: 706-543-4767

Open Monday-Friday 9 am to 5 pm. For Model Ts, As, Bs, Cs and early V8s.

Henry's Model T & A Parts | parts
52 Poole St
Deer Park, Victoria 3023 Australia
03-9363-2869; FAX: 03-9363-5219
E-mail: henrys@optusnet.com.au

Mail order only. Phone orders 7 days a week. Specializing in reproduction parts for Ford Model T and A and early Ford V8 1909-1954. We carry a large range of Model T and A and early Ford V8 parts and distribute Australia wide. Bank card, Visa and MasterCard facilities available.

Hillcrest Hot Rods | custom cars
541 Mercer Rd | street rods
Greenville, PA 16125
PH/FAX: 724-588-3444

See full listing in **Section Two** under **street rods**

Howell's Sheetmetal Co | body panels
PO Box 792 | sheetmetal
Nederland, TX 77627
800-375-6663, 409-727-1999
FAX: 409-727-7127
E-mail: dhowell@fordor.com

Mail order and open shop. Monday-Friday 8 am to 5 pm, Saturday by appointment. Specialize in reproduction sheetmetal, body panels, seat frames, patches, aprons for 1909-1940 Fords. Custom parts from your patterns other than Ford. Web site: www.fordor.com

Joyce's Model A & T Parts | new parts
PO Box 70 | NOS parts
Manchaca, TX 78652-0070 | rebuilt parts
512-282-1196; FAX: 512-479-5091

Specializing in parts, new, used, NOS and rebuilt for Ford Model T 1909-1927 and Ford Model A 1928-1931.

Joe Lagana | parts
Miller Rd
Canterbury, CT 06331
860-546-6000

Mail order and open shop. Monday-Saturday 9 am to 5 pm; other times by appointment. For Model As. No catalogs, send want list.

LeBaron Bonney Co	fabrics
6 Chestnut St, PO Box 6	interior kits
Amesbury, MA 01913	top kits
800-221-5408, 978-388-3811	
FAX: 978-388-1113	
E-mail: lbb-hc@greennet.net	

Antique auto "ready to install" interior kits, top kits and fabrics for over 300 models and variations of Ford (1928-1954) and Mercury (1939-1951) cars and trucks. Free literature with fabric samples and prices available upon request. Free parts and accessories catalog. Worldwide reputation for quality and service. Web site: www.lebaronbonney.com

Mac's Antique Auto Parts	literature
1051 Lincoln Ave, PO Box 238	parts
Lockport, NY 14095-0238	restoration
800-777-0948 US and Canada	supplies
716-433-1500 local and foreign	
FAX: 716-433-1172	
E-mail: mailmacs@aol.com	

Mail order and store. Phone hours: Monday-Friday 8 am to 11 pm; Saturday 8 am to 5 pm. New parts for 1909-1970s Fords from Model T to Mustang and 1909-1948 Ford street rods. 15 free catalogs available. Outside US, $5 each to cover postage. Specify year and model of car to receive correct catalog. Worldwide sales, prompt shipment. MC, Visa, Discover, AmEx, Diners Club, Optima, and COD accepted. Web site: www.macsautoparts.com

W L Wally Mansfield	cars
214 N 13th St	parts
Wymore, NE 68466-1640	trucks
402-645-3546	

See full listing in **Section Two** under **comprehensive parts**

Mark Auto Co Inc	parts
Layton, NJ 07851	restoration
973-948-4157; FAX: 973-948-5458	supplies

Mail and phone orders only. Phone hours: Monday-Thursday 10 am to 2 pm; fax orders may be sent anytime. No counter service. Model T and A Ford parts. A comprehensive selection of restoration supplies. Illustrated master catalog free. Visa, MasterCard. Worldwide dealer inquiries welcomed. Wholesale, retail.

McInnes Antique Auto	parts
PO Box 653	
Niagara-on-the Lake	
ON Canada L0S 1J0	
905-468-7779; FAX: 905-468-0759	
E-mail: mcinnes@netcom.ca	

Mail order and open shop by appointment only. Phone hours: 9 am to 8 pm daily. For 1909-1931 Fords. Price list available on request.

Myers Model A Ford, Mustang & Corvette Parts & Car Trailers	parts
17103 Sterling Rd	
Williamsport, MD 21795	
301-582-2478; FAX: 301-582-5852	
E-mail: myerscorvettes@hotmail.com	

Mail order and open shop. Monday-Friday 5:30 pm to 9:30 pm, Saturday 8 am to 4:30 pm. Sell new and used Model T and A Ford parts and cars. Also Mustang and Ford parts up to 1948 and Corvette parts.

Northeast Ford	parts
Box 66, Rt 9	restoration
East Sullivan, NH 03445	
603-847-9956, 800-562-FORD	
FAX: 603-847-9691	

See full listing in **Section One** under **Ford 1954-up**

Oak Bows	top bows
122 Ramsey Ave	
Chambersburg, PA 17201	
717-264-2602	

See full listing in **Section Two** under **woodwork**

Obsolete Ford Parts Inc	parts
8701 S I-35	
Oklahoma City, OK 73149	
405-631-3933; FAX: 405-634-6815	
E-mail: info@obsoletefordparts.com	

See full listing in **Section One** under **Ford 1954-up**

The Old Car Centre	parts
3-20075 92A Ave	
Langley, BC Canada V1M 3A4	
604-888-4412, 604-888-4055	
FAX: 604-888-7455	
E-mail: oldcarcentre@look.ca	

Mail order and open shop. Monday-Friday 8 am to 5 pm, Saturday 10 am to 4 pm. 1909-1956 Ford cars and pickups, 1937-1964 Chev parts. Specializes in 1928-1956 Fords. Stock and rod parts. 1955-1957 Chevys. A catalog, $3; V8 catalog, $3; 1948-1956 Ford pickup catalog, $3; Rod catalog, $3; Chev catalog, $1.50. Web site: www.oldcarcentre.com

Original Ford Motor Co Literature	collectibles
PO Box 7-AA	literature
Hudson, KY 40145-0007	
502-257-8642; FAX: 502-257-8643	
E-mail: whiteb@bellsouth.net	

See full listing in **Section One** under **Ford 1932-1953**

Precision Babbitt Service	babbitting
4681 Lincoln Ave	engine rebuilding
Beamsville, ON Canada L0R 1B3	
905-563-4364	
E-mail: tkoudys@sprint.ca	

See full listing in **Section Two** under **babbitting**

PV Antique & Classic Ford	parts
1688 Main St	
Tewksbury, MA 01876	
800-MSTANGS orders only	
978-851-9159; FAX: 978-858-3827	
E-mail: pvford@flash.net	

Mail order and open shop. Monday-Friday 9 am to 5 pm, Thursday 9 am to 9 pm, Saturday 9 am to 1 pm. Large inventory in stock of reproduction Model A, 1932-1948 early V8, 1948-1960 F-100 pickups and 1964-1/2 to 1973 Mustang parts and accessories. We ship UPS daily and accept MasterCard and Visa on all orders. Any catalog above, $2 or free with purchase. Web site: www.pvford.com

R&L Model A	parts
54 Clark Dr, Unit D	restorations
East Berlin, CT 06114	service
860-828-7600	

Open shop. Monday-Friday 9 am to 5 pm. A full line of parts and services, full restoration, painting for Model A Fords 1928-1931.

Walter E Rodimon	parts
PO Box 353	
Pike, NH 03780	
603-989-5557	

Mail order. Parts department open by appointment only. Antique original Ford parts bought, sold and traded.

Rootlieb Inc	parts
815 S Soderquist	
PO Box 1810	
Turlock, CA 95381	
209-632-2203; FAX: 209-632-2201	

Reproduction parts manufacturer: 1906-1937 hoods, 1909-1927 fenders, 1909-1931 runningboards, 1909-1929 splash aprons, Model A and T speedster kits and 1909-1916 Model T bodies. Also engine pans. Chevrolet, Ford and Mopar street rod hoods. Free catalog.

S & S Antique Auto	parts
Pine St	
Deposit, NY 13754	
607-467-2929; FAX: 607-467-2109	

See full listing in **Section One** under **Ford 1932-1953**

Smith & Jones Distributing Co Inc	parts
1 Biloxi Sq	
West Columbia, SC 29170	
803-822-8500; FAX: 803-822-8477	

Mail order and open shop. Monday-Friday 8:30 am to 5 pm. A complete line of reproduction parts for 1909-1931 Ford cars and trucks. We now have our complete catalog online for shopping. Web site: www.modela-t-snj.com

Snyder's Antique Auto Parts Inc	parts
12925 Woodworth Rd	
New Springfield, OH 44443	
888-262-5712, 330-549-5313	
FAX: 888-262-5713, 330-549-2211	
E-mail: snyantique@aol.com	

Mail order and open shop. Monday-Friday 8 am to 5 pm, Saturday 8 am to 12 pm. 1909-1931 Model T and A Ford parts. Also custom builds seat springs for any year or make of vehicle. In business over 40 years. Features same day shipping.

Valley Motor Supply	accessories parts
1402 E Second St	
Roswell, NM 88201	
505-622-7450	

See full listing in **Section One** under **Ford 1954-up**

Varco Inc	fitted luggage trunks
8300 S Anderson Rd	
Oklahoma City, OK 73150	
405-732-1637	

Mail order and open shop. Monday to Saturday 8 am to 6 pm. Manufacturer of racks, reinforcing bands, heater covers for Model A Ford; also trunks & fitted luggage for all cars US and foreign. Manufacturer of special size trunks for special interest cars, US & worldwide, also supplier of trunk repair hardware and special trunk racks. Web site: www.varcoinc.com

Vintage Ford Center Inc	accessories parts
302 E Main St	
Berryville, VA 22611	
888-813-FORD (3673)	
FAX: 540-955-0916	
E-mail: mdla@visuallink.com	

Mail order and open shop. Monday-Friday 9 am to 7 pm EST. Specializing in parts and accessories for Ford 1928-1931 Model A. Web site: www.modelastuff.com

Vintage Speed Parts	parts
9103 E Garvey Ave	
Rosemead, CA 91770	
626-280-4546	

Mail order and open shop. Monday-Friday 12 noon to 5 pm, Saturday 9 am to 3 pm. For Model Ts, As, and V8s. SASE required for parts information. Catalog, $6. Specify engine, chassis, etc.

Vintage Trunks	trunks
5 Brownstone Rd	
East Granby, CT 06026	
860-658-0353	
E-mail: john.desousa@snet.net	

See full listing in **Section Two** under **trunks**

Wagon Works	body plans hardware
213 SW Kline	
Ankeny, IA 50021	
515-964-5085	
E-mail: wagonwork2@aol.com	

Mail order only. Depot hack and huckster wagon plans and hardware. Web site: http://members.aol.com/wagonwork2

Pete Watson Enterprises	car dealer restoration
PO Box 488	
Epworth, GA 30541	
706-632-7675	

See full listing in **Section Two** under **restoration shops**

Wescott's Auto Restyling	body parts
19701 SE Hwy 212	
Boring, OR 97009	
800-523-6279; FAX: 503-658-2938	
E-mail: marykarl@gte.net	

See full listing in **Section One** under **Ford 1932-1953**

White Post Restorations	restoration
One Old Car Dr, PO Drawer D	
White Post, VA 22663	
540-837-1140; FAX: 540-837-2368	
E-mail: info@whitepost.com	

See full listing in **Section Two** under **restoration shops**

Wiseman Motor Co Inc	car dealer
Bill Wiseman, Owner	
PO Box 848	
Marion, NC 28752	
828-724-9313	

See full listing in **Section Two** under **car dealers**

1932-1953

600 Racing Inc	5/8 scale replicas
5245 NC Hwy 49 S	
Harrisburg, NC 28075	
704-455-3896; FAX: 704-455-3820	

See full listing in **Section Two** under **racing**

A-1 Street Rods	parts
631 E Las Vegas St	
Colorado Springs, CO 80903	
719-632-4920, 719-577-4588	
FAX: 719-634-6577	

See full listing in **Section Two** under **street rods**

All Ford Parts	accessories parts
1600 Dell Ave, Ste A	
Campbell, CA 95008	
800-532-1932; FAX: 408-866-1934	
E-mail: allford@jps.com	

Specializing in parts and accessories for 1928-1948 Fords. Web site: www.allfordparts.com

Alloy-Fab | bumper brackets
8709 Hwy 99
Vancouver, WA 98665
800-344-2847; FAX: 360-576-0610

Mail order and open shop. Monday-Friday 8:30 am to 5:30 pm. Manufacturer of polished aluminum bumper mounting brackets for customs, street rods, Fords thru 1951, Chevrolets thru 1953, Plymouths and Dodges thru 1951.

American Stamping Corp | frame rails
8719 Caroma
Olive Branch, MS 38654
PH/FAX: 662-895-5300

Mail order and open shop. Monday-Thursday 8 am to 4:30 pm. Specializing in 1932 Ford frame rails.

Antique Auto Fasteners | fasteners / hardware / hose clamps / molding clips
Guy (Chuck) Close
811 Oceanhill Dr
Huntington Beach, CA 92648
714-969-9161, 562-696-3307
E-mail: redjc1@earthlink.net

See full listing in **Section Two** under **hardware**

Antique Ford V8 Parts | parts / shock absorbers
658 Buckley Hwy
Union, CT 06076
860-684-3853

Mail order and open shop by appointment only. Specializing in the rebuilding of Ford shock absorbers and shock related parts for 1928-1948. Also 1932-1948 chassis parts, distributors, water pumps and brake parts.

Antique Radio Doctor | radio repairs
Barry Dalton
196 Kilborn Dr
Grants Pass, OR 97526
541-474-2524
E-mail: radiodoc@rvi.net

See full listing in **Section Two** under **radios**

Apple Hydraulics Inc | brake rebuilding / shock rebuilding
1610 Middle Rd
Calverton, NY 11933-1419
800-882-7753, 631-369-9515
FAX: 631-369-9516
E-mail: info@applehydraulics.com

See full listing in **Section Two** under **suspension parts**

ARASCO | parts
PO Box 24, Dept HA15
Newport, KY 41072
859-441-8363

Mail order and open shop by appointment only. Custom dual or stock exhaust systems. Specializing in flathead Fords.

Arelli Alloy Wheels | custom wheels
164 W Jefferson Blvd
Buena Park, CA 90620
323-733-0403; FAX: 323-733-0423
E-mail: sales@arelli.com

See full listing in **Section Two** under **wheels & wheelcovers**

Atwell-Wilson Motor Museum | museum
Downside Stockley Ln
Calne
Wiltshire SN110NF England
PH/FAX: 01249-813119

See full listing in **Section Six** under **England**

Aussieutes/Old Tin | salvage yard
PO Box 26
Wendouree Victoria 3355 Australia
03 5336 FORD; FAX: 03 5339 9900
E-mail: dave@aussieutes.com

See full listing in **Section Five** under **Australia**

Auto Advisors | appraisals
14 Dudley Rd
Billerica, MA 01821
978-667-0075

See full listing in **Section Two** under **appraisals**

B&C Fiberglass Co | fiberglass bodies / parts
1147 Parkwood Rd
Indiana, PA 15701
724-349-4835; FAX: 724-349-2076

Mail order only. Specializing in the manufacture and sale of fiberglass bodies and parts for 1933-1934 Ford fiberglass coupes.

B & W Antique Auto Parts Inc | accessories / parts
150 W Axton Rd, Unit 2
Bellingham, WA 98226
360-398-9820; FAX: 360-398-9431
E-mail: bwautoparts@bwautoparts.com

Reproduction and NOS parts for 1932-1979 Ford cars and trucks and 1936-1976 Chev cars and trucks. Web site: www.bwautoparts.com

Bill's Model Acres Ford Farm | parts / restoration
RD 1, Box 283, 8th St Rd
Watsontown, PA 17777
570-538-3200

See full listing in **Section One** under **Ford 1903-1931**

Blint Equipment Inc | parts / tractor rebuilding
2204 E Lincolnway
LaPorte, IN 46350
219-362-7021

See full listing in **Section One** under **Ford 1954-up**

Bob's Radio & TV Service | radios
238 Ocean View
Pismo Beach, CA 93449
805-773-8200

See full listing in **Section Two** under **radios**

The Brassworks | radiators
289 Prado Rd
San Luis Obispo, CA 93401
800-342-6759; FAX: 805-544-5615
E-mail: brassworks@thegrid.net

See full listing in **Section Two** under **radiators**

C & G Early Ford Parts | accessories/chrome / emblems & literature / mechanical / weatherstripping / wiring
1941 Commercial St, Dept AH
Escondido, CA 92029-1233
760-740-2400; FAX: 760-740-8700
E-mail: cgford@cgfordparts.com

Since 1978 C & G has offered fine quality, knowledgeable staff, excellent customer service and same day shipping. Over 16,000 quality parts listed in our comprehensive catalogs for 1932-1956 and 1957-1972 cars and pickups; $6 each USA, $9 each foreign ($6 refundable). Online catalogs and ordering at: www.cgfordparts.com

Car Controls Div	**parts**
9107-9 E Garvey Ave Rosemead, CA 91770 626-288-2121	

Mail order and open shop. Daily 12 pm to 5 pm. Phone hours 8 am to 4:30 pm daily. Friction shocks for T, A, V8. Conversion brackets for tube shocks. Catalog $6, refundable with purchase.

Cass County Historical Society	**museum**
1351 W Main Ave, PO Box 719 West Fargo, ND 58078 701-282-2822; FAX: 701-282-7606 E-mail: info@bonanzaville.com	

See full listing in **Section Six** under **North Dakota**

Chandler Classic Cars	**Ford products**
1308 14th St W Bradenton, FL 34205 941-747-3441; FAX: 941-747-9650 E-mail: chandlercars@worldnet.att.net	

See full listing in **Section One** under **Ford 1954-up**

Chernock Enterprises	**trailers**
Airport Rd, PO Box 134 Hazleton, PA 18201 570-455-1752; FAX: 570-455-7585 E-mail: jim@chernock.com	

See full listing in **Section Two** under **trailers**

Class-Tech Corp	**wiring harnesses**
62935 Layton Ave Bend, OR 97701 800-874-9981	

See full listing in **Section Two** under **electrical systems**

Classic Carriages	**repair** **restoration**
267 County Rd 420 Athens, TN 37303 PH/FAX: 423-744-7496	

See full listing in **Section Two** under **restoration shops**

Classic Cars	**cars** **parts**
8926 E Evans Creek Rd Rogue River, OR 97537 PH/FAX: 541-582-8966	

Mail order and open shop. Monday-Saturday 8 am to 5 pm. Specializing in new steel parts for 1928-1934 Ford. American collector car sales.

Classic Wood Mfg	**wood kits** **wood replacement**
1006 N Raleigh St Greensboro, NC 27405 336-691-1344; FAX: 336-273-3074	

See full listing in **Section Two** under **woodwork**

Chuck & Judy Cubel	**wood parts**
PO Box 278 Superior, AZ 85273-0278 520-689-2734; FAX: 520-689-5815, 24 hours E-mail: cubel@theriver.com	

See full listing in **Section One** under **Ford 1903-1931**

Alan Darr Early Ford Parts	**accessories** **parts**
124 E Canyon View Dr Longview, WA 98632 360-425-2463	

Mail order only. 1932-1953. Some original and reproduction parts, accessories, collectibles. New and used flathead speed equipment. No catalog. In business since 1968.

Mike Dennis, Nebraska Mail Order	**parts** **Trippe mounting** **brackets/hardware**
1845 S 48th St Lincoln, NE 68506 402-489-3036; FAX: 402-489-1148	

Ford parts 1926-1970, NOS or used. Mercury original parts, 1939-1965. Classic Trippe driving light brackets with nuts, bolts, wrench. Web site: www.fordoldpart.com

See our ad on this page

Bob Drake Reproductions Inc	**repro parts**
1819 NW Washington Blvd Grants Pass, OR 97526 800-221-3673 FAX: 541-474-0099 E-mail: bobdrake@bobdrake.com	

Mail order and open shop. Monday-Friday 8 am to 4:30 pm. Specializing in reproduction Ford parts for 1932-1948 automobiles and 1932-1966 pickups. Web site: www.bobdrake.com

Durabuilt Automotive Hydraulics	**hose assemblies** **pumps, top cylinders** **valves** **window cylinders**
808 Meadows Ave Canon City, CO 81212 PH/FAX: 719-275-1126	

See full listing in **Section Two** under **tops**

Early Ford Engines | *engine rebuilding* / *parts*
George and Marion Hibbard
Rt 3 Box 448
Claremont, NH 03743
603-542-6269

Open shop. Specializing in engine building for 1928-1953 Fords. Chassis parts and accessories for 1928-1948 Fords available. Most engine overhauls are complete running engines, customer ready and meet judging standards.

Early Ford Parts | *literature* / *parts*
2948 Summer Ave
Memphis, TN 38112
901-323-2179; FAX: 901-323-2195

Mail order and open shop. Monday-Friday 9:30 am to 5:30 pm. New parts for 1928-1959 Ford and Mercury cars and trucks. Catalogs for 1932-1959, $4, specify year and body style. In business full time over 25 years. "Over a million parts." Visa, MasterCard, personal checks accepted.

Early Ford V8 Sales Inc | *parts*
Curtis Industrial Park, Bldg 37
831 Rt 67
Ballston Spa, NY 12020
518-884-2825; FAX: 518-884-2633
E-mail: earlyford@prodigy.net

Mail order and open shop. Specializing in new, reproduction and NOS original engine, chassis and body parts for Ford 1932-1964 passenger and pickup. Web site: www.earlyford.com

Engineering & Mfg Services | *sheetmetal*
Box 24362
Cleveland, OH 44124
216-541-4585

Mail order only. Monday-Friday 8:30 am to 5 pm. Specializing in outer body sheetmetal for 1935-1951 Fords and 1935-1948 Chevrolets.

Fairlane Automotive Specialties | *fiberglass bodies* / *parts*
107 W Railroad St
St Johns, MI 48879
517-224-6460; FAX: 517-224-9488

Mail order and open shop. Monday-Friday 9 am to 5 pm. The leading manufacturer of high quality replacement panels for Ford trucks (1942-1966) and cars (1935-1936 and 1941-1948). Fairlane is well known for parts that fit like NOS. Check out Fairlane's selection of truck parts: hoods, tilt front ends, front and rear fenders, runningboards and more! Replacement parts available for cars include: hoods, runningboards, front and rear fenders, dashes, fender skirts and much more. Also manufactures a superior 1936 roadster body.

F100 Connection | *parts*
2606 Haynie Rd
Custer, WA 98240
800-310-0778; FAX: 360-366-2620
E-mail: f100connect@nas.com

See full listing in **Section One** under **Ford 1954-up**

Firewall Insulators & Quiet Ride Solutions | *air plenums* / *auto insulation* / *firewall insulators* / *gloveboxes* / *sound deadening*
6465 Pacific Ave, Ste 249
Stockton, CA 95207
209-477-4840; FAX: 209-477-0918
E-mail: timcox@quietride.com

See full listing in **Section Two** under **upholstery**

Ford Obsolete | *chassis parts* / *engine parts*
9107-13 Garvey Ave
Rosemead, CA 91770
626-288-2121

See full listing in **Section One** under **Ford 1903-1931**

Ford Truck Enthusiasts Inc | *literature*
PO Box 422
Lilburn, GA 30048
770-806-1955
E-mail: kpayne@ford-trucks.com

See full listing in **Section Two** under **trucks & tractors**

George Frechette | *brake cylinder* / *sleeving*
14 Cedar Dr
Granby, MA 01033
800-528-5235

See full listing in **Section Two** under **brakes**

Garton's Auto | *bicycle sales lit* / *Ford NOS parts* / *sales literature*
401 N 5th St (at 5th & Vine)
Millville, NJ 08332-3129
PH: 856-825-3618

Mail order and open by appointment only. 9 am to 9:30 pm. NOS 1932-1975 Ford and Mercury parts. Send SASE for free sales literature list on Ford V8, Model A, Studebaker or special interest. Genuine Ford, Mercury parts, literature, etc, bought and sold. Specializes in 1929-1979 fenders, grilles, bumpers, radiators, etc. Send SASE for list of original Schwinn sales literature.

Gaslight Auto Parts Inc | *accessories* / *parts*
PO Box 291
Urbana, OH 43078
937-652-2145; FAX: 937-652-2147

See full listing in **Section One** under **Ford 1903-1931**

Leo Gephart Inc | *vintage cars*
7360 E Acoma Dr, Ste 14
Scottsdale, AZ 85260
480-948-2286; FAX: 480-948-2390
E-mail: gephartclassics@earthlink.net

See full listing in **Section Two** under **car dealers**

Bill Gratkowski | *woodgraining*
515 N Petroleum St
Titusville, PA 16354
814-827-1782 days or eves
E-mail: billgrains@csonline.net

See full listing in **Section Two** under **woodgraining**

Green Valentine Inc | *car dealer* / *woodies*
5055 Covington Way
Memphis, TN 38134
901-373-5555; FAX: 901-373-5568

See full listing in **Section Two** under **car dealers**

Hagerty Classic Insurance | *insurance*
PO Box 87
Traverse City, MI 49685
800-922-4050; FAX: 616-941-8227

See full listing in **Section Two** under **insurance**

Half Ton Fun | *NOS parts*
Bob Selzam
166 Toms River Rd
Jackson, NJ 08527
732-928-9421

Mail order and open shop. Specializing in new old stock Ford parts for 1932-1956 pickups and trucks, 1932-1948 passenger cars (mechanical only) and 1932-1953 flathead V8 and 6-cylinder engine and transmission parts. Also stocking new parts such as: heavy duty radiators for V8 and 6-cyl, fiberglass and steel body parts, bed kits and parts, wiring, glass and rubber.

Hillcrest Hot Rods
541 Mercer Rd
Greenville, PA 16125
PH/FAX: 724-588-3444

custom cars
street rods

See full listing in **Section Two** under **street rods**

Bruce Horkey's Wood & Parts
46284 440th St
Windom, MN 56101
507-831-5625; FAX: 507-831-0280
E-mail: woodandparts@yahoo.com

pickup parts

See full listing in **Section Two** under **trucks & tractors**

Hot Rod & Custom Supply
1304 SE 10th St
Cape Coral, FL 33990
941-574-7744; FAX: 941-574-8820

custom parts
engine parts
speed parts

Specializing in 1950s speed and custom parts for Ford/Mercury flathead, speed and custom accessories, flathead air conditioning, engine parts. Web site: www.rodncustom.com

Howell's Sheetmetal Co
PO Box 792
Nederland, TX 77627
800-375-6663, 409-727-1999
FAX: 409-727-7127
E-mail: dhowell@fordor.com

body panels
sheetmetal

See full listing in **Section One** under **Ford 1903-1931**

Hubbard Classic Car Appraisals
1908 Belle Terr
Bakersfield, CA 93304-4352
661-397-7786
E-mail: lynnhubbard@msn.com

appraisals

See full listing in **Section Two** under **appraisals**

William Hulbert Jr
13683 Rt 11, PO Box 151
Adams Center, NY 13606
315-583-5765
E-mail: radio_29chevy@yahoo.com

radios

See full listing in **Section Two** under **radios**

Hyde Products Inc
PO Box 870321
New Orleans, LA 70187-0321
504-649-4041
E-mail: hydeprod@bellsouth.net

hood holders

See full listing in **Section One** under **Chevrolet**

Integrity Machine
383 Pipe Stave Hollow Rd
Mount Sinai, NY 11766
888-446-9670; FAX: 516-476-9675

brake masters
clutch masters
wheel cylinders

See full listing in **Section Two** under **brakes**

International Ford History Project
PO Box 11415
Olympia, WA 98508
360-754-9585
E-mail: ifhp@aol.com

newsletter

See full listing in **Section Four** under **newsletters**

Joblot Automotive Inc
Ford Parts Specialists
98-11 211th St
Queens Village, NY 11429
718-468-8585; FAX: 718-468-8686

parts

Mail order and open shop. Monday-Friday 8:30 am to 4:30 pm. Over 12,000 different new and rebuilt parts. Specializing in the

Ford family of cars and trucks 1928-1969. Engine, brake, transmission and clutch, front and rear end, a full line of rubber, electrical, wiring and ignition. Established in 1956. Three catalogs available: 1928-1948 cars and trucks, 1948/1969 F-1/100 thru F-6/600 trucks, 1949/1969 Ford family of cars. Visa, MC and COD, phone or fax orders accepted. Dealer inquiries invited.

John's F-Fun Hundreds
1575 W Broadway, Unit B
Anaheim, CA 92802
714-563-3100; FAX: 714-563-1592
E-mail: jfun100@aol.com

parts

See full listing in **Section One** under **Ford 1954-up**

Ken's Carburetors
2301 Barnum Ave
Stratford, CT 06615
203-375-9340

carburetors
distributors
parts

Mail order only. Specializing in Ford parts. Mainly rebuilding of flathead carbs and ignition distributors and some NOS and used parts. No body parts. Also glass beading and Ford fuel pump rebuilding services.

Dale King Obsolete Parts
211 Hilltop Dr, PO Box 1099
Liberty, KY 42539
606-787-5031; FAX: 606-787-2130
E-mail: daleking@kih.net

parts

See full listing in **Section One** under **Ford 1954-up**

LeBaron Bonney Co
6 Chestnut St, PO Box 6
Amesbury, MA 01913
800-221-5408, 978-388-3811
FAX: 978-388-1113
E-mail: lbb-hc@greennet.net

fabrics
interior kits
top kits

See full listing in **Section One** under **Ford 1903-1931**

Mac's Antique Auto Parts
1051 Lincoln Ave, PO Box 238
Lockport, NY 14095-0238
800-777-0948 US and Canada
716-433-1500 local and foreign
FAX: 716-433-1172
E-mail: mailmacs@aol.com

literature
parts
restoration
supplies

See full listing in **Section One** under **Ford 1903-1931**

Mack Products
PO Box 856
Moberly, MO 65270
660-263-7444
E-mail: jhummel@mackhils.com

parts
pickup beds

Mail order only. Monday-Friday 8 am to 5 pm. Established in 1973. Die-stamped pickup bed parts, oak bed wood, tailgates. Complete reproduction pickup beds for 1926-1972 Fords and 1928-1972 Chevrolets. Catalog, $1. New items include bed parts for 1933-1947 Dodge, 1941-1959 Studebaker and 1933-1962 Willys.

Mark's 1941-1948 Ford Parts
97 Hoodlum Hill Rd
Binghamton, NY 13905
607-729-1693
E-mail: mkicsak@cs.com

parts

Mail order only. Caters to people who feel 1941-1948 Fords are among the best looking Fords ever produced. Deals in rust-free western sheetmetal and cars. Carries vintique reproduction as well. Specializing in NOS, reproduction and used parts for 1941-1948 Ford and Mercury cars. Reproduction catalog $2; NOS parts list $2, free with orders over $100.

Master Power Brakes
110 Crosslake Park Rd
Mooresville, NC 28117
704-664-8866; FAX: 704-664-8862

brake products
conversion kits

See full listing in **Section One** under **Chevelle/Camaro**

McDonald Obsolete Parts Company
6458 W Eureka Rd
Rockport, IN 47635
800-897-8693 orders (w/part # only),
812-359-4965; FAX: 812-359-5555
E-mail: mcdonald@psci.net

body parts
chassis parts

See full listing in **Section One** under **Ford 1954-up**

Medicine Bow Motors Inc
343 One Horse Creek Rd
Florence, MT 59833
406-273-0002

car dealer

See full listing in **Section Two** under **car dealers**

Miller Obsolete Parts
1329 Campus Dr
Vestal, NY 13850
607-722-5371; FAX: 607-770-9117
E-mail: mmiller3@stny.rr.com

locator service
parts

See full listing in **Section One** under **Ford 1954-up**

N-News Magazine
PO Box 275
East Corinth, VT 05040

magazine

See full listing in **Section Two** under **trucks & tractors**

Narragansett Reproductions
Ed & Miki Pease
107 Woodville Rd, PO Box 51
Wood River Junction, RI 02894
401-364-3839; FAX: 401-364-3830
E-mail: narragansetrepro@aol.com

wire harnesses

See full listing in **Section Two** under **electrical systems**

New Old Stock Ford Parts
639 Glanker St
Memphis, TN 38112
PH/FAX: 901-323-2195, recorder

new parts
shop manuals

New old stock genuine Ford parts, 1930s through 1960s. Send $5 for big list of over 5,000 different part numbers, descriptions and prices.

Northeast Ford
Box 66, Rt 9
East Sullivan, NH 03445
603-847-9956, 800-562-FORD
FAX: 603-847-9691

parts
restoration

See full listing in **Section One** under **Ford 1954-up**

Oak Bows
122 Ramsey Ave
Chambersburg, PA 17201
717-264-2602

top bows

See full listing in **Section Two** under **woodwork**

Obsolete Ford Parts Co
311 E Washington Ave, PO Box 787
Nashville, GA 31639
229-686-2470; FAX: 229-686-7125

parts

See full listing in **Section One** under **Ford 1954-up**

Obsolete Ford Parts Inc
8701 S I-35
Oklahoma City, OK 73149
405-631-3933; FAX: 405-634-6815
E-mail: info@obsoletefordparts.com

parts

See full listing in **Section One** under **Ford 1954-up**

The Old Car Centre
3-20075 92A Ave
Langley, BC Canada V1M 3A4
604-888-4412, 604-888-4055
FAX: 604-888-7455
E-mail: oldcarcentre@look.ca

parts

See full listing in **Section One** under **Ford 1903-1931**

Old Ford Parts
35 4th Ave N
Algona, WA 98001
253-833-8494; FAX: 253-833-2190

parts

Mail order and open shop. Monday-Thursday 8 am to 5 pm, Friday-Saturday 8 am to 2 pm. Specializing in 1932-1948 Ford cars and 1932-1979 Ford trucks parts. Parts, rubber seals, electrical supplies, ie: wiring, bulbs, connectors, trim parts, sheetmetal panels, bumpers, hubcaps, etc.

Original Ford Motor Co Literature
PO Box 7-AA
Hudson, KY 40145-0007
502-257-8642; FAX: 502-257-8643
E-mail: whiteb@bellsouth.net

collectibles
literature

Original Ford literature and collectibles. Send SASE with want list.

P&J Automotive Inc
6262 Riverside Dr
Danville, VA 24541
804-822-2211; FAX: 804-822-2213

bodies
chassis parts

See full listing in **Section Two** under **street rods**

Pick-ups Northwest
9911 Airport Way
Snohomish, WA 98296
360-568-9166; FAX: 360-568-1233

parts
trim

See full listing in **Section One** under **Chevrolet**

Precision Babbitt Service
4681 Lincoln Ave
Beamsville, ON Canada L0R 1B3
905-563-4364
E-mail: tkoudys@sprint.ca

babbitting
engine rebuilding

See full listing in **Section Two** under **babbitting**

Precision Coachworks
19 Winsor Rd
Billerica, MA 01821
978-663-7573
E-mail: precoach@mediaone.net

parts
pickup beds

Mail order and open shop. Daily 8 am to 11 pm. Specializing in reproduction parts and pickup beds for 1935-1940 Ford, 1946-1964 Willys pickup and 1946-1968 Dodge Power Wagon. Web site: www.precisioncoachworks.com

PV Antique & Classic Ford
1688 Main St
Tewksbury, MA 01876
800-MSTANGS orders only
978-851-9159; FAX: 978-858-3827
E-mail: pvford@flash.net

parts

See full listing in **Section One** under **Ford 1903-1931**

R & R Fiberglass & Specialties	body parts

R & R Fiberglass & Specialties
4850 Wilson Dr NW
Cleveland, TN 37312
423-476-2270; FAX: 423-473-9442
E-mail: rrfiberglass@aol.com

See full listing in **Section Two** under **fiberglass parts**

Recks & Relics Ford Trucks	truck parts

Recks & Relics Ford Trucks
2675 Hamilton Mason Rd
Hamilton, OH 45011
513-868-3489; FAX: 513-868-3461
E-mail: truck@choice.net

Ford truck parts for 1928-1979 Ford trucks. Web site: ww4.choice.net/~truck

Red's Headers & Early Ford Speed Equipment	headers mechanical parts

Red's Headers & Early Ford Speed Equipment
22950 Bednar Ln
Fort Bragg, CA 95437-8411
707-964-7733; FAX: 707-964-5434
E-mail: red@reds-headers.com

Mail order and open shop. Monday-Friday 8 am to 4:30 pm. Specializing in headers, mechanical parts and engine machine shop services for 1928-1970 Fords. Headers made and stocked for Model A side valve and ohv, flathead V8; Y-block Fords 272-312 in cars, trucks and T-Birds. Crankshaft grinding and balancing, rod work and engine rebuilding for stock and hot rod Fords, since 1964. Web site: www.reds-headers.com

Renner's Corner	bushings/hardware carb/pump kits gauges/gaskets rebuild service

Renner's Corner
10320 E Austin
Manchester, MI 48158
734-428-8424; FAX: 734-428-1090

Mail order only. Specializing in reproduction of 1932 hard-to-find 4-cylinder and 8-cylinder repair and rebuild kits for fuel pumps, carburetors, fuel gauges, float level gauges, fuel lines and tank gaskets; steering bushings; engine snubbers; side-mount spares; distributor conversions; dry air silencers and more. Some 1928-1931 kits. Carburetor, distributor, fuel gauge and fuel pump rebuild services. Send SASE for complete list. Parts are exactly as Henry built them or better.

Rock Valley Antique Auto Parts	gas tanks

Rock Valley Antique Auto Parts
Box 352, Rt 72 and Rothwell Rd
Stillman Valley, IL 61084
815-645-2271; FAX: 815-645-2740

Deal in stainless steel gas tanks for most antique and street rod cars and pickups. Makes 1931-1940 passenger, 1941-1954 pickup bumpers for Chevrolet. Offers a full line of 1928-1948 reproduction, used and NOS Ford parts. Call or send for our free brochure.

Rocky Mountain V8 Ford Parts	parts

Rocky Mountain V8 Ford Parts
1124 Clark Cir
Colorado Springs, CO 80915
719-597-8375
E-mail: fordyford@juno.com

Mail order and open shop by appointment. Shop address: 1160 Valley St, Colorado Springs, CO. Parts for 1932-1960s Ford products. New, used and reproduction. Buy, sell and trade. Large inventory on hand. Parts cars and trucks in yard. Visa/MC, UPS, COD. Send your want list.

S & S Antique Auto	parts

S & S Antique Auto
Pine St
Deposit, NY 13754
607-467-2929; FAX: 607-467-2109

Mail order and open shop. Monday-Saturday 9 am to 6 pm. Specialize in NOS parts, used and repro for Ford cars and trucks.

Salem Speed Shop	parts speed equipment

Salem Speed Shop
340 Mission St SE
Salem, OR 97302
503-364-4832

Mail order and open shop. Tuesday-Friday 2:30 pm to 5:30 pm. Specializing in speed equipment and standard replacement parts, magneto and distributor service, hood louvering for Ford flathead V8 1932 thru 1953. Established 1950.

Sanders Reproduction Glass	glass

Sanders Reproduction Glass
PO Box 522
Hillsboro, OR 97123
503-648-9184

See full listing in **Section Two** under **glass**

Joe Smith Ford & Hot Rod Parts	parts service

Joe Smith Ford & Hot Rod Parts
51 Lakewood Dr
Marietta, GA 30066
770-426-9850; FAX: 770-426-9854
E-mail: joesmithhotrod@yahoo.com

Mail order and open shop. Monday-Friday 8:30 am to 5:30 pm. 1932-1948 Ford cars, 1932-1952 Ford trucks. Parts and service. Web site: www.joesmithauto.com

Dick Spadaro	fiberglass bodies patch panels rubber products trim

Dick Spadaro
Early Ford Reproductions
PO Box 617, 6599 Rt 158
Altamont, NY 12009
518-861-5367

Mail order and open shop. 9 am to 5 pm EST. Ford V8 to 1948 and pickup to 1956. Supplier of quality accessories and replacement parts and sheetmetal repair panels. Dealer for Gibbon fiberglass bodies. NOS and used parts always in stock. Web site: www.dickspadaro.com

Specialty Ford Parts	engine parts speed parts

Specialty Ford Parts
9103 Garvey Ave
Rosemead, CA 91770
626-280-4546; FAX: 626-288-3311

A, B, C and V8 Ford engine and speed parts. Catalog, $6 USA, specify 4-cylinder or V8.

The V8 Store	accessories parts service

The V8 Store
3010 NE 49th St
Vancouver, WA 98663
360-693-7468; 360-694-7853 nights
FAX: 360-693-0982

See full listing in **Section Two** under **custom cars**

Valley Motor Supply	accessories parts

Valley Motor Supply
1402 E Second St
Roswell, NM 88201
505-622-7450

See full listing in **Section One** under **Ford 1954-up**

Vintage Ford & Chevrolet Parts of Arizona Inc	parts

Vintage Ford & Chevrolet Parts of Arizona Inc
So-Cal Speed Shop
3427 E McDowell Rd
Phoenix, AZ 85008-3845
800-732-0076, 602-275-7990
FAX: 602-267-8439
E-mail: vintageparts@sprintmail.com

See full listing in **Section One** under **Ford 1954-up**

Waldron's Antique Exhaust Inc	exhaust systems

Waldron's Antique Exhaust Inc
25872 M-86, PO Box C
Nottawa, MI 49075
616-467-7185; FAX: 616-467-9041

See full listing in **Section Two** under **exhaust systems**

Pete Watson Enterprises
PO Box 488
Epworth, GA 30541
706-632-7675

car dealer
restoration

See full listing in **Section Two** under **restoration shops**

Wescott's Auto Restyling
19701 SE Hwy 212
Boring, OR 97009
800-523-6279; FAX: 503-658-2938
E-mail: marykarl@gte.net

body parts

Mail order and open shop. Monday-Friday 9 am to 5:30 pm,
Saturday 9 am to 5 pm PST. Specializes in fiberglass replacement fenders and bodies and reproduction body parts for 1926-1948 Ford cars and 1926-1956 Ford pickups.

Kirk F White
PO Box 999
New Smyrna Beach, FL 32170
386-427-6660; FAX: 386-427-7801
E-mail: kirkfwhite@mindspring.com

models
tin toys

See full listing in **Section Two** under **models & toys**

White Post Restorations
One Old Car Dr, PO Drawer D
White Post, VA 22663
540-837-1140; FAX: 540-837-2368
E-mail: info@whitepost.com

restoration

See full listing in **Section Two** under **restoration shops**

Wilk-Bilt Cars
Rt 1 Box 116
Ewing, VA 24248
PH/FAX: 540-445-4501
E-mail: wilkbilt@mounet.com

accessories
parts

Specializing in parts and accessories for Ford 1928-1948 street rods.

James Wood
1102 E Jefferson St
Mishawaka, IN 46545
219-256-0239; FAX: 219-254-2722
E-mail: jimwood67@hotmail.com

appraisals

See full listing in **Section Two** under **appraisals**

WoodArt
1726 Hogar Dr
San Jose, CA 95124
PH/FAX: 408-979-9663
E-mail: ecoughlin@peoplepc.com

wood

Specializing in interior wood for 1932-1948 Ford. Web site:
www.fordwoodart.com

The Woodie Works
245 VT Rt 7A
Arlington, VT 05250
PH/FAX: 802-375-9305
E-mail: dkwoodie@vermontel.net

woodworking

See full listing in **Section Two** under **woodwork**

1954-Up

**12 Volt Stuff, Radio &
Speedometer Repair Co**
10625-A Trade Rd
Richmond, VA 23236
804-423-1055, 888-487-3500 toll free
FAX: 804-423-1059
E-mail: ecs@12voltstuff.com

radios

See full listing in **Section Two** under **radios**

**12 Volt Stuff, Radio &
Speedometer Repair Co**
10625-A Trade Rd
Richmond, VA 23236
804-423-1055, 888-487-3500 toll free
FAX: 804-423-1059
E-mail: ecs@12voltstuff.com

radios

See full listing in **Section Two** under **instruments**

**1958 Thunderbird Convertible
Registry**
Bill Van Ess
6780 Kitson NE
Rockford, MI 49341
616-874-1004; FAX: 616-363-2870
E-mail: billvaness@juno.com

book

See full listing in **Section One** under **Thunderbird**

A-1 Shock Absorber Co
Shockfinders Division
365 Warren Ave, PO Box 2028
Silverthorne, CO 80498
800-344-1966, 970-389-3193 cell
FAX: 970-513-8283

shocks-all types
coil springs
Koni shocks
leaf springs
steering gears

See our ad on the last page

**ABC Auto Upholstery &
Top Company**
1634 Church St
Philadelphia, PA 19124
215-289-0555

upholstery

Mail order and open shop. Monday-Friday 8:30 am to 6 pm.
Upholstery kits for 1954-1959 Fords. NOS vinyls and cloth for
most marques, from late forties to early seventies. Over 30,000
yards of NOS cloth and vinyls in stock at all times.

AKH Wheels
1207 N A St
Ellensburg, WA 98926-2522
509-962-3390
E-mail: akhwheel@eburg.com

Rallye wheels
styled steel wheels
vintage aluminum

See full listing in **Section Two** under **wheels & wheelcovers**

AMK Products Inc
800 Airport Rd
Winchester, VA 22602
540-662-7820; FAX: 540-662-7821

parts

AMK offers a large selection of nuts, bolts, clips, screws, fasteners and kits for 1960s and 1970s. Check out AMK's master kits.
Fasteners feature original head markings and finishes. Catalog
$5 or online at our web site: www.amkproducts.com

Antique Radio Doctor — radio repairs
Barry Dalton
196 Kilborn Dr
Grants Pass, OR 97526
541-474-2524
E-mail: radiodoc@rvi.net

See full listing in **Section Two** under **radios**

ARASCO — parts
PO Box 24, Dept HA15
Newport, KY 41072
859-441-8363

See full listing in **Section One** under **Ford 1932-1953**

Arelli Alloy Wheels — custom wheels
164 W Jefferson Blvd
Buena Park, CA 90620
323-733-0403; FAX: 323-733-0423
E-mail: sales@arelli.com

See full listing in **Section Two** under **wheels & wheelcovers**

Auto Custom Carpet Inc — carpets / floor mats
1429 Noble St, PO Box 1350
Anniston, AL 36201
800-633-2358, 256-236-1118
FAX: 800-516-8274

See full listing in **Section Two** under **carpets**

Auto Krafters Inc — parts
522 S Main St, PO Box 8
Broadway, VA 22815
540-896-5910; FAX: 540-896-6412
E-mail: akraft@shentel.net

Mail order and open shop. Monday-Friday 8:30 am to 6 pm, Saturday 9 am to 12 pm. Specializing in weatherstrip, interior, exterior, engine, wiring, suspension, brakes, hardware, literature. Rebuild parts such as ps control valves for 1964-1973 Mustangs, 1967-1973 Cougars, 1960-1970 Falcons, 1962-1976 Fairlanes/Torinos, 1960-1970 full-size Fords, 1958-1976 T-Birds, 1966-1979 Broncos, 1953-1979 F-Series, 1970-1977 Mavericks, 1960-1979 Rancheros. Aftermarket parts and accessories for 1991-2001 Explorers/Expeditions and 1992-2001 F-Series/Rangers. Online ordering available on our web site: www.autokrafters.com

Autowire Division — alternator conversions / motors / relays & switches
9109 (Rear) E Garvey Ave
Rosemead, CA 91770
626-572-0938; FAX: 626-288-3311

Mail order and open shop. Monday-Friday 9 am to 5 pm. For 1949-1968 Fords, Lincolns and Mercurys. Top motors, relays, window regulators, motors and switches, and alternator conversions for all Fords, 6 and 12 volt.

B & W Antique Auto Parts Inc — accessories / parts
150 W Axton Rd, Unit 2
Bellingham, WA 98226
360-398-9820; FAX: 360-398-9431
E-mail: bwautoparts@bwautoparts.com

See full listing in **Section One** under **Ford 1932-1953**

Bill's Model Acres Ford Farm — parts / restoration
RD 1, Box 283, 8th St Rd
Watsontown, PA 17777
570-538-3200

See full listing in **Section One** under **Ford 1903-1931**

Bill's Speed Shop — body parts
13951 Millersburg Rd
Navarre, OH 44662
330-832-9403; FAX: 330-832-2098

See full listing in **Section One** under **Chevrolet**

Blint Equipment Inc — parts / tractor rebuilding
2204 E Lincolnway
LaPorte, IN 46350
219-362-7021

Mail order and open shop. Monday-Friday 8 am to 5 pm, Saturday 8 am to 12 noon. Rebuild Ford tractors 1939 and up. Also have parts for Ford tractors. Work on other makes too, but specialize in Fords. Also work on some cars and trucks, mostly older models. Have a small stock of Fiat parts and repair older Fiat cars.

Bumper Boyz LLC — bumper repairs / reconditioning / sandblasting
2435 E 54th St
Los Angeles, CA 90058
800-995-1703, 323-587-8976
FAX: 323-587-2013

See full listing in **Section One** under **Chevrolet**

Bob Burgess 1955-56 Ford Parts — parts
793 Alpha-Bellbrook Rd
Bellbrook, OH 45305
937-426-8041
E-mail: bobs19551956@yahoo.com

Mail order and open shop by appointment. Calls taken daily 9 am to 9 pm. Specializing in NOS, used and reproduction parts for 1955-1956 Ford, Lincoln, Mercury. Send double-stamped SASE for free Ford catalog.

Burrell's Service Inc — parts
PO Box 456
Keego Harbor, MI 48320
248-682-2390; FAX: 248-682-2376
E-mail: craigdj@oeonline.com

See full listing in **Section One** under **Chevrolet**

C & G Early Ford Parts — accessories/chrome / emblems & literature / mechanical / weatherstripping / wiring
1941 Commercial St, Dept AH
Escondido, CA 92029-1233
760-740-2400; FAX: 760-740-8700
E-mail: cgford@cgfordparts.com

See full listing in **Section One** under **Ford 1932-1953**

California Thunderbirds — parts
Bill Denzel
1507 Arroyo View Dr
Pasadena, CA 91103
626-792-0720; FAX: 626-792-9937
E-mail: teamdenzel@aol.com

See full listing in **Section One** under **Thunderbird**

Carl's Ford Parts — muscle parts
23219 South St, Box 38
Homeworth, OH 44634
PH/FAX: 330-525-7291
E-mail: fordcobrajet@hotmail.com

See full listing in **Section One** under **Mustang**

Carolina Classics — truck parts
624 E Geer St
Durham, NC 27701
919-682-4211, 800-598-4211
FAX: 919-682-1286

Mail order and open shop. Monday-Friday 8 am to 5:30 pm, Saturday by appointment. 1948-1979 Ford truck parts.

Dennis Carpenter Ford Reproductions — parts
PO Box 26398
Charlotte, NC 28221
704-786-8139; FAX: 704-786-8180

Mail order and counter sales. Monday-Friday 8 am to 5 pm. Manufacture and sell obsolete Ford car and truck parts. Specializing in weatherstripping, antennas, scuff plates, outside door handles and much more. For 1932-1972 Ford cars, 1932-1979 pickups, 1940-1956 Mercury, 1958-1966 T-Birds, 1960-1970 Falcons, 1962-1972 Fairlanes and 1966-1979 Broncos. Catalogs $3, state year and body style.

Cass County Historical Society 1351 W Main Ave, PO Box 719 West Fargo, ND 58078 701-282-2822; FAX: 701-282-7606 E-mail: info@bonanzaville.com	museum

See full listing in **Section Six** under **North Dakota**

Chandler Classic Cars 1308 14th St W Bradenton, FL 34205 941-747-3441; FAX: 941-747-9650 E-mail: chandlercars@worldnet.att.net	Ford products

Specialize in selling Ford products for 1950s and 1960s. Web site: www.c-it.com/chandler

Class-Tech Corp 62935 Layton Ave Bend, OR 97701 800-874-9981	wiring harnesses

See full listing in **Section Two** under **electrical systems**

Classic Auto 251 SW 5th Ct Pompano Beach, FL 33060 PH/FAX: 954-786-1687	restoration

See full listing in **Section Two** under **restoration shops**

Classic Auto Air Mfg Co 2020 W Kennedy Blvd Tampa, FL 33606 813-251-2356, 813-251-4994 FAX: 813-254-7419	air conditioning heating parts

See full listing in **Section One** under **Mustang**

Classic Auto Restoration Service Inc 381 National Dr Rockwall, TX 75032-6556 972-722-9663	restoration

See full listing in **Section One** under **Chevrolet**

Classic Cars 8926 E Evans Creek Rd Rogue River, OR 97537 PH/FAX: 541-582-8966	cars parts

See full listing in **Section One** under **Ford 1932-1953**

Classic Enterprises Box 92 Barron, WI 54812 715-537-5422 office 715-234-4677 products FAX: 715-537-5770 E-mail: lamonte@classicent.com	sheetmetal

See full listing in **Section One** under **Studebaker**

Classic Ford Sales PO Box 60 East Dixfield, ME 04227 207-562-4443; FAX: 207-562-4576 E-mail: sue@classicford.com	salvage yard

See full listing in **Section Five** under **Maine**

Classic Performance Products 8341 Artesia Blvd, Unit C Buena Park, CA 90621 800-522-5004; FAX: 714-522-2500 E-mail: info@classicperform.com	brakes steering suspension

See full listing in **Section One** under **Chevrolet**

Clester's Auto Rubber Seals Inc PO Box 1113 Salisbury, NC 28145 800-457-8223, 704-637-9979 FAX: 704-636-7390	molded rubber parts weatherstripping

See full listing in **Section Two** under **rubber parts**

The Clockworks 1745 Meta Lake Ln Eagle River, WI 54521 800-398-3040; FAX: 715-479-5759 E-mail: clockwks@nnex.net	clock service

See full listing in **Section Two** under **instruments**

Bob Cook Classic Auto Parts Inc 2055 Van Cleave Rd, PO Box 600 Murray, KY 42071-0600 270-753-4000, 800-486-1137 FAX: 270-753-4600	new parts NOS parts reproduced parts

Mail and phone orders. Most Ford vehicles 1955-1972. Catalog price refundable, $5.

Dearborn Classics PO Box 7649 Bend, OR 97708-7649 800-252-7427; FAX: 800-500-7886	accessories restoration parts

The nation's parts source for Ford Ranchero, Falcon, Fairlane and Torino parts and accessories. Moldings, emblems, weatherstripping, interior, engine parts, suspension, brake system and more. Large fully illustrated catalog available or request. Web site: www.dearbornclassics.com

Mike Dennis, Nebraska Mail Order 1845 S 48th St Lincoln, NE 68506 402-489-3036; FAX: 402-489-1148	parts Trippe mounting brackets/hardware

See full listing in **Section One** under **Ford 1932-1953**

Greg Donahue Collector Car Restorations Inc 12900 S Betty Pt Floral City, FL 34436 352-344-4329; FAX: 352-344-0015	parts restoration

Mail order only. Phone hours: Monday-Saturday 9 am to 8 pm. No Sundays or holidays. 1963, 1963-1/2, 1964 Ford Galaxie reproduction and NOS parts: all of the parts needed for any type of Galaxie restoration from the Galaxie restoration authority. Weatherstrip, rubber parts, moldings, carpet, seat covers, dash pads, headliners, exterior and interior chrome, emblems, ornaments, mirrors, mechanical parts, accessories, lenses, sheetmetal, wheelcovers, decals, parts diagrams and shop manuals. We have the largest inventory in the US and handle only 1963 and 1964 Galaxie parts. Current 150-page catalog $5. Also 100-point concours restorations available. Web site: www.gregdonahue.com

Dynamic Racing Transmissions LLC 104-5 Enterprise Dr, Unit 1 North Branford, CT 06471 203-315-0138; FAX: 203-315-0352 E-mail: mightymitejr@aol.com	automatic transmissions

See full listing in **Section Two** under **transmissions**

Early Ford Parts | literature
2948 Summer Ave | parts
Memmphis, TN 38112
901-323-2179; FAX: 901-323-2195

See full listing in **Section One** under **Ford 1932-1953**

Early Ford V8 Sales Inc | parts
Curtis Industrial Park, Bldg 37
831 Rt 67
Ballston Spa, NY 12020
518-884-2825; FAX: 518-884-2633
E-mail: earlyford@prodigy.net

See full listing in **Section One** under **Ford 1932-1953**

Daniel A Evans | literature
2850 John St | parts
Easton, PA 18045
610-258-9542 after 5:30 pm
FAX: 610-252-0370
E-mail: evansd@lafayette.edu

Specializing in NOS and restored hard-to-find parts for 1955-1957 Thunderbirds. Buy, sell, trade Ford dual quad and super-charger parts. Also original literature and Ford dealership items.

F100 Connection | parts
2606 Haynie Rd
Custer, WA 98240
800-310-0778; FAX: 360-366-2620
E-mail: f100connect@nas.com

Mail order only. Specializing in stock and custom parts for 1948-1956 Ford F100 pickups. Web site: www.f100connection.com

Falcon's Forever | parts
PO Box 6531
Albany, CA 94206
510-525-9226; FAX: 510-525-2652
E-mail: dr4falcons@aol.com

Shop open weekends by appointment. Specializing in hard to find parts for 1960-1965 Falcons and Comets. This includes rust-free California sheetmetal, moldings, trim and mechanical parts. Also a supply of new rubber parts.

Faxon Auto Literature | literature
3901 Carter Ave | manuals
Riverside, CA 92501
800-458-2734; FAX: 909-786-4166

See full listing in **Section Two** under **literature dealers**

Feno's T-Bird 55-57 | parts
383 New Britain Ave
Plainville, CT 06062
PH/FAX: 860-747-8711

See full listing in **Section One** under **Thunderbird**

Fifth Avenue Antique Auto Parts | cooling systems
415 Court St | electrical systems
Clay Center, KS 67432 | fuel systems
785-632-3450; FAX: 785-632-6154
E-mail: fifthave@oz-online.net

See full listing in **Section Two** under **electrical systems**

John Filiss | appraisals
45 Kingston Ave
Port Jervis, NY 12771
845-856-2942
E-mail: john@filiss.com

See full listing in **Section Two** under **appraisals**

Finest In Fords | books
Larry Blodget | **Ford 1954-up**
Box 753 | model cars
Ranchero Mirage, CA 92270 | restoration services
E-mail: info@finestinfords.com

See full listing in **Section Four** under **books & publications**

Firewall Insulators & Quiet Ride | air plenums
Solutions | auto insulation
6465 Pacific Ave, Ste 249 | firewall insulators
Stockton, CA 95207 | gloveboxes
209-477-4840; FAX: 209-477-0918 | sound deadening
E-mail: timcox@quietride.com

See full listing in **Section Two** under **upholstery**

Flashback F-100s | parts
2519 Wagon Wheel Rd | parts locators
Reidsville, NC 27320
336-421-3979; FAX: 336-421-5901

Mail order and open shop. Monday-Friday 8 am to midnight, Saturday 10 am to 4 pm. Specializing in 1948-1986 Ford truck parts. We sell new, NOS and good quality used parts that come off trucks from AZ, NM and TX. Also parts locator service.

Ford Parts Store | parts
110 Ford Rd, Box 226
Bryan, OH 43506
419-636-2475; FAX: 419-636-8449
E-mail: fordpart@bright.net

Mail and telephone orders only. Monday-Saturday 9 am to 9 pm, 24 hour fax. Since 1978, specializing in 1952-1970 Ford passenger cars. New and reproduction weatherstripping for doors, windshield, convertible tops, roof rails, wire harnesses, trunk mats, carpet, scuff plates, plastic emblems, chrome scripts, owner's and shop manuals. Appears at 18 major swap meets throughout the year. Catalog available, $3. Secure online ordering. Web site: www.fordpartsstore.com

Ford Powertrain Applications | engines
7702 E 96th St
Puyallup, WA 98371
PH/FAX: 253-848-9503

Monday-Friday 9 am to 6 pm. Specializing in Ford race engines and hp street rod/restoration engines and related hp engine components, Ford Motorsports, Blue Thunder heads and manifolds, FPA custom Tri-Y and shorty Ford headers. Web site: www.fordpowertrain.com

Ford Truck Enthusiasts Inc | literature
PO Box 422
Lilburn, GA 30048
770-806-1955
E-mail: kpayne@ford-trucks.com

See full listing in **Section Two** under **trucks & tractors**

Gear Vendors Inc | overdrive
1717 N Magnolia Ave | transmissions
El Cajon, CA 92020
619-562-0060; FAX: 619-562-1186
E-mail: info@gearvendors.com

See full listing in **Section Two** under **transmissions**

Gearheads Cruiser Products & Services
333 W Ingals Ave
Bismarck, ND 58504
701-223-2269
E-mail: gearheadsnd@aol.com

power steering

Mail order only. We specialize in modern power steering for 1949-1964 Fords, Mercurys, Edsels and T-Birds. This is a fully integrated unit. We also offer disc brake assemblies for 1954-1964 Fords, Mercurys, Edsels and T-Birds. Can be ordered stock height or dropped. Call or e-mail for further information.

Randy Goodling
2046 Mill Rd
Elizabethtown, PA 17022-9401
717-367-6700

parts
parts locating

See full listing in **Section One** under **Mercury**

Grandpa's Radio Shop
26 Queenston Crescent
Kitchener ON Canada N2B 2V5
519-576-2570

radio restoration

1956 Ford "T" and "C" push-buttons for Town & Country radio. Send check or money order for $47 US or $56 Canadian.

Greg's Automotive
Box 1712
Santa Ynez, CA 93460
PH/FAX: 805-688-5675
E-mail: 9pm@silcom.com

accessories
books
literature

See full listing in **Section One** under **Chevrolet**

Half Ton Fun
Bob Selzam
166 Toms River Rd
Jackson, NJ 08527
732-928-9421

NOS parts

See full listing in **Section One** under **Ford 1932-1953**

Bill Heeley
3621 Mt Olney Ln
Olney, MD 20832
301-774-6710

shift assemblies
shift levers

Mail order only. Rebuild/restore original Ford shifters from 1962-1973. Generally have at least one of every Ford V8 4-spd shifters in stock. Five to ten of most, have over 20 varieties of rechromed shift levers.

Henault's Enterprises
8639 Los Cruces Rd
LaGrange, CA 95329
209-852-2476
E-mail: henaults@jps.net

engine parts

Specializing in Y-block Ford core engine parts, blocks, heads, crankshafts, manifolds for 1954-1964 Ford cars and trucks with 272, 292, 312, V8s.

Hidden Valley Auto Parts
21046 N Rio Bravo
Maricopa, AZ 85239
602-252-2122, 602-252-6137
520-568-2945; FAX: 602-258-0951
E-mail: hvap@aol.com

parts

See full listing in **Section One** under **Chevrolet**

Bill Horton
5804 Jones Valley Dr
Huntsville, AL 35802
256-881-6894

vacuum motors

See full listing in **Section One** under **Mercury**

Hot Rod & Custom Supply
1304 SE 10th St
Cape Coral, FL 33990
941-574-7744; FAX: 941-574-8820

custom parts
engine parts
speed parts

See full listing in **Section One** under **Ford 1932-1953**

Instrument Services Inc
11765 Main St
Roscoe, IL 61073
800-558-2674; FAX: 815-623-9180

clocks
gauges
instruments

See full listing in **Section Two** under **instruments**

International Ford History Project
PO Box 11415
Olympia, WA 98508
360-754-9585
E-mail: ifhp@aol.com

newsletter

See full listing in **Section Four** under **newsletters**

Jerry's Classic Cars & Parts Inc
4097 McRay Ave
Springdale, AR 72764
800-828-4584; FAX: 501-750-1682
E-mail: jcc@jerrysclassiccars.com

parts
restoration

Mail order and open shop. Monday-Friday 8 am to 5 pm. Specializing in new, used and reproduction parts for 1957-1959 Ford retractables and convertibles. We also restore 1957s-1959s from good drivers to showroom cars. Web site: www.jerrysclassiccars.com

Joe's Auto Sales
5849-190th St E
Hastings, MN 55033
612-437-6787

parts

Mail order and open shop. Monday-Friday 8 am to 5 pm (closed noon to 1:30 pm weekdays), Saturday 8 am to 12 pm. Specializing in 1939-1989 Ford and Mercury products, sales of used, rebuilt and new parts. Some repair work and parts rebuilding for customers. Rebuild steering columns: auto, standard and tilt.

John's F-Fun Hundreds
1575 W Broadway, Unit B
Anaheim, CA 92802
714-563-3100; FAX: 714-563-1592
E-mail: jfun100@aol.com

parts

Mail order and open shop. Monday-Friday 9 am to 5 pm, Saturday 10 am to 3 pm. Specializing in reproduction original and custom parts for 1948-1979 Ford trucks. Weatherstripping, suspension, emblems, upholstery, catalog on-line at: www.f100.com

K C Obsolete Parts
3343 N 61
Kansas City, KS 66104
913-334-9479; FAX: 913-788-2795

parts

Mail order only. Carries a full line of parts for 1948-1972 Ford pickups and panels. Full line catalog available for $2.

Dale King Obsolete Parts
211 Hilltop Dr, PO Box 1099
Liberty, KY 42539
606-787-5031; FAX: 606-787-2130
E-mail: daleking@kih.net

parts

Specializing in NOS hard to find parts and quality reproductions for Ford, Fairlane, Falcon, Mustang, Ford trucks, Mercury and Comet.

L B Repair
1308 W Benten
Savannah, MO 64485-1549
816-324-3913

restoration

Mail order and open shop. Monday-Saturday 9 am to 7 pm. Specializing in mig welding and subframe installation, all sus-

Section One – Marque Specialists

pension modifications. Special interest: 1953-1956 big window Ford pickups and panels. Drop kit installation on late model pickups, low riders, fiberglass repair, economical restorations.

Lares Manufacturing	power steering equipment

805 S Cleveland
Cambridge, MN 55008
800-334-5749; FAX: 763-754-2853
E-mail: sales@larescorp.com

Mail order and open shop. Monday-Friday 8 am to 4:30 pm CST. Power steering gears, manual steering gears, power steering pumps, power steering control valves and power steering cylinders. Web site: www.larescorp.com

Larry's Thunderbird and Mustang Parts	parts

511 S Raymond Ave
Fullerton, CA 92831
800-854-0393 orders
714-871-6432; FAX: 714-871-1883

See full listing in **Section One** under **Thunderbird**

Lincoln Parts International	parts

707 E 4th St, Bldg G
Perris, CA 92570
800-382-1656, 909-657-5588
FAX: 909-657-4758
E-mail: lincolnparts@pe.net

See full listing in **Section One** under **Lincoln**

Ed Liukkonen	accessories parts

37 Cook Rd
Templeton, MA 01468
978-939-8126

Mail order only. Sale of NOS genuine FoMoCo parts, 1949/1979, for Ford full size, Fairlane, Comet, Mercury, Falcon, Mustang. Some used factory high-performance parts for Ford "muscle cars" also stocked.

Lloyd's Literature	literature

PO Box 491
Newbury, OH 44065
800-292-2665, 440-338-1527
FAX: 440-338-2222
E-mail: lloydslit@aol.com

See full listing in **Section Two** under **literature dealers**

Loyal Ford Mercury Inc	performance parts

2310 Calumet Dr
New Holstein, WI 53061
920-898-4248; FAX: 920-898-9705
E-mail: loyal@loyalfordmercury.com

See full listing in **Section One** under **Mustang**

Mac's Antique Auto Parts	literature parts restoration supplies

1051 Lincoln Ave, PO Box 238
Lockport, NY 14095-0238
800-777-0948 US and Canada
716-433-1500 local and foreign
FAX: 716-433-1172
E-mail: mailmacs@aol.com

See full listing in **Section One** under **Ford 1903-1931**

MAR-K Quality Parts	bed parts customizing parts trim parts

6625 W Wilshire Blvd
Oklahoma City, OK 73132
405-721-7945; FAX: 405-721-8906
E-mail: info@mar-k.com

See full listing in **Section Two** under **trucks & tractors**

The Maverick Connection	literature parts

PO Box 206
Ripley, WV 25271
PH/FAX: 304-372-7825
E-mail: maverickconnection@email.com

Mail order only. Specializing in parts and literature for 1970-1977 Ford Mavericks and Mercury Comets. Web site: www.angelfire.com/ky/maverickconnections/

McDonald Obsolete Parts Company	body parts chassis parts

6458 W Eureka Rd
Rockport, IN 47635
800-897-8693 orders (w/part # only),
812-359-4965; FAX: 812-359-5555
E-mail: mcdonald@psci.net

Mail order only. Specializing in body parts and chassis parts, replacement glass, spotlights and foglights for 1938-present Ford, Mercury, Lincoln and trucks. Inventory is 90% NOS. Also dealers of all major quality reproduced parts. Web site: www.mcdonaldparts.com

Mean Mustang Supply Inc	parts

201 D St
South Charleston, WV 25303
304-746-0300; FAX: 304-746-0395
E-mail: meanstang@aol.com

See full listing in **Section One** under **Mustang**

Melvin's Classic Ford Parts Inc	parts

1521 Dogwood Dr
Conyers, GA 30012
770-761-6800; FAX: 770-761-5777

Mail order and open showroom. Tuesday-Friday 8:30 am to 5:30 pm, Saturday 8:30 am to 4 pm. Specializing in NOS, reproduction and used parts for 1964-1/2 to 1973 Mustang, 1960-1970-1/2 Falcon, 1962-1979 Fairlane, Torino, Ranchero, 1949-1972

Ford car, 1948-1979 Ford trucks, and 1955-1966 Thunderbird. Catalogs-$5, specify vehicle, refundable with first order. Web site: www.melvinsclassicfordparts.com

See our ad on page 91

Miller Obsolete Parts	locator service
1329 Campus Dr	parts
Vestal, NY 13850	
607-722-5371; FAX: 607-770-9117	
E-mail: mmiller3@stny.rr.com	

Mail order only. New original (NOS) parts. 1950s-1990s Ford, Lincoln, Mercury vehicles. 85,000 parts in stock. Free nationwide locator service.

Mostly Mustangs Inc	car dealer
55 Alling St	parts sales
Hamden, CT 06517	restoration
203-562-8804; FAX: 203-562-4891	

See full listing in **Section One** under **Mustang**

Mr G's Enterprises	fasteners
5613 Elliott Reeder Rd	screw kits
Fort Worth, TX 76117	
817-831-3501; FAX: 817-831-0638	
E-mail: mrgs@mrgusa.com	

See full listing in **Section One** under **Mopar**

Mustang of Chicago Inc	new & used parts
1321 W Irving Park Rd	
Bensenville, IL 60106	
630-860-7077	
FAX: 630-860-7120, 24 hrs	
E-mail: cobracars@aol.com	

See full listing in **Section One** under **Mustang**

Mustang Service Center	parts
11610 Vanowen St	service
North Hollywood, CA 91605	
818-765-1196; FAX: 818-765-1349	
E-mail: bo@mustangservicecenter.com	

See full listing in **Section One** under **Mustang**

Mustangs & More	parts
2065 Sperry Ave #C	restoration
Ventura, CA 93003	
800-356-6573; FAX: 805-642-6468	
E-mail: mustmore@aol.com	

See full listing in **Section One** under **Mustang**

Mustangs Plus Inc	racing products
2353 N Wilson Way	restoration
Stockton, CA 95205	
800-999-4289; FAX: 209-944-9980	

See full listing in **Section One** under **Mustang**

Mustangs Unlimited	accessories
185 Adams St	parts
Manchester, CT 06040	
860-647-1965	
E-mail: info@mustangsunlimited.com	

See full listing in **Section One** under **Mustang**

Narragansett Reproductions	wiring harnesses
Ed & Miki Pease	
107 Woodville Rd, PO Box 51	
Wood River Junction, RI 02894	
401-364-3839; FAX: 401-364-3830	
E-mail: narragansetrepro@aol.com	

See full listing in **Section Two** under **electrical systems**

Niagara CHT Productions Inc	swap meets
PO Box 112	
Akron, NY 14001	
716-542-2585	

See full listing in **Section Two** under **auctions & shows**

Normans' Classic Auto Radio	custom sales
8475 68th Way	
Pinellas Park, FL 33781	
727-546-1788	

See full listing in **Section Two** under **radios**

North Yale Auto Parts	salvage yard
Rt 1, Box 707	
Sperry, OK 74073	
800-256-6927 (NYAP), 918-288-7218	
E-mail: nyap@ionet.net	

See full listing in **Section Five** under **Oklahoma**

Northeast Ford	parts
Box 66, Rt 9	restoration
East Sullivan, NH 03445	
603-847-9956, 800-562-FORD	
FAX: 603-847-9691	

Mail order and open shop. Monday-Friday 8 am to 5:30 pm. Ford parts for cars and trucks. Our parts include new, used and quality reproductions from 1928-1979. Catalogues available, from 1932-1979, $3 refundable, must specify year and model. We do inspections and repairs, plus we have a complete restoration facility.

Northwest Classic Falcons Inc   **parts**
1715 NW Pettygrove St
Portland, OR 97209
503-241-9454; FAX: 503-241-1964
E-mail: ron@nwfalcon.com

Mail order and phone order/pickup. Monday-Friday 9 am to 6 pm PST. Specializes in new, reproduction, NOS and good used parts for 1960-1970 Falcon and Comet. Web site: www.nwfalcon.com
See our ad on page 92

NOS Only   **NOS Ford parts**
414 Umbarger Rd, Unit E   **NOS parts**
San Jose, CA 95111
408-227-2353, 408-227-2354
FAX: 408-227-2355
E-mail: nosonly@aol.com

See full listing in **Section Two** under **comprehensive parts**

Obsolete Ford Parts Co   **parts**
311 E Washington Ave, PO Box 787
Nashville, GA 31639
229-686-2470; FAX: 229-686-7125

Mail order and open shop. Monday-Friday 8 am to 5 pm. Comprehensive stock of NOS sheetmetal, trim, chrome, rubber, accessories, literature for 1949-1979 Fords, Falcons, Fairlanes, Ford pickups, Comets, Cougars. Customers' requests by phone or mail accepted. Web site: www.obsoleteford.com

Obsolete Ford Parts Inc   **parts**
8701 S I-35
Oklahoma City, OK 73149
405-631-3933; FAX: 405-634-6815
E-mail: info@obsoletefordparts.com

Mail order and open shop. Monday-Friday 8 am to 6 pm, Saturday 8 am to 1 pm. A full product line for Ford vehicles. We offer (10) different catalogs: 1909-1927 T, 1928-1931 A, 1932-1948 car and pickup, 1948-1979 pickup, 1960-1970 Falcon, 1962-1972 Fairlane, 1955-1972 T-Bird, 1949-1972 full-size Ford car, 1949-1972 Mercury and an all new Street Rod catalog. Web site: www.obsoletefordparts.com

Joe Odehnal   **literature**
2722 N Westnedge   **parts**
Kalamazoo, MI 49004
616-342-5509
E-mail: joe.odehnal@wmich.edu

Mail order only. Used parts for 1957-1959 Ford retractables. Literature and magazine ads for the retractable.

Old Air Products   **air conditioning**
4615 Martin St
Ft Worth, TX 76119
817-531-2665; FAX: 817-531-3257
E-mail: sales@oldairproducts.com

See full listing in **Section One** under **Corvette**

The Old Car Centre   **parts**
3-20075 92A Ave
Langley, BC Canada V1M 3A4
604-888-4412, 604-888-4055
FAX: 604-888-7455
E-mail: oldcarcentre@look.ca

See full listing in **Section One** under **Ford 1903-1931**

The Old Carb Doctor   **carburetors**
1127 Drucilla Church Rd   **fuel pumps**
Nebo, NC 28761
800-945-CARB (2272)
828-659-1428

See full listing in **Section Two** under **carburetors**

Old Dominion Mustang/Camaro   **parts**
509 S Washington Hwy, Rt 1
Ashland, VA 23005
804-798-3348; FAX: 804-798-5105

See full listing in **Section One** under **Mustang**

Original Auto Interiors   **upholstery**
7869 Trumble Rd
Columbus, MI 48063-3915
810-727-2486; FAX: 810-727-4344
E-mail: origauto@tir.com

See full listing in **Section Two** under **upholstery**

Original Falcon, Comet, Ranchero,   **interiors**
Fairlane Interiors   **parts**
6343 Seaview Ave NW   **weatherstripping**
Seattle, WA 98107-2664
888-609-2363 toll free
FAX: 206-781-5046
E-mail: falcon@evergo.net

Mail order and open shop. Monday-Saturday 9 am to 6 pm. Specializing in new old stock upholstery seat sets as well as produces OEM seat sets, door panels, carpets for 1960-1966 Falcons, Comets and Rancheros, Fairlanes as well as thru the 1970s for Rancheros. These models are Sprints, Futuras, Cyclones, Calientes, Mercury S-22 2 and 4-door sedans, convertibles, with a full range of interior goods and weatherstripping. Plus car parts and whole cars. Web site: www.evergo.net/~falcon/

Original Ford Motor Co Literature   **collectibles**
PO Box 7-AA   **literature**
Hudson, KY 40145-0007
502-257-8642; FAX: 502-257-8643
E-mail: whiteb@bellsouth.net

See full listing in **Section One** under **Ford 1932-1953**

P-Ayr Products   **replicas**
719 Delaware St
Leavenworth, KS 66048
913-651-5543; FAX: 913-651-2084
E-mail: sales@payr.com

See full listing in **Section One** under **Chevrolet**

Peninsula Restoration Parts   **parts**
4526 Viewmont Ave
Victoria, BC Canada V8L 4L9
250-727-2678; FAX: 250-727-2693
E-mail: info@peninsularestoration.com

See full listing in **Section One** under **Chevrolet**

Pick-ups Northwest   **parts**
9911 Airport Way   **trim**
Snohomish, WA 98296
360-568-9166; FAX: 360-568-1233

See full listing in **Section One** under **Chevrolet**

Power Brake Booster Exchange Inc   **brake boosters**
4533 SE Division St
Portland, OR 97206
503-238-8882

See full listing in **Section Two** under **brakes**

Recks & Relics Ford Trucks   **truck parts**
2675 Hamilton Mason Rd
Hamilton, OH 45011
513-868-3489; FAX: 513-868-3461
E-mail: truck@choice.net

See full listing in **Section One** under **Ford 1932-1953**

Red's Headers & Early Ford Speed Equipment
22950 Bednar Ln
Fort Bragg, CA 95437-8411
707-964-7733; FAX: 707-964-5434
E-mail: red@reds-headers.com

| headers |
| mechanical parts |

See full listing in **Section One** under **Ford 1932-1953**

Regent Trading Corp
Paul Brensilber
15 Stonehurst Dr
Tenafly, NJ 07670
201-541-7718, NJ
FAX: 212-362-3985, NY

parts

Mail order only. Specializing in door striker plates for Ford trucks and automobiles, for Ford truck 1953-1955, Ford truck 1956, Ford passenger car 1949-1956. Also Ford parts.

S & S Antique Auto
Pine St
Deposit, NY 13754
607-467-2929; FAX: 607-467-2109

parts

See full listing in **Section One** under **Ford 1932-1953**

Sam's Vintage Ford Parts
5105 Washington
Denver, CO 80216
303-295-1709

parts

Mail order and open shop. Monday-Saturday 9 am to 5:30 pm. For V8s, Mustangs and 1949-1970 Fords and Mercurys. Also truck parts.

Sanderson Ford
Jim Ray
6300 N 51 Ave
Glendale, AZ 85301
888-364-3673, 602-842-8663
FAX: 602-842-8637

parts

Mail order and open shop. Monday-Friday 8 am to 6 pm, Saturday 8 am to 4 pm. Specializing in 1965-1973 Mustangs, 1955-1966 Thunderbirds, 1960-1965 Falcons, 1967-1973 Cougars, 1953-1956 F-100, Motorsport parts and late model 5.0 parts. No catalogs. Web site: www.sandersonford.com

Sixties Ford Parts
639 Glanker St
Memphis, TN 38112
PH/FAX: 901-323-2195, recorder

| books |
| new parts |
| shop manuals |

Mail order only. New parts for 1960-1968 Fords, big Ford, Fairlane, Falcon, Thunderbird, trucks. 90 page catalog, $4, specify year and type of Ford as listed above. In business over 25 years. Visa, MasterCard, personal checks accepted.

Sound Move Inc
217 S Main St
Elkhart, IN 46516
800-901-0222, 219-294-5100
FAX: 219-293-4902

radios

See full listing in **Section One** under **Chevrolet**

Special Interest Cars
451 Woody Rd
Oakville, ON Canada L6K 2Y2
905-844-8063; FAX: 905-338-8063
E-mail: sic@istar.ca

| manuals |
| parts |

See full listing in **Section Two** under **comprehensive parts**

Stilwell's Obsolete Car Parts
1617 Wedeking Ave
Evansville, IN 47711
812-425-4794

| body parts |
| interiors |
| parts |

See full listing in **Section One** under **Mustang**

Tags Backeast
PO Box 581
Plainville, CT 06062
860-747-2942
E-mail: dataplt@snet.net

| data plates |
| trim tags |
| cowl tags |

See full listing in **Section Two** under **special services**

Tee-Bird Products Inc
Box 728
Exton, PA 19341
610-363-1725; FAX: 610-363-2691

parts

Mail order and open shop. Monday-Friday 8 am to 5 pm, Saturday morning by appointment. Specializing in a complete line of parts for 1954-1959 Ford, with emphasis on 1955-1956 cars and 1955-1957 Thunderbirds. Offering prompt service, competitive prices and customer satisfaction since 1973. Web site: www.tee-bird.com

Texas Mustang Parts
5774 S University Parks Dr
Waco, TX 76706
800-527-1588; FAX: 254-662-0455
E-mail: mustang@calpha.com

| performance parts |
| restoration |

See full listing in **Section One** under **Mustang**

Thunderbird, Falcon, Fairlane & Comet Connections
728 E Dunlap
Phoenix, AZ 85020
602-997-9285; FAX: 602-997-0624
E-mail: thunderbirdconn@aol.com

| new repros |
| parts |
| used repros |

See full listing in **Section One** under **Thunderbird**

Thunderbird Information eXchange
8421 E Cortez St
Scottsdale, AZ 85260
480-948-3996

newsletter

See full listing in **Section One** under **Thunderbird**

Thunderbirds East
Andy Lovelace
140 Wilmington W Chester Pike
Chadds Ford, PA 19317
610-358-1021; FAX: 610-558-9615

| parts |
| restoration |

See full listing in **Section One** under **Thunderbird**

Universal Transmission Co
23361 Dequindre Rd
Hazel Park, MI 48030
800-882-4327; FAX: 248-398-2581

transmission parts

See full listing in **Section Two** under **transmissions**

Valley Motor Supply
1402 E Second St
Roswell, NM 88201
505-622-7450

| accessories |
| parts |

Mail order and open shop. Monday-Friday 8 am to 5 pm. GM, Ford, Chrysler and tractor products. Some parts for all makes, early to present. Many NOS items.

Vintage Ford & Chevrolet Parts of Arizona Inc
So-Cal Speed Shop
3427 E McDowell Rd
Phoenix, AZ 85008-3845
800-732-0076, 602-275-7990
FAX: 602-267-8439
E-mail: vintageparts@sprintmail.com

parts

Mail order and open showroom. Monday-Friday 9 am to 5 pm, Saturday 8 am to 3 pm. Dealing in 1928-1956 Ford car and truck, 1948-1972 Ford truck, 1947-1972 Chevy truck, 1965-1973 Mustang, 1966-1977 Bronco and hot rods. We offer new and used parts. Web site: www.vintagepartsaz.com

Vintage Gas, Ltd
E-mail: info@vintagegas.com

artwork

See full listing in **Section Two** under **artwork**

White Post Restorations
One Old Car Dr, PO Drawer D
White Post, VA 22663
540-837-1140; FAX: 540-837-2368
E-mail: info@whitepost.com

**brakes
restoration**

See full listing in **Section Two** under **brakes**

White Post Restorations
One Old Car Dr, PO Drawer D
White Post, VA 22663
540-837-1140; FAX: 540-837-2368
E-mail: info@whitepost.com

restoration

See full listing in **Section Two** under **restoration shops**

Dan Williams Toploader Transmissions
206 E Dogwood Dr
Franklin, NC 28734
828-524-9085 noon to midnight
FAX: 828-524-4848

transmissions

Specializing in Ford Toploader transmissions. Sales, service, parts, rebuild kits, Hurst shifters, Lakewood bellhousings. Web site: www.toploadertransmissions.com

A&A Mustang Parts & Mfg Co
105 Fordham Rd
Oak Ridge, TN 37830
423-482-9445
E=-mail: joannantrican@aol.com

**exhaust systems
parts
restorations**

Mail order and open shop. Monday-Friday 8 am to 5 pm. Specializing in single and dual exhaust systems, new and used parts and full restorations for 1964-1/2 to 1973 Mustangs.

American Restorations Unlimited TA
14 Meakin Ave, PO Box 34
Rochelle Park, NJ 07662
201-843-3567; FAX: 201-843-3238
E-mail: amerrest@earthlink.net

**engine
glass
restoration parts
transmission**

See full listing in **Section Two** under **glass**

AMK Products Inc
800 Airport Rd
Winchester, VA 22602
540-662-7820; FAX: 540-662-7821

parts

See full listing in **Section One** under **Ford 1954-up**

Andy's Classic Mustangs
18502 E Sprague
Greenacres, WA 99016
509-924-9824

**parts
service**

Mail order and open shop. Monday-Saturday 8 am to 5 pm. Specializing in Mustangs since 1965. New and used parts. Professional engine rebuilding, carburetors, transmissions, differentials. An authority on Mustangs 1965-1973 as to originality and correctness.

Antique Auto Electric
9109 (Rear) E Garvey Ave
Rosemead, CA 91770
626-572-0938

repro wiring

See full listing in **Section Two** under **electrical systems**

ARS Automotive Research Services
Division of Auto Search International
1702 W Camelback #301
Phoenix, AZ 85015
602-230-7111; FAX: 602-230-7282

**appraisals
research**

See full listing in **Section Two** under **appraisals**

Auto Craftsmen Restoration Inc
27945 Elm Grove
San Antonio, TX 78261
PH/FAX: 830-980-4027

**appraisals
buyer/car locator
old M-B parts
restoration**

See full listing in **Section Two** under **restoration shops**

Auto Krafters Inc
522 S Main St, PO Box 8
Broadway, VA 22815
540-896-5910; FAX: 540-896-6412
E-mail: akraft@shentel.net

parts

See full listing in **Section One** under **Ford 1954-up**

Bel-Kirk Mustang
12760 Bel-Red Rd
Bellevue, WA 98005
425-455-1199; FAX: 425-455-5897

**parts
service**

Mail order and open shop. Monday-Friday 8:30 am to 6 pm, Saturday 10 am to 3 pm. Specializing in parts and service for 1964-1/2 thru 1973 Ford Mustang. Web site: www.belkirkmustang.com

JJ Best & Co
737 Main St, PO Box 10
Chatham, MA 02633
800-USA-1965; FAX: 508-945-6006

financing

See full listing in **Section Two** under **financing**

Tony D Branda Performance
Shelby and Mustang Parts
1434 E Pleasant Valley Blvd
Altoona, PA 16602
814-942-1869; FAX: 814-944-0801
E-mail: cobranda@aol.com

**accessories
decals
emblems
sheetmetal
wheels**

Mail order and open shop. Six days a week 8 am to 5:30 pm. Specializing in Shelby and Mustang parts and accessories for 1965-1970 Shelbys, GT 350 and GT 500. Mustang 1965-1973 parts also available. We deal in parts for restoration such as: decals, emblems, aluminum engine dress-up parts, fiberglass, sheetmetal, wheels, etc.

California Pony Cars
1906 Quaker Ridge Pl
Ontario, CA 91761
909-923-2804; FAX: 909-947-8593
E-mail: 105232.3362@compuserve.com

parts

Manufacturer/wholesaler of reproduction 1964-1/2 to 1973 Mustang parts and restoration supplies. Emblems, suspension, engine, electrical and fiberglass components and 5-speed conversions. Web site: www.calponycars.com

Canadian Mustang
20529 62 Ave
Langley, BC Canada V3A 8R4
604-534-6424; FAX: 604-534-6694
E-mail: parts@canadianmustang.com

parts

Largest and oldest Mustang parts distributor in Canada. Manufacturers, wholesalers and distributors of 1965-1973 Mustang parts. Large Canadian mail order catalog. Web site: www.canadianmustang.com

Carl's Ford Parts
23219 South St, Box 38
Homeworth, OH 44634
PH/FAX: 330-525-7291
E-mail: fordcobrajet@hotmail.com

muscle parts

Specializing in 1960-1970 Ford muscle parts for all Fords and Mercurys. Carburetor rebuilding, parts locating and engine building services for 390, 406, 428, 427 engines. Web site: www.carlsfordparts.com

CBS Performance Automotive
2605-A W Colorado Ave
Colorado Springs, CO 80904
800-685-1492; FAX: 719-578-9485

ignition systems
performance
products

See full listing in **Section Two** under **ignition parts**

CJ Pony Parts Inc
7481 Allentown Blvd
Harrisburg, PA 17112
800-888-6473, 717-657-9252
FAX: 888-888-6573, 717-657-9254
E-mail: creed@redrose.net

parts

Stop by and see our 18,000 sq ft facility including a warehouse, showroom, restoration factility and Mustang graveyard. We've been serving the Mustang restorer since 1985. We sell it all, from tie rods to superchargers. One call does it all. Check out our web site: www.emustang.com

Classic Auto
251 SW 5th Ct
Pompano Beach, FL 33060
PH/FAX: 954-786-1687

restoration

See full listing in **Section Two** under **restoration shops**

Classic Auto Air Mfg Co
2020 W Kennedy Blvd
Tampa, FL 33606
813-251-2356, 813-251-4994
FAX: 813-254-7419

air conditioning
heating
parts

Mail order and open shop. Monday-Friday 9:30 am to 6 pm. Manufactures exact factory or aftermarket parts and complete systems for all 1947-1975 Ford, GM and Chrysler. Show quality rebuilding services and exact hose duplications. Large NOS stock of a/c and heat parts. Specializing in 1965-1973 Mustang/ Cougar, 1949-1979 Rolls-Royce/Bentley and Ford/GM auto temp control systems. Very detailed 1965-1973 Mustang a/c catalog.

Classic Auto Restoration Service Inc
381 National Dr
Rockwall, TX 75032-6556
972-722-9663

restoration

See full listing in **Section One** under **Chevrolet**

Classic Coachworks
735 Frenchtown Rd
Milford, NJ 08848
908-996-3400; FAX: 908-996-0204
E-mail: info@classiccoachworks.net

bodywork
painting
restoration

See full listing in **Section Two** under **restoration shops**

Classic Creations of Central Florida
3620 Hwy 92E
Lakeland, FL 33801
863-665-2322; FAX: 863-666-5348
E-mail: flclassics@aol.com

parts
restoration
service

Monday-Friday 9 am to 6 pm, Saturday 8 am to 2 pm. Full service restoration and repair facility for all of your classic car needs, whether it is complete or partial. Offering complete welding and fabrications, including quarter panels, undercarriage and all exterior metal. Also offering partial or complete interior service and suspension rebuilds. Carrying a full line of new, used and NOS Mustang parts, accessories and collectibles. Web site: www.classiccreationsfl.com

Classic Mustang Inc
24 Robert Porter Rd
Southington, CT 06489
800-243-2742; FAX: 860-276-9986

body parts
carpets
chassis parts
floor pans

Mail order and open shop. Monday thru Friday 9 am-6 pm, Saturday 9 am-3 pm. Specializing in body parts, floor pans, chassis parts, carpets, interiors, exhaust and accessories for 1964 thru 1998 Ford Mustangs. Web site: classic-mustang.com

Classic Mustang Parts of Oklahoma
8801 S Interstate 35
Oklahoma City, OK 73149
405-631-1400; FAX: 405-631-1401
E-mail: mustang@ilovemymustang.com

Mustang parts

Specialize in classic Ford Mustang parts for 1964-1/2 to 1973. Web site: www.ilovemymustang.com
See our ad on page 97

Classics 'n More Inc
939 N Prince St
Lancaster, PA 17603
717-392-0599; FAX 717-392-2371

repairs
restoration

See full listing in **Section Two** under **restoration shops**

Cobra Restorers Ltd
3099 Carter Dr
Kennesaw, GA 30144
770-427-0020; FAX: 770-427-8658

parts
restoration
service

See full listing in **Section One** under **Cobra**

Convertible Service
5126-HA Walnut Grove Ave
San Gabriel, CA 91776
800-333-1140, 626-285-2255
FAX: 626-285-9004

convertible parts
manufacture/
service
top mechanism

See full listing in **Section Two** under **tops**

Bob Cook Classic Auto Parts Inc
2055 Van Cleave Rd, PO Box 600
Murray, KY 42071-0600
270-753-4000, 800-486-1137
FAX: 270-753-4600

new parts
NOS parts
reproduced parts

See full listing in **Section One** under **Ford 1954-up**

Desert Muscle Cars
2853 N Stone Ave
Tucson, AZ 85705
520-882-3010; FAX: 520-628-9332

parts

See full listing in **Section One** under **Chevelle/Camaro**

Dynatech Engineering
PO Box 1446
Alta Loma, CA 91701-8446
805-492-6134
E-mail: dynatechengineering@yahoo.com

motor mounts

See full listing in **Section Two** under **engine parts**

ETC/Every Thing Cars 8727 Clarinda Pico Rivera, CA 90660 562-949-6981	paint repairs restoration welding

See full listing in **Section One** under **Mopar**

Firewall Insulators & Quiet Ride Solutions 6465 Pacific Ave, Ste 249 Stockton, CA 95207 209-477-4840; FAX: 209-477-0918 E-mail: timcox@quietride.com	air plenums auto insulation firewall insulators gloveboxes sound deadening

See full listing in **Section Two** under **upholstery**

Ford Powertrain Applications 7702 E 96th St Puyallup, WA 98371 PH/FAX: 253-848-9503	engines

See full listing in **Section One** under **Ford 1954-up**

Gano Filter 1205 Sandalwood Ln Los Altos, CA 94024 650-968-7017	coolant filters

See full listing in **Section Two** under **radiators**

Glazier's Mustang Barn Inc 531 Wambold Rd Souderton, PA 18964 800-523-6708, 215-723-9674 FAX: 215-723-6277	accessories parts restoration service

Mail order and showroom sales. Monday-Friday 8:30 am to 5 pm; Saturday 9 am to 1 pm; other times by appointment. Prize winning restoration shop. Monday-Thursday 8 am to 5:30 pm; Friday 8 am to 12 noon; other times by appointment. Specializing in

1964-1/2 to 1973 Mustangs and Shelbys. Restorations on other early Fords are considered. Catalog available.

Randy Goodling 2046 Mill Rd Elizabethtown, PA 17022-9401 717-367-6700	parts parts locating

See full listing in **Section One** under **Mercury**

Greg's Automotive Box 1712 Santa Ynez, CA 93460 PH/FAX: 805-688-5675 E-mail: 9pm@silcom.com	accessories books literature

See full listing in **Section One** under **Chevrolet**

Bill Heeley 3621 Mt Olney Ln Olney, MD 20832 301-774-6710	shift assemblies shift levers

See full listing in **Section One** under **Ford 1954-up**

Bill Herndon's Pony Warehouse 20028 Cinnabar Dr Gaithersburg, MD 20879 301-977-0309; FAX: 301-977-1573	accessories parts

Mail order only. Specializing in factory original options and accessories for 1965-1973 Mustangs and Shelbys. One of the largest selections of new old stock parts, including hundreds of hard to find reconditioned original parts and the best available reproduction parts. Quality reconditioning services available for steering wheels, consoles and radios. Your satisfaction guaranteed. We ship anywhere in the USA, Canada and overseas. Visa/MasterCard. Let us be your number one source for quality parts.

Hi-Tech Software
2 Cooks Farm Rd
Montville, NJ 07045
PH/FAX: 973-402-9710
E-mail: harry@htsoftware.com

CD encyclopedia

See full listing in **Section One** under **Corvette**

Kenny's Rod & Kustom
117 Milton Blvd
Newton Falls, OH 44444
330-872-1932; FAX: 330-872-3332

conversion kits
street rod parts

See full listing in **Section Two** under **street rods**

Dale King Obsolete Parts
211 Hilltop Dr, PO Box 1099
Liberty, KY 42539
606-787-5031; FAX: 606-787-2130
E-mail: daleking@kih.net

parts

See full listing in **Section One** under **Ford 1954-up**

**Larry's Thunderbird and
Mustang Parts**
511 S Raymond Ave
Fullerton, CA 92831
800-854-0393 orders
714-871-6432; FAX: 714-871-1883

parts

See full listing in **Section One** under **Thunderbird**

Ed Liukkonen
37 Cook Rd
Templeton, MA 01468
978-939-8126

accessories
parts

See full listing in **Section One** under **Ford 1954-up**

**Long Island Mustang
Restoration Parts**
168 Silverleaf Ln
Islandia, NY 11722
516-232-2388; FAX: 516-272-5201
E-mail: tom@l-i-mustang.com

convertible specialist
rebuilding services
reconditioned
consoles 1965-1970
repro parts

Mail order and open shop. Monday-Saturday 1 pm to 6 pm EST. Specializing in 1964-1/2 to 1973 and 1979-1993 Mustangs (Ford). Convertible specialist, reconditioned consoles, 1,000s new, NOS Ford, finest quality reproduction parts, rebuilding services. Power steering pumps, control valves, slave cylinders, glass beading and general reconditioning. Visa and MasterCard accepted. Web site: www.l-i-mustang.com

---

Loyal Ford Mercury Inc
2310 Calumet Dr
New Holstein, WI 53061
920-898-4248; FAX: 920-898-9705
E-mail: loyal@loyalfordmercury.com

performance parts

Mail order and open shop. Monday-Wednesday 7 am to 8 pm, Thursday-Friday 7 am to 8 pm, Saturday 8 am to 5 pm. We specialize in sales and service of late model hi-performance Ford and Mercury products for Saleen, SVT, Roush, MG Motorsports, Mustangs, Cougars, Explorers, Expeditions, F150s, Cobras, Lightnings and SHOs. We also will upgrade your current vehicle. Web site: www.loyalford.com

---

Mac's Antique Auto Parts
1051 Lincoln Ave, PO Box 238
Lockport, NY 14095-0238
800-777-0948 US and Canada
716-433-1500 local and foreign
FAX: 716-433-1172
E-mail: mailmacs@aol.com

literature
parts
restoration
supplies

See full listing in **Section One** under **Ford 1903-1931**

McDonald Obsolete Parts Company
6458 W Eureka Rd
Rockport, IN 47635
800-897-8693 orders (w/part # only),
812-359-4965; FAX: 812-359-5555
E-mail: mcdonald@psci.net

body parts
chassis parts

See full listing in **Section One** under **Ford 1954-up**

Mean Mustang Supply Inc
201 D St
South Charleston, WV 25303
304-746-0300; FAX: 304-746-0395
E-mail: meanstang@aol.com

parts

Mail order and open shop. Tuesday-Friday 10 am to 5:30 pm EST, Saturday 10 am to 2 pm. Specializing in restoration parts, OEM Ford parts, high-performance parts for Ford Mustang 1964-1/2 to 1999 model years. We offer high quality restoration parts for all years. High-performance parts such as: Ford Motorsport, Eibach, Koni, new Ford parts, Powerdyne and Corbeau seats. Web site: http://members.aol.com/meanstang

---

Mostly Mustangs Inc
55 Alling St
Hamden, CT 06517
203-562-8804; FAX: 203-562-4891

car dealer
parts sales
restoration

Mail order and open shop. Monday-Friday 10 am to 9 pm, Saturday 10 am to 5 pm. Sales, restoration and service of Mustangs and sixties and later Ford products. Discounted new and used parts. Free Mustang parts catalog available.

Mustang Classics
3814 Walnut St
Denver, CO 80205
303-295-3140

parts
restoration
sales
service

Mail order and open shop. Monday-Friday 9 am to 6 pm. Specializing in parts, service, sales and restoration for 1965-1973 Mustang.

Mustang of Chicago Inc
1321 W Irving Park Rd
Bensenville, IL 60106
630-860-7077
FAX: 630-860-7120, 24 hrs
E-mail: cobracars@aol.com

new & used parts

Mail order, retail store and repairs/restorations. Monday-Friday 9 am-6 pm, Wednesday nights until 8 pm, Saturdays 9 am to 2 pm. Since 1980, Chicagoland's #1 source for original Ford, quality aftermarket, and used parts. Certified MCA judge on staff, licensed mechanic on staff, over 20 years' experience with Mustangs. Our latest catalog is $5 to cover postage and handling, refundable with 1st order. Please specify the year and body style of your Mustang. We ship worldwide.

Mustang Service Center
11610 Vanowen St
North Hollywood, CA 91605
818-765-1196; FAX: 818-765-1349
E-mail: bo@mustangservicecenter.com

parts
service

Mail order and open shop. Tuesday-Saturday 8 am to 5 pm. Specializing in NOS Ford and Mustang parts and service. Web site: www.mustangservicecenter.com

---

Mustang Village
8833 Fowler Ave
Pensacola, FL 32534
850-477-8056; FAX: 850-484-4244
E-mail: rmcneal@aol.com

salvage yard

See full listing in **Section Five** under **Florida**

Mustangs & More | parts
2065 Sperry Ave #C | restoration
Ventura, CA 93003
800-356-6573; FAX: 805-642-6468
E-mail: mustmore@aol.com

Mail order and open shop. Monday-Friday 9 am to 5:30 pm,
Saturday 9 am to 1 pm. Specializing in parts and restorations
for 1965-1994 Mustangs, 1962-1973 Fairlanes, 1960-1970
Falcons and 1955-1957 Thunderbirds. Offers the highest quality
parts available, original Ford, reproductions and used, to suit
your budget and needs. 25 years' experience in Ford parts and
restorations enable us to help you with most of your restoration
projects. Quality, service, same day shipping and extensive Ford
knowledge are our marks of excellence. Free catalog.

Mustangs Plus Inc | racing products
2353 N Wilson Way | restoration
Stockton, CA 95205
800-999-4289; FAX: 209-944-9980

Mail order and open shop. Monday-Friday 8 am to 5 pm, Saturday 8 am to noon, closed Sundays. Specializing in restoring,
restomoding and racing products for 1964-1/2 to 1973
Mustangs. Mustangs Plus offers a wide variety of new products
for the classic Mustang owner. Free full color catalog available.
Web site: www.mustangsplus.com

Mustangs Unlimited | accessories
185 Adams St | parts
Manchester, CT 06040
860-647-1965
E-mail: info@mustangsunlimited.com

Mail order and open shop. Monday-Friday 8 am-9 pm, Saturday
8 am to 5 pm, Sunday 11 am-5 pm. Specializing in restoration
parts and accessories for 1965-present Ford Mustang, 1967-
1973 Mercury Cougar and 1980-present Ford trucks. Web site:
www.mustangsunlimited.com

National Parts Depot | accessories
900 SW 38th Ave | parts
Ocala, FL 34474
800-874-7595; FAX: 352-861-8706

Mail order and open shop. Monday-Friday 8 am to 9 pm,
Saturday-Sunday 8 am to 5 pm. Specializing in parts and accessories for 1965-1973 Ford Mustang, 1967-1981 Chevy Camaro,
1955-1957 Ford Thunderbird, 1967-1981 Pontiac Firebird,
1964-1983 Chevy Chevelle, Malibu and 1964-1987 Chevy El
Camino. Web site: www.npdlink.com

Northeast Ford | parts
Box 66, Rt 9 | restoration
East Sullivan, NH 03445
603-847-9956, 800-562-FORD
FAX: 603-847-9691

See full listing in **Section One** under **Ford 1954-up**

OEM Paints Inc | custom aerosol
PO Box 461736 | colors
Escondido, CA 92046-1736
760-747-2100

See full listing in **Section Two** under **paints**

Old Dominion Mustang/Camaro | parts
509 S Washington Hwy, Rt 1
Ashland, VA 23005
804-798-3348; FAX: 804-798-5105

Mail order and open shop. Monday-Friday 9 am to 5 pm,
Saturday 9 am to 3 pm. Specializing in Mustang and Camaro
parts. Web site: www.olddominion.com

Original Falcon, Comet, Ranchero, | interiors
Fairlane Interiors | parts
6343 Seaview Ave NW | weatherstripping
Seattle, WA 98107-2664
888-609-2363 toll free;
FAX: 206-781-5046
E-mail: falcon@evergo.net

See full listing in **Section One** under **Ford 1954-up**

Pony Enterprises | fasteners
PO Box L-1007 | hardware
Langhorne, PA 19047
215-547-2221; FAX: 215-547-7810
E-mail: ponyent@aol.com

Specializing in hardware items (nuts, bolts, screws, rubber bumpers, springs, clips, clamps, plugs, straps, etc) for 1965-1993
Ford Mustangs. We sell items individually packaged in the quantities proper for use or in bulk. We also private label packages
for dealers. Wholesale only. Established in 1981. Member of
SEMA and MCA.

Pony Parts of America | floor boards
1690 Thomas Paine Pkwy | frame rails
Centerville, OH 45459
937-435-4541; FAX: 937-435-4548
E-mail: porshfreek@aol.com

Mail order and open shop. Monday-Friday 7:30 am to 6 pm,
Saturday 9:30 am to 12 pm. Reproduction body parts for
Mustangs. Manufacturer of frame rails and floorboards, 1964-
1/2 to 1970. Also manufacturer of replacement body panels for
Porsche 914 and 911. Web site: http://members.aol.com/
porshfreek/homepage.html

Power Brake Booster Exchange Inc | brake boosters
4533 SE Division St
Portland, OR 97206
503-238-8882

See full listing in **Section Two** under **brakes**

Power Brake X-Change Inc | parts
336 Lamont Pl
Pittsburgh, PA 15232
800-580-5729, 412-441-5729
FAX: 412-441-9333

See full listing in **Section Two** under **brakes**

PV Antique & Classic Ford | parts
1688 Main St
Tewksbury, MA 01876
800-MSTANGS orders only
978-851-9159; FAX: 978-858-3827
E-mail: pvford@flash.net

See full listing in **Section One** under **Ford 1903-1931**

Reproduction Parts Marketing | parts
1920 Alberta Ave | restoration
Saskatoon, SK Canada S7K 1R9 | service
306-652-6668; FAX: 306-652-1123

See full listing in **Section One** under **Chevrolet**

Rode's Restoration | parts
1406 Lohr Rd | restoration
Galion, OH 44833
419-468-5182; FAX: 419-462-1753
E-mail: rodes@bright.net

Mail order and open shop. Rebuilders and manufacturers of
reproduction parts for steering components for 1965-1973
Mustangs, valves, cylinders, steer gears, brackets, pumps, Dana
hoses. Web site: www.rodesrestoration.com

Sam's Vintage Ford Parts 5105 Washington Denver, CO 80216 303-295-1709	parts

See full listing in **Section One** under **Ford 1954-up**

Sanderson Ford Jim Ray 6300 N 51 Ave Glendale, AZ 85301 888-364-3673, 602-842-8663 FAX: 602-842-8637	parts

See full listing in **Section One** under **Ford 1954-up**

Stilwell's Obsolete Car Parts 1617 Wedeking Ave Evansville, IN 47711 812-425-4794	body parts interiors parts

Mail order only. Specializing in 1965-1973 Mustang and Ford NOS and reproduction parts. Bumpers, patch panels, upholstery, original fenders, quarter panels, hoods, etc in stock. We stock the finest upholstery and carpets on the market. Catalog, $3. 25 years as a full time Mustang parts supplier.

Street-Wise Performance Richie Mulligan Box 105 Creek Rd Tranquility, NJ 07879 973-786-7500; FAX: 973-786-7861 E-mail: street-wise@usa.net	differentials new/used parts overhaul kits transmissions

See full listing in **Section Two** under **differentials**

Tags Backeast PO Box 581 Plainville, CT 06062 860-747-2942 E-mail: dataplt@snet.net	data plates trim tags cowl tags

See full listing in **Section Two** under **special services**

Texas Mustang Parts 5774 S University Parks Dr Waco, TX 76706 800-527-1588; FAX: 254-662-0455 E-mail: mustang@calpha.com	performance parts restoration

Mail order and open shop. Monday-Friday 8 am to 5:30 pm, Saturday 8 am to 12 pm CST. Specializing in restoration, performance, handling and restyling for 1964-1973 and 1979-2001 Mustangs. Web site: www.texasmustang.com

USAopoly Inc 565 Westlake St Encinitas, CA 92024 760-634-5910; FAX: 760-634-5923 E-mail: christian@usaopoly.com	Monopoly® game

See full listing in **Section Two** under **models & toys**

Vintage Ford & Chevrolet Parts of Arizona Inc So-Cal Speed Shop 3427 E McDowell Rd Phoenix, AZ 85008-3845 800-732-0076, 602-275-7990 FAX: 602-267-8439 E-mail: vintageparts@sprintmail.com	parts

See full listing in **Section One** under **Ford 1954-up**

Virginia Classic Mustang Inc PO Box 487 Broadway, VA 22815 540-896-2695; FAX: 540-896-9310	accessories parts

Mail order and showroom. Monday-Friday 8 am to 5:30 pm, Saturday 8 am to 1 pm. Specializing in parts and accessories for 1964-1/2 to 1973 Mustang. Our 1964-1/2 to 1973 Mustang parts catalog has over 1,000 photos and 216 pages. Full line of parts available including interior, wheels, weatherstripping, chrome, sheetmetal, engine compartment, suspension, hardware, decals, stereos, literature and detail items. We have been offering super quality parts, fast service and reasonable prices for over 20 years. Web site: www.vamustang.com

Wheel Vintiques Inc 5468 E Lamona Ave Fresno, CA 93727 209-251-6957; FAX: 209-251-1620	hubcaps wheels

See full listing in **Section One** under **Chevrolet**

White Post Restorations One Old Car Dr, PO Drawer D White Post, VA 22663 540-837-1140; FAX: 540-837-2368 E-mail: info@whitepost.com	brakes restoration

See full listing in **Section Two** under **brakes**

White Post Restorations One Old Car Dr, PO Drawer D White Post, VA 22663 540-837-1140; FAX: 540-837-2368 E-mail: info@whitepost.com	restoration

See full listing in **Section Two** under **restoration shops**

Dan Williams Toploader Transmissions 206 E Dogwood Dr Franklin, NC 28734 828-524-9085 noon to midnight FAX: 828-524-4848	transmissions

See full listing in **Section One** under **Ford 1954-up**

1958 Thunderbird Convertible Registry Bill Van Ess 6780 Kitson NE Rockford, MI 49341 616-874-1004; FAX: 616-363-2870 E-mail: billvaness@juno.com	book

Mail order only. A registry of all the remaining 1958 convertibles. 40 pages includes pictures, Square Bird history, production figures and running production changes, frame differences between hardtops and convertibles, current and past owners and history on the remaining cars. If you love Square Birds, you will enjoy this book. $9.75 postpaid.

A Bygone Era Motorcars 6616 Madison Rd Cincinnati, OH 45227 513-831-5520 E-mail: crrchaz@cs.com	appraisals restoration

See full listing in **Section One** under **Rolls-Royce/Bentley**

A-1 Shock Absorber Co Shockfinders Division 365 Warren Ave, PO Box 2028 Silverthorne, CO 80498 800-344-1966, 970-389-3193 cell FAX: 970-513-8283	shocks-all types coil springs Koni shocks leaf springs steering gears

See our ad on the last page

ARASCO   parts
PO Box 24, Dept HA15
Newport, KY 41072
859-441-8363

See full listing in **Section One** under **Ford 1932-1953**

Auto Krafters Inc   parts
522 S Main St, PO Box 8
Broadway, VA 22815
540-896-5910; FAX: 540-896-6412
E-mail: akraft@shentel.net

See full listing in **Section One** under **Ford 1954-up**

B & L Body Shop   restoration
20 O'Shea Ln
Waynesville, NC 28786-4524
828-456-8277

See full listing in **Section Two** under **restoration shops**

Bird Nest   parts
745 SE 9th, PO Box 14865
Portland, OR 97214
503-231-6669, 800-232-6378
USA & Canada toll-free
FAX: 503-234-2473
E-mail: info@tbirdparts.com

Mail order and open shop. Monday-Friday 8 am to 5 pm. Specializes in 1958-1966 Thunderbird parts. New, NOS, reproduction and used parts. Parts out approximately one car per week. 25,000-square foot indoor warehouse. Free catalog. Web site: www.tbirdparts.com

Bob's Bird House   parts
124 Watkin Ave
Chadds Ford, PA 19317
610-358-3420; FAX: 610-558-0729

Mail order and retail store. Tuesday-Friday 9 am to 5 pm, Saturday 9 am to 12 pm. Thunderbird specialist 1958-1966, cars, parts. Buy, sell, trade. New, used and reproduction parts. Catalog available, $3. Web site: www.cybertowne.com/bobsbirdhouse/

California Thunderbirds   parts
Bill Denzel
1507 Arroyo View Dr
Pasadena, CA 91103
626-792-0720; FAX: 626-792-9937
E-mail: teamdenzel@aol.com

Mail order only. New, used and closeout parts plus complete cars. 1955-1957 Ford Thunderbirds.

Dennis Carpenter Ford Reproductions   parts
PO Box 26398
Charlotte, NC 28221
704-786-8139; FAX: 704-786-8180

See full listing in **Section One** under **Ford 1954-up**

Classic Auto   restoration
251 SW 5th Ct
Pompano Beach, FL 33060
PH/FAX: 954-786-1687

See full listing in **Section Two** under **restoration shops**

Classic Auto Supply Company Inc   Thunderbirds
795 High St
Coshocton, OH 43812
800-374-0914; FAX: 800-513-5806

Mail order and open shop. Monday-Friday 8:30 am to 5 pm. Full line parts supplier, restorer and manufacturer of parts for 1955-

1957 Thunderbirds. Free 72 page catalog. Specializing in 1955-1957 Thunderbirds exclusively.

Classic Ford Sales   salvage yard
PO Box 60
East Dixfield, ME 04227
207-562-4443; FAX: 207-562-4576
E-mail: sue@classicford.com

See full listing in **Section Five** under **Maine**

Classic Sheetmetal Inc   body panels
4010 A Hartley St   sheetmetal
Charlotte, NC 28206
800-776-4040, 704-596-5186
FAX: 704-596-3895

Mail order and open shop. Monday-Friday 9 am to 5 pm. Manufacturing sheetmetal body panels for 1955-1971 Thunderbirds. Free catalog. Web site: www.classicsheetmetal.com

Classics 'n More Inc   repairs
939 N Prince St   restoration
Lancaster, PA 17603
717-392-0599; FAX 717-392-2371

See full listing in **Section Two** under **restoration shops**

Classique Cars Unlimited   appraisals
7005 Turkey Bayou Rd, PO Box 249   parts
Lakeshore, MS 39558   repairs
800-543-8691, USA   restorations
228-467-9633; FAX: 228-467-9207
E-mail: parts@datasync.com

See full listing in **Section One** under **Lincoln**

Clean Sweep-Vacuum Windshield   motors
Wiper Motor Rebuilding   repairs
760 Knight Hill Rd   wiper parts
Zillah, WA 98953
509-865-2481; FAX: 509-865-2189
E-mail: dkjaquith@prodigy.net

See full listing in **Section Two** under **windshield wipers**

Bob Cook Classic Auto Parts Inc   new parts
2055 Van Cleave Rd, PO Box 600   NOS parts
Murray, KY 42071-0600   reproduced parts
270-753-4000, 800-486-1137
FAX: 270-753-4600

See full listing in **Section One** under **Ford 1954-up**

Custom Autocraft Inc   restoration
2 Flowerfield, Ste 6   sheetmetal parts
St James, NY 11780
PH/FAX: 631-862-7469

Mail order and open shop. Monday-Friday 9 am to 5:30 pm. Specializing in 1955-1957 Thunderbirds. Concours quality reproduction sheetmetal (18 ga). Braces, rockers, lower rear quarters, doglegs, floor sections (indentations pressed as original), trunk floors, much more. Buy direct from manufacturer. Doing business since 1974. Satisfaction guaranteed. Send SASE for free brochure. See us at Carlisle, PA, Spring Q83, Fall Q48-48A.

Early Ford Parts   literature
2948 Summer Ave   parts
Memphis, TN 38112
901-323-2179; FAX: 901-323-2195

See full listing in **Section One** under **Ford 1932-1953**

Daniel A Evans — literature, parts
2850 John St
Easton, PA 18045
610-258-9542 after 5:30 pm
FAX: 610-252-0370
E-mail: evansd@lafayette.edu

See full listing in **Section One** under **Ford 1954-up**

Feno's T-Bird 55-57 — parts
383 New Britain Ave
Plainville, CT 06062
PH/FAX: 860-747-8711

Specializing in 1955-1957 T-Bird parts, new, used and NOS and repairs. Also certified appraiser in Connecticut.

Firewall Insulators & Quiet Ride Solutions — air plenums, auto insulation, firewall insulators, gloveboxes, sound deadening
6465 Pacific Ave, Ste 249
Stockton, CA 95207
209-477-4840; FAX: 209-477-0918
E-mail: timcox@quietride.com

See full listing in **Section Two** under **upholstery**

Gearheads Cruiser Products & Services — power steering
333 W Ingals Ave
Bismarck, ND 58504
701-223-2269
E-mail: gearheadsnd@aol.com

See full listing in **Section One** under **Ford 1954-up**

Randy Goodling — parts, parts locating
2046 Mill Rd
Elizabethtown, PA 17022-9401
717-367-6700

See full listing in **Section One** under **Mercury**

Hamel's Automotive Inc — restorations
3306 Pleasant Ridge Rd
Wingdale, NY 12594
845-832-9454
E-mail: startnagan@aol.com

See full listing in **Section Two** under **restoration shops**

Hill's Classic Car Restoration — restoration
29670 Bashan Rd
Racine, OH 45771
740-949-2217; FAX: 740-949-1957
E-mail: tbird@eurekanet.com

Shop open 8 am to 5 pm EST. Calls will be taken until 9 pm EST. High quality and concours restoration services for 1955 to 1957 Thunderbirds. Specializing in full body restoration, mechanical, electrical and upholstery. Award winning restorations. Over 23 years' experience. References furnished. Web site: www.hillsresto.com

Hollywood Classic Motorcars Inc — parts, restoration, service
363 Ansin Blvd
Hallandale, FL 33009
954-454-4641; FAX: 954-457-3801

Mail order and open shop. Monday-Friday 9 am to 4 pm. 1955-1966 Thunderbird; buy, sell, restore, repair, parts, service all years. Web site: www.t-bird.net

Bill Horton — vacuum motors
5804 Jones Valley Dr
Huntsville, AL 35802
256-881-6894

See full listing in **Section One** under **Mercury**

Joblot Automotive Inc — parts
Ford Parts Specialists
98-11 211th St
Queens Village, NY 11429
718-468-8585; FAX: 718-468-8686

See full listing in **Section One** under **Ford 1932-1953**

Dale King Obsolete Parts — parts
211 Hilltop Dr, PO Box 1099
Liberty, KY 42539
606-787-5031; FAX: 606-787-2130
E-mail: daleking@kih.net

See full listing in **Section One** under **Ford 1954-up**

Larry's Thunderbird and Mustang Parts — parts
511 S Raymond Ave
Fullerton, CA 92831
800-854-0393 orders
714-871-6432; FAX: 714-871-1883

Mail order and open shop. Monday-Friday 8 am to 6 pm, Saturday 9 am to 1 pm. Specializing in restoration parts and accessories for 1965-1973 Mustangs and 1955-1966 Thunderbirds. In business over 30 years supplying Mustang and Thunderbird enthusiasts with extensive product lines of restoration parts. Offer excellent pricing and availability, with most orders shipped out the same day.

Lincoln Parts International — parts
707 E 4th St, Bldg G
Perris, CA 92570
800-382-1656, 909-657-5588
FAX: 909-657-4758
E-mail: lincolnparts@pe.net

See full listing in **Section One** under **Lincoln**

Ed Liukkonen — accessories, parts
37 Cook Rd
Templeton, MA 01468
978-939-8126

See full listing in **Section One** under **Ford 1954-up**

Long Island Mustang Restoration Parts — convertible specialist, rebuilding services, reconditioned consoles 1965-1970, repro parts
168 Silverleaf Ln
Islandia, NY 11722
516-232-2388; FAX: 516-272-5201
E-mail: tom@l-i-mustang.com

See full listing in **Section One** under **Mustang**

McDonald Obsolete Parts Company — body parts, chassis parts
6458 W Eureka Rd
Rockport, IN 47635
800-897-8693 orders (w/part # only),
812-359-4965; FAX: 812-359-5555
E-mail: mcdonald@psci.net

See full listing in **Section One** under **Ford 1954-up**

Mean Mustang Supply Inc — parts
201 D St
South Charleston, WV 25303
304-746-0300; FAX: 304-746-0395
E-mail: meanstang@aol.com

See full listing in **Section One** under **Mustang**

Mustang Service Center — parts, service
11610 Vanowen St
North Hollywood, CA 91605
818-765-1196; FAX: 818-765-1349
E-mail: bo@mustangservicecenter.com

See full listing in **Section One** under **Mustang**

Mustangs & More	**parts**
2065 Sperry Ave #C	**restoration**
Ventura, CA 93003	
800-356-6573; FAX: 805-642-6468	
E-mail: mustmore@aol.com	

See full listing in **Section One** under **Mustang**

Mustangs Plus Inc	**racing products**
2353 N Wilson Way	**restoration**
Stockton, CA 95205	
800-999-4289; FAX: 209-944-9980	

See full listing in **Section One** under **Mustang**

National Parts Depot	**accessories**
900 SW 38th Ave	**parts**
Ocala, FL 34474	
800-874-7595; FAX: 352-861-8706	

See full listing in **Section One** under **Mustang**

Obsolete Ford Parts Inc	**parts**
8701 S I-35	
Oklahoma City, OK 73149	
405-631-3933; FAX: 405-634-6815	
E-mail: info@obsoletefordparts.com	

See full listing in **Section One** under **Ford 1954-up**

Older Car Restoration	**repro parts**
Martin Lum, Owner	**restoration**
304 S Main St, Box 428	
Mont Alto, PA 17237	
717-749-3383, 717-352-7701	
E-mail: marty@oldercar.com	

See full listing in **Section Two** under **restoration shops**

Original Falcon, Comet, Ranchero,	**interiors**
Fairlane Interiors	**parts**
6343 Seaview Ave NW	**weatherstripping**
Seattle, WA 98107-2664	
888-609-2363 toll free;	
FAX: 206-781-5046	
E-mail: falcon@evergo.net	

See full listing in **Section One** under **Ford 1954-up**

Prestige Thunderbird Inc	**appraisals**
10215 Greenleaf Ave	**radios**
Santa Fe Springs, CA 90670	**repairs**
800-423-4751, 562-944-6237	**restorations**
FAX: 562-941-8677	**tires**
E-mail: tbirds@prestigethunderbird.com	

Mail order and open shop. Monday-Friday 8 am to 5:30 pm, Saturday 8:30 am to 4 pm. Specializes in 1955-1957 Thunderbirds. Offers parts, radios, air conditioners, tires and appraisals, along with restorations and car sales. Parts catalog, $2. Web site: www.prestigethunderbird.com

PV Antique & Classic Ford	**parts**
1688 Main St	
Tewksbury, MA 01876	
800-MSTANGS orders only	
978-851-9159; FAX: 978-858-3827	
E-mail: pvford@flash.net	

See full listing in **Section One** under **Ford 1903-1931**

William H Randel	**appraisals**
PO Box 173	**car locators**
Hatboro, PA 19040	
215-675-8969; FAX: 215-441-0960	
E-mail: tbrdnut@bellatlantic.net	

Mail order and open shop. Monday-Tuesday and Friday-Sunday 9 am to 9 pm. Specializing in locating and appraising for 1955-1957 classic Thunderbird automobiles.

Regal Roadsters Ltd	**replicars**
301 W Beltline Hwy	**restoration**
Madison, WI 53713	
PH/FAX: 608-273-4141	
E-mail: chuck@regaltbird.com	

Mail order and open shop. Monday-Friday 8 am to 5 pm. Specializing in the manufacture of the Regal T-Bird and the restoration of domestic and foreign collectibles. The Regal T-Bird is a full size, authentic, fiberglass bodied reproduction of the famed 1955 and 1956 Ford Thunderbird. We manufacture and sell a variety of kits for the hobbyist, ranging from exact reproductions to personalized street rod versions. Also handcraft turnkey Regal T-Birds to your exacting specifications and deliver worldwide. Also 1955 and 1956 T-Bird fiberglass bodies. Web site: www.regaltbird.com

Sanderson Ford	**parts**
Jim Ray	
6300 N 51 Ave	
Glendale, AZ 85301	
888-364-3673, 602-842-8663	
FAX: 602-842-8637	

See full listing in **Section One** under **Ford 1954-up**

Sixties Ford Parts	**books**
639 Glanker St	**new parts**
Memphis, TN 38112	**shop manuals**
PH/FAX: 901-323-2195, recorder	

See full listing in **Section One** under **Ford 1954-up**

Norman Sudeck Restorations	**restoration**
730 N Electric Ave	
Alhambra, CA 91801	
626-576-7004; FAX: 626-792-9937	

Open shop. Monday-Friday 9:30 am PST, evenings and weekends. You are welcome to visit our shop, please call in advance. High quality and concours restoration services for 1955 to 1957 Thunderbirds. Specializing in mechanical and electrical work plus upholstery. Friendly, knowledgeable staff. Over 25 years' experience, references available.

Sunyaks	**NOS parts**
PO Box 498	**upholstery**
Bound Brook, NJ 08805	**used parts**
908-356-0600	

Mail order and open shop. Monday-Saturday 10 am to 10 pm. Specializing in NOS and restored hard to get parts for 1955-1957 Thunderbirds. Over 1,800 items in our catalog. Specializing in convertible top frames, hardtops, original power steering units, power brakes, power windows, and power seat assemblies, dual quads and NASCAR parts along with upholstery and continental kits. Appraisals, and technical help available.

T-Bird Sanctuary	**parts**
9998 SW Avery	
Tualatin, OR 97062	
503-692-9848; FAX: 503-692-9849	

Mail order and open shop. Monday-Friday 8:30 am to 4:30 pm, Saturday by appointment, closed Sunday, PST. Comprehensive source for NOS, used and reproduction parts for 1958-1979 Thunderbirds. Your T-Bird restoration specialist since 1966. Sheetmetal cut to order. Our parts cars come from the salt-free Northwest and are remarkably well preserved in our mild climate. Same day shipping on most orders. Call in your order on our toll free parts hotline: 800-275-2661.

T-Birds By Nick	**parts**
14649 Lanark St, Unit B	**repair**
Panorama City, CA 91402	
800-669-1961; FAX: 818-780-8493	
E-mail: mail@t-birdsbynick.com	

Mail order parts and repair shop. Monday-Friday 8 am to 5 pm. 18 years' repair experience on Ford Thunderbirds, 1958-1966. Huge inventory of new and used parts. Orders shipped worldwide. Visit our web site: www.t-birdsbynick.com

Section One – Marque Specialists

Tags Backeast	data plates
PO Box 581	trim tags
Plainville, CT 06062	cowl tags
860-747-2942	
E-mail: dataplt@snet.net	

See full listing in **Section Two** under **special services**

Thunderbird Center	parts
23610 John R St	
Hazel Park, MI 48030	
248-548-1721; FAX: 248-548-5531	
E-mail: tbirdcenter@sprintmail.com	

Monday-Friday 9 am to 5 pm. 1955-1956-1957 T-Bird parts
sales, NOS, used, new repro. Everything you may need. Web
site: www.thunderbirdcenter.com

Thunderbird, Falcon, Fairlane &	new repros
Comet Connections	parts
728 E Dunlap	used repros
Phoenix, AZ 85020	
602-997-9285; FAX: 602-997-0624	
E-mail: thunderbirdconn@aol.com	

Mail order and open shop. Monday-Friday 7:30 am to 5 pm,
Saturday 8:30 am to 12 pm MST. In business since 1972.
Specializing in the finest, new, used and reproduced items for
your 1958-1971 T-Birds, 1960-1970 Falcons and Comets and
1962-1969 Fairlanes. We offer only the finest in quality and service. Write for our catalog or call our order number: 800-TTT-
BIRD for your copy. Be sure to specify what model year you
require. All catalogs $3 each. Remember, one call does it all.

Thunderbird Headquarters	accessories
1080 Detroit Ave	literature
Concord, CA 94518	parts
925-825-9550 info; 925-689-1771	upholstery
800-227-2174 parts	
FAX: 800-964-1957 toll free	
E-mail: tbirdhq@tbirdhq.com	

Mail order and counter sales. Monday-Friday 8 am to 5 pm, Saturday 8 am to 11:30 am. Specializing in new and used parts
including rubber weatherstrip, convertible tops, literature, a
complete line of upholstery, carpets and accessories for 1955-
1966 Thunderbirds. Free catalog available on request. Web site:
www.tbirdhq.com

Thunderbird Information eXchange	newsletter
8421 E Cortez St	
Scottsdale, AZ 85260	
480-948-3996	

Specializing in the exchange of information about how to enjoy and
personalize 1989 to 1997 Thunderbird and Cougar automobiles.
The TIX package contains a newsletter with technical tips, want
ads, event listings, production figures and model comparisons. The
TIX package costs $10 (checks payable to Paul Cornell please).

Thunderbird Parts	parts
1051 Lincoln Ave	
Lockport, NY 14094	
800-289-2473, 716-741-2866	
FAX: 716-741-2868	
E-mail: mailmacs@aol.com	

Phone hours Monday-Friday 8 am to 11 pm, Saturday 8 am to 5
pm. Parts for big and small Birds. 1955-1957 free catalog with
184 pages; 1958-1966 free catalog with 240 pages. Web site:
www.macsautoparts.com

Thunderbirds East	parts
Andy Lovelace	restoration
140 Wilmington W Chester Pike	
Chadds Ford, PA 19317	
610-358-1021; FAX: 610-558-9615	

Mail order and open shop. Monday-Friday 8 am to 5 pm, Saturday 8
am to 12 noon. 1955-1956-1957 Thunderbirds and 1967-1980s
Thunderbird parts, new and used. Restorations, partial or complete.

White Post Restorations	brakes
One Old Car Dr, PO Drawer D	restoration
White Post, VA 22663	
540-837-1140; FAX: 540-837-2368	
E-mail: info@whitepost.com	

See full listing in **Section Two** under **brakes**

White Post Restorations	restoration
One Old Car Dr, PO Drawer D	
White Post, VA 22663	
540-837-1140; FAX: 540-837-2368	
E-mail: info@whitepost.com	

See full listing in **Section Two** under **restoration shops**

Pat Wilson's Thunderbird Parts	parts
375 Rt 94	
Fredon Township, NJ 07860	
888-262-1153; FAX: 973-579-2011	
E-mail: wilsontb@nac.net	

Mail order and open shop. Monday-Friday 9 am to 8 pm, Saturday 9 am to 5 pm. Specializing in selling, repairing and rebuilding
new and used Thunderbird parts for 1958-1966. We have rebuilt
seat and window motors. We buy, sell, trade parts and cars and
part out many cars. Member of ITC, VTCI and North Jersey
Thunderbird Club. We accept Visa, MasterCard, UPS COD. Call
or fax for free 2001 catalog. Web site: www.wilsontbird.com
See our ad on this page

Air Cooled Motors 2081 Madelaine Ct Los Altos, CA 94024 PH/FAX: 650-967-2908 E-mail: zmrmn@macconnect.com	car dealers information restoration

Specializing in the preservation and restoration of Franklin, Zimmerman automobiles.

JA Cooley Museum 4233 Park Blvd San Diego, CA 92103 619-296-3112	museum

See full listing in **Section Six** under **California**

Franklin Museum 3420 N Vine Ave Tucson, AZ 85719 520-326-8038 E-mail: hhff2@aol.com	museum

Open October 15-May, Wednesday-Friday 10 am to 4 pm or by appointment. Documents Franklin Company products 1892-1976, with 19 restored or original cars on display in a western desert setting with other make vehicles, art and automobilia. The Tom Hubbard collection of classic Franklins on exhibit. Web site: www.franklincar.org/foundation.htm

Hasslen Co 9581 Jeske Ave NW Annandale, MN 55302 320-274-5576	engine parts

New Franklin gasket sets, engine and trim parts. Series 13 and Series 14 through 16 and Olympic hubcaps. Series 10 reserve and supply fittings. Series 5 through 10 mufflers. Series 16 and 18 door handles. Timing chains for most Franklins, porcelain signs and more. Manufactures Franklin parts. Write your needs.

Hildene Historic Rt 7A, PO Box 377 Manchester, VT 05254 802-362-1788; FAX: 802-362-1564 E-mail: info@hildene.org	museum

See full listing in **Section Six** under **Vermont**

Northeast Classic Car Museum NYS Rt 23, 24 Rexford St Norwich, NY 13815 607-334-AUTO (2886) FAX: 607-336-6745 E-mail: info@classiccarmuseum.org	museum

See full listing in **Section Six** under **New York**

Odyssey Restorations Inc 8080 Central Ave NE Spring Lake Park, MN 55432 763-786-1518; FAX: 763-786-1524	parts restoration

See full listing in **Section Two** under **restoration shops**

A & M SoffSeal Inc 104 May Dr Harrison, OH 45030 800-426-0902 513-367-0028 service/info FAX: 513-367-5506 E-mail: soffseal@soffseal.com	rubber parts weatherstripping

See full listing in **Section Two** under **rubber parts**

American Classic Truck Parts PO Box 409 Aubrey, TX 76227 940-365-9786; FAX: 940-365-3419 E-mail: americanclassic@airmail.net	parts

See full listing in **Section One** under **Chevrolet**

Brothers Truck Parts 801 Parkridge Ave Corona, CA 92880 800-687-6672; FAX: 909-808-9788 E-mail: sales@brotherstrucks.com	accessories parts

See full listing in **Section Two** under **trucks & tractors**

Jim Carter's Antique Truck Parts 1508 E Alton Independence, MO 64055 800-336-1913; FAX: 800-262-3749 E-mail: jimcartertruckparts@ worldnet.att.net	truck parts

See full listing in **Section One** under **Chevrolet**

Chevy Duty Pickup Parts 1 Chevy Duty Dr Kansas City, MO 64150 816-741-8029; FAX: 816-741-5255 E-mail: orders@chevyduty.com	pickup parts

See full listing in **Section One** under **Chevrolet**

Classic Industries Inc Chevy/GMC Truck Parts and Accessories Catalog 17832 Gothard St Huntington Beach, CA 92647 800-854-1280 parts/info FAX: 800-300-3081 E-mail: info@classicindustries.com	accessories parts

See full listing in **Section One** under **Chevrolet**

Classic Performance Products 8341 Artesia Blvd, Unit C Buena Park, CA 90621 800-522-5004; FAX: 714-522-2500 E-mail: info@classicperform.com	brakes steering suspension

See full listing in **Section One** under **Chevrolet**

Dixie Truck Works 10495 Hwy 73 E Mount Pleasant, NC 28124 704-436-2407	parts

See full listing in **Section One** under **Chevrolet**

The Filling Station	literature
990 S Second St	parts
Lebanon, OR 97355-3227	
800-841-6622 orders	
541-258-2114; FAX: 541-258-6968	
E-mail: fssales@fillingstation.com	

See full listing in **Section One** under **Chevrolet**

Firewall Insulators & Quiet Ride Solutions	air plenums
6465 Pacific Ave, Ste 249	auto insulation
Stockton, CA 95207	firewall insulators
209-477-4840; FAX: 209-477-0918	gloveboxes
E-mail: timcox@quietride.com	sound deadening

See full listing in **Section Two** under **upholstery**

Gilbert's Early Chevy Pickup Parts	parts
470 West Rd 1 N	
Chino Valley, AZ 86323	
PH/FAX: 520-636-5337	
E-mail: gilb@goodnet.com	

See full listing in **Section One** under **Chevrolet**

Hamel's Automotive Inc	restorations
3306 Pleasant Ridge Rd	
Wingdale, NY 12594	
845-832-9454	
E-mail: startnagan@aol.com	

See full listing in **Section Two** under **restoration shops**

Hank's Custom Stepside Beds	pickup beds
12693 Clay Station Rd	
Herald, CA 95638	
209-748-2193; FAX: 209-748-2976	
E-mail: truckbeds@softcom.net	

See full listing in **Section Two** under **trucks & tractors**

Heavy Chevy Truck Parts	parts
17445 Heavy Chevy Rd, PO Box 650	
Siloam Springs, AR 72761	
501-524-9575	
FAX: 501-524-4873 or 800-317-2277	
E-mail: heavychevy@heavychevy.com	

See full listing in **Section One** under **Chevrolet**

Impala Bob's Inc	dash pads
4753 E Falcon Dr, Dept HCCA15	emblems
Mesa, AZ 85215	interior kits
800-IMPALAS orders	mechanical parts
480-924-4800 retail store	OEM tires
480-981-1600 office	restoration parts
FAX: 800-716-6237, 480-981-1675	rubber parts
E-mail: info@impalas.com	wiring harnesses

See full listing in **Section One** under **Chevrolet**

LMC Truck	accessories
PO Box 14991	parts
Lenexa, KS 66285	
800-222-5664; FAX: 913-599-0323	

See full listing in **Section One** under **Chevrolet**

Majestic Truck Parts	parts
17726 Dickerson	
Dallas, TX 75252	
972-248-6245; FAX: 972-380-8913	
E-mail: majestictrk@juno.com	

See full listing in **Section One** under **Chevrolet**

Old GMC Trucks.Com	literature
Robert English	parts
PO Box 675	
Franklin, MA 02038-0675	
508-520-3900; FAX: 508-520-7861	
E-mail: oldcarkook@aol.com	

Mail order and open shop. Monday-Friday 9 am to 5 pm. GMC truck parts, NOS, NORS, used, literature, factory training films and materials for pre-1955 GMC light and medium duty. GMC only. 1947-1955 GMC Technical Advisor, National Chevy/GMC Truck Association. Licensed copyright for General Motors. Ship via UPS daily, worldwide. Web site: www.oldgmctrucks.com

Paul's Select Cars & Parts for Porsche®	cars
2280 Gail Dr	parts
Riverside, CA 92509	
909-685-9340; FAX: 909-685-9342	
E-mail: pauls356-s90@webtv.net	

See full listing in **Section One** under **Porsche**

Peninsula Restoration Parts	parts
4526 Viewmont Ave	
Victoria, BC Canada V8L 4L9	
250-727-2678; FAX: 250-727-2693	
E-mail: info@peninsularestoration.com	

See full listing in **Section One** under **Chevrolet**

Scotts Super Trucks	parts
1972 Hwy 592 W	
Penhold, AB Canada T0M 1R0	
403-886-5572; FAX: 403-886-5577	
E-mail: info@scottssupertrucks.com	

See full listing in **Section One** under **Chevrolet**

Trim Parts Inc	trim items
5161 Wolfpen Pleasant Hill	
Milford, OH 45150	
513-831-1472; FAX: 513-248-3402	
E-mail: sales@trimparts.com	

See full listing in **Section One** under **Chevrolet**

The Truck Shop	parts
104 W Marion Ave, PO Box 5035	
Nashville, GA 31639	
800-245-0556 orders	
info: 229-686-3833, 229-686-3396	
FAX: 229-686-3531	

See full listing in **Section One** under **Chevrolet**

GRAHAM

Firewall Insulators & Quiet Ride Solutions	air plenums
6465 Pacific Ave, Ste 249	auto insulation
Stockton, CA 95207	firewall insulators
209-477-4840; FAX: 209-477-0918	gloveboxes
E-mail: timcox@quietride.com	sound deadening

See full listing in **Section Two** under **upholstery**

Antique Motorcycle Restoration | restorations
14611 N Nebraska Ave
Tampa, FL 33613
813-979-9762; FAX: 813-979-9475

Restorations for Harley-Davidson 1936 Knuckleheads.

B & B Cylinder Head Inc | cylinder heads
320 Washington St
West Warwick, RI 02893
401-828-4900; FAX: 401-381-0010
E-mail: bbcyl@choiceone.net

See full listing in **Section Two** under **engine parts**

Bentley Publishers | books manuals
1734 Massachusetts Ave
Cambridge, MA 02138-1804
800-423-4595; FAX: 617-876-9235
E-mail: sales@rb.com

See full listing in **Section Four** under **books & publications**

Francois Bruere | artwork
8 Avenue Olivier Heuze
LeMans 72000 France
(33) 02-4377-1877
FAX: (33) 02-4324-2038
E-mail: francois.bruere@orpheograff.com

See full listing in **Section Two** under **artwork**

Charleston Custom Cycle | parts
211 Washington St
Charleston, IL 61920
217-345-2577; FAX: 217-345-4779

Mail order and open shop. Monday-Friday 10 am to 6 pm, Saturday 10 am to 3 pm. Specializing in NOS parts for Harley-Davidson motorcycles, snowmobiles, golf carts, 1948-1990.

Distinctive Metal Polishing | metal polishing parts
18328 Gault St
Reseda, CA 91335
818-344-2160; FAX: 818-344-8029

Mail order and open shop. Tuesday-Friday 7 am to 5 pm, Monday and Saturday by appointment. Specializing in classic car moldings, automotive parts, marine, aviation, motorcycles. Over 10 years in the custom and production areas. We have automotive and marine price lists as well as Harley-Davidson price lists. Web site: www.dmpolish.com

Geeson Bros Motorcycle Museum & Workshop | museum
2-6 Water Ln
South Witham
Grantham Lincs NG33 5PH England
01572 767280, 01572 768195

See full listing in **Section Six** under **England**

H D Garage | appraisals artwork literature motorcycles
Barry Brown
Comp 8 Bedford Mills RR #2
Westport, ON Canada K0G 1X0
613-273-5036
E-mail: bruffsup@hotmail.com or oldmill@rideau.net

See full listing in **Section Two** under **motorcycles**

Hi-Speed | literature motorcycles parts
John Steel
PO Box 44
Chagrin Falls, OH 44022
PH/FAX: 440-247-6021

Specializing in Harley-Davidson factory limited production racers. XR-750, XRTT, KR, KRTT, VR, RR, MX, CR, CRTT, CRS, WR, XLR, KRTT, ERS, Baja, MX, XLCR, XR-1000 and all others. Complete literature: manuals, sales brochures, parts books, service books, articles, parts, all restoration parts. Videos, restoration, racing. Complete newsletter for all Harley racers. Web site: www.hi-speedmotorcycles.com

Kick-Start Motorcycle Parts Inc | parts
PO Box 9347
Wyoming, MI 49509
616-245-8991

Mail order only. Specializing in rebuilding, replacement and restoration parts for Harley-Davidson flathead and Knucklehead machines, 1929-1973. 272-page catalog, $5.

Liberty Harley-Davidson | accessories parts service
32 E Cuyahoga Falls Ave
Akron, OH 44310
330-535-9900; FAX: 330-535-2354
E-mail: libertyhd@hotmail.com

Open shop. Monday, Wednesday 9 am to 8 pm, Tuesday, Thursday-Friday 9 am to 6 pm, Saturday 9 am to 4 pm, Sunday 10 am to 3 pm. Parts, accessories, motor clothes, service for Harley-Davidson motorcycles. All years, all models. Web site: www.libertyhd.com

Luback & Co | parts
456 W Lincoln Hwy
Chicago Heights, IL 60411-2463
708-481-9685; FAX: 708-481-5837
E-mail: lubackco@aol.com

See full listing in **Section Two** under **motorcycles**

Mid-America Auctions | auctions
2277 W Hwy 36, Ste 324
St Paul, MN 55113
651-633-9655; FAX: 651-633-3212
E-mail: midauction@aol.com

See full listing in **Section Two** under **auctions & shows**

Sammy Miller Motorcycle Museum | museum
Bashley Cross Rd
New Milton
Hampshire BH25 5SZ England
01425 620777; FAX: 01425 619696

See full listing in **Section Six** under **England**

Moto Italia | parts
1060 Petaluma Blvd N
Petaluma, CA 94952
PH/FAX: 707-763-1982

Mail order and open shop. Monday-Friday 8 am to 6 pm, Saturday 9 am to 2 pm. Specializing in parts for Harley-Davidson motorcycles made in Italy from 1961-1978. Model Sprints and two-strokes from 50cc to 250cc. Web site: www.aa.net/~garage/motoital.html

Sturgis Motorcycle Museum and Hall of Fame PO Box 602 Sturgis, SD 57785 605-347-0849; FAX: 605-423-5225 E-mail: sturgismotorcyclemuseum@yahoo.com	museum

See full listing in **Section Six** under **South Dakota**

TK Performance Inc 1508 N Harlan Ave Evansville, IN 47711 812-422-6820; FAX: 812-422-5282	engine building machine work restoration

Mail order and open shop. Monday-Friday 8 am to 5 pm, Saturday 9 am to 1 pm. Complete engine and chassis component building for Harley-Davidsons, all years, makes and models. Ground-up restorations, custom fabricating and machining of parts, complete fabrication of drag bikes and custom show pieces.

USAopoly Inc 565 Westlake St Encinitas, CA 92024 760-634-5910; FAX: 760-634-5923 E-mail: christian@usaopoly.com	Monopoly® game

See full listing in **Section Two** under **models & toys**

Blackhawk Collection 1092 Eagles Nest Pl Danville, CA 94506-3600 925-736-3444; FAX: 925-736-4375 E-mail: info@blackhawkcollection.com	acquisitions sales

See full listing in **Section One** under **Duesenberg**

HONDA

600 Headquarters Miles Chappell PO Box 1262 Felton, CA 95018 831-335-4647 E-mail: z600guru@ix.netcom.com	advice parts service

Mail order and weekend appointments only. Specializing in 1970-1972 Honda 600 sedan and coupe. New and used parts, reproduction parts, hydraulics specialist, free advice since 1981. No COD or credit cards accepted. Look up my Honda 600 part auctions on eBay, user name honda600. Paypal accepted. Web site: www.600miles.com

CSi 1100 S Raymond Ave, Ste H Fullerton, CA 92831 714-879-7955; FAX: 714-879-7310 E-mail: csila@compuserve.com	parts

See full listing in **Section One** under **BMW**

Sammy Miller Motorcycle Museum Bashley Cross Rd New Milton Hampshire BH25 5SZ England 01425 620777; FAX: 01425 619696	museum

See full listing in **Section Six** under **England**

Neuspeed 3300 Corte Manpaso Camarillo, CA 93012 805-388-7171; FAX: 805-388-0030	parts

See full listing in **Section One** under **Audi**

Vintage Auto LLC 605 Pine Knoll Dr Greenville, SC 29609 864-292-8785; FAX: 864-244-5244 E-mail: vintagevuu@aol.com	new/used parts service

See full listing in **Section One** under **Volkswagen**

Wm Albright's Vintage Coach 16593 Arrow Blvd Fontana, CA 92335 909-823-9168, 909-823-0690	car dealer NOS & repro parts tires used parts

Mail order and open shop. Open by appointment only. 30 years same location. Specializing in Hudson, Essex & Terraplane cars. 30 years same business. Also Denman wide white tires. 35 Hudson-Essex-Terraplane cars in inventory. Hudson built cars and parts, restore, buy and sell.

Firewall Insulators & Quiet Ride Solutions 6465 Pacific Ave, Ste 249 Stockton, CA 95207 209-477-4840; FAX: 209-477-0918 E-mail: timcox@quietride.com	air plenums auto insulation firewall insulators gloveboxes sound deadening

See full listing in **Section Two** under **upholstery**

Hudson Motor Car Co Memorabilia Ken Poynter 19638 Huntington Harper Woods, MI 48225 313-886-9292	literature memorabilia novelties signs

Mail order only. Collector of anything pertaining to Hudson, Essex, Terraplane and Dover. Trade and sell duplicates.

K-GAP Automotive Parts PO Box 3065 Santa Fe Springs, CA 90670 PH/FAX: 714-523-0403	repro parts

Hudson, Essex, Terraplane authentic reproduction parts, made in the USA, featuring the products of Metro Moulded Parts. Weatherstrip, runningboard mats, lenses, accessories for 1929-1957. For catalog of parts available, send $2 (refundable with order).

LaCarrera-The Mexican Road Race PO Box 1605 Studio City, CA 91614 323-464-5720; FAX: 323-656-7111 E-mail: lacarrera@earthlink.net	road race

See full listing in **Section Two** under **racing**

Webb's Classic Auto Parts 5084 W State Rd 114 Huntington, IN 46750 219-344-1714; FAX: 219-344-1754	**NOS parts** **reproduction parts** **service manuals** **used parts**

See full listing in **Section One** under **AMC**

Wenner's 5449 Tannery Rd Schnecksville, PA 18078 610-799-5419	**NOS parts**

See full listing in **Section One** under **AMC**

Firewall Insulators & Quiet Ride Solutions 6465 Pacific Ave, Ste 249 Stockton, CA 95207 209-477-4840; FAX: 209-477-0918 E-mail: timcox@quietride.com	**air plenums** **auto insulation** **firewall insulators** **gloveboxes** **sound deadening**

See full listing in **Section Two** under **upholstery**

Charles Noe 64-1/2 Greenwood Ave Bethel, CT 06801 PH/FAX: 203-748-4222 E-mail: mdchas@aol.com	**broker** **parts/auto** **purchases** **parts/auto sales**

See full listing in **Section Two** under **brokers**

Quality Tire Barn Inc 255 Twinsburg Rd Northfield, OH 44067 330-467-1284; FAX: 330-467-1289 (call first) E-mail: donquist@aol.com	**tires**

See full listing in **Section Two** under **tires**

Geeson Bros Motorcycle Museum & Workshop 2-6 Water Ln South Witham Grantham Lincs NG33 5PH England 01572 767280, 01572 768195	**museum**

See full listing in **Section Six** under **England**

H D Garage Barry Brown Comp 8 Bedford Mills RR #2 Westport, ON Canada K0G 1X0 613-273-5036 E-mail: bruffsup@hotmail.com or oldmill@rideau.net	**appraisals** **artwork** **literature** **motorcycles**

See full listing in **Section Two** under **motorcycles**

Kiwi Indian Parts 17399 Sage Ave Riverside, CA 92504 909-780-5400; FAX: 909-780-7722 E-mail: indian@kiwi-indian.com	**parts**

Manufacturers of reproduction parts for Indian motorcycles.
Web site: www.kiwi-indian.com/

Sammy Miller Motorcycle Museum Bashley Cross Rd New Milton Hampshire BH25 5SZ England 01425 620777; FAX: 01425 619696	**museum**

See full listing in **Section Six** under **England**

Randal Aagaard 4207 S 2300 E Salt Lake City, UT 84124 801-272-9979; FAX: 801-273-1742 E-mail: aagaard@netzero.net	**Jaguar**

Mail order only. Specializing in Jaguar and SS 1974 and older.

Dick Ames Stainless Steel Exhaust 4850 Fallcrest Cir Sarasota, FL 34233 941-923-8321; FAX: 941-923-9434 E-mail: dickamesfl@aol.com	**exhaust systems**

Mail order only. Specializing in stainless steel exhaust systems
made in England for Jaguars and Aston Martins. See monthly
ads in *Hemmings*.

The Antique Auto Shop 603 Lytle Ave Elsmere, KY 41018 859-342-8363; FAX: 859-342-9076 E-mail: antaut@aol.com	**brake lines** **brake parts** **weatherstripping**

See full listing in **Section Two** under **brakes**

Apple Hydraulics Inc 1610 Middle Rd Calverton, NY 11933-1419 800-882-7753, 631-369-9515 FAX: 631-369-9516 E-mail: info@applehydraulics.com	**brake rebuilding** **shock rebuilding**

See full listing in **Section Two** under **suspension parts**

Ashton Keynes Vintage Restorations Ltd A Keith Bowley Ashton Keynes, Swindon Wilshire England 01285-861-288; FAX: 01285-860-604	**coachbuilding** **restoration**

See full listing in **Section One** under **Rolls-Royce/Bentley**

Asom Electric 1204 McClellan Dr Los Angeles, CA 90025 310-820-4457; FAX: 310-820-5908	**electrical systems** **rebuilding**

See full listing in **Section Two** under **electrical systems**

Atlantic Enterprises
221 Strand Industrial Dr
Little River, SC 29566
843-399-7565; FAX: 843-399-4600
E-mail: steering@atlantic-ent.com

steering assemblies

See full listing in **Section Two** under **chassis parts**

The Auto Doctor Inc
23125 Telegraph Rd
Southfield, MI 48034
248-355-1505; FAX: 248-355-3460

mechanical parts
service repairs

See full listing in **Section One** under **BMW**

Autosport Inc
2110 W Vernal Pk
Bloomington, IN 47404
812-334-1700; FAX: 812-334-1712

restoration

See full listing in **Section One** under **MG**

BAS Ltd Jaguar Trim Specialist
250 H St, PMB 3000
Blaine, WA 98231
800-661-5377; FAX: 640-990-9988
E-mail: basjag@telus.net

interior parts

Mail order only. Specializing in interior products from the smallest seal to complete interior kits for all Jaguar motor cars, XK to XJ.

Bassett's Jaguar
53 Stilson Rd, PO Box 245
Wyoming, RI 02898
401-539-3010; FAX: 401-539-7861
E-mail: jagwillie@ids.net

parts
restoration
service
upholstery

Mail order and open shop. Monday to Friday 8 am to 5 pm. Specializing in parts, upholstery, restoration and service for Jaguars 1949-present. Also offer our services on other exotic types of cars.

BCP Sport & Classic Co
10525 Airline Dr
Houston, TX 77037
281-448-4739; FAX: 281-448-0189

parts
service

See full listing in **Section One** under **MG**

Best of Britain
RR 1 Box 33
South Ryegate, VT 05069
802-429-2266

car dealer
restoration

Open daily 9 am to 5 pm. Licensed dealer, handling XKEs exclusively. Purchases, sales and complete restoration for XKE Series I, II, III.

BMC Classics Inc
828 N Dixie Freeway
New Smyrna Beach, FL 32168
PH/FAX: 386-426-6405
E-mail: bmcar1@aol.com

parts
repair
restoration

See full listing in **Section Two** under **restoration shops**

BritBooks
PO Box 321
Otego, NY 13825
PH/FAX: 607-988-7956
E-mail: britbooks@britbooks.com

books

See full listing in **Section Four** under **books & publications**

British Auto Parts Ltd
93256 Holland Ln
Marcola, OR 97454
541-933-2880; FAX: 541-933-2302

parts

See full listing in **Section One** under **Morris**

British Auto Shoppe
1909 5th Ave
Moline, IL 61265
309-764-9513; FAX: 309-764-9576

parts
service

See full listing in **Section One** under **MG**

British Auto/USA
92 Londonderry Tpke
Manchester, NH 03104
603-622-1050, 800-452-4787
FAX: 603-622-0849
E-mail: jaguar@britishautousa

parts
upholstery

Mail order and retail store. Monday-Friday 8 am to 5 pm, Saturday 9 am to 12 pm. Large selection of parts and upholstery for all post-war Jaguars. Brake and suspension upgrades also. Part of the SNG Barratt Group. Web site: www.britishautousa.com

British Car Keys
Rt 144 Box 9957
Ellicott City, MD 21042-3647
410-750-2352
E-mail: britishcarkeys@hotmail.com

keys

See full listing in **Section One** under **Austin-Healey**

British Car Magazine
343 Second St, Ste H
Los Altos, CA 94022-3639
650-949-9680; FAX: 650-949-9685
E-mail: editor@britishcar.com

periodical

See full listing in **Section Four** under **periodicals**

British Luxury Automotive Parts
257 Niagara St
Toronto ON Canada M6J 2L7
416-693-8400; FAX: 416-694-3202
Cell: 416-820-4323

new and used parts

Specializing in Jaguar, Rolls-Royce, Aston Martin, Lotus and Range Rover. Alternative soure of new or pre-owned parts, accessories and performance. Used parts of all kinds from engine, a/c, suspension, electrical, body and interior trim. We have leather and wooden pieces that will match yours better than new. Wheels used and new, spoke, disc and alloy in many sizes. All wheels are available as 1 or sets of 4. Please feel free to call for any piece however small. We will be most happy to serve you.

British Miles
9278 Old E Tyburn Rd
Morrisville, PA 19067
215-736-9300; FAX: 215-736-3089

accessories
literature
parts
restoration

See full listing in **Section One** under **MG**

British Motor Co
3825 W 11th Ave
Eugene, OR 97402
800-995-1895; FAX: 541-485-8544

engine rebuilding

Mail order and open shop. Monday-Friday 8 am to 5:30 pm. Specializing in all Jaguar model engine rebuilding. At BMC we understand your desire for the best workmanship available. We use factory parts and commit the time and care necessary to do a superior engine rebuild. Please call if you would like references from some of our satisfied customers.

British Parts International
8101 Hempstead Rd
Houston, TX 77008
800-231-6563 ext 570
FAX: 713-863-8238
E-mail: info@britishparts.com

parts

Since 1982, a leading source of new OEM, NOS, aftermarket, remanufactured and used or salvaged wholesale British car parts for automotive jobbers and installers. Online catalog by make, model and year with pictures of parts. Exclusive US distributor and service agent for Autologic independent Land Rover diagnostic systems. Web site: www.britishparts.com

British Racing Green 30 Aleph Dr Newark, DE 19702 302-368-1117; FAX: 302-368-5910 E-mail: info@brgparts.com	new parts rebuilt parts used parts

See full listing in **Section One** under **MG**

British Restorations 4455 Paul St Philadelphia, PA 19124 215-533-6696	car dealer restoration

Open shop only. Monday-Friday 8 am to 6 pm. Total restoration, including body, mechanical, wood, interior, etc, of all sports and classic cars. Specializing in Jaguars from 1948-1987. Also buys and sells sports and classic cars.

British Sportscars & Classics 4225 Aurora N Seattle, WA 98103-7307 206-634-3990	conversion kits engines transmissions

Mail order and open shop. Monday-Saturday 8:30 am to 5:30 pm. Various conversion kits and installations including 5-speed transmissions, engines, rack and pinion steering, and uprated brakes. Many performance enhancements for original components are available and being developed continuously. All British marques covered but custom conversions of any type considered. Web site: www.britishsportscarsandclassics.com

Francois Bruere 8 Avenue Olivier Heuze LeMans 72000 France (33) 02-4377-1877 FAX: (33) 02-4324-2038 E-mail: francois.bruere@ orpheograff.com	artwork

See full listing in **Section Two** under **artwork**

Bud's Parts for Classic Mercedes-Benz 9130 Hwy 5 Douglasville, GA 30134 800-942-8444; FAX: 770-942-8400	parts restoration service

See full listing in **Section One** under **Mercedes-Benz**

City Imports Ltd 166 Penrod Ct Glen Burnie, MD 21061 410-768-6660; FAX: 410-768-5955 E-mail: cityimports@worldnet.att.net	bodywork car sales restorations

Dealing in the following: Jaguar, MG, Triumph, Rolls-Royce, Bentley, BMW, Mercedes-Benz, Saab, Range Rover. Bodywork, restoration, car sales, regular maintenance. 22 years in the business. Experienced staff mechanics. Web site: www.cityimports.com

Classic Auto Restoration 15445 Ventura Blvd #60 Sherman Oaks, CA 91413 818-905-6267; FAX: 818-906-1249 E-mail: rollsroyce1@earthlink.net	acquisitions restoration sales

See full listing in **Section One** under **Rolls-Royce/Bentley**

Classic Jaguar 9916 Hwy 290 W Austin, TX 78736 512-288-8800; FAX: 512-288-9216 E-mail: danmooney@classicjaguar.com	parts technical support

Mail order and open shop. Monday-Friday 8 am to 5 pm. Classic Jaguar provides Jaguar owners around the world with superla-

tive products and unparalleled levels of customer service and technical support. Web site: www.classicjaguar.com

See our ad on page 112

Classic Showcase 913 Rancheros Dr San Marcos, CA 92069 760-747-9947 restoration/buying 760-747-3188 sales; FAX: 760-747-4021 E-mail: management@ classicshowcase.com	classic vehicles restorations sales

See full listing in **Section Two** under **restoration shops**

Collectors Choice LTD 6400 Springfield-Lodi Rd Dane, WI 53529 608-849-9878; FAX: 608-849-9879 E-mail: collectorschoice1@prodigy.net	parts race preparation restoration service

See full listing in **Section One** under **DeTomaso/Pantera**

Tom Crook Classic Cars 27611 42nd Ave S Auburn, WA 98001 253-941-3454	car dealer

See full listing in **Section Two** under **car dealers**

Dave's Auto Restoration 2285 Rt 307 E Jefferson, OH 44047 PH/FAX: 216-858-2227 E-mail: davesauto@knownet.net	upholstery restoration

See full listing in **Section Two** under **interiors & interior parts**

Doc's Jags 125 Baker Rd Lake Bluff, IL 60044 847-367-5247; FAX: 847-367-6363 E-mail: doc@docsjags.com	appraisals interiors restoration

Open Monday-Sunday by appointment. From January-May each year: Doc's Jags, 7965 E Cholla St, Scottsdale, AZ 85260, PH: 480-951-0777, FAX: 480-951-3339. Largest classic Jaguar selection for sale in the world. All conditions, all models. Restore and maintain all Jaguars. Insurance appraisals are available as well as "expert witness" testimony. Also sell the finest Jaguar Connolly leather interiors in the world. Do NOT sell parts. Web site: www.docsjags.com

Doctor Jaguar Inc 740 W 16th St Costa Mesa, CA 92627 949-646-2816; FAX: 949-574-8097	restoration service

Mail order and open shop. Monday-Friday 8:30 am to 5:30 pm PST. Service, restoration and used parts for all years Jaguar.

Donovan Motorcar Service Inc 4 Holmes Rd Lenox, MA 01240 413-499-6000; FAX: 413-499-6699 E-mail: donmtcar@aol.com	race prep restoration service

Mail order and open shop. Monday-Saturday 8 am to 5:30 pm. Specializing in Jaguar restoration, service and performance improvements. Also all British cars restoration and service. Vintage race preparation and support. Engine machining and rebuilding, foreign and domestic.

Doug's British Car Parts 2487 E Colorado Blvd Pasadena, CA 91107 818-793-2494; FAX: 818-793-4339 E-mail: dougsbritish@msn.com	accessories parts

Mail order and open shop Monday-Saturday 8:30 am to 6 pm. Specializing in new and used auto parts and accessories including

Jaguar XK 120 and Mk VII through XKE, 3.8 Mk II, XJ6, 12, S; MG T Series through MGA to MGB, Midget, Triumph TR2-8, Spitfire, GT6, Austin-Healey 100-4/3000 Mk III BJ8; Rover 2000 TC, 3500S and 1980 3500, Sunbeam Alpine, Hillman and Range Rover.

Doug's British Car Parts 606 Pub St Galloway, OH 43119 614-878-6373; FAX: 614-688-3077 E-mail: braden.13@osu.edu	accessories parts

See full listing in **Section One** under **Triumph**

East Coast Jaguar 802B Naaman's Rd Wilmington, DE 19810 302-475-7200; FAX: 302-475-9258 E-mail: ecjaguar@aol.com	parts service

Mail order and open shop. Monday-Friday 8:30 am to 5:30 pm. Specializing in parts and service for Jaguar XKs to XJs. Deals in remanufactured water pumps and wiper motors for Austin-Healey, BMW, Ferrari, Jaguar/Daimler, Maserati, MG, Mercedes, Morgan, Porsche, Rolls-Royce/Bentley, Rover, Triumph and all European cars.

Eddie's Restorations 4725 Rt 30 Elwood, NJ 08217 609-965-2211	restoration

Shop open Monday-Friday 9 am to 5 pm. Restorations on classic imports, Jaguar XK 120, XK 140, XK 150 and XKE in particular, to factory new specifications, using new metal panels and new parts for rebuilding mechanical components.

English Auto 501 Mt Ephraim Rd Searsport, ME 04974 207-548-2946; FAX: 207-548-6470 E-mail: eauto@mint.net	restoration

See full listing in **Section One** under **Austin-Healey**

European Collectibles Inc 1974 Placentia Ave Costa Mesa, CA 92627-3421 949-650-4718; FAX: 949-650-5881 E-mail: europeancollectibles@ pacbell.net	restoration sales service

See full listing in **Section Two** under **car dealers**

The Fine Car Store 1105 Moana Dr San Diego, CA 92107 619-223-7766; FAX: 619-223-6838	car dealer

See full listing in **Section One** under **Ferrari**

Finish Line 3593 SW 173rd Terr Miramar, FL 33029 954-436-9101; FAX: 954-436-9102 E-mail: e.alibrandi@att.net	parts supplies

See full listing in **Section One** under **Cobra**

Gran Turismo Jaguar 4285 Main St Perry, OH 44081 440-259-5656; FAX: 440-259-5588 E-mail: sales@gtjaguar.com	engine rebuilding performance parts service

Mail order only. The world's largest Jaguar high-performance leader, with 36 years of success, featuring street and race performance parts and services for all Jaguar models from the 1940s-1990s including: 6-speed transmission kits; aluminum flywheels and clutches; suspension, brake and exhaust system upgrades; complete cylinder head and engine rebuilding; engine dynamometer testing; cams and cranks; air, fuel and oil system improvements; excellent customer service. Complete catalog and video available. Web site: www.gtjaguar.com

Section One – Marque Specialists

Grand Prix Classics Inc	racing cars
7456 La Jolla Blvd	sports cars
La Jolla, CA 92037	
858-459-3500; FAX: 858-459-3512	
E-mail: info@grandprixclassics.com	

See full listing in **Section Two** under **racing**

Hastings Enterprises	electrical parts
PO Box 208	
Hampton, VA 23669	
FAX: 757-722-7349	
E-mail: johnh@apluslodging.com	

See full listing in **Section Two** under **electrical systems**

Highway One Classic Automobiles and Highwayone.com	classic automobiles
1035 California Dr	
Burlingame, CA 94010	
650-342-7340; FAX: 650-343-0150	
E-mail: djboscacci@msn.com	

See full listing in **Section One** under **Abarth**

Italy's Famous Exhaust	exhaust systems
2711 183rd St	wheels
Redondo Beach, CA 90278	
E-mail: johnt@famousexhaust.com	

See full listing in **Section Two** under **exhaust systems**

Jaguar Car Keys	original British
9957 Frederick Rd	keys
Ellicott City, MD 21042-3647	
410-750-2352	
E-mail: petegroh@yahoo.com	

Mail order only. Specializing in original British keys for Austin-Healey, Austin, Hillman, Jaguar, Morris, MG, Singer, Triumph, Volvo, Vauxhall and Nash Metropolitan. Wilmot Breeden keys, FRN, FA, FP, FS and FT, letters and number on side of key, $12 each. Rubber headed keys, WASO and British Leyland L swirl keys, $14 each. Can cut by code based on number on ignition switch or three numbers on trunk stem. American key blanks, cost $6 single sided key and $9 for double sided key. All inquiries include a SASE with your daytime telephone number. Web site: www.geocities.com/motorcity/flats/7843/

Jaguar Cars Archives	research
555 MacArthur Blvd	
Mahwah, NJ 07430	
201-818-8144; FAX: 201-818-0281	

See full listing in **Section Four** under **information sources**

Jaguar Heaven	parts
1433 Tillie Lewis Dr	
Stockton, CA 95206	
209-942-4524; FAX: 209-942-3670	

Mail order and open shop. Monday-Friday 8:30 am to 5 pm PST. Specializing in parts for Jaguar cars, Land Rovers and Range Rovers. Web site: www.jaguarheaven.com

Jaguar of Puerto Rico Inc	car dealer
PO Box 13055	parts
San Juan, PR 00908-3055	service
787-723-5177; FAX: 787-723-9488	
E-mail: jaguarpr@hotmail.com	

Open shop only. Monday-Friday 8 am to 6 pm, Saturday 9 am to 4 pm. New Jaguar sales. Used Jaguar parts and service. Selected classic restorations. Sales of new Range Rovers. Web site: www.jaguarpr.com

The Jaguar Warehouse	literature
5389 Ashleigh Rd	parts
Fairfax, VA 22030	
PH/FAX: 703-968-3983	
E-mail: jagware@erols.com	

Parts and literature for Jaguar XK 120, 140, 150 and 1948-1961 Jaguar XKs and sedans. Web site: www.erols.com/jagware

John's Cars Inc	conversion retrofits
800 Jaguar Ln	parts
Dallas, TX 75226	restoration parts
888-281-1529 parts orders only;	service
214-426-4100; FAX: 214-426-3116	

Mail order and open shop. Monday-Friday 8 am to 6 pm. Jaguar XJ series, service, parts, restoration, V8 conversions and kits for DIY conversions, XJ, E-type, TR7, Z car, etc. Rebuilt steering racks, water pumps, brake boosters, etc. GM transmission and alternator retrofits for Jaguars. Upgraded parts with lifetime warranties. Call for free information. Web site: www.johnscars.com

Kensington Motor Group Inc	consignment sales
PO Box 2277	
Sag Harbor, NY 11963	
516-537-1868; FAX: 516-537-2641	
E-mail: kenmotor@aol.com	

See full listing in **Section One** under **Mercedes-Benz**

Shepard Kinsman	sales literature
909 Eastridge	
Miami, FL 33157	
305-255-7067	

See full listing in **Section Two** under **literature dealers**

Chuck Konesky	parts
110 Stolle Rd	
Elma, NY 14059	
716-652-9638	

Mail order only. Call 24 hours a day, seven days a week. For XK 120s, 140s, 150s and E-types. New E-type parts available, but mostly parting out complete cars. Restorable Jaguars for sale.

Lake Oswego Restorations	restoration
19621 S Hazelhurst Ln	sales
West Linn, OR 97068	
PH/FAX: 503-636-7503	

See full listing in **Section One** under **Aston Martin**

Lindley Restorations Ltd	parts
10 S Sanatoga Rd	sales
Pottstown, PA 19464	service
610-326-8484; FAX: 610-326-3845	

Jaguar sales, service, restoration. Refinishing, frame straightening, engine and transmission overhaul, upholstery and structural wood fabrication, repair. Fully equipped to service pre-war to the latest model Jaguar. Over 30 years' experience. Many Jaguar Clubs of North America awards. 30 minutes west of Philadelphia. Pick-up and delivery via enclosed trailer available.

LMARR Disk Ltd	wheel discs
PO Box 910	
Glen Ellen, CA 95442-0910	
707-938-9347; FAX: 707-938-3020	
E-mail: lmarr@attglobal.net	

See full listing in **Section One** under **Rolls-Royce/Bentley**

John A Meering Jaguar Hoses	hoses
6743 Newcastle Ct	
Port Tobacco, MD 20677	
301-609-8557	

Mail order only. Jaguar hoses. Correct size and shape. Heater, radiator and carburetor hoses for XK 120, 140, 150 and Mark 7,

8, 9. Complete sets only. Send SASE for details. Hoses are new, not NOS, and are of modern construction. Also can have made hoses for most post-war British cars.

Moss Motors Ltd 440 Rutherford St Goleta, CA 93117 800-235-6954; FAX: 805-692-2525	accessories parts

See full listing in **Section One** under **MG**

Motorcars Ltd 8101 Hempstead Rd Houston, TX 77008 800-338-5238 ext 570 FAX: 713-863-8238 E-mail: info@motorcarsltd.com	parts

Since 1972, a leading source of new OEM, NOS, aftermarket, remanufactured and used or salvaged British automobile parts at discounted enthusiast prices. Online catalog by make, model and year with pictures of parts. Quality pre-owned British cars, specials, online gift shop, forums for Jaguar and Land Rover and monthly newsletter. Web site: www.motorcarsltd.com

Mr Sport Car Inc 719 W 6th St Papillion, NE 68046 402-592-7559	service

Open shop, Monday-Saturday 8 am to 6 pm. Service for Jaguars, all years. We like XKs, XJs, all MGs, all TRs, Lotus, all 8 & 12-cylinder Ferraris. Have been working on these since 1960.

Muncie Imports & Classics 4401 Old St Rd 3 N Muncie, IN 47303 800-462-4244; FAX: 317-287-9551 E-mail: mic@netdirect.net	repair restoration upholstery

Mail order and open shop. Monday-Friday 7:30 am to 5:30 pm, Saturday 9 am to 1 pm. Specializing in Jaguar and Corvette restoration, service, repair, paint and body. Upholstery for XK 120, 140, 150, Marks and E-types. OSJI factory authorized installer. Web site: www.osjimic.com

Northwest Transmission Parts 13500 US 62 Winchester, OH 45697 800-327-1955 order line 937-442-2811 info; FAX: 937-442-6555	transmission parts

See full listing in **Section Two** under **transmissions**

Omni Specialties 10418 Lorain Ave Cleveland, OH 44111 888-819-6464 (MGMG) 216-251-2269; FAX: 216-251-6083	parts restoration service

See full listing in **Section One** under **MG**

OSJI 4301 Old St Rd 3 N Muncie, IN 47303 800-338-8034; FAX: 765-213-4350 E-mail: osji@net.direct.net	convertible tops interiors rubber seals

For twenty years we have been manufacturers and suppliers of original specification Jaguar interiors, individual Jaguar interior components, rubber seals, convertible tops, top boots, tonneaus, top frame wood components and seat frame wood components. Our product line includes most post WW II Jaguars, from the XK 120s to the XJ6 SIII saloons. We use only the finest genuine leather, genuine Hardura, deep pile wood carpet, wool moquette and ICI vinyl along with well researched patterns to produce with confidence the most accurate original specification Jaguar interiors available anywhere. Web site: www.osjimic.com

Pacific International Auto 1118 Garnet Ave San Diego, CA 92109 619-274-1920; FAX: 619-454-1815	parts sales service

British car specialists. Parts, sales, service, restorations. Hard-to-find parts for Jaguars, MGs, Triumphs. Jaguar XKEs, XK 120s, XK 140s, XK 150s, all sedans.

Paul's Jaguar 4073 NE 5th Terr Oakland Park Fort Lauderdale, FL 33334 954-846-7976; FAX: 954-846-9450 E-mail: paulsjag@aol.com	parts

Mail order only. Phone hours 9 am to 7 pm EST. New and used parts for 1976-1991 Jaguar XJS, XJ-SC, convertibles; 1974-1987 Jaguar XJ6, XJ12, XJ6C and XJ12C models; especially rust-free body panels, new rubber paint kits, replacement authentic Jaguar wood kits, carpets, Connolly leather seat covers, armrest and console recovering service, new door panels, Euro headlamp conversions, new and used Jaguar alloy wheels. Knowledgeable staff, restoration advice, best prices.

Peninsula Imports 3749 Harlem Rd Buffalo, NY 14215 800-999-1209; FAX: 905-847-3021 E-mail: imports@ican.net	accessories parts trim

See full listing in **Section One** under **BMW**

Precision Autoworks 2202 Federal St East Camden, NJ 08105 856-966-0080; FAX: 856-541-0393 E-mail: rplatz007@aol.com	restorations

See full listing in **Section One** under **Mercedes-Benz**

Ragtops & Roadsters 203 S 4th St Perkasie, PA 18944 215-257-1202; FAX: 215-257-2688 E-mail: info@ragtops.com	bodywork/painting British automobiles engine rebuilding vintage race prep

See full listing in **Section One** under **AC**

Regal International Motor Cars Inc PO Box 6819 Hollywood, FL 33081 305-989-9777; FAX: 305-989-9778	car dealer

See full listing in **Section One** under **Rolls-Royce/Bentley**

Reward Service Inc 172 Overhill Rd Stormville, NY 12582 PH/FAX: 845-227-7647	appraisals restoration transportation

Automotive restoration and mechanical rebuilding of Jaguars and other British sports cars for 35 years. Appraisals, personalized transportation in the Northeast and consultation on restoration projects, by appointment. References. International Society of Appraisers' guidelines adhered to.

Rogers Motors 34 Codeyville Rd, PO Box 603 Shutesbury, MA 01072 413-259-1722 E-mail: jollyrogersmo@hotmail.com	used parts

Specializing in used parts for MGA, MGB, Jaguar Mk I, Mk II, S-type, 420 and Volvo Amazons.

Sports Car Haven	**new and used parts**
2-33 Flowerfield Industrial Pk	**race prep**
St James, NY 11780	**restoration**
631-862-8058	**service**
E-mail: sch94@aol.com	

See full listing in **Section One** under **Triumph**

Straight Six Jaguar	**parts**
24321 Hatteras St	**service**
Woodland Hills, CA 91367	
PH/FAX: 818-716-1192	

Specializing in parts and service for Jaguar 1936-1987 and Daimler.

Terry's Jaguar Parts Inc	**parts**
117 E Smith ST	
Benton, IL 62812	
800-851-9438; FAX: 618-438-2371	
E-mail: terryjag@midwest.net	

Mail order and open shop. Specializing in Jaguar parts to present day. New, used and rebuilt parts. Catalog available. Web site: www.terrysjag.com

See our ad on this page

Thoroughbred Motors	**car dealer**
3935 N US 301	**parts**
Sarasota, FL 34234	
941-359-2277; FAX: 941-359-2128	
E-mail: vintagejags@mindspring.com	

Open Monday-Friday 9 am to 5 pm. Jaguar spare parts specialists, 1950-2000 models. Also new parts. Always buying and selling cars. 20 years' experience.

Tillack & Co Ltd	**parts**
630 Mary Ann Dr	**restoration**
Redondo Beach, CA 90278	
310-318-8760; FAX: 310-376-3392	
E-mail: race@tillackco.com	

See full listing in **Section Two** under **restoration shops**

Van Nuys M-B	**parts**
14422 Oxnard St	**restoration**
Van Nuys, CA 91403	**sales**
818-988-5455	**service**

See full listing in **Section One** under **Mercedes-Benz**

Vicarage Jaguar	**parts**
5333 Collins Ave, Ste 704	**restoration**
Miami Beach, FL 33140	
305-866-9511; FAX: 305-866-5738	
E-mail: vicarage@ix.netcom.com	

Mail order and open shop. Monday-Friday 8 am to 5 pm. Specializing in restoration service, upgrades and parts for classic Jaguars. Web site: www.vicarage-jaguar.com

Vintage Jag Works	**consulting**
1390 W Hwy 26	**how-to articles**
Blackfoot, ID 83221	
877-251-5183 toll free order line	
208-684-4767; FAX: 208-684-3386	
E-mail: walt@vintagejag.com	

Mail order and open shop. Monday-Friday 9 am to 5 pm MST and by appointment. Specializing in Jaguar, how-to articles, consulting on repair and restoration by phone and e-mail, parts and memorabilia for Jaguar cars, post WW II-present. XJ performance parts, rebuilt components, 1948-1987. Tip of the Week subscription. Web site: www.vintagejag.com

Vintage Jaguar Spares	**parts**
7804 Billington Ct	
Fort Washington, MD 20744	
301-248-6327; FAX: 301-248-5523	
E-mail: brojag@erols.com	

Mail order only. "Mk IV", Mk V and SS-Jaguar. Price list free.

Von's Austin-Healey Restorations	**parts**
10270 Barberville Rd	**repairs**
Fort Mill, SC 29715	**restoration**
803-548-4590; FAX: 803-548-4816	
E-mail: vons@vnet.net	

See full listing in **Section One** under **Austin-Healey**

Welsh Enterprises Inc	**parts**
223 N 5th St, PO Box 4130	
Steubenville, OH 43952	
800-875-5247; FAX: 888-477-5247	
E-mail: contact@welshent.com	

Monday-Friday 9 am to 5 pm, Saturday 9 am to 1 pm. Over 50,000 square feet of new, reconditioned, rebuilt and NOS Jaguar spares. The largest independent retailer of Jaguar spares for restoration and service. Knowledgeable sales staff, worldwide shipping same day and competitive pricing. Call today for your free catalog. Visit us at our web site: www.welshent.com

See our ad on page 116

Western Jaguar	**parts**
Cordell R Newby	
1625 North Western	
Wenatchee, WA 98801	
509-662-7748; FAX: 509-667-9760	

Mail order only. Specializing in 1949-1951 Mark Vs with comprehensive inventory of new, NOS, reproduction and used parts for 1936-1989 models. Catalog, $3.

White Post Restorations
One Old Car Dr, PO Drawer D
White Post, VA 22663
540-837-1140; FAX: 540-837-2368
E-mail: info@whitepost.com

| | brakes restoration |

See full listing in **Section Two** under **brakes**

White Post Restorations
One Old Car Dr, PO Drawer D
White Post, VA 22663
540-837-1140; FAX: 540-837-2368
E-mail: info@whitepost.com

| | restoration |

See full listing in **Section Two** under **restoration shops**

Wolf Steel
1 Ballerina
Frelighsburg, QC Canada J0J 1C0
450-298-5078; FAX: 450-298-5088
E-mail: allen@alfaparts.net

| | Alfa Romeo body parts |

Mail order and open shop by appointment. Manufacturer and distributor of Alfa Romeo body panels. Specializing in restoration of Jaguars and Alfa Romeos. Web site: www.alfaparts.net

XKs Unlimited
850 Fiero Ln
San Luis Obispo, CA 93401
800-444-5247; FAX: 805-544-1664
E-mail: xksunltd@aol.com

| | instruments parts restorations |

Mail order and open shop. Monday-Friday 8 am to 5 pm. Specializing in Jaguar parts and restoration, Range Rover parts, Stewart-Warner for Jaguar cars 1948-on, Range Rover, Land Rover Defender, Land Rover Discovery 1986-on. We also provide restoration services for most British marques and sports cars. Authorized dealers for Shelby American Cobras, etc. Web site: www.xks.com

Selling Quality Jaguar Parts for over 30 Years!
What all Jaguar Customers Demand...
Competitive Pricing
Same Day Shipping
Knowledgeable Sales Staff
Great Customer Service
Large Inventory of Parts
Welsh Enterprises Delivers!
The Largest Inventory of
NEW, REBUILT, RECONDITIONED, & NOS
Jaguar Spares Found Anywhere
Top Quality, Unbeatable Price, And Welsh Enterprises' Commitment to Satisfying Jaguar Owners Around the World
www.welshent.com
Online Catalogs • Online Ordering • Current Ads
Monthly Flyer • Weekly Specials • Welsh Staff Page
1-800-875-JAGS (5247)
PH: 740-282-8649   FAX: 740-282-1913
223 N. 5th St., Steubenville, OH 43952

Jensen Cars Ltd
140 Franklin Ave
Wyckoff, NJ 07481-3465
201-847-8549, 8 pm-10 pm, EST
FAX: 201-847-8549, 9 am-10 pm

| | parts technical advice |

Jensen Interceptor parts for 1964-1976 Jensen CV8 and Interceptor.

K&D Enterprises
23117 E Echo Lake Rd
Snohomish, WA 98296-5426
425-788-0507; FAX: 360-668-2003
E-mail: tdb@halcyon.com

| | accessories parts restorations |

Parts, services, restoration, accessories solely for the Jensen Interceptor saloon, convertible and coupe models, 1966 and later. Web site: http://interceptor.org

KAISER K FRAZER

A-1 Shock Absorber Co
Shockfinders Division
365 Warren Ave, PO Box 2028
Silverthorne, CO 80498
800-344-1966, 970-389-3193 cell
FAX: 970-513-8283

| | shocks-all types coil springs Koni shocks leaf springs steering gears |

See our ad on the last page

Firewall Insulators & Quiet Ride Solutions
6465 Pacific Ave, Ste 249
Stockton, CA 95207
209-477-4840; FAX: 209-477-0918
E-mail: timcox@quietride.com

| | air plenums auto insulation firewall insulators gloveboxes sound deadening |

See full listing in **Section Two** under **upholstery**

Eugene Gardner
10510 Rico Tatum Rd
Palmetto, GA 30268
770-463-4264, 9 am to 11 pm EST

| | license plates |

See full listing in **Section Two** under **license plates**

K-F-D Services Inc
HC 65, Box 49
Altonah, UT 84002
801-454-3098; FAX: 801-454-3099
E-mail: kfd-services@msn.com

| | parts restoration |

Mail order and open shop. Monday-Saturday 9 am to 4 pm MST. Specializing in restoration parts and service and customized cars for Kaiser, Frazer, Darrin, Henry J, all years.

Shepard Kinsman
909 Eastridge
Miami, FL 33157
305-255-7067

| | sales literature |

See full listing in **Section Two** under **literature dealers**

Walker's Auto Pride Inc
13115 Log Rd, PO Box 134
Peyton, CO 80831
719-749-2668

cars
parts

Open Monday-Saturday 8 am to 5 pm. Kaiser Frazer cars and parts. 108 Kaiser Frazer cars. Specializing in Kaiser Frazer. Full line Kaiser Frazer parts. Parts sales for Kaiser Frazer cars including Henry J. 65 tons of new and used parts available.

Zeug's K-F Parts
1435 Moreno Dr
Simi Valley, CA 93063
805-579-9445 weekends

parts

Mail order only. NOS and used Kaiser Frazer, Henry J and Kaiser Darrin parts. Send $2 for parts list.

Charles S Crail Automobiles
36A Calle Cesar Chavez
Santa Barbara, CA 93103
805-568-1934; FAX: 805-568-1533
E-mail: crailauto@aol.com

auto sales

See full listing in **Section One** under **Rolls-Royce/Bentley**

Rolls-Royce of Beverly Hills
11401 West Pico Blvd
Los Angeles, CA 90064
800-321-9792, 310-477-4262
FAX: 310-473-7498
E-mail: smrr64@aol.com

parts

See full listing in **Section One** under **Rolls-Royce/Bentley**

Drummond Coach and Paint
531 Raleigh Ave
El Cajon, CA 92020
619-579-7229; FAX: 619-579-2128

painting
restoration

See full listing in **Section One** under **Ferrari**

Exoticars USA
6 Washington St
Frenchtown, NJ 08825
908-996-4889
E-mail: exoticars@erols.com

machine work
paint/bodywork
restoration/service
welding/fabrication

See full listing in **Section One** under **Ferrari**

Kreimeyer Co/Auto Legends Inc
3211 N Wilburn Ave
Bethany, OK 73008
PH/FAX: 405-789-9499

antennas/repair
glass/wholesale
parts/wholesale
radios/radio repair

See full listing in **Section One** under **Mercedes-Benz**

**London Stainless Steel
Exhaust Centre**
249-253 Queenstown Rd
London SW8 3NP England
0114420-7622-2120
FAX: 0114420-7627-0991
E-mail: info@quicksilverexhausts.com

exhaust systems

See full listing in **Section Two** under **exhaust systems**

Motorcar Gallery Inc
715 N Federal Hwy
Fort Lauderdale, FL 33304
954-522-9900; FAX: 954-522-9966
E-mail: motorcargallery@aol.com

car dealer

See full listing in **Section One** under **Ferrari**

Motorcars International
528 N Prince Ln
Springfield, MO 65802
417-831-9999; FAX: 417-831-8080
E-mail: sales@motorcars-intl.com

accessories
cars
services
tools

See full listing in **Section One** under **Ferrari**

Garry Roberts & Co
922 Sunset Dr
Costa Mesa, CA 92627
949-650-2690; FAX: 949-650-2730
E-mail: garryroberts@fea.net

cars
parts
service

See full listing in **Section One** under **Ferrari**

Rolls-Royce of Beverly Hills
11401 West Pico Blvd
Los Angeles, CA 90064
800-321-9792, 310-477-4262
FAX: 310-473-7498
E-mail: smrr64@aol.com

parts

See full listing in **Section One** under **Rolls-Royce/Bentley**

White Post Restorations
One Old Car Dr, PO Drawer D
White Post, VA 22663
540-837-1140; FAX: 540-837-2368
E-mail: info@whitepost.com

brakes
restoration

See full listing in **Section Two** under **brakes**

Auto Italia
3350 Woolsey Rd
Windsor, CA 95492
707-528-4825; FAX: 707-569-8717
E-mail: lenny@auto-italia

parts

See full listing in **Section One** under **Fiat**

Bayless Inc
1111 Via Bayless
Marietta, GA 30066-2770
770-928-1446; FAX: 770-928-1342
800-241-1446, order line (US/Canada)
E-mail: baylessfiat@mindspring.com

accessories
parts

See full listing in **Section One** under **Fiat**

Museo Abarth
1111 Via Bayless
Marietta, GA 30066-2770
770-928-1446

| | museum |

See full listing in **Section Six** under **Georgia**

C Obert & Co
2131-D Delaware Ave
Santa Cruz, CA 95060-5706
800-500-3428 orders
831-423-0218; FAX: 831-459-8128
E-mail: fiatplus@aol.com

| | parts |
| | repairs |

See full listing in **Section One** under **Fiat**

Doug Schellinger
13717 W Green Meadow Dr
New Berlin, WI 53151
414-328-1907
E-mail: dsac@execpc.com

	automobilia
	books
	sales literature
	toys

See full listing in **Section One** under **Fiat**

A-1 Shock Absorber Co
Shockfinders Division
365 Warren Ave, PO Box 2028
Silverthorne, CO 80498
800-344-1966, 970-389-3193 cell
FAX: 970-513-8283

	shocks-all types
	coil springs
	Koni shocks
	leaf springs
	steering gears

See our ad on the last page

**Aabar's Cadillac & Lincoln
Salvage & Parts**
9700 NE 23rd St
Oklahoma City, OK 73141
405-769-3318; FAX: 405-769-9542
E-mail: aabar@ilinkusa.net

| | parts |

See full listing in **Section One** under **Cadillac/LaSalle**

Antique Auto Electric
9109 (Rear) E Garvey Ave
Rosemead, CA 91770
626-572-0938

| | repro wiring |

See full listing in **Section Two** under **electrical systems**

Apple Hydraulics Inc
1610 Middle Rd
Calverton, NY 11933-1419
800-882-7753, 631-369-9515
FAX: 631-369-9516
E-mail: info@applehydraulics.com

| | brake rebuilding |
| | shock rebuilding |

See full listing in **Section Two** under **suspension parts**

Autowire Division
9109 (Rear) E Garvey Ave
Rosemead, CA 91770
626-572-0938; FAX: 626-288-3311

	alternator
	conversions
	motors
	relays & switches

See full listing in **Section One** under **Ford 1954-up**

Baker's Auto
196 Providence Pike
Putnam, CT 06260
860-928-7614; FAX: 860-928-0749
E-mail: sales@bakersauto.com

	parts
	repairs
	restoration

Mail order and open shop. Monday-Friday 9 am to 5 pm. Specializing in parts, repairs and restorations for 1961 and newer Lincoln automobiles. Web site: www.bakersauto.com

**Be Happy Automatic
Transmission Parts**
414 Stivers Rd
Hillsboro, OH 45133
937-442-6133; FAX: 937-442-5016

| | trans rebuild kits |

See full listing in **Section Two** under **transmissions**

**Bob's 36-48 Continental
& Zephyr Parts**
10618 N Tee Ct
Fountain Hills, AZ 85268-5723
480-837-0978; FAX: 480-837-0979

	brake parts
	chrome service
	door sills
	instruments/parts
	water pumps

Mail order only. 1936-1948 Continental and Zephyr parts. Rebuilt water pumps, coils, dist, carburetors, NOS rotors, points, dist caps, hubcaps, scripts, stoplight assy, chroming show quality, dashboards, gauges, bumpers, aluminum door sills, stainless screw kits, restored medallions and thousands of other parts. Moved my 27 year collection of Lincoln Zephyr and Continental parts to my 6 car garage in sunny Arizona. Finally organized. Call or write for your needs.

Bob Burgess 1955-56 Ford Parts
793 Alpha-Bellbrook Rd
Bellbrook, OH 45305
937-426-8041
E-mail: bobs19551956@yahoo.com

| | parts |

See full listing in **Section One** under **Ford 1954-up**

John Cashman
8835 Purvis Rd
Lithia, FL 33547-2604
813-737-5466
E-mail: jjlinc@ix.netcom.com

	convertible
	electrics
	new/used parts
	repairs

New, used and rebuilt parts for 1961-1979 Lincolns. Specializing in 1961-1967 four-door convertibles. Have all electric, hydraulic and trim parts in stock from many parts cars and NOS. Also am doing mechanical and electrical work on these cars at my central FL shop near Tampa. Call or go online for details on how my 24 years' experience working on these cars can quickly fix your problems. We ship UPS daily and technical advice is always FREE. Don't forget to visit our web site: www.convertiblelincolns.com

Classic Car Works Ltd
3050 Upper Bethany Rd
Jasper, GA 30143
770-735-3945

| | restoration |

See full listing in **Section Two** under **restoration shops**

Classique Cars Unlimited
7005 Turkey Bayou Rd, PO Box 249
Lakeshore, MS 39558
800-543-8691, USA
228-467-9633; FAX: 228-467-9207
E-mail: parts@datasync.com

	appraisals
	parts
	repairs
	restorations

Mail order/phone order. Monday-Friday 9 am to 6 pm, some Saturdays 9 am to 12 pm CST. 1958-1988 Lincoln and Thunderbird new, used, reproduction parts. Three acres with three buildings full of parts for all your Lincoln and T-Bird needs. Shop work by appointment only. Appraisals for antique, classic, milestone, custom and special interest vehicles. Celebrating our 26th year! Home of the Karen A Williams Collection featuring cars of famous personalities. Catalogs available. Web site: www.classiquecars.com

Clean Sweep-Vacuum Windshield Wiper Motor Rebuilding 760 Knight Hill Rd Zillah, WA 98953 509-865-2481; FAX: 509-865-2189 E-mail: dkjaquith@prodigy.net	motors repairs wiper parts

See full listing in **Section Two** under **windshield wipers**

Color-Ite Refinishing Co Winning Colors 868 Carrington Rd, Rt 69 Bethany, CT 06524 203-393-0240; FAX: 203-393-0873 E-mail: colorite@ctinternet.com	modern finishes restoration service

See full listing in **Section Two** under **paints**

Bob Cook Classic Auto Parts Inc 2055 Van Cleave Rd, PO Box 600 Murray, KY 42071-0600 270-753-4000, 800-486-1137 FAX: 270-753-4600	new parts NOS parts reproduced parts

See full listing in **Section One** under **Ford 1954-up**

Daytona Cams Box 5094 Ormond Beach, FL 32175 800-505-2267; FAX: 904-258-1582 E-mail: info@camshafts.com	camshafts engine parts

See full listing in **Section Two** under **camshafts**

Don's Antique Auto Parts 37337 Niles Blvd Fremont, CA 94536 415-792-4390	new parts used parts

See full listing in **Section Two** under **comprehensive parts**

Firewall Insulators & Quiet Ride Solutions 6465 Pacific Ave, Ste 249 Stockton, CA 95207 209-477-4840; FAX: 209-477-0918 E-mail: timcox@quietride.com	air plenums auto insulation firewall insulators gloveboxes sound deadening

See full listing in **Section Two** under **upholstery**

Mike Gerner, The Lincoln Factory 3636 Scheuneman Rd Gemlake, MN 55110 651-426-8001	car dealer parts restoration

Mail order and open shop. Call first on shop hours. Buys and sells Lincolns, 1936-48 and has parts from over 100 Lincolns. Also does restoration and presently has thirty in personal collection.

R O Hommel 933 Osage Rd Pittsburgh, PA 15243 412-279-8884; FAX: 412-279-8853 E-mail: lc1946@hotmail.com	body tags parts

Mail order only. Used, NOS and reproduction parts for 1942-1948 Lincoln Continentals. Reproduction body tags and patent plates for 1942-1948 Lincolns and Continentals only. Glass parking light lenses reproduced; water pumps rebuilt.

Bill Horton 5804 Jones Valley Dr Huntsville, AL 35802 256-881-6894	vacuum motors

See full listing in **Section One** under **Mercury**

Hot Rod & Custom Supply 1304 SE 10th St Cape Coral, FL 33990 941-574-7744; FAX: 941-574-8820	custom parts engine parts speed parts

See full listing in **Section One** under **Ford 1932-1953**

Jacks Wholesale Division 250 N Robertson Blvd, Ste 405 Beverly Hills, CA 90211-1793 310-839-9417; FAX: 310-839-1046	limousines

Lincoln and Cadillac limousines, Stutz Blackhawk, Rolls-Royce. Web site: www.jwdlimosales.com

Bob Johnson's Auto Literature 92 Blandin Ave Framingham, MA 01702 508-872-9173; FAX: 508-626-0991 E-mail: bjohnson@autopaper.com	brochures literature manuals paint chips

See full listing in **Section Two** under **literature dealers**

LaCarrera-The Mexican Road Race PO Box 1605 Studio City, CA 91614 323-464-5720; FAX: 323-656-7111 E-mail: lacarrera@earthlink.net	road race

See full listing in **Section Two** under **racing**

Lincoln Land Inc Showroom 2025 Gulf-to-Bay Blvd Clearwater, FL 33765 727-443-3646; FAX: 727-443-3632 E-mail: lincolnlandinc.com@ worldnet.att.net	cars parts parts & car display service

Phone orders and open shop. Monday-Friday 9 am to 6 pm, Saturday 10 am to 2 pm. Showroom of parts and 9 car display. 1956-1992 Lincoln Continental cars, parts and service. Daily parts shipments worldwide. Web site: www.lincolnlandinc.com

Lincoln Parts International 707 E 4th St, Bldg G Perris, CA 92570 800-382-1656, 909-657-5588 FAX: 909-657-4758 E-mail: lincolnparts@pe.net	parts

Mail order and open shop. Monday-Friday 8 am to 5 pm, some Saturdays. New, used and reproduction parts for 1961-1990s Lincolns, 1972-1979 Thunderbirds, 1974-1979 Cougars and 1971-1978 Mercury full-size. Quality guaranteed parts. Shipments daily worldwide. Visa, MasterCard, Discover and American Express. Free catalog of Lincoln parts. Web site: www.lincolnpartsintl.com

Lincoln Services Ltd Earle O Brown, Jr 229 Robinhood Ln McMurray, PA 15317 724-941-4567; FAX: 724-942-1940	literature parts

Mail order only. Parts bought, sold or traded for 1936-1948 Lincoln Zephyrs and Continentals, emphasis on HV-12 engine parts. Also Lincoln literature. Free catalog. Also information on membership in the Lincoln Continental Owners Club and/or the Lincoln Zephyr Owners Club.

Lincoln-Rubber Reproductions 9109 E Garvey Ave Rosemead, CA 91770 626-280-4546	parts

Mail order only. For 1940-1948 Continentals. Catalog, $4 USA.

Mark II Enterprises
5225 Canyon Crest Dr, Ste 71-217H
Riverside, CA 92507
909-686-2752; FAX: 909-686-7245
E-mail: markiient@earthlink.net

car covers
parts

See full listing in **Section Two** under **accessories**

Mercury & Ford Molded Rubber
12 Plymouth Ave
Wilmington, MA 01887
978-658-8394

parts

See full listing in **Section One** under **Mercury**

Miller Obsolete Parts
1329 Campus Dr
Vestal, NY 13850
607-722-5371; FAX: 607-770-9117
E-mail: mmiller3@stny.rr.com

locator service
parts

See full listing in **Section One** under **Ford 1954-up**

Narragansett Reproductions
Ed & Miki Pease
107 Woodville Rd, PO Box 51
Wood River Junction, RI 02894
401-364-3839; FAX: 401-364-3830
E-mail: narragansetrepro@aol.com

wiring harnesses

See full listing in **Section Two** under **electrical systems**

Rocky Mountain V8 Ford Parts
1124 Clark Cir
Colorado Springs, CO 80915
719-597-8375
E-mail: fordyford@juno.com

parts

See full listing in **Section One** under **Ford 1932-1953**

Sanders Reproduction Glass
PO Box 522
Hillsboro, OR 97123
503-648-9184

glass

See full listing in **Section Two** under **glass**

Tags Backeast
PO Box 581
Plainville, CT 06062
860-747-2942
E-mail: dataplt@snet.net

data plates
trim tags
cowl tags

See full listing in **Section Two** under **special services**

Pat Walsh Restorations
Box Q
Wakefield, MA 01880
781-246-3266; FAX: 781-224-3311
E-mail: pwalshrest@aol.com

literature
rubber parts

See full listing in **Section Two** under **rubber parts**

Westwind Limousine Sales
2720 W National Rd
Dayton, OH 45414
937-898-9000; FAX: 937-898-9800

limousine sales

Specializing in limousine sales.

White Post Restorations
One Old Car Dr, PO Drawer D
White Post, VA 22663
540-837-1140; FAX: 540-837-2368
E-mail: info@whitepost.com

brakes
restoration

See full listing in **Section Two** under **brakes**

White Post Restorations
One Old Car Dr, PO Drawer D
White Post, VA 22663
540-837-1140; FAX: 540-837-2368
E-mail: info@whitepost.com

restoration

See full listing in **Section Two** under **restoration shops**

LOCOMOBILE

International Towing & Recovery Museum
401 Broad St
Chattanooga, TN 37402
PH/FAX: 423-267-3132

museum

See full listing in **Section Six** under **Tennessee**

Dave Bean Engineering
636 E St Charles St SR3H
San Andreas, CA 95249
209-754-5802; FAX: 209-754-5177
E-mail: admin@davebean.com

parts

Specializing in parts for Lotus. Web site: www.davebean.com

Birkin America
PO Box 120982
Arlington, TX 76012
817-461-7431; FAX: 817-861-5867
E-mail: birkinam@aol.com

cars
replicas

Mail order and open shop. Monday-Saturday 8 am to 5 pm.
Specializing in Lotus Super Seven cars and Lotus Seven replicas.
We are the North American importer for Birkin S-3 cars. These
Birkin cars are replicas of the Lotus Super Seven S-3 cars.
Web site: www.birkinamerica.com

British Luxury Automotive Parts
257 Niagara St
Toronto, ON Canada M6J 2L7
416-693-8400; FAX: 416-694-3202
Cell: 416-820-4323

new and used parts

See full listing in **Section One** under **Jaguar**

French Stuff
PO Box 39772
Glendale, CA 90039-0772
818-244-2498; FAX: 818-500-7628
E-mail: frenchap@gte.net

accessories
engine rebuilding
parts
transaxle rebuilding

See full listing in **Section One** under **Renault**

JAE
375 Pine #26
Goleta, CA 93117
805-967-5767; FAX: 805-967-6183
E-mail: jefforjay@jaeparts.com

parts
service
tech info

Mail order and open shop. Monday-Friday 7:30 am to 5 pm,
Saturday by appointment. Parts, service and tech info for Lotus,
English Ford and English specialist cars (TVR, Elva, Jensen, etc).
Official Lotus Heritage parts dealer. Web site: www.jaeparts.com

Kreimeyer Co/Auto Legends Inc | antennas/repair
3211 N Wilburn Ave | glass/wholesale
Bethany, OK 73008 | parts/wholesale
PH/FAX: 405-789-9499 | radios/radio repair

See full listing in **Section One** under **Mercedes-Benz**

Marcovicci-Wenz Engineering Inc | Cosworth engines
33 Comac Loop
Ronkonkoma, NY 11779
631-467-9040; FAX: 631-467-9041
E-mail: mwerace@compuserve.com

See full listing in **Section Two** under **racing**

RD Enterprises Ltd | parts
290 Raub Rd
Quakertown, PA 18951
215-538-9323; FAX: 215-538-0158
E-mail: rdent@rdent.com

Lotus owners: RD Enterprises has been supplying parts and expert assistance for over 20 years. We have a large inventory of original parts for Elan, Europa, Elite, Esprit and Turbo; engine, suspension, drivetrain, electrics, hydraulics, body seals, badges as well as aftermarket items; CarCapsules, Panasport alloy wheels, Spax adjustable shocks, ColorTune, accessories, books and scale models. Visa, MasterCard accepted. Web site: www.rdent.com

Von's Austin-Healey Restorations | parts
10270 Barberville Rd | repairs
Fort Mill, SC 29715 | restoration
803-548-4590; FAX: 803-548-4816
E-mail: vons@vnet.net

See full listing in **Section One** under **Austin-Healey**

White Post Restorations | brakes
One Old Car Dr, PO Drawer D | restoration
White Post, VA 22663
540-837-1140; FAX: 540-837-2368
E-mail: info@whitepost.com

See full listing in **Section Two** under **brakes**

Firewall Insulators & Quiet Ride | air plenums
Solutions | auto insulation
6465 Pacific Ave, Ste 249 | firewall insulators
Stockton, CA 95207 | gloveboxes
209-477-4840; FAX: 209-477-0918 | sound deadening
E-mail: timcox@quietride.com

See full listing in **Section Two** under **upholstery**

Bassett's Jaguar | parts
53 Stilson Rd, PO Box 245 | restoration
Wyoming, RI 02898 | service
401-539-3010; FAX: 401-539-7861 | upholstery
E-mail: jagwillie@ids.net

See full listing in **Section One** under **Jaguar**

Jerry Bensinger | car dealer
1197 Trails Edge Dr
Hubbard, OH 44425-3353
330-759-5224; FAX: 330-759-5225
E-mail: jbenzr@aol.com

See full listing in **Section Two** under **car dealers**

Chris Davis | bronzes
The Old Vicarage
49 Yates Hay Rd, Malvern Link
Worcestershire, WR14 1LH England
PH/FAX: 01684-560410

See full listing in **Section Two** under **artwork**

Drummond Coach and Paint | painting
531 Raleigh Ave | restoration
El Cajon, CA 92020
619-579-7229; FAX: 619-579-2128

See full listing in **Section One** under **Ferrari**

Exoticars USA | machine work
6 Washington St | paint/bodywork
Frenchtown, NJ 08825 | restoration/service
908-996-4889 | welding/fabrication
E-mail: exoticars@erols.com

See full listing in **Section One** under **Ferrari**

London Stainless Steel | exhaust systems
Exhaust Centre
249-253 Queenstown Rd
London, SW8 3NP England
0114420-7622-2120;
FAX: 0114420-7627-0991
E-mail: info@quicksilverexhausts.com

See full listing in **Section Two** under **exhaust systems**

MIE Corporation | parts
PO Box 1015
Mercer Island, WA 98040
425-455-4449; FAX: 425-688-1903
E-mail: mie@maseratinet.com

Maserati spare parts, $8,000,000 plus in new and used parts, over 30,000 line items in new parts alone. Knowledgeable personnel, computerized for easy ordering. Technical support. Web site: www.maseratinet.com

Garry Roberts & Co | cars
922 Sunset Dr | parts
Costa Mesa, CA 92627 | service
949-650-2690; FAX: 949-650-2730
E-mail: garryroberts@fea.net

See full listing in **Section One** under **Ferrari**

Rosso Bianco Sportscar Museum | museum
Obernauer Str 125
D-63743
Aschaffenburg Germany
06021 21358; FAX: 06021 20636

See full listing in **Section Six** under **Germany**

Tillack & Co Ltd | parts
630 Mary Ann Dr | restoration
Redondo Beach, CA 90278
310-318-8760; FAX: 310-376-3392
E-mail: race@tillackco.com

See full listing in **Section Two** under **restoration shops**

White Post Restorations
One Old Car Dr, PO Drawer D
White Post, VA 22663
540-837-1140; FAX: 540-837-2368
E-mail: info@whitepost.com

brakes
restoration

See full listing in **Section Two** under **brakes**

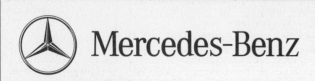

A-1 Shock Absorber Co
Shockfinders Division
365 Warren Ave, PO Box 2028
Silverthorne, CO 80498
800-344-1966, 970-389-3193 cell
FAX: 970-513-8283

shocks-all types
coil springs
Koni shocks
leaf springs
steering gears

See our ad on the last page

Asom Electric
1204 McClellan Dr
Los Angeles, CA 90025
310-820-4457; FAX: 310-820-5908

electrical systems
rebuilding

See full listing in **Section Two** under **electrical systems**

ATVM
97 Mt Royal Ave
Aberdeen, MD 21001
410-272-2252; FAX: 410-272-4940
E-mail: atvm2@prodigy.net

literature
parts

Mail order only. Mercedes-Benz parts and literature for 1934-1972 models.

There's nothing like the way your Classic Mercedes runs after a professional tune-up. Now the same is true for your Classic Becker Radio. Regardless of its age, model, or condition, we can restore your Classic Becker to its optimum performance. Manual antennas, power antennas, classic speakers and grills, dial scales, knobs and chrome trimplates, we have them all! This is all just another part of what we do best, service for you and your Classic Becker Radio at a level only a Factory Representative can.

Sound Advice

BECKER
AUTOMOTIVE SYSTEMS
Becker of North America, Inc
16 Parkway, Upper Saddle River, NJ, USA,07458

Toll Free: **888-423-3537**
E-mail: **info@beckerautosound.com**
web: **www.beckerautosound.com**

Auto Craftsmen Restoration Inc
27945 Elm Grove
San Antonio, TX 78261
PH/FAX: 830-980-4027

appraisals
buyer/car locator
old M-B parts
restoration

See full listing in **Section Two** under **restoration shops**

Autolux Inc
3121 W Coast Hwy, Ste 3D
Newport Beach, CA 92663
949-574-0054; FAX: 949-645-3033

Mercedes parts

Mail order only. Mercedes-Benz replacement parts for Dure-lever heater and vent control levers, attach through vent openings in 20-30 minutes. Chassis #108, #109 and #113. Uni-di door lock diaphragms, Mercedes 1973-1980. AC-DI, repair air conditioning vacuum elements. Chassis #123 and #126. Seat adjustment handles, front and side, chassis #115, #116, #126. Gear replacements for sunroof, seat retractor arms and antenna.

AutoMatch CARS
(Computer Aided Referral Service)
2017 Blvd Napoleon
Louisville, KY 40205
800-962-2771, 502-417-8793 mobile
502-452-1920 office; FAX: 502-479-6222
E-mail: amcars@aol.com or
aautomatch@aol.com

broker
car dealer network
exotic, classic,
new & used car
locator

See full listing in **Section Two** under **car dealers**

Basic Inc
6B Hamilton Business Pk
85 Franklin Rd
Dover, NJ 07801
973-361-5055; FAX: 973-361-6551
E-mail: sales@4basic.com

accessories
seating

Mail order and open shop. Monday-Friday 8 am to 5 pm EST. Specializing in accessories and seating for all Mercedes-Benz cars. SL rear seats, seat reupholstery kits, hardtop hoists and hardtop carts our specialty. Web site: www.4basic.com

Bassett's Jaguar
53 Stilson Rd, PO Box 245
Wyoming, RI 02898
401-539-3010; FAX: 401-539-7861
E-mail: jagwillie@ids.net

parts
restoration
service
upholstery

See full listing in **Section One** under **Jaguar**

Becker of North America Inc
16 Park Way
Upper Saddle River, NJ 07458
888-423-3537; FAX: 201-327-2084
E-mail: info@beckerautosound.com

radio repair

Specializing in Mercedes-Benz radio repair. Web site: www.beckerautosound.com
See our ad on this page

JJ Best & Co
737 Main St, PO Box 10
Chatham, MA 02633
800-USA-1965; FAX: 508-945-6006

financing

See full listing in **Section Two** under **financing**

BMC Classics Inc
828 N Dixie Freeway
New Smyrna Beach, FL 32168
PH/FAX: 386-426-6405
E-mail: bmcar1@aol.com

parts
repair
restoration

See full listing in **Section Two** under **restoration shops**

Brooklyn Motoren Werke Inc 115 Market St Brooklyn, WI 53521 608-455-7441; FAX: 608-455-7442	appraisals parts restoration service

Open shop. Monday-Friday. Restoration, service and parts for post-war Mercedes-Benz. Innovative engineering. Specializing in 300 series.

Bud's Parts for Classic **Mercedes-Benz** 9130 Hwy 5 Douglasville, GA 30134 800-942-8444; FAX: 770-942-8400	parts restoration service

Mail order and open shop. Monday-Friday 8:30 am to 6 pm, Saturday 9 am to 2 pm. Parts, service and complete restoration for 1955-1995 SL and sedan Mercedes at discounted prices.

Concours Cars of Colorado Ltd 2414 W Cucharras St Colorado Springs, CO 80904 719-473-6288; FAX: 719-473-9206	accessories parts service

See full listing in **Section One** under **BMW**

Dave's Auto Restoration 2285 Rt 307 E Jefferson, OH 44047 PH/FAX: 216-858-2227 E-mail: davesauto@knownet.net	upholstery restoration

See full listing in **Section Two** under **interiors & interior parts**

Deutsches Museum Museumsinsel 1 80538 Munchen Germany E-mail: deutsches-museum@ deutsches-museum.de	museum

See full listing in **Section Six** under **Germany**

DTE Motorsports 242 South Rd Brentwood, NH 03833 PH/FAX: 603-642-3766 E-mail: dtemotorsports@aol.com	engines/race prep mechanical services transportation restoration

Specializing in mechanical and component services, engines, transportation, race prep and support for Mercedes-Benz, Ferrari, Porsche, Bugatti and limited production marques. Aircraft mechanical licenses. 30 years in classic car business.

EIS Engines Inc 215 SE Grand Ave Portland, OR 97214 800-547-0002, 503-232-5590 FAX: 503-232-5178 E-mail: edik@att.com	engines

Replacement gas and diesel engines as well as engine parts for Mercedes-Benz vehicles from classic mid-1950s to current.

European Connection 313-1/2 Main St Falmouth, KY 41040 800-395-8636; FAX: 606-654-3700	parts

Mail order only. New and used parts. Over 700 wrecked Mercedes for parts. Lots of NOS. UPS and trucking. Visa, MasterCard and Discover accepted.

EuroTech Services International 108 Milarepa Rd Azalea, OR 97410 541-837-3636; FAX: 541-837-3737 E-mail: jim@eurotech-services.com	parts

Mail order only. A German/American firm serving owners of Mercedes-Benz automobiles. Offers direct surface, air and 3 day

courier procurement for "Germany-only" parts. Also uniquely specialized in sales, service and parts for exceptional Mercedes-Benz vehicles such as Unimog 4x4 trucks/tractors, off-road motorhomes and mobile workshops and auxiliary machinery in world-respected Unimog multi-implement technologies; 4x4 Gelaendewagen, 4x2 trucks, buses and motorhomes. Web site: www.eurotech-services.com

Bob Fatone's Mercedes Used Parts 166 W Main St Niantic, CT 06357 860-739-1923; FAX: 860-691-0669 E-mail: bobfatone@earthlink.net	parts

Mail order or open by appointment only. Specializing in most all used replacement parts, engine, body, chrome, interior, etc, for Mercedes highline chassis #111 coupe and convertible Models 220SE, 250SE, 280SE and some 4-door cars for years 1960-1971. 95% of orders are by mail.

Foreign Motors West 253 N Main St Natick, MA 01760 508-655-5350; FAX: 508-651-0178	car sales

See full listing in **Section One** under **Rolls-Royce/Bentley**

Germany Direct 12325 West Ave San Antonio, TX 78216 888-588-4920; FAX: 210-341-8971	parts

Mail order and open shop. Monday-Friday 9 am to 12 noon and 1 pm to 5 pm. Specializing in parts for Mercedes-Benz 1960s and 1950s models.

Hatch & Sons Automotive Inc 533 Boston Post Rd Wayland, MA 01778 508-358-3500; FAX: 508-358-3578	detailing parts service wood refinishing

Mail order and open shop. Monday-Saturday 8 am to 6 pm. Restoration, auto body, service, detailing, parts, leather work, wood refinishing, sales and consignment for Mercedes-Benz and Porsche exclusively.

Highway One Classic Automobiles **and Highwayone.com** 1035 California Dr Burlingame, CA 94010 650-342-7340; FAX: 650-343-0150 E-mail: djboscacci@msn.com	classic automobiles

See full listing in **Section One** under **Abarth**

Hjeltness Restoration Inc 630 Alpine Way Escondido, CA 92029 760-746-9966; FAX: 760-746-7738	restoration service

See full listing in **Section Two** under **restoration shops**

Horst's Car Care 3160-1/2 N Woodford St Decatur, IL 62526 217-876-1112	engine rebuilding

Open shop only. Monday-Friday 8 am to 5 pm. Mercedes-Benz engine rebuilding, 1950s-1990s.

House of Imports Inc 12203 W Colfax Ave Lakewood, CO 80215 303-232-2540; FAX: 303-232-3260	car dealer

Mail order and open shop. Monday-Saturday 9 am to 6 pm. Buys and sells used Mercedes-Benz. Web site: www.houseofimports.com

International Automobile Archives	sales literature

Kai Jacobsen
Wiesenweg 3b
85757 Karlsfeld Germany
011-49-8131-93158
FAX: 011-49-8131-505973
E-mail: doubledseven@t-online.de

See full listing in **Section Two** under **literature dealers**

International Restoration Specialist Inc	parts restoration sales

PO Box 1303
Mt Airy, NC 27030
336-789-1548

See full listing in **Section Two** under **restoration shops**

Italy's Famous Exhaust	exhaust systems wheels

2711 183rd St
Redondo Beach, CA 90278
E-mail: johnt@famousexhaust.com

See full listing in **Section Two** under **exhaust systems**

JAM Engineering Corp	carburetors

PO Box 2570
Monterey, CA 93942
800-JAM-CORP, 831-372-1787
E-mail: jam@jameng.com

See full listing in **Section Two** under **carburetors**

Kensington Motor Group Inc	consignment sales

PO Box 2277
Sag Harbor, NY 11963
516-537-1868; FAX: 516-537-2641
E-mail: kenmotor@aol.com

Consignment sales of vintage, classic, exotic, sports and luxury motor cars. Promoter of the Hamptons Auto Classic Collector Car Auction in May. Web site: www.kensingtonmotor.com

Kreimeyer Co/Auto Legends Inc	antennas/repair glass/wholesale parts/wholesale radios/radio repair

3211 N Wilburn Ave
Bethany, OK 73008
PH/FAX: 405-789-9499

Specializing in auto glass for all vehicles: antique, classic, domestic, exotic and foreign at wholesale prices. Windshields and back glass for most models. Custom made glass and custom cutting available. Sales and repairs for Becker/Blaupunkt radios and Hirschmann antennas. Specializing in new Mercedes parts, 1950-1995, at wholesale prices. Specializing in 190SL and 300SL parts. Engine, fuel system and transmission service available. First class reproductions. 300SLR reproduction, 300SL sales/parts. Mercedes 1954 300SLR. High-performance 0-60 4.0 seconds! Own a piece of racing history. Photos available.

LaCarrera-The Mexican Road Race	road race

PO Box 1605
Studio City, CA 91614
323-464-5720; FAX: 323-656-7111
E-mail: lacarrera@earthlink.net

See full listing in **Section Two** under **racing**

Lyco Engineering Inc	machine work parts

8645 N Territorial Rd
Plymouth, MI 48170
734-459-7313; FAX: 734-459-2224

Mail order and open shop. Monday-Saturday 9 am to 6 pm. 30 years' experience with Mercedes-Benz 300SL cars, 1954-1964. Complete machine shop. Genuine and reproduction parts in stock. Engine, transmission, running gear, trim, tools, weatherstrips/seals, glass, all brake parts, wheels chromed. Many remanufactured parts on exchange basis. Also extensive inventory of parts for 1952-1962 300 Series coupes and sedans (formerly supplied by Chuck Brahms).

Machina Locksmith	car locks keys

3 Porter St
Watertown, MA 02172-4145
PH/FAX: 617-923-1683

See full listing in **Section Two** under **locks & keys**

Mercedes-Benz Service by Angela & George/ABS Exotic Repair Inc	sales service

700 N Andrews Ave
Fort Lauderdale, FL 33304
954-566-7785; FAX: 954-522-0087
E-mail: mercedeslady@bellsouth.net

Open shop only. Monday-Friday 8:30 am to 7 pm. Specializing in Mercedes-Benz, all models, years. Mercedes-Benz service and parts.

Mercedes-Benz Visitor Center	museum

PO Box 100
Tuscaloosa, AL 35403-0100
888-2TOUR-MB, 205-507-2253
FAX: 205-507-2255

Open year round. Monday-Friday 9 am to 5 pm, Saturday 10 am to 3 pm. Closed 2 weeks for Christmas and New Years and holidays. Houses the only Mercedes-Benz museum outside of Germany. Exhibits include corporate history, including a replica of the world's first motorized vehicle and motorcycle. Also featured are Mercedes-Benz safety developments, racing history and the Alabama-made M-class sport utility vehicle. Several vintage vehicles are displayed, along with numerous audio-visual exhibits. Also housed in the Center is a retail boutique featuring apparel, collectibles and gift items. Exhibition cars of special note: 1956 300SL gullwing, 1907 Mercedes Simplex Spider, M-Class camouflage vehicle from Steven Spielberg's *Lost World*, 1886 Daimler Motorkutsche. Web site: www.mbusi.com

Michael's Classics Inc	Unimogs

954 Montauk Hwy
Bayport, NY 11705
631-363-4200; FAX: 631-363-9226
E-mail: michaelsmogs@aol.com

Specializing in sales and parts of Mercedes-Benz Unimogs, ex-military 4-wheel drive trucks for vintage 1957-1967.

Mid-Jersey Motorama Inc	car dealer

1301 Asbury Ave, PO Box 1395
Asbury Park, NJ 07712
PH/FAX: 732-775-9885
beeper: 732-840-6111
E-mail: sjz1@msn.com

See full listing in **Section One** under **Cadillac/LaSalle**

Millers Incorporated	accessories parts

7412 Count Circle
Huntington Beach, CA 92647
714-375-6565; FAX: 714-847-6606
E-mail: sales@millermbz.com

Mail order and open shop. Monday-Friday 8 am to 5 pm. Specializing in parts and accessories for the classic Mercedes-Benz for 1950s, 1960s and 1970s. Especially Mercedes-Benz 190SLs; 230, 250, 280SLs, 450, 350, 500SL, SLCs; 220, 200 sedans; 250C, 300SD, TD, 380SEC. Web site: www.millermbz.com

James J Montague	parts service

West Rupert, VT 05776
802-394-2929

Mail order and open shop by appointment only. Specializing in pre-1978 Mercedes-Benz gas and diesel cars. Selected pre-1968 foreign sports and exotic cars and pre-WW II US vehicles. Over 25 years' Mercedes-Benz repair and consultation.

Northern Motorsport Ltd PO Box 1028, Rt 5 Wilder, VT 05088 802-296-2099; FAX: 802-295-6599 E-mail: bugatti46@aol.com	repair restoration sales service

See full listing in **Section Two** under **restoration shops**

Northwest Transmission Parts 13500 US 62 Winchester, OH 45697 800-327-1955 order line 937-442-2811 info; FAX: 937-442-6555	transmission parts

See full listing in **Section Two** under **transmissions**

Palo Alto Speedometer Inc 718 Emerson St Palo Alto, CA 94301 650-323-0243; FAX: 650-323-4632 E-mail: pacspeedo@pacbell.net	instruments

Mail order and open shop. Monday-Friday 8 am to 5 pm. Instrument, gauge, clock repair, service and restoration of all makes and models. Web site: www.paspeedo.com

Lyle Pearson Company 351 Auto Dr Boise, ID 83709 800-621-1775; FAX: 208-672-3494 E-mail: partspc@lylepearson.com	accessories literature parts

Mail order and open shop. Monday-Friday 7:30 am to 6 pm MST. Specializing in genuine parts, accessories and literature for Mercedes-Benz, Volvo, Land Rover/Range Rover and Acura. Web site: www.lylepearson.com

Peninsula Imports 3749 Harlem Rd Buffalo, NY 14215 800-999-1209; FAX: 905-847-3021 E-mail: imports@ican.net	accessories parts trim

See full listing in **Section One** under **BMW**

Performance Analysis Co 1345 Oak Ridge Tpke, Ste 258 Oak Ridge, TN 37830 PH/FAX: 865-482-9175 E-mail: george_murphy@ compuserve.com	climate control cruise control

Mail order only. Specializing in climate control, cruise control, electronic modules and specialty parts for Mercedes-Benz automobiles.

John T Poulin Auto Sales/Star Service Center 5th Ave & 111th St North Troy, NY 12182 518-235-8610	car dealer parts restoration service

See full listing in **Section Two** under **car dealers**

Precious Metal Automotive Restoration Co Inc 1601 College Ave SE Grand Rapids, MI 49507 616-243-0220; FAX: 616-243-6646 E-mail: dpayne@iserv.net	broker restoration

Full service 6,500 restoration and service facility devoted to the collectible Mercedes-Benz cars. More than 90 190SL restorations and many 230/250/280SLs, plus 220S/SE coupes and cabriolets and many other models. Cars bought, sold and brokered. Convenient midwest location. Web site: www.preciousauto.com

Precision Autoworks 2202 Federal St East Camden, NJ 08105 856-966-0080; FAX: 856-541-0393 E-mail: rplatz007@aol.com	restorations

Full or partial cosmetic and/or mechanical restorations for all European marques. Specializing in Mercedes-Benz, models post WW II, both for show or drive.

Private Garage LC 8949 SE Bridge Rd, PMB 302 Hobe Sound, FL 33455 561-545-7277; FAX: 561-546-7884	consultant

See full listing in **Section One** under **Ferrari**

Proper Motor Cars Inc 1811 11th Ave N St Petersburg, FL 33713-5794 727-821-8883; FAX: 727-821-0273 E-mail: propermotorcarsinc@ email.msn.com	parts restoration service

See full listing in **Section One** under **Rolls-Royce/Bentley**

RAU Restoration 2027 Pontius Ave Los Angeles, CA 90025 310-445-1128; FAX: 310-575-9715 E-mail: wcrau@rau-autowood.com	woodwork

See full listing in **Section Two** under **woodwork**

Regal International Motor Cars Inc PO Box 6819 Hollywood, FL 33081 305-989-9777; FAX: 305-989-9778	car dealer

See full listing in **Section One** under **Rolls-Royce/Bentley**

Ron's Restorations Inc 2968-B Ask Kay Dr Smyrna, GA 30082 888-416-1057, 770-438-6102 FAX: 770-438-0037	interior trim restoration

Specializing in interior trim replacement, repair and total restorations for all Mercedes-Benz automobiles. Web site: www.ronsrestorations.com

Royal Coach Works Ltd 2146 Lunceford Ln Lilburn, GA 30047 PH/FAX: 770-736-3960 E-mail: royalrow@cs.com	appraisals

See full listing in **Section Two** under **appraisals**

Showroom Auto Sales 960 S Bascom Ave San Jose, CA 95128 408-279-0944; FAX: 408-279-0918	car dealer

Business hours: Monday-Friday 12 noon to 7 pm, Saturday 12 noon to 4 pm. Specializing in 1971 and older classic Mercedes-Benz convertibles. Also specializing in exotics and cars of distinction. Web site: www.showroomcars.com

SL-TECH 230SL-250SL-280SL 1364 Portland Rd, US Rt 1 Arundel/Kennebunkport, ME 04046 207-985-3001; FAX: 207-985-3011 E-mail: gernold@sltechw113.com	parts restoration service

Mail order and open shop. Monday-Friday 8 am to 12 pm, 2 pm to 6 pm, Saturday by appointment. Specializing in parts, service, restoration and convertible top frame repairs for 1963-1971 Mercedes-Benz W113 chassis, 230, 250, 280SL roadsters. Web site: www.sltechw113.com

Sports Leicht Restorations	restoration
16 Maple St	sales
Topsfield, MA 01983	service
978-887-6644; FAX: 978-887-3889	
E-mail: slr190sl@aol.com	

Restoration and service and sales. Specializing in Mercedes. Contact: Alex Dearborn.

Star Classics Inc	parts
7745 E Redfield #300	
Scottsdale, AZ 85260	
800-644-7827, 480-991-7495	
FAX: 480-951-4096	
E-mail: info@starclassics.com	

Mail order and open shop. Monday-Friday 8 am to 5 pm. Parts for Mercedes-Benz of the 1950s. All the collectible models. Hood stars to tailpipe tip. Anything made of rubber, chrome, etc. All lenses and trim items. Component restoration and exchange service available for same day shipping. All engine rebuild parts in stock for these models. Discount plan available. All credit cards accepted. Postwar to 1963. 170 sedan to the Gullwing and the 300S/Sc. Same day worldwide shipping. Web site: www.starclassics.com

See our ad on this page

Star Motors	parts
Neil Dubey	restoration
1694 Union Center Hwy	
Endicott, NY 13760	
607-786-3918 ext 202, 607-754-4272	
FAX: 607-754-5112	
E-mail: n300sel63@aol.com	

Specializing in E service, restorations and parts, new, used and rebuilt for 300SEL, 300SEL 6.3, 450SEL, 450SEL 6.9, Grand 600 (all model years).

Star Quality Parts	accessories
A Silvermine Classics Inc Company	parts
1 Alley Rd	
LaGrangeville, NY 12520	
800-STAR199 (782-7199)	
FAX: 845-223-5394	
E-mail: sales@starqualityparts.com	

Mail order and web only. I specialize in the most comprehensive inventory of new and used parts and accessories for all classic Mercedes-Benz SLs from 1955 through 1989: 190SL, 230SL, 250SL, 280SL, 350-560SLs. In-house experts are on call to help you find the best solutions for your projects. Order on-line or call for your free catalog. Web site: www.starqualityparts.com

Steve's Auto Restorations	restoration
4440 SE 174th Ave	
Portland, OR 97236	
503-665-2222; FAX: 503-665-2225	
E-mail: steve@realsteel.com	

See full listing in **Section Two** under **restoration shops**

Sweeney's Auto & Marine Upholstery Inc	carpets
dba Southampton Auto & Marine Upholstery	interiors
471 N Hwy, PO Box 1479	tops
Southampton, NY 11969	
516-283-2616; FAX: 516-283-2617	

Open Monday-Friday 8 am to 5 pm, Saturday 9 am to 12 pm. Convertible tops, vinyl tops, custom convertibles, carpeting and complete interiors for antique and classic cars. Specializing in Mercedes. Thirty-five years' experience.

Van Nuys M-B	parts
14422 Oxnard St	restoration
Van Nuys, CA 91403	sales
818-988-5455	service

Mail order and open shop. Monday-Saturday 7 am to 6 pm. Specializing in Mercedes-Benz 50s, 60s, 70s parts, sales, service, restoration.

Vintage Sales	sales
Paul Padget	
7641 Reinhold Dr	
Cincinnati, OH 45237	
513-821-2143	

Best by appointment please. Specializing in sales of Mercedes and other specialty cars. Hemmings advertiser since 1962.

White Post Restorations	brakes
One Old Car Dr, PO Drawer D	restoration
White Post, VA 22663	
540-837-1140; FAX: 540-837-2368	
E-mail: info@whitepost.com	

See full listing in **Section Two** under **brakes**

White Post Restorations	restoration
One Old Car Dr, PO Drawer D	
White Post, VA 22663	
540-837-1140; FAX: 540-837-2368	
E-mail: info@whitepost.com	

See full listing in **Section Two** under **restoration shops**

WTH-VMC (formerly Vintage Mercedes Cars Inc)	emblems
921 Sleeping Indian Rd	lenses
Oceanside, CA 92057-2118	manuals
800-WTH-5771 orders only	weatherstrips
760-941-8192, 9 to 4 PST	
FAX: 760-941-6033	
E-mail: wth-vmc@mysiteis.com	

Mail order and shop open by appointment only. Specializes in 380, 500K, 540K, 770K, early 170, 220, 300, others through 1962. Sells lights, lenses, trumpet horns, new rubber, weatherstrip, brake cylinders and kits, exhaust covers, emblems, motor mounts, wiring harnesses, metric screws, wiper blades and motors, manuals. Send $5 for catalog. Visa/MasterCard accepted. Orders only: 800-WTH-5771. Web site: www.mysiteis.com/wth-vmc

Mercer Automobile Company 210 Davis Rd Magnolia, NJ 08049 609-784-4044	parts service

Open Monday-Friday 8 am to 4:30 pm. Parts and service for 1910-1922 Mercer automobiles.

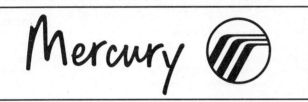

A-1 Shock Absorber Co Shockfinders Division 365 Warren Ave, PO Box 2028 Silverthorne, CO 80498 800-344-1966, 970-389-3193 cell FAX: 970-513-8283	shocks-all types coil springs Koni shocks leaf springs steering gears

See our ad on the last page

Antique Auto Electric 9109 (Rear) E Garvey Ave Rosemead, CA 91770 626-572-0938	repro wiring

See full listing in **Section Two** under **electrical systems**

Apple Hydraulics Inc 1610 Middle Rd Calverton, NY 11933-1419 800-882-7753, 631-369-9515 FAX: 631-369-9516 E-mail: info@applehydraulics.com	brake rebuilding shock rebuilding

See full listing in **Section Two** under **suspension parts**

Auto Krafters Inc 522 S Main St, PO Box 8 Broadway, VA 22815 540-896-5910; FAX: 540-896-6412 E-mail: akraft@shentel.net	parts

See full listing in **Section One** under **Ford 1954-up**

Autowire Division 9109 (Rear) E Garvey Ave Rosemead, CA 91770 626-572-0938; FAX: 626-288-3311	alternator conversions motors relays & switches

See full listing in **Section One** under **Ford 1954-up**

Bob Burgess 1955-56 Ford Parts 793 Alpha-Bellbrook Rd Bellbrook, OH 45305 937-426-8041 E-mail: bobs19551956@yahoo.com	parts

See full listing in **Section One** under **Ford 1954-up**

C & G Early Ford Parts 1941 Commercial St, Dept AH Escondido, CA 92029-1233 760-740-2400; FAX: 760-740-8700 E-mail: cgford@cgfordparts.com	accessories/chrome emblems & literature mechanical weatherstripping wiring

See full listing in **Section One** under **Ford 1932-1953**

Dennis Carpenter Ford Reproductions PO Box 26398 Charlotte, NC 28221 704-786-8139; FAX: 704-786-8180	parts

See full listing in **Section One** under **Ford 1954-up**

Class-Tech Corp 62935 Layton Ave Bend, OR 97701 800-874-9981	wiring harnesses

See full listing in **Section Two** under **electrical systems**

Classic Mercury Parts 1393 Shippee Ln Ojai, CA 93023 805-646-3345; FAX: 805-646-5386 E-mail: mfourez@aol.com	parts

Mail order only. Specializing in new, used, reproduction parts. Emblems, lenses, trunk liners, rubber parts, literature, manuals, stainless and chrome trim for 1949-1956 Mercury. Web site: www.classicmercury.com

Mike Dennis, Nebraska Mail Order 1845 S 48th St Lincoln, NE 68506 402-489-3036; FAX: 402-489-1148	parts Trippe mounting brackets/hardware

See full listing in **Section One** under **Ford 1932-1953**

Falcon Comet Fairlane & Ranchero Interiors 6343 Seaview Ave NW Seattle, WA 98107 888-609-2363; FAX: 206-781-5046 E-mail: falcon@evergo.net	interiors upholstery

See full listing in **Section One** under **Ford 1954-up**

Firewall Insulators & Quiet Ride Solutions 6465 Pacific Ave, Ste 249 Stockton, CA 95207 209-477-4840; FAX: 209-477-0918 E-mail: timcox@quietride.com	air plenums auto insulation firewall insulators gloveboxes sound deadening

See full listing in **Section Two** under **upholstery**

Ford Powertrain Applications 7702 E 96th St Puyallup, WA 98371 PH/FAX: 253-848-9503	engines

See full listing in **Section One** under **Ford 1954-up**

Garton's Auto 401 N 5th St (at 5th & Vine) Millville, NJ 08332-3129 PH: 856-825-3618	bicycle sales lit Ford NOS parts sales literature

See full listing in **Section One** under **Ford 1932-1953**

Gearheads Cruiser Products & Services
333 W Ingals Ave
Bismarck, ND 58504
701-223-2269
E-mail: gearheadsnd@aol.com

power steering

See full listing in **Section One** under **Ford 1954-up**

Randy Goodling
2046 Mill Rd
Elizabethtown, PA 17022-9401
717-367-6700

parts
parts locating

Mail order and open shop by appointment only. Specializing in parts and information on 1967-1973 Mercury Cougars.

Bill Horton
5804 Jones Valley Dr
Huntsville, AL 35802
256-881-6894

vacuum motors

Mail order only. Rebuilder of headlight vacuum motors for 1967-1970 Mercury Cougar, 1967-1971 Thunderbird, 1969-1976 Lincoln, Lincoln Mk III/IV and 1970 Ford Torino. Mail order sales of 1967-1968 Cougar body parts including rechromed bumpers and restored grilles/taillight assemblies.

Hot Rod & Custom Supply
1304 SE 10th St
Cape Coral, FL 33990
941-574-7744; FAX: 941-574-8820

custom parts
engine parts
speed parts

See full listing in **Section One** under **Ford 1932-1953**

Joe's Auto Sales
5849-190th St E
Hastings, MN 55033
612-437-6787

parts

See full listing in **Section One** under **Ford 1954-up**

John's Classic Cougars
11522 E Lakewood Blvd
Holland, MI 49424
616-396-0390; FAX: 616-396-0366
E-mail: jc-cougars@egl.net

accessories
parts

Mail order and open shop. Monday-Friday 9 am to 5 pm, Saturday by appointment. Specializing in new, good used and reproduction parts and accessories for 1967-1973 Mercury Cougars only. Complete Cougar catalog available for $5. "Cougars are our business... not a sideline!" Web site: www.johnsclassiccougars.com

Ken's Cougars
PO Box 5380
Edmond, OK 73083
405-340-1636; FAX: 405-340-5877

parts

Mail order and open shop. Monday-Friday 9 am to 5 pm CST. Specializing in 1967-1973 Mercury Cougar NOS, used and reproduction parts. We also offer complete restoration services. Web site: www.kenscougars.com

Lares Manufacturing
805 S Cleveland
Cambridge, MN 55008
800-334-5749; FAX: 763-754-2853
E-mail: sales@larescorp.com

power steering
equipment

See full listing in **Section One** under **Ford 1954-up**

LeBaron Bonney Co
6 Chestnut St, PO Box 6
Amesbury, MA 01913
800-221-5408, 978-388-3811
FAX: 978-388-1113
E-mail: lbb-hc@greennet.net

fabrics
interior kits
top kits

See full listing in **Section One** under **Ford 1903-1931**

Lincoln Parts International
707 E 4th St, Bldg G
Perris, CA 92570
800-382-1656, 909-657-5588
FAX: 909-657-4758
E-mail: lincolnparts@pe.net

parts

See full listing in **Section One** under **Lincoln**

Ed Liukkonen
37 Cook Rd
Templeton, MA 01468
978-939-8126

accessories
parts

See full listing in **Section One** under **Ford 1954-up**

Loyal Ford Mercury Inc
2310 Calumet Dr
New Holstein, WI 53061
920-898-4248; FAX: 920-898-9705
E-mail: loyal@loyalfordmercury.com

performance parts

See full listing in **Section One** under **Mustang**

Mac's Antique Auto Parts
1051 Lincoln Ave, PO Box 238
Lockport, NY 14095-0238
800-777-0948 US and Canada
716-433-1500 local and foreign
FAX: 716-433-1172
E-mail: mailmacs@aol.com

literature
parts
restoration
supplies

See full listing in **Section One** under **Ford 1903-1931**

Mark's 1941-1948 Ford Parts
97 Hoodlum Hill Rd
Binghamton, NY 13905
607-729-1693
E-mail: mkicsak@cs.com

parts

See full listing in **Section One** under **Ford 1932-1953**

Mercury & Ford Molded Rubber
12 Plymouth Ave
Wilmington, MA 01887
978-658-8394

parts

Mail order and open shop. Specialize in Mercury rubber parts. Sell 1939-1956 Mercury and Ford molded rubber parts. Also some 1939-1948 Mercury used parts and 1939-1941 reproduced metal parts. Can also supply Ford and Ford pickup rubber parts, many years.

Mercury Research Co
639 Glanker St
Memphis, TN 38112
PH/FAX: 901-323-2195, recorder

new parts
shop manuals

Mail, telephone and fax orders. New parts for 1949-1959 Mercury cars. Largest selection of Mercury parts. 75 page catalog, $5. In business over 25 years. Visa, MasterCard, personal checks accepted.

Miller Obsolete Parts
1329 Campus Dr
Vestal, NY 13850
607-722-5371; FAX: 607-770-9117
E-mail: mmiller3@stny.rr.com

locator service
parts

See full listing in **Section One** under **Ford 1954-up**

Mustangs Unlimited
185 Adams St
Manchester, CT 06040
860-647-1965
E-mail: info@mustangsunlimited.com

accessories
parts

See full listing in **Section One** under **Mustang**

Section One – Marque Specialists

Northwest Classic Falcons Inc   parts
1964 NW Pettygrove St
Portland, OR 97209
503-241-9454; FAX: 503-241-1964
E-mail: ron@nwfalcon.com

See full listing in **Section One** under **Ford 1954-up**

Obsolete Ford Parts Co   parts
311 E Washington Ave, PO Box 787
Nashville, GA 31639
229-686-2470; FAX: 229-686-7125

See full listing in **Section One** under **Ford 1954-up**

Obsolete Ford Parts Inc   parts
8701 S I-35
Oklahoma City, OK 73149
405-631-3933; FAX: 405-634-6815
E-mail: info@obsoletefordparts.com

See full listing in **Section One** under **Ford 1954-up**

Original Falcon, Comet, Ranchero,   interiors
Fairlane Interiors   parts
6343 Seaview Ave NW   weatherstripping
Seattle, WA 98107-2664
888-609-2363 toll free
FAX: 206-781-5046
E-mail: falcon@evergo.net

See full listing in **Section One** under **Ford 1954-up**

Power Brake Systems   brake repair
c/o Jerry Cinotti
431 S Sierra Way
San Bernadino, CA 92408
909-884-6980; FAX: 909-884-7872

See full listing in **Section Two** under **brakes**

Rock Valley Antique Auto Parts   gas tanks
Box 352, Rt 72 and Rothwell Rd
Stillman Valley, IL 61084
815-645-2271; FAX: 815-645-2740

See full listing in **Section One** under **Ford 1932-1953**

Rocky Mountain V8 Ford Parts   parts
1124 Clark Cir
Colorado Springs, CO 80915
719-597-8375
E-mail: fordyford@juno.com

See full listing in **Section One** under **Ford 1932-1953**

Sam's Vintage Ford Parts   parts
5105 Washington
Denver, CO 80216
303-295-1709

See full listing in **Section One** under **Ford 1954-up**

Sanders Reproduction Glass   glass
PO Box 522
Hillsboro, OR 97123
503-648-9184

See full listing in **Section Two** under **glass**

Tags Backeast   data plates
PO Box 581   trim tags
Plainville, CT 06062   cowl tags
860-747-2942
E-mail: dataplt@snet.net

See full listing in **Section Two** under **special services**

Pat Walsh Restorations   literature
Box Q   rubber parts
Wakefield, MA 01880
781-246-3266; FAX: 781-224-3311
E-mail: pwalshrest@aol.com

See full listing in **Section Two** under **rubber parts**

White Post Restorations   brakes
One Old Car Dr, PO Drawer D   restoration
White Post, VA 22663
540-837-1140; FAX: 540-837-2368
E-mail: info@whitepost.com

See full listing in **Section Two** under **brakes**

White Post Restorations   restoration
One Old Car Dr, PO Drawer D
White Post, VA 22663
540-837-1140; FAX: 540-837-2368
E-mail: info@whitepost.com

See full listing in **Section Two** under **restoration shops**

Gene Winfield's Rod & Custom   fender skirts
8201 Sierra Hwy   metal repair panels
Mojowe, CA 93501   motor mount kits
661-824-4728

We deal in fiberglass bodies for 41-48 Ford & 50-51 Mercury coupes or convertibles. Auto accessories: Mercury new and used stock parts, motor mount kits, fender skirts, metal repair panels, Winfield hat pins, T-shirts and posters, 8x10 black and white picture of old Winfield custom cars, drop sandals. Send $5 for new catalog (postage incl). We ship COD or Visa & MC.

Merkur

Rapido Group   accessories
80093 Dodson Rd   parts
Tygh Valley, OR 97063
541-544-3333; FAX: 541-544-3100

Mail order and open shop. Monday-Thursday 8 am to 5 pm, Friday 8 am to noon. Accessories and parts (OE, NOS, custom, high-performance) for Merkur XR4Ti and Scorpio, Turbo Thunderbird and SVO Mustang. Web site: www.rapidogroup.com

Metropolitan

British Triumph & Metropolitan   British Leyland
9957 Frederick Rd   Lucas/Girling
Ellicott City, MD 21042-3647   NOS British keys
410-750-2352 evenings   NOS British parts
E-mail: pete_groh@yahoo.com

Mail order only. Keys cut by code: single sided cut, $6; double sided cut, $9. Need number on face of the ignition switch or the three digit number on trunk handle stem. Wilmot Breeden keys; FA, FP, FS and FT original key, $12 each. WASO rubber headed key, $14 each. British Leyland, L swirl for TR7 and TR8, $14 each. With all orders include a SASE and your daytime telephone number. Photocopy of Lucas catalog, $12; Beck catalog, $14. Sample index page with the year/make of your car on request. Buy and sell NOS British parts. Web site: http://britishcarkeys.com

Classic American Parts Inc   parts
14213 Hereford Rd
Neosho, MO 64850
PH/FAX: 800-638-5461
E-mail: classam@clandjop.com

Specializing in auto parts for the Metropolitan 1954-1961. Mail order business specializing only in Metropolitan parts.

Metro Motors   parts
Dale Cheney
1070 E Roland St
Carson City, NV 89701
775-883-7308; FAX: 775-883-3180
E-mail: metroowl@gbis.com

Specializing in parts for Metropolitans. New, used and reconditioned. List available.

Metropolitan Pit Stop   literature
5324-26-28 & 5330 Laurel Canyon Blvd   parts
North Hollywood, CA 91607   restoration
800-PIT-STOP order toll-free
818-769-1515; FAX: 818-769-3500
E-mail: hi-valentine@webtv.net

Mail order and open store. Monday-Friday 10 am to 6 pm. Everything in Metropolitan parts. Repair shop. For 26 years, devoted exclusively to preservation, restoration and repair of Metropolitans. Will buy Metropolitan parts and Metropolitan literature/memorabilia for permanent Metropolitan Historical Collection Museum. Parts catalog free. Web site: http://web.as.net/~kaliboog/metpitstop.htm

Treasure Chest Sales   parts
413 Montgomery
Jackson, MI 49202
517-787-1475

See full listing in **Section One** under **Nash**

Wenner's   NOS parts
5449 Tannery Rd
Schnecksville, PA 18078
610-799-5419

See full listing in **Section One** under **AMC**

1 CAAT Limited Co   restoration
1324 E Harper Ave
Maryville, TN 37804
865-983-7180
E-mail: jhenriks@icx.net

See full listing in **Section Two** under **restoration shops**

A Bygone Era Motorcars   appraisals
6616 Madison Rd   restoration
Cincinnati, OH 45227
513-831-5520
E-mail: crrchaz@cs.com

See full listing in **Section One** under **Rolls-Royce/Bentley**

Abingdon Spares   parts
South St, PO Box 37
Walpole, NH 03608
603-756-4768; FAX: 603-756-9614
orders: 800-225-0251
E-mail: abingdon@sover.net

Mail order and open shop. Monday-Friday 9 am to 5 pm; Saturday 9 am to 12 noon. Selling MGT Series parts (TC, TD, TF models) only. Web site: www.abingdonspares.com

American-Foreign Auto Electric Inc   parts
103 Main St   rebuilding
Souderton, PA 18964
215-723-4877

See full listing in **Section Two** under **electrical systems**

Antique & Classic Car Restoration   restoration
Hwy 107, Box 368
Magdalena, NM 87825

Shop open by appointment only. Specializing in complete frame-up restorations for MG, Paige, Reo and Jaguar.

Apple Hydraulics Inc   brake rebuilding
1610 Middle Rd   shock rebuilding
Calverton, NY 11933-1419
800-882-7753, 631-369-9515
FAX: 631-369-9516
E-mail: info@applehydraulics.com

See full listing in **Section Two** under **suspension parts**

Automotive Artistry   restoration
679 W Streetboro St
Hudson, OH 44236
330-650-1503
E-mail: dale@cmh.net

See full listing in **Section One** under **Triumph**

Autosport Inc   restoration
2110 W Vernal Pk
Bloomington, IN 47404
812-334-1700; FAX: 812-334-1712

Open shop only. Monday-Friday 8:30 am to 5:30 pm. Specializing in mechanical restorations for all MGs, Jaguars, Triumphs, BMWs. Web site: www.autosportinc.com

BCP Sport & Classic Co   parts
10525 Airline Dr   service
Houston, TX 77037
281-448-4739; FAX: 281-448-0189

Mail order and open shop. Specializing in British and German parts and service for MG, Triumph, Jaguar, BMW, Mercedes-Benz, Maserati from 1950-1998. Also buy antique electric fans.

Brit-Tek Ltd   MGB cars
163 Griffin Rd   rustproofing
Deerfield, NH 03037   systems
800-255-5883

MGB performance & restoration parts & accessories. Free catalog. Distributor of Waxoyl rustproofing systems. Web site: www.brittek.com

British Auto Parts Ltd   parts
93256 Holland Ln
Marcola, OR 97454
541-933-2880; FAX: 541-933-2302

See full listing in **Section One** under **Morris**

British Auto Shoppe 1909 5th Ave Moline, IL 61265 309-764-9513; FAX: 309-764-9576	parts service

Mail order and open shop. Monday-Friday 8:30 am to 5:30 pm, Saturday by appointment. Parts (new and used) and service for British cars. Engine rebuild, mechanical restoration and carb rebuilding for MG, Triumph, Austin-Healey, Jaguar, Mini, Morris and Austin. See our cars for sale at: www.britishautoshoppe.com

British Car Keys Rt 144 Box 9957 Ellicott City, MD 21042-3647 410-750-2352 E-mail: britishcarkeys@hotmail.com	keys

See full listing in **Section One** under **Austin-Healey**

British Car Service 2854 N Stone Ave Tucson, AZ 85705 520-882-7026; FAX: 520-882-7053 E-mail: bcs@liveline.com	restoration salvage yard

See full listing in **Section Two** under **restoration shops**

British Car Specialists 2060 N Wilson Way Stockton, CA 95205 209-948-8767; FAX: 209-948-1030 E-mail: healeydoc@aol.com	parts repairs restoration

See full listing in **Section One** under **Austin-Healey**

British Miles 9278 Old E Tyburn Rd Morrisville, PA 19067 215-736-9300; FAX: 215-736-3089	accessories literature parts restoration

Mail order and open shop. Monday-Friday 9 am to 6 pm. Specializing in new and used parts, restorations, repairs and bench rebuilding services for British sports cars, MG, Triumph, Austin-Healey and Jaguar. We also carry tech and workshop manuals, books and accessories. Deals in windshield wiper and lamp parts for kit cars.

See our ad on this page

British Parts NW 4105 SE Lafayette Hwy Dayton, OR 97114 503-864-2001; FAX: 503-864-2081 E-mail: bpnw@onlinemac.com	parts

See full listing in **Section One** under **Triumph**

British Racing Green 30 Aleph Dr Newark, DE 19702 302-368-1117; FAX: 302-368-5910 E-mail: info@brgparts.com	new parts rebuilt parts used parts

Full line of parts for cars made in England (MG), Triumph, Austin-Healey and Jaguar, etc), new, used and rebuilt. Over 35,000 part numbers stocked with 2 acre salvage yard. 30 years' experience. Web site: www.brgparts.com

British Restorations 4455 Paul St Philadelphia, PA 19124 215-533-6696	car dealer restoration

See full listing in **Section One** under **Jaguar**

British Sportscars & Classics 4225 Aurora N Seattle, WA 98103-7307 206-634-3990	conversion kits engines transmissions

See full listing in **Section One** under **Jaguars**

British Wire Wheel 444 Airport Blvd, #114 Watsonville, CA 95077 800-732-9866, 831-763-4200 FAX: 831-763-1780	hubs tires wire wheels

See full listing in **Section One** under **Austin-Healey**

Classic Showcase 913 Rancheros Dr San Marcos, CA 92069 760-747-9947 restoration/buying 760-747-3188 sales; FAX: 760-747-4021 E-mail: management@ classicshowcase.com	classic vehicles restorations sales

See full listing in **Section Two** under **restoration shops**

Classic Wood Mfg 1006 N Raleigh St Greensboro, NC 27405 336-691-1344; FAX: 336-273-3074	wood kits wood replacement

See full listing in **Section Two** under **woodwork**

Doug's British Car Parts 2487 E Colorado Blvd Pasadena, CA 91107 818-793-2494; FAX: 818-793-4339 E-mail: dougsbritish@msn.com	accessories parts

See full listing in **Section One** under **Jaguar**

Doug's British Car Parts 606 Pub St Galloway, OH 43119 614-878-6373; FAX: 614-688-3077 E-mail: braden.13@osu.edu	accessories parts

See full listing in **Section One** under **Triumph**

East Coast Jaguar
802B Naaman's Rd
Wilmington, DE 19810
302-475-7200; FAX: 302-475-9258
E-mail: ecjaguar@aol.com

parts
service

See full listing in **Section One** under **Jaguar**

English Auto
501 Mt Ephraim Rd
Searsport, ME 04974
207-548-2946; FAX: 207-548-6470
E-mail: eauto@mint.net

restoration

See full listing in **Section One** under **Austin-Healey**

Finish Line
3593 SW 173rd Terr
Miramar, FL 33029
954-436-9101; FAX: 954-436-9102
E-mail: e.alibrandi@att.net

parts
supplies

See full listing in **Section One** under **Cobra**

Don Flye
5 Doe Valley Rd
Petersham, MA 01366
978-724-3318

parts

See full listing in **Section One** under **Austin-Healey**

Heritage Motor Centre
Banbury Rd
Gaydon
Warwickshire CV35 0BJ England
01926 641188; FAX: 01926 641555
E-mail: enquiries@
heritagemotorcentre.org.uk

museum

See full listing in **Section Six** under **England**

Heritage Upholstery and Trim
250 H St, PMB 3000
Blaine, WA 98231
604-990-0346; FAX: 604-990-9988

interior kits
trim
upholstery

See full listing in **Section One** under **Austin-Healey**

Jaguar Car Keys
9957 Frederick Rd
Ellicott City, MD 21042-3647
410-750-2352
E-mail: petegroh@yahoo.com

original British
keys

See full listing in **Section One** under **Jaguar**

Kimble Engineering Ltd
Unit 5 Old Mill Creek
Dartmouth
Devon TQ6 0HN England
0044 1803 835757
FAX: 0044 1803 834567
E-mail: johnlkimble@cs.com

aero screens
steering wheels

Mail order only. Specializing in Brooklands steering wheels with many applications and Brooklands aero screens in all forms.

Lake Oswego Restorations
19621 S Hazelhurst Ln
West Linn, OR 97068
PH/FAX: 503-636-7503

restoration
sales

See full listing in **Section One** under **Aston Martin**

M & G Vintage Auto
265 Rt 17, Box 226
Tuxedo Park, NY 10987
845-753-5900; FAX: 845-753-5613

parts
restoration
service
storage

"The Source" for all your MG needs. Largest supplier of new and used MG parts to the trade. We buy, sell, trade cars and parts, 13 car showroom and full shop on premises. We run a fully stocked MG TC/TD/TF, MGA, MGB mail order house. We can expertly rebuild your engine, transmission, carbs and gauges. Fully illustrated catalogs available upon request. Also offer vintage car storage.

McLean's Brit Bits
14 Sagamore Rd
Rye, NH 03870
800-995-2487; FAX: 603-433-0009
E-mail: sam@britbits.com

accessories
parts
sales
service

See full listing in **Section Two** under **car dealers**

Mini Motors Classic Coachworks
2775 Cherry Ave NE
Salem, OR 97303
503-362-3187; FAX: 503-375-9609
E-mail: urbanbugeye@cs.com

parts
restoration
sales
service

See full listing in **Section One** under **Austin-Healey**

Moss Motors Ltd
440 Rutherford St
Goleta, CA 93117
800-235-6954; FAX: 805-692-2525

accessories
parts

Business hours are Monday-Friday 6 am to 7 pm, Saturday and Sunday 7 am to 4 pm Pacific Time. We're the oldest and largest supplier of quality parts and accessories for MG, Triumph, Austin-Healey and Jaguar. Free catalogs for MG, Triumph, Austin-Healey and Jaguar XK 120-150. Free quarterly newsletter with hundreds of sale items, tech articles, club news and events. Toll free ordering with fast, dependable service and locations on both coasts. British Heritage approved supplier. Web site: www.mossmotors.com

Motorhead Ltd
2811-B Old Lee Hwy
Fairfax, VA 22031
800-527-3140; FAX: 703-573-3195

parts
repairs

See full listing in **Section One** under **Austin-Healey**

Motormetrics
6369 Houston Rd
Macon, GA 31216
912-785-0275
E-mail: fzampa@mail.maconstate.edu

used parts

See full listing in **Section One** under **Triumph**

Mouldsworth Motor Museum
Smithy Lane
Mouldsworth
NR Chester
Cheshire CH3 8AR England
01928 731781

museum

See full listing in **Section Six** under **England**

Mr Sport Car Inc
719 W 6th St
Papillion, NE 68046
402-592-7559

service

See full listing in **Section One** under **Jaguar**

| Northwest Import Parts
10042 SW Balmer
Portland, OR 97219
503-245-3806; FAX: 503-245-4193 | parts |

Mail order and open shop. Specialize in new parts for MG cars. Mechanical, interior, rubber, electrical and restoration parts for MGs 1955-1980.

| O'Connor Classic Autos
2569 Scott Blvd
Santa Clara, CA 95050
888-FINE-MGS (346-3647)
FAX: 408-727-3987 | car dealer
parts
restoration |

Mail order and open shop. Monday-Friday 9 am to 5 pm. Restored and unrestored MG cars, including TC, TD, TF, MGA, MGB. Full line of parts and restoration sevices. Web site: www.oconnorclassics.com

| Omni Specialties
10418 Lorain Ave
Cleveland, OH 44111
888-819-6464 (MGMG)
216-251-2269; FAX: 216-251-6083 | parts
restoration
service |

Mail order and open shop. Monday-Friday 9:30 am to 6:30 pm. Specializing in repair, service, parts, restoration for MG, Jaguar, Triumph, Austin-Healey, Lotus and other European classics including BMW, Porsche, VW and Audi. Service and repair for a price that's fair. 35 years' experience.

| Pacific International Auto
1118 Garnet Ave
San Diego, CA 92109
619-274-1920; FAX: 619-454-1815 | parts
sales
service |

See full listing in Section One under Jaguar.

| The Proper MG
97 Tenney St, PO Box 201
Georgetown, MA 01833
800-711-3368; FAX: 978-352-2751
E-mail: propermg@aol.com | parts |

Mail order. Monday-Friday 9 am to 5:30 pm. New and reconditioned parts. Direct importers from England. Retail, toll-free ordering. Fast, dependable service. Competitive prices, free MGB catalog. Specialist in MGB 1962-1980. Web site: www.propermg.com

| The Roadster Factory
328 Killen Rd, PO Box 332
Armagh, PA 15920
800-234-1104; FAX: 814-446-6729 | accessories
parts |

See full listing in Section One under Triumph.

| Rogers Motors
34 Codeyville Rd, PO Box 603
Shutesbury, MA 01072
413-259-1722
E-mail: jollyrogersmo@hotmail.com | used parts |

See full listing in Section One under Jaguar.

| Seven Enterprises Ltd
802 Bluecrab Rd, Ste 100
Newport News, VA 23606
800-992-7007; FAX: 800-296-3327 | accessories
parts |

See full listing in Section One under Austin.

| Shadetree Motors Ltd
3895 Mammoth Cave Ct
Pleasanton, CA 94588
PH/FAX: 925-846-1309
E-mail: kelsey@shadetreemotors.com | parts service |

All aspects of MG parts. Authorized Moss Motors parts distribu-tor. Specialize in all MG parts. $500,000 inventory. Discount pricing. Web site: http://shadetreemotors.com

| Sidecurtain Bags & Accessories
9130 W Broad St
Richmond, VA 23294
804-527-1515; FAX: 804-527-1616
E-mail: kmntr6@aol.com | side curtain bags |

See full listing in Section One under Triumph.

| Sports Car Haven
2-33 Flowerfield Industrial Pk
St James, NY 11780
631-862-8058
E-mail: sch94@aol.com | new and used parts
race prep
restoration
service |

See full listing in Section One under Triumph.

| Sports Car Haven
3414 Bloom Rd, Rt 11
Danville, PA 17821
570-275-5705 | parts
restoration
service |

See full listing in Section Two under restoration shops.

| Sports Car Rentals & Sales
PO Box 265
Batesville, VA 22924
804-823-4442
E-mail: info@sportscarrentals.com | car rentals |

See full listing in Section Two under special services.

| Sports Car Services
2450 Westminster W Rd
Westminster, VT 05158
802-387-4540 | parts
service |

Shop open Monday-Friday 8:30 am to 5:30 pm and some Saturdays. Specializing in service and parts for MG and Austin-Healey.

| Thoroughbred Motors
3935 N US 301
Sarasota, FL 34234
941-359-2277; FAX: 941-359-2128
E-mail: vintagejags@mindspring.com | car dealer
parts |

See full listing in Section One under Jaguar.

| Triple C Motor Accessories
1900 Orange St
York, PA 17404
717-854-4081; FAX: 717-854-6706
E-mail: sales@triple-c.com | accessories
models |

Mail order and open shop. Monday-Friday 9 am to 5 pm. Specializing in regalia, models and accessories for all British marques. Web site: www.triple-c.com

| University Motors Ltd
6490 E Fulton
Ada, MI 49301
616-682-0800; FAX: 616-682-0801 | events
line/bench service
restoration |

Open Monday-Friday 9 am to 6 pm, Saturday 9 am to 1 pm, summers only. Specializing in MG restoration, line and bench service, technical support and events. NAMGBR and MGOC approved workshop. MGCC trade member. British Motor Heritage approved workshop. Web site: www.universitymotorsltd.com

| Victoria British Ltd
Box 14991
Lenexa, KS 66285-4991
800-255-0088, 913-599-3299 | accessories
parts |

Mail order catalog. Monday-Friday 7 am to 9 pm, Saturday-Sunday 9 am to 5 pm. One of the world's largest distributors of parts and accessories for British sports cars. Offering the most complete up-to-date information in our fully illustrated catalogs.

Stocks over 20,000 line items for MG, Triumph, Austin-Healey and Sunbeam. Telephone orders are fast and easy with a reliable on-line computer entry system. As a distributor for British Motor Heritage in the US, the company is able to provide original equipment and authentic reproduction parts. Great prices on high-performance parts, accessories, upholstery, rubber and chrome trim. Web site: www.victoriabritish.com

See our ad on this page

| **Von's Austin-Healey Restorations**
10270 Barberville Rd
Fort Mill, SC 29715
803-548-4590; FAX: 803-548-4816
E-mail: vons@vnet.net | **parts**
repairs
restoration |

See full listing in **Section One** under **Austin-Healey**

| **White Post Restorations**
One Old Car Dr, PO Drawer D
White Post, VA 22663
540-837-1140; FAX: 540-837-2368
E-mail: info@whitepost.com | **brakes**
restoration |

See full listing in **Section Two** under **brakes**

| **White Post Restorations**
One Old Car Dr, PO Drawer D
White Post, VA 22663
540-837-1140; FAX: 540-837-2368
E-mail: info@whitepost.com | **restoration** |

See full listing in **Section Two** under **restoration shops**

MOON

| **Moon Registry**
Carl W Burst III
1600 N Woodlawn
St Louis, MO 63124
314-822-7807
314-822-8688 recorder | **literature**
photographs |

Specializing in all products of the Moon Motor Car Company: Moon, Hol-Tan, Diana, Windsor and Ruxton. Restoration aid, copies of factory photos, owner's manuals, tune-up data, parts location assistance and names of other owners with similar models available at no charge. Please include phone number if writing.

Mopar

| **Accurate Ltd**
7125 Hwy 99 N
Roseburg, OR 97470
PH/FAX: 541-672-2661
E-mail: taswope@jeffnet.org | **muffler products** |

Mail order and open shop. Monday-Friday 8 am to 4:30 pm. Specializing in Mopar exhaust and muffler products. Web site: www.accurateltd.com

| **Antique Auto Fasteners**
Guy (Chuck) Close
811 Oceanhill Dr
Huntington Beach, CA 92648
714-969-9161, 562-696-3307
E-mail: redjc1@earthlink.net | **fasteners**
hardware
hose clamps
molding clips |

See full listing in **Section Two** under **hardware**

| **Antique DeSoto-Plymouth**
4206 Burnett Dr
Murrysville, PA 15668
724-733-1818 eves; FAX: 724-733-9884
E-mail: parts4u@aol.com | **Mopar parts** |

Mail order and open shop by appointment. Phone evenings. New old stock 1938-1960 Chrysler, Plymouth, Dodge, DeSoto parts. Hard-to-find Mopar parts: grilles, bumpers, chrome moldings, etc. Send SASE with list of wants. Satisfaction guaranteed on all we sell. Web site: www.antiquemopar.com

| **Arizona Parts**
320 E Pebble Beach
Tempe, AZ 85282
480-966-6683
800-328-8766, code 88602 | **accessories**
literature
parts |

Mail order only. For 1935-2001 Chrysler Corporation vehicles. 39,000 item computer inventory using Chrysler part numbers with description and application available, (call for cost). New and used parts, accessories and literature stocked. Send SASE for current stock information. Web site: www.arizonaparts.com

Atlas Obsolete Chrysler Parts | parts
10621 Bloomfield St, Unit 32
Los Alamitos, CA 90720
PH/FAX: 562-594-5560
E-mail: atlaschrys@aol.com

Mail order, telephone and open shop sales. Monday-Friday 9 am to 5 pm. NOS and reproduction parts for 1936-1974 Plymouth, Dodge, DeSoto, Chrysler and Imperial. Specializing in engine, driveline, electrical and chassis parts, locks, lenses, literature and rubber. We stock over 10,000 different items. For our latest catalog, send $7 ($14 foreign). Visa and MasterCard welcome. Web site: www.atlasobsolete.com

Barnett & Small Inc | electrical parts
151E Industry Ct
Deer Park, NY 11729
631-242-2100; FAX: 631-242-2101

See full listing in **Section Two** under **electrical systems**

Andy Bernbaum Auto Parts | parts
315 Franklin St
Newton, MA 02458
617-244-1118

Mail order and telephone order. New and NOS parts for 1930-1962 Chrysler, Dodge, Plymouth and DeSoto cars and trucks. Comprehensive parts including mechanical, brake, suspension, weatherstripping, body, drivetrain, electric, trim, accessories and literature. 1930-1962 catalog $4. For later years, call for availability. Visa, MasterCard, Discover, AmEx accepted. Web site: www.oldmopars.com

Brewer's Performance Inc | parts
2580 S St Rt 48
Ludlow Falls, OH 45339-9773
937-698-4259; FAX: 937-698-7109

Specializing in four-speed conversions on 1962-1976 Mopar muscle cars. Rebuilt Hurst shifters, A-833 rebuild kits, rebuilt transmissions, restored pistol grips, new torque shafts, clutch linkage, bellhousings, pedal assemblies, etc. From one small part to complete conversions. Call the 4-speed specialists!

Bumper Boyz LLC | bumper repairs reconditioning sandblasting
2435 E 54th St
Los Angeles, CA 90058
800-995-1703, 323-587-8976
FAX: 323-587-2013

See full listing in **Section One** under **Chevrolet**

Chief Service | parts restoration
Herbert G Baschung
Brunnmatt, PO Box 155
CH-4914 Roggwil Switzerland
PH/FAX: 0041-62-9291777

See full listing in **Section Two** under **restoration shops**

Christian Motorsports Illustrated | performance parts
PO Box 129
Mansfield, PA 16933
570-549-2282; FAX: 570-549-3366

Mail order and open shop. Monday-Friday 9 am to 4 pm. Founded 1976. 3,700 members. 25 years of enthusiast information and parts organization for Mopar enthusiasts, including National Hemi Owners Association, Mopar Muscle Club, Chrysler Performance Parts Association. Bi-monthly publication: *Christian Motorsports Illustrated*, $19.96. Specializing in Chrysler and Mopar performance exhaust parts for 1962-1978 Chrysler, Plymouth, Dodge. Do not need to be a Mopar enthusiast. Dues: none.

Clester's Auto Rubber Seals Inc | molded rubber parts weatherstripping
PO Box 1113
Salisbury, NC 28145
800-457-8223, 704-637-9979
FAX: 704-636-7390

See full listing in **Section Two** under **rubber parts**

Convertible Service | convertible parts manufacture/ service top mechanism
5126-HA Walnut Grove Ave
San Gabriel, CA 91776
800-333-1140, 626-285-2255
FAX: 626-285-9004

See full listing in **Section Two** under **tops**

Dash Specialists | interiors
1910 Redbud Ln
Medford, OR 97504
541-776-0040

See full listing in **Section One** under **Cadillac/LaSalle**

Len Dawson | chrome/trim items electrical parts mechanical parts
15541 Yokeko Dr
Anacortes, WA 98221
FAX: 360-293-1032

Mail order only. One of the world's largest inventories of NOS parts for 1935-1983 Chrysler products. Full line of mechanical and electrical parts, plus thousands of chrome and trim items. Send SASE or 24 hour fax number and Chrysler Corporation part numbers with inquiries.

Daniel N Dietrich | restoration trim parts
RD 1
Kempton, PA 19529
610-756-6078, 610-756-6071

Mail order and open shop. Restores complete car bodies, 1941-1963 Mopar only, back to original factory finish. Also sells exterior chrome, stainless body moldings and trim.

Dynamic Racing Transmissions LLC | automatic transmissions
104-5 Enterprise Dr, Unit 1
North Branford, CT 06471
203-315-0138; FAX: 203-315-0352
E-mail: mightymitejr@aol.com

See full listing in **Section Two** under **transmissions**

Dynatech Engineering | motor mounts
PO Box 1446
Alta Loma, CA 91701-8446
805-492-6134
E-mail: dynatechengineering@yahoo.com

See full listing in **Section Two** under **engine parts**

ETC/Every Thing Cars | paint repairs restoration welding
8727 Clarinda
Pico Rivera, CA 90660
562-949-6981

Shop open by phone appointment only. Monday-Friday 9 am to 6 pm. Deals in body, chassis, engine, trans, brakes, front ends, air conditioning, tune-ups, high-performance, carbs, ignition, detailing, frame-offs and partials. General auto restorations, 1960s-1975. References. R W Nash, owner, technician, craftsman. Reasonable rates. (This business does not sell individual parts).

John Filiss | appraisals
45 Kingston Ave
Port Jervis, NY 12771
845-856-2942
E-mail: john@filiss.com

See full listing in **Section Two** under **appraisals**

Jay M Fisher	mascots
Acken Dr 4-B	sidemount mirrors
Clark, NJ 07066	windwing brackets
732-388-6442	

See full listing in **Section Two** under **accessories**

Gardner Exhaust Systems	exhaust systems
7 Cedar Ln	
Rhinebeck, NY 12572	
845-876-8117; FAX: 845-871-1750	
E-mail: gexhaust@aol.com	

See full listing in **Section Two** under **exhaust systems**

Grand Touring	engine rebuilding
2785 E Regal Park Dr	machine shop
Anaheim, CA 92806	restoration
714-630-0130; FAX: 714-630-6956	suspension

See full listing in **Section Two** under **restoration shops**

Bill Gratkowski	woodgraining
515 N Petroleum St	
Titusville, PA 16354	
814-827-1782 days or eves	
E-mail: billgrains@csonline.net	

See full listing in **Section Two** under **woodgraining**

Jim Harris	cars
16743 39th NE	parts
Seattle, WA 98155	
206-364-6637	
E-mail: jimconniemopar@cs.com	

Mail order and open shop. Cars and parts, Mopar 1927-1975. Specializes in sixties Imperials and Mopar muscle cars. In the hobby since 1974.

Mike Hershenfeld	parts
PO Box 1301	
Bellmore, NY 11710	
PH/FAX: 516-781-PART (7278)	
E-mail: mikesmopar@juno.com	

Mail order only. Specializing in Mopar NOS 1932-1970: engine, fuel, electrical, brakes, lenses, gauges, clutch, ignition, gaskets, cooling, suspension, chrome, literature. Web site: www.mikesmopar.com

Hidden Valley Auto Parts	parts
21046 N Rio Bravo	
Maricopa, AZ 85239	
602-252-2122, 602-252-6137	
520-568-2945; FAX: 602-258-0951	
E-mail: hvap@aol.com	

See full listing in **Section One** under **Chevrolet**

Jeff Johnson Motorsports	literature
PO Box 14327	
Columbus, OH 43214	
614-268-1181; FAX: 614-268-1141	
E-mail: jj@chryslerclassic.com	

Mail order only. Specializing in literature for all Chrysler product cars and trucks.

Bob Johnson's Auto Literature	brochures
92 Blandin Ave	literature
Framingham, MA 01702	manuals
508-872-9173; FAX: 508-626-0991	paint chips
E-mail: bjohnson@autopaper.com	

See full listing in **Section Two** under **literature dealers**

Kramer Automotive Specialties	body parts
PO Box 5	interiors
Herman, PA 16039	sheetmetal
724-285-5566; FAX: 724-285-8898	
E-mail: kramerauto@aol.com	

Mail order only. Monday-Friday, noon to 6 pm. A, B, C and E-body parts, race Hemi, St Hemi, max wedge, body and engine restoration items. 1960s and early 1970s Dodge, Plymouth, Chrysler, with emphasis on factory race cars and muscle cars. Sheetmetal, interiors and chrome in NOS, good used and reproduction.

The Last Precinct Police Museum	museum
15677 Hwy 62 W	
Eureka Springs, AR 72632	
501-253-4948; FAX: 501-253-4949	

See full listing in **Section Six** under **Arkansas**

Layson's Restorations Inc	parts
26164 126th Ave SE	
Kent, WA 98031	
253-630-4088; FAX: 253-630-4065	
E-mail: laysons@foxinternet.net	

Shop open Monday-Friday 9 am to 6 pm PST. Specializing in Dodge, Plymouth, Chrysler automotive parts from 1950 to 1976 for A-body, B-body, C-body, E-body, Chrysler 300 letter cars and more. Manufacturer of many Mopar parts from lenses and bezels to weatherstripping, interiors and sheetmetal. We even have services like plastic chrome, transmission crossmember conversions, woodgrain steering wheel restorations and fuel filler tube conversions. Web site: www.laysons.com

See our ad on page 137

Leo R Lindquist	1950s Hemi parts
1851 US Hwy 14	NORS parts
Balaton, MN 56115-3200	NOS parts
PH/FAX: 507-734-2051	
E-mail: leorob51@frontiernet.net	

Mail order and shop open by appointment. Specializing in 241 to 392 Hemi engines and parts (mainly used); many small pieces available. No high-performance items. Also 1950s Chrysler Corporation vehicles and parts. Engine and transmission rebuilding services available for that era.

Mancini Racing Enterprises	parts
33510 Groesbeck Hwy	
Fraser, MI 48026	
810-294-6670; FAX: 810-294-0390	
E-mail: robc@manciniracing.com	

Mail order and open shop. Monday-Friday 9 am to 6 pm, Saturday 10 am to 3 pm. Specializing in restoration parts and performance parts for 1960 to present Chrysler, Dodge and Plymouth products. Web site: www.manciniracing.com

MikeCo Antique, Kustom &	lenses
Obsolete Auto Parts	parts
4053 Calle Tesoro, Unit C	
Camarillo, CA 93012	
805-482-1725; FAX: 805-987-8524	

Mail order and open shop. Monday-Friday 3:30 pm to 7 pm, Saturday 10 am to 5 pm PST, fax 24 hours. Specializing in lenses, stainless trim, tune-up and electrical, brake parts and weatherstrip for Chrysler product vehicles 1930s-1975. Autolite and Delco electrical parts and weatherstrip for American made vehicles, 1915-1975. Heavy into Chrysler and General Motors with stock of parts for independent makes.

Mike's Auto Parts	NOS Mopar
Box 358	NOS GM
Ridgeland, MS 39158	NOS Ford
601-856-7214	parts for all makes

See full listing in **Section One** under **Chrysler**

Mopar Collector's Guide Magazine PO Box 15489 Baton Rouge, LA 70895-5489 225-274-0609; FAX: 225-274-9033 E-mail: mopar@intersurf.com	magazine

Mail order only. *Mopar Collector's Guide* magazine is the world's largest monthly Mopar only buy, sell, trade publication. Subscribers always advertise free, which pays for subscription. Color racing and restoration articles each month. Extensive price guide. All credit cards accepted. Free T-shirt ($3 s&h) with your subscription when you mention this ad. Subscription: $25/year (12 issues). Web site: www.mcg-pub.com

Mr G's Enterprises 5613 Elliott Reeder Rd Fort Worth, TX 76117 817-831-3501; FAX: 817-831-0638 E-mail: mrgs@mrgusa.com	fasteners screw kits

Mail order and open shop. Monday-Friday 9 am to 5 pm. Specializing in fasteners, screw kits and rechrome plastic for all makes and models. Web site: www.mrgusa.com
See our ad on page 138

NOS Reproductions 22425 Jefferies Rd, RR 3 Komoka ON Canada N0L 1R0 519-471-2740; FAX: 519-471-7675 E-mail: info@nosreproductions.com	parts

Specializing in seat covers, headliners, door panels, weatherstripping and molded carpets for Ford, GM and Chrysler. 1963-1968 Galaxie XL seat skins a specialty.

Obsolete Chrysler NOS Parts 4206 Burnett Dr Murrysville, PA 15668 724-733-1818 eves; FAX: 724-733-9884 E-mail: parts4u@aol.com	literature parts

See full listing in **Section One** under **Chrysler**

Obsolete Parts of Iowa PO Box 233 Earlville, IA 52041 E-mail: finsrus@mwci.net	NOS parts

Mail order only. Specializing in NOS Mopar parts for 1950s, 1960s, 1970s Chrysler, Plymouth, Dodge, DeSoto.

Older Car Restoration Martin Lum, Owner 304 S Main St, Box 428 Mont Alto, PA 17237 717-749-3383, 717-352-7701 E-mail: marty@oldercar.com	repro parts restoration

See full listing in **Section Two** under **restoration shops**

Original Auto Interiors 7869 Trumble Rd Columbus, MI 48063-3915 810-727-2486; FAX: 810-727-4344 E-mail: origauto@tir.com	upholstery

See full listing in **Section Two** under **upholstery**

Phoenix Graphix Inc 5861 S Kyrene Rd #10 Tempe, AZ 85283 800-941-4550	decals stripe kits

See full listing in **Section Two** under **decals**

Plymouth, Dodge, Chrysler, DeSoto Parts 4206 Burnett Dr Murrysville, PA 15668 724-733-1818 eves; FAX: 724-733-9884 E-mail: parts4u@aol.com	NOS parts for DeSoto

See full listing in **Section One** under **DeSoto**

Sam Quinn Cadillac Parts Box 837 Estacada, OR 97023 503-637-3852	parts

See full listing in **Section One** under **Cadillac/LaSalle**

Reproduction Parts Marketing 1920 Alberta Ave Saskatoon, SK Canada S7K 1R9 306-652-6668; FAX: 306-652-1123	parts restoration service

See full listing in **Section One** under **Chevrolet**

Riddle's/Mr Plymouth 20303 8th Ave NW Shoreline, WA 98177-2107 PH/FAX: 206-285-6534 days	decals overdrives parts & info repro parts

Mail order only. Neil Riddle, proprietor. Parts 1940-1954. NOS, used and hard-to-find items a specialty. Send $2 for latest listing of products and reproductions. Technical advisor for Plymouth Owners Club, knowledgeable advice given. Also buy, sell, trade NOS parts. Old Mopar cars and parts locator service.

Mr. G's ENTERPRISES

We do it all Repair, Weld, Rechrome, Paint & Detail Plastic.

Catalog set Printed or on CD, $9.95 Refundable in U.S.A.

Includes Fasteners Screw Kits, Bolt Kits, Etc.

We have 4,000 Parts available for exchange. Other rechroming allow 3-6 weeks. Repaired and/or detailed parts allow more time.

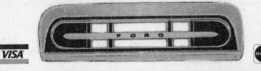

VISA   MasterCard

5613 Elliott Reeder Rd • Fort Worth, Texas 76117
Phone# (817) 831-3501 • Fax# (817) 838-3131
e-mail: mrgs@mrgusa.com   website: wwwmrgusa.com

Special T's Unlimited Inc PO Box 146 Prospect Heights, IL 60070 847-255-5494; FAX: 847-259-7220 E-mail: special_t_bill@yahoo.com	general repair parts restoration service

Mail order and open shop. Shop address: 103 N Wheeling Rd, Prospect Heights, IL 60070. Mopar, specializing in 1956-1972 Plymouth/Dodge parts, repair, service, hi-performance. Repair of moldings, trim, anodizing, engine tuned (swirl pattern) for Sport Fury and Polara 500s. New headlight rings and restored grilles, etc. Engine and transmission changeovers and special detailing. Still service and repair Ford A and T, custom painting and detailing. Max wedge air cleaners, alum bumper brackets, repro Coronet 500 finish panels, chrome, die cast, bumper nameplates, plastic chrome and more.

Ssnake-Oyl Products Inc 114 N Glenwood Blvd Tyler, TX 75702 800-284-7777; FAX: 903-526-4501	carpet underlay firewall insulation seat belt restoration

See full listing in **Section Two** under **interiors & interior parts**

Stencils & Stripes Unlimited Inc 1108 S Crescent Ave #21 Park Ridge, IL 60068 847-692-6893; FAX: 847-692-6895	NOS decals stripe kits

See full listing in **Section Two** under **decals**

Street-Wise Performance Richie Mulligan Box 105 Creek Rd Tranquility, NJ 07879 973-786-7500; FAX: 973-786-7861 E-mail: street-wise@usa.net	differentials new/used parts overhaul kits transmissions

See full listing in **Section Two** under **differentials**

Tags Backeast PO Box 581 Plainville, CT 06062 860-747-2942 E-mail: dataplt@snet.net	data plates trim tags cowl tags

See full listing in **Section Two** under **special services**

Torque Tech Performance Exhaust 1826 Woodland Dr Valdosta, GA 31601 800-408-0016 E-mail: torque@surfsourth.com	exhaust systems

See full listing in **Section Two** under **exhaust systems**

Totally Auto Inc 337 Philmont Ave Feasterville, PA 19053 215-322-2277; FAX: 215-322-4755 E-mail: totalyauto@aol.com	parts restoration service

Mail order and open shop by appointment. Monday-Friday 9 am to 4:30 pm. Chrysler only restoration parts, supplies and services. Offering a full line of restoration parts, clips and fastener kits, NOS and good used, as well as restoration correct spray paints. Our services include zinc and cadmium plating, powder and phosphate coating and component restoration. Why should you use our products and services? Doesn't it make sense to get your restoration parts from an established restoration shop that uses those parts to restore award winning Mopar muscle cars? Web site: www.totallyautoinc.com

Vintage Auto Parts Inc 24300 Hwy 9 Woodinville, WA 98072 800-426-5911, 425-486-0777 FAX: 425-486-0778 E-mail: erics@vapinc.com	cars parts

See full listing in **Section Two** under **comprehensive parts**

White Post Restorations	brakes
One Old Car Dr, PO Drawer D	restoration
White Post, VA 22663	
540-837-1140; FAX: 540-837-2368	
E-mail: info@whitepost.com	

See full listing in **Section Two** under **brakes**

WiperWorks	restoration
PO Box 57	
Sewanee, TN 37375	
PH/FAX: 931-598-9573	

See full listing in **Section One** under **Chevrolet**

Wittenborn's Auto Service Inc	**Mopar**
133 Woodside Ave	**Dodge**
Briarcliff Manor, NY 10510-1717	**Plymouth**
914-941-2744; FAX: 914-769-1327	

Open Monday-Saturday 9 am to 5:30 pm. Dart and Valiant used parts 1961-1976. Also, Volare and Aspen. No muscle car parts. Body, interior, chassis, drivetrain, glass, trim, etc. Repair and service on old and modern cars.

Cantab Motors Ltd	**new & used cars**
37251 E Richardson Ln	**parts**
Purcellville, VA 20132	**service**
540-338-2211, 866-338-7974 for parts	
FAX: 540-338-2944	
E-mail: morgans@cantab-motors.com	

Mail order and open shop. Monday to Friday, weekends by appointment. Morgan sports cars authorized US agents. Specializing in new and used car sales, spare parts, restoration and service, vintage racing preparation for Morgan sports cars. Web site: http://morgans.cantab-motors.com

The CM Booth Collection of Historic Vehicles	**museum**
Falstaff Antiques	
63-67 High St	
Rolvenden Kent TN17 4LP England	
01580-241234	

See full listing in **Section Six** under **England**

Isis Imports Ltd	**cars**
PO Box 2290	**parts**
Gateway Station	**restoration**
San Francisco, CA 94126	
415-433-1344; FAX: 415-788-1850	
E-mail: isis@morgancars-usa.com	

Mail order and open shop daily by appointment. Specializing in Morgan cars, parts, service and restoration. The oldest full service Morgan distributor in the US, providing Morgan cars, service and support since 1968. Web site: www.morgancars-usa.com

Morgan Motor Company Ltd	**motors**
Pickersleigh Road	**parts**
Malvern Link	
Worcester, WR14 2LL England	
0168-4573104; FAX: 0168-4892295	

Mail order and open shop. Monday-Friday 9 to 4. Motor manufacturer and parts supplier for Morgan. Annual catalog. Factory visits welcome by prior appointment.

Morgan Oasis Garage	restoration
N 51 Terrace Rd, PO Box 1010	service
Hoodsport, WA 98548	
360-877-5160	

Mail order and open shop. Monday-Friday 9 am to 6 pm PST. Specializing in service and restoration for Morgan 4-4, Plus 4, Plus 8.

Morgan Spares Ltd	**car sales**
225 Simons Rd	**consulting**
Ancram, NY 12502	**obsolete parts**
518-329-3877; FAX: 518-329-3892	**used parts**
E-mail: morganspares@taconic.net	

Mail order and open shop. Monday-Friday 8 am to 5 pm, Saturday by appointment. Specializing in Morgan +4, 4/4, +8 from 1950-present. Complete body assemblies, sheetmetal, wood, interiors, weather equip, accessories, mechanical, electrical, stainless steel, race and performance items. 24 years of Morgan restoration, service and sales. Genuine Morgan factory parts. Lucas-Girling distributor. Obsolete, used and hard to find parts. Illustrated parts manual. Car sales and sales consulting service. Web site: www.morgan-spares.com

Olde World Restorations	**parts**
2727 Philmont Ave, Ste 350	**restoration**
Huntingdon Valley, PA 19006	
215-947-8720; FAX: 215-947-8722	

Mail order and open shop. Monday-Friday 9 am to 5:30 pm or by appointment. Morgan parts, repairs and restorations.

Ragtops & Roadsters	**bodywork/painting**
203 S 4th St	**British automobiles**
Perkasie, PA 18944	**engine rebuilding**
215-257-1202; FAX: 215-257-2688	**vintage race prep**
E-mail: info@ragtops.com	

See full listing in **Section One** under **AC**

Sports Car Haven	**new and used parts**
2-33 Flowerfield Industrial Pk	**race prep**
St James, NY 11780	**restoration**
631-862-8058	**service**
E-mail: sch94@aol.com	

See full listing in **Section One** under **Triumph**

Triple C Motor Accessories	**accessories**
1900 Orange St	**models**
York, PA 17404	
717-854-4081; FAX: 717-854-6706	
E-mail: sales@triple-c.com	

See full listing in **Section One** under **MG**

Gideon Booth	**car collector**
Rellandsgate, Kings Meaburn	**parts**
Penrith	**restorations**
Cumbria CA10 3BT England	
PH/FAX: 01931 714624	

Mail order and open shop. Daily 9 am to 8 pm. Specializing in Morris cars and trucks for all models 1913-1963. Car collector with 80 Morris vehicles. Reproduces fiberglass body panels, timber frames, exhausts and second hand parts.

British Auto Parts Ltd | parts
93256 Holland Ln
Marcola, OR 97454
541-933-2880; FAX: 541-933-2302

Monday-Friday 8 am to 5 pm. Offering new, used and rebuilt parts for Morris Minor, MG, Triumph and Jaguar. 25 years' of exclusive British experience in supplying the common and hard-to-find for all British cars. Questions and problems welcomed. Daily shipping UPS, bank cards accepted.

Downton | minis
901 Eastgate St | rebuilding
N Elmham
Norfolk NR20 5HE England
+44 1362 667122
FAX: +33 1362 667133
E-mail: downton@compaqnet.co.uk

See full listing in **Section One** under **Austin**

Mini Store | cars
PO Box 7973 | repairs
Van Nuys, CA 91409-7973 | restorations
PH/FAX: 818-893-1421
E-mail: minicoopers@socal.rr.com

See full listing in **Section One** under **Austin**

Patton Orphan Spares | parts
52 Nicole Pl
West Babylon, NY 11704
516-669-2598

See full listing in **Section One** under **Renault**

Seven Enterprises Ltd | accessories
802 Bluecrab Rd, Ste 100 | parts
Newport News, VA 23606
800-992-7007; FAX: 800-296-3327

See full listing in **Section One** under **Austin**

All American Rambler | cars
11661 Martens River Cir #M | manuals
Fountain Valley, CA 92708 | memorabilia
714-662-7200 | parts/tech info
E-mail: rambler411@aol.com

See full listing in **Section One** under **AMC**

Anderson Racing Inc | engine rebuilding
3911 Main St
Grandview, MO 64030
816-765-4881; FAX: 816-765-9897
E-mail: davea@engine-parts.com

See full listing in **Section Two** under **engine rebuilding**

Blaser's Auto, Nash, Rambler, AMC | NOS parts
3200 48th Ave
Moline, IL 61265-6453
309-764-3571; FAX: 309-764-1155
E-mail: blazauto@sprynet.com

See full listing in **Section One** under **AMC**

British Triumph & Metropolitan | British Leyland
9957 Frederick Rd | original British
Ellicott City, MD 21042-3647 | keys
410-750-2352 evenings | WASO
E-mail: pete_groh@yahoo.com | Wilmot Breeden

See full listing in **Section One** under **Metropolitan**

Charles Chambers Parts | parts
Box 60, HC 64
Goldthwaite, TX 76844
E-mail: gonzales@centex.net

Mail order only. Exclusively Nash parts. Good selection of items from ammeters to zerks. SASE required.

Firewall Insulators & Quiet Ride | air plenums
Solutions | auto insulation
6465 Pacific Ave, Ste 249 | firewall insulators
Stockton, CA 95207 | gloveboxes
209-477-4840; FAX: 209-477-0918 | sound deadening
E-mail: timcox@quietride.com

See full listing in **Section Two** under **upholstery**

Galvin's Rambler Parts | parts
7252-R Stockton Blvd
Sacramento, CA 95823
916-424-4202; FAX: 916-424-4240

See full listing in **Section One** under **AMC**

Kennedy American Inc | parts
7100 State Rt 142 SE
West Jefferson, OH 43162
614-879-7283

See full listing in **Section One** under **AMC**

Metropolitan Pit Stop | literature
5324-26-28 & 5330 Laurel Canyon Blvd | parts
North Hollywood, CA 91607 | restoration
800-PIT-STOP order toll-free
818-769-1515; FAX: 818-769-3500
E-mail: hi-valentine@webtv.net

See full listing in **Section One** under **Metropolitan**

South Texas AMC | parts
30115 Hwy 281 N, Ste 126 | restoration
Bulverde, TX 78163
830-980-3165
E-mail: akjamc@juno.com

See full listing in **Section One** under **AMC**

Treasure Chest Sales | parts
413 Montgomery
Jackson, MI 49202
517-787-1475

Mail order and open shop by appointment only. Retail mail order parts source for Nash, Metropolitan and AMC made automobiles, all years, NOS and used.

Webb's Classic Auto Parts | NOS parts
5084 W State Rd 114 | reproduction parts
Huntington, IN 46750 | service manuals
219-344-1714; FAX: 219-344-1754 | used parts

See full listing in **Section One** under **AMC**

Wenner's | NOS parts
5449 Tannery Rd
Schnecksville, PA 18078
610-799-5419

See full listing in **Section One** under **AMC**

KATO USA Inc | models
100 Remington Rd
Schaumburg, IL 60173
847-781-9500; FAX: 847-781-9570

See full listing in **Section One** under **Toyota**

David Casimir Philpa-Augustyn | cars & parts for sale
626-584-6957 | literature for sale

See full listing in **Section One** under **Corvair**

James J Montague | parts
West Rupert, VT 05776 | service
802-394-2929

See full listing in **Section One** under **Mercedes-Benz**

NSU/USA Jim Sykes | literature
717 N 68th St | parts advice
Seattle, WA 98103 | restoration
206-784-5084

Mail order and open shop. Monday-Saturday 1 pm to 7 pm. Any type NSU including motorcycles and Wankels. Restoration and parts advice free with SASE. Over 25 years' experience.

12 Volt Stuff, Radio & Speedometer Repair Co | radios
10625-A Trade Rd
Richmond, VA 23236
804-423-1055, 888-487-3500 toll free
FAX: 804-423-1059
E-mail: ecs@12voltstuff.com

See full listing in **Section Two** under **radios**

12 Volt Stuff, Radio & Speedometer Repair Co | radios
10625-A Trade Rd
Richmond, VA 23236
804-423-1055, 888-487-3500 toll free
FAX: 804-423-1059
E-mail: ecs@12voltstuff.com

See full listing in **Section Two** under **instruments**

The 60 Oldsmobile Club | newsletter
Dick Major
10895 E Hibma Rd
Tustin, MI 49688
616-825-2891; FAX: 616-825-8324
E-mail: dmajor@netonecom.net

Information for 1960 Oldsmobiles. We are a newsletter.

A-1 Shock Absorber Co | shocks-all types
Shockfinders Division | coil springs
365 Warren Ave, PO Box 2028 | Koni shocks
Silverthorne, CO 80498 | leaf springs
800-344-1966, 970-389-3193 cell | steering gears
FAX: 970-513-8283

See our ad on the last page

Anderson Automotive | cars
1604 E Busch Blvd | parts
Tampa, FL 33612
813-932-4611; FAX: 813-932-5025

Mail order and open shop. Monday-Friday 8 am to 5 pm. Parts and complete cars, used and new for 1968-1972 Olds 442, Cutlass only.

Apple Hydraulics Inc | brake rebuilding
1610 Middle Rd | shock rebuilding
Calverton, NY 11933-1419
800-882-7753, 631-369-9515
FAX: 631-369-9516
E-mail: info@applehydraulics.com

See full listing in **Section Two** under **suspension parts**

Art's Antique & Classic Auto Services | restoration
1985 E 5th St #16
Tempe, AZ 85281
480-966-1195

See full listing in **Section One** under **Buick/McLaughlin**

Auto Hardware Specialties | hardware fasteners
3123 McKinley Ave
Sheldon, IA 51201
712-324-2091; FAX: 712-324-2480
E-mail: rweber@rconnect.com

See full listing in **Section One** under **Chevrolet**

Bumper Boyz LLC | bumper repairs
2435 E 54th St | reconditioning
Los Angeles, CA 90058 | sandblasting
800-995-1703, 323-587-8976
FAX: 323-587-2013

See full listing in **Section One** under **Chevrolet**

Cars II | parts
6747 Warren Sharon Rd
Brookfield, OH 44403
330-448-2074; FAX: 330-448-1908

See full listing in **Section One** under **Cadillac/LaSalle**

Chevrolet Parts Obsolete | accessories
PO Box 70027 | parts
Riverside, CA 92513-0027
909-340-2979; FAX: 909-279-4013
E-mail: cpo@att.net

See full listing in **Section One** under **Chevrolet**

Convertible Service
5126-HA Walnut Grove Ave
San Gabriel, CA 91776
800-333-1140, 626-285-2255
FAX: 626-285-9004

convertible parts
manufacture/
service
top mechanism

See full listing in **Section Two** under **tops**

Coopers Vintage Auto Parts
3087 N California St
Burbank, CA 91504
818-567-4140; FAX: 818-567-4101

parts

See full listing in **Section One** under **Cadillac/LaSalle**

The Copper Cooling Works
2455 N 2550 E
Layton, UT 84040
801-544-9939

radiators

See full listing in **Section Two** under **radiators**

D&J GTO Parts
Dan Gregory
11283 Main St
Stoutsville, OH 43154
740-474-4614; FAX: 740-474-2314
E-mail: djgto@hotmail.com

parts

See full listing in **Section One** under **Pontiac**

Dash Specialists
1910 Redbud Ln
Medford, OR 97504
541-776-0040

interiors

See full listing in **Section One** under **Cadillac/LaSalle**

Daytona Cams
Box 5094
Ormond Beach, FL 32175
800-505-2267; FAX: 904-258-1582
E-mail: info@camshafts.com

camshafts
engine parts

See full listing in **Section Two** under **camshafts**

David J Entler Restorations
10903 N Main St Ext
Glen Rock, PA 17327-8373
717-235-2112

woodwork

See full listing in **Section Two** under **woodwork**

**Firewall Insulators & Quiet Ride
Solutions**
6465 Pacific Ave, Ste 249
Stockton, CA 95207
209-477-4840; FAX: 209-477-0918
E-mail: timcox@quietride.com

air plenums
auto insulation
firewall insulators
gloveboxes
sound deadening

See full listing in **Section Two** under **upholstery**

Fusick Automotive Products
22 Thompson Rd Box 655
East Windsor, CT 06088
860-623-1589; FAX: 860-623-3118
E-mail: dj442@ix.netcom.com

restoration parts

Mail order and open shop. Specializing in 1935-1977 Oldsmobile restoration parts. Separate catalogs available for 1935-1960 Oldsmobile, 1961-1977 Cutlass, 442, H/O and 1961-76 88, 98, SF, Toronado. Catalogs, $5 each.

GM Obsolete
909 W Magnolia St
Phoenix, AZ 85007
602-253-8081; FAX: 602-253-8411
E-mail: info@gmobsolete.com

parts

See full listing in **Section One** under **Buick/McLaughlin**

Hampton Coach
6 Chestnut St, PO Box 6
Amesbury, MA 01913
888-388-8726, 978-388-8047
FAX: 978-388-1113
E-mail: lbb-hc@greenet.net

fabrics
interior kits
top kits

See full listing in **Section One** under **Chevrolet**

Inline Tube
33783 Groesbeck Hwy
Fraser, MI 48026
800-385-9452 order
810-294-4093 tech; FAX: 810-294-7349
E-mail: kryta@aol.com

brake cables/clips
brake/fuel lines
choke tubes
engine/vacuum lines
flex hoses/valves

See full listing in **Section Two** under **brakes**

Lectric Limited Inc
7322 S Archer Road
Justice, IL 60458
708-563-0400; FAX: 708-563-0416

parts

See full listing in **Section One** under **Corvette**

LES Auto Parts
Box 81
Dayton, NJ 08810
732-329-6128; FAX: 732-329-1036

parts

See full listing in **Section One** under **Chevrolet**

M & H Electric Fabricators Inc
13537 Alondra Blvd
Santa Fe Springs, CA 90670
562-926-9552; FAX: 562-926-9572
E-mail: sales@wiringharness.com

wiring harnesses

See full listing in **Section Two** under **electrical systems**

Clayton T Nelson
Box 259
Warrenville, IL 60555
630-369-6589

NOS parts

Mail order only. Specializing in NOS parts for Oldsmobile, Mopar and Chevrolet, late 1940s-mid 1970s.

M Parker Autoworks Inc
150 Heller Pl #17W, Dept HCCA02
Bellmawr, NJ 08031
856-933-0801; FAX: 856-933-0805
E-mail: info@factoryfit.com

battery cables
harnesses

See full listing in **Section Two** under **electrical systems**

The Parts Place
217 Paul St
Elburn, IL 60119
630-365-1800; FAX: 630-365-1900
E-mail: sales@thepartsplaceinc.com

parts

See full listing in **Section One** under **Chevrolet**

Garth B Peterson
W 2619 Rockwell Ave
Spokane, WA 99205
509-325-3823 anytime

accessories/chrome
glass/grilles/parts
radios/sheetmetal
steering wheels

See full listing in **Section Two** under **comprehensive parts**

Rodman's Auto Wood Restoration Box 86 Wheeler St Hanna, IN 46340 219-797-3775	**wood kits**

See full listing in **Section One** under **Chevrolet**

Ross' Automotive Machine Co Inc 1763 N Main St Niles, OH 44446 330-544-4466	**racing engines rebuilding**

See full listing in **Section Two** under **engine rebuilding**

Harry Samuel 65 Wisner St Pontiac, MI 48342-1066 248-335-1900 E-mail: samuelinteriors@aol.com	**carpet fabrics interiors upholstery covers**

See full listing in **Section Two** under **interiors & interior parts**

Shiftworks PO Box 25351 Rochester, NY 14625 PH/FAX: 716-383-0574	**shifters**

See full listing in **Section One** under **Chevelle/Camaro**

Stencils & Stripes Unlimited Inc 1108 S Crescent Ave #21 Park Ridge, IL 60068 847-692-6893; FAX: 847-692-6895	**NOS decals stripe kits**

See full listing in **Section Two** under **decals**

Supercars Unlimited 8029 Unit A SW 17th Portland, OR 97219-2857 503-244-8249; FAX: 503-244-9639 E-mail: info@supercarsunlimited.com	**parts**

Mail order only. 9 am to 4 pm PST. Replacement parts and restoration items, mechanical parts (no chrome or sheetmetal) for 1964-1977 Oldsmobile Cutlass, 4-4-2 and Hurst/Olds. Cutlass/4-4-2 is all we do! Web site: www.supercarsunlimited.com

Tags Backeast PO Box 581 Plainville, CT 06062 860-747-2942 E-mail: dataplt@snet.net	**data plates trim tags cowl tags**

See full listing in **Section Two** under **special services**

Tamraz's Parts Discount Warehouse 10022 S Bode Rd Plainfield, IL 60544 630-904-4500; FAX: 630-904-2329	**carpeting upholstery weatherstripping**

See full listing in **Section One** under **Chevelle/Camaro**

Tanson Enterprises 2508 J St, Dept HVA Sacramento, CA 95816-4815 916-448-2950 FAX: 916-443-3269 *88 E-mail: tanson@pipeline.com	**performance parts restoration parts**

Performance and restoration parts, specializing in 1940s and 1950s Oldsmobiles. Heavy duty sway bars, coil springs, early V8 conversions to late automatic transmissions, harmonic balancers, gaskets, rubber parts, windshields, electric wiper conversions, wiring harnesses, floor pans, carpets, pre-bent fuel and brake lines, disc brake conversions and used parts.

Tom's Classic Parts 5207 Sundew Terr Tobyhanna, PA 18466 PH/FAX: 570-894-1459	**parts**

See full listing in **Section One** under **Chevrolet**

Triangle Automotive PO Box 2293 Arcadia, CA 91077 626-357-2377 E-mail: gogmc99@aol.com	**parts**

Mail order only. Specializing in original choice condition body and interior parts and optional equipment for 1965-1977 Olds Cutlass and 442. Also Pontiac GTO, LeMans and Firebird.

White Post Restorations One Old Car Dr, PO Drawer D White Post, VA 22663 540-837-1140; FAX: 540-837-2368 E-mail: info@whitepost.com	**brakes restoration**

See full listing in **Section Two** under **brakes**

White Post Restorations One Old Car Dr, PO Drawer D White Post, VA 22663 540-837-1140; FAX: 540-837-2368 E-mail: info@whitepost.com	**restoration**

See full listing in **Section Two** under **restoration shops**

Year One Inc PO Box 129 Tucker, GA 30085 800-YEAR-ONE (932-7663) 770-493-6568 Atlanta & overseas FAX: 800-680-6806 E-mail: info@yearone.com	**parts**

See full listing in **Section Two** under **comprehensive parts**

Opel GT Source 18211 Zeni Ln Tuolumne, CA 95379 209-928-1110; FAX: 209-928-3298 E-mail: opelgts@opelgtsource.com	**parts technical info**

Mail order. Monday-Friday 8 am to 12 pm, 1 pm to 5 pm PST. Opel parts, technical information, restoration, high-performance, custom body kits, race preparation, specializing in parts for 1968-1975 Opel parts. Offer the largest inventory of new Opel parts in North America. Also have a large selection of used Opel parts as well. Web site: www.opelgtsource.com

Opels Unlimited 1310 Tamarind Ave Rialto, CA 92376 562-690-1051, 909-355-OPEL (6735) FAX: 562-690-3352 E-mail: opelsunl@opelsunl.com	**parts service**

Evenings are best to call, also most Saturdays. The largest Opel parts company in the USA. Over 100 complete cars, service shops, showrooms, club specials, newsletters, videos, tech info, best prices and largest selection anywhere. Over 10,000 sq feet of rust-free sheetmetal, all models from 1955-1981. Life member club includes calendar girls, T-shirts, stickers and key chains.

We beat any price on anything, parts, labor or services. Complete cars shipped anywhere in USA. Over 5,000 new original stock parts available. Take care and happy Opeling. Web site: www.opelsunl.com

Orphan Motorsports 193 Shell Rock Landing Hubert, NC 28539 910-326-3459 E-mail: oms@coastalnet.com	parts

Mail order only. Specializing in new, used and NOS parts for Opels from 1950s to 1975.

Anderson Restoration 1235 Nash Ave Kanawha, IA 50447 641-762-3528	restorations

See full listing in **Section Two** under **restoration shops**

The Antique Auto Shop 603 Lytle Ave Elsmere, KY 41018 859-342-8363; FAX: 859-342-9076 E-mail: antaut@aol.com	brake lines brake parts weatherstripping

See full listing in **Section Two** under **brakes**

Apple Hydraulics Inc 1610 Middle Rd Calverton, NY 11933-1419 800-882-7753, 631-369-9515 FAX: 631-369-9516 E-mail: info@applehydraulics.com	brake rebuilding shock rebuilding

See full listing in **Section Two** under **suspension parts**

EJ Blend 802 8th Ave Irwin, PA 15642-3702 724-863-7624	literature parts

Mail order only. Monday-Friday 9 am to 5 pm. Specializing in Packard parts 1929-1942 and literature for 1933-1934 Twelves.

Robert D Bliss 7 Pineview Ct Monroe, NJ 08831 732-521-4654	electrical parts ignition parts

See full listing in **Section Two** under **electrical systems**

Bob's Radio & TV Service 238 Ocean View Pismo Beach, CA 93449 805-773-8200	radios

See full listing in **Section Two** under **radios**

Bill Boudway 105 Deerfield Dr Canandaigua, NY 14424-2409 716-394-6172 E-mail: gnbboudway@msn.com	restoration info

Mail order only. Copies of restoration information, advertising material and parts lists for Packard Twin Six automobiles 1916-1923. Hershey space #C2G-70.

Brinton's Antique Auto Parts 6826 SW McVey Ave Redmond, OR 97756 541-548-3483; FAX: 541-548-8022	parts

Mail order and open shop. Dismantle Packard cars and chassis and sell the parts taken off them. Sixes, Eights and Super 8s. Also 12-cylinders. Parts for 1920s-1958 Packards.

Classic Cars Inc 52 Maple Terr Hibernia, NJ 07842 973-627-1975; FAX: 973-627-3503	cars parts

Mail order only. Pre WW II Packard parts and Packard cars for 1928-1942. 4-page price sheet of new parts.

The Classic Motorist PO Box 363 Rotterdam Junction, NY 12150-0363	automobilia books & publications Packard

Mail order only. British and American automotive books, art, literature, periodicals, club publications, and motoring accessories. Specializing in custom coachwork and formal car memorabilia. Early auto radio literature and signs. Collector of Classic Era Danbury and Franklin Mint models. Packard enthusiast desiring club, marque and CCCA publications. Please send four stamps for descriptive catalog.

Robert Connole 2525 E 32nd St Davenport, IA 52807 319-355-6266	ignition coils

Mail order only. Packard double coils, 1933-1934 eight-cylinder Northeast, 1934-1939 twelve-cylinder Autolite. All new coils, bases, wires and terminals. Autolite embossed on case for the new 12 coils. Ready to install.

Creative Connections Inc 3407 Hwy 120 Duluth, GA 30096 770-476-7322; FAX: 770-476-7028 E-mail: sales@logolites.com	brake lights logo lights turn signals

See full listing in **Section One** under **Ford 1903-1931**

Tom Crook Classic Cars 27611 42nd Ave S Auburn, WA 98001 253-941-3454	car dealer

See full listing in **Section Two** under **car dealers**

Deters Restorations 6205 Swiss Garden Rd Temperance, MI 48182-1020 734-847-1820	restoration

See full listing in **Section Two** under **restoration shops**

David R Edgerton, Coachworks 9215 St Rt 13 Camden, NY 13316-4933 315-245-3113 E-mail: derods@excite.com	restoration woodworking

See full listing in **Section Two** under **restoration shops**

Firewall Insulators & Quiet Ride Solutions 6465 Pacific Ave, Ste 249 Stockton, CA 95207 209-477-4840; FAX: 209-477-0918 E-mail: timcox@quietride.com	air plenums auto insulation firewall insulators gloveboxes sound deadening

See full listing in **Section Two** under **upholstery**

From Rust To Riches | appraisals
Packard parts
Rolls-Royce parts
Bill McCoskey
PO Box 93
Littlestown, PA 17340
410-346-0660; FAX: 410-346-6499
E-mail: tatrabill@aol.com

See full listing in **Section Two** under **comprehensive parts**

Guild of Automotive Restorers | restoration
sales
service
44 Bridge St, PO Box 1150
Bradford, ON Canada L3Z 2B5
905-775-0499; FAX: 905-775-0944
E-mail: cars@guildclassiccars.com

See full listing in **Section Two** under **restoration shops**

James Hill | ignition parts
source list
935 Sunnyslope St
Emporia, KS 66801
620-342-4826 evenings/weekends
E-mail: jwhill@osprey.net

Mail order only from this address. Packard only, supplying publication: 2001 edition of *Sources of Packard Parts and Services* (The Packard Source List) with 30 pages of source information, 8 pages of name/address listings and 5 pages of fax/e-mail listings. Cost is $5 postpaid in USA and Canada, $7 US funds for airmail to other countries with perfect guarantee. Note: no longer at the Oklahoma address.

L & L Antique Auto Trim | runningboard
moldings
403 Spruce, Box 177
Pierce City, MO 65723
417-476-2871

See full listing in **Section Two** under **special services**

LaVine Restorations Inc | restoration
1349 Beech Rd
Nappanee, IN 46550
219-773-7561; FAX: 219-773-7595
E-mail: lavine@bnin.net

See full listing in **Section Two** under **restoration shops**

Gerald J Lettieri | gaskets
parts
132 Old Main St
Rocky Hill, CT 06067
860-529-7177; FAX: 860-257-3621

See full listing in **Section Two** under **gaskets**

Max Merritt Auto Parts | accessories
parts
PO Box 10
Franklin, IN 46131
317-736-6233; FAX: 317-736-6235

Specializing in NOS, NORS, reproduction and used parts and accessories for Packard automobiles 1930-1956. Stainless steel molding for runningboard trim, hood moldings, and misc other applications for Buick, Cadillac, Chrysler, Dodge, Lincoln, Packard, Pierce-Arrow and others. Authorized dealer of Gas Tank Renu-USA. Most Packard tanks in stock.

ORF Corp | rear end gears
Phil Bray
8858 Ferry Rd
Grosse Ile, MI 48138
734-676-5520; FAX: 734-676-9438
E-mail: carolbray@yahoo.com

Mail order only. Specializing in high speed rear end gears for 1927-1939 Packards, all Duesenberg Js. Will be happy to design a single set for any car. Custom manufacture a gear set for your vehicle. Also produce Packard wire center cowl lacing and hood check straps. Call for price and timing.

Packard Archives | accessories
artwork
automobilia
918 W Co Rd C-2
St Paul, MN 55113-1942
651-484-1184
E-mail: estatecars@earthlink.net

Highest prices paid for Packard automobile dealership and factory memorabilia/collectibles. Cash for dealer giveaways, lapel pins, signs, NOS parts, literature, clocks, filmstrips and movies. Original artwork, accessories, Packard jewelry, rings, watches, awards, pin backs, buttons, advertising promotional items, master salesman awards, metal tin cans and bottles, etc, anything Packard.

Patrician Industries Inc | parts
22644 Nona
Dearborn, MI 48124
313-565-3573
E-mail: packards1@aol.com

Mail order and open shop by appointment only. Handles a full line of new, used and reproduction Packard parts for Packards 1940-1956.

Potomac Packard | wiring harnesses
PO Box 117
Tiger, GA 30576
800-859-9532 orders
706-782-2345 shop; FAX: 706-782-2344

Manufactures and supplies electrical wiring harnesses and equipment for Packards, 1916-1956. Our products are made to exacting standards, using Packard engineering drawings or original wiring harnesses as patterns. All harnesses are made using the correct gauge wire and color code then loomed or overbraided as original. Each wire is identified for easy installation. Our harnesses are 100 points in both appearance and service and satisfaction is assured or money refunded.

Power Brake Systems | brake repair
c/o Jerry Cinotti
431 S Sierra Way
San Bernadino, CA 92408
909-884-6980; FAX: 909-884-7872

See full listing in **Section Two** under **brakes**

Precision Rubber | rubber parts
Box 324
Didsbury, AB Canada T0M 0W0
403-335-9590; FAX: 403-335-9637
E-mail: pat@runningboardmats.com

See full listing in **Section Two** under **rubber parts**

Don Rook | parts
184 Raspberry Ln
Mena, AR 71953
501-394-7555; FAX: 501-394-7618
E-mail: kmrook@voltage.net

See full listing in **Section One** under **Chrysler**

Sierra Grove Packards | conversion kits
425 E Laurel
Sierra Madre, CA 91024
626-355-4023, 714-539-8579
FAX: 626-355-4072

Mail order only. The Ultra-Torc II, a transmission conversion kit to convert Packards to the Chrysler Torqueflite 727 transmission. The kits are for 1951-1954 and 1955-1956 Packards.

Steve's Studebaker-Packard | car dealer
parts
suspension repairs
PO Box 6914
Napa, CA 94581
707-255-8945

Mail order and open shop. Evenings and weekends. Appointment suggested. Specialized Packard services, such as torsion-level suspension and tele-touch electric shift repairs and rebuilding.

Specializing in parts for 1951-1956 Packards and 1953-1966 Studebakers. Packard and Studebaker vehicle sales.

| **Supreme Metal Polishing**
84A Rickenbacker Cir
Livermore, CA 94550
925-449-3490; FAX: 925-449-1475
E-mail: supremet@home.com | **metal working**
parts restoration
plating services
polishing |

See full listing in **Section Two** under **plating & polishing**

| **Tucson Packard/Chirco Automotive**
9101 E 22nd St
Tucson, AZ 85710
520-722-1984; FAX: 520-298-4069
E-mail: tucpackard@aol.com | **accessories**
NORS parts
NOS parts
used parts |

Specializing in rebuilding services, NOS, NORS and used parts and accessories for Packard automobiles, all years and models.

| **John Ulrich**
450 Silver Ave
San Francisco, CA 94112
PH/FAX: 510-223-9587 days | **parts** |

Mail order and open shop by appointment only. Monday-Friday 9 am to 5 pm. Packard parts from 1928-1948. Approximately 20% of the inventory is NOS, the balance is from parted out cars. Strongest part of inventory is 1938-1941 Junior and Senior Series. I buy inventories. I have available sheetmetal, fenders, hoods, wheels, drums, trim, engines, transmissions, differentials, engine parts, switches, dash parts, gauges and 1,000s more parts. I also offer a no hassle guarantee, if not satisfied return within 60 days for refund or exchange.

| **Tom Vagnini**
58 Anthony Rd, RR 3
Pittsfield, MA 01201
413-698-2526 | **used parts** |

Mail order and open shop. Monday-Saturday by appointment. 10 am to 4 pm. Specializing in used parts for Packards 1923-1931.

| **Viking Worldwise Inc**
190 Doe Run Rd
Manheim, PA 17545
866-CJACKETS; FAX: 717-664-5556
E-mail: gkurien@dejazz.com | **leather jackets** |

See full listing in **Section Two** under **apparel**

| **White Post Restorations**
One Old Car Dr, PO Drawer D
White Post, VA 22663
540-837-1140; FAX: 540-837-2368
E-mail: info@whitepost.com | **restoration** |

See full listing in **Section Two** under **restoration shops**

| **Yesterday's Radio**
7759 Edgewood Ln
Seven Hills, OH 44131-5902
PH/FAX: 216-524-2018
E-mail: jerry@yesterdaysradio.com | **interior plastic**
radio parts |

Interior plastic: gearshift knobs, window crank knobs, dash knobs, antenna mounts and knobs, escutcheons and some dash plastic. Chromed die cast door escutcheons. Specializing in radio parts, knobs, push-buttons, push-button caps, escutcheons and related items. A Packard catalog can be downloaded from the web site or mailed upon request. Web site: www.yesterdaysradio.com

PEUGEOT

| **Voss Motors Inc**
4850 37th Ave S
Seattle, WA 98118
888-380-9277 toll free
206-721-3077
E-mail: vossmotors@books4cars.com | **service manuals** |

See full listing in **Section Two** under **literature dealers**

PIERCE-ARROW

| **Apple Hydraulics Inc**
1610 Middle Rd
Calverton, NY 11933-1419
800-882-7753, 631-369-9515
FAX: 631-369-9516
E-mail: info@applehydraulics.com | **brake rebuilding**
shock rebuilding |

See full listing in **Section Two** under **suspension parts**

| **Firewall Insulators & Quiet Ride Solutions**
6465 Pacific Ave, Ste 249
Stockton, CA 95207
209-477-4840; FAX: 209-477-0918
E-mail: timcox@quietride.com | **air plenums**
auto insulation
firewall insulators
gloveboxes
sound deadening |

See full listing in **Section Two** under **upholstery**

| **A-1 Shock Absorber Co**
Shockfinders Division
365 Warren Ave, PO Box 2028
Silverthorne, CO 80498
800-344-1966, 970-389-3193 cell
FAX: 970-513-8283 | **shocks-all types**
coil springs
Koni shocks
leaf springs
steering gears |

See our ad on the last page

| **AKH Wheels**
1207 N A St
Ellensburg, WA 98926-2522
509-962-3390
E-mail: akhwheel@eburg.com | **Rallye wheels**
styled steel wheels
vintage aluminum |

See full listing in **Section Two** under **wheels & wheelcovers**

| **Antique DeSoto-Plymouth**
4206 Burnett Dr
Murrysville, PA 15668
724-733-1818 eves; FAX: 724-733-9884
E-mail: parts4u@aol.com | **Mopar parts** |

See full listing in **Section One** under **Mopar**

Apple Hydraulics Inc | brake rebuilding
1610 Middle Rd | shock rebuilding
Calverton, NY 11933-1419
800-882-7753, 631-369-9515
FAX: 631-369-9516
E-mail: info@applehydraulics.com

See full listing in **Section Two** under **suspension parts**

Atlas Obsolete Chrysler Parts | parts
10621 Bloomfield St, Unit 32
Los Alamitos, CA 90720
PH/FAX: 562-594-5560
E-mail: atlaschrys@aol.com

See full listing in **Section One** under **Mopar**

Auto Body Specialties Inc | accessories
Rt 66 | body parts
Middlefield, CT 06455
888-277-1960 toll free orders only
860-346-4989; FAX: 860-346-4987

See full listing in **Section Two** under **body parts**

Andy Bernbaum Auto Parts | parts
315 Franklin St
Newton, MA 02458
617-244-1118

See full listing in **Section One** under **Mopar**

Brewer's Performance Inc | parts
2580 S St Rt 48
Ludlow Falls, OH 45339-9773
937-698-4259; FAX: 937-698-7109

See full listing in **Section One** under **Mopar**

Coach Builders Muscle Car | interiors
Parts & Services | parts
PO Box 128 | rust remover
Baltimore, MD 21087-0128
410-426-5567

See full listing in **Section One** under **Chevrolet**

Dodge City Vintage Dodge | parts
Vehicles & Parts | restoration
PO Box 1687, 18584 Hwy 108 | research
Jamestown, CA 95327 | vehicles
209-984-5858; FAX: 209-984-3285
E-mail: mike@dodgecityvintage.com

See full listing in **Section One** under **Dodge**

Firewall Insulators & Quiet Ride | air plenums
Solutions | auto insulation
6465 Pacific Ave, Ste 249 | firewall insulators
Stockton, CA 95207 | gloveboxes
209-477-4840; FAX: 209-477-0918 | sound deadening
E-mail: timcox@quietride.com

See full listing in **Section Two** under **upholstery**

Hampton Coach | fabrics
6 Chestnut St, PO Box 6 | interior kits
Amesbury, MA 01913 | top kits
888-388-8726, 978-388-8047
FAX: 978-388-1113
E-mail: lbb-hc@greenet.net

See full listing in **Section One** under **Chevrolet**

Mike Hershenfeld | parts
PO Box 1301
Bellmore, NY 11710
PH/FAX: 516-781-PART (7278)
E-mail: mikesmopar@juno.com

See full listing in **Section One** under **Mopar**

Wayne Hood | NORS parts
228 Revell Rd | NOS parts
Grenada, MS 38901
601-227-8426

See full listing in **Section One** under **Dodge**

Kramer Automotive Specialties | body parts
PO Box 5 | interiors
Herman, PA 16039 | sheetmetal
724-285-5566; FAX: 724-285-8898
E-mail: kramerauto@aol.com

See full listing in **Section One** under **Mopar**

Layson's Restorations Inc | parts
26164 126th Ave SE
Kent, WA 98031
253-630-4088; FAX: 253-630-4065
E-mail: laysons@foxinternet.net

See full listing in **Section One** under **Mopar**

MikeCo Antique, Kustom & | lenses
Obsolete Auto Parts | parts
4053 Calle Tesoro, Unit C
Camarillo, CA 93012
805-482-1725; FAX: 805-987-8524

See full listing in **Section One** under **Mopar**

Mike's Auto Parts | NOS Mopar
Box 358 | NOS GM
Ridgeland, MS 39158 | NOS Ford
601-856-7214 | parts for all makes

See full listing in **Section One** under **Chrysler**

Clayton T Nelson | NOS parts
Box 259
Warrenville, IL 60555
630-369-6589

See full listing in **Section One** under **Oldsmobile**

NOS Reproductions | parts
22425 Jefferies Rd, RR 3
Komoka, ON Canada N0L 1R0
519-471-2740; FAX: 519-471-7675
E-mail: info@nosreproductions.com

See full listing in **Section One** under **Mopar**

Obsolete Chrysler NOS Parts | literature
4206 Burnett Dr | parts
Murrysville, PA 15668
724-733-1818 eves; FAX: 724-733-9884
E-mail: parts4u@aol.com

See full listing in **Section One** under **Chrysler**

Obsolete Parts of Iowa | NOS parts
PO Box 233
Earlville, IA 52041
E-mail: finsrus@mwci.net

See full listing in **Section One** under **Mopar**

Plymouth, Dodge, Chrysler, DeSoto Parts — NOS parts for DeSoto
4206 Burnett Dr
Murrysville, PA 15668
724-733-1818 eves; FAX: 724-733-9884
E-mail: parts4u@aol.com

See full listing in **Section One** under **DeSoto**

Plymouth Parts '46-'48 — parts
PO Box 2502
Grass Valley, CA 95945
530-273-7620
E-mail: jrrnwings@onemain.com

Specialize in used 1946-1948 Plymouth parts.

R & R Fiberglass & Specialties — body parts
4850 Wilson Dr NW
Cleveland, TN 37312
423-476-2270; FAX: 423-473-9442
E-mail: rrfiberglass@aol.com

See full listing in **Section Two** under **fiberglass parts**

Restorations By Julius — restoration
10101-1/2 Canoga Ave
Chatsworth, CA 91311
818-882-2825; FAX: 818-882-2855
E-mail: julius@
restorationsbyjulius.com

Open Tuesday-Friday 8 am to 5 pm. Restoration, repair and sales of 1962-1971 Chrysler, Plymouth and Dodge products. Web site: www.restorationsbyjulius.com

Riddle's/Mr Plymouth — decals / overdrives / parts & info / repro parts
20303 8th Ave NW
Shoreline, WA 98177-2107
PH/FAX: 206-285-6534 days

See full listing in **Section One** under **Mopar**

Roberts Motor Parts — parts
17 Prospect St
West Newbury, MA 01985
978-363-5407; FAX: 978-363-2026
E-mail: sales@robertsmotorparts.com

See full listing in **Section One** under **Chrysler**

Paul Slater Auto Parts — parts
9496 85th St N
Stillwater, MN 55082
651-429-4235

See full listing in **Section One** under **Dodge**

Sound Move Inc — radios
217 S Main St
Elkhart, IN 46516
800-901-0222, 219-294-5100
FAX: 219-293-4902

See full listing in **Section One** under **Chevrolet**

Tags Backeast — data plates / trim tags / cowl tags
PO Box 581
Plainville, CT 06062
860-747-2942
E-mail: dataplt@snet.net

See full listing in **Section Two** under **special services**

Texas Viper Hotline — Prowlers / Vipers
5405 Montclair
Colleyville, TX 76034
817-267-1299; FAX: 972-721-3900
E-mail: dab1213@msn.com

See full listing in **Section One** under **Dodge**

Totally Auto Inc — parts / restoration / service
337 Philmont Ave
Feasterville, PA 19053
215-322-2277; FAX: 215-322-4755
E-mail: totalyauto@aol.com

See full listing in **Section One** under **Mopar**

Weimann's Literature & Collectables — literature
16 Cottage Rd
Harwinton, CT 06791
860-485-0300
FAX: 860-485-1705, 24 hours
E-mail: weimann@snet.net

Mail order or appointment only. Plymouth, Dodge/Dodge truck, DeSoto, Chrysler, Imperial literature. We carry most 1928 to date showroom catalogs, folders, data/trim books, service/shop, parts listing books, plus tech service/sales records/filmstrips, etc. Owner's manuals, accessories, books. Almost anything paper. Color and b&w copying service for Plymouth. We buy, sell, trade. Please send stamped addressed envelope with inquiries.

Bob West Muscle Cars — muscle cars
637 Sellmeyer Ln
Lewisville, TX 75077
972-317-5525

Specializing in 1969-1970 B-body and 1970-1971 E-body only.

White Post Restorations — brakes / restoration
One Old Car Dr, PO Drawer D
White Post, VA 22663
540-837-1140; FAX: 540-837-2368
E-mail: info@whitepost.com

See full listing in **Section Two** under **brakes**

White Post Restorations — restoration
One Old Car Dr, PO Drawer D
White Post, VA 22663
540-837-1140; FAX: 540-837-2368
E-mail: info@whitepost.com

See full listing in **Section Two** under **restoration shops**

Wittenborn's Auto Service Inc — Mopar / Dodge / Plymouth
133 Woodside Ave
Briarcliff Manor, NY 10510-1717
914-941-2744; FAX: 914-769-1327

See full listing in **Section One** under **Mopar**

A-1 Shock Absorber Co — shocks-all types / coil springs / Koni shocks / leaf springs / steering gears
Shockfinders Division
365 Warren Ave, PO Box 2028
Silverthorne, CO 80498
800-344-1966, 970-389-3193 cell
FAX: 970-513-8283

See our ad on the last page

Auto Hardware Specialties	hardware fasteners
3123 McKinley Ave	
Sheldon, IA 51201	
712-324-2091; FAX: 712-324-2480	
E-mail: rweber@rconnect.com	

See full listing in **Section One** under **Chevrolet**

Bill's Birds	new parts
1021 Commack Rd	repro parts
Dix Hills, NY 11746	used parts
631-243-6789, 631-667-3853	
FAX: 631-243-2119	

Mail order and open shop. Monday-Friday, 8:30 am to 5 pm, Saturday 8:30 am to 2 pm. Specializing in Pontiac Firebird parts new & used & 1967 & up repro parts. We also have emblems for Firebird, GTO, LeMans and Tempest and also some big cars, Grand Prix & Bonneville. All emblems are top quality reproductions and some NOS. Licensed by GM.

Boneyard Stan's	cars
Stanley Jones	parts
218 N 69th Ave	
Phoenix, AZ 85043	
623-936-8045; FAX: 623-936-3754	
E-mail: boneyardstans@cs.com	

Mail order and open shop. Daily, call first. Specializing in 1950-1980s Pontiac cars and parts. Also have many other types of cars and will locate cars and parts. Shipping anywhere, US, Canada, overseas. Web site: www.boneyardstan.com

Camaro Specialties	parts
112 Elm St	restoration
East Aurora, NY 14052	
716-652-7086; FAX: 716-652-2279	
E-mail: camarospecial@wzrd.com	

See full listing in **Section One** under **Chevelle/Camaro**

Chevrolet Parts Obsolete	accessories
PO Box 70027	parts
Riverside, CA 92513-0027	
909-340-2979; FAX: 909-279-4013	
E-mail: cpo@att.net	

See full listing in **Section One** under **Chevrolet**

Chief Service	parts
Herbert G Baschung	restoration
Brunnmatt, PO Box 155	
CH-4914 Roggwil Switzerland	
PH/FAX: 0041-62-9291777	

See full listing in **Section Two** under **restoration shops**

Classic Industries Inc	accessories
Firebird Parts and Accessories Catalog	parts
17832 Gothard St	
Huntington Beach, CA 92647	
800-854-1280 parts/info	
FAX: 800-300-3081 toll free	
E-mail: info@classicindustries.com	

Largest selection of Firebird/Trans Am parts and accessories ever assembled in one catalog. Well over 400 full color pages of the finest quality restoration products and late model accessories. Only $5, refunded on first order. Call our 24-hour toll-free catalog hotline, 888-GM-CATALOG, and receive the industry's most comprehensive parts catalog from the undisputed leader in the industry, Classic Industries. Web site: www.classicindustries.com

Coach Builders Muscle Car Parts & Services	interiors
PO Box 128	parts
Baltimore, MD 21087-0128	rust remover
410-426-5567	

See full listing in **Section One** under **Chevrolet**

Competitive Automotive Inc	parts
2095 W Shore Rd (Rt 117)	restoration
Warwick, RI 02889	
401-739-6262, 401-739-6288	
FAX: 401-739-1497	

See full listing in **Section One** under **Chevelle/Camaro**

Convertible Service	convertible parts
5126-HA Walnut Grove Ave	manufacture/
San Gabriel, CA 91776	service
800-333-1140, 626-285-2255	top mechanism
FAX: 626-285-9004	

See full listing in **Section Two** under **tops**

CPR	new parts
431 S Sierra Way	reproduction parts
San Bernardino, CA 92408	used parts
909-884-6980; FAX: 909-884-7872	

All mechanical, brake, rubber, trim, suspension, new, used and reproduction parts for Pontiac 1927-present. Parts lists are available, phone or mail request.

D&J GTO Parts	parts
Dan Gregory	
11283 Main St	
Stoutsville, OH 43154	
740-474-4614; FAX: 740-474-2314	
E-mail: djgto@hotmail.com	

Specializing in Pontiac GTO, LeMans, Tempest parts (new and used) and restorable cars. Web site: www.djgto.com

East West Auto Parts Inc	European import
4605 Dawson Rd	parts
Tulsa, OK 74115	GM parts
800-447-2886; FAX: 918-832-7900	

See full listing in **Section Five** under **Oklahoma**

David J Entler Restorations	woodwork
10903 N Main St Ext	
Glen Rock, PA 17327-8373	
717-235-2112	

See full listing in **Section Two** under **woodwork**

ETC/Every Thing Cars	paint
8727 Clarinda	repairs
Pico Rivera, CA 90660	restoration
562-949-6981	welding

See full listing in **Section One** under **Mopar**

Firewall Insulators & Quiet Ride Solutions	air plenums
6465 Pacific Ave, Ste 249	auto insulation
Stockton, CA 95207	firewall insulators
209-477-4840; FAX: 209-477-0918	gloveboxes
E-mail: timcox@quietride.com	sound deadening

See full listing in **Section Two** under **upholstery**

Hampton Coach	fabrics
6 Chestnut St, PO Box 6	interior kits
Amesbury, MA 01913	top kits
888-388-8726, 978-388-8047	
FAX: 978-388-1113	
E-mail: lbb-hc@greenet.net	

See full listing in **Section One** under **Chevrolet**

Hjeltness Restoration Inc
630 Alpine Way
Escondido, CA 92029
760-746-9966; FAX: 760-746-7738

restoration
service

See full listing in **Section Two** under **restoration shops**

Indian Adventures Inc
121 South St, PO Box 206
Foxboro, MA 02035
508-359-4660; FAX: 508-359-5435

parts

See full listing in **Section Two** under **comprehensive parts**

Inline Tube
33783 Groesbeck Hwy
Fraser, MI 48026
800-385-9452 order
810-294-4093 tech; FAX: 810-294-7349
E-mail: kryta@aol.com

brake cables/clips
brake & fuel lines
choke tubes
engine/vacuum lines
flex hoses/valves

See full listing in **Section Two** under **brakes**

The Judge's Chambers
114 Prince George Dr
Hampton, VA 23669
757-838-2059 evenings
E-mail: thejudge@pcdocs.net

automobilia
parts

Mail order only. Parts for 1969-1971 Pontiac GTO Judge, including stripe kits/decals, spoilers, glovebox emblems, hood tachometers, Ram Air systems, GTO and Judge memorabilia and videos. Royal Pontiac memorabilia. Also, appraisals and services. Web site: www.thejudgeschambers.net

Dave Kauzlarich
60442 N Tranquility Rd
Lacombe, LA 70445
504-882-3000
E-mail: fierog97j@aol.com

literature
memorabilia

See full listing in **Section Two** under **literature dealers**

Kurt Kelsey
Antique Pontiac Parts
14083 P Ave
Iowa Falls, IA 50126
PH/FAX: 641-648-9086

parts dealer

Mail order and open shop. Call ahead for directions. Also usually several Pontiacs for sale. Large stock of antique and obsolete Pontiac parts. Fast, personalized service.

Lectric Limited Inc
7322 S Archer Road
Justice, IL 60458
708-563-0400; FAX: 708-563-0416

parts

See full listing in **Section One** under **Corvette**

LES Auto Parts
Box 81
Dayton, NJ 08810
732-329-6128; FAX: 732-329-1036

parts

See full listing in **Section One** under **Chevrolet**

M & H Electric Fabricators Inc
13537 Alondra Blvd
Santa Fe Springs, CA 90670
562-926-9552; FAX: 562-926-9572
E-mail: sales@wiringharness.com

wiring harnesses

See full listing in **Section Two** under **electrical systems**

Mecham Design, Performance
12637 N 66th Dr
Glendale, AZ 85304
623-486-3155
E-mail: demecham@uswest.net

parts

See full listing in **Section One** under **Chevrolet**

National Parts Depot
900 SW 38th Ave
Ocala, FL 34474
800-874-7595; FAX: 352-861-8706

accessories
parts

See full listing in **Section One** under **Mustang**

**Next Generation Restoration and
Performance by Year One**
PO Box 2023
Tucker, GA 30084
800-921-9214; FAX: 800-680-6806
E-mail: info@nextgenparts.com

parts

See full listing in **Section One** under **Chevelle/Camaro**

Old Coach Works Restoration Inc
1206 Badger St
Yorkville, IL 60560-1701
630-553-0414; FAX: 630-553-1053
E-mail: oldcoachworks@msn.com

appraisals
restoration

See full listing in **Section Two** under **restoration shops**

Original Auto Interiors
7869 Trumble Rd
Columbus, MI 48063-3915
810-727-2486; FAX: 810-727-4344
E-mail: origauto@tir.com

upholstery

See full listing in **Section Two** under **upholstery**

Original Parts Group Inc
17892 Gothard St
Huntington Beach, CA 92647
800-243-8355 US/Canada
714-841-5363; FAX: 714-847-8159

accessories
parts

Mail order and open shop. Monday-Friday 7:30 am to 5 pm, Saturday 10 am to 3 pm Pacific time. Manufacturer and distributor of original and reproduction 1964-1973 GTO, Tempest, LeMans, 1964-1987 Chevelle, El Camino and 1970-1987 Monte Carlo parts and accessories: emblems, interior trim, moldings, sheetmetal, electrical, engine parts, dash pads, door panels, seat upholstery, chrome trim parts, weatherstripping, gaskets, body seals, underbody bushings and much more along with an extensive line of obsolete GM items.

M Parker Autoworks Inc
150 Heller Pl #17W, Dept HCCA02
Bellmawr, NJ 08031
856-933-0801; FAX: 856-933-0805
E-mail: info@factoryfit.com

battery cables
harnesses

See full listing in **Section Two** under **electrical systems**

The Parts Place
217 Paul St
Elburn, IL 60119
630-365-1800; FAX: 630-365-1900
E-mail: sales@thepartsplaceinc.com

parts

See full listing in **Section One** under **Chevrolet**

Parts Unlimited Inc — interiors, weatherstrips
Cliff Carr
12101 Westport Rd
Louisville, KY 40245-1789
800-342-0610, 502-425-3766
FAX: 502-425-7910, 502-232-9784
E-mail: contactpui@aol.com

See full listing in **Section One** under **Chevrolet**

Performance Years Pontiac — parts
2880 Bergey Rd, Unit O
Hatfield, PA 19440
215-712-7400; FAX: 215-712-9968
E-mail: sales@performanceyears.com

Mail order only. Pontiac parts for GTO, Tempest, LeMans, Firebird, Trans Am, Grand Prix, Catalina, Bonneville, 1955-1977. Web site: http://performanceyears.com

Phoenix Graphix Inc — decals, stripe kits
5861 S Kyrene Rd #10
Tempe, AZ 85283
800-941-4550

See full listing in **Section Two** under **decals**

PMD Specialties — component restoration, OEM/used/NOS parts, restoration specialist, verification/appraisals
20498 82nd Ave
Langley, BC Canada V2Y 2A9
604-888-4100; FAX: 604-513-1188
E-mail: pmdgto@home.com

Our expertise lies mainly in the GTO (1964-1974), Grand Prix (1962, 1969-1972), Trans Am (1970-1973), American and Canadian full-size Pontiacs (1962), engine parts for 1960-1981. Some NOS GM parts. Tri-power, Ram Air specialist. Body, chassis, driveline parts. Complete, partial, component restorations. Specific cars/parts search. Usually available for consultation on Monday 9 am to 4 pm, Thursdays 9 am to 5 pm, Saturdays 1 pm to 5 pm PST, please call/fax needs/wants prior to consultation. We appreciate your patience as we try to fill your needs.

Ponti-Action Racing — engine builders
PO Box 354
Medfield, MA 02052
888-RAM-AIRS; FAX: 508-359-5485
E-mail: gtogeezer@media.net

Pontiac engine builders.

Pontiac Engines Custom Built — custom built engines
E-mail: pontiacgregg@earthlink.net

Mail order and open shop. Monday-Saturday 9 am to 5 pm. Specializing in custom built Pontiac engines ready to drop in for 1960-1999 Pontiac cars. Call for other make motors. Engines custom built or yours custom rebuilt, street or strip, ported heads, balanced to 1/2 gram, etc, all engines dialed in, short blocks and heads available. Free catalog. Web site: www.pontiacengines.net

Precision Pontiac — parts, repairs
2719 Columbus Ave
Columbus, OH 43209
614-258-3500; FAX: 614-258-0060
E-mail: peter.serio@gte.net

Mail order only. Specializing in engine detail, shifters rebuilt and rechromed, 1965-1967 rally gauges, factory options, used small parts. Original Pontiac vacuum gauges and tachometers restored and for sale. Web site: www.precisionpontiac.com

Precision Rubber — rubber parts
Box 324
Didsbury, AB Canada T0M 0W0
403-335-9590; FAX: 403-335-9637
E-mail: pat@runningboardmats.com

See full listing in **Section Two** under **rubber parts**

Replica Plastics — fiberglass parts
260 S Oates St, Box 1147
Dothan, AL 36302
800-873-5871; FAX: 334-792-1175
E-mail: stone@ala.net

See full listing in **Section Two** under **fiberglass parts**

Rodman's Auto Wood Restoration — wood kits
Box 86 Wheeler St
Hanna, IN 46340
219-797-3775

See full listing in **Section One** under **Chevrolet**

Harry Samuel — carpet, fabrics, interiors, upholstery covers
65 Wisner St
Pontiac, MI 48342-1066
248-335-1900
E-mail: samuelinteriors@aol.com

See full listing in **Section Two** under **interiors & interior parts**

Shiftworks — shifters
PO Box 25351
Rochester, NY 14625
PH/FAX: 716-383-0574

See full listing in **Section One** under **Chevelle/Camaro**

Sonic Motors Inc — parts
9110 Hickory Ridge Rd
Holly, MI 48442
810-750-1421; FAX: 810-750-7440

Specializing in Pontiac GTO specialty parts, NOS, services for 1960-1973 big Pontiacs, 1964-1974 GTOs, 1967-1969 Firebirds and 1970-1981 Trans Ams. Web site: www.sonicrepro.com

Sound Move Inc — radios
217 S Main St
Elkhart, IN 46516
800-901-0222, 219-294-5100
FAX: 219-293-4902

See full listing in **Section One** under **Chevrolet**

Ssnake-Oyl Products Inc — carpet underlay, firewall insulation, seat belt restoration
114 N Glenwood Blvd
Tyler, TX 75702
800-284-7777; FAX: 903-526-4501

See full listing in **Section Two** under **interiors & interior parts**

Stencils & Stripes Unlimited Inc — NOS decals, stripe kits
1108 S Crescent Ave #21
Park Ridge, IL 60068
847-692-6893; FAX: 847-692-6895

See full listing in **Section Two** under **decals**

Steve's Antiques/POR-15 — bicycles, POR-15 distributor
Steve Verhoeven
5609 S 4300 W
Hooper, UT 84315
888-817-6715 toll-free, 801-985-4835
E-mail: steve@stevesantiques.com

See full listing in **Section Two** under **rustproofing**

Street-Wise Performance — differentials, new/used parts, overhaul kits, transmissions
Richie Mulligan
Box 105 Creek Rd
Tranquility, NJ 07879
973-786-7500; FAX: 973-786-7861
E-mail: street-wise@usa.net

See full listing in **Section Two** under **transmissions**

Tags Backeast   data plates
PO Box 581   trim tags
Plainville, CT 06062   cowl tags
860-747-2942
E-mail: dataplt@snet.net

See full listing in **Section Two** under **special services**

Tom's Classic Parts   parts
5207 Sundew Terr
Tobyhanna, PA 18466
PH/FAX: 570-894-1459

See full listing in **Section One** under **Chevrolet**

Torque Tech Performance Exhaust   exhaust systems
1826 Woodland Dr
Valdosta, GA 31601
800-408-0016
E-mail: torque@surfsouth.com

See full listing in **Section Two** under **exhaust systems**

Waldron's Antique Exhaust Inc   exhaust systems
25872 M-86, PO Box C
Nottawa, MI 49075
616-467-7185; FAX: 616-467-9041

See full listing in **Section Two** under **exhaust systems**

Jim Wangers   memorabilia
1309 Melrose Way
Vista, CA 92083
760-941-9303; FAX: 760-941-9305
E-mail: info@jimwangers.com

Mail order only. Specializing in Pontiac memorabilia. Publishes *Glory Days*, Jim Wanger's award winning book describing the Glory Days of Pontiac and Detroit. Web site: www.jimwangers.com

White Post Restorations   brakes
One Old Car Dr, PO Drawer D   restoration
White Post, VA 22663
540-837-1140; FAX: 540-837-2368
E-mail: info@whitepost.com

See full listing in **Section Two** under **brakes**

356 Enterprises   parts
Vic & Barbara Skirmants
27244 Ryan Rd
Warren, MI 48092
810-575-9544; FAX: 810-558-3616
E-mail: skirmants@home.com

Mail order and open shop. Specializing in Porsche 356s made from 1948-1965. Engines, transmissions, suspension, brakes, all mechanical parts. Specializing in vintage racing and performance parts and services, including close ratio gear sets and transmission modifications for racing. Web site: www.356enterprises.com

The Auto Doctor Inc   mechanical parts
23125 Telegraph Rd   service repairs
Southfield, MI 48034
248-355-1505; FAX: 248-355-3460

See full listing in **Section One** under **BMW**

Auto Quest Investment Cars Inc   car dealer
710 W 7th St, PO Box 22
Tifton, GA 31793
912-382-4750; FAX: 912-382-4752
E-mail: info@auto-quest.com

See full listing in **Section Two** under **car dealers**

AutoMatch CARS   broker
(Computer Aided Referral Service)   car dealer network
2017 Blvd Napoleon   exotic, classic,
Louisville, KY 40205   new & used car
800-962-2771, 502-417-8793 mobile   locator
502-452-1920 office
FAX: 502-479-6222
E-mail: amcars@aol.com or
aautomatch@aol.com

See full listing in **Section Two** under **car dealers**

Best Deal   accessories
8171 Monroe St   parts
Stanton, CA 90680
800-354-9202; FAX: 714-995-5918
E-mail: bestdeal@deltnet.com

Open shop. Tuesday-Friday 9 am to 5 pm, Saturday 9 am to 3 pm. Catalog of new and used Porsche parts and accessories available. 25 years in the business of selling new and used parts for 356, 911, 914, 924 and 944. Web site: http://users.deltanet.com/~bestdeal

BMC Classics Inc   parts
828 N Dixie Freeway   repair
New Smyrna Beach, FL 32168   restoration
PH/FAX: 386-426-6405
E-mail: bmcar1@aol.com

See full listing in **Section Two** under **restoration shops**

Bud's Parts for Classic   parts
Mercedes-Benz   restoration
9130 Hwy 5   service
Douglasville, GA 30134
800-942-8444; FAX: 770-942-8400

See full listing in **Section One** under **Mercedes-Benz**

Classic Coachworks   bodywork
735 Frenchtown Rd   painting
Milford, NJ 08848   restoration
908-996-3400; FAX: 908-996-0204
E-mail: info@classiccoachworks.net

See full listing in **Section Two** under **restoration shops**

Classic Showcase   classic vehicles
913 Rancheros Dr   restorations
San Marcos, CA 92069   sales
760-747-9947 restoration/buying
760-747-3188 sales
FAX: 760-747-4021
E-mail: management@classicshowcase.com

See full listing in **Section Two** under **restoration shops**

Dave's Auto Restoration   upholstery
2285 Rt 307 E   restoration
Jefferson, OH 44047
PH/FAX: 216-858-2227
E-mail: davesauto@knownet.net

See full listing in **Section Two** under **interiors & interior parts**

Driven By Design
8440 Carmel Valley Rd
Carmel, CA 93923
800-366-1393, 831-625-1393
FAX: 831-625-9342
E-mail: drbydesign@earthlink.net

information
products
services

Mail order and open shop. Monday-Friday 9:30 am to 6 pm.
Specializing in Porsche information, products and services,
videos/books for all years. Inspection videos for the 356, 911,
930, $39.95. Produce and distribute a video *How To Buy a Better
Used Car*. Publishes *The Directory*, a resource book for Porsche
parts suppliers (worldwide), $26.95.

European Collectibles Inc
1974 Placentia Ave
Costa Mesa, CA 92627-3421
949-650-4718; FAX: 949-650-5881
E-mail: europeancollectibles@
pacbell.net

restoration
sales
service

See full listing in **Section Two** under **car dealers**

Excellence Magazine
42 Digital Dr #5
Novato, CA 94949
415-382-0580; FAX: 415-382-0587

magazine

See full listing in **Section Four** under **periodicals**

Grand Prix Classics Inc
7456 La Jolla Blvd
La Jolla, CA 92037
858-459-3500; FAX: 858-459-3512
E-mail: info@grandprixclassics.com

racing cars
sports cars

See full listing in **Section Two** under **racing**

Hatch & Sons Automotive Inc
533 Boston Post Rd
Wayland, MA 01778
508-358-3500; FAX: 508-358-3578

detailing
parts
service
wood refinishing

See full listing in **Section One** under **Mercedes-Benz**

International Mercantile
PO Box 2818
Del Mar, CA 92014-2818
800-356-0012, 760-438-2205
FAX: 760-438-1428
E-mail: morhous@msn.com

rubber parts

Since 1971. Full service in-house design, machine shop and fabricating facility dedicated to the 356, 912 and early 911. All
products are made in the US, of the highest quality. All products
equal OEM or exceed original specifications. New products
monthly. Please write or call for latest brochure. Web site:
www.im356-911.com

Klasse 356 Inc
311 Liberty St
Allentown, PA 18102
800-634-7862; FAX: 610-432-8027
E-mail: parts@klasse356.com

cars
parts
restoration

Mail order and open shop. Monday-Friday, 8 am to 5 pm EST. Cars
and parts (new and used) as well as restoration for Porsche 356.

Machina Locksmith
3 Porter St
Watertown, MA 02172-4145
PH/FAX: 617-923-1683

car locks
keys

See full listing in **Section Two** under **locks & keys**

Mid America Direct
PO Box 1368
Effingham, IL 62401
217-347-5591; FAX: 217-347-2952

accessories
parts

See full listing in **Section One** under **Corvette**

**Thomas Montanari
Automotive Artist**
51 Lamb-Hope Rd
Hopewell, NJ 08525
609-466-7753; FAX: 609-466-7939
E-mail: tmontanari@aol.com

illustrations
paintings
prints

See full listing in **Section Two** under **artwork**

Motorcars International
528 N Prince Ln
Springfield, MO 65802
417-831-9999; FAX: 417-831-8080
E-mail: sales@motorcars-intl.com

accessories
cars
services
tools

See full listing in **Section One** under **Ferrari**

Muncie Imports & Classics
4401 Old St Rd 3 N
Muncie, IN 47303
800-462-4244; FAX: 317-287-9551
E-mail: mic@netdirect.net

repair
restoration
upholstery

See full listing in **Section One** under **Jaguar**

Palo Alto Speedometer Inc
718 Emerson St
Palo Alto, CA 94301
650-323-0243; FAX: 650-323-4632
E-mail: pacspeedo@pacbell.net

instruments

See full listing in **Section One** under **Mercedes-Benz**

PAR Porsche Specialists
310 Main St
New Rochelle, NY 10801
914-637-8800, 800-367-7270
FAX: 914-637-6078
E-mail: parcars@bestweb.net

accessories
car dealer
parts

Mail order and open shop. Monday-Friday 8:30 am to 5:30 pm;
Saturday 9 am to 1 pm. Porsche specialist in both new and used
parts and accessories. Pre-owned Porsches, 1950-present, 356,
911, 928, 944 and Boxster. Sold on consignment. Over 100 cars
available at any one time. Distributor of Recaro automotive seats
and office chairs. Web site: www.parcars.com

**Paul's Select Cars & Parts for
Porsche®**
2280 Gail Dr
Riverside, CA 92509
909-685-9340; FAX: 909-685-9342
E-mail: pauls356-s90@webtv.net

cars
parts

Dry California, rust-free experience parts for most air cooled
Porsches. Call us last for that hard-to-find part. Good prices as
always. New interest: GMC Syclone and Typhoon Turbo trucks
and body parts available.

People Kars
290 Third Ave Ext
Rensselaer, NY 12144
518-465-0477; FAX: 518-465-0614
E-mail: peoplekars@aol.com

models/more
VW toys

See full listing in **Section One** under **Volkswagen**

Perfect Panels of America	body panels
1690 Thomas Paine Pkwy	
Centerville, OH 45459	
937-435-4541; FAX: 937-435-4548	
E-mail: porshfreek@aol.com	

Mail order and open shop. Monday-Friday 7:30 am to 6 pm, Saturday 9:30 am to 12 pm. Manufacturer of replacement body panels for Porsche 914 and 911. 914: hinge plate, hinge bolts, left and right roll panels, complete right suspension consoles, left and right door steps, battery tray, battery tray support, battery hold clamp, jack tubes, jack supports, left and right inner rockers. 911: left and right outer rockers, left and right inner rockers, jack tubes, jack plates. Web site: http://members.aol.com/porshfreek/homepage.html

Pony Parts of America	floor boards
1690 Thomas Paine Pkwy	frame rails
Centerville, OH 45459	
937-435-4541; FAX: 937-435-4548	
E-mail: porshfreek@aol.com	

See full listing in **Section One** under **Mustang**

Precision Autoworks	restorations
2202 Federal St	
East Camden, NJ 08105	
856-966-0080; FAX: 856-541-0393	
E-mail: rplatz007@aol.com	

See full listing in **Section One** under **Mercedes-Benz**

Showroom Auto Sales	car dealer
960 S Bascom Ave	
San Jose, CA 95128	
408-279-0944; FAX: 408-279-0918	

See full listing in **Section One** under **Mercedes-Benz**

Spyder Enterprises Inc	accessories
RFD 1682	artwork
Laurel Hollow, NY 11791-9644	automobilia
516-367-1616; FAX: 516-367-3260	books
E-mail: singer356@aol.com	

See full listing in **Section Two** under **automobilia**

Stoddard Imported Cars Inc	parts
38845 Mentor Ave	
Willoughby, OH 44094-7932	
440-951-1040 in Ohio & overseas;	
800-342-1414; FAX: 440-946-9410	
E-mail: sicars@ix.netcom.com	

International Porsche parts mail order. Extensive inventory for all model Porsches with emphasis on vintage Porsche 356, 911 and 914. Catalogs available for all models. Visit our web site: www.stoddard.com

Stormin Norman's Bug Shop	repair
201 Commerce Dr #3	restoration
Fort Collins, CO 80524	
970-493-5873	

See full listing in **Section One** under **Volkswagen**

Stuttgart Automotive Inc	parts
1690 Thomas Paine Pkwy	service
Centerville, OH 45459	
937-435-4541; FAX: 937-435-4548	
E-mail: porshfreek@aol.com	

Mail order and open shop. For 1955-1999 Porsches. Complete service. Many obsolete parts in stock for 356 Series. Also manufacturer of replacement body panels for 911, 914 and Mustang. Web site: http://members.aol.com/porshfreek/homepage.html

Translog Motorsports	car dealer
619-635 W Poplar St	parts
York, PA 17404	restoration
PH/FAX: 717-846-1885	
E-mail: translogm@aol.com	

Mail order and open shop. Monday-Saturday 9 am to 6 pm. Engine, transmission and body modifications to your specifications. Specializing in restoring Porsches. Large inventory of used and new Porsche parts. Custom built Porsches. Specializing in 914-6 GT replicas, parts duplicated from the Sunoco 914-6 GT.

White Post Restorations	brakes
One Old Car Dr, PO Drawer D	restoration
White Post, VA 22663	
540-837-1140; FAX: 540-837-2368	
E-mail: info@whitepost.com	

See full listing in **Section Two** under **brakes**

Willhoit Auto Restoration	engine rebuilding
1360 Gladys Ave	restoration
Long Beach, CA 90804	
562-439-3333; FAX: 562-439-3956	

Mail order and open shop. Monday-Friday 8 am to 5 pm. Complete in-house restoration services for all models of Porsche 356 (including 4 cam). Including: show quality painting, metalwork and rust repair, engine and transaxle rebuilding, interior installation, car appraisals and pre-purchase inspections. Also a very large used parts inventory. Web site: www.willhoitautorestoration.com

Zim's Autotechnik	parts
1804 Reliance Pkwy	service
Bedford, TX 76021	
800-356-2964; FAX: 817-545-2002	
E-mail: zimips@allzim.com	

Mail order and open shop. Monday-Friday 8 am to 5:30 pm, Saturday 9 am to 1 pm CST. Porsche (only) service and parts. We specialize in the maintenance and repair of Porsche automobiles, Zim's has a large inventory of parts including hard to find parts for older vehicles. We have been in business for over 29 years. Web site: www.allzim.com

4-CV Service	accessories
3301 Shetland Rd	parts
Beavercreek, OH 45434	
E-mail: mike7353@aol.com	

Mail order only. NOS and used parts, accessories and information for restorers of Renault 4-CVs and related vehicles. Some Dauphine mechanical parts. Thirty-eight years' experience with all models of 1948-1961 4-CVs. For information, contact Michael Self at above address or e-mail.

David Casimir Philpa-Augustyn	cars & parts for sale
626-584-6957	literature for sale

See full listing in **Section One** under **Corvair**

French Stuff	accessories
PO Box 39772	engine rebuilding
Glendale, CA 90039-0772	parts
818-244-2498; FAX: 818-500-7628	transaxle rebuilding
E-mail: frenchap@gte.net	

Wholesale and mail order 24 hrs, phone and fax. Will call counter 4 pm to 8 pm PST for local pickups. Direct importers, office in Paris. Established in 1958. Stock and high-performance parts and accessories for all models Renault, Alpine, Matra, Panhard, Deutsch-Bonnet. Technical literature. Lotus Europas S1/S2: engines, transaxles, stock and high-performance parts. V6 PRV engines and 5-speed transaxles for DeLorean and Peugeot. Engines and transaxle rebuilding all Renault models. Specialized R5 Turbo, Alpine, Gordini, V6.

Jacques Rear Engine Renault Parts	**parts**
13839 Hwy 8 Business	
El Cajon, CA 92021	
619-561-6687; FAX: 619-561-1656	
E-mail: renaultj@pacbell.net	

Mail order and open shop. Monday-Saturday, some Sundays, home business. Renaults from the late 1940s, 1950s, 1960s and early 1970s. We stock full line of parts for new (and some used) rear engine Renaults. Rebuilt parts, brake suspension, engine, trim, body, interior, books, spcls. In stock parts, 4CV, Dauphine, Caravelle, R8, R10, even the smallest parts.

Patton Orphan Spares	**parts**
52 Nicole Pl	
West Babylon, NY 11704	
516-669-2598	

Mail order only. Sell spare parts for orphan makes such as Renault Dauphines, Austin A40s and Morris Minor 1000s. Spares are mechanical parts primarily, new and used. Factory shop and parts manuals for same automobiles for sale. Also Renault Alliances and Encores, 1983-1987.

A Bygone Era Motorcars	**appraisals**
6616 Madison Rd	**restoration**
Cincinnati, OH 45227	
513-831-5520	
E-mail: crrchaz@cs.com	

Mail order and open shop. Monday-Friday 8 am to 5 pm or by appointment. Specializing in Rolls-Royce and Bentley restorations and appraisals for Wraith, Derby Bentley and post-war models, especially coachbuilt bodied cars. Also offering pre-purchase inspections and insurance appraisals. 15 year member of RROC.

Albers Rolls-Royce	**car dealer**
360 S First St	**parts**
Zionsville, IN 46077	
317-873-2360, 317-873-2560	
FAX: 317-873-6860	

Monday-Friday 8 am to 5 pm. America's oldest exclusive authorized Rolls-Royce/Bentley dealer. New and pre-owned motor cars available. Largest stock of parts in North America from pre-war to current series. We are now in our 4th decade of service "where total commitment to the product does make a difference". Please supply your chassis/identification number when ordering parts.

Apple Hydraulics Inc	**brake rebuilding**
1610 Middle Rd	**shock rebuilding**
Calverton, NY 11933-1419	
800-882-7753, 631-369-9515	
FAX: 631-369-9516	
E-mail: info@applehydraulics.com	

See full listing in **Section Two** under **suspension parts**

Ashton Keynes Vintage Restorations Ltd	**coachbuilding**
A Keith Bowley	**restoration**
Ashton Keynes, Swindon	
Wilshire England	
01285-861-288; FAX: 01285-860-604	

Coachbuilders and restorers of vintage and classic cars. Panel work, painting and electrical and mechanical restorations. Specializing in Rolls-Royce, Bentley, Jaguar and all classic marques. Engine reconditioning, white metaling and line boring, specialist machining.

Atlantic Enterprises	**steering assemblies**
221 Strand Industrial Dr	
Little River, SC 29566	
843-399-7565; FAX: 843-399-4600	
E-mail: steering@atlantic-ent.com	

See full listing in **Section Two** under **chassis parts**

Atwell-Wilson Motor Museum	**museum**
Downside Stockley Ln	
Calne	
Wiltshire SN110NF England	
PH/FAX: 01249-813119	

See full listing in **Section Six** under **England**

Auto Craftsmen Restoration Inc	**appraisals**
27945 Elm Grove	**buyer/car locator**
San Antonio, TX 78261	**old M-B parts**
PH/FAX: 830-980-4027	**restoration**

See full listing in **Section Two** under **restoration shops**

Bassett Classic Restoration	**parts**
2616 Sharon St, Ste D	**restoration**
Kenner, LA 70062-4934	**service**
PH/FAX: 504-469-2982	

Mail order and open shop. Concours quality, affordable woodwork repair, reveneering and refinishing are our specialty. Console cup holders to match interior woodwork. Complete restorations to partial repairs. Parts, sales and service. We have restored RROC National First Place and Senior Award winning motor cars. Rolls-Royce and Bentley motor cars exclusively. Satisfying discriminating customers for 29 years. References available.

Betws-Y-Coed Motor Museum	**museum**
Betws-Y-Coed	
Conwy Valley	
Gwynedd LL24 0AH England	
01690710760	

See full listing in **Section Six** under **England**

Blackhawk Collection	**acquisitions**
1092 Eagles Nest Pl	**sales**
Danville, CA 94506-3600	
925-736-3444; FAX: 925-736-4375	
E-mail: info@blackhawkcollection.com	

See full listing in **Section One** under **Duesenberg**

Borla East	**exhaust systems**
600 A Lincoln Blvd	
Middlesex, NJ 08846	
732-469-9666	

Mail order and open shop. Monday-Friday 9 am to 5 pm. Custom exhaust systems in 304 stainless steel or mild steel. For any car, but specializes in Rolls-Royce, Jaguar and Mercedes-Benz.

| The Brassworks
289 Prado Rd
San Luis Obispo, CA 93401
800-342-6759; FAX: 805-544-5615
E-mail: brassworks@thegrid.net | radiators |

See full listing in **Section Two** under **radiators**

| British Auto/USA
92 Londonderry Tpke
Manchester, NH 03104
603-622-1050, 800-452-4787
FAX: 603-622-0849
E-mail: jaguar@britishautousa | parts
upholstery |

See full listing in **Section One** under **Jaguar**

| British Luxury Automotive Parts
257 Niagara St
Toronto, ON Canada M6J 2L7
416-693-8400; FAX: 416-694-3202
Cell: 416-820-4323 | new & used parts |

See full listing in **Section One** under **Jaguar**

| Michael Chapman
Priorsleigh, Mill Ln
Cleeve Prior
Worcestershire WR11 5JZ England
0044-1789-773897
FAX: 0044-1789-773588 | automobilia |

See full listing in **Section Two** under **automobilia**

| Classic Auto Restoration
15445 Ventura Blvd #60
Sherman Oaks, CA 91413
818-905-6267; FAX: 818-906-1249
E-mail: rollsroyce1@earthlink.net | acquisitions
restoration
sales |

Open by appointment only. Rolls-Royce, Bentley and fine classic automobile restoration, appraisals, acquisitions and sales. Picture vehicle rental services. Specializing in classic and exotic automobiles. Custom fabrication and preparation of all makes and models to the motion picture and television industry.

| Coachbuilt Motors
907 E Hudson St
Columbus, OH 43211
614-261-1541
E-mail: coachbuilt907@aol.com | repairs |

Mail order and open shop. Tuesday-Friday 8 am to 5:30 pm, Saturday by appointment. Rolls-Royce mail order and repair service shop. Web site: www.coachbuiltmotors.com

| Charles S Crail Automobiles
36A Calle Cesar Chavez
Santa Barbara, CA 93103
805-568-1934; FAX: 805-568-1533
E-mail: crailauto@aol.com | auto sales |

Auto sales for pre and post-war classic European marques such as Rolls-Royce, Bentley, Delahaye, Delage, Aston Martin, BMW, etc.

| Enfield Auto Restoration Inc
4 Print Shop Rd
Enfield, CT 06082
860-749-7917; FAX: 860-749-2836 | panel beating
restorations
Rolls-Royce parts
woodworking |

See full listing in **Section Two** under **restoration shops**

| English Auto
501 Mt Ephraim Rd
Searsport, ME 04974
207-548-2946; FAX: 207-548-6470
E-mail: eauto@mint.net | restoration |

See full listing in **Section One** under **Austin-Healey**

| The Enthusiasts Shop
John Parnell
PO Box 485
Madisonville, LA 70447
985-845-7033; FAX: 985-845-1628 | cars
pre-war parts
transportation |

Mail order only. Specializing in Rolls-Royce and Bentley cars and pre-war parts. Buying, selling literature for pre-1966 Rolls-Royce and Bentleys. Also do inspections and transportation. Will purchase cars in any condition or location. Finder's fees paid. Pre-war abandoned restoration projects and incomplete cars wanted. References gladly furnished.

| Foreign Motors West
253 N Main St
Natick, MA 01760
508-655-5350; FAX: 508-651-0178 | car sales |

Mail order and open shop. Monday-Friday 8 am to 6 pm, Saturday 8 am to noon. Specializing in Rolls-Royce/Bentley, Mercedes-Benz, BMW, Land Rover, Peugeot for all years and models.

| From Rust To Riches
Bill McCoskey
PO Box 93
Littlestown, PA 17340
410-346-0660; FAX: 410-346-6499
E-mail: tatrabill@aol.com | appraisals
Packard parts
Rolls-Royce parts |

See full listing in **Section Two** under **comprehensive parts**

| Glazier Pattern & Coachworks
3720 Loramie-Washington Rd
Houston, OH 45333
937-492-7355; FAX: 937-492-9987
E-mail: s.glazier.fam@juno.com | coachwork
interior woodwork
restoration of wood
bodied cars |

See full listing in **Section One** under **Chrysler**

| Guild of Automotive Restorers
44 Bridge St, PO Box 1150
Bradford, ON Canada L3Z 2B5
905-775-0499; FAX: 905-775-0944
E-mail: cars@guildclassiccars.com | restoration
sales
service |

See full listing in **Section Two** under **restoration shops**

| Tony Handler Inc
2028 Cotner Ave
Los Angeles, CA 90025
310-473-7773; FAX: 310-479-1197 | parts |

Mail order and open shop. Monday-Friday 8 am to 6 pm, Saturday-Sunday by appointment. World's largest stock of used parts for post-war Rolls-Royce and Bentley cars. Technical advice and personalized service. Restoration candidates and rebuildable Rolls-Royce and Bentleys. Web site: www.rolsfix.com

| Heritage Upholstery and Trim
250 H St, PMB 3000
Blaine, WA 98231
604-990-0346; FAX: 604-990-9988 | interior kits
trim
upholstery |

See full listing in **Section One** under **Austin-Healey**

| Jacks Wholesale Division
250 N Robertson Blvd, Ste 405
Beverly Hills, CA 90211-1793
310-839-9417; FAX: 310-839-1046 | limousines |

See full listing in **Section One** under **Lincoln**

| Jersey Motor Museum
St Peter's Village
Jersey JE3 7AG Channel Islands
01534-482966 | museum |

See full listing in **Section Six** under **Channel Islands**

David M King, Automotive Books — literature
5 Brouwer Ln
Rockville Centre, NY 11570
516-766-1561; FAX: 516-766-7502
E-mail: rollskingusa@yahoo.com

Mail order only. Automotive books. Buyer and seller of books on all makes plus racing, biographies, auto travel and annuals. Specializing in literature, books, catalogs, ads, manuals, etc, for Rolls-Royces and Bentleys. Publishers of the *Rolls-Royce Review, The Journal of Rolls-Royce and Bentley Book and Literature Collecting.*

Kreimeyer Co/Auto Legends Inc — antennas/repair glass/wholesale parts/wholesale radios/radio repair
3211 N Wilburn Ave
Bethany, OK 73008
PH/FAX: 405-789-9499

See full listing in **Section One** under **Mercedes-Benz**

Leatherique Professional Leather Restoration & Preservation Products — leather cleaning conditioning & professional restoration products
PO Box 2678
Orange Park, FL 32065
904-272-0992; FAX: 904-272-1534
E-mail: lrpltd@bellsouth.net

Manufacturers of internationally famous, professional quality rejuvenator oil. Contains proteins and collagens to actually nourish and maintain leather to luxurious suppleness. Ph correct cleaners, professional quality co-polymer custom color match leather dyes for leather/vinyl, crack filler, prepping agent, canvas top/carpet dye. Family owned and operated over 40 years. Visit our web site: www.leatherique.com

LMARR Disk Ltd — wheel discs
PO Box 910
Glen Ellen, CA 95442-0910
707-938-9347; FAX: 707-938-3020
E-mail: lmarr@attglobal.net

Mail order only. Specializing in wheel discs for pre-war Rolls-Royce, PI, PII, PIII, 20/25, 25/30, Wraith, Bentley 3-1/2, 4-1/4, Speed 6, 8 litre, Bentley rear wheelcover, Alfa, Bugatti, Delage D8, Lagonda, Jaguar Mk IV, Hispano-Suiza, Lincoln, Voisin. Web site: www.lmarr.com

Mid-Jersey Motorama Inc — car dealer
1301 Asbury Ave, PO Box 1395
Asbury Park, NJ 07712
PH/FAX: 732-775-9885
beeper: 732-840-6111
E-mail: sjz1@msn.com

See full listing in **Section One** under **Cadillac/LaSalle**

Motorcar Gallery Inc — car dealer
715 N Federal Hwy
Fort Lauderdale, FL 33304
954-522-9900; FAX: 954-522-9966
E-mail: motorcargallery@aol.com

See full listing in **Section One** under **Ferrari**

The Museum of Science & Industry in Manchester — museum
Liverpool Rd
Castlefield
Manchester M34FP England
+44 (0) 161-832-2244
FAX: +44 (0) 161-606-0186
E-mail: info@msim.org.uk

See full listing in **Section Six** under **England**

Northern Motorsport Ltd — repair restoration sales service
PO Box 1028, Rt 5
Wilder, VT 05088
802-296-2099; FAX: 802-295-6599
E-mail: bugatti46@aol.com

See full listing in **Section Two** under **restoration shops**

Northwest Transmission Parts — transmission parts
13500 US 62
Winchester, OH 45697
800-327-1955 order line
937-442-2811 info; FAX: 937-442-6555

See full listing in **Section Two** under **transmissions**

Oregon Crewe Cutters Inc — parts
1665 Redwood Ave
Grants Pass, OR 97527
541-479-5663; FAX: 541-479-6339

Mail order and open shop. Monday-Friday 8 am to 5 pm. World's largest stock of used parts for post-war Rolls-Royce and Bentley cars. Technical advice and personalized service. Web site: www.rolsfix.com

Powers Parts Inc — literature parts
425 Pine Ave, PO Box 796
Anna Maria, FL 34216
941-778-7270; FAX: 941-778-0289
E-mail: powersinc@aol.com

Mail order and open shop. Monday-Friday 9 am to 4 pm. New and used parts and literature for 1933-1939 Bentleys, Rolls-Royces and WW II small horsepower Rolls-Royces.

Precision Autoworks — restorations
2202 Federal St
East Camden, NJ 08105
856-966-0080; FAX: 856-541-0393
E-mail: rplatz007@aol.com

See full listing in **Section One** under **Mercedes-Benz**

Proper Motor Cars Inc — parts restoration service
1811 11th Ave N
St Petersburg, FL 33713-5794
727-821-8883; FAX: 727-821-0273
E-mail: propermotorcarsinc@email.msn.com

Mail order and open shop. Monday-Friday 8 am to 4:30 pm. Restoration and maintenance of Rolls-Royces and Bentleys. Also restoration and maintenance of vintage sports and racing cars. All types of restoration. Mercedes-Benz, Ferrari and other European cars serviced and restored. Largest stock of Rolls-Royce new and used parts in the Southeast. Bosch authorized service.

RAU Restoration — woodwork
2027 Pontius Ave
Los Angeles, CA 90025
310-445-1128; FAX: 310-575-9715
E-mail: wcrau@rau-autowood.com

See full listing in **Section Two** under **woodwork**

Regal International Motor Cars Inc — car dealer
PO Box 6819
Hollywood, FL 33081
305-989-9777; FAX: 305-989-9778

Deals in Rolls-Royce, Mercedes, Jaguar, Avanti, special interest cars.

Rolls-Royce Foundation 505 Fishing Creek Rd Lewisberry, PA 17339 717-932-9900; FAX: 717-932-9925 E-mail: rds@flightsystems.com	library literature museum

Founded 1978. 1,800 members. Research library and educational museum dedicated to Rolls-Royce and Bentley motor cars. 501c3 charitable organization. Publishes *Hyphen* twice yearly. Sells manuals, literature and parts through its stores. Dues: $15/year. Web site: www.rollsroycefoundation.com

Rolls-Royce of Beverly Hills 11401 West Pico Blvd Los Angeles, CA 90064 800-321-9792, 310-477-4262 FAX: 310-473-7498 E-mail: smrr64@aol.com	parts

Mail order and open shop. Monday-Friday 8 am to 5:30 pm. Specializing in Rolls-Royce and Bentley parts of all years. We have recently started handling parts for pre WW II models too. Web site: www.rollsroycebeverlyhills.com

Royal Coach Works Ltd 2146 Lunceford Ln Lilburn, GA 30047 PH/FAX: 770-736-3960 E-mail: royalrow@cs.com	appraisals

See full listing in **Section Two** under **appraisals**

Rajam Srinivasan 35-11 92nd St Queens, NY 11372 917-705-4812; FAX: 718-205-0637 E-mail: rajam_s@hotmail.com	accessories parts

Mail order and open shop. Deals in Rolls-Royce and Bentley parts and accessories. I have been doing this the last two years. I have 15 years of experience in Rolls-Royce and Bentley. Proper service. Lowest and reasonable price is our motto.

Supreme Metal Polishing 84A Rickenbacker Cir Livermore, CA 94550 925-449-3490; FAX: 925-449-1475 E-mail: supremet@home.com	metal working parts restoration plating services polishing

See full listing in **Section Two** under **plating & polishing**

Teddy's Garage 8530 Louise Ave Northridge, CA 91325 818-341-0505	parts restoration service

Mail order and open shop. Monday-Friday 8 am to 6 pm. Restores, services and repairs Rolls-Royces, Bentleys, Jaguars, MGs and other fine British automobiles. We have a large stock of parts for pre-1966 Rolls and Bentley cars. If we don't have it, we will get it. Finest workmanship for finest cars.

Van Nuys M-B 14422 Oxnard St Van Nuys, CA 91403 818-988-5455	parts restoration sales service

See full listing in **Section One** under **Mercedes-Benz**

Vantage Motorworks Inc 1898 NE 151 St N Miami, FL 33162 305-940-1161; FAX: 305-949-7481	restoration sales service

Open shop only. Monday-Saturday 8 am to 5 pm. Rolls-Royce/Bentley sales, service, restoration for postwar Rolls-Royce and Bentleys, particular emphasis on S/Cloud series, 1956-1967.

White Post Restorations One Old Car Dr, PO Drawer D White Post, VA 22663 540-837-1140; FAX: 540-837-2368 E-mail: info@whitepost.com	brakes restoration

See full listing in **Section Two** under **brakes**

White Post Restorations One Old Car Dr, PO Drawer D White Post, VA 22663 540-837-1140; FAX: 540-837-2368 E-mail: info@whitepost.com	restoration

See full listing in **Section Two** under **restoration shops**

Wolfson Engineering 512 Pkwy W Las Vegas, NV 89106 PH/FAX: 702-384-4196	mech engineering

See full listing in **Section Two** under **special services**

Atlantic British Ltd Halfmoon Light Industrial Park 6 Enterprise Ave Clifton Park, NY 12065 800-533-2210; FAX: 518-664-6641 E-mail: ab@roverparts.com	accessories parts

North America's largest independent mail order Rover parts and accessories distributor. Free catalog available for Land Rover, Range Rover, Discovery, Defender and Sterling vehicles. Web site: www.atlanticbritish.com

British Luxury Automotive Parts 257 Niagara St Toronto, ON Canada M6J 2L7 416-693-8400; FAX: 416-694-3202 Cell: 416-820-4323	new & used parts

See full listing in **Section One** under **Jaguar**

British Motor Co 3825 W 11th Ave Eugene, OR 97402 800-995-1895; FAX: 541-485-8544	engine rebuilding

See full listing in **Section One** under **Jaguar**

British Pacific Ltd 26007 Huntington Ln, Unit 2 Valencia, CA 91355 800-554-4133; FAX: 661-257-9765 E-mail: britpac@aol.com	parts

Mail order and retail counter. Monday-Friday 9 am to 5 pm. Exclusively Land Rover parts 1958-1997. Catalogs available for Series II, IIA, III; Defender, Discovery, Range Rover. Genuine, OEM and aftermarket parts and accessories. Web site: www.britishpacific.com

British Parts International 8101 Hempstead Rd Houston, TX 77008 800-231-6563 ext 570 FAX: 713-863-8238 E-mail: info@britishparts.com	parts

See full listing in **Section One** under **Jaguar**

Classic Jaguar 9916 Hwy 290 W Austin, TX 78736 512-288-8800; FAX: 512-288-9216 E-mail: danmooney@classicjaguar.com	parts technical support

See full listing in **Section One** under **Jaguar**

Foreign Motors West 253 N Main St Natick, MA 01760 508-655-5350; FAX: 508-651-0178	car sales

See full listing in **Section One** under **Rolls-Royce/Bentley**

Heritage Motor Centre Banbury Rd Gaydon Warwickshire CV35 0BJ England 01926 641188; FAX: 01926 641555 E-mail: enquiries@ heritagemotorcentre.org.uk	museum

See full listing in **Section Six** under **England**

Jaguar Heaven 1433 Tillie Lewis Dr Stockton, CA 95206 209-942-4524; FAX: 209-942-3670	parts

See full listing in **Section One** under **Jaguar**

Jaguar of Puerto Rico Inc PO Box 13055 San Juan, PR 00908-3055 787-723-5177; FAX: 787-723-9488 E-mail: jaguarpr@hotmail.com	car dealer parts service

See full listing in **Section One** under **Jaguar**

Mid-Jersey Motorama Inc 1301 Asbury Ave, PO Box 1395 Asbury Park, NJ 07712 PH/FAX: 732-775-9885 beeper: 732-840-6111 E-mail: sjz1@msn.com	car dealer

See full listing in **Section One** under **Cadillac/LaSalle**

Motorcars Ltd 8101 Hempstead Rd Houston, TX 77008 800-338-5238 ext 570 FAX: 713-863-8238 E-mail: info@motorcarsltd.com	parts

See full listing in **Section One** under **Jaguar**

Lyle Pearson Company 351 Auto Dr Boise, ID 83709 800-621-1775; FAX: 208-672-3494 E-mail: partspc@lylepearson.com	accessories literature parts

See full listing in **Section One** under **Mercedes-Benz**

Rovers West 1815 E 19th St, Unit 2 Tucson, AZ 85719 520-670-9377; FAX: 520-670-9080 E-mail: roverswest@aol.com	accessories parts

Mail/phone order. Monday-Friday 10 am to 6 pm, weekends by appointment. Specializing in new and used parts, high-performance parts, off-road accessories and optional equipment for Land Rover, Range Rovers, Rover 2000, 3500S, SD-1 Rovers. Web site: www.roverswest.com

Spectral Kinetics 17 Church St Garnerville, NY 10923 845-947-3126; FAX: 845-947-3126 E-mail: harve86@altglobal.net	parts restoration

Mail order and open shop by appointment. Specializes in the sale of new and used Rover sedan parts, particularly the 2000, 3500S and SD1 models. Also specializes in early Range Rovers. Rebuilding and restoration services. "We sell parts for what we drive."

XKs Unlimited 850 Fiero Ln San Luis Obispo, CA 93401 800-444-5247; FAX: 805-544-1664 E-mail: xksunltd@aol.com	instruments parts restorations

See full listing in **Section One** under **Jaguar**

The Auto Doctor Inc 23125 Telegraph Rd Southfield, MI 48034 248-355-1505; FAX: 248-355-3460	mechanical parts service repairs

See full listing in **Section One** under **BMW**

Irving Galis 357 Atlantic Ave Marblehead, MA 01945	books dealer items literature

Mail order only. 1) Out-of-print automobile books, emphasis on early Saabs; 2) Saab literature, books and dealer items list. Send SASE (each list).

Rayce Inc 3637 NE 2nd St Gainesville, FL 32609 800-426-2221, 352-335-8900 FAX: 352-335-8930	parts

See full listing in **Section One** under **Alfa Romeo**

White Post Restorations One Old Car Dr, PO Drawer D White Post, VA 22663 540-837-1140; FAX: 540-837-2368 E-mail: info@whitepost.com	brakes restoration

See full listing in **Section Two** under **brakes**

Miller Energy Inc 3200 South Clinton Ave S Plainfield, NJ 07080 908-755-6700; FAX: 908-755-0312 E-mail allyon@aol.com	engine parts

Mail order only. Level gauge, sight glass for Stanley steam engine.

Stanley Museum
School St
Kingfield, ME 04947
207-265-2729; FAX: 207-265-4700
E-mail: stanleym@somtel.com

museum

See full listing in **Section Six** under **Maine**

Vintage Steam Products
396 North Rd
Chester, NJ 07930-2327
973-584-3319
E-mail: arthart@att.net

**parts
supplies**

Mail order only. Specializing in reproduction parts and supplies for Stanleys and other early steam powered automobiles.

Arthur W Aseltine
18215 Challenge Cut-Off Rd
Forbestown, CA 95941
530-675-2773; FAX: 530-675-9134
E-mail: awa@lostsierra.net

**parts
research
restoration**

Mail order and open shop. Monday-Friday 8 am to 5:30 pm; Saturday and Sunday by appointment. Total or partial restoration of Stearns, Stearns-Knight, Daimler, Minerva and other sleeve-valve motorcars. 40 years' experience with sleeve-valve motors. All work guaranteed. Web site: www.aseltine-associates.com

1956 Studebaker Golden Hawk Owners Register
31700 Wekiva River Rd
Sorrento, FL 32776-9233
E-mail: 56sghor@prodigy.net

**information
exchange**

Established January 1, 1989. Our purpose is to: track the remaining 1956 Golden Hawks, help owners maintain and restore their cars and help buyers make intelligent purchases. Publish a newsletter called *56J Only* (for owners only). We maintain a web site for online information, correspondence and registration. Web site: http://pages.prodigy.net/56sghor

A-1 Shock Absorber Co
Shockfinders Division
365 Warren Ave, PO Box 2028
Silverthorne, CO 80498
800-344-1966, 970-389-3193 cell
FAX: 970-513-8283

**shocks-all types
coil springs
Koni shocks
leaf springs
steering gears**

See our ad on the last page

Apple Hydraulics Inc
1610 Middle Rd
Calverton, NY 11933-1419
800-882-7753, 631-369-9515
FAX: 631-369-9516
E-mail: info@applehydraulics.com

**brake rebuilding
shock rebuilding**

See full listing in **Section Two** under **suspension parts**

Chief Service
Herbert G Baschung
Brunnmatt, PO Box 155
CH-4914 Roggwil Switzerland
PH/FAX: 0041-62-9291777

**parts
restoration**

See full listing in **Section Two** under **restoration shops**

Classic Enterprises
Box 92
Barron, WI 54812
715-537-5422 office
715-234-4677 products
FAX: 715-537-5770
E-mail: lamonte@classicent.com

sheetmetal

Manufacturer of top quality sheetmetal restoration reproductions. Specializes in restoration reproductions (sheetmetal) for Studebakers and 1946-1986 Willys Jeeps. Floor panels for 1957-1958 Fords. We either meet or exceed all metal gauge requirements. All products are backed by a 30-day satisfaction guarantee. MasterCard, Visa, AmEx. Web site: www.classicent.com

Dakota Studebaker Parts
39408 280th St
Armour, SD 57313
605-724-2527
E-mail: dakstude1@unitelsd.com

parts

Mail order only. Specialize in parts for Studebaker trucks, pickups and cars 1936-1964.

Dennis DuPont
77 Island Pond Rd
Derry, NH 03038
603-434-9290

**automobilia
literature
parts**

Mail order only. Sell NOS and used parts for Studebaker from mid 1930s-1966. Also have Studebaker literature, ads and automobilia. Buy Studebaker NOS parts, literature and automobilia. If it says Studebaker, we are interested.

Firewall Insulators & Quiet Ride Solutions
6465 Pacific Ave, Ste 249
Stockton, CA 95207
209-477-4840; FAX: 209-477-0918
E-mail: timcox@quietride.com

**air plenums
auto insulation
firewall insulators
gloveboxes
sound deadening**

See full listing in **Section Two** under **upholstery**

Eugene Gardner
10510 Rico Tatum Rd
Palmetto, GA 30268
770-463-4264, 9 am to 11 pm EST

license plates

See full listing in **Section Two** under **license plates**

Garton's Auto
401 N 5th St (at 5th & Vine)
Millville, NJ 08332-3129
PH: 856-825-3618

**bicycle sales lit
Ford NOS parts
sales literature**

See full listing in **Section One** under **Ford 1932-1953**

Kelley's Korner
22 14th St
Bristol, TN 37620
423-968-5583

**parts
repair**

Mail order and open shop. Monday-Saturday 9 am to 5 pm. Studebaker repair, parts for Studebaker cars and trucks 1925-1966. Engine rebuilds, brake overhauls, front end work, electrical work and wiring harnesses.

Loga Enterprises | interior parts
5399 Old Town Hall Rd
Eau Claire, WI 54701
715-832-7302
E-mail: logaent@cs.com

Mail order only. Specializing in Studebaker 1937-1966 for interior panels, firewall liners, headliners, kick pads, truck headliners, trunk mats, carpets, gloveboxes. Also door boards, firewall pads, hood pads, door clips, custom interior panels.

Old Coach Works Restoration Inc | appraisals / restoration
1206 Badger St
Yorkville, IL 60560-1701
630-553-0414; FAX: 630-553-1053
E-mail: oldcoachworks@msn.com

See full listing in **Section Two** under **restoration shops**

Phil's Studebaker | NOS parts / used parts
11250 Harrison Rd
Osceola, IN 46561-9375
219-674-0084
E-mail: stude67a@aol.com

Mail order. For 1947-1966 Studebakers. NOS, reproduction and excellent used Studebaker parts and accessories.

Steve's Studebaker-Packard | car dealer / parts / suspension repairs
PO Box 6914
Napa, CA 94581
707-255-8945

See full listing in **Section One** under **Packard**

Studebaker International | parts
97 N 150 W
Greenfield, IN 46140
317-462-3124; FAX: 317-462-8891

Mail order and open shop. Monday-Friday 8 am to 5 pm. Specializing in Studebakers.

Studebaker National Museum | museum
525 S Main St
South Bend, IN 46601
219-235-9714, 888-391-5600
FAX: 219-235-5522
E-mail: stumuseum@skyenet.net

See full listing in **Section Six** under **Indiana**

Studebakers West | mechanical / rebuilding / transmission parts / wiring harnesses
335A Convention Way
Redwood City, CA 94063
650-366-8787

Mail order and open shop. Monday-Friday 9 am to 12 noon and 1 pm to 5 pm; Saturday 9 am to 12 noon. Mechanical, chassis, engine, transmission and new wiring harnesses. Over 13,000 part numbers in stock. "Studebakers are our business, our only business."

Volunteer Studebaker | parts / parts locator
228 Marquiss Cir
Clinton, TN 37716
615-457-3002; FAX: 775-514-1386
E-mail: studebaker_joe@msn.com

Mail order only. Specializing in parts, new and used, for 1939-1966 Studebakers, Avanti, Avanti II.

White Post Restorations | brakes / restoration
One Old Car Dr, PO Drawer D
White Post, VA 22663
540-837-1140; FAX: 540-837-2368
E-mail: info@whitepost.com

See full listing in **Section Two** under **brakes**

Grand Touring | engine rebuilding / machine shop / restoration / suspension
2785 E Regal Park Dr
Anaheim, CA 92806
714-630-0130; FAX: 714-630-6956

See full listing in **Section Two** under **restoration shops**

Classic Sunbeam Auto Parts Inc | body parts / carpets / electrical parts / upholstery
2 Tavano Rd
Ossining, NY 10562
800-24-SUNBEAM
E-mail: classicsun@aol.com

Mail order only. Phone hours: Monday-Saturday 10 am to 10 pm. New OEM quality reproductions of running parts, trim, upholstery, carpets, tops, electrical and body parts for 1959-1967 Alpines and Tigers. 24 page catalog. Web site: www.classicsunbeam.com

Kip Motor Company Inc | literature / parts / restoration
2127 Crown Rd
Dallas, TX 75229
972-243-0440; FAX: 972-243-2387
E-mail: kipmotor@aol.com

See full listing in **Section One** under **Austin**

Sports Car Haven | new and used parts / race prep / restoration / service
2-33 Flowerfield Industrial Pk
St James, NY 11780
631-862-8058
E-mail: sch94@aol.com

See full listing in **Section One** under **Triumph**

Sunbeam Specialties | parts / restoration supplies
PO Box 771
Los Gatos, CA 95031
408-371-1642; FAX: 408-371-8070
E-mail: sunsp19@pacbell.net

Mail order and open shop. Monday-Friday 8 am to 5 pm. Carries an extensive supply of mechanical, hydraulic and soft trim and restoration supplies for Sunbeam Alpine and Tiger cars. Will ship overseas. Fast service. Web site: www.rootes.com

Victoria British Ltd | accessories / parts
Box 14991
Lenexa, KS 66285-4991
800-255-0088, 913-599-3299

See full listing in **Section One** under **MG**

TALBOT

Dragone Classic Motorcars
1797 Main St
Bridgeport, CT 06604
203-335-4643; FAX: 203-335-9798

car dealer

See full listing in **Section Two** under **car dealers**

TERRAPLANE

Firewall Insulators & Quiet Ride Solutions
6465 Pacific Ave, Ste 249
Stockton, CA 95207
209-477-4840; FAX: 209-477-0918
E-mail: timcox@quietride.com

air plenums
auto insulation
firewall insulators
gloveboxes
sound deadening

See full listing in **Section Two** under **upholstery**

K-GAP
Automotive Parts
PO Box 3065
Santa Fe Springs, CA 90670
PH/FAX: 714-523-0403

repro parts

See full listing in **Section One** under **Hudson**

 TOYOTA

CSi
1100 S Raymond Ave, Ste H
Fullerton, CA 92831
714-879-7955; FAX: 714-879-7310
E-mail: csila@compuserve.com

parts

See full listing in **Section One** under **BMW**

KATO USA Inc
100 Remington Rd
Schaumburg, IL 60173
847-781-9500; FAX: 847-781-9570

models

1/43 scale automobile models of Nissan 300ZX and Toyota Supra. Available through hobby dealers or direct order. Web site: www.katousa.com

Keiser Motors
1169 Dell Ave #A
Campbell, CA 95008
408-374-7303

Gelaendewagens
Land Cruisers

Specializing in Toyota Land Cruisers, FJ40, FJ55, FJ60, FJ80. Specializing in Mercedes Gelaendewagen 4-wheel drives. Web site: www.keisermotors.com

Land Cruiser Solutions Inc
20 Thornell Rd
Newton, NH 03858
603-382-3555; FAX: 603-378-0431
E-mail: twbii@aol.com

accessories
restoration
services

Mail order and open shop. Monday-Friday 8 am to 5 pm EST, Saturday 9 am to 12 noon by appointment. Toyota Land Cruiser parts and accessories. Providing maintenance and service for all Land Cruisers. Specializing in full restorations, engine and transmission conversions, suspensions, power steering, interiors, frame components, wiring harnesses, and custom paint finishes. Original supplier of the aluminum body tub for the FJ40 and FJ45. Complete and rare Land Cruisers for sale. We ship worldwide. Web site: www.landcruisersolutions.com

Specter Off-Road Inc
21600 Nordhoff St, Dept HM
Chatsworth, CA 91311
818-882-1238; FAX: 818-882-7144
E-mail: sor@sor.com

accessories
parts

Mail order and open shop. Monday-Friday 9 am to 6 pm PST, closed Saturday and Sunday. Toyota Land Cruiser parts & accessories. Complete line of new, used, unique and hard to find Land Cruiser items. 50,000 sq ft warehouse. We invite you to visit our showroom and museum with many rare Land Cruisers on display. 500 page catalog available with price list, $7.50 USA, $30 foreign. Web site: www.sor.com

 TRIUMPH

A Bygone Era Motorcars
6616 Madison Rd
Cincinnati, OH 45227
513-831-5520
E-mail: crrchaz@cs.com

appraisals
restoration

See full listing in **Section One** under **Rolls-Royce/Bentley**

American-Foreign Auto Electric Inc
103 Main St
Souderton, PA 18964
215-723-4877

parts
rebuilding

See full listing in **Section Two** under **electrical systems**

Apple Hydraulics Inc
1610 Middle Rd
Calverton, NY 11933-1419
800-882-7753, 631-369-9515
FAX: 631-369-9516
E-mail: info@applehydraulics.com

brake rebuilding
shock rebuilding

See full listing in **Section Two** under **suspension parts**

Atlantic Enterprises
221 Strand Industrial Dr
Little River, SC 29566
843-399-7565; FAX: 843-399-4600
E-mail: steering@atlantic-ent.com

steering assemblies

See full listing in **Section Two** under **chassis parts**

Automotive Artistry
679 W Streetboro St
Hudson, OH 44236
330-650-1503
E-mail: dale@cmh.net

restoration

Open shop only. Monday-Friday 8 am to 5 pm. Restoration of sports cars, all years and makes. Partial or body-off. Complete services offered, mechanical, body, upholstery and painting.

Section One – Marque Specialists

Autosport Inc
2110 W Vernal Pk
Bloomington, IN 47404
812-334-1700; FAX: 812-334-1712

restoration

See full listing in **Section One** under **MG**

BCP Sport & Classic Co
10525 Airline Dr
Houston, TX 77037
281-448-4739; FAX: 281-448-0189

parts
service

See full listing in **Section One** under **MG**

British Auto Parts Ltd
93256 Holland Ln
Marcola, OR 97454
541-933-2880; FAX: 541-933-2302

parts

See full listing in **Section One** under **Morris**

British Auto Shoppe
1909 5th Ave
Moline, IL 61265
309-764-9513; FAX: 309-764-9576

parts
service

See full listing in **Section One** under **MG**

British Car Keys
Rt 144 Box 9957
Ellicott City, MD 21042-3647
410-750-2352
E-mail: britishcarkeys@hotmail.com

keys

See full listing in **Section One** under **Austin-Healey**

British Car Magazine
343 Second St, Ste H
Los Altos, CA 94022-3639
650-949-9680; FAX: 650-949-9685
E-mail: editor@britishcar.com

periodical

See full listing in **Section Four** under **periodicals**

British Car Service
2854 N Stone Ave
Tucson, AZ 85705
520-882-7026; FAX: 520-882-7053
E-mail: bcs@liveline.com

restoration
salvage yard

See full listing in **Section Two** under **restoration shops**

British Car Specialists
2060 N Wilson Way
Stockton, CA 95205
209-948-8767; FAX: 209-948-1030
E-mail: healeydoc@aol.com

parts
repairs
restoration

See full listing in **Section One** under **Austin-Healey**

British Miles
9278 Old E Tyburn Rd
Morrisville, PA 19067
215-736-9300; FAX: 215-736-3089

accessories
literature
parts
restoration

See full listing in **Section One** under **MG**

British Parts NW
4105 SE Lafayette Hwy
Dayton, OR 97114
503-864-2001; FAX: 503-864-2081
E-mail: bpnw@onlinemac.com

parts

Mail/phone orders only. Monday-Friday 8 am to 5 pm. Direct importer for Triumph, Jaguar, MGA, B (engine parts only) and Austin-Healey 100-4 through 3000 (engine parts only). Carry a full line of polyurethane bushings for TR4A-6, Spitfire, GT6 and TR7, 8. High-performance engine parts for all Triumph engines plus MG are also available. Web site: www.bpnorthwest.com

---

British Racing Green
30 Aleph Dr
Newark, DE 19702
302-368-1117; FAX: 302-368-5910
E-mail: info@brgparts.com

new parts
rebuilt parts
used parts

See full listing in **Section One** under **MG**

British Restorations
4455 Paul St
Philadelphia, PA 19124
215-533-6696

car dealer
restoration

See full listing in **Section One** under **Jaguar**

British Sportscars & Classics
4225 Aurora N
Seattle, WA 98103-7307
206-634-3990

conversion kits
engines
transmissions

See full listing in **Section One** under **Jaguars**

British Triumph & Metropolitan
9957 Frederick Rd
Ellicott City, MD 21042-3647
410-750-2352 evenings
E-mail: pete_groh@yahoo.com

British Leyland
original British
keys
WASO
Wilmot Breeden

See full listing in **Section One** under **Metropolitan**

British Wire Wheel
444 Airport Blvd, #114
Watsonville, CA 95077
800-732-9866, 831-763-4200
FAX: 831-763-1780

hubs
tires
wire wheels

See full listing in **Section One** under **Austin-Healey**

Doug's British Car Parts
2487 E Colorado Blvd
Pasadena, CA 91107
818-793-2494; FAX: 818-793-4339
E-mail: dougsbritish@msn.com

accessories
parts

See full listing in **Section One** under **Jaguar**

Doug's British Car Parts
606 Pub St
Galloway, OH 43119
614-878-6373; FAX: 614-688-3077
E-mail: braden.13@osu.edu

accessories
parts

Mail order only. Specializing in parts and accessories for Triumph 1950-81, MG 1950-80, Austin-Healey 1955-67, Jaguar 1950 to present. I have NOS and used, also new Moss parts at discount prices.

Eightparts
1815 E 19th St Unit 2
Tucson, AZ 85719
520-670-9377; FAX: 520-670-9080
E-mail: roverswest@aol.com

accessories
parts

Mail/phone order. Monday-Friday 10 am to 6 pm, weekends by appointment. Specializing in new and used parts, high-performance, accessories and optional equipment for TR8 and Stag. Also Triumph TR7 parts. Web site: www.roverswest.com

---

Don Flye
5 Doe Valley Rd
Petersham, MA 01366
978-724-3318

parts

See full listing in **Section One** under **Austin-Healey**

| **Heritage Motor Centre**
Banbury Rd
Gaydon
Warwickshire CV35 0BJ England
01926 641188; FAX: 01926 641555
E-mail: enquiries@
heritagemotorcentre.org.uk | **museum** |

See full listing in **Section Six** under **England**

| **Heritage Upholstery and Trim**
250 H St, PMB 3000
Blaine, WA 98231
604-990-0346; FAX: 604-990-9988 | **interior kits**
trim
upholstery |

See full listing in **Section One** under **Austin-Healey**

| **John's Cars Inc**
800 Jaguar Ln
Dallas, TX 75226
888-281-1529 parts orders only
214-426-4100; FAX: 214-426-3116 | **conversion retrofits**
parts
restoration
service |

See full listing in **Section One** under **Jaguar**

| **Morgan Spares Ltd**
225 Simons Rd
Ancram, NY 12502
518-329-3877; FAX: 518-329-3892
E-mail: morganspares@taconic.net | **car sales**
consulting
obsolete parts
used parts |

See full listing in **Section One** under **Morgan**

| **Moss Motors Ltd**
440 Rutherford St
Goleta, CA 93117
800-235-6954; FAX: 805-692-2525 | **accessories**
parts |

See full listing in **Section One** under **MG**

| **Motorhead Ltd**
2811-B Old Lee Hwy
Fairfax, VA 22031
800-527-3140; FAX: 703-573-3195 | **parts**
repairs |

See full listing in **Section One** under **Austin-Healey**

| **Motormetrics**
6369 Houston Rd
Macon, GA 31216
912-785-0275
E-mail: fzampa@mail.maconstate.edu | **used parts** |

Mail order only. Used parts for MG Midget, TR3, and X-19.

| **Mr Sport Car Inc**
719 W 6th St
Papillion, NE 68046
402-592-7559 | **service** |

See full listing in **Section One** under **Jaguar**

| **Omni Specialties**
10418 Lorain Ave
Cleveland, OH 44111
888-819-6464 (MGMG)
216-251-2269; FAX: 216-251-6083 | **parts**
restoration
service |

See full listing in **Section One** under **MG**

| **Pacific International Auto**
1118 Garnet Ave
San Diego, CA 92109
619-274-1920; FAX: 619-454-1815 | **parts**
sales
service |

See full listing in **Section One** under **Jaguar**

| **The Roadster Factory**
328 Killen Rd, PO Box 332
Armagh, PA 15920
800-234-1104; FAX: 814-446-6729 | **accessories**
parts |

Telephone orders Monday-Thursday 8 am to 9 pm; Friday-Saturday 8 am to 6 pm EST; counter sales Monday-Saturday 8 am to 6 pm. Original components and accessories for Triumph TR2 through TR8, Spitfire, GT6 and MGB. Manufacturer of high quality replacement parts. Minor components to rebuilt units and nuts and bolts to body shells. Company owned and operated by Triumph and MGB enthusiasts since 1978. Free catalogs. Web site: www.the-roadster-factory.com

| **Sidecurtain Bags & Accessories**
9130 W Broad St
Richmond, VA 23294
804-527-1515; FAX: 804-527-1616
E-mail: kmntr6@aol.com | **side curtain bags** |

Mail order only. Specializing in side curtain bags, convertible top bags and tool bags for Triumph TR3, MGA, Jaguar, etc. Web site: www.sidecurtain.com

| **Sports Car Haven**
2-33 Flowerfield Industrial Pk
St James, NY 11780
631-862-8058
E-mail: sch94@aol.com | **new and used parts**
race prep
restoration
service |

Mail order and open shop. Monday-Friday 9 am to 6 pm, Saturday 9 am to 2 pm. Over 30 years' experience in service, restorations, race prep and parts for British and other sports cars. SCCA and vintage race car preparation. Triumph engine thrust washer problems solved. Authorized Moss distributor.

| **Sports Car Haven**
3414 Bloom Rd, Rt 11
Danville, PA 17821
570-275-5705 | **parts**
restoration
service |

See full listing in **Section Two** under **restoration shops**

| **Sports Car Rentals & Sales**
PO Box 265
Batesville, VA 22924
804-823-4442
E-mail: info@sportscarrentals.com | **car rentals** |

See full listing in **Section Two** under **special services**

| **Triple C Motor Accessories**
1900 Orange St
York, PA 17404
717-854-4081; FAX: 717-854-6706
E-mail: sales@triple-c.com | **accessories**
models |

See full listing in **Section One** under **MG**

| **Triumph World Magazine**
PO Box 75
Tadworth
Surrey KT20 7XF England
01737 814311; FAX: 01737 814591
E-mail: triumphworld@chpltd.com | **periodical** |

Triumph World magazine is a bi-monthly, top quality magazine devoted entirely to the ever-popular classic cars produced under the Triumph banner, such famous sports car models that carry the marque name to the four corners of the globe. The TR range, Spitfire and Stag plus those other unique models that epitomize the best of British styling and engineering. Subscription: $39/year (6 issues). Web site: www.chpltd.com

| **Victoria British Ltd**
Box 14991
Lenexa, KS 66285-4991
800-255-0088, 913-599-3299 | **accessories**
parts |

See full listing in **Section One** under **MG**

White Post Restorations | brakes
One Old Car Dr, PO Drawer D | restoration
White Post, VA 22663
540-837-1140; FAX: 540-837-2368
E-mail: info@whitepost.com

See full listing in **Section Two** under **brakes**

Classic Motor Works | parts
100 Station St
Johnstown, PA 15905
814-288-6911; FAX: 814-288-4455
E-mail: birdcmw@aol.com

New and used parts for TVR sports cars from Grantura to 280i.

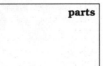

From Rust To Riches | appraisals
Bill McCoskey | Packard parts
PO Box 93 | Rolls-Royce parts
Littlestown, PA 17340
410-346-0660; FAX: 410-346-6499
E-mail: tatrabill@aol.com

See full listing in **Section Two** under **comprehensive parts**

4 ever 4 | car dealer
Rt 10 | parts
Marlow, NH 03456 | service
877-4EVER4-VW, 603-446-7820

Mail order and open shop. Tuesday-Friday 9 am to 6 pm, Thursday 9 am to 8 pm, Saturday by prior appointment only. Specializing in Volkswagen parts and services for air cooled vehicles. Purchases and sells vehicles, toys, parts and literature, full service shop, many NOS parts and thousands of tagged and tested used parts, UPS daily. Involved with VW since 1967. A friendly, one man business. No catalog. We love all Vanagons. Web site: www.4evr4-vw-aircl-allvans.com

Concours Cars of Colorado Ltd | accessories
2414 W Cucharras St | parts
Colorado Springs, CO 80904 | service
719-473-6288; FAX: 719-473-9206

See full listing in **Section One** under **BMW**

David Casimir Philpa-Augustyn | cars & parts for sale
626-584-6957 | literature for sale

See full listing in **Section One** under **Corvair**

Discount Auto Parts | salvage yard
4703 Broadway SE
Albuquerque, NM 87105
505-877-6782

See full listing in **Section Five** under **New Mexico**

Melissa & Jerry Jess | accessories
3121 E Yucca St | literature
Phoenix, AZ 85028 | models
602-867-7672
E-mail: vwstuff@qwest.net

Mail order only. Specializing in Volkswagen, models, literature, accessories and more for 1939-1966 all air cooled VWs. Web site: http://vwstuff.vwspeed.com

John's Car Corner | body/mech parts
Rt 5, PO Box 85 | car dealer
Westminster, VT 05158 | repairs/restoration
802-722-3180; FAX: 802-722-3181

Mail order and open shop. Monday-Friday 8 am to 5 pm, Saturday 9 am to 12 pm. Millions of new and used parts for Volkswagen and Audi, all years and all models. Over 30 years in business.

Karmann Ghia Parts & Restoration | parts
PO Box 997
Ventura, CA 93002
800-927-2787; FAX: 805-641-3333
E-mail: info@karmannghia.com

Mail order. Wholesale/retail. Parts, new and used for Volkswagen Karmann Ghias, all years. Manufacturers and importers for all parts (except engine and transmission) for all years of Karmann Ghias. Web site: www.karmannghia.com

Last Chance Repair & Restoration | repairs
1242 Myers Rd, PO Box 362A | restoration
Shaftsbury, VT 05262
802-447-7040

See full listing in **Section Two** under **restoration shops**

Mid America Direct | accessories
PO Box 1368 | parts
Effingham, IL 62401
217-347-5591; FAX: 217-347-2952

See full listing in **Section One** under **Corvette**

Neuspeed | parts
3300 Corte Manpaso
Camarillo, CA 93012
805-388-7171; FAX: 805-388-0030

See full listing in **Section One** under **Audi**

People Kars | models/more
290 Third Ave Ext | VW toys
Rensselaer, NY 12144
518-465-0477; FAX: 518-465-0614
E-mail: peoplekars@aol.com

Mail order and shows. Specializing in toys, models and collectibles for all types and years of Volkswagens. People Kars feature VW models from Vitesse, Solido, Mini Champs, Shabak, Siku and more plus an extensive collection of older discontinued models, toys and promotional pieces, all with the VW enthusiast in mind. In addition to Volkswagen scale miniatures, People Kars now offers a variety of Porsche and select European vehicle marques including German micro cars. Please contact us for our current catalog/list or visit us on the web at: www.peoplekars.com

Quality Tire Barn Inc 255 Twinsburg Rd Northfield, OH 44067 330-467-1284 FAX: 330-467-1289 (call first) E-mail: donquist@aol.com	tires

See full listing in **Section Two** under **tires**

The Real Source PO Box 1248 Effingham, IL 62401 800-LUV-BUGG (588-2844), Dept VS1 FAX: 217-347-2952 E-mail: mail@800luvbugg.com	accessories parts

The Real Source of parts and accessories for your VW Beetle! This free full-color catalog features restoration, maintenance and performance parts plus styling enhancements and lifestyle accessories for yesterday's air-cooled Bug and today's 1998-2001 Beetle.

Rocky Mountain Motorworks Inc 1003 Tamarac Pkwy Woodland Park, CO 80863 800-258-1996; FAX: 800-544-1084 E-mail: sales@motorworks.com	accessories parts

Monday-Friday 7 am-7 pm, Saturday 9 am-4 pm MST. Catalog/Internet company. Thousands of exceptional quality VW and BMW parts and accessories. Expansive new and used parts with retail and wholesale divisions. Lifetime warranty on all parts, risk-free guarantee and same day shipping guarantee. Free catalog. Web site: www.motorworks.com

Stormin Norman's Bug Shop 201 Commerce Dr #3 Fort Collins, CO 80524 970-493-5873	repair restoration

Open Tuesday-Friday 8 am to 5:30 pm. Repair and complete restoration services for Volkswagen Beetles.

V-Dub's 'R' Us 5705 Gordon Dr Harrisburg, PA 17112 717-540-9972 E-mail: jamessieg@aol.com	literature parts toys

Mail order. Used, NOS and repro parts for air-cooled Volkswagens. Sheetmetal, rubber parts, chrome trim, cabriolet parts, restored steering wheels. VW toys and literature. Restoration supplies and assistance. We use what we sell.

Vintage Auto LLC 605 Pine Knoll Dr Greenville, SC 29609 864-292-8785; FAX: 864-244-5244 E-mail: vintagevuu@aol.com	new/used parts service

Mail order and open shop. Monday-Friday 8 am to 6 pm, Saturday 9 am to 1 pm. Volkswagen and Honda service, new and used parts, preowned cars. All years and models. We offer all stock and custom parts for VWs, both air and water cooled. Service all Hondas. Have 50+ parts cars to sell used parts off of. 20+ preowned VWs and Hondas. Web site: vintageonline.com

Volkswagen Collectors c/o Jerry Jess 3121 E Yucca St Phoenix, AZ 85028-2616 PH/FAX: 602-867-7672 E-mail: vwstuff@qwest.net	literature memorabilia toys

Mail order only. Collectors of Volkswagen. Toys, literature, memorabilia, cars and accessories. Buy, sell and trade VWs and have been for 21+ years. Also locate or sell your VW for free. Send $1 for catalog. Wanted: 1966 and older VW buses, looking for Empi, Judson, Speedwell factory workshop manuals and Bentley. Web site: http://vwstuff.vwspeed.com

West Coast Metric Inc 24002 Frampton Ave Harbor City, CA 90710 310-325-0005; FAX: 310-325-9733 E-mail: wcm@westcoastmetric.com	carpet kits door panels emblems plastic parts rubber parts

Mail order and walk-ins welcome. Monday-Friday 7 am to 5 pm PST. Manufacturer and importer of quality rubber and plastic parts for 1946-2001 Volkswagens, including Bug, Bus, Ghia, Type 3, Thing, Vanagon and new Beetles. We have over 5,000 parts and accessories to properly restore your VW. Featuring: carpet kits, door and window rubber, emblems, lenses, mirrors, seat belts and more. Web site: www.westcoastmetric.com

VOLVO

A-1 Shock Absorber Co Shockfinders Division 365 Warren Ave, PO Box 2028 Silverthorne, CO 80498 800-344-1966, 970-389-3193 cell FAX: 970-513-8283	shocks-all types coil springs Koni shocks leaf springs steering gears

See our ad on the last page

Dan's Volvo Service 6615 S MacDill Ave Tampa, FL 33611 813-831-1616	restoration

Open Monday-Friday 9 am to 5 pm. Complete repair and restoration service on all vintage PV544, 122-S, 1800-S Volvos, parts.

Foreign Autotech 3235 C Sunset Ln Hatboro, PA 19040 215-441-4421; FAX: 215-441-4490 E-mail: fap1800@aol.com	parts

Specializing in new, reproduction and used parts for Volvo P1800, P, S, E and ES Models 1961-1973. As the world's largest supplier of P1800 parts we are continually developing reproduction parts that have long been out of production. Our engineering skills (proven by our domination of the 1997 and 1998 Volvo Historics Vintage Racing Championships) enable us to exceed the quality of OEM parts. In addition to vast stocks of new parts, we have used parts from over 150 donor cars. Web site: www.foreignautotech.com

David Hueppchen N 6808 Hwy OJ, PO Box 540 Plymouth, WI 53073 920-893-2531; FAX: 920-893-6800 E-mail: ojrallye@excel.net	parts service

Mail order and open shop. Monday-Friday 9 am to 12 pm, 2 pm to 6 pm. New and used parts, service by appointment for Volvo 122, 140, 1800, 240 and 262C Bertone coupe. Over 40 driver and parts cars on hand. Restoration, vintage race preparation also done. Importer of high tech Swedish headers, cams and much more for Volvo ohv and sohc motors. Web site: www.vclassics.com/ojrallye.htm

Italy's Famous Exhaust 2711 183rd St Redondo Beach, CA 90278 E-mail: johnt@famousexhaust.com	exhaust systems wheels

See full listing in **Section Two** under **exhaust systems**

Jaguar Car Keys
9957 Frederick Rd
Ellicott City, MD 21042-3647
410-750-2352
E-mail: petegroh@yahoo.com

original British
keys

See full listing in **Section One** under **Jaguar**

Shepard Kinsman
909 Eastridge
Miami, FL 33157
305-255-7067

sales literature

See full listing in **Section Two** under **literature dealers**

Lyle Pearson Company
351 Auto Dr
Boise, ID 83709
800-621-1775; FAX: 208-672-3494
E-mail: partspc@lylepearson.com

accessories
literature
parts

See full listing in **Section One** under **Mercedes-Benz**

R E Pierce
47 Stone Rd
Wendell Depot, MA 01380
978-544-7442; FAX: 978-544-2978
E-mail: robin@billsgate.com

parts
restoration

Tires to roof rack restorations on 122s, P-1800s and 140s. 18 years of collecting and restoring classic Volvos. 78 parts cars and stock piles of used parts. Free estimates, reasonable prices. Located in north central MA, near Orange/Athol. Call for an appointment.

Rayce Inc
3637 NE 2nd St
Gainesville, FL 32609
800-426-2221, 352-335-8900
FAX: 352-335-8930

parts

See full listing in **Section One** under **Alfa Romeo**

Revolvstore The Volvo Place
5275 E Drexel Rd
Tucson, AZ 85706
800-288-6586; FAX: 520-574-3629
E-mail: revolvstore@revolvstore.com

Volvo parts

See full listing in **Section Five** under **Arizona**

Rogers Motors
34 Codeyville Rd, PO Box 603
Shutesbury, MA 01072
413-259-1722
E-mail: jollyrogersmo@hotmail.com

used parts

See full listing in **Section One** under **Jaguar**

Michael A Stahl
PO Box 18036
Huntsville, AL 35804
205-882-6457
E-mail: stahlcon@aol.com

parts

See full listing in **Section One** under **Cadillac/LaSalle**

Swedish Classics Inc
PO Box 557
Oxford, MD 21654
800-258-4422; FAX: 410-226-5543
E-mail: sales@swedishclassics.com

parts

Restoration and repair parts for vintage Volvos, specializing in rubber, steel and mechanical restoration parts. New catalog available! Web site: www.swedishclassics.com

Vintage Sales
Paul Padget
7641 Reinhold Dr
Cincinnati, OH 45237
513-821-2143

sales

See full listing in **Section One** under **Mercedes-Benz**

Voluparts Inc
751 Trabert Ave NW
Atlanta, GA 30318
404-352-3402; FAX: 404-352-1077
E-mail: voluparts@mindspring.com

parts

Mail order and open shop. Monday-Friday 9 am to 6 pm. 18,000 square foot warehouse. New, used and rebuilt Volvo parts. Web site: www.voluparts.com

Volvo Shop Inc
5220 New Milford Rd
Ravenna, OH 44266
330-297-1297; FAX: 330-297-6206
E-mail: volvocarl@aol.com

parts
restoration

Volvos from mid 1950s-1990s. Have new and used parts for P1800, 544, 122, 140, 240, 700, 900 Series, also complete cars for parts or restoration. We also do mechanical repair on all above listed Volvos.

Tom's Cars
1400 Kingsdale Ave
Redondo Beach, CA 90278
310-370-5501; FAX: 310-371-3237

parts
restoration

Mail order and open shop. Monday-Saturday 8 am to 5 pm. Specializing in Wills Sainte Claire parts and restoration for all 1921-1926.

Brian's 4wd Parts LLC
428 N Harbor St
Branford, CT 06405
203-481-5873; FAX: 203-481-3995
E-mail: willysgp@aol.com

literature
parts

Mail order and open shop. Monday-Friday 9 am to 5 pm, weekends by chance or appointment. Parts and literature for Jeep vehicles produced by Willys, Kaiser and AMC. New, used, rebuilt and NOS parts available. Full or partial restoration services available for any year or make Jeep vehicle. Single component or full rebuild to your satisfaction. Active buyers of Jeep literature, vehicles and collectibles. New Jeep enthusiasts always welcome.

Classic Enterprises
Box 92
Barron, WI 54812
715-537-5422 office, 715-234-4677 products; FAX: 715-537-5770
E-mail: lamonte@classicent.com

sheetmetal

See full listing in **Section One** under **Studebaker**

| **Commonwealth Automotive Restorations** 1725 Hewins St Ashley Falls, MA 01222 413-229-3196 | **body rebuilding parts restoration** |

Mail order and open shop. Monday-Saturday 8 am to 8 pm, Sunday by appointment. Specializing in complete body, mechanical work, turnkey vehicles built to order, civilian, military, parts and supplies. Jeep body rebuilding service one of many specialties.

| **Firewall Insulators & Quiet Ride Solutions** 6465 Pacific Ave, Ste 249 Stockton, CA 95207 209-477-4840; FAX: 209-477-0918 E-mail: timcox@quietride.com | **air plenums auto insulation firewall insulators gloveboxes sound deadening** |

See full listing in **Section Two** under **upholstery**

| **The Jeepster Man** 238 Ramtown Greenville Rd Howell, NJ 07731 732-458-3966; FAX: 732-458-9289 | **literature parts** |

Mail order and open shop. Monday-Friday 9 am to 5 pm; Saturday 9 am to 12 noon. Large selection of Jeep and Jeepster parts. Send 75¢ SASE and model designation for free list. Shop manuals for all Willys vehicles. Contact The Jeepster Man for all hard to find parts. New items, horn rings, car covers, sunvisors, choke cables, o/s mirrors.

| **Obsolete Jeep® & Willys® Parts** Division of Florida 4 Wheel Drive & Truck Parts 6110 17th St E Bradenton, FL 34203 941-756-7844; PH/FAX: 941-756-7757 | **literature parts** |

Mail order and open shop. Monday-Friday 11 am to 6 pm. Jeep/Willys parts. New, used, rebuilt, NOS, hard-to-find, manuals.

Bought out many dealers, dismantled many vehicles. Shipping nationwide daily. Try us! Web site: www.florida4wheeldrive.com

| **Precision Coachworks** 19 Winsor Rd Billerica, MA 01821 978-663-7573 E-mail: precoach@mediaone.net | **parts pickup beds** |

See full listing in **Section One** under **Ford 1932-1953**

| **Whippet Resource Center** John Olson 1241 23000 Rd Parsons, KS 67357 620-421-0643 | **literature memorabilia** |

Specializing in literature, information, memorabilia for Whippet cars and trucks, all years, 1926-1931. Providing information about Whippets, buying literature and memorabilia about Whippets.

| **The Willys Man** Ron Ladley 1850 Valley Forge Rd Lansdale, PA 19446 610-584-1665; FAX: 610-584-8537 | **literature parts vehicles** |

Mail order and open shop. Weeknights and weekends. Supplier and adviser of 1933-1942 Willys cars, trucks, parts and literature for over 35 years (no post-war Willys Jeep parts or fwd parts).

| **Willys Wood** 35336 Chaucer Dr North Ridgeville, OH 44039 440-327-2916 | **wood parts** |

Mail order only. Replacement body wood for 1933/1936, 1940/1941 Willys coupes, steel or fiberglass, stock or chopped. Kits or individual pieces available.

| **Willys Works Inc** 1933 W Gardner Ln Tucson, AZ 85705 520-888-5082 | **car dealer parts restoration service** |

Mail order and open shop. Tuesday-Friday 10 am to 6 pm, Saturday 9 am to 4 pm. Primarily mechanical parts and Jeep universal, utility wagon and pickup, vintage and modern.

Zimmer

| **Zimmer Neo-Classic Motor Car Co** 1415 W Genesee St Syracuse, NY 13204 315-422-7011 ext 125 FAX: 315-422-1721 E-mail: azimmer@syracusenewtimes.com | **manufacturing** |

Mail order and open shop. Monday-Friday 9 am to 5 pm. Specializing in Zimmer Golden Spirit vintage autos for 1979-2001 Zimmers. Manufacturing 1997-2001 Zimmer Golden Spirit motor cars. Deals in Zimmer Golden Spirit and Zimmer Quicksilver. Web site: www.zimmermotorcars.com
See our ad on this page

Tourguide:
Marque Specialists

Planning a trip? Or perhaps you would just like to know what old-car resources are in your home territory. In either case, the tourguide to Section One will help.

This tourguide offers you an alphabetical listing of marque specialists with open shops by state and foreign country. Simply turn to the page number indicated for complete information on the object of your visit, including hours of operation, complete address, and phone number.

Alabama

77 Good Old Days Garage Inc, Birmingham
124 Mercedes-Benz Visitor Center, Tuscaloosa

Arizona

24 Art's Antique & Classic Auto Services, Tempe
149 Boneyard Stan's, Phoenix
51 Desert Muscle Cars, Tucson
105 Franklin Museum, Tucson
25 GM Obsolete, Phoenix
16 Heinze Enterprise, Scottsdale
42 Hidden Valley Auto Parts, Maricopa
44 Mecham Design, Performance, Glendale
59 Performance Chevy, Phoenix
94 Sanderson Ford, Glendale
21 Southwest Avanti Sales & Service, Phoenix
126 Star Classics Inc, Scottsdale
104 Thunderbird, Falcon, Fairlane & Comet Connections, Phoenix
95 Vintage Ford & Chevrolet Parts of Arizona Inc, Phoenix
168 Willys Works Inc, Tucson

Arkansas

42 Heavy Chevy Truck Parts, Siloam Springs
90 Jerry's Classic Cars & Parts Inc, Springdale
64 Don Rook, Mena

California

21 2002 AD, Sun Valley
15 All American Rambler, Fountain Valley
160 Arthur W Aseltine, Forbestown
87 Autowire Division, Rosemead
152 Best Deal, Stanton
158 British Pacific Ltd, Valencia
19 British Wire Wheel, Watsonville
25 Buick Bonery, Sacramento
35 Bumper Boyz LLC, Los Angeles
28 Cadillac King, Pacoima
28 California Collectors' Classics (CCC), San Bernardino
81 Car Controls Div, Rosemead
75 Caribou Imports Inc, Lake Forest
51 Chevyland Parts & Accessories, Rancho Cordova
29 Ed Cholakian Enterprises Inc, Sylmar
25 Classic Buicks Inc, Chino
29 Coopers Vintage Auto Parts, Burbank
57 Corvette Pacifica, Atascadero

57 Corvette Service, North Hollywood
22 CSi, Fullerton
40 Danchuk Mfg, Santa Ana
68 DeLorean One, Chatsworth
107 Distinctive Metal Polishing, Reseda
111 Doctor Jaguar Inc, Costa Mesa
70 Dodge City Vintage Dodge Vehicles & Parts, Jamestown
111 Doug's British Car Parts, Pasadena
153 Driven By Design, Carmel
58 EC Products Design Inc, Atascadero
52 The El Camino Store, Goleta
77 Ford Obsolete, Rosemead
16 Gordon Imports Inc, Santa Fe Springs
58 Guldstrand Engineering Inc, Burbank
69 Hall Pantera, Paramount
156 Tony Handler Inc, Los Angeles
13 Highway One Classic Automobiles and Highwayone.com, Burlingame
155 Jacques Rear Engine Renault Parts, El Cajon
120 JAE, Goleta
113 Jaguar Heaven, Stockton
90 John's F-Fun Hundreds, Anaheim
102 Larry's Thunderbird and Mustang Parts, Fullerton
119 Lincoln Parts International, Perris
130 Metropolitan Pit Stop, North Hollywood
45 Mike's Chevy Parts, Canoga Park
136 MikeCo Antique, Kustom & Obsolete Auto Parts, Camarillo
124 Millers Incorporated, Huntington Beach
132 Moss Motors Ltd, Goleta
107 Moto Italia, Petaluma
67 Motorsport Auto, Orange
98 Mustang Service Center, North Hollywood
99 Mustangs & More, Ventura
99 Mustangs Plus Inc, Stockton
18 Neuspeed, Camarillo
75 C Obert & Co, Santa Cruz
133 O'Connor Classic Autos, Santa Clara
46 Old Chevy Parts Store, San Marcos
150 Original Parts Group Inc, Huntington Beach
125 Palo Alto Speedometer Inc, Palo Alto
69 Pantera Parts Connection, Mountain View
31 Piru Cads, Piru
103 Prestige Thunderbird Inc, Santa Fe Springs
85 Red's Headers & Early Ford Speed Equipment, Fort Bragg
48 Restoration Specialties, Lompoc
148 Restorations By Julius, Chatsworth
158 Rolls-Royce of Beverly Hills, Los Angeles
125 Showroom Auto Sales, San Jose
162 Specter Off-Road Inc, Chatsworth
53 Steve's Camaros, San Bruno
161 Studebakers West, Redwood City
103 Norman Sudeck Restorations, Alhambra
161 Sunbeam Specialties, Los Gatos
103 T-Birds By Nick, Panorama City
158 Teddy's Garage, Northridge
104 Thunderbird Headquarters, Concord
167 Tom's Cars, Redondo Beach
53 True Connections, Riverside
126 Van Nuys M-B, Van Nuys
79 Vintage Speed Parts, Rosemead
166 West Coast Metric Inc, Harbor City
154 Willhoit Auto Restoration, Long Beach
116 XKs Unlimited, San Luis Obispo

Colorado

76 Antique Automotive Engineering Inc, Denver
123 House of Imports Inc, Lakewood
98 Mustang Classics, Denver
69 Pantera Performance Center, Castle Rock
94 Sam's Vintage Ford Parts, Denver
166 Stormin Norman's Bug Shop, Fort Collins
117 Walker's Auto Pride Inc, Peyton

Connecticut

- 14 Alfas Unlimited Inc, Norfolk
- 118 Baker's Auto, Putnam
- 167 Brian's 4wd Parts LLC, Branford
- 96 Classic Mustang Inc, Southington
- 142 Fusick Automotive Products, East Windsor
- 77 Joe Lagana, Canterbury
- 98 Mostly Mustangs Inc, Hamden
- 99 Mustangs Unlimited, Manchester
- 47 PRO Antique Auto Parts, Windsor Locks
- 78 R&L Model A, East Berlin

Delaware

- 112 East Coast Jaguar, Wilmington

Florida

- 15 American Performance Products, Cocoa
- 141 Anderson Automotive, Tampa
- 35 Bow Tie Chevy Association, Orlando
- 96 Classic Auto Air Mfg Co, Tampa
- 38 Classic Chevy International, Orlando
- 96 Classic Creations of Central Florida, Lakeland
- 166 Dan's Volvo Service, Tampa
- 102 Hollywood Classic Motorcars Inc, Hallandale
- 119 Lincoln Land Inc Showroom, Clearwater
- 75 Linearossa International Inc, Ft Lauderdale
- 124 Mercedes-Benz Service by Angela & George/ABS Exotic Repair Inc, Fort Lauderdale
- 99 National Parts Depot, Ocala
- 168 Obsolete Jeep® & Willys® Parts, Bradenton
- 157 Powers Parts Inc, Anna Maria
- 157 Proper Motor Cars Inc, St Petersburg
- 60 Rogers Corvette Center, Maitland
- 115 Thoroughbred Motors, Sarasota
- 158 Vantage Motorworks Inc, N Miami
- 115 Vicarage Jaguar, Miami Beach
- 54 Worldwide Camaro Association, Orlando

Georgia

- 123 Bud's Parts for Classic Mercedes-Benz, Douglasville
- 65 Cobra Restorers Ltd, Kennesaw
- 77 Hancock's Engine Rebuilders and Balancing Service, Athens
- 91 Melvin's Classic Ford Parts Inc, Conyers
- 93 Obsolete Ford Parts Co, Nashville
- 53 Rick's First Generation Camaro Parts & Accessories, Athens
- 85 Joe Smith Ford & Hot Rod Parts, Marietta
- 49 The Truck Shop, Nashville
- 167 Voluparts Inc, Atlanta

Idaho

- 125 Lyle Pearson Company, Boise
- 115 Vintage Jag Works, Blackfoot

Illinois

- 15 Blaser's Auto, Nash, Rambler, AMC, Moline
- 76 Bob's Antique Auto Parts Inc, Rockford
- 131 British Auto Shoppe, Moline
- 107 Charleston Custom Cycle, Charleston
- 56 Chicago Corvette Supply, Justice
- 57 D&M Corvette Specialists Ltd, Downers Grove
- 123 Horst's Car Care, Decatur
- 43 Kessler's Antique Cars & Body Shop, Olney
- 45 Midwest Restoration Parts, Des Plaines
- 98 Mustang of Chicago, Bensenville
- 138 Special T's Unlimited Inc, Prospect Heights
- 115 Terry's Jaguar Parts Inc, Benton

Indiana

- 130 Autosport Inc, Bloomington

- 87 Blint Equipment Inc, LaPorte
- 114 Muncie Imports & Classics, Muncie
- 46 The Paddock® Inc, Knightstown
- 60 Jack Podell Fuel Injection Spec, South Bend
- 49 Sound Move Inc, Elkhart
- 161 Studebaker International, Greenfield
- 108 TK Performance Inc, Evansville
- 16 Webb's Classic Auto Parts, Huntington

Iowa

- 150 Kurt Kelsey, Iowa Falls
- 44 Merv's Classic Chevy Parts, Iowa Falls
- 71 Vintage Power Wagons Inc, Fairfield

Kentucky

- 45 Nova Parts, Mount Washington

Louisiana

- 155 Bassett Classic Restoration, Kenner

Maine

- 76 Bryant's Antique Auto Parts, Hampden
- 125 SL-TECH 230SL-250SL-280SL, Arundel/Kennebunkport

Maryland

- 67 Banzai Motorworks, Upper Marlboro
- 57 Corvette Specialties of MD Inc, Eldersburg
- 29 Driving Passion Ltd USA, Clarksville
- 20 Healey Surgeons Inc, Takoma Park
- 78 Myers Model A Ford, Mustang & Corvette Parts & Car Trailers, Williamsport

Massachusetts

- 168 Commonwealth Automotive Restorations, Ashley Falls
- 111 Donovan Motorcar Service Inc, Lenox
- 156 Foreign Motors West, Natick
- 77 Freeman's Garage, Norton
- 123 Hatch & Sons Automotive Inc, Wayland
- 43 J & K Old Chevy Stuff, Plymouth
- 63 Jeepsamerica, Weymouth
- 128 Mercury & Ford Molded Rubber, Wilmington
- 106 Old GMC Trucks.Com, Franklin
- 84 Precision Coachworks, Billerica
- 78 PV Antique & Classic Ford, Tewksbury
- 61 Wild Bill's Corvette & Hi-Performance Center Inc, Wrentham

Michigan

- 152 356 Enterprises, Warren
- 22 The Auto Doctor Inc, Southfield
- 57 Corvette Rubber Company, Cadillac
- 82 Fairlane Automotive Specialties, St Johns
- 128 John's Classic Cougars, Holland
- 124 Lyco Engineering Inc, Plymouth
- 136 Mancini Racing Enterprises, Fraser
- 59 Michigan Corvette Recyclers, Riga
- 21 Nostalgic Motor Cars, Wixom
- 104 Thunderbird Center, Hazel Park
- 133 University Motors Ltd, Ada

Minnesota

- 76 Classtique Upholstery & Top Co, Isanti
- 119 Mike Gerner, The Lincoln Factory, Gemlake
- 90 Joe's Auto Sales, Hastings
- 91 Lares Manufacturing, Cambridge

Mississippi

- 80 American Stamping Corp, Olive Branch
- 70 Wayne Hood, Grenada
- 46 Oldenbetter Restorations Inc, Saucier

Missouri

- **76** Battlefield Antique, Battlefield
- **36** Chevy Duty Pickup Parts, Kansas City
- **90** L B Repair, Savannah
- **74** Motorcars International, Springfield

Nebraska

- **114** Mr Sport Car Inc, Papillion

New Hampshire

- **165** 4 ever 4, Marlow
- **130** Abingdon Spares, Walpole
- **22** Bavarian Autosport, Portsmouth
- **110** British Auto/USA, Manchester
- **82** Early Ford Engines, Claremont
- **162** Land Cruiser Solutions Inc, Newton
- **92** Northeast Ford, East Sullivan

New Jersey

- **55** Antique Cars, Parts & Trains, Millville
- **122** Basic Inc, Dover
- **155** Borla East, Middlesex
- **56** Conte's Corvettes & Classics, Vineland
- **57** Corvette Cosmetics, Shamong
- **112** Eddie's Restorations, Elwood
- **41** Fifties Forever, Garfield
- **82** Half Ton Fun, Jackson
- **168** The Jeepster Man, Howell
- **43** LES Auto Parts, Dayton
- **127** Mercer Automobile Company, Mercer
- **103** Sunyaks, Bound Brook
- **104** Pat Wilson's Thunderbird Parts, Fredon Township

New Mexico

- **94** Valley Motor Supply, Roswell

New York

- **35** Baldwin/Chevy, Baldwin
- **149** Bill's Birds, Dix Hills
- **101** Custom Autocraft Inc, St James
- **40** Dave's Auto Machine & Parts, Ischua
- **82** Early Ford V8 Sales Inc, Ballston Spa
- **58** Elmer's Auto Parts Inc, Webster
- **77** Ford Parts Specialists, Queens Village
- **83** Joblot Automotive Inc, Queens Village
- **98** Long Island Mustang Restoration Parts, Islandia
- **78** Mac's Antique Auto Parts, Lockport
- **59** Marcel's Corvette Shop Inc, Mechanicville
- **139** Morgan Spares Ltd, Ancram
- **153** PAR Porsche Specialists, New Rochelle
- **23** Peninsula Imports, Buffalo
- **158** Rajam Srinivasan, Queens
- **85** S & S Antique Auto, Deposit
- **85** Dick Spadaro, Altamont
- **164** Sports Car Haven, St James
- **126** Sweeney's Auto & Marine Upholstery Inc, Southampton
- **139** Wittenborn's Auto Service Inc, Briarcliff Manor
- **168** Zimmer Neo-Classic Motor Car Co, Syracuse

North Carolina

- **33** 60 Chev Sam, Hamptonville
- **87** Carolina Classics, Durham
- **67** Dennis Carpenter Cushman Reproductions, Charlotte
- **87** Dennis Carpenter Ford Reproductions, Charlotte
- **101** Classic Sheetmetal Inc, Charlotte
- **40** Dixie Truck Works, Mount Pleasant
- **89** Flashback F-100s, Reidsville
- **59** Morrison Motor Co Inc, Concord
- **49** Tri-Five Classics, Browns Summit

Ohio

- **155** A Bygone Era Motorcars, Cincinnati
- **162** Automotive Artistry, Hudson
- **24** Bicknell Engine Company, Enon
- **35** Bill's Speed Shop , Navarre
- **28** Cars II, Brookfield
- **101** Classic Auto Supply Company Inc, Coshocton
- **156** Coachbuilt Motors, Columbus
- **77** Gaslight Auto Parts Inc, Urbana
- **102** Hill's Classic Car Restoration, Racine
- **15** Kennedy American Inc, West Jefferson
- **107** Liberty Harley-Davidson, Akron
- **31** Mahoning Auto, North Jackson
- **133** Omni Specialties, Cleveland
- **154** Perfect Panels of America, Centerville
- **99** Pony Parts of America, Centerville
- **99** Rode's Restoration, Galion
- **79** Snyder's Antique Auto Parts Inc, New Springfield
- **154** Stuttgart Automotive Inc, Centerville
- **49** Trim Parts Inc, Milford
- **115** Welsh Enterprises Inc, Steubenville
- **16** Wymer Classic AMC, Fremont

Oklahoma

- **27** Aabar's Cadillac & Lincoln Salvage & Parts, Oklahoma City
- **128** Ken's Cougars, Edmond
- **93** Obsolete Ford Parts Inc, Oklahoma City
- **79** Varco Inc, Oklahoma City

Oregon

- **134** Accurate Ltd, Roseburg
- **101** Bird Nest, Portland
- **144** Brinton's Antique Auto Parts, Redmond
- **140** British Auto Parts Ltd, Marcola
- **110** British Motor Co, Eugene
- **81** Classic Cars, Rogue River
- **38** Cliff's Classic Chevrolet Parts Co, Portland
- **81** Bob Drake Reproductions Inc, Grants Pass
- **41** The Filling Station, Lebanon
- **15** For Ramblers Only, Portland
- **52** Gold Eagle Classics, Aloha
- **20** Mini Motors Classic Coachworks, Salem
- **133** Northwest Import Parts, Portland
- **46** Old Car Parts, Portland
- **157** Oregon Crewe Cutters Inc, Grants Pass
- **129** Rapido Group, Tygh Valley
- **85** Salem Speed Shop, Salem
- **103** T-Bird Sanctuary, Tualatin
- **86** Wescott's Auto Restyling, Boring

Pennsylvania

- **86** ABC Auto Upholstery & Top Company, Philadelphia
- **76** Bill's Model Acres Ford Farm, Watsontown
- **101** Bob's Bird House, Chadds Ford
- **95** Tony D Branda Performance, Altoona
- **131** British Miles, Morrisville
- **111** British Restorations, Philadelphia
- **35** C & P Chevy Parts, Kulpsville
- **135** Christian Motorsports Illustrated, Mansfield
- **96** CJ Pony Parts Inc, Harrisburg
- **54** Corvair Ranch Inc, Gettysburg
- **57** Corvette World, Greensburg
- **57** County Corvette, West Chester
- **135** Daniel N Dietrich, Kempton
- **58** Dobbins Restoration Publishing, Hatboro
- **40** Mike Drago Chevy Parts, Easton
- **40** East Coast Chevy Inc, Doylestown
- **97** Glazier's Mustang Barn Inc, Souderton
- **31** Holcombe Cadillac Parts, Bensalem
- **153** Klasse 356 Inc, Allentown

44 Lutty's Chevy Warehouse, Cheswick
64 Obsolete Chrysler NOS Parts, Murrysville
139 Olde World Restorations, Huntingdon Valley
13 Ragtops & Roadsters, Perkasie
103 William H Randel, Hatboro
164 The Roadster Factory, Armagh
60 Bob Sottile's Hobby Car Auto Sales Inc, Martinsburg
18 Steelwings, Ivyland
61 Stoudt Auto Sales, Reading
94 Tee-Bird Products Inc, Exton
104 Thunderbirds East, Chadds Ford
154 Translog Motorsports, York
133 Triple C Motor Accessories, York
168 The Willys Man, Lansdale

Puerto Rico

113 Jaguar of Puerto Rico Inc, San Juan

Rhode Island

110 Bassett's Jaguar, Wyoming
51 Competitive Automotive Inc, Warwick

South Carolina

79 Smith & Jones Distributing Co Inc, West Columbia
166 Vintage Auto LLC, Greenville
21 Von's Austin-Healey Restorations, Fort Mill

Tennessee

95 A&A Mustang Parts & Mfg Co, Oak Ridge
82 Early Ford Parts, Memphis
160 Kelley's Korner, Bristol
50 Volunteer State Chevy Parts LLC, Greenbrier

Texas

34 American Classic Truck Parts, Aubrey
130 BCP Sport & Classic Co, Houston
120 Birkin America, Arlington
38 Classic Auto Restoration Service Inc, Rockwall
111 Classic Jaguar, Austin
72 Edsel Associates, Fort Worth
123 Germany Direct, San Antonio
58 Gulf Coast Corvette, Humble
31 Honest John's Caddy Corner, Justin
77 Howell's Sheetmetal Co, Nederland
113 John's Cars Inc, Dallas
18 Kip Motor Company Inc, Dallas
137 Mr G's Enterprises, Fort Worth
59 Old Air Products, Ft Worth
14 Orion Motors European Parts Inc, Houston
16 South Texas AMC, Bulverde
100 Texas Mustang Parts, Waco
154 Zim's Autotechnik, Bedford

Utah

116 K-F-D Services Inc, Altonah

Vermont

110 Best of Britain, South Ryegate
165 John's Car Corner, Westminster
133 Sports Car Services, Westminster

Virginia

87 Auto Krafters Inc, Broadway
139 Cantab Motors Ltd, Purcellville
99 Old Dominion Mustang/Camaro, Ashland
71 S&P Creations, Newport News
19 Seven Enterprises Ltd, Newport News
61 Still Cruisin' Corvettes, Haymarket
79 Vintage Ford Center Inc, Berryville
100 Virginia Classic Mustang Inc, Broadway

61 Virginia Vettes Parts & Sales, Williamsburg

Washington

80 Alloy-Fab, Vancouver
95 Andy's Classic Mustangs, Greenacres
95 Bel-Kirk Mustang, Bellevue
111 British Sportscars & Classics, Seattle
25 Buick Specialists, Kent
56 Corvette & High-Performance, Olympia
136 Jim Harris, Seattle
136 Layson's Restorations Inc, Kent
139 Morgan Oasis Garage, Hoodsport
141 NSU/USA Jim Sykes, Seattle
84 Old Ford Parts, Algona
93 Original Falcon, Comet, Ranchero, Fairlane Interiors, Seattle
47 Pick-ups Northwest, Snohomish

West Virginia

98 Mean Mustang Supply Inc, South Charleston

Wisconsin

123 Brooklyn Motoren Werke Inc, Brooklyn
35 Butch's Trim, Big Bend
68 Collectors Choice LTD, Dane
40 CPX-RTS Auto Parts, Milwaukee
20 Fourintune Garage Inc, Cedarburg
166 David Hueppchen, Plymouth
43 Lee's Classic Chevy Sales, Glenbeulah
98 Loyal Ford Mercury Inc, New Holstein
103 Regal Roadsters Ltd, Madison

Canada

34 All Chevy/Canadian Impala, Parksville, BC
78 The Old Car Centre, Langley, BC
47 Peninsula Restoration Parts, Victoria, BC
48 Reproduction Parts Marketing, Saskatoon, SK
48 Scotts Super Trucks, Penhold, AB

England

139 Gideon Booth, Cumbria
139 Morgan Motor Company Ltd, Worcester
67 Barry Thorne, Surrey

Sweden

32 TA Motor AB, Lulea
61 Lars Tidblom Automobil, Sundbyberg

Section Two
Generalists

3,792 listings

In this section, vendors who offer parts, literature, services or other items for a variety of makes and models are listed under general categories. As in Section One, if a vendor provides several services or products, an abbreviated subsidiary listing will appear in all of the appropriate sections with a cross reference to the main listing located in the category with the greatest concentration of the vendor's business.

The taglines located in the right-hand box of each listing provide a quick guide to what the vendor primarily offers.

This section of the Almanac is intended to serve owners of virtually every car make being collected. Restorers or collectors interested in parts or services for specific car marques should check Section One also, which presents vendor listings by marque specialty.

accessories

Aardvark International
PO Box 509
Whittier, CA 90608
562-699-8887; FAX: 562-699-2288
E-mail: usa@talbotco.com

CIBIE lighting
Fiamm horns
Talbot mirrors

Specializing in Talbot™ sport mirrors for Alfa Romeo, Aston Martin, Austin-Healey, BMW, Cobra, Cooper, DeTomaso, Facel Vega, Ferrari, Fiat, Jaguar, Lamborghini, Lancia, Lotus, Maserati, Mercedes-Benz, MG, NSU, Opel, Porsche, Sunbeam, Triumph, TVR, Volkswagen, Iso, McLaren, Brabham and various race cars. Many models in chrome finish or aluminum. Housings are hand-spun to perfection. Three different mounting systems are available. Mirror elements are flat or convex "first surface" glass. Talbot™ mirrors are the finest money can buy and are stamped with the correct Talbot™ markings. CIBIE headlights and auxiliary lights, USA distributor. Fiamm air horns distributor.

AC Enterprises
13387 Gladstone Ave
Sylmar, CA 91342
818-367-8337

gloveboxes

Gloveboxes for most cars and trucks. Will work to sketch for custom application. SASE please.

Accessoryland Truckin' Supplies
10723 Rt 61 S
Dubuque, IA 52003
319-556-5482; FAX: 319-556-9087
E-mail: unityspotlights@aol.com or
chevygmcparts@aol.com

accessories
foglights/spotlights
mounting brackets
parts

See full listing in **Section One** under **Chevrolet**

Addison Generator Inc
21 W Main St Rear
Freehold, NJ 07728
732-431-2438; FAX: 732-431-4503

auto parts
repairs
supplies

See full listing in **Section Two** under **electrical systems**

American Performance Products
675 S Industry Rd
Cocoa, FL 32926
321-632-8299; FAX: 321-632-5119
E-mail: amc@oldcarparts.com

parts

See full listing in **Section One** under **AMC**

Anderson's Car Door Monograms
32700 Coastsite #102
Rancho Palos Verdes, CA 90275
800-881-9049, 310-377-1007

car door monograms

Mail order only. Car door monograms, three initials pre-spaced for foolproof installation. Die cut from 3-M cast vinyl. Looks just like hand lettered enamel. Available in script, block, old English or in a circle. Colors: gold, silver, black, white, blue, red. Set of two three-letter monograms, $27.50 prepaid. To order, put three initials on a piece of paper, underline initial of last name which will appear in the center. Free literature. Unconditional money back guarantee.

Andover Restraints Inc
PO Box 2651
Columbia, MD 21045
410-381-6700; FAX: 410-381-6703
E-mail: andoauto@clark.net

seat belts

See full listing in **Section Two** under **interiors & interior parts**

Aremco Products Inc
707-B Executive Blvd
Valley Cottage, NY 10989
845-268-0039; FAX: 845-268-0041
E-mail: aremco@aremco.com

compounds

Mail order only. Aremco's new Pyromax line features high temperature sealers, adhesives and paints for repairing and coating pits, holes and cracks in engine blocks, cylinder heads, manifolds, headers and other exhaust components. Product trade names include Pyro-Putty, Pyro-Paint, Pyro-Weld and Pyro-Seal. Web site: www.aremco.com

Atlantic British Ltd
Halfmoon Light Industrial Park
6 Enterprise Ave
Clifton Park, NY 12065
800-533-2210; FAX: 518-664-6641
E-mail: ab@roverparts.com

accessories
parts

See full listing in **Section One** under **Rover/Land Rover**

Auto Etc Neon
PO Box 531992
Harlingen, TX 78553
PH/FAX: 956-425-7487

signs
time pieces

See full listing in **Section One** under **Corvette**

AutoGuide.net
150 Consumers Rd, Ste 403
Toronto, ON Canada M2J 1P9
416-499-8351
E-mail: info@autoguide.net

automotive
directory

See full listing in **Section Four** under **information sources**

AutoLifters
3450 N Rock Rd, Bldg 500, Ste 507
Wichita, KS 67226
800-759-0703; FAX: 316-630-0015

lifts

See full listing in **Section Two** under **tools**

C E Babcock
619 Waterside Way
Sarasota, FL 34242
941-349-4990; FAX: 941-349-5751

1941, 1942, 1946, 1947 Cadillac parts

See full listing in **Section One** under **Cadillac/LaSalle**

Backyard Buddy Corp
140 Dana St
Warren, OH 44483
800-837-9353, 330-395-9372
FAX: 330-392-9311

automotive lift

Mail order and display area. Manufacture a complete line of automotive lifts, 4-post and 2-post. The 4-post, 7,000 lb is ideal for the home hobbist, used for storage and service. Convenience options including drip pans, casters and jack platforms, all American made in our own plants. Worldwide shipping. Check our web site or calling our 800 number puts you in direct contact with our manufacturing facility. Web site: www.backyardbuddy.com

Barnett & Small Inc
151E Industry Ct
Deer Park, NY 11729
631-242-2100; FAX: 631-242-2101

electrical parts

See full listing in **Section Two** under **electrical systems**

Battlefield Antique
5054 S Broadview
Battlefield, MO 65619
417-882-7923
E-mail: battlefielda@aol.com

parts

See full listing in **Section One** under **Ford 1903-1931**

Bavarian Autosport
275 Constitution Ave
Portsmouth, NH 03801
800-535-2002; FAX: 800-507-2002

accessories
parts

See full listing in **Section One** under **BMW**

Baxter Auto Parts
9444 N Whitaker Rd (corporate office)
Portland, OR 97217
800-765-3785; FAX: 503-246-4590

accessories
parts

See full listing in **Section Two** under **comprehensive parts**

Big Boys Toys
Richard Boutin
Rt 67A, Box 174A
North Bennington, VT 05257
800-286-1721; FAX: 802-447-0962

accessories
bodywork
tires
wheels

Automotive specialty store, customizing trucks and cars. Specialty wheels, bodywork. Lund, Dee Zee, Deflecta, American Racing, Rancho, Western, Smitty built, Holley, Cooper tires and specialty tires.

Billie Inc
PO Box 1161
Ashburn, VA 20146-1161
800-878-6328; FAX: 703-858-0102

garage diaper
mats

See full listing in **Section Two** under **car care products**

Blast From the Past
21006 Cornhusker Rd
Gretna, NE 68028
402-332-5050; FAX: 402-332-5029
E-mail: blast2past@aol.com

neon clocks
neon signs

See full listing in **Section Two** under **automobilia**

Blue Ribbon Motoring
8055 Clairemont Mesa Blvd
San Diego, CA 92111
858-569-8111

car covers
floor mats
seat covers

Specializing in automotive accessories (car covers, floor mats, seat covers, etc) for all vehicles. Web site: www.autoanything.com

Blue Ridge Mountain Cookery Inc
130 Green St, PO Box 70
Waynesboro, PA 17268
800-266-5377, 717-762-1211
FAX: 717-762-1966
E-mail: cookers@classiccookers.com

barbeque grills

Mail order and open shop. Monday-Friday 8 am to 5 pm. Stainless steel BBQ grills for the trailer hitches of vehicles for SUVs or any vehicle with a hitch. We also manufacture commercial barbeque grills and custom built residential. Web site: www.classiccookers.com

Bonneville Sports Inc
3544 Enterprise Dr
Anaheim, CA 92807
888-999-7258, 714-666-1966
FAX: 714-666-1955
E-mail: bonspeed@aol.com

accessories
clothing

See full listing in **Section Two** under **apparel**

Buick Bonery
6970 Stamper Way
Sacramento, CA 95828
916-381-5271; FAX: 916-381-0702
E-mail: buickbonery@webtv.net

parts

See full listing in **Section One** under **Buick/McLaughlin**

C & G Early Ford Parts
1941 Commercial St, Dept AH
Escondido, CA 92029-1233
760-740-2400; FAX: 760-740-8700
E-mail: cgford@cgfordparts.com

accessories/chrome
emblems
literature
mechanical
weatherstripping

See full listing in **Section One** under **Ford 1932-1953**

CBS Performance Automotive
2605-A W Colorado Ave
Colorado Springs, CO 80904
800-685-1492; FAX: 719-578-9485

ignition systems
performance products

See full listing in **Section Two** under **ignition parts**

Michael Chapman
Priorsleigh, Mill Ln
Cleeve Prior
Worcestershire, WR11 5JZ England
0044-1789-773897
FAX: 0044-1789-773588

automobilia

See full listing in **Section Two** under **automobilia**

Classic Autopart Repro Service
789 Furlong Rd
Sebastopol, CA 95472
PH/FAX: 707-824-0657
E-mail: quotes@brassauto.com

parts

See full listing in **Section Two** under **brass cars/parts**

Classic Chevrolet Parts Inc | parts
8723 S I-35
Oklahoma City, OK 73149
405-631-4400; FAX: 405-631-5999
E-mail: info@classicchevroletparts.com

See full listing in **Section One** under **Chevrolet**

Classic Impressions Inc | accessories
PO Box 691167
Houston, TX 77379
800-252-3435; FAX: 281-251-2020
E-mail: sales@classicimpressions.com

Mail order only. Deals in automotive bank checks, leather checkbook covers and wallets, automotive logo etched glass, automotive mouse pads. Web site: www.classicimpressions.com

C'NC Sheetmetal | car casters / patterns
11790 FM 3270
Tyler, TX 75708
800-668-1691; FAX: 903-877-2060
E-mail: cncsmetal@aol.com

See full listing in **Section Two** under **restoration aids**

Collectibles For You | memorabilia
6001 Canyon Rd
Harrisburg, PA 17111
717-558-2653; FAX: 717-558-7325
E-mail: cllect4you@aol.com

See full listing in **Section Two** under **automobilia**

Comfy/Inter-American Sheepskins Inc | floor mats / seat covers
1346 Centinela Ave
West Los Angeles, CA 90025-1901
800-521-4014; FAX: 310-442-6080
E-mail: sales@comfysheep.com

See full listing in **Section Two** under **interiors & interior parts**

Corvette & High-Performance | accessories / parts
Division of Classic &
High-Performance Inc
2840 Black Lake Blvd SW #D
Olympia, WA 98512
360-754-7890

See full listing in **Section One** under **Corvette**

Corvette America | accessories / interiors / parts
Rt 322, PO Box 324
Boalsburg, PA 16827
800-458-3475
814-364-2141 foreign
FAX: 814-364-9615, 24 hours
E-mail: vettebox@corvetteamerica.com

See full listing in **Section One** under **Corvette**

Corvette Central | accessories / parts
13550 Three Oaks Rd, Dept HM
Sawyer, MI 49125
616-426-3342; FAX: 616-426-4108
E-mail: mail@corvettecentral.com

See full listing in **Section One** under **Corvette**

Corvette Specialties of MD Inc | parts / restoration / service
1912 Liberty Rd
Eldersburg, MD 21784
410-795-3180; FAX: 410-795-3247

See full listing in **Section One** under **Corvette**

Cruising International Inc | automobilia / belt buckles / decals/lapel pins / license plates / novelties
1000 N Beach St
Daytona Beach, FL 32117
386-254-8753; FAX: 386-255-2460
E-mail: sales@cruising-intl.com

See full listing in **Section Two** under **license plates**

Crutchfield Corp | car stereos
1 Crutchfield Park
Charlottesville, VA 22911
800-955-9009; FAX: 804-817-1010
E-mail: sales@crutchfield.com

See full listing in **Section Two** under **radios**

Custom Autosound Mfg | accessories / CD players / custom radios / speaker upgrades
808 W Vermont Ave
Anaheim, CA 92805
800-888-8637; FAX: 714-533-0361
E-mail: info@customautosound.com

Monday-Friday 8 am to 5 pm. Manufacturer and distributor. Custom radios, AM-FM cassettes, CDs, speakers and accys. "No modification fit" for all classic Chevys, Fords, Mopar, GM, AMC, imports and more. New hideaway AM-FM CD controller audio system, RF controlled 50' range, perfect for street rods, classics, secret audio. Web site: www.customautosound.com

See our ad on page 335

Custom Solutions & Services | badges / keychains / software
2218 Pleasant View Ct
Deer Creek, IL 61733-9672
309-447-6320
E-mail: jscharfcss@juno.com

See full listing in **Section Four** under **information sources**

Dare Classics | leather handles / leather straps / luggage / trunks
8984 Sierra St
Elk Grove, CA 95624
916-212-6018; FAX: 916-686-5434
E-mail: olliedare@hotmail.com

Mail order only. Reproduce or design custom luggage and trunks for antique and classic automobiles. Repair and restore original luggage and trunks. Manufacture custom leather handles and straps per customer specifications.

DashCovers of Florida | accessories / car covers / carpets
1301 W Copans Rd, Ste F-8-9
Pompano Beach, FL 33064
800-441-3274; FAX: 954-970-9119
E-mail: danny@dashcover.com

Custom floor mats, molded carpets, dash covers, wood kits, automatic universal rear sunshade, custom sunshades and seat covers. Web site: www.dashcover.com

Dashhugger | dashboard covers
PO Box 933
Clovis, CA 93613
559-298-4529; FAX: 559-298-3428
E-mail: info@dashhugger.com

See full listing in **Section Two** under **interiors & interior parts**

Davies Corvette | accessories / parts
7141 US Hwy 19
New Port Richey, FL 34653
800-236-2383, 727-842-8000
FAX: 727-846-8216
E-mail: davies@corvetteparts.com

See full listing in **Section One** under **Corvette**

Don's Hot Rod Shop Inc
2811 N Stone Ave
Tucson, AZ 85705
520-884-8892; FAX: 520-628-1682

accessories
parts

See full listing in **Section Two** under **street rods**

Double Park Lifts
6352 N Hillside
Wichita, KS 67219
800-754-8786; FAX: 316-744-9221
E-mail: lewis216@southwind.net

service lifts

See full listing in **Section Two** under **storage**

Eckler's Quality Parts & Accessories for Corvettes
5140 S Washington Ave
Titusville, FL 32780
800-327-4868; FAX: 407-383-2059
E-mail: ecklers@ecklers.net

accessories
parts

See full listing in **Section One** under **Corvette**

Enthusiast's Specialties
350 Old Connecticut Path
Framingham, MA 01701
800-718-3999; FAX: 508-872-4914
E-mail: alvis1934@aol.com

automobilia

See full listing in **Section Two** under **automobilia**

Explicit Concepts Customs & Minis
Livonia, MI 48150
313-617-5433
E-mail: vabruno@explicitconcepts.net

aftermarket
restyling

See full listing in **Section Two** under **custom cars**

Jay M Fisher
Acken Dr 4-B
Clark, NJ 07066
732-388-6442

mascots
sidemount mirrors
windwing brackets

Mail order only. Manufacturer of sidemount mirrors, 1900-1970, inside mirror restoration, windwing brackets, radiator caps, mascots, small parts fabrication, leather straps, restoration of any mirrors. Catalog, $2 cash plus 55¢ SASE.

For Ramblers Only
2324 SE 34th Ave
Portland, OR 97214
503-232-0497
E-mail: ramblers@teleport.com

accessories
parts

See full listing in **Section One** under **AMC**

Fred's Classic Auto Radio & Clocks
7908 Gilette
Lenexa, KS 66215
913-599-2303

clock repair
radio repair

See full listing in **Section Two** under **radios**

Gano Filter
1205 Sandalwood Ln
Los Altos, CA 94024
650-968-7017

coolant filters

See full listing in **Section Two** under **radiators**

Gaslight Auto Parts Inc
PO Box 291
Urbana, OH 43078
937-652-2145; FAX: 937-652-2147

accessories
parts

See full listing in **Section One** under **Ford 1903-1931**

Gasoline Alley LLC
1700E Iron Ave, PO Box 737
Salina, KS 67402
800-326-8372, 785-822-1003
FAX: 785-827-9337
E-mail: morrison@midusa.net

drip pans

Mail order only. Manufacture Perma-Pan drip pans which feature a DuPont Tedlar® top surface making the easiest cleaning pan on the market. Also sell Coustasheet, a vibration damping and sound barrier material that can make cars 10-15 dB quieter. Web site: www.gasolinealleyllc.com

Griot's Garage
3500-A 20th St E
Tacoma, WA 98424
800-345-5789; FAX: 888-252-2252
E-mail: info@griotsgarage.com

car care products
paint
tools

See full listing in **Section Two** under **tools**

Hale's Products
906 19th St
Wheatland, WY 82201
800-333-0989

license plates

See full listing in **Section Two** under **license plates**

Hampton Coach
6 Chestnut St, PO Box 6
Amesbury, MA 01913
888-388-8726, 978-388-8047
FAX: 978-388-1113
E-mail: lbb-hc@greenet.net

fabrics
interior kits
top kits

See full listing in **Section One** under **Chevrolet**

Haneline Products Co
PO Box 430
Morongo Valley, CA 92256
760-363-6597; FAX: 760-363-7321

electrical/gauges
instrument panels
power windows
stainless parts

Mail order only. Manufacture bolt-in retro instrument panels. Engine turned stainless steel accessories. Cars and trucks 1920s-1980s. Trim parts, door sills, firewalls, distributor-Teleflex, Westach, Classic, S-W, VDO, Auto Meter, Dakota Digital gauges, electric life power windows, door locks, keyless entry. Painless Wiring, Ididit, Le Carra, Vintage Air, Hot Rod Air and others.

Ned R Healy & Company Inc
17602 Griffin Ln, PO Box 2120
Huntington Beach, CA 92647
714-848-2251
E-mail: sales@nedrhealy.com

accessories
parts

Wholesale distributor of accessories, parts, shop supplies and die cast cars to new car dealerships. Web site: www.nedrhealy.com

Hi-Tech Aluminum & Automotive Products Inc
100 Industrial Ave, PO Box 1609
Cedartown, GA 30125
800-541-4946
E-mail: htechaluminum@aol.com

accessories
windshield wipers

See full listing in **Section Two** under **windshield wipers**

Hot Rod Coffee
1314 Rollins Rd
Burlingame, CA 94010
650-348-8269; FAX: 650-340-9473
E-mail: hotrodcoffee@pacbell.net

gourmet coffee

Mail order only. Hot rod coffee for car guys, gourmet roasted, specially blended, coffee for hot rodders. Try some, you'll love it. Makes a great car guy gift.

William Hulbert Jr — radios
13683 Rt 11, PO Box 151
Adams Center, NY 13606
315-583-5765
E-mail: radio_29chevy@yahoo.com

See full listing in **Section Two** under **radios**

Hunters Custom Automotive — accessories engine parts fiberglass products
975 Main St
Nashville, TN 37206
615-227-6584; FAX: 615-227-4897

Mail order and open shop. Monday-Saturday 8 am to 5 pm. Dealing in street rod accessories, sport truck accessories, four wheel drive and off-road, hi-performance engine parts, fiberglass products, wheel and tire specialty store. All types speed/custom accessories for SUV's and Jeeps.

Melissa & Jerry Jess — accessories literature models
3121 E Yucca St
Phoenix, AZ 85028
602-867-7672
E-mail: vwstuff@qwest.net

See full listing in **Section One** under **Volkswagen**

JLM — power window lifts
Maud Rd, PO Box 1348
Palmer, AK 99645
907-745-4670; FAX: 907-745-5510
E-mail: jlmob@alaska.net

See full listing in **Section Two** under **glass**

K&S Industries — display cases
1801 Union Center Hwy
Endicott, NY 13760
PH/FAX: 888-PICK-KNS
E-mail: pleximan@888pickkns.com

See full listing in **Section Two** under **models & toys**

Karl's Collectibles — banks collectibles logo design
41 Chestnut St
Lewiston, ME 04240
800-636-0457, 207-784-0098
FAX: 207-795-0295
E-mail: karl@designsbyskip.com

See full listing in **Section Two** under **models & toys**

Klasse 356 Inc — cars parts restoration
311 Liberty St
Allentown, PA 18102
800-634-7862; FAX: 610-432-8027
E-mail: parts@klasse356.com

See full listing in **Section One** under **Porsche**

LeBaron Bonney Co — fabrics interior kits top kits
6 Chestnut St, PO Box 6
Amesbury, MA 01913
800-221-5408, 978-388-3811
FAX: 978-388-1113
E-mail: lbb-hc@greennet.net

See full listing in **Section One** under **Ford 1903-1931**

LHI Inc — rechargeable flashlight
1280 B Huff Ln, PO Box 9280
Jackson Hole, WY 83002-9280
800-328-9069, FAX: 307-733-1495
E-mail: sales@dashlite.com

Rechargeable flashlights for the car. Our flashlight fits in the cigarette lighter or accessory outlet and recharges as you drive.

"Dashlight Flashlight" fits all cigarette outlets in all makes and models. Web site: www.dashlite.com

Lord Byron Inc — fender covers
420 Sackett Point Rd
North Haven, CT 06473
203-287-9881; FAX: 203-288-9456

See full listing in **Section Two** under **car covers**

M & R Products — hardware tie-downs
1940 SW Blvd
Vineland, NJ 08360
800-524-2560, 609-696-9450
FAX: 609-696-4999
E-mail: mrproducts@mrproducts.com

Tie-downs: automotive, motorcycle and utility. Related hardware (D-rings, track systems) and racing safety equipment (harnesses, window net and collars). Web site: www.mrproducts.com

Marcel's Corvette Shop Inc — sales service parts
1000 Waterford Rd
Mechanicville, NY 12118
518-664-7344; FAX: 518-664-2908
E-mail: marcel@marcelscorvette.com

See full listing in **Section One** under **Corvette**

Mark II Enterprises — car covers parts
5225 Canyon Crest Dr, Ste 71-217H
Riverside, CA 92507
909-686-2752; FAX: 909-686-7245
E-mail: markiient@earthlink.net

1956-1957 Continental Mark II parts. Large inventory of NOS, NORS, used and rebuilt parts for Mark II and Lincolns of the 50s. Covers: car cover closeout, 100s below cost, $50-$125, 8 fabrics, special orders, guaranteed lowest price, custom tailored by world's largest manufacturer, 45,000 patterns. Located in Riverside, at same address since 1956. 45+ cars for parts. Major credit cards accepted. Web site: www.markii.com

McLean's Brit Bits — accessories parts sales service
14 Sagamore Rd
Rye, NH 03870
800-995-2487; FAX: 603-433-0009
E-mail: sam@britbits.com

See full listing in **Section Two** under **car dealers**

Mid America Direct — accessories parts
PO Box 1368
Effingham, IL 62401
217-347-5591; FAX: 217-347-2952

See full listing in **Section One** under **Corvette**

Midwest Hot Rods Inc — street rods service shops upholstery
10 E Main St (Rt 126)
Plainfield, IL 60544
815-254-7637; FAX: 815-254-7640
E-mail: mwhr@aol.com

See full listing in **Section Two** under **street rods**

Mild to Wild Classics — parts repairs restoration
1300 3rd St NW
Albuquerque, NM 87102
505-244-1139; FAX: 505-244-1164

See full listing in **Section Two** under **street rods**

Millers Incorporated
7412 Count Cir
Huntington Beach, CA 92647
714-375-6565; FAX: 714-847-6606
E-mail: sales@millermbz.com

accessories
parts

See full listing in **Section One** under **Mercedes-Benz**

Moss Motors Ltd
440 Rutherford St
Goleta, CA 93117
800-235-6954; FAX: 805-692-2525

accessories
parts

See full listing in **Section One** under **MG**

Motorsport Auto
1139 W Collins Ave
Orange, CA 92667
800-633-6331, 714-639-2620
FAX: 714-639-7460
E-mail: motorsport@worldnet.att.net

parts

See full listing in **Section One** under **Datsun**

MotorWeek
11767 Owings Mills Blvd
Owings Mills, MD 21117
410-356-5600; FAX: 410-581-4113
E-mail: motorweek@mpt.org

TV program

See full listing in **Section Four** under **information sources**

Neumaclassic
Ayacucho 1292
Rosario Sta Fe 2000 Argentina
+54 341 425-0040
FAX: +54 341 421-9629
E-mail: bcdcs@bcd.com.ar

tires

See full listing in **Section Two** under **tires**

NMW Products
35 Orlando Dr
Raritan, NJ 08869
908-256-3800

dollies

Mail order and open shop. Monday-Friday 8 am to 4:30 pm.
Manufacturer of car dollies/engine shop dollies.

O'Brien Truckers
29 A Young Rd
Charlton, MA 01507-1599
508-248-1555; FAX: 508-248-6179
E-mail: obt@ziplink.net

accessories
belt buckles
plaques
valve covers

See full listing in **Section Two** under **plaques**

Obsolete Ford Parts Inc
8701 S I-35
Oklahoma City, OK 73149
405-631-3933; FAX: 405-634-6815
E-mail: info@obsoletefordparts.com

parts

See full listing in **Section One** under **Ford 1954-up**

OJ Rallye Automotive
N 6808 Hwy OJ, PO Box 540
Plymouth, WI 53073
920-893-2531; FAX: 920-893-6800
E-mail: ojrallye@excel.net

accessories
car care products
lighting parts

See full listing in **Section Two** under **lighting equipment**

P&J Products
988 Gordon Ln
Birmingham, MI 48009
888-647-1879

car skates
trailer dollies

Dealing in car skates for moving cars, boats, trailers easily in
any direction. Great for storage. 6,000 lbs capacity for 4 skates.

$145/set of 4, $135/set of 4 when 2 or more sets are ordered.
Satisfaction or your money back. Web site: www.carskates.com

PE/Snappin Turtle Tie-Down Straps
641 Bethlehem Pike
Colmar, PA 18951
800-TIE-DOWN; FAX: 215-822-0161

locks
tie-down straps
winches

See full listing in **Section Two** under **trailers**

Performance Automotive Inc
1696 New London Tpke, PO Box 10
Glastonbury, CT 06033
860-633-7868; FAX: 860-657-9110
E-mail: pai@pcnet.com

accessories
car care

See full listing in **Section Two** under **car care products**

Performance Automotive Warehouse
21001 Nordhoff St
Chatsworth, CA 91311
818-678-3000; FAX: 818-678-3001

accessories
engine parts

See full listing in **Section Two** under **engine parts**

Premier Designs Historic Costume
15512 St Rt 613
Van Buren, OH 45889
800-427-0907; FAX: 419-299-3919
E-mail: premier@bright.net

clothing

See full listing in **Section Two** under **apparel**

Pro's Pick Rod & Custom
4210 Dixie Hwy
Erlanger, KY 41018
PH/FAX: 859-727-9600
E-mail: gary@prospick.com

parts

See full listing in **Section Two** under **street rods**

Pulfer & Williams
213 Forest Rd, PO Box 67
Hancock, NH 03449-0067
603-525-3532; FAX: 603-525-4293
E-mail: dorwill@webtv.net

mascots
nameplates
radiator emblems

See full listing in **Section Two** under **radiator emblems & mascots**

Quik-Shelter
PO Box 1123
Orange, CT 06477
800-211-3730; FAX: 203-937-8897
E-mail: info@quikshelter.com

temporary garages

See full listing in **Section Two** under **car covers**

RB's Obsolete Automotive
7711 Lake Ballinger Way
Edmonds, WA 98026-9163
425-670-6739; FAX: 425-670-9151
E-mail: rbobsole@gte.net

parts

See full listing in **Section Two** under **comprehensive parts**

The Real Source
PO Box 1248
Effingham, IL 62401
800-LUV-BUGG (588-2844), Dept VS1
FAX: 217-347-2952
E-mail: mail@800luvbugg.com

accessories
parts

See full listing in **Section One** under **Volkswagen**

Re-Flex Border Marker 138 Grant St Lexington, MA 02173 781-862-1343	border markers **posts**

See full listing in **Section Two** under **hardware**

Rick's First Generation Camaro **Parts & Accessories** 420 Athena Dr Athens, GA 30601 800-359-7717; FAX: 877-548-8581 E-mail: firstgen@negia.net	accessories **parts**

See full listing in **Section One** under **Chevelle/Camaro**

Rocky Mountain Motorworks Inc 1003 Tamarac Pkwy Woodland Park, CO 80863 800-258-1996; FAX: 800-544-1084 E-mail: sales@motorworks.com	accessories **parts**

See full listing in **Section One** under **Volkswagen**

The Rod Factory 3131 N 31st Ave Phoenix, AZ 85017 602-269-0031 E-mail: laserjet@amug.org	accessories **suspension parts**

See full listing in **Section Two** under **street rods**

Ron's Restorations Inc 2968-B Ask Kay Dr Smyrna, GA 30082 888-416-1057, 770-438-6102 FAX: 770-438-0037	interior trim **restoration**

See full listing in **Section One** under **Mercedes-Benz**

Scotts Manufacturing 25520 Ave Stanford #304 Valencia, CA 91355 800-544-5596; FAX: 661-295-9342	electric fans **fan electronics**

See full listing in **Section Two** under **electrical systems**

Sherco Auto Supply 3700 NW 124th Ave, Ste 114 Coral Springs, FL 33065 954-344-1993; FAX: 954-344-2664 E-mail: parts@sherco-auto.com	bulbs electrical wire **fuses**

See full listing in **Section Two** under **electrical systems**

Sidecurtain Bags & Accessories 9130 W Broad St Richmond, VA 23294 804-527-1515; FAX: 804-527-1616 E-mail: kmntr6@aol.com	side curtain bags

See full listing in **Section One** under **Triumph**

Smartire Systems Inc 13151 Vanier Pl, Ste 150 Richmond, BC Canada V6V 2J1 604-276-9884; FAX: 604-276-2350 E-mail: info@smartire.com	gauges

Smartire develops and markets the world's most technically advanced tire pressure and contained air temperature monitoring systems for all sectors of the automotive and transportation industries. Web site: www.smartire.com

Smith & Jones Distributing Co Inc 1 Biloxi Sq West Columbia, SC 29170 803-822-8500; FAX: 803-822-8477	parts

See full listing in **Section One** under **Ford 1903-1931**

So-Cal Speed Engineering PO Box 1421 Costa Mesa, CA 92628 714-979-7964	headers

See full listing in **Section Two** under **exhaust systems**

Sonic Motors Inc 9110 Hickory Ridge Rd Holly, MI 48442 810-750-1421; FAX: 810-750-7440	parts

See full listing in **Section One** under **Pontiac**

Specialty Cars Inc 17211 Roseton Ave Artesia, CA 90701 562-924-6904; FAX: 562-402-9544	parts **street rods**

See full listing in **Section Two** under **street rods**

Specialty Wheels Ltd 19310 NE San Rafael St Portland, OR 97230 503-491-8848; FAX: 503-491-8828 E-mail: wheelzrus@msn.com	wheels

See full listing in **Section Two** under **wheels & wheelcovers**

Specter Off-Road Inc 21600 Nordhoff St, Dept HM Chatsworth, CA 91311 818-882-1238; FAX: 818-882-7144 E-mail: sor@sor.com	accessories **parts**

See full listing in **Section One** under **Toyota**

Sterling Specialties 42 Ponderosa Ln Monroe, NY 10950 845-782-7614	car care products

See full listing in **Section Two** under **car care products**

Stinger by Axe Hwy 177 N, PO Box 296 Council Grove, KS 66846 800-854-4850; FAX: 316-767-5482 E-mail: axeequipment@tctelco.net	lifts

See full listing in **Section Two** under **storage care products**

Superior Equipment 326 S Meridian Valley Center, KS 67147 800-526-9992; FAX: 316-755-4391 E-mail: mail@superlifts.com	auto lifts **shop tools**

See full listing in **Section Two** under **tools**

Te Puke Vintage Auto Barn 26 Young Rd Te Puke New Zealand PH/FAX: 07 5736547	parts restoration **sales**

See full listing in **Section Two** under **restoration shops**

Section Two – Generalists

Thunderbird, Falcon, Fairlane & Comet Connections
728 E Dunlap
Phoenix, AZ 85020
602-997-9285; FAX: 602-997-0624
E-mail: thunderbirdconn@aol.com

new repros
parts
used repros

See full listing in **Section One** under **Thunderbird**

Tuxedo Turntables by Tuxedo Enterprises
4914 Gassner Rd, PO Box 580
Brookshire, TX 77423
888-TUXEDO-T (889-3368)

display turntables

Mail order and open shop by appointment only. Specializing in display turntables for show cars and other items (manufacture and sales), cars, motorcycles, airplanes, etc. Web site: www.tuxedoenterprises.com

Valco Cincinnati Consumer Products Inc
411 Circle Freeway Dr
Cincinnati, OH 45246
513-874-6550; FAX: 513-874-3612

adhesives
detailing products
sealants
tools

See full listing in **Section Two** under **tools**

Valenti Classics Inc
355 S Hwy 41
Caledonia, WI 53108
262-835-2070; FAX: 262-835-2575
E-mail: vci@valenticlassics.com

collectibles
restoration
sales
service

See full listing in **Section Two** under **car dealers**

Vintage Ford Center Inc
302 E Main St
Berryville, VA 22611
888-813-FORD (3673)
FAX: 540-955-0916
E-mail: mdla@visuallink.com

accessories
parts

See full listing in **Section One** under **Ford 1903-1931**

Visibolts From Classic Safety Products
7131 Hickory Run
Waunakee, WI 53597
888-212-2163; FAX: 608-824-9200
E-mail: clovis@www.visibolts.com

accessories

See full listing in **Section Two** under **lighting equipment**

Volunteer State Chevy Parts LLC
2414 Hwy 41 S, PO Box 10
Greenbrier, TN 37073
615-643-4583; FAX: 615-643-5100

accessories
parts

See full listing in **Section One** under **Chevrolet**

VPA International
369 E Blaine St
Corona, CA 92879
909-273-1033; FAX: 909-273-1041
E-mail: vpaintl@aol.com

alarm systems
door lock systems
power windows

Mail order and open shop. Monday-Friday 9:30 am to 3 pm Pacific time. VPA International manufactures and supplies the automotive aftermarket industry with automotive power accessories such as power windows and door lock systems, remote keyless entry, alarm systems, customized applications like the door poppers and shaved door handles. Web site: www.auto-accessories.com

Jim Wangers
1309 Melrose Way
Vista, CA 92083
760-941-9303; FAX: 760-941-9305
E-mail: info@jimwangers.com

memorabilia

See full listing in **Section One** under **Pontiac**

The Wheel Shoppe Inc
13635 SE Division St
Portland, OR 97236
503-761-5119; FAX: 503-761-5190
E-mail: rogeradams@
thewheelshoppe.com

parts
steering wheels

See full listing in **Section Two** under **steering wheels**

Wholesale Express
830 W 3rd St
Eddy, TX 76524
254-859-5364; FAX: 254-859-5407
E-mail: tommy@wacool.net

buffing supplies
sandblasters

We are a manufacturer of sandblasters and we sell buffing supplies. Web site: www.buffnstuff.com

Wirth's Custom Automotive
505 Conner St, PO Box 5
Prairie du Rocher, IL 62277
618-284-3359
E-mail: roywirth@htc.net

custom accessories
fender skirts
spinner hubcaps

Mail order only. 1940s, 1950s and 1960s custom accessories, Lake pipes, dummy spotlights, Smithy mufflers, spinner hubcaps, fender skirts, dice and skull items and much more. Web site: www.wirthscustomauto.com

Wooddash.com
438 Calle San Pablo, Unit B
Camarillo, CA 93012
805-987-2086; FAX: 805-389-5375
E-mail: mrchrome@west.net

dashes
steering wheels

See full listing in **Section Two** under **woodgraining**

www.albertsgifts.com
3001 Penn Ave
Pittsburgh, PA 15201
800-233-2800, 412-683-2900
FAX: 412-683-3110
E-mail: info@aimgifts.com

bike plates
license plates

See full listing in **Section Two** under **license plates**

Xtreme Class CC
Philip Patrick
25607 McDonald
Dearborn Heights, MI 48125
313-477-6799; FAX: 313-291-5744
E-mail: xtremeclass@aol.com

interior work
stereo installation

Custom stereo installation, suspension work and some interior work. Web site: www.xtremeclass.com

air conditioning

Cal West Auto Air & Radiators Inc
24309 Creekside Rd #119
Valencia, CA 91355
800-535-2034; FAX: 661-254-6120
E-mail: mike@calwest-radiators.com

a/c units/condensers
fan shrouds
gas tanks
heaters/radiators
radios/wheels

See full listing in **Section Two** under **radiators**

The Car Shop
10449 Rt 39
Springville, NY 14141
716-592-2060; FAX: 716-592-5766
E-mail: carshop77@aol.com

parts
service

See full listing in **Section Two** under **street rods**

Dagel's Street Rods
1048 W Collins Ave
Orange, CA 92867
714-288-1445; FAX: 714-288-1400

parts
street rods

See full listing in **Section Two** under **street rods**

Gas Tank and Radiator Rebuilders
20123 Hwy 362
Waller, TX 77484
800-723-3759
E-mail: donhart@donhart.com

abrasive blasting
gas tank rebuilding
heaters
radiator repair

See full listing in **Section Two** under **fuel system parts**

Alan Grove Components Inc
27070 Metcalf Rd
Louisburg, KS 66053
913-837-4368; FAX: 913-837-5721

a/c components

See full listing in **Section Two** under **street rods**

Holcombe Cadillac Parts
2933 Century Ln
Bensalem, PA 19020
215-245-4560; FAX: 215-633-9916
E-mail: holcars@aol.com

parts

See full listing in **Section One** under **Cadillac/LaSalle**

Long Island Corvette Supply Inc
1445 Strong Ave
Copiague, NY 11726-3227
631-225-3000; FAX: 631-225-5030
E-mail: info@licorvette.com

parts

See full listing in **Section One** under **Corvette**

Performance Analysis Co
1345 Oak Ridge Tpke, Ste 258
Oak Ridge, TN 37830
PH/FAX: 865-482-9175
E-mail: george_murphy@
compuserve.com

climate control
cruise control

See full listing in **Section One** under **Mercedes-Benz**

A Petrik
Restoration & Rebuilding Service
504 Edmonds Ave NE
Renton, WA 98056-3636
425-466-5590, 425-255-4852
E-mail: rnrserv@qwest.net or
rnrserv@hotmail.com

heater control
valve rebuilding
windshield
regulators

See full listing in **Section Two** under **heaters**

Tubes-n-Hoses by TKM
955 76th St SW
Byron Center, MI 49315
FAX: 616-878-4949

hose assemblies
tubes

Mail order and open shop. Monday-Friday 8 am to 5 pm Eastern time. All metal and rubber vehicle fluid lines: power steering, air conditioning, oil cooler, transmission, fuel and brake lines.

Wilk-Bilt Cars
Rt 1, Box 116
Ewing, VA 24248
PH/FAX: 540-445-4501
E-mail: wilkbilt@mounet.com

accessories
parts

See full listing in **Section One** under **Ford 1932-1953**

anti-theft

Bathurst Company
6101 Pine Meadows Dr
Loveland, OH 45140
513-722-9940; FAX: 513-722-9941
E-mail: kipkeywest@aol.com

auto accessories
battery accessories

See full listing in **Section Two** under **electrical systems**

Brakelock USA
PO Box 101715
Cape Coral, FL 33910
PH/FAX: 941-772-4490
E-mail: tony@brakelock.com

security systems

Mail order only. Brakelock vehicle security system: this device is a US patented mechanical security system which locks all the wheels on your vehicle. Turn the key and depress the brake pedal, the system is activated and the vehicle will not move. May be installed by any competent mechanic in about one hour. Web site: www.brakelock.com

Jacobs Electronics
500 N Baird St
Midland, TX 79701
915-685-3345, 800-627-8800
FAX: 915-687-5951
E-mail: retsales@marshill.com

ignition systems

See full listing in **Section Two** under **ignition parts**

Miltronics Mfg Inc
95 Krif Rd
Keene, NH 03431
603-352-3333 business line
800-NH-ALERT or
800-828-9089 order lines

detection system

Driveway Alert enhances your living by monitoring driveways, entry ways, back yards, pool areas, etc. Use this wireless, monitoring and detection system to safeguard your world. Be alerted when someone enters your property. The basic system is made up of an infra-red sensor transmitter which detects and/or senses the activity and a receiver which receives the transmission and alerts the household. The systems can be built up with more than one sensor or receiver for complete detection and reception throughout home and property. Call the manufacturer. Military wireless detection system manufacturer selling systems factory direct. Call today and be protected tomorrow. Web site: www.drivewayalert.com

Stevens Car Care Products Inc
36542 Vine St
East Lake, OH 44095
440-953-2900; FAX: 440-953-4473
E-mail: info@stevenscarcare.com

car alarms
rust deterrents

Mail order and open shop. Monday-Friday 8 am to 5:30 pm, Saturday 8 am to 1 pm. Defiance remote car alarms and keyless entry systems, Rusterminator, electronic rust deterrent systems, Stevens advanced formula detailing chemicals, tri-poly glaze paint sealant, waves, car wash, dressings, terminator, interior shampoo and odor eliminator, clay bar, extraction machines, wash mitts, complete detailing chemicals, supplies and equipment. Web site: www.stevenscarcare.com

Thunderbolt Traders Inc 6900 N Dixie Dr Dayton, OH 45414-3297 513-890-3344; FAX: 513-890-9403 E-mail: tbolt@erinet.com	battery cables

See full listing in **Section One** under **Edsel**

VPA International 369 E Blaine St Corona, CA 92879 909-273-1033; FAX: 909-273-1041 E-mail: vpaintl@aol.com	alarm systems door lock systems power windows

See full listing in **Section Two** under **accessories**

apparel

Bud Bagdasarian Studios 5136 Finney Ct Carmichael, CA 95608 916-965-6675; FAX: 916-966-9186	hats mugs T-shirts

Mail order only. Printing hundreds of different cars and hot rods onto T-shirts, mugs, hats for any make or model in stock or you may send us any picture of your own that can be transferred to T-shirts, mugs, hats, etc. Web site: www.burnoutgear.com

Bell Motorsports/Pyrotect 3227 14th Ave Oakland, CA 94602 800-669-2355; FAX: 510-261-2355 E-mail: bob@bellmotorsports.com	harnesses safety equipment

Mail order and open shop. Monday-Friday 8:30 am to 5:30 pm Pacific time. Deals in safety equipment and harnesses. Web site: www.pyrotect.com

Bonneville Speed & Supply PO Box 3924 Tustin, CA 92781 714-666-1966; FAX: 714-666-1955 E-mail: bonspeed@aol.com	memorabilia vintage clothing

Mail order and open shop. Monday-Friday 9 am to 5 pm. The leader in hot rod and vintage drag racing clothing and memorabilia. Many posters and vintage signs, die cast and T-shirts. Web site: www.bonnevillesports.com

Bonneville Sports Inc 3544 Enterprise Dr Anaheim, CA 92807 888-999-7258, 714-666-1966 FAX: 714-666-1955 E-mail: bonspeed@aol.com	accessories clothing

Color catalog packed with custom clothing and cool car stuff for you, your car and your garage. Not only do we create the finest automotive apparel in the world, we manufacture and source the best in garage goodies and automobilia. Now have Tony Nancy vintage drag racing, Posie and Troy Trepanier T-shirts and more. Also have a great catalog showroom in Anaheim, just 15 minutes from Disneyland. Web site: www.bonnevillesports.com

California Car Cover Co 9525 DeSoto Chatsworth, CA 91311 800-423-5525; FAX: 818-998-2442	accessories apparel car covers tools

See full listing in **Section Two** under **car covers**

Horseplayactionwear.com 211 N Catherine Bay City, MI 48706 517-892-5509, 800-447-7669 FAX: 517-671-1003 E-mail: horsplay@concentric.net	apparel decals gifts

Mail order and open shop. Monday-Friday 9 am to 5 pm. Wearing apparel, stickers and gifts. Horsepower related items, all makes and models, any year. T-shirts, sweatshirts, caps, denim shirts, jackets, coffee mugs and more. Screen printed, embroidered, custom work for clubs and businesses available. Items for cars, trucks, bikes, pwc, boats, anything that goes fast and has horsepower. Racers wanted. Web site: www.horseplayactionwear.com

Mercedes-Benz Visitor Center PO Box 100 Tuscaloosa, AL 35403-0100 888-2TOUR-MB, 205-507-2253 FAX: 205-507-2255	museum

See full listing in **Section One** under **Mercedes-Benz**

Motorcars International 528 N Prince Ln Springfield, MO 65802 417-831-9999; FAX: 417-831-8080 E-mail: sales@motorcars-intl.com	accessories cars services tools

See full listing in **Section One** under **Ferrari**

O'Brien Truckers 29 A Young Rd Charlton, MA 01507-1599 508-248-1555; FAX: 508-248-6179 E-mail: obt@ziplink.net	accessories belt buckles plaques valve covers

See full listing in **Section Two** under **plaques**

Old Cabot Village 465 Cabot St Beverly, MA 01915 978-922-7142; FAX: 978-922-6917 E-mail: oldcabot@mediaone.net	neckties

Mail order only. Specializing in automotive neckties, hot rod, custom and racing. Web site: www.racinties.com

Premier Designs Historic Costume 15512 St Rt 613 Van Buren, OH 45889 800-427-0907; FAX: 419-299-3919 E-mail: premier@bright.net	clothing

Mail order only. Historic clothing for women and men. Victorian to 1920s. Products include dusters, motor caps, knickers, shirts, collars, ladies blouses, jackets and skirts, and many more items. Web site: www.premierclothing.com

Viking Worldwise Inc 190 Doe Run Rd Manheim, PA 17545 866-CJACKETS; FAX: 717-664-5556 E-mail: gkurien@dejazz.com	leather jackets

Mail order and open shop. Monday-Friday 9 am to 6 pm, Saturday by appointment/chance Eastern time. Apparel custom leather jackets. Top quality custom leather jackets made of lambskin, fully lined, with your logo, design, car, hobby, inlaid in full color leather. No minimums. Quantities from 1 to 1,000. Imagine your club logo, car, etc. inlaid in leather on a custom leather jacket made just for you. Prices range from $325-$450 on average, depending on design. Racing teams and corporate orders our specialty. Web site: www.cjackets.com

Vintage Shop Coats
40 Fourth St #106
Petaluma, CA 94952
925-837-7869; FAX: 707-762-7901

shop coats

Classic shop coats. Web site: www.vintageshopcoats.com

appraisals

1866 Estimate
PO Box 322
Springfield, NJ 07081
1-866-ESTIMATE
E-mail: info@1866estimate.com

appraisals

Specializing in vehicle value appraisals for classic, custom and antique vehicles. Nationwide autobody network. Web site: www.1866estimate.com

AAAC-Antique Automobile Appraisal & Consulting
PO Box 700153
Plymouth, MI 48170
PH/FAX: 734-453-7644
E-mail: aaac@ameritech.net

appraisals
Cadillac parts
consulting

See full listing in **Section One** under **Cadillac/LaSalle**

AAG-Auto Appraisal Group Inc
PO Box 7034
Charlottesville, VA 22906
800-848-2886, 804-295-1722
FAX: 804-295-7918
E-mail: aag@autoappraisal.com

appraisals

Nationwide company. Pre-purchase inspections, insurance documentation, property settlements, museums. IRS accepted. Official appraisers, world's largest private collection, Harold LeMay estate. AAG certified agents provide services in: California, Connecticut, Florida, Georgia, Illinois, Kentucky, Maryland, Massachusetts, Mississippi, Missouri, New Jersey, New York, North Carolina, Ohio, Pennsylvania, Texas, Utah, Vermont, Virginia, Washington, Wisconsin. Extensive information gathering, originality and historical research, current market comparable analysis, factual reporting. Web site: www.autoappraisal.com

Accurate Auto Appraisers
1362 Hopkins St
Berkeley, CA 94702
800-733-4937, 510-528-9377
FAX: 510-527-7803

appraisals

Qualifications include: ten years as owner-manager of automotive leasing and rental business, including responsibility for determining resale value and depreciation; fifteen years as owner-operator of complete automotive service facility, including estimations; forty years as a craftsman in metal finishing and paint restoration; experience as buyer and seller at automotive auctions; thirty years as licensed automotive dealer in California; International Automotive Appraisers Association certified, member #5105289377. Web site: www.accuratevalue.com

Alt Auto Sales
Box 364
Regina SK Canada S4P 3A1
306-545-7119, 306-757-0369

car dealer

See full listing in **Section Two** under **car dealers**

AMC Classic Appraisers
7963 Depew St
Arvada, CO 80003
303-428-8760; FAX: 303-428-1070

appraisals

Mail order and open shop. Monday-Saturday 10 am to 7 pm. Collector car appraisals and on site evaluations. All cars 1900-present, includes stock, custom, modified cars, trucks, motorcycles, all makes and models. Certified Master Appraiser, IAAA member, #1006050095.

John Analla's Auto Appraisal Service
8952 Geraldine Ave
San Diego, CA 92123-2915
858-278-4084; FAX: 858-278-7435
E-mail: ja.analla@excite.com

appraisals

Appraisals for foreign and domestic with special emphasis on classics and collectibles. Exotics, limousines, hot rods, motorhomes, motorcycles, boats, Senior Certified member of the American Society of Appraisers, advisory board member of NADA, Classic Collectible and Special Interest Car Appraisal Guide. California business license #80061238. Twenty-one years as an appraiser, performing appraisals for banks, credit unions, divorce estates, litigation, insurance disputes, US government, etc. Web site: www.appraisers.org/sandiego/

Antique & Classic Auto Appraisal
Robert F Keefe
18812 Monteverde Dr
Springhill, FL 34610
PH/FAX: 727-856-5168

appraisals
consultant

Appraiser and consultant for antique, classic and special interest vehicles. 30 years' involvement in the old car field. Associate member of the International Society of Appraisers. Pre-purchase and travel available.

A-One Auto Appraisals
19 Hope Ln
Narragansett, RI 02882
401-783-7701, RI; 407-668-9610, FL

appraisals

Auto appraisals on all types antique, street rods, customs and special interest. License #472. New England area and Florida.

Appraisals R Us ET
Ed Thornton
15 Davis Dr
Alton, ON Canada L0N 1A0
519-942-0436

appraisals

Appraiser and consultant of any type or vintage of automobile or truck which includes street rods and fire apparatus. Over thirty years in the old car hobby. A complete portfolio of quality typed reports supplemented with pictures.

Archer & Associates
1807 East Ave
Hayward, CA 94541
510-581-4911
FAX: 510-537-7864

appraisals
consultant
expert witness
promotion
sales/purchasing

See full listing in **Section Two** under **auctions & shows**

Armstrong's Classic Auto Appraisals
3298 E Old State Rd
Schenectady, NY 12303
518-355-1387

appraisals
insurance

Phone hours: Monday-Friday 10 am to 4 pm Eastern time. Auto appraisals for vehicles 25 years or older, street rods, classics, customs, replicas and other specialty vehicles including foreign vehicles. I also specialize in classic car insurance, New York state only.

ARS Automotive Research Services
Division of Auto Search International
1702 W Camelback #301
Phoenix, AZ 85015
602-230-7111; FAX: 602-230-7282

appraisals
research

Mail order and open shop. Daily 10 am to 10 pm Pacific time, central Phoenix location. Appraisals and research. Free phone consultation. Don't sell, settle, donate or buy until you verify. All years cars, light trucks, street rods and customs too. Member NADA Advisory Board and Society of Automotive Historians. 15 years' full-time vehicle research experience. No conflicts of interest. Excellent reference library. Data packages prepared. Affordable rates. Can travel. From pre-purchase inspections to qualified expert witness testimony, our detailed reports and substantiated comprehensive appraisals stand tall under any circumstance, including total loss insurance claim mediation, fires and unrecovered thefts. Also available as neutral umpire for disputed claims. Collectible vehicle specialists since 1987.

Auto Advisors 14 Dudley Rd Billerica, MA 01821 978-667-0075	**appraisals**

Licensed appraiser for cars, trucks and motorcycles. Specializing in appraisals for antique and classic cars of all types and models. Also work with court approved divorces and estates.

Auto Appraisal Service 2208 N Leg Rd Augusta, GA 30909 706-736-7070; FAX: 706-736-7080	**appraisals**

Monday-Friday 10 am to 3 pm. Auto and truck appraisals. IAAA member, #1005130097.

Auto Consultants & **Appraisal Service** Charles J Kozelka PO Box 111 Macedonia, OH 44056 330-467-0748; FAX: 330-467-3725	**appraisals**

Professional appraisals for antique, classic, special interest and late model vehicles. Video appraisals at extra charge. Certified automobile accident and vehicle theft investigator. Expert witness and court testimony. Pre-purchase inspections or liquidation evaluations our specialty. Technical assistance on vehicle transactions, restorations or any auto related service. Consultant for commercial advertising, promotions, entertainment, special events, etc. Vehicle locator and broker service available.

Auto World Sales 2245 Q St Lincoln, NE 68503 402-435-7111; FAX: 402-435-7131 E-mail: autowwkh@navix.net	**appraisals** **sales**

Monday-Saturday 9 am to 6 pm. Sale of older rust-free pickups, 1970-1990. Hand-picked from the Southwest, out of the "rust belt." Offer professional appraisals on classic and collectible cars and pickups, in a four-state area. Member of the International Auto Appraisers Association since 1995, member #1006030095. Web site: www.carseekers.com

Auto-Line Enterprises Inc 2 Lyons Rd Armonk, NY 10504 914-681-1757; FAX: 914-273-5159 E-mail: autocashny@aol.com	**appraisals** **broker services**

Mail and telephone orders. Appraisal and broker services provided by an experienced dealer with over 28 years in the business. All types of classics, antiques and special interest autos included. Purchase and sale consulting services available. Web site: www.autocashofnewyork.com

Automobile Appraisal Service & **Special Interest Autos** 10097 Manchester Rd, Ste 203 St Louis, MO 63122 PH/FAX: 314-821-4015	**appraiser**

Appraisals of antique, classic, special interest, vintage, milestone, sport, muscle, street rods and street machines, customs,

reproductions, replicas and kit cars, foreign and late model cars, trucks and trailers, RVs, SUVs, motorcycles, manufactured homes, machinery and equipment for buying, selling, insurance coverage, claims, loans, value before the accident, estate and gift taxes, charitable donations, bankruptcy. Consignment sales. Broker, arbitrator, trial consultant and expert witness testimony. International Society of Appraisers (certified appraiser).

Automobile Classics Appraisal **Services** 5385 S Cook Rd College Park, GA 30349 404-761-0350; FAX: 404-761-3703 E-mail: johnboy30349@aol.com	**appraisals**

Mail order and open shop. Monday-Saturday 9 am to 9 pm. Independent certified appraisals since 1973: everyday drivers, antiques, muscle, classics, custom and street rods. Diminution of value, prior-to value, insurance value covering estates, marriage/business settlements, pre-sale/pre-purchase. Credentials and rate sheet upon request.

Automobilia Auctions Inc 132 Old Main St Rocky Hill, CT 06067 860-529-7177; FAX: 860-257-3621	**appraisals** **auctions**

See full listing in **Section Two** under **auctions & shows**

Automotive Legal Service Inc PO Box 626 Dresher, PA 19025 800-487-4947, 215-659-4947 FAX: 215-657-5843 E-mail: autolegal@aol.com	**appraisals**

State licensed automotive appraisal specialists. Antique, classic, exotic, kit, muscle car, pro street, street rod, cars, vans, trucks, original, restored, modified, incomplete, hard to value, insurance claims and restoration disputes, arbitration, litigation our specialty. Member Collector Car and Truck, NADA, OCPG Advisory Panels, National Muscle Car Association Regional director, qualified expert witness 160 times, also current model Accident Investigation/Reconstruction Lemon Law. Quality references, maximum credibility, reasonable rates, travel USA. Free consultation. Web site: www.angelfire.com/pa3/autolegalservice/index.html

AVM Automotive Consulting Box 338 Montvale, NJ 07645-0338 201-391-5194; FAX: 978-383-4776 E-mail: avmtony@yahoo.com	**appraisals** **consultant**

Open 9 am to 9 pm weekdays. Specializing in appraisals, pre-purchase inspections and consulting for antique, classic and custom vehicles and equipment. Will travel or by mail. Writing appraisals for over 20 years for legal and estate settlements. Automotive products and business consulting with 30 years' experience. Services are available for individuals, attorneys and corporations. Member of the International Automotive Appraisers Association (member #1000071994) makes prompt inspections possible worldwide.

Bastian Automotive Restoration 4170 Finch Ave Fairfield, OH 45014 PH/FAX: 513-738-4268	**appraisals** **restoration**

See full listing in **Section Two** under **restoration shops**

Dave Bayowski 3686 Niles Carver Rd Mineral Ridge, OH 44440 PH/FAX: 330-544-0242	**appraisals**

Auto appraisals for antique, classic, custom and street rod. ISA, IAAA (member #1002180098). 30 years' experience in restoration, consulting and appraising.

Bill's Collector Cars
6478 County Rd #1
South Point, OH 45680
740-894-5175

appraisals
car dealer

See full listing in **Section Two** under **car dealers**

Blair Collectors & Consultants
2821 SW 167th Pl
Seattle, WA 98166
206-242-6745, 206-246-1305
E-mail: blairhall33@aol.com

appraisals
consultant
literature

Mail order and open shop. Monday-Friday 9 am to 10 pm Pacific time. Collector car appraisals, cars and parts locating service, technical and restoration/customizing advice, car importing advice and assistance, data packages for all cars, buy/sell literature. Covers vintage, classic, muscle, street rods and imports. Professional engineer with over 40 years' experience.

Brandeberry Antique Auto Appraisal
401 First Ave
Gallipolis, OH 45631
740-446-3225

appraiser

Appraisals by mail or in person. 25 years' experience.

Bryant's Antique Auto Parts
851 Western Ave
Hampden, ME 04444
207-862-4019

appraisals
chassis/engine parts
sheetmetal
wiring harnesses

See full listing in **Section One** under **Ford 1903-1931**

C&V Classic Restorations
420 East St
Webb City, MO 64870
800-464-8592; FAX: 417-673-7544
E-mail: info@cvclassic.com

appraisals
restorations

See full listing in **Section Two** under **restoration shops**

Car Critic
202 Woodshire Ln
Naples, FL 34105
941-435-1157; FAX: 941-261-4864
E-mail: carcritic@earthlink.net

appraisals
inspections

See full listing in **Section Two** under **car & parts locators**

Car Values Plus
40 Plank Rd
Newburgh, NY 12550
845-561-3594; FAX: 845-561-1745
E-mail: jim@hvaa.com

appraisals

Online appraisals for collector cars. Web site is always open: www.carvaluesplus.com

Chicago Car Exchange
14085 W Rockland Rd
Libertyville, IL 60048
847-680-1950; FAX: 847-680-1961
E-mail: oldtoys@wwa.com

appraisals
car dealer
car locator
financing
storage

See full listing in **Section Two** under **car dealers**

Charles W Clarke,
Automotive Consultants
17 Saddle Ridge Dr
West Simsbury, CT 06092-2118
PH/FAX: 860-658-2714

appraisals
car dealer
consultant

See full listing in **Section Two** under **consultants**

Classic Auto Appraisals
3497 Simpson Rd SE
Rochester, MN 55904
507-289-7111
E-mail: ashie@rconnect.com

appraisals

Appraisals for special interest, antique, milestones, muscle and classic cars. Our specialty: 1950s, 1960s rods and customs. For insurance coverage, estates, loan valuation, charitable contributions, marriage, business/settlements, pre-sale, pre-purchase inspections.

Classic Auto Appraiser
24316 Carlton Ct
Laguna Niguel, CA 92677
800-454-1313; FAX: 949-425-1533
E-mail: classicauto64@home.com

appraisals

Mail order and open shop. Appraisals of custom cars, show cars, street rods and classics.

Classic Auto Restoration
437 Greene St
Buffalo, NY 14212
716-896-6663
E-mail: jp@classicbuff.com

appraisals
plating
polishing
restoration

See full listing in **Section Two** under **restoration shops**

Classic Car Appraisal Service
Atlanta Office
1400 Lake Ridge Ct
Roswell, GA 30076
770-993-5622

appraiser

Open by appointment only. Donald R Peterson, president. Have appraised more than 11,000 collector cars since opening in 1974. Packard, Rolls-Royce and other CCCA Classics are our specialty. Member of CCCA, AACA, HCCA, VMCCA, MCS, RROC, PAC and SAH. A copy of our credentials will be mailed at your request. We also do diminished value appraisals, pre-purchase examinations and have served as an expert witness on dozens of occasions.

Classic Car Appraisals
37 Wyndwood Rd
West Hartford, CT 06107
PH/FAX: 860-236-0125
E-mail: tjakups@
classiccarappraisals.net

appraisals

Postwar American stock automobiles. Complete evaluation of car, operational check and photos. Certified and accepted by insurance companies, courts, IRS. Serving all of Connecticut. Web site: www.classiccarappraisals.net

Classic Car Research
29508 Southfield Rd, Ste 106
Southfield, MI 48076
248-557-2880; FAX: 248-557-3511
E-mail: kawifreek@msn.com

appraisals
consultant
part locating

Appraisal and pre-purchase inspections, will travel. Established in 1985. IAAA member (#1001070097), NADA Board and ASA candidate member. Michigan's most certified appraiser specializing in American and exotic cars. Also new and used parts for Corvettes, muscle cars and classic Kawasaki motorcycles. Web site: www.jmkclassiccars.com

Classic Carriage House
5552 E Washington
Phoenix, AZ 85034
602-275-6825; FAX: 602-244-1538

restoration

See full listing in **Section Two** under **restoration shops**

Classic Motors
PO Box 1321
Shirley, MA 01464
978-425-4614

| appraisals |
| car dealer |
| consulting |

See full listing in **Section Two** under **car dealers**

Classique Cars Unlimited
7005 Turkey Bayou Rd, PO Box 249
Lakeshore, MS 39558
800-543-8691, USA
228-467-9633; FAX: 228-467-9207
E-mail: parts@datasync.com

| appraisals |
| parts |
| repairs |
| restorations |

See full listing in **Section One** under **Lincoln**

Collector Car & Truck Market Guide
41 N Main St
North Grafton, MA 01536
508-839-6707; FAX: 508-839-6266
E-mail: vmr@vmrintl.com

| price guide |

See full listing in **Section Four** under **periodicals**

Collector's Carousel
84 Warren Ave
Westbrook, ME 04092
207-854-0343; FAX: 207-856-6913

| appraisals |
| sales |
| service |

See full listing in **Section Two** under **car dealers**

Robert W Cook Corvette Art
8047 Moss Meadows Dr
Dallas, TX 75231
214-349-6232; FAX: 214-692-7286
E-mail: prelim@cs.com

| appraisals |
| artwork |

See full listing in **Section Two** under **artwork**

Lance S Coren, CAA, CMA
20545 Eastwood Ave
Torrance, CA 90503-3611
310-370-4114; FAX: 310-371-4120
E-mail: lscent@hotmail.com

| appraisals |

Mail order and open by appointment only. The only FIA and ORDINEX Certified Automotive Appraiser in the western United States. Material damage appraisals, actual cash evaluations. Exotic, classic and race cars. American Bar Association and IRS qualified. Insurance, bank, charity, museum, court evaluations. Expert witness testimony. Arbitration and mediation. Auto manufacturer and United Nations acknowledged expert. Celebrity clientele. 20 years' experience. Servicing the United States, Europe and Japan. Senior member: Society of Automotive Appraisers, International Automotive Appraisers Association, Automotive Arbitration Council. Web site: www.theautoappraiser.com

---

Corvette Enterprise Brokerage
The Power Broker-Mike Kitain
52 Van Houten Ave
Passaic Park, NJ 07055-5512
973-472-7021

| appraisals |
| broker |
| car locator |
| investment |
| planning |

See full listing in **Section One** under **Corvette**

Creative Automotive Consultants
PO Box 2221
San Rafael, CA 94912-2221
415-892-3331; FAX: 415-892-3339
E-mail: cars4cac@earthlink.net

| appraisals |
| car locator |
| promotion |
| DMV |

See full listing in **Section Two** under **consultants**

Customs & Classics
PO Box 737
Clayton, CA 94517
925-672-7230; FAX: 925-672-5512
E-mail: japolk@jps.net

| appraisals |

Appraisal services for antique, collectible and modern automobiles. Web site: www.customsclassics.com

---

Dearborn Automobile Co
16 Maple St (at Rt 1)
Topsfield, MA 01983
978-887-6644; FAX: 978-887-3889
E-mail: slr190sl@aol.com

| appraisals |
| car dealer |

Open Monday-Friday 9 am to 5 pm, Saturday 9 am to 12 noon. All types of rare Mercedes bought, sold and brokered, appraisals. Specializing in Mercedes 1949-1971. Appraiser for estates and insurance.

Robert DeMars Ltd
Auto Appraisers/Historians
222 Lakeview Ave, Ste 160/256
West Palm Beach, FL 33401
561-832-0171; FAX: 561-738-5284
E-mail: carapraisr@aol.com

| appraisals |
| auto historians |
| auto locating |
| research library |
| resto consultants |

Appraisers/Historians: telephone consultation worldwide for fast information and recommendations! NADA consultant. Available in person, by mail, e-mail and fax. We're the 30 year pioneers of the field of collector car appraisal, traveling the world. Low mileage, antique, classic, sports, muscle car, race car, Pebble Beach Concours and prototype "Dream Cars" a specialty. Clients and inspectors thru US, Europe, Japan, South America. As historians and performance/race drivers with a large research library, we appreciate fine machinery and monitor the "Now Market" for trends and values. Pebble Beach, CA/Palm Beach, FL. Please note new main office and phone. Web site: www.robertdemarsltd.com

---

Russ Dentico's Sales &
Auto Appraisal Consulting
PO Box 566
Trenton, MI 48183
734-675-3306; FAX: 734-675-8908

| appraisals |

Open Tuesday-Friday 11 am to 5 pm. Appraisal service for attorney estate service, Corvettes, street rods and special interest vehicles, salvage appraisal service (licensed salvage and used car dealer). IAAA member (#1005020095). 31 years' experience. Insurance company endorsed, Detroit, MI and Toledo, OH areas.

Richard H Feibusch
211 Dimmick Ave
Venice, CA 90291
310-392-6605; FAX: 310-396-1933
E-mail: rfeibusch@loop.com

| appraisals |

Appraiser and automotive journalist. Recognized by the IRS, Probate Court and all major insurance companies. Antiques, classics, special interest, foreign, rods, customs and kit/home-built cars. British car specialist. Los Angeles area only.

FEN Enterprises of New York Inc
1090 Rt 376, PO Box 1559
Wappingers Falls, NY 12590
845-462-5959, 845-462-5094
FAX: 845-462-8450
E-mail: fenenterprises@aol.com

| parts |
| restoration |

See full listing in **Section One** under **Cadillac/LaSalle**

Fiesta's Classic Car Center
3901 N Kings Hwy
St Louis, MO 63115
314-385-4567

| appraisals |
| consignment sales |
| storage |

See full listing in **Section Two** under **storage**

John Filiss
45 Kingston Ave
Port Jervis, NY 12771
845-856-2942
E-mail: john@filiss.com

appraisals

Mail order and open shop by appointment. Specialize in low-cost, professional appraisals for insurance purposes, also divorces and estate settlements. Web site: www.motionalmemories.com

Florida Inspection Associates
PO Box 1308
Largo, FL 33770
888-342-4678 toll free, 727-588-0331
FAX: 727-588-0580
E-mail: bills@fiainspectors.com

appraisals

FIA has provided certified appraisals and inspections since 1987. Offer nationwide service on all makes, models and years of motor vehicles, recreation or motorcycles. IAAA certified master appraiser Bill Schultz, member #1008010096. 450 locations nationwide. Forensic mechanics also offered. Web site: www.fiainspectors.com

Green Mountain Vintage Auto
20 Bramley Way
Bellows Falls, VT 05101
PH/FAX: 802-463-3141
E-mail: vintauto@sover.net

damage appraisals
vehicle evaluations

Call or e-mail your needs. Specializing in pre-1950s vehicle evaluations. Damage appraisals for all models.

The Gullwing Garage Ltd
Bricklin SVI Specialists
5 Cimorelli Dr
New Windsor, NY 12553-6201
845-561-0019 anytime

appraisals
literature
parts
service

See full listing in **Section One** under **Bricklin**

Hand's Elderly Auto Care
2000 Galveston St
Grand Prairie, TX 75051
PH/FAX: 972-642-4288

repair
restoration

See full listing in **Section Two** under **restoration shops**

Hawthorne's Happy Motoring
Box 1332
Coaldale AB Canada T1M 1N2
PH/FAX: 403-345-2101

appraisals
parts

Open shop. Monday-Saturday, year round, 7 am to 5 pm. Auto restoration supplies, auto appraisals, broker of antique and special interest vehicles.

John H Heldreth & Associates
919 W Main St, Ste L-4
Lakeview Plaza
Hendersonville, TN 37075
615-824-5994; FAX: 615-822-4919

appraisals

Open Monday-Friday 8:30 am to 5 pm, outside appointments by phone. Appraisals for all makes and models. IAAA member, #1006010095.

Don Hoelscher, Auto Appraiser
52 Waynesboro Ct
St Charles, MO 63304
636-939-9667; FAX: 801-459-1621, UT
E-mail: dhoelsch@mail.win.org

appraisals

By appointment only. Appraisals of classic, antique, special interest/collector cars, trucks and other vehicles, all years and models. Web site: www.geocities.com/donhoelscherautoappraisals/

Hubbard and Associates
Appraisers of Collectible Autos
80 W Bellevue Dr #200
Pasadena, CA 91105
626-568-0122; FAX: 626-568-1510

appraisals

Office hours Monday-Friday 9 am to 5 pm by appointment only. Appraisals for insurance, probate, marriage dissolution and pre-purchase inspections. Licensed, Board certified, Senior member American Society of Appraisers. Professional resume and references upon request. Twenty years' experience. Expert witness, arbitration and litigation.

Hubbard Classic Car Appraisals
1908 Belle Terr
Bakersfield, CA 93304-4352
661-397-7786
E-mail: lynnhubbard@msn.com

appraisals

Open shop by appointment only, at your site or mine. Automobile appraisals for all marques. Specializing in Corvette, street rod and custom. Knowledgeable in mechanical and safety aspects, do a full safety 23-point inspection on each appraisal, free inspection. I'm an inspector with National Street Rod Association, appraiser certified with International Association of Automobile Appraisers, member SEMA and NADA.

International Automotive Appraisers Assoc
Box 338
Montvale, NJ 07645
201-391-3251; FAX: 978-383-4776
E-mail: automotiveappraiser@yahoo.com

appraisals

Incorporated in New Jersey on September 1, 1994. Publications, organizations and the courts recognize and approve its policies. Recognized professional automotive appraisers from Canada and the US including Puerto Rico and Hawaii comprise the membership. *The Auto Appraiser News* is the official newsletter of the IAAA. It devotes total content to automotive appraisers, appraisals and the industry that they serve. A roster that lists members, their expertise and their geographic locations is available to organizations and insurers. Goals include educating and training appraisers and promoting professionalism among them. The IAAA is in the process of documenting standards and practices of automotive appraisers. Web site: www.auto-appraisers.com

Jesser's Auto Clinic
26 West St
Akron, OH 44303
330-376-8181; FAX: 330-384-9129

appraisals

Open shop. Monday-Friday 10 am to 4 pm. By appointment and on-site appraisals. Bonded and insured, over 15 years' experience. Personal, professional, certified appraisals and pre-purchase inspections. All portfolios done in triplicate with full color photographs. For all domestic and foreign models. Stated insurance values, loan appraisals, appraisals for any purpose. Insurance arbitrator, expert witness. Member, advisor, board member NADA Exotics and Collectibles. Member International Automotive Appraisers Association (member #100231294). Active memberships in AACA, CCCA, VMCCA, MCS, BCA, MCA, OCA, WPC, PAC, PIMCC, CTC, CLC, CCI, POCI, LCOC, HOG and twenty others. Up-to-date, well maintained reference library. Web site: www.jessersclassickeys.com

John's Auto Classics
6135 N 79 Dr
Glendale, AZ 85303
602-999-0845

appraisals

Appraisals for antique, classic and collectibles. Appraisals for banks, insurance companies and personal use. Specializing in Cadillacs.

K & K Vintage Motorcars LC	restoration
9848 SW Frwy	sales
Houston, TX 77074	service
713-541-2281; FAX: 713-541-2286	
E-mail: vintagemotorcars@ev1.net	

See full listing in **Section Two** under **restoration shops**

J A Kennedy Inc	appraisals
1727 Hartford Tpke	
North Haven, CT 06473	
203-239-2227	

Specializing in appraisals of both damage and value for antique, classic and special interest cars.

Ken's Cougars	parts
PO Box 5380	
Edmond, OK 73083	
405-340-1636; FAX: 405-340-5877	

See full listing in **Section One** under **Mercury**

Kruse International	auction
5540 County Rd 11-A, PO Box 190	
Auburn, IN 46706	
800-968-4444; FAX: 219-925-5467	

See full listing in **Section Two** under **auctions & shows**

Laigle Motorsporte Ltd	appraisals
5707 Schumacher Ln	
Houston, TX 77057	
713-781-6900; FAX: 713-781-6556	
E-mail: laigle@usa.net	

Certified appraiser for special interest automobiles. Member IAAA (#100171294), board member NADA Galleria area, Houston, TX. Insurance appraisals. Expert witness, legal consultant.

Landry Classic MotorCars	appraisals
34 Goodhue Ave	
Chicopee, MA 01020	
413-592-2746; FAX: 413-594-8378	
oldcar@map.com	

Open 7 days by appointment only. Specializing in all types of professional appraisals including stated value, pre-purchase inspections for all collector cars and trucks. Licensed and certified in several states. Member of 13 national clubs.

Col Glenn Larson	appraisals
4415 Canyon Dr	auctioneer
Amarillo, TX 79110	
806-358-9797; FAX: 806-467-0280	
E-mail: colonel@arn.net	

Certified appraisals for collector cars. Collector car auctioneer. Over 10 years' experience. References available. IAAA member, #1010010097.

Larson Motor Co	appraisals
Russell Larson	restoration
4415 Canyon Dr	sales
Amarillo, TX 79110	
806-358-9797	

See full listing in **Section Two** under **car dealers**

Bob Lichty Content & Consulting	appraisals
1330 Fulton Rd NW	consultant
Canton, OH 44703	promoter
330-456-7869; FAX: 330-456-7883	
E-mail: rrubin@neo.rr.com	

Appraisals, pre-purchase inspections, estates, insurance. Consultant to publishers, dot-coms, museums, event promotion.

AAG certified. SEMA/ARMO member. Donation placement assistance. F&F cereal car collector. Author *AACA History*.

M & L Automobile Appraisal	appraisals
2662 Palm Terr	
Deland, FL 32720	
904-734-1761	
386-734-1761 (effective 11/01)	

Open daily by appointment. Florida licensed to appraise antique, classic, special interest, custom/altered automobiles, motorcycles, custom trailers and toys for insurance coverage, loan valuation, estate settlements or disputes.

M & M Automobile Appraisers Inc	appraisals
584 Broomspun St	broker
Henderson, NV 89015	consultant
702-568-5120; FAX: 702-568-5158	
E-mail: mmautoappr@earthlink.net	

Appraise special interest, collectible and antique automobiles for insurance coverage, loan valuation, marriage or business dissolutions and value disputes. Expert witness insurance arbitration and investment consultation.

Randall Marcus Vintage Automobiles	appraisals
706 Hanshaw Rd	broker
Ithaca, NY 14850	car locator
607-257-5939; FAX: 607-272-8806	consultant
E-mail: randysvintageautos@	
bgdmlaw.com	

See full listing in **Section Two** under **brokers**

Gerry Martel's Classic Carriages	appraisals
173 Main St	
Fitchburg, MA 01420	
978-343-6382; FAX: 978-342-1939	

Appraisals for all collector cars. IAAA member (#1005050095). 20 years' experience.

Bill McCoskey	accident/damage
PO Box 93	investigations
Littlestown, PA 17340	appraisals
410-346-0660; FAX: 410-346-6499	
E-mail: billmccoskey@aol.com	

Certified value appraisals, diminution in value claims, insurance claim arbitration service and effective expert witness court testimony. Forensic mechanical examinations and reconstructions. Accident damage investigations. Pre-claim value reconstruction and appraisal-by-mail service available. Over 25 years in the antique and classic car business and hobby, rare European cars a specialty. Well-equipped restoration shop on premises.

Memory Lane Motors	car dealer
562 County Rd 121	restoration
Fenelon Falls, ON Canada K0M 1N0	service
705-887-CARS; FAX: 705-887-4028	

See full listing in **Section Two** under **restoration shops**

Memory Lane Motors Inc	appraisals
1231 Rt 176	car dealer
Lake Bluff, IL 60044	storage
847-362-4600	

See full listing in **Section Two** under **car dealers**

Dennis Mitosinka's Classic Cars and Appraisals Service	appraisals
619 E Fourth St	books
Santa Ana, CA 92701	
714-953-5303; FAX: 714-953-1810	
E-mail: mitoclassics@earthlink.net	

Appraisals of all types of autos. For the most professional service, for disputes in value, litigation, insurance, donations, diminished value purchases or sales. Call for cost estimates. Certified appraiser with over 31 years' experience. Also large selection of auto books, mostly out of print.

Old Car Co	**appraisals**
Rich House	
3112 Eaglewood Pl	
St Charles, MO 63303	
314-926-2789	

Appraisal service for classic cars, hot rods, antique cars and collector cars. Reliable, experienced and up to date. We come to you. IAAA member, #1011120097. We do appraisals within 100 mile radius of St Louis, Missouri.

Paradise Classic Auto Appraisal	**appraisals**
5894 Cornell	**transport**
Taylor, MI 48180	
313-291-2758	

Auto appraisal and transporting. IAAA member, #1008010095.

CT Peters Inc Appraisers	**appraisals**
2A W Front St	
Red Bank, NJ 07701	
732-747-9450 Red Bank	
732-528-9451 Brielle	
E-mail: ctp2120@aol.com	

Mail order and open shop. Monday-Friday 9 am to 5 pm. Antique, classic and vintage motorcars appraised throughout the tri-state area since 1976, for insurance, fair market and estate values. Appointments at your premises available or send photographs for appraisal by mail. References available. Also offer fast, effective, discreet methods of selling investment quality automobiles through our exclusive tri-state area computer client mailing list.

Prairie Auto	**appraisals**
Jeremiah Larson	**car dealers**
7087 Orchid Ln	
Maple Grove, MN 55311	
612-420-8600; FAX: 612-420-8637	
E-mail: jer4cars@aol.com	

See full listing in **Section Two** under **car dealers**

Prestige Thunderbird Inc	**appraisals**
10215 Greenleaf Ave	**radios**
Santa Fe Springs, CA 90670	**repairs**
800-423-4751, 562-944-6237	**restorations**
FAX: 562-941-8677	**tires**
E-mail: tbirds@prestigethunderbird.com	

See full listing in **Section One** under **Thunderbird**

Rader's Relics	**appraisals**
1896 Kentucky Ave	**car dealer**
Winter Park, FL 32789	
407-647-1940; FAX: 407-647-1930	
E-mail: therelic@bellsouth.net	

See full listing in **Section Two** under **car dealers**

William H Randel	**appraisals**
PO Box 173	**car locators**
Hatboro, PA 19040	
215-675-8969; FAX: 215-441-0960	
E-mail: tbrdnut@bellatlantic.net	

See full listing in **Section One** under **Thunderbird**

The Rappa Group	**appraisals**
174 Brady Ave	
Hawthorne, NY 10532	
914-747-7010; FAX: 914-747-7013	
E-mail: djrappa@rappa.com	

Antique, classic, custom, street rod and exotic vehicle insurance and appraisals. IAAA member, #1000241294. Web site: www.rappa.com

Reinholds Restorations	**appraisals**
c/o Rick Reinhold	**repairs**
PO Box 178, 255 N Ridge Rd	**restoration**
Reinholds, PA 17569-0178	
717-336-5617; FAX: 717-336-7050	

See full listing in **Section Two** under **restoration shops**

Reward Service Inc	**appraisals**
172 Overhill Rd	**restoration**
Stormville, NY 12582	**transportation**
PH/FAX: 845-227-7647	

See full listing in **Section One** under **Jaguar**

RM Classic Cars	**auctions**
5 W Forest Ave	
Ypsilanti, MI 48197	
734-547-2400; FAX: 734-547-9424	
E-mail: michigan@rmcars.com	

See full listing in **Section Two** under **auctions & shows**

Douglas D Roark	**appraisals**
34000 N 1850 E Rd	
Rossville, IL 60963-7040	
217-765-4781	

Appraisals of antique, classic and special interest vehicles, for purposes of insurance value or pre-purchase inspection.

Royal Coach Works Ltd	**appraisals**
2146 Lunceford Ln	
Lilburn, GA 30047	
PH/FAX: 770-736-3960	
E-mail: royalrow@cs.com	

Restorations by appointment. Appraisals for pre-purchase and insurance. IAAA member (#1005140098). Restorations, woodwork, maintenance, parts for Rolls-Royce to 1985, Aston to 1992, Mercedes 600 to 1975.

Richard C Ryder	**appraisals**
828 Prow Ct	
Sacramento, CA 95822	
916-442-3424 anytime	
916-600-4825 mobile	
FAX: 916-442-4939	
E-mail: rydvntrzcwnet.com	

Collector car evaluations for individuals, insurance, lenders, legal or government agencies.

James T Sandoro	**appraisals**
24 Myrtle Ave	**consultant**
Buffalo, NY 14204	
716-855-1931	

Confidential automotive consultant, appraiser, expert witness, trial consultant. 38 years' full time experience. Unique qualifications. Retained by the largest collections, museums, government agencies, restoration shops. I can give you an overview and act as an expert on your behalf as well as a trial consultant regarding collector vehicles, motorcycles, memorabilia, etc. I only testify in cases I believe in. My referrals are from other appraisers, dealers and restorers. Available anywhere in the world.

Bernard A Siegal ASA
Automotive Restoration Services
PO Box 140722
Dallas, TX 75214
214-827-2678; FAX: 214-826-0000

appraisals

Monday-Saturday 9 am to 6 pm Central time. Appraisals for all marques and all years. Valuation for insurance, pre-purchase inspection, physical damage appraisals, loss of value, divorces, estate settlements. One of ten Senior members of the American Society of Appraisers accredited and tested in this field. Eight areas of certification by Automotive Service Excellence. Licensed Texas adjuster. All valuation reports conform to USPAP standards.

RL Smith Sales Inc
Gregory S Smith, President
466 Hays Rd
Rensselaer, NY 12144-4701
518-449-4240; FAX: 518-463-1288
E-mail: gsmith9215@aol.com

appraisals

Mail order and open shop. Monday-Saturday 9 am to 7 pm Eastern time. Appraisals, Albany, NY, area. Estates, collector, insurance and donation, expert witness, all types of vehicles. IAAA certified member (#1002050098). Realistic work, fairly priced. Web site: www.rlsmithsales.com

Specialized Street Rods
18101 Redondo Cir #M
Huntington Beach, CA 92648
714-841-2114; FAX: 714-841-2447
E-mail: specstrrods@earthlink.net

street rods

See full listing in **Section Two** under **street rods**

Steele's Appraisal
Shore Dr, Box 276
Maynard, MA 01754
978-897-8984

appraisals

Mail order and open shop. Seven days 5 pm to 8 pm. Travel the New England area to view and appraise antique and special interest autos to prevent sight-unseen purchases by out-of-the-area buyers.

Sterling Restorations Inc
1705 Eastwood Dr
Sterling, IL 61081
815-625-2260; FAX: 815-625-0799

appraisals
restorations

See full listing in **Section Two** under **restorations shops**

Still Cruisin' Corvettes
5759 Benford Dr
Haymarket, VA 20169
703-754-1960; FAX: 703-754-1222
E-mail: chuckberge@starpower.net

appraisals
repairs
restoration

See full listing in **Section One** under **Corvette**

Timeless Masterpieces
221 Freeport Dr
Bloomingdale, IL 60108
630-893-1058 evenings

appraisals
consultant

Appraisals, consulting, research, historian of pre-1975 antique, classic, vintage automobiles. Auction/agent representation. Write or call for information. Established 1976.

Sol W Toder
808 Hillaire Dr
Pittsburgh, PA 15243
412-279-6180

appraisals

Appraisals of inventory and equipment of salvage yards. Also experienced court qualified expert witness in matters regarding the auto salvage industry. Automobiles and member of advisory board. NADA. IAAA member, #1007190096.

Top Hat John
PO Box 46024
Mt Clemens, MI 48046-6024
810-465-1933; FAX: 810-493-1953

appraisals

Appraisal service by Top Hat John, automotive historian, custom classic, special interest. Prior to purchase or sale, insurance coverage, settlement, investment portfolio. References. Local or travel. Able to identify, negotiate and close sale if necessary. Detail oriented. Member Society of Automotive Historians. Web site: www.tophatjohn.com

Lou Trepanier, Appraiser #1
250 Highland St
Taunton, MA 02780
508-823-6512; FAX: 508-285-4841

appraisals
consultant

Stated value appraisals, antique, classic, customs and exotics. Consultant to hobbyists and businesses, licensed and appointed and sworn arbitrator for insurance, financial or legals. 40 years in automotive services. Guaranteed neutral umpire service for disputed claims.

USA Auto Appraisers
5062 S 108th St, Ste 225
Omaha, NE 68137
402-681-2968; FAX: 402-861-8772

appraisals

Mail order and open shop by appointment. Appraise late model, classic, antique, street rods and custom cars. Stated value insurance appraisals our specialty. E-mail appraisals nationwide. Automotive legal consultant, court tested expert witness, any legality. Bankruptcy, divorce, tax issues, estates, quality of repair or diminution of value issues. 20 years' of automotive experience. Member NADA Classic and Collectable Board. Calls returned anywhere. 24-hour phone. We can help. Web site: www.usaautoappraisers.com

USAppraisal
754 Walker Rd, PO Box 472
Great Falls, VA 22066-0472
703-759-9100; FAX: 703-759-9099
E-mail: dhkinney@usappraisal.com

appraisals

Open 7 days by appointment. Appraisals for all makes and models of automobiles and trucks of all years. Available nationwide. 25 years' collector car experience. All appraisals and record keeping conform to USPAP standards. David H Kinney, ASA, Accredited Senior member, American Society of Appraisers. For further information visit our web site: www.usappraisal.com

Valenti Classics Inc
355 S Hwy 41
Caledonia, WI 53108
262-835-2070; FAX: 262-835-2575
E-mail: vci@valenticlassics.com

collectibles
restoration
sales
service

See full listing in **Section Two** under **car dealers**

Vehicle Appraisers Inc
59 Wheeler Ave
Milford, CT 06460
203-877-1066
E-mail: vehicle@snet.net

appraisals

Appointment only. Licensed since 1975 in all 50 states to do appraisals of both value and damage. Have performed over 10,000 appraisals. One of the largest private automotive libraries in the eastern United States with crash books as far back as 1947. Answer any questions at no charge. Write, phone or e-mail. Private and commercial accepted.

Vehicle Preservation Society
PO Box 9800
San Diego, CA 92169
619-449-1010; FAX: 619-449-6388
E-mail: vehicles@vps.cc

appraisals

Established 1989. Formed to provide all services promoting the hobby and supported by an international membership. Services offered include certified appraisals and condition reports on any vehicle worldwide. VPS is qualified by the IRS, USPAP and the American Bar Association to perform all classic and special interest vehicle valuations. VPS represents vehicle owners for insurance, umpire and arbitration disputes. Vehicle insurance, bank, charity, museum and court valuations since 1967. Our member services are unlimited and have been published in *Hemmings Motor News*, February 1999. Private lifetime memberships are only $95. Ask for free fax info. Web site: www.vehicles.org

Vintage Auto Ent	**appraisals**
PO Box 2183	**auctioneer**
Manchester Center, VT 05255	
802-362-4719; FAX: 802-362-3007	
E-mail: dbrownell@sprynet.com	

All makes and years. Will travel internationally. Collections and estates a specialty. Serving individuals, banks, insurance companies, institutions for over 30 years. Experienced in cars and fine automobilia.

C Wells Appraisals	**appraisals**
1220 Redwood Ln	
Selma, CA 93662	
559-896-2607	
E-mail: cwellsclassic@aol.com	

Specializing in appraisals for 1940s, 1950s, 1960s autos. Member of IAAA, #1004020099.

James Wood	**appraisals**
1102 E Jefferson St	
Mishawaka, IN 46545	
219-256-0239; FAX: 219-254-2722	
E-mail: jimwood67@hotmail.com	

Specializing in street rods, muscle cars, Corvettes, 1932-1948 Fords. Certified appraisals for automobiles. IAAA (member #1004270097), ASA, ISA, NIADA, IIADA, AAA, NADA Appraisal Guides, advisory board.

Yesterday's Auto Sales	**appraisals**
2800 Lyndale Ave S	**car dealer**
Minneapolis, MN 55408	
612-872-9733; FAX: 612-872-1386	
E-mail: al-hagen@yesterdaysauto.com	

See full listing in **Section Two** under **car dealers**

artwork

Anderson's Car Door Monograms	**car door monograms**
32700 Coastsite #102	
Rancho Palos Verdes, CA 90275	
800-881-9049, 310-377-1007	

See full listing in **Section Two** under **accessories**

Antique Car Paintings	**color prints**
6889 Fairwood	**ink drawings**
Dearborn Heights, MI 48127	**original**
313-274-7774	**illustrations**

Mail order and open shop. Monday-Saturday 9 am to 5 pm. Retired Ford Motor Co artist with 50 years' experience. Have painted 1,205 original paintings of old cars. Also full color prints of 1932 Fords, 1936 Fords, Model As and 40 Fords, 1932 Duesenberg roadster, 1930 Cadillac roadster, 1934 Packard touring, 1930 Rolls-Royce touring.

Auto Art by Paul G McLaughlin	**artwork**
2720 Tennessee NE	**toys**
Albuquerque, NM 87110	
505-296-2554	

Mail order only. Automotive art in pen and ink, pencil, oil and watercolor. Photographs, toys and other auto memorabilia.

Automotive Art Specialties	**drawings**
Dan McCrary	**paintings**
PO Box 18795	**prints**
Charlotte, NC 28218	
704-372-2899; FAX: 704-375-8686	
E-mail: mccrarydan@aol.com	

Any day by appointment. Original water color paintings, drawings and limited edition prints on a wide variety of automotive subjects.

Automotive Fine Art	**artwork**
37986 Tralee Trail	
Northville, MI 48167	
248-476-9529	

Mail order and studio open by appointment only. Specializing in original, dramatic works of automotive art in permanent medium. Signed and numbered print editions of classic automobiles by artist Tom Hale. Variety of automotive posters available.

Automotive Fine Art Society Journal	**periodical**
PO Box 325, Dept HMN	
Lake Orion, MI 48361-0325	
PH/FAX: 810-814-0627	

See full listing in **Section Four** under **periodicals**

Barnett Design Inc	**models**
PO Box 160	
Twin Lakes, WI 53181	
262-877-9343; FAX: 262-877-9320	

See full listing in **Section Two** under **models & toys**

Blackhawk Editions	**automotive prints**
1092 Eagles Nest Pl	
Danville, CA 94506	
925-736-3444; FAX: 925-736-4375	
E-mail: auto@blackhawkart.com	

Publishers of limited edition automotive canvas and paper prints of historic motor racing scenes. Web site: www.blackhawkart.com

John E Boehm	**artwork**
T/A Boehm Design Ltd	
PO Box 9096	
Silver Spring, MD 20916	
301-649-6449	

Automotive art renderings of antique, classic, special interest and other historic and modern day automobiles. Artist drawings of buildings (both residential and commercial with or without cars). Also original automotive styling, designs for individual need or for corporations and art illustrations for publicity or promotional uses.

Francois Bruere	**artwork**
8 Avenue Olivier Heuze	
LeMans 72000 France	
(33) 02-4377-1877	
FAX: (33) 02-4324-2038	
E-mail: francois.bruere@	
orpheograff.com	

Specializing in artwork, hyperrealism paintings, limited editions for Harley-Davidson, Ferrari, Jaguar, American cars and ACO. Official painter for the 24 hours of LeMans races (exhibitions in Europe, USA, Japan, ask for dates and catalogues). Web site: www.orpheograff.com

Car Collectables	**banks**
32 White Birch Rd	**Christmas cards**
Madison, CT 06443	**note cards**
PH/FAX: 203-245-9203	

Mail order only. Company geared specifically to meet the interests of collectors, restorers and all those who appreciate vintage automobiles. Offer holiday greeting cards, beautifully illustrated in full color, as well as note cards, metal car coin banks and many other fine gift items, all with antique car motifs.

Cardmakers	cards
66 High Bridge Rd	
Lyme, NH 03768	
603-795-4422; FAX: 603-795-4222	
E-mail: info@cardmakers.com	

See full listing in **Section Two** under **automobilia**

Ceramicar	auto-related ceramics
679 Lapla Rd	
Kingston, NY 12401	
PH/FAX: 845-338-2199	

Manufacture ceramic automobile cookie jars. Handmade in the USA. Signed and dated in limited editions of 200. Body styles are not model or year specific. They are fantasy cars that combine typical design elements of the 1930s, 1940s and 1950s. Styles include taxis, police and fire chief's cars, convertibles, ice cream, pick-up and delivery trucks. Big (14"x9"x9"), colorful and chromy, prices average around $300. Personalization available. Please call or write for a price list and dazzling photo.

Chief Studios	artwork novelties
1903 Greenview Pl SW	
Rochester, MN 55902	
507-271-7435	

Mail order only. Specializing in graphic designs, motorsport designs for T-shirts, posters. Chief Studio designs, muscle cars, drag racing (NHRA, IHRA approved).

Classic Car Publications	calendars
292 S Mount Zion Rd	
Milltown, IN 47145	
812-633-7826	

Mail order only. Personalized calendars of your car photos. Send 6 photos repeated for $17.95 or 12 photos, $24.95. Send check or money order (includes s&h), include name, address, phone and name to appear on calendar.

Robert W Cook Corvette Art	appraisals artwork
8047 Moss Meadows Dr	
Dallas, TX 75231	
214-349-6232; FAX: 214-692-7286	
E-mail: prelim@cs.com	

Mail order only. Specializing in automotive art (watercolor prints), Corvette consulting and Corvette appraisals for 1953-1982 Corvettes only. Web site: www.robertwcook.com

Chris Davis	bronzes
The Old Vicarage	
49 Yates Hay Rd, Malvern Link	
Worcestershire, WR14 1LH England	
PH/FAX: 01684-560410	

Bronze automotive sculptures including Maserati 250F and Aston Martin DBR1. Web site: www.motorart.co.uk

Driven By Desire	automobilia car dealer models
300 N Fraley St	
Kane, PA 16735	
814-837-7590; FAX: 814-837-6850	
E-mail: driven@penn.com	

See full listing in **Section Two** under **car dealers**

Gaylord Sales	automobilia automotive art mascots
Frank Ranghelli	
125 Dugan Ln	
Toms River, NJ 08753	
732-349-9213; FAX: 732-341-5353	
E-mail: fgaylordsales@aol.com	

See full listing in **Section Two** under **radiator emblems & mascots**

Guenther Graphics	artwork
PO Box 266	
LeClaire, IA 52753	
PH/FAX: 319-289-9010	
E-mail: artwork@guenthergraphics.com	

Mail order and open shop. Monday-Saturday 8 am to 8 pm Central time. Specializing in automotive and racing art, full service illustration, fine art and commercial services, online gallery and samples. Hand-rendered full color artwork of your vehicle, unframed and framed. Computer rendered artwork of your vehicle with specific sponsor logos and colors for sponsor presentation proposals. Brochures, flyers, business cards, newsletters, logos, posters and T-shirt designs for individuals and clubs. Cars, trucks, motorcycles, boats, planes, trailers, pitcarts, buildings, homes, products and more can be illustrated. Call Douglas Guenther for quotes. To view samples visit our web site: www.guenthergraphics.com

Harbort Automotive Art	artwork
805 7th St NW	
Minot, ND 58703	
701-838-1808	
E-mail: bsbort@minot.com	

Mail order only. Automotive art featuring a variety of American muscle cars. Web site: www.harbort.com

Hot Rod Art	artwork
5880 Traffic Way	
Atascadero, CA 93422	
805-462-1934; FAX: 805-462-8621	
E-mail: vonblekl@pacbell.net	

Over 30 artists' work in stock featuring junkyard scenes, dealerships, drive-ins, etc. Street rods, muscle cars and 1930s to 1970s specialty autos. Check out our web site: www.hotrodart.com

Wayne Huffaker, Automobilia Artist	artwork
925 S Mason Rd, Dept 168	
Katy, TX 77450	
281-579-8516	

Mail order only. Automobilia art, limited edition prints and commission auto art. Specialize in period service station, diner, restaurant scenes highlighting cars and trucks of the 1930s-1950s. Also have car-airplane art series.

Hurst Racing Tires/ **Traction By Hurst**	drag tires slicks
190 East Ave A, PO Box 278	
Wendell, ID 83355	
208-536-6236	

See full listing in **Section Two** under **tires**

Ideal Signs	lettering painting striping
4033 Ridgeway Rd	
Manchester, NJ 08759	
732-657-0100; FAX: 732-323-0390	
E-mail: idealsigns1@aol.com	

Lettering, striping, painting cars, trucks, race cars and other signs and banners.

Imaginographx
PO Box 95
Hawthorne, NJ 07506
800-848-9459
E-mail: imaginographx@netscape.net

automotive portraits
automotive prints
idea renderings
logo designs

Photo realistic prints of your car; redesigned, restored or customized, without getting your hands dirty. Send your ideas with car photos and have them materialize in print. Great for pre-project stage or old memory restoration. Photos unharmed. Professional work by award winning artist/designer. Web site: www.imaginographx.com

Jack Juratovic
819 Absequami Trail
Lake Orion, MI 48362
PH/FAX: 248-814-0627

artwork
magazine

Mail order only. Fine art, limited edition auto art, corporate and private commissions. Publish *Automotive Art* magazine, *AFAS Journal*.

Kaiser Illustration
133 Troy-Schenectady Rd
Watervliet, NY 12189
PH/FAX: 518-272-0754
E-mail: brucekaiser@worldnet.att.net

automotive art
design
illustration

Mail order only. Kaiser Illustration offers Limited Edition automotive art prints by artist Bruce Kaiser. Also specialize in automotive commercial advertising, design, illustration and commissioned art. Web site: www.kaiserillustration.com

Dale Klee
25322 Eureka Ave
Wyoming, MN 55092
651-464-2200; FAX: 651-464-7688
E-mail: daleklee@oldcarart.com

fine art prints

Limited edition fine art prints with a rustic old car theme. Color brochures available. Prices range from $45-$75 per print. Web site: www.oldcarart.com

LA Ltd Design Graphics
822A S McDuffie St
Anderson, SC 29624
PH/FAX: 864-231-7715

artwork
design
greeting cards

See full listing in **Section Two** under **automobilia**

Legendary Motorcars LLC
34 Tuckahoe Rd, PMB #350
Marmora, NJ 08223
609-399-2401; FAX: 609-399-2512

model cars

See full listing in **Section Two** under **models & toys**

McIntyre Auctions
PO Box 60
East Dixfield, ME 04227
800-894-4300, 207-562-4443
FAX: 207-562-4576
E-mail: sue@classicford.com

auctions
automobilia
literature
petroliana

See full listing in **Section Two** under **auctions & shows**

Thomas Montanari
Automotive Artist
51 Lamb-Hope Rd
Hopewell, NJ 08525
609-466-7753; FAX: 609-466-7939
E-mail: tmontanari@aol.com

illustrations
paintings
prints

Mail order and open shop. Monday-Saturday 10 am to 5 pm. The aficionado who desires a one of a kind can commission Thom to produce an original painting of their collectible car. His illustrations, paintings and prints are found in corporate collections and private collections throughout the United States and Europe. Web site: www.avantimotorsports.com

Museum of Transportation
Larz Anderson Park
15 Newton St
Brookline, MA 02445
617-522-6547; FAX: 617-524-0170

museum

See full listing in **Section Six** under **Massachusetts**

Packard Archives
918 W Co Rd C-2
St Paul, MN 55113-1942
651-484-1184
E-mail: estatecars@earthlink.net

accessories
artwork
automobilia

See full listing in **Section One** under **Packard**

Paragon Models & Art
3570 North Rd
North Fort Myers, FL 33917
941-567-0047; FAX: 941-567-1344
E-mail: info@myhotrod.com

artwork
models

See full listing in **Section Two** under **automobilia**

Pelham Prints
2819 N 3rd St
Clinton, IA 52732-1717
563-242-0280

drawings
note cards

Mail order only. Antique or classic autos illustrated for note cards. Also pen and ink and scratchboard drawings of antique and classic autos. Write for free information.

Hugo Prado Limited Edition
Corvette Art Prints
PO Box 18437
Chicago, IL 60618-0437
PH/FAX: 773-681-7770
E-mail: vetteart@aol.com

fine art prints

See full listing in **Section One** under **Corvette**

Red Lion Racing
8318 Avenida Castro
Cucamonga, CA 91730
909-987-9818; FAX: 909-987-6538
E-mail: rlracing@cris.com

photographs
posters

Mail order and open shop anytime. Deal in reproduction auto, air and boat racing posters from the past. Also vintage auto racing photographs, 1912-1935. Poster catalog available for $3, refundable with your first order. Vintage auto racing photo catalog, *Ironmen/Ironcars*, is $10, also refundable with order. Web site: www.visref.com/redlion

Reni Studio
475 E Westfield Ave
Roselle Park, NJ 07204
PH/FAX: 908-245-1218
E-mail: renistudio@aol.com

crystal/glass/
mirror/metal/wood
carving
etching
portraiture

Auto portraiture, auto customizing art, fine engraving, fine and abrasive blasting, carving on glass, crystal, mirror, metal and wood monogramming and personalization, ID numbers engraved. Specialty original artwork. Also computer generated art. Commercial, residential, custom, decorative, restoration, signage.

Frank Riley Automotive Art
PO Box 95
Hawthorne, NJ 07506
800-848-9459
E-mail: rileystudio@netscape.net

automotive prints

Mail order only. Limited edition automotive prints by award winning artist. Museum quality printing on the best acid-free paper available. A beautiful investment, available framed or unframed. Brochure of all prints available upon request. Web site: www.frankriley.com/rileyprints.htm

Legends Live Forever.

They don't fade away.

Like your first road trip with your best friends, or that
'32 Ford your dad always talked about. You'll never forget
the GTO you saved up for by bagging groceries, or that
starry night in the Mustang.

The images and memories are here...In the great road
machines from days gone by. Legendary. Captured forever.

Check them out, online, at www.vintagegas.com.

vintagegas.com

RT-Designs USA — artwork
PO Box 2061
Salisbury, NC 28145
704-279-9301; FAX: 704-279-8019
E-mail: rtoth@salisbury.net

Automotive art: art, prints, paintings, sculpture, desk accessories of cars and other transportation art. All my original designs. Web site: www.roberttoth.com

Jack Schmitt Studio — paintings / prints
PO Box 1761
San Juan Capistrano, CA 92693
E-mail: jack_schmitt@msn.com

Gasoline classics, over 80 limited edition and open edition prints of carefully and accurately detailed paintings of vintage gasoline stations and classic cars from the 1930s-1960s. Catalog, $2, refundable on first purchase.

Jay Texter — photography
417 Haines Mill Rd
Allentown, PA 18104
610-821-0963
E-mail: jaytexter@ot.com

See full listing in **Section Two** under **photography**

Peter Tytla Artist — photographic collages
PO Box 43
East Lyme, CT 06333-0043
860-739-7105

Both mail order and open shop. Every day 9 am to 9 pm. Artwork/automotive art. Specializing in humorous photographic collages of rusty cars from the 1920s and 1930s. It takes 200 to 400 separate original photographs to create one image. 28 images available in four sizes, starting at $25. Framing (museum quality) approximately 25% below retail. Also specialize in personalization. I can put you, your family, car and dog, etc, in one of the images and it will appear that you are in it (only an additional $25).

Vintage Automotive Art — artwork / automobilia / literature dealers
PO Box 3702
Beverly Hills, CA 90212
310-278-0882; FAX: 310-278-0883
E-mail: artline1@pacbell.net

See full listing in **Section Two** under **automobilia**

Vintage Gas, Ltd — artwork
E-mail: info@vintagegas.com

Legends Live Forever. The images and memories are here... In the great road machines from days gone by. Legendary and captured forever in beautiful, precise renderings. These archival quality, limited edition lithographs of the classic cars from the 1970s and earlier are reasonably priced, and available framed or unframed. Check them out online at: www.vintagegas.com
See our ad on page 194

Walneck's Inc — motorcycles / murals / posters
7923 Janes Ave
Woodridge, IL 60517
630-985-4995; FAX: 630-985-2750

Posters and many size wall murals, up to 10' in length of many classic motorcycles. Some color posters. Penetrating oil. Call, fax or write for our free catalog of products.

Brady Ward-Scale Autoworks — models
313 Bridge St #4
Manchester, NH 03104-5045
PH/FAX: 603-623-5925

See full listing in **Section Two** under **models & toys**

Weber's Nostalgia Supermarket — collectibles / gas pump supplies / old photos / signs
6611 Anglin Dr
Fort Worth, TX 76119
817-534-6611; FAX: 817-534-3316

See full listing in **Section Two** under **novelties**

auctions & shows

Amherst Antique Auto Show — swap meets
157 Hollis Rd
Amherst, NH 03031
603-673-2093, NH
FAX: 617-641-0647, MA

Antique swap and sell meets. Last Sunday of each month, April-October (7 shows), open 6 am, since 1960. Largest in New Hampshire. 505 dealers, 150 show car spaces. Free admission, $5 site parking. Good food, beautiful grounds. Come have fun. Web site: www.amherstnhautoshow.com/

Archer & Associates — appraisals / consultant / expert witness / promotion / sales/purchasing
1807 East Ave
Hayward, CA 94541
510-581-4911
FAX: 510-537-7864

Office hours: Monday-Saturday 9 am to 10 pm. Call for appointment. Collector car consignment sales held three times annually at the San Mateo, CA Expo Center in February, June and October. Automotive historian, collector, expert witness, maximum qualifications. Nationwide service.

"The Auction" – Las Vegas — auction / dealer / events / expo / sales
3535 Las Vegas Blvd S
Las Vegas, NV 89109
702-794-3174; FAX: 702-369-7430
E-mail: info@vegasauction.com

Antique, classic and collector car auction and exposition sale, held at the Imperial Palace Hotel and Casino in Las Vegas, Nevada. For more information, contact Rob Williams, General Manager of The Auction. Web site: www.vegasauction.com

Auctioneer Phil Jacquier Inc — auctions
18 Klaus Anderson Rd
Southwick, MA 01077
413-569-6421; FAX: 413-569-6599
E-mail: info@jacquierauctions.com

Open shop only. Hours vary. Has been in the auction business for 30 years and can handle auctions of any type. Offers a complete, efficient service and consultation costs you nothing. Call or fax us your full address and types of auctions you attend to be on our mailing list, or log onto our web page to check out our auction calendar. Web site: www.jacquierauctions.com

Automobilia Auctions Inc — appraisals / auctions
132 Old Main St
Rocky Hill, CT 06067
860-529-7177; FAX: 860-257-3621

Mail order and open shop by appointment. No-reserve consignment auctions of automobilia, literature, petroliana, mascots, signs and other quality vintage auto collector's items from 1900-1970. Estates and appraisals a specialty.

Barrett-Jackson Auction Co LLC — auctions
3020 N Scottsdale Rd
Scottsdale, AZ 85251
480-421-6694; FAX: 480-421-6697
E-mail: info@barrett-jackson.com

Barrett-Jackson Auction is more than an auction, it is an automotive event. The world's greatest classic car auction which is held annually in January. The dates set for 2002 are January 16-20. Featuring classic, collectible, sports muscle, antique, fifties and sixties automobiles. Exposition of rare collectible cars are also shown. Web site: www.barrett-jackson.com

| **Bloomington Gold® Corvettes USA**
PO Box 457
Marengo, IL 60152
815-568-1960; FAX: 815-568-8650
E-mail: bginfo@bloomingtongold.com | **Corvette show** |

See full listing in **Section One** under **Corvette**

| **British Invasion Inc**
433 Mountain Rd
Stowe, VT 05672
802-253-5320; FAX: 802-253-8944
E-mail: englandinn@aol.com | **shows** |

Specializing in British classic and sports car shows for all cars manufactured in Great Britain. Web site: www.britishinvasion.com

| **Carlisle Productions**
1000 Bryn Mawr Rd
Carlisle, PA 17013-1588
717-243-7855; FAX: 717-243-0255
E-mail: cp@epix.net | **auctions**
car shows
flea markets |

2002 Carlisle collector car events, held at the Carlisle Pennsylvania Fairgrounds: Spring Carlisle, April 18-21; Custom Compact Power Jam, May 3-5; Import-Kit/Replicar Nationals, May 17-19; All-Ford Nationals, May 31-June 2; All-Truck Nationals, June 14-16; All-GM Nationals, June 28-30; All Chrysler Nationals, July 12-14; Summer Carlisle, July 26-28; Corvettes at Carlisle, August 23-25; Fall Carlisle, October 3-6. Call, fax, write or e-mail for a free event brochure. For a complete listing of all Carlisle events: www.carsatcarlisle.com

See our ad on this page

| **Central Florida Auto Festival**
& Toy Expo
1420 N Galloway Rd
Lakeland, FL 33810
863-686-8320 | **auto festival**
toy expo |

Central Florida Auto Festival and Toy Expo, February 9th-10th, 2002, USA International Speedway, Lakeland, FL, Exit 20 off I-4. 1,400 space swap meet and toy show, 900 show cars. 8 am to 4 pm both days. Admission $4, free parking. Call for information.

| **Chewning's Auto Literature**
2011 Elm Tree Terr
Buford, GA 30518
770-945-9795
E-mail: cchewy69@aol.com | **literature**
manuals |

See full listing in **Section Two** under **literature dealers**

| **Coys of Kensington**
2-4 Queen's Gate Mews
London SW7 5QJ England
0207-584-7444; FAX: 0207-584-2733
E-mail: auctions@
coys-of-kensington.co.uk
or sales@coys-of-kensington.co.uk | **auctions** |

Founded in 1919, one of Europe's oldest and best known specialists in the sale of historic motor cars. In addition to our many international auctions held annually, Coys' London showrooms always have a vast selection of both pre and post-war collectors' motor cars. Will travel anywhere in the world to obtain a classic motor car. For further information, please do not hesitate to contact us. Web site: www.coys.co.uk

| **George Cross & Sons Inc**
PO Box 3923
Tustin, CA 92781
714-538-7091; FAX: 714-538-7080
E-mail: pomonasm@pacbell.net | **car show**
swap meet |

George Cross & Sons Inc promotes The West Coast's Largest Antique Auto, Corvette, Porsche, Street Rod and Volkswagen Car Show and Swap Meet, 8 times a year, at Farplex in Pomona, California.

| **Cruisin for MDA**
969 Halifax Rd
Holts Summit, MO 65043
PH/FAX: 573-896-8330
E-mail: strobox@aol.com | **monthly cruise** |

Founded 2000. 10 members. This is a monthly cruise in downtown Jefferson City, MO. March-October, free to all, with swap meet. Dues: none.

| **Five Star Transport**
691 W Merrick Rd
Valley Stream, NY 11580
800-464-9965, 516-285-1077
FAX: 516-285-3729 | **transport** |

See full listing in **Section Two** under **transport**

| **Henry Ford Museum**
& Greenfield Village
20900 Oakwood Blvd
Dearborn, MI 48121-1970
313-271-1620; FAX: 313-982-6247 | **museum** |

See full listing in **Section Six** under **Michigan**

Fowlkes Realty & Auction Co
500 Hale St, PO Box 471
Newman Grove, NE 68758
800-275-5522; FAX: 402-447-6000
E-mail: fowlkes@megavision.com

appraisals
auctions

Classic and antique auctions and appraisals throughout the Midwest. Over 25 years' experience. Web site: www.fowlkesrealtyandauction.com

Gearhead Auction.com
32451 Park Ln
Garden City, MI 48135
734-422-7614; FAX: 734-422-9253
E-mail: info@gearheadauction.com

auctions

Specializing in auctions for all things mechanical. Web site: www.gearheadauction.com

Greater New York Automobile Dealers Association
18-10 Whitestone Expressway
Whitestone, NY 11357
718-746-5300; FAX: 718-746-9333
E-mail: darlene@autoshowny.com

book

See full listing in **Section Four** under **books & publications**

Harley Rendezvous Classic
1142 Batter St
Pattersonville, NY 12137
518-864-5659; FAX: 518-864-5917
E-mail: frank@harleyrendezvous.com

motorcycle events

See full listing in **Section Two** under **motorcycles**

Hot August Nights
1425 E Greg St
Sparks, NV 89431
775-356-1956; FAX: 775-356-1957
E-mail: info@hotaugustnights.net

car event

Founded 1986. 500+ members. Members must volunteer a minimum of 8 hours during the event. Members receive: polo shirt, hat, monthly 20 page newsletter, passes (access) to certain events; parties for members throughout the year. Publishes *Hot Flashes* monthly, $12/year. 20 page publication that features information on the Hot August Nights event, membership and car participant information, nostalgia highlights, automotive history. Nostalgic classic car event featuring cruising, show-n-shines, parade, free entertainment, drag races, swap meet, nostalgia fair, prom, sockhop, poker run, poker walk and much more. Dues: $25. Web site: www.hotaugustnights.net

International Classic Auctions
1265 S Gilbert Rd
Gilbert, AZ 85296
800-243-1957; FAX: 480-963-1277
E-mail: icaruth@hotmail.com

auctions

Web site: www.icaauctions.com

Iowa Gas Swap Meet
1739 E Grand Ave
Des Moines, IA 50316
515-276-2099, 515-251-8811
FAX: 515-265-5170
E-mail: iowagasjon@aol.com

auction
swap meet

Founded 1986. Largest oil, gas and auto related advertising collectibles show, swap meet and auctions. Held annually in August in Des Moines. Annual publication mailed following each year's event. Registration fee: $18/year. Web site: www.iowagas.com

Klassic Kolor Auctions
PO Box 55243
Hayward, CA 94545-0243
510-795-2776; FAX: 510-441-6050
E-mail: gentle_ben@easyriders.com

auction "color"
broadcaster
master of ceremonies

Michael Ben-Edward is a broadcaster, actor and the voice of *Easyriders Video Tapes* (Gentle Ben). Specializing in auction ring "color" of vintage and classic motorcycles, automobiles and airplanes.

Kruse International
5540 County Rd 11-A, PO Box 190
Auburn, IN 46706
800-968-4444; FAX: 219-925-5467

auctions

Open daily 8 am to 5 pm. Largest collector car auction company in the world. Also provide appraisals, private treaties. Conducts over 25 collector car events around the country. Call for free color brochure. Web site: www.kruseinternational.com

Col Glenn Larson
4415 Canyon Dr
Amarillo, TX 79110
806-358-9797; FAX: 806-467-0280
E-mail: colonel@arn.net

appraisals
auctioneer

See full listing in **Section Two** under **appraisals**

The Latest Scoop –
Auto Enthusiast Magazine
PO Box 7477
Loveland, CO 80537-0477
970-686-6155
E-mail: scoopautoevents@aol.com

periodical

See full listing in **Section Four** under **periodicals**

M & S Enterprises
PO Box 2055
Valparaiso, IN 46384-2055
219-464-9918

auction

Held in August (two weeks before Labor Day). Annual Midwest Corvette and Chevy show, swap and auction. Big swap meet, 42 class Chevy show, giant foodfest, beer garden and more. Call for free brochure.

McIntyre Auctions
PO Box 60
East Dixfield, ME 04227
800-894-4300, 207-562-4443
FAX: 207-562-4576
E-mail: sue@classicford.com

auctions
automobilia
literature
petroliana

Mail order and open shop. Monday-Friday 9 am to 5 pm, closed Saturday. Established January 15, 1976. Specializing in automobilia, toys, literature and petroliana. Call for details. Web site: www.classicford.com

Dana Mecum Auctions Inc
Box 422
Marengo, IL 60152
815-568-8888; FAX: 815-568-6615
E-mail: info@mecumauction.com

collector car
auctions

Mail order and open shop. Monday-Friday 9 am to 5 pm, Saturday by appointment. Over 30 main auction events nationwide annually. Professional full service automobile auction service. Specializing in auctioning of Corvettes, hot rods and muscle cars. Purveyor of 1950s, 1960s, sports, classics and vintage race cars. Offices located in Marengo, Illinois. Web site: www.mecumauction.com

**Michigan Antique
& Collectible Festivals**
2156 N Rudy Ct
Midland, MI 48642
989-687-9001; FAX: 989-687-7116

*auto show
swap meet*

Monday-Friday 7 pm to 9 pm. Held at Midland, Michigan, fair-grounds, 2001 dates: September 22-23; 2002 dates: June 1-2, July 27-28, September 21-22; 2003 dates: May 31-June 1, July 26-27, September 27-28. Featuring Michigan's largest special interest auto sales lot. For sale (and show) autos register at gate. Swap spaces by advance only. Write or call for information. Web site: www.miantiquefestival.com

Mid-America Auctions
2277 W Hwy 36, Ste 324
St Paul, MN 55113
651-633-9655; FAX: 651-633-3212
E-mail: midauction@aol.com

auctions

Classic, collector and special interest automobile auctions. Motorcycle auctions, automobile and motorcycle appraisals. Web site: www.midamerica-auctions.com

Museum of Transportation
Larz Anderson Park
15 Newton St
Brookline, MA 02445
617-522-6547; FAX: 617-524-0170

museum

See full listing in **Section Six** under **Massachusetts**

Niagara CHT Productions Inc
PO Box 112
Akron, NY 14001
716-542-2585

swap meets

"Niagara" gigantic auto swap meet and car shows; June 23-24, 2001, Niagara County fairgrounds, Lockport, New York.

Nostalgia Productions Inc
268 Hillcrest Blvd
St Ignace, MI 49781
906-643-8087; FAX: 906-643-9784
E-mail: edreavie@nostalgia-prod.com

*shows
swap meets*

Production of auto, truck, toy shows, swap meets and cruise nights. From pedal cars to 18 wheelers. Web sites: www.nostalgia-prod.com or www.auto-shows.com

NW Cruisers
5701 Orchard St W #EE2
Tacoma, WA 98467
253-474-3395; FAX: 253-474-2205
E-mail: touche214@aol.com

cruz-ins

Founded 2000. 18 members. Host for the Cruz-in at Freddie's in Fife, WA on Friday nights, charity show in September and Father's Day Cruz-in (*Hemmings*). Cruz-in for 1900-2002 cars, trucks, motor-cycles, race cars, street rods, classics at Freddie's Club Casino. Dues: none. Web site: www.geocities.com/nw_cruisers/main.html

Old Bridge Township Raceway Park
230 Pension Rd
Englishtown, NJ 07726
732-446-7800; FAX: 732-446-1373
E-mail: etownrcwy@aol.com

*shows
swap meets*

A facility that presents auto shows and swap meets. Web site: www.etownraceway.com

**Old Gold Retold Inc
Florida Swap Meets**
6250 Tennessee Ave
New Port Richey, FL 34653
800-438-8559; FAX: 727-846-8922
E-mail: swapmet@gte.net

*auction
car show
swap meet*

Automotive swap meet, car show, car corral, 1st Sunday of each month except for July/August. Visit us at our web site: www.floridaswapmeets.net

Old Rhinebeck Aerodrome
Stone Church & Norton Rd
Rhinebeck, NY 12572
845-752-3200; FAX: 845-758-6481

museum

See full listing in **Section Six** under **New York**

Palm Springs Exotic Car Auctions
602 E Sunny Dunes Rd
Palm Springs, CA 92264
760-320-3290; FAX: 760-323-7031
E-mail: classicauction@msn.com

auctions

Sale of 350 antique, classic and special interest autos. Held at the Palm Springs Convention Center, last weekend in February and 3rd weekend in November each year. Web site: www.classic-caruction.com

Pate Swap Meet
Registrar
7751 Oak Vista
Houston, TX 77087
713-649-0922

swap meet

Third largest swap meet in US. Held every April at the Texas Motor Speedway in Fort Worth, TX.

Lloyd Ralston Gallery
350 Long Beach Blvd
Stratford, CT 06615
203-386-9399; FAX: 203-386-9519
E-mail: lrgallery@aol.com

toys

See full listing in **Section Two** under **models & toys**

RM Classic Cars
5 W Forest Ave
Ypsilanti, MI 48197
734-547-2400; FAX: 734-547-9424
E-mail: michigan@rmcars.com

auctions

Specializing in collector car auctions for all makes and models. Collector car sales. Web site: www.rmcars.com

Route 66 Corvette Show
2419 A W Jefferson
Joliet, IL 60435
815-722-8388; FAX: 815-733-8389
E-mail: acs@corvetteshow.com

car show

A major Corvette show event that includes: drag racing, autocross, swap meet, driving schools and fun. Web site: www.corvetteshow.com

Alfred P Sloan Museum
1221 E Kearsley St
Flint, MI 48503
810-237-3450; FAX: 810-237-3451

museum

See full listing in **Section Six** under **Michigan**

Sparrow Auction Co
59 Wheeler Ave
Milford, CT 06460
203-877-1066
E-mail: sparrowauction@hotmail.com

auction company

Both mail order and open shop by appointment. Full service auction company specializing in the auction of anything for and related to automobiles including automobiles, models, parts, literature and salvage. Will travel anywhere or you may consign items to our local auctions. We will also prepare and place items on eBay. Experience in the auction of insurance salvage and the auction of salvage yards.

Springfield Swap Meet & Car Show	**swap meet**
492 W 2nd St, Ste 204	
Xenia, OH 45385	
937-376-0111; FAX: 937-372-1171	
E-mail: wirth4@siscom.net	

Calendar of events: fall show, September 7-9, 2001; winter show, November 10-11, 2001. Cars and Parts Springfield swap meet and car show at Clark County Fairgrounds, I-70 Exit 59, Springfield, OH. Hundreds of vendors, cars for sale and show cars. Ohio's largest event of its type. Call or write to the above address for info and/or free brochure. Web site: www.ohioswapmeet.com

Start/Finish Productions	**swap meets**
PO Box 2124	
Vernon, CT 06066-5124	
860-871-6376	

Autoparts Swap n' Sell. All automotive swap meet, 300 vendors, one million parts, 12x15 ft space. Antique, classic, special interest. January 19-20, 2002, Eastern States Expo, indoors, Springfield, MA, 30,000 attend.

Towe Auto Museum	**museum**
2200 Front St	
Sacramento, CA 95818	
916-442-6802; FAX: 916-442-2646	
E-mail: khartley@toweautomuseum.org	

See full listing in **Section Six** under **California**

Trunzo's Antique Cars	**antique cars**
4213 Ohio River Blvd	**auctions**
Pittsburgh, PA 15202	**restorations**
412-734-0717	

Auctions and events. Complete and partial restorations. Antique cars bought and sold.

Zephyrhills Festivals and Auction Inc	**auction**
PO Box 996	**swap meet**
Odessa, FL 33556-0996	
813-258-6726 office	
813-782-0835 park	
FAX: 813-258-3779	

Giant automotive, antique and collectibles swap meet, with car corral, collector car auction, dirt track vintage auto racing and classic car show. Four day events (Thursday-Sunday) held twice each year. Fall event in November, two weekends before Thanksgiving (17th year in 2001); winter event in February, weekend after President's Day (28th year in 2002). Call for information on selling cars or becoming a bidder. Web site: www.zephyrhillsswapmeet.com

automobilia

Accent Models Inc	**die cast models**
PO Box 295	
Denville, NJ 07834	
973-887-8403; FAX: 973-887-5088	

See full listing in **Section Two** under **models & toys**

American Classics Unlimited Inc	**automobilia**
PO Box 192-V	**models**
Oak Lawn, IL 60454-0192	**toys**
PH/FAX: 708-424-9223	

See full listing in **Section Two** under **models & toys**

Auctioneer Phil Jacquier Inc	**auctions**
18 Klaus Anderson Rd	
Southwick, MA 01077	
413-569-6421; FAX: 413-569-6599	
E-mail: info@jacquierauctions.com	

See full listing in **Section Two** under **auctions & shows**

Auto Art by Paul G McLaughlin	**artwork**
2720 Tennessee NE	**toys**
Albuquerque, NM 87110	
505-296-2554	

See full listing in **Section Two** under **artwork**

The Auto Collections at the Imperial Palace	**museum**
3535 Las Vegas Blvd S	
Las Vegas, NV 89109	
702-794-3174; FAX: 702-369-7430	
E-mail: info@autocollections.com	

See full listing in **Section Six** under **Nevada**

Auto Etc Neon	**signs**
PO Box 531992	**time pieces**
Harlingen, TX 78553	
PH/FAX: 956-425-7487	

See full listing in **Section One** under **Corvette**

Auto Motif Inc	**automobilia**
2941 Atlanta Rd SE	**models**
Smyrna, GA 30080-3654	**signs**
770-435-5025; FAX: 413-521-5298	
E-mail: automotifinc@aol.com	

Mail order and open shop. Tuesday-Saturday 10 am to 6 pm. Automobilia retailer, ie: kits, models, books, magazines, glassware, posters, key rings, reproduction signs and more.

Auto Zone	**books**
33202 Woodward Ave	**magazines**
Birmingham, MI 48009	**models**
800-647-7288; FAX: 248-646-5381	**videos**
E-mail: info@azautozone.com	

See full listing in **Section Two** under **models & toys**

AutoGuide.net	**automotive**
150 Consumers Rd, Ste 403	**directory**
Toronto, ON Canada M2J 1P9	
416-499-8351	
E-mail: info@autoguide.net	

See full listing in **Section Four** under **information sources**

Autohobbies	**memorabilia**
Jim & Nancy Schaut	**toys**
7147 W Angela Dr	
Glendale, AZ 85308	
623-878-4293	
E-mail: nancy@autohobbies.com	

Mail order and Internet only. We buy collections. We sell antique toys, auto advertising and racing memorabilia. Web site: http://autohobbies.com

Automobilia	**gas pumps**
200 N Emporia	**models**
Wichita, KS 67202	**signs**
PH/FAX: 316-264-9986	
E-mail: automobilia@juno.com	

Mail order and open shop. Monday-Saturday 10 am to 5:30 pm. Automobilia has been in operation for 21 years. We carry gas pumps and restoration supplies, all types of signs, clocks, neon, pedal cars, model kits, T-shirts, books, decals, die cast cars, hats, license tags and frames. Sorry, no catalog available at this time. Check us out at our web site: www.automobiliausa.com

Automobilia	models
Division of Lustron Industries	
18 Windgate Dr	
New City, NY 10956	
PH/FAX: 845-639-6806	
E-mail: lustron@worldnet.att.net	

See full listing in **Section Two** under **models & toys**

Automobilia Auctions Inc	appraisals
132 Old Main St	auctions
Rocky Hill, CT 06067	
860-529-7177; FAX: 860-257-3621	

See full listing in **Section Two** under **auctions & shows**

Automobilia International	automobilia
PO Box 606	
Peapack, NJ 07977	
732-469-9666	

By appointment only. Buying and selling automobilia of all kinds. Especially auto racing. Yearly auctions.

Automotive Art Specialties	drawings
Dan McCrary	paintings
PO Box 18795	prints
Charlotte, NC 28218	
704-372-2899; FAX: 704-375-8686	
E-mail: mccrarydan@aol.com	

See full listing in **Section Two** under **artwork**

Barnett Design Inc	models
PO Box 160	
Twin Lakes, WI 53181	
262-877-9343; FAX: 262-877-9320	

See full listing in **Section Two** under **models & toys**

Berliner Classic Motorcars Inc	automobilia
1975 Stirling Rd	car dealer
Dania Beach, FL 33004	motorcycles
954-923-7271; FAX: 954-926-3306	
E-mail: info@berlinerclassiccars.com	

See full listing in **Section Two** under **car dealers**

Big Boys' Toys Inc	neon clocks
1214 E Bunn Ave #13	
Springfield, IL 62703	
217-585-9939; FAX: 217-585-9941	

Mail order only. Neon clocks, stylized with antique auto, gasoline and sodaware images.

Blast From the Past	neon clocks
21006 Cornhusker Rd	neon signs
Gretna, NE 68028	
402-332-5050; FAX: 402-332-5029	
E-mail: blast2past@aol.com	

Mail order and open shop. Monday-Friday 9 am to 5 pm. Custom neon signs and clocks are our specialty. Manufacture and distribute nostalgic neons of all types, todays highest quality with the look of yesterday. Satisfaction guaranteed. Great for garage, office, showroom, etc. Many old auto themes. Also custom restoration services for old soda machines, gas pumps, pedal cars, etc. Original advertising signs (auto dealership neon and non-neon, soda, gas/oil) also bought, sold, traded. Your one stop nostalgic shop. Web site: http://pmadt.com/blastpast

John E Boehm	artwork
T/A Boehm Design Ltd	
PO Box 9096	
Silver Spring, MD 20916	
301-649-6449	

See full listing in **Section Two** under **artwork**

British Only Motorcycles and	literature
Parts Inc	memorabilia
32451 Park Ln	motorcycles
Garden City, MI 48135	parts
734-421-0303; FAX: 734-422-9253	
E-mail: info@britishonly.com	

See full listing in **Section Two** under **motorcycles**

C&N Reproductions Inc	pedal cars
1341 Ashover Ct	
Bloomfield Hills, MI 48304	
248-853-0215; FAX: 248-852-1999	
E-mail: ckcn@ix.netcom.com	

Mail order and open shop. Monday-Friday 9 am to 4 pm. Deals in pedal cars, pedal planes and parts. Web site: www.pedalcar.com

Caddytown™/Pawl Engineering Co	memorabilia
4960 Arrowhead, PO Box 240105	parts
West Bloomfield, MI 48324	toys
PH/FAX: 248-682-2007	
E-mail: pawl@earthlink.net	

See full listing in **Section One** under **Cadillac/LaSalle**

The Can Corner	audio tapes
PO Box VA 1173	
Linwood, PA 19061	

Mail order only. Have been providing old car commercials on audio tape for the past 20 years. Now has over 100 1 hour tapes (each different). Will research history of old time radio shows with car ads on them. Have list to send free with any order of old commercials upon request. Have over 3,000 different old time commercials from 1932 to 1975 and many modern such as DeSoto, Chrysler, Hudson, Nash, Studebaker, Willys, etc. Also has complete radio shows, prices upon request.

Cardmakers	cards
66 High Bridge Rd	
Lyme, NH 03768	
603-795-4422; FAX: 603-795-4222	
E-mail: info@cardmakers.com	

Mail order only. Publishes special holiday greeting cards for automobile enthusiasts. Web site: www.automobilecard.com or www.cardmakers.com

Castle Display Case Co	models
102 W Garfield Ave	
New Castle, PA 16105-2544	
724-654-6358	

See full listing in **Section Two** under **models & toys**

Central Florida Auto Festival	auto festival
& Toy Expo	toy expo
1420 N Galloway Rd	
Lakeland, FL 33810	
863-686-8320	

See full listing in **Section Two** under **auctions & shows**

Michael Chapman   automobilia
Priorsleigh, Mill Ln
Cleeve Prior
Worcestershire, WR11 5JZ England
0044-1789-773897
FAX: 0044-1789-773588

Mail order and open shop by prior appointment only. Specialize in Rolls-Royce/Bentley, Hispano and quality vehicle parts. Finest selection veteran, Edwardian, vintage lamps, horns, emblems, instruments, books, badges, tools, mascots, etc, all makes, 1890-1980. The finest selection in Europe. No inquiry is too large or too small. Also high-wheeler bicycles and cycling memorabilia sometimes available.

Chewning's Auto Literature   literature
2011 Elm Tree Terr   manuals
Buford, GA 30518
770-945-9795
E-mail: cchewy69@aol.com

See full listing in **Section Two** under **literature dealers**

Classic Car Publications   calendars
292 S Mount Zion Rd
Milltown, IN 47145
812-633-7826

See full listing in **Section Two** under **artwork**

Classic Impressions Inc   accessories
PO Box 691167
Houston, TX 77379
800-252-3435; FAX: 281-251-2020
E-mail: sales@classicimpressions.com

See full listing in **Section Two** under **accessories**

Classic Mercury Parts   parts
1393 Shippee Ln
Ojai, CA 93023
805-646-3345; FAX: 805-646-5386
E-mail: mfourez@aol.com

See full listing in **Section One** under **Mercury**

The Classic Motorist   automobilia
PO Box 363   books & publications
Rotterdam Junction, NY 12150-0363

See full listing in **Section One** under **Packard**

Coker Tire   tires
1317 Chestnut St
Chattanooga, TN 37402
800-251-6336 toll free
423-265-6368 local & international
FAX: 423-756-5607

See full listing in **Section Two** under **tires**

Collectibles For You   memorabilia
6001 Canyon Rd
Harrisburg, PA 17111
717-558-2653; FAX: 717-558-7325
E-mail: cllect4you@aol.com

Mail order only. Porcelain reproduction auto signs, copper automotive printers' blocks, auto pins and jewelry. Coca-Cola, Pepsi and 1950s collectibles.

Creative Products of Minnesota Inc   mailbox
400 N Seeley Ave
Dunnell, MN 56127
507-695-2301; FAX: 507-695-2302
E-mail: crprod@frontiernet.net

Mail order only. Fiberglass mailbox of a 1930s style coupe car and 1930s style coupe pickup.

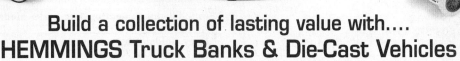

Cruising International Inc	automobilia
1000 N Beach St	belt buckles
Daytona Beach, FL 32117	decals/lapel pins
386-254-8753; FAX: 386-255-2460	license plates
E-mail: sales@cruising-intl.com	novelties

See full listing in **Section Two** under **license plates**

Chris Davis	bronzes
The Old Vicarage	
49 Yates Hay Rd, Malvern Link	
Worcestershire, WR14 1LH England	
PH/FAX: 01684-560410	

See full listing in **Section Two** under **artwork**

DeLorean Literature	collectibles
3116 Welsh Rd	literature
Philadelphia, PA 19136-1810	
215-338-6142; PH/FAX: 888-392-4832	
ext 291-291-1979 (* for fax)	
E-mail: delorean.literature@excite.com	

See full listing in **Section One** under **DeLorean**

DETAILS License Plate Restoration	license plates
74 Montague City Rd	
Greenfield, MA 01301	
413-774-6982	
E-mail: jeri@valinet.com	

See full listing in **Section Two** under **license plates**

Driven By Desire	automobilia
300 N Fraley St	car dealer
Kane, PA 16735	models
814-837-7590; FAX: 814-837-6850	
E-mail: driven@penn.com	

See full listing in **Section Two** under **car dealers**

Emblemagic Co	decorative
PO Box 420	emblems
Grand River, OH 44045-0420	plastic insert
440-209-0792	emblems
E-mail: emblemagic@aol.com	

See full listing in **Section Two** under **grille emblem badges**

Enthusiast's Specialties	automobilia
350 Old Connecticut Path	
Framingham, MA 01701	
800-718-3999; FAX: 508-872-4914	
E-mail: alvis1934@aol.com	

Mail order only. Import fine English hampers (picnic baskets). Also supply logo cap tire valves, vintage motorsport photography, grille badges, lapel pins and "country of origin" magnetic plates. Single issues and complete years of *Road & Track* and *Car & Driver* as well as back issues of *Autocar* (England). Specializing in European marques, European manfacturer inquiries invited. Web site: www.classic-sportscar.com

Eurosport Daytona Inc	license plates
355 Tomoka Ave	
Ormond Beach, FL 32174-6222	
800-874-8044, 904-672-7199	
FAX: 904-673-0821	

See full listing in **Section Two** under **license plates**

Daniel A Evans	literature
2850 John St	parts
Easton, PA 18045	
610-258-9542 after 5:30 pm	
FAX: 610-252-0370	
E-mail: evansd@lafayette.edu	

See full listing in **Section One** under **Ford 1954-up**

EWA & Miniature Cars USA Inc	books
205 US Hwy 22	models
Green Brook, NJ 08812-1909	subscriptions
732-424-7811; FAX: 732-424-7814	videos
E-mail: ewa@ewacars.com	

See full listing in **Section Two** under **models & toys**

Fill Er Up	automobilia
Brian Steiner	petroliana
2613 Old Philadelphia Pike	
PO Box 406	
Bird In Hand, PA 17505	
717-397-2519	

Mail order and open shop. Wednesday-Saturday 10 am to 5 pm. Automobilia, petroliana, new and old collectables. Located in center of Amish farmlands. Books, gas pumps, signs, clocks, automotive art and antiques.

Gaylord Sales	automobilia
Frank Ranghelli	automotive art
125 Dugan Ln	mascots
Toms River, NJ 08753	
732-349-9213; FAX: 732-341-5353	
E-mail: fgaylordsales@aol.com	

See full listing in **Section Two** under **radiator emblems & mascots**

Get It On Paper	automobilia
Gary Weickart, President	literature
185 Maple St	toys
Islip, NY 11751	
631-581-3897	

Mail order and open shop. Every Saturday 12 noon to 5 pm. Offer sales brochures, original ads, shop manuals and owner's manuals for your old cars and trucks. Also a nice selection of automotive books and magazines, models, toys, license plates, old advertising signs and the occasional old car. We need to acquire your model kit collection (either built or unbuilt). Call or send your list with prices for an immediate answer.

GMP (Georgia Marketing & Promotions)	die cast replicas
PO Box 570	
Winder, GA 30680	
800-536-1637, 770-307-1042	
FAX: 770-867-0786	
E-mail: peachgmp@peachgmp.com	

See full listing in **Section Two** under **models & toys**

Jerry Goldsmith Promos	models
4634 Cleveland Heights	
Lakeland, FL 33813	
863-644-7013, 863-646-8490	
PH/FAX: 863-644-5013	
E-mail: shirley.goldsmith@gte.net	

Mail order and open shop. Tuesday-Saturday 10 am to 6 pm. Corvette and Chevrolet promotional models from 1953-present. Also other automobilia. Same day shipping. Price list available upon request. Visa/MC.

Grandpa's Attic	toys
112 E Washington	
Goshen, IN 46528	
219-534-2778	

See full listing in **Section Two** under **models & toys**

The Gullwing Garage Ltd	appraisals
Bricklin SVI Specialists	literature
5 Cimorelli Dr	parts
New Windsor, NY 12553-6201	service
845-561-0019 anytime	

See full listing in **Section One** under **Bricklin**

Hale's Products 906 19th St Wheatland, WY 82201 800-333-0989	**license plates**

See full listing in **Section Two** under **license plates**

Richard Hamilton 28 E 46th St Indianapolis, IN 46205 317-283-1902	**sales literature**

See full listing in **Section Two** under **literature dealers**

Historic Video Archives PO Box 189-VA Cedar Knolls, NJ 07927-0189	**videotapes**

Mail order only. The greatest (often the only) source of original TV commercials and promo films on video for antique and classic cars 1935-1970. Tremendous selection, choose from over 1,000 titles! Auto racing, vintage TV shows, movies, documentaries, cartoons, newsreels, all kinds of rare footage. Tapes that cannot be found at local video stores, at prices the public can afford. Send $3 for our big illustrated catalog. Web site: www.historicvideoarchives.com

Horseplayactionwear.com 211 N Catherine Bay City, MI 48706 517-892-5509, 800-447-7669 FAX: 517-671-1003 E-mail: horsplay@concentric.net	**apparel** **decals** **gifts**

See full listing in **Section Two** under **apparel**

Hot Rod Coffee 1314 Rollins Rd Burlingame, CA 94010 650-348-8269; FAX: 650-340-9473 E-mail: hotrodcoffee@pacbell.net	**gourmet coffee**

See full listing in **Section Two** under **accessories**

Hot Rod Memories PO Box 280040 Northridge, CA 91328-0040 818-886-7637; FAX: 818-349-1403 E-mail: sales@hotrodmemories.com	**videos**

See full listing in **Section Four** under **information sources**

Hot Rod Nostalgia™ PO Box 249 West Point, CA 95255-0249 209-293-2114; FAX: 209-293-2120 E-mail: hvaa@hotrodnostalgia.com	**"magalog"**

See full listing in **Section Four** under **books & publications**

Hot Rod Things PO Box 898 Washougal, WA 98671 360-835-8661; FAX: 360-835-7215 E-mail: dave@hotrodthings.com	**posters** **T-shirts**

Mail order only. Hot Rod Things produces high quality reproductions of movie posters and lobby cards with a focus on hot rod and other automotive theme films from the 1930s through the 1960s. All images are available in 11x17 prints, 27x41 prints or printed on a T-shirt. Web site: www.hotrodthings.com

Hudson Motor Car Co Memorabilia Ken Poynter 19638 Huntington Harper Woods, MI 48225 313-886-9292	**literature** **memorabilia** **novelties** **signs**

See full listing in **Section One** under **Hudson**

Wayne Huffaker, Automobilia Artist 925 S Mason Rd, Dept 168 Katy, TX 77450 281-579-8516	**artwork**

See full listing in **Section Two** under **artwork**

Melissa & Jerry Jess 3121 E Yucca St Phoenix, AZ 85028 602-867-7672 E-mail: vwstuff@qwest.net	**accessories** **literature** **models**

See full listing in **Section One** under **Volkswagen**

Jesser's Classic Keys 26 West St, Dept HVA Akron, OH 44303-2344 330-376-8181; FAX: 330-384-9129	**automobilia** **keys**

See full listing in **Section Two** under **locks & keys**

Jack Juratovic 819 Absequami Trail Lake Orion, MI 48362 PH/FAX: 248-814-0627	**artwork** **magazine**

See full listing in **Section Two** under **artwork**

K&S Industries 1801 Union Center Hwy Endicott, NY 13760 PH/FAX: 888-PICK-KNS E-mail: pleximan@888pickkns.com	**display cases**

See full listing in **Section Two** under **models & toys**

Kaiser Illustration 133 Troy-Schenectady Rd Watervliet, NY 12189 PH/FAX: 518-272-0754 E-mail: brucekaiser@worldnet.att.net	**automotive art** **design** **illustration**

See full listing in **Section Two** under **artwork**

Karl's Collectibles 41 Chestnut St Lewiston, ME 04240 800-636-0457, 207-784-0098 FAX: 207-795-0295 E-mail: karl@designsbyskip.com	**banks** **collectibles** **logo design**

See full listing in **Section Two** under **models & toys**

David M King, Automotive Books 5 Brouwer Ln Rockville Centre, NY 11570 516-766-1561; FAX: 516-766-7502 E-mail: rollskingusa@yahoo.com	**literature**

See full listing in **Section One** under **Rolls-Royce/Bentley**

KJ Classic Metal Designs PO Box 663 Winder, GA 30680 770-867-4452; FAX: 770-586-0163 E-mail: kjclassic@mindspring.com	**toys**

Mail order only. Collectible toys made from pressed steel. 1969 Chevy pickup, 1960s delivery van and Buddy L and Metalcraft. Web site: www.kjclassic.com

The Klemantaski Collection 65 High Ridge Rd, Ste 219 Stamford, CT 06905 PH/FAX: 203-968-2970 E-mail: klemcoll@aol.com	**books photography**

See full listing in **Section Two** under **photography**

LA Ltd Design Graphics 822A S McDuffie St Anderson, SC 29624 PH/FAX: 864-231-7715	**artwork design greeting cards**

Christmas and all-occasion greeting cards featuring scenes with 1/43 scale die cast miniature cars and trucks, realistic detail. Also design old car event logos, produce newsletters and flyers, etc.

LaCarrera-The Mexican Road Race PO Box 1605 Studio City, CA 91614 323-464-5720; FAX: 323-656-7111 E-mail: lacarrera@earthlink.net	**road race**

See full listing in **Section Two** under **racing**

l'art et l'automobile Red Horse Plaza 74 Montauk Hwy East Hampton, NY 11937 516-329-8580; FAX: 516-329-8589 E-mail: jvautoart@aol.com	**artwork memorabilia**

Retail store and mail order. Specializing in automotive paintings, lithos, posters, models, toys, objects, sculptures, new and old books and memorabilia from the beginning of the automotive era to present. A unique place for the automotive enthusiast. Web site: www.arteauto.com

Legendary Motorcars LLC 34 Tuckahoe Rd, PMB #350 Marmora, NJ 08223 609-399-2401; FAX: 609-399-2512	**model cars**

See full listing in **Section Two** under **models & toys**

Dave Lincoln Box 331 Yorklyn, DE 19736 610-444-4144, PA E-mail: tagbarn@msn.com	**license plates**

See full listing in **Section Two** under **license plates**

Lone Wolf 9375 Bearwalk Path Brooksville, FL 34613 352-596-9949 E-mail: lonewolfwhistle@bigfoot.com	**wolf whistles**

Ding dong bells, all brass cups are polished. Wolf whistles, stainless steel. Also air horn kits and buyer/seller of used horns and whistles. Web site: www.lonewolfwhistle.com

George & Denise Long 891 E Court St Marion, NC 28752 828-652-9229 (24 hrs w/recorder)	**automobilia**

Mail order only. Broad range of automobilia, all makes, general to obscure. Emphasis on cars with promotional model cars, also other toy vehicle replicas, tin, rubber, die cast, plastic, ranging from Matchbox to pedal cars and large variety of discontinued model kits. Vast assortment with majority old and very little new items. Huge stock of automobile dealership/service station premiums such as porcelain signs, jewelry, banks, key chains, ashtrays, rulers, literature, trinkets, give-away novelties, etc; also miscellaneous NASCAR.

Larry Machacek PO Box 515 Porter, TX 77365 281-429-2505	**decals license plates novelties**

Sell self-adhesive vinyl decal reproductions of 1951-1975 Texas safety inspection stickers ($20 each), plus original Texas license plates (1917-1975) at various prices. Also sell reproduction WW II gasoline windshield ration stickers and posters from era photographs of cars.

Manchester Motor Car Co 319 Main St Manchester, CT 06040 860-643-5874; FAX: 860-643-6190 E-mail: mmcollc@aol.com	**automobilia parts petroliana restorations**

See full listing in **Section Two** under **comprehensive parts**

Max Neon Design Group 19807 Sussex Dr St Clair Shores, MI 48081-3257 810-773-5000; FAX: 810-772-6224	**custom face logos glass light-up clocks neon clocks**

Mail order only. Designer, manufacturer, distributor of replica neon and glass light-up clocks depicting automotive, petro, motorcycle, etc, face logos. Custom face logos for individual or corporate clients also available. Web site: www.maxneon.com

McCoy's Memorabilia 35583 N 1830 E Rossville, IL 60963-7175 PH/FAX: 217-748-6513 E-mail: indy500@soltec.net	**memorabilia racing literature**

See full listing in **Section Two** under **literature dealers**

McIntyre Auctions PO Box 60 East Dixfield, ME 04227 800-894-4300, 207-562-4443 FAX: 207-562-4576 E-mail: sue@classicford.com	**auctions automobilia literature petroliana**

See full listing in **Section Two** under **auctions & shows**

Mild to Wild Classics 1300 3rd St NW Albuquerque, NM 87102 505-244-1139; FAX: 505-244-1164	**parts repairs restoration**

See full listing in **Section Two** under **street rods**

Milestone Motorcars Mark Tyra 3317 Nevel Meade Dr Prospect, KY 40059 502-228-5945; FAX: 502-228-1856 E-mail: coolcars@ milestonemotorcars.com	**die cast cars**

See full listing in **Section Two** under **models & toys**

MITCHCO 1922 N Los Robles Ave Pasadena, CA 91104-1105 626-401-4303	**rubber stamps**

Mail order only. If you can't put the classic in your garage, you can put it on your business cards, checks or note cards with Cool Car Stamps by MITCHCO. Automobile rubber stamps of classic and vintage cars. Catalogue of images, $2 (refundable with first order). Wholesale and custom inquiries welcome.

Section Two – Generalists

Moroso Motorsports Park PO Box 31907 Palm Beach Gardens, FL 33420 561-622-1400; FAX: 561-626-2053 E-mail: mail@ morosomotorsportspark.com	**race track**

See full listing in **Section Two** under **racing**

MotoMedia PO Box 489 Lansdowne, PA 19050 PH/FAX: 610-623-6930 E-mail: motomedia@earthlink.net	**books** **magazines**

See full listing in **Section Two** under **literature dealers**

MotorCam Media 138 N Alling Rd Tallmadge, OH 44278 800-240-1777; FAX: 330-633-3249 E-mail: carvideo@motorcam.com	**automotive videos**

See full listing in **Section Two** under **videos**

MotorLit.com PO Box 4907 Mesa, AZ 85211-4907 480-969-0102 E-mail: info@motorlit.com	**books** **manuals** **memorabilia**

See full listing in **Section Two** under **literature dealers**

Mouldsworth Motor Museum Smithy Lane Mouldsworth NR Chester Cheshire CH3 8AR England 01928 731781	**museum**

See full listing in **Section Six** under **England**

Museum of Transportation Larz Anderson Park 15 Newton St Brookline, MA 02445 617-522-6547; FAX: 617-524-0170	**museum**

See full listing in **Section Six** under **Massachusetts**

NATMUS Roadside Market 1000 Gordon M Buehrig Pl Auburn, IN 46706 PH/FAX: 219-925-9100 E-mail: natmus@ctlnet.com	**automobilia**

Mail order and open shop. Daily 9 am to 5 pm. Books, models, toys, apparel, videos, publications, gifts, sculptures, etc, etc. General automobilia. Our shop is located at the National Automotive and Truck Museum of the United States (NATMUS).

Neumaclassic Ayacucho 1292 Rosario Sta Fe 2000 Argentina +54 341 425-0040 FAX: +54 341 421-9629 E-mail: bcdcs@bcd.com.ar	**tires**

See full listing in **Section Two** under **tires**

Dave Newell's Chevrobilia PO Box 588 Orinda, CA 94563 510-223-4725	**literature** **memorabilia**

See full listing in **Section One** under **Chevrolet**

NJ Nostalgia Hobby 401 Park Ave Scotch Plains, NJ 07076 908-322-2676; FAX: 908-322-4079 E-mail: njhobby@aol.com	**automobilia**

Both mail order and open shop. Wednesday 10-6, Thursday-Friday 12-8, Saturday 10-6. Automobilia: 1960s slot cars, H/O to 1/24, Aurora Model Motoring & 1/32 scale slot car specialist. Over 20 different brands in stock.

North Yorkshire Motor Museum D T Mathewson Roxby Garage, Pickering Rd Thornton-le-Dale, North Yorkshire England 01751 474455; FAX: 01944 758188	**museum**

See full listing in **Section Six** under **England**

Nostalgic Images Inc **(formerly NEO)** 1898 Spruce St Defiance, OH 43512 419-784-1728; FAX: 419-782-9459 E-mail: nii17@hotmail.com	**collectibles** **memorabilia** **signs**

Over 300 styles of collector metal signs. Approx size 12"x17." Most signs $6 or less. Quantity pricing available. Harley-Davidson, Ford, Chevy, Coca-Cola, Elvis and more. Ship USA and overseas. Please visit our web site for collector close-outs also. Web site: www.nostalgicimages.com

O'Brien Truckers 29 A Young Rd Charlton, MA 01507-1599 508-248-1555; FAX: 508-248-6179 E-mail: obt@ziplink.net	**accessories** **belt buckles** **plaques** **valve covers**

See full listing in **Section Two** under **plaques**

Ohio Jukebox Co 6211 Cubbison Rd Cumberland, OH 43732 740-638-5059 E-mail: offy@se-guernsey.net	**jukeboxes**

See full listing in **Section Two** under **novelties**

Oil Company Collectibles Inc PO Box 556 LaGrange, OH 44050 440-355-6608; FAX: 440-355-4955 E-mail: scottpcm@aol.com	**books** **gasoline globes** **signs**

Largest supplier and buyer of original gasoline pump globes in the world. Original gasoline globes, signs, etc. Buy and sell original gasoline globes, signs and related collectibles. We carry related books on same subject too. Web site: www.gasglobes.com

Old Cabot Village 465 Cabot St Beverly, MA 01915 978-922-7142; FAX: 978-922-6917 E-mail: oldcabot@mediaone.net	**neckties**

See full listing in **Section Two** under **apparel**

Old Gold Retold Inc **Florida Swap Meets** 6250 Tennessee Ave New Port Richey, FL 34653 800-438-8559; FAX: 727-846-8922 E-mail: swapmet@gte.net	**auction** **car show** **swap meet**

See full listing in **Section Two** under **auctions & shows**

On Mark International Inc   replicas
8923 S 43rd W Ave
Tulsa, OK 74132
888-373-2092, 918-446-7906
FAX: 918-445-1532
E-mail: onmark@igeotec.net

See full listing in **Section Two** under **models & toys**

Packard Archives   accessories
918 W Co Rd C-2   artwork
St Paul, MN 55113-1942   automobilia
651-484-1184
E-mail: estatecars@earthlink.net

See full listing in **Section One** under **Packard**

Paragon Models & Art   artwork
3570 North Rd   models
North Fort Myers, FL 33917
941-567-0047; FAX: 941-567-1344
E-mail: info@myhotrod.com

Mail order only. Automotive and truck collectibles, cool stuff.
Web site: www.myhotrod.com

Past Gas Company   automobilia
308 Willard St   gas pumps
Cocoa, FL 32922
321-636-0449; FAX: 321-636-1006

Restored gas pumps, Coke machines, neon clocks, etc. Eco
Tireflator parts, Fry visible parts. Complete gas pump restoration
catalog, $2.

Past Lane Auto   racing memorabilia
PO Box 69
Athol Springs, NY 14010
716-649-4108; FAX: 716-646-1969

Mail order only. Deals in racing memorabilia, decals, posters,
photos, movies, books and apparel.

People Kars   models/more
290 Third Ave Ext   VW toys
Rensselaer, NY 12144
518-465-0477; FAX: 518-465-0614
E-mail: peoplekars@aol.com

See full listing in **Section One** under **Volkswagen**

Petersen Automotive Museum   museum
6060 Wilshire Blvd
Los Angeles, CA 90036
213-930-CARS (2277)
FAX: 323-930-6642

See full listing in **Section Six** under **California**

Hugo Prado Limited Edition   fine art prints
Corvette Art Prints
PO Box 18437
Chicago, IL 60618-0437
PH/FAX: 773-681-7770
E-mail: vetteart@aol.com

See full listing in **Section One** under **Corvette**

Premier Designs Historic Costume   clothing
15512 St Rt 613
Van Buren, OH 45889
800-427-0907; FAX: 419-299-3919
E-mail: premier@bright.net

See full listing in **Section Two** under **apparel**

Lloyd Ralston Gallery   toys
350 Long Beach Blvd
Stratford, CT 06615
203-386-9399; FAX: 203-386-9519
E-mail: lrgallery@aol.com

See full listing in **Section Two** under **models & toys**

Red Lion Racing   photographs
8318 Avenida Castro   posters
Cucamonga, CA 91730
909-987-9818; FAX: 909-987-6538
E-mail: rlracing@cris.com

See full listing in **Section Two** under **artwork**

Replicarz   books
166 Spruce St   kits
Rutland, VT 05701   models
802-747-7151   videos
E-mail: replicarz@aol.com

See full listing in **Section Two** under **racing**

Frank Riley Automotive Art   automotive prints
PO Box 95
Hawthorne, NJ 07506
800-848-9459
E-mail: rileystudio@netscape.net

See full listing in **Section Two** under **artwork**

RT-Designs USA   artwork
PO Box 2061
Salisbury, NC 28145
704-279-9301; FAX: 704-279-8019
E-mail: rtoth@salisbury.net

See full listing in **Section Two** under **artwork**

Doug Schellinger   automobilia
13717 W Green Meadow Dr   books
New Berlin, WI 53151   sales literature
414-328-1907   toys
E-mail: dsac@execpc.com

See full listing in **Section One** under **Fiat**

Jack Schmitt Studio   paintings
PO Box 1761   prints
San Juan Capistrano, CA 92693
E-mail: jack_schmitt@msn.com

See full listing in **Section Two** under **artwork**

Ron Scobie Enterprises   gas pump parts
7676 120th St N
Hugo, MN 55038
651-653-6503
E-mail: rscobie@gaspump.com

See full listing in **Section Two** under **petroliana**

Scott Signal Co   stoplights
8368 W Farm Rd 84
Willard, MO 65781
417-742-5040

Mail order and open shop. Daily 8 am to 8 pm. Stoplights, walk/
don't walk, parking meters, sequencer kits, poles. 2-page color
brochure, $3. Web site: www.trafficlights.com

Showcase Express	display systems
17862 Metzler Ln	
Huntington Beach, CA 92647	
714-842-5564 ext 29	
FAX: 714-842-6534	
E-mail: carl@sonos1.com	

See full listing in **Section Two** under **models & toys**

SIGNPAST	signs
3202 E Birch Ave, Ste 14	
Arkansas City, KS 67005	
316-442-1626	
E-mail: skj@horizon.hit.net	

Mail order and open shop by appointment. Large reproductions of antique auto, oil and other advertising signs, including several available nowhere else. Over 100 available. Send SASE for details and free photos. Web site: www.signpast.com

Henri Simar J R	books
Rue du College, BP 172	literature
B-4800 Verviers Belgium	
32-87335501; FAX: 32-87335122	

See full listing in **Section Two** under **literature dealers**

Skopos Motor Museum	museum
Alexandra Hills, Alexandra Rd	
Batley	
West Yorkshire WA7 6JA England	
01924-444423	

See full listing in **Section Six** under **England**

Robert H Snyder	literature
PO Drawer 821	parts
Yonkers, NY 10702	
914-476-8500	
FAX: 914-476-8573, 24 hours	
E-mail: cohascodpc@earthlink.net	

See full listing in **Section One** under **Cadillac/LaSalle**

Sparrow Auction Co	auction company
59 Wheeler Ave	
Milford, CT 06460	
203-877-1066	
E-mail: sparrowauction@hotmail.com	

See full listing in **Section Two** under **auctions & shows**

Speedzone	die cast models
1750 Broadway	
New Hyde Park, NY 11040	
516-354-8178; FAX: 516-354-0692	
E-mail: sales@speedzoneusa.com	

See full listing in **Section Two** under **models & toys**

Spirit Enterprises	automobilia
4325 Sunset Dr	stereo systems
Lockport, NY 14094	
716-434-9938 showroom	
716-434-0077 warehouse	
E-mail: sprtntrprs@cs.com	

Mail order and open shop. Daily 8 am to 8 pm. Hard-to-find car kits from 1950s-1970s, plus new releases. Specializing in stereo systems for high-performance, American made cars. Over 4,000 model cars and die cast in stock at all times.

Spyder Enterprises Inc	accessories
RFD 1682	artwork
Laurel Hollow, NY 11791-9644	automobilia
516-367-1616; FAX: 516-367-3260	books
E-mail: singer356@aol.com	

Authentic vintage posters, memorabilia, cars, books & literature, old models, photos, race programs, stamps, signatures, etc.

Active buyer and seller of original items relating to Porsche (356 & Spyder), Ferrari (1948-1967), Siata 208-S and Racing (Formula 1, 2 and Sports Racing, 1950-1960s). Manufacturer of finest quality leather accessories for the Porsche 356 and Siata 208-S. SASE with 3 oz postage for free 29-page list; the finest selection of posters of this era anywhere in the world!

TCMB Models & Stuff	models
8207 Clinton Ave S	
Bloomington, MN 55420-2315	
952-884-3997; FAX: 952-884-2827	
E-mail: info@tcmbmodels.com	

See full listing in **Section Two** under **models & toys**

Jay Texter	photography
417 Haines Mill Rd	
Allentown, PA 18104	
610-821-0963	
E-mail: jaytexter@ot.com	

See full listing in **Section Two** under **photography**

Edward Tilley Automotive	automobilia
Collectibles	literature
PO Box 4233	parts
Cary, NC 27519-4233	
919-460-8262	
E-mail: edandsusan@aol.com	

Mail order only. Buy and sell promotional models, out of print books, automobilia, literature, auto related toys and vintage racing collectibles. Since 1979. See our online catalog at http://members.aol.com/edandsusan/automobilia.html

Town & Country Toys	banks
227 Midvale Dr, PO Box 574	Ertl cars
Marshall, WI 53559	mini license plates
608-655-4961	
E-mail: dejaeger@itis.com	

See full listing in **Section Two** under **models & toys**

Al Trommers-Rare Auto Literature	automobilia/lit
614 Vanburenville Rd	hubcaps
Middletown, NY 10940-7242	wheelcovers

See full listing in **Section Two** under **literature dealers**

Peter Tytla Artist	photographic
PO Box 43	collages
East Lyme, CT 06333-0043	
860-739-7105	

See full listing in **Section Two** under **artwork**

Vic's Place Inc	restoration parts
123 N 2nd St	
Guthrie, OK 73044	
PH/FAX: 405-282-5586	
E-mail: vics@telepath.com	

See full listing in **Section Two** under **petroliana**

Vintage Auto Ent	appraisals
PO Box 2183	auctioneer
Manchester Center, VT 05255	
802-362-4719; FAX: 802-362-3007	
E-mail: dbrownell@sprynet.com	

See full listing in **Section Two** under **appraisals**

Vintage Automotive Art	artwork
PO Box 3702	automobilia
Beverly Hills, CA 90212	literature dealers
310-278-0882; FAX: 310-278-0883	
E-mail: artline1@pacbell.net	

Mail order and open shop by appointment only. Posters, photography, paintings, drawings and trophies. Mostly dealing in racing. Formula One memorabilia, Italian and American coachbuilder drawings. All works date from 1900-1979. Rare auto books and hot rod memorabilia. Web site: www.1gallery.com

Vintage Books	books
6613 E Mill Plain	literature
Vancouver, WA 98661	
360-694-9519; FAX: 360-694-7644	
E-mail: books@vintage-books.com	

See full listing in **Section Two** under **literature dealers**

Vintage Gas, Ltd	artwork
E-mail: info@vintagegas.com	

See full listing in **Section Two** under **artwork**

Vintage Jag Works	consulting
1390 W Hwy 26	how-to articles
Blackfoot, ID 83221	
877-251-5183 toll free order line	
208-684-4767; FAX: 208-684-3386	
E-mail: walt@vintagejag.com	

See full listing in **Section One** under **Jaguar**

Vintage Restorations	accessories
The Old Bakery	instruments
Windmill Street, Tunbridge Wells	
Kent, TN2 4UU England	
UK 1892-525-899	
FAX: UK 1892-525499	
E-mail: instruments@	
vintagerestorations.com	

See full listing in **Section Two** under **instruments**

Mary Weinheimer	color charts
103 Highgate Terr	
Bergenfield, NJ 07621	
201-384-7661; FAX: 201-439-7662	
E-mail: marychevy@aol.com	

Mail order and open shop by appointment only. Deals in paint color charts and related information. Assorted charts by DuPont, Sherwin Williams, Ditzler, Arco, etc, for cars and trucks 1940-1980s, domestic and imports.

West Michigan Die-Cast Cars	die cast cars
2523 W Kinney Rd	
Ludington, MI 49431	
616-843-4278	
E-mail: wmpc@t-one.net	

See full listing in **Section Two** under **models & toys**

Kirk F White	models
PO Box 999	tin toys
New Smyrna Beach, FL 32170	
386-427-6660; FAX: 386-427-7801	
E-mail: kirkfwhite@mindspring.com	

See full listing in **Section Two** under **models & toys**

Clarence Young Autohobby	antique toy vehicles
300-1 Reems Creek Rd	dealer promos
Weaverville, NC 28787	exclusive metal cars
PH/FAX: 828-645-5243	exclusive resin cars
E-mail: cya@carhobby.com	

See full listing in **Section Two** under **models & toys**

Zephyrhills Festivals and Auction Inc	auction
PO Box 996	swap meet
Odessa, FL 33556-0996	
813-258-6726 office	
813-782-0835 park	
FAX: 813-258-3779	

See full listing in **Section Two** under **auctions & shows**

babbitting

Antique Automotive Engineering Inc	babbitt service
3560 Chestnut Pl	engine restoration
Denver, CO 80216	
303-296-7332, 800-846-7332	
E-mail: ed@antiqueautoengr.com	

See full listing in **Section One** under **Ford 1903-1931**

The Babbitt Pot	engine rebuilding
Zigmont G Billus	rebabbitting &
1693 St Rt 4	boring of bearings
Fort Edward, NY 12828	
518-747-4277	

Mail order and open shop. Monday-Friday 9 am to 5 pm, Saturday by appointment. Babbitt bearing specialist and antique engine rebuilder for 25 years, using the best materials and best effort.

Harkin Machine Shop	engine rebuilding
903 43rd St NE	rebabbitting
Watertown, SD 57201	
605-886-7880	

See full listing in **Section Two** under **engine rebuilding**

Paul's Rod & Bearing Ltd	babbitting
PO Box 29098	
Parkville, MO 64152-0398	
816-587-4747; FAX: 816-587-4312	

Mail order and open shop. Monday-Thursday 6 am to 4:30 pm, closed Friday. Babbitting of rods and main bearings for antique cars.

Precision Babbitt Service	babbitting
4681 Lincoln Ave	engine rebuilding
Beamsville, ON Canada L0R 1B3	
905-563-4364	
E-mail: tkoudys@sprint.ca	

Mail order and open shop. Evenings and Saturdays. Complete custom engine rebuilding. Babbitt bearings poured and machined for any application, using certified tin-base alloy. Specializes in, but not limited to, Model T, A, B and V8. All work done in shop.

Vintage Motor and Machine	auto components
Gene French	fixtures
1513 Webster Ct	industrial
Fort Collins, CO 80524	components
970-498-9224	

See full listing in **Section Two** under **machine work**

batteries

Antique Auto Battery	batteries
2320 Old Mill Rd	battery cables
Hudson, OH 44236	
800-426-7580, 330-425-2395	
FAX: 330-425-4642	
E-mail: info@antiqueautobattery.com	

The world's only manufacturer of hard rubber raised letter Antique Batteries licensed by The Big Three that offers complete coverage of accurate reproduction batteries for all models. All with hard rubber script cases, correct caps and the tar tops have our famous nonsticky Poly Tar®. Finest quality dry charged factory fresh batteries available for your cars and trucks. Complete line of cables hend alternators, 6-volt and 8-volt. MasterCard, Visa, American Express, Discover or COD. Web site: www.antiqueautobattery.com

Battery Ignition Co Inc
91 Meadow St
Hartford, CT 06114
860-296-4215; FAX: 860-947-3259
E-mail: biscokid@aol.com

parts
rebuilding
rebushing

See full listing in **Section Two** under **carburetors**

C & G Early Ford Parts
1941 Commercial St, Dept AH
Escondido, CA 92029-1233
760-740-2400; FAX: 760-740-8700
E-mail: cgford@cgfordparts.com

accessories/chrome
emblems
literature
mechanical
weatherstripping

See full listing in **Section One** under **Ford 1932-1953**

Cole's Ign & Mfg
52 Legionaire Dr
Rochester, NY 14617
PH/FAX: 716-342-9613

battery cables
ignition wire sets

See full listing in **Section Two** under **ignition parts**

George's Auto & Tractor Sales Inc
1450 N Warren Rd
North Jackson, OH 44451
330-538-3020; FAX: 330-538-3033
E-mail: gmyuhas1450@cs.com

Blue Dots/car dealer
Dri-Wash metal
polish
upholstery cleaner
New Castle batteries

See full listing in **Section Two** under **car dealers**

SS Specialties
15777 SE Ruby Dr
Milwaukie, OR 97267
503-250-0498; FAX: 503-654-8868

batteries

Mail order and open shop. Monday-Saturday 7 am to 7 pm. Odyssey dry cell batteries for cars, boats, street rods, motorcycles, watercraft, ATVs and commercial usage.

bicycles — no

bearings

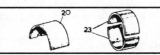

Allied Bearing Sales
8962 Ellis Ave
Los Angeles, CA 90034
800-421-3658 nationwide
310-837-0752; FAX: 310-837-0755

bearings
seals

Mail order and open shop. Monday-Friday 8 am to 4 pm. Supply all types of bearings for automotive applications, except engine bearings. Ball, cylindrical roller and tapered roller bearings and seals. Many part numbers are for obsolete or classic cars. Foreign and domestic. Many obsolete seals also in stock.

Antique Auto Parts Cellar
6 Chauncy St, PO Box 3
South Weymouth, MA 02190
781-335-1579; FAX: 781-335-1925
E-mail: our1932@aol.com

brake/chassis/
engine parts
fuel pumps/kits
gaskets
water pumps

See full listing in **Section Two** under **comprehensive parts**

C & G Early Ford Parts
1941 Commercial St, Dept AH
Escondido, CA 92029-1233
760-740-2400; FAX: 760-740-8700
E-mail: cgford@cgfordparts.com

accessories/chrome
emblems
literature
mechanical
weatherstripping

See full listing in **Section One** under **Ford 1932-1953**

Daytona Turbo Action Camshafts
1109 US #1, PO Box 5094
Ormond Beach, FL 32175
888-RARE-CAM, 800-505-CAMS
386-676-7478; FAX: 386-258-1582
E-mail: info@camshafts.com

camshafts
engine parts

Phone and mail order. Monday-Friday 9 am to 9 pm. Specializing in obsolete engine parts and custom ground camshafts for postwar US cars and trucks. Visa, MC, Discover. Web site: www.camshafts.com

OlCar Bearing Co
135 James Creek Rd
Southern Pines, NC 28387
910-693-3324; FAX: 910-693-1943
E-mail: brgdr@earthlink.net

bearings
seals

Mail order only. Bearings and seals for: axles, clutch, differential, pinion, transmission, steering knuckle and wheels. All years, most model cars and trucks.

Paul's Rod & Bearing Ltd
PO Box 29098
Parkville, MO 64152-0398
816-587-4747; FAX: 816-587-4312

babbitting

See full listing in **Section Two** under **babbitting**

QA1 Precision Products Inc
21730 Hanover Ave
Lakeville, MN 55044
800-721-7761; FAX: 952-985-5679
E-mail: ehaines@qa1.net

suspension parts

See full listing in **Section Two** under **suspension parts**

South Shore Bearing Dist
111 Copeland St
Quincy, MA 02169
617-471-7800; FAX: 617-479-9192

bearings
grease seals

Mail order and open shop. Monday-Friday 8 am to 5 pm, Saturday 8 am to 12 pm. Bearings, oil and grease seals for cars and trucks.

Taylor Auto Parts
PO Box 650
Esparto, CA 95627
530-787-1929

bearings
brakes
gaskets
seals

See full listing in **Section Two** under **comprehensive parts**

bicycles

British Cycling Museum
The Old Station
Camelford
Cornwall PL32 9TZ England
PH/FAX: 01840-212811

museum

See full listing in **Section Six** under **England**

Gaylord Sales
Frank Ranghelli
125 Dugan Ln
Toms River, NJ 08753
732-349-9213; FAX: 732-341-5353
E-mail: fgaylordsales@aol.com

automobilia
automotive art
mascots

See full listing in **Section Two** under **radiator emblems & mascots**

National Cycle Collection
The Automobile Palace Temple St
Llandrindod Wells Powys
Mid Wales LD1 5DL Wales
PH/FAX: 01597-825531

museum

See full listing in **Section Six** under **Wales**

Skopos Motor Museum
Alexandra Hills, Alexandra Rd
Batley
West Yorkshire WA7 6JA England
01924-444423

museum

See full listing in **Section Six** under **England**

Slim's Garage
PO Box 49
Seminary, MS 39479-0049
PH/FAX: 601-722-9861

garden tractors

See full listing in **Section Two** under **trucks & tractors**

www.albertsgifts.com
3001 Penn Ave
Pittsburgh, PA 15201
800-233-2800, 412-683-2900
FAX: 412-683-3110
E-mail: info@aimgifts.com

bike plates
license plates

See full listing in **Section Two** under **license plates**

body parts

60 Chev Sam
2912 Wright Rd
Hamptonville, NC 27020
336-468-1745

parts

See full listing in **Section One** under **Chevrolet**

A/Altered Hot Rod Parts
PO Box 851
Emporia, KS 66801
620-343-1796

body parts

See full listing in **Section One** under **Ford 1903-1931**

ADP Hollander
14800 28th Ave N #190
Plymouth, MN 55447
800-761-9266; FAX: 800-825-1124
E-mail: info@hollander-auto-parts.com

interchange info
manuals

See full listing in **Section Two** under **car & parts locators**

American Performance Products
675 S Industry Rd
Cocoa, FL 32926
321-632-8299; FAX: 321-632-5119
E-mail: amc@oldcarparts.com

parts

See full listing in **Section One** under **AMC**

AMK Products Inc
800 Airport Rd
Winchester, VA 22602
540-662-7820; FAX: 540-662-7821

parts

See full listing in **Section One** under **Ford 1954-up**

Anderson Automotive
1604 E Busch Blvd
Tampa, FL 33612
813-932-4611; FAX: 813-932-5025

cars
parts

See full listing in **Section One** under **Oldsmobile**

Andy's Classic Mustangs
18502 E Sprague
Greenacres, WA 99016
509-924-9824

parts
service

See full listing in **Section One** under **Mustang**

Antique Auto Parts Sales
40 Iron Mtn W
Hartford, KY 42347
270-264-1483, 270-298-7684
E-mail: aapsales@aol.com

patch panels

Patch panels for 1935-up GM, Ford and Chrysler. All types of
rust repair panels and replacement panels.

Auto Body Specialties Inc
Rt 66
Middlefield, CT 06455
888-277-1960 toll free orders only
860-346-4989; FAX: 860-346-4987

accessories
body parts

Mail order and open shop. Monday, Tuesday 9 am to 6 pm;
Wednesday, Friday 9 am to 5 pm; Thursday 9 am to 7 pm;
Saturday 9 am to 3 pm. Body parts and accessories, reproduction, original and used for GM, Ford, Chrysler 1950-present
cars, pickups and vans. Web site: www.autobodyspecialt.com

AutoFashions Restoration & Parts
Pittsboro, NC 27312
919-542-5566
E-mail: autofashions@mindspring.com

auto parts
auto sales
handcrafts
restoration

By appointment only. New, used, and reconditioned auto parts,
auto sales and auto restoration. Inventive handcrafts on web
site: http://home.mindspring.com/~autofashions

Big Boys Toys
Richard Boutin
Rt 67A, Box 174A
North Bennington, VT 05257
800-286-1721; FAX: 802-447-0962

accessories
bodywork
tires
wheels

See full listing in **Section Two** under **accessories**

Bill's Speed Shop
13951 Millersburg Rd
Navarre, OH 44662
330-832-9403; FAX: 330-832-2098

body parts

See full listing in **Section One** under **Chevrolet**

Bob's Bird House
124 Watkin Ave
Chadds Ford, PA 19317
610-358-3420; FAX: 610-558-0729

parts

See full listing in **Section One** under **Thunderbird**

Bob's Brickyard Inc
1030 N Hickory Ridge Tr
Milford, MI 48380
248-685-9508; FAX: 248-685-8662
E-mail: bobsbrick@aol.com

parts

See full listing in **Section One** under **Bricklin**

Section Two – Generalists

Gideon Booth | car collector
Rellandsgate, Kings Meaburn | parts
Penrith | restorations
Cumbria CA10 3BT England
PH/FAX: 01931 714624

See full listing in **Section One** under **Morris**

The Buckle Man | buckles
Douglas D Drake
28 Monroe Ave
Pittsford, NY 14534
716-381-4604

See full listing in **Section Two** under **hardware**

Caddy Central | cars
11117 Tippett Rd | locating service
Clinton, MD 20735 | parts
301-234-0135; FAX: 301-234-0140
E-mail: cadlocator@juno.com

See full listing in **Section One** under **Cadillac/LaSalle**

California Pony Cars | parts
1906 Quaker Ridge Pl
Ontario, CA 91761
909-923-2804; FAX: 909-947-8593
E-mail: 105232.3362@compuserve.com

See full listing in **Section One** under **Mustang**

Canadian Mustang | parts
20529 62 Ave
Langley, BC Canada V3A 8R4
604-534-6424; FAX: 604-534-6694
E-mail: parts@canadianmustang.com

See full listing in **Section One** under **Mustang**

Cars II | parts
6747 Warren Sharon Rd
Brookfield, OH 44403
330-448-2074; FAX: 330-448-1908

See full listing in **Section One** under **Cadillac/LaSalle**

Jim Carter's Antique Truck Parts | truck parts
1508 E Alton
Independence, MO 64055
800-336-1913; FAX: 800-262-3749
E-mail: jimcartertruckparts@
worldnet.att.net

See full listing in **Section One** under **Chevrolet**

Chevelle World Inc | parts
PO Box 926
Noble, OK 73068
405-872-0379; FAX: 405-872-0385

See full listing in **Section One** under **Chevelle/Camaro**

Cheyenne Pickup Parts | body panels
Box 959 | bumpers
Noble, OK 73068 | carpet
405-872-3399; FAX: 405-872-0385 | weatherstripping
E-mail: sales@cheyennepickup.com

See full listing in **Section One** under **Chevrolet**

Ed Cholakian Enterprises Inc | museum
dba All Cadillacs of the 40s and 50s | parts
12811 Foothill Blvd
Sylmar, CA 91342
800-808-1147, 818-361-1147
FAX: 818-361-9738

See full listing in **Section One** under **Cadillac/LaSalle**

Class Glass & Performance Inc | body parts
101 Winston St
Cumberland, MD 21502
800-774-3456 toll free
301-777-3456; FAX: 301-777-7044

See full listing in **Section Two** under **fiberglass parts**

Classic Chevrolet Parts Inc | parts
8723 S I-35
Oklahoma City, OK 73149
405-631-4400; FAX: 405-631-5999
E-mail: info@classicchevroletparts.com

See full listing in **Section One** under **Chevrolet**

Classic Ford Sales | salvage yard
PO Box 60
East Dixfield, ME 04227
207-562-4443; FAX: 207-562-4576
E-mail: sue@classicford.com

See full listing in **Section Five** under **Maine**

Classic Mustang Inc | body parts
24 Robert Porter Rd | carpets
Southington, CT 06489 | chassis parts
800-243-2742; FAX: 860-276-9986 | floor pans

See full listing in **Section One** under **Mustang**

Classic Sheetmetal Inc | body panels
4010 A Hartley St | sheetmetal
Charlotte, NC 28206
800-776-4040, 704-596-5186
FAX: 704-596-3895

See full listing in **Section One** under **Thunderbird**

CR Plastics Inc | bumper filler parts
2790 NE 7th Ave
Pompano Beach, FL 33064
800-551-3155

See full listing in **Section One** under **Cadillac/LaSalle**

Dakota Studebaker Parts | parts
39408 280th St
Armour, SD 57313
605-724-2527
E-mail: dakstude1@unitelsd.com

See full listing in **Section One** under **Studebaker**

Dave's Auto Machine & Parts | accessories
Rt 16 | machine work
Ischua, NY 14743 | parts
716-557-2402

See full listing in **Section One** under **Chevrolet**

Desert Dog Auto Parts Inc | body parts
542 W Washington St
Woodstock, IL 60098
815-337-9594; FAX: 815-337-9597
E-mail: ddog@desertdogautoparts.com

Mail order and open shop. Monday-Friday 8 am to 5 pm. Anything American, 1950-1980s. Specializing in rust-free sheetmetal, pit-free chrome, bumper restoration program. Accept Visa, Discover, MasterCard and ship worldwide. Web site: www.desertdogautoparts.com

Section Two – Generalists

Desert Valley Auto Parts 2227 W Happy Valley Rd Phoenix, AZ 85027 800-905-8024 623-780-8024; FAX: 623-582-9141 E-mail: sales@dvap.com	salvage yard

See full listing in **Section Five** under **Arizona**

Daniel N Dietrich RD 1 Kempton, PA 19529 610-756-6078, 610-756-6071	restoration trim parts

See full listing in **Section One** under **Mopar**

Mike Drago Chevy Parts 141 E St Joseph St Easton, PA 18042 PH/FAX: 610-252-5701 E-mail: dragomdcp@aol.com	Chevrolet parts

See full listing in **Section One** under **Chevrolet**

Bob Drake Reproductions Inc 1819 NW Washington Blvd Grants Pass, OR 97526 800-221-3673; FAX: 541-474-0099 E-mail: bobdrake@bobdrake.com	repro parts

See full listing in **Section One** under **Ford 1932-1953**

Driving Passion Ltd USA Marc Tuwiner 7132 Chilton Ct Clarksville, MD 21029 PH/FAX: 301-596-9078 E-mail: lm7132@aol.com	cars parts salvage yard

See full listing in **Section One** under **Cadillac/LaSalle**

East West Auto Parts Inc 4605 Dawson Rd Tulsa, OK 74115 800-447-2886; FAX: 918-832-7900	European import parts GM parts

See full listing in **Section Five** under **Oklahoma**

Eckler's Quality Parts & Accessories for Corvettes 5140 S Washington Ave Titusville, FL 32780 800-327-4868; FAX: 407-383-2059 E-mail: ecklers@ecklers.net	accessories parts

See full listing in **Section One** under **Corvette**

Fairlane Automotive Specialties 210 E Walker St St Johns, MI 48879 517-224-6460	fiberglass bodies parts

See full listing in **Section One** under **Ford 1932-1953**

FEN Enterprises of New York Inc 1090 Rt 376, PO Box 1559 Wappingers Falls, NY 12590 845-462-5959, 845-462-5094 FAX: 845-462-8450 E-mail: fenenterprises@aol.com	parts restoration

See full listing in **Section One** under **Cadillac/LaSalle**

Gaslight Auto Parts Inc PO Box 291 Urbana, OH 43078 937-652-2145; FAX: 937-652-2147	accessories parts

See full listing in **Section One** under **Ford 1903-1931**

J Giles Automotive 703 Morgan Ave Pascagoula, MS 39567-2116 228-769-1012; FAX: 228-769-8904 E-mail: jgauto@datasync.com	car & parts locator exporter

See full listing in **Section Two** under **car & parts locators**

Goodmark Industries Inc 625 E Old Norcross Rd Lawrenceville, GA 30045 770-339-8557; FAX: 770-339-7562	sheetmetal trim

See full listing in **Section Two** under **sheetmetal**

Gulf Coast Corvette 15100 Lee Rd #101 Humble, TX 77396 800-546-2111 order line 281-441-2111 info line FAX: 281-441-3057	parts

See full listing in **Section One** under **Corvette**

Halpin Used Auto & Truck Parts 1093 Rt 123 Mayfield, NY 12117 518-863-4906 E-mail: junkyard2064@webtv.net	NOS auto parts NOS truck parts used auto parts used truck parts

See full listing in **Section Five** under **New York**

Harmon's Incorporated Hwy 27 N, PO Box 100 Geneva, IN 46740 219-368-7221; FAX: 219-368-9396 E-mail: harmons@harmons.com	interiors parts

See full listing in **Section One** under **Chevrolet**

Hoffman Automotive Distributor US Hwy #1, Box 818 Hilliard, FL 32046 904-845-4421	parts

Mail order and open shop. Monday-Friday 9 am to 5 pm, Saturday 9 am to 2 pm. Started business in 1969. Sell NOS and reproduction parts, 1955-1972 Chevy parts and are currently branching out to Mustang parts, 1968-1972.

Holcombe Cadillac Parts 2933 Century Ln Bensalem, PA 19020 215-245-4560; FAX: 215-633-9916 E-mail: holcars@aol.com	parts

See full listing in **Section One** under **Cadillac/LaSalle**

Hollywood Classic Motorcars Inc 363 Ansin Blvd Hallandale, FL 33009 954-454-4641; FAX: 954-457-3801	parts restoration service

See full listing in **Section One** under **Thunderbird**

Howell's Sheetmetal Co PO Box 792 Nederland, TX 77627 800-375-6663, 409-727-1999 FAX: 409-727-7127 E-mail: dhowell@fordor.com	body panels sheetmetal

See full listing in **Section One** under **Ford 1903-1931**

Impala Bob's Inc — dash pads, emblems, interior kits, mechanical parts, OEM tires, restoration parts, rubber parts, wiring harnesses
4753 E Falcon Dr, Dept HCCA15
Mesa, AZ 85215
800-IMPALAS orders
480-924-4800 retail store
480-981-1600 office
FAX: 800-716-6237, 480-981-1675
E-mail: info@impalas.com
See full listing in **Section One** under **Chevrolet**

Imperial Motors — parts
PO Box 496
Campobello, SC 29322
864-895-3474; FAX: 864-895-1248
See full listing in **Section One** under **Chrysler**

Jefferis Autobody — windshield glass kit
269 Tank Farm Rd
San Luis Obispo, CA 93401
800-807-1937; FAX: 805-543-4757
See full listing in **Section Two** under **glass**

K&D Enterprises — accessories, parts, restorations
23117 E Echo Lake Rd
Snohomish, WA 98296-5426
425-788-0507; FAX: 360-668-2003
E-mail: tdb@halcyon.com
See full listing in **Section One** under **Jensen**

K-F-D Services Inc — parts, restoration
HC 65, Box 49
Altonah, UT 84002
801-454-3098; FAX: 801-454-3099
E-mail: kfd-services@msn.com
See full listing in **Section One** under **Kaiser Frazer**

Klasse 356 Inc — cars, parts, restoration
311 Liberty St
Allentown, PA 18102
800-634-7862; FAX: 610-432-8027
E-mail: parts@klasse356.com
See full listing in **Section One** under **Porsche**

L & L Antique Auto Trim — runningboard moldings
403 Spruce, Box 177
Pierce City, MO 65723
417-476-2871
See full listing in **Section Two** under **special services**

Majestic Truck Parts — parts
17726 Dickerson
Dallas, TX 75252
972-248-6245; FAX: 972-380-8913
E-mail: majestictrk@juno.com
See full listing in **Section One** under **Chevrolet**

Marcel's Corvette Shop Inc — sales, service, parts
1000 Waterford Rd
Mechanicville, NY 12118
518-664-7344; FAX: 518-664-2908
E-mail: marcel@marcelscorvette.com
See full listing in **Section One** under **Corvette**

Merv's Classic Chevy Parts — parts
1330 Washington Ave
Iowa Falls, IA 50126
641-648-3168; PH/FAX: 641-648-9675
See full listing in **Section One** under **Chevrolet**

Mill Supply Inc — clips, fasteners, panels
PO Box 28400
Cleveland, OH 44128
800-888-5072; FAX: 888-781-2700
E-mail: info@millsupply.com
See full listing in **Section Two** under **sheetmetal**

Motorsport Auto — parts
1139 W Collins Ave
Orange, CA 92667
800-633-6331, 714-639-2620
FAX: 714-639-7460
E-mail: motorsport@worldnet.att.net
See full listing in **Section One** under **Datsun**

National Spring Co Inc — spring parts, spring services
1402 N Magnolia Ave
El Cajon, CA 92020
619-441-1901; FAX: 619-441-2460
See full listing in **Section Two** under **suspension parts**

Northwest Classic Falcons Inc — parts
1964 NW Pettygrove St
Portland, OR 97209
503-241-9454; FAX: 503-241-1964
E-mail: ron@nwfalcon.com
See full listing in **Section One** under **Ford 1954-up**

NOS Only — NOS Ford parts, NOS parts
414 Umbarger Rd, Unit E
San Jose, CA 95111
408-227-2353, 408-227-2354
FAX: 408-227-2355
E-mail: nosonly@aol.com
See full listing in **Section Two** under **comprehensive parts**

Obsolete Ford Parts Inc — parts
8701 S I-35
Oklahoma City, OK 73149
405-631-3933; FAX: 405-634-6815
E-mail: info@obsoletefordparts.com
See full listing in **Section One** under **Ford 1954-up**

Paragon Reproductions Inc — Corvette repro parts
8040 S Jennings Rd
Swartz Creek, MI 48473
800-882-4688; FAX: 810-655-6667
E-mail: sales@corvette-paragon.com
See full listing in **Section One** under **Corvette**

Paul's Select Cars & Parts for Porsche® — cars, parts
2280 Gail Dr
Riverside, CA 92509
909-685-9340; FAX: 909-685-9342
E-mail: pauls356-s90@webtv.net
See full listing in **Section One** under **Porsche**

Perfect Panels of America — body panels
1690 Thomas Paine Pkwy
Centerville, OH 45459
937-435-4541; FAX: 937-435-4548
E-mail: porshfreek@aol.com
See full listing in **Section One** under **Porsche**

Pony Parts of America
1690 Thomas Paine Pkwy
Centerville, OH 45459
937-435-4541; FAX: 937-435-4548
E-mail: porshfreek@aol.com

floor boards
frame rails

See full listing in **Section One** under **Mustang**

Pro's Pick Rod & Custom
4210 Dixie Hwy
Erlanger, KY 41018
PH/FAX: 859-727-9600
E-mail: gary@prospick.com

parts

See full listing in **Section Two** under **street rods**

Raybuck Autobody Parts
RD 4, Box 170
Punxsutawney, PA 15767
814-938-5248; FAX: 814-938-4250

body parts

Mail order and open shop. Monday-Friday 8 am to 5 pm. New high quality reproduction body parts for pickups, vans and jeeps.

Robert's Custom Metal
24 Lark Industrial Pkwy #D
Smithfield, RI 02828
401-949-2361

metal fabrication
welding
woodwork

See full listing in **Section Two** under **sheetmetal**

Rocker King
804 Chicago Ave
Waukesha, WI 53188-3511
262-549-9583; FAX: 262-549-9643
E-mail: sonoma@execpc.com

body parts
sheetmetal parts

See full listing in **Section Two** under **sheetmetal**

Rodster Inc
128 Center St #B
El Segundo, CA 90245
310-322-2767; FAX: 310-322-2761

conversion kits

See full listing in **Section Two** under **street rods**

Rolling Steel Body Parts
7913 Chardon Rd, Rt 6
Kirtland, OH 44094
888-765-5460, 440-256-8383
FAX: 440-256-8994
E-mail: sales@rollingsteelbodyparts.com

body parts

Dealing in body parts and panels. Steel repair body panels that fit 1947-up cars and trucks. Featuring made in USA parts. Web site: www.rollingsteelbodyparts.com

Rust Busters
PO Box 341
Clackamas, OR 97015
503-223-3203
E-mail: info@rustbusters.com

rust repair

See full listing in **Section Two** under **restoration shops**

S & S Antique Auto
Pine St
Deposit, NY 13754
607-467-2929; FAX: 607-467-2109

parts

See full listing in **Section One** under **Ford 1932-1953**

Sherman & Associates Inc
61166 Van Dyke Rd
Washington, MI 48094
810-677-6800; FAX: 810-677-6801

body panels
body parts
fenders/floors
quarter panels

Mail order and open shop. Monday-Friday 8:30 am to 5 pm, Saturday 9 am to 12 pm Eastern time. Specialize in restoration body parts and panels for Ford, GM, Chrysler, imports and light trucks, 1949-up. Have complete fenders, quarters and hoods plus patch panels for spot repair of damaged or rusted areas. Our product line includes components for vintage restorations and late model crash repairs, plus general maintenance and customization items including heater cores, radiators, runningboards, fender flares, trim rings, rear spoilers, step-type truck bumpers and other add-on accessories. To assure prompt service we have moved to a new 110,000 sq ft facility to house all our products under one roof. Web site: www.shermanparts.com

Paul Slater Auto Parts
9496 85th St N
Stillwater, MN 55082
651-429-4235

parts

See full listing in **Section One** under **Dodge**

Smith & Jones Distributing Co Inc
1 Biloxi Sq
West Columbia, SC 29170
803-822-8500; FAX: 803-822-8477

parts

See full listing in **Section One** under **Ford 1903-1931**

Smooth Line
2562 Riddle Run Rd
Tarentum, PA 15084
724-274-6002; FAX: 724-274-6121

body panels
removable hardtops

See full listing in **Section Two** under **tops**

Stilwell's Obsolete Car Parts
1617 Wedeking Ave
Evansville, IN 47711
812-425-4794

body parts
interiors
parts

See full listing in **Section One** under **Mustang**

Tom's Obsolete Chevy Parts
14 Delta Dr
Pawtucket, RI 02860
401-723-7580; FAX: 401-724-7568

parts

See full listing in **Section One** under **Chevrolet**

Tucson Packard/Chirco Automotive
9101 E 22nd St
Tucson, AZ 85710
520-722-1984; FAX: 520-298-4069
E-mail: tucpackard@aol.com

accessories
NORS parts
NOS parts
used parts

See full listing in **Section One** under **Packard**

John Ulrich
450 Silver Ave
San Francisco, CA 94112
PH/FAX: 510-223-9587 days

parts

See full listing in **Section One** under **Packard**

Tom Vagnini
58 Anthony Rd, RR 3
Pittsfield, MA 01201
413-698-2526

used parts

See full listing in **Section One** under **Packard**

Volvo Shop Inc
5220 New Milford Rd
Ravenna, OH 44266
330-297-1297; FAX: 330-297-6206
E-mail: volvocarl@aol.com

parts
restoration

See full listing in **Section One** under **Volvo**

Wales Antique Chevy Truck Parts | parts
143 Center
Carleton, MI 48117
734-654-8836

See full listing in **Section One** under **Chevrolet**

Pat Wilson's Thunderbird Parts | parts
375 Rt 94
Fredon Township, NJ 07860
888-262-1153; FAX: 973-579-2011
E-mail: wilsontb@nac.net

See full listing in **Section One** under **Thunderbird**

Zephyrhills Festivals | auction
and Auction Inc | swap meet
PO Box 996
Odessa, FL 33556-0996
813-258-6726 office
813-782-0835 park
FAX: 813-258-3779

See full listing in **Section Two** under **auctions & shows**

bodywork

Ace Antique Auto Restoration | air conditioning
65 S Service Rd | body rebuilding
Plainview, NY 11803 | restoration
516-752-6065; FAX: 516-752-1484 | wiring harnesses

See full listing in **Section Two** under **restoration shops**

ACE Automotive Cleaning | sandblasting
Equipment Co | equipment
897 S Washington, Ste 232
Holland, MI 49423
616-772-3260; FAX: 616-772-3261

See full listing in **Section Two** under **rust removal & stripping**

Adler's Antique Autos Inc | auto preservation
801 NY Rt 43 | Chevrolet knowledge
Stephentown, NY 12168 | parts
518-733-5749 | repair
E-mail: advdesign1@aol.com | restoration

See full listing in **Section Two** under **restoration shops**

Antique & Classic Car Restoration | restoration
Hwy 107, Box 368
Magdalena, NM 87825

See full listing in **Section One** under **MG**

Auto Restoration by William R Hahn | custom work
8837 Beebles Rd | restorations
Allison Park, PA 15101
412-367-2538, 724-935-3790

See full listing in **Section Two** under **restoration shops**

Bayliss Automobile Restorations | repainting
2/15 Bon Mace Close, Berkeley Vale | repairs
Via Gosford NSW 2261 Australia | sheetmetal work
61-2-43885253; FAX: 61-2-43893152
E-mail: bayrest@ozemail.com.au

See full listing in **Section Two** under **restoration shops**

Big Boys Toys | accessories
Richard Boutin | bodywork
Rt 67A, Box 174A | tires
North Bennington, VT 05257 | wheels
800-286-1721; FAX: 802-447-0962

See full listing in **Section Two** under **accessories**

Bob's Brickyard Inc | parts
1030 N Hickory Ridge Tr
Milford, MI 48380
248-685-9508; FAX: 248-685-8662
E-mail: bobsbrick@aol.com

See full listing in **Section One** under **Bricklin**

City Imports Ltd | bodywork
166 Penrod Ct | car sales
Glen Burnie, MD 21061 | restorations
410-768-6660; FAX: 410-768-5955

See full listing in **Section One** under **Jaguar**

Classic Auto Works | cars
7301-1 Singleton Bend Rd | parts
Travis Peak, TX 78654 | repairs
PH/FAX: 512-267-3707
E-mail: classica@concentric.net

See full listing in **Section Two** under **street rods**

Classic Garage | bodywork
120 Monmouth St | paint
Red Bank, NJ 07701 | restoration
732-741-2450; FAX: 732-741-4134

See full listing in **Section Two** under **restoration shops**

Classic Sheetmetal Inc | body panels
4010 A Hartley St | sheetmetal
Charlotte, NC 28206
800-776-4040, 704-596-5186
FAX: 704-596-3895

See full listing in **Section One** under **Thunderbird**

County Corvette | restoration
315 Westtown Rd | sales
West Chester, PA 19382 | service
610-696-7888; FAX: 610-696-9114

See full listing in **Section One** under **Corvette**

Cover-It | all-weather shelters
17 Wood St
West Haven, CT 06516-3843
800-932-9344; FAX: 203-931-4754
E-mail: info@coverit.com

See full listing in **Section Two** under **car covers**

Customs & Classics Inc | bodywork
4674 S Brown St | painting
Murray, UT 84107 | restoration
801-288-1863; FAX: 801-288-1623 | street rods
E-mail: kelley@customsandclassics.com

See full listing in **Section Two** under **restoration shops**

DeLorean One | bodywork
20229 Nordhoff St | parts
Chatsworth, CA 91311 | service
818-341-1796; FAX: 818-998-6381

See full listing in **Section One** under **DeLorean**

East Coast Chevy Inc
Ol '55 Chevy Parts
4154A Skyron Dr
Doylestown, PA 18938
215-348-5568; FAX: 215-348-0560

custom work
parts
restoration

See full listing in **Section One** under **Chevrolet**

Engineering & Mfg Services
Box 24362
Cleveland, OH 44124
216-541-4585

sheetmetal

See full listing in **Section One** under **Ford 1932-1953**

Extreme Motorsports Painting Ltd
300 Old Reading Pike
Stowe, PA 19464
610-326-4425; FAX: 610-326-8522
E-mail: extrememail@aol.com

bodywork
painting

See full listing in **Section Two** under **painting**

Foreign Autotech
3235 C Sunset Ln
Hatboro, PA 19040
215-441-4421; FAX: 215-441-4490
E-mail: fap1800@aol.com

parts

See full listing in **Section One** under **Volvo**

Fuller's Restoration Inc
Old Airport Rd
Manchester Center, VT 05255
802-362-3643; FAX: 802-362-3360
E-mail: chevy@vermontel.net

repairs
restoration

See full listing in **Section Two** under **restoration shops**

Grey Hills Auto Restoration
51 Vail Rd, PO Box 630
Blairstown, NJ 07825
9908-362-8232; FAX: 908-362-6796
E-mail: info@greyhillsauto.com

restoration
service

See full listing in **Section Two** under **restoration shops**

Hatfield Restorations
PO Box 846
Canton, TX 75103
903-567-6742; FAX: 903-567-0645
E-mail: pathat@vzinet.com

restoration

See full listing in **Section Two** under **restoration shops**

Hi-Town Automotive
PO Box 381
High Point, NC 27261
336-259-1063; FAX: 336-869-5282
E-mail: lstamey@northstate.net

street rod repairs

See full listing in **Section Two** under **street rods**

Hyde Auto Body
44-1/2 S Squirrel Rd
Auburn Hills, MI 48326
PH/FAX: 248-852-7832
E-mail: bodyman8@juno.com

refinishing
restoration

See full listing in **Section Two** under **restoration shops**

Imaginographx
PO Box 95
Hawthorne, NJ 07506
800-848-9459
E-mail: imaginographx@netscape.net

automotive portraits
automotive prints
idea renderings
logo designs

See full listing in **Section Two** under **artwork**

JCM Industries
2 Westwood Dr
Danbury, CT 06811
800-752-0245

wax hardener

See full listing in **Section Two** under **car care products**

Jefferis Autobody
269 Tank Farm Rd
San Luis Obispo, CA 93401
800-807-1937; FAX: 805-543-4757

windshield glass kit

See full listing in **Section Two** under **glass**

Keilen's Auto Restoring
580 Kelley Blvd (R)
North Attleboro, MA 02760
508-699-7768

restoration

See full listing in **Section Two** under **restoration shops**

LEX-AIRE Nationwide Sales
34 Hutchinson Rd
Arlington, MA 02474
800-LEX-AIRE; FAX: 562-691-9374

painting equipment
turbine systems

See full listing in **Section Two** under **tools**

**Libbey's Classic Car
Restoration Center**
137 N Quinsigamond Ave
Shrewsbury, MA 01545
PH/FAX: 508-792-1560

bodywork
restoration
service

See full listing in **Section Two** under **restoration shops**

Mastermind Inc
32155 Joshua Dr
Wildomar, CA 92595
PH/FAX: 909-674-0509
E-mail: mike@mastermindinc.net

new/used parts
restoration

See full listing in **Section One** under **Cadillac/LaSalle**

McCann Auto
630 North St, PO Box 1025
Houlton, ME 04730
207-532-2206; FAX: 207-532-6748
E-mail: mccadani@javanet.com

custom work
restoration
sandblasting

See full listing in **Section Two** under **restoration shops**

Mill Supply Inc
PO Box 28400
Cleveland, OH 44128
800-888-5072; FAX: 888-781-2700
E-mail: info@millsupply.com

clips
fasteners
panels

See full listing in **Section Two** under **sheetmetal**

New Era Motors
11611 NE 50th Ave, Unit 6
Vancouver, WA 98686
360-573-8788; FAX: 360-573-7461

restoration

See full listing in **Section Two** under **woodwork**

R E Pierce parts
47 Stone Rd restoration
Wendell Depot, MA 01380
978-544-7442; FAX: 978-544-2978
E-mail: robin@billsgate.com

See full listing in **Section One** under **Volvo**

Prestige Automotive Inc restoration
30295 Moravian Tr
Tippecanoe, OH 44699
740-922-3542
E-mail: blacklabs@tusco.net

See full listing in **Section Two** under **restoration shops**

Restorations Unlimited II Inc restoration
304 Jandus Rd
Cary, IL 60013
847-639-5818

See full listing in **Section Two** under **restoration shops**

Rick's Relics bodywork
Wheeler Rd painting
Pittsburg, NH 03592 restoration
603-538-6612
E-mail: relics@aspi.net

See full listing in **Section Two** under **restoration shops**

Rod-1 Shop street rods
210 Clinton Ave
Pitman, NJ 08071
609-228-7631; FAX: 609-582-5770
E-mail: atboz@webtv.net

See full listing in **Section Two** under **street rods**

Rust Busters rust repair
PO Box 341
Clackamas, OR 97015
503-223-3203
E-mail: info@rustbusters.com

See full listing in **Section Two** under **restoration shops**

RX Autoworks restoration
983 W 1st St
North Vancouver, BC Canada V7P 1A4
604-986-0102, 877-986-0102 toll free
FAX: 604-986-0175

See full listing in **Section Two** under **restoration shops**

T Schmidt rust removers
827 N Vernon
Dearborn, MI 48128-1542
313-562-7161

See full listing in **Section Two** under **rust removal & stripping**

Steck Manufacturing Co Inc tools
1115 S Broadway
Dayton, OH 45408
800-227-8325; FAX: 937-222-6666
E-mail: steckmfgco@earthlink.net

See full listing in **Section Two** under **tools**

Stone Barn Inc restoration
202 Rt 46, Box 117
Vienna, NJ 07880
908-637-4444; FAX: 908-637-4290

See full listing in **Section Two** under **restoration shops**

Strange Motion Rod & customizing
Custom Construction Inc design
14696 N 350th Ave fabrication
Cambridge, IL 61238
309-927-3346
E-mail: strangemtn@cin.net

See full listing in **Section Two** under **street rods**

Tower Paint Co Inc paint
Box 2345
Oshkosh, WI 54903-2345
920-235-6520; FAX: 920-235-6521
E-mail: info@towerpaint.com

See full listing in **Section Two** under **paints**

Widmann's Garage repairs
346 Bunting Ave restorations
Hamilton, NJ 08611
609-392-1553; FAX: 609-392-1709
E-mail: widsgarage@aol.com

See full listing in **Section Two** under **restoration shops**

Willhoit Auto Restoration engine rebuilding
1360 Gladys Ave restoration
Long Beach, CA 90804
562-439-3333; FAX: 562-439-3956

See full listing in **Section One** under **Porsche**

Willow Automotive Service bodywork
Box 4640, Rt 212 painting
Willow, NY 12495 restorations
845-679-4679

See full listing in **Section Two** under **restoration shops**

brakes

Accurate Machine Products suspension
20417 Earl St components
Torrance, CA 90503
310-370-4075; FAX: 310-370-1035
E-mail: petrusg@ix.netcom.com

See full listing in **Section Two** under **suspension parts**

All British Car Parts Inc parts
2847 Moores Rd
Baldwin, MD 21013
410-692-9572; FAX: 410-692-5654
E-mail: lucasguy@home.com

See full listing in **Section Two** under **electrical systems**

Allied Power Brake Co brakes
8730 Michigan Ave
Detroit, MI 48210
313-584-8208

Mail order and open shop. Monday-Friday 8 am to 5 pm. Power brake specialists.

American Street Rod hoses
3340 Sunrise Blvd D-1 tubing
Rancho Cordova, CA 95742
916-638-3275

See full listing in **Section Two** under **street rods**

Angeli Machine Co 417 N Varney St Burbank, CA 91502 818-846-5359 E-mail: angelimach@aol.com	machine work

See full listing in **Section Two** under **machine work**

Antique Auto Parts Cellar 6 Chauncy St, PO Box 3 South Weymouth, MA 02190 781-335-1579; FAX: 781-335-1925 E-mail: our1932@aol.com	brake/chassis/ engine parts fuel pumps/kits gaskets water pumps

See full listing in **Section Two** under **comprehensive parts**

The Antique Auto Shop 603 Lytle Ave Elsmere, KY 41018 859-342-8363; FAX: 859-342-9076 E-mail: antaut@aol.com	brake lines brake parts weatherstripping

Mail order and open shop. Monday-Friday 6 am to 4 pm. Specialize in Packards, Jaguar and Corvettes. Brake parts and brake lines for all makes and models 1975 and older. Weatherstripping for most older cars. Web site: www.antiqueautoshop.com

See our ad on this page

Apple Hydraulics Inc 1610 Middle Rd Calverton, NY 11933-1419 800-882-7753, 631-369-9515 FAX: 631-369-9516 E-mail: info@applehydraulics.com	brake rebuilding shock rebuilding

See full listing in **Section Two** under **suspension parts**

Atlas Obsolete Chrysler Parts 10621 Bloomfield St, Unit 32 Los Alamitos, CA 90720 PH/FAX: 562-594-5560 E-mail: atlaschrys@aol.com	parts

See full listing in **Section One** under **Mopar**

Automotive Friction 4621 SE 27th Ave Portland, OR 97202 800-545-9088; FAX: 503-234-1026	brakes clutches water pumps

See full listing in **Section Two** under **clutches**

Baer Brake Systems 3108 W Thomas Rd #1201 Phoenix, AZ 85017 602-233-1411; FAX: 602-352-8445 E-mail: brakes@baer.com	brakes

Performance brake systems and products, 1955 thru current models. Web site: www.baer.com

Bronx Automotive 501 Tiffany St Bronx, NY 10474 718-589-2979	parts

See full listing in **Section Two** under **ignition parts**

C & G Early Ford Parts 1941 Commercial St, Dept AH Escondido, CA 92029-1233 760-740-2400; FAX: 760-740-8700 E-mail: cgford@cgfordparts.com	accessories/chrome emblems literature mechanical weatherstripping

See full listing in **Section One** under **Ford 1932-1953**

California Pony Cars 1906 Quaker Ridge Pl Ontario, CA 91761 909-923-2804; FAX: 909-947-8593 E-mail: 105232.3362@compuserve.com	parts

See full listing in **Section One** under **Mustang**

Canadian Mustang 20529 62 Ave Langley, BC Canada V3A 8R4 604-534-6424; FAX: 604-534-6694 E-mail: parts@canadianmustang.com	parts

See full listing in **Section One** under **Mustang**

Carson's Antique Auto Parts 235 Shawfarm Rd Holliston, MA 01746 508-429-2269; FAX: 508-429-0761 E-mail: w1066@gis.net	parts

See full listing in **Section Two** under **engine parts**

Chassis Engineering Inc 119 N 2nd St, Box 70 West Branch, IA 52358 319-643-2645; FAX: 319-643-2801	brakes chassis parts suspension parts

See full listing in **Section Two** under **chassis parts**

Chev's of the 40's 2027 B St, Dept Z Washougal, WA 98671 800-999-CHEV (2438) FAX: 360-835-7988	parts

See full listing in **Section One** under **Chevrolet**

Classic Chevrolet Parts Inc 8723 S I-35 Oklahoma City, OK 73149 405-631-4400; FAX: 405-631-5999 E-mail: info@classicchevroletparts.com	parts

See full listing in **Section One** under **Chevrolet**

Classic Tube Division of Classic & Performance Spec Inc 80 Rotech Dr Lancaster, NY 14086 800-TUBES-11 (882-3711) 716-759-1800; FAX: 716-759-1014 E-mail: classictube@aol.com	brake lines choke tubes fuel lines transmission lines vacuum lines

Pre-bent brake, fuel, transmission, choke, vacuum lines manufactured in stainless or OE steel with stainless (an exclusive) or OE steel fittings. Stainless braided hoses, power steering and fuel injection lines too. All lines are manufactured on computerized CNC state-of-the-art tube benders for 100% accuracy. Applications, for domestic or foreign cars and trucks, available from stock or made to your custom specifications. We lead the industry in the most accurate and largest selection of lines. Make your car or truck safer. Web site: www.classictube.com
See our ad on this page

CPR 431 S Sierra Way San Bernardino, CA 92408 909-884-6980; FAX: 909-884-7872	new parts reproduction parts used parts

See full listing in **Section One** under **Pontiac**

Dr Vette 14364 SW 139th Ct Miami, FL 33186 800-262-9595; FAX: 305-253-3641	brakes fuel system parts repairs

See full listing in **Section One** under **Corvettes**

Engineered Components Inc PO Box 841 Vernon, CT 06066 860-872-7046; FAX: 860-870-4841	disc brakes power boosters rebuild kits

Mail order and open shop. Monday-Friday 9 am to 5 pm. Deals in disc brake conversions for early Ford thru 1953, Chevy passenger cars thru 1964, Ford through 1964 and Chevy pickups thru 1959. We also offer power booster conversions and rear drum brake rebuild kits. Web site: www.ecihotrodbrakes.com

George Frechette 14 Cedar Dr Granby, MA 01033 800-528-5235	brake cylinder sleeving

Sleeving of brake cylinders with stainless steel for most makes and models of older cars and motorcycles.

Art Houser's Rear End Service 128 N Main St Topton, PA 19562 888-560-2127; FAX: 610-641-0163 E-mail: houser@rearman.com	rear end parts service

See full listing in **Section Two** under **differentials**

Inline Tube 33783 Groesbeck Hwy Fraser, MI 48026 800-385-9452 order 810-294-4093 tech FAX: 810-294-7349 E-mail: kryta@aol.com	brake cables/clips brake/fuel lines choke tubes engine lines flex hoses/valves vacuum lines

Mail order and open shop. Monday-Friday 9 am to 6 pm. Manufacture pre-bent brake lines, fuel lines, vacuum and transmission lines for any American auto. Also manufacturer of stainless parking brake cables for any American auto. All cables are available in aircraft quality stainless steel and are manufactured identical to the factory original, in appearance, application and fit. Custom applications welcome. Web site: www.inlinetube.com

Integrity Machine 383 Pipe Stave Hollow Rd Mount Sinai, NY 11766 888-446-9670; FAX: 516-476-9675	brake masters clutch masters wheel cylinders

Mail order and open shop. Monday-Friday 8 am to 5 pm. Deal in brake masters, clutch masters, wheel cylinders, clutch slave cylinders, sleeved with brass to original sizes. Complete rebuilding also available. Caliper rebuilding available. Visa, M/C.

Kanter Auto Products 76 Monroe St Boonton, NJ 07005 800-526-1096; 201-334-9575 FAX: 201-334-5423	car covers carpet sets front end kits parts

See full listing in **Section Two** under **comprehensive parts**

KC's Rods & Customs 3500 Aloma Ave, Ste D-16 Winter Park, FL 32792 877-750-6350; FAX: 407-673-9131 E-mail: bobbyb@bellsouth.net	brakes exhaust systems restoration

See full listing in **Section Two** under **street rods**

Muskegon Brake & Dist Co 848 E Broadway Muskegon, MI 49444 231-733-0874; FAX: 231-733-0635	brakes springs suspensions

Mail order and open shop. Monday-Friday 7:30 am to 5:30 pm, Saturday 9 am to 12 pm. Retail/wholesale service. Dealers wel-

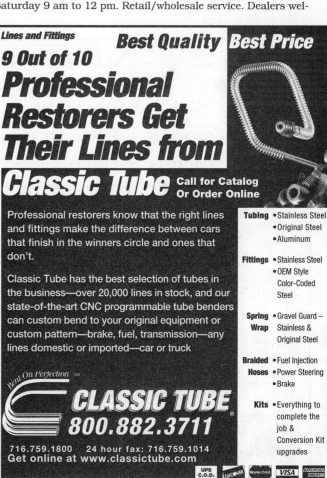

come. Brakes, suspension and springs for most vehicles. Specializing in these parts and services for Corvettes. Sleeving of all brake cylinders. Manufacture leaf springs for all makes and models. Located in Muskegon, MI, since 1945. Accept all major credit cards. Can ship almost anywhere. Web site: www.muskegonbrake.com

Northwestern Auto Supply Inc	parts
1101 S Division	
Grand Rapids, MI 49507	
800-704-1078, 616-241-1714	
FAX: 616-241-0924	

See full listing in **Section Two** under **engine parts**

Power Brake Booster Exchange Inc	brake boosters
4533 SE Division St	
Portland, OR 97206	
503-238-8882	

Mail order and open shop. Monday-Friday 9 am to 5 pm. Power brake booster rebuilder, 1959-1990. Plating available, 1 year warranty. Power brake booster only without master cylinder, call "Booster" Dewey.

See our ad on this page

Power Brake Systems	brake repair
c/o Jerry Cinotti	
431 S Sierra Way	
San Bernadino, CA 92408	
909-884-6980; FAX: 909-884-7872	

Mail order and open shop. Monday-Friday 8 am to 5 pm. Brakes: Bendix, Treadle-Vac and Delco Moraine power units rebuilt, 1953-1960, all units are complete, disassembled, parts cleaned and inspected, all units are pressure tested and vacuum tested to ensure total quality, all work guaranteed.

Power Brake X-Change Inc	parts
336 Lamont Pl	
Pittsburgh, PA 15232	
800-580-5729, 412-441-5729	
FAX: 412-441-9333	

Mail order and open shop. Monday-Friday 8 am to 4 pm. Remanufacturer of power manual gearboxes, pumps, control valves, cylinders with new chrome shafts, rack and pinions. Brake boosters, Hydro Vacs, Treadle-Vacs, Hydro Boosts, vacuum pumps and antilock brakes.

Rochester Clutch & Brake Co	brakes clutches
35 Niagara St	
Rochester, NY 14605	
716-232-2579; FAX: 716-232-3279	

Mail order and open shop. Monday-Friday 7:30 am to 4 pm. Specializing in clutch and brake remanufacturing, all vehicles and machines. All antiques and vintage racing. Special materials. Custom applications. 60 years' experience.

Sierra Specialty Auto	cylinder rebuilding
3494 Chandler Rd	
Quincy, CA 95971	
800-4-BRASS-1; FAX: 530-283-4845	
E-mail: joe@brakecylinder.com	

Mail order only. Brake and clutch cylinders sleeved with brass. Cars, trucks, tractors, motorcycles. Complete rebuilding available for most cylinders. Guaranteed. Also one-wire conversions and rebuild kits for Delco 10DN, 10SI and 12SI alternators. Web site: www.brakecylinder.com

Speed Bleeder Products Co — brake parts
12 S 751 Carpenter St
Lemont, IL 60439
630-739-4620; FAX: 630-739-9626
E-mail: speedbleeder@ameritech.net

Mail order and open shop. Open 24-7. Specializing in automotive brake bleeder screws with a built-in check valve for any vehicle with hydraulic brakes. There are over 17 sizes to fit any vehicle past and present. Web site: www.speedbleeder.com

Straight Six Jaguar — parts / service
24321 Hatteras St
Woodland Hills, CA 91367
PH/FAX: 818-716-1192

See full listing in **Section One** under **Jaguar**

Taylor Auto Parts — bearings / brakes / gaskets / seals
PO Box 650
Esparto, CA 95627
530-787-1929

See full listing in **Section Two** under **comprehensive parts**

Vintage Auto Parts Inc — cars / parts
24300 Hwy 9
Woodinville, WA 98072
800-426-5911, 425-486-0777
FAX: 425-486-0778
E-mail: erics@vapinc.com

See full listing in **Section Two** under **comprehensive parts**

Volunteer Studebaker — parts / parts locator
228 Marquiss Cir
Clinton, TN 37716
615-457-3002; FAX: 775-514-1386
E-mail: studebaker_joe@msn.com

See full listing in **Section One** under **Studebaker**

Wheeler's Classic Parts — parts
104 S Bowles
West Harrison, IN 47060
812-637-2194
E-mail: info@partsforclassics.com

Deals in antique and classic cars parts (1930-1970) including fuel, suspension, brakes, cooling, shocks, clutch, electrical, ignition, door regulators/channel, rebuilding services, some body, chrome and glass. Web site: www.partsforclassics.com

White Post Restorations — brakes / restoration
One Old Car Dr, PO Drawer D
White Post, VA 22663
540-837-1140; FAX: 540-837-2368
E-mail: info@whitepost.com

Brakes sleeved and rebuilt: masters, wheels, clutches, slaves, calipers, boosters, and shoes relined. Better than new. Quick service. Lifetime written warranty. Web site: www.whitepost.com
See our ad on page 359

brass cars/parts

Blaak Radiateurenbedryf — radiators
Blaaksedyk oost 19
Heinenoord 3274LA Netherlands
31-186-601732; FAX: 31-186-603044
E-mail: info@blaak.com

See full listing in **Section Two** under **radiators**

Classic Autopart Repro Service — parts
789 Furlong Rd
Sebastopol, CA 95472
PH/FAX: 707-824-0657
E-mail: quotes@brassauto.com

Brass era pre-1916 auto part manufacturer and restorer. We make all parts for brass era cars. Web site: www.brassauto.com

Lyme Pond Restorations — restoration
PO Box 202
Barnard, VT 05031
802-457-4657

See full listing in **Section Two** under **restoration shops**

Ben McAdam — electrical parts
500 Clover Ln
Wheeling, WV 26003
304-242-3388, 304-242-0855
E-mail: antiquebenny@aol.com

See full listing in **Section Two** under **ignition parts**

Skills Unlimited Inc — radiators
7172 CR 33
Tiffin, OH 44883
PH/FAX: 419-992-4680
419-448-4639 shop
E-mail: smith@friendlynet.com

See full listing in **Section Two** under **radiators**

Zephyrhills Festivals and Auction Inc — auction / swap meet
PO Box 996
Odessa, FL 33556-0996
813-258-6726 office
813-782-0835 park
FAX: 813-258-3779

See full listing in **Section Two** under **auctions & shows**

brokers

Auto Consultants & Appraisal Service — appraisals
Charles J Kozelka
PO Box 111
Macedonia, OH 44056
330-467-0748; FAX: 330-467-3725

See full listing in **Section Two** under **appraisals**

Auto-Line Enterprises Inc — appraisals / broker services
2 Lyons Rd
Armonk, NY 10504
914-681-1757; FAX: 914-273-5159
E-mail: autocashny@aol.com

See full listing in **Section Two** under **appraisals**

Charles W Clarke, Automotive Consultants — appraisals / car dealer consultant
17 Saddle Ridge Dr
West Simsbury, CT 06092-2118
PH/FAX: 860-658-2714

See full listing in **Section Two** under **consultants**

Classic Auto Brokers
18812 Monteverde Dr
Springhill, FL 34610
PH/FAX: 727-856-5168

appraiser
broker

Brokering only top quality vehicles. Specializing in Mustang, Shelby, Thunderbird and all quality collectibles.

Classic Car Research
29508 Southfield Rd, Ste 106
Southfield, MI 48076
248-557-2880; FAX: 248-557-3511
E-mail: kawifreek@msn.com

appraisals
consultant
part locating

See full listing in **Section Two** under **appraisals**

Corvette Enterprise Brokerage
The Power Broker-Mike Kitain
52 Van Houten Ave
Passaic Park, NJ 07055-5512
973-472-7021

appraisals
broker
car locator
investment
planning

See full listing in **Section One** under **Corvette**

Mark Gillett
PO Box 9177
Dallas, TX 75209
PH/FAX: 214-902-9258
011-525-559-6240 Mexico City, Mexico
E-mail: autonet@onramp.net

car locator
sales

See full listing in **Section Two** under **car dealers**

The Gullwing Garage Ltd
Bricklin SVI Specialists
5 Cimorelli Dr
New Windsor, NY 12553-6201
845-561-0019 anytime

appraisals
literature
parts
service

See full listing in **Section One** under **Bricklin**

Kruse International
5540 County Rd 11-A, PO Box 190
Auburn, IN 46706
800-968-4444; FAX: 219-925-5467

auction

See full listing in **Section Two** under **auctions & shows**

M & M Automobile Appraisers Inc
584 Broomspun St
Henderson, NV 89015
702-568-5120; FAX: 702-568-5158
E-mail: mmautoappr@earthlink.net

appraisals
broker
consultant

See full listing in **Section Two** under **appraisals**

Randall Marcus Vintage Automobiles
706 Hanshaw Rd
Ithaca, NY 14850
607-257-5939; FAX: 607-272-8806
E-mail: randysvintageautos@
bgdmlaw.com

appraisals
broker
car locator
consultant

Vintage cars bought and sold. Pre-purchase inspections and valuations performed. Consultation provided on acquisition and liquidation of collections. Specializing in all pre-1930 automobiles and vintage British sports and touring cars, 1930s through 1960s.

Bill McCoskey
PO Box 93
Littlestown, PA 17340
410-346-0660; FAX: 410-346-6499
E-mail: billmccoskey@aol.com

accident/damage
investigations
appraisals

See full listing in **Section Two** under **appraisals**

Memory Lane Motors Inc
1231 Rt 176
Lake Bluff, IL 60044
847-362-4600

appraisals
car dealer
storage

See full listing in **Section Two** under **car dealers**

Charlie Merrill
1041 Kenyon Rd
Twin Falls, ID 83301
208-736-0949

broker
car dealer
car locator

Mail order and open shop. Sell good restorable cars and brokerage of cars for others. Also search for particular cars of all makes.

Charles Noe
64-1/2 Greenwood Ave
Bethel, CT 06801
PH/FAX: 203-748-4222
E-mail: mdchas@aol.com

broker
parts/auto purchases
parts/auto sales

Specialize in 1932-1933 Chevrolet and 1973-1979 Chevrolet pickup parts and cars. Listing service for all automobile makes. Always looking for quality cars and car parts. Also pedal cars, pedal car parts, vintage toys and trains.

Precious Metal Automotive Restoration Co Inc
1601 College Ave SE
Grand Rapids, MI 49507
616-243-0220; FAX: 616-243-6646
E-mail: dpayne@iserv.net

broker
restoration

See full listing in **Section One** under **Mercedes-Benz**

RM Classic Cars
5 W Forest Ave
Ypsilanti, MI 48197
734-547-2400; FAX: 734-547-9424
E-mail: michigan@rmcars.com

auctions

See full listing in **Section Two** under **auctions & shows**

Vintage Auto Ent
PO Box 2183
Manchester Center, VT 05255
802-362-4719; FAX: 802-362-3007
E-mail: dbrownell@sprynet.com

appraisals
auctioneer

See full listing in **Section Two** under **appraisals**

camshafts

Air Flow Research
10490 Ilex Ave
Pacoima, CA 91331
818-890-0616; FAX: 818-890-0490

cylinder heads

See full listing in **Section One** under **Chevrolet**

Atlas Engine Rebuilding Co Inc
24251 Frampton Ave
Harbor City, CA 90710
310-325-6898; FAX: 310-325-7701

engine rebuilding
machine work

See full listing in **Section Two** under **engine rebuilding**

Cam-Pro
PO Box 3305
Great Falls, MT 59403
800-525-2581, 406-771-0300

camshaft repair
engine parts

Mail order and open shop. Monday-Saturday 10 am to 5 pm. Camshaft grinding and repair. Lifter resurfacing. New cams, lifters and other engine parts.

Section Two – Generalists

Daytona Cams Box 5094 Ormond Beach, FL 32175 800-505-2267; FAX: 904-258-1582 E-mail: info@camshafts.com	**camshafts** **engine parts**

Camshafts and new engine parts for most US built cars and light trucks. Web site: www.daytonacams.com

Daytona Turbo Action Camshafts 1109 US #1, PO Box 5094 Ormond Beach, FL 32175 888-RARE-CAM, 800-505-CAMS 386-676-7478; FAX: 386-258-1582 E-mail: info@camshafts.com	**camshafts** **engine parts**

See full listing in **Section Two** under **bearings**

Maximum Torque Specialties PO Box 925 Delavan, WI 53115 262-740-1118; FAX: 262-740-1161 E-mail: mts@elknet.net	**high-perf parts** **restoration parts**

See full listing in **Section One** under **Cadillac/LaSalle**

No 1 Performance 1775 S Redwood Rd Salt Lake City, UT 84104 800-453-8250; FAX: 801-975-9653	**engine kits** **parts**

See full listing in **Section Two** under **engine parts**

Skip's Auto Parts Skip Bollinger 1500 Northaven Dr Gladstone, MO 64118 816-455-2337; FAX: 816-459-7547 E-mail: carpartman@aol.com	**chassis parts** **ignition parts** **water pumps**

See full listing in **Section Two** under **water pumps**

car & parts locators

A-1 Street Rods 631 E Las Vegas St Colorado Springs, CO 80903 719-632-4920, 719-577-4588 FAX: 719-634-6577	**parts**

See full listing in **Section Two** under **street rods**

AAAC-Antique Automobile **Appraisal & Consulting** PO Box 700153 Plymouth, MI 48170 PH/FAX: 734-453-7644 E-mail: aaac@ameritech.net	**appraisals** **Cadillac parts** **consulting**

See full listing in **Section One** under **Cadillac/LaSalle**

ADP Hollander 14800 28th Ave N #190 Plymouth, MN 55447 800-761-9266; FAX: 800-825-1124 E-mail: info@hollander-auto-parts.com	**interchange info** **manuals**

Looking for parts for your classic car? Increase your search possibilities with *Hollander Interchange Classic Search Manuals* from ADP Hollander, the most complete and accurate source for indexing interchangeable parts among vehicles. Trusted by automotive professionals for more than 60 years, *Hollander Interchange Classic Search Manuals* are perfect for classic car enthusiasts and do-it-yourself mechanics. Web site: www.hollander-auto-parts.com

All British Car Parts Inc 2847 Moores Rd Baldwin, MD 21013 410-692-9572; FAX: 410-692-5654 E-mail: lucasguy@home.com	**parts**

See full listing in **Section Two** under **electrical systems**

Amherst Antique Auto Show 157 Hollis Rd Amherst, NH 03031 603-673-2093, NH FAX: 617-641-0647, MA	**swap meets**

See full listing in **Section Two** under **auctions & shows**

AutoMatch CARS (Computer Aided Referral Service) 2017 Blvd Napoleon Louisville, KY 40205 800-962-2771, 502-417-8793 mobile 502-452-1920 office FAX: 502-479-6222 E-mail: amcars@aol.com or aautomatch@aol.com	**broker** **car dealer network** **exotic, classic, new** **& used car locator**

See full listing in **Section Two** under **car dealers**

The Autoworks Ltd 90 Center Ave Westwood, NJ 07675 201-358-0200; FAX: 201-358-0442	**restoration** **sales** **service**

See full listing in **Section Two** under **service shops**

AVM Automotive Consulting Box 338 Montvale, NJ 07645-0338 201-391-5194; FAX: 978-383-4776 E-mail: avmtony@yahoo.com	**appraisals** **consultant**

See full listing in **Section Two** under **appraisals**

British Car Service 2854 N Stone Ave Tucson, AZ 85705 520-882-7026; FAX: 520-882-7053 E-mail: bcs@liveline.com	**restoration** **salvage yard**

See full listing in **Section Two** under **restoration shops**

British Luxury Automotive Parts 257 Niagara St Toronto, ON Canada M6J 2L7 416-693-8400; FAX: 416-694-3202 Cell: 416-820-4323	**new and used parts**

See full listing in **Section One** under **Jaguar**

Caddy Central 11117 Tippett Rd Clinton, MD 20735 301-234-0135; FAX: 301-234-0140 E-mail: cadlocator@juno.com	**cars** **locating service** **parts**

See full listing in **Section One** under **Cadillac/LaSalle**

Car Critic 202 Woodshire Ln Naples, FL 34105 941-435-1157; FAX: 941-261-4864 E-mail: carcritic@earthlink.net	**appraisals** **inspections**

Mail order and open shop. Daily 8 am to 8 pm. Perform nationwide pre-purchase inspections, certified appraisals, mechanical failure analysis, off lease inspections prior to or immediately after lease termination, physical damage appraisals for insurance companies, diminution (loss) of value, automobile fire investigations, accident scene inspections, investigations and photographs and civil expert testimonial. This work is performed on automobiles, trucks, motorcycles, boats and watercraft. Perform repair facility fraud investigations as well as local evaluations for attorneys, banks and consumers. Member of IAAA, IATN, ASE. Web site: www.carcritic.net

Checker Motors 1314 Rollins Rd Burlingame, CA 94010 650-340-8669; FAX: 650-340-9473 E-mail: tonyleo@pacbell.net	cars parts rentals

Specializing in Checker taxi cabs, Checker Marathons and Checker station wagons. Cars for sale or rent for movies, commercials or print ads. Checker locator service for cars and parts.

Chicago Car Exchange 14085 W Rockland Rd Libertyville, IL 60048 847-680-1950; FAX: 847-680-1961 E-mail: oldtoys@wwa.com	appraisals car dealer car locator financing storage

See full listing in **Section Two** under **car dealers**

Classic Car Research 29508 Southfield Rd, Ste 106 Southfield, MI 48076 248-557-2880; FAX: 248-557-3511 E-mail: kawifreek@msn.com	appraisals consultant part locating

See full listing in **Section Two** under **appraisals**

Daytona Cams Box 5094 Ormond Beach, FL 32175 800-505-2267; FAX: 904-258-1582 E-mail: info@camshafts.com	camshafts engine parts

See full listing in **Section Two** under **camshafts**

DeLorean One 20229 Nordhoff St Chatsworth, CA 91311 818-341-1796; FAX: 818-998-6381	bodywork parts service

See full listing in **Section One** under **DeLorean**

Desert Valley Auto Parts 2227 W Happy Valley Rd Phoenix, AZ 85027 800-905-8024 623-780-8024; FAX: 623-582-9141 E-mail: sales@dvap.com	salvage yard

See full listing in **Section Five** under **Arizona**

Dodge City Vintage Dodge Vehicles & Parts 18584 Hwy 108, PO Box 1687 Jamestown, CA 95327 209-984-5858; FAX: 209-984-3285 E-mail: mike@dodgecityvintage.com	parts restoration research vehicles

See full listing in **Section One** under **Dodge**

Driving Passion Ltd USA Marc Tuwiner 7132 Chilton Ct Clarksville, MD 21029 PH/FAX: 301-596-9078 E-mail: lm7132@aol.com	cars parts salvage yard

See full listing in **Section One** under **Cadillac/LaSalle**

David Elliott 11796 Franklin Minocqua, WI 54548 715-356-1335	auto transport car locator

See full listing in **Section Two** under **transport**

Richard H Feibusch 211 Dimmick Ave Venice, CA 90291 310-392-6605; FAX: 310-396-1933 E-mail: rfeibusch@loop.com	appraisals

See full listing in **Section Two** under **appraisals**

Finders Service 454-458 W Lincoln Hwy Chicago Heights, IL 60411-2463 708-481-9685; FAX: 708-481-5837 E-mail: findersvc@aol.com	parts finders

Mail order only. Our dedication is to save history accurately. Offers free information and order form packet sent by USPS mail if given complete name, address, city, state, country and mailing code. OEM new and used genuine parts, accessories, literature, service manuals, catalogs, tools, keys and locks, American and European all years and makes 1900-1995 including government, army and navy parts. Research Service Department hours: Monday-Friday 11 am to 4 pm. Web site: www.usaworks.com/findersvc

Fort Wayne Clutch & Driveline 2424 Goshen Rd Fort Wayne, IN 46808 219-484-8505; FAX: 219-484-8605 E-mail: clutches@skyenet.net	axles axleshafts clutches driveshafts

See full listing in **Section Two** under **clutches**

J Giles Automotive 703 Morgan Ave Pascagoula, MS 39567-2116 228-769-1012; FAX: 228-769-8904 E-mail: jgauto@datasync.com	car & parts locator exporter

Arrange shipment of all vehicles to any port. For foreign clients, locate, inspect, purchase and ship all types of vehicles. Full spares support for all years, makes and models for foreign and domestic clients. Worldwide references.

Mark Gillett PO Box 9177 Dallas, TX 75209 PH/FAX: 214-902-9258 011-525-559-6240 Mexico City, Mexico E-mail: autonet@onramp.net	car locator sales

See full listing in **Section Two** under **car dealers**

Halpin Used Auto & Truck Parts 1093 Rt 123 Mayfield, NY 12117 518-863-4906 E-mail: junkyard2064@webtv.net	NOS auto parts NOS truck parts used auto parts used truck parts

See full listing in **Section Five** under **New York**

Happy Daze Classic Cars 257 Morris Ct Fond Du Lac, WI 54935 920-922-8450	car dealer

See full listing in **Section Two** under **car dealers**

Hawthorne's Happy Motoring Box 1332 Coaldale AB Canada T1M 1N2 PH/FAX: 403-345-2101	appraisals parts

See full listing in **Section Two** under **appraisals**

Gary Hill Auto Service
150 E St Joseph St
Arcadia, CA 91006
626-447-2576; FAX: 626-447-1461

restoration
service

See full listing in **Section Two** under **racing**

Jacques Rear Engine Renault Parts
13839 Hwy 8 Business
El Cajon, CA 92021
619-561-6687; FAX: 619-561-1656
E-mail: renaultj@pacbell.net

parts

See full listing in **Section One** under **Renault**

Landry Classic MotorCars
34 Goodhue Ave
Chicopee, MA 01020
413-592-2746; FAX: 413-594-8378
oldcar@map.com

appraisals

See full listing in **Section Two** under **appraisals**

Dave Lincoln
Box 331
Yorklyn, DE 19736
610-444-4144, PA
E-mail: tagbarn@msn.com

license plates

See full listing in **Section Two** under **license plates**

Randall Marcus Vintage Automobiles
706 Hanshaw Rd
Ithaca, NY 14850
607-257-5939; FAX: 607-272-8806
E-mail: randysvintageautos@
bgdmlaw.com

appraisals
broker
car locator
consultant

See full listing in **Section Two** under **brokers**

McLean's Brit Bits
14 Sagamore Rd
Rye, NH 03870
800-995-2487; FAX: 603-433-0009
E-mail: sam@britbits.com

accessories
parts
sales
service

See full listing in **Section Two** under **car dealers**

Charlie Merrill
1041 Kenyon Rd
Twin Falls, ID 83301
208-736-0949

broker
car dealer
car locator

See full listing in **Section Two** under **brokers**

National Parts Locator Service
636 East 6th St #81
Ogden, UT 84404-2415
877-672-7875, 801-627-7210

parts locator

Mail order only. Locate parts, accessories, literature, services, novelties, interior, upholstery, memorabilia for automobiles, trucks and motorcycles, foreign and domestic, from 1895-present. Looking for an automobile, truck or a motorcycle? National and international locator directory. How to buy a used automobile? Auctions? Anything automotive, challenge us. Web site: www.nationalpartslocatorservice.com

Pilkington Glass Search
1975 Galaxie St
Columbus, OH 43207
800-848-1351; FAX: 614-443-0709

glass parts

See full listing in **Section Two** under **glass**

**Precious Metal Automotive
Restoration Co Inc**
1601 College Ave SE
Grand Rapids, MI 49507
616-243-0220; FAX: 616-243-6646
E-mail: dpayne@iserv.net

broker
restoration

See full listing in **Section One** under **Mercedes-Benz**

William H Randel
PO Box 173
Hatboro, PA 19040
215-675-8969; FAX: 215-441-0960
E-mail: tbrdnut@bellatlantic.net

appraisals
car locators

See full listing in **Section One** under **Thunderbird**

Rapido Group
80093 Dodson Rd
Tygh Valley, OR 97063
541-544-3333; FAX: 541-544-3100

accessories
parts

See full listing in **Section One** under **Merkur**

Stone Barn Inc
202 Rt 46, Box 117
Vienna, NJ 07880
908-637-4444; FAX: 908-637-4290

restoration

See full listing in **Section Two** under **restoration shops**

T-Bird Sanctuary
9997 SW Avery
Tualatin, OR 97062
503-692-9848; FAX: 503-692-9849

parts

See full listing in **Section One** under **Thunderbird**

Timeless Masterpieces
221 Freeport Dr
Bloomingdale, IL 60108
630-893-1058 evenings

appraisals
consultant

See full listing in **Section Two** under **appraisals**

car care products

**ACE Automotive Cleaning
Equipment Co**
897 S Washington, Ste 232
Holland, MI 49423
616-772-3260; FAX: 616-772-3261

sandblasting
equipment

See full listing in **Section Two** under **rust removal & stripping**

Auto Chic/Liquid Glass
6B Hamilton Business Pk
85 Franklin Rd
Dover, NJ 07801
973-989-9220; FAX: 973-989-9234
E-mail: sales@autochic.com

car covers

See full listing in **Section Two** under **car covers**

Backyard Buddy Corp
140 Dana St
Warren, OH 44483
800-837-9353, 330-395-9372
FAX: 330-392-9311

automotive lift

See full listing in **Section Two** under **accessories**

Section Two – Generalists

Section Two – Generalists

Bavarian Autosport
275 Constitution Ave
Portsmouth, NH 03801
800-535-2002; FAX: 800-507-2002

| accessories parts |

See full listing in **Section One** under **BMW**

Bill & Brad's Tropical Formula
811 Howard Ct
Clearwater, FL 33756
727-442-6711
E-mail: bradwade@gte.net

| car wash cheater spray paste wax |

Mail order and open shop. Professional detailer making special car care products. Web site: www.billandbrads.com

Billie Inc
PO Box 1161
Ashburn, VA 20146-1161
800-878-6328; FAX: 703-858-0102

| garage diaper mats |

Mail and phone orders. 24 hours, 7 days a week. Non-leak super absorbent under-the-car mat. Sold as individual mats and economical 30 foot rolls.

See our ad on page 379

Leon Blackledge Sales Co
156 N School Ln
Souderton, PA 18964-1153
800-525-7515, 215-734-4270
FAX: 215-723-7004

| polish |

Markets Wonder Tool, the only dual headed orbital polisher-sander. Complete line of Duragloss® and Wax Shop® polishes and cleaners. "Mr. Moly" (0.05 micron particle size molybdenum disulphide) engine treatment, "you will feel the difference", Becker automotive audio systems. German engineering at its finest.

Brit-Tek Ltd
163 Griffin Rd
Deerfield, NH 03037
800-255-5883

| MGB cars rustproofing systems |

See full listing in **Section One** under **MG**

**Buenger Enterprises/
GoldenRod Dehumidifier**
3600 S Harbor Blvd
Oxnard, CA 93035
800-451-6797; FAX: 805-985-1534

| dehumidifiers |

Mail order only. The GoldenRod dehumidifier protects your prized auto from dampness, rust and mildew. It is easy to install, maintenance free and operates for pennies a day. Our product is UL listed, made in the USA and guaranteed for ten years. You've spent so much time restoring your old car, why not protect it with the GoldenRod?

**Buffalo Milke Automotive
Polishing Products Inc**
PO Box 1955
Pleasanton, CA 94566
888-462-8332; FAX: 925-417-7445
E-mail: buffalomilke@buffalomilke.com

| spray wax |

Buffalo Milke® instant spray wax. Three products in one: cleaner, detailer and wax. Cleans and protects both paint and chrome surfaces. Leaves no white residue or powder on rubber, textured or grainy trim parts. No harsh abrasives, cover large areas quickly, excellent on clear coat, any painted surface as well as chrome, glass and plexi-glass. Lasts through several washings, hides minor spider webbing and scratches. Money back guarantee. Proudly made in the USA. Web site: www.buffalomilke.com

California Car Cover Co
9525 DeSoto
Chatsworth, CA 91311
800-423-5525; FAX: 818-998-2442

| accessories apparel car covers tools |

See full listing in **Section Two** under **car covers**

Caswell Electroplating in Miniature
4336 Rt 31
Palmyra, NY 14522
315-597-5140, 315-597-6378
FAX: 315-597-1457
E-mail: sales@caswellplating.com

| plating kits |

See full listing in **Section Two** under **plating & polishing**

**Color-Plus Leather
Restoration System**
106 Harrier Ct, 3767 Sunrise Lake
Milford, PA 18337-9315
570-686-3158; FAX: 570-686-4161
E-mail: jpcolorplus@pikeonline.net

| leather conditioning leather dye |

See full listing in **Section Two** under **leather restoration**

**Comfy/Inter-American
Sheepskins Inc**
1346 Centinela Ave
West Los Angeles, CA 90025-1901
800-521-4014; FAX: 310-442-6080
E-mail: sales@comfysheep.com

| floor mats seat covers |

See full listing in **Section Two** under **interiors & interior parts**

Competition Chemicals Inc
715 Railroad St, PO Box 820
Iowa Falls, IA 50126
641-648-5121; FAX: 641-648-9816

| polish |

See full listing in **Section Two** under **plating & polishing**

Cover-It
17 Wood St
West Haven, CT 06516-3843
800-932-9344; FAX: 203-931-4754
E-mail: info@coverit.com

| all-weather shelters |

See full listing in **Section Two** under **car covers**

Cyclo Industries LLC
10190 Riverside Dr
Palm Beach Gardens, FL 33410
800-843-7813, 561-775-9600
FAX: 561-622-1055
E-mail: cyclo@cyclo.com

| cleaners lubricants |

Offer a complete line of professionally formulated, time tested cleaners, lubricants and additives in dynamic packages. Products designed for the complete maintenance and enhanced performance of motor vehicles, marine, home and industrial applications. For almost 40 years the Cyclo brand of products have been tested and preferred by professional mechanics to maintain and extend the use and performance of cars, trucks, plane and industrial machinery. Offering a full line of service chemicals including a variety of cleaners, lubricants and additives. Call or write for more information. Web site: www.cyclo.com

Dashhugger
PO Box 933
Clovis, CA 93613
559-298-4529; FAX: 559-298-3428
E-mail: info@dashhugger.com

| dashboard covers |

See full listing in **Section Two** under **interiors & interior parts**

Double Park Lifts
6352 N Hillside
Wichita, KS 67219
800-754-8786; FAX: 316-744-9221
E-mail: lewis216@southwind.net

| service lifts |

See full listing in **Section Two** under **storage**

Dri-Wash 'n Guard Independent Distributor PO Box 1331 Palm Desert, CA 92261 800-428-1883, 760-346-1984 FAX: 760-568-6354 E-mail: driwasherik@aol.com	**automotive care products boat care products**

Cleans and protects virtually everything you own without using water; DWG International's waterless and water saving technologies make it simple, efficient and economical. Dri-Wash 'n Guard cleans, seals, protects and polishes without scratching any non-porous surface, fine automobiles, RVs, boats, airplanes and equipment. A full line of carpet, fabric and upholstery, leather and vinyl, metal polish and home products are also available. Don't overlook the health care and body product lines now available. Monthly publication, *InfoGram.*

Emgee/Clean Tools 10 Plaza Dr Westmont, IL 60559 630-887-7707; FAX: 630-887-1347	**drying product**

The Absorber, an all purpose drying product that is compact and reusable. The Absorber dries faster and absorbs 50% more water than other drying products. A safe, non-abrasive, lintless material that is resistant to grease, oil and most chemicals. The Absorber is machine washable and will last for years. Revolutionary new product (cleaning and waxing product): the Glosser™, is the easy new waterless way to give your car that last minute quick detail. No water or toweling required. The Glosser™ is the first cleaning tool that contains cleaners and waxes in a triceraphilic™ microfiber wipe that adds gloss to cars, trucks, boats, motorcycles, RVs and much more.

Fast Lane Products PO Box 7000-50 Palos Verdes Peninsula, CA 90274 800-327-8669; FAX: 310-541-2235 E-mail: info@fastlaneproducts.com	**chamois cleaners & waxes drain tubs hand wringers**

Mail order only. Monday-Friday 9 am to 5 pm Pacific time. Commercial quality hand wringers, drain tubs, premium synthetic chamois, and superb Harly wax products for easy maintenance of cars, trucks, airplanes and boats. Web site: www.fastlaneproducts.com

FHS Supply Inc PO Box 9 Clover, SC 29710 800-742-8484; FAX: 803-222-7285 E-mail: fhsoil@aol.com	**oil**

See full listing in **Section Two** under **lubricants**

The Finished Look PO Box 191413 Sacramento, CA 95819-1413 800-827-6715; FAX: 916-451-3984 E-mail: info@thefinishedlook.com	**POR-15 products**

See full listing in **Section Two** under **rustproofing**

Frost Auto Restoration Techniques Ltd Crawford St Rochdale OL16 5NU United Kingdom 44-1706-658619 FAX: 44-1706-860338 E-mail: order@frost.co.uk	**car care products paints tools**

See full listing in **Section Two** under **tools**

Gasoline Alley LLC 1700E Iron Ave, PO Box 737 Salina, KS 67402 800-326-8372, 785-822-1003 FAX: 785-827-9337 E-mail: morrison@midusa.net	**drip pans**

See full listing in **Section Two** under **accessories**

Gliptone Manufacturing Inc 1595 A-6 Ocean Ave Bohemia, NY 11716 631-737-1130, FAX: 631-589-5487 E-mail: wmessina@gliptone.com or rcaporaco@gliptone.com	**car care products**

Deals in car care products. Web site: www.gliptone.com

Green-Stuff Metal Polish PO Box 7071 Knoxville, TN 37921 865-382-1286 E-mail: greenstuffpolish@aol.com	**metal polish**

See full listing in **Section Two** under **plating & polishing**

Griot's Garage 3500-A 20th St E Tacoma, WA 98424 800-345-5789; FAX: 888-252-2252 E-mail: info@griotsgarage.com	**car care products paint tools**

See full listing in **Section Two** under **tools**

Jack P Gross Assoc/Scott Manufacturing Inc 163 Helenwood Detour Rd, PO Box 97 Helenwood, TN 37755 423-569-6088; FAX: 423-569-6428 E-mail: scottmfg@highland.net	**air hose products water hose products**

See full listing in **Section Two** under **service shops**

Iverson Automotive 14704 Karyl Dr Minnetonka, MN 55345 800-325-0480; FAX: 952-938-5707	**polishes pot metal restoration**

See full listing in **Section Two** under **plating & polishing**

JCM Industries 2 Westwood Dr Danbury, CT 06811 800-752-0245	**wax hardener**

Mail order only. Offering a hardener for car waxes. Makes car finishes hard as a rock. It's like putting two coats of wax on a car or truck.

Koala International PO Box 255 Uwchland, PA 19480 610-458-8395; FAX: 610-458-8735 E-mail: sales@koala-products.com	**convertible cleaners & protectants plastic coating plastic polish**

Products include the following: vinyl cleaners and semi-permanent protectants for convertibles. Clear sealer coating for renewing aged, brittle, interior panels. Prevents top surfaces from crumbling. Plastic polish removes scratches and hazing from lenses, bezels, instrument clusters and paint, permanently. Dealer inquiries welcome. Web site: www.koala-products.com

Section Two – Generalists

KozaK® Auto Drywash® Inc
6 S Lyon St
Batavia, NY 14020
800-237-9927, 716-343-8111
FAX: 716-343-3732
E-mail: info@kozak.com

| | cloths |

Mail order and open shop. Manufacturer of KozaK® Drywash® brand cleaning cloths for cars and furniture. Also new printing services available with mailing services (i.e. Cheshire® labeling and inserting). You'll never drive a dirty car again. KozaK® safety cleans and polishes your car without water. Sold and guaranteed since 1926. Call Ed Harding, President, for info. Web site: www.kozak.com

Leatherique Professional Leather Restoration & Preservation Products
PO Box 2678
Orange Park, FL 32065
904-272-0992; FAX: 904-272-1534
E-mail: lrpltd@bellsouth.net

| | leather cleaning conditioning & professional restoration products |

See full listing in **Section One** under **Rolls-Royce/Bentley**

Liquid Glass Enterprises Inc
PO Box 1170
Teaneck, NJ 07666
201-387-6755; FAX: 201-387-2168
E-mail: lheywang@ix.netcom.com

| | car care products |

Car care products. Manufacturer of the Liquid Glass Total Appearance System. This includes Liquid Glass polish, car wash and pre-cleaner. Also Connoisseur's choice line of protectants and cleaners. Web site: www.liquidglass.com

M & R Products
1940 SW Blvd
Vineland, NJ 08360
800-524-2560, 609-696-9450
FAX: 609-696-4999
E-mail: mrproducts@mrproducts.com

| | hardware tie-downs |

See full listing in **Section Two** under **accessories**

Mac's Custom Tie-Downs
105 Sanderson Rd
Chehalis, WA 98532
800-666-1586 orders
360-748-1180; FAX: 360-748-1185

| | automotive tie-downs |

See full listing in **Section Two** under **trailers**

Malm Chem Corp
PO Box 300, Dept HVA
Pound Ridge, NY 10576
914-764-5775; FAX: 914-764-5785
E-mail: jkolin@cloud9.net

| | polish wax |

Dealing in auto wax, polishes and tools for their application. Web site: www.malms.com

Murphy's Motoring Accessories Inc
PO Box 618
Greendale, WI 53129-0618
800-529-8315, 414-529-8333
FAX: 414-529-0616
E-mail: mma@execpc.com

| | car covers |

See full listing in **Section Two** under **car covers**

Neumaclassic
Ayacucho 1292
Rosario Sta Fe 2000 Argentina
+54 341 425-0040
FAX: +54 341 421-9629
E-mail: bcdcs@bcd.com.ar

| | tires |

See full listing in **Section Two** under **tires**

Northern Tool & Equipment
PO Box 1219
Burnsville, MN 55337-0219
800-533-5545

| | engines generators hydraulics |

See full listing in **Section Two** under **tools**

OJ Rallye Automotive
N 6808 Hwy OJ, PO Box 540
Plymouth, WI 53073
920-893-2531; FAX: 920-893-6800
E-mail: ojrallye@excel.net

| | accessories car care products lighting parts |

See full listing in **Section Two** under **lighting equipment**

Performance Automotive Inc
1696 New London Tpke, PO Box 10
Glastonbury, CT 06033
860-633-7868; FAX: 860-657-9110
E-mail: pai@pcnet.com

| | accessories car care |

Dealing in accessories and car care products, retail/wholesale, detailing and concours preparation. Enthusiasts serving enthusiasts, providing total car care. Web site: www.perfauto.com

Prezerve
1101 Arapahoe, Ste 3
Lincoln, NE 68502
888-774-4184; FAX: 402-420-7777
E-mail: prezerve@prezerveit.com

| | additives |

Mail order only. Chem-Tec Corp has developed Prezerve™, an additive designed to stabilize automotive fluids during storage. Packaged as a set of three. Prezerve fights the effects of oil, gasoline and anti-freeze breakdown. Web site: www.prezerveit.com

Protective Products Corp
Box 246
Johnston, IA 50131
888-772-1277; FAX: 515-334-7533
E-mail: ppc1@aol.com

| | chemical products |

See full listing in **Section Two** under **restoration aids**

T Schmidt
827 N Vernon
Dearborn, MI 48128-1542
313-562-7161

| | rust removers |

See full listing in **Section Two** under **rust removal & stripping**

Standard Abrasives Motorsports Division
4201 Guardian St
Simi Valley, CA 93063
800-383-6001; 805-520-5800 ext 371
FAX: 805-577-7398
E-mail: tech@sa-motorsports.com

| | abrasives |

See full listing in **Section Two** under **restoration aids**

Sterling Specialties
42 Ponderosa Ln
Monroe, NY 10950
845-782-7614

| | car care products |

Mail and phone orders. Oil drain valves by Fumoto, Kozak cloths, AMS/oil synthetic lubricants, Semichrome. Free brochure.

Stevens Car Care Products Inc
36542 Vine St
East Lake, OH 44095
440-953-2900; FAX: 440-953-4473
E-mail: info@stevenscarcare.com

| | car alarms rust deterrents |

See full listing in **Section Two** under **anti-theft**

Stoner Inc 1070 Robert Fulton Hwy Quarryville, PA 17566 717-786-7355; FAX: 717-786-8819 E-mail: sales@stonersolutions.com	cleaners lubricants

Mail order and open shop. Phone Monday-Friday 8 am to 8 pm. Specialty auto detailing cleaners, lubricants and appearance dressing for auto enthusiasts and detailers. More Shine Less Time™ detail dressing for tires, plastic, vinyl, rubber and trim. Web site: www.stonersolutions.com

Superior Equipment 326 S Meridian Valley Center, KS 67147 800-526-9992; FAX: 316-755-4391 E-mail: mail@superlifts.com	auto lifts shop tools

See full listing in **Section Two** under **tools**

Thermax Inc 5385 Alpha Ave Reno, NV 89506 888-THERMAX (843-7629) FAX: 775-972-3478	interior detailing

Since 1971, Thermax has pioneered the cleaning industry as it is known today. The Therminator models are manufactured for fast, easy cleaning of vehicle interiors. Improve the quality of your interior, save time by using Thermax and make more money in the process. The Thermax distributor can show you the advantage of the Therminator line. Call today and receive a free demonstration which allows you to see the latest in cleaning technology. Web site: www.thermaxvac.com

Tower Paint Co Inc Box 2345 Oshkosh, WI 54903-2345 920-235-6520; FAX: 920-235-6521 E-mail: info@towerpaint.com	paint

See full listing in **Section Two** under **paints**

Ultimate Appearance Ltd 113 Arabian Tr Smithfield, VA 23430 888-446-3078; FAX: 757-255-2620	cleaners detailing products detailing services polish/wax

Mail order and open shop. Stocking exclusive detailing products. IBIZ world class products, Novus plastic polish line, Stoner professional, P21s, Lexol, Sprayway, 303 products, Wenol, Clay Magic, brushes and mitts, car covers, floor mats and Pinnacle. Detailing seminars by appointment. Auto detailing services provided. Catalog available. MasterCard, Visa, Discover and American Express accepted.

Valco Cincinnati Consumer Products Inc 411 Circle Freeway Dr Cincinnati, OH 45246 513-874-6550; FAX: 513-874-3612	adhesives detailing products sealants tools

See full listing in **Section Two** under **tools**

Ziebart/Tidy Car 803 Mt Royal Blvd Pittsburgh, PA 15223 412-486-4711	accessories detailing rustproofing

See full listing in **Section Two** under **rustproofing**

car covers

The Gilbert Auto Cover — Keeps Out Dust Damp and Light

Auto Chic/Liquid Glass 6B Hamilton Business Pk 85 Franklin Rd Dover, NJ 07801 973-989-9220; FAX: 973-989-9234 E-mail: sales@autochic.com	car covers

Mail order and open shop. Monday-Friday 8 am to 5 pm Eastern time. Manufacturer of custom and standard size car and truck covers. Sales division of Liquid Glass products. Web site: www.autochic.com

California Car Cover Co 9525 DeSoto Chatsworth, CA 91311 800-423-5525; FAX: 818-998-2442	accessories apparel car covers tools

Specialize in protecting your valuable automotive investments. Offer covers made from six different materials to ensure your getting the best possible cover for your application and we have nearly 30,000 precision master patterns from which to build a custom fit cover from. Other items in our line include specialty tools and accessories for your garage, a wide assortment of car care products, novelty items and apparel. Catalog free for the asking. Web site: www.calcarcover.com

Car Cover Company 146 W Pomona Ave Monrovia, CA 91016 626-357-7718; FAX: 626-930-9248	car covers

Mail order and open shop. Monday-Friday 9 am to 5 pm. Manufacturer of custom car covers for muscle cars and classics. Specializing in selling wholesale to mail order houses. Can make or get any car cover pattern for any car, provided our customers can use these patterns on an ongoing basis.

Classic Motoring Accessories 146 W Pomona Ave Monrovia, CA 91016 800-327-3045, 626-357-8264 FAX: 626-930-9248	accessories car covers

Mail order and open shop. Monday-Friday 9 am to 5 pm. Manufactures own custom car covers for muscle cars and classics. Our retail prices are lower than our competitors. Also have thousands of chrome goodies, silver and gold jewelry with diamonds, fans, overheating equipment, Heartbeat of America jackets, valve covers and much more. Please send for our free 64-page catalog.

Cover-It 17 Wood St West Haven, CT 06516-3843 800-932-9344; FAX: 203-931-4754 E-mail: info@coverit.com	all-weather shelters

Mail order and open shop. Monday-Friday 8 am to 6 pm, Saturday 8 am to 4 pm. Our all-weather shelters provide protection for cars, boats, trucks, RVs, motorcycles, docks, pools, paint booths, sandblasting, workshops, industrial contracts, greenhouses and more! Shelters withstand wind, rain, snow, sap and sun. From 4' to 72' wide, any length made with heavy duty galvanized steel frame with a waterproof UV treated "Rip-Stop" cover. Portable, assemble quickly and easily. The perfect solution for covering anything and everything year-round, economically and securely. Web site: www.coverit.com

DashCovers of Florida 1301 W Copans Rd, Ste F-8-9 Pompano Beach, FL 33064 800-441-3274; FAX: 954-970-9119 E-mail: danny@dashcover.com	accessories carpets car covers

See full listing in **Section Two** under **accessories**

Lord Byron Inc 420 Sackett Point Rd North Haven, CT 06473 203-287-9881; FAX: 203-288-9456	**fender covers**

Specializing in official GM licensed auto fender covers. Manufacture custom printed auto fender covers and can manufacture covers with custom logos for specialty car clubs and parts suppliers. In addition, we market our own line of official licensed GM fender covers.

Mark II Enterprises 5225 Canyon Crest Dr, Ste 71-217H Riverside, CA 92507 909-686-2752; FAX: 909-686-7245 E-mail: markiient@earthlink.net	**car covers** **parts**

See full listing in **Section Two** under **accessories**

Murphy's Motoring Accessories Inc PO Box 618 Greendale, WI 53129-0618 800-529-8315, 414-529-8333 FAX: 414-529-0616 E-mail: mma@execpc.com	**car covers**

Specialist in custom-fit covers for cars, trucks, vans and SUVs from 1900-present. Eight fabrics including flannel, Weather-Shield™ and Kimberly-Clark's EVOLUTION®, NOAH® and DUSTOP®. More than 40,000 patterns. For very rare vehicles, have a simple procedure for making one-of-a-kind covers from your measurements and photos. Other product lines include tonneau covers, carpeting, floor mats, dash savers, fender covers, front end masks, dusters, water blades and other car care and protection products.

Performance Automotive Inc 1696 New London Tpke, PO Box 10 Glastonbury, CT 06033 860-633-7868; FAX: 860-657-9110 E-mail: pai@pcnet.com	**accessories** **car care**

See full listing in **Section Two** under **car care products**

Pine Ridge Ent 13165 Center Bath, MI 48808 800-522-7224; FAX: 517-641-6444 E-mail: carbag@voyager.net	**storage bags**

Mail order only. Deals in car storage bags. Web site: www.carbag.com

Quik-Shelter PO Box 1123 Orange, CT 06477 800-211-3730; FAX: 203-937-8897 E-mail: info@quikshelter.com	**temporary garages**

Manufacturer of all purpose garages, screen houses and greenhouses; made of heavy duty galvanized metal tubing with a rip scrim fabric cover. Any size available. Many styles to choose from. Easy assembly, all bolt together. Dealers and exporters welcome (sell these diversified money making products). Web site: www.quikshelter.com

RD Enterprises Ltd 290 Raub Rd Quakertown, PA 18951 215-538-9323; FAX: 215-538-0158 E-mail: rdent@rdent.com	**parts**

See full listing in **Section One** under **Lotus**

Sailorette's Nautical Nook 451 Davy Ln Wilmington, IL 60481 815-476-1644; FAX: 815-476-2524	**covers** **interiors**

See full listing in **Section Two** under **upholstery**

Rajam Srinivasan 35-11 92nd St Queens, NY 11372 917-705-4812; FAX: 718-205-0637 E-mail: rajam_s@hotmail.com	**accessories** **parts**

See full listing in **Section One** under **Rolls-Royce/Bentley**

Ultimate Appearance Ltd 113 Arabian Tr Smithfield, VA 23430 888-446-3078; FAX: 757-255-2620	**detailing products**

See full listing in **Section Two** under **car care products**

Van Raalte & Co LLC 5621 Garden Valley Rd Garden Valley, CA 95633 800-286-0030; FAX: 530-333-2034 E-mail: info@ezup4u.com	**canopies**

Mail order and open shop. Monday-Friday 8 am to 6 pm. EZ-Up instant shelter canopies, Camptime tables. Web site: www.ezup4u.com

car dealers

2002 AD 11066 Tuxford St Sun Valley, CA 91352 800-420-0223; FAX: 818-768-2697 E-mail: bmwsales@2002ad.com	**cars** **parts** **restoration**

See full listing in **Section One** under **BMW**

Albers Rolls-Royce 190 W Sycamore Zionsville, IN 46077 317-873-2360, 317-873-2560 FAX: 317-873-6860	**car dealer** **parts**

See full listing in **Section One** under **Rolls-Royce/Bentley**

Alfas Unlimited Inc 89 Greenwoods Rd W, Rt 44 Norfolk, CT 06058 860-542-5351; FAX: 860-542-5993 E-mail: alfasun@esslink.com	**engine rebuilding** **parts** **restoration** **service**

See full listing in **Section One** under **Alfa Romeo**

Alt Auto Sales Box 364 Regina SK Canada S4P 3A1 306-545-7119, 306-757-0369	**car dealer**

Shop open by appointment only. Collector car dealership, listing service and appraisals. Specializes in luxury cars from 1954 to 1976.

Antique & Classic Automobiles Royce A Emerson Carlisle St, Ext D Hanover, PA 17331 717-637-8344, 717-632-9182	**car dealer**

Shop open Monday-Friday 8 am to 8 pm. 30 years' dealing in fine, clean automobiles. Mostly Cadillac convertibles.

Appleton Garage PO Box B West Rockport, ME 04865 207-594-2062	**car dealer** **parts** **wheelcovers**

See full listing in **Section Two** under **wheels & wheelcovers**

Auto Quest Investment Cars Inc 710 W 7th St, PO Box 22 Tifton, GA 31793 912-382-4750; FAX: 912-382-4752 E-mail: info@auto-quest.com	car dealer

Open Monday-Friday 8:30 am to 5 pm. Dealer since 1932 of domestic and foreign classic and exotic vehicles. 90 plus vehicles on display at the dealership. Worldwide shipping available. The extensive web site has prices and color photos of every vehicle in stock and is updated every business day. Dealership and cabin shop is located 600 yards east of Exit 62 on I-75, US 319, US 82 and GA 520 at Tifton, GA. Web site: www.auto-quest.com

Auto World Sales 2245 Q St Lincoln, NE 68503 402-435-7111; FAX: 402-435-7131 E-mail: autowwkh@navix.net	appraisals sales

See full listing in **Section Two** under **appraisals**

AutoFashions Restoration & Parts Pittsboro, NC 27312 919-542-5566 E-mail: autofashions@mindspring.com	auto parts auto sales handcrafts restoration

See full listing in **Section Two** under **restoration shops**

Auto-Line Enterprises Inc 2 Lyons Rd Armonk, NY 10504 914-681-1757; FAX: 914-273-5159 E-mail: autocashny@aol.com	appraisals broker services

See full listing in **Section Two** under **appraisals**

AutoMatch CARS (Computer Aided Referral Service) 2017 Blvd Napoleon Louisville, KY 40205 800-962-2771, 502-417-8793 mobile 502-452-1920 office FAX: 502-479-6222 E-mail: amcars@aol.com or aautomatch@aol.com	broker car dealer network exotic, classic, new & used car locator

Buy, sell, trade, locate and consign all makes. Specializing in exotic and special interest. Over 1,000 representatives around the world help you save time, money and hassle on all of your automotive needs. Free listing for your car at: www.automatchcars.com

Jerry Bensinger 1197 Trails Edge Dr Hubbard, OH 44425-3353 330-759-5224; FAX: 330-759-5225 E-mail: jbenzr@aol.com	car dealer

Monday-Friday 9 am to 5 pm. Sale of very nice or restorable Ferraris, Maseratis, Jaguars, Astons, Austin-Healeys, etc. International shipping, references, 20 years in business with regularly satisfied customers.

Berliner Classic Motorcars Inc 1975 Stirling Rd Dania Beach, FL 33004 954-923-7271; FAX: 954-926-3306 E-mail: info@berlinerclassiccars.com	automobilia car dealer motorcycles

Mail order and open showroom. Monday-Friday 9 am to 5 pm, some Saturdays 10 am to 1 pm. Licensed dealer that buys and sells classic and antique automobiles, classic motorcycles and a wide variety of memorabilia. 15,000 square foot showroom located in south Fort Lauderdale, Florida, minutes from the airport and interstate. We have it all, drivers to #1 judged show condition cars, American and European, jukeboxes, Coca-Cola items, gas pumps, music boxes, etc. Accept items on consignment and for storage. Experienced in exporting. Party and special events facility. Web site: www.berlinerclassiccars.com

Bill's Collector Cars 6478 County Rd #1 South Point, OH 45680 740-894-5175	appraisals car dealer

Open Monday-Saturday 10 am to 6 pm, evenings and Sundays by appointment. Appraisals for estates, banks and individuals. Over 35 years' experience. Honesty and integrity in all our dealings with the old car hobby.

Birkin America PO Box 120982 Arlington, TX 76012 817-461-7431; FAX: 817-861-5867 E-mail: birkinam@aol.com	cars replicas

See full listing in **Section One** under **Lotus**

Blackhawk Collection 1092 Eagle Nest Pl Danville, CA 94506 925-736-3444; FAX: 925-736-4375 E-mail: info@blackhawkcollection.com	cars

Specializing in purchasing and selling of one-of-a-kind classic cars. Pebble Beach and Hershey Exposition sales. Web site: www.blackhawkcollection.com

Bud's Chevrolets, Corvettes, ZR1s 1415 Commerce Dr, PO Box 128 St Marys, OH 45885 800-688-2837; FAX: 419-394-4781	car dealer

See full listing in **Section One** under **Corvette**

Cars of the Times 1218 Crest Ln, Ste 16 Duncanville, TX 75137 972-572-6677 E-mail: cottjb@swbell.net	car dealer street rods

Open shop only. Monday-Friday 10 am to 5 pm, other hours by appointment. Specializing in classics, street rods, muscle cars and more, pre-1972 vehicles (later model cars at times). Buy, sell, trade, consignment. Web site: www.carsofthetimes.com

Chicago Car Exchange 14085 W Rockland Rd Libertyville, IL 60048 847-680-1950; FAX: 847-680-1961 E-mail: oldtoys@wwa.com	appraisals car dealer car locator financing storage

Open shop. Monday-Friday 10 am to 6 pm, Saturday 10 am to 5 pm. 20,000 square foot showroom with over 150 collectable cars. Buy, sell, consign, appraise, locate, detail and store collector cars. Strive to give accurate representations of cars to long distance buyers. Establishes long-standing, working relationships with clients. Specialties are pre-war, vintage, muscle, Mercedes, Cadillac, Pontiac and Hudson. Financing available. Worldwide shipping. Phone/fax for current inventory list. Web site: www.chicagocarexchange.com

City Imports Ltd 166 Penrod Ct Glen Burnie, MD 21061 410-768-6660; FAX: 410-768-5955	bodywork car sales restorations

See full listing in **Section One** under **Jaguar**

Charles W Clarke, Automotive Consultants 17 Saddle Ridge Dr West Simsbury, CT 06092-2118 PH/FAX: 860-658-2714	appraisals car dealer consultant

See full listing in **Section Two** under **consultants**

Classic Cars	cars
8926 E Evans Creek Rd	parts
Rogue River, OR 97537	
PH/FAX: 541-582-8966	

See full listing in **Section One** under **Ford 1932-1953**

Classic Cars & Parts	car dealer
Division of AKV Auto/Mike Chmilarski	parts
622 Rt 109	
Lindenhurst, NY 11757	
516-888-3914	

Mail order and open shop. Buy, sell and trade General Motors cars and parts. Specializing in 1959-1972. Also late model special interest vehicles for sale, all marques.

Classic Cars Inc	cars
52 Maple Terr	parts
Hibernia, NJ 07842	
973-627-1975; FAX: 973-627-3503	

See full listing in **Section One** under **Packard**

Classic Motors	appraisals
PO Box 1321	car dealer
Shirley, MA 01464	consulting
978-425-4614	

Open by appointment only. Antique, classic and special interest vehicles. Specialize in the sale of brass-era cars. Also, we do appraisals and pre-purchase inspection on all makes, models and years.

Coach Builders Limited Inc	car dealer
1410 S Main St, PO Box 1978	conv conversion
High Springs, FL 32655	
904-454-2060; FAX: 904-454-4080	

See full listing in **Section Two** under **restoration shops**

Collector's Carousel	appraisals
84 Warren Ave	sales
Westbrook, ME 04092	service
207-854-0343; FAX: 207-856-6913	

Antique auto sales, service and appraisals.

Contemporary and Investment	buy/sell/trade
Automobiles	mechanical work
4115 Poplar Springs Rd	memorabilia
Gainesville, GA 30507	
770-539-9111; FAX: 770-539-9818	
E-mail: contemporaryauto@	
mindspring.com	

See full listing in **Section Two** under **street rods**

Frank Corrente's Cadillac	car dealer
Corner Inc	
7614 Sunset Blvd	
Hollywood, CA 90046	
323-850-1881; FAX: 323-850-1884	
E-mail: corrente@ix.netcom.com	

See full listing in **Section One** under **Cadillac/LaSalle**

County Corvette	restoration
315 Westtown Rd	sales
West Chester, PA 19382	service
610-696-7888; FAX: 610-696-9114	

See full listing in **Section One** under **Corvette**

Tom Crook Classic Cars	car dealer
27611 42nd Ave S	
Auburn, WA 98001	
253-941-3454	

Specializing in classic car sales for Packards, Cadillacs, Duesenberg, Jaguar, Ford and all classics 1925-1948.

D&M Corvette Specialists Ltd	car dealer
1804 Ogden Ave	parts
Downers Grove, IL 60515	restoration
630-968-0031; FAX: 630-968-0465	sales
E-mail: sales@dmcorvette.com	service

See full listing in **Section One** under **Corvette**

Dragone Classic Motorcars	car dealer
1797 Main St	
Bridgeport, CT 06604	
203-335-4643; FAX: 203-335-9798	

Open shop only. Monday-Friday 9 to 5. Saturday 9 to 3. High quality antique, classic and exotic cars such as Delahaye, Delage, Alfa Romeo, Bugatti, Hispano-Suiza, Isotta-Fraschini and quality early brass era cars. Always a fine selection.

Driven By Desire	automobilia
300 N Fraley St	car dealer
Kane, PA 16735	models
814-837-7590; FAX: 814-837-6850	
E-mail: driven@penn.com	

Mail order and open shop. Monday-Thursday 1 pm to 6 pm, Friday 1 pm to 8 pm, Saturday 12 pm to 5 pm. Collector car sales, mostly 1960s. The area's largest selection of foreign and domestic model car and truck kits, paint, supplies, etc. Die cast metal models, specializing in 1/18 scale, books, posters, and general automobilia. Stock car racing items: jackets, T-shirts, fan flags and more. Web site: www.users.penn.com/~driven/dxd.html

Duffy's Collectible Cars	car dealer
250 Classic Car Ct SW	
Cedar Rapids, IA 52404	
319-364-7000; FAX: 319-364-4036	
E-mail: sales@duffys.com	

Mail order and open shop. Monday-Friday 8:30 am to 5 pm, Saturday 8:30 am to 4:30 pm, closed Sundays. Gift shop and tours. Collector car sales and service. Specializing in cars from 1930-1970. Fully restored hardtops and convertibles. 100 car showroom. Sales, finance, storage, delivery and appraisals. Celebrating our 58th year. Web site: www.duffys.com

Malcolm C Elder & Son	car dealer
The Motor Shed	motorcycles
Middle Aston, Bicester	
Oxfordshire OX25 5QL England	
PH/FAX: 01869 340999	
E-mail: malcolmcelderson@	
btinternet.com	

Shop open Monday-Saturday 9:30 am to 5 pm; other times by appointment. Closed on Sunday. Home phone: Steeple Aston, 01869 340606. Also deal in vintage and classic motorcycles, tires. Exceedingly wide range of cars stocked, 1890s to 1980s. Complete range of marques, models and prices. Over 100 cars on display. Web site: www.vintageandclassiccars.co.uk

The Enthusiasts Shop	cars
John Parnell	pre-war parts
PO Box 485	transportation
Madisonville, LA 70447	
985-845-7033; FAX: 985-845-1628	

See full listing in **Section One** under **Rolls-Royce/Bentley**

European Collectibles Inc
1974 Placentia Ave
Costa Mesa, CA 92627-3421
949-650-4718; FAX: 949-650-5881
E-mail: europeancollectibles@
pacbell.net

restoration
sales
service

Open shop only. Monday-Friday 9 am to 5 pm, Saturday 10 am to 2 pm, closed Sundays. Specializing in European and British 1950s and 1960s classic sports cars, Porsche, Jaguar, Austin-Healey, Ferrari 246, Aston Martin, Mercedes-Benz, Triumph and MG. Sales, service and complete ground-up restorations. Web site: www.europeancollectibles.com

The Fine Car Store
1105 Moana Dr
San Diego, CA 92107
619-223-7766; FAX: 619-223-6838

cars

See full listing in **Section One** under **Ferrari**

Five Star Transport
691 W Merrick Rd
Valley Stream, NY 11580
800-464-9965, 516-285-1077
FAX: 516-285-3729

transport

See full listing in **Section Two** under **transport**

Freeman's Garage
29 Ford Rd
Norton, MA 02766
508-285-6500; FAX: 508-285-6566

parts
restoration
sales
service

See full listing in **Section One** under **Ford 1903-1931**

Freman's Auto
138 Kountz Rd
Whitehall, MT 59759
406-287-5436; FAX: 406-287-9103

car dealer
restoration shop
salvage yard

Mail order only. Sell parts for all makes and models, 1950-1980, over 25,000 cars. Worldwide shipping. Some complete cars available. Restoration services available.

George's Auto & Tractor Sales Inc
1450 N Warren Rd
North Jackson, OH 44451
330-538-3020; FAX: 330-538-3033
E-mail: gmyuhas1450@cs.com

Blue Dots/car dealer
Dri-Wash metal
polish
upholstery cleaner
New Castle batteries

Mail order and open shop. Monday-Friday 9 am to 5 pm. Blue Dots. New Castle batteries, special interest autos. Dri-Wash leather and vinyl treatment, Dri-Wash 'n Guard waterless car wash and protective glaze. Fluid film rust and corrosion preventative.

Leo Gephart Inc
7360 E Acoma Dr, Ste 14
Scottsdale, AZ 85260
480-948-2286; FAX: 480-948-2390
E-mail: gephartclassics@earthlink.net

vintage cars

Mail order and open shop. Monday-Friday 9 am to 5 pm, Saturday 9 am to 12 pm. We are primarily a vintage car store, for over 50 years but we have some J and SJ Duesenberg parts and early V8 Ford about 1932-1934 radios and a smidgen of Packard and Cadillac and miscellaneous. Also some automobile memorabilia.

Mark Gillett
PO Box 9177
Dallas, TX 75209
PH/FAX: 214-902-9258
011-525-559-6240 Mexico City, Mexico
E-mail: autonet@onramp.net

car locator
sales

Open by appointment only. Sales and locating of specialty cars and vintage race cars. Specializing in finding old, dead race cars. Extensive contacts in Latin America.

Green Valentine Inc
5055 Covington Way
Memphis, TN 38134
901-373-5555; FAX: 901-373-5568

car dealer
woodies

Specializing in wood station wagons, wood convertibles for any brand.

Grumpy's Old Cars
396 Marsh St
San Luis Obispo, CA 93401
805-549-7875; FAX: 805-549-7877
E-mail: slohot@hotmail.com

car dealer

Open shop Monday-Friday 9:30 am to 6 pm, Saturday-Sunday 10 am to 5 pm. We buy and sell special interest, collector, classic, hot rods and old cars.

Happy Daze Classic Cars
257 Morris Ct
Fond Du Lac, WI 54935
920-922-8450

car dealer

Mail order and open shop. Cars shown by appointment only. Buy, sell and trade outstanding collectible cars from the 1930s-early 1970s. All cars are displayed in our indoor, heated, sales facility. Specializing in rust-free, low mileage originals and cars which have undergone frame-off restorations.

J & K Old Chevy Stuff
Ship Pond Rd
Plymouth, MA 02360
508-224-7616
kblaze58@aol.com

car dealer
parts
sheetmetal

See full listing in **Section One** under **Chevrolet**

John's Car Corner
Rt 5, PO Box 85
Westminster, VT 05158
802-722-3180; FAX: 802-722-3181

body/mech parts
car dealer
repairs/restoration

See full listing in **Section One** under **Volkswagen**

K & K Vintage Motorcars LC
9848 SW Frwy
Houston, TX 77074
713-541-2281; FAX: 713-541-2286
E-mail: vintagemotorcars@ev1.net

restoration
sales
service

See full listing in **Section Two** under **restoration shops**

Larson Motor Co
Russell Larson
4415 Canyon Dr
Amarillo, TX 79110
806-358-9797

appraisals
restoration
sales

Mail order and open shop. Monday-Friday 9 am to 4 pm. Sales, service and restoration of collector cars. Certified appraisals. Over 40 years' experience. IAAA member, #1002110097.

Bill McCoskey
PO Box 93
Littlestown, PA 17340
410-346-0660; FAX: 410-346-6499
E-mail: billmccoskey@aol.com

accident/damage
investigations
appraisals

See full listing in **Section Two** under **appraisals**

McLean's Brit Bits
14 Sagamore Rd
Rye, NH 03870
800-995-2487; FAX: 603-433-0009
E-mail: sam@britbits.com

accessories
parts
sales
service

Mail order and open shop. Monday-Saturday 9 am to 6 pm, Sunday by appointment. Specializing in sales, service, new and used parts and accessories for MGs, Austin-Healeys, Triumphs,

Sunbeams, Morris Minors, Daimlers, Lotuses, Land Rovers and Hillmans. Web site: www.britbits.com

Medicine Bow Motors Inc	car dealer
343 One Horse Creek Rd	
Florence, MT 59833	
406-273-0002	

Specializing in 1946-1951 Ford car parts. Handle 1950s custom goodies. Builders of street rods, customs and quality restorations.

Memory Lane Motors	car dealer
562 County Rd 121	restoration
Fenelon Falls, ON Canada K0M 1N0	service
705-887-CARS; FAX: 705-887-4028	

See full listing in **Section Two** under **restoration shops**

Memory Lane Motors Inc	appraisals
1231 Rt 176	car dealer
Lake Bluff, IL 60044	storage
847-362-4600	

Open shop only. Monday-Saturday 9 am to 5 pm. Buy, sell, trade and consign antique and classic cars. Also do vehicle appraisals and provide storage for automobiles. Web site: www.memorylanemotors.com

Dennis Mitosinka's Classic Cars	appraisals
and Appraisals Service	books
619 E Fourth St	
Santa Ana, CA 92701	
714-953-5303; FAX: 714-953-1810	
E-mail: mitoclassics@earthlink.net	

See full listing in **Section Two** under **appraisals**

Morrison Motor Co Inc	car dealer
1170 Old Charlotte Rd	
Concord, NC 28025	
704-782-7716; FAX: 704-788-9514	
E-mail: morrisonmotors@unet.net	

See full listing in **Section One** under **Corvette**

Motorcar Gallery Inc	car dealer
715 N Federal Hwy	
Fort Lauderdale, FL 33304	
954-522-9900; FAX: 954-522-9966	
E-mail: motorcargallery@aol.com	

See full listing in **Section One** under **Ferrari**

Mountain Fuel	car dealer
Russell Van Aken	machinery
Gilboa, NY 12076	parts

Mail order and open shop. Weekends during the day. 50 years as a car dealer. SASE required.

J C Nadeau	car dealer
306 Notre Dame St N	
Thetford Mines, QC Canada G6G 2S4	
418-338-1106 after 6 pm	

Mail order only. Antique cars and parts bought and sold.

Ohio Limo and Coach Sales	car dealer
PO Box 681	
Bellefontaine, OH 43311	
937-592-3746; FAX: 937-593-3299	
E-mail: ohiolimo@ohiolimo.com	

Open by appointment. Dealer of specialty vehicles including limousines, convertibles and sports cars. Web site: www.ohiolimo.com

John T Poulin	car dealer
Auto Sales/Star Service Center	parts
5th Ave & 111th St	restoration service
North Troy, NY 12182	
518-235-8610	

Mail order and open shop. Monday-Saturday 9 am to 6 pm. Specializing in sales of Mercedes-Benz and has a repair shop for all service and restoration of Mercedes with many used and new parts. Been in business of Mercedes-Benz for 45 years (complete car care). 1950s-1990s Mercedes and BMW used cars.

Prairie Auto	appraisals
Jeremiah Larson	car dealers
7087 Orchid Ln	
Maple Grove, MN 55311	
612-420-8600; FAX: 612-420-8637	
E-mail: jer4cars@aol.com	

Antique and collectible autos, 1930-1972. Also late model sales and appraisals on all aspects automotive related: diminished value, arbitration, insurance purposes. IAAA member, #100201294.

Prestige Motors	car dealer
120 N Bessie Rd	
Spokane, WA 99212	
509-927-1041	

Investment quality, special interest car dealer. Handle antiques, muscle cars, street rods, sports cars and classics.

Proteam Corvette Sales Inc	car collection
PO Box 606	car dealer
Napoleon, OH 43545-0606	
888-592-5086, 419-592-5086	
FAX: 419-592-4242	
E-mail: proteam@proteam-corvette.com	

See full listing in **Section One** under **Corvette**

Rader's Relics	appraisals
1896 Kentucky Ave	car dealer
Winter Park, FL 32789	
407-647-1940; FAX: 407-647-1930	
E-mail: therelic@bellsouth.net	

Mail order and open shop. Call ahead for appointment. 24 years in business near I-4 and Fairbanks. Home of the two year buy-back warranty. Consider our greatest asset a good reputation locally and internationally. A 10% deposit holds any car for 30 days and is fully refundable if you come see the car and don't like it for any reason. Buying, selling and appraising antiques and classics. Keeping an inventory of about 12 cars at all times.

William H Randel	appraisals
PO Box 173	car locators
Hatboro, PA 19040	
215-675-8969; FAX: 215-441-0960	
E-mail: tbrdnut@bellatlantic.net	

See full listing in **Section One** under **Thunderbird**

RARE Corvettes	cars
Joe Calcagno	parts
Box 1080	
Soquel, CA 95073	
831-475-4442; FAX: 831-475-1115	

See full listing in **Section One** under **Corvette**

Regal International Motor Cars Inc	car dealer
PO Box 6819	
Hollywood, FL 33081	
305-989-9777; FAX: 305-989-9778	

See full listing in **Section One** under **Rolls-Royce/Bentley**

Retrospect Automotive
980 E Jericho Tpk
Huntington Station, NY 11746
631-421-0255; FAX: 631-421-0473

	accessories
---	car sales
	parts

Mail order and open shop. Monday-Saturday 8 am to 6 pm. Parts and accessories, classic car sales of domestic cars, muscle cars of the 1950s-1972.

Reynolds Museum Ltd
4110-57th St
Wetaskiwin, AB Canada T9A 2B6
780-352-6201; FAX: 780-352-4666
E-mail: srsl@incentre.net

museum

Open daily. Stanley G Reynolds, President. Located on Highway 2A in Wetaskiwin. Exhibits include antique airplanes, cars, tractors, steam engines, trucks, fire engines and military vehicles museum. 900 1912-1949 parts cars (many restorable), trucks and tractors for sale.

RM Classic Cars
5 W Forest Ave
Ypsilanti, MI 48197
734-547-2400; FAX: 734-547-9424
E-mail: michigan@rmcars.com

auctions

See full listing in **Section Two** under **auctions & shows**

Rogers Corvette Center
8675 N Orlando Ave
Maitland, FL 32751
407-628-8300; FAX: 407-628-8388
E-mail: sales@rogerscorvette.com

car dealer

See full listing in **Section One** under **Corvette**

Spyder Enterprises Inc
RFD 1682
Laurel Hollow, NY 11791-9644
516-367-1616; FAX: 516-367-3260
E-mail: singer356@aol.com

| accessories |
| artwork |
| automobilia |
| books |

See full listing in **Section Two** under **automobilia**

Thoroughbred Motors
3935 N US 301
Sarasota, FL 34234
941-359-2277; FAX: 941-359-2128
E-mail: vintagejags@mindspring.com

| car dealer |
| parts |

See full listing in **Section One** under **Jaguar**

Translog Motorsports
619-635 W Poplar St
York, PA 17404
PH/FAX: 717-846-1885
E-mail: translogm@aol.com

| car dealer |
| parts |
| restoration |

See full listing in **Section One** under **Porsche**

U S Oldies & Classics
Vunt 3
Holsbeek 3220 Belgium
32-16446611; FAX: 32-16446520

car dealer

Open by appointment only. Specializing in classic American made automobiles, 1900-1976, especially Cadillac, Chrysler, Corvette, Lincoln, Oldsmobile, Packard, in very good to perfect condition.

Valenti Classics Inc
355 S Hwy 41
Caledonia, WI 53108
262-835-2070; FAX: 262-835-2575
E-mail: vci@valenticlassics.com

| collectibles |
| restoration |
| sales |
| service |

Mail order and open shop. Monday-Saturday 8 am to 6 pm.

Sales, service and restoration of classic and collectible automobiles. Also sell gas related signs, pumps and collectibles. Business is family owned and operated. Antique mall also at same location. Web site: www.valenticlassics.com

Vintage Auto Parts
PO Box 323
Temple, PA 19560-0323
610-939-9593

| car dealer |
| new/used parts |

See full listing in **Section One** under **BMW**

Westchester Vintage Coach Inc
Box 252
Yonkers, NY 10705
914-693-1624

car dealer

Antique car sales. Appraisals only.

Willhoit Auto Restoration
1360 Gladys Ave
Long Beach, CA 90804
562-439-3333; FAX: 562-439-3956

| engine rebuilding |
| restoration |

See full listing in **Section One** under **Porsche**

Wiseman Motor Co Inc
Bill Wiseman, Owner
PO Box 848
Marion, NC 28752
828-724-9313

car dealer

Buying and selling antique and classic cars. Model A Fords and early V8s a specialty. Our 35th year.

Yesterday's Auto Sales
2800 Lyndale Ave S
Minneapolis, MN 55408
612-872-9733; FAX: 612-872-1386
E-mail: al-hagen@yesterdaysauto.com

| appraisals |
| car dealer |

Open Monday-Friday 10 am to 4 pm, Saturday 10 am to 2 pm. Since 1983, have been a full-time collector car dealer. Inventory includes cars foreign and domestic, from the 1960s back to the 1920s. Located in an historic two story building near downtown Minneapolis. Web site: www.yesterdaysauto.com

carburetors

Advanced Plating & Powder Coating
1425 Cowan Ct
Nashville, TN 37207
615-227-6900; FAX: 615-262-7935
E-mail: gochrome@aol.com

| chrome plating |
| polishing |
| repair service |

See full listing in **Section Two** under **plating & polishing**

American Street Rod
3340 Sunrise Blvd D-1
Rancho Cordova, CA 95742
916-638-3275

| hoses |
| tubing |

See full listing in **Section Two** under **street rods**

Andy's Classic Mustangs
18502 E Sprague
Greenacres, WA 99016
509-924-9824

| parts |
| service |

See full listing in **Section One** under **Mustang**

Antique Auto Parts Cellar 6 Chauncy St, PO Box 3 South Weymouth, MA 02190 781-335-1579; FAX: 781-335-1925 E-mail: our1932@aol.com	brake/chassis/ engine parts fuel pumps/kits gaskets water pumps

See full listing in **Section Two** under **comprehensive parts**

Arch Carburetor 583 Central Ave Newark, NJ 07107 973-482-2755 E-mail: mmfried@quixnet.net	carburetors

Mail order and open shop. Monday-Friday 7:30 am to 3 pm, Saturday 8 am to 12 pm. Rebuilding and restoration of carburetors. Web site: www.archcarburetor.com

Battery Ignition Co Inc 91 Meadow St Hartford, CT 06114 860-296-4215; FAX: 860-947-3259 E-mail: biscokid@aol.com	parts rebuilding rebushing

Mail order and open shop. Monday-Friday 8:30 am to 5 pm, Thursday until 8 pm. Since 1926 offering parts, rebuilding and rebushing services for most domestic carburetors, including automotive, marine, industrial and antique applications. Also available, search services for hard to find fuel system and electrical parts. Web site: www.users.neca.com/biscokid

C & G Early Ford Parts 1941 Commercial St, Dept AH Escondido, CA 92029-1233 760-740-2400; FAX: 760-740-8700 E-mail: cgford@cgfordparts.com	accessories/chrome emblems literature mechanical weatherstripping

See full listing in **Section One** under **Ford 1932-1953**

The Carburetor Refactory 815 Harbour Way S #5 Richmond, CA 94804 510-237-1277; FAX: 510-237-2092 E-mail: info@carbkits.com	parts rebuilding rebushing

Mail order (UPS) and open shop. Monday-Thursday 9 am to 5:30 pm. Rebuild and rebush American, Japanese and European carburetors. Also sell parts for those carburetors including throttle shafts, butterflies, rebuild kits, TPS, Varajet, pull-offs, etc. Web site: www.carbkits.com

The Carburetor Shop 204 E 15th St Eldon, MO 65026 573-392-7378 FAX: 573-392-7176 (24 hours, 7 days)	carburetors carburetor kits carburetor repair carburetor restoration

Open shop. Phone hours: Monday-Thursday 8 am to 5 pm. Over 150,000 carburetors on hand 1900-1974. Rebuilding, restoration available. We guarantee our work. Manufacturer of rebuilding kits with following coverage: 1974-1925, 99.9%; 1924-1912, 80%; 1911-1904, 25%. Other carburetors parts available with purchase of repair kit. Also huge library of original carburetor literature for sale. MasterCard and Visa accepted (no fee). Web site: www.thecarburetorshop.com

Carl's Ford Parts 23219 South St, Box 38 Homeworth, OH 44634 PH/FAX: 330-525-7291 E-mail: fordcobrajet@hotmail.com	muscle parts

See full listing in **Section One** under **Mustang**

Carobu Engineering 1017 W 18th St Costa Mesa, CA 92627 949-722-9307; FAX: 949-631-3184 E-mail: tate@carobu.com	dyno testing engine rebuilding exhaust systems

See full listing in **Section Two** under **engine rebuilding**

Carson's Antique Auto Parts 235 Shawfarm Rd Holliston, MA 01746 508-429-2269; FAX: 508-429-0761 E-mail: w1066@gis.net	parts

See full listing in **Section Two** under **engine parts**

Chicago Corvette Supply 7322 S Archer Rd Justice, IL 60458 708-458-2500; FAX: 708-458-2662	parts

See full listing in **Section One** under **Corvette**

Corvair Underground PO Box 339 Dundee, OR 97115 800-825-8247, 503-434-1648 FAX: 503-434-1626	parts

See full listing in **Section One** under **Corvair**

Demon Carburetion 1450 McDonald Rd Dahlonega, GA 30533 706-864-8544; FAX: 706-864-2206	carburetors

Carburetor manufacturer. Web site: www.gpt300.com

Ferris Auto Electric Ltd 106 Lakeshore Dr North Bay, ON Canada P1A 2A6 705-474-4560; FAX: 705-474-9453	parts service

See full listing in **Section Two** under **electrical systems**

Ignition Distributor Service 19042 SE 161st Renton, WA 98058 425-255-8052 E-mail: pjo@uswest.net	rebuild carbs rebuild distributors rebuild Turbos

See full listing in **Section Two** under **ignition parts**

J & C's Parts 7127 Ward Rd North Tonawanda, NY 14120 716-693-4090; FAX: 716-695-7144	parts

See full listing in **Section One** under **Buick/McLaughlin**

JAM Engineering Corp PO Box 2570 Monterey, CA 93942 800-JAM-CORP, 831-372-1787 E-mail: jam@jameng.com	carburetors

Mail order only. Design and manufacture of 50 State Legal Weber and Holley carburetor replacement packages. Kits include linkage, air cleaner adapters, hardware and more. Specializing in BMW and Mercedes-Benz. Web site: www.jameng.com

Ken's Carburetors 2301 Barnum Ave Stratford, CT 06615 203-375-9340	carburetors distributors parts

See full listing in **Section One** under **Ford 1932-1953**

The Old Carb Doctor
1127 Drucilla Church Rd
Nebo, NC 28761
800-945-CARB (2272)
828-659-1428

carburetors
fuel pumps

Mail order shop only. Please call Monday-Saturday 8 am to 7 pm. Carburetors completely restored from core supplied by customer. Castings resurfaced and repaired, shafts rebushed and resealed, rust removal, steel and brass refinished. Guaranteed full service restoration at reasonable rates, 1900-1980. Mechanical screw together fuel pumps of the same vintage also restored. Sorry, no parts or cores for sale.

Rick's Carburetor Repair
135 Blissville Rd, PO Box 46
Hydeville, VT 05750
802-265-3006
E-mail: robinric@sover.net

carburetor
rebuilding

Mail order and open shop. Monday-Friday 8 am to 5 pm, Saturday 8 am to 12 pm; mail order calls anytime. Dealing in carburetor rebuilding, classic cars through present day. Guaranteed quality workmanship, 25 years' experience, competitive prices, fast turnaround via UPS service or US postal service.

Straight Six Jaguar
24321 Hatteras St
Woodland Hills, CA 91367
PH/FAX: 818-716-1192

parts
service

See full listing in **Section One** under **Jaguar**

Sugarbush Products Inc
117 Bristol Rd
Chalfont, PA 18914
215-822-1495; FAX: 215-997-2519
E-mail: wechsler@voicenet.com

carburetors

Mail order and open shop. Monday-Friday 8 am to 5 pm. NOS and used carburetors bought and sold. Deal in vintage carburetors only.

---

carpets

Accurate Auto Tops &
Upholstery Inc
Miller Rd & W Chester Pike
Edgemont, PA 19028
610-356-1515; FAX: 610-353-8230

tops
upholstery

See full listing in **Section Two** under **upholstery**

All Seams Fine
23 Union St
Waterbury, VT 05676
800-244-7326 (SEAM), 802-244-8843

interior restorations

See full listing in **Section Two** under **upholstery**

Auto Custom Carpet Inc
1429 Noble St, PO Box 1350
Anniston, AL 36201
800-633-2358, 256-236-1118
FAX: 800-516-8274

carpets
floor mats

Auto Custom Parts Inc, the world's leading manufacturer of aftermarket floor coverings, has a product line covering vehicles from 1947-2000. Available from ACC is complete line of molded carpet sets, cut and sew carpet sets, vinyl floor coverings, trunk mats and custom floor mats. Furthermore, ACC products meet or exceed OEM specifications. Web site: www.accmats.com

Auto-Mat Co
69 Hazel St
Hicksville, NY 11801
800-645-7258 orders
516-938-7373; FAX: 516-931-8438
E-mail: browner5@ix.netcom.com

accessories
carpet sets
interiors
tops
upholstery

See full listing in **Section Two** under **interiors & interior parts**

Bud's Auto Carpets
PO Box 97
Leominster, MA 01453
800-545-8547, 978-534-4894
FAX: 978-534-0677
E-mail: manager@plasticsmall.com

automotive
carpeting

We sell automotive carpeting, 1950s to present year autos. Web site: www.plasticsmall.com/auto

CARS Inc
1964 W 11 Mile Rd
Berkley, MI 48072
248-398-7100; FAX: 248-398-7078
E-mail: carsinc@worldnet.att.net

interiors

See full listing in **Section Two** under **interiors & interior parts**

Clark's Corvair Parts Inc
Rt 2, #400 Mohawk Tr
Shelburne Falls, MA 01370
413-625-9776; FAX: 413-625-8498
E-mail: clarks@corvair.com

accessories
interiors
literature
parts
sheetmetal

See full listing in **Section One** under **Corvair**

Classic Chevrolet Parts Inc
8723 S I-35
Oklahoma City, OK 73149
405-631-4400; FAX: 405-631-5999
E-mail: info@classicchevroletparts.com

parts

See full listing in **Section One** under **Chevrolet**

Classic Mustang Inc
24 Robert Porter Rd
Southington, CT 06489
800-243-2742; FAX: 860-276-9986

body parts
carpets
chassis parts
floor pans

See full listing in **Section One** under **Mustang**

Custom Auto Interiors
by Ron Mangus
18127 Marygold Ave
Bloomington, CA 92316
909-877-9342; FAX: 909-877-1741
E-mail: customautointeriors@
hotmail.com

accessories
carpet kits
die cast collectibles
seat frames

See full listing in **Section Two** under **interiors & interior parts**

Custom Interiors
PO Box 51174
Indian Orchard, MA 01151
413-589-9176; FAX: 413-589-9178
E-mail: ci@customseatcovers.com

carpets
custom seat covers
interior parts

See full listing in **Section Two** under **interiors & interior parts**

DashCovers of Florida
1301 W Copans Rd, Ste F-8-9
Pompano Beach, FL 33064
800-441-3274; FAX: 954-970-9119
E-mail: danny@dashcover.com

accessories
carpets
car covers

See full listing in **Section Two** under **accessories**

Hampton Coach
6 Chestnut St, PO Box 6
Amesbury, MA 01913
888-388-8726, 978-388-8047
FAX: 978-388-1113
E-mail: lbb-hc@greenet.net

> fabrics
> interior kits
> top kits

See full listing in **Section One** under **Chevrolet**

Dave Knittel Upholstery
850 E Teton #7
Tucson, AZ 85706
PH/FAX: 520-746-1588

> interiors
> tops
> upholstery

See full listing in **Section Two** under **upholstery**

LeBaron Bonney Co
6 Chestnut St, PO Box 6
Amesbury, MA 01913
800-221-5408, 978-388-3811
FAX: 978-388-1113
E-mail: lbb-hc@greenet.net

> fabrics
> interior kits
> top kits

See full listing in **Section One** under **Ford 1903-1931**

Linearossa International Inc
3931 SW 47th Ave
Ft Lauderdale, FL 33314
954-327-9888; FAX: 954-791-6555

> parts

See full listing in **Section One** under **Fiat**

Melvin's Classic Ford Parts Inc
1521 Dogwood Dr
Conyers, GA 30012
770-761-6800; FAX: 770-761-5777

> parts

See full listing in **Section One** under **Ford 1954-up**

Murphy's Motoring Accessories Inc
PO Box 618
Greendale, WI 53129-0618
800-529-8315, 414-529-8333
FAX: 414-529-0616
E-mail: mma@execpc.com

> car covers

See full listing in **Section Two** under **car covers**

Obsolete Ford Parts Inc
8701 S I-35
Oklahoma City, OK 73149
405-631-3933; FAX: 405-634-6815
E-mail: info@obsoletefordparts.com

> parts

See full listing in **Section One** under **Ford 1954-up**

Sailorette's Nautical Nook
451 Davy Ln
Wilmington, IL 60481
815-476-1644; FAX: 815-476-2524

> covers
> interiors

See full listing in **Section Two** under **upholstery**

Tamraz's Parts Discount Warehouse
10022 S Bode Rd
Plainfield, IL 60544
630-904-4500; FAX: 630-904-2329

> carpeting
> upholstery
> weatherstripping

See full listing in **Section One** under **Chevelle/Camaro**

Thermax Inc
5385 Alpha Ave
Reno, NV 89506
888-THERMAX (843-7629)
FAX: 775-972-3478

> interior detailing

See full listing in **Section Two** under **car care products**

West Coast Metric Inc
24002 Frampton Ave
Harbor City, CA 90710
310-325-0005; FAX: 310-325-9733
E-mail: wcm@westcoastmetric.com

> carpet kits
> door panels
> emblems
> plastic parts
> rubber parts

See full listing in **Section One** under **Volkswagen**

castings

Air Flow Research
10490 Ilex Ave
Pacoima, CA 91331
818-890-0616; FAX: 818-890-0490

> cylinder heads

See full listing in **Section One** under **Chevrolet**

ASC&P International
PO Box 255
Uwchland, PA 19480
610-458-8395; FAX: 610-458-8735

> custom molding
> fiberglass
> plastic

See full listing in **Section Two** under **fiberglass parts**

Dwight H Bennett
1330 Ximeno Ave
Long Beach, CA 90804
PH/FAX: 562-498-6488

> emblem repair
> hardware repair
> mascot repair
> plaque repair

See full listing in **Section Two** under **grille emblem badges**

Casting Salvage Technologies
26 Potomac Creek Dr
Fredricksburg, VA 22405
800-833-8814 national
540-659-3797 local
FAX: 540-659-9453

> repairs

Mail order and open shop. Monday-Saturday 8 am to 5 pm. We specialize in the testing and repair of automobile, motorcycle and marine castings. Both cast iron and aluminum as well as engine rebuilding services. Motor blocks, cylinder heads, exhaust manifolds, etc.

Chevi Shop Custom Casting
338 Main Ave, Box 75
Milledgeville, IL 61051
815-225-7565; FAX: 815-225-7616
E-mail: synka@cin.net

> custom castings
> parts

See full listing in **Section One** under **Chevrolet**

Bob Drake Reproductions Inc
1819 NW Washington Blvd
Grants Pass, OR 97526
800-221-3673; FAX: 541-474-0099
E-mail: bobdrake@bobdrake.com

> repro parts

See full listing in **Section One** under **Ford 1932-1953**

Fini-Finish Metal Finishing
24657 Mound Rd
Warren, MI 48091
810-758-0050; FAX: 810-758-0054
E-mail: info@fini-finish.com

> plating
> polishing
> pot metal repair

See full listing in **Section Two** under **plating & polishing**

Harter Industries Inc
PO Box 502
Holmdel, NJ 07733
732-566-7055; FAX: 732-566-6977
E-mail: harter101@aol.com

> parts
> restoration

See full listing in **Section Two** under **comprehensive parts**

KJ Classic Metal Designs | toys
PO Box 663
Winder, GA 30680
770-867-4452; FAX: 770-586-0163
E-mail: kjclassic@mindspring.com

See full listing in **Section Two** under **automobilia**

Model Engineering | new parts casting
Gene or Jeff Sanders
3284 S Main St
Akron, OH 44319
330-644-3450; FAX: 330-644-0088

Casting new parts from drawings or the original part. Making wood and metal patterns, models, molds, casting parts in aluminum, bronze, iron and steel. Machine shop and pattern shop services, polish and plating service. Web site: www.modelengineeringco.com

North GA Patterns | castings patterns
Rt 2 Box 2154
Oak Valley Rd
Toccoa, GA 30577
706-886-0183; FAX: 706-886-5483

Broken or beyond repair? Engine blocks, heads, manifolds, brake drums, any cast part large or small. Can make patterns for parts and get new castings in any type metal.

Richardson Restorations | custom work repairs restoration
352 S I St
Tulare, CA 93274
559-688-5002
E-mail: cal5002@aol.com

See full listing in **Section Two** under **restoration shops**

Verdone's Custom Stainless Casting | casting polishing
31 Stricklerstown Loop Rd
Newmanstown, PA 17073
717-949-3341; FAX: 717-949-2782

Mail order only. Deals in custom casting for antique cars. Casting to order in stainless steel only. We cast and polish, you do drilling and tapping. Many patterns on hand for many years and makes of cars. Small stuff.

chassis parts

AXLE

60 Chev Sam | parts
2912 Wright Rd
Hamptonville, NC 27020
336-468-1745

See full listing in **Section One** under **Chevrolet**

A-1 Shock Absorber Co | shocks-all types coil springs Koni shocks leaf springs steering gears
Shockfinders Division
365 Warren Ave, PO Box 2028
Silverthorne, CO 80498
800-344-1966, 970-389-3193 cell
FAX: 970-513-8283

See our ad on the last page

American Stamping Corp | frame rails
8719 Caroma
Olive Branch, MS 38654
PH/FAX: 662-895-5300

See full listing in **Section One** under **Ford 1932-1953**

Anderson Automotive | cars parts
1604 E Busch Blvd
Tampa, FL 33612
813-932-4611; FAX: 813-932-5025

See full listing in **Section One** under **Oldsmobile**

Antique Auto Parts Cellar | brake/chassis/ engine parts fuel pumps/kits gaskets water pumps
6 Chauncy St, PO Box 3
South Weymouth, MA 02190
781-335-1579; FAX: 781-335-1925
E-mail: our1932@aol.com

See full listing in **Section Two** under **comprehensive parts**

Atlantic Enterprises | steering assemblies
221 Strand Industrial Dr
Little River, SC 29566
843-399-7565; FAX: 843-399-4600
E-mail: steering@atlantic-ent.com

Mail order and open shop. Monday-Friday 8 am to 5 pm. Specializing in rebuilt rack and pinion steering assemblies for Jaguar, Aston Martin, Jensen, Triumph, Rover, Rolls-Royce, Bentley. Web site: www.atlantic-ent.com

Atlas Obsolete Chrysler Parts | parts
10621 Bloomfield St, Unit 32
Los Alamitos, CA 90720
PH/FAX: 562-594-5560
E-mail: atlaschrys@aol.com

See full listing in **Section One** under **Mopar**

Bronx Automotive | parts
501 Tiffany St
Bronx, NY 10474
718-589-2979

See full listing in **Section Two** under **ignition parts**

Bryant's Antique Auto Parts | appraisals chassis/engine parts sheetmetal wiring harnesses
851 Western Ave
Hampden, ME 04444
207-862-4019

See full listing in **Section One** under **Ford 1903-1931**

The Car Shop | parts service
10449 Rt 39
Springville, NY 14141
716-592-2060; FAX: 716-592-5766
E-mail: carshop77@aol.com

See full listing in **Section Two** under **street rods**

Car-Line Manufacturing & Distribution Inc | chassis parts engine parts sheetmetal
1250 Gulf St, PO Box 1192
Beaumont, TX 77701
409-833-9757; FAX: 409-835-2468
E-mail: car-line@car-line.net

See full listing in **Section Two** under **sheetmetal**

Chassis Engineering Inc | brakes chassis parts suspension parts
119 N 2nd St, Box 70
West Branch, IA 52358
319-643-2645; FAX: 319-643-2801

Mail order only. Monday-Friday 8 am to 4:30 pm. We have manufactured chassis components for street rods for over 30 years. Suspensions, brakes, engine and transmission mounting kits. Frames, springs and many related chassis parts for 1928-1948 Fords, 1935-1954 Chevrolets, 1933-1934 Dodge and Plymouths.

The Chopper Rod Shop
20851 Missouri Ave, PO Box 185
Elmer, MO 63538
PH/FAX: 660-825-4572
E-mail: choprods@usa.net

chopped tops
street rods

See full listing in **Section Two** under **street rods**

Classic Chevrolet Parts Inc
8723 S I-35
Oklahoma City, OK 73149
405-631-4400; FAX: 405-631-5999
E-mail: info@classicchevroletparts.com

parts

See full listing in **Section One** under **Chevrolet**

Classic Mustang Inc
24 Robert Porter Rd
Southington, CT 06489
800-243-2742; FAX: 860-276-9986

body parts
carpets
chassis parts
floor pans

See full listing in **Section One** under **Mustang**

Early Ford V8 Sales Inc
Curtis Industrial Park, Bldg 37
831 Rt 67
Ballston Spa, NY 12020
518-884-2825; FAX: 518-884-2633
E-mail: earlyford@prodigy.net

parts

See full listing in **Section One** under **Ford 1932-1953**

Eckler's Quality Parts & Accessories for Corvettes
5140 S Washington Ave
Titusville, FL 32780
800-327-4868; FAX: 407-383-2059
E-mail: ecklers@ecklers.net

accessories
parts

See full listing in **Section One** under **Corvette**

Energy Suspension
1131 Via Callejon
San Clemente, CA 92673
949-361-3935; FAX: 949-361-3940
E-mail: hyperflex@energysuspension.com

suspension parts

See full listing in **Section Two** under **suspension parts**

ESPO Springs 'n Things
701 Pine Tree Rd
Danville, PA 17821
800-903-9019; FAX: 570-672-0368
E-mail: springsnthings@aol.com

chassis parts
suspension parts

See full listing in **Section Two** under **suspension parts**

Greer Enterprises
1981 Greenbrook Blvd
Richland, WA 99352
509-627-3411
E-mail: greenent@owt.com

parts

Mail order and open shop. Monday-Friday 1 pm to 9 pm. Specializing in 1928-1948 Ford street rod and reproduction parts.

Guldstrand Engineering Inc
912 Chestnut St
Burbank, CA 91506
818-558-1499; FAX: 818-558-1449
E-mail: gss@guldstrand.com

parts

See full listing in **Section One** under **Corvette**

Gulf Coast Corvette
15100 Lee Rd #101
Humble, TX 77396
800-546-2111 order line
281-441-2111 info line
FAX: 281-441-3057

parts

See full listing in **Section One** under **Corvette**

Hoffman Automotive Distributor
US Hwy #1, Box 818
Hilliard, FL 32046
904-845-4421

parts

See full listing in **Section Two** under **body parts**

Horton
244 Woolwich St S
Breslau, ON Canada N0B 1M0
519-648-2150; FAX: 519-648-3355
E-mail: mail@horton.on.ca

parts

See full listing in **Section Two** under **street rods**

House of Powder Inc
Rt 71 & 1st St, PO Box 110
Standard, IL 61363
815-339-2648

powder coating
sandblasting

See full listing in **Section Two** under **service shops**

Innovative Rod Products
28 Bruce Way
Moundhouse, NV 89706
PH/FAX: 775-246-1718
E-mail: rick@innovativerod.com

body components
chassis parts

Mail order and open shop. Monday-Friday 8 am to 5 pm. Manufacturing of chassis and body components. Web site: www.innovativerod.com

Jackson's Oldtime Parts
4502 Grand Ave
Duluth, MN 55807
888-399-7278, 218-624-5791
E-mail: sales@oldtimeparts.com

parts

See full listing in **Section Two** under **engine parts**

JECC Inc
PO Box 616
West Paterson, NJ 07424
973-890-9682; FAX: 973-812-2724

chassis parts
gaskets
transmissions

See full listing in **Section One** under **Buick/McLaughlin**

Kenask Spring Co
307 Manhattan Ave
Jersey City, NJ 07307
201-653-4589

springs

See full listing in **Section Two** under **suspension parts**

Roger Kraus Racing
2896 Grove Way
Castro Valley, CA 94546
510-582-5031; FAX: 510-886-5605

shocks
tires
wheels

See full listing in **Section Two** under **tires**

Lonny's Fabrication
44279 Cabo St
Temecula, CA 92592
909-699-4582

custom fabrication
welding

See full listing in **Section Two** under **manufacturing**

Section Two – Generalists

Majestic Truck Parts   parts
17726 Dickerson
Dallas, TX 75252
972-248-6245; FAX: 972-380-8913
E-mail: majestictrk@juno.com

See full listing in **Section One** under **Chevrolet**

Mancini Racing Enterprises   parts
33510 Groesbeck Hwy
Fraser, MI 48026
810-294-6670; FAX: 810-294-0390
E-mail: robc@manciniracing.com

See full listing in **Section One** under **Mopar**

Donald McKinsey   fuel pumps
PO Box 94H   ignition parts
Wilkinson, IN 46186   literature
765-785-6284   spark plugs

See full listing in **Section Two** under **ignition parts**

Northern Auto Parts Warehouse Inc   parts
PO Box 3147
Sioux City, IA 51102
800-831-0884; FAX: 712-258-0088
E-mail: sales@northernautoparts.com

See full listing in **Section Two** under **engine parts**

Northwestern Auto Supply Inc   parts
1101 S Division
Grand Rapids, MI 49507
800-704-1078, 616-241-1714
FAX: 616-241-0924

See full listing in **Section Two** under **engine parts**

Obsolete Ford Parts Inc   parts
8701 S I-35
Oklahoma City, OK 73149
405-631-3933; FAX: 405-634-6815
E-mail: info@obsoletefordparts.com

See full listing in **Section One** under **Ford 1954-up**

P&J Automotive Inc   bodies
6262 Riverside Dr   chassis parts
Danville, VA 24541
804-822-2211; FAX: 804-822-2213

See full listing in **Section Two** under **street rods**

Performance Coatings   ceramic coatings
9768 Feagin Rd   engine parts
Jonesboro, GA 30236   suspension parts
770-478-2775; FAX: 770-478-1926
Email: gemobpci@mindspring.com

See full listing in **Section Two** under **exhaust systems**

Pole Position Racing Products   parts
2021 E 74th Ave, Unit J
Denver, CO 80229
303-286-8555; FAX: 303-286-8666
E-mail: sales@polepositionrp.com

Manufacturer of upper and lower control arms (adjustable), camber, caster, toe gauges, etc.

Power Steering Services Inc   pumps
2347 E Kearney St   rack & pinion
Springfield, MO 65803   steering gearboxes
417-864-6676; FAX: 417-864-7103
E-mail: chip@powersteering.com

See full listing in **Section Two** under **suspension parts**

R&L Model A   parts
54 Clark Dr, Unit D   restorations
East Berlin, CT 06114   service
860-828-7600

See full listing in **Section One** under **Ford 1903-1931**

RARE Corvettes   cars
Joe Calcagno   parts
Box 1080
Soquel, CA 95073
831-475-4442; FAX: 831-475-1115

See full listing in **Section One** under **Corvette**

Rochester Clutch & Brake Co   brakes
35 Niagara St   clutches
Rochester, NY 14605
716-232-2579; FAX: 716-232-3279

See full listing in **Section Two** under **brakes**

The Rod Factory   accessories
3131 N 31st Ave   suspension parts
Phoenix, AZ 85017
602-269-0031
E-mail: laserjet@amug.org

See full listing in **Section Two** under **street rods**

Rolling Steel Body Parts   body parts
7913 Chardon Rd, Rt 6
Kirtland, OH 44094
888-765-5460, 440-256-8383
FAX: 440-256-8994
E-mail: sales@rollingsteelbodyparts.com

See full listing in **Section Two** under **body parts**

Donald E Schneider Marinette &   parts
Menominee Auto Club
RR 1, N7340 Miles Rd
Porterfield, WI 54159
715-732-4958

See full listing in **Section Two** under **comprehensive parts**

Smith & Jones Distributing Co Inc   parts
1 Biloxi Sq
West Columbia, SC 29170
803-822-8500; FAX: 803-822-8477

See full listing in **Section One** under **Ford 1903-1931**

Joe Smith Ford & Hot Rod Parts   parts
51 Lakewood Dr   service
Marietta, GA 30066
770-426-9850; FAX: 770-426-9854
E-mail: joesmithhotrod@yahoo.com

See full listing in **Section One** under **Ford 1932-1953**

Steelman/JS Products   tools
5440-B S Procyon Ave
Las Vegas, NV 89118
800-255-7011; FAX: 702-362-5084
E-mail: jsprodnlv@aol.com

See full listing in **Section Two** under **tools**

Tanson Enterprises   performance parts
2508 J St, Dept HVA   restoration parts
Sacramento, CA 95816-4815
916-448-2950
FAX: 916-443-3269 *88
E-mail: tanson@pipeline.com

See full listing in **Section One** under **Oldsmobile**

Tucson Packard/Chirco Automotive
9101 E 22nd St
Tucson, AZ 85710
520-722-1984; FAX: 520-298-4069
E-mail: tucpackard@aol.com

accessories
NORS parts
NOS parts
used parts

See full listing in **Section One** under **Packard**

Tom Vagnini
58 Anthony Rd, RR 3
Pittsfield, MA 01201
413-698-2526

used parts

See full listing in **Section One** under **Packard**

Vintage Auto Parts Inc
24300 Hwy 9
Woodinville, WA 98072
800-426-5911, 425-486-0777
FAX: 425-486-0778
E-mail: erics@vapinc.com

cars
parts

See full listing in **Section Two** under **comprehensive parts**

cleaning products

Gent-l-Kleen Products Inc
3445 Board Rd
York, PA 17402-9409
717-767-6881; FAX: 717-767-6888
E-mail: info@gent-l-kleen.com

hand cleaners
soaps

Deals in hand cleaners and soaps. Web site: www.gent-l-kleen.com

clutches

Antique Auto Parts Cellar
6 Chauncy St, PO Box 3
South Weymouth, MA 02190
781-335-1579; FAX: 781-335-1925
E-mail: our1932@aol.com

brake/chassis/
engine parts
fuel pumps/kits
gaskets
water pumps

See full listing in **Section Two** under **comprehensive parts**

Automotive Friction
4621 SE 27th Ave
Portland, OR 97202
800-545-9088; FAX: 503-234-1026

brakes
clutches
water pumps

Mail order and open shop. Monday-Friday 8 am to 5 pm Pacific time. Rebuilding clutches, brakes and water pumps.

Automotive Restorations Inc
Stephen Babinsky
4 Center St
Bernardsville, NJ 07924
908-766-6688; FAX: 908-766-6684
E-mail: autorestnj@aol.com

clutch rebuilding
mechanical services
restorations

See full listing in **Section Two** under **restoration shops**

Dave Bean Engineering
636 E St Charles St SR3H
San Andreas, CA 95249
209-754-5802; FAX: 209-754-5177
E-mail: admin@davebean.com

parts

See full listing in **Section One** under **Lotus**

Fort Wayne Clutch & Driveline
2424 Goshen Rd
Fort Wayne, IN 46808
219-484-8505; FAX: 219-484-8605
E-mail: clutches@skyenet.net

axles
axleshafts
clutches
driveshafts

Mail order and open shop. Monday-Friday 8 am to 5 pm, Saturday 8:30 am to 12:30 pm. Wide variety of clutches, clutch parts, driveshafts, driveshaft parts, axleshafts and axleshaft parts. Specialize in antiques, obsolete, foreign and just plain hard to find parts. Carry a wide stock of parts for everything from lawn mowers to earth movers. A staff of professionals with over 100 years' experience. Large portion of our business is done through mail order. Ship worldwide. If we do not stock the part you are looking for, we can usually make it. Web site: www.fortwayneclutch.com

No 1 Performance
1775 S Redwood Rd
Salt Lake City, UT 84104
800-453-8250; FAX: 801-975-9653

engine kits
parts

See full listing in **Section Two** under **engine parts**

Orion Motors European Parts Inc
10722 Jones Rd
Houston, TX 77065
800-736-6410, 281-894-1982
FAX: 281-849-1997
E-mail: orion-yugo@yugoparts.com

parts

See full listing in **Section One** under **Alfa Romeo**

coachbuilders & designers

Ashton Keynes Vintage Restorations Ltd
A Keith Bowley
Ashton Keynes, Swindon
Wilshire England
01285-861-288; FAX: 01285-860-604

coachbuilding
restoration

See full listing in **Section One** under **Rolls-Royce/Bentley**

Backyard Buddy Corp
140 Dana St
Warren, OH 44483
800-837-9353, 330-395-9372
FAX: 330-392-9311

automotive lift

See full listing in **Section Two** under **accessories**

Bayliss Automobile Restorations
2/15 Bon Mace Close, Berkeley Vale
Via Gosford NSW 2261 Australia
61-2-43885253; FAX: 61-2-43893152
E-mail: bayrest@ozemail.com.au

repainting
repairs
sheetmetal work

See full listing in **Section Two** under **restoration shops**

Caddytown™/Pawl Engineering Co
4960 Arrowhead, PO Box 240105
West Bloomfield, MI 48324
PH/FAX: 248-682-2007
E-mail: pawl@earthlink.net

memorabilia
parts
toys

See full listing in **Section One** under **Cadillac/LaSalle**

Classic Auto Appraiser
24316 Carlton Ct
Laguna Niguel, CA 92677
800-454-1313; FAX: 949-425-1533
E-mail: classicauto64@home.com

appraisals

See full listing in **Section Two** under **appraisals**

| Classic Coachworks Rod & Custom
7492 S Division Ave
Grand Rapids, MI 49548
616-455-8110
E-mail: classiccoachal@aol.com | parts
repairs
restoration |

See full listing in **Section Two** under **street rods**

| Dagel's Street Rods
1048 W Collins Ave
Orange, CA 92867
714-288-1445; FAX: 714-288-1400 | parts
street rods |

See full listing in **Section Two** under **street rods**

| Deters Restorations
6205 Swiss Garden Rd
Temperance, MI 48182-1020
734-847-1820 | restoration |

See full listing in **Section Two** under **restoration shops**

| Jack Juratovic
819 Absequami Trail
Lake Orion, MI 48362
PH/FAX: 248-814-0627 | artwork
magazine |

See full listing in **Section Two** under **artwork**

| Mastercraft Body Works Inc
3602 Ovilla Rd
Ovilla, TX 75154
972-617-0507; FAX: 972-617-3252
E-mail: schovanetz@aol.com | bodywork
fabrication
rust work |

Open shop. Monday-Friday 8 am to 5:30 pm, Saturday by appointment. Fabrication of aluminum and metal parts from door skin to complete bodies. Rust work, bodywork and paint. Two separate buildings. Located 20 miles south of Dallas, same location since 1979. Specialize in exotic and luxury vehicles.

| New Era Motors
11611 NE 50th Ave, Unit 6
Vancouver, WA 98686
360-573-8788; FAX: 360-573-7461 | restoration |

See full listing in **Section Two** under **woodwork**

| Odyssey Restorations Inc
8080 Central Ave NE
Spring Lake Park, MN 55432
763-786-1518; FAX: 763-786-1524 | parts
restoration |

See full listing in **Section Two** under **restoration shops**

| Thompson Hill Metalcraft
23 Thompson Hill Rd
Berwick, ME 03901
207-698-5756
E-mail: wpeach@thompsonhill.com | metal forming
panel beating
welding |

See full listing in **Section Two** under **sheetmetal**

| Brady Ward-Scale Autoworks
313 Bridge St #4
Manchester, NH 03104-5045
PH/FAX: 603-623-5925 | models |

See full listing in **Section Two** under **models & toys**

| The Woodie Works
245 VT Rt 7A
Arlington, VT 05250
PH/FAX: 802-375-9305
E-mail: dkwoodie@vermontel.net | woodworking |

See full listing in **Section Two** under **woodwork**

comprehensive parts

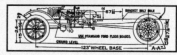

| ADP Hollander
14800 28th Ave N #190
Plymouth, MN 55447
800-761-9266; FAX: 800-825-1124
E-mail: info@hollander-auto-parts.com | interchange info
manuals |

See full listing in **Section Two** under **car & parts locators**

| American Performance Products
675 S Industry Rd
Cocoa, FL 32926
321-632-8299; FAX: 321-632-5119
E-mail: amc@oldcarparts.com | parts |

See full listing in **Section One** under **AMC**

| Antique Auto Parts
PO Box 64, 60 View Dr
Elkview, WV 25071
304-965-1821 | parts
parts cars |

Mail order and open shop. Monday-Friday 9 am to dusk, Saturday 9 am to 5 pm. Antique parts for all makes and models, plus 120 parts cars from 1935-1972. Parting out 100 cars and trucks from 1935-1972. Over 25 years in business.

| Antique Auto Parts Cellar
6 Chauncy St, PO Box 3
South Weymouth, MA 02190
781-335-1579; FAX: 781-335-1925
E-mail: our1932@aol.com | brake/chassis/
engine parts
fuel pumps/kits
gaskets
water pumps |

Mail order and open shop. Monday-Friday 9 am to 5 pm. Supply new, new old stock and our own reproduction quality mechanical parts for US cars and trucks from 1910-1991. Revulcanizing motor mounts (100+ different ones, plus thousands of NOS), fuel pumps and kits, water pumps, motor parts: pistons, rings, valves, guides, tappets, timing components (more than 20 of our own manufacture), gaskets (more than 200 cut on our own dies); bearings and seals; brake and suspension parts; rebuilding services on starters, generators, tank senders, distributors, vacuum advances, clutches. Providing the hobby with guaranteed parts and services since 1975. Brush on engine paint for most American vehicles. Fuel tank sealer high temp manifold paint. Web site: www.then-now.com

See our ad on page 244

| Atlantic British Ltd
Halfmoon Light Industrial Park
6 Enterprise Ave
Clifton Park, NY 12065
800-533-2210; FAX: 518-664-6641
E-mail: ab@roverparts.com | accessories
parts |

See full listing in **Section One** under **Rover/Land Rover**

| C E Babcock
619 Waterside Way
Sarasota, FL 34242
941-349-4990; FAX: 941-349-5751 | 1941, 1942, 1946,
1947 Cadillac parts |

See full listing in **Section One** under **Cadillac/LaSalle**

| Battlefield Antique
5054 S Broadview
Battlefield, MO 65619
417-882-7923
E-mail: battlefielda@aol.com | parts |

See full listing in **Section One** under **Ford 1903-1931**

Bavarian Autosport
275 Constitution Ave
Portsmouth, NH 03801
800-535-2002; FAX: 800-507-2002

accessories
parts

See full listing in **Section One** under **BMW**

Baxter Auto Parts
9444 N Whitaker Rd (corporate office)
Portland, OR 97217
800-765-3785; FAX: 503-246-4590
E-mail: see our web site

accessories
parts

Mail order and open shop. Monday-Friday 8 am to 9 pm, Saturday 8 am to 6 pm, Sunday 9 am to 5 pm Pacific time. Deals in performance and hard parts and accessories for import and domestic cars and trucks. Professionals since 1936. We are a chain of retail stores in the Pacific Northwest, offering mail order through our toll free number. Web site: www.baxterautoparts.com

Blaser's Auto, Nash, Rambler, AMC
3200 48th Ave
Moline, IL 61265-6453
309-764-3571; FAX: 309-764-1155
E-mail: blazauto@sprynet.com

NOS parts

See full listing in **Section One** under **AMC**

Chris' Parts Cars
1409 Rt 179
Lambertville, NJ 08530-3413
609-397-9045

cars
parts

Cars seen by appointment only. Complete cars from 1940s, 1950s and 1960s, many are restorable, over 200 parts cars. Would rather sell complete cars, not parts, on most. Prices range from $75-$475. I am retired, these are cars collected through my auto body repair business of thirty-five years. It is very hard to reach me by phone, better to write and SASE for an answer.

Classic Cars & Parts
Division of AKV Auto/Mike Chmilarski
622 Rt 109
Lindenhurst, NY 11757
516-888-3914

car dealer
parts

See full listing in **Section Two** under **car dealers**

Collector's Auto Supply
PO Box 1541
Peachland, BC Canada V0H 1X9
888-772-7848, 250-767-1974
FAX: 250-767-3340
E-mail: car@telus.net

parts

New and used parts for most makes 1909 to 1979. NOS Mopar and GM parts a specialty. See our web site for NOS listings by year. Illustrated tune-up parts catalogs for most domestic and foreign ignition systems also on line. US mailing address: 1510 Main St, PO Box 2076, Oroville, WA 98844; proprietor: Jim Carpenter. Web site: www.collectorsauto.com

Corvette World
RD 9, Box 770, Dept H
Greensburg, PA 15601
724-837-8600; FAX: 724-837-4420
E-mail: cvworld@sgi.net

accessories
parts

See full listing in **Section One** under **Corvette**

Joe Curto Inc
22-09 126th St
College Point, NY 11356
718-762-SUSU
FAX: 718-762-6287 (h)

English
carburetors
English parts
repairs

Mail order and open shop. Monday-Friday 9 am to 6:30 pm Eastern time. Large stocks of SU and British Stromberg parts, new and used. Comprehensive rebuilding service, as well as a

knowledgeable staff to serve you. 25 years in the British car trade, well versed in the ins and outs of Lucas, Girling and Lockheed systems. Offer full rebuilding of water pumps, starters, generators, wiper motors, calipers, servos. Also do repairs and restorations on your vehicle. Web site: www.joecurtoinc.com

Davies Corvette	accessories
7141 US Hwy 19	parts
New Port Richey, FL 34653	
800-236-2383, 727-842-8000	
FAX: 727-846-8216	
E-mail: davies@corvetteparts.com	

See full listing in **Section One** under **Corvette**

Daytona Turbo Action Camshafts	camshafts
1109 US #1, PO Box 5094	engine parts
Ormond Beach, FL 32175	
888-RARE-CAM, 800-505-CAMS	
386-676-7478; FAX: 386-258-1582	
E-mail: info@camshafts.com	

See full listing in **Section Two** under **bearings**

Dearborn Classics	accessories
PO Box 7649	restoration parts
Bend, OR 97708-7649	
800-252-7427; FAX: 800-500-7886	

See full listing in **Section One** under **Ford 1954-up**

Greg Donahue Collector Car Restorations Inc	parts
12900 S Betty Pt	restoration
Floral City, FL 34436	
352-344-4329; FAX: 352-344-0015	

See full listing in **Section One** under **Ford 1954-up**

Don's Antique Auto Parts	new parts
37337 Niles Blvd	used parts
Fremont, CA 94536	
415-792-4390	

Mail order and open shop. Monday-Saturday 9:30 am to 6 pm. Deal in American parts up to 1954 for most cars and trucks. Specialize in 1936-1948 Lincoln Zephyrs and Continentals. New, used and rebuilt parts.

For Ramblers Only	accessories
2324 SE 34th Ave	parts
Portland, OR 97214	
503-232-0497	
E-mail: ramblers@teleport.com	

See full listing in **Section One** under **AMC**

From Rust To Riches	appraisals
Bill McCoskey	Packard parts
PO Box 93	Rolls-Royce parts
Littlestown, PA 17340	
410-346-0660; FAX: 410-346-6499	
E-mail: tatrabill@aol.com	

Mail order parts only. Specialists in American and European cars including Packard, Rolls-Royce, Bentley, Studebaker and more obscure European car parts, Tatra cars and parts. Expert certified appraiser. Over 30 years in the old car hobby and business.

J Giles Automotive	car & parts locator
703 Morgan Ave	exporter
Pascagoula, MS 39567-2116	
228-769-1012; FAX: 228-769-8904	
E-mail: jgauto@datasync.com	

See full listing in **Section Two** under **car & parts locators**

Gowen Auto Parts	parts
Rt 2, PO Box 249	
Coffeyville, KS 67337	
316-251-4237	

Mail order and open shop. Antique and classic parts, 1910s-1970s. Mostly engine, brake and suspension parts. Also classic rebuilt short blocks.

Harter Industries Inc	parts
PO Box 502	restoration
Holmdel, NJ 07733	
732-566-7055; FAX: 732-566-6977	
E-mail: harter101@aol.com	

Mail order and shop open by appointment only. Restoration and replacement of almost any cast, machined, small formed sheet-metal or wood part for antique and classic cars. "We work from your old part, a borrowed part or a carefully dimensioned sketch or photograph." Service for car owners and restorers. Call or write to help solve hard-to-find parts problems.

IMCADO Manufacturing Co	leather equipment
50 Winthrop Ave, PO Box 87	
Umatilla, FL 32784-0087	
352-669-3308	

Mail order and open shop. Monday-Friday 9 am to 5 pm. Complete line of leather equipment for any motorcar ever built from 1896-on. Hood belts, top straps, crank holsters, fan belts, axle straps, gaiters, joint boots, etc. Original replacement authenticated and approved, prime grade cowhide with select hardware. 12-month warranty.

Indian Adventures Inc	parts
121 South St, PO Box 206	
Foxboro, MA 02035	
508-359-4660; FAX: 508-359-5435	

Authorized retailers only. Specialty and reproduction parts for 1960s and 1970s Pontiacs including engine cradles, throttle shafts, license pockets, frame repair kits, rear end dollies, carburetor rebuild kits and other restoration helpers. Web site: www.chiefmanyhorses.com

Interesting Parts Inc	appraisals
Paul TerHorst	gaskets
27526 N Owens Rd	parts
Mundelein, IL 60060-9608	storage
PH/FAX: 847-949-1030	transport
847-558-9732 cell	
E-mail: pterhorst@interaccess.com	

Mail order and open shop by appointment only. Local transportation and storage service. Classic parts especially for Packard, Cadillac, Auburn, etc. Also reproduction gaskets and appraisal services.

Joyce's Model A & T Parts	new parts
PO Box 70	NOS parts
Manchaca, TX 78652-0070	rebuilt parts
512-282-1196; FAX: 512-479-5091	

See full listing in **Section One** under **Ford 1903-1931**

Kanter Auto Products	car covers
76 Monroe St	carpet sets
Boonton, NJ 07005	front end kits
800-526-1096; 201-334-9575	parts
FAX: 201-334-5423	

Monday-Friday 8:30 am to 5 pm, Saturday 9 am to 2 pm. Helping you keep fun on the American road since 1960. Catalog featuring front end kits, brakes, engine parts, interior/exterior trim, carpet sets, exhaust, fuel and water pumps, suspension parts, weatherstripping, electrical parts, books and manuals, transmission parts, carburetors and more for 1930-1990 domestic cars and trucks. Web site: www.kanter.com

Klasse 356 Inc 311 Liberty St Allentown, PA 18102 800-634-7862; FAX: 610-432-8027 E-mail: parts@klasse356.com	cars parts restoration

See full listing in **Section One** under **Porsche**

Leo R Lindquist 1851 US Hwy 14 Balaton, MN 56115-3200 PH/FAX: 507-734-2051 E-mail: leorob51@frontiernet.net	1950s Hemi parts NORS parts NOS parts

See full listing in **Section One** under **Mopar**

Long Island Mustang **Restoration Parts** 168 Silverleaf Ln Islandia, NY 11722 516-232-2388; FAX: 516-272-5201 E-mail: tom@l-i-mustang.com	convertible specialist rebuilding services reconditioned consoles 1965-1970 repro parts

See full listing in **Section One** under **Mustang**

M & T Manufacturing Co 30 Hopkins Ln Peace Dale, RI 02883 401-789-0472; FAX: 401-789-5650 E-mail: sales@mtmfg.com	convertible hold-down cables wooden top bows

See full listing in **Section Two** under **woodwork**

Manchester Motor Car Co 319 Main St Manchester, CT 06040 860-643-5874; FAX: 860-643-6190 E-mail: mmcollc@aol.com	automobilia parts petroliana restorations

Mail order and open shop. Monday-Wednesday and Friday 9 am to 5 pm, Thursday 9 am to 9 pm, Saturday 9 am to 3 pm. Operates as a dealership for antique, classic and muscle American cars and light trucks. Supply NOS, NORS, used, new and reproduction parts, automobilia and petroliana, antique tools and toys and literature and manuals. Complete restoration facility, doing body and mechanical work as well as interior, tops and detailing. Also offer an extensive parts locator and vehicle locator service. Car clubs are invited to have meetings in our vintage shop. Web site: www.manchestermotorcar.com

W L Wally Mansfield 214 N 13th St Wymore, NE 68466-1640 402-645-3546	cars parts trucks

Mail order and open shop by appointment only. Pre-war cars, trucks and parts. Specializing in Model T and A, NOS and good used parts. Also 1925-1948 Chevrolet, 1914-1948 Ford and 1920-1926 Dodge, all makes to 1950.

Mark Auto Co Inc Layton, NJ 07851 973-948-4157; FAX: 973-948-5458	parts restoration supplies

See full listing in **Section One** under **Ford 1903-1931**

Mustang Classics 3814 Walnut St Denver, CO 80205 303-295-3140	parts restoration sales service

See full listing in **Section One** under **Mustang**

Mustang of Chicago Inc 1321 W Irving Park Rd Bensenville, IL 60106 630-860-7077 FAX: 630-860-7120, 24 hrs E-mail: cobracars@aol.com	new & used parts

See full listing in **Section One** under **Mustang**

National Parts Locator Service 636 East 6th St #81 Ogden, UT 84404-2415 877-672-7875, 801-627-7210	parts locator

See full listing in **Section Two** under **car & parts locators**

Next Generation Restoration and **Performance by Year One** PO Box 2023 Tucker, GA 30084 800-921-9214; FAX: 800-680-6806 E-mail: info@nextgenparts.com	parts

See full listing in **Section One** under **Chevelle/Camaro**

NOS Only 414 Umbarger Rd, Unit E San Jose, CA 95111 408-227-2353, 408-227-2354 FAX: 408-227-2355 E-mail: nosonly@aol.com	NOS Ford parts NOS parts

Retail and mail order. Monday-Friday 9 am to 6 pm Pacific time. Specializing in new and obsolete Ford, Lincoln, Mercury parts from 1955 to current year. Car, truck and van parts. Authorized distributor of Dennis Carpenter repro.

Obsolete Auto Parts Co P/L 143 Comleroy Rd, PO Box 5 Kurrajong, NSW 2758 Australia 61-2-45-731424 FAX: 61-2-45-732106 E-mail: obsolete@pnc.com.au	parts parts locating service

Mail order and open shop. Monday-Saturday 9 am to 5 pm. AJ Noonan, owner. 1900-1960s new and used parts for English, European and American vehicles. Largest varied range of items in southern hemisphere. Parts locating service. Many rare items in stock. Fast, efficient international service provided. Information sheet, $1 US. Web site: www.antiqueautoparts.au.com

Old Ford Parts 35 4th Ave N Algona, WA 98001 253-833-8494; FAX: 253-833-2190	parts

See full listing in **Section One** under **Ford 1932-1953**

Original Parts Group Inc 17892 Gothard St Huntington Beach, CA 92647 800-243-8355 US/Canada 714-841-5363; FAX: 714-847-8159	accessories parts

See full listing in **Section One** under **Pontiac**

Parts House 2912 Hunter St Fort Worth, TX 76112 817-451-2708 E-mail: theparts@flash.net	brake shoes/drums fenders sheetmetal repair panels

Mail, e-mail, telephone orders and open shop. Cars and light trucks: 1920-1975. Suspension/steering, brake shoes, drums, engine headgaskets, 1900-1975; engine (internal) components, 1930-1954. Engine (external) water pumps, fuel pumps, generators, starters, 1930-1962. Large supply of NORS, NOS sheetmetal repair panels, fenders, quarter panels, rocker panels, 1941-1970. NOS Buick, Olds fenders, 1940-1948. Specializing in Chevrolet pickups, 1941-1972, all sheetmetal parts.

Garth B Peterson W 2619 Rockwell Ave Spokane, WA 99205 509-325-3823 anytime	accessories/chrome glass/grilles/parts radios/sheetmetal steering wheels

Tremendous supply of NOS/used Hudson, Essex, Terraplane, Dover, Nash, Rambler, Metropolitan, AMC parts, accessories and sheetmetal. Extra endeavors to fullfill your critical needs, any way possible. Also new/used parts and accessories for all 1930-1970 cars. Original car radios and hood ornaments for all cars. We try to do the impossible for you. SASE please.

Pre-Sixties Cars and Parts Ltd 75 Victoria Rd South Guelph, ON Canada N1E 5P7 800-364-7710; FAX: 519-766-4497	appraisals auto sales/locator body repairs parts

Mail order and open shop. Monday-Saturday 9 am to 6 pm. Central source for parts to fit North American cars, 1920s-1970s. Established 20 years. Auto locator service, flatbed service, auto appraisals, inspections, auto body repairs and refinishing, mechanical repairs and auto sales. Large and varied stock of parts. Buy and sell job lots of new or rebuilt parts.

Sam Quinn Cadillac Parts Box 837 Estacada, OR 97023 503-637-3852	parts

See full listing in **Section One** under **Cadillac/LaSalle**.

RB's Obsolete Automotive 7711 Lake Ballinger Way Edmonds, WA 98026-9163 425-670-6739; FAX: 425-670-9151 E-mail: rbobsole@gte.net	parts

Mail order: Monday-Friday 7 am to 5 pm. Retail store: Tuesday-Friday 9 am to 5 pm, Saturday 9 am to 3 pm Pacific time.

Aftermarket products for street rods, classics, antiques and special interest vehicles. Specializing in Chevrolet and Ford cars and pickups. Visit us at NSRA and Goodguys events across the country. Web site: www.rbsobsolete.com

R-D-T Plans and Parts PO Box 2272 Merced, CA 95344-0272 209-383-4441	car parts trailer plans

See full listing in **Section Two** under **trailers**

The Real Source PO Box 1248 Effingham, IL 62401 800-LUV-BUGG (588-2844), Dept VS1 FAX: 217-347-2952 E-mail: mail@800luvbugg.com	accessories parts

See full listing in **Section One** under **Volkswagen**

Reproduction Parts Marketing 1920 Alberta Ave Saskatoon, SK Canada S7K 1R9 306-652-6668; FAX: 306-652-1123	parts restoration service

See full listing in **Section One** under **Chevrolet**

Restoration Specialties and Supply Inc 148 Minnow Creek Ln, PO Box 328 Windber, PA 15963 814-467-9842; FAX: 814-467-5323 E-mail: info@restorationspecialties.com	parts

Mail order and open shop. Monday-Friday 9 am to 5 pm. Weatherstripping, clips, fasteners, mattings, screws and bolts. Family owned corporation with each order receiving the prompt attention it deserves. 75% of all orders are shipped the same day as

Section Two – Generalists

received. Illustrated catalog available, $3.50 US and Canada, $6 overseas. Web site: www.restorationspecialties.com

Restoration Supply Company 2060 Palisade Dr Reno, NV 89509 775-825-5663; FAX: 775-825-9330 E-mail: restoration@rsc.reno.nv.us	accessories restoration supplies

See full listing in **Section Two** under **restoration aids**

Roaring Twenties Antiques Rt 1 Box 104-D Madison, VA 22727 703-948-3744, 703-948-6290 FAX: 703-948-3744 E-mail: info@roaring-twenties.com	automobilia gasoline collectibles parts signs

Open Thursday-Monday 10 am to 5 pm, Sunday 12 pm to 5 pm. Automobilia, car parts, signs, service station and gasoline collectibles, collectible toy cars and trucks, interesting and unique memorabilia for sale. Rt 29 N, 2 miles south of scenic Madison, Virginia. In the foothills of the Blue Ridge, 26 miles north of Charlottesville, 90 miles south of Washington, DC. Web site: www.roaring-twenties.com

Donald E Schneider Marinette & Menominee Auto Club RR 1, N7340 Miles Rd Porterfield, WI 54159 715-732-4958	parts

Mail order and open shop by appointment only. NOS parts for 1930-1969 cars and trucks. No body parts. Club parts being sold to finance club library.

Special Interest Cars 451 Woody Rd Oakville, ON Canada L6K 2Y2 905-844-8063; FAX: 905-338-8063 E-mail: sic@istar.com	manuals parts

Mail order and open shop. Monday-Friday 8 am to 5:30 pm. Canada's largest obsolete automotive warehouse specializing in hard to find steering and brake parts. Currently supply 50-60 dealers. Large stock of import brake, ignition, water pumps, clutches, suspension, etc by Lucas, Quinton Hazel and other makes for sale enbloc or will break up for quantity sales wholesale. Also an obsolete Ford warehouse, inquire for all your needs. Lots of NOS sales literature, shop and owner's manuals.

Speed & Spares America 167D Portland Rd, Units 7/8 Weymouth, Dorset DT4 9BQ England +44 (0) 1305 766293 FAX: +44 (0) 1305 761304 E-mail: sales@speedandspares.co.uk	parts racing equipment

Mail order and open shop. Supplies parts and racing equipment. NOS and replacement parts and racing equipment for 1950-present GMCs, Fords, Chryslers and AMC/Jeeps. Web site: www.speedandspares.co.uk

Star Classics Inc 7745 E Redfield #300 Scottsdale, AZ 85260 800-644-7827, 480-991-7495 FAX: 480-951-4096 E-mail: info@starclassics.com	parts

See full listing in **Section One** under **Mercedes-Benz**

Studebakers West 335A Convention Way Redwood City, CA 94063 650-366-8787	mechanical rebuilding transmission parts wiring harnesses

See full listing in **Section One** under **Studebaker**

Taylor Auto Parts PO Box 650 Esparto, CA 95627 530-787-1929; FAX: 530-787-1921	bearings brakes gaskets seals

Mail order and open shop. Monday-Saturday 9 am to 5 pm. Specializing in NOS mechanical parts for domestic vehicles, 1920s-1970s. Large inventory of ignition, brakes, bearings, seals, fuel and water pumps, electrical, chassis, engine parts and gaskets.

Thunderbird Headquarters 1080 Detroit Ave Concord, CA 94518 925-825-9550 info; 925-689-1771 800-227-2174 parts FAX: 800-964-1957 toll free E-mail: tbirdhq@tbirdhq.com	accessories literature parts upholstery

See full listing in **Section One** under **Thunderbird**

Tubes-n-Hoses by TKM 955 76th St SW Byron Center, MI 49315 FAX: 616-878-4949	hose assemblies tubes

See full listing in **Section Two** under **air conditioning**

Jim Tucker "The Heater Valve Guy" 29597 Paso Robles Rd Valley Center, CA 92082 760-749-3488 E-mail: jthcv@juno.com	carburetors heater valves trans gears U-joints

Mail order and open shop by appointment. Specializing in new Ranco and Harrison thermostatically controlled heater control valves. Also rebuild your original heater valve, 1949-1963, all makes. Vacuum and mechanical valves for cars 1963-1975 also on hand. Carburetors for all makes 1946-1970 (rebuilt) in stock. Transmission gears and U-joints also on hand, for 1948-1963 cars. In business full time for 18 years. Advertising in *Hemmings Motor News*.

Vintage Auto Parts Inc 24300 Hwy 9 Woodinville, WA 98072 800-426-5911, 425-486-0777 FAX: 425-486-0778 E-mail: erics@vapinc.com	cars parts

Mail order and open shop. Monday-Friday 8 am to 5 pm Pacific time. The world's most complete inventory of new old stock parts for all American cars and trucks, 1915-1970. Engine, clutch, transmission, driveline, differential, bearings, seals, brake drums, cylinders, linings, chassis, body, trim and much, much more. Specializing in NOS parts for over 40 years. Ship worldwide. Catalogs on web site: www.vapinc.com

Year One Inc PO Box 129 Tucker, GA 30085 800-YEAR-ONE (932-7663) 770-493-6568 Atlanta & overseas FAX: 800-680-6806 E-mail: info@yearone.com	parts

Serving the enthusiast since 1981, Year One specializes in restoration and performance parts and accessories. Catalogs are available for 1964-1972 Chevelle, El Camino, and Monte Carlo; 1967-1981 Camaro; 1962-1974 Chevy II/Nova; 1958-1972 Impala and full-size Chevy; 1966-1974 Dodge/Plymouth B/E-bodies; 1966-1974 Dodge/Plymouth A/C-bodies; 1964-1972 Skylark/GS; 1964-1972 Cutlass/442; 1964-1972 GTO/LeMans; 1967-1981 Firebird; each catalog is $7.50 with a $7.50 refund on your first order. The following FREE catalogs are also available: 1967-1987 Chevy/GMC truck, Next Generation 1982-present Camaro/Firebird; Next Generation 1979-present Mustang. Web site: www.yearone.com

Zim's Autotechnik
1804 Reliance Pkwy
Bedford, TX 76021
800-356-2964; FAX: 817-545-2002
E-mail: zimips@allzim.com

parts
service

See full listing in **Section One** under **Porsche**

consultants

**AAAC-Antique Automobile
Appraisal & Consulting**
PO Box 700153
Plymouth, MI 48170
PH/FAX: 734-453-7644
E-mail: aaac@ameritech.net

appraisals
Cadillac parts
consulting

See full listing in **Section One** under **Cadillac/LaSalle**

AAG-Auto Appraisal Group Inc
PO Box 7034
Charlottesville, VA 22906
800-848-2886; FAX: 804-295-7918
E-mail: aag@autoappraisal.com

appraisals

See full listing in **Section Two** under **appraisals**

Archer & Associates
1807 East Ave
Hayward, CA 94541
510-581-4911
FAX: 510-537-7864

appraisals
consultant
expert witness
promotion
sales/purchasing

See full listing in **Section Two** under **auctions & shows**

ARS Automotive Research Services
Division of Auto Search International
1702 W Camelback #301
Phoenix, AZ 85015
602-230-7111; FAX: 602-230-7282

appraisals
research

See full listing in **Section Two** under **appraisals**

Auctioneer Phil Jacquier Inc
18 Klaus Anderson Rd
Southwick, MA 01077
413-569-6421; FAX: 413-569-6599
E-mail: info@jacquierauctions.com

auctions

See full listing in **Section Two** under **auctions & shows**

**Auto Consultants &
Appraisal Service**
Charles J Kozelka
PO Box 111
Macedonia, OH 44056
330-467-0748; FAX: 330-467-3725

appraisals

See full listing in **Section Two** under **appraisals**

Auto-Line Enterprises Inc
2 Lyons Rd
Armonk, NY 10504
914-681-1757; FAX: 914-273-5159
E-mail: autocashny@aol.com

appraisals
broker services

See full listing in **Section Two** under **appraisals**

**Automobile Appraisal Service &
Special Interest Autos**
10097 Manchester Rd, Ste 203
St Louis, MO 63122
PH/FAX: 314-821-4015

appraiser

See full listing in **Section Two** under **appraisals**

Automotive Legal Service Inc
PO Box 626
Dresher, PA 19025
800-487-4947, 215-659-4947
FAX: 215-657-5843
E-mail: autolegal@aol.com

appraisals

See full listing in **Section Two** under **appraisals**

The Autoworks Ltd
90 Center Ave
Westwood, NJ 07675
201-358-0200; FAX: 201-358-0442

restoration
sales
service

See full listing in **Section Two** under **service shops**

AVM Automotive Consulting
Box 338
Montvale, NJ 07645-0338
201-391-5194; FAX: 978-383-4776
E-mail: avmtony@yahoo.com

appraisals
consultant

See full listing in **Section Two** under **appraisals**

Blair Collectors & Consultants
2821 SW 167th Pl
Seattle, WA 98166
206-242-6745, 206-246-1305
E-mail: blairhall33@aol.com

appraisals
consultant
literature

See full listing in **Section Two** under **appraisals**

The Can Corner
PO Box VA 1173
Linwood, PA 19061

audio tapes

See full listing in **Section Two** under **automobilia**

Car Critic
202 Woodshire Ln
Naples, FL 34105
941-435-1157; FAX: 941-261-4864
E-mail: carcritic@earthlink.net

appraisals
inspections

See full listing in **Section Two** under **car & parts locators**

Car Values Plus
40 Plank Rd
Newburgh, NY 12550
845-561-3594; FAX: 845-561-1745
E-mail: jim@hvaa.com

appraisals

See full listing in **Section Two** under **appraisals**

**Charles W Clarke,
Automotive Consultants**
17 Saddle Ridge Dr
West Simsbury, CT 06092-2118
PH/FAX: 860-658-2714

appraisals
car dealer
consultant

Appraisals, consulting. Connecticut, Hartford area based, can travel. Personal service and fees tailored to your needs. 40 years' automotive experience, appraisals, brokering, locating, etc. Connecticut licensed appraiser.

Classic Car Appraisals
37 Wyndwood Rd
West Hartford, CT 06107
PH/FAX: 860-236-0125
E-mail: tjakups@
classiccarappraisals.net

appraisals

See full listing in **Section Two** under **appraisals**

Section Two – Generalists

Clean Air Performance Professionals (CAPP) 84 Hoy Ave Fords, NJ 08863 732-738-7859; FAX: 732-738-7625 E-mail: stellacapp@earthlink.net	legislative watch organization

See full listing in **Section Three** under **legislative watch organizations**

Robert W Cook Corvette Art 8047 Moss Meadows Dr Dallas, TX 75231 214-349-6232; FAX: 214-692-7286 E-mail: prelim@cs.com	appraisals artwork

See full listing in **Section Two** under **artwork**

Lance S Coren, CAA, CMA 20545 Eastwood Ave Torrance, CA 90503-3611 310-370-4114; FAX: 310-371-4120 E-mail: lscent@hotmail.com	appraisals

See full listing in **Section Two** under **appraisals**

Corvette Enterprise Brokerage The Power Broker-Mike Kitain 52 Van Houten Ave Passaic Park, NJ 07055-5512 973-472-7021	appraisals broker consultant investment planning

See full listing in **Section One** under **Corvette**

Creative Automotive Consultants PO Box 2221 San Rafael, CA 94912-2221 415-892-3331; FAX: 415-892-3339 E-mail: cars4cac@earthlink.net	appraisals car locator promotion DMV

All hours by appointment. Appraisals for all collector vehicles. Period vehicles for the visual arts industry and special events. We need listings of all age and type vehicles. Auction coordination and support. 21 years' experience. Expert witness testimony. Also DMV registration service and vehicle verification. Web site: www.creative-automotive.com

Robert DeMars Ltd Auto Appraisers/Historians 222 Lakeview Ave, Ste 160/256 West Palm Beach, FL 33401 561-832-0171; FAX: 561-738-5284 E-mail: carapraisr@aol.com	appraisals auto historians auto locating research library resto consultants

See full listing in **Section Two** under **appraisals**

Mark Gillett PO Box 9177 Dallas, TX 75209 PH/FAX: 214-902-9258 011-525-559-6240 Mexico City, Mexico E-mail: autonet@onramp.net	car locator sales

See full listing in **Section Two** under **car dealers**

Eliot James Enterprises Inc PO Box 3986 Dana Point, CA 92629-8986 949-661-0889; FAX: 949-661-1901	development info

See full listing in **Section Four** under **books & publications**

Jesser's Auto Clinic 26 West St Akron, OH 44303 330-376-8181; FAX: 330-384-9129	appraisals

See full listing in **Section Two** under **appraisals**

Landry Classic MotorCars 34 Goodhue Ave Chicopee, MA 01020 413-592-2746; FAX: 413-594-8378 oldcar@map.com	appraisals

See full listing in **Section Two** under **appraisals**

M & M Automobile Appraisers Inc 584 Broomspun St Henderson, NV 89015 702-568-5120; FAX: 702-568-5158 E-mail: mmautoappr@earthlink.net	appraisals broker consultant

See full listing in **Section Two** under **appraisals**

Randall Marcus Vintage Automobiles 706 Hanshaw Rd Ithaca, NY 14850 607-257-5939; FAX: 607-272-8806 E-mail: randysvintageautos@ bgdmlaw.com	appraisals broker car locator consultant

See full listing in **Section Two** under **brokers**

Cathie Marples & The Marples Team Real Estate Broker 1555 Riverlake Rd, Ste N Discovery Bay, CA 94514 925-634-7774; FAX: 925-634-0902 E-mail: qikturn@aol.com	real estate brokers

Located in Contra Costa County along the California Delta within 90 minutes of San Jose and San Francisco. Direct boating access to San Francisco, Sacramento and the world. Web site: www.marplesteam.com

Bill McCoskey PO Box 93 Littlestown, PA 17340 410-346-0660; FAX: 410-346-6499 E-mail: billmccoskey@aol.com	accident/damage investigations appraisals

See full listing in **Section Two** under **appraisals**

Dennis Mitosinka's Classic Cars and Appraisals Service 619 E Fourth St Santa Ana, CA 92701 714-953-5303; FAX: 714-953-1810 E-mail: mitoclassics@earthlink.net	appraisals books

See full listing in **Section Two** under **appraisals**

Morgan Spares Ltd 225 Simons Rd Ancram, NY 12502 518-329-3877; FAX: 518-329-3892 E-mail: morganspares@taconic.net	car sales consulting obsolete parts used parts

See full listing in **Section One** under **Morgan**

Reward Service Inc 172 Overhill Rd Stormville, NY 12582 PH/FAX: 845-227-7647	appraisals restoration transportation

See full listing in **Section One** under **Jaguar**

Spyder Enterprises Inc RFD 1682 Laurel Hollow, NY 11791-9644 516-367-1616; FAX: 516-367-3260 E-mail: singer356@aol.com	accessories artwork automobilia books

See full listing in **Section Two** under **automobilia**

JC Taylor Antique Automobile Insurance Agency
320 S 69th St
Upper Darby, PA 19082
800-345-8290

insurance

See full listing in **Section Two** under **insurance**

Timeless Masterpieces
221 Freeport Dr
Bloomingdale, IL 60108
630-893-1058 evenings

appraisals consultant

See full listing in **Section Two** under **appraisals**

USAppraisal
754 Walker Rd, PO Box 472
Great Falls, VA 22066-0472
703-759-9100; FAX: 703-759-9099
E-mail: dhkinney@usappraisal.com

appraisals

See full listing in **Section Two** under **appraisals**

Vintage Jag Works
1390 W Hwy 26
Blackfoot, ID 83221
877-251-5183 toll free order line
208-684-4767; FAX: 208-684-3386
E-mail: walt@vintagejag.com

consulting how-to articles

See full listing in **Section One** under **Jaguar**

Wolfson Engineering
512 Parkway W
Las Vegas, NV 89106
PH/FAX: 702-384-4196

mech engineering

See full listing in **Section Two** under **special services**

---

custom cars

American Autowire/Factory Fit®
150 Heller Pl #17W, Dept HCCA02
Bellmawr, NJ 08031
800-482-9473; FAX: 856-933-0805
E-mail: info@americanautowire.com

battery cables electrical systems switches/ components

See full listing in **Section Two** under **street rods**

Amherst Antique Auto Show
157 Hollis Rd
Amherst, NH 03031
603-673-2093, NH
FAX: 617-641-0647, MA

swap meets

See full listing in **Section Two** under **auctions & shows**

Automobile Classics Appraisal Services
5385 S Cook Rd
College Park, GA 30349
404-761-0350; FAX: 404-761-3703
E-mail: johnboy30349@aol.com

appraisals

See full listing in **Section Two** under **appraisals**

Belmont's Rod & Custom Shop
138 Bussey St
Dedham, MA 02026
781-326-9599, 781-326-3270

speed equipment transmissions

See full listing in **Section Two** under **street rods**

Berkshire Auto's Time Was
10 Front St, Box 347
Collinsville, CT 06022
860-693-2332
E-mail: obteddi3@aol.com

restoration

See full listing in **Section Two** under **restoration shops**

Bob's Rod & Custom
866 W 3200 S
Nibley, UT 84321
435-752-7467
E-mail: bobsrod@cache.net

car assembly fabrication interiors

See full listing in **Section Two** under **street rods**

Boop Photography
2347 Derry St
Harrisburg, PA 17104-2728
717-564-8533
E-mail: booper@home.com

photography

See full listing in **Section Two** under **photography**

Brooks Performance Coatings
17819 SW Fisner Rd
Sherwood, OR 97140
503-524-4048

powder coatings

See full listing in **Section Two** under **special services**

Cars of the Times
1218 Crest Ln, Ste 16
Duncanville, TX 75137
972-572-6677
E-mail: cottjb@swbell.net

car dealer street rods

See full listing in **Section Two** under **car dealers**

The Chopper Rod Shop
20851 Missouri Ave, PO Box 185
Elmer, MO 63538
PH/FAX: 660-825-4572
E-mail: choprods@usa.net

chopped tops street rods

See full listing in **Section Two** under **street rods**

Classic Auto Appraiser
24316 Carlton Ct
Laguna Niguel, CA 92677
800-454-1313; FAX: 949-425-1533
E-mail: classicauto64@home.com

appraisals

See full listing in **Section Two** under **appraisals**

Classic Coachworks Rod & Custom
7492 S Division Ave
Grand Rapids, MI 49548
616-455-8110
E-mail: classiccoachal@aol.com

parts repairs restoration

See full listing in **Section Two** under **street rods**

Concours d'Elegance Upholstery
1607 Pine Ridge
Bushkill, PA 18324
888-ELEG-UPH
PH/FAX: 570-588-0969
E-mail: concoursuph@enter.net

upholstery

See full listing in **Section Two** under **upholstery**

Section Two – Generalists

Contemporary and Investment Automobiles
4115 Poplar Springs Rd
Gainesville, GA 30507
770-539-9111; FAX: 770-539-9818
E-mail: contemporaryauto@
mindspring.com

buy/sell/trade
mechanical work
memorabilia

See full listing in **Section Two** under **street rods**

Dagel's Street Rods
1048 W Collins Ave
Orange, CA 92867
714-288-1445; FAX: 714-288-1400

parts
street rods

See full listing in **Section Two** under **street rods**

Engine Master Conversions Ltd
32 W Strathmore Ave
Pontiac, MI 48340
248-745-0272

rwd conversions

See full listing in **Section Two** under **street rods**

Explicit Concepts Customs & Minis
Livonia, MI 48150
313-617-5433
E-mail: vabruno@explicitconcepts.net

aftermarket
restyling

Mail order and open shop by appointment only. Specializing in custom aftermarket restyling and sponsored show vehicles and car club for all trucks and cars from lowering to custom body-work including graphics. Deals in APC, Belltech, Airlift, low-grow neon, cool glow neon, Stoner, Optima battery, limited alloy wheels, NGK, Real Stuff neon, B&B Graphics, Accent Your Vibe clothing, Hemmings. SEMA members since 2000. Web site: www.explicitconcepts.net

Grumpy's Old Cars
396 Marsh St
San Luis Obispo, CA 93401
805-549-7875; FAX: 805-549-7877
E-mail: slohot@hotmail.com

car dealer

See full listing in **Section Two** under **car dealers**

Guldstrand Engineering Inc
912 Chestnut St
Burbank, CA 91506
818-558-1499; FAX: 818-558-1449
E-mail: gss@guldstrand.com

parts

See full listing in **Section One** under **Corvette**

Hillcrest Hot Rods
541 Mercer Rd
Greenville, PA 16125
PH/FAX: 724-588-3444

custom cars
street rods

See full listing in **Section Two** under **street rods**

Hunters Custom Automotive
975 Main St
Nashville, TN 37206
615-227-6584; FAX: 615-227-4897

accessories
engine parts
fiberglass products

See full listing in **Section Two** under **accessories**

ididit inc
610 S Maumee St
Tecumseh, MI 49286
517-424-0577; FAX: 517-424-7293
E-mail: sales@ididitinc.com

steering columns

See full listing in **Section Two** under **steering columns**

Keilen's Auto Restoring
580 Kelley Blvd (R)
North Attleboro, MA 02760
508-699-7768

restoration

See full listing in **Section Two** under **restoration shops**

K-F-D Services Inc
HC 65, Box 49
Altonah, UT 84002
801-454-3098; FAX: 801-454-3099
E-mail: kfd-services@msn.com

parts
restoration

See full listing in **Section One** under **Kaiser Frazer**

Dave Knittel Upholstery
850 E Teton #7
Tucson, AZ 85706
PH/FAX: 520-746-1588

interiors
tops
upholstery

See full listing in **Section Two** under **upholstery**

Lone Wolf
9375 Bearwalk Path
Brooksville, FL 34613
352-596-9949
E-mail: lonewolfwhistle@bigfoot.com

wolf whistles

See full listing in **Section Two** under **automobilia**

Lyme Pond Restorations
PO Box 202
Barnard, VT 05031
802-457-4657

restoration

See full listing in **Section Two** under **restoration shops**

Mastercraft Body Works Inc
3602 Ovilla Rd
Ovilla, TX 75154
972-617-0507; FAX: 972-617-3252
E-mail: schovanetz@aol.com

bodywork
fabrication
rust work

See full listing in **Section Two** under **coachbuilders & designers**

Mild to Wild Classics
1300 3rd St NW
Albuquerque, NM 87102
505-244-1139; FAX: 505-244-1164

parts
repairs
restoration

See full listing in **Section Two** under **street rods**

Niagara CHT Productions Inc
PO Box 112
Akron, NY 14001
716-542-2585

swap meets

See full listing in **Section Two** under **auctions & shows**

Prestige Motors
120 N Bessie Rd
Spokane, WA 99212
509-927-1041

car dealer

See full listing in **Section Two** under **car dealers**

Prototype Research & Dev Ltd
David Carlaw
230 Albert Ln
Campbellford, ON Canada K0L 1L0
705-653-4525; FAX: 705-653-4800
E-mail: davidcarlaw@hotmail.com

fiberglass bodies

See full listing in **Section One** under **Chevrolet**

Ray's Upholstering
600 N St Frances Cabrini Ave
Scranton, PA 18504
800-296-RAYS; FAX: 570-963-0415

partial/total
restoration

See full listing in **Section Two** under **restoration shops**

Ridgefield Auto Upholstery
34 Bailey Ave
Ridgefield, CT 06877
203-438-7583; FAX: 203-438-2666

interiors
tops

See full listing in **Section Two** under **interiors & interior parts**

Rod-1 Shop
210 Clinton Ave
Pitman, NJ 08071
609-228-7631; FAX: 609-582-5770
E-mail: atboz@webtv.net

street rods

See full listing in **Section Two** under **street rods**

**Strange Motion Rod &
Custom Construction Inc**
14696 N 350th Ave
Cambridge, IL 61238
309-927-3346
E-mail: strangemtn@cin.net

customizing
design
fabrication

See full listing in **Section Two** under **street rods**

Thompson Hill Metalcraft
23 Thompson Hill Rd
Berwick, ME 03901
207-698-5756
E-mail: wpeach@thompsonhill.com

metal forming
panel beating
welding

See full listing in **Section Two** under **sheetmetal**

Thunderbolt Traders Inc
6900 N Dixie Dr
Dayton, OH 45414-3297
513-890-3344; FAX: 513-890-9403
E-mail: tbolt@erinet.com

battery cables

See full listing in **Section One** under **Edsel**

Tricks Custom Hot Rods
7126 Wall Triana Hwy
Madison, AL 35757
256-722-8222

paint
restorations

See full listing in **Section Two** under **painting**

The V8 Store
3010 NE 49th St
Vancouver, WA 98663
360-693-7468; FAX: 360-693-0982
360-694-7853 nights

accessories
parts
service

Mail order and open shop. Monday-Friday 7:30 am to 5 pm,
nights and Saturdays by appointment. Rod and custom supply
store specializing in authentic fifties accessories. Also have both
used and NOS engine, drivetrain, body parts, flathead speed
equipment. Have added the complete line of Offenhauser performance products.

Webber Engineering LLC
1 Alice Ct
Pawcatuck, CT 06379
860-599-8895; FAX: 860-599-8609
E-mail: kwebbereng@aol.com

street rods
welding

See full listing in **Section Two** under **sheetmetal**

Wirth's Custom Automotive
505 Conner St, PO Box 5
Prairie du Rocher, IL 62277
618-284-3359
E-mail: roywirth@htc.net

custom accessories
fender skirts
spinner hubcaps

See full listing in **Section Two** under **accessories**

decals

Anderson's Car Door Monograms
32700 Coastsite #102
Rancho Palos Verdes, CA 90275
800-881-9049, 310-377-1007

car door monograms

See full listing in **Section Two** under **accessories**

Auto Nostalgia Enr
332 St Joseph
Mont St Gregoire, QC Canada J0J 1K0
PH/FAX: 450-346-3644
E-mail: autonostalgia@vif.com

literature
manuals
models
tractor decals

See full listing in **Section Two** under **models & toys**

Automobilia
200 N Emporia
Wichita, KS 67202
PH/FAX: 316-264-9986
E-mail: automobilia@juno.com

gas pumps
models
signs

See full listing in **Section Two** under **automobilia**

C & G Early Ford Parts
1941 Commercial St, Dept AH
Escondido, CA 92029-1233
760-740-2400; FAX: 760-740-8700
E-mail: cgford@cgfordparts.com

accessories/chrome
emblems
literature
mechanical
weatherstripping

See full listing in **Section One** under **Ford 1932-1953**

Classic Chevrolet Parts Inc
8723 S I-35
Oklahoma City, OK 73149
405-631-4400; FAX: 405-631-5999
E-mail: info@classicchevroletparts.com

parts

See full listing in **Section One** under **Chevrolet**

Del's Decals
6150 Baldwin St
Hudsonville, MI 49426

decals

Mail order only. Engine compartment decals for the air cleaner,
oil filter, valve cover, etc. SASE for free list, please state make.

Eurosport Daytona Inc
355 Tomoka Ave
Ormond Beach, FL 32174-6222
800-874-8044, 904-672-7199
FAX: 904-673-0821

license plates

See full listing in **Section Two** under **license plates**

Hi-Speed
John Steel
PO Box 44
Chagrin Falls, OH 44022
PH/FAX: 440-247-6021

literature
motorcycles
parts

See full listing in **Section One** under **Harley-Davidson**

Horseplayactionwear.com
211 N Catherine
Bay City, MI 48706
517-892-5509, 800-447-7669
FAX: 517-671-1003
E-mail: horsplay@concentric.net

apparel
decals
gifts

See full listing in **Section Two** under **apparel**

Larry Machacek
PO Box 515
Porter, TX 77365
281-429-2505

decals
license plates
novelties

See full listing in **Section Two** under **automobilia**

Operations Plus
PO Box 26347
Santa Ana, CA 92799
PH/FAX: 714-962-2776
E-mail: aquacel@earthlink.net

accessories
parts

See full listing in **Section One** under **Cobra**

Jim Osborn Reproductions Inc
101 Ridgecrest Dr
Lawrenceville, GA 30245
770-962-7556; FAX: 770-962-5881
E-mail: dosborn@
osborn-reproduction.com

decals
manuals

Mail order and open shop. Monday-Friday 8 am to 5 pm. Largest selection of restoration decals, owner's and shop manuals. All new catalog, $5. Web site: www.osborn-reproduction.com

Past Lane Auto
PO Box 69
Athol Springs, NY 14010
716-649-4108; FAX: 716-646-1969

racing memorabilia

See full listing in **Section Two** under **automobilia**

Phoenix Graphix Inc
5861 S Kyrene Rd #10
Tempe, AZ 85283
800-941-4550

decals
stripe kits

"Any decal, any car, any year!" Specialists in 1964-2000 Trans-Am, Z-28, Mustang, Plymouth and Dodge decals. Carry all lines, including Turbo and Special Edition packages. Affordable. High quality and original appearance. GM licensed manufacturer. Established 1985. Web site: www.phoenixgraphix.com

Stencils & Stripes Unlimited Inc
1108 S Crescent Ave #21
Park Ridge, IL 60068
847-692-6893; FAX: 847-692-6895

NOS decals
stripe kits

Mail order only. Offer reproduction paint and stripe kits along with NOS decals and stripes. Kits are available for Camaro, Chevelle, El Camino, Corvette, Nova, Olds 442, Dodge, Plymouth, Pontiac T/A, GTO and H/O models, AMC plus Ford. All reproduction kits use special high-performance vinyls. Specializing in reproduction paint stencil, decals and stripes for 1967-up GM, Ford, Chrysler and GMC. Licensed by GM. Web site: www.stencilsandstripes.com

un-du Products Inc
12784 Perimeter Dr, Ste B-100
Dallas, TX 75228
972-279-6633; FAX: 972-279-6644
E-mail: mfoley@un-du.com

decal remover

Mail order and open shop. un-du sticker- and decal remover removes stickers and decals from all surfaces without damage. Re-use stickers when dry. Web site: www.un-du.com

differentials

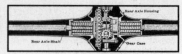

American Transmissions
7145 E Earll Dr
Scottsdale, AZ 85251
480-946-5391; FAX: 480-425-8997
E-mail: amer1trans@aol.com

differentials
transmissions

See full listing in **Section Two** under **transmissions**

Art Houser's Rear End Service
128 N Main St
Topton, PA 19562
888-560-2127; FAX: 610-641-0163
E-mail: houser@rearman.com

rear end parts
service

Mail order and shop open by appointment only. Deals in rear parts and service for most auto, truck, 4x4, SUV, van, RV. Used and rebuilt transmissions. Also used classic and muscle car parts. Web site: www.rearman.com
See our ad on page 247

Rearend Specialties
1040 DiGiulio, Ste 350
Santa Clara, CA 95050
408-988-3619; FAX: 408-988-1105

parts
service

Deals in parts and service for most differentials. Most parts in stock: rings and pinions, bearings, posi units, axles. Usually same day repairs. 1-year warranty in most cases.

Street-Wise Performance
Richie Mulligan
Box 105 Creek Rd
Tranquility, NJ 07879
973-786-7500; FAX: 973-786-7861
E-mail: street-wise@usa.net

differentials
new/used parts
overhaul kits
transmissions

Mail order and open shop. Monday-Saturday 9 am to 6 pm. Strictly sticks and posi power. Experience the excitement of a clutch vehicle with positraction. Always on hand, many 3, 4 and 5-speeds, totally rebuilt, guaranteed, with shifters and other conversion parts. Plus most 1955-1980s posi rear applications, any ratio, built/fabricated to order. Visa, MC, Discover. Spring/Fall Englishtown swap meet spaces: RK 58-60. Web site: www.street-wiseperformance.com

driveshafts

Denny's Driveshafts
1189 Military Rd
Kenmore, NY 14217
716-875-6640; FAX: 716-875-6743
E-mail: dds@olm1.com

driveshafts

Mail order and open shop. Monday-Friday 9 am to 5 pm. Deals in steel and aluminum driveshafts for street rods, race cars and 4-wheel drive trucks. Web site: www.dennysdriveshaft.com

electrical systems

Addison Generator Inc
21 W Main St Rear
Freehold, NJ 07728
732-431-2438; FAX: 732-431-4503

auto parts
repairs
supplies

Mail order and open shop. Monday-Friday 8 am to 5 pm. Rebuild or repair of: starters, generators, alternators for all makes and models, cars, trucks and tractors. One wire alternators and a complete line of auto parts and supplies.

All British Car Parts Inc 2847 Moores Rd Baldwin, MD 21013 410-692-9572; FAX: 410-692-5654 E-mail: lucasguy@home.com	parts

Buy and sell new and new old stock Lucas, Girling, Lockheed. Current, discontinued, NLA, super sessions, hard to find items. Lamps, lenses, switches, ignitions, starters, alternators, brake hydraulics and components, virtually anything Lucas, Girling, Lockheed, post 1950-today. Fax your obsolete Lucas, Girling list for offer.

American Autowire/Factory Fit® 150 Heller Pl #17W, Dept HCCA02 Bellmawr, NJ 08031 800-482-9473; FAX: 856-933-0805 E-mail: info@americanautowire.com	battery cables electrical systems switches/ components

See full listing in **Section Two** under **street rods**

American-Foreign Auto Electric Inc 103 Main St Souderton, PA 18964 215-723-4877	parts rebuilding

Open shop. Monday-Friday 8 am to 5 pm, Saturday by appointment. Authorized Lucas service station. Parts and expertise to rebuild vintage starters and generators as well as late style alternators and starters.

Antique Auto Electric 9109 (Rear) E Garvey Ave Rosemead, CA 91770 626-572-0938	repro wiring

Open Monday-Friday 9 am to 5 pm. For all years and models. Specializing in 1908-1948 Fords, Mercurys and Lincolns, SASE required for catalog and information. New alternator conversion catalogs for As and V8s, $6. Specify catalog desired.

Antique Radio Service 12 Shawmut Ave Cochituate, MA 01778 800-201-2635; FAX: 508-653-2418 E-mail: richardfoster@prodigy.net	radio service

See full listing in **Section Two** under **radios**

Asom Electric 1204 McClellan Dr Los Angeles, CA 90025 310-820-4457; FAX: 310-820-5908	electrical systems rebuilding

Auto electrical rebuilding for all Bosch, Lucas, Delco, French Motorola. Deal in Jaguar, Rolls-Royce, BMW, Range Rover, Mercedes-Benz.

Barnett & Small Inc 151E Industry Ct Deer Park, NY 11729 631-242-2100; FAX: 631-242-2101	electrical parts

Antique auto parts, all NOS. Also generators, voltage regulators, starters, speedometers, carburetors and electric wiper motors. Mopar gauges and horns. 47 years in business. Auto parts dealers.

Bathurst Company 6101 Pine Meadows Dr Loveland, OH 45140 513-722-9940; FAX: 513-722-9941 E-mail: kipkeywest@aol.com	auto accessories battery accessories

Mail and phone orders. The battery disconnect switches (4 models available) are for the protection of the mechanic when work-

ing on a vehicle. Fire and theft protection to your auto, tractor, boat and RV. Also, the switches help keep your battery from discharging. Visa and MasterCard welcome. Dealer inquiries. Web site: www.bathurstcompany.com

See our ad on this page

Blaser's Auto, Nash, Rambler, AMC 3200 48th Ave Moline, IL 61265-6453 309-764-3571; FAX: 309-764-1155 E-mail: blazauto@sprynet.com	NOS parts

See full listing in **Section One** under **AMC**

Robert D Bliss 7 Pineview Ct Monroe, NJ 08831 732-521-4654	electrical parts ignition parts

Mail order and open shop. Monday-Friday after 6 pm, Saturday and Sunday all day. New distributor caps, rotors, points, condensers, voltage regulators, headlight, ignition, starter, stoplight switches, horn relays, generator and starter parts from 1920-1970; headlight relays, headlight bulbs, ignition wire sets.

British Wiring Inc 20449 Ithaca Rd Olympia Fields, IL 60461 PH/FAX: 708-481-9050 E-mail: britishwiring@ameritech.net	wiring accessories wiring harnesses

See full listing in **Section Two** under **wiring harnesses**

C & G Early Ford Parts 1941 Commercial St, Dept AH Escondido, CA 92029-1233 760-740-2400; FAX: 760-740-8700 E-mail: cgford@cgfordparts.com	accessories/chrome emblems literature mechanical weatherstripping

See full listing in **Section One** under **Ford 1932-1953**

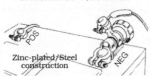

Certified Auto Electric Inc
225 Northfield Rd
Bedford, OH 44146
440-439-1100; FAX: 440-439-2163
E-mail: earli@apk.net

**generators
parts
rebuilding service
starters**

Mail order and open shop. Monday-Friday 8 am to 5 pm,
Saturday 9 am to 12 pm Eastern time. Rebuilding electrical
parts for all makes and models, ie: generators, starters, alternators. Generator to alternator conversions, 6-volt, 8-volt, 12-volt
and 24-volt. Chrome units available. Web site:
www.mall-express.com/cert-auto-elect

Class-Tech Corp
62935 Layton Ave
Bend, OR 97701
800-874-9981

wiring harnesses

Mail order only. Authentic reproduction Ford wiring harnesses
through the early 1960s, this includes Mercury, pickups, and
1955-1957 T-Birds. Dealer inquiries welcome.

Robert Connole
2525 E 32nd St
Davenport, IA 52807
319-355-6266

ignition coils

See full listing in **Section One** under **Packard**

Development Associates
12791-G Newport Ave
Tustin, CA 92780
714-730-6843; FAX: 714-730-6863
E-mail: devassoc@yahoo.com

electrical parts

Mail order. Monday-Friday 9 am to 6 pm. Retail and wholesale
advanced electronic sequencers for 1965-1968 Thunderbirds
and 1967-1968 Cougars. These units replace the original elec-
tro-mechanical motor and cam switch assembly no longer available from Ford. These improved units are compatible in form
and fit and offer substantial ownership benefits in terms of performance, reliability and installation ease. This company, with
over 28 years of hardware/software and systems experience,
also offers its services for development of custom automotive
electronics. Web site: www.geocities.com/devassoc/

DW Electrochemicals Ltd
97 Newkirk Rd N, Unit 3
Richmond Hill, ON Canada L4C 3G4
905-508-7500; FAX: 905-508-7502
E-mail: dwel@stabilant.com

contact enhancer

Stabiliant 22 Contact Enhancer is a long-term resident, active
contact treatment. It is easy to use, cost-effective, and substantially improves the reliability and conductivity of connectors.
Stabiliant 22 will work on low-power-level sensors and computer
module connections to high amperage lighting and starting connections. Web site: www.stabiliant.com

Ferris Auto Electric Ltd
106 Lakeshore Dr
North Bay, ON Canada P1A 2A6
705-474-4560; FAX: 705-474-9453

**parts
service**

Mail order and open shop. Monday-Friday 8 am to 5:30 pm. For
your antique vehicle requirements, specializing in custom wiring
harnesses, either braided or plastic wire, rebuilding of generators,
starters, alternators, carburetors, distributors or magnetos and
speedometers. Speedometer cables and casings made to order.

Fifth Avenue Antique Auto Parts
415 Court St
Clay Center, KS 67432
785-632-3450; FAX: 785-632-6154
E-mail: fifthave@oz-online.net

**cooling systems
electrical systems
fuel systems**

Mail order and open shop. Monday-Friday 9 am to 5:30 pm,
Saturday 9 am to noon. Fifth Avenue specializes in electrical,
cooling and fuel systems for all types of antique and classic vehi-

cles. They have successfully prepared cars entered in the Great
American Race since 1989. They have also completed numerous
projects for the Hollywood movie studios, the most recent was
for the movie "LA Confidential." Send $3 for current catalog.

Ron Francis' Wire Works
167 Keystone Rd
Chester, PA 19013
800-292-1940 orders, 610-485-1937
E-mail: rfwwx@aol.com

**fuel injection
harnesses
wiring accessories
wiring kits**

See full listing in **Section Two** under **wiring harnesses**

Fun Projects Inc
PMB 164
2460 W Main St -D
St Charles, IL 60175
630-584-1471
E-mail: piewagon@funprojects.com

**electrical parts
mechanical parts**

Mail order only. Design and manufacture of electrical parts for vintage cars. Make voltage regulators for Ford cars, 1919-1939 and
other cars on special order. Early brass era Model T Ford parts.
Pinion bearings, Model T horns. Web site: www.funprojects.com

Green Mountain Vintage Auto
20 Bramley Way
Bellows Falls, VT 05101
PH/FAX: 802-463-3141
E-mail: vintauto@sover.net

**damage appraisals
vehicle evaluations**

See full listing in **Section Two** under **appraisals**

Haneline Products Co
PO Box 430
Morongo Valley, CA 92256
760-363-6597; FAX: 760-363-7321

**gauges
instrument panels
stainless parts
trim parts**

See full listing in **Section Two** under **accessories**

Harnesses Unlimited
PO Box 435
Wayne, PA 19087
610-688-3998

**wiring harnesses
wiring supplies**

Mail order only. USA manufacturer of wiring harness systems
that use cloth braided and lacquered wire. Each system comes
with installation instructions and wiring schematics. All makes
except Ford, Lincoln and Mercury. Also offering wiring supplies
and harness braiding service. Catalog or information, $5. If call-
ing by phone, leave message, all calls are returned.

Hastings Enterprises
PO Box 208
Hampton, VA 23669
FAX: 757-722-7349
E-mail: johnh@apluslodging.com

electrical parts

Mail order only. New old stock Lucas electrical parts for British
cars. Mostly 1950s thru 1970s, some for other years.

J & C's Parts
7127 Ward Rd
North Tonawanda, NY 14120
716-693-4090; FAX: 716-695-7144

parts

See full listing in **Section One** under **Buick/McLaughlin**

L & N Olde Car Co
9992 Kinsman Rd, PO Box 378
Newbury, OH 44065
440-564-7204; FAX: 440-564-8187

restoration

See full listing in **Section Two** under **restoration shops**

Last Chance Repair & Restoration
1242 Myers Rd, PO Box 362A
Shaftsbury, VT 05262
802-447-7040

**repairs
restoration**

See full listing in **Section Two** under **restoration shops**

M & H Electric Fabricators Inc | **wiring harnesses**
13537 Alondra Blvd
Santa Fe Springs, CA 90670
562-926-9552; FAX: 562-926-9572
E-mail: sales@wiringharness.com

Mail order and open shop. Monday-Friday 8 am to 4:30 pm. We deal in the manufacturing of exact reproduction wiring harnesses for most GM vehicles from 1955-1976. Call for applications and pricing. Web site: www.wiringharness.com

Jack Marcheski | **12/6-volt converters rebuilding repair**
100 Dry Creek Rd
Hollister, CA 95023
831-637-3453
E-mail: jmar1@hollinet.com

Mail order and open shop anytime. Gas gauge sending unit repair, rebuilding; also 12/6-volt converters.

Ben McAdam | **electrical parts**
500 Clover Ln
Wheeling, WV 26003
304-242-3388, 304-242-0855
E-mail: antiquebenny@aol.com

See full listing in **Section Two** under **ignition parts**

Motorsport Auto | **parts**
1139 W Collins Ave
Orange, CA 92667
800-633-6331, 714-639-2620
FAX: 714-639-7460
E-mail: motorsport@worldnet.att.net

See full listing in **Section One** under **Datsun**

Narragansett Reproductions | **wiring harnesses**
Ed & Miki Pease
107 Woodville Rd, PO Box 51
Wood River Junction, RI 02894
401-364-3839; FAX: 401-364-3830
E-mail: narragansetrepro@aol.com

Mail order only. Phone hours 10 am to 5 pm Eastern time. Lincoln parts 1936-1957, Ford parts 1932-1960. Wiring harnesses for all makes and models from 1900 to 1980. Authentic, reproduction wiring harnesses manufactured in our plant. Send $2 for catalog, stating year and model of vehicle. Web site: www.myclassiccar.com/motormart/narragansett.shtml

M Parker Autoworks Inc | **battery cables harnesses**
150 Heller Pl #17W, Dept HCCA02
Bellmawr, NJ 08031
856-933-0801; FAX: 856-933-0805
E-mail: info@factoryfit.com

Mail order and open shop. Monday-Friday 8 am to 5 pm. Largest manufacturer of replacement wiring harnesses, battery cables, etc, for 1947-1982 GM cars and trucks. All Factory Fit harnesses are built to original GM specifications with emphasis on quality and originality using original GM components and specs. High-performance alternator and HEI modifications are available. Factory Fit harnesses are supported by a knowledgeable technical support staff and backed by a money back guarantee. Visa, MC, COD accepted. Catalog, $4. Dealer inquiries welcome. Web site: www.factoryfit.com

Performance Analysis Co | **climate control cruise control**
1345 Oak Ridge Tpke, Ste 258
Oak Ridge, TN 37830
PH/FAX: 865-482-9175
E-mail: george_murphy@compuserve.com

See full listing in **Section One** under **Mercedes-Benz**

J Pinto | **electric motors relay repair solenoid repair switch repair**
2306 Memphis St
Philadelphia, PA 19125
215-739-1132
E-mail: lectri@yahoo.com

Electric motors and all switches, relays, solenoids (including overdrive) restored, 6 and 12 volt. Stay original. OEM specs or better. "We can when others can't."™ 50+ years' experience: w/wiper, w/washer, headlight, fan, blower, conv top, horns, power window, locks, seat, antenna. No charge if unrestorable. Free 3-day shipping West, Midwest. Send to: J Pinto at above address.

Potomac Packard | **wiring harnesses**
PO Box 117
Tiger, GA 30576
800-859-9532 orders
706-782-2345 shop
FAX: 706-782-2344

See full listing in **Section One** under **Packard**

Rhode Island Wiring Services Inc | **wiring harnesses**
567 Liberty Ln, Box 434
W Kingston, RI 02892
401-789-1955; FAX: 401-783-0091
E-mail: info@riwire.com

Mail order and open shop. Monday-Friday 9 am to 5 pm. Exact reproduction wiring harnesses using braided or plastic wire, depending on original. Web site: www.riwire.com

Rockland Auto Electric | **electrical parts**
88 S Main St
Pearl River, NY 10965
914-735-3362, 914-735-3372

Mail order and open shop. Monday-Friday 8 am to 5:30 pm, Saturday 8 am to 1 pm. Rebuild starters, generators and alternators for all years and makes of automobiles and other motor vehicles. Full line of voltage regulators and solenoids. Chrome starters and alternators also available.

S&M Electro-Tech Inc | **electrical parts**
8836 Xylite St NE
Blaine, MN 55449
763-780-2861
E-mail: turnswitch@turnswitch.com

Mail order and open shop. Monday-Friday 9 am to 5 pm, Saturday 9:30 am to 2 pm. Electrical parts and services for American cars including wiring harnesses, turn signals, radio repair, AM-FM stereo radio conversions. Web site: www.turnswitch.com

Scotts Manufacturing | **electric fans fan electronics**
25520 Ave Stanford #304
Valencia, CA 91355
800-544-5596; FAX: 661-295-9342

Deal in custom built electric cooling fans, 7" to 16" radiator cooling fans in 6, 12 and 24-volt. Also transmission and engine oil coolers with electric fans. Fan electronics, low profile 2" mini fans. Replacement parts for electric fans. Web site: http://home.earthlink.net/~scottsfans

Sherco Auto Supply | **bulbs electrical wire fuses**
3700 NW 124th Ave, Ste 114
Coral Springs, FL 33065
954-344-1993; FAX: 954-344-2664
E-mail: parts@sherco-auto.com

Mail order only. Electrical wire and connectors, bulbs, fuses, chemicals and other supply items. Web site: www.autosupply.ws

Section Two – Generalists

Sierra Specialty Auto
3494 Chandler Rd
Quincy, CA 95971
800-4-BRASS-1; FAX: 530-283-4845
E-mail: joe@brakecylinder.com

cylinder rebuilding

See full listing in **Section Two** under **brakes**

Silicone Wire Systems
3462 Kirkwood Dr
San Jose, CA 95117-1549
E-mail: sethracer@aol.com

ignition wire sets

See full listing in **Section One** under **Corvair**

Ed Strain Inc
6555 44th St #2006
Pinellas Park, FL 33781
800-266-1623, 727-521-1597

magnetos

See full listing in **Section Two** under **special services**

JF Sullivan Company
14 Clarendon Rd
Auburn, MA 01501
508-792-9500

*electrical parts
repairs*

See full listing in **Section Two** under **fuel system parts**

Sunburst Technology
PO Box 598
Lithia Springs, GA 30122
FAX: 770-942-6091
E-mail: sunburst2000@juno.com

*electronic technical
consultant*

See full listing in **Section Four** under **information sources**

Tucson Packard/Chirco Automotive
9101 E 22nd St
Tucson, AZ 85710
520-722-1984; FAX: 520-298-4069
E-mail: tucpackard@aol.com

*accessories
NORS parts
NOS parts
used parts*

See full listing in **Section One** under **Packard**

Vintage Ford Center Inc
302 E Main St
Berryville, VA 22611
888-813-FORD (3673)
FAX: 540-955-0916
E-mail: mdla@visuallink.com

*accessories
parts*

See full listing in **Section One** under **Ford 1903-1931**

**Visibolts From Classic
Safety Products**
7131 Hickory Run
Waunakee, WI 53597
888-212-2163; FAX: 608-824-9200
E-mail: clovis@www.visibolts.com

accessories

See full listing in **Section Two** under **lighting equipment**

YnZ's Yesterdays Parts
333 E Stuart Ave A, Dept AA
Redlands, CA 92374
909-798-1498; FAX: 909-335-6237

wiring harnesses

Mail order only. For over 2,500 different makes and models. Copies of original wiring harnesses using lacquer coated, braided wire. Simplified number coded instructions. Satisfaction guaranteed. Catalog, $2.

engine parts

60 Chev Sam
2912 Wright Rd
Hamptonville, NC 27020
336-468-1745

parts

See full listing in **Section One** under **Chevrolet**

Advanced Plating & Powder Coating
1425 Cowan Ct
Nashville, TN 37207
615-227-6900; FAX: 615-262-7935
E-mail: gochrome@aol.com

*chrome plating
polishing
repair service*

See full listing in **Section Two** under **plating & polishing**

American Restorations Unlimited TA
14 Meakin Ave, PO Box 34
Rochelle Park, NJ 07662
201-843-3567; FAX: 201-843-3238
E-mail: amerrest@earthlink.net

*engine
glass
restoration parts
transmission*

See full listing in **Section Two** under **glass**

Anderson Racing Inc
3911 Main St
Grandview, MO 64030
816-765-4881; FAX: 816-765-9897
E-mail: davea@engine-parts.com

engine rebuilding

See full listing in **Section Two** under **engine rebuilding**

Antique Auto Parts Cellar
6 Chauncy St, PO Box 3
South Weymouth, MA 02190
781-335-1579; FAX: 781-335-1925
E-mail: our1932@aol.com

*brake/chassis/
engine parts
fuel pumps/kits
gaskets
water pumps*

See full listing in **Section Two** under **comprehensive parts**

Atlas Engine Rebuilding Co Inc
24251 Frampton Ave
Harbor City, CA 90710
310-325-6898; FAX: 310-325-7701

*engine rebuilding
machine work*

See full listing in **Section Two** under **engine rebuilding**

Atlas Obsolete Chrysler Parts
10621 Bloomfield St, Unit 32
Los Alamitos, CA 90720
PH/FAX: 562-594-5560
E-mail: atlaschrys@aol.com

parts

See full listing in **Section One** under **Mopar**

B & B Cylinder Head Inc
320 Washington St
West Warwick, RI 02893
401-828-4900; FAX: 401-381-0010
E-mail: bbcyl@choiceone.net

cylinder heads

Mail order and open shop. Monday-Friday 8 am to 4:30 pm. Cylinder heads, restoration, fabrication, high-performance, no-lead conversions. Antique, obsolete to late model high tech. Custom engines built completely. Motorcycles, trucks, etc.

Baxter Auto Parts
9444 N Whitaker Rd (corporate office)
Portland, OR 97217
800-765-3785; FAX: 503-246-4590

*accessories
parts*

See full listing in **Section Two** under **comprehensive parts**

Bayless Inc — accessories, parts
1111 Via Bayless
Marietta, GA 30066-2770
770-928-1446; FAX: 770-928-1342
800-241-1446, order line (US & Canada)
E-mail: baylessfiat@mindspring.com

See full listing in **Section One** under **Fiat**

Dave Bean Engineering — parts
636 E St Charles St SR3H
San Andreas, CA 95249
209-754-5802; FAX: 209-754-5177
E-mail: admin@davebean.com

See full listing in **Section One** under **Lotus**

Blaser's Auto, Nash, Rambler, AMC — NOS parts
3200 48th Ave
Moline, IL 61265-6453
309-764-3571; FAX: 309-764-1155
E-mail: blazauto@sprynet.com

See full listing in **Section One** under **AMC**

Bob's Bird House — parts
124 Watkin Ave
Chadds Ford, PA 19317
610-358-3420; FAX: 610-558-0729

See full listing in **Section One** under **Thunderbird**

Bronx Automotive — parts
501 Tiffany St
Bronx, NY 10474
718-589-2979

See full listing in **Section Two** under **ignition parts**

Bryant's Antique Auto Parts — appraisals, chassis/engine parts, sheetmetal, wiring harnesses
851 Western Ave
Hampden, ME 04444
207-862-4019

See full listing in **Section One** under **Ford 1903-1931**

C & G Early Ford Parts — accessories/chrome, emblems, literature, mechanical, weatherstripping
1941 Commercial St, Dept AH
Escondido, CA 92029-1233
760-740-2400; FAX: 760-740-8700
E-mail: cgford@cgfordparts.com

See full listing in **Section One** under **Ford 1932-1953**

Cam-Pro — camshaft repair, engine parts
PO Box 3305
Great Falls, MT 59403
800-525-2581, 406-771-0300

See full listing in **Section Two** under **camshafts**

Car-Line Manufacturing & Distribution Inc — chassis parts, engine parts, sheetmetal
1250 Gulf St, PO Box 1192
Beaumont, TX 77701
409-833-9757; FAX: 409-835-2468
E-mail: car-line@car-line.net

See full listing in **Section Two** under **sheetmetal**

Carl's Ford Parts — muscle parts
23219 South St, Box 38
Homeworth, OH 44634
PH/FAX: 330-525-7291
E-mail: fordcobrajet@hotmail.com

See full listing in **Section One** under **Mustang**

Carobu Engineering — dyno testing, engine rebuilding, exhaust systems
1017 W 18th St
Costa Mesa, CA 92627
949-722-9307; FAX: 949-631-3184
E-mail: tate@carobu.com

See full listing in **Section Two** under **engine rebuilding**

Carson's Antique Auto Parts — parts
235 Shawfarm Rd
Holliston, MA 01746
508-429-2269; FAX: 508-429-0761
E-mail: w1066@gis.net

Mail order only. Monday-Saturday 9 am to 6 pm Eastern time. Specializing in Auburn, Buick, Cadillac, Chevrolet, Chrysler, Cord, DeSoto, Dodge, Essex, Graham, Graham-Paige, Hudson, Hupmobile, International, Oldsmobile, Overland, Plymouth, Pontiac, Studebaker, Whippet mechanical, ignition, brake, headlight parts, lenses, runningboard moldings, seals, gaskets and transmission gears. Web site: www.webmerchants.com/carson

Casting Salvage Technologies — repairs
26 Potomac Creek Dr
Fredricksburg, VA 22405
800-833-8814 national
540-659-3797 local
FAX: 540-659-9453

See full listing in **Section Two** under **castings**

Stan Chernoff — mechanical parts, restoration parts, technical info, trim parts
1215 Greenwood Ave
Torrance, CA 90503
310-320-4554; FAX: 310-328-7867
E-mail: az589@lafn.org

See full listing in **Section One** under **Datsun**

Ed Cholakian Enterprises Inc — museum, parts
dba All Cadillacs of the 40s and 50s
12811 Foothill Blvd
Sylmar, CA 91342
800-808-1147, 818-361-1147
FAX: 818-361-9738

See full listing in **Section One** under **Cadillac/LaSalle**

Classic Chevrolet Parts Inc — parts
8723 S I-35
Oklahoma City, OK 73149
405-631-4400; FAX: 405-631-5999
E-mail: info@classicchevroletparts.com

See full listing in **Section One** under **Chevrolet**

Corvair Underground — parts
PO Box 339
Dundee, OR 97115
800-825-8247, 503-434-1648
FAX: 503-434-1626

See full listing in **Section One** under **Corvair**

CPR — new parts, reproduction parts, used parts
431 S Sierra Way
San Bernardino, CA 92408
909-884-6980; FAX: 909-884-7872

See full listing in **Section One** under **Pontiac**

Custom Plating — bumper specialist, chrome plating, parts
3030 Alta Ridge Way
Snellville, GA 30078
770-736-1118; FAX: 770-736-6620
E-mail: customplating@mediaone.net

See full listing in **Section Two** under **plating & polishing**

Dakota Studebaker Parts
39408 280th St
Armour, SD 57313
605-724-2527
E-mail: dakstude1@unitelsd.com

parts

See full listing in **Section One** under **Studebaker**

Dave's Auto Machine & Parts
Rt 16
Ischua, NY 14743
716-557-2402

accessories
machine work
parts

See full listing in **Section One** under **Chevrolet**

Daytona Turbo Action Camshafts
1109 US #1, PO Box 5094
Ormond Beach, FL 32175
888-RARE-CAM, 800-505-CAMS
386-676-7478; FAX: 386-258-1582
E-mail: info@camshafts.com

camshafts
engine parts

See full listing in **Section Two** under **bearings**

Don's Hot Rod Shop Inc
2811 N Stone Ave
Tucson, AZ 85705
520-884-8892; FAX: 520-628-1682

accessories
parts

See full listing in **Section Two** under **street rods**

Dynatech Engineering
PO Box 1446
Alta Loma, CA 91701-8446
805-492-6134
E-mail: dynatechengineering@
yahoo.com

motor mounts

Mail order only. Leading provider of muscle car motor mounts. Dynatech's patented lock-up design. Allows the engine to float on the insulators during normal driving then lock-up during hard acceleration. These mounts improve launch characteristics and eliminate the need for harsh solid mounts. When installed they look like standard OEM mounts. Call or write for a free *Mitymounts* catalog.

Early Ford V8 Sales Inc
Curtis Industrial Park, Bldg 37
831 Rt 67
Ballston Spa, NY 12020
518-884-2825; FAX: 518-884-2633
E-mail: earlyford@prodigy.net

parts

See full listing in **Section One** under **Ford 1932-1953**

Egge Machine Company Inc
11707 Slauson Ave
Santa Fe Springs, CA 90670-2217
800-866-3443, 562-945-3419
FAX: 562-693-1635
E-mail: info@egge.com

bearings
gaskets
pistons/rings
timing components
valvetrain

Order desk open Monday-Thursday 7 am to 4 pm Pacific time, Friday 7:30 am to 3:30 pm Pacific time. Your source for obsolete engine parts! 1900s through 1970s. Web site: www.egge.com
See our ad inside the front cover

EIS Engines Inc
215 SE Grand Ave
Portland, OR 97214
800-547-0002, 503-232-5590
FAX: 503-232-5178
E-mail: edik@att.com

engines

See full listing in **Section One** under **Mercedes-Benz**

Engines Direct
7830 E Gelding, Bldg 200
Scottsdale, AZ 85260
800-998-2100; FAX: 480-998-6070

engines
parts

See full listing in **Section Two** under **engine rebuilding**

Ford Powertrain Applications
7702 E 96th St
Puyallup, WA 98371
PH/FAX: 253-848-9503

engines

See full listing in **Section One** under **Ford 1954-up**

Foreign Autotech
3235 C Sunset Ln
Hatboro, PA 19040
215-441-4421; FAX: 215-441-4490
E-mail: fap1800@aol.com

parts

See full listing in **Section One** under **Volvo**

AT Francis/Blue Thunder
255 N El Cielo #499
Palm Springs, CA 92262
760-328-9259; FAX: 760-328-2505

parts

Specializing in the manufacture and wholesale distribution of performance, appearance and restoration types of engine parts including manifolds, cylinder heads, racing engine dampers, main cap girdles and valve covers for Ford related performance applications. All items available via Blue Thunder dealers only. Web site: www.bluethunderauto.com

Good Old Days Garage Inc
2341 Farley Pl
Birmingham, AL 35226
205-822-4569; FAX: 205-823-1944

engine building
Firestone tires
parts
service

See full listing in **Section One** under **Ford 1903-1931**

Halpin Used Auto & Truck Parts
1093 Rt 123
Mayfield, NY 12117
518-863-4906
E-mail: junkyard2064@webtv.net

NOS auto parts
NOS truck parts
used auto parts
used truck parts

See full listing in **Section Five** under **New York**

Horst's Car Care
3160-1/2 N Woodford St
Decatur, IL 62526
217-876-1112

engine rebuilding

See full listing in **Section One** under **Mercedes-Benz**

Jackson's Oldtime Parts
4502 Grand Ave
Duluth, MN 55807
888-399-7278, 218-624-5791
E-mail: sales@oldtimeparts.com

parts

Mail order and open shop. Monday-Friday 8 am to 5:30 pm, Saturday 9 am to 1 pm. Large automotive parts store which purchases the older automotive parts from other automotive parts stores, warehouse distributors and aftermarket manufacturers. Sell the parts that an automotive parts store considers obsolete as it is no longer listed in current catalogs. Sell NOS engine, chassis, brake and drivetrain parts which are old, obsolete or no longer in production from 1930-1985. Web site: www.oldtimeparts.com

Jeepsamerica
367 Washington St
Weymouth, MA 02189
781-331-4333; FAX: 781-331-6947
E-mail: mconsiglio1@yahoo.com

parts
service

See full listing in **Section One** under **Chrysler**

Jet-Hot Coatings/MCCI 55 E Front St, Ste A-200 Bridgeport, PA 19405 800-432-3379 E-mail: sales@jet-hot.com	**high-temp coatings**

See full listing in **Section Two** under **exhaust systems**

Joyce's Model A & T Parts PO Box 70 Manchaca, TX 78652-0070 512-282-1196; FAX: 512-479-5091	**new parts** **NOS parts** **rebuilt parts**

See full listing in **Section One** under **Ford 1903-1931**

Kanter Auto Products 76 Monroe St Boonton, NJ 07005 800-526-1096; 201-334-9575 FAX: 201-334-5423	**car covers** **carpet sets** **front end kits** **parts**

See full listing in **Section Two** under **comprehensive parts**

Ken's Carburetors 2301 Barnum Ave Stratford, CT 06615 203-375-9340	**carburetors** **distributors** **parts**

See full listing in **Section One** under **Ford 1932-1953**

Lincoln Services Ltd Earle O Brown, Jr 229 Robinhood Ln McMurray, PA 15317 724-941-4567; FAX: 724-942-1940	**literature** **parts**

See full listing in **Section One** under **Lincoln**

Lindskog Balancing 1170 Massachusetts Ave Boxborough, MA 01719-1415 978-263-2040; FAX: 978-263-4035	**engine balancing**

See full listing in **Section Two** under **engine rebuilding**

Linearossa International Inc 3931 SW 47th Ave Ft Lauderdale, FL 33314 954-327-9888; FAX: 954-791-6555	**parts**

See full listing in **Section One** under **Fiat**

Mancini Racing Enterprises 33510 Groesbeck Hwy Fraser, MI 48026 810-294-6670; FAX: 810-294-0390 E-mail: robc@manciniracing.com	**parts**

See full listing in **Section One** under **Mopar**

Maximum Torque Specialties PO Box 925 Delavan, WI 53115 262-740-1118; FAX: 262-740-1161 E-mail: mts@elknet.net	**high-perf parts** **restoration parts**

See full listing in **Section One** under **Cadillac/LaSalle**

Michigan Corvette Recyclers 11995 US 223, PO Box 98 Riga, MI 49276 800-533-4650; FAX: 517-486-4124 E-mail: mcr@cass.net	**Corvette parts** **new/used parts** **salvage**

See full listing in **Section One** under **Corvette**

Miller Energy Inc 3200 South Clinton Ave S Plainfield, NJ 07080 908-755-6700; FAX: 908-755-0312 E-mail: allyon@aol.com	**engine parts**

See full listing in **Section One** under **Stanley**

Millers Incorporated 7412 Count Cir Huntington Beach, CA 92647 714-375-6565; FAX: 714-847-6606 E-mail: sales@millermbz.com	**accessories** **parts**

See full listing in **Section One** under **Mercedes-Benz**

Moline Engine Service Inc 3227 23rd Ave Moline, IL 61265 309-764-9735	**engine parts** **engine rebuilding** **restoration**

See full listing in **Section Two** under **engine rebuilding**

No 1 Performance 1775 S Redwood Rd Salt Lake City, UT 84104 800-453-8250; FAX: 801-975-9653	**engine kits** **parts**

Deals in engine kits, parts, radiators, clutches and crankshafts. We have a large variety in stock for all types of applications. Call today for the pricing and delivery option that best suits your needs.

Noble Racing Inc 1058 Dry Ridge Rd Versailles, KY 40383 859-879-1123; FAX: 859-879-3743 E-mail: nobleracing@iwebworks.com	**accessories** **parts**

Performance parts and accessories. Engines and machine work. Eagle Specialty Products dealer for crankshafts, connecting rods and rotating assemblies. Web site: www.nobleracing.com

Northern Auto Parts Warehouse Inc PO Box 3147 Sioux City, IA 51102 800-831-0884; FAX: 712-258-0088 E-mail: sales@northernautoparts.com	**parts**

Hundreds of engine rebuild kits available. Plus carbs, manifolds, oil pumps, etc from stock to performance. You have the vehicle, we have the parts. Web site: www.northernautoparts.com

Northwestern Auto Supply Inc 1101 S Division Grand Rapids, MI 49507 800-704-1078, 616-241-1714 FAX: 616-241-0924	**parts**

Mail order and retail store. Monday-Friday 8 am to 5:30 pm, Saturday by appointment. An old time parts store that enjoys servicing the old, classic and current car enthusiast. Deal in mechanical parts such as engine, brake, ignition, chassis and drivetrain. When ordering ask for Sam.

NOS Only 414 Umbarger Rd, Unit E San Jose, CA 95111 408-227-2353, 408-227-2354 FAX: 408-227-2355 E-mail: nosonly@aol.com	**NOS Ford parts** **NOS parts**

See full listing in **Section Two** under **comprehensive parts**

Nova Parts PO Box 985 Mount Washington, KY 40047 502-239-8487; FAX: 502-231-1397	**NOS parts** **reproduction parts** **used parts**

See full listing in **Section One** under **Chevrolet**

Section Two – Generalists

Obsolete Chevrolet Parts Co
PO Box 68
Nashville, GA 31639-0068
800-248-8785; FAX: 229-686-3056
E-mail: obschevy@surfsouth.com

| engine parts |
| radiators |
| rubber parts |
| transmissions |

See full listing in **Section One** under **Chevrolet**

Obsolete Ford Parts Inc
8701 S I-35
Oklahoma City, OK 73149
405-631-3933; FAX: 405-634-6815
E-mail: info@obsoletefordparts.com

parts

See full listing in **Section One** under **Ford 1954-up**

Obsolete Jeep® & Willys® Parts
Division of Florida 4 Wheel Drive &
Truck Parts
6110 17th St E
Bradenton, FL 34203
941-756-7844; PH/FAX: 941-756-7757

| literature |
| parts |

See full listing in **Section One** under **Willys**

Olson's Gaskets
3059 Opdal Rd E
Port Orchard, WA 98366
PH/FAX: 360-871-1207
E-mail: info@olsonsgaskets.com

gaskets

See full listing in **Section Two** under **gaskets**

The Paddock® Inc
221 W Main, PO Box 30
Knightstown, IN 46148
800-428-4319; FAX: 800-286-4040
E-mail: paddock@paddockparts.com

| accessories |
| parts |

See full listing in **Section One** under **Chevrolet**

Paragon Reproductions Inc
8040 S Jennings Rd
Swartz Creek, MI 48473
800-882-4688; FAX: 810-655-6667
E-mail: sales@corvette-paragon.com

| Corvette repro |
| parts |

See full listing in **Section One** under **Corvette**

Parts House
2912 Hunter St
Fort Worth, TX 76112
817-451-2708
E-mail: theparts@flash.net

| brake shoes/drums |
| fenders |
| sheetmetal repair |
| panels |

See full listing in **Section Two** under **comprehensive parts**

Partwerks of Chicago
718 S Prairie Rd
New Lenox, IL 60451
815-462-3000; FAX: 815-462-3006
E-mail: partwerks9@aol.com

| parts |
| service |

Mail order and open shop. Monday-Saturday 8 am to 6 pm.
Parts and services for all German autos.

Performance Automotive Warehouse
21001 Nordhoff St
Chatsworth, CA 91311
818-678-3000; FAX: 818-678-3001

| accessories |
| engine parts |

Mail order and open shop. Seven days a week 8:30 am to 5:30
pm Pacific time. Deal in stock and high-performance engine
parts and accessories for 1963 and later domestic L-6, V6 and
V8 engines. Complete 1,200 page catalog available. Also a full
line of early Chrysler 331, 354, 392 engine parts and accessories. 48 page color catalog available. Web site:
www.pawengineparts.com

Performance Chevy
2995 W Whitton
Phoenix, AZ 85017
800-203-6621; FAX: 602-254-1094

| engine parts |
| restoration |

See full listing in **Section One** under **Corvette**

Performance Coatings
9768 Feagin Rd
Jonesboro, GA 30236
770-478-2775; FAX: 770-478-1926
Email: gemobpci@mindspring.com

| ceramic coatings |
| engine parts |
| suspension parts |

See full listing in **Section Two** under **exhaust systems**

Pontiac Engines Custom Built
E-mail: pontiacgregg@earthlink.net

| custom built |
| engines |

See full listing in **Section One** under **Pontiac**

Red Bird Racing
6640 Valley St
Coeur d'Alene, ID 83815
208-762-5305

parts

See full listing in **Section One** under **Chevrolet**

Rochester Clutch & Brake Co
35 Niagara St
Rochester, NY 14605
716-232-2579; FAX: 716-232-3279

| brakes |
| clutches |

See full listing in **Section Two** under **brakes**

Ross Racing Pistons
625 S Douglas St
El Segundo, CA 90250
310-536-0100; FAX: 310-536-0333

pistons

Mail order and open shop. Monday-Friday 8 am to 4:30 pm. We
specialize in manufacturing custom pistons to fit every auto
enthusiasts' specific needs. Web site: www.rosspistons.com

**Donald E Schneider Marinette &
Menominee Auto Club**
RR 1, N7340 Miles Rd
Porterfield, WI 54159
715-732-4958

parts

See full listing in **Section Two** under **comprehensive parts**

Scotts Manufacturing
25520 Ave Stanford #304
Valencia, CA 91355
800-544-5596; FAX: 661-295-9342

| electric fans |
| fan electronics |

See full listing in **Section Two** under **electrical systems**

Joe Smith Ford & Hot Rod Parts
51 Lakewood Dr
Marietta, GA 30066
770-426-9850; FAX: 770-426-9854
E-mail: joesmithhotrod@yahoo.com

| parts |
| service |

See full listing in **Section One** under **Ford 1932-1953**

Rajam Srinivasan
35-11 92nd St
Queens, NY 11372
917-705-4812; FAX: 718-205-0637
E-mail: rajam_s@hotmail.com

| accessories |
| parts |

See full listing in **Section One** under **Rolls-Royce/Bentley**

Straight Six Jaguar
24321 Hatteras St
Woodland Hills, CA 91367
PH/FAX: 818-716-1192

parts
service

See full listing in **Section One** under **Jaguar**

Superior Pump Exchange Co
12901 Crenshaw Blvd
Hawthorne, CA 90250-5511
310-676-4995; FAX: 310-676-9430
E-mail: autoh20@aol.com

water pumps

Mail order and open shop. Monday-Friday 8 am to 4 pm. Quality remanufactured automotive and industrial water pumps. Large inventory, all makes, models and years. Cars, trucks, forklifts, welders, farm equipment, etc.

TA Motor AB
Torpslingan 21
Lulea S 97347 Sweden
+46-920-18888; FAX: +46-920-18821

accessories
parts

See full listing in **Section One** under **Cadillac/LaSalle**

Tanson Enterprises
2508 J St, Dept HVA
Sacramento, CA 95816-4815
916-448-2950
FAX: 916-443-3269 *88
E-mail: tanson@pipeline.com

performance parts
restoration parts

See full listing in **Section One** under **Oldsmobile**

Tatom Custom Engines
PO Box 2504
Mt Vernon, WA 98273
360-424-8314; FAX: 360-424-6717
E-mail: flatheads@tatom.com

engine rebuilding
machine shop

See full listing in **Section Two** under **engine rebuilding**

T-Bird Sanctuary
9997 SW Avery
Tualatin, OR 97062
503-692-9848; FAX: 503-692-9849

parts

See full listing in **Section One** under **Thunderbird**

Valley Head Service Inc
19340 Londelius St
Northridge, CA 91324
818-993-7000; FAX: 818-993-9712

engine rebuilding
machine work

See full listing in **Section Two** under **engine rebuilding**

Vibratech Inc (Fluidampr)
11980 Walden Ave
Alden, NY 14004
716-937-3603; FAX: 716-937-4692

performance parts

Manufacture Fluidamprs-performance harmonic dampers, they are used in high-performance street and race applications.

Vintage Auto Parts Inc
24300 Hwy 9
Woodinville, WA 98072
800-426-5911, 425-486-0777
FAX: 425-486-0778
E-mail: erics@vapinc.com

cars
parts

See full listing in **Section Two** under **comprehensive parts**

Vintage Ford Center Inc
302 E Main St
Berryville, VA 22611
888-813-FORD (3673)
FAX: 540-955-0916
E-mail: mdla@visuallink.com

accessories
parts

See full listing in **Section One** under **Ford 1903-1931**

Volunteer Studebaker
228 Marquiss Cir
Clinton, TN 37716
615-457-3002; FAX: 775-514-1386
E-mail: studebaker_joe@msn.com

parts
parts locator

See full listing in **Section One** under **Studebaker**

Paul Weaver's Garage
680 Sylvan Way
Bremerton, WA 98310-2844
360-373-7870
E-mail: pjmarilyn@aol.com

rings

Piston rings for cars, trucks and tractors through 1980. Please specify oversize, quantity and widths.

Winslow Mfg Co
5700 Dean Ave
Raleigh, NC 27604
919-790-9713

parts rebuilding

Mail order only. Proprietorship specializing in the rebuilding and reconstruction of worn machinery and automobile parts with original rubber bushings. New material is high strength silicone. Harmonic balancer and flexible coupling rebuilding.

engine rebuilding

300 Below Inc
2101 E Olive St
Decatur, IL 62526
800-550-2796; FAX: 217-423-3075
E-mail: cryo300@midwest.net

cryogenic tempering
machine work
welding

See full listing in **Section Two** under **special services**

356 Enterprises
Vic & Barbara Skirmants
27244 Ryan Rd
Warren, MI 48092
810-575-9544; FAX: 810-558-3616
E-mail: skirmants@home.com

parts

See full listing in **Section One** under **Porsche**

Aldrich Auto Supply Inc
95 Prospect St
Hatfield, MA 01038
800-533-2306, 413-247-0230

engine rebuilding

Mail order and open shop. Monday-Friday 8 am to 5:30 pm. Auto engine rebuilding shop specializing in unleaded gas conversions and complete overhauls of classic, vintage and hi-performance engines. Also repair of cracked aluminum and cast iron engine components.

Anderson Racing Inc
3911 Main St
Grandview, MO 64030
816-765-4881; FAX: 816-765-9897
E-mail: davea@engine-parts.com

engine rebuilding

Engine rebuilding. Turnkey engines only. Web site: www.engine-parts.com

Andy's Classic Mustangs
18502 E Sprague
Greenacres, WA 99016
509-924-9824

parts
service

See full listing in **Section One** under **Mustang**

Antique Automotive Engineering Inc
3560 Chestnut Pl
Denver, CO 80216
303-296-7332, 800-846-7332
E-mail: ed@antiqueautoengr.com

babbitt service
engine restoration

See full listing in **Section One** under **Ford 1903-1931**

Atlas Engine Rebuilding Co Inc
24251 Frampton Ave
Harbor City, CA 90710
310-325-6898; FAX: 310-325-7701

engine rebuilding
machine work

Open shop only. Monday-Friday 8 am to 5 pm. In business for over 35 years. Complete engine rebuilding and machine shop. Crankshaft grinding and camshaft grinding. All internal engine parts.

Automotive Restorations Inc
Stephen Babinsky
4 Center St
Bernardsville, NJ 07924
908-766-6688; FAX: 908-766-6684
E-mail: autorestnj@aol.com

clutch rebuilding
mechanical services
restorations

See full listing in **Section Two** under **restoration shops**

B & B Cylinder Head Inc
320 Washington St
West Warwick, RI 02893
401-828-4900; FAX: 401-381-0010
E-mail: bbcyl@choiceone.net

cylinder heads

See full listing in **Section Two** under **engine parts**

The Babbitt Pot
Zigmont G Billus
1693 St Rt 4
Fort Edward, NY 12828
518-747-4277

engine rebuilding
rebabbitting &
boring of bearings

See full listing in **Section Two** under **babbitting**

Bicknell Engine Company
7055 Dayton Rd
Enon, OH 45323
937-864-5224

parts
repair
restoration

See full listing in **Section One** under **Buick/McLaughlin**

BPE Racing Heads
702 Dunn Way
Placentia, CA 92870
714-572-6072; FAX: 714-572-6073
E-mail: steve@bpeheads.com

cylinder heads

See full listing in **Section Two** under **machine work**

Cam-Pro
PO Box 3305
Great Falls, MT 59403
800-525-2581, 406-771-0300

camshaft repair
engine parts

See full listing in **Section Two** under **camshafts**

Carobu Engineering
1017 W 18th St
Costa Mesa, CA 92627
949-722-9307; FAX: 949-631-3184
E-mail: tate@carobu.com

dyno testing
engine rebuilding
exhaust systems

Open shop only. Monday-Friday 9 am to 5 pm. Engine rebuilding, dyno testing and exhaust system design. Web site: www.carobu.com

---

County Corvette
315 Westtown Rd
West Chester, PA 19382
610-696-7888; FAX: 610-696-9114

restoration
sales
service

See full listing in **Section One** under **Corvette**

Damper Doctor
1055 Parkview Ave
Redding, CA 96001
530-246-2984; FAX: 530-246-2987
E-mail: damperdoc@aol.com

harmonic balancers

Mail order and open shop. Monday-Friday 8 am to 5 pm Pacific time. Specializing in harmonic balancer repairs and rebuilding. Web site: www.members/damperdoctor.com

---

Done Right Engine & Machine Inc
12955 York Delta, Unit J
North Royalton, OH 44133
440-582-1366; FAX: 440-582-2005

engine rebuilding
machine shop

Complete engine rebuilding and machine shop services, specializing in antique and classic engines. Complete turnkey engines along with removal and installation service. Custom built engines to meet customer's needs.

Donovan Motorcar Service Inc
4 Holmes Rd
Lenox, MA 01240
413-499-6000; FAX: 413-499-6699
E-mail: donmtcar@aol.com

race prep
restoration
service

See full listing in **Section One** under **Jaguar**

DTE Motorsports
242 South Rd
Brentwood, NH 03833
PH/FAX: 603-642-3766
E-mail: dtemotorsports@aol.com

engines/race prep
mechanical services
transportation
restoration

See full listing in **Section One** under **Mercedes-Benz**

EIS Engines Inc
215 SE Grand Ave
Portland, OR 97214
800-547-0002, 503-232-5590
FAX: 503-232-5178
E-mail: edik@att.com

engines

See full listing in **Section One** under **Mercedes-Benz**

Engines Direct
7830 E Gelding, Bldg 200
Scottsdale, AZ 85260
800-998-2100; FAX: 480-998-6070

engines
parts

Mail order and open shop. Monday-Friday 8 am to 5 pm. Deals in new and remanufactured domestic, import, performance and marine engines. Mopar performance parts at 10% over cost. Full performance automatic transmissions and electronic overdrive conversion kits. Web site: www.enginesdirect.com

---

Grand Touring
2785 E Regal Park Dr
Anaheim, CA 92806
714-630-0130; FAX: 714-630-6956

engine rebuilding
machine shop
restoration
suspension

See full listing in **Section Two** under **restoration shops**

Grey Hills Auto Restoration
51 Vail Rd, PO Box 630
Blairstown, NJ 07825
908-362-8232; FAX: 908-362-6796
E-mail: info@greyhillsauto.com

restoration
service

See full listing in **Section Two** under **restoration shops**

Harkin Machine Shop
903 43rd St NE
Watertown, SD 57201
605-886-7880

engine rebuilding
rebabbitting

Mail order and open shop. Monday-Friday 8 am to 6 pm. Rebabbitting engine bearings and complete rebuilding of antique car engines.

Gary Hill Auto Service
150 E St Joseph St
Arcadia, CA 91006
626-447-2576; FAX: 626-447-1461

restoration
service

See full listing in **Section Two** under **racing**

Hi-Town Automotive
PO Box 381
High Point, NC 27261
336-259-1063; FAX: 336-869-5282
E-mail: lstamey@northstate.net

street rod repairs

See full listing in **Section Two** under **street rods**

Horst's Car Care
3160-1/2 N Woodford St
Decatur, IL 62526
217-876-1112

engine rebuilding

See full listing in **Section One** under **Mercedes-Benz**

Hot Heads Research & Racing Inc
276 Walker's Hollow Tr
Lowgap, NC 27024
336-352-4866; FAX: 336-352-3892
E-mail: info@hothemiheads.com

parts

See full listing in **Section One** under **Chrysler**

Indian Adventures Inc
121 South St, PO Box 206
Foxboro, MA 02035
508-359-4660; FAX: 508-359-5435

parts

See full listing in **Section Two** under **comprehensive parts**

Koffel's Place II
740 River Rd
Huron, OH 44839
419-433-4410; FAX: 419-433-2166

engine rebuilding
machine shop

Mail order and open shop. Monday-Friday 8 am to 6 pm, Wednesday 8 am to 9 pm. Two locations providing quality service and parts. Engine building for racing, collector cars, street rods, antique cars and boats. Complete in-house machine shop services and dyno testing.

Krem Engineering
10204 Perry Hwy
Meadville, PA 16335
814-724-4806; FAX: 814-337-2992
E-mail: info@krem-enterprises.com

engine rebuilding
repairs
restoration

See full listing in **Section Two** under **restoration shops**

Last Chance Repair & Restoration
1242 Myers Rd, PO Box 362A
Shaftsbury, VT 05262
802-447-7040

repairs
restoration

See full listing in **Section Two** under **restoration shops**

Libbey's Classic Car Restoration Center
137 N Quinsigamond Ave
Shrewsbury, MA 01545
PH/FAX: 508-792-1560

bodywork
restoration
service

See full listing in **Section Two** under **restoration shops**

Lindley Restorations Ltd
10 S Sanatoga Rd
Pottstown, PA 19464
610-326-8484; FAX: 610-326-3845

parts
sales
service

See full listing in **Section One** under **Jaguar**

Lindskog Balancing
1170 Massachusetts Ave
Boxborough, MA 01719-1415
978-263-2040; FAX: 978-263-4035

engine balancing

Complete engine balancing and individual engine component balancing. Antique work is our specialty.

Miles Auto Parts & Machine
7596 Dixie Hwy
Louisville, KY 40258
502-935-5583; FAX: 502-935-0849
E-mail: milesmachine58@cs.com

engine rebuilding

Engine rebuilding of antique, stock, performance, cars, trucks, tractors and stationary.

Moline Engine Service Inc
3227 23rd Ave
Moline, IL 61265
309-764-9735

engine parts
engine rebuilding
restoration

Open Monday-Friday 9 am to 5 pm. Restoring and improving the performance of your most favored vehicles for over 50 years. Complete machine shop, engine rebuilding, balancing, c/s grinding and welding, cylinder boring, valve jobs. We love restoring older motors and 1928 Chevrolets. We have finished crankshafts and cores (over 250), cylinder heads, connecting rods, etc, for late 1940s to 1980s. Call with casting number. Bring us your car or engine.

Morgan Oasis Garage
N 51 Terrace Rd, PO Box 1010
Hoodsport, WA 98548
360-877-5160

restoration
service

See full listing in **Section One** under **Morgan**

Myk's Tools
365 Sunnyvale St
Coos Bay, OR 97420
541-267-6957; FAX: 541-267-5967
E-mail: mykel@harborside.com

engine hoists
engine removal tool

See full listing in **Section Two** under **tools**

Noble Racing Inc
1058 Dry Ridge Rd
Versailles, KY 40383
859-879-1123; FAX: 859-879-3743
E-mail: nobleracing@iwebworks.com

accessories
parts

See full listing in **Section Two** under **engine parts**

Northern Auto Parts Warehouse Inc
PO Box 3147
Sioux City, IA 51102
800-831-0884; FAX: 712-258-0088
E-mail: sales@northernautoparts.com

parts

See full listing in **Section Two** under **engine parts**

Section Two – Generalists

Odyssey Restorations Inc 8080 Central Ave NE Spring Lake Park, MN 55432 763-786-1518; FAX: 763-786-1524	parts restoration

See full listing in **Section Two** under **restoration shops**

Partwerks of Chicago 718 S Prairie Rd New Lenox, IL 60451 815-462-3000; FAX: 815-462-3006 E-mail: partwerks9@aol.com	parts service

See full listing in **Section Two** under **engine parts**

Ponti-Action Racing PO Box 354 Medfield, MA 02052 888-RAM-AIRS; FAX: 508-359-5485 E-mail: gtogeezer@media.net	engine builders

See full listing in **Section One** under **Pontiac**

Pontiac Engines Custom Built E-mail: pontiacgregg@earthlink.net	custom built engines

See full listing in **Section One** under **Pontiac**

Precision Babbitt Service 4681 Lincoln Ave Beamsville, ON Canada L0R 1B3 905-563-4364 E-mail: tkoudys@sprint.ca	babbitting engine rebuilding

See full listing in **Section Two** under **babbitting**

Prestige Automotive Inc 30295 Moravian Tr Tippecanoe, OH 44699 740-922-3542 E-mail: blacklabs@tusco.net	restoration

See full listing in **Section Two** under **restoration shops**

R & L Engines Inc 308 Durham Rd Dover, NH 03820 603-742-8812; FAX: 603-742-8137	engine rebuilding restorations

Mail order and open shop. Monday-Friday 8 am to 5 pm, Saturday 8 am to 12 noon. Deal in specialty engine rebuilding, antique restoration, classic, street rod, high-performance and marine. Web site: www.rlengines.com

Roadrunner Tire & Auto 4850 Hwy 377 S Fort Worth, TX 76116 817-244-4924	restoration speedometer repair

See full listing in **Section Two** under **restoration shops**

Ross' Automotive Machine Co Inc 1763 N Main St Niles, OH 44446 330-544-4466	racing engines rebuilding

Mail order and open shop. Specializing in 1949-1964 Olds motors. Deal in 1949-1970 Chev, Olds, Buick, Pontiac. Stock rebuilds, unleaded conversions, racing engines, balancing, dyno testing, etc. We are a 6 man racing engine shop with the most modern equipment including dyno and ultrasonic testing. Capable of very close tolerance machining as we build NASCAR motors and are especially interested in 1949-1964 Olds motors.

Ross Racing Pistons 625 S Douglas St El Segundo, CA 90250 310-536-0100; FAX: 310-536-0333	pistons

See full listing in **Section Two** under **engine parts**

Scotts Manufacturing 25520 Ave Stanford #304 Valencia, CA 91355 800-544-5596; FAX: 661-295-9342	electric fans fan electronics

See full listing in **Section Two** under **electrical systems**

Shepard's Automotive Div of Fine Ride Industries 4131 S Main St Akron, OH 44319 330-644-2000; FAX: 330-644-6522 E-mail: shepardsauto@aol.com	appraisals engine remanufacturing

Specialist remanufacturing antique motors. Rebuilding standard/performance engines. Known worldwide for our remanufactured Cadillac-Hemis-Packards, max wedge motors and long list of many others. Specialist 1920s-1970s power plants. Work performed in-house with two hi-tech machine shops. Motors are show quality and pre-run on test stand to assure guarantee. 51 years of engine building. "Best on the block."

Stone Barn Inc 202 Rt 46, Box 117 Vienna, NJ 07880 908-637-4444; FAX: 908-637-4290	restoration

See full listing in **Section Two** under **restoration shops**

Studebakers West 335A Convention Way Redwood City, CA 94063 650-366-8787	mechanical rebuilding transmission parts wiring harnesses

See full listing in **Section One** under **Studebaker**

Tatom Custom Engines PO Box 2504 Mt Vernon, WA 98273 360-424-8314; FAX: 360-424-6717 E-mail: flatheads@tatom.com	engine rebuilding machine shop

In business for over 10 years. Engine restoration and the construction of vintage, specialty, hi-performance and race engines. Full service machine shop including cast iron repair. Substantial number of major brand speed equipment parts available. Call for catalog. Web site: www.tatom.com

Teddy's Garage 8530 Louise Ave Northridge, CA 91325 818-341-0505	parts restoration service

See full listing in **Section One** under **Rolls-Royce/Bentley**

Thul Auto Parts Inc 225 Roosevelt Ave Plainfield, NJ 07060 800-276-8485, 908-754-3333 FAX: 908-756-0239 E-mail: thulauto@juno.com	boring machine work rebabbitting vintage auto parts

Open Monday-Friday 8 am to 5:30 pm. Rebabbitting, crankshaft grinding and build up, align boring, resleeving, reboring, large general machine shop. Some old engines and parts, cracked blocks and heads repaired. Resleeving, reboring, crack repairs, large general machine shop. Custom engine and cylinder head rebuilding. Featuring computer aided engine design and sealed power parts with a 100,000 mile factory warranty. Web site: www.thulautoparts.com

Valley Head Service Inc
19340 Londelius St
Northridge, CA 91324
818-993-7000; FAX: 818-993-9712

engine rebuilding
machine work

Mail order and open shop. Monday-Friday 9 am to 5 pm. Rebuilding engines and machine work for antique, collector and muscle cars. Web site: www.valleyhead.com

Vintage Motor and Machine
Gene French
1513 Webster Ct
Fort Collins, CO 80524
970-498-9224

auto components
fixtures
industrial
components

See full listing in **Section Two** under **machine work**

Willow Automotive Service
Box 4640, Rt 212
Willow, NY 12495
845-679-4679

bodywork
painting
restorations

See full listing in **Section Two** under **restoration shops**

Zim's Autotechnik
1804 Reliance Pkwy
Bedford, TX 76021
800-356-2964; FAX: 817-545-2002
E-mail: zimips@allzim.com

parts
service

See full listing in **Section One** under **Porsche**

exhaust systems

A&A Mustang Parts & Mfg Co
105 Fordham Rd
Oak Ridge, TN 37830
423-482-9445
E-mail: joannantrican@aol.com

exhaust systems
parts
restorations

See full listing in **Section One** under **Mustang**

Accurate Ltd
7125 Hwy 99 N
Roseburg, OR 97470
PH/FAX: 541-672-2661
E-mail: taswope@jeffnet.org

muffler products

See full listing in **Section One** under **Mopar**

Aremco Products Inc
707-B Executive Blvd
Valley Cottage, NY 10989
845-268-0039; FAX: 845-268-0041
E-mail: aremco@aremco.com

compounds

See full listing in **Section Two** under **accessories**

Gideon Booth
Rellandsgate, Kings Meaburn
Penrith
Cumbria CA10 3BT England
PH/FAX: 01931 714624

car collector
parts
restorations

See full listing in **Section One** under **Morris**

Borla East
600 A Lincoln Blvd
Middlesex, NJ 08846
732-469-9666

exhaust systems

See full listing in **Section One** under **Rolls-Royce/Bentley**

Carobu Engineering
1017 W 18th St
Costa Mesa, CA 92627
949-722-9307; FAX: 949-631-3184
E-mail: tate@carobu.com

dyno testing
engine rebuilding
exhaust systems

See full listing in **Section Two** under **engine rebuilding**

Cars of the Past Restorations Inc
11180 Kinsman Rd
Newbury, OH 44065
440-564-2277

restoration

See full listing in **Section Two** under **restoration shops**

Corvette Central
13550 Three Oaks Rd, Dept HM
Sawyer, MI 49125
616-426-3342; FAX: 616-426-4108
E-mail: mail@corvettecentral.com

accessories
parts

See full listing in **Section One** under **Corvette**

Custom Exhaust Specialties Inc
61533 American Loop #3
Bend, OR 97702
541-330-5931; FAX: 541-330-8311
E-mail: customexhaust@bendcable.com

exhaust systems

Here at Custom Exhaust we specialize in Mandrel bending from 1.50" to 4.00." With our years of experience, commitment and state of the art equipment, we can help perfect your performance exhaust system for showing, racing or just getting around town. We also offer custom header and custom flange services. Web site: www.4customexhaust.com

Exhaust Tech
6466 Gayhart St
Commerce, CA 90040
323-724-9184; FAX: 323-724-2999
E-mail: rsimons250@aol.com

exhaust systems

Web site: www.exhausttech.com

Jim Fortin
95 Weston St
Brockton, MA 02301-3334
508-586-4855
E-mail: het1@aol.com

exhaust systems

Mail order and open shop by appointment only. Phone hours: Monday-Friday noon to midnight; weekends by chance. Prefer e-mail or telephone calls, however, all letters with SASE answered. Exhaust systems manufactured for most cars and light trucks from 1909-muscle car era. Pipes manufactured in heavy steel, inquire for aluminized or stainless steel. Most mufflers aluminized. Have large amount of NORS mufflers available from mid 1950s-late 1960s. We also have carburetor heat tubes for 1920s, 1930s Buicks. Lower radiator water connector tubes available for Mopar, GM, Ford, Hudson, Packard. Guaranteed satisfaction on all parts sold. Established 1967. At 55, I've been exhausting myself for over 35 years.

Gardner Exhaust Systems
7 Cedar Ln
Rhinebeck, NY 12572
845-876-8117; FAX: 845-871-1750
E-mail: gexhaust@aol.com

exhaust systems

Specializing in reproduction GM and Mopar muscle car exhaust systems for 1964-1972 GTOs, 1965-1972 Novas, 1967-1974

Camaros, 1967-1974 Firebirds, 1964-1972 Chevelles, 1965-1972 Buick GSs, 1965-1972 Oldsmobile 442s, 1968-1972 El Caminos, 1986-1987 Buick Grand Nationals, 1968-1970 Mopar B-bodies. Web site: www.gardnerexhaust.com

Gulf Coast Corvette 15100 Lee Rd #101 Humble, TX 77396 800-546-2111 order line 281-441-2111 info line FAX: 281-441-3057	**parts**

See full listing in **Section One** under **Corvette**

Headers by "Ed" Inc 2710-JZ 16th Ave S Minneapolis, MN 55407 612-729-2802; FAX: 612-729-5638	**headers**

Mail order and open shop. Monday-Friday 8:30 am to 5 pm. Pre-1975 V8 car headers. V8/Allison V12 vertical exit pull/Mudbog headers. Header kits, header parts for over one hundred different 4, 6, V6, V8, V12 engines. Very informative header catalog, $5.50. Informative header parts catalog (learn how to build headers better than any you can buy), $3.95. 90 minute header design audio cassette (with reference charts), will make you a header design expert, $10.95. Since 1962. Web site: www.headersbyed.com

See our ad on this page

High Performance Coatings 14788 S Heritagecrest Way Bluffdale, UT 84065 800-456-4721, 801-501-8303 FAX: 801-501-8315 E-mail: hpcsales@hpcoatings.com	**coatings**

Mail order and open shop. Monday-Friday 8 am to 5 pm. Specializing in all cars and motorcycles exhaust system coatings,

thermal barrier coatings, dry film lubricative coatings, corrosion resistant coatings. Web site: www.hpcoatings.com

Italy's Famous Exhaust 2711 183rd St Redondo Beach, CA 90278 E-mail: johnt@famousexhaust.com	**exhaust systems** **wheels**

Mail order only. Dealing in Daytona free flow exhaust systems and Campagnolo wheels. Exclusive global distributor for FAZA. Web site: www.famousexhaust.com

Jet-Hot Coatings/MCCI 55 E Front St, Ste A-200 Bridgeport, PA 19405 800-432-3379 E-mail: sales@jet-hot.com	**high-temp coatings**

We provide high-temperature coatings for vehicles of every sort: street, performance, racing, restoration, air/snow/water, two-wheels, four wheels or no wheels at all! Web site: www.jet-hot.com
See our ad on page 327

KC's Rods & Customs 3500 Aloma Ave, Ste D-16 Winter Park, FL 32792 877-750-6350; FAX: 407-673-9131 E-mail: bobbyb@bellsouth.net	**brakes** **exhaust systems** **restoration**

See full listing in **Section Two** under **street rods**

London Stainless Steel **Exhaust Centre** 249-253 Queenstown Rd London, SW8 3NP England 0114420-7622-2120 FAX: 0114420-7627-0991 E-mail: info@quicksilverexhausts.com	**exhaust systems**

Mail order and open shop. Monday-Friday 8:30 am to 5:30 pm. The widest range of stainless steel exhausts anywhere, fast UPS delivery. Web site: www.quicksilverexhausts.com

Pace Setter Performance Products 2841 W Clarendon Ave Phoenix, AZ 85017 602-266-1964; FAX: 602-650-1136	**exhaust systems** **fluid transfer hose** **intake tubes** **shifters**

Manufacture and open shop. Monday-Friday 8 am to 4:30 pm Mountain time. Exhaust systems for import cars and trucks, including Triumph, Austin-Healey, MG, VW, Nissan and Honda. Web site: www.pacesetterexhaust.com

Performance Coatings 9768 Feagin Rd Jonesboro, GA 30236 770-478-2775; FAX: 770-478-1926 Email: gemobpci@mindspring.com	**ceramic coatings** **engine parts** **suspension parts**

Deal in metallic ceramic coatings for exhaust components. Powder coatings for chassis, suspension and engine components. Web site: www.headercoatings.com

Porcelain Patch & Glaze Co Inc 966 86th Ave Oakland, CA 94621 510-635-2188	**porcelain** **enameling**

Open Monday-Friday 9 am to 3 pm. Specializing in porcelain enameling of intake and exhaust manifolds. Welding and repairs available. UPS orders.

Power Effects®
1800H Industrial Park Dr
Grand Haven, MI 49417
877-3POWRFX (376-9739) toll free
616-847-4200; FAX: 616-847-4210

exhaust systems

Power Effects® performance components and engineered systems are designed for cars, sport trucks, sport utility vehicles and street rods. Flange mounted cast aluminum exhaust components and mandrel bent tubing provide maximum flexibility and ease of installation. Aluminum tuneable Power Capsules™ replace conventional mufflers offering superior air flow and a deep, rich-sounding exhaust. Aluminum Power Tips™ finish off the tailpipe end and are available to fit 2-1/4, 2-1/2, 2-3/4 and 3 inch tubing using our flanges. Web site: www.powereffects.com

Prairie Auto Porcelain
1424 90th St W
Northfield, MN 55057
507-645-5325; FAX: 507-645-0987

porcelain coatings

Manifold coating specialists, authentic porcelain coatings for classic car manifolds, Packard, Cadillac, Cord, Duesenberg, Lincoln, Pierce-Arrow, Jaguar, etc. Show quality, driver guaranteed. Also ceramic heat barrier coatings for later model cars. Weld repairs available. Web site: www.prairieauto.com

Red Bird Racing
6640 Valley St
Coeur d'Alene, ID 83815
208-762-5305

parts

See full listing in **Section One** under **Chevrolet**

Red's Headers & Early Ford Speed Equipment
22950 Bednar Ln
Fort Bragg, CA 95437-8411
707-964-7733; FAX: 707-964-5434
E-mail: red@reds-headers.com

headers
mechanical parts

See full listing in **Section One** under **Ford 1932-1953**

Rod Shop Performance Center Inc
1126 Rockledge Rd
Attalla, AL 35954
256-538-0376
E-mail: rodshop@
rodshopperformance.com

exhaust systems

Mail order only. High quality stainless steel exhaust components including a full line of patented Hi-Flow® mufflers, exhaust tips and extensions, clamps, tubing, hangers and bends. Custom work available. Web site: www.rodshopperformance.com

So-Cal Speed Engineering
PO Box 1421
Costa Mesa, CA 92628
714-979-7964

headers

Mail order only. Lakes style megaphone headers.

Stahl Headers Inc
1515 Mount Rose Ave
York, PA 17403
717-846-1632; FAX: 717-854-9486
E-mail: judys@stahlheaders.com

exhaust systems

Mail order only. Manufacturer of high-performance exhaust systems (headers). Exhaust parts and accessories. Web site: www.stahlheaders.com
See our ad on this page

Thermal Tech Coatings Inc
312 E Poythress St, Ste A
Hopewell, VA 23860
877-754-9795; FAX: 804-452-1825
E-mail: webmaster@
thermaltechcoatings.com

coatings

Mail order and open shop. Monday-Friday 8:30 am to 5:30 pm. Deals in coatings for metal parts. Coating services offered include thermal barriers, reflective and dissipative, powder coatings and dry film lubricants. Web site: www.thermaltechcoatings.com

Torque Tech Performance Exhaust
1826 Woodland Dr
Valdosta, GA 31601
800-408-0016
E-mail: torque@surfsourth.com

exhaust systems

Specializing in huge performance exhaust systems for American muscle cars, GM and Mopar. Web site: www.torquetechexh.com

Waldron's Antique Exhaust Inc
25872 M-86, PO Box C
Nottawa, MI 49075
800-503-9428, 616-467-7185
FAX: 616-467-9041

exhaust systems

Mail order and open shop. Monday-Friday 9 am to 5 pm. New exhaust systems for 1920s-1980s cars. Oldest and most complete old car exhaust system supplier in the USA.

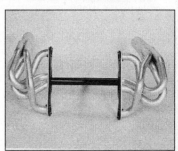

fans

Flex-a-lite
PO Box 580
Milton, WA 98354
253-922-2700; FAX: 253-922-0226
E-mail: flex@flex-a-lite.com

fans

Dealing in high-performance cooling fans, both electric and belt-driven. Transmission and engine oil coolers. Web site: www.flex-a-lite.com

GRIFFIN Radiator
100 Hurricane Creek Rd
Piedmont, SC 29673
800-RACE-RAD (722-3723)
864-845-5000; FAX: 864-845-5001
E-mail: griffinrad@aol.com

radiators

See full listing in **Section Two** under **radiators**

fiberglass parts

A/Altered Hot Rod Parts
PO Box 851
Emporia, KS 66801
620-343-1796

body parts

See full listing in **Section One** under **Ford 1903-1931**

Accessoryland Truckin' Supplies
10723 Rt 61 S
Dubuque, IA 52003
319-556-5482; FAX: 319-556-9087
E-mail: unityspotlights@aol.com or
chevygmcparts@aol.com

**accessories
foglights/spotlights
mounting brackets
parts**

See full listing in **Section One** under **Chevrolet**

ASC&P International
PO Box 255
Uwchland, PA 19480
610-458-8395; FAX: 610-458-8735

**custom molding
fiberglass
plastic**

Reproduction of plastic and fiberglass. Short run production is a specialty. Hardness range from rubber to rigid. Your first step in the reproduction business.

Tony D Branda Performance
Shelby and Mustang Parts
1434 E Pleasant Valley Blvd
Altoona, PA 16602
814-942-1869; FAX: 814-944-0801
E-mail: cobranda@aol.com

**accessories
decals
emblems
sheetmetal
wheels**

See full listing in **Section One** under **Mustang**

Champion Luggage Trailers
9471 Hemlock Cir
Shreveport, LA 71118
318-688-2787

luggage trailer kits

See full listing in **Section Two** under **trailers**

Class Glass & Performance Inc
101 Winston St
Cumberland, MD 21502
800-774-3456 toll free
301-777-3456; FAX: 301-777-7044

body parts

Mail order and open shop. Monday-Friday 8 am to 4:30 pm. Street rod 32 Chevy, T bucket racing, 33 Willys, 57 Turner.

Hoods, fenders, body parts, 1932-2001 Chevrolet, Dodge, Ford, Dodge pickup, Studebaker pickup.

Corvette Central
13550 Three Oaks Rd, Dept HM
Sawyer, MI 49125
616-426-3342; FAX: 616-426-4108
E-mail: mail@corvettecentral.com

**accessories
parts**

See full listing in **Section One** under **Corvette**

Greer Enterprises
1981 Greenbrook Blvd
Richland, WA 99352
509-627-3411
E-mail: greenent@owt.com

parts

See full listing in **Section Two** under **chassis parts**

Grossmueller's Classic Corvette
55 Sitgreaves St
Phillipsburg, NJ 08865
908-213-8832; FAX: 908-213-7088
E-mail: wfg@gccorvettes.com

**NOS parts
used parts**

See full listing in **Section One** under **Corvette**

Long Island Corvette Supply Inc
1445 Strong Ave
Copiague, NY 11726-3227
631-225-3000; FAX: 631-225-5030
E-mail: info@licorvette.com

parts

See full listing in **Section One** under **Corvette**

Obsolete Ford Parts Inc
8701 S I-35
Oklahoma City, OK 73149
405-631-3933; FAX: 405-634-6815
E-mail: info@obsoletefordparts.com

parts

See full listing in **Section One** under **Ford 1954-up**

P&J Automotive Inc
6262 Riverside Dr
Danville, VA 24541
804-822-2211; FAX: 804-822-2213

**bodies
chassis parts**

See full listing in **Section Two** under **street rods**

R & R Fiberglass & Specialties
4850 Wilson Dr NW
Cleveland, TN 37312
423-476-2270; FAX: 423-473-9442
E-mail: rrfiberglass@aol.com

body parts

Dealing in fiberglass, fenders, runningboards, grille shells and misc fiberglass body parts for Ford, Chevy, Plymouth, Dodge, Ford 1923-1948 car/1928-1956 truck, Chevy 1931-1950 car/1933-1972 truck, Plymouth and Dodge 1931-1948 car/1933-1953 truck. Also aluminum grille insert for Plymouth and Dodge 1932-1936 car and 1933-1938 Dodge truck.

Regal Roadsters Ltd
301 W Beltline Hwy
Madison, WI 53713
PH/FAX: 608-273-4141
E-mail: chuck@regaltbird.com

**replicars
restoration**

See full listing in **Section One** under **Thunderbird**

Replica Plastics
260 S Oates St, Box 1147
Dothan, AL 36302
800-873-5871; FAX: 334-792-1175
E-mail: stone@ala.net

fiberglass parts

Mail order and open shop. Monday-Friday 7 am to 6 pm. Dealing in fiberglass quarter panel extensions. Furnish over 400 fiberglass replacement panels for all GM cars. Ship worldwide, same day. Web site: www.replica-plastics.com

Rodster Inc 128 Center St #B El Segundo, CA 90245 310-322-2767; FAX: 310-322-2761	**conversion kits**

See full listing in **Section Two** under **street rods**

Smooth Line 2562 Riddle Run Rd Tarentum, PA 15084 724-274-6002; FAX: 724-274-6121	**body panels** **removable hardtops**

See full listing in **Section Two** under **tops**

Wescott's Auto Restyling 19701 SE Hwy 212 Boring, OR 97009 800-523-6279; FAX: 503-658-2938 E-mail: marykarl@gte.net	**body parts**

See full listing in **Section One** under **Ford 1932-1953**

Wild Bill's Corvette & **Hi-Performance Center Inc** 446 Dedham St Wrentham, MA 02093 508-384-7373; FAX: 508-384-9366 E-mail: wildbillscorvette@ worldnet.att.net	**parts** **rebuilding** **service**

See full listing in **Section One** under **Corvette**

Gene Winfield's Rod & Custom 8201 Sierra Hwy Mojowe, CA 93501 661-824-4728	**fender skirts** **metal repair panels** **motor mount kits**

See full listing in **Section One** under **Mercury**

Rush Performance Fitters 1450 McDonald Rd Dahlonega, GA 30533 706-864-8544; FAX: 706-864-2206	**air filters**

Manufacturer of reusable air filters. Web site: www.gtp300.com

JJ Best & Co 737 Main St, PO Box 10 Chatham, MA 02633 800-USA-1965; FAX: 508-945-6006	**financing**

Open Monday-Friday 8 am to 9 pm, Saturday 10 am to 4 pm Eastern time. Specializing in financing antique, classic, exotic, kit, muscle, rod and sport automobiles. Great low rates and long terms, 5-12 years. Will take an application on the phone or through the web site and usually let a customer know within 5 minutes of approval or denial. Very familiar with most cars from 1901-1996 and will offer financing up to 90% of market value. Web site: www.jjbest.com

First National Bank of Sumner 101-N Christy Ave Sumner, IL 62466 618-936-2396; FAX: 618-936-9079 E-mail: hobbes@wworld.com	**financing**

Offering simple interest loan financing for the purchase of antique and collector automobiles. Web site: www.fnbsumner.com

Midbanc Financial Services PO Box 20402 Columbus, OH 43220 614-442-7701; FAX: 614-442-7704 E-mail: patricia@midbanc.com	**financing**

Financing for collectible automobiles. Web site: www.midbanc.com

JC Taylor Antique Automobile **Insurance Agency** 320 S 69th St Upper Darby, PA 19082 800-345-8290	**insurance**

See full listing in **Section Two** under **insurance**

Bob's Speedometer Service 32411 Grand River Ave Farmington, MI 48336 800-592-9673; FAX: 248-473-5517	**gauges** **speedometers** **tachometers**

See full listing in **Section Two** under **instruments**

Ceramicar 679 Lapla Rd Kingston, NY 12401 PH/FAX: 845-338-2199	**auto-related** **ceramics**

See full listing in **Section Two** under **artwork**

Connecticut Fire Museum PO Box 297 Warehouse Point, CT 06088 860-623-4732	**museum**

See full listing in **Section Six** under **Connecticut**

Ben McAdam 500 Clover Ln Wheeling, WV 26003 304-242-3388, 304-242-0855 E-mail: antiquebenny@aol.com	**electrical parts**

See full listing in **Section Two** under **ignition parts**

Reinholds Restorations c/o Rick Reinhold PO Box 178, 255 N Ridge Rd Reinholds, PA 17569-0178 717-336-5617; FAX: 717-336-7050	**appraisals** **repairs** **restoration**

See full listing in **Section Two** under **restoration shops**

Sandringham House **Museum & Grounds** Sandringham Nr King's Lynn Norfolk PE356EN England 01553-772675; FAX: 01485-541571	**museum**

See full listing in **Section Six** under **England**

Harold Warp Pioneer Village Foundation
PO Box 68
Minden, NE 68959-0068
308-832-1181; FAX: 308-832-2750
800-445-4447 (out of state)
E-mail: pioneervllge@nebi.com

museum

See full listing in **Section Six** under **Nebraska**

Wheels O' Time Museum
PO Box 9636
Peoria, IL 61612-9636
309-243-9020
E-mail: wotmuseum@aol.com

museum

See full listing in **Section Six** under **Illinois**

fuel system parts

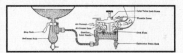

American Street Rod
3340 Sunrise Blvd D-1
Rancho Cordova, CA 95742
916-638-3275

hoses
tubing

See full listing in **Section Two** under **street rods**

Antique Auto Parts Cellar
6 Chauncy St, PO Box 3
South Weymouth, MA 02190
781-335-1579; FAX: 781-335-1925
E-mail: our1932@aol.com

brake/chassis/
engine parts
fuel pumps/kits
gaskets
water pumps

See full listing in **Section Two** under **comprehensive parts**

Atlas Obsolete Chrysler Parts
10621 Bloomfield St, Unit 32
Los Alamitos, CA 90720
PH/FAX: 562-594-5560
E-mail: atlaschrys@aol.com

parts

See full listing in **Section One** under **Mopar**

C & G Early Ford Parts
1941 Commercial St, Dept AH
Escondido, CA 92029-1233
760-740-2400; FAX: 760-740-8700
E-mail: cgford@cgfordparts.com

accessories/chrome
emblems
literature
mechanical
weatherstripping

See full listing in **Section One** under **Ford 1932-1953**

Chicago Corvette Supply
7322 S Archer Rd
Justice, IL 60458
708-458-2500; FAX: 708-458-2662

parts

See full listing in **Section One** under **Corvette**

Classic Tube
Division of Classic & Performance
Spec Inc
80 Rotech Dr
Lancaster, NY 14086
800-TUBES-11 (882-3711)
716-759-1800; FAX: 716-759-1014
E-mail: classictube@aol.com

brake lines
choke tubes
fuel lines
transmission lines
vacuum lines

See full listing in **Section Two** under **brakes**

Dr Vette
14364 SW 139th Ct
Miami, FL 33186
800-262-9595; FAX: 305-253-3641

brakes
fuel system parts
repairs

See full listing in **Section One** under **Corvettes**

Ferris Auto Electric Ltd
106 Lakeshore Dr
North Bay, ON Canada P1A 2A6
705-474-4560; FAX: 705-474-9453

parts
service

See full listing in **Section Two** under **electrical systems**

Flotamex Automotive Inc
3050 Bank One Center
1717 Main St
Dallas, TX 75201
214-939-5502; FAX: 214-939-6100
E-mail: flomexjec3@aol.com

sending units

Mail order only. Deals in fuel level sending units. Web site: www.flotamex.com

Ron Francis' Wire Works
167 Keystone Rd
Chester, PA 19013
800-292-1940 orders, 610-485-1937
E-mail: rfwwx@aol.com

fuel injection
harnesses
wiring accessories
wiring kits

See full listing in **Section Two** under **wiring harnesses**

Gas Tank and Radiator Rebuilders
20123 Hwy 362
Waller, TX 77484
800-723-3759
E-mail: donhart@donhart.com

abrasive blasting
gas tank rebuilding
heaters
radiator repair

Gas tank rebuilding and restoration, radiator, heater, air conditioning condenser and heat exchanger repair, rebuilding and restoration. New gas tanks, radiators, heaters and air conditioning condensers and evaporators. Oil pan and transmission pan repair and restoration. Abrasive blasting and rust removal. Antique and vintage specialists. Professional service, environmentally conscious and fully insured. Three locations to serve you: Rockville, MD; Houston, TX; Stockton, CA. Web site: www.radiatorshops.com/gastanks

Gas Tank Renu USA
12727 Greenfield
Detroit, MI 48227
800-997-3688; FAX: 313-273-4759
E-mail: danrenu@aol.com

fuel tank repair

Repair of fuel tanks for automotive and marine industries. Lifetime warranty on any vehicle less than 3/4 ton. Web site: www.gastankrenu.com

Jack P Gross Assoc/Scott Manufacturing Inc
163 Helenwood Detour Rd, PO Box 97
Helenwood, TN 37755
423-569-6088; FAX: 423-569-6428
E-mail: scottmfg@highland.net

air hose products
water hose products

See full listing in **Section Two** under **service shops**

Hotchkiss Vacuum Tank Service
2102 S Brentwood Pl
Essexville, MI 48732-1489
517-894-2073

repair kits
restoration

Mail order only. Restoration of the vacuum fuel feed system tank, repair kits, gaskets and parts.

Kanter Auto Products
76 Monroe St
Boonton, NJ 07005
800-526-1096; 201-334-9575
FAX: 201-334-5423

car covers
carpet sets
front end kits
parts

See full listing in **Section Two** under **comprehensive parts**

Section Two – Generalists

Ken's Carburetors 2301 Barnum Ave Stratford, CT 06615 203-375-9340	carburetors distributors parts

See full listing in **Section One** under **Ford 1932-1953**

Mac's Radiator Service & Gas Tank Renu LA 9681 Alondra Blvd Bellflower, CA 90706 800-901-8265; 562-920-1871 FAX: 562-920-8491 E-mail: bruce@macs-radiator.com	gas tanks radiators

See full listing in **Section Two** under **radiators**

Jack Marcheski 100 Dry Creek Rd Hollister, CA 95023 831-637-3453 E-mail: jmar1@hollinet.com	12/6-volt converters rebuilding repair

See full listing in **Section Two** under **electrical systems**

Marren Motor Sports Inc 49 Burtville Ave #3A Derby, CT 06418 203-732-4565 E-mail: tim.marren@snet.net	fuel injectors fuel pumps

Mail order and open shop. Monday-Friday 9 am to 5 pm Eastern time. Deals in fuel injectors, fuel injector service, fuel management systems, carburetor to fuel injection conversions, fuel pumps, filters, dampers and miscellaneous fuel components. Web site: www.injector.com

Donald McKinsey PO Box 94H Wilkinson, IN 46186 765-785-6284	fuel pumps ignition parts literature spark plugs

See full listing in **Section Two** under **ignition parts**

Partwerks of Chicago 718 S Prairie Rd New Lenox, IL 60451 815-462-3000; FAX: 815-462-3006 E-mail: partwerks9@aol.com	parts service

See full listing in **Section Two** under **engine parts**

Jack Podell Fuel Injection Spec 106 Wakewa Ave South Bend, IN 46617 219-232-6430; FAX: 219-234-8632 E-mail: podellsfi@aol.com	fuel system parts fuel system rebuilding

See full listing in **Section One** under **Corvette**

Prezerve 1101 Arapahoe, Ste 3 Lincoln, NE 68502 888-774-4184; FAX: 402-420-7777 E-mail: prezerve@prezerveit.com	additives

See full listing in **Section Two** under **car care products**

Radiator & Gas Tank Specialist 20123 Hwy 362, PO Box 758 Waller, TX 77484 800-723-3759; FAX: 936-372-5032 E-mail: donhart@donhart.com	gas tanks heaters radiators

See full listing in **Section Two** under **radiators**

Renner's Corner 10320 E Austin Manchester, MI 48158 734-428-8424; FAX: 734-428-1090	bushings/hardware carb/pump kits gauges/gaskets rebuild service

See full listing in **Section One** under **Ford 1932-1953**

Skip's Auto Parts Skip Bollinger 1500 Northaven Dr Gladstone, MO 64118 816-455-2337; FAX: 816-459-7547 E-mail: carpartman@aol.com	chassis parts ignition parts water pumps

See full listing in **Section Two** under **water pumps**

JF Sullivan Company 14 Clarendon Rd Auburn, MA 01501 508-792-9500	electrical parts repairs

Mail order and open shop. Monday-Friday 10 am to 6 pm. Manufacturers and rebuilders of all types of gasoline tank sending units and electrical component repairs.

Wheeler's Classic Parts 104 S Bowles West Harrison, IN 47060 812-637-2194 E-mail: info@partsforclassics.com	parts

See full listing in **Section Two** under **brakes**

Zim's Autotechnik 1804 Reliance Pkwy Bedford, TX 76021 800-356-2964; FAX: 817-545-2002 E-mail: zimips@allzim.com	parts service

See full listing in **Section One** under **Porsche**

gaskets

Antique Auto Parts Cellar 6 Chauncy St, PO Box 3 South Weymouth, MA 02190 781-335-1579; FAX: 781-335-1925 E-mail: our1932@aol.com	brake/chassis/ engine parts fuel pumps/kits gaskets water pumps

See full listing in **Section Two** under **comprehensive parts**

Aremco Products Inc 707-B Executive Blvd Valley Cottage, NY 10989 845-268-0039; FAX: 845-268-0041 E-mail: aremco@aremco.com	compounds

See full listing in **Section Two** under **accessories**

Best Gasket Inc 11558 Washington Blvd Unit F Whittier, CA 90606 888-333-BEST, 562-699-6631 FAX: 562-699-5034 E-mail: best1@inreach.com	gaskets

Mail order and open shop. Monday-Friday 8 am to 4 pm Pacific time. Manufacturer of gaskets for domestic automotive and light duty truck engines from the Model A to the V8s of the 1960s. Sell wholesale only. $500 initial stock order required to buy direct. Also do custom work.

Gideon Booth
Rellandsgate, Kings Meaburn
Penrith
Cumbria CA10 3BT England
PH/FAX: 01931 714624

car collector
parts
restorations

See full listing in **Section One** under **Morris**

C & G Early Ford Parts
1941 Commercial St, Dept AH
Escondido, CA 92029-1233
760-740-2400; FAX: 760-740-8700
E-mail: cgford@cgfordparts.com

accessories/chrome
emblems
literature
mechanical
weatherstripping

See full listing in **Section One** under **Ford 1932-1953**

Carson's Antique Auto Parts
235 Shawfarm Rd
Holliston, MA 01746
508-429-2269; FAX: 508-429-0761
E-mail: w1066@gis.net

parts

See full listing in **Section Two** under **engine parts**

Clean Seal Inc
PO Box 2919
South Bend, IN 46680-2919
800-366-3682; FAX: 219-299-8044
E-mail: cleanseal@cleanseal.com

rubber seals

Dealing in extruded rubber seals. Web site: www.cleanseal.com

Corvair Underground
PO Box 339
Dundee, OR 97115
800-825-8247, 503-434-1648
FAX: 503-434-1626

parts

See full listing in **Section One** under **Corvair**

JECC Inc
PO Box 616
West Paterson, NJ 07424
973-890-9682; FAX: 973-812-2724

chassis parts
gaskets
transmissions

See full listing in **Section One** under **Buick/McLaughlin**

Gerald J Lettieri
132 Old Main St
Rocky Hill, CT 06067
860-529-7177; FAX: 860-257-3621

gaskets
parts

Gaskets, head, manifold, oil pan, full engine sets, copper O-rings. Large NOS inventory. Over 30 years of satisfied service.

Molina Gaskets
23126 Mariposa Ave
Torrance, CA 90502
310-539-1883; FAX: 310-539-3886

head gaskets

Specializing in copper and asbestos head gaskets, custom made for any car, tractor or marine engine.

Northern Auto Parts Warehouse Inc
PO Box 3147
Sioux City, IA 51102
800-831-0884; FAX: 712-258-0088
E-mail: sales@northernautoparts.com

parts

See full listing in **Section Two** under **engine parts**

Olson's Gaskets
3059 Opdal Rd E
Port Orchard, WA 98366
PH/FAX: 360-871-1207
E-mail: info@olsonsgaskets.com

gaskets

Mail and phone orders. Monday-Friday, 24 hr machine. Engine gaskets, NOS, new production, handmaking service. Full sets,

head gaskets, manifolds, etc, for cars, trucks, tractors, etc. Visa/MasterCard. Web site: www.olsonsgaskets.com

Powers Parts Co
Roy F Powers
1354 Ridge Rd
Fabius, NY 13063
315-683-5376

gaskets

Mail order and open shop. 6 days by chance, call first. NOS gaskets, car, truck, tractor, industrial. Light on classics.

Rubber Age LM Mfg Inc
13418 Halldale Ave
Gardena, CA 90249
310-329-2888; FAX: 310-532-4988
E-mail: rubberage@aol.com

rubber parts

See full listing in **Section Two** under **rubber parts**

Standard Abrasives
Motorsports Division
4201 Guardian St
Simi Valley, CA 93063
800-383-6001; 805-520-5800 ext 371
FAX: 805-577-7398
E-mail: tech@sa-motorsports.com

abrasives

See full listing in **Section Two** under **restoration aids**

glass

Airplane Plastics
9785 Julie Ct
Tipp City, OH 45371
937-669-2677; FAX: 937-669-2777

plastic
transparencies

Dealing in custom plastic transparencies. Windshields, headlamp shields, aircraft canopies. Restorations: customs, street rods, aircrafts and boats.

American Restorations Unlimited TA
14 Meakin Ave, PO Box 34
Rochelle Park, NJ 07662
201-843-3567; FAX: 201-843-3238
E-mail: amerrest@earthlink.net

engine
glass
restoration parts
transmission

Mail order and open shop. Monday-Saturday 8 am to 8 pm. Going on our 20th year keeping legends on the road. Represent over 175 manufacturers of restorations parts from 1928-1980s. Specialize in the following categories: glass-flat glass, curved for all American cars and trucks, T-tops for all years, we can even supply flat dash glass; transmission parts, parts and kits for automatic transmissions, 1940-1965 and up, also standard transmission parts starting with 1935. We now can rebuild your automatic or standard transmission; engine parts and rebuilding as well as complete gas tank restoration.

Blaser's Auto, Nash, Rambler, AMC
3200 48th Ave
Moline, IL 61265-6453
309-764-3571; FAX: 309-764-1155
E-mail: blazauto@sprynet.com

NOS parts

See full listing in **Section One** under **AMC**

Bob's Classic Auto Glass
21170 Hwy 36
Blachly, OR 97412
800-624-2130

glass

Daily 9 am to 9 pm. Flat auto glass for all makes and models, 1920-1960. No foreign. Also available: curved back windows for 1940-1948 Chevys, 1941-1948 Fords. Reproduced in clear, green, grey and bronze.

Custom Cut Auto Glass/ Southern Glass Inc 2605 Beltway 8 Pasadena, TX 77503 800-803-7778, 281-487-7778 FAX: 281-487-7779	**glass**

Mail order and open shop. Monday-Thursday 8 am to 5 pm, Friday 8 am to 4 pm. Windshields and glass for street rods and early model cars. V-bolt windshields, 1-piece side glasses for cars and trucks.

Bob Fatone's Mercedes Used Parts 166 W Main St Niantic, CT 06357 860-739-1923; FAX: 860-691-0669 E-mail: bobfatone@earthlink.net	**parts**

See full listing in **Section One** under **Mercedes-Benz**

The Glass House 446 W Arrow Hwy #4 San Dimas, CA 91773 909-592-1078; FAX: 909-592-5099	**glass**

Auto glass and related parts for antique auto, street rods, 1950s, 1960s cars. Complete installation also available.

Hometown Auto Glass 160 Kingsley Rd, PO Box 288 Burnt Hills, NY 12027 518-399-0164; FAX: 518-399-0173	**glass**

Open shop only. Monday-Friday 8:30 am to 6 pm, Saturday by appointment only. We custom cut flat glass in a variety of colors, windshields and backlights.

Jefferis Autobody 269 Tank Farm Rd San Luis Obispo, CA 93401 800-807-1937; FAX: 805-543-4757	**windshield glass kit**

Monday-Friday 8 am to 5 pm Pacific time. Glass: vintage or street rod, clear, green, gray or bronze tint. Safety laminated DOT approved, complete kits or pieces. One-piece curved windshield 1937-1940 Ford. Home of the V-Butt windshield. Shipped UPS, special packing, fully insured. Visa, MasterCard, Discover.

JLM Maud Rd, PO Box 1348 Palmer, AK 99645 907-745-4670; FAX: 907-745-5510 E-mail: jlmob@alaska.net	**power window lifts**

Mail order only. Power window lifts for all cars with flat glass. 12v conversion units. Web site: www.alaska.net/~jlmob

W L Wally Mansfield 214 N 13th St Wymore, NE 68466-1640 402-645-3546	**cars parts trucks**

See full listing in **Section Two** under **comprehensive parts**

N/C Industries Antique Auto Parts 301 S Thomas Ave, PO Box 254 Sayre, PA 18840 570-888-6216; FAX: 570-888-1821 E-mail: kdb@cyber-quest.com	**windshield frames**

Mail order and open shop. Monday-Friday 8 am to 5 pm. Specializing in windshield frames for almost all makes and models of cars and trucks. 1933-1934 Plymouth and Dodge parts.

OEM Glass Inc Rt 9 E, PO Box 362 Bloomington, IL 61702 800-283-2122, 309-662-2122 FAX: 309-663-7474	**auto glass**

Mail order only. Auto and truck glass for 1920-1976 cars and trucks. Specializing in original logos and date codes for show cars.

Pilkington Glass Search 1975 Galaxie St Columbus, OH 43207 800-848-1351; FAX: 614-443-0709	**glass parts**

Mail order and open shop. Monday-Friday 8 am to 6 pm Eastern time. Glass Search carries an inventory of over 70,000 glass parts. We have the auto glass you need. Original classic parts per original specifications. Corvette, Buick, Chevy, Olds, just to name a few. We also can supply original glass parts for Ferrari, Jaguar, Rolls-Royce and a number of exotic vehicles. Need a part cut to pattern? We can supply that also. Pilkington's Glass Search team is always ready to serve you. Web site: www.glasssearch.com

Redden's Auto Glass Engraving 7219 W 75 S Lafayette, IN 47909-9263 765-572-2293 E-mail: redden78@gte.net	**engraving**

Open by appointment only. Engrave any automobile, boat, truck, RV glass (excluding windshields) using a high speed drill. Equipment is portable so work can be done at customer's residence. Can engrave any design that can be photocopied.

The Reflected Image 21 W Wind Dr Northford, CT 06472 PH/FAX: 203-484-0760 E-mail: scott@reflectedimage.com	**mirror reproduction mirror resilvering**

See full listing in **Section Two** under **special services**

Rick's Relics Wheeler Rd Pittsburg, NH 03592 603-538-6612 E-mail: relics@aspi.net	**bodywork painting restoration**

See full listing in **Section Two** under **restoration shops**

Sanders Reproduction Glass PO Box 522 Hillsboro, OR 97123 503-648-9184	**glass**

Mail order only. Daily 8 am to 12 pm. Specializing in superior quality flat laminated safety glass for 1930s, 1940s, 1950s cars. Cut to original patterns, authentically detailed with sandblasted script, dated month and year, rounded polished edges and inlaid black edging. Meticulous craftsmanship is evident on every piece. Specializing in Fords, Lincolns and Mercs. Officially licensed product of Ford Motor Co.

Specialty Power Window 2087 Collier Rd Forsyth, GA 31029 800-634-9801; FAX: 912-994-3124	**power window kits windshield wiper kit**

See full listing in **Section Two** under **street rods**

Vintage Glass USA 326 S River Rd, PO Box 336 Tolland, CT 06084 800-889-3826, 860-872-0018	**auto glass**

Mail order and open shop. Monday-Friday 9 am to 5 pm Eastern time. Auto glass, flat and curved for American cars and trucks, 1915-1970.

Section Two – Generalists

grille emblem badges

Dwight H Bennett
1330 Ximeno Ave
Long Beach, CA 90804
PH/FAX: 562-498-6488

emblem repair
hardware repair
mascot repair
plaque repair

Mail order and open shop by arrangement, 7 days. Deals in repair, restoration and reproduction of metal cast and/or fabricated objects that other people say are irreparable such as: emblems, enameled emblems, chrome strips, trim, mascots, hardware, photo etched plaques, silkscreen plaques, white metal repair, door handles, knobs, etc. Also does prototyping and custom one-off pieces.

C & G Early Ford Parts
1941 Commercial St, Dept AH
Escondido, CA 92029-1233
760-740-2400; FAX: 760-740-8700
E-mail: cgford@cgfordparts.com

accessories/chrome
emblems
literature
mechanical
weatherstripping

See full listing in **Section One** under **Ford 1932-1953**

Classic Chevrolet Parts Inc
8723 S I-35
Oklahoma City, OK 73149
405-631-4400; FAX: 405-631-5999
E-mail: info@classicchevroletparts.com

parts

See full listing in **Section One** under **Chevrolet**

Comet Products
Cherry Parke 101-B
Cherry Hill, NJ 08002
856-795-4810; FAX: 856-354-6313

accessories
emblems

Mail order only. Manufacturer of car emblem badges for the front car grille. Over 500 types are available: countries, states, autos, auto clubs, military, fraternal organizations, etc. Also makes lapel pins, belt buckles, key chains, key fobs, decals, patches, country of origin ovals. Catalog, $3. Dept HV.

Concours Quality Auto Restoration
32535 Pipeline Rd
Gresham, OR 97080
503-663-4335; FAX: 503-663-3435

pot metal restoration
repro gloveboxes

See full listing in **Section Two** under **restoration shops**

D&D Automobilia
813 Ragers Hill Rd
South Fork, PA 15956
814-539-5653

plastic parts
steering wheels

See full listing in **Section Two** under **steering wheels**

Emblemagic Co
PO Box 420
Grand River, OH 44045-0420
440-209-0792
E-mail: emblemagic@aol.com

decorative
emblems
plastic insert
emblems

Sell, restore, reproduce clear top plastic insert emblems used on grille, trunk, interior and exterior, wheel hubs, etc. Also sell and restore cloisonne, enamel radiator badges or decorative emblems.

Enthusiast's Specialties
350 Old Connecticut Path
Framingham, MA 01701
800-718-3999; FAX: 508-872-4914
E-mail: alvis1934@aol.com

automobilia

See full listing in **Section Two** under **automobilia**

Mascots Unlimited
PO Box 666
Old Saybrook, CT 06475
PH/FAX: 860-388-1511
E-mail: rpearl@cyberzone.net

grille ornaments
hood ornaments

See full listing in **Section Two** under **radiator emblems & mascots**

Obsolete Ford Parts Inc
8701 S I-35
Oklahoma City, OK 73149
405-631-3933; FAX: 405-634-6815
E-mail: info@obsoletefordparts.com

parts

See full listing in **Section One** under **Ford 1954-up**

hardware

Antique Auto Fasteners
Guy (Chuck) Close
811 Oceanhill Dr
Huntington Beach, CA 92648
714-969-9161, 562-696-3307
E-mail: redjc1@earthlink.net

fasteners
hardware
hose clamps
molding clips

Mail order and open shop. Fasteners for upholstery and cloth tops. Molding trim clips and bolts. Match samples for most cars thru 1965. Stainless capped bumper bolts. Brass Sherman hose clamps. NOS Swiss and Ferro lock mechanisms for 1935-1936 Mopar, 1935-1949 Ford closed cars; miscellaneous springs; 1934-1955 inside door handles; 1939-1947 GM trunk handles. Striker plates, special screws and bolts, trim hardware, speed nuts, hinge pins, door checkstraps, pedal pads, assist straps and robe ropes. Illustrated catalog, $4. SASE.
See our ad on page 277

Auto Hardware Specialties
3123 McKinley Ave
Sheldon, IA 51201
712-324-2091; FAX: 712-324-2480
E-mail: rweber@rconnect.com

hardware fasteners

See full listing in **Section One** under **Chevrolet**

Dwight H Bennett
1330 Ximeno Ave
Long Beach, CA 90804
PH/FAX: 562-498-6488

emblem repair
hardware repair
mascot repair
plaque repair

See full listing in **Section Two** under **grille emblem badges**

Big Flats Rivet Co
35 Sunny Dell Cir
Horseheads, NY 14845
607-562-3501; FAX: 607-562-3711
E-mail: jim@bigflatsrivet.com

rivets
tools for riveting

Mail order only. Rivets and installation tools for all makes of antique autos. Round tire valve nuts (brass) for Fords and other early cars. Web site: www.bigflatsrivet.com

The Buckle Man
Douglas D Drake
28 Monroe Ave
Pittsford, NY 14534
716-381-4604

buckles

Strap buckles for all types of needs (I do not sell leather straps, only the buckles for your straps). These are NOS buckles, brass, nickel and black for all your restoration needs: sidemount and mirror tie downs, top and windshield strap buckles, trunk strap buckles, spring cover buckles, trunk and luggage strap buckles, etc. Whether it is for a brass era car or a classic, try The Buckle Man. Over 125 buckle styles, 10,000 in stock. Send Xerox copy of your needs and I will match to my stock.

C & G Early Ford Parts
1941 Commercial St, Dept AH
Escondido, CA 92029-1233
760-740-2400; FAX: 760-740-8700
E-mail: cgford@cgfordparts.com

| accessories/chrome |
| emblems |
| literature |
| mechanical |
| weatherstripping |

See full listing in **Section One** under **Ford 1932-1953**

Concours Quality Auto Restoration
32535 Pipeline Rd
Gresham, OR 97080
503-663-4335; FAX: 503-663-3435

| pot metal restoration |
| repro gloveboxes |

See full listing in **Section Two** under **restoration shops**

Fast Lane Products
PO Box 7000-50
Palos Verdes Peninsula, CA 90274
800-327-8669; FAX: 310-541-2235
E-mail: info@fastlaneproducts.com

| chamois |
| cleaners & waxes |
| drain tubs |
| hand wringers |

See full listing in **Section Two** under **car care products**

King Bolt Co
4680 N Grand Ave
Covina, CA 91724
626-339-8400; FAX: 626-339-8210

| hardware |

Mail order and open shop. Monday-Friday 8 am to 6 pm, Saturday 8 am to 5 pm. Deals in USS, SAE, metric-steel, grade 8, stainless, chrome nuts, bolts, screws, washers, pins, springs, clips, clamps, Heli coils, rod ends, Dzus, ARP, anchors, stainless braided hose and fittings, LEDs, switches, hitches, taps, dies, drilles, tools, etc.

M & R Products
1940 SW Blvd
Vineland, NJ 08360
800-524-2560, 609-696-9450
FAX: 609-696-4999
E-mail: mrproducts@mrproducts.com

| hardware |
| tie-downs |

See full listing in **Section Two** under **accessories**

Mr G's Enterprises
5613 Elliott Reeder Rd
Fort Worth, TX 76117
817-831-3501; FAX: 817-831-0638
E-mail: mrgs@mrgusa.com

| fasteners |
| screw kits |

See full listing in **Section One** under **Mopar**

MSC Fasteners
104 Oakdale Dr
Zelienople, PA 16063
800-359-7166, 724-452-8003
FAX: 724-452-1145
E-mail: msc999@ccia.com

| hardware |

Mail order only. Stainless steel and brass fasteners, ie: nuts, bolts, screws, washers, cotter pins, solid and threaded rod, clevis pins in American and metric sizes, best discounts anywhere. Web site: www.mscfasteners.com

Old Ford Parts
35 4th Ave N
Algona, WA 98001
253-833-8494; FAX: 253-833-2190

| parts |

See full listing in **Section One** under **Ford 1932-1953**

Section Two – Generalists

Pennsylvania Metal Cleaning 200 17th St Monaca, PA 15061-1969 724-728-5535	derusting stainless fasteners stripping

See full listing in **Section Two** under **rust removal & stripping**

Re-Flex Border Marker 138 Grant St Lexington, MA 02173 781-862-1343	border markers posts

Mail order only. Flexible border markers and posts for marking driveways, parking areas, work areas or anywhere that must be made more visible.

Restoration Supply Company 2060 Palisade Dr Reno, NV 89509 775-825-5663; FAX: 775-825-9330 E-mail: restoration@rsc.reno.nv.us	accessories restoration supplies

See full listing in **Section Two** under **restoration aids**

Specialty Fasteners 183 Blanchard Way Tecumseh, ON Canada N8N 2L9 519-727-4848; FAX: 519-727-4844 E-mail: lancastr@wincom.net	fasteners

Specializing in chrome and polished stainless fasteners. Engine kits for classics made to order. All sizes and materials. No catalogs. Motorcycle fasteners available. Specialize in Harley-Davidson.

Steelman/JS Products 5440-B S Procyon Ave Las Vegas, NV 89118 800-255-7011; FAX: 702-362-5084 E-mail: jsprodnlv@aol.com	tools

See full listing in **Section Two** under **tools**

Totally Stainless PO Box 3249 Gettysburg, PA 17325 717-677-8811; FAX: 717-677-4525 E-mail: info@totallystainless.com	stainless hardware

Mail order only. Stainless steel bolts, screws, nuts, washers, clamps and more. Offers the largest selection of US and metric fasteners available. Over 6,000 ready to install assembly kits are available. Web site: www.totallystainless.com

Visibolts From Classic Safety Products 7131 Hickory Run Waunakee, WI 53597 888-212-2163; FAX: 608-824-9200 E-mail: clovis@www.visibolts.com	accessories

See full listing in **Section Two** under **lighting equipment**

heaters

Autolux Inc 3121 W Coast Hwy, Ste 3D Newport Beach, CA 92663 949-574-0054; FAX: 949-645-3033	Mercedes parts

See full listing in **Section One** under **Mercedes-Benz**

Blaak Radiateurenbedryf Blaaksedyk oost 19 Heinenoord 3274LA Netherlands 31-186-601732; FAX: 31-186-603044 E-mail: info@blaak.com	radiators

See full listing in **Section Two** under **radiators**

Gas Tank and Radiator Rebuilders 20123 Hwy 362 Waller, TX 77484 800-723-3759 E-mail: donhart@donhart.com	abrasive blasting gas tank rebuilding heaters radiator repair

See full listing in **Section Two** under **fuel system parts**

Jack P Gross Assoc/Scott Manufacturing Inc 163 Helenwood Detour Rd, PO Box 97 Helenwood, TN 37755 423-569-6088; FAX: 423-569-6428 E-mail: scottmfg@highland.net	air hose products water hose products

See full listing in **Section Two** under **service shops**

A Petrik Restoration & Rebuilding Service 504 Edmonds Ave NE Renton, WA 98056-3636 425-466-5590, 425-255-4852 E-mail: rnrserv@qwest.net or rnrserv@hotmail.com	heater control valve rebuilding windshield regulators

Rebuilding of all Ranco and Harrison (thermostatic type) heater control valves, late 1930s into the 1960s, cars and trucks. Established 1972. Also complete restoration on windshield regulators: 1930s-1940s trucks and passenger cars. Our name says it all, Restoration & Rebuilding Service, that's all we do. No parts available. Web site: www.heatercontrolvalve.com (it figures).

Radiator & Gas Tank Specialist 20123 Hwy 362, PO Box 758 Waller, TX 77484 800-723-3759; FAX: 936-372-5032 E-mail: donhart@donhart.com	gas tanks heaters radiators

See full listing in **Section Two** under **radiators**

hubcaps

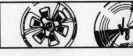

Binder's Auto Restoration and Salvage 1 Mile Maud Rd, PO Box 1144 Palmer, AK 99645 907-745-4670; FAX: 907-745-5510	salvage yard

See full listing in **Section Five** under **Alaska**

C & G Early Ford Parts 1941 Commercial St, Dept AH Escondido, CA 92029-1233 760-740-2400; FAX: 760-740-8700 E-mail: cgford@cgfordparts.com	accessories/chrome emblems literature mechanical weatherstripping

See full listing in **Section One** under **Ford 1932-1953**

Classic Chevrolet Parts Inc 8723 S I-35 Oklahoma City, OK 73149 405-631-4400; FAX: 405-631-5999 E-mail: info@classicchevroletparts.com	parts

See full listing in **Section One** under **Chevrolet**

Hubcap Mike 2465 N Batavia Orange, CA 92865 714-685-8801; FAX: 714-685-8804	**hubcaps** **wheelcovers**

We have the world's largest selection of hubcaps and wheelcovers covering 1940 to present. We offer same day shipping to anywhere in the world plus 30 day customer satisfaction guarantee.

Obsolete Ford Parts Inc 8701 S I-35 Oklahoma City, OK 73149 405-631-3933; FAX: 405-634-6815 E-mail: info@obsoletefordparts.com	**parts**

See full listing in **Section One** under **Ford 1954-up**

Al Trommers-Rare Auto Literature 614 Vanburenville Rd Middletown, NY 10940-7242	**automobilia/lit** **hubcaps** **wheelcovers**

See full listing in **Section Two** under **literature dealers**

Wirth's Custom Automotive 505 Conner St, PO Box 5 Prairie du Rocher, IL 62277 618-284-3359 E-mail: roywirth@htc.net	**custom accessories** **fender skirts** **spinner hubcaps**

See full listing in **Section Two** under **accessories**

ignition parts

Antique Auto Parts Cellar 6 Chauncy St, PO Box 3 South Weymouth, MA 02190 781-335-1579; FAX: 781-335-1925 E-mail: our1932@aol.com	**brake/chassis/** **engine parts** **fuel pumps/kits** **gaskets** **water pumps**

See full listing in **Section Two** under **comprehensive parts**

Atlas Obsolete Chrysler Parts 10621 Bloomfield St, Unit 32 Los Alamitos, CA 90720 PH/FAX: 562-594-5560 E-mail: atlaschrys@aol.com	**parts**

See full listing in **Section One** under **Mopar**

Battery Ignition Co Inc 91 Meadow St Hartford, CT 06114 860-296-4215; FAX: 860-947-3259 E-mail: biscokid@aol.com	**parts** **rebuilding** **rebushing**

See full listing in **Section Two** under **carburetors**

Baxter Auto Parts 9444 N Whitaker Rd (corporate office) Portland, OR 97217 800-765-3785; FAX: 503-246-4590	**accessories** **parts**

See full listing in **Section Two** under **comprehensive parts**

Dave Bean Engineering 636 E St Charles St SR3H San Andreas, CA 95249 209-754-5802; FAX: 209-754-5177 E-mail: admin@davebean.com	**parts**

See full listing in **Section One** under **Lotus**

Blaser's Auto, Nash, Rambler, AMC 3200 48th Ave Moline, IL 61265-6453 309-764-3571; FAX: 309-764-1155 E-mail: blazauto@sprynet.com	**NOS parts**

See full listing in **Section One** under **AMC**

Robert D Bliss 7 Pineview Ct Monroe, NJ 08831 732-521-4654	**electrical parts** **ignition parts**

See full listing in **Section Two** under **electrical systems**

Bronx Automotive 501 Tiffany St Bronx, NY 10474 718-589-2979	**parts**

Mail order only. Mostly parts for 1930-1970. Taillight lenses, ignition parts, fuel pumps, brakes, suspension parts, engine parts, other assorted parts. Carb kits, brake wheel cylinders and kits. Early high-performance manifolds, cams, carbs, valve covers, etc.

C & G Early Ford Parts 1941 Commercial St, Dept AH Escondido, CA 92029-1233 760-740-2400; FAX: 760-740-8700 E-mail: cgford@cgfordparts.com	**accessories/chrome** **emblems** **literature** **mechanical** **weatherstripping**

See full listing in **Section One** under **Ford 1932-1953**

CBS Performance Automotive 2605-A W Colorado Ave Colorado Springs, CO 80904 800-685-1492; FAX: 719-578-9485	**ignition systems** **performance products**

Mail order and open shop. Monday-Saturday 8 am to 6 pm. Never change points again! CBS Performance is your supplier for the Ignitor by Pertronix. The Ignitor replaces your points and condenser with an electronic ignition system that fits neatly inside your stock distributor cap. The Ignitor is available for most vehicles between 1956 and 1974 and is only $79. Call for more information. Web site: www.cbsperformance.com

Classic Chevrolet Parts Inc 8723 S I-35 Oklahoma City, OK 73149 405-631-4400; FAX: 405-631-5999 E-mail: info@classicchevroletparts.com	**parts**

See full listing in **Section One** under **Chevrolet**

Cole's Ign & Mfg 52 Legionaire Dr Rochester, NY 14617 PH/FAX: 716-342-9613	**battery cables** **ignition wire sets**

Ignition wire sets, custom made battery cables and ground straps, light wire supplies, brass hose clamps, Rajah terminals, air cleaner elements (dry type), auto loom, magneto ends, armored cab and more.

Collector's Auto Supply PO Box 1541 Peachland, BC Canada V0H 1X9 888-772-7848, 250-767-1974 FAX: 250-767-3340 E-mail: car@telus.net	**parts**

See full listing in **Section Two** under **comprehensive parts**

Robert Connole 2525 E 32nd St Davenport, IA 52807 319-355-6266	**ignition coils**

See full listing in **Section One** under **Packard**

Danspeed
5831 Date Ave
Rialto, CA 92377
909-873-5804, FAX: 909-875-7610
E-mail: danspeedtwo@aol.com

filters
gauges
ignition parts

See full listing in **Section Two** under **instruments**

Ferris Auto Electric Ltd
106 Lakeshore Dr
North Bay, ON Canada P1A 2A6
705-474-4560; FAX: 705-474-9453

parts
service

See full listing in **Section Two** under **electrical systems**

Green Mountain Vintage Auto
20 Bramley Way
Bellows Falls, VT 05101
PH/FAX: 802-463-3141
E-mail: vintauto@sover.net

damage appraisals
vehicle evaluations

See full listing in **Section Two** under **appraisals**

James Hill
935 Sunnyslope St
Emporia, KS 66801
620-342-4826 evenings/weekends
E-mail: jwhill@osprey.net

ignition parts
source list

See full listing in **Section One** under **Packard**

Ignition Distributor Service
19042 SE 161st
Renton, WA 98058
425-255-8052
E-mail: pjo@uswest.net

rebuild carbs
rebuild distributors
rebuild Turbos

Mail order only. Phone hours: Monday-Friday 8 am to 12 pm Pacific time. Rebuilding and modifying of Rochester Q-Zet carburetors, GM Turbo 350/400 transmissions and any year/make of American ignition distributor. Many parts and core assemblies available. Vacuum advances, points, condensers, etc.

J & C's Parts
7127 Ward Rd
North Tonawanda, NY 14120
716-693-4090; FAX: 716-695-7144

parts

See full listing in **Section One** under **Buick/McLaughlin**

Jacobs Electronics
500 N Baird St
Midland, TX 79701
915-685-3345, 800-627-8800
FAX: 915-687-5951
E-mail: jacobssales@caprok.net

ignition systems

Mail order, international and dosmetic dealers. High-performance ignition systems, including timing controls, anti-theft and nitrous safety systems. Web site: www.jacobselectronics.com

Kenneth L Johnson
550 Industrial Dr
Carmel, IN 46032
317-844-8154

distributor caps
parts
rotors

Hose clamps NOS original solid brass, double wire, Corbon spring wire self-tightening, strap. 1900 to 1980s. We know all your correct sizes. Quality parts for classics, Cadillac, LaSalle, Packard, Lincoln, Marmons 8- and 16-cyl, Pierce-Arrow plus others. Original Garlock water pump packing rings, cars, trucks, tractors, we know most all your correct sizes. Ignitions, mid 1920s-up. Distributor caps, rotors, points, voltage regulators, generator cut-outs, 4-, 6-, 8-, 12-, 16-cyl.

Ben McAdam
500 Clover Ln
Wheeling, WV 26003
304-242-3388, 304-242-0855
E-mail: antiquebenny@aol.com

electrical parts

Mail and phone order anytime. Open shop by appointment. Ignition parts 1913-1965. Electrical parts and points, distributor caps, rotors, condensers, generator and starter brushes. Abbott through Wolseley.

Donald McKinsey
PO Box 94H
Wilkinson, IN 46186
765-785-6284

fuel pumps
ignition parts
spark plugs

Mail order only. Obsolete spark plugs, obsolete shocks, 6-volt electric fuel pumps, some literature and voltage regulators. Also miscellaneous items.

MikeCo Antique, Kustom & Obsolete Auto Parts
4053 Calle Tesoro, Unit C
Camarillo, CA 93012
805-482-1725; FAX: 805-987-8524

lenses
parts

See full listing in **Section One** under **Mopar**

MSD Ignition
1490 Henry Brennan Dr
El Paso, TX 79936
915-857-5200; FAX: 915-857-3344
E-mail: msdign@msdignition.com

ignition parts

Manufacturer of high-performance ignition systems and accessories. Web site: www.msdignition.com

Northwestern Auto Supply Inc
1101 S Division
Grand Rapids, MI 49507
800-704-1078, 616-241-1714
FAX: 616-241-0924

parts

See full listing in **Section Two** under **engine parts**

Obsolete Ford Parts Inc
8701 S I-35
Oklahoma City, OK 73149
405-631-3933; FAX: 405-634-6815
E-mail: info@obsoletefordparts.com

parts

See full listing in **Section One** under **Ford 1954-up**

PerTronix Inc
440 E Arrow Hwy
San Dimas, CA 91773
909-599-5955; FAX: 909-599-6424
E-mail: rsherer@pertronix.com

electronic ignition

Manufacturer of the Ignitor® and Ignitor® II electronic ignition, retro-fit replacement for breaker points. Also Flame-Thrower® high performance coils, spark plug wires (Magx2 and Stock-Look) and HEI distributors. Web site: www.pertronix.com

Renner's Corner
10320 E Austin
Manchester, MI 48158
734-428-8424; FAX: 734-428-1090

bushings/hardware
carb/pump kits
gauges/gaskets
rebuild service

See full listing in **Section One** under **Ford 1932-1953**

Donald E Schneider Marinette & Menominee Auto Club
RR 1, N7340 Miles Rd
Porterfield, WI 54159
715-732-4958

parts

See full listing in **Section Two** under **comprehensive parts**

Silicone Wire Systems 3462 Kirkwood Dr San Jose, CA 95117-1549 E-mail: sethracer@aol.com	ignition wire sets

See full listing in **Section One** under **Corvair**

Skip's Auto Parts Skip Bollinger 1500 Northaven Dr Gladstone, MO 64118 816-455-2337; FAX: 816-459-7547 E-mail: carpartman@aol.com	chassis parts ignition parts water pumps

See full listing in **Section Two** under **water pumps**

Special Interest Autos 602 A St NE Ardmore, OK 73401 580-226-0270; FAX: 580-226-0233	parts restoration

See full listing in **Section Two** under **restoration shops**

Speed Service Inc 3049 W Irving Park Rd Chicago, IL 60618 773-478-1616; FAX: 773-478-1645	distributors engine rebuilding magnetos

Mail order and open shop. Monday-Saturday 9 am to 7 pm. Distributor and Vertex magneto specialists. Distributors rebuilt, no matter how old. We can also custom make magnetos and distributors. Complete competition engine rebuilding.

Ed Strain Inc 6555 44th St #2006 Pinellas Park, FL 33781 800-266-1623, 727-521-1597	magnetos

See full listing in **Section Two** under **special services**

Sunburst Technology PO Box 598 Lithia Springs, GA 30122 FAX: 770-942-6091 E-mail: sunburst2000@juno.com	electronic technical consultant

See full listing in **Section Four** under **information sources**

Taylor Auto Parts PO Box 650 Esparto, CA 95627 530-787-1929	bearings brakes gaskets seals

See full listing in **Section Two** under **comprehensive parts**

Vintage Auto Parts Inc 24300 Hwy 9 Woodinville, WA 98072 800-426-5911, 425-486-0777 FAX: 425-486-0778 E-mail: erics@vapinc.com	cars parts

See full listing in **Section Two** under **comprehensive parts**

instruments

12 Volt Stuff, Radio & Speedometer Repair Co 10625-A Trade Rd Richmond, VA 23236 804-423-1055, 888-487-3500 toll free FAX: 804-423-1059 E-mail: ecs@12voltstuff.com	radios

Mail order and open shop. Monday-Friday 8 am to 5:30 pm. Specializing in the repair of digital Buick, Cadillac, Corvette, Riviera, Toronado instrument clusters and EEC electronic climate controls, 1982-up. GM, Ford, Chrysler VDO mechanical and analog electronic speedometers, tachometers and odometer repair, 1965-up. Cable ratio adapters, boxes and electronic VSS (Drac) converters custom made. Exchange units available for nationwide next day air delivery. MasterCard, Visa, Discover, American Express and COD. We warranty the entire unit, not just the parts we use. On-site dyno for vehicle speed calibration. Web site: www.12voltstuff.com

Advanced Racing Technologies Inc 17 N Cross Rd Staatsburg, NY 12580 PH/FAX: 845-889-4499 E-mail: advancedracing@ compuserve.com	wheel alignment

See full listing in **Section Two** under **racing**

Atlas Obsolete Chrysler Parts 10621 Bloomfield St, Unit 32 Los Alamitos, CA 90720 PH/FAX: 562-594-5560 E-mail: atlaschrys@aol.com	parts

See full listing in **Section One** under **Mopar**

Backwoods Auto 487 Esperance Rd Esperance, NY 12066 518-875-6538 E-mail: backwoods_auto@hotmail.com	motorcycles repairs

See full listing in **Section Two** under **motorcycles**

Barnett & Small Inc 151E Industry Ct Deer Park, NY 11729 631-242-2100; FAX: 631-242-2101	electrical parts

See full listing in **Section Two** under **electrical systems**

Bill's Speedometer Shop 109 Twinbrook Pl Sidney, OH 45365 937-492-7800 E-mail: wheidemann@woh.rr.com	repairs restoration

Repair and restoration of speedometers for all cars 1900-1972. Cables and ratio drives to correct readings. Many NOS parts to make your speedometer look and feel great. Many heads, cables and drives for brass era cars.

Bob's Speedometer Service 32411 Grand River Ave Farmington, MI 48336 800-592-9673; FAX: 248-473-5517	gauges speedometers tachometers

Mail order and open shop. Monday-Friday 8 am to 5 pm Eastern time. Speedometers, tachometers, clocks, gauges, clusters, gas tank sending units, GM cruise controls, cables and castings, ratio boxes for automobiles, trucks, customs, hot rods, boats, military, fire engines, motorcycles, bicycles, complete repair, restoration and customizing, 1883-present. Web site: www.bobsspeedometer.com

See our ad on this page

The Clockworks 1745 Meta Lake Ln Eagle River, WI 54521 800-398-3040; FAX: 715-479-5759 E-mail: clockwks@nnex.net	clock service

Automobile clock service and quartz conversions. All makes and models, 1930s-1980s, serviced from $39.95. Quartz conversions from $59.95. Most service completed within 24 hours. MasterCard and Visa welcome. Over 15,000 serviced since 1988. Web site: www.clockwks.com

Corvette Clocks by Roger 24 Leisure Ln Jackson, TN 38305 901-664-6120; FAX: 901-664-1627	repair restoration

Mail order and open shop. Monday-Friday 8 am to 5 pm. Specializing in the repair/restoration of 53-82 Corvette speedometers, tachometers, small gauges, complete instrument clusters, glovebox doors, clocks both mechanical and quartz conversions, wiper motors, headlight motors and radios, Corvette Clocks by Roger has an established reputation in the Corvette world for excellence in this field. We also stock KHE radios. Should you have questions, our staff is ready to assist you.

D&D Instruments Inc 770 Kasota Ave Minneapolis, MN 55414 612-378-1224; FAX: 612-378-1445 E-mail: cselby@ddinstruments.com	gauges instruments

Specializing in the repair and restoration of instruments and gauges for all makes and models of domestic and foreign cars and trucks. Web site: www.ddspeedometer.com

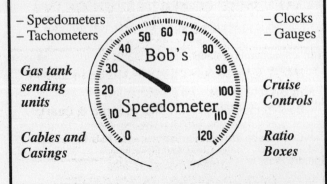

LET US DO IT, WE KNOW HOW! LET US DO IT, WE KNOW HOW!

Bob's Speedometer

Bob's Speedometer
32411 Grand River Ave.   *Est. 1929*
Farmington, MI 48336
www.bobspeedometer.com

1-800-592-9673
(248) 473-9006
FAX: (248) 473-5517
bobspeedometer@aol.com

Clusters

– Speedometers
– Tachometers

– Clocks
– Gauges

Gas tank sending units

Cruise Controls

Cables and Casings

Ratio Boxes

**Automobiles • Trucks • Military Vehicles • Boats
Fire Engines • Motorcycles • Bicycles**

Complete Repair, Restoration and Custom

We Buy!

LET US DO IT, WE KNOW HOW! LET US DO IT, WE KNOW HOW!

Danspeed 5831 Date Ave Rialto, CA 92377 909-873-5804, FAX: 909-875-7610 E-mail: danspeedtwo@aol.com	filters gauges ignition parts

Mail order only. K&N filters, Tavia, Hypertech computer chips, MSD ignition, autometer gauges, Stage 8 locking fasteners. We have carried these six lines since 1990 and we have a complete inventory in stock.

Development Associates 12791-G Newport Ave Tustin, CA 92780 714-730-6843; FAX: 714-730-6863 E-mail: devassoc@yahoo.com	electrical parts

See full listing in **Section Two** under **electrical systems**

Dials For Cars/Scott Young 332 Devon Dr San Rafael, CA 94903 415-472-5126	instruments

Mail order only. Furnishing dash glass and metal instrument dial restoration for over 20 years. Dash glass silkscreened (numbers on glass) for speedometers, clocks and radios. In-stock dash glass for over 200 cars in the 1930s, 1940s and early 1950s. Authentic metal dial restoration (numbers on metal). Our process is appropriate for show cars or cars of value.

Electronic Safety Products Inc 6350 Westhaven Dr, Ste N Indianapolis, IN 46254 800-683-6654, 317-295-4142 E-mail: drivalert@aol.com	safety devices

Mail order and open shop. Monday-Friday 8 am to 5 pm. Electronic automotive safety devices, ie: Sam, fatigue monitor; deer alert, digital backup warning system. Web site: www.driverfatigue.com

Fifth Avenue Antique Auto Parts 415 Court St Clay Center, KS 67432 785-632-3450; FAX: 785-632-6154 E-mail: fifthave@oz-online.net	cooling systems electrical systems fuel systems

See full listing in **Section Two** under **electrical systems**

Fred's Classic Auto Radio & Clocks 7908 Gilette Lenexa, KS 66215 913-599-2303	clock repair radio repair

See full listing in **Section Two** under **radios**

Haneline Products Co PO Box 430 Morongo Valley, CA 92256 760-363-6597; FAX: 760-363-7321	gauges instrument panels stainless parts trim parts

See full listing in **Section Two** under **accessories**

Harter Industries Inc PO Box 502 Holmdel, NJ 07733 732-566-7055; FAX: 732-566-6977 E-mail: harter101@aol.com	parts restoration

See full listing in **Section Two** under **comprehensive parts**

<table>
<tr><td>Instrument Services Inc
11765 Main St
Roscoe, IL 61073
800-558-2674; FAX: 815-623-9180</td><td align="right">clocks
gauges
instruments</td></tr>
</table>

Mail order and open shop. Monday-Friday 8 am to 4:30 pm. Restore and service all makes and models of foreign and domestic clocks, speedos, tachs, clusters, gas tank sending units and GM cruise controls. Car, truck, motorcycle, tractor and marine. Do-it-yourself original electric and quartz conversion kits with free how-to video. Complete Corvette clocks, 1968-1982. Thousands of NOS clocks in stock. Free catalog.
See our ad on this page

<table>
<tr><td>David Lindquist,
Automobile Clock Repair
12427 Penn St
Whittier, CA 90602
562-698-4445</td><td align="right">clock repair</td></tr>
</table>

Mail order and open shop. Monday-Friday 1 pm to 7 pm Pacific time. Automobile clock repair services and automobile clock sales. Quartz conversions on most 1956-up domestic automobile clocks.

<table>
<tr><td>Jack Marcheski
100 Dry Creek Rd
Hollister, CA 95023
831-637-3453
E-mail: jmar1@hollinet.com</td><td align="right">12/6-volt converters
rebuilding
repair</td></tr>
</table>

See full listing in **Section Two** under **electrical systems**

<table>
<tr><td>Palo Alto Speedometer Inc
718 Emerson St
Palo Alto, CA 94301
650-323-0243; FAX: 650-323-4632
E-mail: pacspeedo@pacbell.net</td><td align="right">instruments</td></tr>
</table>

See full listing in **Section One** under **Mercedes-Benz**

<table>
<tr><td>Reynolds Speedometer Repair
2631 River Reach Dr
Naples, FL 34104
941-643-4103</td><td align="right">repair
restoration
sales</td></tr>
</table>

Mail order and open shop. Quality repair and restoration of American and European speedometers, tachometers, cables, gauges, dial and glass refinishing, plating. NOS and restored units for sale.

<table>
<tr><td>Roadrunner Tire & Auto
4850 Hwy 377 S
Fort Worth, TX 76116
817-244-4924</td><td align="right">restoration
speedometer repair</td></tr>
</table>

See full listing in **Section Two** under **restoration shops**

<table>
<tr><td>Speed-o-Tac
3328 Silver Spur Ct
Thousand Oaks, CA 91360
805-492-6600</td><td align="right">repairs
restoration</td></tr>
</table>

Mail order and open shop. 6 days 9 am to 5 pm. Dealing in repair, service and restoration of vintage and classic mechanical speedometers and tachometers, including the following: Stewart-Warner, SS White, Waltham, AC Delco, GM, King Seeley, Ford, Chrysler, Motometer US, Motometer European; all VDO instruments: Porsche, M-B, BMW, VW, etc. Cables and ratio boxes made to order (to correct cable input to the speedometer). SASE for free data sheet to determine ratio needs. Call before shipping instrument for repair.

<table>
<tr><td>The Temperature Gauge Guy
172 Laurel Hill Dr
S Burlington, VT 05403
802-862-6374</td><td align="right">temperature gauges</td></tr>
</table>

Temperature gauge problems? We are continuing the same reliable service of over 35 years, just a new captain at the helm. Still no radiator caps or electrics, still guaranteed service.

<table>
<tr><td>Vintage Restorations
The Old Bakery
Windmill Street, Tunbridge Wells
Kent, TN2 4UU England
UK 1892-525-899
FAX: UK 1892-525499
E-mail: instruments@
vintagerestorations.com</td><td align="right">accessories
instruments</td></tr>
</table>

Mail order and open shop by appointment only. Specializing in the complete restoration, supply and fabrication of instruments and dashboard accessories, mostly for European sports and exotic cars such as Alfa Romeo, Alvis, Aston Martin, Bentley, Bugatti, Ferrari, Maserati, MG, Rolls-Royce and Riley. Master-Card and Visa accepted. Send for leaflet or look us up on the web site: www.mgcars.org.uk/vr/

<table>
<tr><td>Westberg Manufacturing Inc
3400 Westach Way
Sonoma, CA 95476
800-400-7024
707-938-2121
FAX: 707-938-4968
E-mail: westach@juno.com</td><td align="right">gauges/instruments
tachometers</td></tr>
</table>

Mail order and open shop. Dual 2-1/16 gauges available. In business 57 years. Web site: www.westach.com

<table>
<tr><td>The Wheel Shoppe Inc
13635 SE Division St
Portland, OR 97236
503-761-5119
FAX: 503-761-5190
E-mail: rogeradams@
thewheelshoppe.com</td><td align="right">parts
steering wheels</td></tr>
</table>

See full listing in **Section Two** under **steering wheels**

XKs Unlimited
850 Fiero Ln
San Luis Obispo, CA 93401
800-444-5247; FAX: 805-544-1664
E-mail: xksunltd@aol.com

instruments
parts
restorations

See full listing in **Section One** under **Jaguar**

insulation

Design Engineering Inc
36960 Detroit Rd
Avon, OH 44011
440-934-0800; FAX: 440-934-0067
E-mail: sales@designengineering.com

insulation

Mail order only. Deals in thermal management and heat protection products such as insulation material, exhaust wrap and hoses and wiring protection. Web site: www.designengineering.com

insurance

American Collectors Insurance Inc
498 Kings Hwy N, PO Box 8343
Haddonfield, NJ 08033
800-360-2277, 856-779-7212
FAX: 856-779-7289
E-mail: aci1americancollectors.net

insurance

Collector vehicle insurance, outstanding, low cost, agreed value insurance for collector vehicles, antiques, street rods, muscle cars and motorcycles. If it is 15 years or older, we could save you money. For 25 years collectors have been insuring their vehicles with us. Please call or visit our web site: www.americancollectorsins.com

Armstrong's Classic Auto Appraisals
3298 E Old State Rd
Schenectady, NY 12303
518-355-1387

appraisals
insurance

See full listing in **Section Two** under **appraisals**

ARS Automotive Research Services
Division of Auto Search International
1702 W Camelback #301
Phoenix, AZ 85015
602-230-7111; FAX: 602-230-7282

appraisals
research

See full listing in **Section Two** under **appraisals**

Automobile Classics Appraisal Services
5385 S Cook Rd
College Park, GA 30349
404-761-0350; FAX: 404-761-3703
E-mail: johnboy30349@aol.com

appraisals

See full listing in **Section Two** under **appraisals**

Automotive Legal Service Inc
PO Box 626
Dresher, PA 19025
800-487-4947, 215-659-4947
FAX: 215-657-5843
E-mail: autolegal@aol.com

appraisals

See full listing in **Section Two** under **appraisals**

Car Values Plus
40 Plank Rd
Newburgh, NY 12550
845-561-3594; FAX: 845-561-1745
E-mail: jim@hvaa.com

appraisals

See full listing in **Section Two** under **appraisals**

Classic Car Lobby
Henri Simar Jr
Rue Des Combattants, 81
4800 Verviers Belgium
32-87335501; FAX: 32-87335122

insurance

Mail order and open shop. Monday-Saturday 9 am to 12 pm, 2 pm to 6 pm, closed Sunday. Specialist for classic car insurance and insurance broker.

Collector Car Insurance Inc
PO Box 414
Leo, IN 46765
219-627-3355, 800-787-7637
FAX: 219-627-6317

insurance

Automobile insurance for the specialty car market. Street rods, customs, antiques, exotics, Limited Edition vehicles up to 2001.

Environmentally Safe Products Inc
313 W Golden Ln
New Oxford, PA 17350
800-289-5693; FAX: 717-624-7089
E-mail: heidiz@low-e.com

insulation

See full listing in **Section Two** under **street rods**

Great American Insurance
Classic Collectors Program
PO Box 429569
Cincinnati, OH 45242-9569
800-252-5233; FAX: 513-530-8405
E-mail: classiccollectors@yahoo.com

insurance

Collectible auto insurance for antiques, classics, exotics, street rods, replicas, military vehicles and antique fire engines. Web site: www.classiccollectors.com

Grundy Worldwide
PO Box 1957
Horsham, PA 19044
800-338-4005; FAX: 215-674-5685

insurance

Collector vehicle insurance for collectible automobiles with no model, year limitation, no mileage limitation. Underwritten by A++ rated carrier, finest industry standards set and maintained. Available in all 50 states. Call today. Web site: www.grundy.com

Hagerty Classic Insurance
PO Box 87
Traverse City, MI 49685
800-922-4050; FAX: 616-941-8227

insurance

Provides agreed value coverage, superior service and exceptionally competitive rates for antique, classic, limited edition and special interest vehicles. Offers flexible mileage, usage and underwriting guidelines and a variety of appropriate liability packages to meet your needs. Trust your classic to nothing less than Hagerty Classic Insurance. For a quote, call or visit our web site: www.hagerty.com

Jesser's Auto Clinic
26 West St
Akron, OH 44303
330-376-8181; FAX: 330-384-9129

appraisals

See full listing in **Section Two** under **appraisals**

M & L Automobile Appraisal | appraisals
2662 Palm Terr
Deland, FL 32720
904-734-1761
386-734-1761 (effective 11/01)

See full listing in **Section Two** under **appraisals**

Motorsports Insurance Services | insurance
12240 Venice Blvd, Ste 30
Los Angeles, CA 90066
310-301-0333; FAX: 310-578-1309
E-mail: info@
motorsports-insurance.com

We specialize in all forms of insurance, servicing the motorsports community and automotive industry. Commercial businesses, as well as individuals. Web site: www.motorsports-insurance.com

CT Peters Inc Appraisers | appraisals
2A W Front St
Red Bank, NJ 07701
732-747-9450 Red Bank
732-528-9451 Brielle
E-mail: ctp2120@aol.com

See full listing in **Section Two** under **appraisals**

Pete Reinthaler Insurance | insurance
PO Box 2004
Bellaire, TX 77402-2004
800-689-1127, 713-669-1127
FAX: 713-864-2068
E-mail: par2004@ev1.net

Mail order and open shop. Monday-Friday 8:30 am to 5 pm. Antique auto insurance for all types of cars.

JC Taylor Antique Automobile Insurance Agency | insurance
320 S 69th St
Upper Darby, PA 19082
800-345-8290

Classic, antique, collector or modified automobile insurance. Web site: www.jctaylor.com

Tri-County Calabasas Insurance | insurance
Bob Rosenberg
23961 Craftsman Rd, Ste L
Calabasas, CA 91302
818-223-8383; FAX: 818-223-8181
E-mail: brosenberg@tcinsurance.com

Specializing in insurance for street rods, custom cars and collector cars. Web site: www.tcinsurance.com

Tri-State Insurance | insurance
(Member of Continental Western Group)
1 Roundwind Rd
Luverne, MN 56156
800-533-0303; FAX: 800-232-9925

Deals in insurance. Web site: www.tsic.com

Visibolts From Classic Safety Products | accessories
7131 Hickory Run
Waunakee, WI 53597
888-212-2163; FAX: 608-824-9200
E-mail: clovis@www.visibolts.com

See full listing in **Section Two** under **lighting equipment**

Zehr Insurance Brokers Ltd | insurance
65 Huron St
New Hamburg, ON Canada N0B 2G0
519-662-1710; FAX: 519-662-2025
E-mail: info@zehrinsurance.com

Mail order and open shop. Monday-Friday 9 am to 5 pm. Special rated auto insurance for antique, classic, special interest automobiles plus all lines of general insurance in Ontario. Web site: www.zehrinsurance.com

interiors & interior parts

AAC Restorations | seat springs
Rt 1 Box 409
Mount Clare, WV 26408
304-622-2849

See full listing in **Section Two** under **upholstery**

ABC Auto Upholstery & Top Company | upholstery
1634 Church St
Philadelphia, PA 19124
215-289-0555

See full listing in **Section One** under **Ford 1954-up**

Accurate Auto Tops & Upholstery Inc | tops / upholstery
Miller Rd & W Chester Pike
Edgemont, PA 19028
610-356-1515; FAX: 610-353-8230

See full listing in **Section Two** under **upholstery**

All Seams Fine | interior restorations
23 Union St
Waterbury, VT 05676
800-244-7326 (SEAM), 802-244-8843

See full listing in **Section Two** under **upholstery**

American Plastic Chrome | replating plastic
8812 Hannan Rd
Wayne, MI 48184-1557
313-721-1967 days
313-261-4454 eves

See full listing in **Section Two** under **plastic parts**

Andover Restraints Inc | seat belts
PO Box 2651
Columbia, MD 21045
410-381-6700; FAX: 410-381-6703
E-mail: andoauto@clark.net

Mail order and open shop. Monday-Friday 9 am to 6 pm Eastern time. Seat belts for most cars and trucks including retrofits for domestic and imported vehicles prior to seat belts being factory installed. Retail, wholesale. Web site: www.andoauto.com

Arrow Fastener Co Inc | nail guns / rivet tools / staple guns
271 Mayhill St
Saddle Brook, NJ 07663

See full listing in **Section Two** under **tools**

Auto Custom Carpet Inc | carpets / floor mats
1429 Noble St, PO Box 1350
Anniston, AL 36201
800-633-2358, 256-236-1118
FAX: 800-516-8274

See full listing in **Section Two** under **carpets**

Auto-Mat Co	accessories
69 Hazel St	carpet sets
Hicksville, NY 11801	interiors
800-645-7258 orders	tops
516-938-7373; FAX: 516-931-8438	upholstery
E-mail: browner5@ix.netcom.com	

Mail order and open shop. Monday-Friday 8 am to 5 pm, Saturday 8 am to 1 pm. Specializing in auto interior restorations and accessories for all years and models, foreign and domestic, cars and trucks since 1956. Work can be done on cars (or just seats) in our large installation department, or ready made products can be shipped for do-it-yourself installation. Carpet sets, upholstery kits, seat covers, door panels, dashes, tops, headliners, trunk mats, rubber mats, personalized carpet mats, steering wheels, sheepskins, car covers, Recaro seats and more. Send $1 for catalog or visit our showroom. Web site: www.autointeriors.net

Auto Upholstery Unlimited	upholstery supplies
36 Glenmoor Dr	
East Haven, CT 06512	
203-467-6433; FAX: 203-484-5199	

Mail order only. Supplying original equipment NOS seat fabrics and vinyls, snaps and fasteners. Send sample of material needed and SASE for free match. Yardage available.

Automotive Interiors	carpets
PO Box 492	floor mats
Wilbraham, MA 01095	interiors
PH/FAX: 413-796-3950	
E-mail: info@automotiveinteriors.com	

Mail order and internet only. Automotive interiors (custom, slip-on, animal print), molded carpets, headliners, floor mats, cargo liners, dash covers and other miscellaneous accessories. Web site: www.automotiveinteriors.com

BAS Ltd Jaguar Trim Specialist	interior parts
250 H St, PMB 3000	
Blaine, WA 98231	
800-661-5377; FAX: 640-990-9988	
E-mail: basjag@telus.net	

See full listing in **Section One** under **Jaguar**

Berkshire Auto's Time Was	restoration
10 Front St, Box 347	
Collinsville, CT 06022	
860-693-2332	
E-mail: obteddi3@aol.com	

See full listing in **Section Two** under **restoration shops**

Bob's Bird House	parts
124 Watkin Ave	
Chadds Ford, PA 19317	
610-358-3420; FAX: 610-558-0729	

See full listing in **Section One** under **Thunderbird**

Bob's Classic Auto Glass	glass
21170 Hwy 36	
Blachly, OR 97412	
800-624-2130	

See full listing in **Section Two** under **glass**

Bob's Rod & Custom	car assembly
866 W 3200 S	fabrication
Nibley, UT 84321	interiors
435-752-7467	
E-mail: bobsrod@cache.net	

See full listing in **Section Two** under **street rods**

Buenger Enterprises/	dehumidifiers
GoldenRod Dehumidifier	
3600 S Harbor Blvd	
Oxnard, CA 93035	
800-451-6797; FAX: 805-985-1534	

See full listing in **Section Two** under **car care products**

Canadian Mustang	parts
20529 62 Ave	
Langley, BC Canada V3A 8R4	
604-534-6424; FAX: 604-534-6694	
E-mail: parts@canadianmustang.com	

See full listing in **Section One** under **Mustang**

CARS Inc	interiors
1964 W 11 Mile Rd	
Berkley, MI 48072	
248-398-7100; FAX: 248-398-7078	
E-mail: carsinc@veriomail.com	

Mail order and open shop. Monday-Friday 8:30 am to 5:30 pm, Saturday 8:30 am to 2 pm. Original style interiors, parts and heavy gauge sheetmetal products for 1955-1972 full-size Chevys, 1964-1972 Chevelle and El Camino, 1967-1976 Camaro, 1962-1972 Nova, 1970-1972 Monte Carlo, 1955-1957 Cameos and 1967-1972 Chevy pickups. Web site: www.carsinc.com

Cascade Audio Engineering	soundproofing
19135 Kiowa Rd	materials
Bend, OR 97702	
541-389-6821; FAX: 541-389-5273	
E-mail: cae@hwy97.net	

Mail order and open shop. We manufacture high performance, lightweight sound deadening materials and thermal control products, engineered for a variety of automotive applications. Web site: www.cascadeaudio.com

Cerullo Performance Seating	seating
2853 Metropolitan Pl	
Pomona, CA 91767	
909-392-5561; FAX: 909-392-8544	
E-mail: cerullo@tstonramp.com	

Mail order and open shop. Monday-Friday 8 am to 3:30 pm. Seating for sports cars, trucks, SUVs and street rods. Web site: www.cerullo.com

Stan Chernoff	mechanical parts
1215 Greenwood Ave	restoration parts
Torrance, CA 90503	technical info
310-320-4554; FAX: 310-328-7867	trim parts
E-mail: az589@lafn.org	

See full listing in **Section One** under **Datsun**

Chevelle World Inc	parts
PO Box 926	
Noble, OK 73068	
405-872-0379; FAX: 405-872-0385	

See full listing in **Section One** under **Chevelle/Camaro**

Cheyenne Pickup Parts	body panels
Box 959	bumpers
Noble, OK 73068	carpet
405-872-3399; FAX: 405-872-0385	weatherstripping
E-mail: sales@cheyennepickup.com	

See full listing in **Section One** under **Chevrolet**

Classic Chevrolet Parts Inc	parts
8723 S I-35	
Oklahoma City, OK 73149	
405-631-4400; FAX: 405-631-5999	
E-mail: info@classicchevroletparts.com	

See full listing in **Section One** under **Chevrolet**

Classic Creations of Central Florida
3620 Hwy 92E
Lakeland, FL 33801
863-665-2322; FAX: 863-666-5348
E-mail: flclassics@aol.com

parts
restoration
service

See full listing in **Section One** under **Mustang**

Classtique Upholstery Supply
PO Box 278-H
Isanti, MN 55040
763-444-4025, 763-444-3768
FAX: 763-444-9980

carpet sets
headliners

Mail order and store sales. Dealing in ready to install carpet sets, headliners, convertible tops and many related parts for most American cars 1950s-1970s. All GM, Ford, Chrysler, etc cars. Advise year and body style of car, send samples if possible for match. Established 1959. Free catalog on request.

Classtique Upholstery & Top Co
PO Box 278 HK
Isanti, MN 55040
763-444-4025; FAX: 763-444-9980

top kits
upholstery kits

See full listing in **Section One** under **Ford 1903-1931**

Color-Plus Leather Restoration System
106 Harrier Ct, 3767 Sunrise Lake
Milford, PA 18337-9315
570-686-3158; FAX: 570-686-4161
E-mail: jpcolorplus@pikeonline.net

leather conditioning
leather dye

See full listing in **Section Two** under **leather restoration**

Comfy/Inter-American Sheepskins Inc
1346 Centinela Ave
West Los Angeles, CA 90025-1901
800-521-4014; FAX: 310-442-6080
E-mail: sales@comfysheep.com

floor mats
seat covers

Mail order and open shop. Monday-Friday 7:30 am to 5 pm, Saturday 10 am to 4 pm. Specializing in sheepskin seat covers and sheepskin floor mats for most all automobiles and airplanes. Also offer sheepskin accessories: heel pads, seat belt covers, steering wheel covers, wash mitts. Web site: www.comfysheep.com

Concours Quality Auto Restoration
32535 Pipeline Rd
Gresham, OR 97080
503-663-4335; FAX: 503-663-3435

pot metal restoration
repro gloveboxes

See full listing in **Section Two** under **restoration shops**

Corbeau USA
727 W 14881 S
Bluffdale, UT 84065
801-255-3737; FAX: 801-255-3222
E-mail: info@corbeau.com

bucket seats

Custom bucket seats for street, race and off-road vehicles. Available in cloth, leather and vinyl. Web site: www.corbeau.com

Dom Corey Upholstery & Antique Auto
1 Arsene Way
Fairhaven Business Park
Fairhaven, MA 02719
508-997-6555

carpets/seats
conv tops
dash covers
door panels
headliners
upholstery

Mail order and open shop. Monday-Friday 8:30 am to 5 pm Eastern time. Specializing in vehicle interiors, both new and old (1902-1998). Custom design interiors and redo originals as needed. Mostly car show and muscle cars as well as 1920s-1950s. Seats, carpets, door panels, headliners, convertible tops, dash covers, tonneau covers, motorcycles, trucks, Land Rovers, boat tops, etc.

Corvair Ranch Inc
1079 Bon-Ox Rd
Gettysburg, PA 17325
717-624-2805; FAX: 717-624-1196

auto sales
parts
restoration
service

See full listing in **Section One** under **Corvair**

Corvette America
Rt 322, PO Box 324
Boalsburg, PA 16827
800-458-3475
814-364-2141 foreign
FAX: 814-364-9615, 24 hours
E-mail: vettebox@corvetteamerica.com

accessories
interiors
parts

See full listing in **Section One** under **Corvette**

Corvette Specialties of MD Inc
1912 Liberty Rd
Eldersburg, MD 21784
410-795-3180; FAX: 410-795-3247

parts
restoration
service

See full listing in **Section One** under **Corvette**

Corvette World
RD 9, Box 770, Dept H
Greensburg, PA 15601
724-837-8600; FAX: 724-837-4420
E-mail: cvworld@sgi.net

accessories
parts

See full listing in **Section One** under **Corvette**

Custom Auto Interiors by Ron Mangus
18127 Marygold Ave
Bloomington, CA 92316
909-877-9342; FAX: 909-877-1741
E-mail: customautointeriors@hotmail.com

accessories
carpet kits
die cast collectibles
seat frames

Mail order and open shop. Monday-Friday 9 am to 5 pm, Saturday by appointment only. Custom hot rod interiors and accessories. Call today for information about our book, *Custom Auto Interiors* by Don Taylor and Ron Mangus. If you are looking for seat frames, carpet kits, steering wheel wraps or die cast collectibles, call or e-mail for more information. Web site: www.customautointeriors.com

Custom Interiors
PO Box 51174
Indian Orchard, MA 01151
413-589-9176; FAX: 413-589-9178
E-mail: ci@customseatcovers.com

carpets
custom seat covers
interior parts

Interior parts for all makes and models from 1928 to 2001. We specialize in custom seat covers and carpets. Web site: www.customseatcovers.com

D&D Automobilia
813 Ragers Hill Rd
South Fork, PA 15956
814-539-5653

plastic parts
steering wheels

See full listing in **Section Two** under **steering wheels**

D&D Plastic Chrome Plating
925 Markey Dr
Bryan, OH 43506
419-260-2723; FAX: 419-636-3534
E-mail: hl20@webtv.net

plating

We metalize plastic and fiberglass parts for most makes and models of cars. We specialize in interior parts such as dash bezels, armrests, consoles, some outside parts for show cars.

Section Two – Generalists

Dash Graining by Mel Erikson 31 Meadow Rd Kings Park, NY 11754 631-544-1102; FAX: 631-544-1107	dashboard restoration

See full listing in **Section Two** under **woodgraining**

Dash Specialists 1910 Redbud Ln Medford, OR 97504 541-776-0040	interiors

See full listing in **Section One** under **Cadillac/LaSalle**

Dashhugger PO Box 933 Clovis, CA 93613 559-298-4529; FAX: 559-298-3428 E-mail: info@dashhugger.com	dashboard covers

Mail order only. High quality dashboard covers for all makes and models of cars, trucks and vans. Web site: www.dashhugger.com

Dashtop by Palco Ind Inc 5980 Alpha Ave Reno, NV 89506 775-677-0766; FAX: 775-677-8248	dashboard covers door panels

Open Monday-Friday 7 am to 4 pm Pacific time. Manufacturer of molded plastic dashboard covers designed to fit over existing dashboards, replacement door panels, replacement padded armrests and other plastic interior and exterior components. Web site: www.dashtop.com

Dave's Auto Restoration 2285 Rt 307 E Jefferson, OH 44047 PH/FAX: 216-858-2227 E-mail: davesauto@knownet.net	upholstery restoration

Open shop. Monday-Friday 8:30 am to 5:30 pm. Specializing in automotive upholstery for all makes and models, Porsche, Jaguar, Mercedes, Rolls-Royce, Bentley, Packard, Ferrari, Pierce-Arrow, Duesenberg and Auburn, Cord, 1900-present. Reconditioned Porsche Targa tops by mail order. Web site: www.geocities.com/davesautorest

Dearborn Classics PO Box 7649 Bend, OR 97708-7649 800-252-7427; FAX: 800-500-7886	accessories restoration parts

See full listing in **Section One** under **Ford 1954-up**

Diamond Trim Gary Nolan 10 Furbacher Ln #7 Aurora, ON Canada L4G 6W1 905-726-3221; FAX: 905-726-3277 E-mail: garynolan@diamondtrim.com	interiors

Automotive interior and top restoration, finest imported leathers, wools and canvas award winning interiors since 1983, quality concours workmanship guaranteed. Antique, classic, vintage and exotic. Web site: www.diamondtrim.com

Dodge City Vintage Dodge **Vehicles & Parts** 18584 Hwy 108, PO Box 1687 Jamestown, CA 95327 209-984-5858; FAX: 209-984-3285 E-mail: mike@dodgecityvintage.com	parts restoration research vehicles

See full listing in **Section One** under **Dodge**

Greg Donahue Collector Car **Restorations Inc** 12900 S Betty Pt Floral City, FL 34436 352-344-4329; FAX: 352-344-0015	parts restoration

See full listing in **Section One** under **Ford 1954-up**

Douglass Interior Products 2000 124th Ave NE Bellevue, WA 98005 800-722-7272, 425-455-2120 FAX: 425-451-4779 E-mail: rbd@dipi.com	leather hides vinyl

Deal in genuine leather hides, wide selection of colors in stock. All top selection European cowhide. Average size 55 sq ft. Also carry trim weight leather in selected colors. Vinyl, carpet and sheepskin, all in stock. Natural wool headliner fabrics and synthetic headliner material in a range of colors. Web site: www.dipi.com
See our ad on page 289

Mike Drago Chevy Parts 141 E St Joseph St Easton, PA 18042 PH/FAX: 610-252-5701 E-mail: dragomdcp@aol.com	Chevrolet parts

See full listing in **Section One** under **Chevrolet**

East Coast Chevy Inc Ol '55 Chevy Parts 4154A Skyron Dr Doylestown, PA 18938 215-348-5568; FAX: 215-348-0560	custom work parts restoration

See full listing in **Section One** under **Chevrolet**

The El Camino Store 57 B Depot Rd Goleta, CA 93117 805-681-8164; FAX: 805-681-8166 E-mail: ec@elcaminostore.com	parts

See full listing in **Section One** under **Chevelle/Camaro**

Emblemagic Co PO Box 420 Grand River, OH 44045-0420 440-209-0792 E-mail: emblemagic@aol.com	decorative emblems plastic insert emblems

See full listing in **Section Two** under **grille emblem badges**

Bob Fatone's Mercedes Used Parts 166 W Main St Niantic, CT 06357 860-739-1923; FAX: 860-691-0669 E-mail: bobfatone@earthlink.net	parts

See full listing in **Section One** under **Mercedes-Benz**

Walter A Finner 11131 Etiwanda Ave Northridge, CA 91326 818-363-6076	woodgraining

See full listing in **Section Two** under **woodgraining**

$\mathcal{F}$INE SCOTTISH LEATHER, FROM ANDREW MUIRHEAD & SON LTD., IS NOW AVAILABLE FOR THE DISCRIMINATING AUTO ENTHUSIAST. EXCLUSIVELY FROM DOUGLASS INTERIOR PRODUCTS.

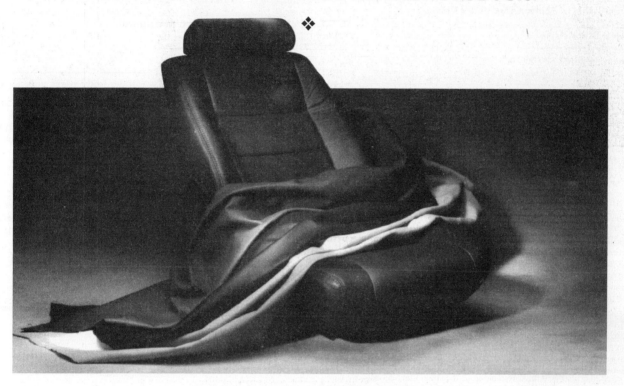

Selected from the top 5% of all European hides, Douglass Fine Scottish Leather™ is renowned for its stunning beauty and durability. Chosen, for example, more than any other leather by the world's leading airlines and aircraft manufacturers.

Renowned, too, for exceptional value. Large, clean hides provide superior cutting yields, at competitive square foot costs.

Finished at Scotland's famous Andrew Muirhead & Son tannery, our leather is full top grain, and aniline dyed for a deep, rich finish.

Our TRIM-WEIGHT™ leather, whose thin profile is ideal for hard-to-fit areas like glareshields and arm caps, is particularly suited for automobile applications. And consider our economical new Columbia™ multi-purpose synthetic fabric; it has a soft, leather-like appearance and extraordinary durability. We also carry woven-wool headliner fabrics that are easy-fitting and stretchable.

Most Douglass products are in stock and available for immediate shipment. For pricing information and complimentary samples, please call us at 800-722-7272.

DOUGLASS
INTERIOR PRODUCTS

425-455-2120. Or toll-free at 800-722-7272. www.dipi.com

Corporate Offices • 2000 124th Avenue N.E. • Bellevue, Washington 98005 • Telephone 800-722-7272 or 425-455-2120 • Fax 425-451-4779
East Coast Offices • Jet Center – Suite 350, 1100 Lee Wagener Blvd. • Ft. Lauderdale, Florida 33315 • Telephone 954-359-3610 • Fax 954-359-7812

Firewall Insulators & Quiet Ride Solutions
6465 Pacific Ave, Ste 249
Stockton, CA 95207
209-477-4840; FAX: 209-477-0918
E-mail: timcox@quietride.com

| air plenums |
| auto insulation |
| firewall insulators |
| gloveboxes |
| sound deadening |

See full listing in **Section Two** under **upholstery**

Foreign Autotech
3235 C Sunset Ln
Hatboro, PA 19040
215-441-4421; FAX: 215-441-4490
E-mail: fap1800@aol.com

parts

See full listing in **Section One** under **Volvo**

Golden State Parts
3493 Arrowhead Dr
Carson City, NV 89706
800-235-5717; FAX: 888-723-2495

parts

See full listing in **Section One** under **Chevrolet**

Hampton Coach
6 Chestnut St, PO Box 6
Amesbury, MA 01913
888-388-8726, 978-388-8047
FAX: 978-388-1113
E-mail: lbb-hc@greenet.net

fabrics
interior kits
top kits

See full listing in **Section One** under **Chevrolet**

Harmon's Incorporated
Hwy 27 N, PO Box 100
Geneva, IN 46740
219-368-7221; FAX: 219-368-9396
E-mail: harmons@harmons.com

interiors
parts

See full listing in **Section One** under **Chevrolet**

Hawthorne's Happy Motoring
Box 1332
Coaldale AB Canada T1M 1N2
PH/FAX: 403-345-2101

appraisals
parts

See full listing in **Section Two** under **appraisals**

Bill Hirsch Auto Parts
396 Littleton Ave
Newark, NJ 07103
973-642-2404; FAX: 973-642-6161
E-mail: hirschauto@aol.com

enamel lacquer
hubcaps
top material

See full listing in **Section Two** under **paints**

Hoffman Automotive Distributor
US Hwy #1, Box 818
Hilliard, FL 32046
904-845-4421

parts

See full listing in **Section Two** under **body parts**

Hollywood Classic Motorcars Inc
363 Ansin Blvd
Hallandale, FL 33009
954-454-4641; FAX: 954-457-3801

parts
restoration
service

See full listing in **Section One** under **Thunderbird**

Itsashoka Innovations
1215 Frazier Rd, PO Box 743
Albertville, AL 35950
256-891-4343; FAX: 256-891-0922

entry systems
hood kits
interior trim

See full listing in **Section Two** under **manufacturing**

Jeepsamerica
367 Washington St
Weymouth, MA 02189
781-331-4333; FAX: 781-331-6947
E-mail: mconsiglio1@yahoo.com

parts
service

See full listing in **Section One** under **Chrysler**

Jerry's Classic Cars & Parts Inc
4097 McRay Ave
Springdale, AR 72764
800-828-4584; FAX: 501-750-1682
E-mail: jcc@jerrysclassiccars.com

parts
restoration

See full listing in **Section One** under **Ford 1954-up**

Just Dashes Inc
5941 Lemona Ave
Van Nuys, CA 91411
800-247-DASH, 818-780-9005
FAX: 818-780-9014
E-mail: sales@justdashes.com

armrests
dash pads
door panels
headrests

Worldwide mail order and open shop. Monday-Friday 8 am to 5 pm. Manufactures and restores dash pads, molded door panels, dielectric heat stamped door panels, armrests and consoles using OEM materials and an exclusive thermo-forming process. Also available: reproduction, OEM, NOS and used dash pads. Specializing in vehicles 1954 and up. All work guaranteed. Web site: www.justdashes.com

K&D Enterprises
23117 E Echo Lake Rd
Snohomish, WA 98296-5426
425-788-0507; FAX: 360-668-2003
E-mail: tdb@halcyon.com

accessories
parts
restorations

See full listing in **Section One** under **Jensen**

Keleen Leathers Inc
10526 W Cermak Rd
Westchester, IL 60154
708-409-9800; FAX: 708-409-9801
E-mail: keleenlea@aol.com

                                        leather hides

Leather hides from automotive leather specialists. Have been serving automobile restorers for twenty years with top quality hides at the most competitive prices. Call us with your questions, whether you want to custom tan an exact match of your original leather or select from our hundreds of stock colors.

Dave Knittel Upholstery
850 E Teton #7
Tucson, AZ 85706
PH/FAX: 520-746-1588

                                        interiors
                                        tops
                                        upholstery

See full listing in **Section Two** under **upholstery**

Koala International
PO Box 255
Uwchland, PA 19480
610-458-8395; FAX: 610-458-8735
E-mail: sales@koala-products.com

                                        convertible cleaners
                                        & protectants
                                        plastic coating
                                        plastic polish

See full listing in **Section Two** under **car care products**

LeBaron Bonney Co
6 Chestnut St, PO Box 6
Amesbury, MA 01913
800-221-5408, 978-388-3811
FAX: 978-388-1113
E-mail: lbb-hc@greennet.net

                                        fabrics
                                        interior kits
                                        top kits

See full listing in **Section One** under **Ford 1903-1931**

Loga Enterprises
5399 Old Town Hall Rd
Eau Claire, WI 54701
715-832-7302
E-mail: logaent@cs.com

                                        interior parts

See full listing in **Section One** under **Studebaker**

Lutty's Chevy Warehouse
RD 2, 2385 Saxonburg Blvd
Cheswick, PA 15024
724-265-2988; FAX: 724-265-4773
E-mail: luttys@nauticom.net

                                        reproduction parts

See full listing in **Section One** under **Chevrolet**

Marcel's Corvette Shop Inc
1000 Waterford Rd
Mechanicville, NY 12118
518-664-7344; FAX: 518-664-2908
E-mail: marcel@marcelscorvette.com

                                        sales
                                        service
                                        parts

See full listing in **Section One** under **Corvette**

Melvin's Classic Ford Parts Inc
1521 Dogwood Dr
Conyers, GA 30012
770-761-6800; FAX: 770-761-5777

                                        parts

See full listing in **Section One** under **Ford 1954-up**

Muncie Imports & Classics
4401 Old St Rd 3 N
Muncie, IN 47303
800-462-4244; FAX: 317-287-9551
E-mail: mic@netdirect.net

                                        repair
                                        restoration
                                        upholstery

See full listing in **Section One** under **Jaguar**

Nova Parts
PO Box 985
Mount Washington, KY 40047
502-239-8487; FAX: 502-231-1397

                                        NOS parts
                                        reproduction parts
                                        used parts

See full listing in **Section One** under **Chevrolet**

Original Parts Group Inc
17892 Gothard St
Huntington Beach, CA 92647
800-243-8355 US/Canada
714-841-5363; FAX: 714-847-8159

                                        accessories
                                        parts

See full listing in **Section One** under **Pontiac**

OSJI
4301 Old St Rd 3 N
Muncie, IN 47303
800-338-8034; FAX: 765-213-4350
E-mail: osji@net.direct.net

                                        convertible tops
                                        interiors
                                        rubber seals

See full listing in **Section One** under **Jaguar**

The Paddock® Inc
221 W Main, PO Box 30
Knightstown, IN 46148
800-428-4319; FAX: 800-286-4040
E-mail: paddock@paddockparts.com

                                        accessories
                                        parts

See full listing in **Section One** under **Chevrolet**

Parts House
2912 Hunter St
Fort Worth, TX 76112
817-451-2708
E-mail: theparts@flash.net

                                        brake shoes/drums
                                        fenders
                                        sheetmetal repair
                                        panels

See full listing in **Section Two** under **comprehensive parts**

Parts Unlimited Inc
Cliff Carr
12101 Westport Rd
Louisville, KY 40245-1789
800-342-0610, 502-425-3766
FAX: 502-425-7910, 502-232-9784
E-mail: contactpui@aol.com

                                        interiors
                                        weatherstrips

See full listing in **Section One** under **Chevrolet**

Partwerks of Chicago
718 S Prairie Rd
New Lenox, IL 60451
815-462-3000; FAX: 815-462-3006
E-mail: partwerks9@aol.com

                                        parts
                                        service

See full listing in **Section Two** under **engine parts**

Paul's Jaguar
4073 NE 5th Terr
Oakland Park
Fort Lauderdale, FL 33334
954-846-7976; FAX: 954-846-9450
E-mail: paulsjag@aol.com

                                        parts

See full listing in **Section One** under **Jaguar**

RAU Restoration
2027 Pontius Ave
Los Angeles, CA 90025
310-445-1128; FAX: 310-575-9715
E-mail: wcrau@rau-autowood.com

                                        woodwork

See full listing in **Section Two** under **woodwork**

Section Two – Generalists

Ray's Upholstering
600 N St Frances Cabrini Ave
Scranton, PA 18504
800-296-RAYS; FAX: 570-963-0415

| partial/total restoration |

See full listing in **Section Two** under **restoration shops**

The Reflected Image
21 W Wind Dr
Northford, CT 06472
PH/FAX: 203-484-0760
E-mail: scott@reflectedimage.com

| mirror reproduction mirror resilvering |

See full listing in **Section Two** under **special services**

REM Automotive Inc
2610 N Brandt Rd
Annville, PA 17003
717-838-4242; FAX: 717-838-5091
E-mail: remautoinc@aol.com

| interior parts molded hood insulation trunk lining |

Supply manufactured soft good parts throughout the United States and Canada. Parts are die cut for precision fit for most all domestic cars. Production, warehousing and shipping is all done in our facility. Renowned for our ability to fabricate, in-house, nearly everything we sell, as well as develop customer generated special projects. At REM, the emphasis is on quality, products and delivery to the customer.

Restoration Specialties
John Sarena
124 North F St
Lompoc, CA 93436
805-736-2627
E-mail: showtimechevys@msn.com

| interiors restoration |

See full listing in **Section One** under **Chevrolet**

Ridgefield Auto Upholstery
34 Bailey Ave
Ridgefield, CT 06877
203-438-7583; FAX: 203-438-2666

| interiors tops |

Mail order and open shop. Monday-Friday 8 am to 6 pm, Saturday 8 am to noon. Foreign and domestic, antique to present, complete or partial interior replacement or restoration, convertible top, repair and replacement, custom made and ready made. One man shop assures strict attention to quality and detail. Custom work a speciality.

Rocky Mountain Motorworks Inc
1003 Tamarac Pkwy
Woodland Park, CO 80863
800-258-1996; FAX: 800-544-1084
E-mail: sales@motorworks.com

| accessories parts |

See full listing in **Section One** under **Volkswagen**

Rod Doors
PO Box 2160
Chico, CA 95927
530-896-1513; FAX: 530-896-1518
E-mail: sales@roddoors.com

| door panels interior parts |

Mail order only. Deals in designer door panels and interior parts for street rods and classic trucks. Web site: www.roddoors.com

---

Sailorette's Nautical Nook
451 Davy Ln
Wilmington, IL 60481
815-476-1644; FAX: 815-476-2524

| covers interiors |

See full listing in **Section Two** under **upholstery**

Harry Samuel
65 Wisner St
Pontiac, MI 48342-1066
248-335-1900
E-mail: samuelinteriors@aol.com

| carpet fabrics interiors upholstery covers |

Mail and phone orders. Soft trim for 1950-1977 Buick, Cadillac, Chevrolet, Ford, Lincoln, Mercury, Mopar, Oldsmobile and (specializing in) Pontiac. Cut, sewn and molded carpets for above cars plus NOS factory original carpets for 1961-1964 Buicks, Oldsmobiles and Pontiacs. Original seat upholstery covers for 1960-1965 Bonneville, Catalina Ventura, 2+2 and Grand Prix. Headliners, package trays, hood pads, trunk kits, vinyl and cloth yardage and more for all GM cars, some Chrysler and Ford cars. Web site: www.autointeriorsbyharrysamuel.com

---

Robert H Snyder
PO Drawer 821
Yonkers, NY 10702
914-476-8500
FAX: 914-476-8573, 24 hours
E-mail: cohascodpc@earthlink.net

| literature parts |

See full listing in **Section One** under **Cadillac/LaSalle**

Ssnake-Oyl Products Inc
114 N Glenwood Blvd
Tyler, TX 75702
800-284-7777; FAX: 903-526-4501

| carpet underlay firewall insulation seat belt restoration |

Seat belts restored to show quality condition. NOS seat belts, automotive insulation systems underlayment, water shields and firewall insulation. Specializing in seat belt restoration for 1950s, 1960s and 1970s. Visit our web site: www.ssnake-oyl.com

---

Sta-Dri Pouches/Beach Filler Products Inc
7682 Glenville Rd
Glen Rock, PA 17327
800-BEACH85; FAX: 717-235-4858
E-mail: beach@blazenet.net

| corrosion protection mildew protection moisture protection |

See full listing in **Section Two** under **storage care products**

Stilwell's Obsolete Car Parts
1617 Wedeking Ave
Evansville, IN 47711
812-425-4794

| body parts interiors parts |

See full listing in **Section One** under **Mustang**

Swedish Classics Inc
PO Box 557
Oxford, MD 21654
800-258-4422; FAX: 410-226-5543
E-mail: sales@swedishclassics.com

| parts |

See full listing in **Section One** under **Volvo**

Sweeney's Auto & Marine Upholstery Inc
dba Southampton Auto & Marine Upholstery
471 N Hwy, PO Box 1479
Southampton, NY 11969
516-283-2616; FAX: 516-283-2617

| carpets interiors tops |

See full listing in **Section One** under **Mercedes-Benz**

Thermax Inc
5385 Alpha Ave
Reno, NV 89506
888-THERMAX (843-7629)
FAX: 775-972-3478

| interior detailing |

See full listing in **Section Two** under **car care products**

Section Two – Generalists

Thunderbird Headquarters 1080 Detroit Ave Concord, CA 94518 925-825-9550 info; 925-689-1771 800-227-2174 parts FAX: 800-964-1957 toll free E-mail: tbirdhq@tbirdhq.com	**accessories** **literature** **parts** **upholstery**

See full listing in **Section One** under **Thunderbird**

Translog Motorsports 619-635 W Poplar St York, PA 17404 PH/FAX: 717-846-1885 E-mail: translogm@aol.com	**car dealer** **parts** **restoration**

See full listing in **Section One** under **Porsche**

Vicarage Jaguar 5333 Collins Ave, Ste 704 Miami Beach, FL 33140 305-866-9511; FAX: 305-866-5738 E-mail: vicarage@ix.netcom.com	**parts** **restoration**

See full listing in **Section One** under **Jaguar**

Wild Bill's Corvette & **Hi-Performance Center Inc** 446 Dedham St Wrentham, MA 02093 508-384-7373; FAX: 508-384-9366 E-mail: wildbillscorvette@ worldnet.att.net	**parts** **rebuilding** **service**

See full listing in **Section One** under **Corvette**

Willow Grove Auto Top 43 N York Rd Willow Grove, PA 19090 215-659-3276	**interiors** **tops** **upholstery**

Open shop only. Monday-Friday 8:30 am to 5:30 pm, Saturday by appointment. Auto interiors, auto tops & custom upholstery. Web site: www.wgautotop.com

Pat Wilson's Thunderbird Parts 375 Rt 94 Fredon Township, NJ 07860 888-262-1153; FAX: 973-579-2011 E-mail: wilsontb@nac.net	**parts**

See full listing in **Section One** under **Thunderbird**

Woolies (I&C Woolstenholmes Ltd) Whitley Way, Northfields Ind Estate Market Deeping Nr Peterborough, PE6 8AR England 0044-1778-347347 FAX: 0044-1778-341847 E-mail: info@woolies-trim.co.uk	**accessories** **trim** **upholstery**

Mail order and open shop. Monday-Friday 8:30 am to 5 pm, other times by appointment. Woolies trim, wing pipings, window channels, headlinings, leather/cloth and vinyls, duck and mohair hoodings, moquettes, carpets, felt and Hardura off-the-roll, Bedford cords, rubber and sponge extrusions, fasteners and draught excluders. Also extruded aluminum sections, leather renovation kits and black/polished pressed aluminum number plates, 3-1/2 inch and 3-1/8 inch digit size and goggles. Catalog, $3 (in bills). Web site: www.woolies-trim.co.uk

kit cars & replicars

AAdvanced Transmissions 15 Parker St Worcester, MA 01610 508-752-9674; FAX: 508-842-0672	**rear axle service** **restoration** **ring/pinion** **parts/sales/** **rebuilding/service**

See full listing in **Section Two** under **transmissions**

Bayliss Automobile Restorations 2/15 Bon Mace Close, Berkeley Vale Via Gosford NSW 2261 Australia 61-2-43885253; FAX: 61-2-43893152 E-mail: bayrest@ozemail.com.au	**repainting** **repairs** **sheetmetal work**

See full listing in **Section Two** under **restoration shops**

Birkin America PO Box 120982 Arlington, TX 76012 817-461-7431; FAX: 817-861-5867 E-mail: birkinam@aol.com	**cars** **replicas**

See full listing in **Section One** under **Lotus**

Classic Tube Division of Classic & Performance Spec Inc 80 Rotech Dr Lancaster, NY 14086 800-TUBES-11 (882-3711) 716-759-1800; FAX: 716-759-1014 E-mail: classictube@aol.com	**brake lines** **choke tubes** **fuel lines** **transmission lines** **vacuum lines**

See full listing in **Section Two** under **brakes**

Contemporary and Investment **Automobiles** 4115 Poplar Springs Rd Gainesville, GA 30507 770-539-9111; FAX: 770-539-9818 E-mail: contemporaryauto@ mindspring.com	**buy/sell/trade** **mechanical work** **memorabilia**

See full listing in **Section Two** under **street rods**

EVA Sports Cars RR 1 Vankleek Hill, ON Canada K0B 1R0 613-678-3377; FAX: 613-678-6110	**kit cars**

Open five days a week, Saturday by appointment. Cobra 427 replicar, space frame chassis, custom twin A-arm front suspension, NASCAR 4-bar rear set-up with Panhard rod. Partially assembled cars for $10,000. The Diva, 1950s style roadster, fiberglass body and tube steel space frame. In-house A-arm top and lower front suspension, 5-link rear, uses Chevy 350 cu in small block motor and vintage style model with Aero screens now available.

Fairlane Automotive Specialties 210 E Walker St St Johns, MI 48879 517-224-6460	**fiberglass bodies** **parts**

See full listing in **Section One** under **Ford 1932-1953**

Lee's Street Rods RR 3 Box 3061A Rome, PA 18837 570-247-2326 E-mail: lka41@epix.net	**accessories** **parts** **restoration**

See full listing in **Section Two** under **street rods**

Little Old Cars
3410 Fulton Dr NW
Canton, OH 44718
216-455-4685

| | model cars |

See full listing in **Section Two** under **models & toys**

Mild to Wild Classics
1300 3rd St NW
Albuquerque, NM 87102
505-244-1139; FAX: 505-244-1164

| | parts repairs restoration |

See full listing in **Section Two** under **street rods**

Operations Plus
PO Box 26347
Santa Ana, CA 92799
PH/FAX: 714-962-2776
E-mail: aquacel@earthlink.net

| | accessories parts |

See full listing in **Section One** under **Cobra**

Power Effects®
1800H Industrial Park Dr
Grand Haven, MI 49417
877-3POWRFX (376-9739) toll free
616-847-4200; FAX: 616-847-4210

| | exhaust systems |

See full listing in **Section Two** under **exhaust systems**

Prototype Research & Dev Ltd
David Carlaw
230 Albert Ln
Campbellford, ON Canada K0L 1L0
705-653-4525; FAX: 705-653-4800
E-mail: davidcarlaw@hotmail.com

| | fiberglass bodies |

See full listing in **Section One** under **Chevrolet**

Regal Roadsters Ltd
301 W Beltline Hwy
Madison, WI 53713
PH/FAX: 608-273-4141
E-mail: chuck@regaltbird.com

| | replicars restoration |

See full listing in **Section One** under **Thunderbird**

Rod Shop Performance Center Inc
1126 Rockledge Rd
Attalla, AL 35954
256-538-0376
E-mail: rodshop@
rodshopperformance.com

| | exhaust systems |

See full listing in **Section Two** under **exhaust systems**

Rodster Inc
128 Center St #B
El Segundo, CA 90245
310-322-2767; FAX: 310-322-2761

| | conversion kits |

See full listing in **Section Two** under **street rods**

Specialty Power Window
2087 Collier Rd
Forsyth, GA 31029
800-634-9801; FAX: 912-994-3124

| | power window kits windshield wiper kit |

See full listing in **Section Two** under **street rods**

Webber Engineering LLC
1 Alice Ct
Pawcatuck, CT 06379
860-599-8895; FAX: 860-599-8609
E-mail: kwebbereng@aol.com

| | street rods welding |

See full listing in **Section Two** under **sheetmetal**

leather restoration

All Seams Fine
23 Union St
Waterbury, VT 05676
800-244-7326 (SEAM), 802-244-8843

| | interior restorations |

See full listing in **Section Two** under **upholstery**

Auto-Mat Co
69 Hazel St
Hicksville, NY 11801
800-645-7258 orders
516-938-7373; FAX: 516-931-8438
E-mail: browner5@ix.netcom.com

| | accessories carpet sets interiors tops upholstery |

See full listing in **Section Two** under **interiors & interior parts**

Bassett Classic Restoration
2616 Sharon St, Ste D
Kenner, LA 70062-4934
PH/FAX: 504-469-2982

| | parts restoration service |

See full listing in **Section One** under **Rolls-Royce/Bentley**

Cerullo Performance Seating
2853 Metropolitan Pl
Pomona, CA 91767
909-392-5561; FAX: 909-392-8544
E-mail: cerullo@tstonramp.com

| | seating |

See full listing in **Section Two** under **interiors & interior parts**

Color-Plus Leather Restoration System | **leather conditioning leather dye**
106 Harrier Ct, 3767 Sunrise Lake
Milford, PA 18337-9315
570-686-3158; FAX: 570-686-4161
E-mail: jpcolorplus@pikeonline.net

Mail order only. Leather and vinyl restoration products and colorants. SOFFENER™, complete leather conditioner, restores old leather to glove-like softness. Maintains and preserves new leather. SURFLEX™, water-base colorant for leather and vinyl, user-friendly. Achieve professional results. Custom color matching is our specialty. Call for free 18-page booklet. Complete how-to, product descriptions and price list. Web site: www.colorplus.com

See our ad on page 294

Diamond Trim | **interiors**
Gary Nolan
10 Furbacher Ln #7
Aurora, ON Canada L4G 6W1
905-726-3221; FAX: 905-726-3277
E-mail: garynolan@diamondtrim.com

See full listing in **Section Two** under **interiors & interior parts**

Gliptone Manufacturing Inc | **car care products**
1595 A-6 Ocean Ave
Bohemia, NY 11716
631-737-1130, FAX: 631-589-5487
E-mail: wmessina@gliptone.com or rcaporaco@gliptone.com

See full listing in **Section Two** under **car care products**

Imperial Restorations POR-15 Products | **coatings**
7550 E Rice Rd
Gardner, IL 60424
800-576-5822; FAX: 815-237-8707
E-mail: imprest@btc-skynet.net

See full listing in **Section Two** under **rustproofing**

Karmann Ghia Parts & Restoration | **parts**
PO Box 997
Ventura, CA 93002
800-927-2787; FAX: 805-641-3333
E-mail: info@karmannghia.com

See full listing in **Section One** under **Volkswagen**

Keleen Leathers Inc | **leather hides**
10526 W Cermak Rd
Westchester, IL 60154
708-409-9800; FAX: 708-409-9801

See full listing in **Section Two** under **interiors & interior parts**

Leatherique Professional Leather Restoration & Preservation Products | **leather cleaning conditioning & professional restoration products**
PO Box 2678
Orange Park, FL 32065
904-272-0992; FAX: 904-272-1534
E-mail: lrpltd@bellsouth.net

See full listing in **Section One** under **Rolls-Royce/Bentley**

Paul's Jaguar | **parts**
4073 NE 5th Terr
Oakland Park
Fort Lauderdale, FL 33334
954-846-7976; FAX: 954-846-9450
E-mail: paulsjag@aol.com

See full listing in **Section One** under **Jaguar**

license plates

Cruising International Inc | **automobilia belt buckles decals/lapel pins license plates novelties**
1000 N Beach St
Daytona Beach, FL 32117
386-254-8753; FAX: 386-255-2460
E-mail: sales@cruising-intl.com

Manufacturer, wholesaler and exporter of license plates, hat pins, key chains, porcelain signs, belt buckles, decals and automotive novelties. Stock and custom orders. Please call for our catalog. Wir sprechen deutsch! Web site: www.cruising-intl.com

Norman D'Amico | **license plates**
44 Middle Rd
Clarksburg, MA 01247
413-663-6886

Mail order and open shop. License plates of all states, years, types and countries. Also driving licenses, registrations, plate color and data information charts, etc. Miscellaneous license plate frames.

Darryl's | **restoration**
266 Main St
Duryea, PA 18642
PH/FAX: 570-451-1600

Mail order only. Show quality license plate restoration with all damage, dents, tears, holes, rust, etc, repaired to new condition and painted in original colors, numbers will duplicate originals not brush painted or taped off. This is the finest restoration available. Car, truck, motorcycle, bicycle, reflective number, plates and duplications. Our plates have an automotive quality hand polished and waxed finish. Call or write for more information. Web site: www.darrylsplates.com

Dave's Auto Machine & Parts | **accessories machine work parts**
Rt 16
Ischua, NY 14743
716-557-2402

See full listing in **Section One** under **Chevrolet**

DETAILS License Plate Restoration | **license plates**
74 Montague City Rd
Greenfield, MA 01301
413-774-6982
E-mail: jeri@valinet.com

We restore license plates to better than new condition. You send them in the mail with a check for $60 each which includes shipping. We buff and polish them to show quality or you may request a flat or semi-gloss finish. If the plates are damaged, we send estimates. Web site: www.licenseplaterestoration.com

Richard Diehl | **license plates**
5965 W Colgate Pl
Denver, CO 80227
303-985-7481

Mail order only. License plates, buy, sell, trade.

Duane's License Plate Restoration | **license plates**
1621 Craig St
Lansing, MI 48906
517-371-3225
E-mail: michplates@webtv.net

Mail order and open shop. Monday-Friday 8 am to 5:30 pm. Selling Michigan license plates or restoring your license plates.

Section Two – Generalists

| Eurosign Metalwerke Inc
PO Box 93-6331
Margate, FL 33093
954-979-1448; FAX: 954-970-0430 | license plates |

Mail order only. Leading manufacturer of antique license plates from the United States and around the world featuring: Euro rectangular and oval plates, USA plates from 1900s-on and a wide variety of license plate frames and plate holders. Our antique replica plates are stamped in metal and look so good that thousands of *Hemmings'* readers have been satisfied customers. Our plates are also used in Hollywood movies, TV shows and commercials. Web site: www.euro-sign.com

| Eurosport Daytona Inc
355 Tomoka Ave
Ormond Beach, FL 32174-6222
800-874-8044, 904-672-7199
FAX: 904-673-0821 | license plates |

The manufacturer of classic and vanity license plates, frames and accessories. Specializing in laser cut Lazer-Tags™, stainless steel and authentic Euro plates. The largest selection of license plates available in the USA.

| Eugene Gardner
10510 Rico Tatum Rd
Palmetto, GA 30268
770-463-4264 | license plates |

Mail order and open shop by appointment only. Phone hours: 9 am to 11pm Eastern time. License plates bought, sold and traded. Discounts on large orders. Send SASE for The License Plate Club information.

| Get It On Paper
Gary Weickart, President
185 Maple St
Islip, NY 11751
631-581-3897 | automobilia
literature
toys |

See full listing in **Section Two** under **automobilia**

| Hale's Products
906 19th St
Wheatland, WY 82201
800-333-0989 | license plates |

Mail order only. Specializing in 1960s Wyoming license plates (car and truck). Cars: 1967 red/white, 1968 brown/gold and extras. "Real cowboy plates", plain $8; mounted with barbed wire, $18.

| Howard Hinz
Box 216
Vero Beach, FL 32961
561-567-9121; FAX: 561-567-0986
E-mail: flp8s@webtv.net | license plates |

Sell Florida license plates only, 1913-1980.

| Richard Hurlburt
27 West St
Greenfield, MA 01301
413-773-3235 | license plates
parts
toys |

Mail order and open shop. Auto related collectibles and toys. New and used parts for 1972-1979 Datsun model 620 pickup trucks. Also antique, classic, aircraft-related items, advertising signs, vehicle literature. Large stock of 1903-1980 USA, Canada, and foreign license plates. Send wants with SASE.

| Dave Lincoln
Box 331
Yorklyn, DE 19736
610-444-4144, PA
E-mail: tagbarn@msn.com | license plates |

Mail order and open shop by appointment. License plates, USA/foreign. All years and types. Buy, sell, swap. Thousands avail-able. Porcelains a specialty. Recent plates sold in bulk. YOM, birth year, etc. SASE with specific requests. Collections, accumulations wanted. Will travel.

| George & Denise Long
891 E Court St
Marion, NC 28752
828-652-9229 (24 hrs w/recorder) | automobilia |

See full listing in **Section Two** under **automobilia**

| Larry Machacek
PO Box 515
Porter, TX 77365
281-429-2505 | decals
license plates
novelties |

See full listing in **Section Two** under **automobilia**

| Skimino Enterprises
129 Skimino Rd
Williamsburg, VA 23188-2229
757-565-1422 | body parts
license plates
mechanical parts |

Mail order and open shop. Daily 9 am to 1 pm. Specializing in body parts, mechanical parts, Virginia license plates, towing and recovery. Update parts weekly.

| Town & Country Toys
227 Midvale Dr, PO Box 574
Marshall, WI 53559
608-655-4961
E-mail: dejaeger@itis.com | banks
Ertl cars
mini license plates |

See full listing in **Section Two** under **models & toys**

| www.albertsgifts.com
3001 Penn Ave
Pittsburgh, PA 15201
800-233-2800, 412-683-2900
FAX: 412-683-3110
E-mail: info@aimgifts.com | bike plates
license plates |

Mail order only. American made souvenir license plates and bike plates. Web site: www.albertsgifts.com

lighting equipment

| All British Car Parts Inc
2847 Moores Rd
Baldwin, MD 21013
410-692-9572; FAX: 410-692-5654
E-mail: lucasguy@home.com | parts |

See full listing in **Section Two** under **electrical systems**

| Robert D Bliss
7 Pineview Ct
Monroe, NJ 08831
732-521-4654 | electrical parts
ignition parts |

See full listing in **Section Two** under **electrical systems**

| Collins Metal Spinning
6371 W 100 S
New Palestine, IN 46163
317-894-3008 | headlight rims |

Mail order and open shop. Monday-Saturday 8:30 am to 4:30 pm; other times by appointment. Anything round in brass, copper, aluminum and steel.

Development Associates | electrical parts
12791-G Newport Ave
Tustin, CA 92780
714-730-6843; FAX: 714-730-6863
E-mail: devassoc@yahoo.com

See full listing in **Section Two** under **electrical systems**

W F Harris Lighting | work lights
PO Box 5023
Monroe, NC 28111-5023
704-283-7477; FAX: 704-283-6880

Mail order only. Automotive work lights. Underhood and under-dash task lights, larger work lights with accessories including rolling light/tool tray and rolling light cart that can be propped up for work on sides of vehicles.

Headlight Headquarters | lights parts
Donald I Axelrod
35 Timson St
Lynn, MA 01902
781-598-0523

Mail order and open shop by appointment only. Headlights and headlight parts for 1914-1939 automobiles. No Ford. SASE required.

Wayne Hood | NORS parts NOS parts
228 Revell Rd
Grenada, MS 38901
601-227-8426

See full listing in **Section One** under **Dodge**

OJ Rallye Automotive | accessories car care products lighting parts
N 6808 Hwy OJ, PO Box 540
Plymouth, WI 53073
920-893-2531; FAX: 920-893-6800
E-mail: ojrallye@excel.net

Mail order and open shop. Monday-Friday, 9 am to 12 pm, 2 pm to 6 pm. World's largest assortment of European lighting part numbers in stock. Carello, Cibie, Hella, Lucas, Marchal and other pre-war to current high tech fog, driving and headlight parts, bulbs and kits available in 6, 12 and 24-volt. Restoration of lamps is also offered. Other quality accessories and car care products sold, retail and wholesale. Web site: www.vclassics.com/ojrallye.htm

Sherco Auto Supply | bulbs electrical wire fuses
3700 NW 124th Ave, Ste 114
Coral Springs, FL 33065
954-344-1993; FAX: 954-344-2664
E-mail: parts@sherco-auto.com

See full listing in **Section Two** under **electrical systems**

Steelman/JS Products | tools
5440-B S Procyon Ave
Las Vegas, NV 89118
800-255-7011; FAX: 702-362-5084
E-mail: jsprodnlv@aol.com

See full listing in **Section Two** under **tools**

Visibolts From Classic Safety Products | accessories
7131 Hickory Run
Waunakee, WI 53597
888-212-2163; FAX: 608-824-9200
E-mail: clovis@www.visibolts.com

Mail order only. LED/illuminated bumper style bolts and accessories for any car or truck to add safety and style. Visibolts were awarded Best New Product Under $100 by the National Street Rod Association. Visibolts appear original when not lit, showing no color. No wiring harness modification necessary. Available in red, amber and white. Web site: www.visibolts.com

limousine rentals

Jacks Wholesale Division | limousines
250 N Robertson Blvd, Ste 405
Beverly Hills, CA 90211-1793
310-839-9417; FAX: 310-839-1046

See full listing in **Section One** under **Lincoln**

Westwind Limousine Sales | limousine sales
2720 W National Rd
Dayton, OH 45414
937-898-9000; FAX: 937-898-9800

See full listing in **Section One** under **Lincoln**

literature dealers

Applegate and Applegate | owner's manuals sales literature
Box 129
Mount Gretna, PA 17064-0129

See full listing in **Section One** under **Corvette**

The Auto Buff, Books & Collectibles | books literature manuals
13809 Ventura Blvd
Sherman Oaks, CA 91423
E-mail: autobuffbooks@mindspring.com

Mail order only. Automotive literature including out-of-print books, owner's manuals, shop manuals and sales literature covering antique and modern cars from racing to restoration.

Auto Nostalgia Enr | literature manuals models tractor decals
332 St Joseph
Mont St Gregoire, QC Canada J0J 1K0
PH/FAX: 450-346-3644
E-mail: autonostalgia@vif.com

See full listing in **Section Two** under **models & toys**

Auto-West Advertising | sales literature
Gary Hinkle
PO Box 3875
Modesto, CA 95352
209-524-9541, 209-522-4777

Mail order and open shop by appointment only. Specialize in all US and foreign postwar literature, postcards and owner's manuals.

Auto World Books | literature magazines research service
Box 562
Camarillo, CA 93011
805-987-5570

Mail order only. Car and truck literature, manuals and magazines, US and foreign. Free research service.

Irv Bishko Literature | literature
14550 Watt Rd
Novelty, OH 44072
440-338-4811; FAX: 440-338-2222
E-mail: bishkobook@aol.com

Shop manuals, parts books, sales brochures, owner's manuals, dealer albums, color/upholstery and data books, etc. Wide selection of domestic and foreign literature for cars and trucks, 1900-present. Phone or e-mail. See our web site: www.autobooksbishko.com

Blair Collectors & Consultants
2821 SW 167th Pl
Seattle, WA 98166
206-242-6745, 206-246-1305
E-mail: blairhall33@aol.com

appraisals
consultant
literature

See full listing in **Section Two** under **appraisals**

EJ Blend
802 8th Ave
Irwin, PA 15642-3702
724-863-7624

literature
parts

See full listing in **Section One** under **Packard**

M K Boatright
629 Santa Monica
Corpus Christi, TX 78411
361-852-6639; FAX: 361-853-7168

books
literature
models

Mail order only. Sales albums, model cars, library books and other miscellaneous literature for US and foreign cars and trucks, 1930s-1980s.

Bill Boudway
105 Deerfield Dr
Canandaigua, NY 14424-2409
716-394-6172
E-mail: gnbboudway@msn.com

restoration info

See full listing in **Section One** under **Packard**

Bricklin Literature
3116 Welsh Rd
Philadelphia, PA 19136-1810
888-392-4832, Ext 215-338-6142
E-mail: bricklin.literature@excite.com

collectibles
literature

See full listing in **Section One** under **Bricklin**

BritBooks
PO Box 321
Otego, NY 13825
PH/FAX: 607-988-7956
E-mail: britbooks@britbooks.com

books

See full listing in **Section Four** under **books & publications**

The Can Corner
PO Box VA 1173
Linwood, PA 19061

audio tapes

See full listing in **Section Two** under **automobilia**

Ken Case
5706 E 5th Pl
Tulsa, OK 74112
918-835-5872

gas globes
literature
signs

Mail order only. Literature for all types of cars and trucks. Also gas and oil related items including signs, globes, cans, road maps, etc.

Chewning's Auto Literature
2011 Elm Tree Terr
Buford, GA 30518
770-945-9795
E-mail: cchewy69@aol.com

literature
manuals

Mail order only. Specializing in literature for all makes and models. Shop manuals, owner's manuals, sales catalogs, parts books, license plates, automobilia, petroliana, etc. Also buy automotive literature. Send list or call for a prompt, courteous reply.

Classic Auto Literature
1592 Seacrest Rd
Nanoose Bay BC Canada V9P 9B5
250-468-9522

manuals/models
parts catalogs
posters/videos
sales brochures

Mail orders our specialty. Suppliers of all types of automotive literature. Shop, owner's and body manuals; parts catalogs; sales brochures; magazine ads; posters; wiring diagrams; dealer albums and facts books. Also, automotive videos, die casts, plastic models and some related memorabilia. Canadian requests please include SASE.

Crank'en Hope Publications
382 Sloan Alley
Blairsville, PA 15717-1481
724-459-8853; FAX: 724-459-8860
E-mail: cranken@yourinter.net

assembly manuals
body manuals
parts books
shop manuals

Mail order and open shop. Monday-Friday 9 am to 9 pm Eastern time. Shop manuals, parts books, body manuals, Chevrolet assembly manuals and more. Retail and wholesale. If visiting our shop, please phone ahead for hours. Accept Visa and MasterCard. For our most recent catalog please include 3 first class stamps or $1 cash to cover postage. Extend discounts to clubs, libraries and organizations.

DeLorean Literature
3116 Welsh Rd
Philadelphia, PA 19136-1810
215-338-6142; PH/FAX: 888-392-4832
ext 291-291-1979 (* for fax)
E-mail: delorean.literature@excite.com

collectibles
literature

See full listing in **Section One** under **DeLorean**

Daniel N Dietrich
RD 1
Kempton, PA 19529
610-756-6078, 610-756-6071

restoration
trim parts

See full listing in **Section One** under **Mopar**

Driven By Desire
300 N Fraley St
Kane, PA 16735
814-837-7590; FAX: 814-837-6850
E-mail: driven@penn.com

automobilia
car dealer
models

See full listing in **Section Two** under **car dealers**

Dennis DuPont
77 Island Pond Rd
Derry, NH 03038
603-434-9290

automobilia
literature
parts

See full listing in **Section One** under **Studebaker**

Faxon Auto Literature
3901 Carter Ave
Riverside, CA 92501
800-458-2734; FAX: 909-786-4166

literature
manuals

Open Monday-Friday 6 am to 6 pm, Saturday 8:30 am to 1:30 pm. Find all of your manuals and literature with one free call. You can own the best manuals and literature for your vehicle. Familiar with every manual and most of the literature that exists and will match the correct book to your needs from the most complete inventory in the world. Money back guarantee. Inquiries use 909-786-4177. Visa, MasterCard, American Express and Discover welcome; also CODs, money order, or check.

Steve Fields' Automobilia
Steve Fields
1021 Laguna St #4
Santa Barbara, CA 93101
805-965-3280; FAX: 805-965-5680
E-mail: jsfields@earthlink.net

books

Mail order and open shop by appointment. Specializing in out-of-print automotive history books. Racing, sports cars, import and exotic cars. Also race programs and race posters.

Ford Truck Enthusiasts Inc PO Box 422 Lilburn, GA 30048 770-806-1955 E-mail: kpayne@ford-trucks.com	**literature**

See full listing in **Section Two** under **trucks & tractors**

Irving Galis 357 Atlantic Ave Marblehead, MA 01945	**books** **dealer items** **literature**

See full listing in **Section One** under **Saab**

Get It On Paper Gary Weickart, President 185 Maple St Islip, NY 11751 631-581-3897	**automobilia** **literature** **toys**

See full listing in **Section Two** under **automobilia**

Richard Hamilton 28 E 46th St Indianapolis, IN 46205 317-283-1902	**sales literature**

Mail order only. Dealing in sales literature for Australian, British, Canadian, French, Indian, Mexican, Japanese and US cars. Also offer books, press kits, ads, models and magazines. Have Ferrari and other exotic literature (Bitter, Excalibur, etc).

Justin Hartley 17 Fox Meadow Ln West Hartford, CT 06107-1216 860-523-0056, 860-604-9950 cell FAX: 860-233-8840 E-mail: cadillacbooks@home.com	**reprinted literature**

See full listing in **Section One** under **Cadillac/LaSalle**

James Hill 935 Sunnyslope St Emporia, KS 66801 620-342-4826 evenings/weekends E-mail: jwhill@osprey.net	**ignition parts** **source list**

See full listing in **Section One** under **Packard**

Hi-Speed John Steel PO Box 44 Chagrin Falls, OH 44022 PH/FAX: 440-247-6021	**literature** **motorcycles** **parts**

See full listing in **Section One** under **Harley-Davidson**

Historic Video Archives PO Box 189-VA Cedar Knolls, NJ 07927-0189	**videotapes**

See full listing in **Section Two** under **automobilia**

Hudson Motor Car Co Memorabilia Ken Poynter 19638 Huntington Harper Woods, MI 48225 313-886-9292	**literature** **memorabilia** **novelties** **signs**

See full listing in **Section One** under **Hudson**

International Automobile Archives Kai Jacobsen Wiesenweg 3b 85757 Karlsfeld Germany 011-49-8131-93158 FAX: 011-49-8131-505973 E-mail: doubledseven@t-online.de	**sales literature**

Mail order and open shop. Automotive sales literature of the post-war period from all countries of the world. Also technical data

Section Two – Generalists

available for nearly every car from 1947 until today. Specialize in sports and exotic cars. Comprehensive list, $5 airmail.

International Ford History Project	**newsletter**
PO Box 11415	
Olympia, WA 98508	
360-754-9585	
E-mail: ifhp@aol.com	

See full listing in **Section Four** under **newsletters**

Jeff Johnson Motorsports	**literature**
PO Box 14327	
Columbus, OH 43214	
614-268-1181; FAX: 614-268-1141	

See full listing in **Section One** under **Mopar**

Bob Johnson's Auto Literature	**brochures**
92 Blandin Ave	**literature**
Framingham, MA 01702	**manuals**
508-872-9173; FAX: 508-626-0991	**paint chips**
E-mail: bjohnson@autopaper.com	

Most complete selection of sales brochures, owner's manuals, repair manuals, parts books, showroom albums, color and upholstery books, paint chips for auto, truck, farm, construction. Buy collections or single items. Web site: www.autopaper.com
See our ad on this page

Dave Kauzlarich	**literature**
60442 N Tranquility Rd	**memorabilia**
Lacombe, LA 70445	
504-882-3000	
E-mail: fierog97j@aol.com	

Mail order only. Buying, selling and trading 1984-1988 Pontiac and Fiero literature and memorabilia.

David M King, Automotive Books	**literature**
5 Brouwer Ln	
Rockville Centre, NY 11570	
516-766-1561; FAX: 516-766-7502	
E-mail: rollskingusa@yahoo.com	

See full listing in **Section One** under **Rolls-Royce/Bentley**

Shepard Kinsman	**sales literature**
909 Eastridge	
Miami, FL 33157	
305-255-7067	

Large 1931-1980 domestic and foreign collection being sold. Marque lists available.

Kosters Motorboghandel	**owner's manuals**
Ostergade 9	**shop manuals**
8900 Randers Denmark	
45-86-42-6613; FAX: 45-86-42-0813	

Mail order and open shop. Specialize in European shop manuals and owner's manuals for cars and motorcycles, from turn-of-the-century onwards.

Lincoln Services Ltd	**literature**
Earle O Brown, Jr	**parts**
229 Robinhood Ln	
McMurray, PA 15317	
724-941-4567; FAX: 724-942-1940	

See full listing in **Section One** under **Lincoln**

Lloyd's Literature	**literature**
PO Box 491	
Newbury, OH 44065	
800-292-2665, 440-338-1527	
FAX: 440-338-2222	
E-mail: lloydslit@aol.com	

Shop manuals, owner's manuals, sales literature, parts books, dealer albums. Specialize in automobile literature for all US and foreign cars and trucks 1915-1999. Fast dependable service. Online store and e-mail service too. Web site: www.lloydsautolit.com

George & Denise Long	**automobilia**
891 E Court St	
Marion, NC 28752	
828-652-9229 (24 hrs w/recorder)	

See full listing in **Section Two** under **automobilia**

The Maverick Connection	**literature**
137 Valley Dr	**parts**
Ripley, WV 25271	
PH/FAX: 304-372-7825	
E-mail: maverickconnection@email.com	

See full listing in **Section One** under **Ford 1954-up**

McCoy's Memorabilia	**memorabilia**
35583 N 1830 E	**racing literature**
Rossville, IL 60963-7175	
PH/FAX: 217-748-6513	
E-mail: indy500@soltec.net	

Mail order. Buying and selling Indy 500 and other auto race literature, memorabilia and vintage auto magazines, will do computer search for information on auto races, race cars, race car drivers, vintage autos, tech info. Check out my eBay auction sites; eBay User ID: indy500nut

McFarland & Company Inc Publishers	books
Box 611	
Jefferson, NC 28640	
336-246-4460; FAX: 336-246-5018	
E-mail: info@mcfarlandpub.com	

See full listing in **Section Four** under **books & publications**

Ken McGee Auto Literature	literature
PO Box 464	
Goderich, ON Canada N7A 4C7	
888-275-2666 orders, toll-free	
519-524-5821; FAX: 519-524-9679	
E-mail: kenmcgeebooks@odyssey.on.ca	

Largest stock of original North American car and truck literature in Canada. Specializing in pre-war. Car and truck original literature from 1897-1999. Sales brochures, parts and shop manuals, owner's manuals, data books, dealer albums, etc. Major credit cards accepted. Next day shipping. If selling your collection, please write us, thank you. Web site: www.kenmcgeeautobooks.com

McIntyre Auctions	auctions automobilia literature petroliana
PO Box 60	
East Dixfield, ME 04227	
800-894-4300, 207-562-4443	
FAX: 207-562-4576	
E-mail: sue@classicford.com	

See full listing in **Section Two** under **auctions & shows**

Donald McKinsey	fuel pumps ignition parts literature spark plugs
PO Box 94H	
Wilkinson, IN 46186	
765-785-6284	

See full listing in **Section Two** under **ignition parts**

McLellan's Automotive History	books factory literature magazines memorabilia press kits/programs sales literature
Robert and Sharon McLellan	
9111 Longstaff Dr	
Houston, TX 77031-2711	
713-772-3285; FAX: 713-772-3287	
E-mail: mclellans@	
mclellansautomotive.com	

Mail order only. High quality rare books, sales literature, press kits, magazines, programs, factory literature, dealer literature and memorabilia bought and sold. Domestic and foreign. 1900-present. Racing, classics, antiques, sports cars, commercial, professional and recreational vehicles. Guaranteed original and in excellent condition. World's largest web site for automotive literature with over 40,000 items described and priced. Source of information for over 42 years. Free shipping. Web site: www.mclellansautomotive.com

Walter Miller	literature
6710 Brooklawn Pkwy	
Syracuse, NY 13211	
315-432-8282; FAX: 315-432-8256	
E-mail: info@autolit.com	

Mail order only. Over two million pieces of original literature in stock. World's largest selection of original US and foreign automobile, truck, motorcycle sales brochures, repair manuals, owner's manuals, parts books and showroom items. I am a serious buyer and travel to purchase literature. Web site: www.autolit.com

Dennis Mitosinka's Classic Cars and Appraisals Service	appraisals books
619 E Fourth St	
Santa Ana, CA 92701	
714-953-5303; FAX: 714-953-1810	
E-mail: mitoclassics@earthlink.net	

See full listing in **Section Two** under **appraisals**

MotoMedia	books magazines
PO Box 489	
Lansdowne, PA 19050	
PH/FAX: 610-623-6930	
E-mail: motomedia@earthlink.net	

Mail order and flea market sales. More than 20,000 carefully selected issues and 300 books in stock. General interest and racing a specialty. Visa and MasterCard accepted. $2.50 for current lists.

MotorCam Media	automotive videos
138 N Alling Rd	
Tallmadge, OH 44278	
800-240-1777; FAX: 330-633-3249	
E-mail: carvideo@motorcam.com	

See full listing in **Section Two** under **videos**

MotorLit.com	books manuals memorabilia
PO Box 4907	
Mesa, AZ 85211-4907	
480-969-0102	
E-mail: info@motorlit.com	

Mail order only. Online catalog of rare and out-of-print automobilia books, marque histories, biographies, auto racing books, programs, yearbooks, posters, photos, models and memorabilia. Also original shop and owner's manuals, sales literature, paint chips, tune-up specification and chassis lubrication charts, wiring diagrams, parts catalogs, carburetor service bulletins and other technical publications. Web site: www.motorlit.com

Dave Newell's Chevrobilia	literature memorabilia
PO Box 588	
Orinda, CA 94563	
510-223-4725	

See full listing in **Section One** under **Chevrolet**

Obsolete Jeep® & Willys® Parts	literature parts
Division of Florida 4 Wheel Drive & Truck Parts	
6110 17th St E	
Bradenton, FL 34203	
941-756-7844; PH/FAX: 941-756-7757	

See full listing in **Section One** under **Willys**

Old GMC Trucks.Com	literature parts
Robert English	
PO Box 675	
Franklin, MA 02038-0675	
508-520-3900; FAX: 508-520-7861	
E-mail: oldcarkook@aol.com	

See full listing in **Section One** under **GMC**

Original Ford Motor Co Literature	collectibles literature
PO Box 7-AA	
Hudson, KY 40145-0007	
502-257-8642; FAX: 502-257-8643	
E-mail: whiteb@bellsouth.net	

See full listing in **Section One** under **Ford 1932-1953**

Jim Osborn Reproductions Inc	decals manuals
101 Ridgecrest Dr	
Lawrenceville, GA 30245	
770-962-7556; FAX: 770-962-5881	
E-mail: dosborn@	
osborn-reproduction.com	

See full listing in **Section Two** under **decals**

Packard Archives
918 W Co Rd C-2
St Paul, MN 55113-1942
651-484-1184
E-mail: estatecars@earthlink.net

accessories
artwork
automobilia

See full listing in **Section One** under **Packard**

Parts of the Past
PO Box 602
Waukesha, WI 53187
262-679-4212; FAX: 262-679-4461

literature

Shop manuals, owner's manuals, sales literature for most
1930s-1990s American cars, trucks. Call or send SASE with
needs for quote. Visa/MasterCard accepted.

Portrayal Press
PO Box 1190
Andover, NJ 07821
PH/FAX: 973-579-5781
E-mail: info@portrayal.com

books
manuals

See full listing in **Section Two** under **military vehicles**

Bert Provisor
23175 Western Crest Dr
Gavilan Hills, CA 92570
909-657-1884

body/owner's/shop
manuals
showroom albums

Shop, body, parts and owner's manuals, showroom albums,
data/facts books, wiring diagrams, service bulletins, color chips,
accessories, warranties. *National Service Data, Motors,* and some
sales literature. Largest selection of original manuals west of the
Mississippi. SASE only.

Samlerborsen
Jacobys Alle 2-4
DK 1806 Frederiksberg C Denmark
+45-33254022; FAX: +45-33250622

books
toys

Open shop only. Monday-Friday 12 pm to 5:30 pm. Deals in
motorbooks, models and toys, new and second-hand, Tekno,
Dinky, Corgi, Solido, etc. Publisher of the book *Tekno Made in
Denmark* by Dorte Johansen. Web site: www.samlerboersen.dk

**Schiff European Automotive
Literature Inc**
881 Dyer Ave
Cranston, RI 02920
401-946-4711; FAX: 401-946-5785
E-mail: seal11@aol.com

literature

Mail order, phone and fax orders, in store. Monday-Friday 8 am
to 3 pm, Saturday 8 am to 11 am. Barry Schiff, owner. Owner's
manuals, parts catalogs and workshop manuals for all foreign
cars. Web site: www.schiffeuropean.com

E J Serafin
Valley Rd
Matinecock, NY 11560

manuals

See full listing in **Section One** under **Cadillac/LaSalle**

Henri Simar J R
Rue du College, BP 172
B-4800 Verviers Belgium
32-87335501; FAX: 32-87335122

books
literature

Mail order. Deal in sales literature, handbooks, workshop manuals, books, posters, magazines. I am collecting all MG, Mini,
Lotus, John Player Special, James Bond items.

Robert H Snyder
PO Drawer 821
Yonkers, NY 10702
914-476-8500
FAX: 914-476-8573, 24 hours
E-mail: cohascodpc@earthlink.net

literature
parts

See full listing in **Section One** under **Cadillac/LaSalle**

Sparrow Auction Co
59 Wheeler Ave
Milford, CT 06460
203-877-1066
E-mail: sparrowauction@hotmail.com

auction company

See full listing in **Section Two** under **auctions & shows**

Spyder Enterprises Inc
RFD 1682
Laurel Hollow, NY 11791-9644
516-367-1616; FAX: 516-367-3260
E-mail: singer356@aol.com

accessories
artwork
automobilia
books

See full listing in **Section Two** under **automobilia**

**Edward Tilley Automotive
Collectibles**
PO Box 4233
Cary, NC 27519-4233
919-460-8262
E-mail: edandsusan@aol.com

automobilia
literature
parts

See full listing in **Section Two** under **automobilia**

TMC Publications
5817 Park Heights Ave
Baltimore, MD 21215-3931
410-367-4490; FAX: 410-466-3566
E-mail: carolyny@tmcpubl.com

literature
manuals

See full listing in **Section Four** under **books & publications**

Transport Books at DRB Motors Inc
16 Elrose Ave
Toronto, ON Canada M9M 2H6
800-665-2665, 416-744-7675
FAX: 416-744-7696
E-mail: info@transportbooks.com

books
manuals
periodicals
videos

See full listing in **Section Four** under **books & publications**

Al Trommers-Rare Auto Literature
614 Vanburenville Rd
Middletown, NY 10940-7242

automobilia/lit
hubcaps
wheelcovers

Mail order only. Shop open by written request only, include SASE.
Specializing in thousands of hard and soft cover auto books, tons of
old auto magazines and club publications. Lots of Chilton Motors'
repair manuals, lots of NOS original literature, brochures, shop
manuals, owner's manuals, postcards, license plates, hubcaps,
wheelcovers, music, records and tapes from when your car was
new, doo whopps, rock and roll, jazz, etc. Automotive literature and
hubcaps are our specialty. Originals and reissues, plus much more.

Vintage Automotive Art
PO Box 3702
Beverly Hills, CA 90212
310-278-0882; FAX: 310-278-0883
E-mail: artline1@pacbell.net

artwork
automobilia
literature dealers

See full listing in **Section Two** under **automobilia**

Vintage Books
6613 E Mill Plain
Vancouver, WA 98661
360-694-9519; FAX: 360-694-7644
E-mail: books@vintage-books.com

books
literature

Mail order and open shop. Monday-Saturday 10 am to 6 pm.
General stock bookstore specializing in automotive literature. We

have a large selection of books (general and marque history, restoration, etc), plus shop manuals and owner's manuals. Online also: paint chips, sales literature and magazines. Secure web site: www.vintage-books.com

Voss Motors Inc	service manuals
4850 37th Ave S	
Seattle, WA 98118	
888-380-9277 toll-free	
206-721-3077	
E-mail: vossmotors@books4cars.com	

Mail order and open shop. Monday-Friday and Sunday 9 am to 9 pm. Service manuals for all automobiles and light trucks, both domestic and import, including obscure and hard-to-find. Reasonable prices with excellent personalized service. Web site: www.books4cars.com

Mary Weinheimer	color charts
103 Highgate Terr	
Bergenfield, NJ 07621	
201-384-7661; FAX: 201-439-7662	
E-mail: marychevy@aol.com	

See full listing in **Section Two** under **automobilia**

Colonel Bill White	literature
Auto Literature Sales	
PO Box 7-AA	
Hudson, KY 40145-0007	
502-257-8642; FAX: 502-257-8643	
E-mail: whiteb@bellsouth.net	

Automobile and truck sales literature, owner's manuals.

Wymer Classic AMC	NOS/used parts
Mark & George Wymer	owner's manuals
340 N Justice St	repairs
Fremont, OH 43420	service manuals
419-332-4291	
419-334-6945 after 5 pm	

See full listing in **Section One** under **AMC**

Clarence Young Autohobby	antique toy vehicles
300-1 Reems Creek Rd	dealer promos
Weaverville, NC 28787	exclusive metal cars
PH/FAX: 828-645-5243	exclusive resin cars
E-mail: cya@carhobby.com	

See full listing in **Section Two** under **models & toys**

locks & keys

Antique Auto Keys	keys
Douglas Vogel	locks
PO Box 335	
Dexter, MI 48130	
734-424-9336; FAX: 734-424-9337	

Mail order only. Original keys and locks for 1900-1975 cars, keys cut from code or original lock. Large inventory of old locks and cylinders.

Atlas Obsolete Chrysler Parts	parts
10621 Bloomfield St, Unit 32	
Los Alamitos, CA 90720	
PH/FAX: 562-594-5560	
E-mail: atlaschrys@aol.com	

See full listing in **Section One** under **Mopar**

AUTOTEC	lock work
12915 Eastbrook Pl	
Brookfield, WI 53005-6520	
262-797-9988; FAX: 262-797-7999	

Mail order and open shop by appointment. Best time to call is 8 pm to 10 pm Central time. Foreign and domestic vehicle lock work exclusively. Repairs, recoding, making keys. This is a full-time occupation. In business since 1982. Large inventory.

C & G Early Ford Parts	accessories/chrome
1941 Commercial St, Dept AH	emblems
Escondido, CA 92029-1233	literature
760-740-2400; FAX: 760-740-8700	mechanical
E-mail: cgford@cgfordparts.com	weatherstripping

See full listing in **Section One** under **Ford 1932-1953**

Classic Chevrolet Parts Inc	parts
8723 S I-35	
Oklahoma City, OK 73149	
405-631-4400; FAX: 405-631-5999	
E-mail: info@classicchevroletparts.com	

See full listing in **Section One** under **Chevrolet**

Jarvis Old Car Locks & Keys	repairs
Box 2245	
Alderwood Manor, WA 98036	
425-776-2804	

Mail order only. Repair work done on old car locks. Many cylinders and handles from 1930s thru 1950s. Original key blanks. Codes changed.

Jesser's Classic Keys	automobilia
26 West St, Dept HVA	keys
Akron, OH 44303-2344	
330-376-8181; FAX: 330-384-9129	

Mail order, car shows and open shop: 10 am to 4 pm five days; mail order: 9 am to 9 pm Eastern time seven days. Complete line of NOS keys and gold plated keys for all American cars and trucks from 1900-date. Keys stamped and cut by code. Have many of those hard-to-find keys and lock cylinders, please inquire and include year, make and model. Also carry automobilia, key rings, grille badges, belt buckles, pins, money clips and more. Visa, MasterCard, AmEx, Discover. Web site: www.jessersclassickeys.com

Machina Locksmith	car locks
3 Porter St	keys
Watertown, MA 02172-4145	
PH/FAX: 617-923-1683	

All vehicle lockwork, car locks in stock. Hi-security keys and by code.

Obsolete Ford Parts Inc	parts
8701 S I-35	
Oklahoma City, OK 73149	
405-631-3933; FAX: 405-634-6815	
E-mail: info@obsoletefordparts.com	

See full listing in **Section One** under **Ford 1954-up**

Uhlenhopp Lock	lock restoration
29983 Superior Rd	NOS locks
Clarksville, IA 50619	rebuilding
319-278-4355	rekeying

Mail order and open shop.

VPA International	alarm systems
369 E Blaine St	door lock systems
Corona, CA 92879	power windows
909-273-1033; FAX: 909-273-1041	
E-mail: vpaintl@aol.com	

See full listing in **Section Two** under **accessories**

lubricants

Cam2 Oil Products Company
380 W Butler Ave
New Britain, PA 18901
800-338-2262; FAX: 215-340-2265
E-mail: cam2oil@aol.com

antifreeze
lubricants

Lubricants, antifreeze, automotive aftermarket. Web site: www.cam2.com

CRC Industries
885 Louis Dr
Warminster, PA 18974
PH/FAX: 215-674-4300

additives
greases
lubricants

Maintenance chemicals, lubricants, greases, gear oils, functional fluids, leak stoppers, leather care and additives. Web site: www.crcindustries.com

FHS Supply Inc
PO Box 9
Clover, SC 29710
800-742-8484; FAX: 803-222-7285
E-mail: fhsoil@aol.com

oil

Mail order and open shop. Monday-Friday 9 am to 5 pm. Smokeless oil for older cars and trucks with worn engines. Money back guarantee to prevent oil smoking. Web site: http://members.aol.com/fhsoil

Frost Auto Restoration Techniques Ltd
Crawford St
Rochdale OL16 5NU United Kingdom
44-1706-658619
FAX: 44-1706-860338
E-mail: order@frost.co.uk

car care products
paints
tools

See full listing in **Section Two** under **tools**

Mr Moly
PO Box 12542
Rochester, NY 14612
PH/FAX: 716-266-3737
E-mail: mrmoly@frontiernet.net

lubricants

Specialty lubricants based on molybdenum disulphide. Web site: www.mrmoly.com

Prezerve
1101 Arapahoe, Ste 3
Lincoln, NE 68502
888-774-4184; FAX: 402-420-7777
E-mail: prezerve@prezerveit.com

additives

See full listing in **Section Two** under **car care products**

Sterling Specialties
42 Ponderosa Ln
Monroe, NY 10950
845-782-7614

car care products

See full listing in **Section Two** under **car care products**

Stoner Inc
1070 Robert Fulton Hwy
Quarryville, PA 17566
717-786-7355; FAX: 717-786-8819
E-mail: sales@stonersolutions.com

cleaners
lubricants

See full listing in **Section Two** under **car care products**

Thermal Tech Coatings Inc
312 E Poythress St, Ste A
Hopewell, VA 23860
877-754-9795; FAX: 804-452-1825
E-mail: webmaster@
thermaltechcoatings.com

coatings

See full listing in **Section Two** under **exhaust systems**

VACO Inc
PO Box 6
Florence, MA 01062
413-586-0978; FAX: 413-586-1020
E-mail: ampcolubes@rcn.com

lubricators

Mail order only selling the original AMPCO top cylinder lubricators. NOS manufactured in the 1940s. Some original NOS carburetor plates available for 1920-1960 cars. Web site: www.ampcolubes.com

Valco Cincinnati Consumer Products Inc
411 Circle Freeway Dr
Cincinnati, OH 45246
513-874-6550; FAX: 513-874-3612

adhesives
detailing products
sealants
tools

See full listing in **Section Two** under **tools**

WD-40 Company
PO Box 80607
San Diego, CA 92138
619-275-1400; FAX: 619-275-5823

lubricants

Open shop only. Many locations. WD-40 multi-purpose lubricant, 3-in-one drip oil, Lava heavy duty hand cleaner. Web site: www.wd40.com

machine work

Angeli Machine Co
417 N Varney St
Burbank, CA 91502
818-846-5359
E-mail: angelimach@aol.com

machine work

Monday-Friday 9 am to 5 pm. Master and wheel cylinder resleeving with stainless steel and other machine shop services.

Atlas Engine Rebuilding Co Inc
24251 Frampton Ave
Harbor City, CA 90710
310-325-6898; FAX: 310-325-7701

engine rebuilding
machine work

See full listing in **Section Two** under **engine rebuilding**

Automotive Restorations Inc
Stephen Babinsky
4 Center St
Bernardsville, NJ 07924
908-766-6688; FAX: 908-766-6684
E-mail: autorestnj@aol.com

clutch rebuilding
mechanical services
restorations

See full listing in **Section Two** under **restoration shops**

The Babbitt Pot
Zigmont G Billus
1693 St Rt 4
Fort Edward, NY 12828
518-747-4277

engine rebuilding
rebabbitting &
boring of bearings

See full listing in **Section Two** under **babbitting**

Bob's Automotive Machine — engine parts, machine shop
30 Harrison Ave
Harrison, NJ 07029
973-483-0059; FAX: 973-483-6092

Mail order and open shop. Monday-Friday 9 am to 6 pm, Saturday 9 am to 12 noon. Specializing in early 1960s Ford engine parts. Area's most complete machine shop service from boring to balancing, to complete engine dynamometer analysis.

BPE Racing Heads — cylinder heads
702 Dunn Way
Placentia, CA 92870
714-572-6072; FAX: 714-572-6073
E-mail: steve@bpeheads.com

Mail order and open shop. Monday-Friday 9 am to 6 pm. Cylinder head and manifold porting and polishing: automotive, motorcycle, 2-valve, multi-valve, aluminum, cast iron, stock, aftermarket, domestic, import. Cylinder head restoration: seats and guides installed, welding, thread restoration. Air flow testing: heads, manifolds, mufflers, intercoolers, air cleaners, etc. Can build fixtures for your project. Cast aluminum manifold restoration and fabrication: cut, splice, weld, install injector bosses. Problem specialists: emergency repairs, tight deadlines, special projects, tough challenges and limited runs. Web site: www.bpeheads.com

Cam-Pro — camshaft repair, engine parts
PO Box 3305
Great Falls, MT 59403
800-525-2581, 406-771-0300

See full listing in **Section Two** under **camshafts**

Done Right Engine & Machine Inc — engine rebuilding, machine shop
12955 York Delta Unit J
North Royalton, OH 44133
440-582-1366; FAX: 440-582-2005

See full listing in **Section Two** under **engine rebuilding**

Economy Racing Components Inc — machine work, welding, wheels/tires
7550 Negley Rd
Henderson, KY 42420
PH/FAX: 270-826-3159
E-mail: erc@henderson.net

See full listing in **Section Two** under **special services**

EIS Engines Inc — engines
215 SE Grand Ave
Portland, OR 97214
800-547-0002, 503-232-5590
FAX: 503-232-5178
E-mail: edik@att.com

See full listing in **Section One** under **Mercedes-Benz**

George's Speed Shop — machine shop, race engine building, race engine parts
716 Brantly Ave
Dayton, OH 45404
937-233-0353; FAX: 937-236-3501

See full listing in **Section Two** under **racing**

Harter Industries Inc — parts, restoration
PO Box 502
Holmdel, NJ 07733
732-566-7055; FAX: 732-566-6977
E-mail: harter101@aol.com

See full listing in **Section Two** under **comprehensive parts**

Innovative Rod Products — body components, chassis parts
28 Bruce Way
Moundhouse, NV 89706
PH/FAX: 775-246-1718
E-mail: rick@innovativerod.com

See full listing in **Section Two** under **chassis parts**

Jackson & Wardick Hot Rods — metal shaping
749 Croton Lake Rd
Bedford Corners, NY 10549-4230
914-666-2057
E-mail: wardj@bestweb.net

See full listing in **Section Two** under **street rods**

Koffel's Place II — engine rebuilding, machine shop
740 River Rd
Huron, OH 44839
419-433-4410; FAX: 419-433-2166

See full listing in **Section Two** under **engine rebuilding**

Krem Engineering — engine rebuilding, repairs, restoration
10204 Perry Hwy
Meadville, PA 16335
814-724-4806; FAX: 814-337-2992
E-mail: info@krem-enterprises.com

See full listing in **Section Two** under **restoration shops**

Lindskog Balancing — engine balancing
1170 Massachusetts Ave
Boxborough, MA 01719-1415
978-263-2040; FAX: 978-263-4035

See full listing in **Section Two** under **engine rebuilding**

Maximum Torque Specialties — high-perf parts, restoration parts
PO Box 925
Delavan, WI 53115
262-740-1118; FAX: 262-740-1161
E-mail: mts@elknet.net

See full listing in **Section One** under **Cadillac/LaSalle**

Mid Valley Engineering — machine work, parts, restoration
16637 N 21st St
Phoenix, AZ 85022
602-482-1251; FAX: 602-788-0812

See full listing in **Section Two** under **transmissions**

Noble Racing Inc — accessories, parts
1058 Dry Ridge Rd
Versailles, KY 40383
859-879-1123; FAX: 859-879-3743
E-mail: nobleracing@iwebworks.com

See full listing in **Section Two** under **engine parts**

Olson's Gaskets — gaskets
3059 Opdal Rd E
Port Orchard, WA 98366
PH/FAX: 360-871-1207
E-mail: info@olsonsgaskets.com

See full listing in **Section Two** under **gaskets**

R & L Engines Inc — engine rebuilding, restorations
308 Durham Rd
Dover, NH 03820
603-742-8812; FAX: 603-742-8137

See full listing in **Section Two** under **engine rebuilding**

RB's Prototype Model & Machine Co — machine work
44 Marva Ln
Stamford, CT 06903
203-329-2715; FAX: 203-329-8029
E-mail: rbprototype@aol.com

See full listing in **Section Two** under **service shops**

Section Two – Generalists

| **Rochester Clutch & Brake Co**
35 Niagara St
Rochester, NY 14605
716-232-2579; FAX: 716-232-3279 | brakes
clutches |

See full listing in **Section Two** under **brakes**

| **Rode's Restoration**
1406 Lohr Rd
Galion, OH 44833
419-468-5182; FAX: 419-462-1753
E-mail: rodes@bright.net | parts
restoration |

See full listing in **Section One** under **Mustang**

| **Simons Balancing & Machine Inc**
1987 Ashley River Rd
Charleston, SC 29407
843-766-3911; FAX: 843-766-9003 | machine work |

Balancing, boring, crank grinding, flywheel work, line boring, rod work, valve work.

| **Tatom Custom Engines**
PO Box 2504
Mt Vernon, WA 98273
360-424-8314; FAX: 360-424-6717
E-mail: flatheads@tatom.com | engine rebuilding
machine shop |

See full listing in **Section Two** under **engine rebuilding**

| **Thul Auto Parts Inc**
225 Roosevelt Ave
Plainfield, NJ 07060
800-276-8485, 908-754-3333
FAX: 908-756-0239
E-mail: thulauto@juno.com | boring
machine work
rebabbitting
vintage auto parts |

See full listing in **Section Two** under **engine rebuilding**

| **Valley Head Service Inc**
19340 Londelius St
Northridge, CA 91324
818-993-7000; FAX: 818-993-9712 | engine rebuilding
machine work |

See full listing in **Section Two** under **engine rebuilding**

| **Vintage Motor and Machine**
Gene French
1513 Webster Ct
Fort Collins, CO 80524
970-498-9224 | auto components
fixtures
industrial
components |

Mail order and open shop. Monday-Friday 7:30 am to 5 pm, Saturday 8 am to 12 pm. Manufacture babbitt bearing molds and fixtures for Model A and T Fords as well as other vehicles. Perform rebabbitting for most automotive and light industrial applications and general machine shop services including lathe, mill surface grinding and electric discharge machining. Design and building of injection and compression molds and short run production of industrial and automotive components.

| **Willow Automotive Service**
Box 4640, Rt 212
Willow, NY 12495
845-679-4679 | bodywork
painting
restorations |

See full listing in **Section Two** under **restoration shops**

manufacturing

| **A&A Mustang Parts & Mfg Co**
105 Fordham Rd
Oak Ridge, TN 37830
423-482-9445
E-mail: joannantrican@aol.com | exhaust systems
parts
restorations |

See full listing in **Section One** under **Mustang**

| **Advanced Plating & Powder Coating**
1425 Cowan Ct
Nashville, TN 37207
615-227-6900; FAX: 615-262-7935
E-mail: gochrome@aol.com | chrome plating
polishing
repair service |

See full listing in **Section Two** under **plating & polishing**

| **Advanced Racing Technologies Inc**
17 N Cross Rd
Staatsburg, NY 12580
PH/FAX: 845-889-4499
E-mail: advancedracing@
compuserve.com | wheel alignment |

See full listing in **Section Two** under **racing**

| **Alum-Line Inc**
US Hwy 9 W, PO Box 59
Cresco, IA 52136
800-446-1407; FAX: 563-547-5366
E-mail: alumline@powerbank.net | fabrication
manufacturing |

See full listing in **Section Two** under **trailers**

| **Angeli Machine Co**
417 N Varney St
Burbank, CA 91502
818-846-5359
E-mail: angelimach@aol.com | machine work |

See full listing in **Section Two** under **machine work**

| **ASC&P International**
PO Box 255
Uwchland, PA 19480
610-458-8395; FAX: 610-458-8735 | custom molding
fiberglass
plastic |

See full listing in **Section Two** under **fiberglass parts**

| **Baer Brake Systems**
3108 W Thomas Rd #1201
Phoenix, AZ 85017
602-233-1411; FAX: 602-352-8445
E-mail: brakes@baer.com | brakes |

See full listing in **Section Two** under **brakes**

| **Blast From the Past**
21006 Cornhusker Rd
Gretna, NE 68028
402-332-5050; FAX: 402-332-5029
E-mail: blast2past@aol.com | neon clocks
neon signs |

See full listing in **Section Two** under **automobilia**

| **Brookville Roadster Inc**
718 Albert Rd
Brookville, OH 45309
937-833-4605; FAX: 937-833-4785
E-mail: kenny@brookville-roadster.com | roadster bodies |

Mail order and open shop. Monday-Friday 8 am to 4:30 pm, Saturday 8 am to 12 pm. Specializing in the reproduction of 1928-1932 steel roadster bodies. Web site: www.brookville-roadster.com

Chassis Engineering Inc 119 N 2nd St, Box 70 West Branch, IA 52358 319-643-2645; FAX: 319-643-2801	brakes chassis parts suspension parts

See full listing in **Section Two** under **chassis parts**

Clark & Clark Specialty Products Inc 568 Central Ave Holland, MI 49423 616-396-4157; FAX: 616-396-0983 E-mail: obertro@macatawa.org	manufacturing

Open 9 am to 5 pm Eastern time. Specializing in the development and manufacturing of short-run (100-5,000 annual volume) products. Supply about 100 sports car (MG, Jaguar, Miata, etc) parts and accessories to catalog sellers and retail shops. From polyethylene transmission covers to brass logo tire valve caps. Plastics, metals, composites, wood, upholstered goods. Rotational molding, injection molding, thermoforming, casting, stamping, laser cutting, weldments, CNC routing and machining, screw machine turnings, etc. Wholesale only. Always looking for product ideas, automotive or otherwise.

DashCovers of Florida 1301 W Copans Rd, Ste F-8-9 Pompano Beach, FL 33064 800-441-3274; FAX: 954-970-9119 E-mail: danny@dashcover.com	accessories carpets car covers

See full listing in **Section Two** under **accessories**

Dashtop by Palco Ind Inc 5980 Alpha Ave Reno, NV 89506 775-677-0766; FAX: 775-677-8248	dashboard covers door panels

See full listing in **Section Two** under **interiors & interior parts**

Dodge City Vintage Dodge Vehicles & Parts 18584 Hwy 108, PO Box 1687 Jamestown, CA 95327 209-984-5858; FAX: 209-984-3285 E-mail: mike@dodgecityvintage.com	parts restoration research vehicles

See full listing in **Section One** under **Dodge**

Golden Mile Sales Inc J DeAngelo 2439 S Bradford St Allentown, PA 18103-5821 PH/FAX: 610-791-4497, 24 hours E-mail: abguy@enter.net	NORS parts NOS parts sheetmetal

See full listing in **Section One** under **American Austin/Bantam**

GRIFFIN Radiator 100 Hurricane Creek Rd Piedmont, SC 29673 800-RACE-RAD (722-3723) 864-845-5000; FAX: 864-845-5001 E-mail: griffinrad@aol.com	radiators

See full listing in **Section Two** under **radiators**

Alan Grove Components Inc 27070 Metcalf Rd Louisburg, KS 66053 913-837-4368; FAX: 913-837-5721	a/c components

See full listing in **Section Two** under **street rods**

Hi-Tech Aluminum & Automotive Products Inc 100 Industrial Ave, PO Box 1609 Cedartown, GA 30125 800-541-4946 E-mail: htechaluminum@aol.com	accessories windshield wipers

See full listing in **Section Two** under **windshield wipers**

Hillsboro Trailers 220 Industrial Rd Hillsboro, KS 67063 800-835-0209 E-mail: hii@gplains.com	trailers

See full listing in **Section Two** under **trailers**

Hurst Racing Tires/ Traction By Hurst 190 East Ave A, PO Box 278 Wendell, ID 83355 208-536-6236	drag tires slicks

See full listing in **Section Two** under **tires**

Hyde Products Inc PO Box 870321 New Orleans, LA 70187-0321 504-649-4041 E-mail: hydeprod@bellsouth.net	hood holders

See full listing in **Section One** under **Chevrolet**

Imtek Environmental Corporation PO Box 2066 Alpharetta, GA 30023 770-667-8621; FAX: 770-667-8683 E-mail: imtek@no-odor.com	ammonia removal products odor control products

Manufacturer of environmentally friendly odor and pollution control products for consumer and commercial applications. Over 100 types of unique environmentally friendly products such as: odor control products, ammonia removal products, water softeners. Web site: www.no-odor.com

Itsashoka Innovations 1215 Frazier Rd, PO Box 743 Albertville, AL 35950 256-891-4343; FAX: 256-891-0922	entry systems hood kits interior trim

Emergency entry systems for door, hood, trunk. Manufacturer of billet aluminum parts for street rods, knobs, bezels, trunk kits, hood kits, interior trim. Also item built for specialty use as item built to spec.

PK Lindsay Co Inc 63 Nottingham Rd Deerfield, NH 03037 800-258-3576; FAX: 800-843-2974 E-mail: sales@pklindsay.com	paint removal rust removal

See full listing in **Section Two** under **rust removal & stripping**

Lonny's Fabrication 44279 Cabo St Temecula, CA 92592 909-699-4582	custom fabrication welding

Specializing in custom fabrication, welding and chassis work for hot rods, etc, mainly 1930-1939 Ford cars.

National Spring Co Inc 1402 N Magnolia Ave El Cajon, CA 92020 619-441-1901; FAX: 619-441-2460	spring parts spring services

See full listing in **Section Two** under **suspension parts**

Prototype Research & Dev Ltd — fiberglass bodies
David Carlaw
230 Albert Ln
Campbellford, ON Canada K0L 1L0
705-653-4525; FAX: 705-653-4800
E-mail: davidcarlaw@hotmail.com

See full listing in **Section One** under **Chevrolet**

Rod Shop Performance Center Inc — exhaust systems
1126 Rockledge Rd
Attalla, AL 35954
256-538-0376
E-mail: rodshop@
rodshopperformance.com

See full listing in **Section Two** under **exhaust systems**

Rode's Restoration — parts / restoration
1406 Lohr Rd
Galion, OH 44833
419-468-5182; FAX: 419-462-1753
E-mail: rodes@bright.net

See full listing in **Section One** under **Mustang**

Rolling Steel Body Parts — body parts
7913 Chardon Rd, Rt 6
Kirtland, OH 44094
888-765-5460, 440-256-8383
FAX: 440-256-8994
E-mail: sales@rollingsteelbodyparts.com

See full listing in **Section Two** under **body parts**

Rubber Age LM Mfg Inc — rubber parts
13418 Halldale Ave
Gardena, CA 90249
310-329-2888; FAX: 310-532-4988
E-mail: rubberage@aol.com

See full listing in **Section Two** under **rubber parts**

Team Simpson Racing — safety products
328 FM 306
New Braunfels, TX 78130
830-625-1774; FAX: 830-625-3269

Mail order, direct sales, resellers, internet. Motorsport safety products. Simpson World Race Fan Stores: Mooresville, NC; Torrance, CA; Indianapolis, IN; Hershey, PA; Charlotte, NC. Web site: www.simpsonraceproducts.com

Ultra Shield Race Products — race car seats / safety equipment
19313 Hwy 69 S
Flint, TX 75762
903-894-3550; FAX: 903-894-3212
E-mail: sales@ultrashieldrace.com

Manufactures safety equipment, race car seats, etc. Web site: www.ultrashieldrace.com

Wholesale Express — buffing supplies / sandblasters
830 W 3rd St
Eddy, TX 76524
254-859-5364; FAX: 254-859-5407
E-mail: tommy@wacool.net

See full listing in **Section Two** under **accessories**

Zimmer Neo-Classic Motor Car Co — manufacturing
1415 W Genesee St
Syracuse, NY 13204
315-422-7011 ext 125
FAX: 315-422-1721
E-mail: azimmer@
syracusenewtimes.com

See full listing in **Section One** under **Zimmer**

military vehicles

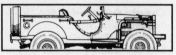

Automobilia — models
Division of Lustron Industries
18 Windgate Dr
New City, NY 10956
PH/FAX: 845-639-6806
E-mail: lustron@worldnet.att.net

See full listing in **Section Two** under **models & toys**

The Beachwood Canvas Works — canvas covers / parts / tops / upholstery
PO Box 137
Island Heights, NJ 08732
732-929-3168; FAX: 732-929-3479
E-mail: beachwood@adelphia.net

Research and reproduction of canvas tops, seat cushions, enclosures, decals, wiring harnesses, top bows and other antique four-wheel drive products to original manfacturers' specifications. Supply antique military and civilian Jeep and truck parts and canvas. Web site: www.beachwoodcanvas.com

Brian's 4wd Parts LLC — literature / parts
428 N Harbor St
Branford, CT 06405
203-481-5873; FAX: 203-481-3995
E-mail: willysgp@aol.com

See full listing in **Section One** under **Willys**

Cobbaton Combat Collection — museum
Chittlehampton
Umberleigh
N Devon EX37 9RZ England
01769-540740; FAX: 01769-540141
E-mail: info@cobbatoncombat.co.uk

Over 50 mainly WW II British and Canadian vehicles and artillery pieces plus thousands of smaller items, from tanks to ration books, all undercover, plus building dedicated to the home front. Militaria and souvenir shop, NAAFI cafeteria and children's play vehicles. Vehicles and spares to sell, also film and location hire. Web site: www.cobbatoncombat.co.uk

Commonwealth Automotive Restorations — body rebuilding / parts / restoration
1725 Hewins St
Ashley Falls, MA 01222
413-229-3196

See full listing in **Section One** under **Willys**

Dusty Memories and Faded Glory — rentals
118 Oxford Hts Rd
Somerset, PA 15501-1134
814-443-2393; FAX: 814-443-9452

Rental of military vehicles, trucks and tractors for veterans' organizations, movies, commercials and shows.

Firewall Insulators & Quiet Ride Solutions — air plenums / auto insulation / firewall insulators / gloveboxes / sound deadening
6465 Pacific Ave, Ste 249
Stockton, CA 95207
209-477-4840; FAX: 209-477-0918
E-mail: timcox@quietride.com

See full listing in **Section Two** under **upholstery**

Historical Military Armor Museum — museum
2330 Crystal St
Anderson, IN 46012
765-649-TANK; FAX: 765-642-0262

See full listing in **Section Six** under **Indiana**

| Kick-Start Motorcycle Parts Inc
PO Box 9347
Wyoming, MI 49509
616-245-8991 | parts |

See full listing in **Section One** under **Harley-Davidson**

| Nelson's Surplus Jeeps and Parts
1024 E Park Ave
Columbiana, OH 44408
330-482-5191 | heater kits
parts
tires |

Phone hours: Monday-Friday 9 am to 12 noon Eastern time; shop hours: Saturday 10:30 am to 3 pm Eastern time; other times by appointment. Specializing in military Jeeps, parts and all sizes of US military tread tires.

| Portrayal Press
PO Box 1190
Andover, NJ 07821
PH/FAX: 973-579-5781
E-mail: info@portrayal.com | books
manuals |

Mail order only. Publishes and sells manuals and books for older Jeeps, Dodge military trucks and other military trucks (WW II to modern) and tracked military vehicles such as tanks. 56-page full-size catalog mailed first class for $3 (overseas $5). Dennis R Spence, owner. Web site: www.portrayal.com

| Richardson Restorations
352 S I St
Tulare, CA 93274
559-688-5002
E-mail: cal5002@aol.com | custom work
repairs
restoration |

See full listing in **Section Two** under **restoration shops**

| Skopos Motor Museum
Alexandra Hills, Alexandra Rd
Batley
West Yorkshire WA7 6JA England
01924-444423 | museum |

See full listing in **Section Six** under **England**

| Wallace W Wade Specialty Tires
530 Regal Row, PO Box 560906
Dallas, TX 75356
800-666-TYRE, 214-688-0091
FAX: 214-634-8465
E-mail: wwwadest@earthlink.net | tires |

See full listing in **Section Two** under **tires**

models & toys

| Accent Models Inc
PO Box 295
Denville, NJ 07834
973-887-8403; FAX: 973-887-5088 | die cast models |

Mail order only. Die cast, white metal and promotional model cars and collector's items. Major credit cards accepted. Catalog $2, refundable.

| The Airplane Shop
24 Stewart Pl #4
Fairfield, NJ 07004
973-244-1203; FAX: 973-244-1227
E-mail: info@airplaneshop.com | collectibles
models |

The world's largest source of commercial and military aviation models and collectibles. Web site: www.airplaneshop.com

| American Classics Unlimited Inc
PO Box 192-V
Oak Lawn, IL 60454-0192
PH/FAX: 708-424-9223 | automobilia
models
toys |

Mail order and car shows. The Collectors Outlet Store, location: 9713 SW Hwy, Oak Lawn, IL 60453. Visit our store for the finest die cast models kits, dealer promotional model cars, promotional model trucks/banks, paints and accessories. Scales from 1/160th to 1/12th are carried along with current boxed Matchbox #1-75 issues. Sorry, no catalog available. Not in the area? Call with your needs.

| Asheville DieCast
1434 Brevard Rd
Asheville, NC 28806-9560
800-343-4685, 888-343-4685
828-667-9690; FAX: 828-667-1110
E-mail: sales@ashevillediecast.com | banks
models |

Internet, mail order and store. Monday-Friday 9 am to 5:30 pm, Saturday 9 am to 5 pm. Large selection of collectible banks, replica signs and vehicle replicas. Brand name products such as: Armour Airplane replicas, Ande Rooney porcelain/steel signs, Brooklin, Corgi, desktop wood airplane replicas, eagle's collectibles, First Gear gearbox, Jada toys, Liberty Classics, Lledo, Maisto, plastic gas vehicle promotionals, Racing Champions Ertl, Redbox, Spec Cast, Welly and Yat Ming. Web site: http://ashevillediecast.com

| Astro Models
13856 Roxanne Rd
Sterling Heights, MI 48312-5673
810-268-3479
E-mail: paully@home.com | accessories
parts |

Mail order only. Deal in model car parts and hand cast accessories, GMC Typhoon decals, Mag wheels, full size drag strip decals, flying eyeball decals and patches. 1/24, 1/25 scale only.

| Auctioneer Phil Jacquier Inc
18 Klaus Anderson Rd
Southwick, MA 01077
413-569-6421; FAX: 413-569-6599
E-mail: info@jacquierauctions.com | auctions |

See full listing in **Section Two** under **auctions & shows**

| Auto Motif Inc
2941 Atlanta Rd SE
Smyrna, GA 30080-3654
770-435-5025; FAX: 413-521-5298
E-mail: automotifinc@aol.com | automobilia
models
signs |

See full listing in **Section Two** under **automobilia**

| Auto Muzeuma Haris (Bross)
Testverek
1117 Budapest
XI, Moricz Zsigmond Korter 12
Hungary
01 (1) 3656893 | museum |

See full listing in **Section Six** under **Hungary**

| Auto Nostalgia Enr
332 St Joseph
Mont St Gregoire, QC Canada J0J 1K0
PH/FAX: 450-346-3644
E-mail: autonostalgia@vif.com | literature
manuals
models
tractor decals |

Mail order and open shop. Tuesday-Saturday 9 am to 8 pm, closed Sundays and Mondays. Automotive literature, shop manuals, parts lists, car books, tractor manuals, owner's manuals, sales catalogs, new and used. Also models, plastic, die cast, all makes, white metal. Hobby shop for collectors of real vehicles and models. New and old toys and literature. Buy, sell, trade. Credit cards ok. Web site: www.vif.com/users/autonostalgia/

Auto Zone
33202 Woodward Ave
Birmingham, MI 48009
800-647-7288; FAX: 248-646-5381
E-mail: info@azautozone.com

books
magazines
models
videos

Mail order and open shop. Monday-Friday 10 am to 8 pm, Saturday 10 am to 7 pm, closed Sundays. Metro Detroit's largest selection of automobilia including a large selection of books covering all makes and subjects. More than 120 different magazines from around the world. Die cast models from 1:87th scale to 1:12th scale including Brooklin, Minichamps, Brumm, Best/Bang and Kyosho as well as plastic kits, promos, videos, clothing and collectibles. The store for the auto enthusiast. Web site: www.azautozone.com

Autohobbies
Jim & Nancy Schaut
7147 W Angela Dr
Glendale, AZ 85308
623-878-4293
E-mail: nancy@autohobbies.com

memorabilia
toys

See full listing in **Section Two** under **automobilia**

Automobilia
200 N Emporia
Wichita, KS 67202
PH/FAX: 316-264-9986
E-mail: automobilia@juno.com

gas pumps
models
signs

See full listing in **Section Two** under **automobilia**

Automobilia
Division of Lustron Industries
18 Windgate Dr
New City, NY 10956
PH/FAX: 845-639-6806
E-mail: lustron@worldnet.att.net

models

Mail order only. 1/43 scale die cast models of classic and historic European cars with emphasis on race cars. These are models of cars from the turn of the century through the 1980s. Also offer convenience of automatic shipments and extra savings to club members.

Autophile Car Books
850 Eglinton Ave E
Toronto, ON Canada M4G 2L1
PH/FAX: 416-425-1555
E-mail: info@autophile.ca

books
models

See full listing in **Section Four** under **books & publications**

Barnett Design Inc
PO Box 160
Twin Lakes, WI 53181
262-877-9343; FAX: 262-877-9320

models

Mail order and open shop Monday-Friday by appointment only. Large 1/10 scale stylized models. Limited Edition of 100 Schlemmer Dry Lakes roadsters, cover car on the first issue of Hot Rod magazine (1948). Still have a few left. This model features the original flames with hand painted stripes and numbers, $450 plus s&h. Web site: www.barnettmodels.com

Bonneville Speed & Supply
PO Box 3924
Tustin, CA 92781
714-666-1966; FAX: 714-666-1955
E-mail: bonspeed@aol.com

memorabilia
vintage clothing

See full listing in **Section Two** under **apparel**

Bonneville Sports Inc
3544 Enterprise Dr
Anaheim, CA 92807
888-999-7258, 714-666-1966
FAX: 714-666-1955
E-mail: bonspeed@aol.com

accessories
clothing

See full listing in **Section Two** under **apparel**

British Only Motorcycles and Parts Inc
32451 Park Ln
Garden City, MI 48135
734-421-0303; FAX: 734-422-9253
E-mail: info@britishonly.com

literature
memorabilia
motorcycles
parts

See full listing in **Section Two** under **motorcycles**

C&N Reproductions Inc
1341 Ashover Ct
Bloomfield Hills, MI 48304
248-853-0215; FAX: 248-852-1999
E-mail: ckcn@ix.netcom.com

pedal cars

See full listing in **Section Two** under **automobilia**

Caddytown™/Pawl Engineering Co
4960 Arrowhead, PO Box 240105
West Bloomfield, MI 48324
PH/FAX: 248-682-2007
E-mail: pawl@earthlink.net

memorabilia
parts
toys

See full listing in **Section One** under **Cadillac/LaSalle**

Car Collectables
32 White Birch Rd
Madison, CT 06443
PH/FAX: 203-245-9203

banks
Christmas cards
note cards

See full listing in **Section Two** under **artwork**

Castle Display Case Co
102 W Garfield Ave
New Castle, PA 16105-2544
724-654-6358

models

Mail order only. Handmade oak display cases made for model cars, trucks, trains, farm tractors, etc. Large selection of vertical and horizontal sizes available.

Central Florida Auto Festival & Toy Expo
1420 N Galloway Rd
Lakeland, FL 33810
863-686-8320

auto festival
toy expo

See full listing in **Section Two** under **auctions & shows**

Ceramicar
679 Lapla Rd
Kingston, NY 12401
PH/FAX: 845-338-2199

auto-related
ceramics

See full listing in **Section Two** under **artwork**

DeLorean Literature
3116 Welsh Rd
Philadelphia, PA 19136-1810
215-338-6142; PH/FAX: 888-392-4832
ext 291-291-1979 (* for fax)
E-mail: delorean.literature@excite.com

collectibles
literature

See full listing in **Section One** under **DeLorean**

Section Two – Generalists

Diecast & More   die cast models
11709 Oakland Dr   toys
Schoolcraft, MI 49087
616-679-4002
E-mail: lstrong639@aol.com

Mail order only. 1/18, 1/24 Ertl toys, Maisto, Burago, Racing Champions, Road Champs, all makes and models. Also car buckles, car necklaces, car earrings and all types of plastic model kits. Hot Wheels, Matchbox cars, old and new, loose and in packages. Also Coke collectables and gas station memorabilia. Send want list or for request list. Send LSASE (2 oz) for list of inventory cars. Allow 2 weeks for shipping.

Dominion Models   models
PO Box 515
Salem, VA 24153
PH/FAX: 540-375-3750
E-mail: dominionmodels@aol.com

Mail order only. Specialize in 1/43rd scale die cast and white metal models of American cars. Free illustrated brochure available.

EWA & Miniature Cars USA Inc   books
205 US Hwy 22   models
Green Brook, NJ 08812-1909   subscriptions
732-424-7811; FAX: 732-424-7814   videos
E-mail: ewa@ewacars.com

Mail order and showroom. Publishes *Classic & Sportscar*, monthly publication filled with timely news, previews of upcoming events, auction news & event information. Includes huge classified section. Published in England. Featuring 15,000 different scale models from 400 manufacturers. Subscription: $69/year. Also available are subscriptions for 40 foreign automobile magazines, including back issues and 3,000 different auto books. Also 600 auto videos. Almost 16,000 different products. Huge 128-page color catalog $4. Web site: www.ewacars.com

Finest In Fords   books
Larry Blodget   Ford 1954-up
Box 753   model cars
Ranchero Mirage, CA 92270   restoration services
E-mail: info@finestinfords.com

See full listing in **Section Four** under **books & publications**

Get It On Paper   automobilia
Gary Weickart, President   literature
185 Maple St   toys
Islip, NY 11751
631-581-3897

See full listing in **Section Two** under **automobilia**

GMP (Georgia Marketing & Promotions)   die cast replicas
PO Box 570
Winder, GA 30680
800-536-1637, 770-307-1042
FAX: 770-867-0786
E-mail: peachgmp@peachgmp.com

GMP has been providing top quality, limited production die cast replicas to the collector for over eight years. Our reputation for attention to detail and accuracy continues to grow with each new project. Our replicas include vintage dirt cars, vintage midgets, winged sprints, muscle cars, vintage road racing and upcoming front engine dragsters. Web site: www.peachgmp.com

Jerry Goldsmith Promos   models
4634 Cleveland Heights
Lakeland, FL 33813
863-644-7013, 863-646-8490
PH/FAX: 863-644-5013
E-mail: shirley.goldsmith@gte.net

See full listing in **Section Two** under **automobilia**

Grandpa's Attic   toys
112 E Washington
Goshen, IN 46528
219-534-2778

Mail order and open shop. Monday-Friday 9:30 am to 5 pm, Saturday until 3 pm. Specializing in die cast collector toys.

H D Garage   appraisals
Barry Brown   artwork
Comp 8 Bedford Mills, RR #2   literature
Westport, ON Canada K0G 1X0   motorcycles
613-273-5036
E-mail: bruffsup@hotmail.com or
oldmill@rideau.net

See full listing in **Section Two** under **motorcycles**

Richard Hamilton   sales literature
28 E 46th St
Indianapolis, IN 46205
317-283-1902

See full listing in **Section Two** under **literature dealers**

Hobby Express Inc   die cast models
309 Mars-Valencia Rd   kits
Mars, PA 16046
724-625-1550; FAX: 724-625-8599
E-mail: hobby@nauticom.net

Mail order and open shop. Monday-Friday 10 am to 9 pm, Saturday 10 am to 6 pm. Deals in die cast, plastic kits of classic, muscle and current cars and trucks. Web site: www.hobbyexpressinc.com

Hotchkiss Mfg/Clear Case   display cases
PO Box 810
Merlin, OR 97532
800-444-5005; FAX: 541-476-0268
E-mail: hotchkiss@chatlink.com

Quality wood and acrylic display cases for collector cars, trains, ships and dolls. Web site: www.chatlink.com/~hotchkiss

International House of Toys   toys
16582 Jamesville Rd
Muskego, WI 53150
414-422-9505; FAX: 414-422-9507

Mail order and open shop. Monday-Friday 10 am to 6 pm, Saturday 10 am to 4 pm. Specializing in die cast toys.

Melissa & Jerry Jess   accessories
3121 E Yucca St   literature
Phoenix, AZ 85028   models
602-867-7672
E-mail: vwstuff@qwest.net

See full listing in **Section One** under **Volkswagen**

K&S Industries   display cases
1801 Union Center Hwy
Endicott, NY 13760
PH/FAX: 888-PICK-KNS
E-mail: pleximan@888pickkns.com

Mail order only. Monday-Friday 9 am to 5 pm Eastern time. Acrylic display cases for model cars. Web site: www.888pickkns.com

Karl's Collectibles   banks
41 Chestnut St   collectibles
Lewiston, ME 04240   logo design
800-636-0457, 207-784-0098
FAX: 207-795-0295
E-mail: karl@designsbyskip.com

Mail order and open shop. Monday-Friday 9 am to 5 pm. Die cast banks and collectibles, as well as custom logo and printing needs. Design, market and broker collectibles, specializing in the motorcycle trade but not exclusive. Now offer screen printing at very reasonable prices. Design logos for new companies as well as companies looking for that new look. Web site: www.karlscollectibles.com

KJ Classic Metal Designs   *toys*
PO Box 663
Winder, GA 30680
770-867-4452; FAX: 770-586-0163
E-mail: kjclassic@mindspring.com

See full listing in **Section Two** under **automobilia**

LA Ltd Design Graphics   *artwork / design / greeting cards*
822A S McDuffie St
Anderson, SC 29624
PH/FAX: 864-231-7715

See full listing in **Section Two** under **automobilia**

The Last Precinct Police Museum   *museum*
15677 Hwy 62 W
Eureka Springs, AR 72632
501-253-4948; FAX: 501-253-4949

See full listing in **Section Six** under **Arkansas**

Legendary Motorcars LLC   *model cars*
34 Tuckahoe Rd, PMB #350
Marmora, NJ 08223
609-399-2401; FAX: 609-399-2512

Producer of hand built model cars for the connoisseur collector. Very limited production. 1/43rd scale, retail price $259. Third issue is a 1967 Cadillac Eldorado in a steel top and padded top version. Telephone, fax or write for more information.

Lilliput Motor Co, LLC   *tin toys*
321 S Main St
Yerington, NV 89447
775-463-5181; FAX: 775-463-1582
E-mail: lilliput@tele-net.net

Deal in mechanical toys, vintage, tin plate and die cast. Exclusive distributor Schuco, Paya and Gonio in North America. Web site: www.lilliputmotorcompany.com

Little Old Cars   *model cars*
3410 Fulton Dr NW
Canton, OH 44718
216-455-4685

Mail order and open shop. Monday-Friday 4 pm to 10 pm, Saturday-Sunday 8 am to 10 pm. Specializing in promotional model cars, 1950s-up. Also unbuilt kits. Buy, sell and trade. All correspondences welcome. No catalog available. Please include SASE for immediate response.

Mercedes-Benz Visitor Center   *museum*
PO Box 100
Tuscaloosa, AL 35403-0100
888-2TOUR-MB, 205-507-2253
FAX: 205-507-2255

See full listing in **Section One** under **Mercedes-Benz**

Midwestern KlipperKarts   *model cars*
67742 CR 23
New Paris, IN 46553
219-831-5200; FAX: 219-831-5210
E-mail: bhoward@midwesternklipperkarts.com

80 different models and body styles of mini cars. Prowlers, Vipers, 1957 Chevy, 1957 Thunderbird, NASCARS, Dodge Dakota and Ram, Kenworth Peterbuilt, Model Ts, Model As. We also do promotional displays. Web site: www.klipperkarts.com

Milestone Motorcars   *die cast cars*
Mark Tyra
3317 Nevel Meade Dr
Prospect, KY 40059
502-228-5945; FAX: 502-228-1856
E-mail: coolcars@milestonemotorcars.com

Call us Wednesday/Thursday, e-mail, or send $2 for latest listing. Diecast 1:18th scale models. Over 1,000 cars available on our web site. We specialize in Limited Editions and hard to find discontinued cars. Visit our web site: www.milestonemotorcars.com

Model Engineering   *new parts casting*
Gene or Jeff Sanders
3284 S Main St
Akron, OH 44319
330-644-3450; FAX: 330-644-0088

See full listing in **Section Two** under **castings**

Neil's Wheels Inc   *toys*
Box 354
Old Bethpage, NY 11804-0354
516-293-9659; FAX: 516-420-0483
E-mail: nw@neilswheels.com

We specialize in Matchbox toys, Matchbox collectibles, AHL and the Magic Box display system since 1980. Web site: www.neilswheels.com

On Mark International Inc   *replicas*
8923 S 43rd W Ave
Tulsa, OK 74132
888-373-2092, 918-446-7906
FAX: 918-445-1532
E-mail: onmark@igeotec.net

Producer of die cast replica trucks and planes. Web site: www.onmarkint.com

Pedal Toys   *pedal toys*
210 South St
Dodge Center, MN 55927
800-770-5638
E-mail: smms@clear.lakes.co

Specializing in the reproduction of toy pedal cars, trucks, planes, trikes and wagons. These pedal cars are all metal construction, geared to 2-6 year old children. Blasts from the past 1940s and 1950s pedal toys. Web site: www.sominn.co

People Kars   *models/more VW toys*
290 Third Ave Ext
Rensselaer, NY 12144
518-465-0477; FAX: 518-465-0614
E-mail: peoplekars@aol.com

See full listing in **Section One** under **Volkswagen**

PM Research Inc   *books / models*
4110 Niles Hill Rd
Wellsville, NY 14895
716-593-3169; FAX: 716-593-5637
E-mail: pmrgang@pmresearchinc.com

PM Research manufactures a large line of model stationary steam engine kits, model boilers and operating model machine shop tools. Model pipe and machined or unmachined pipe fittings available as well as a line of "Stirling" hot air engines. Large selection of related books. Send for catalog at above address, Dept 98, only $3. Or visit our web site: www.pmreasearchinc.com

Hugo Prado Limited Edition Corvette Art Prints   *fine art prints*
PO Box 18437
Chicago, IL 60618-0437
PH/FAX: 773-681-7770
E-mail: vetteart@aol.com

See full listing in **Section One** under **Corvette**

Lloyd Ralston Gallery
350 Long Beach Blvd
Stratford, CT 06615
203-386-9399; FAX: 203-386-9519
E-mail: lrgallery@aol.com

toys

Open Monday-Friday 10 am to 4 pm. Auction gallery specializing in old toys and trains. We buy and sell vintage toy trains, die cast autos, and soldiers. Web site: www.lloydralstontoys.com

Rideable Antique Bicycle Replicas
2329 Eagle Ave
Alameda, CA 94501
510-769-0980; FAX: 510-521-7145
E-mail: hiwheel@barrongroup.com

bicycles
spokes
tires

See full listing in **Section Two** under **motorcycles**

Frank Riley Automotive Art
PO Box 95
Hawthorne, NJ 07506
800-848-9459
E-mail: rileystudio@netscape.net

automotive prints

See full listing in **Section Two** under **artwork**

Route 1 Scale Models
421 E Washington St
North Attleboro, MA 02760
508-695-0588; FAX: 508-699-8649
E-mail: rt1models@naisp.net

models

Located on Route 1, North Attleboro, MA. Specializing in hand-built fire truck models (Ashton Models) and unique handbuilt construction models.

Samlerborsen
Jacobys Alle 2-4
DK 1806 Frederiksberg C Denmark
+45-33254022; FAX: +45-33250622

books
toys

See full listing in **Section Two** under **literature dealers**

Scott Signal Co
8368 W Farm Rd 84
Willard, MO 65781
417-742-5040

stoplights

See full listing in **Section Two** under **automobilia**

Showcase Express
17862 Metzler Ln
Huntington Beach, CA 92647
714-842-5564 ext 29
FAX: 714-842-6534
E-mail: carl@sonos1.com

display systems

Mail order and open shop. Monday-Friday 8 am to 5 pm. Showcase Express display system, expandable system that grows with your collection. Includes dustproof windows and end caps. Three sizes fit: 64th, 43rd and 25th. Optional raceway background, step shelf and Monza track. Versatile system displays cars, trains, any collectible. Web site: www.showcase-express.com

Sinclair's Mini-Auto
PO Box 8403-HVAA
Erie, PA 16505
PH/FAX: 814-838-2274, 24 hours

miniature cars

Established 1964, this is the oldest firm in the models-by-mail business and exclusive distributor-western hemisphere for VF Modellautomobiles of Germany who make hand-crafted miniatures in 1:43 and 1:24 scale at $165 up. Many Cadillacs, including hearses, flower cars and ambulances; Rolls, Lincolns, James Bond cars. Other lines include: MiniMarque 43, Durham, Conquest-Madison, Design Studio, Stylish Cars Duesenbergs and many more. Catalog $2 (with $4 rebate coupon).

Spec Cast
428 6th Ave NW, Box 368
Dyersville, IA 52040-0368
319-875-8706; FAX: 319-875-8056
E-mail: info@speccast.com

models

Spec Cast manufactures accurate replica scale die cast models of street rods, pickups and panel deliveries that can be customized to use as promotional items. Web site: www.speccast.com

Speedzone
1750 Broadway
New Hyde Park, NY 11040
516-354-8178; FAX: 516-354-0692
E-mail: sales@speedzoneusa.com

die cast models

Deals in die cast collectibles of street cars, NASCAR, Formula I, IRL and CART. Web site: www.speedzoneusa.com

Spyder Enterprises Inc
RFD 1682
Laurel Hollow, NY 11791-9644
516-367-1616; FAX: 516-367-3260
E-mail: singer356@aol.com

accessories
artwork
automobilia
books

See full listing in **Section Two** under **automobilia**

TCMB Models & Stuff
8207 Clinton Ave S
Bloomington, MN 55420-2315
952-884-3997; FAX: 952-884-2827
E-mail: info@tcmbmodels.com

models

Mail order only. Metal model kits, 1/25 scale vehicle banks and 1/43rd scale vehicles. Accept Visa, MasterCard, American Express and Discover cards. Web site: www.tcmbmodels.com

Edward Tilley Automotive Collectibles
PO Box 4233
Cary, NC 27519-4233
919-460-8262
E-mail: edandsusan@aol.com

automobilia
literature
parts

See full listing in **Section Two** under **automobilia**

Town & Country Toys
227 Midvale Dr, PO Box 574
Marshall, WI 53559
608-655-4961
E-mail: dejaeger@itis.com

banks
Ertl cars
mini license plates

Mail order and open shop. Tuesday 7 pm to 9 pm and Saturday afternoons. Dealing in 1/18th scale die cast Ertl cars. Originator and supplier of Ertl's Mach 1s. Farm toys, truck and airplane banks, engraved miniature license plates. Send for list, specify interest.

USAopoly Inc
565 Westlake St
Encinitas, CA 92024
760-634-5910; FAX: 760-634-5923
E-mail: christian@usaopoly.com

Monopoly® game

Mail order only. Special editions of the Monopoly® game: Corvette, Harley-Davidson, Dale Earnhardt and Mustang. Web site: www.usaopoly.com

Vanda Die Cast
1107 E Bell Rd #2
Phoenix, AZ 85022
877-856-2674 toll free
FAX: 602-493-8656

die cast models

Collectible scale model die cast vehicles, racing die cast and memorabilia. NASCAR, Indy, NHRA and Sprints. Collections bought. Web site: www.vandaenterprises.com

Section Two – Generalists

Jim Wangers   memorabilia
1309 Melrose Way
Vista, CA 92083
760-941-9303; FAX: 760-941-9305
E-mail: info@jimwangers.com

See full listing in **Section One** under **Pontiac**

Brady Ward-Scale Autoworks   models
313 Bridge St #4
Manchester, NH 03104-5045
PH/FAX: 603-623-5925

Mail order-workshop open by appointment only. Fine 1/8 scale
custom-built model cars with custom paint and interiors, specializing in the classic Alfa Romeo 8C2300, Bugatti 50T, and
Ferrari F40, Testarossa, 643 F1. Also selling super detail trans
kits and accessories for the Pocher 1/8 scale kits and Randy
Owens Classic F1 prints, featuring Gilles Villeneuve, Monaco,
and Long Beach USGP. Web site: www.scaleautoworks.com

West Michigan Die-Cast Cars   die cast cars
2523 W Kinney Rd
Ludington, MI 49431
616-843-4278
E-mail: wmpc@t-one.net

Deal in 1/18th scale die cast cars, airplanes. Web site:
www.t-one.net/~wmpc/

Wheels O' Time Museum   museum
PO Box 9636
Peoria, IL 61612-9636
309-243-9020
E-mail: wotmuseum@aol.com

See full listing in **Section Six** under **Illinois**

Kirk F White   models
PO Box 999   tin toys
New Smyrna Beach, FL 32170
386-427-6660; FAX: 386-427-7801
E-mail: kirkfwhite@mindspring.com

Mail order and open shop by appointment only. Early gas
engined racing cars of all types. Early historied hot rods, racing
memorabilia, fine large scale racing models. All types of early
European transportation tin toys.

Clarence Young Autohobby   antique toy vehicles
300-1 Reems Creek Rd   dealer promos
Weaverville, NC 28787   exclusive metal cars
PH/FAX: 828-645-5243   exclusive resin cars
E-mail: cya@carhobby.com

Mail order and open shop by appointment. Obsolete dealer promotionals, model kits and antique toy vehicles. Manufacturer of
1/25th metal cars and resin cars. Showroom sales materials.
Web site: www.carhobby.com

motorcycles

AMC Classic Appraisers   appraisals
7963 Depew St
Arvada, CO 80003
303-428-8760; FAX: 303-428-1070

See full listing in **Section Two** under **appraisals**

Auto Advisors   appraisals
14 Dudley Rd
Billerica, MA 01821
978-667-0075

See full listing in **Section Two** under **appraisals**

Auto Muzeuma Haris (Bross)   museum
Testverek
1117 Budapest
XI, Moricz Zsigmond Korter 12
Hungary
01 (1) 3656893

See full listing in **Section Six** under **Hungary**

Backwoods Auto   motorcycles
487 Esperance Rd   repairs
Esperance, NY 12066
518-875-6538
E-mail: backwoods_auto@hotmail.com

Mail order and open shop. Monday-Saturday. Vintage American
motorcycles, early British motorcycles, antique auto repairs, parts
fabrication, early electric repairs, instrument repairs. Web site:
http://hammer.prohosting.com/~backwood/backwoods.html

Berliner Classic Motorcars Inc   automobilia
1975 Stirling Rd   car dealer
Dania Beach, FL 33004   motorcycles
954-923-7271; FAX: 954-926-3306
E-mail: info@berlinerclassiccars.com

See full listing in **Section Two** under **car dealers**

Bimmer Magazine   magazine
42 Digital Dr #5
Novato, CA 94949
415-382-0580; FAX: 415-382-0587

See full listing in **Section Four** under **periodicals**

BPE Racing Heads   cylinder heads
702 Dunn Way
Placentia, CA 92870
714-572-6072; FAX: 714-572-6073
E-mail: steve@bpeheads.com

See full listing in **Section Two** under **machine work**

British Only Motorcycles and   literature
Parts Inc   memorabilia
32451 Park Ln   motorcycles
Garden City, MI 48135   parts
734-421-0303; FAX: 734-422-9253
E-mail: info@britishonly.com

Mail order only. Dealing in British motorcycles and parts. Literature and memorabilia for all motorcycles. Online auction site at:
gearheadauction.com. Web site: www.britishonly.com

British Wiring Inc   wiring accessories
20449 Ithaca Rd   wiring harnesses
Olympia Fields, IL 60461
PH/FAX: 708-481-9050
E-mail: britishwiring@ameritech.net

See full listing in **Section Two** under **wiring harnesses**

Brooks Performance Coatings   powder coatings
17819 SW Fisner Rd
Sherwood, OR 97140
503-524-4048

See full listing in **Section Two** under **special services**

Caswell Electroplating in Miniature   plating kits
4336 Rt 31
Palmyra, NY 14522
315-597-5140, 315-597-6378
FAX: 315-597-1457
E-mail: sales@caswellplating.com

See full listing in **Section Two** under **plating & polishing**

Champion Luggage Trailers | luggage trailer kits
9471 Hemlock Cir
Shreveport, LA 71118
318-688-2787

See full listing in **Section Two** under **trailers**

Classic Car Research | appraisals
29508 Southfield Rd, Ste 106 | consultant
Southfield, MI 48076 | part locating
248-557-2880; FAX: 248-557-3511
E-mail: kawifreek@msn.com

See full listing in **Section Two** under **appraisals**

Coker Tire | tires
1317 Chestnut St
Chattanooga, TN 37402
800-251-6336 toll free
423-265-6368 local & international
FAX: 423-756-5607

See full listing in **Section Two** under **tires**

Malcolm C Elder & Son | car dealer
The Motor Shed | motorcycles
Middle Aston, Bicester
Oxfordshire OX25 5QL England
PH/FAX: 01869 340999
E-mail: malcolmcelderson@
btinternet.com

See full listing in **Section Two** under **car dealers**

Extreme Motorsports Painting Ltd | bodywork
300 Old Reading Pike | painting
Stowe, PA 19464
610-326-4425; FAX: 610-326-8522
E-mail: extrememail@aol.com

See full listing in **Section Two** under **painting**

Finders Service | parts finders
454-458 W Lincoln Hwy
Chicago Heights, IL 60411-2463
708-481-9685; FAX: 708-481-5837
E-mail: finderssvc@aol.com

See full listing in **Section Two** under **car & parts locators**

Geeson Bros Motorcycle Museum | museum
& Workshop
2-6 Water Ln
South Witham
Grantham Lincs NG33 5PH England
01572 767280, 01572 768195

See full listing in **Section Six** under **England**

J Giles Automotive | car & parts locator
703 Morgan Ave | exporter
Pascagoula, MS 39567-2116
228-769-1012; FAX: 228-769-8904
E-mail: jgauto@datasync.com

See full listing in **Section Two** under **car & parts locators**

Guenther Graphics | artwork
PO Box 266
LeClaire, IA 52753
PH/FAX: 319-289-9010
E-mail: artwork@guenthergraphics.com

See full listing in **Section Two** under **artwork**

H D Garage | appraisals
Barry Brown | artwork
Comp 8 Bedford Mills RR #2 | literature
Westport, ON Canada K0G 1X0 | motorcycles
613-273-5036
E-mail: bruffsup@hotmail.com or
oldmill@rideau.net

Rare pre-WW II motorcycles and related literature and artworks (bronzes, paintings, miniatures, etc), Brough-Superior, Crocker, early Harley (especially racers) and American 4-cylinder specialist. Parts information and restoration and location services for these and others. OHC Norton collector and specialist. Continental European racing bikes, etc sought, top dollar paid and finder's fee. Also appraisals.

Harley Rendezvous Classic | motorcycle events
1142 Batter St
Pattersonville, NY 12137
518-864-5659; FAX: 518-864-5917
E-mail: frank@harleyrendezvous.com

Specializing in motorcycle events and swap meets.

Hi-Speed | literature
John Steel | motorcycles
PO Box 44 | parts
Chagrin Falls, OH 44022
PH/FAX: 440-247-6021

See full listing in **Section One** under **Harley-Davidson**

Hosking Cycle Works | motorcycle parts
136 Hosking Ln
Accord, NY 12404
845-626-4231; FAX: 845-626-3245
E-mail: cycle@ulster.net

ROKON RT and MX 340 motorcycle parts. Service and parts books. Anything for vintage racing or show restorations of ROKON motorcycles. Web site: www.hoskingcycle.com

Jesser's Auto Clinic | appraisals
26 West St
Akron, OH 44303
330-376-8181; FAX: 330-384-9129

See full listing in **Section Two** under **appraisals**

Kick-Start Motorcycle Parts Inc | parts
PO Box 9347
Wyoming, MI 49509
616-245-8991

See full listing in **Section One** under **Harley-Davidson**

Liberty Harley-Davidson | accessories
32 E Cuyahoga Falls Ave | parts
Akron, OH 44310 | service
330-535-9900; FAX: 330-535-2354
E-mail: libertyhd@hotmail.com

See full listing in **Section One** under **Harley-Davidson**

Luback & Co | parts
456 W Lincoln Hwy
Chicago Heights, IL 60411-2463
708-481-9685; FAX: 708-481-5837
E-mail: lubackco@aol.com

Open Monday-Saturday 11 am to 4 pm. We only locate 1920-1996 motorcycle OEM, official equipment manufacture new and used genuine parts, accessories and tools. Web site: www.usaworks.com/finderssvc

M & R Products
1940 SW Blvd
Vineland, NJ 08360
800-524-2560, 609-696-9450
FAX: 609-696-4999
E-mail: mrproducts@mrproducts.com

hardware
tie-downs

See full listing in **Section Two** under **accessories**

Mid-America Auctions
2277 W Hwy 36, Ste 324
St Paul, MN 55113
651-633-9655; FAX: 651-633-3212
E-mail: midauction@aol.com

auctions

See full listing in **Section Two** under **auctions & shows**

Moores Cycle Supply
49 Custer St
West Hartford, CT 06110
860-953-1689; FAX: 860-953-4366

motorcycles
parts

Mail order and open shop. Monday-Friday 12 noon to 8 pm, Saturday 2 pm to 5 pm. Deal in motorcycles, parts for Triumphs, BSA, Norton motorcycles.

Moto Guzzi, Harper's
32401 Stringtown Rd
Greenwood, MO 64034
800-752-9735, 816-697-3411
FAX: 816-566-3413
E-mail: harpermoto@att.net

accessories
bikes
parts

Mail order and open shop. Monday-Friday 9 am to 5 pm, Saturday 9 am to 1 pm, closed Sundays and all holidays. Exploding with lots of stock. New, used, antique, classic and hard-to-find Moto Guzzi bikes and parts. Lots of NOS too. Aftermarket accessories for the Moto Guzzi motorcycle. Only $3 for aftermarket catalog. Bike flyer available, listing most of the bikes we have for sale. Ship bikes and parts worldwide. Visa, MasterCard, American Express. Web site: www.harpermotoguzzi.com

Motorcycle Museum (Motorrad Museum)
Lengericher Str
49479 Ibbenburen Germany
05451-6454

museum

See full listing in **Section Six** under **Germany**

National Parts Locator Service
636 East 6th St #81
Ogden, UT 84404-2415
877-672-7875, 801-627-7210

parts locator

See full listing in **Section Two** under **car & parts locators**

North Yorkshire Motor Museum
D T Mathewson
Roxby Garage, Pickering Rd
Thornton-le-Dale, North Yorkshire
England
01751 474455; FAX: 01944 758188

museum

See full listing in **Section Six** under **England**

Redi-Strip Company
100 W Central Ave
Roselle, IL 60172
630-529-2442; FAX: 630-529-3626

abrasive media
baking soda blasting
paint removal
rust removal

See full listing in **Section Two** under **rust removal & stripping**

Reinholds Restorations
c/o Rick Reinhold
PO Box 178, 255 N Ridge Rd
Reinholds, PA 17569-0178
717-336-5617; FAX: 717-336-7050

appraisals
repairs
restoration

See full listing in **Section Two** under **restoration shops**

Rideable Antique Bicycle Replicas
2329 Eagle Ave
Alameda, CA 94501
510-769-0980; FAX: 510-521-7145
E-mail: hiwheel@barrongroup.com

bicycles
spokes
tires

Mail order only. Specializing in 1880 full-size antique high wheel bicycles, 15 different models from 1870-1895. Solid rubber tires for pedal cars, tea carts, buggy wheel, gasoline cart. 1880 replica catalogs. Bicycle oil lamps. Schwinn Stingray replica parts, spring forks, frames, etc. Spokes, any size, motorcycle, antique bicycle. Web site: www.hiwheel.com

Sanders Antique Auto Restoration
1120 22nd St
Rockford, IL 61108
815-226-0535

restoration

See full listing in **Section Two** under **restoration shops**

Slim's Garage
PO Box 49
Seminary, MS 39479-0049
PH/FAX: 601-722-9861

garden tractors

See full listing in **Section Two** under **trucks & tractors**

TK Performance Inc
1508 N Harlan Ave
Evansville, IN 47711
812-422-6820; FAX: 812-422-5282

engine building
machine work
restoration

See full listing in **Section One** under **Harley-Davidson**

Toys n' Such
437 Dawson St
Sault Sainte Marie, MI 49783
906-635-0356
E-mail: rtraut@portup.com

parts

Mail order only. For English cycles, 1940s-1960s, some German and Italian parts from same years, along with dealer brochures. Also buying toy motorcycles and race cars. Mopar parts for sale, NOS, 1940s-1960s; also dealer brochures for sale. US and European, including Canadian.

Walneck's Inc
7923 Janes Ave
Woodridge, IL 60517
630-985-4995; FAX: 630-985-2750

motorcycles
murals
posters

See full listing in **Section Two** under **artwork**

Harold Warp Pioneer Village Foundation
PO Box 68
Minden, NE 68959-0068
308-832-1181; FAX: 308-832-2750
800-445-4447 (out of state)
E-mail: pioneervllge@nebi.com

museum

See full listing in **Section Six** under **Nebraska**

Xanders' Britbikes
1280 Stringtown Rd
Grove City, OH 43123
614-871-9001; FAX: 775-890-3407
E-mail: norton@earthling.net

motorcycle parts

Mail order service. Specialists in parts, accessories and machine work for Norton Twins and unit Triumph and BSA. Bikes and parts bought and sold. Parts quotes gladly given by e-mail.

novelties

Accent Models Inc — die cast models
PO Box 295
Denville, NJ 07834
973-887-8403; FAX: 973-887-5088

See full listing in **Section Two** under **models & toys**

American Arrow Corp — mascots / wire wheel rebuilding
105 Kinross
Clawson, MI 48017
248-435-6115; FAX: 248-435-4670
E-mail: dsommer@greatid.com

Manufacturer of classic era parts since 1966. Pilot Ray turning lights, stainless steel mascots, metal edge windwings, tonneau windshields, new and rebuilt wire wheels and much more. Also fired porcelain license plates, art quality trophies and awards, fine art transportation collectibles and lighted Lalique mascots. Call or send for catalog. Web site: www.donsommer.com

---

Anderson's Car Door Monograms — car door monograms
32700 Coastsite #102
Rancho Palos Verdes, CA 90275
800-881-9049, 310-377-1007

See full listing in **Section Two** under **accessories**

Antique Refinishing Service — gas pumps / soda machines
19955 E Williamette Ln
Aurora, CO 80015
303-680-1909
E-mail: antiquevend@earthlink.com

See full listing in **Section Two** under **petroliana**

Auto Etc Neon — signs / time pieces
PO Box 531992
Harlingen, TX 78553
PH/FAX: 956-425-7487

See full listing in **Section One** under **Corvette**

Bonneville Sports Inc — accessories / clothing
3544 Enterprise Dr
Anaheim, CA 92807
888-999-7258, 714-666-1966
FAX: 714-666-1955
E-mail: bonspeed@aol.com

See full listing in **Section Two** under **apparel**

Castle Display Case Co — models
102 W Garfield Ave
New Castle, PA 16105-2544
724-654-6358

See full listing in **Section Two** under **models & toys**

Ceramicar — auto-related ceramics
679 Lapla Rd
Kingston, NY 12401
PH/FAX: 845-338-2199

See full listing in **Section Two** under **artwork**

Chief Studios — artwork / novelties
1903 Greenview Pl SW
Rochester, MN 55902
507-271-7435

See full listing in **Section Two** under **artwork**

Collectibles For You — memorabilia
6001 Canyon Rd
Harrisburg, PA 17111
717-558-2653; FAX: 717-558-7325
E-mail: cllect4you@aol.com

See full listing in **Section Two** under **automobilia**

Cruising International Inc — automobilia / belt buckles / decals/lapel pins / license plates / novelties
1000 N Beach St
Daytona Beach, FL 32117
386-254-8753; FAX: 386-255-2460
E-mail: sales@cruising-intl.com

See full listing in **Section Two** under **license plates**

Diecast & More — die cast models / toys
11709 Oakland Dr
Schoolcraft, MI 49087
616-679-4002
E-mail: lstrong639@aol.com

See full listing in **Section Two** under **models & toys**

Eurosport Daytona Inc — license plates
355 Tomoka Ave
Ormond Beach, FL 32174-6222
800-874-8044, 904-672-7199
FAX: 904-673-0821

See full listing in **Section Two** under **license plates**

Excitement Inc — decor items
1203 5th Ave
Rock Island, IL 61201
309-794-3022

Specialize in street clocks and street lights. Items vary from year to year.

Golden Rods — jewelry
7007 S Indian River Dr
Fort Pierce, FL 34982
877-716-2277 toll free, 561-466-8573
FAX: 561-466-4292
E-mail: foxs@metrolink.net

Jewelry for car lovers. We manufacture 14 kt gold and sterling silver street rod, classic, antique car jewelry. We also have a licensed Chevrolet and Corvette line. Additionally, we are the East Coast source for Speedo Larry Henley custom Rat Fink sculptures. Web site: www.goldenrodsjewelry.com

---

Hale's Products — license plates
906 19th St
Wheatland, WY 82201
800-333-0989

See full listing in **Section Two** under **license plates**

Historic Video Archives — videotapes
PO Box 189-VA
Cedar Knolls, NJ 07927-0189

See full listing in **Section Two** under **automobilia**

Hot Rod Coffee — gourmet coffee
1314 Rollins Rd
Burlingame, CA 94010
650-348-8269; FAX: 650-340-9473
E-mail: hotrodcoffee@pacbell.net

See full listing in **Section Two** under **accessories**

Hotchkiss Mfg/Clear Case PO Box 810 Merlin, OR 97532 800-444-5005; FAX: 541-476-0268 E-mail: hotchkiss@chatlink.com	display cases

See full listing in **Section Two** under **models & toys**

K&S Industries 1801 Union Center Hwy Endicott, NY 13760 PH/FAX: 888-PICK-KNS E-mail: pleximan@888pickkns.com	display cases

See full listing in **Section Two** under **models & toys**

Karl's Collectibles 41 Chestnut St Lewiston, ME 04240 800-636-0457, 207-784-0098 FAX: 207-795-0295 E-mail: karl@designsbyskip.com	banks collectibles logo design

See full listing in **Section Two** under **models & toys**

Lone Wolf 9375 Bearwalk Path Brooksville, FL 34613 352-596-9949 E-mail: lonewolfwhistle@bigfoot.com	wolf whistles

See full listing in **Section Two** under **automobilia**

Larry Machacek PO Box 515 Porter, TX 77365 281-429-2505	decals license plates novelties

See full listing in **Section Two** under **automobilia**

Mascots Unlimited PO Box 666 Old Saybrook, CT 06475 PH/FAX: 860-388-1511 E-mail: rpearl@cyberzone.net	grille ornaments hood ornaments

See full listing in **Section Two** under **radiator emblems & mascots**

MITCHCO 1922 N Los Robles Ave Pasadena, CA 91104-1105 626-401-4303	rubber stamps

See full listing in **Section Two** under **automobilia**

Monikers 26 W 213 Durfee Rd Wheaton, IL 60187 800-587-9015; FAX: 630-260-0204 E-mail: donbeacom@monikers.net	screensavers

Car clubs and car museums sell screensavers featuring your marque. Car clubs sell screensavers to members as a fundraiser. Museums sell screensavers in your gift shop. You supply the photos, we do the rest. Web site: www.monikers.net

MotorWeek 11767 Owings Mills Blvd Owings Mills, MD 21117 410-356-5600; FAX: 410-581-4113 E-mail: motorweek@mpt.org	TV program

See full listing in **Section Four** under **information sources**

Neonetics Inc 9631B Liberty Rd Randallstown, MD 21133 410-521-1962; FAX: 410-521-1543 E-mail: neonman@neonetics.com	neon art

We specialize in collector's neon art for auto enthusiasts. We make a variety of lighted art highlighting 1950s cars and diners. Web site: www.neon4less.com

Ohio Jukebox Co 6211 Cubbison Rd Cumberland, OH 43732 740-638-5059 E-mail: offy@se-guernsey.net	jukeboxes

Mail order and open shop. Monday-Friday 9 am to 5 pm Central time. Specialize in 1950 jukeboxes. Buy, sell, repair. 5-year warranty. Web site: www.ohioseeburgrepair.com

Old Cabot Village 465 Cabot St Beverly, MA 01915 978-922-7142; FAX: 978-922-6917 E-mail: oldcabot@mediaone.net	neckties

See full listing in **Section Two** under **apparel**

Past Lane Auto PO Box 69 Athol Springs, NY 14010 716-649-4108; FAX: 716-646-1969	racing memorabilia

See full listing in **Section Two** under **automobilia**

Re-Flex Border Marker 138 Grant St Lexington, MA 02173 781-862-1343	border markers posts

See full listing in **Section Two** under **hardware**

Rideable Antique Bicycle Replicas 2329 Eagle Ave Alameda, CA 94501 510-769-0980; FAX: 510-521-7145 E-mail: hiwheel@barrongroup.com	bicycles spokes tires

See full listing in **Section Two** under **motorcycles**

Scott Signal Co 8368 W Farm Rd 84 Willard, MO 65781 417-742-5040	stoplights

See full listing in **Section Two** under **automobilia**

SIGNPAST 3202 E Birch Ave, Ste 14 Arkansas City, KS 67005 316-442-1626 E-mail: skj@horizon.hit.net	signs

See full listing in **Section Two** under **automobilia**

Sky Signs Balloons Ltd Box 887 Valley Forge, PA 19481 800-582-4095, 610-933-6952 FAX: 610-935-7808 E-mail: skysigns@netreach.net	balloons

Phone and fax orders. Monday-Friday 8:30 am to 5 pm. Stand out from the crowd. Giant blimps and balloons. Use indoors or outdoors. Advertise your name, logo or product line. Make product replicas, animals, character shapes, seasonal decorations and banners. Web site: www.skysignsballoons.com

Peter Tytla Artist
PO Box 43
East Lyme, CT 06333-0043
860-739-7105

| photographic |
| collages |

See full listing in **Section Two** under **artwork**

Weber's Nostalgia Supermarket
6611 Anglin Dr
Fort Worth, TX 76119
817-534-6611; FAX: 817-534-3316

| collectibles |
| gas pump supplies |
| old photos |
| signs |

Mail order and open shop. Monday-Friday 9 am to 5 pm. Specializing in gas pump restoration, supplies, ie: globes, signs, decals, hoses, nozzles, glass, rubber, etc. Also large selection of game-room decor and old photos. Ship immediately, worldwide. Dealer inquiries welcome. Catalog free with order or $4, refundable.

West Michigan Die-Cast Cars
2523 W Kinney Rd
Ludington, MI 49431
616-843-4278
E-mail: wmpc@t-one.net

| die cast cars |

See full listing in **Section Two** under **models & toys**

painting

Ace Antique Auto Restoration
65 S Service Rd
Plainview, NY 11803
516-752-6065; FAX: 516-752-1484

| air conditioning |
| body rebuilding |
| restoration |
| wiring harnesses |

See full listing in **Section Two** under **restoration shops**

Antique & Classic Car Restoration
Hwy 107, Box 368
Magdalena, NM 87825

| restoration |

See full listing in **Section One** under **MG**

Auto Restoration by William R Hahn
8837 Beebles Rd
Allison Park, PA 15101
412-367-2538, 724-935-3790

| custom work |
| restorations |

See full listing in **Section Two** under **restoration shops**

Automotion Classics Inc
100 N Strong Ave
Lindenhurst, NY 11757
631-225-0485

| painting |
| restoration |
| sandblasting |

See full listing in **Section Two** under **restoration shops**

BDI Automotive Design/Brandon
13985 Madison Pk
Morningview, KY 41063
859-363-0086; FAX: 859-363-0081
E-mail: bdi@fuse.net

| lettering |
| painting |
| pinstriping |

See full listing in **Section Two** under **striping**

Cars of the Past Restorations Inc
11180 Kinsman Rd
Newbury, OH 44065
440-564-2277

| restoration |

See full listing in **Section Two** under **restoration shops**

CJ Spray Inc
370 Airport Rd
South St Paul, MN 55075
800-328-4827 ext 1240
FAX: 651-450-5671

| painting equipment |

Mail order and open shop. Monday-Friday 8 am to 5 pm Central time. Spray painting equipment.

Classic Auto Rebuilders/CAR
Box 9796
Fargo, ND 58106

| painting |
| plating |
| restoration |
| woodwork |

See full listing in **Section Two** under **restoration shops**

County Auto Restoration
6 Gavin Rd
Mt Vernon, NH 03057
603-673-4840
E-mail: CountyAutoRest@aol.com

| bodywork |
| brakes |
| restoration |
| woodwork |

See full listing in **Section Two** under **restoration shops**

Customs & Classics Inc
4674 S Brown St
Murray, UT 84107
801-288-1863; FAX: 801-288-1623
E-mail: kelley@customsandclassics.com

| bodywork |
| painting |
| restoration |
| street rods |

See full listing in **Section Two** under **restoration shops**

Extreme Motorsports Painting Ltd
300 Old Reading Pike
Stowe, PA 19464
610-326-4425; FAX: 610-326-8522
E-mail: extrememail@aol.com

| bodywork |
| painting |

Mail order and open shop. Monday-Friday 9 am to 4 pm Eastern time, Saturdays by appointment. We are a custom paint and body shop who specializes in classic, antique and motorsport cars, trucks and motorcycles. We work with steel, aluminum, fiberglass or carbon fiber. Web site: www.extremepainting.com

Walter A Finner
11131 Etiwanda Ave
Northridge, CA 91326
818-363-6076

| woodgraining |

See full listing in **Section Two** under **woodgraining**

Grey Hills Auto Restoration
51 Vail Rd, PO Box 630
Blairstown, NJ 07825
908-362-8232; FAX: 908-362-6796
E-mail: info@greyhillsauto.com

| restoration |
| service |

See full listing in **Section Two** under **restoration shops**

High Performance Coatings
14788 S Heritagecrest Way
Bluffdale, UT 84065
800-456-4721, 801-501-8303
FAX: 801-501-8315
E-mail: hpcsales@hpcoatings.com

| coatings |

See full listing in **Section Two** under **exhaust systems**

Hyde Auto Body
44-1/2 S Squirrel Rd
Auburn Hills, MI 48326
PH/FAX: 248-852-7832
E-mail: bodyman8@juno.com

| refinishing |
| restoration |

See full listing in **Section Two** under **restoration shops**

L & N Olde Car Co	restoration
9992 Kinsman Rd, PO Box 378	
Newbury, OH 44065	
440-564-7204; FAX: 440-564-8187	

See full listing in **Section Two** under **restoration shops**

Lake Buchanan Industries Inc	blasting cabinet
400 Carlson Cir	
Buchanan Dam, TX 78609	
888-552-5278 toll-free	
512-793-2867; FAX: 512-793-2869	
E-mail: lbi:@tstar.net	

See full listing in **Section Two** under **tools**

LEX-AIRE Nationwide Sales	painting equipment
34 Hutchinson Rd	turbine systems
Arlington, MA 02474	
800-LEX-AIRE; FAX: 562-691-9374	

See full listing in **Section Two** under **tools**

Pilgrim's Auto Restorations	bodywork
3888 Hill Rd	metal fabrication
Lakeport, CA 95453	paint
707-262-1062; FAX: 707-263-6956	restoration
E-mail: pilgrims@pacific.net	

See full listing in **Section Two** under **restoration shops**

Prestige Automotive Inc	restoration
30295 Moravian Tr	
Tippecanoe, OH 44699	
740-922-3542	
E-mail: blacklabs@tusco.net	

See full listing in **Section Two** under **restoration shops**

Redi-Strip Company	abrasive media
100 W Central Ave	baking soda blasting
Roselle, IL 60172	paint removal
630-529-2442; FAX: 630-529-3626	rust removal

See full listing in **Section Two** under **rust removal & stripping**

Restorations Unlimited II Inc	restoration
304 Jandus Rd	
Cary, IL 60013	
847-639-5818	

See full listing in **Section Two** under **restoration shops**

Rick's Relics	bodywork
Wheeler Rd	painting
Pittsburg, NH 03592	restoration
603-538-6612	
E-mail: relics@aspi.net	

See full listing in **Section Two** under **restoration shops**

Ed Rouze	painting guide book
746 N Memorial	
Prattville, AL 36067	
334-365-2381	

Mail order only. Author of comprehensive how-to automobile painting guide, *Paint Your Car Like A Pro*. Details every step from start to finish, written in easy to understand language. Also author of *555 Restoration, Performance & Appearance Tips*, a compilation of 555 restoration tips in a 120-page book using the same easy to read format, covers everything from air compressors to welding.

Steck Manufacturing Co Inc	tools
1115 S Broadway	
Dayton, OH 45408	
800-227-8325; FAX: 937-222-6666	
E-mail: steckmfgco@earthlink.net	

See full listing in **Section Two** under **tools**

Stencils & Stripes Unlimited Inc	NOS decals
1108 S Crescent Ave #21	stripe kits
Park Ridge, IL 60068	
847-692-6893; FAX: 847-692-6895	

See full listing in **Section Two** under **decals**

TP Tools & Equipment	abrasive blasters
7075 Rt 446, PO Box 649	air compressors
Canfield, OH 44406	tools
330-533-3384 local, 800-321-9260	welders

See full listing in **Section Two** under **restoration aids**

Tricks Custom Hot Rods	paint
7126 Wall Triana Hwy	restorations
Madison, AL 35757	
256-722-8222	

Auto restoration, hot rods, fab work on chassis, bodies, engines. Complete restorations, stock or radical. Extreme paint. Master auto builder.

Verne's Chrome Plating Inc	chrome plating
1559 El Segundo Blvd	polishing
Gardena, CA 90249	powder coating
323-754-4126; FAX: 323-754-3873	

See full listing in **Section Two** under **plating & polishing**

Mary Weinheimer	color charts
103 Highgate Terr	
Bergenfield, NJ 07621	
201-384-7661; FAX: 201-439-7662	
E-mail: marychevy@aol.com	

See full listing in **Section Two** under **automobilia**

paints

American Restoration Services	paints
373 Glen Eagles Way	transmission oil
Simi Valley, CA 93065	
PH/FAX: 805-583-5189	

See full listing in **Section One** under **Chrysler**

Antique Auto Parts Cellar	brake/chassis/
6 Chauncy St, PO Box 3	engine parts
South Weymouth, MA 02190	fuel pumps/kits
781-335-1579; FAX: 781-335-1925	gaskets
E-mail: our1932@aol.com	water pumps

See full listing in **Section Two** under **comprehensive parts**

Automotive Paints Unlimited	acrylic enamels
4585 Semora Rd	acrylic lacquers
Roxboro, NC 27573	paints
336-599-5155	polyurethanes

Mail order and open shop. Monday-Friday 9 am to 5 pm. Supplier of paints for vehicles, 1904-present. In business since 1976. The paint place.

Bryn Dana International
PO Box 1233
Havertown, PA 19083
610-789-8031; FAX: 610-789-8041

coatings

Specializing in coatings for recoloring leather and plastic for all models. Web site: www.bryndana.com

Classic Auto Works
7301-1 Singleton Bend Rd
Travis Peak, TX 78654
PH/FAX: 512-267-3707
E-mail: classica@concentric.net

cars
parts
repairs

See full listing in **Section Two** under **street rods**

Color-Ite Refinishing Co
Winning Colors
868 Carrington Rd, Rt 69
Bethany, CT 06524
203-393-0240; FAX: 203-393-0873
E-mail: colorite@ctinternet.com

modern finishes
restoration service

Mail order and open shop. Monday-Friday 9 am to 5 pm; Saturday 9 am to 2 pm. Original paint colors in modern finishes. Restorations and sales of original 1940-1948 Lincoln Continentals, full or partial restorations, specializing in early Lincolns. Also, master chip booklets for selected models. Focus has changed from restorations to the paint and leather finishes. Manufacturers are Sherwin-Williams for the paint and SEM for the leather/vinyl colorants. Web site: www.color-ite.com

The Eastwood Company
263 Shoemaker Rd
Pottstown, PA 19464
800-345-1178; FAX: 610-323-6269

automotive tools
powder coating
welding supplies

See full listing in **Section Two** under **tools**

Hibernia Auto Restorations Inc
52 Maple Terr
Hibernia, NJ 07842
973-627-1882; FAX: 973-627-3503

lacquer
restoration

See full listing in **Section Two** under **restoration shops**

Bill Hirsch Auto Parts
396 Littleton Ave
Newark, NJ 07103
973-642-2404; FAX: 973-642-6161
E-mail: hirschauto@aol.com

enamel lacquer
hubcaps
top material

Mail order and open shop. Monday-Friday 8 am to 4 pm. Manufacturer of hubcaps for Cadillac, Chevrolet, Buick, Packard, Ford. Engine enamels for most American cars, exhaust and manifold paints, gas tank sealer, gas preservative, miracle rustproof paint, leather, broadcloth, Bedford cloth, top material, carpet, carpet sets, car covers, convertible tops, much more. Web site: www.hirschauto.com

Imperial Restorations
POR-15 Products
7550 E Rice Rd
Gardner, IL 60424
800-576-5822; FAX: 815-237-8707
E-mail: imprest@btc-skynet.net

coatings

See full listing in **Section Two** under **rustproofing**

JCM Industries
2 Westwood Dr
Danbury, CT 06811
800-752-0245

wax hardener

See full listing in **Section Two** under **car care products**

Magnet Paints
336 Bayview Ave
Amityville, NY 11701
800-922-9981; FAX: 718-253-4430
E-mail: magneter@ix.netcom.com

clear coats
paints
primers

Deal in high-performance automotive refinish and industrial maintenance paints, primers, clear coats and specialty products. Finishes include acrylic urethanes, acrylic enamels and synthetics. Web site: www.magnetpaints.com

Maintenance Specialties Company
21 Valley Forge Rd, PO Box 251
New Castle, DE 19720
800-777-6715; FAX: 302-328-2315

rustproofing paints

See full listing in **Section Two** under **rustproofing**

OEM Paints Inc
PO Box 461736
Escondido, CA 92046-1736
760-747-2100

custom aerosol
colors

Offer unique, innovative and Ecoformulated™ custom aerosols that meet highest standards of quality and performance. These are the latest and hottest upscale finishes for those who demand authenticity. Experience popular original equipment colors manufactured with todays technology. Best of all they are made in the USA and licensed by major automotive manufacturers. Web site: www.oempaints.com

Tar Heel Parts Inc
PO Box 2604
Matthews, NC 28106-2604
800-322-1957, 704-753-9114 (local)
FAX: 704-753-9117
E-mail: buffing@tarheelparts.com

buffing supplies

See full listing in **Section Two** under **plating & polishing**

Tower Paint Co Inc
Box 2345
Oshkosh, WI 54903-2345
920-235-6520; FAX: 920-235-6521
E-mail: info@towerpaint.com

paint

Paint and custom spray cans using DuPont and PPG finishes for 1930-present for auto's engine, frame, interior and exterior. Web site: www.towerpaint.com

petroliana

Antique Refinishing Service
19955 E Williamette Ln
Aurora, CO 80015
303-680-1909
E-mail: antiquevend@earthlink.com

gas pumps
soda machines

Mail order only. Deals in the restoration of 1920 to 1960 gasoline pumps and soda pop machines. Parts, decals, machine locating, repairs in the state of Colorado.

Asheville DieCast
1434 Brevard Rd
Asheville, NC 28806-9560
800-343-4685, 888-343-4685
828-667-9690; FAX: 828-667-1110
E-mail: sales@ashevillediecast.com

banks
models

See full listing in **Section Two** under **models & toys**

Section Two – Generalists

Auto Motif Inc
2941 Atlanta Rd SE
Smyrna, GA 30080-3654
770-435-5025; FAX: 413-521-5298
E-mail: automotifinc@aol.com

automobilia
models
signs

See full listing in **Section Two** under **automobilia**

Automobilia
200 N Emporia
Wichita, KS 67202
PH/FAX: 316-264-9986
E-mail: automobilia@juno.com

gas pumps
models
signs

See full listing in **Section Two** under **automobilia**

Automobilia Auctions Inc
132 Old Main St
Rocky Hill, CT 06067
860-529-7177; FAX: 860-257-3621

appraisals
auctions

See full listing in **Section Two** under **auctions & shows**

Berliner Classic Motorcars Inc
1975 Stirling Rd
Dania Beach, FL 33004
954-923-7271; FAX: 954-926-3306
E-mail: info@berlinerclassiccars.com

automobilia
car dealer
motorcycles

See full listing in **Section Two** under **car dealers**

Blast From the Past
21006 Cornhusker Rd
Gretna, NE 68028
402-332-5050; FAX: 402-332-5029
E-mail: blast2past@aol.com

neon clocks
neon signs

See full listing in **Section Two** under **automobilia**

**Central Florida Auto Festival
& Toy Expo**
1420 N Galloway Rd
Lakeland, FL 33810
863-686-8320

auto festival
toy expo

See full listing in **Section Two** under **auctions & shows**

"Check The Oil!" Magazine
PO Box 937
Powell, OH 43065-0937
614-848-5038; FAX: 614-436-4760
E-mail: ctomagazine@aol.com

magazine

Bi-monthly publication for enthusiasts and collectors of the
memorabilia and history of the petroleum industry. Anything
associated with the oil and gas business of days gone by, eg: gas
pumps, globes, signs, maps, oil bottles, etc. Subscription:
$21.95/year US, $30/year Canada, $37/year overseas.

Chewning's Auto Literature
2011 Elm Tree Terr
Buford, GA 30518
770-945-9795
E-mail: cchewy69@aol.com

literature
manuals

See full listing in **Section Two** under **literature dealers**

Collectibles For You
6001 Canyon Rd
Harrisburg, PA 17111
717-558-2653; FAX: 717-558-7325
E-mail: cllect4you@aol.com

memorabilia

See full listing in **Section Two** under **automobilia**

Dave Lincoln
Box 331
Yorklyn, DE 19736
610-444-4144, PA
E-mail: tagbarn@msn.com

license plates

See full listing in **Section Two** under **license plates**

George & Denise Long
891 E Court St
Marion, NC 28752
828-652-9229 (24 hrs w/recorder)

automobilia

See full listing in **Section Two** under **automobilia**

Manchester Motor Car Co
319 Main St
Manchester, CT 06040
860-643-5874; FAX: 860-643-6190
E-mail: mmcollc@aol.com

automobilia
parts
petroliana
restorations

See full listing in **Section Two** under **comprehensive parts**

Oil Co Collectibles Inc
PO Box 556
LaGrange, OH 44050
440-355-6608; FAX: 440-355-4955
E-mail: scottpcm@aol.com

gas globes
magazine
signs

See full listing in **Section Two** under **automobilia**

Petro Classics
8829 W Camino De Oro
Peoria, AZ 85382
602-825-9070; FAX: 602-825-7030
E-mail: bj@petroclassics.com

collectibles
restoration

Mail order only. Monday-Saturday 9 am to 5 pm. Deal in petroliana restoration, Pepsi-Cola collectibles, amusement rides and
pedal cars. Web site: www.petroclassics.com

Frank Riley Automotive Art
PO Box 95
Hawthorne, NJ 07506
800-848-9459
E-mail: rileystudio@netscape.net

automotive prints

See full listing in **Section Two** under **artwork**

Jack Schmitt Studio
PO Box 1761
San Juan Capistrano, CA 92693
E-mail: jack_schmitt@msn.com

paintings
prints

See full listing in **Section Two** under **artwork**

Ron Scobie Enterprises
7676 120th St N
Hugo, MN 55038
651-653-6503
E-mail: rscobie@gaspump.com

gas pump parts

Manufacturing parts for antique gasoline pumps and air meters.
Also make "Master" oil bottle spouts from the original machines.
Web site: www.gaspump.com

Scott Signal Co
8368 W Farm Rd 84
Willard, MO 65781
417-742-5040

stoplights

See full listing in **Section Two** under **automobilia**

SIGNPAST 3202 E Birch Ave, Ste 14 Arkansas City, KS 67005 316-442-1626 E-mail: skj@horizon.hit.net	signs

See full listing in **Section Two** under **automobilia**

Time Passages Ltd PO Box 65596 West Des Moines, IA 50265 515-223-5105; FAX: 515-223-5149 E-mail: timepass@netins.net	vintage gas pumps

Mail order and open shop. Monday-Saturday 9 am to 5:30 pm. Specializing in restoration parts and supplies for vintage gasoline pumps. We carry unrestored and restored pumps, globes, signs, decals, ID tags, molded, cast, spun and stamped parts. Books, art prints and photographs. We also provide appraisals, design and decor, movie props and restaurant decor. Mail order parts catalogs, $4 each. Web site: www.time-pass.com

Town & Country Toys 227 Midvale Dr, PO Box 574 Marshall, WI 53559 608-655-4961 E-mail: dejaeger@itis.com	banks Ertl cars mini license plates

See full listing in **Section Two** under **models & toys**

Vic's Place Inc 123 N 2nd St Guthrie, OK 73044 PH/FAX: 405-282-5586 E-mail: vics@telepath.com	restoration parts

Shop open Monday-Saturday 8 am to 5 pm. Restoration parts for all makes of gas pumps. 40-page color catalog available. Restoration and original pumps available. 10,000 square foot shop. Web site: www.vicsplace.com

photography

3-D Imagery Inc 2149 S Yukon Way Lakewood, CO 80227 303-989-4557	DVD

3-D Imagery Inc is one of the first companies to master film to DVD. It is now affordable to author and master DVDs. Put your car on a DVD! Web site: www.3-DI.com
See our ad on this page

Bud Bagdasarian Studios 5136 Finney Ct Carmichael, CA 95608 916-965-6675; FAX: 916-966-9186	hats mugs T-shirts

See full listing in **Section Two** under **apparel**

Boop Photography 2347 Derry St Harrisburg, PA 17104-2728 717-564-8533 E-mail: booper@home.com	photography

Mail order and open shop. Sunday-Saturday 9 am to 9 pm Eastern time. Automotive photography, drag racing, classics, street rods. Former car club photographer. Nikon equipment. 10 years' experience. Degree in photography. Will have automotive photography displayed at Carlisle show.

Classic Car Publications 292 S Mount Zion Rd Milltown, IN 47145 812-633-7826	calendars

See full listing in **Section Two** under **artwork**

Richard Hamilton 28 E 46th St Indianapolis, IN 46205 317-283-1902	sales literature

See full listing in **Section Two** under **literature dealers**

Hot Rod Nostalgia™ PO Box 249 West Point, CA 95255-0249 209-293-2114; FAX: 209-293-2120 E-mail: hvaa@hotrodnostalgia.com	"magalog"

See full listing in **Section Four** under **books & publications**

Imaginographx PO Box 95 Hawthorne, NJ 07506 800-848-9459 E-mail: imaginographx@netscape.net	automotive portraits automotive prints idea renderings logo designs

See full listing in **Section Two** under **artwork**

The Klemantaski Collection 65 High Ridge Rd, Ste 219 Stamford, CT 06905 PH/FAX: 203-968-2970 E-mail: klemcoll@aol.com	books photography

Mail order only. Motor racing photography by Louis Klemantaski, Nigel Snowdon, Robert Daley, Alan R Smith, Colin Waldeck and Edward Eves. Also publish books of our photographs. Supply enthusiasts, collectors, authors and publishers worldwide.

LA Ltd Design Graphics
822A S McDuffie St
Anderson, SC 29624
PH/FAX: 864-231-7715

artwork
design
greeting cards

See full listing in **Section Two** under **automobilia**

Maximum Downforce
Gary Toriello
120 E Clinton Ave
Bergenfield, NJ 07621
201-384-0529; FAX: 201-384-5062
E-mail: racerx@maximumdownforce.com

photography

Deals in automotive photography and web site design. Web site: www.maximumdownforce.com

MPH Interactive Designs
7766 W 450 S
Williamsport, IN 47993
765-491-9604; FAX: 765-893-4017
E-mail: park@mphinteractive.net

photography
research
writing

See full listing in **Section Four** under **information sources**

Practical Images
PO Box 245
Haddam, CT 06438-0245
860-704-0525
E-mail: services@practimages.com

int'l VHS video
conversions
photo scanning
photography

International VHS video conversions ($20 in the USA, mail order only). Freelance photography for advertisements, personal, legal, insurance, etc. Disc jockey services available for background music and special occasions, etc. Please write or call for more information. Web site: www.practimages.com

Red Lion Racing
8318 Avenida Castro
Cucamonga, CA 91730
909-987-9818; FAX: 909-987-6538
E-mail: rlracing@cris.com

photographs
posters

See full listing in **Section Two** under **artwork**

Richard Spiegelman Productions Inc
19 Guild Hall Dr
Scarborough, ON Canada M1R 3Z7
416-759-1644
E-mail: carphoto@sympatico.com or
carphoto@yahoo.com

photography
slides

See full listing in **Section Four** under **information sources**

Jay Texter
417 Haines Mill Rd
Allentown, PA 18104
610-821-0963
E-mail: jaytexter@ot.com

photography

Automotive and motorsport photography, editorial, advertising or private commissions. Traditional or electronic output. Immortalize your vehicle or mobilia collection with a sense of style. Quality and craftsmanship guaranteed. Web site: www.jaytexter.com

Peter Tytla Artist
PO Box 43
East Lyme, CT 06333-0043
860-739-7105

photographic
collages

See full listing in **Section Two** under **artwork**

Vermont Visual Experts
8 Scottsdale Rd
South Burlington, VT 05403
802-862-3768
E-mail: vermontvisualexperts@att.net

photography

On location fine art automobile photography, car shows, and digital photography. Auto web site design.

Vintage Automotive Art
PO Box 3702
Beverly Hills, CA 90212
310-278-0882; FAX: 310-278-0883
E-mail: artline1@pacbell.net

artwork
automobilia
literature dealers

See full listing in **Section Two** under **automobilia**

plaques

Bud Bagdasarian Studios
5136 Finney Ct
Carmichael, CA 95608
916-965-6675; FAX: 916-966-9186

hats
mugs
T-shirts

See full listing in **Section Two** under **apparel**

Nostalgic Reflections
PO Box 350
Veradale, WA 99037
PH/FAX: 509-226-3522
E-mail: jmt1@peoplepc.com

custom etched
plates
dash glass/decals
porcelain radiator
medallions/scripts

Mail order and open shop. Monday-Saturday 8 am to 6 pm. Reproduction serial plates, decals, door sill plates, porcelain medallions, instrument faces, dash glass, special castings and plating, radiator scripts. Web site: www.nostalgicreflections.com

O'Brien Truckers
29 A Young Rd
Charlton, MA 01507-1599
508-248-1555; FAX: 508-248-6179
E-mail: obt@ziplink.net

accessories
belt buckles
plaques
valve covers

Mail order only. Cast aluminum car club plaques, belt buckles and key chains. Air cleaners and nostalgic engine accessories. Complete line of No Club Lone Wolf items, license plate toppers, valley covers, Hemi valve covers, lake pipe caps and many other nostalgic accessories.

plastic parts

American Plastic Chrome
8812 Hannan Rd
Wayne, MI 48184-1557
313-721-1967 days
313-261-4454 eves

replating plastic

Specializing in replating plastic interior parts for most cars from late 50s to early 70s using the original vacuum metalizing process. This multi-step process will restore your plastic parts to their original shine and brilliance. Replating instrument gauge cluster bezels, armrest bases, domelight bezels, etc, for most cars from late 50s to early 70s.

ASC&P International
PO Box 255
Uwchland, PA 19480
610-458-8395; FAX: 610-458-8735

custom molding
fiberglass
plastic

See full listing in **Section Two** under **fiberglass parts**

Autolux Inc
3121 W Coast Hwy, Ste 3D
Newport Beach, CA 92663
949-574-0054; FAX: 949-645-3033

Mercedes parts

See full listing in **Section One** under **Mercedes-Benz**

C & G Early Ford Parts
1941 Commercial St, Dept AH
Escondido, CA 92029-1233
760-740-2400; FAX: 760-740-8700
E-mail: cgford@cgfordparts.com

| accessories/chrome |
| emblems |
| literature |
| mechanical |
| weatherstripping |

See full listing in **Section One** under **Ford 1932-1953**

CR Plastics Inc
2790 NE 7th Ave
Pompano Beach, FL 33064
800-551-3155

bumper filler parts

See full listing in **Section One** under **Cadillac/LaSalle**

D&D Automobilia
813 Ragers Hill Rd
South Fork, PA 15956
814-539-5653

plastic parts
steering wheels

See full listing in **Section Two** under **steering wheels**

Dashtop by Palco Ind Inc
5980 Alpha Ave
Reno, NV 89506
775-677-0766; FAX: 775-677-8248

dashboard covers
door panels

See full listing in **Section Two** under **interiors & interior parts**

Emblemagic Co
PO Box 420
Grand River, OH 44045-0420
440-209-0792
E-mail: emblemagic@aol.com

decorative
emblems
plastic insert
emblems

See full listing in **Section Two** under **grille emblem badges**

Rod Doors
PO Box 2160
Chico, CA 95927
530-896-1513; FAX: 530-896-1518
E-mail: sales@roddoors.com

door panels
interior parts

See full listing in **Section Two** under **interiors & interior parts**

Special T's Unlimited Inc
PO Box 146
Prospect Heights, IL 60070
847-255-5494; FAX: 847-259-7220
E-mail: special_t_bill@yahoo.com

general repair
parts
restoration
service

See full listing in **Section One** under **Mopar**

West Coast Metric Inc
24002 Frampton Ave
Harbor City, CA 90710
310-325-0005; FAX: 310-325-9733
E-mail: wcm@westcoastmetric.com

carpet kits
door panels
emblems
plastic parts
rubber parts

See full listing in **Section One** under **Volkswagen**

Yesterday's Radio
7759 Edgewood Ln
Seven Hills, OH 44131-5902
PH/FAX: 216-524-2018
E-mail: jerry@yesterdaysradio.com

interior plastic
radio parts

See full listing in **Section One** under **Packard**

plating & polishing

A & A Plating Inc
9400 E Wilson Rd
Independence, MO 64053
816-833-0045; FAX: 816-254-1517

plating
polishing

Mail order and open shop. Monday-Friday 7 am to 6 pm, Saturday 8 am to 12 pm. Chrome, nickel and copper plating for steel, aluminum, die cast and brass, cast iron, pot metal. Polishing of stainless steel, brass, aluminum, copper, nickel and silver.

ACPlating
Division of SUM Inc
317 Mt Vernon
Bakersfield, CA 93307
661-324-5454; FAX: 661-324-5381

plating

Mail order and open shop. Monday-Friday 8 am to 4:30 pm Pacific time. Founded in 1975, ACPlating has focused on providing the professional and amateur auto restorer the avenue to return all their brightwork to better than new condition. Stainless steel, pot metal, steel bumpers and brass parts are all meticulously stripped, straightened, hand polished, copper plated, copper buffed, pitfilled, then nickel and chrome plated. For all your high quality needs in metal finishing visit ACPlating. Web site: www.ac-plating.com

Advanced Plating & Powder Coating
1425 Cowan Ct
Nashville, TN 37207
615-227-6900; FAX: 615-262-7935
E-mail: gochrome@aol.com

chrome plating
polishing
repair service

Mail order and open shop. Monday-Friday 8 am to 4:30 pm, Saturday 8 am to 12 noon. Restoration of antique car parts, bumpers, grilles, aluminum, polishing, chrome plating, gold, black chrome, acid copper, copper, nickel and powder coating. Repair service is available. Over 39 years' experience. Free catalog. Full line of chrome GM parts, intakes, carbs, valve covers, etc. Web site: www.advancedplating.com

American Plastic Chrome
8812 Hannan Rd
Wayne, MI 48184-1557
313-721-1967 days
313-261-4454 eves

replating plastic

See full listing in **Section Two** under **plastic parts**

ANC Restoration
Chris Palmerie
254 New Haven Ave
Waterbury, CT 06708
203-574-2249, 203-558-1488
E-mail: cpwp2@javanet.com

restorations

Mail order and open shop. Monday-Saturday, answering service available 24 hours. Antique auto restoration, buffing, dent removal, stainless steel and aluminum for antique vehicles, all makes and models, preferably before 1970s. Total restorations, partial restorations including engine compartment, undercarriage, trunk compartments and interiors.

Ano-Brite Inc
6945 Farmdale Ave
North Hollywood, CA 91605
818-982-0997; FAX: 818-982-0804
E-mail: anobrite@anobrite.com

anodizing
polishing
restoration
welding

Mail order and open shop. Monday-Friday 8:30 am to 4:30 pm. Deal in aluminum and stainless steel trim restoration, anodizing, straightening, polishing and welding. Web site: www.anobrite.com

Caswell Electroplating in Miniature
4336 Rt 31
Palmyra, NY 14522
315-597-5140, 315-597-6378
FAX: 315-597-1457
E-mail: sales@caswellplating.com

plating kits

Professional quality plating kits for chrome, nickel, black oxide, anodizing, zinc and chromating, silver and gold, copper, cadmium, brass. Tanks, heaters, chemicals and manuals. Complete line of professional buffing and polishing tools and supplies. Web site: www.caswellplating.com

Chevi Shop Custom Casting
338 Main Ave, Box 75
Milledgeville, IL 61051
815-225-7565; FAX: 815-225-7616
E-mail: synka@cin.net

*custom castings
parts*

See full listing in **Section One** under **Chevrolet**

Circle N Stainless
1517 NW 33rd
Lawton, OK 73505
580-355-9366
E-mail: neald@juno.com

*stainless steel
trim restoration*

See full listing in **Section Two** under **special services**

Classic Auto Rebuilders/CAR
Box 9796
Fargo, ND 58106

*painting
plating
restoration
woodwork*

See full listing in **Section Two** under **restoration shops**

Classic Auto Restoration
437 Greene St
Buffalo, NY 14212
716-896-6663
E-mail: jp@classicbuff.com

*appraisals
plating
polishing
restoration*

See full listing in **Section Two** under **restoration shops**

Competition Chemicals Inc
715 Railroad St, PO Box 820
Iowa Falls, IA 50126
641-648-5121; FAX: 641-648-9816

polish

Mail order only. Deals in Simichrome polish. Web site: www.simichromepolish.com

Custom Plating
3030 Alta Ridge Way
Snellville, GA 30078
770-736-1118; FAX: 770-736-6620
E-mail: customplating@mediaone.net

*bumper specialist
chrome plating
parts*

Chrome plating of bumpers, engine parts, suspension parts, interior and exterior parts, pot metal. Polishing and straightening of aluminum and stainless trim. 40 years' experience. Antique bumper specialist.

CustomChrome Plating Inc
963 Mechanic St, PO Box 125
Grafton, OH 44044
440-926-3116

*electroplating
plating
polishing*

Mail order and open shop. Monday-Thursday 8 am to 5 pm, Friday 8 am to 4 pm. Polishing, buffing and electroplating. Chrome, nickel, copper plating on customer's parts.

D&D Plastic Chrome Plating
925 Markey Dr
Bryan, OH 43506
419-260-2723; FAX: 419-636-3534
E-mail: hl20@webtv.net

plating

See full listing in **Section Two** under **interiors & interior parts**

Dalmar
11759 S Cleveland Ave, Ste 28
Ft Myers, FL 33907
941-275-6540; FAX: 941-275-1731
E-mail: dalmar@peganet.com

*electroplating
plating supplies*

Electroplating and electroforming equipment, chemicals, supplies and kits. Featuring chrome, nickel, gold, copper, silver, brass, bronze and cadmium plating. Our kits will plate on metallic and non-metallic surfaces. Manufacture both brush and tank plating kits. Free catalog. Complete catalog and prices on our web site: www.dalmarplating.com

Distinctive Metal Polishing
18328 Gault St
Reseda, CA 91335
818-344-2160; FAX: 818-344-8029

*metal polishing
parts*

See full listing in **Section One** under **Harley-Davidson**

Fini-Finish Metal Finishing
24657 Mound Rd
Warren, MI 48091
810-758-0050; FAX: 810-758-0054
E-mail: info@fini-finish.com

*plating
polishing
pot metal repair*

Polishing and buffing on all metals. Copper, nickel, chrome and cadmium plating on all metals. Repair work on pot metal (zinc die cast) our specialty. Web site: www.fini-finish.com

Foss Plating Co Inc
8140 Secura Way
Santa Fe Springs, CA 90670
562-945-3451; FAX: 562-698-2326
E-mail: fosspl8@gte.net

chrome plating

Open shop only. Custom refinishing of all chrome plated auto accessories.

Green-Stuff Metal Polish
PO Box 7071
Knoxville, TN 37921
865-382-1286
E-mail: greenstuffpolish@aol.com

metal polish

Mail order only. Green-Stuff Metal Polish: the miracle polish for all things metal. Clean, polish and protect aluminum, chrome, brass, silver, copper and stainless steel. Your satisfaction is guaranteed by our double your money back guarantee. Web site: www.green-stuff-polish.com

Iverson Automotive
14704 Karyl Dr
Minnetonka, MN 55345
800-325-0480; FAX: 952-938-5707

*polishes
pot metal
restoration*

Mail order and open shop. Monday-Saturday 8:30 am to 6:30 pm Stainless, pot metal and aluminum trim restoration. Have developed a 10-step state of the art process to put the life and luster back into dented, scratched and deteriorated auto trim. There is a critical difference between polishing auto trim and restoring auto trim, anyone can polish. Also manufacture stainless, aluminum and chrome polishes called "Iverson Automotive Secret Sauce." Do all the work myself and guarantee your satisfaction.

J & L Industries
6 Gem Ave
Los Gatos, CA 95032
408-356-3943

polishing

Mail order only. Dealing in stainless trim straightening and polishing. Also aluminum castings polished.

Section Two – Generalists

JET-HOT® High-Temp Coatings
Breathe New Life into Old Parts

Nothing beats *JET-HOT* if you want to protect or restore original equipment. It's the world's leading high-tech header coating and the first choice of restorers, rodders, racers and auto enthusiasts.

• *JET-HOT* extends component life ten times or more by protecting against rust and thermal fatigue. It won't chip, fade or burn off at temperatures up to 1,300°F.

• *JET-HOT* sterling silver (shown on the partially restored header below) offers the richest sheen ever achieved with a high-tech coating. These coatings also come in other great-looking colors, like the cast-iron finish shown on the partially restored manifold below.

• *JET-HOT* is extremely cost effective. It saves you money over the long haul.

• *JET-HOT* keeps headers cool. It knocks down engine-bay temperatures by 25°F or more.

• When applied to the interior and exterior of headers, *JET-HOT* boosts power. Racers have reported gains of up to 3%.

Header restored with JET-HOT Sterling Silver

• *JET-HOT* backs its coatings with a guarantee of satisfaction, plus a 3-year warranty on used parts and lifetime protection against new parts rusting through.

Manifold restored with JET-HOT Cast-Iron Gray

Isn't your car worth more than a can of paint?

Condition of parts before restoration

Martin's of Philadelphia
7327 State Rd
Philadelphia, PA 19136-4112
215-331-5565; FAX: 215-331-7113
E-mail: chromeo@Iopener.net or
coffeeglen@aol.com

buffing
copper plating
metal grinding

Simply stated, Martin's of Philadelphia produces the most beautiful "SHOW CHROME" plating in the world! Not my words, but the opinion of thousands. We do potmetal, stainless steel, brass, aluminum, etc. Complete repair facilities; continuing 135 year family tradition in metal crafting and 40 years in business. Coming soon, "LEVEL FORM," designed to restore the unrestorable!

Master Plating
2109 Newton Ave
San Diego, CA 92113
619-232-3092; FAX: 619-232-3094

plating
restoration

Repair/restoration of plated parts of all makes and models. Repair and polishing of stainless steel and aluminum, re-engraving of faded logos. Replate with copper, nickel, chrome, to show quality (100 point or very close). Website: www.masterplating.com

Paul's Chrome Plating Inc
90 Pattison St
Evans City, PA 16033
800-245-8679, 724-538-3367
FAX: 724-538-3403
E-mail: pcp@fyi.net

repair
restoration

Mail order and open shop. Monday-Friday 8 am to 5 pm, Saturday by appointment only. Triple plate rechroming, repair and restoration of all metal parts, including pot metal (zinc die cast).

Pot Metal Restorations
4794 C Woodlane Cir
Tallahassee, FL 32303
850-562-3847; FAX: 850-562-0538

pot metal restoring
& rechroming

Mail order and open shop. Monday-Friday 8 am to 5 pm. Pitted pot metal restoration and rechroming.

Qual Krom-Great Lakes Plant
4725-A Iroquois Ave
Erie, PA 16511
800-673-2427; FAX: 814-899-8632

plating
repairs
restoration

Mail order and open shop. Monday-Friday 8 am to 5 pm, Saturday by appointment. Custom restoration plating of your parts, guaranteed show quality only. Do all repairs necessary to restore your steel, zinc die castings and stainless steel parts. Web site: www.qualkrom.com

The Reflected Image
21 W Wind Dr
Northford, CT 06472
PH/FAX: 203-484-0760
E-mail: scott@reflectedimage.com

mirror reproduction
mirror resilvering

See full listing in **Section Two** under **special services**

Samson Technology Corporation
6825 SW 21st Ct #3
Davie, FL 33317
800-256-0692; FAX: 954-916-9338
E-mail: sales@samson24k.com

plating systems

Mail order and open shop. Monday-Friday 8:30 am to 5 pm. Manufacturers of portable and tank electroplating systems as well as the JetCover, the retractable car cover. Also offers a complete line of electroplating and buffing supplies. Portable anodizing and bright chrome plating systems. Web site: www.samson24k.com

Special T's Unlimited Inc
PO Box 146
Prospect Heights, IL 60070
847-255-5494; FAX: 847-259-7220
E-mail: special_t_bill@yahoo.com

general repair
parts
restoration
service

See full listing in **Section One** under **Mopar**

Speed & Sport Chrome Plating Inc
404 Broadway
Houston, TX 77012
713-921-0235

chrome plating

Mail order and open shop. Monday-Friday 8 am - 5:30 pm Central time. Antique cars and trucks, muscle cars, race cars, show cars, street cars. Specializing in chrome plating on all the above. 15 day service, all work guaranteed. Triple show chrome.

Standard Abrasives
Motorsports Division
4201 Guardian St
Simi Valley, CA 93063
800-383-6001; 805-520-5800 ext 371
FAX: 805-577-7398
E-mail: tech@sa-motorsports.com

abrasives

See full listing in **Section Two** under **restoration aids**

Star Chrome
4009 Ogden Ave
Chicago, IL 60623
312-521-9000

plating
polishing

Mail order and open shop. Monday-Saturday 6 am to 12 noon. Chrome, gold, and nickel plating and polishing for antique and classic cars, street rods and motorcycles. Specializing in pot metal repair and restoration of the highest quality. Work taken only in the morning. All work show quality and guaranteed. In business since 1970.

Supreme Metal Polishing
84A Rickenbacker Cir
Livermore, CA 94550
925-449-3490; FAX: 925-449-1475
E-mail: supremet@home.com

metal working
parts restoration
plating services
polishing

Priceless parts finished to impeccable standards. Special attention to reflective clarity and trueness of linear reflections. Delicate finishing of precision machined parts. 28 years of show winners ranging from "America's most beautiful roadster" to 1998 Pebble Beach Best of Show. Serving both private and professional restorers and enthusiasts. References available upon request.

Tar Heel Parts Inc
PO Box 2604
Matthews, NC 28106-2604
800-322-1957, 704-753-9114 (local)
FAX: 704-753-9117
E-mail: buffing@tarheelparts.com

buffing supplies

Mail order only. Buffing specialty and auto restoration supply company. Offer Baldor buffers, buffing supplies, arbors and mandrels, abrasives, flanging pliers, Seymour paints, sandblasters, bead blast cabinets, and more. Please call for more information and a complimentary catalog. Web site: www.tarheelparts.com

Verne's Chrome Plating Inc
1559 El Segundo Blvd
Gardena, CA 90249
323-754-4126; FAX: 323-754-3873

chrome plating
polishing
powder coating

Restoration quality polishing and chrome plating. We are not a big bumper outfit or production shop, we are a small restoration shop. In business since 1959.

Wholesale Express
830 W 3rd St
Eddy, TX 76524
254-859-5364; FAX: 254-859-5407
E-mail: tommy@wacool.net

buffing supplies
sandblasters

See full listing in **Section Two** under **accessories**

racing

300 Below Inc
2101 E Olive St
Decatur, IL 62526
800-550-2796; FAX: 217-423-3075
E-mail: cryo300@midwest.net

cryogenic tempering
machine work
welding

See full listing in **Section Two** under **special services**

356 Enterprises
Vic & Barbara Skirmants
27244 Ryan Rd
Warren, MI 48092
810-575-9544; FAX: 810-558-3616
E-mail: skirmants@home.com

parts

See full listing in **Section One** under **Porsche**

600 Racing Inc
5245 NC Hwy 49 S
Harrisburg, NC 28075
704-455-3896; FAX: 704-455-3820

5/8 scale replicas

Mail order and open shop. Monday-Saturday 8 am to 6 pm. Exclusive manufacturer of Legends Cars, which are 5/8 scale replicas of 1932-1940 Fords, Chevys and Dodge NASCAR stock cars. Legends Cars compete in more than 1,500 races every year and are fun and affordable race cars. Web site: www.600racing.com

Advanced Racing Technologies Inc
17 N Cross Rd
Staatsburg, NY 12580
PH/FAX: 845-889-4499
E-mail: advancedracing@compuserve.com

wheel alignment

Portable laser and electronic wheel alignment. Web site: www.advancedracing.com

Air Flow Research
10490 Ilex Ave
Pacoima, CA 91331
818-890-0616; FAX: 818-890-0490

cylinder heads

See full listing in **Section One** under **Chevrolet**

American Autowire/Factory Fit®
150 Heller Pl #17W, Dept HCCA02
Bellmawr, NJ 08031
800-482-9473; FAX: 856-933-0805
E-mail: info@americanautowire.com

battery cables
electrical systems
switches/
components

See full listing in **Section Two** under **street rods**

Skip Barber Racing School
29 Brook St
Lakeville, CT 06039
800-221-1131; FAX: 860-435-1321
E-mail: speed@skipbarber.com

racing school

The Skip Barber Racing School, the world's largest, offers on-track racing programs for experienced vintage competitors and aspiring racers alike, ranging from the 3-hour *Introduction to Racing (sm)* to the industry standard *Three Day Racing School (sm)*. Classes are taught in open-wheel Formula Dodge race cars and are available nationwide. Also offer advanced street driving schools, teaching street-based defensive driving techniques. Call for details. Web site: www.skipbarber.com

Bell Motorsports/Pyrotect
3227 14th Ave
Oakland, CA 94602
800-669-2355; FAX: 510-261-2355
E-mail: bob@bellmotorsports.com

harnesses
safety equipment

See full listing in **Section Two** under **apparel**

Belmont's Rod & Custom Shop
138 Bussey St
Dedham, MA 02026
781-326-9599, 781-326-3270

speed equipment
transmissions

See full listing in **Section Two** under **street rods**

Birkin America
PO Box 120982
Arlington, TX 76012
817-461-7431; FAX: 817-861-5867
E-mail: birkinam@aol.com

cars
replicas

See full listing in **Section One** under **Lotus**

Boop Photography
2347 Derry St
Harrisburg, PA 17104-2728
717-564-8533
E-mail: booper@home.com

photography

See full listing in **Section Two** under **photography**

British Only Motorcycles and Parts Inc
32451 Park Ln
Garden City, MI 48135
734-421-0303; FAX: 734-422-9253
E-mail: info@britishonly.com

literature
memorabilia
motorcycles
parts

See full listing in **Section Two** under **motorcycles**

Coffey Classic Transmissions
310 Aviator Dr
Fort Worth, TX 76179
817-439-1611

transmissions

See full listing in **Section Two** under **transmissions**

Corvette Service
11629 Vanowen St
North Hollywood, CA 91605
818-765-9117

race prep
repairs

See full listing in **Section One** under **Corvette**

Danspeed
5831 Date Ave
Rialto, CA 92377
909-873-5804, FAX: 909-875-7610
E-mail: danspeedtwo@aol.com

filters
gauges
ignition parts

See full listing in **Section Two** under **instruments**

Robert DeMars Ltd
Auto Appraisers/Historians
222 Lakeview Ave, Ste 160/256
West Palm Beach, FL 33401
561-832-0171; FAX: 561-738-5284
E-mail: carapraisr@aol.com

appraisals
auto historians
auto locating
research library
resto consultants

See full listing in **Section Two** under **appraisals**

Diamond Back Classics   tires
Bill Chapman
4753 Hwy 90
Conway, SC 29526
888-922-1642; FAX: 843-399-3091
E-mail: diamondbackclassics@
worldnet.att.net

See full listing in **Section Two** under **tires**

Don's Hot Rod Shop Inc   accessories
2811 N Stone Ave   parts
Tucson, AZ 85705
520-884-8892; FAX: 520-628-1682

See full listing in **Section Two** under **street rods**

Donington Grand Prix Collection   museum
Donington Park
Castle Donington, Derby
Derbyshire DE74 2RP England
01332 811027; Fax: 01332 812829
E-mail: enquiries@
doningtoncollection.co.uk

See full listing in **Section Six** under **England**

Economy Racing Components Inc   machine work
7550 Negley Rd   welding
Henderson, KY 42420   wheels/tires
PH/FAX: 270-826-3159
E-mail: erc@henderson.net

See full listing in **Section Two** under **special services**

Engines Direct   engines
7830 E Gelding, Bldg 200   parts
Scottsdale, AZ 85260
800-998-2100; FAX: 480-998-6070

See full listing in **Section Two** under **engine rebuilding**

Environmentally Safe Products Inc   insulation
313 W Golden Ln
New Oxford, PA 17350
800-289-5693; FAX: 717-624-7089
E-mail: heidiz@low-e.com

See full listing in **Section Two** under **street rods**

FB Performance Transmissions   transmissions
85 Cleveland Ave
Bay Shore, NY 11706
631-242-0008; FAX: 631-243-3054
E-mail: fbperf@trim.net

See full listing in **Section Two** under **transmissions**

George's Speed Shop   machine shop
716 Brantly Ave   race engine building
Dayton, OH 45404   race engine parts
937-233-0353; FAX: 937-236-3501

Open shop only. Stock to full race engine parts and building.
Full machine shop service. Two in-house dyno cells.

GMP (Georgia Marketing   die cast replicas
& Promotions)
PO Box 570
Winder, GA 30680
800-536-1637, 770-307-1042
FAX: 770-867-0786
E-mail: peachgmp@peachgmp.com

See full listing in **Section Two** under **models & toys**

Grand Prix Classics Inc   racing cars
7456 La Jolla Blvd   sports cars
La Jolla, CA 92037
858-459-3500; FAX: 858-459-3512
E-mail: info@grandprixclassics.com

In business for twenty years and specialize in the buying and
selling of historic sports cars and racing cars. On display in our
facility you will find 10-15 historically significant cars. Active
participants in historic racing events worldwide. If you have a
car to sell or are looking for a special car to buy, feel free to contact us. Learn more about us by looking at our web page. Web
site: www.grandprixclassics.com

GRIFFIN Radiator   radiators
100 Hurricane Creek Rd
Piedmont, SC 29673
800-RACE-RAD (722-3723)
864-845-5000; FAX: 864-845-5001
E-mail: griffinrad@aol.com

See full listing in **Section Two** under **radiators**

Guenther Graphics   artwork
PO Box 266
LeClaire, IA 52753
PH/FAX: 319-289-9010
E-mail: artwork@guenthergraphics.com

See full listing in **Section Two** under **artwork**

Gary Hill Auto Service   restoration
150 E St Joseph St   service
Arcadia, CA 91006
626-447-2576; FAX: 626-447-1461

Mail order and open shop. Monday-Friday 8 am to 5 pm. Routine
service repairs and complete restorations, full time parts sourcing
for all domestic brands made between 1920-1975. Specialists in
1960s-1970s muscle cars, racing, drag racing, road course and
performance off-road.

Historic Video Archives   videotapes
PO Box 189-VA
Cedar Knolls, NJ 07927-0189

See full listing in **Section Two** under **automobilia**

Horseplayactionwear.com   apparel
211 N Catherine   decals
Bay City, MI 48706   gifts
517-892-5509, 800-447-7669
FAX: 517-671-1003
E-mail: horsplay@concentric.net

See full listing in **Section Two** under **apparel**

Hot Rod Memories   videos
PO Box 280040
Northridge, CA 91328-0040
818-886-7637; FAX: 818-349-1403
E-mail: sales@hotrodmemories.com

See full listing in **Section Four** under **information sources**

Hot Rod Nostalgia™   "magalog"
PO Box 249
West Point, CA 95255-0249
209-293-2114; FAX: 209-293-2120
E-mail: hvaa@hotrodnostalgia.com

See full listing in **Section Four** under **books & publications**

Hunters Custom Automotive   accessories
975 Main St   engine parts
Nashville, TN 37206   fiberglass products
615-227-6584; FAX: 615-227-4897

See full listing in **Section Two** under **accessories**

Hurst Racing Tires/
Traction By Hurst — drag tires slicks
190 East Ave A, PO Box 278
Wendell, ID 83355
208-536-6236

See full listing in **Section Two** under **tires**

Ideal Signs — lettering painting striping
4033 Ridgeway Rd
Manchester, NJ 08759
732-657-0100; FAX: 732-323-0390
E-mail: idealsigns1@aol.com

See full listing in **Section Two** under **artwork**

International Motor Racing
Research Center at Watkins Glen — research
610 S Decatur St
Watkins Glen, NY 14891
607-535-9044; FAX: 607-535-9039
E-mail: research@racingarchives.org

See full listing in **Section Four** under **research & reference libraries**

King Bolt Co — hardware
4680 N Grand Ave
Covina, CA 91724
626-339-8400; FAX: 626-339-8210

See full listing in **Section Two** under **hardware**

Koffel's Place II — engine rebuilding machine shop
740 River Rd
Huron, OH 44839
419-433-4410; FAX: 419-433-2166

See full listing in **Section Two** under **engine rebuilding**

Krem Engineering — engine rebuilding repairs restoration
10204 Perry Hwy
Meadville, PA 16335
814-724-4806; FAX: 814-337-2992
E-mail: info@krem-enterprises.com

See full listing in **Section Two** under **restoration shops**

Kwiklift Inc — accessories lifts
610 N Walnut
Broken Arrow, OK 74012
800-961-5438; FAX: 918-259-1170
E-mail: sales@kwiklift.com

See full listing in **Section Two** under **tools**

LaCarrera-The Mexican Road Race — road race
PO Box 1605
Studio City, CA 91614
323-464-5720; FAX: 323-656-7111
E-mail: lacarrera@earthlink.net

Founded 1988. 2,500 members. Info, catalog and rules regarding LaCarrera Panamerica, the 14th annual Mexican Road Race. Dues: none. Web site: www.mexicanroadrace.com

---

Mancini Racing Enterprises — parts
33510 Groesbeck Hwy
Fraser, MI 48026
810-294-6670; FAX: 810-294-0390
E-mail: robc@manciniracing.com

See full listing in **Section One** under **Mopar**

Marcovicci-Wenz Engineering Inc — Cosworth engines
33 Comac Loop
Ronkonkoma, NY 11779
631-467-9040; FAX: 631-467-9041
E-mail: mwerace@compuserve.com

Mail order and open shop. Monday-Saturday 8 am to 6 pm. Vintage engine rebuilders, specializing in engine parts and services for road racing motors of the 1960s, 1970s and 1980s. Also Cosworth and Ferrari. Complete dyno facility.

Maximum Downforce — photography
Gary Toriello
120 E Clinton Ave
Bergenfield, NJ 07621
201-384-0529; FAX: 201-384-5062
E-mail: racerx@
maximumdownforce.com

See full listing in **Section Two** under **photography**

McCoy's Memorabilia — memorabilia racing literature
35583 N 1830 E
Rossville, IL 60963-7175
PH/FAX: 217-748-6513
E-mail: indy500@soltec.net

See full listing in **Section Two** under **literature dealers**

Mid Valley Engineering — machine work parts restoration
16637 N 21st St
Phoenix, AZ 85022
602-482-1251; FAX: 602-788-0812

See full listing in **Section Two** under **transmissions**

Moroso Motorsports Park — race track
PO Box 31907
Palm Beach Gardens, FL 33420
561-622-1400; FAX: 561-626-2053
E-mail: mail@
morosomotorsportspark.com

Daily 9 am to 5 pm. Multi-purpose year round race track with a 2.25 mile road course and 1/4 mile NHRA drag strip. Weekly races Wednesday, Friday and Saturday and special events monthly that feature car shows, swap meets and restoration market place. Exhibition cars include Jet Funny cars, dragsters, trucks, top fuel, pro mods. Web site: www.morosomotorsportspark.com

---

MotorLit.com — books manuals memorabilia
PO Box 4907
Mesa, AZ 85211-4907
480-969-0102
E-mail: info@motorlit.com

See full listing in **Section Two** under **literature dealers**

Noble Racing Inc — accessories parts
1058 Dry Ridge Rd
Versailles, KY 40383
859-879-1123; FAX: 859-879-3743
E-mail: nobleracing@iwebworks.com

See full listing in **Section Two** under **engine parts**

Performance Automotive Warehouse — accessories engine parts
21001 Nordhoff St
Chatsworth, CA 91311
818-678-3000; FAX: 818-678-3001

See full listing in **Section Two** under **engine parts**

QA1 Precision Products Inc — suspension parts
21730 Hanover Ave
Lakeville, MN 55044
800-721-7761; FAX: 952-985-5679
E-mail: ehaines@qa1.net

See full listing in **Section Two** under **suspension parts**

Section Two – Generalists

Racing Consultants 11361 152nd St Jupiter, FL 33478 561-745-9366; FAX: 561-743-7314 E-mail: richie@raceconsultant.com	consultants marketing

Mail order only. Race team marketing and promotions, sponsorship procurement.

Red Lion Racing 8318 Avenida Castro Cucamonga, CA 91730 909-987-9818; FAX: 909-987-6538 E-mail: rlracing@cris.com	photographs posters

See full listing in **Section Two** under **artwork**

Replicarz 166 Spruce St Rutland, VT 05701 802-747-7151 E-mail: replicarz@aol.com	books kits models videos

Mail order only. Die cast miniature models, plastic model kits, books, videos. Specialize in racing, current and Vintage Formula 1, Indy, DTM, WSC, LeMans and more.

Ross' Automotive Machine Co Inc 1763 N Main St Niles, OH 44446 330-544-4466	racing engines rebuilding

See full listing in **Section Two** under **engine rebuilding**

Ross Racing Pistons 625 S Douglas St El Segundo, CA 90250 310-536-0100; FAX: 310-536-0333	pistons

See full listing in **Section Two** under **engine parts**

RPM Catalog PO Box 12031 Kansas City, KS 66109 913-788-3219; FAX: 913-788-9682 E-mail: dale@dalewilch.com	parts speed equipment

Catalog listing of used race car and hot rod cars, parts and equipment. Subscription: $20/year. Web site: www.rpmcatalog.com

Simons Balancing & Machine Inc 1987 Ashley River Rd Charleston, SC 29407 843-766-3911; FAX: 843-766-9003	machine work

See full listing in **Section Two** under **machine work**

Specialty Cars Inc 17211 Roseton Ave Artesia, CA 90701 562-924-6904; FAX: 562-402-9544	parts street rods

See full listing in **Section Two** under **street rods**

Speed & Spares America 167D Portland Rd, Units 7/8 Weymouth, Dorset DT4 9BQ England +44 (0) 1305 766293 FAX: +44 (0) 1305 761304 E-mail: sales@speedandspares.co.uk	parts racing equipment

See full listing in **Section Two** under **comprehensive parts**

Speedzone 1750 Broadway New Hyde Park, NY 11040 516-354-8178; FAX: 516-354-0692 E-mail: sales@speedzoneusa.com	die cast models

See full listing in **Section Two** under **models & toys**

Spyder Enterprises Inc RFD 1682 Laurel Hollow, NY 11791-9644 516-367-1616; FAX: 516-367-3260 E-mail: singer356@aol.com	accessories artwork automobilia books

See full listing in **Section Two** under **automobilia**

Edward Tilley Automotive Collectibles PO Box 4233 Cary, NC 27519-4233 919-460-8262 E-mail: edandsusan@aol.com	automobilia literature parts

See full listing in **Section Two** under **automobilia**

Towe Auto Museum 2200 Front St Sacramento, CA 95818 916-442-6802; FAX: 916-442-2646 E-mail: khartley@toweautomuseum.org	museum

See full listing in **Section Six** under **California**

Vibratech Inc (Fluidampr) 11980 Walden Ave Alden, NY 14004 716-937-3603; FAX: 716-937-4692	performance parts

See full listing in **Section Two** under **engine parts**

Vicarage Jaguar 5333 Collins Ave, Ste 704 Miami Beach, FL 33140 305-866-9511; FAX: 305-866-5738 E-mail: vicarage@ix.netcom.com	parts restoration

See full listing in **Section One** under **Jaguar**

radiator emblems & mascots

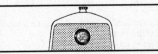

Dwight H Bennett 1330 Ximeno Ave Long Beach, CA 90804 PH/FAX: 562-498-6488	emblem repair hardware repair mascot repair plaque repair

See full listing in **Section Two** under **grille emblem badges**

Brass Script Arthur Evans 32 Richmond-Belvidere Rd Bangor, PA 18013-9544 610-588-7541	brass script

Brass script for antique car radiators. Over 800 original scripts. SASE required for pencil rub and price.

C & G Early Ford Parts 1941 Commercial St, Dept AH Escondido, CA 92029-1233 760-740-2400; FAX: 760-740-8700 E-mail: cgford@cgfordparts.com	accessories/chrome emblems literature mechanical weatherstripping

See full listing in **Section One** under **Ford 1932-1953**

Classic Chevrolet Parts Inc | parts
8723 S I-35
Oklahoma City, OK 73149
405-631-4400; FAX: 405-631-5999
E-mail: info@classicchevroletparts.com

See full listing in **Section One** under **Chevrolet**

Jay M Fisher | mascots
Acken Dr 4-B | sidemount mirrors
Clark, NJ 07066 | windwing brackets
732-388-6442

See full listing in **Section Two** under **accessories**

Gaylord Sales | automobilia
Frank Ranghelli | automotive art
125 Dugan Ln | mascots
Toms River, NJ 08753
732-349-9213; FAX: 732-341-5353
E-mail: fgaylordsales@aol.com

Mail order, car shows (Carlisle, Hershey, etc). Mascots, automotive art: paintings, bronzes, collector posters, all forms of automobilia. Have been doing the above for 26 years. Always interested in purchasing items.

Mike Z Kleba | hood ornaments
PO Box 70 | radiator caps
Mallorytown, ON Canada K0E 1R0
613-923-5934

Mascots, radiator caps and hood ornaments, collector, repair-restore, buy, swap, sell.

Mascots Unlimited | grille ornaments
PO Box 666 | hood ornaments
Old Saybrook, CT 06475
PH/FAX: 860-388-1511
E-mail: rpearl@cyberzone.net

Mail order and open shop by appointment only. Deals in hood ornaments, grille ornaments (not OEM), aftermarket only. Dogs, horses, figures and wild animals. Cast bronze, chrome plated or enamelled. Very high quality.

Obsolete Ford Parts Inc | parts
8701 S I-35
Oklahoma City, OK 73149
405-631-3933; FAX: 405-634-6815
E-mail: info@obsoletefordparts.com

See full listing in **Section One** under **Ford 1954-up**

Pulfer & Williams | mascots
213 Forest Rd, PO Box 67 | nameplates
Hancock, NH 03449-0067 | radiator emblems
603-525-3532; FAX: 603-525-4293
E-mail: dorwill@webtv.net

Mail order only. Manufacture emblems, nameplates, handles reproduction mascots.

Verdone's Custom Stainless Casting | casting
31 Stricklerstown Loop Rd | polishing
Newmanstown, PA 17073
717-949-3341; FAX: 717-949-2782

See full listing in **Section Two** under **castings**

radiators

American Honeycomb | manufacturing
Radiator Mfg Co | repairs
Neil Thomas
171 Hwy 34
Holmdel, NJ 07733
718-948-7772 days; 732-741-8743 eves

Mail order and open shop. Monday-Friday 9 am to 4 pm Eastern time. Manufacturer of cartridge type and cellular antique radiators. Also manufacture odd one-of-a-kind radiators and refurbish antique radiators. Exhibited in national and private airplane and automobile museums. Send for free color brochure.
See our ad on this page

Blaak Radiateurenbedryf | radiators
Blaaksedyk oost 19
Heinenoord 3274LA Netherlands
31-186-601732; FAX: 31-186-603044
E-mail: info@blaak.com

Mail order and open shop. Monday-Friday 8:30 am to 5:30 pm. Specializing in pre-1940 radiators. All types of cellular and cartridge honeycomb cores. Web site: www.blaak.com

The Brassworks | radiators
289 Prado Rd
San Luis Obispo, CA 93401
800-342-6759; FAX: 805-544-5615
E-mail: brassworks@thegrid.net

Mail order and open shop. Monday-Friday 8 am to 5 pm. Manufacture all foreign and domestic radiators, 1890s-up. Model T to SPAD XIII airplanes and everything in between. All work guaranteed. Ship worldwide.

| Cal West Auto Air & Radiators Inc
24309 Creekside Rd #119
Valencia, CA 91355
800-535-2034; FAX: 661-254-6120
E-mail: mike@calwest-radiators.com | a/c units/condensers
fan shrouds
gas tanks
heaters/radiators
radios/wheels |
|---|---|

Mail order and open shop. Monday-Saturday; 24 hrs/7 days for emergencies. Radiators (new, recored and custom), air conditioning condensers and heaters. 1955-1957 Chevy, Camaro, Corvette, Mustang and T-Bird radiators. Antique radiators available. Custom catalog available. Automotive products online. Web site: www.calwest-radiators.com

| Chev's of the 40's
2027 B St, Dept Z
Washougal, WA 98671
800-999-CHEV (2438)
FAX: 360-835-7988	parts

See full listing in **Section One** under **Chevrolet**

| Classic Chevrolet Parts Inc
8723 S I-35
Oklahoma City, OK 73149
405-631-4400; FAX: 405-631-5999
E-mail: info@classicchevroletparts.com	parts

See full listing in **Section One** under **Chevrolet**

| The Copper Cooling Works
2455 N 2550 E
Layton, UT 84040
801-544-9939	radiators

Mail order only. Build new, exact copies of the disc and tube radiators used on the early chain drive cars. Started in 1966 and have had many new radiators on top winning cars throughout the world. Specializing in Cadillac and Oldsmobile.

| DeWitts Reproductions
11672 Hyne Rd
Brighton, MI 48114
810-220-0181; FAX: 810-220-0182
E-mail: dewitts@ismi.net	radiators

See full listing in **Section One** under **Corvette**

| The Filling Station
990 S Second St
Lebanon, OR 97355-3227
800-841-6622 orders
541-258-2114; FAX: 541-258-6968
E-mail: fssales@fillingstation.com | literature
parts |
|---|---|

See full listing in **Section One** under **Chevrolet**

| Gano Filter
1205 Sandalwood Ln
Los Altos, CA 94024
650-968-7017	coolant filters

Mail order only. In-line coolant filter, prevents radiator clogging. Permanent, easily cleaned accessory. Available in brass or transparent, durable thermoplastic. Kits include necessary clamps and instructions for proper installation. Plastic kits: $30 each or 2/$56; brass kits: $37 or 2/$70. Also available: heater core filters in brass, $17 each. All prices include shipping. Satisfaction guaranteed or money back. Free information and wholesale prices on request.

| Gas Tank and Radiator Rebuilders
20123 Hwy 362
Waller, TX 77484
800-723-3759
E-mail: donhart@donhart.com | abrasive blasting
gas tank rebuilding
heaters
radiator repair |
|---|---|

See full listing in **Section Two** under **fuel system parts**

| GRIFFIN Radiator
100 Hurricane Creek Rd
Piedmont, SC 29673
800-RACE-RAD (722-3723)
864-845-5000; FAX: 864-845-5001
E-mail: griffinrad@aol.com	radiators

Mail order and open shop. Monday-Friday 8 am to 5 pm. Manufacturer of high-performance direct replacement and custom designed all aluminum radiators for street rods, vintage, classic, muscle, late model, kit and exotic cars and trucks. Custom aluminum shrouds. Quality and durability delivered with a sense of urgency and focused on customer service. Two-year warranty. Built to your exact specifications and with the same performance as GRIFFIN radiators for NASCAR and other racing series. Free catalog. Web site: http://griffinrad.com

| Highland Radiator Inc
Rt 9 W
Highland, NY 12528
845-691-7020; FAX: 845-691-2489 | parts
service |
|---|---|

Mail order and open shop. Monday-Friday 8 am to 5 pm. Complete auto radiator repair and services facility. Specializing in antique, classic, special interest and all types of automotive radiators. Expertly repaired, restored, rebuilt or recored, quality craftsmanship. Honeycomb cores available. 42 years' experience.

| Horton
244 Woolwich St S
Breslau, ON Canada N0B 1M0
519-648-2150; FAX: 519-648-3355
E-mail: mail@horton.on.ca	parts

See full listing in **Section Two** under **street rods**

| Mac's Radiator Service &
Gas Tank Renu LA
9681 Alondra Blvd
Bellflower, CA 90706
800-901-8265, 562-920-1871
FAX: 562-920-8491
E-mail: bruce@macs-radiator.com | gas tanks
radiators |
|---|---|

Mail order and open shop. Monday-Saturday 8 am to 5 pm. New gas tanks, gas tank restoration, extra capacity gas tanks for trucks and vans, Griffin all aluminum racing radiators, copper/ brass radiators, plastic tank radiators, motorcycle tank restoration, gas tank sending units rebuilding. Web site: www.macs-radiator.com

| No 1 Performance
1775 S Redwood Rd
Salt Lake City, UT 84104
800-453-8250; FAX: 801-975-9653 | engine kits
parts |
|---|---|

See full listing in **Section Two** under **engine parts**

| Obsolete Chevrolet Parts Co
PO Box 68
Nashville, GA 31639-0068
800-248-8785; FAX: 229-686-3056
E-mail: obschevy@surfsouth.com | engine parts
radiators
rubber parts
transmissions |
|---|---|

See full listing in **Section One** under **Chevrolet**

| Obsolete Ford Parts Inc
8701 S I-35
Oklahoma City, OK 73149
405-631-3933; FAX: 405-634-6815
E-mail: info@obsoletefordparts.com	parts

See full listing in **Section One** under **Ford 1954-up**

| Powell Radiator Service
1277 W Main St, Box 427
Wilmington, OH 45177
937-382-2096	restoration

Mail order and open shop. Monday-Friday 8 am to 5 pm Eastern time. Show quality restorations on any type or year of radiator (except aluminum). Some old radiators in stock needing restoration but available for sale or restoration.

Prezerve	**additives**
1101 Arapahoe, Ste 3	
Lincoln, NE 68502	
888-774-4184; FAX: 402-420-7777	
E-mail: prezerve@prezerveit.com	

See full listing in **Section Two** under **car care products**

Rad Cap Products	**radiator caps**
5236 Pacheco Blvd	
Pacheco, CA 94553	
925-689-6214; FAX: 925-689-0145	

Mail order and open shop. Monday-Friday 9 am to 5 pm Pacific time. We manufacture a sacrifical anode radiator cap to combat the harmful effects of electrolysis which is found in all engines and cooling systems. Electrolysis is costing collectors thousands of dollars every year in unwanted costly repairs. Web site: www.radcaps.com

Radiator & Gas Tank Specialist	**gas tanks**
20123 Hwy 362, PO Box 758	**heaters**
Waller, TX 77484	**radiators**
800-723-3759; FAX: 936-372-5032	
E-mail: donhart@donhart.com	

Radiators, gas tanks, heaters, air conditioning condensers repaired, restored, rebuilt, new. Vintage and antique specialists. California, Texas and Maryland. Web site: www.radiatorshops.com/gastanks

Glen Ray Radiators Inc	**rebuilding**
2105 Sixth St	**recoring**
Wausau, WI 54401	
800-537-3775	

Mail order and open shop. Monday-Friday 7 am to 5:30 pm. Radiator rebuilding and recoring.

Raybuck Autobody Parts	**body parts**
RD 4, Box 170	
Punxsutawney, PA 15767	
814-938-5248; FAX: 814-938-4250	

See full listing in **Section Two** under **body parts**

Skills Unlimited Inc	**radiators**
7172 CR 33	
Tiffin, OH 44883	
PH/FAX: 419-992-4680	
419-448-4639 shop	
E-mail: smith@friendlynet.com	

Mail order and open shop. Monday-Saturday 8 am to 8 pm. Deals in replacement of authentic vintage radiator cores and complete radiators, including shells and tanks.

radios

12 Volt Stuff, Radio &	**radios**
Speedometer Repair Co	
10625-A Trade Rd	
Richmond, VA 23236	
804-423-1055, 888-487-3500 toll free	
FAX: 804-423-1059	
E-mail: ecs@12voltstuff.com	

Mail order and open shop. Monday-Friday 8 am to 5:30 pm. Automobile radio restorations from 1965 and up. Wonderbar, 8-tracks, cassette and CD players rebuilt. Delco, Bose amps and speakers, OEM and aftermarket. Authorized Ford, Lincoln, Visteon exchange center. Custom installation available for FM conversion and remote CD players. We warranty the entire unit, not just the parts we use. Exchange units available for nation-

wide next day air delivery. MasterCard, Visa, Discover, American Express and COD. Web site: www.12voltstuff.com

Antique Automobile Radio Inc	**radio accessories**
700 Tampa Rd	**radio parts**
Palm Harbor, FL 34683	**stereo conversions**
800-933-4926, 727-785-8733	
FAX: 727-789-0283	
E-mail: sales@	
antiqueautomobileradio.com	

Mail order and open shop. Monday-Friday 8 am to 4:30 pm Eastern time. Manufacture over 60 types of radio vibrators, power inverters (to operate 12-volt accessories on 6-volt systems) and FM conversion kits. Stocks speakers, tubes, transformers, antennas, dial glass. 3,500+ radios in inventory. Visa, Master-Card, Discover. Free catalog. Dealer inquiries invited. Web site: www.antiqueautomobileradio.com

Antique Radio Doctor	**radio repairs**
Barry Dalton	
196 Kilborn Dr	
Grants Pass, OR 97526	
541-474-2524	
E-mail: radiodoc@rvi.net	

Mail order only. Deal in the repair of vintage auto radios, 1930-1965, GM, Ford, Mopar. Free estimate of repairs. Rapid turnaround. Please, no tape decks. Specializing in vacuum tube gear.

Antique Radio Service	**radio service**
12 Shawmut Ave	
Cochituate, MA 01778	
800-201-2635; FAX: 508-653-2418	
E-mail: richardfoster@prodigy.net	

Antique auto radios 1926-1962, sales, service, restoration, FM conversions, speaker recores. Radios bought.

Becker of North America Inc 16 Park Way Upper Saddle River, NJ 07458 888-423-3537; FAX: 201-327-2084 E-mail: info@beckerautosound.com	radio repair

See full listing in **Section One** under **Mercedes-Benz**

Bob's Radio & TV Service 238 Ocean View Pismo Beach, CA 93449 805-773-8200	radios

Mail order and open shop with radio museum. Monday-Friday and most Saturdays 8 am to 5:30 pm. Vintage car radio restorations and FM additions, stereo conversions, 1932-1970, most models, American only. Flat rates to repair/overhaul. Vintage home radios are also welcome. No parts for sale. Visa and MasterCard accepted. Web site: www.bobsradio.com

Classic Car Radio Service® 25 Maple Rd, PO Box 764 Woodacre, CA 94973 415-488-4596; FAX: 415-488-1512 E-mail: healy@classicradio.com	radio repair radio restoration

Radio repair and restoration. Five year, parts and labor, written transferrable guarantee. The only true bargain is quality. Don't spoil the "pride of your car", insist on authentic restoration maintaining the value and integrity of your classic automobile. The best sound, the best performance. MasterCard and Visa accepted. The original Classic Car Radio Service®. Web site: www.classicradio.com/

Classic Chevrolet Parts Inc 8723 S I-35 Oklahoma City, OK 73149 405-631-4400; FAX: 405-631-5999 E-mail: info@classicchevroletparts.com	parts

See full listing in **Section One** under **Chevrolet**

Corvette Clocks by Roger 24 Leisure Ln Jackson, TN 38305 901-664-6120; FAX: 901-664-1627	repair restoration

See full listing in **Section Two** under **instruments**

Crutchfield Corp 1 Crutchfield Park Charlottesville, VA 22911 800-955-9009; FAX: 804-817-1010 E-mail: sales@crutchfield.com	car stereos

Car stereo components and systems, mobile video, home theater systems, and audio/video components, A/V-PC convergence products, car security, telephones, and more. "Easy fit" vehicle guide, plus free-with-purchase guidebooks on hook-up and installation of car & home products. Toll-free technical support for life. FREE catalog. Web site: www.crutchfield.com

Custom Autosound Mfg 808 W Vermont Ave Anaheim, CA 92805 800-888-8637; FAX: 714-533-0361 E-mail: info@custom-autosound.com	accessories CD players custom radios speaker upgrades

See full listing in **Section Two** under **accessories**

Elliott's Car Radio 313 Linfield Rd Parkerford, PA 19457 610-495-6360; FAX: 610-495-7723 E-mail: elliottradio@aol.com	radio repairs

Mail order. Monday-Friday 9 am to 5 pm. Specializing in the repair of car radios and tape decks. Repair and sales of car radios 1958-1990. Radio and speaker wiring for GM 1960-1990.

Fred's Classic Auto Radio & Clocks 7908 Gilette Lenexa, KS 66215 913-599-2303	clock repair radio repair

Mail order and open shop. Monday-Friday 9 am to 6 pm Central time. Specializing in radio and clock repair for 1932-1979 American cars and trucks. Also sell parts for do-it-yourselfers such as vibrators, tubes, speakers and knobs.

Jim Gensch 1810 Juliet St Paul, MN 55105 651-690-2029	radios repair vibrators

Mail order and open shop by appointment only. Vintage car and home radio repair, 1920s-1960. Hundreds of restored car radios in stock through the 1970s.

Grandpa's Radio Shop 26 Queenston Crescent Kitchener, ON Canada N2B 2V5 519-576-2570	radio restoration

See full listing in **Section One** under **Ford 1954-up**

William Hulbert Jr 13683 Rt 11, PO Box 151 Adams Center, NY 13606 315-583-5765 E-mail: radio_29chevy@yahoo.com	radios

Radios, pre-1959. Restored sets for sale or restore yours. Dead sets taken on trade. One year guarantee after you've installed it in your car and are using it. Will also trade for parts for my own cars and trucks.

Jukebox Friday Night 110 Beech St Cochran, GA 31014 478-934-8866	parts repairs restoration

Mail order only. Repair, restore, parts for home and car radios. Repair, parts for juke boxes. Electronic parts: tubes, vibrators, transformers.

Leo Gephart Inc 7360 E Acoma Dr, Ste 14 Scottsdale, AZ 85260 480-948-2286; FAX: 480-948-2390 E-mail: gephartclassics@earthlink.net	vintage cars

See full listing in **Section Two** under **car dealers**

Marquette Radio 7852 W Sycamore Dr Orland Park, IL 60462 708-633-0545 E-mail: alsvir@ameritech.net	radios tape players

Mail order and open shop. Original 1963-1985 factory AM-FM radios and tape players.

Michigan Corvette Recyclers 11995 US 223, PO Box 98 Riga, MI 49276 800-533-4650; FAX: 517-486-4124 E-mail: mcr@cass.net	Corvette parts new/used parts salvage

See full listing in **Section One** under **Corvette**

Mountain Vintage Radio Repair 7 KeKeTaw Ln Columbia, NJ 07832 908-362-9650 E-mail: mountainradio@goes.com	radio repair

Mail order only. Radio repair for all makes.

Normans' Classic Auto Radio | custom sales
8475 68th Way
Pinellas Park, FL 33781
727-546-1788

Mail order and open by appointment. Radio sales of custom AM/FM cassette radios that fit and fill original dash openings without modifications. Prices start at $159. Also CD changers, stereo conversions and FM converters.

Obsolete Ford Parts Inc | parts
8701 S I-35
Oklahoma City, OK 73149
405-631-3933; FAX: 405-634-6815
E-mail: info@obsoletefordparts.com

See full listing in **Section One** under **Ford 1954-up**

Prestige Thunderbird Inc | appraisals / radios / repairs / restorations / tires
10215 Greenleaf Ave
Santa Fe Springs, CA 90670
800-423-4751, 562-944-6237
FAX: 562-941-8677
E-mail: tbirds@prestigethunderbird.com

See full listing in **Section One** under **Thunderbird**

S&M Electro-Tech Inc | electrical parts
8836 Xylite St NE
Blaine, MN 55449
763-780-2861
E-mail: turnswitch@turnswitch.com

See full listing in **Section Two** under **electrical systems**

Spirit Enterprises | automobilia / stereo systems
4325 Sunset Dr
Lockport, NY 14094
716-434-9938 showroom
716-434-0077 warehouse
E-mail: sprtntrprs@cs.com

See full listing in **Section Two** under **automobilia**

JF Sullivan Company | electrical parts / repairs
14 Clarendon Rd
Auburn, MA 01501
508-792-9500

See full listing in **Section Two** under **fuel system parts**

Vintage Radio Shop | parts / radios / repairs
Wilford Wilkes Sr
101 Swoope St, Box 103
Brisbin, PA 16620
814-378-8526; FAX: 814-378-6149

Mail order or open by appointment. Exclusively European auto radios, 1940s-1970. Tube or transistor. Blaupunkt, Becker, Telefunken, Radiomobile, etc. The only shop catering to these specialized auto radios exclusively. Repairs, restoration. Stocking new dial faces, knobs, push-buttons, etc. Visa/MC. All work done myself personally.

Yesterday's Radio | interior plastic / radio parts
7759 Edgewood Ln
Seven Hills, OH 44131-5902
PH/FAX: 216-524-2018
E-mail: jerry@yesterdaysradio.com

See full listing in **Section One** under **Packard**

George Zaha | FM conversions / radios / speakers
4900 Green Hollow Dr
Orion, MI 48359
248-393-1732 evenings

Radios repaired, sold and purchased since 1934. Over 50 years of service guarantees you the best quality at the best prices. FM conversions, vibrators, speaker reconing, massive stock of radios and NOS parts inventory. Complete sales and service facility. All work fully guaranteed one year.

restoration aids

ACE Automotive Cleaning Equipment Co | sandblasting / equipment
897 S Washington, Ste 232
Holland, MI 49423
616-772-3260; FAX: 616-772-3261

See full listing in **Section Two** under **rust removal & stripping**

Amherst Antique Auto Show | swap meets
157 Hollis Rd
Amherst, NH 03031
603-673-2093, NH
FAX: 617-641-0647, MA

See full listing in **Section Two** under **auctions & shows**

Antique Radio Service | radio service
12 Shawmut Ave
Cochituate, MA 01778
800-201-2635; FAX: 508-653-2418
E-mail: richardfoster@prodigy.net

See full listing in **Section Two** under **radios**

Apple Hydraulics Inc | brake rebuilding / shock rebuilding
1610 Middle Rd
Calverton, NY 11933-1419
800-882-7753, 631-369-9515
FAX: 631-369-9516
E-mail: info@applehydraulics.com

See full listing in **Section Two** under **suspension parts**

Aremco Products Inc | compounds
707-B Executive Blvd
Valley Cottage, NY 10989
845-268-0039; FAX: 845-268-0041
E-mail: aremco@aremco.com

See full listing in **Section Two** under **accessories**

Atlantic British Ltd | accessories / parts
Halfmoon Light Industrial Park
6 Enterprise Ave
Clifton Park, NY 12065
800-533-2210; FAX: 518-664-6641
E-mail: ab@roverparts.com

See full listing in **Section One** under **Rover/Land Rover**

Bob's Brickyard Inc | parts
1030 N Hickory Ridge Tr
Milford, MI 48380
248-685-9508; FAX: 248-685-8662
E-mail: bobsbrick@aol.com

See full listing in **Section One** under **Bricklin**

Section Two – Generalists

Bonk's Automotive Inc   automotive tools
4480 Lazelda Dr
Milan, MI 48160
800-207-6906; FAX: 734-434-0845
E-mail: bonkers@bonkauto.com

See full listing in **Section Two** under **tools**

British Wiring Inc   wiring accessories
20449 Ithaca Rd   wiring harnesses
Olympia Fields, IL 60461
PH/FAX: 708-481-9050
E-mail: britishwiring@ameritech.net

See full listing in **Section Two** under **electrical systems**

The Buckle Man   buckles
Douglas D Drake
28 Monroe Ave
Pittsford, NY 14534
716-381-4604

See full listing in **Section Two** under **hardware**

Buenger Enterprises/   dehumidifiers
GoldenRod Dehumidifier
3600 S Harbor Blvd
Oxnard, CA 93035
800-451-6797; FAX: 805-985-1534

See full listing in **Section Two** under **car care products**

C & P Chevy Parts   parts
50 Schoolhouse Rd, PO Box 348VA   restoration supplies
Kulpsville, PA 19443
215-721-4300, 800-235-2475
FAX: 215-721-4539

See full listing in **Section One** under **Chevrolet**

CARS Inc   interiors
1964 W 11 Mile Rd
Berkley, MI 48072
248-398-7100; FAX: 248-398-7078
E-mail: carsinc@worldnet.att.net

See full listing in **Section Two** under **interiors & interior parts**

Caswell Electroplating in Miniature   plating kits
4336 Rt 31
Palmyra, NY 14522
315-597-5140, 315-597-6378
FAX: 315-597-1457
E-mail: sales@caswellplating.com

See full listing in **Section Two** under **plating & polishing**

Stan Chernoff   mechanical parts
1215 Greenwood Ave   restoration parts
Torrance, CA 90503   technical info
310-320-4554; FAX: 310-328-7867   trim parts
E-mail: az589@lafn.org

See full listing in **Section One** under **Datsun**

Classic Auto Literature   manuals/models
1592 Seacrest Rd   parts catalogs
Nanoose Bay BC Canada V9P 9B5   posters/videos
250-468-9522   sales brochures

See full listing in **Section Two** under **literature dealers**

Classic Mercury Parts   parts
1393 Shippee Ln
Ojai, CA 93023
805-646-3345; FAX: 805-646-5386
E-mail: mfourez@aol.com

See full listing in **Section One** under **Mercury**

C'NC Sheetmetal   car casters
11790 FM 3270   patterns
Tyler, TX 75708
800-668-1691; FAX: 903-877-2060
E-mail: cncsmetal@aol.com

Car casters for 4-1/2", 4-3/4", 5" and 5-1/2" 5-hole bolt patterns
and custom bolt patterns are available. Web site:
www.fannincreekcnc.com

Color-Plus Leather   leather conditioning
Restoration System   leather dye
106 Harrier Ct, 3767 Sunrise Lake
Milford, PA 18337-9315
570-686-3158; FAX: 570-686-4161
E-mail: jpcolorplus@pikeonline.net

See full listing in **Section Two** under **leather restoration**

Cover-It   all-weather shelters
17 Wood St
West Haven, CT 06516-3843
800-932-9344; FAX: 203-931-4754
E-mail: info@coverit.com

See full listing in **Section Two** under **car covers**

Dalmar   electroplating
11759 S Cleveland Ave, Ste 28   plating supplies
Ft Myers, FL 33907
941-275-6540; FAX: 941-275-1731
E-mail: dalmar@peganet.com

See full listing in **Section Two** under **plating & polishing**

Daytona MIG   plasma cutters
1821 Holsonback Dr   welders
Daytona Beach, FL 32117
800-331-9353; FAX: 904-274-1237
E-mail: ask@daytonamig.com

See full listing in **Section Two** under **tools**

Development Associates   electrical parts
12791-G Newport Ave
Tustin, CA 92780
714-730-6843; FAX: 714-730-6863
E-mail: devassoc@yahoo.com

See full listing in **Section Two** under **electrical systems**

Mike Drago Chevy Parts   Chevrolet parts
141 E St Joseph St
Easton, PA 18042
PH/FAX: 610-252-5701
E-mail: dragomdcp@aol.com

See full listing in **Section One** under **Chevrolet**

Dri-Wash 'n Guard   automotive care
Independent Distributor   products
PO Box 1331   boat care products
Palm Desert, CA 92261
800-428-1883, 760-346-1984
FAX: 760-568-6354
E-mail: driwasherik@aol.com

See full listing in **Section Two** under **car care products**

DW Electrochemicals Ltd   contact enhancer
97 Newkirk Rd N, Unit 3
Richmond Hill, ON Canada L4C 3G4
905-508-7500; FAX: 905-508-7502
E-mail: dwel@stabilant.com

See full listing in **Section Two** under **electrical systems**

The Eastwood Company | automotive tools / powder coating / welding supplies
263 Shoemaker Rd
Pottstown, PA 19464
800-345-1178; FAX: 610-323-6269

See full listing in **Section Two** under **tools**

The Finished Look | POR-15 products
PO Box 191413
Sacramento, CA 95819-1413
800-827-6715; FAX: 916-451-3984
E-mail: info@thefinishedlook.com

See full listing in **Section Two** under **rustproofing**

Frost Auto Restoration Techniques Ltd | car care products / paints / tools
Crawford St
Rochdale OL16 5NU United Kingdom
44-1706-658619
FAX: 44-1706-860338
E-mail: order@frost.co.uk

See full listing in **Section Two** under **tools**

The Garden of Speedin | books
4645 Q Ruffner St
San Diego, CA 92111
800-MOTORHEAD
FAX: 858-467-0777
E-mail: cars@gardenofspeed.com

See full listing in **Section Four** under **information sources**

Gasoline Alley LLC | drip pans
1700E Iron Ave, PO Box 737
Salina, KS 67402
800-326-8372, 785-822-1003
FAX: 785-827-9337
E-mail: morrison@midusa.net

See full listing in **Section Two** under **accessories**

The Glass House | glass
446 W Arrow Hwy #4
San Dimas, CA 91773
909-592-1078; FAX: 909-592-5099

See full listing in **Section Two** under **glass**

Green Oak Enterprises Inc | car dollies
12166 Andresen Dr
South Lyon, MI 48178
888-721-9595

See full listing in **Section Two** under **tools**

House of Powder Inc | powder coating / sandblasting
Rt 71 & 1st St, PO Box 110
Standard, IL 61363
815-339-2648

See full listing in **Section Two** under **service shops**

Imaginographx | automotive portraits / automotive prints / idea renderings / logo designs
PO Box 95
Hawthorne, NJ 07506
800-848-9459
E-mail: imaginographx@netscape.net

See full listing in **Section Two** under **artwork**

Imperial Restorations POR-15 Products | coatings
7550 E Rice Rd
Gardner, IL 60424
800-576-5822; FAX: 815-237-8707
E-mail: imprest@btc-skynet.net

See full listing in **Section Two** under **rustproofing**

Independence Porcelain Enamel | manifolds
703 S Cottage
Independence, MO 64050
816-252-8180; FAX: 816-252-8181
E-mail: info@ipe-porcelain.com

Mail order and open shop. Monday-Friday 8 am to 4 pm. Porcelain coating automobile manifolds. Web site: www.ipe-porcelain.com

J & G Auto Parts | clips / fasteners / weatherstripping
3050 Wild Run Rd
Pennsburg, PA 18073
215-679-4683 after 5 pm

Supply clips, fasteners and weatherstripping for restorations. Attends all major car shows and flea markets.

JCM Industries | wax hardener
2 Westwood Dr
Danbury, CT 06811
800-752-0245

See full listing in **Section Two** under **car care products**

Jersey Late Greats Inc | documentation / service / restoration details
PO Box 1294
Hightstown, NJ 08520
609-448-0526

See full listing in **Section One** under **Chevrolet**

Jet-Hot Coatings/MCCI | high-temp coatings
55 E Front St, Ste A-200
Bridgeport, PA 19405
800-432-3379
E-mail: sales@jet-hot.com

See full listing in **Section Two** under **exhaust systems**

Ken's Cougars | parts
PO Box 5380
Edmond, OK 73083
405-340-1636; FAX: 405-340-5877

See full listing in **Section One** under **Mercury**

Kenask Spring Co | springs
307 Manhattan Ave
Jersey City, NJ 07307
201-653-4589

See full listing in **Section Two** under **suspension parts**

Koala International | convertible cleaners & protectants / plastic coating / plastic polish
PO Box 255
Uwchland, PA 19480
610-458-8395; FAX: 610-458-8735
E-mail: sales@koala-products.com

See full listing in **Section Two** under **car care products**

Kwiklift Inc | accessories / lifts
610 N Walnut
Broken Arrow, OK 74012
800-961-5438; FAX: 918-259-1170
E-mail: sales@kwiklift.com

See full listing in **Section Two** under **tools**

Section Two – Generalists

Lake Buchanan Industries Inc
400 Carlson Cir
Buchanan Dam, TX 78609
888-552-5278 toll-free
512-793-2867; FAX: 512-793-2869
E-mail: lbi:@tstar.net
| blasting cabinet |

See full listing in **Section Two** under **tools**

Leatherique Professional Leather Restoration & Preservation Products
PO Box 2678
Orange Park, FL 32065
904-272-0992; FAX: 904-272-1534
E-mail: lrpltd@bellsouth.net
| leather cleaning conditioning & professional restoration products |

See full listing in **Section One** under **Rolls-Royce/Bentley**

LEX-AIRE Nationwide Sales
34 Hutchinson Rd
Arlington, MA 02474
800-LEX-AIRE; FAX: 562-691-9374
| painting equipment turbine systems |

See full listing in **Section Two** under **tools**

PK Lindsay Co Inc
63 Nottingham Rd
Deerfield, NH 03037
800-258-3576; FAX: 800-843-2974
E-mail: sales@pklindsay.com
| paint removal rust removal |

See full listing in **Section Two** under **rust removal & stripping**

Loga Enterprises
5399 Old Town Hall Rd
Eau Claire, WI 54701
715-832-7302
E-mail: logaent@cs.com
| interior parts |

See full listing in **Section One** under **Studebaker**

Maintenance Specialties Company
21 Valley Forge Rd, PO Box 251
New Castle, DE 19720
800-777-6715; FAX: 302-328-2315
| rustproofing paints |

See full listing in **Section Two** under **rustproofing**

Malm Chem Corp
PO Box 300, Dept HVA
Pound Ridge, NY 10576
914-764-5775; FAX: 914-764-5785
E-mail: jkolin@cloud9.net
| polish wax |

See full listing in **Section Two** under **car care products**

The Masters Company
30 Willow Dr, Ste A
Fort Thomas, KY 41075-2035
800-385-5811; FAX: 859-441-6765
E-mail: rmasters3@home.com
| parts tools |

See full listing in **Section Two** under **tools**

Mild to Wild Classics
1300 3rd St NW
Albuquerque, NM 87102
505-244-1139; FAX: 505-244-1164
| parts repairs restoration |

See full listing in **Section Two** under **street rods**

Moroso Motorsports Park
PO Box 31907
Palm Beach Gardens, FL 33420
561-622-1400; FAX: 561-626-2053
E-mail: mail@
morosomotorsportspark.com
| race track |

See full listing in **Section Two** under **racing**

MotorLit.com
PO Box 4907
Mesa, AZ 85211-4907
480-969-0102
E-mail: info@motorlit.com
| books manuals memorabilia |

See full listing in **Section Two** under **literature dealers**

MSC Fasteners
104 Oakdale Dr
Zelienople, PA 16063
800-359-7166, 724-452-8003
FAX: 724-452-1145
E-mail: msc999@ccia.com
| hardware |

See full listing in **Section Two** under **hardware**

Muscle Express
135 Hibiscus St
Jupiter, FL 33458
800-323-3043 order line
561-744-3043 tech line
| parts |

See full listing in **Section One** under **Chevelle/Camaro**

Myk's Tools
365 Sunnyvale St
Coos Bay, OR 97420
541-267-6957; FAX: 541-267-5967
E-mail: mykel@harborside.com
| engine hoists engine removal tool |

See full listing in **Section Two** under **tools**

OEM Glass Inc
Rt 9 E, PO Box 362
Bloomington, IL 61702
800-283-2122, 309-662-2122
FAX: 309-663-7474
| auto glass |

See full listing in **Section Two** under **glass**

Original Parts Group Inc
17892 Gothard St
Huntington Beach, CA 92647
800-243-8355 US/Canada
714-841-5363; FAX: 714-847-8159
| accessories parts |

See full listing in **Section One** under **Pontiac**

Pennsylvania Metal Cleaning
200 17th St
Monaca, PA 15061-1969
724-728-5535
| derusting stainless fasteners stripping |

See full listing in **Section Two** under **rust removal & stripping**

Bill Peters
41 Vassar Pl
Rockville Centre, NY 11570
516-766-8397
| steering wheel restoration |

See full listing in **Section Two** under **steering wheels**

J Pinto
2306 Memphis St
Philadelphia, PA 19125
215-739-1132
E-mail: lectri@yahoo.com
| electric motors relay repair solenoid repair switch repair |

See full listing in **Section Two** under **electrical systems**

Poly All Fast Set International Inc
44 Bridge St, PO Box 1150
Bradford, ON Canada L3Z 2B5
905-778-9010; FAX: 905-778-9011
E-mail: info@polyall.com
| sealants wood care products |

A new product, Poly All 2000, repairs rotten wood, use on fiberglass, use on metal to seal. Web site: www.polyall.com

Protective Products Corp   chemical products
Box 246
Johnston, IA 50131
888-772-1277; FAX: 515-334-7533
E-mail: ppc1@aol.com

Unique chemical products which greatly reduce the labor time in restoration and surface care products which produce prize winning results. PPC products are currently used by many of the national leading shops and nationally recognized show car winners. Web site: http://ppcexcels.com/

Rapido Group   accessories
80093 Dodson Rd   parts
Tygh Valley, OR 97063
541-544-3333; FAX: 541-544-3100

See full listing in **Section One** under **Merkur**

RB's Obsolete Automotive   parts
7711 Lake Ballinger Way
Edmonds, WA 98026-9163
425-670-6739; FAX: 425-670-9151
E-mail: rbobsole@gte.net

See full listing in **Section Two** under **comprehensive parts**

REM Automotive Inc   interior parts
2610 N Brandt Rd   molded hood
Annville, PA 17003   insulation
717-838-4242; FAX: 717-838-5091   trunk lining
E-mail: remautoinc@aol.com

See full listing in **Section Two** under **interiors & interior parts**

Restoration Supply Company   accessories
2060 Palisade Dr   restoration supplies
Reno, NV 89509
775-825-5663; FAX: 775-825-9330
E-mail: restoration@rsc.reno.nv.us

Mail order only. Deal in authentic hard to find restoration supplies and accessories for the automobile and marine enthusiast.

Ed Rouze   painting guide book
746 N Memorial
Prattville, AL 36067
334-365-2381

See full listing in **Section Two** under **painting**

Rust Busters   rust repair
PO Box 341
Clackamas, OR 97015
503-223-3203
E-mail: info@rustbusters.com

See full listing in **Section Two** under **restoration shops**

Samson Technology Corporation   plating systems
6825 SW 21st Ct #3
Davie, FL 33317
800-256-0692; FAX: 954-916-9338
E-mail: sales@samson24k.com

See full listing in **Section Two** under **plating & polishing**

T Schmidt   rust removers
827 N Vernon
Dearborn, MI 48128-1542
313-562-7161

See full listing in **Section Two** under **rust removal & stripping**

Ron Scobie Enterprises   gas pump parts
7676 120th St N
Hugo, MN 55038
651-653-6503
E-mail: rscobie@gaspump.com

See full listing in **Section Two** under **petroliana**

Smithy Company   tools
170 Aprill Dr, PO Box 1517
Ann Arbor, MI 48106
800-476-4849; FAX: 800-431-8892

See full listing in **Section Two** under **tools**

Specialty Wheels Ltd   wheels
19310 NE San Rafael St
Portland, OR 97230
503-491-8848; FAX: 503-491-8828
E-mail: wheelzrus@msn.com

See full listing in **Section Two** under **wheels & wheelcovers**

Sta-Dri Pouches/Beach Filler   corrosion protection
Products Inc   mildew protection
7682 Glenville Rd   moisture protection
Glen Rock, PA 17327
800-BEACH85; FAX: 717-235-4858
E-mail: beach@blazenet.net

See full listing in **Section Two** under **storage care products**

Standard Abrasives   abrasives
Motorsports Division
4201 Guardian St
Simi Valley, CA 93063
800-383-6001; 805-520-5800 ext 371
FAX: 805-577-7398
E-mail: tech@sa-motorsports.com

Mail order only. Monday-Friday 8 am to 5 pm Pacific time. Specialty abrasives and surface conditioning products to make work easier, cleaner and more productive on a variety of restoration and customization applications including frame work, bodywork, wheels and trim. Product kits available. Call for free catalog. Web site: www.sa-motorsports.com

Stevens Car Care Products Inc   car alarms
36542 Vine St   rust deterrents
East Lake, OH 44095
440-953-2900; FAX: 440-953-4473
E-mail: info@stevenscarcare.com

See full listing in **Section Two** under **anti-theft**

Sunchaser Tools   metal-finishing kit
3202 E Foothill Blvd   video
Pasadena, CA 91107
626-795-1588; FAX: 626-795-6494

See our ad inside the back cover

Tar Heel Parts Inc   buffing supplies
PO Box 2604
Matthews, NC 28106-2604
800-322-1957, 704-753-9114 (local)
FAX: 704-753-9117
E-mail: buffing@tarheelparts.com

See full listing in **Section Two** under **plating & polishing**

This Old Truck Magazine
PO Box 500
Missouri City, TX 77459
888-760-8108 subscriptions
937-767-1433 publishing office
FAX: 937-767-2726
E-mail: antique@antiquepower.com

magazine

See full listing in **Section Four** under **periodicals**

**Thunderbird, Falcon, Fairlane &
Comet Connections**
728 E Dunlap
Phoenix, AZ 85020
602-997-9285; FAX: 602-997-0624
E-mail: thunderbirdconn@aol.com

new repros parts used repros

See full listing in **Section One** under **Thunderbird**

TMC Publications
5817 Park Heights Ave
Baltimore, MD 21215-3931
410-367-4490; FAX: 410-466-3566
E-mail: carolyny@tmcpubl.com

literature manuals

See full listing in **Section Four** under **books & publications**

Tower Paint Co Inc
Box 2345
Oshkosh, WI 54903-2345
920-235-6520; FAX: 920-235-6521
E-mail: info@towerpaint.com

paint

See full listing in **Section Two** under **paints**

Keeping History Alive

This Old Truck

- Color Features
- Classic Restorations & Tips
- Detailed Histories
- Technical Information
- Product & Book Reviews
- Commercial & Classified Ads
- Best of all ...FREE ads for SUBSCRIBERS

FREE ISSUE

JOIN US TODAY & RECEIVE A FREE ISSUE

Visit us at www.thisoldtruck.com

1-888-760-8108

☑ Yes! Rush my FREE issue today and start my subscription to *This Old Truck*.
☐ INSTANT SAVINGS — I'm paying $24.95 today and SAVING $2.00!
☐ Payment Enclosed   ☐ Visa   ☐ MasterCard
Card # _____   Exp. Date _____
☐ Bill me later for the full price of $26.95.   (U.S. funds only.) (Overseas: $39.95)
Name _____
Address _____
City _____ State _____ Zip _____

Mail to: *This Old Truck*, P.O. Box 500, Missouri City, TX 77459
or FAX to (281) 261-5999   G01HMA

TP Tools & Equipment
7075 Rt 446, PO Box 649
Canfield, OH 44406
330-533-3384 local, 800-321-9260

abrasive blasters air compressors tools welders

Mail order and open shop. Monday-Friday 8:30 am to 6 pm, Saturday 8:30 am to 1:30 pm. Glass bead cabinets, abrasives, parts and supplies. Champion, Quincy and Campbell Hausfeld air compressors, HVLP paint systems and spray guns, Baldor Buffers, Hobart and Lincoln Welders. Plus, air tools, hydraulic presses, engine stands and cranes, parts washers, plasma cutters, metalworking equipment and more! We have the tools you need. Free 136-page catalog. Web site: www.tptools.com

Ultimate Appearance Ltd
113 Arabian Trail
Smithfield, VA 23430
888-446-3078; FAX: 757-255-2620

cleaners detailing products detailing services polish/wax

See full listing in **Section Two** under **car care products**

Vintage Glass USA
326 S River Rd, PO Box 336
Tolland, CT 06084
800-889-3826, 860-872-0018

auto glass

See full listing in **Section Two** under **glass**

Voss Motors Inc
4850 37th Ave S
Seattle, WA 98118
888-380-9277 toll-free
206-721-3077
E-mail: vossmotors@books4cars.com

service manuals

See full listing in **Section Two** under **literature dealers**

Williams Lowbuck Tools Inc
4175 California Ave
Norco, CA 91760
909-735-7848; FAX: 909-735-1210
E-mail: wlowbuck@aol.com

tools

See full listing in **Section Two** under **tools**

Wymer Classic AMC
Mark & George Wymer
340 N Justice St
Fremont, OH 43420
419-332-4291
419-334-6945 after 5 pm

NOS/used parts owner's manuals repairs service manuals

See full listing in **Section One** under **AMC**

restoration shops

1 CAAT Limited Co
1324 E Harper Ave
Maryville, TN 37804
865-983-7180
E-mail: jhenriks@icx.net

restoration

Maintenance and restoration for classic British motorcars. "1 Car at a Time."

2002 AD
11066 Tuxford St
Sun Valley, CA 91352
800-420-0223; FAX: 818-768-2697
E-mail: bmwsales@2002ad.com

cars parts restoration

See full listing in **Section One** under **BMW**

A&A Mustang Parts & Mfg Co
105 Fordham Rd
Oak Ridge, TN 37830
423-482-9445
E-mail: joannantrican@aol.com

| exhaust systems |
| parts |
| restorations |

See full listing in **Section One** under **Mustang**

AAdvanced Transmissions
15 Parker St
Worcester, MA 01610
508-752-9674; FAX: 508-842-0672

| rear axle service |
| restoration |
| ring/pinion |
| parts/sales/ |
| rebuilding/service |

See full listing in **Section Two** under **transmissions**

Ace Antique Auto Restoration
65 S Service Rd
Plainview, NY 11803
516-752-6065; FAX: 516-752-1484

| air conditioning |
| body rebuilding |
| restoration |
| wiring harnesses |

Mail order and open shop. Monday-Friday 8 am to 5 pm. Partial and complete restoration services. Fabrication, body rebuilding, paint, powertrain rebuilding, glass interior and chrome plating, air conditioning installation, wiring harnesses. Web site: www.aceautobody.com

Adams Custom Engines Inc
806 Glendale Ave
Sparks, NV 89431-5720
775-358-8070; FAX: 775-358-8040

| restorations |

Mail order. Shop open Monday-Friday 8 am to 5 pm. Full and partial restorations of antique and classic automobiles. 30 years' experience. Specializing in woodgraining. Quality work for the most discriminating, national award winning work. 352 body-off restorations since 1965.

Adler's Antique Autos Inc
801 NY Rt 43
Stephentown, NY 12168
518-733-5749
E-mail: advdesign1@aol.com

| auto preservation |
| Chevrolet knowledge |
| parts |
| repair |
| restoration |

Open Monday-Friday 9 am to 5 pm; other hours and days by appointment. Chevrolet car and truck specialist. Factory authentic restoration, both body and mechanical. MIG welding, panel fabrication, sandblasting and painting are done to factory or the owner's specifications. Over 600 GM vehicles in stock for parts salvage as well as potential restoration projects, dating back to 1934. Dealer for Chevrolet truck reproduction parts. Expert on Chevrolet Advance Design trucks, 1947-1955. See work we've done 28 years ago still going strong. All parts and work guaranteed. Author of *Notes From the Corrosion Lab* and Chevrolet historian.

Alfas Unlimited Inc
89 Greenwoods Rd W, Rt 44
Norfolk, CT 06058
860-542-5351; FAX: 860-542-5993
E-mail: alfasun@esslink.com

| engine rebuilding |
| parts |
| restoration |
| service |

See full listing in **Section One** under **Alfa Romeo**

ANC Restoration
Chris Palmerie
254 New Haven Ave
Waterbury, CT 06708
203-574-2249, 203-558-1488
E-mail: cpwp2@javanet.com

| restorations |

See full listing in **Section Two** under **plating & polishing**

Anderson Restoration
1235 Nash Ave
Kanawha, IA 50447
641-762-3528

| restorations |

Open shop only. Monday-Saturday 5:30 am to 4:30 pm. Complete or partial restorations to show quality of antique and clas-

sic automobiles. References available. 1928, 1932 and 1939 Packards, two 1911s, 1914, 1916, 1956 and 1965 Fords, 1904 Sandusky Courier, all AACA Silver Platter winners.

Antique Auto Restoration
Randy Reed, Owner
1975 Del Monte Blvd
Seaside, CA 93955
408-393-9411; FAX: 408-393-1041

| restoration |

Full or partial restorations or service. Experienced in British, German, Italian and American makes. Visit us when on the Monterey Peninsula for golfing, racing or the Concours. Web site: www.antiqueautorestoration.com

The Antique Auto Shop
603 Lytle Ave
Elsmere, KY 41018
859-342-8363; FAX: 859-342-9076
E-mail: antaut@aol.com

| mechanical service |
| restoration |

Open Monday-Friday 6 am to 4 pm. Full or partial restoration on antique, classic and sport cars from body-off the frame show cars to partial and component restoration. Paint, body and mechanical service. Same location 25 years. Appraisals by appointment. Custom car covers. Web site: www.antiqueautoshop.com

Antique & Classic Car Restoration
Hwy 107, Box 368
Magdalena, NM 87825

| restoration |

See full listing in **Section One** under **MG**

Art's Antique & Classic Auto Services
1985 E 5th St #16
Tempe, AZ 85281
480-966-1195

| restoration |

See full listing in **Section One** under **Buick/McLaughlin**

Auto Craftsmen Restoration Inc
27945 Elm Grove
San Antonio, TX 78261
PH/FAX: 830-980-4027

| appraisals |
| buyer/car locator |
| old M-B parts |
| restoration |

Mail order and open shop. Monday-Friday 8 am to 5 pm. Specializing in Mercedes-Benz and Rolls-Royce, Mustang convertibles, others considered. Top winning show cars have been restored by this shop.

Auto Restoration by William R Hahn
8837 Beebles Rd
Allison Park, PA 15101
412-367-2538, 724-935-3790

| custom work |
| restorations |

Open Monday-Friday 8 am to 5 pm, Saturday and evenings by appointment. Ground-up or partial restorations on all years, domestic and foreign vehicles. Will hand build the dream car you deserve, to your choice of concours quality, points correct or driver. Every level includes show quality with exceptional roadability. All are built to last long enough to become a family heirloom. Qualifications include National award winners. Over 25 years specializing in restoration. Detail oriented.

AutoFashions Restoration & Parts
Pittsboro, NC 27312
919-542-5566
E-mail: autofashions@mindspring.com

| auto parts |
| auto sales |
| handcrafts |
| restoration |

See full listing in **Section Two** under **body parts**

Automotion Classics Inc
100 N Strong Ave
Lindenhurst, NY 11757
631-225-0485

| painting |
| restoration |
| sandblasting |

Full restorations of all makes and models of classic automobiles, media and sandblasting, fabrications, custom painting and welding.

Section Two – Generalists

Automotive Restorations Inc
Stephen Babinsky
4 Center St
Bernardsville, NJ 07924
908-766-6688; FAX: 908-766-6684
E-mail: autorestnj@aol.com

| clutch rebuilding |
| mechanical services |
| restorations |

Mail order and open shop. Monday-Saturday 8 am to 6 pm, closed Sundays. Partial and full restorations. Specializing in 1930s classic cars and specialized services, ie: cast iron welding, repair of manifolds, heads, blocks, etc, and clutch rebuilding and relining, radiator core manufacture and repair, full mechanical services, etc.

The Autoworks Ltd
90 Center Ave
Westwood, NJ 07675
201-358-0200; FAX: 201-358-0442

| restoration |
| sales |
| service |

See full listing in **Section Two** under **service shops**

Avanti Auto Service
Rt 322, 67 Conchester Hwy
Glen Mills, PA 19342-1506
610-558-9999

| repair |
| restoration |

Open shop only. Monday-Friday 9 am to 6 pm. General auto repair serving all makes, models and years. Mechanical restoration, front end alignment, computer service, brakes, shocks, tires, etc. 20 years' experience. Specializing in Pantera, Avanti, Corvette and others.

B & L Body Shop
20 O'Shea Ln
Waynesville, NC 28786-4524
828-456-8277

| restoration |

Complete restoration of antique autos. Call first for confirmation. Established in 1968.

Back-In-Time Automotive Restorations
57 Cannonball Rd
Pompton Lakes, NJ 07442
PH/FAX: 973-616-6300

| restoration |

Open Monday-Friday 8 am to 6 pm, Saturday by appointment. Body and mechanical restoration, metal fabrication, show paint, upholstery and electrical, machine shop on premises, problem solvers. In-house babbitt work.

Backwoods Auto
487 Esperance Rd
Esperance, NY 12066
518-875-6538
E-mail: backwoods_auto@hotmail.com

| motorcycles |
| repairs |

See full listing in **Section Two** under **motorcycles**

Banzai Motorworks
8039-B Penn Randall Pl
Upper Marlboro, MD 20772
PH/FAX: 301-420-4200
E-mail: zspert@olg.com

| parts |
| pre-purchase |
| insp/consultation |
| repairs/restoration |
| service |

See full listing in **Section One** under **Datsun**

Bassett Classic Restoration
2616 Sharon St, Ste D
Kenner, LA 70062-4934
PH/FAX: 504-469-2982

| parts |
| restoration |
| service |

See full listing in **Section One** under **Rolls-Royce/Bentley**

Bastian Automotive Restoration
4170 Finch Ave
Fairfield, OH 45014
PH/FAX: 513-738-4268

| appraisals |
| restoration |

Open Monday-Friday 8 am to 5 pm, Saturday 9 am to 1 pm. National show winning restorations of antique, classic, muscle

and vintage race automobiles. Vintage automobile repair and authentic rewiring. Chrysler Town & Countrys our specialty. Our automobiles have won Best of Class and People's Choice awards at National Concours d'Elegance, AACA and CCCA National awards. Certified appraisals available by appointment. International Automobile Appraisers Association, member #1003160096.

Bayliss Automobile Restorations
2/15 Bon Mace Close, Berkeley Vale
Via Gosford NSW 2261 Australia
61-2-43885253; FAX: 61-2-43893152
E-mail: bayrest@ozemail.com.au

| repainting |
| repairs |
| sheetmetal work |

Repairing, rebodying and repainting of vintage, thoroughbred and classic cars. Body panels and sheetmetal work fabricated to your specifications (or to original) in steel or aluminum. All mechanical and upholstery work also undertaken. Home of the Amardo Clubman. Handbuilt, modern, wide-bodied Lotus 7 lookalike, kit or complete.

Berkshire Auto's Time Was
10 Front St, Box 347
Collinsville, CT 06022
860-693-2332
E-mail: obteddi3@aol.com

| restoration |

Specializing in repair of street rods, custom or classic cars including insurance claim work. Our frame work is second to none. Can custom mix any color in urethane paint. Motto: "Repair, not total, your old car." Also full body-off or partial restorations with impeccable detail for competition or personal pleasure.

Bill's Model Acres Ford Farm
RD 1, Box 283, 8th St Rd
Watsontown, PA 17777
570-538-3200

| parts |
| restoration |

See full listing in **Section One** under **Ford 1903-1931**

Billie Inc
PO Box 1161
Ashburn, VA 20146-1161
800-878-6328; FAX: 703-858-0102

| garage diaper |
| mats |

See full listing in **Section Two** under **car care products**

Blackheart Enterprises Ltd
305-12 Knickerbocker Ave
Bohemia, NY 11716
516-752-6065; FAX: 516-694-1078

| parts |
| restoration |

See full listing in **Section One** under **Checker**

BMC Classics Inc
828 N Dixie Freeway
New Smyrna Beach, FL 32168
PH/FAX: 386-426-6405
E-mail: bmcar1@aol.com

| parts |
| repair |
| restoration |

Open shop. Monday-Friday 8 am to 5:30 pm, Saturday 8 am to 12 pm. Restorations, repairs, service, parts. Specializing in Jaguar, Austin-Healey, Triumph, Mercedes, Porsche from 1950s-1980s. Web site: www.dreamsonwheels.com

Bob's Speedometer Service
32411 Grand River Ave
Farmington, MI 48336
800-592-9673; FAX: 248-473-5517

| gauges |
| speedometers |
| tachometers |

See full listing in **Section Two** under **instruments**

Bonnet to Boot 7217 Geyser Ave Reseda, CA 91335 818-757-7050; FAX: 818-340-8674 E-mail: bonnettoboot@earthlink.net	**restoration**

Mail order and open shop. Restoration shop. Service and parts for Bentley, Jaguar and Rolls-Royce. Original British license plates. Color-Tune tool dealer.

Brian's 4wd Parts LLC 428 N Harbor St Branford, CT 06405 203-481-5873; FAX: 203-481-3995 E-mail: willysgp@aol.com	**literature** **parts**

See full listing in **Section One** under **Willys**

British Auto/USA 92 Londonderry Tpke Manchester, NH 03104 603-622-1050, 800-452-4787 FAX: 603-622-0849 E-mail: jaguar@britishautousa	**parts** **upholstery**

See full listing in **Section One** under **Jaguar**

British Car Service 2854 N Stone Ave Tucson, AZ 85705 520-882-7026; FAX: 520-882-7053 E-mail: bcs@liveline.com	**restoration** **salvage yard**

Mail order and open shop. Monday-Friday 8 am to 5:30 pm, Saturday 9 am to 3 pm. Specializing in rust-free British cars and parts from the 1950s to the present. We also offer complete machine shop services and distributor rebuilding as well as a full service maintenance and restoration facility for British cars.

New parts for all British and European cars available. Now in our 27th year. E-mail inquiries encouraged or see our web site: www.britishcarservice.com

C&V Classic Restorations 420 East St Webb City, MO 64870 800-464-8592; FAX: 417-673-7544 E-mail: info@cvclassic.com	**appraisals** **restorations**

Restorations, complete frame-off, original or custom, 18 years' experience, show quality work, satisfaction guaranteed. Appraisals. Web site: www.cvclassic.com

Cars of the Past Restorations Inc 11180 Kinsman Rd Newbury, OH 44065 440-564-2277	**restoration**

Shop open Monday-Friday 8 am to 6 pm. Complete or partial restorations on antiques, classics, special interest, exotics and trucks. Custom painting and graphics, custom pipe bending on all types of exhaust, including stainless steel. 1955-1957 Chevys, Corvettes, 1955-1957 T-Birds and trucks are our specialties.

Central Alabama Restorations LLC Ed Rouze Owner 1665 McQueen Smith Rd S Prattville, AL 36066-7500 334-361-7433	**appraisals** **restoration**

Complete restoration work. Full-time, 9-man shop. Two new modern buildings. Partials or complete restorations. Rust fabrication, welding, painting, blasting, bodywork, interiors, appraisals. Reliable and honest. Quality workmanship, fair rates. Many National winners. Restorations are our only business.

Section Two – Generalists

Chief Service
Herbert G Baschung
Brunnmatt, PO Box 155
CH-4914 Roggwil Switzerland
PH/FAX: 0041-62-9291777

> parts
> **restoration**

Mail order and open shop by appointment only. Specializing in restoration, full or partial, plus parts, new and used for pre-1960 GM, Ford, Mopar and Studebaker. Complete or partial restoration for all pre-1960 US makes to period perfect condition. Buy, trade, sell cars, parts, literature and memorabilia, 1930-1960. Can locate your dream car.

City Imports Ltd
166 Penrod Ct
Glen Burnie, MD 21061
410-768-6660; FAX: 410-768-5955

> **bodywork**
> **car sales**
> **restorations**

See full listing in **Section One** under **Jaguar**

Classic Auto
251 SW 5th Ct
Pompano Beach, FL 33060
PH/FAX: 954-786-1687

> **restoration**

Restoration of autos, specializing in Ford products, Mustangs and T-Birds. Also street rods, custom cars, custom painting.

Classic Auto Rebuilders/CAR
Box 9796
Fargo, ND 58106

> **painting**
> **plating**
> **restoration**
> **woodwork**

Mail order and open shop by appointment only. Complete and partial restorations, plating, castings, welding, painting, convertible conversions, trim work, woodwork, customizing and metal work and parts fabrication. Complete coach and limousine building.

Classic Auto Restoration
15445 Ventura Blvd #60
Sherman Oaks, CA 91413
818-905-6267; FAX: 818-906-1249
E-mail: rollsroyce1@earthlink.net

> **acquisitions**
> **restoration**
> **sales**

See full listing in **Section One** under **Rolls-Royce/Bentley**

Classic Auto Restoration
437 Greene St
Buffalo, NY 14212
716-896-6663
E-mail: jp@classicbuff.com

> **appraisals**
> **plating**
> **polishing**
> **restoration**

Mail order only. Chrome plating, potmetal repair, stainless steel repair and polishing, aluminum polishing, top show quality for over 25 years by United Custom Plating Ltd, 905-791-0990. Also do appraisals. Web site: www.classicbuff.com

Classic Auto Restoration Service Inc
381 National Dr
Rockwall, TX 75032-6556
972-722-9663

> **restoration**

See full listing in **Section One** under **Chevrolet**

Classic Car Radio Service®
25 Maple Rd, PO Box 764
Woodacre, CA 94973
415-488-4596; FAX: 415-488-1512
E-mail: healy@classicradio.com

> **radio repair**
> **radio restoration**

See full listing in **Section Two** under **radios**

Classic Car Works Ltd
3050 Upper Bethany Rd
Jasper, GA 30143
770-735-3945

> **restoration**

Monday-Saturday 8 am to 6 pm. Service and restoration of all antique, classic and sports cars, American and foreign. Specialize in Buicks and all English cars for all years and models. Electrical and mechanical problems solved. Expert paint, body and interior work. All convertible tops repaired and replaced.

Classic Carriage House
5552 E Washington
Phoenix, AZ 85034
602-275-6825; FAX: 602-244-1538

> **restoration**

Restoration, sales and appraisals by Craig Jackson, certified by Internal Society of Appraisers.

Classic Carriages
267 County Rd 420
Athens, TN 37303
PH/FAX: 423-744-7496

> **repair**
> **restoration**

Open shop. Monday-Saturday 9 am to 5 pm. Deal in restoration and repair of antique and classic autos and the building of street rods. 1932-1953 flathead Fords and 1950s style hot rods are a specialty, as well as engine conversions and complete chassis work. Will consider all projects.

Classic Coachworks
735 Frenchtown Rd
Milford, NJ 08848
908-996-3400; FAX: 908-996-0204
E-mail: info@classiccoachworks.net

> **bodywork**
> **painting**
> **restoration**

Open Monday-Saturday by appointment only. Restoration and restyling facility specializing in cars from 1950-present. All work performed by certified craftsmen and supervised by a certified master craftsman. ASE certified and I-Car certified master repair/refinish technicians. I-Car Gold Class repair facility. Bodywork, painting and restorations for 1950s-present Corvette, Mustang, T-Bird, Mercedes, Rolls-Royce and Porsche. Collision work to all years, makes and models. Web site: www.classiccoachworks.net

Classic Coachworks Rod & Custom
7492 S Division Ave
Grand Rapids, MI 49548
616-455-8110
E-mail: classiccoachal@aol.com

> **parts**
> **repairs**
> **restoration**

See full listing in **Section Two** under **street rods**

Classic Creations of Central Florida
3620 Hwy 92E
Lakeland, FL 33801
863-665-2322; FAX: 863-666-5348
E-mail: flclassics@aol.com

> **parts**
> **restoration**
> **service**

See full listing in **Section One** under **Mustang**

Classic Garage
120 Monmouth St
Red Bank, NJ 07701
732-741-2450; FAX: 732-741-4134

> **bodywork**
> **paint**
> **restoration**

Open shop Monday-Friday 8 am to 5 pm, Saturday by appointment. Complete or partial restoration, service and repair on antique, classic and special interest vehicles. Full in-house mechanical, electrical, body and paint work performed by experienced craftsmen.

Classic Jaguar
9916 Hwy 290 W
Austin, TX 78736
512-288-8800; FAX: 512-288-9216
E-mail: danmooney@classicjaguar.com

> **parts**
> **technical support**

See full listing in **Section One** under **Jaguar**

Section Two – Generalists

Classic Motors
PO Box 1011
San Mateo, CA 94403
650-342-4117; FAX: 650-340-9473
E-mail: tonyleo@pacbell.net

appraisals
locator service
movie rentals
parts/restoration

Mail order and open shop. Monday-Friday 9 am to 6 pm. Automotive restoration. Specializing in convertibles and collector cars. Appraisals, service and parts for convertibles and collector cars. Corvette parts locator service. Collectable car and truck locator service. Movie car and prop rental service specializing in convertibles, sports cars and Corvettes.

Classic Showcase
913 Rancheros Dr
San Marcos, CA 92069
760-747-9947 restoration/buying
760-747-3188 sales
FAX: 760-747-4021
E-mail: management@
classicshowcase.com

classic vehicles
restorations
sales

Buy-Restore-Sell hours: Monday-Friday 8 am to 4 pm by appointment. Restoration facility address above, showroom address: 955 Rancheros Dr, San Marcos, CA 92069. Specializing in restoration and sales of British, German and Italian classic vehicles. Restorations are taken to show level or daily driver. Specialize in Jaguar, Austin-Healey, MG, Triumph, Mercedes, Porsche, BMW, Ferrari, Alfa Romeo, Fiat and microcars. References available upon request. Worldwide shipping available as well. Web site: www.classicshowcase.com

Classics and Customs
14024 Honeywell Rd
Largo, FL 33771
888-221-1847 toll-free
727-536-8372

appraisals
guide
painting
restoration
rust repairs

Open Monday-Friday 8 am to 6 pm, Saturday by appointment. Partial and complete frame-up restorations. Specializing in 1950s-1960s GM products including traditional sheetmetal fabricating, metal finishing and welding. Award-winning body and finish work. Show quality detailing. Also publish the most comprehensive tip and technique book ever written covering all aspects of antique auto restoration, *Secrets of the Pros*. Because of the limited printing, supply going fast. Call now.

Classics 'n More Inc
939 N Prince St
Lancaster, PA 17603
717-392-0599; FAX 717-392-2371

repairs
restoration

Shop open Monday-Friday 8 am to 4 pm. Restoration shop, classics, antiques, Corvettes, T-Birds, Mustangs, Triumphs, VWs and others. Specialize in automotive restoration for cars of the thirties to cars and trucks of the seventies. Also Packards 1939 to 1947, Ford retractables and Model As. Deal in all phases of automotive repair, frame-up restoration to everyday driver cars.

Coach Builders Limited Inc
1410 S Main St, PO Box 1978
High Springs, FL 32655
904-454-2060; FAX: 904-454-4080

car dealer
conv conversion

Monday-Friday 8 am to 5 pm. Convertible conversions of Cadillac Eldorado.

Coachbuilt Motors
907 E Hudson St
Columbus, OH 43211
614-261-1541
E-mail: coachbuilt907@aol.com

repairs

See full listing in **Section One** under **Rolls-Royce/Bentley**

Cobra Restorers Ltd
3099 Carter Dr
Kennesaw, GA 30144
770-427-0020; FAX: 770-427-8658

parts
restoration
service

See full listing in **Section One** under **Cobra**

Collector's Carousel
84 Warren Ave
Westbrook, ME 04092
207-854-0343; FAX: 207-856-6913

appraisals
sales
service

See full listing in **Section Two** under **car dealers**

Color-Ite Refinishing Co
Winning Colors
868 Carrington Rd, Rt 69
Bethany, CT 06524
203-393-0240; FAX: 203-393-0873
E-mail: colorite@ctinternet.com

modern finishes
restoration service

See full listing in **Section Two** under **paints**

Concours Quality Auto Restoration
32535 Pipeline Rd
Gresham, OR 97080
503-663-4335; FAX: 503-663-3435

pot metal restoration
repro gloveboxes

Mail order and open shop. Monday-Saturday 8 am to 6 pm or leave message. Specializing in pot metal welding, repair and restoration. Also glovebox reproduction, all cars with original style and color interior flocking.

Corvette Specialties of MD Inc
1912 Liberty Rd
Eldersburg, MD 21784
410-795-3180; FAX: 410-795-3247

parts
restoration
service

See full listing in **Section One** under **Corvette**

County Auto Restoration
6 Gavin Rd
Mt Vernon, NH 03057
603-673-4840
E-mail: CountyAutoRest@aol.com

bodywork
brakes
restoration
woodwork

Open shop. Monday-Friday 8 am to 5 pm, Saturday by appointment. Small shop specializing in total frame-up or partial restoration on antique cars and trucks, foreign or domestic. Sheetmetal panel and part fabrication, painting, woodwork, woodgraining and upholstering. Also service antique vehicles. Over 40 years' experience. References upon request.

Custom Autocraft Inc
2 Flowerfield, Ste 6
St James, NY 11780
PH/FAX: 631-862-7469

restoration
sheetmetal parts

See full listing in **Section One** under **Thunderbird**

Customs & Classics Inc
4674 S Brown St
Murray, UT 84107
801-288-1863; FAX: 801-288-1623
E-mail: kelley@customsandclassics.com

bodywork
painting
restoration
street rods

Open shop only. Monday-Friday 7 am to 4 pm. Antique and classic full service restorations, street rod engineering. Web site: www.customsandclassics.com

D&D Instruments Inc
770 Kasota Ave
Minneapolis, MN 55414
612-378-1224; FAX: 612-378-1445
E-mail: cselby@ddinstruments.com

gauges
instruments

See full listing in **Section Two** under **instruments**

Section Two – Generalists

D&D Plastic Chrome Plating	**plating**
925 Markey Dr	
Bryan, OH 43506	
419-260-2723; FAX: 419-636-3534	
E-mail: hl20@webtv.net	

See full listing in **Section Two** under **interiors & interior parts**

D&M Corvette Specialists Ltd	**car dealer**
1804 Ogden Ave	**parts**
Downers Grove, IL 60515	**restoration**
630-968-0031; FAX: 630-968-0465	**sales**
E-mail: sales@dmcorvette.com	**service**

See full listing in **Section One** under **Corvette**

Dan's Volvo Service	**restoration**
6615 S MacDill Ave	
Tampa, FL 33611	
813-831-1616	

See full listing in **Section One** under **Volvo**

Dash Graining by Mel Erikson	**dashboard**
31 Meadow Rd	**restoration**
Kings Park, NY 11754	
631-544-1102; FAX: 631-544-1107	

See full listing in **Section Two** under **woodgraining**

Davies Corvette	**accessories**
7141 US Hwy 19	**parts**
New Port Richey, FL 34653	
800-236-2383, 727-842-8000	
FAX: 727-846-8216	
E-mail: davies@corvetteparts.com	

See full listing in **Section One** under **Corvette**

DBM Classic Auto	**restoration**
Rt 3 Box 657	
Andalusia, AL 36420	
334-222-3673; FAX: 334-222-1256	
E-mail: goldie@alaweb.com	

Mail order and open shop. Open 7 days a week 8 am to 5 pm. Restoration of classic vehicles. Engine, trans upgrade assemblies, r&r interior to original or custom, r&r body and frame to repair or replace sheetmetal or suspension upgrades, rotator equipment to mount car assembly to repair floor pans and braces, original and custom painting.

DeLorean One	**bodywork**
20229 Nordhoff St	**parts**
Chatsworth, CA 91311	**service**
818-341-1796; FAX: 818-998-6381	

See full listing in **Section One** under **DeLorean**

DETAILS License Plate Restoration	**license plates**
74 Montague City Rd	
Greenfield, MA 01301	
413-774-6982	
E-mail: jeri@valinet.com	

See full listing in **Section Two** under **license plates**

Deters Restorations	**restoration**
6205 Swiss Garden Rd	
Temperance, MI 48182-1020	
734-847-1820	

Mail order and open shop. Monday-Friday 7 am to 5 pm, Saturday 9 am to 2 pm. Antique, special interest and street rod restorations complete and partial. Sheetmetal fabrication.

DiSchiavi Enterprises Inc	**restoration**
1248 Yardville Allentown Rd	
Allentown, NJ 08501	
609-259-0787	

Complete and partial restoration of antique, classic, sports and exotic automobiles. Specializing in 1953-2002 Chevrolet Corvettes. Restore to NCRS, NCCC and Bloomington Gold standards. Excellence in custom painting and coachwork. 35-year reputation for unsurpassed quality at an affordable price.

Distinctive Metal Polishing	**metal polishing**
18328 Gault St	**parts**
Reseda, CA 91335	
818-344-2160; FAX: 818-344-8029	

See full listing in **Section One** under **Harley-Davidson**

Dobbins Restoration Publishing	**literature**
16 E Montgomery Avenue	**parts**
Hatboro, PA 19040	**restoration**
215-443-0779	

See full listing in **Section One** under **Corvette**

Doc's Jags	**appraisals**
125 Baker Rd	**interiors**
Lake Bluff, IL 60044	**restoration**
847-367-5247; FAX: 847-367-6363	
E-mail: doc@docsjags.com	

See full listing in **Section One** under **Jaguar**

Doctor Jaguar Inc	**restoration**
740 W 16th St	**service**
Costa Mesa, CA 92627	
949-646-2816; FAX: 949-574-8097	

See full listing in **Section One** under **Jaguar**

Dodge City Vintage Dodge Vehicles & Parts	**parts**
18584 Hwy 108, PO Box 1687	**restoration**
Jamestown, CA 95327	**research**
209-984-5858; FAX: 209-984-3285	**vehicles**
E-mail: mike@dodgecityvintage.com	

See full listing in **Section One** under **Dodge**

Done Right Engine & Machine Inc	**engine rebuilding**
12955 York Delta Unit J	**machine shop**
North Royalton, OH 44133	
440-582-1366; FAX: 440-582-2005	

See full listing in **Section Two** under **engine rebuilding**

Donovan Motorcar Service Inc	**race prep**
4 Holmes Rd	**restoration**
Lenox, MA 01240	**service**
413-499-6000; FAX: 413-499-6699	
E-mail: donmtcar@aol.com	

See full listing in **Section One** under **Jaguar**

DTE Motorsports	**engines/race prep**
242 South Rd	**mechanical services**
Brentwood, NH 03833	**transportation**
PH/FAX: 603-642-3766	**restoration**
E-mail: dtemotorsports@aol.com	

See full listing in **Section One** under **Mercedes-Benz**

East Coast Chevy Inc	**custom work**
Ol '55 Chevy Parts	**parts**
4154A Skyron Dr	**restoration**
Doylestown, PA 18938	
215-348-5568; FAX: 215-348-0560	

See full listing in **Section One** under **Chevrolet**

Eddie's Restorations 4725 Rt 30 Elwood, NJ 08217 609-965-2211	restoration

See full listing in **Section One** under **Jaguar**

David R Edgerton Coachworks 9215 St Rt 13 Camden, NY 13316-4933 315-245-3113 E-mail: derods@excite.com	restoration woodworking

Open Monday-Friday 9 am to 5 pm or by appointment. Classic auto restoration. Twenty years' experience utilizing the most technologically advanced materials combined with old fashioned craftsmanship to produce high point, show winning restorations of full classics. The finest metal working, fabrication, woodworking and mechanical work available. Absolutely the highest attention to detail and originality. Full or partial projects considered. Investment quality automobiles available.

Enfield Auto Restoration Inc 4 Print Shop Rd Enfield, CT 06082 860-749-7917; FAX: 860-749-2836	panel beating restorations Rolls-Royce parts woodworking

Mail order and open shop. Monday-Friday 8 am to 5:30 pm. Full service. Restoration, panel beating, fabrication services, woodworking, bodywork and paint, maintenance sales and services, wire-on leather service and coach building. Springfield Rolls-Royce parts.

European Collectibles Inc 1974 Placentia Ave Costa Mesa, CA 92627-3421 949-650-4718; FAX: 949-650-5881 E-mail: europeancollectibles@ pacbell.net	restoration sales service

See full listing in **Section Two** under **car dealers**

FEN Enterprises of New York Inc 1090 Rt 376, PO Box 1559 Wappingers Falls, NY 12590 845-462-5959, 845-462-5094 FAX: 845-462-8450 E-mail: fenenterprises@aol.com	parts restoration

See full listing in **Section One** under **Cadillac/LaSalle**

Finest In Fords Larry Blodget Box 753 Ranchero Mirage, CA 92270 E-mail: info@finestinfords.com	books Ford 1954-up model cars restoration services

See full listing in **Section Four** under **books & publications**

Flatlander's Hot Rod 1005 W 45th St Norfolk, VA 23508 757-440-1932; FAX: 757-423-8601	chassis mfg hot rods parts street rods

See full listing in **Section Two** under **street rods**

Fourintune Garage Inc W63 N147 Washington Ave Cedarburg, WI 53012 262-375-0876; FAX: 262-675-2874	restoration

See full listing in **Section One** under **Austin-Healey**

George Frechette 14 Cedar Dr Granby, MA 01033 800-528-5235	brake cylinder sleeving

See full listing in **Section Two** under **brakes**

Freeman's Garage 29 Ford Rd Norton, MA 02766 508-285-6500; FAX: 508-285-6566	parts restoration sales service

See full listing in **Section One** under **Ford 1903-1931**

Freman's Auto 138 Kountz Rd Whitehall, MT 59759 406-287-5436; FAX: 406-287-9103	car dealer restoration shop salvage yard

See full listing in **Section Two** under **car dealers**

Fuller's Restoration Inc Old Airport Rd Manchester Center, VT 05255 802-362-3643; FAX: 802-362-3360 E-mail: chevy@vermontel.net	repairs restoration

Open shop only. Monday-Friday 8 am to 5 pm. Rust, collision and restoration, all makes and models, free estimates.

Gary's Steering Wheel Restoration 2677 Ritner Hwy Carlisle, PA 17013 717-243-5646; FAX: 717-243-5072 E-mail: wheelrest@aol.com	repairs

See full listing in **Section Two** under **steering wheels**

Mike Gerner, The Lincoln Factory 3636 Scheuneman Rd Gemlake, MN 55110 651-426-8001	car dealer parts restoration

See full listing in **Section One** under **Lincoln**

Grand Touring 2785 E Regal Park Dr Anaheim, CA 92806 714-630-0130; FAX: 714-630-6956	engine rebuilding machine shop restoration suspension

Open shop. Monday-Friday 8 am to 5 pm. Complete in-house restoration facilities offering engine building and dyno testing, interior, paint and machine shop services. Twenty-five years' experience. Specializing in all GM, Mopar, Packard, Stutz and vintage race cars. From body-off restorations to simple repairs, we provide the best craftsmanship available. Enclosed transportation services available. Our restorations have been featured in the top automotive publications and have won major Concours events including Pebble Beach.

Grey Hills Auto Restoration 51 Vail Rd, PO Box 630 Blairstown, NJ 07825 908-362-8232; FAX: 908-362-6796 E-mail: info@greyhillsauto.com	restoration service

Offering services for all makes and models, antique, classic, collector, muscle cars and street rods. Web site: www.greyhillsauto.com

Grossmueller's Classic Corvette 55 Sitgreaves St Phillipsburg, NJ 08865 908-213-8832; FAX: 908-213-7088 E-mail: wfg@gccorvettes.com	NOS parts used parts

See full listing in **Section One** under **Corvette**

Guild of Automotive Restorers | restoration
44 Bridge St, PO Box 1150 | sales
Bradford, ON Canada L3Z 2B5 | service
905-775-0499; FAX: 905-775-0944
E-mail: cars@guildclassiccars.com

Dedicated to the restoration and sale of the world's great cars. Services include true coachbuilding, ash framing, panel beating, mechanical and trim parts fabrication, engine rebuilding, paint and upholstering. Restore and service automobiles with an emphasis on the full classics of the 1920s and 1930s. From complete frame-off restorations to small repairs and service. The Guild offers fine quality workmanship. Service a wide variety of cars including Bugatti, Rolls-Royce, Bentley, Packard, Pierce-Arrow, GM, Ford and many more. Web site: www.guildclassiccars.com

Hamel's Automotive Inc | restorations
3306 Pleasant Ridge Rd
Wingdale, NY 12594
845-832-9454
E-mail: startnagan@aol.com

Specializing in restoration of antique automobiles. Professional quality service for over 20 years. Full frame-off or partial restoration. Call Doug at above phone number.

Hand's Elderly Auto Care | repair
2000 Galveston St | restoration
Grand Prairie, TX 75051
PH/FAX: 972-642-4288

Mail order and open shop. Monday-Friday 8 am to 5 pm. Maintaining, repairing and restoring antique automobiles, turn of the century to the 1950s. Specializing in Cadillac and Chevrolet. Web site: www.flash.net/~oldcars

Harbor Auto Restoration | restoration
315 SW 15th Ave
Pompano Beach, FL 33069
954-785-7887; FAX: 954-785-7388
E-mail: harbor@harbor-auto.com

Open Monday-Friday 7 am to 3:30 pm. A family owned and operated state of the art facility. Specializing in total or partial restoration of foreign, domestic, classic, street rod and muscle vehicles with hundreds of nationally acclaimed competition victories to our credit. Web site: www.harbor-auto.com
See our ad on this page

Hatfield Restorations | restoration
PO Box 846
Canton, TX 75103
903-567-6742; FAX: 903-567-0645
E-mail: pathat@vzinet.com

Open shop only. Monday-Friday 8 am to 5 pm. Complete or partial restorations. Street rod design and construction. Woodwork and metal fabrication. Quality workmanship and attention to detail. We invite you to come by and visit the shop. Also do interior work.

Hibernia Auto Restorations Inc | lacquer
52 Maple Terr | restoration
Hibernia, NJ 07842
973-627-1882; FAX: 973-627-3503

Open Monday-Friday 7 am to 5 pm. Restoration of any collectible car, full or partial restoration. Nitrocellulose and acrylic lacquer for sale.

Hjeltness Restoration Inc | restoration
630 Alpine Way | service
Escondido, CA 92029
760-746-9966; FAX: 760-746-7738

Specializing in the restoration, service and repair of Mercedes 300SL and other classic automobiles. Internationally recognized for our attention to authenticity and detail.

Hollywood Classic Motorcars Inc | parts
363 Ansin Blvd | restoration
Hallandale, FL 33009 | service
954-454-4641; FAX: 954-457-3801

See full listing in **Section One** under **Thunderbird**

The Horn Shop | horn restoration
7129 Oriskany Rd
Rome, NY 13440

Mail order only. Rebuild the motor section of your antique auto, motorcycle or boat horn. Mechanical and electrical repairs, includes the rewinding of the field coils and armature. If your horn is damaged beyond repair or missing completely, we will try to locate the correct horn for your marque's year and model. For inspection and written estimate of repairs, send the horn motor section, $10 and a SASE.

Hyde Auto Body | refinishing
44-1/2 S Squirrel Rd | restoration
Auburn Hills, MI 48326
PH/FAX: 248-852-7832
E-mail: bodyman8@juno.com

Open shop only. Monday-Friday 9 am to 6 pm, Saturday 9 am to 1 pm. Classic auto restoration and refinishing. Web site: www.hydeautobody.com

International Restoration Specialist Inc | restoration
PO Box 1303 | sales
Mt Airy, NC 27030
336-789-1548

Restoration of exotics including Jaguar, Ferrari, Triumph, Mercedes, Rolls-Royce/Bentley, Porsche, Pantera, Bugatti and other fine collector cars. They perform top quality full ground-up and partial restorations in house on all marques. Consistently receiving National honors, including Grand National 1st Place AACA, Regional Best of Show Awards, JCNA Regional and National Concours Awards and prestigious invitational appearances. Restoration, sales and purchases of fine automobiles are worthy of International Restoration Specialist Inc.

Jerry's Classic Cars & Parts Inc 4097 McRay Ave Springdale, AR 72764 800-828-4584; FAX: 501-750-1682 E-mail: jcc@jerrysclassiccars.com	**parts** **restoration**

See full listing in **Section One** under **Ford 1954-up**

John's Car Corner Rt 5, PO Box 85 Westminster, VT 05158 802-722-3180; FAX: 802-722-3181	**body/mech parts** **car dealer** **repairs/restoration**

See full listing in **Section One** under **Volkswagen**

JWF Restorations Inc 11955 SW Faircrest St Portland, OR 97225-4615 503-643-3225; FAX: 503-646-4009	**restoration**

See full listing in **Section One** under **AC**

K&D Enterprises 23117 E Echo Lake Rd Snohomish, WA 98296-5426 425-788-0507; FAX: 360-668-2003 E-mail: tdb@halcyon.com	**accessories** **parts** **restorations**

See full listing in **Section One** under **Jensen**

K & K Vintage Motorcars LC 9848 SW Frwy Houston, TX 77074 713-541-2281; FAX: 713-541-2286 E-mail: vintagemotorcars@ev1.net	**restoration** **sales** **service**

Open Monday-Friday 9 am to 5 pm, Saturday by appointment. Sales, service and restoration of classic and exotic cars. Specializing in Maserati, Jaguar, MGs, Fords and all other makes of domestic and foreign pre or post-war. Over 20 years' experience. Worldwide references upon request.

KC's Rods & Customs 3500 Aloma Ave, Ste D-16 Winter Park, FL 32792 877-750-6350; FAX: 407-673-9131 E-mail: bobbyb@bellsouth.net	**brakes** **exhaust systems** **restoration**

See full listing in **Section Two** under **street rods**

K-F-D Services Inc HC 65, Box 49 Altonah, UT 84002 801-454-3098; FAX: 801-454-3099 E-mail: kfd-services@msn.com	**parts** **restoration**

See full listing in **Section One** under **Kaiser Frazer**

Keilen's Auto Restoring 580 Kelley Blvd (R) North Attleboro, MA 02760 508-699-7768	**restoration**

Open shop only. Monday-Friday 8 am to 5 pm, Saturday 8 am to 12 noon. Restoring all years and makes of cars and trucks, all types of painting and customizing, street rods and mechanical repairs.

Kelley's Korner 22 14th St Bristol, TN 37620 423-968-5583	**parts** **repair**

See full listing in **Section One** under **Studebaker**

Ken's Cougars PO Box 5380 Edmond, OK 73083 405-340-1636; FAX: 405-340-5877	**parts**

See full listing in **Section One** under **Mercury**

Ken's Klassics Inc 20803 St Hwy 60 Muscoda, WI 53573-5466 608-739-4242; FAX: 608-739-4241 E-mail: klassics@mwt.net	**car sales** **restoration**

Shop open Monday-Friday 8 am to 5 pm, Saturday by appointment. Established in 1981. A complement of eight experienced craftsmen specializing in complete and partial restorations of classic, collectible and special interest vehicles. Meticulous workmanship performed at reasonable rates and honest billings. Certified PPG show quality paint and refinishing services. National show and pleasure car restorations. References gladly given. Inquire for shop informational portfolio. Visitors to our beautiful facility are always welcome.

Krem Engineering 10204 Perry Hwy Meadville, PA 16335 814-724-4806; FAX: 814-337-2992 E-mail: info@krem-enterprises.com	**engine rebuilding** **repairs** **restoration**

Mail order and open shop. Monday-Friday 8 am to 5 pm. Restoration problems are what we do best, the stuff no one else can or wants to do. Can make or repair the uncommon, non-existent or

difficult components. Also do problem engine and driveline rebuilds. Use original manufacturing practices and procedures whenever possible. Thirty years' experience. Automobile, airplane, train, boat, tractor or machine. Web site: www.krem-enterprises.com

L B Repair
1308 W Benten
Savannah, MO 64485-1549
816-324-3913

restoration

See full listing in **Section One** under **Ford 1954-up**

L & N Olde Car Co
9992 Kinsman Rd, PO Box 378
Newbury, OH 44065
440-564-7204; FAX: 440-564-8187

restoration

Complete or partial restoration. Specializing in collector and show automobiles. Concours or to custom specifications, show quality paint and finish, sheetmetal and aluminum fabrication. Wood fabrication and coachwork, mechanical, electrical, lead work. Machine work and parts fabrication. Maintenance work and repairs. Serving our customers since 1976.
See our ad on this page

Land Cruiser Solutions Inc
20 Thornell Rd
Newton, NH 03858
603-382-3555; FAX: 603-378-0431
E-mail: twbii@aol.com

accessories
restoration
services

See full listing in **Section One** under **Toyota**

Larson Motor Co
Russell Larson
4415 Canyon Dr
Amarillo, TX 79110
806-358-9797

appraisals
restoration
sales

See full listing in **Section Two** under **car dealers**

Last Chance Repair & Restoration
1242 Myers Rd, PO Box 362A
Shaftsbury, VT 05262
802-447-7040

repairs
restoration

Mail order and open shop. Monday-Friday 7 am to 3:30 pm. Chassis preparations and restoration. Special interest in Ford pickups and old VW Beetles. Parts and vehicles for sale or located. Five years' Great American Race experience. Emphasis on reliability.

LaVine Restorations Inc
1349 Beech Rd
Nappanee, IN 46550
219-773-7561; FAX: 219-773-7595
E-mail: lavine@bnin.net

restoration

Shop open Monday-Friday 8 am to 5 pm, Saturday by appointment. Specializing in professional national show restorations and pleasure car restorations. Antique, classic, special interest and street rod. Also specializing in Packards. 27 years in business.

Lee's Street Rods
RR 3 Box 3061A
Rome, PA 18837
570-247-2326
E-mail: lka41@epix.net

accessories
parts
restoration

See full listing in **Section Two** under **street rods**

Libbey's Classic Car Restoration Center
137 N Quinsigamond Ave
Shrewsbury, MA 01545
PH/FAX: 508-792-1560

bodywork
restoration
service

Open shop. Monday-Friday 9 am to 6 pm, some Saturdays 9 am to 12 noon. Complete and partial restoration, service, problem solving, mechanical, electrical and bodywork for all types of classic and special interest cars and antiques. Have done restorations on several Duesenbergs (two CCAC 100 pt cars), as well as Stanley Steamers, Packards, T-Birds, Mustangs and Cadillacs.

Jeff Lilly Restoration Inc
11125 FM 1560
Helotes, TX 78023
210-695-5151; FAX: 210-695-1719

classic car
restoration
street rod building

Classic cars and custom street rods built on an hourly basis. Separate buildings for mechanical, body, painting, upholstery, assembly, creates organization, efficiency and a cleaner finished product of highest quality. Organized disassembly process to find all the parts needed for your classic. 3/16 gaps between body panels with stunning paint will complement your cars physique. Our work appears monthly in national magazines for your review in choosing us as your restoration company. Visit our web site for a complete shop tour. Web site: www.jefflilly.com

Lindley Restorations Ltd
10 S Sanatoga Rd
Pottstown, PA 19464
610-326-8484; FAX: 610-326-3845

parts
sales
service

See full listing in **Section One** under **Jaguar**

Lindskog Balancing
1170 Massachusetts Ave
Boxborough, MA 01719-1415
978-263-2040; FAX: 978-263-4035

engine balancing

See full listing in **Section Two** under **engine rebuilding**

Lyme Pond Restorations
PO Box 202
Barnard, VT 05031
802-457-4657

restoration

Open shop only. Monday-Friday 8 am to 5 pm. A small shop offering complete restoration services, mechanical, bodywork, upholstery. Rust repairs, convertible tops, British cars our specialty. All makes and models of automobiles, trucks and motorcycles accepted. Impossible projects encouraged.

| Manchester Motor Car Co
319 Main St
Manchester, CT 06040
860-643-5874; FAX: 860-643-6190
E-mail: mmcollc@aol.com | automobilia
parts
petroliana
restorations |

See full listing in **Section Two** under **comprehensive parts**

| Master Plating
2109 Newton Ave
San Diego, CA 92113
619-232-3092; FAX: 619-232-3094 | plating
restoration |

See full listing in **Section Two** under **plating & polishing**

| Mastermind Inc
32155 Joshua Dr
Wildomar, CA 92595
PH/FAX: 909-674-0509
E-mail: mike@mastermindinc.net | new/used parts
restoration |

See full listing in **Section One** under **Cadillac/LaSalle**

| The Masters Company
30 Willow Dr, Ste A
Fort Thomas, KY 41075-2035
800-385-5811; FAX: 859-441-6765
E-mail: rmasters3@home.com | parts
tools |

See full listing in **Section Two** under **tools**

| McCann Auto
630 North St, PO Box 1025
Houlton, ME 04730
207-532-2206; FAX: 207-532-6748
E-mail: mccadani@javanet.com | custom work
restoration
sandblasting |

Open shop only. Monday-Friday 8 am to 5 pm. Full service collision and restoration facility. Over 25 years' experience in complete or partial restoration of classic, antique, or special interest cars and trucks. Quality custom work, including but not limited to sheetmetal fabrication, sandblasting, and coachwork. Pickup and delivery available upon request. Web site: www.mccannauto.com

| Memory Lane Motors
562 County Rd 121
Fenelon Falls, ON Canada K0M 1N0
705-887-CARS; FAX: 705-887-4028 | car dealer
restoration
service |

Mail order and open shop. Monday-Friday 8 am to 5 pm, Saturday 8:30 am to noon usually. Interesting older autos, talked about enthusiastically. Bought, sold, serviced, recreated. Restore antique and classic vehicles, mechanical and body repair, Krown rust control center, float vehicles on a ramp truck. Used motor vehicles for sale. Insurance appraisals and custom exhaust.

| Memoryville USA Inc
2220 N Bishop Ave
Rolla, MO 65401
573-364-1810; FAX: 573-364-6975
E-mail: memoryvl@fidnet.com | restoration |

Mail order and open shop. Monday-Friday 8 am to 4:30 pm. Can restore any automobile, partial or complete, either for driving or to show quality, in one of the largest established restoration shops in the United States. Restoration is done in our shop by highly skilled craftsmen, with over 25 years' experience, who specialize in all phases of restoration work including mechanical, woodworking, painting, upholstering, pinstriping, woodgraining and parts fabrication. For more information, write or call for our free brochure.

| Alan Mest Early Model Auto Repair
17212 Gramercy Pl
Gardena, CA 90247
310-532-8657, 310-372-1039
FAX: 310-376-6009 | mechanical repair
restoration |

Shop open six days 9 am to 6 pm. Repair and restoration of all pre-1955 American made autos.

| Mid Valley Engineering
16637 N 21st St
Phoenix, AZ 85022
602-482-1251; FAX: 602-788-0812 | machine work
parts
restoration |

See full listing in **Section Two** under **transmissions**

| Midwest Hot Rods Inc
10 E Main St (Rt 126)
Plainfield, IL 60544
815-254-7637; FAX: 815-254-7640
E-mail: mwhr@aol.com | street rods
service shops
upholstery |

See full listing in **Section Two** under **street rods**

| Mike's Chevy Parts
7716 Deering Ave
Canoga Park, CA 91304
818-346-0070; FAX: 818-713-0715
E-mail: mikeschevyparts@aol.com | front end repair
parts |

See full listing in **Section One** under **Chevrolet**

| Mild to Wild Classics
1300 3rd St NW
Albuquerque, NM 87102
505-244-1139; FAX: 505-244-1164 | parts
repairs
restoration |

See full listing in **Section Two** under **street rods**

| Morgan Oasis Garage
N 51 Terrace Rd, PO Box 1010
Hoodsport, WA 98548
360-877-5160 | restoration
service |

See full listing in **Section One** under **Morgan**

| Morgan Spares Ltd
225 Simons Rd
Ancram, NY 12502
518-329-3877; FAX: 518-329-3892
E-mail: morganspares@taconic.net | car sales
consulting
obsolete parts
used parts |

See full listing in **Section One** under **Morgan**

| Mostly Mustangs Inc
55 Alling St
Hamden, CT 06517
203-562-8804; FAX: 203-562-4891 | car dealer
parts sales
restoration |

See full listing in **Section One** under **Mustang**

| Muncie Imports & Classics
4401 Old St Rd 3 N
Muncie, IN 47303
800-462-4244; FAX: 317-287-9551
E-mail: mic@netdirect.net | repair
restoration
upholstery |

See full listing in **Section One** under **Jaguar**

| Muscle Express
135 Hibiscus St
Jupiter, FL 33458
800-323-3043 order line
561-744-3043 tech line | parts |

See full listing in **Section One** under **Chevelle/Camaro**

Section Two – Generalists

Mustang Classics
3814 Walnut St
Denver, CO 80205
303-295-3140

parts
restoration
sales
service

See full listing in **Section One** under **Mustang**

Mustangs & More
2065 Sperry Ave #C
Ventura, CA 93003
800-356-6573; FAX: 805-642-6468
E-mail: mustmore@aol.com

parts
restoration

See full listing in **Section One** under **Mustang**

NCA Automotive
4532 W Palm Ln
Phoenix, AZ 85035
PH/FAX: 602-278-6070
E-mail: ncaltec@netscape.net

restoration

Stainless steel restoration, straightening and polishing. Also aluminum.

New Era Motors
11611 NE 50th Ave, Unit 6
Vancouver, WA 98686
360-573-8788; FAX: 360-573-7461

restoration

See full listing in **Section Two** under **woodwork**

Northern Motorsport Ltd
Rt 5, PO Box 1028
Wilder, VT 05088
802-296-2099; FAX: 802-295-6599
E-mail: bugatti46@aol.com

repair
restoration
sales
service

Open shop. Monday-Friday 8 am to 6 pm. Specialize in service, repair and mechanical restoration of pre-1970s Rolls-Royces, Bentleys, Mercedes, Bugattis and Packards. Full service shop providing service and repairs to current model year European automobiles as well as our beloved antiques. With machine tools on premises, we can fabricate some parts. References and pictures upon request. Contact: Mike Zack. Also sell European and antique automobiles. Web site: www.northernmotorsportltd.com

Odyssey Restorations Inc
8080 Central Ave NE
Spring Lake Park, MN 55432
763-786-1518; FAX: 763-786-1524

parts
restoration

Mail order and open shop. Monday-Friday 8 am to 5 pm, Saturday by appointment. Specializing in concours restorations of brass and CCCA Classic cars, exotic engine and driveline restorations and major tour prep. Difficult, rare, early projects a specialty. Consistent major Concours winners and worldwide tour participants. Parts and services for Franklin automobiles 1902-1934.

Old Coach Works Restoration Inc
1206 Badger St
Yorkville, IL 60560-1701
630-553-0414; FAX: 630-553-1053
E-mail: oldcoachworks@msn.com

appraisals
restoration

Open shop only. Monday-Friday 7 am to 5 pm, Saturday by appointment. Specializing in complete or partial restoration service on all antique, classic or special interest automobiles. Also enjoy sports cars, street rods and an occasional motorcycle. 25 years at the same location. Nationwide pickup and delivery available. Call for a free brochure. Appraisal service also available. Web site: www.oldcoachworks.com

Oldenbetter Restorations Inc
22530 Hwy 49, PO Box 1000
Saucier, MS 39574-1000
228-831-2650
E-mail: oldenbeter@yahoo.com

repairs
restorations

See full listing in **Section One** under **Chevrolet**

Older Car Restoration
Martin Lum, Owner
304 S Main St, Box 428
Mont Alto, PA 17237
717-749-3383, 717-352-7701
E-mail: marty@oldercar.com

repro parts
restoration

Mail order and open shop. Monday-Friday 8 am to 5 pm. Partial or total restorations on all kinds of cars. Offers a line of 1928-1931 Mopar reproduction parts. Chrysler, Dodge, DeSoto, Plymouth parts, service, mechanical and cosmetic restorations, chrome plating and appraisals also available. Also reproduction parts for 1950s DeSotos. Web site: www.oldercar.com

Bob Ore Restorations
4725 Iroquois Ave
Erie, PA 16511
814-898-3933; FAX: 814-899-8632

chemical stripping
chrome plating
restoration

Open Monday-Friday 8 am to 5 pm, Saturday 8 am to 11:30 am. Specializing in complete or partial restoration, service and maintenance of all automobiles. In house chemical stripping and show quality chrome plating. Enclosed transport, references available. 25 years' experience.

Bill Peters
41 Vassar Pl
Rockville Centre, NY 11570
516-766-8397

steering wheel
restoration

See full listing in **Section Two** under **steering wheels**

R E Pierce
47 Stone Rd
Wendell Depot, MA 01380
978-544-7442; FAX: 978-544-2978
E-mail: robin@billsgate.com

parts
restoration

See full listing in **Section One** under **Volvo**

Pilgrim's Auto Restorations
3888 Hill Rd
Lakeport, CA 95453
707-262-1062; FAX: 707-263-6956
E-mail: pilgrims@pacific.net

bodywork
metal fabrication
paint
restoration

Shop open Monday-Friday 8 am to 5 pm, Saturday 8 am to 12 noon. Offer restoration, metal fabrication, body and paint. Web site: www.autorestore.com

Precious Metal Automotive Restoration Co Inc
1601 College Ave SE
Grand Rapids, MI 49507
616-243-0220; FAX: 616-243-6646
E-mail: dpayne@iserv.net

broker
restoration

See full listing in **Section One** under **Mercedes-Benz**

Prestige Automotive Inc
30295 Moravian Tr
Tippecanoe, OH 44699
740-922-3542
E-mail: blacklabs@tusco.net

restoration

Monday-Friday 9 am to 6 pm Eastern time. Restorations of Mopar muscle cars and other interesting classics. Full restoration facility, mechanical, trim, body and paint.

Al Prueitt & Sons Inc
8 Winter Ave, PO Box 158
Glen Rock, PA 17327
800-766-0035, 717-428-1305
FAX: 717-235-4428

| restoration upholstery woodwork |

Shop open Monday-Friday 8 am to 4:30 pm. Complete restorations, upholstery, wood refinishing for antique and classic cars. Expert paint and bodywork, all types of mechanical work. Rolls-Royce service. Family run business with over thirty years' experience restoring cars of all makes. Please visit our shop anytime.

R & L Engines Inc
308 Durham Rd
Dover, NH 03820
603-742-8812; FAX: 603-742-8137

| engine rebuilding restorations |

See full listing in **Section Two** under **engine rebuilding**

R&L Model A
54 Clark Dr, Unit D
East Berlin, CT 06114
860-828-7600

| parts restorations service |

See full listing in **Section One** under **Ford 1903-1931**

Ray's Upholstering
600 N St Frances Cabrini Ave
Scranton, PA 18504
800-296-RAYS; FAX: 570-963-0415

| partial/total restoration |

Open Monday-Friday 8 am to 5 pm. Restore antique, classic and specialized automobiles. Partial or total restorations. Our specialty are custom interiors for antiques and street rods in leather and imitation suede.

Realistic Auto Restorations Inc
2519 6th Ave S
St Petersburg, FL 33712
727-327-5162; FAX: 727-327-1877
E-mail: jsamu58686@aol.com

| restoration |

Complete or partial restorations on antique, special interest, foreign and domestic autos. Specialists in sheetmetal fabrication, paint and body, mechanics, upholstery, woodwork, wiring and stainless steel repair, etc. Family owned and operated since 1978. Many Concours and National trophy winners. No job too small.

Redding Corp
Box 477
George's Mills, NH 03751
603-763-2566; FAX: 603-763-5682

| restoration |

Open Monday-Friday 8 am to 4 pm. Offering general restoration ranging from dependable drivers to show. Any make. Estimates cheerfully provided, references available.

Regal Roadsters Ltd
301 W Beltline Hwy
Madison, WI 53713
PH/FAX: 608-273-4141
E-mail: chuck@regaltbird.com

| replicars restoration |

See full listing in **Section One** under **Thunderbird**

Reinholds Restorations
c/o Rick Reinhold
PO Box 178, 255 N Ridge Rd
Reinholds, PA 17569-0178
717-336-5617; FAX: 717-336-7050

| appraisals repairs restoration |

Open shop only. Monday-Friday 8 am to 5 pm, Saturdays and evenings by appointment. Complete quality restorations, repairs, service, appraisals, cars, trucks, fire engines, motorcycles. Anything, wood working, engine rebuilding, gas tank tumble cleaning, woodgraining.

Restoration Specialties
John Sarena
124 North F St
Lompoc, CA 93436
805-736-2627
E-mail: showtimechevys@msn.com

| interiors restoration |

See full listing in **Section One** under **Chevrolet**

Restorations Unlimited II Inc
304 Jandus Rd
Cary, IL 60013
847-639-5818

| restoration |

Open shop only. Monday-Friday 7 am to 5 pm, Saturday by appointment. A full service restoration center performing all phases in-house. Paint, upholstery, panel forming. Concours preparation. Restorations of foreign and domestic, aluminum, steel and glass. Have a history of winning cars at Pebble Beach, Meadowbrook, LCOC, AACA. Call us for that special project. Celebrating our 31st year in the restoration business. Web site: www.dwinc.com/ruii/

Richard's Auto Restoration
RD 3, Box 83A
Wyoming, PA 18644
570-333-4191

| restoration |

Mail order and open shop. Monday-Friday 7:30 am to 3:30 pm. Sandblasting and glass beadwork done.

Richardson Restorations
352 S I St
Tulare, CA 93274
559-688-5002
E-mail: cal5002@aol.com

| custom work repairs restoration |

Restoration of antique and classic autos. Fabrication of custom rods, subframing, top chops and restyling. Sand casting of small parts. Rusted out panel replacement. Reasonable hourly rate. Personalized service. Web site: www.richardsonresto.bigstep.com

Rick's Relics
Wheeler Rd
Pittsburg, NH 03592
603-538-6612
E-mail: relics@aspi.net

| bodywork painting restoration |

Shop open Monday-Saturday 8 am to 5 pm. Complete and partial restorations for antique, classic and special interest cars. Painting, glass work, wiring, bodywork with lead. All makes, foreign and domestic. 36 years' experience in the trade.

Roadrunner Tire & Auto
4850 Hwy 377 S
Fort Worth, TX 76116
817-244-4924

| restoration speedometer repair |

Mail order and open shop. Monday-Friday 7:30 am to 5:30 pm Central time. Mechanical restoration, engine rebuilding, suspension, brakes. Also mail order speedometer repair. Have had 14 Great Race entries, all finished.

Rod-1 Shop
210 Clinton Ave
Pitman, NJ 08071
609-228-7631; FAX: 609-582-5770
E-mail: atboz@webtv.net

| street rods |

See full listing in **Section Two** under **street rods**

Ron's Restorations Inc
2968-B Ask Kay Dr
Smyrna, GA 30082
888-416-1057, 770-438-6102
FAX: 770-438-0037

| interior trim restoration |

See full listing in **Section One** under **Mercedes-Benz**

RPM Catalog
PO Box 12031
Kansas City, KS 66109
913-788-3219; FAX: 913-788-9682
E-mail: dale@dalewilch.com

parts
speed equipment

See full listing in **Section Two** under **racing**

Rust Busters
PO Box 341
Clackamas, OR 97015
503-223-3203
E-mail: info@rustbusters.com

rust repair

Mail order and open shop. Monday-Friday 7 am to 3:30 pm. Rust Busters makes a machine that repairs rust holes in older and newer cars without using patch panels, fiberglass or bondo, sprays, pure metal. See ad in *Hemmings Motor News* under Services Offered.

RX Autoworks
983 W 1st St
North Vancouver, BC Canada V7P 1A4
604-986-0102, 877-986-0102 toll free
FAX: 604-986-0175

restoration

Open shop only. Monday-Friday 9 am to 5 pm, Saturday by appointment. Vintage and classic auto restorations. At RX Autoworks our attention to quality and detail has produced many award winning restorations on vintage and classic automobiles, including several class wins at Pebble Beach. Choosing a qualified restoration facility is the single most important factor in the outcome of your classic car restoration.

Sanders Antique Auto Restoration
1120 22nd St
Rockford, IL 61108
815-226-0535

restoration

Open Monday-Friday 8 am to 4:30 pm. Partial and complete restorations plus some repair. Most of our work is antique and classic cars, but we enjoy special interest and sports cars, street rods and motorcycles.

Schaeffer & Long
210 Davis Rd
Magnolia, NJ 08049
609-784-4044

restoration

Open Monday-Friday 8 am to 4:30 pm. Restorations, complete or partial. In business since 1968.

SL-TECH 230SL-250SL-280SL
1364 Portland Rd, US Rt 1
Arundel/Kennebunkport, ME 04046
207-985-3001; FAX: 207-985-3011
E-mail: gernold@sltechw113.com

parts
restoration
service

See full listing in **Section One** under **Mercedes-Benz**

Chris Smith's Creative Workshop
Motorcar Restoration
118 NW Park St
Dania, FL 33004
954-920-3303; FAX: 954-920-9950
E-mail: restor1st@aol.com

parts
restoration
service

Mail order and open shop. Monday-Friday 9 am to 5 pm. First quality ground-up, frame-off restorations. Parts, wood, steel and aluminum fabrication. Upholstery and trim. Complete in-house service specializing in Mercedes, Ferrari, Porsche, Lamborghini, antiques and special interest autos. Immersion paint and rust removal. Sandblasting parts, fabrication, detail, race car prep. Also large reference library. Web site: www.restoreautomobiles.com

Special Interest Autos
602 A St NE
Ardmore, OK 73401
580-226-0270; FAX: 580-226-0233

parts
restoration

Mail order and open shop. Monday-Friday 9 to 5. Small, family-operated business with fast, courteous and dependable service. Also specialize in high quality restoration for distributors, starters and generators. Electrical parts and restoration for all 1910-1970s makes and models.

Special T's Unlimited Inc
PO Box 146
Prospect Heights, IL 60070
847-255-5494; FAX: 847-259-7220
E-mail: special_t_bill@yahoo.com

general repair
parts
restoration
service

See full listing in **Section One** under **Mopar**

Sports Car Haven
3414 Bloom Rd, Rt 11
Danville, PA 17821
570-275-5705

parts
restoration
service

Mail order and open shop. Monday-Friday 9 am to 5 pm, Saturday 9 am to 11:30 am. Specializing in parts, new, used and rebuilt. Also repairs, restoration, competition preparation for Austin-Healey, MG, Triumph and Jaguar.

Sterling Restorations Inc
1705 Eastwood Dr
Sterling, IL 61081
815-625-2260; FAX: 815-625-0799

appraisals
restorations

Open shop only. Monday-Friday 8 am to 4:30 pm, Saturday by appointment. Restoration of antique and classic autos. Appraisal service, member of International Automotive Appraisers Association (#1002040099).

Steve's Auto Restorations
4440 SE 174th Ave
Portland, OR 97236
503-665-2222; FAX: 503-665-2225
E-mail: steve@realsteel.com

restoration

Mail order and open shop. Monday-Friday 7 am to 4:30 pm. Complete ground-up show quality restorations on antiques and classics, specializing in 300SL Mercedes, pre-war Mercedes, one-off and production run classics. Street rod design and construction. Mechanical, bodywork, paint, wiring, upholstery, metal fabrication. Resilvering of headlight reflectors. Complete light restoration, Halogen conversions, headlight lens, bulb and gasket sales. New "real steel" 33-34 roadster and cabriolet bodies, sheetmetal also available. Web sites: www.realsteel.com or www.stevesautorestorations.com

Still Cruisin' Corvettes
5759 Benford Dr
Haymarket, VA 20169
703-754-1960; FAX: 703-754-1222
E-mail: chuckberge@starpower.net

appraisals
repairs
restoration

See full listing in **Section One** under **Corvette**

Stockton Wheel Service
648 W Fremont St
Stockton, CA 95203
209-464-7771, 800-395-9433
FAX: 209-464-4725
E-mail: sales@stocktonwheel.com

wheel repair

See full listing in **Section Two** under **wheels & wheelcovers**

LearnAutos

Stone Barn Inc
202 Rt 46, Box 117
Vienna, NJ 07880
908-637-4444; FAX: 908-637-4290

restoration

Restoration of antique, classic, exotic and special interest automobiles.

Stormin Norman's Bug Shop
201 Commerce Dr #3
Fort Collins, CO 80524
970-493-5873

repair
restoration

See full listing in **Section One** under **Volkswagen**

Supreme Metal Polishing
84A Rickenbacker Cir
Livermore, CA 94550
925-449-3490; FAX: 925-449-1475
E-mail: supremet@home.com

metal working
parts restoration
plating services
polishing

See full listing in **Section Two** under **plating & polishing**

Te Puke Vintage Auto Barn
26 Young Rd
Te Puke New Zealand
PH/FAX: 07 5736547

parts
restoration
sales

Mail order and open shop. Daily 9 am to 5 pm. Car display, restoration and sales of old cars. Specialize in cars from the 1920s-1970s. Have parts and restore any make, do not have a preference.

Teddy's Garage
8530 Louise Ave
Northridge, CA 91325
818-341-0505

parts
restoration
service

See full listing in **Section One** under **Rolls-Royce/Bentley**

Hemmings
Rods & Performance

A bi-monthly publication dedicated to today's Street Rod, Racing and Performance Market...

Subscribe Today!

6 issues –
Only $17.95

$23.95 in Canada, GST included, US funds only. Vermont add 5% sales tax.

**Call 1-800-227-4373 ext. 550 (toll-free)
or 802-447-9550**
to use your MC/VISA/Discover/AmEx, or send payment to

Hemmings Rods & Performance

PO Box 2000-S27128, Bennington, Vermont 05201
Order Online at:
www.hemmingsrodsandperformance.com/gifts

Telstar Mustang-Shelby-Cobra Restorations
1300-1400 S Kimball St
Mitchell, SD 57301
605-996-6550

restorations

Open shop every day, anytime on request. Complete restorations on Shelbys, Boss 302s, Boss 429s, AC Cobras, fastbacks, GTs, convertibles. 37 years in the business. Restored over 200 vehicles in the past 17 years.

Thunderbirds East
Andy Lovelace
140 Wilmington W Chester Pike
Chadds Ford, PA 19317
610-358-1021; FAX: 610-558-9615

parts
restoration

See full listing in **Section One** under **Thunderbird**

Tillack & Co Ltd
630 Mary Ann Dr
Redondo Beach, CA 90278
310-318-8760; FAX: 310-376-3392
E-mail: race@tillackco.com

parts
restoration

Est 1979 as full service restoration shop. Specializing in Italian and English exotics, Ferrari, Jaguar, Porsche, 356, Cisitalia, Lamborghini, Maserati. Fully licensed auto dealership. Full restoration, parts, custom welding, machining and fabrication, race prep. Tax deferred exchanges and collection management. Web site: www.tillackco.com

Translog Motorsports
619-635 W Poplar St
York, PA 17404
PH/FAX: 717-846-1885
E-mail: translogm@aol.com

car dealer
parts
restoration

See full listing in **Section One** under **Porsche**

Tricks Custom Hot Rods
7126 Wall Triana Hwy
Madison, AL 35757
256-722-8222

paint
restorations

See full listing in **Section Two** under **painting**

Trunzo's Antique Cars
4213 Ohio River Blvd
Pittsburgh, PA 15202
412-734-0717

antique cars
auctions
restorations

See full listing in **Section Two** under **auctions & shows**

Glenn Vaughn Restoration Services Inc
550 N Greenferry
Post Falls, ID 83854
208-773-3525; FAX: 208-773-3526

restoration

Automobile restoration, complete or partial, show car or driver restorations. Located in a low overhead area, so our labor rates are very competitive, while our focus is on efficiency, quality and integrity. Ask for Glenn Vaughn, formerly with Hill and Vaughn.

Verne's Chrome Plating Inc
1559 El Segundo Blvd
Gardena, CA 90249
323-754-4126; FAX: 323-754-3873

chrome plating
polishing
powder coating

See full listing in **Section Two** under **plating & polishing**

Pete Watson Enterprises PO Box 488 Epworth, GA 30541 706-632-7675	car dealer restoration

Shop open by appointment only. Specializing in Fords.

West Coast Classics Inc 795 W San Jose Ave Claremont, CA 91711 909-624-7156	car sales

Car sales and antique and collector car toys for sale. Also fender skirts, hubcaps, parts and motors.

White Post Restorations One Old Car Dr, PO Drawer D White Post, VA 22663 540-837-1140; FAX: 540-837-2368 E-mail: info@whitepost.com	restoration

Restorations of cars 25 years old and older by one of the largest, complete shops in the US, established in 1940. All professional, highly skilled technicians. Call us now for a complete frame-up show or driving quality restoration. Web site: www.whitepost.com

See our ad on this page

Widmann's Garage 346 Bunting Ave Hamilton, NJ 08611 609-392-1553; FAX: 609-392-1709 E-mail: widsgarage@aol.com	repairs restorations

Open Monday-Saturday 9 am to 5:30 pm. Deal in repairs and restorations of antiques, classics, customs and street rods. Specializing in trucks of all types. Web site: www.widmannsgarage.com

Wild Bill's Corvette & Hi-Performance Center Inc 446 Dedham St Wrentham, MA 02093 508-384-7373; FAX: 508-384-9366 E-mail: wildbillscorvette@ worldnet.att.net	parts rebuilding service

See full listing in **Section One** under **Corvette**

Willhoit Auto Restoration 1360 Gladys Ave Long Beach, CA 90804 562-439-3333; FAX: 562-439-3956	engine rebuilding restoration

See full listing in **Section One** under **Porsche**

Willow Automotive Service Box 4640, Rt 212 Willow, NY 12495 845-679-4679	bodywork painting restorations

Open shop Monday-Saturday by appointment. Antique, classic, muscle, exotic and foreign. Scheduled maintenance to ground-up restoration. Bodywork, metal fabrication, painting, in-house machine shop, woodwork service available, full mechanical shop. Assured attention to detail, call Arthur for services.

Wilson's Classic Auto 417 Kaufman Rt 150, PO Box 58 Congerville, IL 61729 309-448-2408; FAX: 309-448-2409	restoration

Open shop only. Monday-Friday 8 am to 5 pm, Saturday 8 am to 12 pm. Award winning restorations, total or partial. We care more about quality than low price. Give us a call.

WTH Service and Restorations Inc 6561 Commerce Ct Warrenton, VA 20187-2300 540-349-3034; FAX: 540-349-9652 E-mail: wthauto@wthrestorations.com	restoration

Open Monday-Thursday 7 am to 5 pm Eastern time. High quality restorations, antique and classic automobiles, tractors and aircraft. E-mail us today and receive our newsletter via the internet.

WW Motor Cars & Parts Inc 132 N Main St, PO Box 667 Broadway, VA 22815 540-896-8243; FAX: 540-896-8244	restoration

Open Monday-Thursday 7 am to 5:30 pm, Friday and Saturday by appointment. Complete or partial restorations of antique and classic automobiles and trucks. Our goal is to perform restoration work of national award-winning caliber, whether for a trailer only show car or just a good driver. Top quality work, guaranteed. Also offer consignment sales.

Wymer Classic AMC Mark & George Wymer 340 N Justice St Fremont, OH 43420 419-332-4291 419-334-6945 after 5 pm	NOS/used parts owner's manuals repairs service manuals

See full listing in **Section One** under **AMC**

rubber parts

A & M SoffSeal Inc
104 May Dr
Harrison, OH 45030
800-426-0902; FAX: 513-367-5506
513-367-0028 service/info
E-mail: soffseal@soffseal.com

| rubber parts |
| weatherstripping |

Manufacture the highest quality weatherstripping and rubber detail. Product line includes weatherstripping for GM cars, GM, GMC, Ford and Dodge trucks, A, B and E-body performance Chrysler plus an unlimited selection for street rods and customs. SoffSeal's USA made weatherstripping, pedal pads, extrusions, gasket materials are engineered with sun and ozone resistant materials and backed by our 100% lifetime satisfaction guarantee and can be purchased directly from SoffSeal or from one of our worldwide distributors. Web site: www.soffseal.com

Atlas Obsolete Chrysler Parts
10621 Bloomfield St, Unit 32
Los Alamitos, CA 90720
PH/FAX: 562-594-5560
E-mail: atlaschrys@aol.com

| parts |

See full listing in **Section One** under **Mopar**

Autolux Inc
3121 W Coast Hwy, Ste 3D
Newport Beach, CA 92663
949-574-0054; FAX: 949-645-3033

| Mercedes parts |

See full listing in **Section One** under **Mercedes-Benz**

Brothers Truck Parts
801 Parkridge Ave
Corona, CA 92880
800-687-6672; FAX: 909-808-9788
E-mail: sales@brotherstrucks.com

| accessories |
| parts |

See full listing in **Section Two** under **trucks & tractors**

C & G Early Ford Parts
1941 Commercial St, Dept AH
Escondido, CA 92029-1233
760-740-2400; FAX: 760-740-8700
E-mail: cgford@cgfordparts.com

| accessories/chrome |
| emblems |
| literature |
| mechanical |
| weatherstripping |

See full listing in **Section One** under **Ford 1932-1953**

Chev's of the 40's
2027 B St, Dept Z
Washougal, WA 98671
800-999-CHEV (2438)
FAX: 360-835-7988

| parts |

See full listing in **Section One** under **Chevrolet**

Chevelle World Inc
PO Box 926
Noble, OK 73068
405-872-0379; FAX: 405-872-0385

| parts |

See full listing in **Section One** under **Chevelle/Camaro**

Cheyenne Pickup Parts
Box 959
Noble, OK 73068
405-872-3399; FAX: 405-872-0385
E-mail: sales@cheyennepickup.com

| body panels |
| bumpers |
| carpet |
| weatherstripping |

See full listing in **Section One** under **Chevrolet**

Classic Chevrolet Parts Inc
8723 S I-35
Oklahoma City, OK 73149
405-631-4400; FAX: 405-631-5999
E-mail: info@classicchevroletparts.com

| parts |

See full listing in **Section One** under **Chevrolet**

Classic Mercury Parts
1393 Shippee Ln
Ojai, CA 93023
805-646-3345; FAX: 805-646-5386
E-mail: mfourez@aol.com

| parts |

See full listing in **Section One** under **Mercury**

Clester's Auto Rubber Seals Inc
PO Box 1113
Salisbury, NC 28145
800-457-8223, 704-637-9979
FAX: 704-636-7390

| molded rubber |
| parts |
| weatherstripping |

Mail order and open shop. Monday-Friday 8:30 am to 5 pm. Manufacture rubber weatherstripping (ie: windshield seals, door seals, trunk seals), molded rubber parts and other products for Chevrolet, Ford and Mopar cars and trucks. Also International Harvester pickups and Travelalls, Studebaker cars and trucks. Web site: www.clestersauto.com

Corvette Rubber Company
H-10640 W Cadillac Rd
Cadillac, MI 49601
888-216-9412 toll-free
616-779-2888; FAX: 616-779-9833

| rubber products |
| weatherstripping |

See full listing in **Section One** under **Corvette**

CPR
431 S Sierra Way
San Bernardino, CA 92408
909-884-6980; FAX: 909-884-7872

| new parts |
| reproduction parts |
| used parts |

See full listing in **Section One** under **Pontiac**

CR Plastics Inc
2790 NE 7th Ave
Pompano Beach, FL 33064
800-551-3155

| bumper filler parts |

See full listing in **Section One** under **Cadillac/LaSalle**

Bob Drake Reproductions Inc
1819 NW Washington Blvd
Grants Pass, OR 97526
800-221-3673; FAX: 541-474-0099
E-mail: bobdrake@bobdrake.com

| repro parts |

See full listing in **Section One** under **Ford 1932-1953**

The El Camino Store
57 B Depot Rd
Goleta, CA 93117
805-681-8164; FAX: 805-681-8166
E-mail: ec@elcaminostore.com

| parts |

See full listing in **Section One** under **Chevelle/Camaro**

The Filling Station
990 S Second St
Lebanon, OR 97355-3227
800-841-6622 orders
541-258-2114; FAX: 541-258-6968
E-mail: fssales@fillingstation.com

| literature |
| parts |

See full listing in **Section One** under **Chevrolet**

Flashback F-100s
2519 Wagon Wheel Rd
Reidsville, NC 27320
336-421-3979; FAX: 336-421-5901

parts
parts locators

See full listing in **Section One** under **Ford 1954-up**

Golden State Parts
3493 Arrowhead Dr
Carson City, NV 89706
800-235-5717; FAX: 888-723-2495

parts

See full listing in **Section One** under **Chevrolet**

Greer Enterprises
1981 Greenbrook Blvd
Richland, WA 99352
509-627-3411
E-mail: greenent@owt.com

parts

See full listing in **Section Two** under **chassis parts**

Harmon's Incorporated
Hwy 27 N, PO Box 100
Geneva, IN 46740
219-368-7221; FAX: 219-368-9396
E-mail: harmons@harmons.com

interiors
parts

See full listing in **Section One** under **Chevrolet**

Hoffman Automotive Distributor
US Hwy #1, Box 818
Hilliard, FL 32046
904-845-4421

parts

See full listing in **Section Two** under **body parts**

Holcombe Cadillac Parts
2933 Century Ln
Bensalem, PA 19020
215-245-4560; FAX: 215-633-9916
E-mail: holcars@aol.com

parts

See full listing in **Section One** under **Cadillac/LaSalle**

Impala Bob's Inc
4753 E Falcon Dr, Dept HCCA15
Mesa, AZ 85215
800-IMPALAS orders
480-924-4800 retail store
480-981-1600 office
FAX: 800-716-6237, 480-981-1675
E-mail: info@impalas.com

dash pads
emblems
interior kits
mechanical parts
OEM tires
restoration parts
rubber parts
wiring harnesses

See full listing in **Section One** under **Chevrolet**

International Mercantile
PO Box 2818
Del Mar, CA 92014-2818
800-356-0012, 760-438-2205
FAX: 760-438-1428
E-mail: morhous@msn.com

rubber parts

See full listing in **Section One** under **Porsche**

J & G Auto Parts
3050 Wild Run Rd
Pennsburg, PA 18073
215-679-4683 after 5 pm

clips
fasteners
weatherstripping

See full listing in **Section Two** under **restoration aids**

Jerry's Classic Cars & Parts Inc
4097 McRay Ave
Springdale, AR 72764
800-828-4584; FAX: 501-750-1682
E-mail: jcc@jerrysclassiccars.com

parts
restoration

See full listing in **Section One** under **Ford 1954-up**

Karr Rubber Manufacturing
133 Lomita St
El Segundo, CA 90245
800-955-5277, 310-322-1993
FAX: 310-640-6872
E-mail: g7r7i7f@aol.com

rubber parts

Manufacturer of thousands of extrusion shapes. Can custom make almost any molded parts based upon customer samples, including door seals, roof rails, vent window seals, shift boots, grommets, etc. Web site: www.karrubber.com

---

K C Obsolete Parts
3343 N 61
Kansas City, KS 66104
913-334-9479; FAX: 913-788-2795

parts

See full listing in **Section One** under **Ford 1954-up**

LMC Truck
PO Box 14991
Lenexa, KS 66285
800-222-5664; FAX: 913-599-0323

accessories
parts

See full listing in **Section One** under **Chevrolet**

The Maverick Connection
137 Valley Dr
Ripley, WV 25271
PH/FAX: 304-372-7825
E-mail: maverickconnection@email.com

literature
parts

See full listing in **Section One** under **Ford 1954-up**

Mercury & Ford Molded Rubber
12 Plymouth Ave
Wilmington, MA 01887
978-658-8394

parts

See full listing in **Section One** under **Mercury**

Merv's Classic Chevy Parts
1330 Washington Ave
Iowa Falls, IA 50126
641-648-3168; PH/FAX: 641-648-9675

parts

See full listing in **Section One** under **Chevrolet**

Mike's Chevy Parts
7716 Deering Ave
Canoga Park, CA 91304
818-346-0070; FAX: 818-713-0715
E-mail: mikeschevyparts@aol.com

front end repair
parts

See full listing in **Section One** under **Chevrolet**

MikeCo Antique, Kustom & Obsolete Auto Parts
4053 Calle Tesoro, Unit C
Camarillo, CA 93012
805-482-1725; FAX: 805-987-8524

lenses
parts

See full listing in **Section One** under **Mopar**

Obsolete Ford Parts Inc
8701 S I-35
Oklahoma City, OK 73149
405-631-3933; FAX: 405-634-6815
E-mail: info@obsoletefordparts.com

parts

See full listing in **Section One** under **Ford 1954-up**

Obsolete Jeep® & Willys® Parts
Division of Florida 4 Wheel Drive &
Truck Parts
6110 17th St E
Bradenton, FL 34203
941-756-7844; PH/FAX: 941-756-7757

literature
parts

See full listing in **Section One** under **Willys**

The Paddock® Inc
221 W Main, PO Box 30
Knightstown, IN 46148
800-428-4319; FAX: 800-286-4040
E-mail: paddock@paddockparts.com

accessories
parts

See full listing in **Section One** under **Chevrolet**

Precision Rubber
Box 324
Didsbury, AB Canada T0M 0W0
403-335-9590; FAX: 403-335-9637
E-mail: pat@runningboardmats.com

rubber parts

Specializing in the reproduction of runningboard mats for all
vintage vehicles (as original). Street rod mats can be custom
designed and color coordinated to match your vehicle. Also specialize in runningboard metal repair and mat installation. Web
site: www.runningboardmats.com

Raybuck Autobody Parts
RD 4, Box 170
Punxsutawney, PA 15767
814-938-5248; FAX: 814-938-4250

body parts

See full listing in **Section Two** under **body parts**

Rubber Age LM Mfg Inc
13418 Halldale Ave
Gardena, CA 90249
310-329-2888; FAX: 310-532-4988
E-mail: rubberage@aol.com

rubber parts

Mail order and open shop. Monday-Friday 7:30 am to 4 pm.
Custom manufacturer of molded rubber components as well as
non-metallic die cut products.

Spectrum Rubber & Panels
4/4 Appin Place
St Mary's 2760, PO Box 328
Dunheved, Sydney Australia
61 (2) 9623-5333
FAX: 61 (2) 9833-1041, 24 hours
E-mail: sales@spectrumrubber.com.au

parts

Mail order and open shop. Monday-Friday 8:30 am to 5 pm. Specializing in mail order. Extrusions, molded rubber parts, door
and screen seals, body hardware, engine and suspension
mounts. Also sheetmetal body panels and rust repair sections.
Inhouse rubber moldings, small run specialists. Post samples,
fax drawings. Prompt quotations. Vintage to mid-1980s for all
Australian Holden and Ford. Major British, many Japanese and
American models. When in Sydney, come and visit. Web site:
www.spectrumrubber.com.au

Steele Rubber Products Inc
6180 Hwy 150 E
Denver, NC 28037
800-544-8665; 704-483-9343
FAX: 704-483-6650

repro rubber parts

Mail order and open shop. Monday-Friday 8 am to 5 pm; orders
accepted 24 hours. "Top quality US rubber, first in detailed and
faithful to original." For 1925-mid 70s American cars except
Ford. Web site: www.steelerubber.com
See our ad on this page

| Swedish Classics Inc
PO Box 557
Oxford, MD 21654
800-258-4422; FAX: 410-226-5543
E-mail: sales@swedishclassics.com | parts |

See full listing in **Section One** under **Volvo**

| Tubes-n-Hoses by TKM
955 76th St SW
Byron Center, MI 49315
FAX: 616-878-4949 | hose assemblies
tubes |

See full listing in **Section Two** under **air conditioning**

| Wales Antique Chevy Truck Parts
143 Center
Carleton, MI 48117
734-654-8836 | parts |

See full listing in **Section One** under **Chevrolet**

| Pat Walsh Restorations
Box Q
Wakefield, MA 01880
781-246-3266; FAX: 781-224-3311
E-mail: pwalshrest@aol.com | literature
rubber parts |

Mail order and open shop. Monday-Friday 8 am to 5 pm. No Holidays. Specializing in weatherseals, floor mats, NOS, rubber, service manuals, parts books, trunk mats, interiors, carpets, trunk interiors, window seals, glass runs and settings, other restoration items 1900-1980s.

| Wefco Rubber Manufacturing
Company Inc
21000 Osborne St, Ste 2
Canoga Park, CA 91304-1758
818-886-8872; FAX: 818-886-8875 | rubber extrusions |

Mail order and open shop. Monday-Friday 7 am to 4 pm. Extrusions: rubber and soft sponge. Send sample or drawing of parts needed and 1/2-inch sample or drawing of extrusion needed. No job too big or too small.

| West Coast Metric Inc
24002 Frampton Ave
Harbor City, CA 90710
310-325-0005; FAX: 310-325-9733
E-mail: wcm@westcoastmetric.com | carpet kits
door panels
emblems
plastic parts
rubber parts |

See full listing in **Section One** under **Volkswagen**

rust removal & stripping

| ACE Automotive Cleaning
Equipment Co
897 S Washington, Ste 232
Holland, MI 49423
616-772-3260; FAX: 616-772-3261 | sandblasting
equipment |

Mail order only. Sandblasting equipment and parts cleaners.

| ACPlating
Division of SUM Inc
317 Mt Vernon
Bakersfield, CA 93307
661-324-5454; FAX: 661-324-5381 | plating |

See full listing in **Section Two** under **plating & polishing**

| Advanced Plating & Powder Coating
1425 Cowan Ct
Nashville, TN 37207
615-227-6900; FAX: 615-262-7935
E-mail: gochrome@aol.com | chrome plating
polishing
repair service |

See full listing in **Section Two** under **plating & polishing**

| Automotion Classics Inc
100 N Strong Ave
Lindenhurst, NY 11757
631-225-0485 | painting
restoration
sandblasting |

See full listing in **Section Two** under **restoration shops**

| B & L Body Shop
20 O'Shea Ln
Waynesville, NC 28786-4524
828-456-8277 | restoration |

See full listing in **Section Two** under **restoration shops**

| Bel Air Restorations
312 Hug Cemetery Rd
Pocahontas, IL 62275
618-669-2758
E-mail: blaster@frontiernet.net | priming
rust removal |

Open shop only. Monday-Friday 8 am to 5 pm Central time. Fine silica blasting of auto body, frames, trailers and machinery. Rust and painted metal taken down to bare metal ready for prime. We also do priming. Prep work for your restoration our specialty.

| Fini-Finish Metal Finishing
24657 Mound Rd
Warren, MI 48091
810-758-0050; FAX: 810-758-0054
E-mail: info@fini-finish.com | plating
polishing
pot metal repair |

See full listing in **Section Two** under **plating & polishing**

| The Finished Look
PO Box 191413
Sacramento, CA 95819-1413
800-827-6715; FAX: 916-451-3984
E-mail: info@thefinishedlook.com | POR-15 products |

See full listing in **Section Two** under **rustproofing**

| Guyson Corp of USA
W J Grande Industrial Park
Saratoga Springs, NY 12866-9044
518-587-7894; FAX: 518-587-7840
E-mail: jetsinfo@guyson.com | restoration aids |

Manufacturer of blast cleaning and surface finishing cabinets, both manually operated and automatic. Web site: www.guyson.com/jetstream.htm

| Lake Buchanan Industries Inc
400 Carlson Cir
Buchanan Dam, TX 78609
888-552-5278 toll-free
512-793-2867; FAX: 512-793-2869
E-mail: lbi:@tstar.net | blasting cabinet |

See full listing in **Section Two** under **tools**

| PK Lindsay Co Inc
63 Nottingham Rd
Deerfield, NH 03037
800-258-3576; FAX: 800-843-2974
E-mail: sales@pklindsay.com | paint removal
rust removal |

Mail order only. Manufacturer of portable abrasive blasters used in the automobile restoration industry. Commonly used to remove rust/corrosion from frames or paint from fenders. Also manufacture portable air compressors. Web site: www.pklindsay.com

Section Two – Generalists

Maintenance Specialties Company	rustproofing paints
21 Valley Forge Rd, PO Box 251	
New Castle, DE 19720	
800-777-6715; FAX: 302-328-2315	

See full listing in **Section Two** under **rustproofing**

Painting & Stripping Corp	powder coating
10051 Greenleaf Ave	stripping
Santa Fe Springs, CA 90670	
562-946-1521; FAX: 562-946-8039	

Open shop only. Monday-Friday 7 am to 3:30 pm. All cars and trucks. Service only. Motorcycles. Any metal parts. Stripping and powder coating.

Paul's Chrome Plating Inc	repair
90 Pattison St	restoration
Evans City, PA 16033	
800-245-8679, 724-538-3367	
FAX: 724-538-3403	
E-mail: pcp@fyi.net	

See full listing in **Section Two** under **plating & polishing**

Pennsylvania Metal Cleaning	derusting
200 17th St	stainless fasteners
Monaca, PA 15061-1969	stripping
724-728-5535	

Mail order and open shop. Monday-Friday 8 am to 5 pm, Saturday 8 am to noon. Opened in 1978. Can strip and derust anything from a bolt to a body, using non-destructive alkaline system. Tanks are 20 feet in length. Individuals, commercial or industrial. Extensive selection of stainless steel nuts, bolts, washers, screws, cotter pins, wood screws and nails. Specialty items include exhaust system clamps. Model A bumper end bolts and door hinge screws in stainless steel. Please call or write, all inquiries answered.

Pro-Strip	paint removal
2415 W State Blvd	rust removal
Fort Wayne, IN 46808	
219-436-2828; FAX: 219-432-1941	
E-mail: prostrip@tk7.net	

Mail order and open shop. Monday-Friday 7 am to 5 pm. Providing service since 1985. Offer complete rust and paint removal from individual parts to complete automobiles. State of the art methods of paint and rust removal. Can also custom powder coat your part in a wide variety of colors, wrinkle finishes and textures, also buffing and polishing on metal. Powder coating items up to 19-1/2´ long. Also custom powder coat candy colors and fluorescents. Cast iron repair, blocks, heads, manifolds. Web site: www.prostrip.com

Professional Metal Refinishing Inc	rust removal
2415 W State Blvd	
Fort Wayne, IN 46808	
219-436-2828; FAX: 219-432-1941	
E-mail: mail@prostrip.com	

Specializing in plastic media blasting, derusting, degreasing, specialty powder service for metal objects. Web site: www.prostrip.com

Redi-Strip Company	abrasive media
Box 72199	baking soda blasting
Roselle, IL 60172	paint removal
630-529-2442; FAX: 630-529-3626	rust removal

Mail order and open shop. Monday-Friday 8 am to 5 pm, Saturday 8:30 am to 11:30 am. Non-destructive chemical paint and alkaline electrolytic immersion process rust removal. Also non-abrasive blasting removes paint and coatings from delicate substrates. Abrasive blasting removes rust and etch and texturize surfaces. Baking soda safely removes paints from fiberglass, aluminum and steel.

Richard's Auto Restoration	restoration
RD 3, Box 83A	
Wyoming, PA 18644	
570-333-4191	

See full listing in **Section Two** under **restoration shops**

Riverbend Abrasive Blasting	blasting
44308 St Rt 36 W	painting
Coshocton, OH 43812-9741	polishing
614-622-0867	restoration

Mail order and open shop. Monday-Friday 9 am to 5 pm, Saturday by appointment. Multi-media abrasive blasting, stainless steel trim restoration, metal buffing and polishing, vehicle restoration, painting and powdercoating. Emphasis on fine unhurried workmanship.

Rust Busters	rust repair
PO Box 341	
Clackamas, OR 97015	
503-223-3203	
E-mail: info@rustbusters.com	

See full listing in **Section Two** under **restoration shops**

T Schmidt	rust removers
827 N Vernon	
Dearborn, MI 48128-1542	
313-562-7161	

Mail order only. Deal in Oxisolv rust removers, metal preps, degreasers, wire wheel cleaners and parts washers.

Tar Heel Parts Inc	buffing supplies
PO Box 2604	
Matthews, NC 28106-2604	
800-322-1957, 704-753-9114 (local)	
FAX: 704-753-9117	
E-mail: buffing@tarheelparts.com	

See full listing in **Section Two** under **plating & polishing**

TP Tools & Equipment	abrasive blasters
7075 Rt 446, PO Box 649	air compressors
Canfield, OH 44406	tools
330-533-3384 local, 800-321-9260	welders

See full listing in **Section Two** under **restoration aids**

Tri-State Metal Cleaning	cleaning
4725 Iroquois Ave	rust removal
Erie, PA 16511	stripping
814-898-3933; FAX: 814-899-8632	

Mail order and open shop. Monday-Friday 8 am to 5 pm. Large capacity tanks, 18´ long x 8´ wide x 6´ deep, to remove many years of accumulated grime, paint and rust from bodies, engines and frames. When we do the dirty work, hundreds of labor hours of hand cleaning and stripping are eliminated.

WD-40 Company	lubricants
PO Box 80607	
San Diego, CA 92138	
619-275-1400; FAX: 619-275-5823	

See full listing in **Section Two** under **lubricants**

Ziebart/Tidy Car	accessories
803 Mt Royal Blvd	detailing
Pittsburgh, PA 15223	rustproofing
412-486-4711	

See full listing in **Section Two** under **rustproofing**

rustproofing

Bel Air Restorations   priming
312 Hug Cemetery Rd   rust removal
Pocahontas, IL 62275
618-669-2758
E-mail: blaster@frontiernet.net

See full listing in **Section Two** under **rust removal & stripping**

The Finished Look   POR-15 products
PO Box 191413
Sacramento, CA 95819-1413
800-827-6715; FAX: 916-451-3984
E-mail: info@thefinishedlook.com

West Coast distributor of POR-15 restoration products. Stop
rust, rust preventive coatings, gas tank sealer, heat paints,
engine enamels, cleaners/degreaser and rust remover. Web site:
www.thefinishedlook.com

Graf International   rust preventative
4336 Willick Rd
Niagara Falls, ON Canada L2E 6S6
905-295-3118; FAX: 905-295-6610

Instead of rust, Noverox. Noverox Formula anti-rust does not con-
tain pollutants such as lead, zinc, chromates, mineral acids. It is
non-flammable. Noverox does not damage painted surfaces. Rust
preventative and neutralizer. Paint right over rust. Kills rust.

High Performance Coatings   coatings
14788 S Heritagecrest Way
Bluffdale, UT 84065
800-456-4721, 801-501-8303
FAX: 801-501-8315
E-mail: hpcsales@hpcoatings.com

See full listing in **Section Two** under **exhaust systems**

Imperial Restorations   coatings
POR-15 Products
7550 E Rice Rd
Gardner, IL 60424
800-576-5822; FAX: 815-237-8707
E-mail: imprest@btc-skynet.net

Mail order and open shop by appointment only. Special coatings
for frames, floors, inside doors or anything rusty; engine enamels, high temp coatings, multifunctional protective coatings that
provide enhanced durability. Web site: www.getrust.com

Maintenance Specialties Company   rustproofing paints
21 Valley Forge Rd, PO Box 251
New Castle, DE 19720
800-777-6715; FAX: 302-328-2315

Mail order only. 24 hour order line. We sell the complete POR-15
line of rustproofing paints and chemicals. All orders ship for $4.
Check out our web site or request a free catalog. Web site:
www.rustpaint.com

Memory Lane Motors   car dealer
562 County Rd 121   restoration
Fenelon Falls, ON Canada K0M 1N0   service
705-887-CARS; FAX: 705-887-4028

See full listing in **Section Two** under **restoration shops**

Rust Busters   rust repair
PO Box 341
Clackamas, OR 97015
503-223-3203
E-mail: info@rustbusters.com

See full listing in **Section Two** under **restoration shops**

Stevens Car Care Products Inc   car alarms
36542 Vine St   rust deterrents
East Lake, OH 44095
440-953-2900; FAX: 440-953-4473
E-mail: info@stevenscarcare.com

See full listing in **Section Two** under **anti-theft**

Steve's Antiques/POR-15   bicycles
Steve Verhoeven   POR-15 distributor
5609 S 4300 W
Hooper, UT 84315
888-817-6715 toll-free, 801-985-4835
E-mail: steve@stevesantiques.com

Stop rust permanently. Distributor POR-15 products. Rust
Inhibitor coatings, engine parts, degreasers, gas tank sealers,
fuel preservatives, exhaust coatings, epoxy putties, much more.
Also gas pumps and parts. Original and reproduction antique
advertising signs. 1950s and 1960s Schwinns, specializing in
Schwinn Stingrays. Call for a free catalog.

Ziebart/Tidy Car   accessories
803 Mt Royal Blvd   detailing
Pittsburgh, PA 15223   rustproofing
412-486-4711

Open Monday-Friday 8 am to 5 pm, Saturday 9 am to 12 noon.
Treat rusted metal with rust inhibitors then rust protect the
entire vehicle. Also detail restored and unrestored cars and
trucks along with custom accessories.

service shops

2002 AD   cars
11066 Tuxford St   parts
Sun Valley, CA 91352   restoration
800-420-0223; FAX: 818-768-2697
E-mail: bmwsales@2002ad.com

See full listing in **Section One** under **BMW**

Advanced Plating & Powder Coating   chrome plating
1425 Cowan Ct   polishing
Nashville, TN 37207   repair service
615-227-6900; FAX: 615-262-7935
E-mail: gochrome@aol.com

See full listing in **Section Two** under **plating & polishing**

Antique Radio Service   radio service
12 Shawmut Ave
Cochituate, MA 01778
800-201-2635; FAX: 508-653-2418
E-mail: richardfoster@prodigy.net

See full listing in **Section Two** under **radios**

Arch Carburetor   carburetors
583 Central Ave
Newark, NJ 07107
973-482-2755
E-mail: mmfried@quixnet.net

See full listing in **Section Two** under **carburetors**

The Autoworks Ltd   restoration
90 Center Ave   sales
Westwood, NJ 07675   service
201-358-0200; FAX: 201-358-0442

Open shop. Monday-Friday 6 am to 5 pm. Deal in service, consignment sales, partial or complete restoration on classic, vintage and collector British marques, any year, any model.

Section Two – Generalists

The Babbitt Pot
Zigmont G Billus
1693 St Rt 4
Fort Edward, NY 12828
518-747-4277

engine rebuilding
rebabbitting &
boring of bearings

See full listing in **Section Two** under **babbitting**

Banzai Motorworks
8039-B Penn Randall Pl
Upper Marlboro, MD 20772
PH/FAX: 301-420-4200
E-mail: zspert@olg.com

parts
pre-purchase
insp/consultation
repairs/restoration
service

See full listing in **Section One** under **Datsun**

Bassett Classic Restoration
2616 Sharon St, Ste D
Kenner, LA 70062-4934
PH/FAX: 504-469-2982

parts
restoration
service

See full listing in **Section One** under **Rolls-Royce/Bentley**

Bicknell Engine Company
7055 Dayton Rd
Enon, OH 45323
937-864-5224

parts
repair
restoration

See full listing in **Section One** under **Buick/McLaughlin**

Bob's Speedometer Service
32411 Grand River Ave
Farmington, MI 48336
800-592-9673; FAX: 248-473-5517

gauges
speedometers
tachometers

See full listing in **Section Two** under **instruments**

Classic Car Works Ltd
3050 Upper Bethany Rd
Jasper, GA 30143
770-735-3945

restoration

See full listing in **Section Two** under **restoration shops**

Classic Carriages
267 County Rd 420
Athens, TN 37303
PH/FAX: 423-744-7496

repair
restoration

See full listing in **Section Two** under **restoration shops**

Classic Creations of Central Florida
3620 Hwy 92E
Lakeland, FL 33801
863-665-2322; FAX: 863-666-5348
E-mail: flclassics@aol.com

parts
restoration
service

See full listing in **Section One** under **Mustang**

Classic Garage
120 Monmouth St
Red Bank, NJ 07701
732-741-2450; FAX: 732-741-4134

bodywork
paint
restoration

See full listing in **Section Two** under **restoration shops**

Classic Jaguar
9916 Hwy 290 W
Austin, TX 78736
512-288-8800; FAX: 512-288-9216
E-mail: danmooney@classicjaguar.com

parts
technical support

See full listing in **Section One** under **Jaguar**

Coachbuilt Motors
907 E Hudson St
Columbus, OH 43211
614-261-1541
E-mail: coachbuilt907@aol.com

repairs

See full listing in **Section One** under **Rolls-Royce/Bentley**

Coffey Classic Transmissions
310 Aviator Dr
Fort Worth, TX 76179
817-439-1611

transmissions

See full listing in **Section Two** under **transmissions**

D&D Instruments Inc
770 Kasota Ave
Minneapolis, MN 55414
612-378-1224; FAX: 612-378-1445
E-mail: cselby@ddinstruments.com

gauges
instruments

See full listing in **Section Two** under **instruments**

D&M Corvette Specialists Ltd
1804 Ogden Ave
Downers Grove, IL 60515
630-968-0031; FAX: 630-968-0465
E-mail: sales@dmcorvette.com

car dealer
parts
restoration
sales
service

See full listing in **Section One** under **Corvette**

Doc's Jags
125 Baker Rd
Lake Bluff, IL 60044
847-367-5247; FAX: 847-367-6363
E-mail: doc@docsjags.com

appraisals
interiors
restoration

See full listing in **Section One** under **Jaguar**

**Dodge City Vintage Dodge
Vehicles & Parts**
18584 Hwy 108, PO Box 1687
Jamestown, CA 95327
209-984-5858; FAX: 209-984-3285
E-mail: mike@dodgecityvintage.com

parts
restoration
research
vehicles

See full listing in **Section One** under **Dodge**

Done Right Engine & Machine Inc
12955 York Delta Unit J
North Royalton, OH 44133
440-582-1366; FAX: 440-582-2005

engine rebuilding
machine shop

See full listing in **Section Two** under **engine rebuilding**

DTE Motorsports
242 South Rd
Brentwood, NH 03833
PH/FAX: 603-642-3766
E-mail: dtemotorsports@aol.com

engines/race prep
mechanical services
transportation
restoration

See full listing in **Section One** under **Mercedes-Benz**

FB Performance Transmissions
85 Cleveland Ave
Bay Shore, NY 11706
631-242-0008; FAX: 631-243-3054
E-mail: fbperf@trim.net

transmissions

See full listing in **Section Two** under **transmissions**

Freeman's Garage
29 Ford Rd
Norton, MA 02766
508-285-6500; FAX: 508-285-6566

parts
restoration
sales
service

See full listing in **Section One** under **Ford 1903-1931**

Golden Mile Sales Inc
J DeAngelo
2439 S Bradford St
Allentown, PA 18103-5821
PH/FAX: 610-791-4497, 24 hours
E-mail: abguy@enter.net

> NORS parts
> NOS parts
> sheetmetal

See full listing in **Section One** under **American Austin/Bantam**

Jack P Gross Assoc/Scott Manufacturing Inc
163 Helenwood Detour Rd, PO Box 97
Helenwood, TN 37755
423-569-6088; FAX: 423-569-6428
E-mail: scottmfg@highland.net

> air hose products
> water hose products

Mail order and open shop. Monday-Friday 8 am to 5 pm. Leading supplier of air and water hose products. We are able to furnish regular as well as custom hose assembly needs.

Gary Hill Auto Service
150 E St Joseph St
Arcadia, CA 91006
626-447-2576; FAX: 626-447-1461

> restoration
> service

See full listing in **Section Two** under **racing**

House of Powder Inc
Rt 71 & 1st St, PO Box 110
Standard, IL 61363
815-339-2648

> powder coating
> sandblasting

Mail order and open shop. Monday-Friday 8 am to 5 pm, Saturday 8 am to 12 pm. Services which include powder coating, aluma-coating and sandblasting for all makes of cars, trucks, motorcycles, etc.

Hyde Auto Body
44-1/2 S Squirrel Rd
Auburn Hills, MI 48326
PH/FAX: 248-852-7832
E-mail: bodyman8@juno.com

> refinishing
> restoration

See full listing in **Section Two** under **restoration shops**

Kelley's Korner
22 14th St
Bristol, TN 37620
423-968-5583

> parts
> repair

See full listing in **Section One** under **Studebaker**

Kenask Spring Co
307 Manhattan Ave
Jersey City, NJ 07307
201-653-4589

> springs

See full listing in **Section Two** under **suspension parts**

Land Cruiser Solutions Inc
20 Thornell Rd
Newton, NH 03858
603-382-3555; FAX: 603-378-0431
E-mail: twbii@aol.com

> accessories
> restoration
> services

See full listing in **Section One** under **Toyota**

Memoryville USA Inc
2220 N Bishop Ave
Rolla, MO 65401
573-364-1810; FAX: 573-364-6975
E-mail: memoryvl@fidnet.com

> restoration

See full listing in **Section Two** under **restoration shops**

Mike's Chevy Parts
7716 Deering Ave
Canoga Park, CA 91304
818-346-0070; FAX: 818-713-0715
E-mail: mikeschevyparts@aol.com

> front end repair
> parts

See full listing in **Section One** under **Chevrolet**

Mild to Wild Classics
1300 3rd St NW
Albuquerque, NM 87102
505-244-1139; FAX: 505-244-1164

> parts
> repairs
> restoration

See full listing in **Section Two** under **street rods**

Model Engineering
Gene or Jeff Sanders
3284 S Main St
Akron, OH 44319
330-644-3450; FAX: 330-644-0088

> new parts casting

See full listing in **Section Two** under **castings**

Morgan Oasis Garage
N 51 Terrace Rd, PO Box 1010
Hoodsport, WA 98548
360-877-5160

> restoration
> service

See full listing in **Section One** under **Morgan**

Mustang Classics
3814 Walnut St
Denver, CO 80205
303-295-3140

> parts
> restoration
> sales
> service

See full listing in **Section One** under **Mustang**

The Old Carb Doctor
1127 Drucilla Church Rd
Nebo, NC 28761
800-945-CARB (2272)
828-659-1428

> carburetors
> fuel pumps

See full listing in **Section Two** under **carburetors**

Oldenbetter Restorations Inc
22530 Hwy 49, PO Box 1000
Saucier, MS 39574-1000
228-831-2650
E-mail: oldenbeter@yahoo.com

> repairs
> restorations

See full listing in **Section One** under **Chevrolet**

Bill Peters
41 Vassar Pl
Rockville Centre, NY 11570
516-766-8397

> steering wheel
> restoration

See full listing in **Section Two** under **steering wheels**

A Petrik
Restoration & Rebuilding Service
504 Edmonds Ave NE
Renton, WA 98056-3636
425-466-5590, 425-255-4852
E-mail: rnrserv@qwest.net or
rnrserv@hotmail.com

> heater control
> valve rebuilding
> windshield
> regulators

See full listing in **Section Two** under **heaters**

John T Poulin
Auto Sales/Star Service Center
5th Ave & 111th St
North Troy, NY 12182
518-235-8610

> car dealer
> parts
> restoration service

See full listing in **Section Two** under **car dealers**

R & L Engines Inc
308 Durham Rd
Dover, NH 03820
603-742-8812; FAX: 603-742-8137

engine rebuilding
restorations

See full listing in **Section Two** under **engine rebuilding**

R&L Model A
54 Clark Dr, Unit D
East Berlin, CT 06114
860-828-7600

parts
restorations
service

See full listing in **Section One** under **Ford 1903-1931**

RB's Prototype Model & Machine Co
44 Marva Ln
Stamford, CT 06903
203-329-2715; FAX: 203-329-8029
E-mail: rbprototype@aol.com

machine work

Mail order and open shop. Monday-Friday 8 am to 6 pm Eastern time. Fabricating or machining parts to rebuild parts for automobiles. Custom machine work (no engine internals). Duplicating small parts for cars (radio knobs, handles, springs, bushings, plastic parts, etc). Billet aluminum work. Dashes, air cleaners, valve covers, etc. One of a kind work. No job too small or large.

Ron's Restorations Inc
2968-B Ask Kay Dr
Smyrna, GA 30082
888-416-1057, 770-438-6102
FAX: 770-438-0037

interior trim
restoration

See full listing in **Section One** under **Mercedes-Benz**

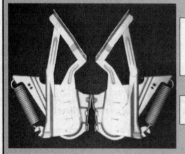
Rust Busters
PO Box 341
Clackamas, OR 97015
503-223-3203
E-mail: info@rustbusters.com

rust repair

See full listing in **Section Two** under **restoration shops**

Simons Balancing & Machine Inc
1987 Ashley River Rd
Charleston, SC 29407
843-766-3911; FAX: 843-766-9003

machine work

See full listing in **Section Two** under **machine work**

SMS Auto Restoration Services
1320 Rt 9
Champlain, NY 12919
450-638-2324; FAX: 450-638-0400

hood hinges

Hood hinge rebuilding service. Web site: www.sms-auto.com
See our ad on this page

Speed & Sport Chrome Plating Inc
404 Broadway
Houston, TX 77012
713-921-0235

chrome plating

See full listing in **Section Two** under **plating & polishing**

Steering Systems
Disivion of A-1 Shock Absorber Co
365 Warren Ave, PO Box 2028
Silverthorne, CO 80498
800-344-1966, 970-389-3193 cell
FAX: 970-513-8283

steering cylinders
steering gears
steering pumps
steering valves

See our ad on the last page

Still Cruisin' Corvettes
5759 Benford Dr
Haymarket, VA 20169
703-754-1960; FAX: 703-754-1222
E-mail: chuckberge@starpower.net

appraisals
repairs
restoration

See full listing in **Section One** under **Corvette**

Teddy's Garage
8530 Louise Ave
Northridge, CA 91325
818-341-0505

parts
restoration
service

See full listing in **Section One** under **Rolls-Royce/Bentley**

Ultimate Appearance Ltd
113 Arabian Tr
Smithfield, VA 23430
888-446-3078; FAX: 757-255-2620

detailing products

See full listing in **Section Two** under **car care products**

Volvo Shop Inc
5220 New Milford Rd
Ravenna, OH 44266
330-297-1297; FAX: 330-297-6206
E-mail: volvocarl@aol.com

parts
restoration

See full listing in **Section One** under **Volvo**

White Post Restorations
One Old Car Dr, PO Drawer D
White Post, VA 22663
540-837-1140; FAX: 540-837-2368
E-mail: info@whitepost.com

brakes
restoration

See full listing in **Section Two** under **brakes**

White Post Restorations	**restoration**
One Old Car Dr, PO Drawer D
White Post, VA 22663
540-837-1140; FAX: 540-837-2368
E-mail: info@whitepost.com	

See full listing in **Section Two** under **restoration shops**

| **Widmann's Garage** | **repairs**
restorations |
|---|---|
| 346 Bunting Ave
Hamilton, NJ 08611
609-392-1553; FAX: 609-392-1709
E-mail: widsgarage@aol.com | |

See full listing in **Section Two** under **restoration shops**

| **Wittenborn's Auto Service Inc** | **Mopar**
Dodge
Plymouth |
|---|---|
| 133 Woodside Ave
Briarcliff Manor, NY 10510-1717
914-941-2744; FAX: 914-769-1327 | |

See full listing in **Section One** under **Mopar**

sheetmetal

| **Accessoryland Truckin' Supplies** | **accessories**
foglights/spotlights
mounting brackets
parts |
|---|---|
| 10723 Rt 61 S
Dubuque, IA 52003
319-556-5482; FAX: 319-556-9087
E-mail: unityspotlights@aol.com or
chevygmcparts@aol.com | |

See full listing in **Section One** under **Chevrolet**

Antique Auto Parts Sales	**patch panels**
40 Iron Mtn W
Hartford, KY 42347
270-264-1483, 270-298-7684
E-mail: aapsales@aol.com	

See full listing in **Section Two** under **body parts**

| **C E Babcock** | **1941, 1942, 1946,**
1947 Cadillac parts |
|---|---|
| 619 Waterside Way
Sarasota, FL 34242
941-349-4990; FAX: 941-349-5751 | |

See full listing in **Section One** under **Cadillac/LaSalle**

Battlefield Antique	**parts**
5054 S Broadview
Battlefield, MO 65619
417-882-7923
E-mail: battlefielda@aol.com	

See full listing in **Section One** under **Ford 1903-1931**

| **Tony D Branda Performance** | **accessories**
decals
emblems
sheetmetal
wheels |
|---|---|
| Shelby and Mustang Parts
1434 E Pleasant Valley Blvd
Altoona, PA 16602
814-942-1869; FAX: 814-944-0801
E-mail: cobranda@aol.com | |

See full listing in **Section One** under **Mustang**

| **C & P Chevy Parts** | **parts**
restoration supplies |
|---|---|
| 50 Schoolhouse Rd, PO Box 348VA
Kulpsville, PA 19443
215-721-4300, 800-235-2475
FAX: 215-721-4539 | |

See full listing in **Section One** under **Chevrolet**

| **Car-Line Manufacturing &**
Distribution Inc | **chassis parts**
engine parts
sheetmetal |
|---|---|
| 1250 Gulf St, PO Box 1192
Beaumont, TX 77701
409-833-9757; FAX: 409-835-2468
E-mail: car-line@car-line.net | |

Mail order and open shop. Monday-Friday 8 am to 5 pm. Manufacturing USA sheetmetal, wood and seat springs for Model T and A Fords, 1909-1931. Also carry a full line of engine and chassis parts. Some V8 parts (metal, seat springs). Catalog available.

CARS Inc	**interiors**
1964 W 11 Mile Rd
Berkley, MI 48072
248-398-7100; FAX: 248-398-7078
E-mail: carsinc@worldnet.att.net	

See full listing in **Section Two** under **interiors & interior parts**

| **Clark's Corvair Parts Inc** | **accessories**
interiors
literature
parts
sheetmetal |
|---|---|
| Rt 2, #400 Mohawk Tr
Shelburne Falls, MA 01370
413-625-9776; FAX: 413-625-8498
E-mail: clarks@corvair.com | |

See full listing in **Section One** under **Corvair**

Classic Chevrolet Parts Inc	**parts**
8723 S I-35
Oklahoma City, OK 73149
405-631-4400; FAX: 405-631-5999
E-mail: info@classicchevroletparts.com	

See full listing in **Section One** under **Chevrolet**

Classic Enterprises	**sheetmetal**
Box 92
Barron, WI 54812
715-537-5422 office
715-234-4677 products
FAX: 715-537-5770
E-mail: lamonte@classicent.com	

See full listing in **Section One** under **Studebaker**

| **Classic Sheetmetal Inc** | **body panels**
sheetmetal |
|---|---|
| 4010 A Hartley St
Charlotte, NC 28206
800-776-4040, 704-596-5186
FAX: 704-596-3895 | |

See full listing in **Section One** under **Thunderbird**

| **Commonwealth Automotive**
Restorations | **body rebuilding**
parts
restoration |
|---|---|
| 1725 Hewins St
Ashley Falls, MA 01222
413-229-3196 | |

See full listing in **Section One** under **Willys**

| **County Auto Restoration** | **bodywork**
brakes
restoration
woodwork |
|---|---|
| 6 Gavin Rd
Mt Vernon, NH 03057
603-673-4840
E-mail: CountyAutoRest@aol.com | |

See full listing in **Section Two** under **restoration shops**

| **Custom Autocraft Inc** | **restoration**
sheetmetal parts |
|---|---|
| 2 Flowerfield, Ste 6
St James, NY 11780
PH/FAX: 631-862-7469 | |

See full listing in **Section One** under **Thunderbird**

Danchuk Mfg
3201 S Standard Ave
Santa Ana, CA 92705
714-751-1957; FAX: 714-850-1957
E-mail: info@danchuk.com

accessories
parts
restoration

See full listing in **Section One** under **Chevrolet**

The El Camino Store
57 B Depot Rd
Goleta, CA 93117
805-681-8164; FAX: 805-681-8166
E-mail: ec@elcaminostore.com

parts

See full listing in **Section One** under **Chevelle/Camaro**

Golden State Parts
3493 Arrowhead Dr
Carson City, NV 89706
800-235-5717; FAX: 888-723-2495

parts

See full listing in **Section One** under **Chevrolet**

Goodmark Industries Inc
625 E Old Norcross Rd
Lawrenceville, GA 30045
770-339-8557; FAX: 770-339-7562

sheetmetal
trim

Shop open Monday-Friday 9 am to 6 pm Eastern time. Reproduction sheetmetal and trim for GM and Chrysler muscle cars and classic GM trucks. Also offers steel cowl induction hoods for 1967-2001 GMC and Chevrolet trucks and 1960s and 1970s Chevrolet cars. Web site: www.goodmarkindustries.com

Grizzly Industrial Inc
2406 Reach Rd
Williamsport, PA 17701
800-523-4777; FAX: 800-438-5901
E-mail: csr@grizzly.com

tools

See full listing in **Section Two** under **tools**

Howell's Sheetmetal Co
PO Box 792
Nederland, TX 77627
800-375-6663, 409-727-1999
FAX: 409-727-7127
E-mail: dhowell@fordor.com

body panels
sheetmetal

See full listing in **Section One** under **Ford 1903-1931**

Imperial Motors
PO Box 496
Campobello, SC 29322
864-895-3474; FAX: 864-895-1248

parts

See full listing in **Section One** under **Chrysler**

Innovative Rod Products
28 Bruce Way
Moundhouse, NV 89706
PH/FAX: 775-246-1718
E-mail: rick@innovativerod.com

body components
chassis parts

See full listing in **Section Two** under **chassis parts**

J & K Old Chevy Stuff
Ship Pond Rd
Plymouth, MA 02360
508-224-7616
kblaze58@aol.com

car dealer
parts
sheetmetal

See full listing in **Section One** under **Chevrolet**

Jackson & Wardick Hot Rods
749 Croton Lake Rd
Bedford Corners, NY 10549-4230
914-666-2057
E-mail: wardj@bestweb.net

metal shaping

See full listing in **Section Two** under **street rods**

L & N Olde Car Co
9992 Kinsman Rd, PO Box 378
Newbury, OH 44065
440-564-7204; FAX: 440-564-8187

restoration

See full listing in **Section Two** under **restoration shops**

The Maverick Connection
137 Valley Dr
Ripley, WV 25271
PH/FAX: 304-372-7825
E-mail: maverickconnection@email.com

literature
parts

See full listing in **Section One** under **Ford 1954-up**

McCann Auto
630 North St, PO Box 1025
Houlton, ME 04730
207-532-2206; FAX: 207-532-6748
E-mail: mccadani@javanet.com

custom work
restoration
sandblasting

See full listing in **Section Two** under **restoration shops**

Melvin's Classic Ford Parts Inc
1521 Dogwood Dr
Conyers, GA 30012
770-761-6800; FAX: 770-761-5777

parts

See full listing in **Section One** under **Ford 1954-up**

Merv's Classic Chevy Parts
1330 Washington Ave
Iowa Falls, IA 50126
641-648-3168; PH/FAX: 641-648-9675

parts

See full listing in **Section One** under **Chevrolet**

Mill Supply Inc
PO Box 28400
Cleveland, OH 44128
800-888-5072; FAX: 888-781-2700
E-mail: info@millsupply.com

clips
fasteners
panels

Replacement panels and supplies for collision and rust repair. Carry the widest selection of replacement panels for your car, truck or van. Plus, a variety of fasteners, clips and body shop supplies. Call or write for specific information. Complete 192 page catalog, $4. Web site: www.rustrepair.com

Millers Incorporated
7412 Count Cir
Huntington Beach, CA 92647
714-375-6565; FAX: 714-847-6606
E-mail: sales@millermbz.com

accessories
parts

See full listing in **Section One** under **Mercedes-Benz**

Obsolete Ford Parts Inc
8701 S I-35
Oklahoma City, OK 73149
405-631-3933; FAX: 405-634-6815
E-mail: info@obsoletefordparts.com

parts

See full listing in **Section One** under **Ford 1954-up**

| Parts House
2912 Hunter St
Fort Worth, TX 76112
817-451-2708
E-mail: theparts@flash.net | brake shoes/drums
fenders
sheetmetal repair
panels |

See full listing in **Section Two** under **comprehensive parts**

| Pilgrim's Auto Restorations
3888 Hill Rd
Lakeport, CA 95453
707-262-1062; FAX: 707-263-6956
E-mail: pilgrims@pacific.net | bodywork
metal fabrication
paint
restoration |

See full listing in **Section Two** under **restoration shops**

| Raybuck Autobody Parts
RD 4, Box 170
Punxsutawney, PA 15767
814-938-5248; FAX: 814-938-4250 | body parts |

See full listing in **Section Two** under **body parts**

| Robert's Custom Metal
24 Lark Industrial Pkwy #D
Smithfield, RI 02828
401-949-2361 | metal fabrication
welding
woodwork |

Open shop. Monday-Friday 8 am to 6 pm, Saturday by appointment only. A small shop that specializes in metal fabrication, welding, woodwork, bodywork and coachbuilding. Restoration of rare parts or fabrication of rare and new parts for custom, classic and antiques. Specializing in early 1900s Cadillac. No job too small or too big. Quality workmanship, fair rates. Give Bob a call and check out our web site: www.crazyhorseinc.com

| Rocker King
804 Chicago Ave
Waukesha, WI 53188-3511
262-549-9583; FAX: 262-549-9643
E-mail: sonoma@execpc.com | body parts
sheetmetal parts |

Phone sales seven days a week, 9 am to 9 pm. Mail order inquiries include SASE. Sells reproduction rocker panels, dog legs, door skins, quarter panel and fender sections for cars made from 1940-1964 and trucks from 1946-1966. Web site: www.execpc.com/~sonoma/

| Rolling Steel Body Parts
7913 Chardon Rd, Rt 6
Kirtland, OH 44094
888-765-5460, 440-256-8383
FAX: 440-256-8994
E-mail: sales@rollingsteelbodyparts.com | body parts |

See full listing in **Section Two** under **body parts**

| Royals' Garage
16-24 Calhoun St
Torrington, CT 06790
860-489-4500 | NOS parts
used parts |

See full listing in **Section One** under **Corvette**

| Rust Busters
PO Box 341
Clackamas, OR 97015
503-223-3203
E-mail: info@rustbusters.com | rust repair |

See full listing in **Section Two** under **restoration shops**

| RX Autoworks
983 W 1st St
North Vancouver, BC Canada V7P 1A4
604-986-0102, 877-986-0102 toll free
FAX: 604-986-0175 | restoration |

See full listing in **Section Two** under **restoration shops**

| Thompson Hill Metalcraft
23 Thompson Hill Rd
Berwick, ME 03901
207-698-5756
E-mail: wpeach@thompsonhill.com | metal forming
panel beating
welding |

Open shop only. Monday-Friday 9 am to 5 pm. Panel beating, metal forming, metal finishing and welding. Aluminum and steel. Hand-builts, customs and antiques. Web site: www.thompsonhill.com

See our ad on this page

| John Ulrich
450 Silver Ave
San Francisco, CA 94112
PH/FAX: 510-223-9587 days | parts |

See full listing in **Section One** under **Packard**

| Webber Engineering LLC
1 Alice Ct
Pawcatuck, CT 06379
860-599-8895; FAX: 860-599-8609
E-mail: kwebbereng@aol.com | street rods
welding |

Mail order and open shop. Monday-Friday 8 am to 5 pm Eastern time. Deals in metal restoration, aluminum welding, street rod building and turnkey cars.

| Pat Wilson's Thunderbird Parts
375 Rt 94
Fredon Township, NJ 07860
888-262-1153; FAX: 973-579-2011
E-mail: wilsontb@nac.net | parts |

See full listing in **Section One** under **Thunderbird**

Section Two – Generalists

special services

300 Below Inc
2101 E Olive St
Decatur, IL 62526
800-550-2796; FAX: 217-423-3075
E-mail: cryo300@midwest.net

cryogenic tempering
machine work
welding

Open shop only. Monday-Friday 8 am to 5 pm. Specializing in deep cryogenic tempering of engines, transmissions, ring and pinions, axles and Turbochargers and brake rotor and brake drums for race cars, sports cars, muscle cars or any type of application where wear and breakage need to be reduced. Broken parts can often be welded, machined and then treated through our process. Web site: www.300below.com

A AAAdvantage Auto Transport Inc
8920 S Hardy
Tempe, AZ 85284
800-233-4875
E-mail: webinfo@aaaadv.com

transport

See full listing in **Section Two** under **transport**

AIS Gator Exports Inc
201 Springsong Rd
Lithia, FL 33547
813-689-2790; FAX: 813-685-1222
E-mail: h.conrad@worldnet.att.net

export

Shipping of various vehicles worldwide.

ANC Restoration
Chris Palmerie
254 New Haven Ave
Waterbury, CT 06708
203-574-2249, 203-558-1488
E-mail: cpwp2@javanet.com

restorations

See full listing in **Section Two** under **plating & polishing**

Ano-Brite Inc
6945 Farmdale Ave
North Hollywood, CA 91605
818-982-0997; FAX: 818-982-0804
E-mail: anobrite@anobrite.com

anodizing
polishing
restoration
welding

See full listing in **Section Two** under **plating & polishing**

Arch Carburetor
583 Central Ave
Newark, NJ 07107
973-482-2755
E-mail: mmfried@quixnet.net

carburetors

See full listing in **Section Two** under **carburetors**

Authentic Automotive
529 Buttercup Tr
Mesquite, TX 75149
972-289-6373; FAX: 972-289-4303

power steering

See full listing in **Section One** under **Chevrolet**

Automotive Legal Service Inc
PO Box 626
Dresher, PA 19025
800-487-4947, 215-659-4947
FAX: 215-657-5843
E-mail: autolegal@aol.com

appraisals

See full listing in **Section Two** under **appraisals**

Skip Barber Racing School
29 Brook St
Lakeville, CT 06039
800-221-1131; FAX: 860-435-1321
E-mail: speed@skipbarber.com

racing school

See full listing in **Section Two** under **racing**

Bob's Classic Auto Glass
21170 Hwy 36
Blachly, OR 97412
800-624-2130

glass

See full listing in **Section Two** under **glass**

John E Boehm
T/A Boehm Design Ltd
PO Box 9096
Silver Spring, MD 20916
301-649-6449

artwork

See full listing in **Section Two** under **artwork**

Brian's 4wd Parts LLC
428 N Harbor St
Branford, CT 06405
203-481-5873; FAX: 203-481-3995
E-mail: willysgp@aol.com

literature
parts

See full listing in **Section One** under **Willys**

Brooks Performance Coatings
17819 SW Elsner Rd
Sherwood, OR 97140
503-524-4048

powder coatings

Open shop only. Monday-Saturday 10 am to 5 pm. Coatings for the custom auto, restoration, racing, automotive and motorcycle industry, including class A powder and thermal ceramic coatings.

Car Critic
202 Woodshire Ln
Naples, FL 34105
941-435-1157; FAX: 941-261-4864
E-mail: carcritic@earthlink.net

appraisals
inspections

See full listing in **Section Two** under **car & parts locators**

Chief Studios
1903 Greenview Pl SW
Rochester, MN 55902
507-271-7435

artwork
novelties

See full listing in **Section Two** under **artwork**

Circle N Stainless
1517 NW 33rd
Lawton, OK 73505
580-355-9366
E-mail: neald@juno.com

stainless steel
trim restoration

Mail order and open shop. Monday-Saturday 7 am to 8 pm. Restoration of stainless steel trim, no heavy buffer lines, all smoothing is done by hand sanding. No payment due until parts are returned and inspected.

Classic Car Appraisals
37 Wyndwood Rd
West Hartford, CT 06107
PH/FAX: 860-236-0125
E-mail: tjakups@
classiccarappraisals.net

appraisals

See full listing in **Section Two** under **appraisals**

Classic Car Publications 292 S Mount Zion Rd Milltown, IN 47145 812-633-7826	calendars

See full listing in **Section Two** under **artwork**

The Clockworks 1745 Meta Lake Ln Eagle River, WI 54521 800-398-3040; FAX: 715-479-5759 E-mail: clockwks@nnex.net	clock service

See full listing in **Section Two** under **instruments**

Custom Auto Interiors **by Ron Mangus** 18127 Marygold Ave Bloomington, CA 92316 909-877-9342; FAX: 909-877-1741 E-mail: customautointeriors@ hotmail.com	accessories carpet kits die cast collectibles seat frames

See full listing in **Section Two** under **interiors & interior parts**

Custom Solutions & Services 2218 Pleasant View Ct Deer Creek, IL 61733-9672 309-447-6320 E-mail: jscharfcss@juno.com	badges keychains software

See full listing in **Section Four** under **information sources**

Dash Graining by Mel Erikson 31 Meadow Rd Kings Park, NY 11754 631-544-1102; FAX: 631-544-1107	dashboard restoration

See full listing in **Section Two** under **woodgraining**

Dashhugger PO Box 933 Clovis, CA 93613 559-298-4529; FAX: 559-298-3428 E-mail: info@dashhugger.com	dashboard covers

See full listing in **Section Two** under **interiors & interior parts**

DETAILS License Plate Restoration 74 Montague City Rd Greenfield, MA 01301 413-774-6982 E-mail: jeri@valinet.com	license plates

See full listing in **Section Two** under **license plates**

Economy Racing Components Inc 7550 Negley Rd Henderson, KY 42420 PH/FAX: 270-826-3159 E-mail: erc@henderson.net	machine work welding wheels/tires

Wheels, tires and parts for mini Sprints and modified Midget race cars. Also does custom machine work and welding. Web site: www.cincy-racing/erc

Explicit Concepts Customs & Minis Livonia, MI 48150 313-617-5433 E-mail: vabruno@explicitconcepts.net	aftermarket restyling

See full listing in **Section Two** under **custom cars**

FB Performance Transmissions 85 Cleveland Ave Bay Shore, NY 11706 631-242-0008; FAX: 631-243-3054 E-mail: fbperf@trim.net	transmissions

See full listing in **Section Two** under **transmissions**

FHS Supply Inc PO Box 9 Clover, SC 29710 800-742-8484; FAX: 803-222-7285 E-mail: fhsoil@aol.com	oil

See full listing in **Section Two** under **lubricants**

First National Bank of Sumner PO Box 145 Sumner, IL 62466 618-936-2396; FAX: 618-936-9079 E-mail: hobbes@wworld.com	financing

See full listing in **Section Two** under **financing**

Five Star Transport 691 W Merrick Rd Valley Stream, NY 11580 800-464-9965, 516-285-1077 FAX: 516-285-3729	transport

See full listing in **Section Two** under **transport**

Fowlkes Realty & Auction Co 500 Hale St, PO Box 471 Newman Grove, NE 68758 800-275-5522; FAX: 402-447-6000 E-mail: fowlkes@megavision.com	appraisals auctions

See full listing in **Section Two** under **auctions & shows**

Fred's Classic Auto Radio & Clocks 7908 Gilette Lenexa, KS 66215 913-599-2303	clock repair radio repair

See full listing in **Section Two** under **radios**

The Generation Gap 123 Peachtree Park Byron, GA 31008 478-956-2678; FAX: 478-956-2608	antiques sales

Open Monday-Saturday 9 am to 7 pm, Sunday 12 noon to 6 pm. Specializing in sales of antique, classic and special interest autos for the past 28 years. Now located in our new 15,000 sq ft showroom on I-75 at Exit 46 under the big peach in Byron, GA. Offering quality antiques and great prices on Wells Cargo trailers. Be sure and visit our unique showrooms, we are half classic cars and half quality antiques. Web site: www.thegenerationgap.com

Hodges Custom Haulers 9076 Scale Rd Benton, KY 42025 800-851-7229; FAX: 270-898-2356	truck beds

See full listing in **Section Two** under **trailers**

Hot Rod Coffee 1314 Rollins Rd Burlingame, CA 94010 650-348-8269; FAX: 650-340-9473 E-mail: hotrodcoffee@pacbell.net	gourmet coffee

See full listing in **Section Two** under **accessories**

Imtek Environmental Corporation
PO Box 2066
Alpharetta, GA 30023
770-667-8621; FAX: 770-667-8683
E-mail: imtek@no-odor.com

ammonia removal
products
odor control
products

See full listing in **Section Two** under **manufacturing**

Jersey Late Greats Inc
PO Box 1294
Hightstown, NJ 08520
609-448-0526

documentation
service
restoration details

See full listing in **Section One** under **Chevrolet**

Katen and Associates Inc
405 Greenbriar Rd
Lexington, KY 40503-2637
PH/FAX: 859-278-0758
E-mail: kenkaten@aol.com

welding

Micro-tig welding of small steel and stainless steel components. No part too small.

Klassic Kolor Auctions
PO Box 55243
Hayward, CA 94545-0243
510-795-2776; FAX: 510-441-6050
E-mail: gentle_ben@easyriders.com

auction "color"
broadcaster
master of ceremonies

See full listing in **Section Two** under **auctions & shows**

L & L Antique Auto Trim
403 Spruce, Box 177
Pierce City, MO 65723
417-476-2871

runningboard
moldings

Mail order only. Dealing in runningboard moldings. Grip moldings and tread strip moldings also available.

Lee's Street Rods
RR 3 Box 3061A
Rome, PA 18837
570-247-2326
E-mail: lka41@epix.net

accessories
parts
restoration

See full listing in **Section Two** under **street rods**

M & L Automobile Appraisal
2662 Palm Terr
Deland, FL 32720
904-734-1761
386-734-1761 (effective 11/01)

appraisals

See full listing in **Section Two** under **appraisals**

Mar-Ke Woodgraining
1102 Hilltop Dr
Loveland, CO 80537
970-663-7803; FAX: 970-663-1138

woodgraining

See full listing in **Section Two** under **woodgraining**

Maximum Downforce
Gary Toriello
120 E Clinton Ave
Bergenfield, NJ 07621
201-384-0529; FAX: 201-384-5062
E-mail: racerx@
maximumdownforce.com

photography

See full listing in **Section Two** under **photography**

National Spring Co Inc
1402 N Magnolia Ave
El Cajon, CA 92020
619-441-1901; FAX: 619-441-2460

spring parts
spring services

See full listing in **Section Two** under **suspension parts**

NCA Automotive
4532 W Palm Ln
Phoenix, AZ 85035
PH/FAX: 602-278-6070
E-mail: ncaltec@netscape.net

restoration

See full listing in **Section Two** under **restoration shops**

Nu-Chrome Corp
161 Graham Rd
Fall River, MA 02720
508-324-0002; FAX: 508-324-0004
E-mail: chromeplating00@aol.com

metal fabrication
plating
restoration

25 years experience in the restoration and plating of antique car parts. Metal fabrication shop, pot metal specialists, triple chrome plating process, gold plating available. Quality guaranteed, professional support available. Contact us for advice or a cost estimate. Web site: www.nu-chrome.com
See our ad on page 355

CT Peters Inc Appraisers
2A W Front St
Red Bank, NJ 07701
732-747-9450 Red Bank
732-528-9451 Brielle
E-mail: ctp2120@aol.com

appraisals

See full listing in **Section Two** under **appraisals**

A Petrik
Restoration & Rebuilding Service
504 Edmonds Ave NE
Renton, WA 98056-3636
425-466-5590, 425-255-4852
E-mail: rnrserv@qwest.net or
rnrserv@hotmail.com

heater control
valve rebuilding
windshield
regulators

See full listing in **Section Two** under **heaters**

Power Steering Services Inc
2347 E Kearney St
Springfield, MO 65803
417-864-6676; FAX: 417-864-7103
E-mail: chip@powersteering.com

pumps
rack & pinion
steering gearboxes

See full listing in **Section Two** under **suspension parts**

Practical Images
PO Box 245
Haddam, CT 06438-0245
860-704-0525
E-mail: services@practimages.com

int'l VHS video
conversions
photo scanning
photography

See full listing in **Section Two** under **photography**

Premier Designs Historic Costume
15512 St Rt 613
Van Buren, OH 45889
800-427-0907; FAX: 419-299-3919
E-mail: premier@bright.net

clothing

See full listing in **Section Two** under **apparel**

Professional Metal Refinishing Inc
2415 W State Blvd
Fort Wayne, IN 46808
219-436-2828; FAX: 219-432-1941
E-mail: mail@prostrip.com

rust removal

See full listing in **Section Two** under **rust removal & stripping**

Redi-Strip Company
100 W Central Ave
Roselle, IL 60172
630-529-2442; FAX: 630-529-3626

abrasive media
baking soda blasting
paint removal
rust removal

See full listing in **Section Two** under **rust removal & stripping**

The Reflected Image — mirror reproduction / mirror resilvering
21 W Wind Dr
Northford, CT 06472
PH/FAX: 203-484-0760
E-mail: scott@reflectedimage.com

Mail order only. Mirror resilvering, dial gauge restoration, coin-op mirror reproduction, glass and mirror sand carving and personalization products. Web site: www.reflectedimage.com

Samson Technology Corporation — plating systems
6825 SW 21st Ct #3
Davie, FL 33317
800-256-0692; FAX: 954-916-9338
E-mail: sales@samson24k.com

See full listing in **Section Two** under **plating & polishing**

Showcase Express — display systems
17862 Metzler Ln
Huntington Beach, CA 92647
714-842-5564 ext 29
FAX: 714-842-6534
E-mail: carl@sonos1.com

See full listing in **Section Two** under **models & toys**

Slim's Garage — garden tractors
PO Box 49
Seminary, MS 39479-0049
PH/FAX: 601-722-9861

See full listing in **Section Two** under **trucks & tractors**

Smartire Systems Inc — gauges
13151 Vanier Pl, Ste 150
Richmond, BC Canada V6V 2J1
604-276-9884; FAX: 604-276-2350
E-mail: info@smartire.com

See full listing in **Section Two** under **accessories**

SMS Auto Restoration Services — hood hinges
1320 Rt 9
Champlain, NY 12919
450-638-2324; FAX: 450-638-0400

See full listing in **Section Two** under **service shops**

Speed & Sport Chrome Plating Inc — chrome plating
404 Broadway
Houston, TX 77012
713-921-0235

See full listing in **Section Two** under **plating & polishing**

Sports Car Rentals & Sales — car rentals
PO Box 265
Batesville, VA 22924
804-823-4442
E-mail: info@sportscarrentals.com

Mail order and open shop. Open 24 hours, 7 days a week. Renting and selling of classic convertible sports cars in the Charlottesville, VA area. Our sports car fleet includes: Austin-Healey, MGA, MGB, MG Midget, and Triumph TR3. Surprise someone special on their birthday or anniversary with a sports car rental! All our rentals include 200 free miles per day. Renters must be over 25 years of age. Pick-up and delivery available. Reduced rates available for weekly rentals. We can also assist you with your purchase or sale of any sports car! Web site: www.sportscarrentals.com

Star Quality Parts — accessories / parts
A Silvermine Classics Inc Company
1 Alley Rd
LaGrangeville, NY 12520
800-STAR199 (782-7199)
FAX: 845-223-5394
E-mail: sales@starqualityparts.com

See full listing in **Section One** under **Mercedes-Benz**

Steering Systems — steering cylinders / steering gears / steering pumps / steering valves
Disivion of A-1 Shock Absorber Co
365 Warren Ave, PO Box 2028
Silverthorne, CO 80498
800-344-1966, 970-389-3193 cell
FAX: 970-513-8283

Rebuilt manual and power steering gears, pumps and cylinders for all domestic cars and trucks. Many units are available on an exchange basis. Our warranty covers repair or replacement for one year. Great service and quality. Call Monday-Friday 9 am to 6 pm Mountain time and most Saturdays. Web site: www.shockfinders.com

See our ad on the last page

Stockton Wheel Service — wheel repair
648 W Fremont St
Stockton, CA 95203
209-464-7771, 800-395-9433
FAX: 209-464-4725
E-mail: sales@stocktonwheel.com

See full listing in **Section Two** under **wheels & wheelcovers**

Ed Strain Inc — magnetos
6555 44th St #2006
Pinellas Park, FL 33781
800-266-1623, 727-521-1597

Open Monday-Friday 8 am to 2 pm. Magnetos rebuilt, restored, repaired, coil winding. Home of obsolete technology.

JF Sullivan Company — electrical parts / repairs
14 Clarendon Rd
Auburn, MA 01501
508-792-9500

See full listing in **Section Two** under **fuel system parts**

Tags Backeast — data plates / trim tags / cowl tags
PO Box 581
Plainville, CT 06062
860-747-2942
E-mail: dataplt@snet.net

Mail order only. Restoration of data plates, trim tags for 1952-1969 Ford family; 1960-1974 Mopars; 1930s-1970s GM family. Legitimate authentic cars only. Web site: www.datatags.com

Jay Texter — photography
417 Haines Mill Rd
Allentown, PA 18104
610-821-0963
E-mail: jaytexter@ot.com

See full listing in **Section Two** under **photography**

TMC Publications — literature / manuals
5817 Park Heights Ave
Baltimore, MD 21215-3931
410-367-4490; FAX: 410-466-3566
E-mail: carolyny@tmcpubl.com

See full listing in **Section Four** under **books & publications**

Toronto Vintage Vehicles 536 Pefferlaw Rd Pefferlaw, ON Canada L0E 1N0 705-437-3817; FAX: 705-437-2722 E-mail: havebus@ils.net	vehicles for movies

We supply picture vehicles to the film industry (commercials, movies, TV series, etc). We have access to over 1,100 vehicles covering all years and most models. All of our vehicles are privately owned. We also specialize in vintage buses. Web site: www.havebus.com

Lou Trepanier, Appraiser #1 250 Highland St Taunton, MA 02780 508-823-6512; FAX: 508-285-4841	appraisals consultant

See full listing in **Section Two** under **appraisals**

Valley Wire Wheel Service 14731 Lull St Van Nuys, CA 91405 818-785-7237; FAX: 818-994-2042 E-mail: valleywirewheel@aol.com	wheel restoration wheels

See full listing in **Section Two** under **wheels & wheelcovers**

Verdone's Custom Stainless Casting 31 Stricklerstown Loop Rd Newmanstown, PA 17073 717-949-3341; FAX: 717-949-2782	casting polishing

See full listing in **Section Two** under **castings**

F Todd Warner's Mahogany Bay 2642 Commerce Blvd Mound, MN 55364 952-495-0007; FAX: 952-495-1237 E-mail: sales@mahoganybay.net	wooden boat restoration

Wooden boat restoration, sales (we buy classic boats), service. Financing available. Transportation worldwide. Appraisal consulting, expert finishing. Established 1975. Large inventory of the finest selection of custom runabouts, utilities and launches. Web site: www.mahoganybay.net

Wholesale Express 830 W 3rd St Eddy, TX 76524 254-859-5364; FAX: 254-859-5407 E-mail: tommy@wacool.net	buffing supplies sandblasters

See full listing in **Section Two** under **accessories**

Wild About Wheels 274 Great Rd Acton, MA 01720-4702 978-264-9921; 800-538-0539 (orders) FAX: 978-264-9547 E-mail: globaltv@tiac.net	video tapes

Mail order only. Wild About Wheels TV and Video produces award winning automotive television and video programming including *Wild About Wheels*, *Motortrend Television* and *Wheels*. Web store has over 100 automotive videos, most produced by Wild About Wheels. Automotive corporate services are also a large part of our business including event coverage, marketing and training videos. Web site: www.wildaboutwheels.com

Winslow Mfg Co 5700 Dean Ave Raleigh, NC 27604 919-790-9713	parts rebuilding

See full listing in **Section Two** under **engine parts**

Wolfson Engineering 512 Parkway W Las Vegas, NV 89106 PH/FAX: 702-384-4196	mech engineering

Mail order and open shop by appointment. Major and minor mechanical engineering projects, modifications, research and development, designs, welding, fabrication. Difficult new and used parts secured. Specialist in Rolls-Royce and American muscle cars. Member SAE, Society of Automotive Engineers and 30 year member RROC. Not accepting assignments with Asian cars or computer related electronics.

steering columns

ididit inc 610 S Maumee St Tecumseh, MI 49286 517-424-0577; FAX: 517-424-7293 E-mail: sales@ididitinc.com	steering columns

Monday-Friday 8:30 am to 5:30 pm, Saturday 10 am to 2 pm Eastern time. Specializing in steering columns for street rods, 1930s to 1969 cars and 1930-1972 trucks. Also steering accessories (of all kinds), steering wheels, U-joints and steering gearboxes. Web site: www.ididitinc.com

steering wheels

Automotive Specialties 11240 E Sligh Ave Seffner, FL 33584 800-676-1928	restoration

Steering wheel restoration, woodgrain dash and molding restoration.

Classic Chevrolet Parts Inc 8723 S I-35 Oklahoma City, OK 73149 405-631-4400; FAX: 405-631-5999 E-mail: info@classicchevroletparts.com	parts

See full listing in **Section One** under **Chevrolet**

D&D Automobilia 813 Ragers Hill Rd South Fork, PA 15956 814-539-5653	plastic parts steering wheels

Mail order and open shop. Monday-Friday 8 am to 5 pm. Recasting steering wheels, dash and gearshift knobs and other plastic parts. All colors, clear, transparents, woodgrain, marbles and new speckled marble.

JB Donaldson Co 2533 W Cypress Phoenix, AZ 85009 602-278-4505; FAX: 602-278-1112	castings steering wheels wood parts

Show quality plastic steering wheel recastings for Cadillac, Buick, Packard and other makes steering wheels. Woody parts and complete kits for GM, Buicks and Packards 1937-1953. Web site: www.jbdonaldsonco.com

Gary's Steering Wheel Restoration 2677 Ritner Hwy Carlisle, PA 17013 717-243-5646; FAX: 717-243-5072 E-mail: wheelrest@aol.com	repairs

Mail order and open shop. Monday-Friday 9 am to 6 pm, Saturday by appointment. Repair all types of plastic steering wheels.

Specialize in woodgrain wheels, Corvette, GTO, AMX, Road-runner, Challenger, also inlay type wheels, Cadillac, Oldsmobile, T-Bird and Ford. Repair cracks using an acrylic plastic and then primer and seal, then top coated with four coats of acrylic ure-thane paint. Show quality work. Free estimates. Your satisfaction guaranteed. Since 1981, see us at Carlisle Spring, Summer, and Fall meets at space K-189, Ford H-126, Mopar H-56, Corvette D-129. Web site: www.dealonwheels.com/parts/garys/

Grant Products Inc 700 Allen Ave Glendale, CA 91201 818-247-2910; FAX: 818-241-4683 E-mail: customerservice@ grantproducts.com	**steering wheels**

Manufacturer of a complete line of custom steering wheels. Sell wholesale only. Web site: www.grantproducts.com

Kimble Engineering Ltd Unit 5 Old Mill Creek Dartmouth Devon TQ6 0HN England 0044 1803 835757 FAX: 0044 1803 834567 E-mail: johnlkimble@cs.com	**aero screens** **steering wheels**

See full listing in **Section One** under **MG**

Koch's 26943 Ruether Ave, Unit M Canyon Country, CA 91351 661-252-9264; FAX: 661-252-2834 E-mail: customerservice@kochs.com	**restoration**

Mail order and open shop. Monday-Friday 8 am to 5 pm. Steering wheel restorations. Web site: www.kochs.com

Obsolete Ford Parts Inc 8701 S I-35 Oklahoma City, OK 73149 405-631-3933; FAX: 405-634-6815 E-mail: info@obsoletefordparts.com	**parts**

See full listing in **Section One** under **Ford 1954-up**

Bill Peters 41 Vassar Pl Rockville Centre, NY 11570 516-766-8397	**steering wheel** **restoration**

Mail order and open shop. Monday-Saturday reasonable hours. Steering wheel restoration, recasting, color and clear. For Auburn, Cord, Chrysler, Cadillac V16-V8, Chevrolet, Willys, Pontiac, Packard, Rolls/Bentley, Studebaker, Mercedes-Benz, Lincoln. All wheels, A-Z, Concours quality, domestic, imports. Woodgrain, modern, custom fabrication, truck, marine, aircraft.

The Wheel Shoppe Inc 13635 SE Division St Portland, OR 97236 503-761-5119; FAX: 503-761-5190 E-mail: rogeradams@ thewheelshoppe.com	**parts** **steering wheels**

Mail order and open shop. Tuesday-Friday 10 am to 5 pm, Saturday 10 am to 2 pm. The Wheel Shoppe banjo steering wheel, street rod parts, wheels and accessories. Web site: www.thewheelshoppe.com

Wooddash.com 438 Calle San Pablo, Unit B Camarillo, CA 93012 805-987-2086; FAX: 805-389-5375 E-mail: mrchrome@west.net	**dashes** **steering wheels**

See full listing in **Section Two** under **woodgraining**

storage

Chicago Car Exchange 14085 W Rockland Rd Libertyville, IL 60048 847-680-1950; FAX: 847-680-1961 E-mail: oldtoys@wwa.com	**appraisals** **car dealer** **car locator** **financing** **storage**

See full listing in **Section Two** under **car dealers**

C'NC Sheetmetal 11790 FM 3270 Tyler, TX 75708 800-668-1691; FAX: 903-877-2060 E-mail: cncsmetal@aol.com	**car casters** **patterns**

See full listing in **Section Two** under **restoration aids**

DeWitts Reproductions 11672 Hyne Rd Brighton, MI 48114 810-220-0181; FAX: 810-220-0182 E-mail: dewitts@ismi.net	**radiators**

See full listing in **Section One** under **Corvette**

Double Park Lifts 6352 N Hillside Wichita, KS 67219 800-754-8786; FAX: 316-744-9221 E-mail: lewis216@southwind.net	**service lifts**

Manufacturer of 4-post automotive storage and/or service lifts. Lift is portable with caster kit option. Also manufactures lifts for enclosed car trailers. Custom lifts available too. Web site: www.doublepark.net

Exotic Car Transport Inc PO Box 91 Ocoee, FL 34761 800-766-8797; FAX: 407-654-9951 E-mail: info@exoticcartransport.com	**transport**

See full listing in **Section Two** under **transport**

Family Sports Storage Inc 4400 Killarney Park Dr Burton, MI 48529 810-743-5670	**storage**

Open by appointment only. 32 years.

Fiesta's Classic Car Center 3901 N Kings Hwy St Louis, MO 63115 314-385-4567	**appraisals** **consignment sales** **storage**

Open daily except holidays. Specializing in clean, secure storage. Your classic is protected by a 24 hour state-of-the-art security system. Conveniently located in the center of the USA. Can assist in preparation and transportation to car shows and auctions. Consignment sales showroom available. Will build to suit multi-car garages per your specifications. Base rate for 2001 is $50 per month per vehicle.

Grizzly Industrial Inc 2406 Reach Rd Williamsport, PA 17701 800-523-4777; FAX: 800-438-5901 E-mail: csr@grizzly.com	**tools**

See full listing in **Section Two** under **tools**

Highway Products Inc 7905 Agate Rd White City, OR 97503 800-TOOLBOX; FAX: 800-465-9545 E-mail: toolbox@cdsnet.net	**toolboxes**

Mail order and open shop. Monday-Friday 6:30 am to 5 pm
Pacific time. Manufacturer of toolboxes from pickups to semis in
steel, aluminum and stainless steel. Also a manufacturer of the
Highwayman RV tow body, aluminum flatbeds and custom
boxes. Web site: www.800toolbox.com

Interesting Parts Inc Paul TerHorst 27526 N Owens Rd Mundelein, IL 60060-9608 PH/FAX: 847-949-1030 847-558-9732 cell E-mail: pterhorst@interaccess.com	**appraisals** **gaskets** **parts** **storage** **transport**

See full listing in **Section Two** under **comprehensive parts**

Interstate Towing Service 6029 Geary Blvd San Francisco, CA 94121 415-221-1117, 24 hours FAX: 415-221-1060 E-mail: interstow@earthlink.net	**transport**

See full listing in **Section Two** under **transport**

Kaddies Inc PO Box 342 Walnut Creek, CA 94597 925-934-4488; FAX: 925-934-4492 E-mail: tshette@pacbell.net	**portable storage** **tool kaddies**

Portable storage, labor saving and efficiency products. Tool
Kaddies are double wall polyethylene cabinets. Dolly style porta-
bility, lockable and extremely durable and chemical resistant.
Web site: www.kaddiesinc.com

Lester Building Systems 1111 2nd Ave S Lester Prairie, MN 55354 800-826-4439; FAX: 320-395-2969 E-mail: info@lesterbuildingsystems.com	**wood frame** **buildings**

Lester Building Systems manufactures pre-engineered wood
frame buildings for a variety of end uses including garages,
hobby shops and storage facilities. Flexible designs, fast construction and lower in-place costs are only a few of the advan-
tages of choosing a Lester® building. Call us or visit our web site
today: www.lesterbuildings.com

Memory Lane Motors Inc 1231 Rt 176 Lake Bluff, IL 60044 847-362-4600	**appraisals** **car dealer** **storage**

See full listing in **Section Two** under **car dealers**

Miracle Steel Structures 505 N Hwy 169, Ste 500 Minneapolis, MN 55441-6420 800-521-0386, 763-593-1000 FAX: 763-544-1835 E-mail: buildings@miracletruss.com	**steel buildings**

Pre-engineered, construct yourself steel buildings for people to
build their own garage, repair/workshop, storage, etc. Web site:
www.miracletruss.com

P&J Products 988 Gordon Ln Birmingham, MI 48009 888-647-1879	**car skates** **trailer dollies**

See full listing in **Section Two** under **accessories**

Quik-Shelter PO Box 1123 Orange, CT 06477 800-211-3730; FAX: 203-937-8897 E-mail: info@quikshelter.com	**temporary garages**

See full listing in **Section Two** under **car covers**

RD Enterprises Ltd 290 Raub Rd Quakertown, PA 18951 215-538-9323; FAX: 215-538-0158 E-mail: rdent@rdent.com	**parts**

See full listing in **Section One** under **Lotus**

Superior Equipment 326 S Meridian Valley Center, KS 67147 800-526-9992; FAX: 316-755-4391 E-mail: mail@superlifts.com	**auto lifts** **shop tools**

See full listing in **Section Two** under **tools**

storage care products

Archway Press Inc 19 W 44th St New York, NY 10036 800-374-4766; FAX: 212-869-5215 E-mail: archway@mindspring.com	**garage blueprints**

See full listing in **Section Four** under **books & publications**

Billie Inc PO Box 1161 Ashburn, VA 20146-1161 800-878-6328; FAX: 703-858-0102	**garage diaper mats**

See full listing in **Section Two** under **car care products**

Buenger Enterprises/ **GoldenRod Dehumidifier** 3600 S Harbor Blvd Oxnard, CA 93035 800-451-6797; FAX: 805-985-1534	**dehumidifiers**

See full listing in **Section Two** under **car care products**

Double Park Lifts 6352 N Hillside Wichita, KS 67219 800-754-8786; FAX: 316-744-9221 E-mail: lewis216@southwind.net	**service lifts**

See full listing in **Section Two** under **storage**

Dri-Wash 'n Guard Independent Distributor PO Box 1331 Palm Desert, CA 92261 800-428-1883, 760-346-1984 FAX: 760-568-6354 E-mail: driwasherik@aol.com	**automotive care products** **boat care products**

See full listing in **Section Two** under **car care products**

Green Oak Enterprises Inc 12166 Andresen Dr South Lyon, MI 48178 888-721-9595	**car dollies**

See full listing in **Section Two** under **tools**

Highway Products Inc 7905 Agate Rd White City, OR 97503 800-TOOLBOX; FAX: 800-465-9545 E-mail: toolbox@cdsnet.net	**toolboxes**

See full listing in **Section Two** under **storage**

Murphy's Motoring Accessories Inc PO Box 618 Greendale, WI 53129-0618 800-529-8315, 414-529-8333 FAX: 414-529-0616 E-mail: mma@execpc.com	**car covers**

See full listing in **Section Two** under **car covers**

P&J Products 988 Gordon Ln Birmingham, MI 48009 888-647-1879	**car skates trailer dollies**

See full listing in **Section Two** under **accessories**

Quik-Shelter PO Box 1123 Orange, CT 06477 800-211-3730 FAX: 203-937-8897 E-mail: info@quikshelter.com	**temporary garages**

See full listing in **Section Two** under **car covers**

Sta-Dri Pouches/Beach Filler **Products Inc** 7682 Glenville Rd Glen Rock, PA 17327 800-BEACH85 FAX: 717-235-4858 E-mail: beach@blazenet.net	**corrosion protection** **mildew protection** **moisture protection**

Sta-Dri Pouches protect your investment from moisture, mildew and corrosion. Rust, mildew and corrosion can damage your auto's interior, especially while storing, put Sta-Dri Pouches on the seats, dashboard and engine compartment. Can be regenerated. Visa and MasterCard accepted. Web site: www.sta-dri.com

Stinger by Axe Hwy 177 N, PO Box 296 Council Grove, KS 66846 800-854-4850 FAX: 316-767-5482 E-mail: axeequipment@tctelco.net	**lifts**

Manufacturer of a complete line of classic and race car storage systems. Residential and trailer auto lifts designed for the discriminating restorer/collector/racer. Line of residential lifts includes three different models. Trailer lifts are custom made to accommodate any trailer needs. All lifts are electric over hydraulic and are powder coat painted for a lifetime of use. Structure of lifts has a lifetime warranty. Showcase your vehicle(s) on a Stinger by Axe Lift. Web site: www.stingerlifts.com

Section Two – Generalists

Van Raalte & Co LLC
5621 Garden Valley Rd
Garden Valley, CA 95633
800-286-0030; FAX: 530-333-2034
E-mail: info@ezup4u.com

canopies

See full listing in **Section Two** under **car covers**

street rods

A-1 Street Rods
631 E Las Vegas St
Colorado Springs, CO 80903
719-632-4920, 719-577-4588
FAX: 719-634-6577

parts

Mail order and open shop. Monday-Friday 9:30 am to 5:30 pm, Saturday 9:30 am to 1 pm. Specialize in Chevrolet 1937-1957 and Ford 1928-1948 parts. Sell antique and classic car parts, street rod parts, accessories, rubber parts, chassis parts and cars.

A-One Auto Appraisals
19 Hope Ln
Narragansett, RI 02882
401-783-7701, RI; 407-668-9610, FL

appraisals

See full listing in **Section Two** under **appraisals**

A/Altered Hot Rod Parts
PO Box 851
Emporia, KS 66801
620-343-1796

body parts

See full listing in **Section One** under **Ford 1903-1931**

AAdvanced Transmissions
15 Parker St
Worcester, MA 01610
508-752-9674; FAX: 508-842-0672

rear axle service
restoration
ring/pinion
parts/sales/
rebuilding/service

See full listing in **Section Two** under **transmissions**

Addison Generator Inc
21 W Main St Rear
Freehold, NJ 07728
732-431-2438; FAX: 732-431-4503

auto parts
repairs
supplies

See full listing in **Section Two** under **electrical systems**

Alloy-Fab
8709 Hwy 99
Vancouver, WA 98665
800-344-2847; FAX: 360-576-0610

bumper brackets

See full listing in **Section One** under **Ford 1932-1953**

American Autowire/Factory Fit®
150 Heller Pl #17W, Dept HCCA02
Bellmawr, NJ 08031
800-482-9473; FAX: 856-933-0805
E-mail: info@americanautowire.com

battery cables
electrical systems
switches/
components

Premier manufacturer of cutting edge automotive electrical systems covering street rods, street machines, race cars, custom cars and original equipment segments of the car market. Primary emphasis is on technically superior complete panel systems incorporating late model innovations in the easiest to install system on the market. Full line of accessory wiring kits and related components. Technical support and money back guarantee. Visa and MasterCard accepted. Dealer inquiries welcome. Web site: www.americanautowire.com

American Street Rod
3340 Sunrise Blvd D-1
Rancho Cordova, CA 95742
916-638-3275

hoses
tubing

Mail order and open shop. Monday-Friday 8 am to 5 pm, Saturday 9 am to 1 pm. Hot rod plumbing. Stainless braided hoses and AN fittings, full plumbing shop, custom hoses made, stainless steel tubing, tubing benders and 37 degree flaring tools. Largest inventory in the northwestern United States. We ship everywhere. Web site: www.amstreetrod.com

Antique Automotive Engineering Inc
3560 Chestnut Pl
Denver, CO 80216
303-296-7332, 800-846-7332
E-mail: ed@antiqueautoengr.com

babbitt service
engine restoration

See full listing in **Section One** under **Ford 1903-1931**

**Automobile Appraisal Service &
Special Interest Autos**
10097 Manchester Rd, Ste 203
St Louis, MO 63122
PH/FAX: 314-821-4015

appraiser

See full listing in **Section Two** under **appraisals**

**Automobile Classics Appraisal
Services**
5385 S Cook Rd
College Park, GA 30349
404-761-0350; FAX: 404-761-3703
E-mail: johnboy30349@aol.com

appraisals

See full listing in **Section Two** under **appraisals**

BDI Automotive Design/Brandon
13985 Madison Pk
Morningview, KY 41063
859-363-0086; FAX: 859-363-0081
E-mail: bdi@fuse.net

lettering
painting
pinstriping

See full listing in **Section Two** under **striping**

Belmont's Rod & Custom Shop
138 Bussey St
Dedham, MA 02026
781-326-9599, 781-326-3270

speed equipment
transmissions

Mail order and open shop. Monday-Saturday 10 am to 8 pm. Specializing in high-performance new and used speed equipment for all makes and models. Transmission adapters, intakes, etc.

Berkshire Auto's Time Was
10 Front St, Box 347
Collinsville, CT 06022
860-693-2332
E-mail: obteddi3@aol.com

restoration

See full listing in **Section Two** under **restoration shops**

Bob's Classic Auto Glass
21170 Hwy 36
Blachly, OR 97412
800-624-2130

glass

See full listing in **Section Two** under **glass**

Bob's Rod & Custom
866 W 3200 S
Nibley, UT 84321
435-752-7467
E-mail: bobsrod@cache.net

car assembly
fabrication
interiors

Deals in car assembly and fabrication, electrical, interiors and upholstery, custom built air cleaners. Web site: www.cache.net/bobsrod

Section Two – Generalists

Bonneville Speed & Supply
PO Box 3924
Tustin, CA 92781
714-666-1966; FAX: 714-666-1955
E-mail: bonspeed@aol.com

memorabilia
vintage clothing

See full listing in **Section Two** under **apparel**

Boop Photography
2347 Derry St
Harrisburg, PA 17104-2728
717-564-8533
E-mail: booper@home.com

photography

See full listing in **Section Two** under **photography**

BPE Racing Heads
702 Dunn Way
Placentia, CA 92870
714-572-6072; FAX: 714-572-6073
E-mail: steve@bpeheads.com

cylinder heads

See full listing in **Section Two** under **machine work**

The Car Shop
10449 Rt 39
Springville, NY 14141
716-592-2060; FAX: 716-592-5766
E-mail: carshop77@aol.com

parts
service

Both mail order and open shop. Monday-Friday 9 am to 9 pm, Saturday 9 am to 4 pm, Sunday 9 am to 12 pm. Deals in rod, custom and performance parts and service. Web site: www.thecarshop-ny.com

Cars of the Times
1218 Crest Ln, Ste 16
Duncanville, TX 75137
972-572-6677
E-mail: cottjb@swbell.net

car dealer
street rods

See full listing in **Section Two** under **car dealers**

CBS Performance Automotive
2605-A W Colorado Ave
Colorado Springs, CO 80904
800-685-1492; FAX: 719-578-9485

ignition systems
performance products

See full listing in **Section Two** under **ignition parts**

Champion Luggage Trailers
9471 Hemlock Cir
Shreveport, LA 71118
318-688-2787

luggage trailer kits

See full listing in **Section Two** under **trailers**

The Chopper Rod Shop
20851 Missouri Ave, PO Box 185
Elmer, MO 63538
PH/FAX: 660-825-4572
E-mail: choprods@usa.net

chopped tops
street rods

Open shop only. Specializing in 1960 and older cars and trucks built as hot rods. Chopped tops are my specialty. Custom body modifications and complete chassis work. Turnkey cars built and project cars for sale and parts for sale. Web site: www.chopperrodshop.com

Class Glass & Performance Inc
101 Winston St
Cumberland, MD 21502
800-774-3456 toll free
301-777-3456; FAX: 301-777-7044

body parts

See full listing in **Section Two** under **fiberglass parts**

Classic Auto Appraiser
24316 Carlton Ct
Laguna Niguel, CA 92677
800-454-1313; FAX: 949-425-1533
E-mail: classicauto64@home.com

appraisals

See full listing in **Section Two** under **appraisals**

Classic Auto Works
7301-1 Singleton Bend Rd
Travis Peak, TX 78654
PH/FAX: 512-267-3707
E-mail: classica@concentric.net

cars
parts
repairs

Mail order and open shop. Monday-Friday 10:30 am to 6:30 pm. We are a full service street rod shop dealing in street rods and custom cars from parts and repair to turnkey. We also offer complete paint and body service.

Classic Carriages
267 County Rd 420
Athens, TN 37303
PH/FAX: 423-744-7496

repair
restoration

See full listing in **Section Two** under **restoration shops**

Classic Coachworks Rod & Custom
7492 S Division Ave
Grand Rapids, MI 49548
616-455-8110
E-mail: classiccoachal@aol.com

parts
repairs
restoration

Mail order and open shop. Monday-Friday 8:30 am to 5:30 pm, Saturday 9 am to 1 pm. All years and makes rod, custom or show projects. Also repairs and partials, restorations. We are dealers for all major brand rod parts and restoration parts. In business since 1973. We do appraisals.

Coffey Classic Transmissions
310 Aviator Dr
Fort Worth, TX 76179
817-439-1611

transmissions

See full listing in **Section Two** under **transmissions**

Collector's Carousel
84 Warren Ave
Westbrook, ME 04092
207-854-0343; FAX: 207-856-6913

appraisals
sales
service

See full listing in **Section Two** under **car dealers**

Contemporary and Investment Automobiles
4115 Poplar Springs Rd
Gainesville, GA 30507
770-539-9111; FAX: 770-539-9818
E-mail: contemporaryauto@mindspring.com

buy/sell/trade
mechanical work
memorabilia

Buy, sell, trade, consign antique, classic, muscle, sport, kit, street rod, custom, race, any type of special interest cars, trucks and motorcycles. Over 120 cars in our enclosed facility in a northern suburb of Atlanta, GA. Also have a good selection of memorabilia. Do mechanical, body, paint, restoration and build street rods in our Georgia facility.

Custom Cut Auto Glass/ Southern Glass Inc
2605 Beltway 8
Pasadena, TX 77503
800-803-7778, 281-487-7778
FAX: 281-487-7779

glass

See full listing in **Section Two** under **glass**

Customs & Classics Inc
4674 S Brown St
Murray, UT 84107
801-288-1863; FAX: 801-288-1623
E-mail: kelley@customsandclassics.com

bodywork
painting
restoration
street rods

See full listing in **Section Two** under **restoration shops**

Dagel's Street Rods
1048 W Collins Ave
Orange, CA 92867
714-288-1445; FAX: 714-288-1400

parts
street rods

Mail order and open shop. Monday-Friday 9 am to 5 pm, Saturday 9 am to 12 pm. Deals in street rods, fifties and sixties cars and trucks. I sell parts and build complete turnkey cars and trucks. Dealer for Vintage Air, Zoops, Ididit, Borgeson, Painless Wiring, Lokar and many more.

**Russ Dentico's Sales &
Auto Appraisal Consulting**
PO Box 566
Trenton, MI 48183
734-675-3306; FAX: 734-675-8908

appraisals

See full listing in **Section Two** under **appraisals**

Deters Restorations
6205 Swiss Garden Rd
Temperance, MI 48182-1020
734-847-1820

restoration

See full listing in **Section Two** under **restoration shops**

Diamond Back Classics
Bill Chapman
4753 Hwy 90
Conway, SC 29526
888-922-1642; FAX: 843-399-3091
E-mail: diamondbackclassics@
worldnet.att.net

tires

See full listing in **Section Two** under **tires**

Don's Hot Rod Shop Inc
2811 N Stone Ave
Tucson, AZ 85705
520-884-8892; FAX: 520-628-1682

accessories
parts

Deals in high performance auto parts, street rod parts, gauges, chrome accessories, steering wheels, racing helmets, carbs, cams, headers and much more.

Energy Suspension
1131 Via Callejon
San Clemente, CA 92673
949-361-3935; FAX: 949-361-3940
E-mail: hyperflex@
energysuspension.com

suspension parts

See full listing in **Section Two** under **suspension parts**

Engine Master Conversions Ltd
32 W Strathmore Ave
Pontiac, MI 48340
248-745-0272

rwd conversions

Mail order only. We produce and retail rear wheel drive conversions for the Northstar 4.6L 32-valve V8 for use in street rods and classic cars.

Environmentally Safe Products Inc
313 W Golden Ln
New Oxford, PA 17350
800-289-5693; FAX: 717-624-7089
E-mail: heidiz@low-e.com

insulation

E-Z Cool stops heat, deadens sound and will not absorb moisture. A reflective insulation made with 1/4" polyethylene foam with 99% pure aluminum facing on both sides, it may be used in the firewall, floorboard, under headliners, in door panels, trunks and under the hood. Web site: www.reflectiveinsulation.com

EVA Sports Cars
RR 1
Vankleek Hill, ON Canada K0B 1R0
613-678-3377; FAX: 613-678-6110

kit cars

See full listing in **Section Two** under **kit cars & replicars**

Extreme Motorsports Painting Ltd
300 Old Reading Pike
Stowe, PA 19464
610-326-4425; FAX: 610-326-8522
E-mail: extrememail@aol.com

bodywork
painting

See full listing in **Section Two** under **painting**

Fairlane Automotive Specialties
210 E Walker St
St Johns, MI 48879
517-224-6460

fiberglass bodies
parts

See full listing in **Section One** under **Ford 1932-1953**

**Firewall Insulators & Quiet Ride
Solutions**
6465 Pacific Ave, Ste 249
Stockton, CA 95207
209-477-4840; FAX: 209-477-0918
E-mail: timcox@quietride.com

air plenums
auto insulation
firewall insulators
gloveboxes
sound deadening

See full listing in **Section Two** under **upholstery**

Flatlander's Hot Rods
1005 W 45th St
Norfolk, VA 23508
757-440-1932; FAX: 757-423-8601

chassis mfg
hot rods
parts
street rods

Open daily. Traditional and nostalgic hot rod parts. Manufacturer of 1932 Ford 5-w coupe and roadster bodies as well as complete chassis for 1928-1934 Ford cars and trucks. Also manufacture hot rod tubular axles and many related components for street rods 1928-1948. MasterCard, Visa, worldwide shipping. Our 23rd year. Catalog $3.

Fort Wayne Clutch & Driveline
2424 Goshen Rd
Fort Wayne, IN 46808
219-484-8505; FAX: 219-484-8605
E-mail: clutches@skyenet.net

axles
axleshafts
clutches
driveshafts

See full listing in **Section Two** under **clutches**

Freedom Street Rods
5890 Traffic Way
Atascadero, CA 93422
805-462-1934; FAX: 805-462-8621
E-mail: vonblekl@pacbell.net

parts

We stock all major lines of street rod, custom and early Ford and GM reproduction parts. 38 years in business. Check us for best prices, let our experience work for you. Web site: www.freedomstreetrods.com

The Glass House	glass
446 W Arrow Hwy #4	
San Dimas, CA 91773	
909-592-1078; FAX: 909-592-5099	

See full listing in **Section Two** under **glass**

Alan Grove Components Inc	a/c components
27070 Metcalf Rd	
Louisburg, KS 66053	
913-837-4368; FAX: 913-837-5721	

Mail order only. Manufacturer of a/c compressor, alternator and power steering pump brackets. Web site: www.alangrovecomponents.com

Grumpy's Old Cars	car dealer
396 Marsh St	
San Luis Obispo, CA 93401	
805-549-7875; FAX: 805-549-7877	
E-mail: slohot@hotmail.com	

See full listing in **Section Two** under **car dealers**

Guenther Graphics	artwork
PO Box 266	
LeClaire, IA 52753	
PH/FAX: 319-289-9010	
E-mail: artwork@guenthergraphics.com	

See full listing in **Section Two** under **artwork**

Haneline Products Co	gauges
PO Box 430	instrument panels
Morongo Valley, CA 92256	stainless parts
760-363-6597; FAX: 760-363-7321	trim parts

See full listing in **Section Two** under **accessories**

Hatfield Restorations	restoration
PO Box 846	
Canton, TX 75103	
903-567-6742; FAX: 903-567-0645	
E-mail: pathat@vzinet.com	

See full listing in **Section Two** under **restoration shops**

Hi-Town Automotive	street rod repairs
PO Box 381	
High Point, NC 27261	
336-259-1063; FAX: 336-869-5282	
E-mail: lstamey@northstate.net	

Mail order and open shop by appointment only. Repair and fabrication of street rod cars and parts.

High Performance Coatings	coatings
14788 S Heritagecrest Way	
Bluffdale, UT 84065	
800-456-4721, 801-501-8303	
FAX: 801-501-8315	
E-mail: hpcsales@hpcoatings.com	

See full listing in **Section Two** under **exhaust systems**

Hillcrest Hot Rods	custom cars
541 Mercer Rd	street rods
Greenville, PA 16125	
PH/FAX: 724-588-3444	

Open shop only. Monday-Saturday 9 am to 5 pm. Specializing in street rods and custom cars for 1903-60s. From small jobs to turnkey cars.

Horton	parts
244 Woolwich St S	
Breslau, ON Canada N0B 1M0	
519-648-2150; FAX: 519-648-3355	
E-mail: mail@horton.on.ca	

Mail order and open shop. Monday-Friday 8 am to 5 pm, Saturday by appointment. Deals in street rod parts and frames. Web site: www.horton.on.ca

The Hot Rod Shop	car dealer
16741 State Rd 1	chassis conversion
Spencerville, IN 46788	
219-627-5474; FAX: 219-627-6317	

Street rod and collector car dealer. 1941-1948 Ford to GM chassis conversion kit.

House of Powder Inc	powder coating
Rt 71 & 1st St, PO Box 110	sandblasting
Standard, IL 61363	
815-339-2648	

See full listing in **Section Two** under **service shops**

Hubbard Classic Car Appraisals	appraisals
1908 Belle Terr	
Bakersfield, CA 93304-4352	
661-397-7786	
E-mail: lynnhubbard@msn.com	

See full listing in **Section Two** under **appraisals**

Hunters Custom Automotive	accessories
975 Main St	engine parts
Nashville, TN 37206	fiberglass products
615-227-6584; FAX: 615-227-4897	

See full listing in **Section Two** under **accessories**

384 Section Two — Generalists   street rods

Hyde Products Inc PO Box 870321 New Orleans, LA 70187-0321 504-649-4041 E-mail: hydeprod@bellsouth.net	hood holders

See full listing in **Section One** under **Chevrolet**

ididit inc 610 S Maumee St Tecumseh, MI 49286 517-424-0577; FAX: 517-424-7293 E-mail: sales@ididitinc.com	steering columns

See full listing in **Section Two** under **steering columns**

Innovative Rod Products 28 Bruce Way Moundhouse, NV 89706 PH/FAX: 775-246-1718 E-mail: rick@innovativerod.com	body components chassis parts

See full listing in **Section Two** under **chassis parts**

Jackson & Wardick Hot Rods 749 Croton Lake Rd Bedford Corners, NY 10549-4230 914-666-2057 E-mail: wardj@bestweb.net	metal shaping

Open shop. Monday-Saturday 9 am to 5 pm. Metal shaping and finishing.

Jefferis Autobody 269 Tank Farm Rd San Luis Obispo, CA 93401 800-807-1937; FAX: 805-543-4757	windshield glass kit

See full listing in **Section Two** under **glass**

JLM Maud Rd, PO Box 1348 Palmer, AK 99645 907-745-4670; FAX: 907-745-5510 E-mail: jlmob@alaska.net	power window lifts

See full listing in **Section Two** under **glass**

KC's Rods & Customs 3500 Aloma Ave, Ste D-16 Winter Park, FL 32792 877-750-6350; FAX: 407-673-9131 E-mail: bobbyb@bellsouth.net	brakes exhaust systems restoration

Mail order and open shop. Monday-Saturday 8 am to 5 pm. Building and restoration of street rods, hot rods, muscle cars, customs & classic autos. Specialist in disc brake conversions for all cars and stainless steel exhaust. Major dealer for American Racing wheels. Web site: www.kcsrods.com

Keilen's Auto Restoring 580 Kelley Blvd (R) North Attleboro, MA 02760 508-699-7768	restoration

See full listing in **Section Two** under **restoration shops**

Kenny's Rod & Kustom 117 Milton Blvd Newton Falls, OH 44444 330-872-1932; FAX: 330-872-3332	conversion kits street rod parts

Mail order and open shop. Monday-Friday 9 am to 6 pm, Saturday 10 am to 2 pm. Specializing in the sale, retail/wholesale of street rod parts. We specialize in Mustang II front end conversion kits for cars of the 1930s, 1940s and 1950s.

King Bolt Co 4680 N Grand Ave Covina, CA 91724 626-339-8400; FAX: 626-339-8210	hardware

See full listing in **Section Two** under **hardware**

Koffel's Place II 740 River Rd Huron, OH 44839 419-433-4410; FAX: 419-433-2166	engine rebuilding machine shop

See full listing in **Section Two** under **engine rebuilding**

Kwiklift Inc 610 N Walnut Broken Arrow, OK 74012 800-961-5438; FAX: 918-259-1170 E-mail: sales@kwiklift.com	accessories lifts

See full listing in **Section Two** under **tools**

LaVine Restorations Inc 1349 Beech Rd Nappanee, IN 46550 219-773-7561; FAX: 219-773-7595 E-mail: lavine@bnin.net	restoration

See full listing in **Section Two** under **restoration shops**

Lee's Street Rods RR 3 Box 3061A Rome, PA 18837 570-247-2326 E-mail: lka41@epix.net	accessories parts restoration

Mail order and open shop. Monday-Friday 8 am to 5 pm, Saturday 8 am to 12 pm. Complete shop for street rods, kit cars, race cars and total restorations on antique and classic autos. A one stop shop for parts, upholstery, engine, speed equipment, etc, and accessories. Autos bought and sold.

Lone Wolf 9375 Bearwalk Path Brooksville, FL 34613 352-596-9949 E-mail: lonewolfwhistle@bigfoot.com	wolf whistles

See full listing in **Section Two** under **automobilia**

Mastercraft Body Works Inc 3602 Ovilla Rd Ovilla, TX 75154 972-617-0507; FAX: 972-617-3252 E-mail: schovanetz@aol.com	bodywork fabrication rust work

See full listing in **Section Two** under **coachbuilders & designers**

The Masters Company 30 Willow Dr, Ste A Fort Thomas, KY 41075-2035 800-385-5811; FAX: 859-441-6765 E-mail: rmasters3@home.com	parts tools

See full listing in **Section Two** under **tools**

Charlie Merrill 1041 Kenyon Rd Twin Falls, ID 83301 208-736-0949	broker car dealer car locator

See full listing in **Section Two** under **brokers**

Section Two – Generalists

Midwest Hot Rods Inc 10 E Main St (Rt 126) Plainfield, IL 60544 815-254-7637; FAX: 815-254-7640 E-mail: mwhr@aol.com	street rods service shops upholstery

Mail order and open shop. Monday-Wednesday and Friday 9 am to 6 pm, Thursday 9 am to 8 pm, Saturday 10 am to 2 pm. Street rods, muscle cars, upholstery shop, service shop, metal fabrication, sell parts, restorations. Web site: www.midwesthotrods.com

Mild to Wild Classics 1300 3rd St NW Albuquerque, NM 87102 505-244-1139; FAX: 505-244-1164	parts repairs restoration

Deals in parts and service for hot rod builders, classic and vintage restorations, modifications, repairs, offers a wild ride for a mild price. Building the past to the present since 1994. Web site: www.mildtowildclassics.com

MSC Fasteners 104 Oakdale Dr Zelienople, PA 16063 800-359-7166, 724-452-8003 FAX: 724-452-1145 E-mail: msc999@ccia.com	hardware

See full listing in **Section Two** under **hardware**

NCA Automotive 4532 W Palm Ln Phoenix, AZ 85035 PH/FAX: 602-278-6070 E-mail: ncaltec@netscape.net	restoration

See full listing in **Section Two** under **restoration shops**

Nostalgia Productions Inc 268 Hillcrest Blvd St Ignace, MI 49781 906-643-8087; FAX: 906-643-9784 E-mail: edreavie@nostalgia-prod.com	shows swap meets

See full listing in **Section Two** under **auctions & shows**

Obsolete Ford Parts Inc 8701 S I-35 Oklahoma City, OK 73149 405-631-3933; FAX: 405-634-6815 E-mail: info@obsoletefordparts.com	parts

See full listing in **Section One** under **Ford 1954-up**

Old Cabot Village 465 Cabot St Beverly, MA 01915 978-922-7142; FAX: 978-922-6917 E-mail: oldcabot@mediaone.net	neckties

See full listing in **Section Two** under **apparel**

P&J Automotive Inc 6262 Riverside Dr Danville, VA 24541 804-822-2211; FAX: 804-822-2213	bodies chassis parts

Mail order and open shop. Monday-Friday 8 am to 5 pm, other hours by appointment. Specializing in fiberglass car bodies and chassis parts for 1932, 1933, 1934, 1939/1940, 1940 Fords and 1951 Mercurys. Builders of turnkey street rods.

Paintwerks by Jeff Tischler PO Box 488 Tranquility, NJ 07879 PH/FAX: 973-579-9619 E-mail: paintwerks@webtv.net	pinstriping

See full listing in **Section Two** under **striping**

Paragon Models & Art 3570 North Rd North Fort Myers, FL 33917 941-567-0047; FAX: 941-567-1344 E-mail: info@myhotrod.com	artwork models

See full listing in **Section Two** under **automobilia**

Performance Automotive Warehouse 21001 Nordhoff St Chatsworth, CA 91311 818-678-3000; FAX: 818-678-3001	accessories engine parts

See full listing in **Section Two** under **engine parts**

Jack Podell Fuel Injection Spec 106 Wakewa Ave South Bend, IN 46617 219-232-6430; FAX: 219-234-8632 E-mail: podellsfi@aol.com	fuel system parts fuel system rebuilding

See full listing in **Section One** under **Corvette**

Pontiac Engines Custom Built E-mail: pontiacgregg@earthlink.net	custom built engines

See full listing in **Section One** under **Pontiac**

Power Effects® 1800H Industrial Park Dr Grand Haven, MI 49417 877-3POWRFX (376-9739) toll free 616-847-4200; FAX: 616-847-4210	exhaust systems

See full listing in **Section Two** under **exhaust systems**

Prestige Motors 120 N Bessie Rd Spokane, WA 99212 509-927-1041	car dealer

See full listing in **Section Two** under **car dealers**

Pro's Pick Rod & Custom 4210 Dixie Hwy Erlanger, KY 41018 PH/FAX: 859-727-9600 E-mail: gary@prospick.com	parts

Mail order and open shop. Tuesday-Friday 10 am to 7 pm, Saturday 10 am to 6 pm. Frame and suspension parts, body and body parts, interior parts, engine and driveline parts for street rods, hot rods and customs, 1950s and older. Web site: www.prospick.com

R/T Street Rods 230 E Landis St Coopersburg, PA 18036 610-282-1726; FAX: 610-282-1233	street rods

Open shop only. Monday-Friday 10 am to 8 pm, Saturday 9 am to 5 pm. Sale of turnkey street rods with an inventory of 60 cars at our location. Also are stocking dealer for 65 street rod manufacturers. We can sell the complete car or everything you need to build it. Web site: www.rtstreetrods.com

RB's Obsolete Automotive	parts

7711 Lake Ballinger Way
Edmonds, WA 98026-9163
425-670-6739; FAX: 425-670-9151
E-mail: rbobsole@gte.net

See full listing in **Section Two** under **comprehensive parts**

Red's Headers & Early Ford Speed Equipment	headers mechanical parts

22950 Bednar Ln
Fort Bragg, CA 95437-8411
707-964-7733; FAX: 707-964-5434
E-mail: red@reds-headers.com

See full listing in **Section One** under **Ford 1932-1953**

Rock Valley Antique Auto Parts	gas tanks

Rt 72 and Rothwell Rd, Box 352
Stillman Valley, IL 61084
815-645-2271; FAX: 815-645-2740

See full listing in **Section One** under **Ford 1932-1953**

Rod-1 Shop	street rods

210 Clinton Ave
Pitman, NJ 08071
609-228-7631; FAX: 609-582-5770
E-mail: atboz@webtv.net

Open shop only. Monday-Friday 7 am to 5 pm, weekends by appointment. Street rods, restorations of 1930, 1940, 1950 and 1960 cars, original or customs and muscle cars, turnkey or partial. Welding, wiring, performance, chassis modifications, front end installations, sheetmetal work and bodywork.

Rod Doors	door panels interior parts

PO Box 2160
Chico, CA 95927
530-896-1513; FAX: 530-896-1518
E-mail: sales@roddoors.com

See full listing in **Section Two** under **interiors & interior parts**

The Rod Factory	accessories suspension parts

3131 N 31st Ave
Phoenix, AZ 85017
602-269-0031
E-mail: laserjet@amug.org

Mail order and open shop. Monday-Friday 8 am to 5 pm, Saturday 9 am to noon Mountain time. Specializing in reproduction frames and suspension upgrades, accessories for 1928-1948 Ford car, 1928-1957 Ford truck, 1934-1954 Chevy car, 1936-1959 Chevy truck. Web site: www.rodfactory.com

Rod Shop Performance Center Inc	exhaust systems

1126 Rockledge Rd
Attalla, AL 35954
256-538-0376
E-mail: rodshop@rodshopperformance.com

See full listing in **Section Two** under **exhaust systems**

Rodster Inc	conversion kits

128 Center St #B
El Segundo, CA 90245
310-322-2767; FAX: 310-322-2761

Rodster street rods: the crowd pleasin', EZ buildin', EZ ownin' and EZ cruisin' rods you build on 1983-1994 Chevy S-10 Blazers. Roadster and sedan delivery kits available from $2,995-$7,695. Web site: www.rodster.com

Rollin' Review Magazine	magazine

PO Box 910
Alcoa, TN 37701
800-434-4132; FAX: 865-681-0174
E-mail: editorrrm@aol.com

See full listing in **Section Four** under **periodicals**

Rust Busters	rust repair

PO Box 341
Clackamas, OR 97015
503-223-3203
E-mail: info@rustbusters.com

See full listing in **Section Two** under **restoration shops**

Sanders Antique Auto Restoration	restoration

1120 22nd St
Rockford, IL 61108
815-226-0535

See full listing in **Section Two** under **restoration shops**

Joe Smith Ford & Hot Rod Parts	parts service

51 Lakewood Dr
Marietta, GA 30066
770-426-9850; FAX: 770-426-9854
E-mail: joesmithhotrod@yahoo.com

See full listing in **Section One** under **Ford 1932-1953**

So-Cal Speed Engineering	headers

PO Box 1421
Costa Mesa, CA 92628
714-979-7964

See full listing in **Section Two** under **exhaust systems**

Sparrow Auction Co	auction company

59 Wheeler Ave
Milford, CT 06460
203-877-1066
E-mail: sparrowauction@hotmail.com

See full listing in **Section Two** under **auctions & shows**

Specialized Street Rods	street rods

18101 Redondo Cir #M
Huntington Beach, CA 92648
714-841-2114; FAX: 714-841-2447
E-mail: specstrrods@earthlink.net

Shop open Monday-Friday 8 am to 5 pm, Saturday 8 am to 12 pm. Specializing in building street rods. Have been doing for 40 years.

Specialty Cars Inc	parts street rods

17211 Roseton Ave
Artesia, CA 90701
562-924-6904; FAX: 562-402-9544

Mail order and open shop. Monday-Thursday 8 am to 5:30 pm, Friday 10 am to 3 pm. Deals in all types of street rods. We make chassis, suspension parts and steering parts. We build complete turnkey cars. We repair and service street rods and race cars.

Specialty Power Window	power window kits windshield wiper kit

2087 Collier Rd
Forsyth, GA 31029
800-634-9801; FAX: 912-994-3124

Mail order and open shop. Monday-Friday 8 am to 5 pm Eastern time. Complete power window kits and windshield wiper kits for street rods, cars, trucks and kit cars. Web site: www.specialtypowerwindows.com

Steve's Auto Restorations — restoration
4440 SE 174th Ave
Portland, OR 97236
503-665-2222; FAX: 503-665-2225
E-mail: steve@realsteel.com

See full listing in **Section Two** under **restoration shops**

Stockton Wheel Service — wheel repair
648 W Fremont St
Stockton, CA 95203
209-464-7771, 800-395-9433
FAX: 209-464-4725
E-mail: sales@stocktonwheel.com

See full listing in **Section Two** under **wheels & wheelcovers**

Strange Motion Rod & Custom Construction Inc — customizing / design / fabrication
14696 N 350th Ave
Cambridge, IL 61238
309-927-3346
E-mail: strangemtn@cin.net

Award winning street rod and custom design, fabrication, concepts, paint and body. Full custom twin rail tubular chassis work. On-site upholstery shop. Parts distribution for all major brands. UPS shipping daily. Work has appeared in over 45 magazines worldwide.

Street Rod Engineering Inc — street rods
1960 Commander Dr
Lake Havasu City, AZ 86403
520-855-5616; FAX: 520-505-3740
E-mail: strodeng@pair.com

Web site: www.streetrodengineering.com

The Street Rod Place — fabrication / parts / repair
565-F Nucla Way
Aurora, CO 80011
303-367-8200

Open shop only. Monday-Friday 7 am to 4:30 pm, half day Saturday. Street rod repair, fabrication and construction, also street rod parts.

Tatom Custom Engines — engine rebuilding / machine shop
PO Box 2504
Mt Vernon, WA 98273
360-424-8314; FAX: 360-424-6717
E-mail: flatheads@tatom.com

See full listing in **Section Two** under **engine rebuilding**

Thompson Hill Metalcraft — metal forming / panel beating / welding
23 Thompson Hill Rd
Berwick, ME 03901
207-698-5756
E-mail: wpeach@thompsonhill.com

See full listing in **Section Two** under **sheetmetal**

Thunderbolt Traders Inc — battery cables
6900 N Dixie Dr
Dayton, OH 45414-3297
513-890-3344; FAX: 513-890-9403
E-mail: tbolt@erinet.com

See full listing in **Section One** under **Edsel**

Vibratech Inc (Fluidampr) — performance parts
11980 Walden Ave
Alden, NY 14004
716-937-3603; FAX: 716-937-4692

See full listing in **Section Two** under **engine parts**

Visibolts From Classic Safety Products — accessories
7131 Hickory Run
Waunakee, WI 53597
888-212-2163; FAX: 608-824-9200
E-mail: clovis@www.visibolts.com

See full listing in **Section Two** under **lighting equipment**

Webber Engineering LLC — street rods / welding
1 Alice Ct
Pawcatuck, CT 06379
860-599-8895; FAX: 860-599-8609
E-mail: kwebbereng@aol.com

See full listing in **Section Two** under **sheetmetal**

Wescott's Auto Restyling — body parts
19701 SE Hwy 212
Boring, OR 97009
800-523-6279; FAX: 503-658-2938
E-mail: marykarl@gte.net

See full listing in **Section One** under **Ford 1932-1953**

Kirk F White — models / tin toys
PO Box 999
New Smyrna Beach, FL 32170
386-427-6660; FAX: 386-427-7801
E-mail: kirkfwhite@mindspring.com

See full listing in **Section Two** under **models & toys**

Wilk-Bilt Cars — accessories / parts
Rt 1, Box 116
Ewing, VA 24248
PH/FAX: 540-445-4501
E-mail: wilkbilt@mounet.com

See full listing in **Section One** under **Ford 1932-1953**

Williams — parts / street rods
14770 Cooks Mill Rd
Humboldt, IL 61931
217-235-1758; FAX: 217-235-6258
E-mail: wilwel@advant.net or willtt@advant.net

Deals in street rods, customs, fabricates a full line of parts, builds cars in any stage, installs, fabrication work, chassis builder, retail store.

Wirth's Custom Automotive — custom accessories / fender skirts / spinner hubcaps
505 Conner St, PO Box 5
Prairie du Rocher, IL 62277
618-284-3359
E-mail: roywirth@htc.net

See full listing in **Section Two** under **accessories**

striping

BDI Automotive Design/Brandon — lettering / painting / pinstriping
13985 Madison Pk
Morningview, KY 41063
859-363-0086; FAX: 859-363-0081
E-mail: bdi@fuse.net

Open shop by appointment only, 8 am to 9 pm. Custom paint, lettering, pinstriping, graphics, new and used wheels for street rods, etc.

Section Two – Generalists

Ideal Signs
4033 Ridgeway Rd
Manchester, NJ 08759
732-657-0100; FAX: 732-323-0390
E-mail: idealsigns1@aol.com

lettering
painting
striping

See full listing in **Section Two** under **artwork**

Paintwerks by Jeff Tischler
PO Box 488
Tranquility, NJ 07879
PH/FAX: 973-579-9619
E-mail: paintwerks@webtv.net

pinstriping

Shop open by appointment only. Custom hand-painted pinstriping and monogramming. Specializing in street rods, kustoms, classic automobiles and motorcycles. Some traveling possible. Located in Newton, NJ, area. 28 years' experience.

The Pinstriper
19 Hope Ln
Narragansett, RI 02882
401-783-7701, RI; 407-668-9610, FL

pinstriping

Mail order and open shop. Saturday 10 am to 6 pm. Specialist in hand painted pinstripes, scroll or straight line. Your place or mine. 30+ years' experience; FL, RI, CT, MA.

Stencils & Stripes Unlimited Inc
1108 S Crescent Ave #21
Park Ridge, IL 60068
847-692-6893; FAX: 847-692-6895

NOS decals
stripe kits

See full listing in **Section Two** under **decals**

suspension parts

A-1 Shock Absorber Co
Shockfinders Division
365 Warren Ave, PO Box 2028
Silverthorne, CO 80498
800-344-1966, 970-389-3193 cell
FAX: 970-513-8283

shocks-all types
coil springs
Koni shocks
leaf springs
steering gears

Call Monday-Friday 9 am to 6 pm Mountain time and most Saturdays. Hard-to-find shock and spring specialists since 1936. We customize extra heavy duty, spring assist, air shocks, heavy duty shocks, steering dampners and Delco spiral shocks to fit any vehicle. Our specialty is the XHD shocks that have a 50% larger piston to give you better stability and control while maintaining a comfortable ride. Spring assist and air shocks add 1,000 lbs of lift. Coil and leaf springs are made to OEM specs or heavier, raised or lowered, lever shock rebuilding, Koni shock distributor, rebuilt power and manual steering gears, pumps, control valves and cylinders, many in stock. Great service and quality product. Web site: www.shockfinders.com
See our ad on the last page

Accurate Machine Products
20417 Earl St
Torrance, CA 90503
310-370-4075; FAX: 310-370-1035
E-mail: petrusg@ix.netcom.com

suspension
components

Specializing in suspension components, brake upgrades for Shelby Cobra, originals and replicas. Web site: www.cobraracing.com

Antique Auto Parts Cellar
6 Chauncy St, PO Box 3
South Weymouth, MA 02190
781-335-1579; FAX: 781-335-1925
E-mail: our1932@aol.com

brake/chassis/
engine parts
fuel pumps/kits
gaskets
water pumps

See full listing in **Section Two** under **comprehensive parts**

Apple Hydraulics Inc
1610 Middle Rd
Calverton, NY 11933-1419
800-882-7753, 631-369-9515
FAX: 631-369-9516
E-mail: info@applehydraulics.com

brake rebuilding
shock rebuilding

Mail order and open shop. Monday-Friday 8 am to 4:30 pm. Shock absorbers rebuilt, knee-action and lever type. Largest USA rebuilder of Delco, Armstrong, Girling, Houdaille, American, British and other vintage shocks 1909-1974. Brake cylinders sleeved and completely rebuilt, service includes brake masters, boosters, servos, wheel cylinders, and calipers. Fast service. Visa, MasterCard, COD orders welcome. Free catalog. Web site: www.applehydraulics.com

Atlas Obsolete Chrysler Parts
10621 Bloomfield St, Unit 32
Los Alamitos, CA 90720
PH/FAX: 562-594-5560
E-mail: atlaschrys@aol.com

parts

See full listing in **Section One** under **Mopar**

Baer Brake Systems
3108 W Thomas Rd #1201
Phoenix, AZ 85017
602-233-1411; FAX: 602-352-8445
E-mail: brakes@baer.com

brakes

See full listing in **Section Two** under **brakes**

Blaser's Auto, Nash, Rambler, AMC
3200 48th Ave
Moline, IL 61265-6453
309-764-3571; FAX: 309-764-1155
E-mail: blazauto@sprynet.com

NOS parts

See full listing in **Section One** under **AMC**

Bonk's Automotive Inc
4480 Lazelda Dr
Milan, MI 48160
800-207-6906; FAX: 734-434-0845
E-mail: bonkers@bonkauto.com

automotive tools

See full listing in **Section Two** under **tools**

C & G Early Ford Parts
1941 Commercial St, Dept AH
Escondido, CA 92029-1233
760-740-2400; FAX: 760-740-8700
E-mail: cgford@cgfordparts.com

accessories/chrome
emblems
literature
mechanical
weatherstripping

See full listing in **Section One** under **Ford 1932-1953**

California Pony Cars
1906 Quaker Ridge Pl
Ontario, CA 91761
909-923-2804; FAX: 909-947-8593
E-mail: 105232.3362@compuserve.com

parts

See full listing in **Section One** under **Mustang**

Chassis Engineering Inc
119 N 2nd St, Box 70
West Branch, IA 52358
319-643-2645; FAX: 319-643-2801

brakes
chassis parts
suspension parts

See full listing in **Section Two** under **chassis parts**

Chicago Corvette Supply
7322 S Archer Rd
Justice, IL 60458
708-458-2500; FAX: 708-458-2662

parts

See full listing in **Section One** under **Corvette**

Classic Chevrolet Parts Inc	parts
8723 S I-35	
Oklahoma City, OK 73149	
405-631-4400; FAX: 405-631-5999	
E-mail: info@classicchevroletparts.com	

See full listing in **Section One** under **Chevrolet**

Coil Spring Specialties	custom coil springs
632 W Bertrand	
St Mary's, KS 66536	
785-437-2025; FAX: 785-437-2266	
E-mail: info@coilsprings.com	

Mail order only. Deal in custom coil springs for all makes and models. Specializing in classic and muscle car applications. 100% calibrate to factory specifications so you get the right spring the first time. Can also custom make springs for any special application you may require.

See our ad on this page

Corvette America	accessories
Rt 322, PO Box 324	interiors
Boalsburg, PA 16827	parts
800-458-3475	
814-364-2141, foreign	
FAX: 814-364-9615, 24 hours	
E-mail: vettebox@corvetteamerica.com	

See full listing in **Section One** under **Corvette**

Corvette World	accessories
RD 9, Box 770, Dept H	parts
Greensburg, PA 15601	
724-837-8600; FAX: 724-837-4420	
E-mail: cvworld@sgi.net	

See full listing in **Section One** under **Corvette**

Greg Donahue Collector Car	parts
Restorations Inc	restoration
12900 S Betty Pt	
Floral City, FL 34436	
352-344-4329; FAX: 352-344-0015	

See full listing in **Section One** under **Ford 1954-up**

Dr Vette	brakes
14364 SW 139th Ct	fuel system parts
Miami, FL 33186	repairs
800-262-9595; FAX: 305-253-3641	

See full listing in **Section One** under **Corvettes**

Eaton Detroit Spring Service Co	bushings
1555 Michigan Ave	coil springs
Detroit, MI 48216	leaf springs
313-963-3839; FAX: 313-963-7047	shackles
E-mail: sales@eatonsprings.com	U-bolts

Mail order and open shop. Monday-Friday 8 am to 5:30 pm. Supply any leaf or coil spring for American cars and trucks from the 1902 curved dash Oldsmobile to present. With a library of over 20,000 OEM blueprints, can manufacture to OEM specs or custom make to your specs. Complete line of shackles, bushings and U-bolts. Web Site: www.eatonsprings.com

Energy Suspension	suspension parts
1131 Via Callejon	
San Clemente, CA 92673	
949-361-3935; FAX: 949-361-3940	
E-mail: hyperflex@	
energysuspension.com	

Polyurethane suspension components and mounts for a variety of cars and trucks. Products include control arm bushings, leaf spring bushings, sway bar bushings, bump stops, motor and transmission mounts and much more. Web site: www.energysuspension.com

ESPO Springs 'n Things	chassis parts
701 Pine Tree Rd	suspension parts
Danville, PA 17821	
800-903-9019; FAX: 570-672-0368	
E-mail: springsnthings@aol.com	

Mail order. Monday-Friday 8 am to 5:30 pm. Suspension parts, new leaf springs, coil springs, shackle kits, bushings, U-bolts, front end parts, most makes, models and years, generally 1950s to present with an expanding inventory of leafs/accessories for 1930s and 1940s. Leafs start at $90 pr, coils start at $50 pr. Visa, MasterCard, Discover or COD accepted. Shipped UPS. Web site: www.espo.com

Explicit Concepts Customs & Minis	aftermarket
Livonia, MI 48150	restyling
313-617-5433	
E-mail: vabruno@explicitconcepts.net	

See full listing in **Section Two** under **custom cars**

Five Points Classic Auto Shocks	shock absorbers
2911 A S Main	
Santa Ana, CA 92707	
714-979-0451; FAX: 714-241-3454	

Mail order and open shop. Monday-Friday 9 am to 5 pm. New hydraulic and gas charged shocks for all makes of cars and trucks, 1938-1975. Rebuild lever type shocks for all makes and models. Rebuild certain tubular shocks.

For Ramblers Only	accessories
2324 SE 34th Ave	parts
Portland, OR 97214	
503-232-0497	
E-mail: ramblers@teleport.com	

See full listing in **Section One** under **AMC**

Section Two – Generalists

Horton   parts
244 Woolwich St S
Breslau, ON Canada N0B 1M0
519-648-2150; FAX: 519-648-3355
E-mail: mail@horton.on.ca

See full listing in **Section Two** under **street rods**

K C Obsolete Parts   parts
3343 N 61
Kansas City, KS 66104
913-334-9479; FAX: 913-788-2795

See full listing in **Section One** under **Ford 1954-up**

Kenask Spring Co   springs
307 Manhattan Ave
Jersey City, NJ 07307
201-653-4589

Mail order and open shop. Monday-Saturday 9 am to 4 pm. Dealing in auto and truck leaf springs and coil springs, also all parts related to springs. Rubbers, bushings, U-bolts, shackles, hangers, pins, bolts, insulators, etc. Also install what we sell.

Roger Kraus Racing   shocks
2896 Grove Way   tires
Castro Valley, CA 94546   wheels
510-582-5031; FAX: 510-886-5605

See full listing in **Section Two** under **tires**

L B Repair   restoration
1308 W Benten
Savannah, MO 64485-1549
816-324-3913

See full listing in **Section One** under **Ford 1954-up**

Linearossa International Inc   parts
3931 SW 47th Ave
Ft Lauderdale, FL 33314
954-327-9888; FAX: 954-791-6555

See full listing in **Section One** under **Fiat**

LMC Truck   accessories
PO Box 14991   parts
Lenexa, KS 66285
800-222-5664; FAX: 913-599-0323

See full listing in **Section One** under **Chevrolet**

Mullins & Teardrop Reproductions   trailers
3330-B Mary Ln
Auburn, CA 95602
530-878-0407

See full listing in **Section Two** under **trailers**

Muskegon Brake & Dist Co   brakes
848 E Broadway   springs
Muskegon, MI 49444   suspensions
231-733-0874; FAX: 231-733-0635

See full listing in **Section Two** under **brakes**

Mustangs Plus Inc   racing products
2353 N Wilson Way   restoration
Stockton, CA 95205
800-999-4289; FAX: 209-944-9980

See full listing in **Section One** under **Mustang**

National Spring Co Inc   spring parts
1402 N Magnolia Ave   spring services
El Cajon, CA 92020
619-441-1901; FAX: 619-441-2460

Mail order and open shop. Monday-Friday 8 am to 6 pm, Saturday by appointment. Established 1947. Auto and truck leaf and coil spring parts and service for all years and makes of vehicles. We custom make springs for your vehicle per your front and rear weights and for the particular use of the vehicle.
See our ad on this page

Northwest Classic Falcons Inc   parts
1964 NW Pettygrove St
Portland, OR 97209
503-241-9454; FAX: 503-241-1964
E-mail: ron@nwfalcon.com

See full listing in **Section One** under **Ford 1954-up**

Nova Parts   NOS parts
PO Box 985   reproduction parts
Mount Washington, KY 40047   used parts
502-239-8487; FAX: 502-231-1397

See full listing in **Section One** under **Chevrolet**

Obsolete Ford Parts Inc   parts
8701 S I-35
Oklahoma City, OK 73149
405-631-3933; FAX: 405-634-6815
E-mail: info@obsoletefordparts.com

See full listing in **Section One** under **Ford 1954-up**

Performance Coatings   ceramic coatings
9768 Feagin Rd   engine parts
Jonesboro, GA 30236   suspension parts
770-478-2775; FAX: 770-478-1926
Email: gemobpci@mindspring.com

See full listing in **Section Two** under **exhaust systems**

Pole Position Racing Products   parts
2021 E 74th Ave, Unit J
Denver, CO 80229
303-286-8555; FAX: 303-286-8666
E-mail: sales@polepositionrp.com

See full listing in **Section Two** under **chassis parts**

Power Steering Services Inc   pumps
2347 E Kearney St   rack & pinion
Springfield, MO 65803   steering gearboxes
417-864-6676; FAX: 417-864-7103
E-mail: chip@powersteering.com

Rebuilt and new steering gearboxes for cars and trucks. Both power and manual steering gears available. Also quick ratio steering gear conversions for GM power steering gearboxes. New Borgeson steering universal joints and shafts. Power steering pumps. Ship everywhere. Web site: www.powersteering.com

Pro's Pick Rod & Custom   parts
4210 Dixie Hwy
Erlanger, KY 41018
PH/FAX: 859-727-9600
E-mail: gary@prospick.com

See full listing in **Section Two** under **street rods**

QA1 Precision Products Inc   suspension parts
21730 Hanover Ave
Lakeville, MN 55044
800-721-7761; FAX: 952-985-5679
E-mail: ehaines@qa1.net

High performance shock absorbers, struts, K-members, A-arms, springs, rod end and spherical bearings and related suspension components. Web site: www.qa1.net

RARE Corvettes   cars
Joe Calcagno   parts
Box 1080
Soquel, CA 95073
831-475-4442; FAX: 831-475-1115

See full listing in **Section One** under **Corvette**

Rare Parts Inc   suspension parts
621 Wilshire Ave
Stockton, CA 95203
209-948-6005; FAX: 209-948-2851
E-mail: rparts@rareparts.com

Mail order and open shop. Five days a week 8 am to 5 pm. Purchase and manufacture suspension parts for vehicles from 1930-1994. Distribute through all W/D, jobbers and auto repair/restoration businesses. Yes, we can manufacture! Give us your needs.

Red Bird Racing   parts
6640 Valley St
Coeur d'Alene, ID 83815
208-762-5305

See full listing in **Section One** under **Chevrolet**

Rick's First Generation Camaro   accessories
Parts & Accessories   parts
420 Athena Dr
Athens, GA 30601
8800-359-7717; FAX: 877-548-8581
E-mail: firstgen@negia.net

See full listing in **Section One** under **Chevelle/Camaro**

The Rod Factory   accessories
3131 N 31st Ave   suspension parts
Phoenix, AZ 85017
602-269-0031
E-mail: laserjet@amug.org

See full listing in **Section Two** under **street rods**

Solow Suspension   suspension parts
7731 NE 33rd Dr
Portland, OR 97211
503-288-5951; FAX: 503-288-5991
E-mail: dropshop99@hevanet.com

See full listing in **Section One** under **Chevrolet**

Specialty Cars Inc   parts
17211 Roseton Ave   street rods
Artesia, CA 90701
562-924-6904; FAX: 562-402-9544

See full listing in **Section Two** under **street rods**

Star Classics Inc   parts
7745 E Redfield #300
Scottsdale, AZ 85260
800-644-7827, 480-991-7495
FAX: 480-951-4096
E-mail: info@starclassics.com

See full listing in **Section One** under **Mercedes-Benz**

Steering Systems   steering cylinders
Disivion of A-1 Shock Absorber Co   steering gears
365 Warren Ave, PO Box 2028   steering pumps
Silverthorne, CO 80498   steering valves
800-344-1966, 970-389-3193 cell
FAX: 970-513-8283

See our ad on the last page

TA Motor AB   accessories
Torpslingan 21   parts
Lulea S 97347 Sweden
+46-920-18888; FAX: +46-920-18821

See full listing in **Section One** under **Cadillac/LaSalle**

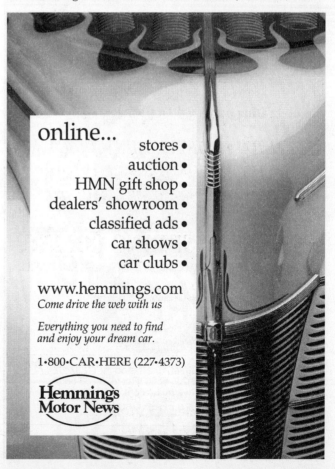

online...
stores •
auction •
HMN gift shop •
dealers' showroom •
classified ads •
car shows •
car clubs •

www.hemmings.com
Come drive the web with us

Everything you need to find and enjoy your dream car.

1•800•CAR•HERE (227•4373)

Hemmings Motor News

Section Two – Generalists

Thunderbird Headquarters
1080 Detroit Ave
Concord, CA 94518
925-825-9550 info; 925-689-1771
800-227-2174 parts
FAX: 800-964-1957 toll free
E-mail: tbirdhq@tbirdhq.com

accessories
literature
parts
upholstery

See full listing in **Section One** under **Thunderbird**

Vehicle Spring Service
7582 Industrial Way
Stanton, CA 90680
714-379-8077; FAX: 714-897-1892

springs
suspensions

Both mail order and open shop. Monday-Friday 8 am to 5 pm,
Saturday 8 am to 12 pm. Complete spring shop facility. Sell and
rebuild springs. New leaf springs and coils for all vehicles.
Custom rearching and rebuildling of leaf springs. Custom air
suspension conversions for RV and work vehicles.

Wheeler's Classic Parts
104 S Bowles
West Harrison, IN 47060
812-637-2194
E-mail: info@partsforclassics.com

parts

See full listing in **Section Two** under **brakes**

Xtreme Class CC
Philip Patrick
25607 McDonald
Dearborn Heights, MI 48125
313-477-6799; FAX: 313-291-5744
E-mail: xtremeclass@aol.com

interior work
stereo installation

See full listing in **Section Two** under **accessories**

Fine Tires for Collector Vehicles!

Coker Tire

1317 Chestnut Street, Chattanooga, TN 37402
Local & Int'l (423)265-6368 Fax (423)756-5607
www.coker.com
Call for a FREE Catalog!
1-800-251-6336
Code C177HMA0

tires

Big Boys Toys
Richard Boutin
Rt 67A, Box 174A
North Bennington, VT 05257
800-286-1721; FAX: 802-447-0962

accessories
bodywork
tires
wheels

See full listing in **Section Two** under **accessories**

Coker Tire
1317 Chestnut St
Chattanooga, TN 37402
800-251-6336 toll free
423-265-6368 local & international
FAX: 423-756-5607

tires

Call for a free catalog featuring authentic, original equipment
tires, tubes and flaps for Model Ts to muscle cars. Vintage
brands such as Firestone, Firestone Wide Oval, BF Goodrich
Silvertowns, Vintage Michelin and US Royal. Also available, the
world's first true wide whitewall radial tire as well as muscle car
and street rod wheels. Helpful sales staff, toll-free number and
major credit cards accepted. Web site: www.coker.com
See our ad on this page

Diamond Back Classics
Bill Chapman
4753 Hwy 90
Conway, SC 29526
888-922-1642; FAX: 843-399-3091
E-mail: diamondbackclassics@
worldnet.att.net

tires

Dealing in tires, steel belted radial wide white, redline/goldline/
whiteline, low rider, street rod, racing tires. Web site:
www.widewhitewalltires.com
See our ad on page 393

Greg's Wheel & Tire
11032 S Trudie Ave
Whittier, CA 90604
562-947-2346
E-mail: valvestems@aol.com

tools
valve stems

See full listing in **Section Two** under **wheels & wheelcovers**

**Hurst Racing Tires/
Traction By Hurst**
190 East Ave A, PO Box 278
Wendell, ID 83355
208-536-6236

drag tires
slicks

Deals in nostalgic slicks and cheater slicks, oval racing dirt and
asphalt, drag tires and McCoy artwork. Dealer for So-Cal Speed
Shop. Business started in 1961.

Kelsey Tire Inc
PO Box 564
Camdenton, MO 65020
800-325-0091; FAX: 800-845-7581
E-mail: kelsey@kelseytire.com

auto tires

Specializing in Goodyear and General vintage auto tires. Web
site: www.kelseytire.com

Roger Kraus Racing
2896 Grove Way
Castro Valley, CA 94546
510-582-5031; FAX: 510-886-5605

shocks
tires
wheels

Specialize in vintage race tires. Dunlop vintage, Goodyear vintage,
Englebert, Michelin, Avon and Hoosier. Wheels by American, PS
Engineering, Panasport, Jongbloed. Web site:
www.rogerkrausracing.com

Neumaclassic   tires
Ayacucho 1292
Rosario Sta Fe 2000 Argentina
+54 341 425-0040
FAX: +54 341 421-9629
E-mail: bcdcs@bcd.com.ar

Supplier of vintage and classic tires to the collector car hobby.
Web site: www.neumaclassic.com.ar

Performance Designed   valve stems
11032 S Trudie Ave
Whittier, CA 90604
562-947-2346
E-mail: valvestems@aol.com

We manufacture billet aluminum tire valve stems for street,
strip, show and off-road, in 6 colors: chrome, clear, red, blue,
black and gold.

Prestige Thunderbird Inc   appraisals
10215 Greenleaf Ave   radios
Santa Fe Springs, CA 90670   repairs
800-423-4751, 562-944-6237   restorations
FAX: 562-941-8677   tires
E-mail: tbirds@prestigethunderbird.com

See full listing in **Section One** under **Thunderbird**

Quality Tire Barn Inc   tires
255 Twinsburg Rd
Northfield, OH 44067
330-467-1284
FAX: 330-467-1289 (call first)
E-mail: donquist@aol.com

Specializing in hard-to-get antique auto and truck tires from
1930-1960, 30 Sayors and Schoville 4-door vans, 30 Jordan 4-
door, 29 Chrysler 4-door, 31 Hupmobile and electric Volkswagens.

Rideable Antique Bicycle Replicas   bicycles
2329 Eagle Ave   spokes
Alameda, CA 94501   tires
510-769-0980; FAX: 510-521-7145
E-mail: hiwheel@barrongroup.com

See full listing in **Section Two** under **motorcycles**

Smartire Systems Inc   gauges
13151 Vanier Pl, Ste 150
Richmond, BC Canada V6V 2J1
604-276-9884; FAX: 604-276-2350
E-mail: info@smartire.com

See full listing in **Section Two** under **accessories**

The Tire Source Inc   race tires
2828 30th St
Boulder, CO 80301
303-443-3021; 800-422-8473
FAX: 303-449-9842

Mail order and open shop. Monday-Friday 8-5:30, Saturday 8-2.
Dealing in Goodyear vintage race tires.

Tire & Wheel Emporium   tires
6416-C Franklin Blvd
Sacramento, CA 95823
916-424-4700; FAX: 916-424-1012
E-mail: wheelbrokers@earthlink.net

Mail order and open shop. Monday-Friday 8:30 am to 5:30 pm,
Saturday 9 am to 3 pm. Wide whitewall radial tires in 70 sizes,
vintage style wheels, aftermarket wheelcovers, Ford and Chevy
fender skirts, miscellaneous accessories. Web site:
www.tireandwheelbrokers.com

Section Two – Generalists

Universal Vintage Tire Co | tires
2994 Elizabethtown Rd
Hershey, PA 17033
800-233-3827; FAX: 717-534-0719

Mail order and open shop. Monday-Friday 8 am to 5 pm. Established 1968. Knowledgeable sales staff. Tires for vintage and classic automobiles. Also tubes with metal valve stems, authentic hardware and brass runningboard trim. Web site: www.universaltire.com

Wallace W Wade Specialty Tires | tires
530 Regal Row, PO Box 560906
Dallas, TX 75356
800-666-TYRE, 214-688-0091
FAX: 214-634-8465
E-mail: wwwadest@earthlink.net

Mail order and open shop. Monday-Friday 8:30 am to 5:30 pm, most Saturdays, appointments preferred. Antique, vintage and classic auto tires in many brands, plus obsolete Michelin tires, military ND tires. Tire chains, repair materials for tires, metal valve caps and brass valve stem covers, patches, boots. Antique truck tires, vintage tractor tires, tires for cannons, pedal car tires, turf and lawn tires, vintage racing tires. Checker flags and pennants, race track flags, car club pennants. Flags for all countries. Web site: www.wallacewade.com

 tools

A & I Supply | tools
401 Radio City Dr
N Pekin, IL 61554
800-260-2647; FAX: 309-382-1420

Mail order and open shop. Monday-Friday 8 am to 5 pm, Saturday 9 am to 1 pm. Stock your shop with 15,000 different tools and equipment. Name brand hand tools, body shop tools, air tools, power tools, air compressors, abrasives specialty tools, sheetmetal equipment and all type of shop equipment.

Accessible Systems Inc | lifts
440 Matson Rd
Jonesborough, TN 37659
423-975-8907; FAX: 423-975-8908
E-mail: sales@accessiblesystems.com

Open shop. Monday-Saturday 8 am to 6 pm. Rotating lifts, tilters and accessories. Web site: www.accessiblesystems.com

Arrow Fastener Co Inc | nail guns / rivet tools / staple guns
271 Mayhill St
Saddle Brook, NJ 07663

Manufacturer of precision built staplers, rivet tools, staple and nail guns, hot melt glue guns, staples, nails, adhesives and rivets. Web site: www.arrowfastener.com

AutoLifters | lifts
3450 N Rock Rd, Bldg 500, Ste 507
Wichita, KS 67226
800-759-0703; FAX: 316-630-0015

Backyard Buddy Corp | automotive lift
140 Dana St
Warren, OH 44483
800-837-9353, 330-395-9372
FAX: 330-392-9311

See full listing in **Section Two** under **accessories**

Bonk's Automotive Inc | automotive tools
4480 Lazelda Dr
Milan, MI 48160
800-207-6906; FAX: 734-434-0845
E-mail: bonkers@bonkauto.com

Universal automotive work stand, power lift transmission stand and specialty automotive tools. Web site: www.bonkauto.com

California Car Cover Co | accessories / apparel / car covers / tools
9525 DeSoto
Chatsworth, CA 91311
800-423-5525; FAX: 818-998-2442

See full listing in **Section Two** under **car covers**

C'NC Sheetmetal | car casters / patterns
11790 FM 3270
Tyler, TX 75708
800-668-1691; FAX: 903-877-2060
E-mail: cncsmetal@aol.com

See full listing in **Section Two** under **restoration aids**

Custom Bandsaw Blades | bandsaw blades
103 N High St
Muncie, IN 47308-0543
800-378-0761; FAX: 317-289-2889
E-mail: aemmjgray@aol.com

Mail order and open shop. Monday-Friday 8 am to 4 pm Eastern time. Bandsaw blades made to custom lengths to fit any machine. Large selection of blade material in stock.

Danspeed | filters / gauges / ignition parts
5831 Date Ave
Rialto, CA 92377
909-873-5804, FAX: 909-875-7610
E-mail: danspeedtwo@aol.com

See full listing in **Section Two** under **instruments**

Daytona MIG | plasma cutters / welders
1821 Holsonback Dr
Daytona Beach, FL 32117
800-331-9353; FAX: 904-274-1237
E-mail: ask@daytonamig.com

Mail order sales for 15 years and now online. The pioneers in providing welding and plasma cutting equipment to the auto hobbyist/restorer and professional body shops. From portable machines to industrial heavy duty equipment, all consumables and accessories. Our technical sales department will help you choose the correct machine for your projects. Our technicians will help you maintain your equipment and achieve your project goals. Nobody offers you more. Web site: www.daytonamig.com

The Eastwood Company | automotive tools / powder coating / welding supplies
263 Shoemaker Rd
Pottstown, PA 19464
800-345-1178; FAX: 610-323-6269

Extensive offering of unique automotive tools and supplies for restoring or customizing collector vehicles. Products include hot coat powder coating, specialty coatings, buffing, welding supplies and more. Web site: www.eastwoodcompany.com

Enthusiast's Specialties | automobilia
350 Old Connecticut Path
Framingham, MA 01701
800-718-3999; FAX: 508-872-4914
E-mail: alvis1934@aol.com

See full listing in **Section Two** under **automobilia**

Section Two – Generalists

Fast Lane Products
PO Box 7000-50
Palos Verdes Peninsula, CA 90274
800-327-8669; FAX: 310-541-2235
E-mail: info@fastlaneproducts.com

chamois
cleaners & waxes
drain tubs
hand wringers

See full listing in **Section Two** under **car care products**

Frost Auto Restoration
Techniques Ltd
Crawford St
Rochdale OL16 5NU United Kingdom
44-1706-658619
FAX: 44-1706-860338
E-mail: order@frost.co.uk

car care products
paints
tools

Mail order and open shop. Monday-Friday 8:30 am to 5 pm. Deals in specialist tools, paints, car care products, machinery and equipment for auto restoration and fabrication. Web site: www.frost.co.uk

Goodson Shop Supplies
156 Galewski Dr
Winona, MN 55987
800-533-8010; FAX: 507-452-2907
E-mail: orderdesk@goodson.com

tools

Mail order and open shop. Monday-Friday 8 am to 5 pm. Goodson stocks and sells over 8,000 tools and supplies for rebuilding import, aluminum and domestic cylinder heads, short blocks, flywheels, crankshafts and brakes. Web site: www.goodson.com

Green Oak Enterprises Inc
12166 Andresen Dr
South Lyon, MI 48178
888-721-9595

car dollies

Mail order only. Aluminum car dolly sets. Web site under construction: www.car-dolly.com

Griot's Garage
3500-A 20th St E
Tacoma, WA 98424
800-345-5789; FAX: 888-252-2252

car care products
paint
tools

Offering the finest in products for the automotive enthusiast. Premium car care, the finest in detailing supplies, garage organizational items, quality US and European tools, non-lifting concrete floor paint, unique automotive accessories. Over 2,500 products for your car, motorcycle and garage. Call today for a free handbook. Web site: www.griotsgarage.com

Grizzly Industrial Inc
2406 Reach Rd
Williamsport, PA 17701
800-523-4777; FAX: 800-438-5901
E-mail: csr@grizzly.com

tools

Grizzly Industrial Inc is proud to announce the publication of its year 2001 catalog. This free catalog with 436 pages features many new and exciting woodworking and metalworking tools and accessories. Grizzly's huge product selection caters to all ability levels of woodworkers and metalworkers from the home hobby shop to the industrial production shop. All products featured in this catalog are also available on Grizzly's expansive web site at: www.grizzly.com

HTP America Inc
3200 Nordic Rd
Arlington Heights, IL 60005-4729
800-USA-WELD toll free
FAX: 877-HTPS-FAX
E-mail: sales@htpweld.com

welding tools

Mail order and open shop. Monday-Friday 9 am to 5:30 pm. Selling mig welders, plasma cutters, metalworking tools, welding supplies and related equipment to body shops, garages, home restorers, street rodders and hobbyists. Web site: www.htpweld.com

Jacobs Electronics
500 N Baird St
Midland, TX 79701
915-685-3345, 800-627-8800
FAX: 915-687-5951
E-mail: retsales@marshill.com

ignition systems

See full listing in **Section Two** under **ignition parts**

Kaddies Inc
PO Box 342
Walnut Creek, CA 94597
925-934-4488; FAX: 925-934-4492
E-mail: tshette@pacbell.net

portable storage
tool kaddies

See full listing in **Section Two** under **storage**

Kingsbury Dolly Co Inc
128 Kingsbury Rd
Walpole, NH 03608
800-413-6559; FAX: 603-756-4767
E-mail: sales@kingdolly.com

dollies

Save your back. Move heavy objects quick and easy with Kingsbury Shop Dollies. Motors, transmissions, anything heavy and if you need to move a car, you can do that too. Multi-purpose shop tool allows you to easily move up to 4,000 pounds with 4 dollies. Great for project cars, restoration jobs and more. Satisfaction guaranteed or your money back. 2-year warranty. Web site: www.kingdolly.com

Kwiklift Inc
610 N Walnut
Broken Arrow, OK 74012
800-961-5438; FAX: 918-259-1170
E-mail: sales@kwiklift.com

accessories
lifts

Mail order and open shop. Monday-Friday 8 am to 6 pm Central time. Kwiklift manufactures and sells a series of portable auto and industrial lifts and accessories. Prices start at just $995. Web site: www.kwiklift.com

Lake Buchanan Industries Inc
400 Carlson Cir
Buchanan Dam, TX 78609
888-552-5278 toll-free
512-793-2867; FAX: 512-793-2869
E-mail: lbi:@tstar.net

blasting cabinet

Mail order and open shop. Monday-Friday 8 am to 5 pm. Offering the Barrel Blaster™, an affordable abrasive blasting cabinet for the automotive restorer, only $299. Web site: www.barrelblaster.com

LEX-AIRE Nationwide Sales
34 Hutchinson Rd
Arlington, MA 02474
800-LEX-AIRE; FAX: 562-691-9374

painting equipment
turbine systems

HVLP spray painting equipment, complete HVLP turbine systems, HVLP spray guns for air compressors. Web site: www.lexaire.com

PK Lindsay Co Inc
63 Nottingham Rd
Deerfield, NH 03037
800-258-3576; FAX: 800-843-2974
E-mail: sales@pklindsay.com

paint removal
rust removal

See full listing in **Section Two** under **rust removal & stripping**

Mac's Custom Tie-Downs
105 Sanderson Rd
Chehalis, WA 98532
800-666-1586 orders
360-748-1180; FAX: 360-748-1185

automotive
tie-downs

See full listing in **Section Two** under **trailers**

Malm Chem Corp	**polish**
PO Box 300, Dept HVA	**wax**
Pound Ridge, NY 10576	
914-764-5775; FAX: 914-764-5785	
E-mail: jkolin@cloud9.net	

See full listing in **Section Two** under **car care products**

The Masters Company	**parts**
30 Willow Dr, Ste A	**tools**
Fort Thomas, KY 41075-2035	
800-385-5811; FAX: 859-441-6765	
E-mail: rmasters3@home.com	

Deal in automotive shop equipment, distributor testers, engine and gas analyzers, etc. Buy, sell, repair, trade parts.

Mill Supply Inc	**clips**
PO Box 28400	**fasteners**
Cleveland, OH 44128	**panels**
800-888-5072; FAX: 888-781-2700	
E-mail: info@millsupply.com	

See full listing in **Section Two** under **sheetmetal**

Myk's Tools	**engine hoists**
365 Sunnyvale St	**engine removal tool**
Coos Bay, OR 97420	
541-267-6957; FAX: 541-267-5967	
E-mail: mykel@harborside.com	

Mike Pothoff, the owner of Myk's Tools, has been in the metal fabrication industry for 38 years. He has been producing the pivot plate since 1991 and has thousands in use worldwide. Special adapters can be made for applications that may not be covered in the current product line. The engine hoist, Pivot Plate, is used to remove and replace a complete V8 engine and transmission from all older cars and trucks as well as street rods and race cars. It will work on Ford flathead V8s, Corvette fuel injection and electronic fuel injected engines of Ford and GM too. It also works on the Jaguar six-cylinder engine. Web site: www.myks-tool.com

Northern Tool & Equipment	**engines**
PO Box 1219	**generators**
Burnsville, MN 55337-0219	**hydraulics**
800-533-5545	

Mail order and open shop. Where the pros and handymen shop. It's your #1 source for generators and engines, name brand power, air and hand tools, air compressors and welders, log splitters and chainsaws, lawn and garden equipment and accessories, pressure washers and spraying equipment, trailers, trailer parts and winches, hydraulics and more. Save up to 50%. Web site: www.northerntool.com

PE/Snappin Turtle Tie-Down Straps	**locks**
641 Bethlehem Pike	**tie-down straps**
Colmar, PA 18951	**winches**
800-TIE-DOWN; FAX: 215-822-0161	

See full listing in **Section Two** under **trailers**

Pole Position Racing Products	**parts**
2021 E 74th Ave, Unit J	
Denver, CO 80229	
303-286-8555; FAX: 303-286-8666	
E-mail: sales@polepositionrp.com	

See full listing in **Section Two** under **chassis parts**

Production Tool Supply of Ohio	**abrasives**
10801 Brookpark Rd	**compressors**
Cleveland, OH 44130	**cutting tools**
216-265-0000 local	**hand tools**
800-362-0142 nationwide	**machinery**
FAX: 216-265-0094	**shop supplies**
E-mail: cleveland.mgr@ptf-tools.com	

Mail order and open shop. Monday-Friday 8 am to 5 pm, Saturday 8 am to 12 noon. Full stocking distributor of over 190,000 tools of all kinds, available at discounts of up to 70% off list prices. 1,600-plus page catalog available free. Deal in tools, abrasives, machine tools, compressors, cutting tools, woodworking tools, hand tools, shop supplies. Visa, MasterCard and COD shipments daily. UPS free for orders over $50. Call or e-mail for free catalog.

RD Enterprises Ltd	**parts**
290 Raub Rd	
Quakertown, PA 18951	
215-538-9323; FAX: 215-538-0158	
E-mail: rdent@rdent.com	

See full listing in **Section One** under **Lotus**

Re-Flex Border Marker	**border markers**
138 Grant St	**posts**
Lexington, MA 02173	
781-862-1343	

See full listing in **Section Two** under **hardware**

RJ Tool & Supply	**abrasives**
917 State Ave	**instruments**
Cincinnati, OH 45204	**tools**
513-921-1356; FAX: 513-921-3592	
E-mail: robert@rjtool.com	

Automotive specialty tools, abrasives, precision instruments, pneumatic tools and accessories. Web site: www.rjtool.com

Sherco Auto Supply	**bulbs**
3700 NW 124th Ave, Ste 114	**electrical wire**
Coral Springs, FL 33065	**fuses**
954-344-1993; FAX: 954-344-2664	
E-mail: parts@sherco-auto.com	

See full listing in **Section Two** under **electrical systems**

Smithy Company	**tools**
170 Aprill Dr, PO Box 1517	
Ann Arbor, MI 48106	
800-476-4849; FAX: 800-431-8892	

Machine tools for the garage mechanic: latches, mills, drills, combination machines, tooling and accessories. Web site: www.smithy.com

Steck Manufacturing Co Inc	**tools**
1115 S Broadway	
Dayton, OH 45408	
800-227-8325; FAX: 937-222-6666	
E-mail: steckmfgco@earthlink.net	

Mail order and open shop. Monday-Friday 8 am to 4 pm. Hand tools for collision repair, body restoration and painting. Also manufacture affordable 4-wheel alignment equipment and heavy pulling equipment. Web site: www.steckmfg.com

Steelman/JS Products	**tools**
5440-B S Procyon Ave	
Las Vegas, NV 89118	
800-255-7011; FAX: 702-362-5084	
E-mail: jsprodnlv@aol.com	

Mail order and open shop. Monday-Friday 8 am to 5 pm. We manufacture and sell electronic listening tools for the engine and chassis of an automobile. We make Krypton lights that fit into very tiny places, a hands-free flashlight and a special lighted screwdriver set and a lighted socket. Drop forged plier sets with a lifetime warranty. Many other unique one of a kind products.

| Superior Equipment
326 S Meridian
Valley Center, KS 67147
800-526-9992; FAX: 316-755-4391
E-mail: mail@superlifts.com | auto lifts
shop tools |

Mail order and open shop. Monday-Friday 8 am to 5 pm Central time. Auto lifts, service equipment and shop tools. Web site: www.superlifts.com

| TP Tools & Equipment
7075 Rt 446, PO Box 649
Canfield, OH 44406
330-533-3384 local, 800-321-9260 | abrasive blasters
air compressors
tools
welders |

See full listing in **Section Two** under **restoration aids**

| Tru-Cut Automotive
75 Elm Ave
Salem, OH 44460-2627
800-634-7267; FAX: 330-332-5326
E-mail: trucut@mindspring.com | car ramps
jacks
lug wrenches |

Mail order only. Makers of domestic lift and support products such as Ultra-Ramps™, car ramps, jack stands, scissor jacks, lug wrenches and garage accessories. Web site: www.autoramps.com

| Valco Cincinnati Consumer Products Inc
411 Circle Freeway Dr
Cincinnati, OH 45246
513-874-6550; FAX: 513-874-3612 | adhesives
detailing products
sealants
tools |

Sole manufacturer of the Tube-Grip™, a patented 14-gauge steel tool which applies 10 times more pressure to a flexible tube than squeezing by hand, it allows you to squeeze 96% of the material out of the tube. In addition, Valco offers a complete line of high quality sealants, adhesives, detailers, lubricants and thread lockers for automotive applications. Web site: www.valco-cp.com

| WD-40 Company
PO Box 80607
San Diego, CA 92138
619-275-1400; FAX: 619-275-5823 | lubricants |

See full listing in **Section Two** under **lubricants**

| WELD USA
862 Farmington Ave #230
Bristol, CT 06010
860-826-6662, 800-WELD-USA
FAX: 860-826-5500 | metal working
tools
welders
welding accessories |

E-commerce only. On-line ordering 24 hours a day 7 days a week. The fabricator's source for affordable welding accessories, consumables, torch outfits, metalworking tools, clamps, abrasives, safety equipment and more. Visa, MasterCard accepted. Web site: www.weldusa.com

| Williams Lowbuck Tools Inc
4175 California Ave
Norco, CA 91760
909-735-7848; FAX: 909-735-1210
E-mail: wlowbuck@aol.com | tools |

Mail order and open shop. Monday-Friday 9 am to 4 pm. Deal in metal fabricating tools for tubing and sheetmetal. Web site: www.lowbucktools.com

Get-Away!

tops

| Accurate Auto Tops & Upholstery Inc
Miller Rd & W Chester Pike
Edgemont, PA 19028
610-356-1515; FAX: 610-353-8230 | tops
upholstery |

See full listing in **Section Two** under **upholstery**

| Auto-Mat Co
69 Hazel St
Hicksville, NY 11801
800-645-7258 orders
516-938-7373; FAX: 516-931-8438
E-mail: browner5@ix.netcom.com | accessories
carpet sets
interiors
tops
upholstery |

See full listing in **Section Two** under **interiors & interior parts**

| California Convertible Co
1950 Lindsley Park Dr
San Marcos, CA 92069-3337
760-739-9833 | top frames and
parts |

Mail order and open shop. Monday-Friday 8 am to 4:30 pm. For American convertibles only. Top frame parts.

| Classtique Upholstery Supply
PO Box 278-H
Isanti, MN 55040
763-444-4025, 763-444-3768
FAX: 763-444-9980 | carpet sets
headliners |

See full listing in **Section Two** under **interiors & interior parts**

| Classtique Upholstery & Top Co
PO Box 278 HK
Isanti, MN 55040
763-444-4025; FAX: 763-444-9980 | top kits
upholstery kits |

See full listing in **Section One** under **Ford 1903-1931**

| Concours d'Elegance Upholstery
1607 Pine Ridge
Bushkill, PA 18324
888-ELEG-UPH
PH/FAX: 570-588-0969
E-mail: concoursuph@enter.net | upholstery |

See full listing in **Section Two** under **upholstery**

| Convertible Service
5126-HA Walnut Grove Ave
San Gabriel, CA 91776
800-333-1140, 626-285-2255
FAX: 626-285-9004 | convertible parts
manufacture &
service
top mechanism |

For domestic cars from 1946-present. Manufacture and sell convertible top mechanism replacement parts. 6 and 12-volt electric and hydraulic top motors, hydraulic top lift cylinders and window lift cylinders, hose assemblies, top latches, relays, top switches, folding top frames. Distributor for Metro Molded Parts. Convertible top weatherstripping sets and weatherstripping and rubber parts in general. Most parts shipped same day. Overnight delivery available. Send $1 (to cover postage) and we'll send you our catalog of convertible parts. Web site: www.convertibleparts.com

| Dom Corey Upholstery & Antique Auto
1 Arsene Way
Fairhaven Business Park
Fairhaven, MA 02719
508-997-6555 | carpets/seats
conv tops
dash covers
door panels
headliners
upholstery |

See full listing in **Section Two** under **interiors & interior parts**

Durabuilt Automotive Hydraulics
808 Meadows Ave
Canon City, CO 81212
PH/FAX: 719-275-1126

| hose assemblies pumps, top cylinders valves window cylinders |

For over 12 years we have provided quality hydraulic products to restoration shops, car owners and museums. Our components are on daily drivers and show-winning vehicles throughout the world. Manufacture new pumps, valves, window cylinders, top cylinders and hose assemblies. Our rebuilt original pumps and valves perform and look like new. Can help with any 1930s-1990s American or European vehicle. All backed by the best warranty and competitive pricing.

Hampton Coach
6 Chestnut St, PO Box 6
Amesbury, MA 01913
888-388-8726, 978-388-8047
FAX: 978-388-1113
E-mail: lbb-hc@greenet.net

| fabrics interior kits top kits |

See full listing in **Section One** under **Chevrolet**

Hydro-E-Lectric
5475 Williamsburg Dr, Unit 8
Punta Gorda, FL 33982
800-343-4261; FAX: 941-639-0376

| convertible top parts power window parts |

Carry canvas and vinyl tops, carpets, weatherstrip and a full line of convertible top and power window parts for US and foreign cars from 1946-present day. All parts are new. Please call for information. Web site: www.hydroe.com
See our ad on this page

Koala International
PO Box 255
Uwchland, PA 19480
610-458-8395; FAX: 610-458-8735
E-mail: sales@koala-products.com

| convertible cleaners & protectants plastic coating plastic polish |

See full listing in **Section Two** under **car care products**

LeBaron Bonney Co
6 Chestnut St, PO Box 6
Amesbury, MA 01913
800-221-5408, 978-388-3811
FAX: 978-388-1113
E-mail: lbb-hc@greenet.net

| fabrics interior kits top kits |

See full listing in **Section One** under **Ford 1903-1931**

Markel's Auto Upholstery
1163 S Robertson Blvd
Los Angeles, CA 90035
310-274-1501

| upholstery |

See full listing in **Section Two** under **upholstery**

Ray's Upholstering
600 N St Frances Cabrini Ave
Scranton, PA 18504
800-296-RAYS; FAX: 570-963-0415

| partial/total restoration |

See full listing in **Section Two** under **restoration shops**

Ridgefield Auto Upholstery
34 Bailey Ave
Ridgefield, CT 06877
203-438-7583; FAX: 203-438-2666

| interiors tops |

See full listing in **Section Two** under **interiors & interior parts**

SL-TECH 230SL-250SL-280SL
1364 Portland Rd, US Rt 1
Arundel/Kennebunkport, ME 04046
207-985-3001; FAX: 207-985-3011
E-mail: gernold@sltechw113.com

| parts restoration service |

See full listing in **Section One** under **Mercedes-Benz**

Smooth Line
2562 Riddle Run Rd
Tarentum, PA 15084
724-274-6002; FAX: 724-274-6121

| body panels removable hardtops |

Mail order only. Monday-Friday 9 am to 5 pm. World's largest selection of removable hardtops for sports cars. Change your convertible into a GT coupe in minutes. Enjoy the best of both. Quiet and secure. New restoration body panels now available. Save. Austin-Healey, Fiats, Triumph, Datsun Z, MG, A, B, Midget. High-performance composites end rust forever. Premium quality. Fully guaranteed. Web site: www.smoothline.com

The Bill Stevenson Company
PO Box 5037
Kent, WA 98064-5368
253-852-0584; FAX: 253-854-7520

| hood insulation |

Mail order and open shop. 1941-1986 hood insulation. Fast service.

Ultimate Appearance Ltd
113 Arabian Trail
Smithfield, VA 23430
888-446-3078; FAX: 757-255-2620

| cleaners detailing products detailing services polish/wax |

See full listing in **Section Two** under **car care products**

Willow Grove Auto Top
43 N York Rd
Willow Grove, PA 19090
215-659-3276

| interiors tops upholstery |

See full listing in **Section Two** under **interiors & interior parts**

trailers

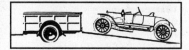

Alum-Line Inc | fabrication
US Hwy 9 W, PO Box 59 | manufacturing
Cresco, IA 52136
800-446-1407; FAX: 563-547-5366
E-mail: alumline@powerbank.net

All aluminum open and enclosed car trailers. Aluminum truck beds and bodies, aluminum toolboxes. Fabrication and manufacturing. Web site: www.alum-line.com

Beam Distributors Trailer Sales | trailers
769 River Hwy
Mooresville, NC 28117
704-892-9853; FAX: 704-660-0137
E-mail: info@beamtrailersales.com

Dealer United Express Line enclosed trailers. Large stock of enclosed trailers for all your automotive needs. Serving the old car hobby since 1968. Web site: www.beamtrailersales.com

C & C Manufacturing Co | trailers
300 S Church St
Hazleton, PA 18201
570-454-0819; FAX: 570-454-5131

Mail order and open shop. Specializing in the manufacturing of custom car carriers to transport antique automobiles for the past 30 years.

Champion Luggage Trailers | luggage trailer kits
9471 Hemlock Cir
Shreveport, LA 71118
318-688-2787

Mail order only. Fiberglass luggage trailer kit, complete except wheels, tires or taillights. Ford bolt pattern, all hardware installed, sealed plywood floor, will hold some personal mobility scooters, EZ-up canopy.

Chernock Enterprises | trailers
Airport Rd, PO Box 134
Hazleton, PA 18201
570-455-1752; FAX: 570-455-7585
E-mail: jim@chernock.com

Enclosed and open car trailers, cargo and concession trailers custom built. International orders welcome. Factory authorized dealer for Carmate, Cargo Express vintage trailers, Trailex aluminum trailers. Web site: www.chernock.com

Classic Trailers | open & enclosed
21900 US 12 | trailers
Sturgis, MI 49091
616-651-9319; 800-826-1960
E-mail: info@classicmfg.com

Monday-Friday 8 to 5. Manufacturer of open and enclosed auto trailers to meet the needs of your classic car. Call for dealer nearest you. Web site: http://classicmfg.com

D & D Trailers Inc | accessories
100 Lexington Ave | trailers
Trenton, NJ 08618
800-533-0442, 609-771-0001
FAX: 609-771-4479

Mail order and open shop. Monday-Saturday 8 am to 4:30 pm, other times by appointment. Custom built car carriers and utility trailers. Distributor of Wells Cargo enclosed trailers. Also carry tie-downs, winches and trailer parts. Registered trade name DEANDE™.

Tommy Gale Trailer Sales & Service | trailers
Glassport-Elizabeth Rd
Elizabeth, PA 15037
412-384-3640; FAX: 412-384-8532

Open shop only. Monday-Friday 8:30 am to 5 pm, Saturday 8:30 am to 12:30 pm. Specialize in enclosed race, classic car, gooseneck and custom trailers. Open trailer from 5´x8´ to 53´ long.

George's Auto & Tractor Sales Inc | Blue Dots/car dealer
1450 N Warren Rd | Dri-Wash metal
North Jackson, OH 44451 | polish
330-538-3020; FAX: 330-538-3033 | upholstery cleaner
E-mail: gmyuhas1450@cs.com | New Castle batteries

See full listing in **Section Two** under **car dealers**

Haulmark Industries Inc | trailers
14054 CR #4, PO Box 281
Bristol, IN 46507
219-825-5867; FAX: 219-825-9816
E-mail: sales@haulmark.com

Manufacturer of enclosed trailers for vintage automobiles. Web site: www.haulmark.com

Highway Products Inc | toolboxes
7905 Agate Rd
White City, OR 97503
800-TOOLBOX; FAX: 800-465-9545
E-mail: toolbox@cdsnet.net

See full listing in **Section Two** under **storage**

Hillsboro Trailers | trailers
220 Industrial Rd
Hillsboro, KS 67063
800-835-0209
E-mail: hii@gplains.com

Car trailers and cargo trailers. All aluminum construction, fully enclosed. Web site: www.gplains.com/hillsboro

Hodges Custom Haulers | truck beds
9076 Scale Rd
Benton, KY 42025
800-851-7229; FAX: 270-898-2356

Mail order and open shop. Monday-Friday 8 am to 5 pm. Specializing in truck beds for hauling antique cars.

Lazy B Trailer Sales Inc | parts
6040 St Rt 45 | repairs
Bristolville, OH 44402 | service
330-889-2353; FAX: 330-889-9630
E-mail: danny@lazybtrailers.com

Mail order and open shop. Monday-Friday 8 am to 5 pm, Saturday 9 am to 4 pm. Dealing in new and used steel and aluminum trailers, both open and enclosed. Have a complete parts and service facility capable of providing minor to major repairs and the capability to ship most parts directly to you. Can custom build a trailer to suit your needs. Call us for a quote. Web site: www.lazybtrailers.com

Bruce Litton Trailer Sales | car haulers
PO Box 34174
Indianapolis, IN 46234
317-293-7007; FAX: 317-293-7009
E-mail: info@brucelitton.com

Mail order and open shop. Monday-Friday 8:30 am to 5:30 pm Eastern time. Custom enclosed car haulers and truck conversion motorhomes. Web site: www.brucelitton.com

Mac's Custom Tie-Downs | **automotive**
105 Sanderson Rd | **tie-downs**
Chehalis, WA 98532
800-666-1586 orders
360-748-1180; FAX: 360-748-1185

A full range of tie-down equipment for all loads. Specializing in automotive tie-downs. Custom orders welcome. Web site: www.macscustomtiedowns.com

Mobile Structures Inc/MSI Trailers | **trailers**
2405 Cassopolis St, PO Box 1405
Elkhart, IN 46514
800-348-8541; FAX: 219-264-4399
E-mail: msibill@acninc.net

Specializing in car and cargo trailers. Also have race, vendor and office trailers, modular buildings. Distributor for Haulmark, Pace American and United Expressline offering units in widths of 5´, 6´, 7´, 8´ and 8-1/2´ and in lengths from 8´ to 50´. Web site: www.mobilestructures.com

Mullins & Teardrop Reproductions | **trailers**
3330-B Mary Ln
Auburn, CA 95602
530-878-0407

Mail order and open shop. Specializing in antique trailers for Mullins and teardrop. Catalog $1.

Nyles Haulmark Trailer Sales | **car carriers**
352 Macedon Center Rd
Fairport, NY 14450
716-223-6433

Open Monday-Friday 9 am to 5 pm, Saturday 9 am to 12 pm. Enclosed and open car carriers for vintage autos, race cars, snowmobiles. Major lines: Haulmark, Cargo Mate.

P&J Products | **car skates**
988 Gordon Ln | **trailer dollies**
Birmingham, MI 48009
888-647-1879

See full listing in **Section Two** under **accessories**

PE/Snappin Turtle Tie-Down Straps | **locks**
641 Bethlehem Pike | **tie-down straps**
Colmar, PA 18951 | **winches**
800-TIE-DOWN; FAX: 215-822-0161

Mail order only. Tie-down straps, D-rings, wheel clocks, trailer hitches, trailer locks and electric winches. Specialize in antique and classic car tie-downs. Over 18 years serving the hobby. Call us for fast, friendly service. Web site: www.1800tiedown.com

Performance Shop | **trailers**
Ray Thorp
2078 Pleasant Valley Rd
Newark, DE 19702
302-368-9534; FAX: 302-368-0760

Open daily 7 am to 7 pm. Designing trailers, Lite car trailers, Hefty Hauler car trailers, E-Z Up Hauler, a tilting deck car trailer, features no ramps. Will build it your way, any size.

R-D-T Plans and Parts | **car parts**
PO Box 2272 | **trailer plans**
Merced, CA 95344-0272
209-383-4441

Mail order and open shop. Monday-Friday 8 am to 5 pm. Trailer plans designed and sold. Also miscellaneous car parts for Packards, Cadillacs, Fords, Chevrolet and American underslung cars, along with Ferrari.

Sloan's Kwik Load Inc | **trailers**
15225 State Hwy 56
Sherman, TX 75092
903-893-7133; FAX: 903-868-0448
E-mail: dsloan@gte.com

Trailer manufacturing and sales. Open, air, rollback trailers. Web site: www.kwikload.com

Timber Wolf Trailers Inc | **trailers**
Division of Leland Engineering
13861 County Rd 4
Bristol, IN 46507-1529
800-837-9653; FAX: 219-825-8774
E-mail: info@timberwolftrailers.com

Manufacturer of cargo trailers, race car trailers, car haulers and custom trailers. Web site: www.timberwolftrailers.com

Trailer World Inc | **trailers**
800 Three Springs Rd
Bowling Green, KY 42104
270-843-4587, 800-872-2833
FAX: 502-781-8221

Mail order and open shop. Sales Monday-Friday 7:30 am to 5:30 pm, Saturday 8 am to 2 pm. Factory Monday-Friday 8 am to 5 pm. Brands: TWI aluminum and steel open; United; Storm, US Cargo enclosed car, vendor and cargo trailers. Web site: www.trailerworld.com

Trailers of New England Inc | **trailers**
Boston Rd Rt 20
Palmer, MA 01069
413-289-1211; FAX: 413-289-1292
E-mail: dskarp@
trailersofnewengland.com

Mail order and open shop. Monday-Friday 8:30 am to 5 pm, Saturday 8:30 am to 12 noon. Specializing in Wells Cargo enclosed trailers, open trailers, trailer design and customizing,

trailer parts, hitches and tie-down products. We now carry travel trailers. Web site: www.trailersofnewengland.com

Trailersource   trailers
117 Barber Rd SE
Marietta, GA 30060
800-241-4275; FAX: 404-426-8850

Open Monday-Friday 8:30 to 5:30, Saturday 10 to 2. Sell car haulers, cargo, concession, living quarters. Pace American, Avenger and others in steel and aluminum. Full service shop. In business since 1974. Delivery nationwide. Cars hauled, rental trailers. Custom designs a specialty.

Trailex Inc   aluminum & steel trailers
1 Industrial Park Dr, PO Box 553
Canfield, OH 44406
330-533-6814
800-282-5042, 877-TRAILEX toll-free
FAX: 330-533-9118
E-mail: trailex1@aol.com

Open Monday-Friday 8 am to 5 pm, Saturday 8 am to 12 noon. Trailers made from heat treated aluminum extrusions, anodized for lasting beauty. Also aluminum auto tow dollys. 10 different product lines of the world's only all aluminum, bolted, anodized trailers including our all new enclosed aluminum car trailer. A full line of steel trailers also available. We are the manufacturer, not just another dealer. Web site: www.trailex.com

Transport Designs Inc   trailers
240 Streibeigh Ln
Montoursville, PA 17754
570-368-1403; FAX: 570-368-2398
E-mail: boys4@csrlink.net

Factory direct sales. Monday-Friday 8 am to 5 pm, Saturday by appointment. Tag-a-long, goosenecks and semi-trailer styles. Enclosed only. Specializing in custom fabrication. Web site: www.transportdesigns.com

Wells Cargo Inc   trailers
1503 W McNaughton St, PO Box 728
Elkhart, IN 46515-0728
219-264-9661, 800-348-7553
FAX: 219-264-5938
E-mail: info@wellscargo.com

Open shop only. Monday-Friday 8 am to 5 pm, Saturday 8 am to 11 am. Manufacturing and selling of enclosed, steel structured trailers for hauling all types of collector automobiles. Web site: www.wellscargo.com

See our ad on this page

356 Enterprises   parts
Vic & Barbara Skirmants
27244 Ryan Rd
Warren, MI 48092
810-575-9544; FAX: 810-558-3616
E-mail: skirmants@home.com

See full listing in **Section One** under **Porsche**

4-Speeds by Darrell   transmissions
3 Water St, PO Box 110
Vermilion, IL 61955
217-275-3743; FAX: 217-275-3515

Mail order and open shop. Monday-Friday 8 am to 5 pm, Saturday 8 am to 12 noon Central time. Rebuilt transmissions. Show quality Borg-Warner T-10, M-21 and M-22, including all related parts. Specializes in build date transmissions for Corvette, Chevy 1958-up, Chevelle, Camaro, Buick, Pontiac and Oldsmobile.

Section Two – Generalists

| AAdvanced Transmissions
15 Parker St
Worcester, MA 01610
508-752-9674; FAX: 508-842-0672 | rear axle service
restoration
ring/pinion
parts/sales/
rebuilding/service |

Mail order and open shop. Monday-Saturday 9 am to 6 pm. Standard transmission rebuilding since 1968. Rebuilt 3/4/5-speeds in stock. Muncie, Borg-Warner, Ford Toploader, GM Saginaw specialists. Complete units in stock. Worldwide sales, service. Customer cores accepted. RPS daily. AMC to Z-28.

| American Restoration Services
373 Glen Eagles Way
Simi Valley, CA 93065
PH/FAX: 805-583-5189 | paints
transmission oil |

See full listing in **Section One** under **Chrysler**

| American Transmissions
7145 E Earll Dr
Scottsdale, AZ 85251
480-946-5391; FAX: 480-425-8997
E-mail: amer1trans@aol.com | differentials
transmissions |

Open shop only. Monday-Friday 8 am to 5 pm. A state of the art facility for the restoration of automatic and standard shift transmissions from 1935 to present day. Web site: www.americantransmissions.com

| Be Happy Automatic
Transmission Parts
414 Stivers Rd
Hillsboro, OH 45133
937-442-6133; FAX: 937-442-5016 | trans rebuild kits |

Mail order only. Owner operated by David and Mona Crone. Dealing in automatic transmission rebuild kits, external dry-up kits and hard parts, 1940-1965. NOS, NORS, good used, Dynaflow, Dual Path, Flightpitch, Hydramatic, Jetaway, Slim Jim, Roto 5, Powerglide, Turboglide, Powerflite, Torqueflite, 3-band, Ultramatic, etc. Technical assistance, exploded views, troubleshooting and repair literature. Orders for individual gaskets, seals, etc welcome. Free wholesale price list. We're open late for our West Coast customers. MasterCard, Visa, Discover, CODs accepted.

| Bicknell Engine Company
7055 Dayton Rd
Enon, OH 45323
937-864-5224 | parts
repair
restoration |

See full listing in **Section One** under **Buick/McLaughlin**

| Blaser's Auto, Nash, Rambler, AMC
3200 48th Ave
Moline, IL 61265-6453
309-764-3571; FAX: 309-764-1155
E-mail: blazauto@sprynet.com | NOS parts |

See full listing in **Section One** under **AMC**

| Bonk's Automotive Inc
4480 Lazelda Dr
Milan, MI 48160
800-207-6906; FAX: 734-434-0845
E-mail: bonkers@bonkauto.com | automotive tools |

See full listing in **Section Two** under **tools**

| Classic Tube
Division of Classic &
Performance Spec Inc
80 Rotech Dr
Lancaster, NY 14086
800-TUBES-11 (882-3711)
716-759-1800; FAX: 716-759-1014
E-mail: classictube@aol.com | brake lines
choke tubes
fuel lines
transmission lines
vacuum lines |

See full listing in **Section Two** under **brakes**

| Coffey Classic Transmissions
310 Aviator Dr
Fort Worth, TX 76179
817-439-1611 | transmissions |

Mail order and open shop. Monday-Friday 9 am to 5 pm Central time. Specializing in transmission parts and service for early model classic standard and automatic transmissions. Classic, vintage and racing transmissions, parts and service.

| Dynamic Racing Transmissions LLC
104-5 Enterprise Dr, Unit 1
North Branford, CT 06471
203-315-0138; FAX: 203-315-0352
E-mail: mightymitejr@aol.com | automatic
transmissions |

Mail order and open shop. Monday-Friday 8 am to 5 pm. Saturday or other times by appointment only. Specializing in building a wide variety of high performance automatics for domestic, rear wheel drive, from 1960s muscle cars to street rods and mega horsepower modern drag cars. Web site: www.dynamicracingtrans.com

| David Edwards-Transmission Parts
56 Dale St, PO Box 245
Needham Heights, MA 02494-0245
PH/FAX: 781-449-2065
E-mail: autotran2@aol.com | auto trans kits
auto trans parts |

Mail order only. SASE not required. Phone hours: Monday-Friday 6 pm to 11:30 pm, Saturday-Sunday by chance. For all automatic transmissions from 1946 to the present except Flightpitch and Ultramatics. Kits, bands, pumps, bushings, washers, drums and other miscellaneous parts in stock. Daily UPS shipments. Web site: http://members.aol.com/autotran

| Energy Suspension
1131 Via Callejon
San Clemente, CA 92673
949-361-3935; FAX: 949-361-3940
E-mail: hyperflex@
energysuspension.com | suspension parts |

See full listing in **Section Two** under **suspension parts**

| Engines Direct
7830 E Gelding, Bldg 200
Scottsdale, AZ 85260
800-998-2100; FAX: 480-998-6070 | engines
parts |

See full listing in **Section Two** under **engine rebuilding**

| Fatsco Transmission Parts
337 Changebridge Rd, PO Box 635
Pinebrook, NJ 07058
800-524-0485; FAX: 973-227-5414
E-mail: fatsco@att.net | parts |

Mail order and open shop. Monday-Friday 8 am to 5 pm. Automatic transmission parts, 1946 to date for all American made cars and light trucks and foreign models with American automatics. Web site: www.fatsco.com

SERVICE COAL — *More Heat Less Waste*

FB Performance Transmissions | transmissions
85 Cleveland Ave
Bay Shore, NY 11706
631-242-0008; FAX: 631-243-3054
E-mail: fbperf@trim.net

Mail order and open shop. Monday-Friday 9 am to 5:30 pm. Deals in high performance and racing transmissions. Web site: www.fbperformance.com

Gear Vendors Inc | overdrive transmissions
1717 N Magnolia Ave
El Cajon, CA 92020
619-562-0060; FAX: 619-562-1186
E-mail: info@gearvendors.com

Manufacturer of under/overdrive brand of auxiliary overdrive transmissions. Web site: www.gearvendors.com

Art Houser's Rear End Service | rear end parts service
128 N Main St
Topton, PA 19562
888-560-2127; FAX: 610-641-0163
E-mail: houser@rearman.com

See full listing in **Section Two** under **differentials**

Ignition Distributor Service | rebuild carbs rebuild distributors rebuild Turbos
19042 SE 161st
Renton, WA 98058
425-255-8052
E-mail: pjo@uswest.net

See full listing in **Section Two** under **ignition parts**

Joyce's Model A & T Parts | new parts NOS parts rebuilt parts
PO Box 70
Manchaca, TX 78652-0070
512-282-1196; FAX: 512-479-5091

See full listing in **Section One** under **Ford 1903-1931**

Lindley Restorations Ltd | parts sales service
10 S Sanatoga Rd
Pottstown, PA 19464
610-326-8484; FAX: 610-326-3845

See full listing in **Section One** under **Jaguar**

Mid Valley Engineering | machine work parts restoration
16637 N 21st St
Phoenix, AZ 85022
602-482-1251; FAX: 602-788-0812

Mail order and open shop. Monday-Friday 8 am to 5 pm, Saturday by appointment. Large inventory of new and antique Hewland parts. Complete fabrication and machine shop facilities for race car restoration. MVE Shur shifter side door pat pen for T-10 transmissions.

Northwest Transmission Parts | transmission parts
13500 US 62
Winchester, OH 45697
800-327-1955 order line
937-442-2811 info
FAX: 937-442-6555

Automatic and standard shift parts back to 1933. Gears, shafts, bearings, kits for automatics, bands, pumps, drums, bushings, etc. Also parts for Mercedes, Rolls-Royce and Jaguar automatics in stock. Automatic transmission flywheels. Motor and transmission mounts back to 1933.

Obsolete Chevrolet Parts Co | engine parts radiators rubber parts transmissions
PO Box 68
Nashville, GA 31639-0068
800-248-8785; FAX: 229-686-3056
E-mail: obschevy@surfsouth.com

See full listing in **Section One** under **Chevrolet**

Orion Motors European Parts Inc | parts
10722 Jones Rd
Houston, TX 77065
800-736-6410, 281-894-1982
FAX: 281-849-1997
E-mail: orion-yugo@yugoparts.com

See full listing in **Section One** under **Alfa Romeo**

P-Ayr Products | replicas
719 Delaware St
Leavenworth, KS 66048
913-651-5543; FAX: 913-651-2084
E-mail: sales@payr.com

See full listing in **Section One** under **Chevrolet**

Phoenix Transmission Products | torque converters transmissions
1304 Mineral Wells Hwy
Weatherford, TX 76086
817-599-7680; FAX: 817-599-3161
E-mail: phx1tran@airmail.net

Mail order and open shop. Monday-Friday 7 am to 5 pm. Specializing in automatic transmissions and torque converters, especially automatic overdrives. Web site: www.phoenixtrans.com

Sierra Grove Packards | conversion kits
425 E Laurel
Sierra Madre, CA 91024
626-355-4023, 714-539-8579
FAX: 626-355-4072

See full listing in **Section One** under **Packard**

Street-Wise Performance | differentials new/used parts overhaul kits transmissions
Richie Mulligan
Box 105 Creek Rd
Tranquility, NJ 07879
973-786-7500; FAX: 973-786-7861
E-mail: street-wise@usa.net

Mail order and open shop. Monday-Saturday 9 am to 6 pm. Strictly sticks and posi power. Experience the excitement of a clutch vehicle with positraction. Always on hand, many 3, 4 and 5-speeds, totally rebuilt, guaranteed, with shifters and other conversion parts. Plus most 1955-1980s posi rear applications, any ratio, built/fabricated to order. Visa, MC, Discover. Spring/Fall Englishtown swap meet spaces: RK 58-60. Web site: www.street-wiseperformance.com

John Ulrich | parts
450 Silver Ave
San Francisco, CA 94112
PH/FAX: 510-223-9587 days

See full listing in **Section One** under **Packard**

Section Two – Generalists

Universal Transmission Co 23361 Dequindre Rd Hazel Park, MI 48030 800-882-4327; FAX: 248-398-2581	transmission parts

Dealing in standard transmission parts for American cars from Model A till tomorrow. A family owned business since 1948. Wholesale/retail.

See our ad on this page

Vicarage Jaguar 5333 Collins Ave, Ste 704 Miami Beach, FL 33140 305-866-9511; FAX: 305-866-5738 E-mail: vicarage@ix.netcom.com	parts restoration

See full listing in **Section One** under **Jaguar**

Dan Williams Toploader Transmissions 206 E Dogwood Dr Franklin, NC 28734 828-524-9085 noon to midnight FAX: 828-524-4848	transmissions

See full listing in **Section One** under **Ford 1954-up**

transport

A AAAdvantage Auto Transport Inc 8920 S Hardy Tempe, AZ 85284 800-233-4875 E-mail: webinfo@aaaadv.com	transport

Mail order and open shop. Monday-Friday 7 am to 5 pm, Saturday 9 am to 12 pm, Mountain time. Transport of vehicles across the state or across the globe. Open or enclosed transport trucks. Provide the specialized care your car deserves. Web site: www.aaaadv.com

See our ad on page 405

Auto Transport Services 5367 Fargo Rd Avoca, MI 48006 810-324-2598 FAX: 810-324-6094	transport

Transporting automobiles.

Autobahn Transportation Service Inc 12799 Archer Ave Chicago, IL 60439 630-257-1184 FAX: 630-257-1865	vehicle relocation

Your only source for vehicle relocation. Insurance available up to $5,000,000 per vehicle. International service available. Award winning service. Enclosed trailers, tracking systems.

See our ad on page 405

California Jaguar	auto transport
29109 Triunfo Dr	
Agoura, CA 91301	
800-335-2482; FAX: 818-707-3062	

Coast to coast, door to door, open or enclosed transport. Cars, motorcycles, trucks, parts, boats.

David Elliott	auto transport
11796 Franklin	car locator
Minocqua, WI 54548	
715-356-1335	

Auto transport and locator of western cars and parts. Transport cars from Wisconsin to Utah, Colorado, Arizona, Nevada, New Mexico, Texas, California or points near or between. Locator of all years western cars and trucks. Specializing in 1960s-1970s project cars and body shells.

Exotic Car Transport Inc	transport
880 C Maguire Rd	
Ocoee, FL 34761	
800-766-8797; FAX: 407-654-9951	
E-mail: info@exoticcartransport.com	

Nationwide transporter of exotic, vintage and luxury automobiles on enclosed carriers. Indoor storage available. Web site: www.exoticcartransport.com

Five Star Transport	transport
691 W Merrick Rd	
Valley Stream, NY 11580	
800-464-9965, 516-285-1077	
FAX: 516-285-3729	

Mail order and open shop. Monday-Saturday 7 am to 7 pm. Towing, transport flatbed and trailer. Cars, trucks, equipment. ICC and DOT authority. NY, NJ, PA, CT, MA, RI, VT, ME, MD, DE, VA. Classics, antique, muscle, vans, exotic.

Tommy Gale Trailer Sales & Service	trailers
Glassport-Elizabeth Rd	
Elizabeth, PA 15037	
412-464-0119; FAX: 412-384-8532	

See full listing in **Section Two** under **trailers**

Hodges Custom Haulers	truck beds
9076 Scale Rd	
Benton, KY 42025	
800-851-7229; FAX: 270-898-2356	

See full listing in **Section Two** under **trailers**

Intercity Lines Inc	transport
River Rd, Box 1299	
Warren, MA 01083	
800-221-3936; FAX: 413-436-9422	
E-mail: info@intercitylines.com	

Open Monday-Friday 9 am to 6 pm, Saturday 9 am to 12 noon. Specializing in enclosed transportation of collector cars throughout all 48 states and Canada. Web site: www.intercitylines.com

Interesting Parts Inc	appraisals
Paul TerHorst	gaskets
27526 N Owens Rd	parts
Mundelein, IL 60060-9608	storage
PH/FAX: 847-949-1030	transport
847-558-9732 cell	
E-mail: pterhorst@interaccess.com	

See full listing in **Section Two** under **comprehensive parts**

Interstate Towing Service   transport
6029 Geary Blvd
San Francisco, CA 94121
415-221-1117, 24 hours
FAX: 415-221-1060
E-mail: interstow@earthlink.net

Open Monday-Friday 8 am to 5 pm. Local and long distance transportation of antique, classic and collectible automobiles. 25 years' experience. Inoperable, driveable. We also offer enclosed storage.

Bruce Litton Trailer Sales   car haulers
PO Box 34174
Indianapolis, IN 46234
317-293-7007; FAX: 317-293-7009
E-mail: info@brucelitton.com

See full listing in **Section Two** under **trailers**

Mac's Custom Tie-Downs   automotive
105 Sanderson Rd   tie-downs
Chehalis, WA 98532
800-666-1586 orders
360-748-1180; FAX: 360-748-1185

See full listing in **Section Two** under **trailers**

Mac's Euro Motorcars & Transport   Alfa Romeos
1520 Burr Oak Rd   parts
Homewood, IL 60430   transport
708-799-3469

See full listing in **Section One** under **Alfa Romeo**

Paradise Classic Auto Appraisal   appraisals
5894 Cornell   transport
Taylor, MI 48180
313-291-2758

See full listing in **Section Two** under **appraisals**

Section Two – Generalists

Passport Transport Ltd	transport
37 Progess Pkwy	
St Louis, MO 63043	
800-325-4267; FAX: 314-878-7295	

Nationwide enclosed transportation of antique, classic and special interest cars. Over 100,000 vehicles transported nationwide since we "invented" this business in 1970. To provide the best service possible, we custom design and build our air-ride trailers specifically to handle the unique requirements of these vehicles. Passport Transport, the first and still the finest in enclosed auto transportation.

See our ad on page 406

Peterson Auto Transport	transport
866-467-1280; 303-467-1280	
E-mail:	
robyn@petersonautotransport.com	
Website:	
www.petersonautotransport.com	

See our ad on this page

Reliable Carriers	automotive transportation
3324 E Atlanta Ave	
Phoenix, AZ 85040	
800-528-5709; FAX: 602-243-3620	

Specializing in automotive transportation of prototypes and collectibles. Several added features on trucks prevent damage. Insured for full value of vehicles, up to $1,000,000 per load. Not the cheapest, but the best.

See our ad on page 406

Reward Service Inc	appraisals restoration transportation
172 Overhill Rd	
Stormville, NY 12582	
PH/FAX: 845-227-7647	

See full listing in **Section One** under **Jaguar**

Sea Expo Freight Services Inc   transporter
32 Somerville Rd
Hewitt, NJ 07421
888-733-9766, 201-973-5700
FAX: 973-728-6060
E-mail: w.tmurphy@seaexpo.com

International transporter of motor vehicles, project cargo, car parts, general goods (export and import) worldwide.

Thomas C Sunday Inc   transport
PO Box 217
New Kingstown, PA 17072
800-541-6601; FAX: 717-697-0727

Coast to coast enclosed automobile transportation, weekly service, including the Pacific Northwest, door-to-door service, liftgate loading, competitive rates. Fully insured, special events, shows, races, auctions, etc. Web site: www.thomascsundayinc.com
See our ad on page 407

trucks & tractors

Addison Generator Inc   auto parts
21 W Main St Rear   repairs
Freehold, NJ 07728   supplies
732-431-2438; FAX: 732-431-4503

See full listing in **Section Two** under **electrical systems**

AMC Classic Appraisers   appraisals
7963 Depew St
Arvada, CO 80003
303-428-8760; FAX: 303-428-1070

See full listing in **Section Two** under **appraisals**

American Classic Truck Parts   parts
PO Box 409
Aubrey, TX 76227
940-365-9786; FAX: 940-365-3419
E-mail: americanclassic@airmail.net

See full listing in **Section One** under **Chevrolet**

Automobile Appraisal Service & Special Interest Autos   appraiser
10097 Manchester Rd, Ste 203
St Louis, MO 63122
PH/FAX: 314-821-4015

See full listing in **Section Two** under **appraisals**

Blint Equipment Inc   parts
2204 E Lincolnway   tractor rebuilding
LaPorte, IN 46350
219-362-7021

See full listing in **Section One** under **Ford 1954-up**

Brothers Truck Parts   accessories
801 Parkridge Ave   parts
Corona, CA 92880
800-687-6672; FAX: 909-808-9788
E-mail: sales@brotherstrucks.com

Mail order and open shop. Monday-Friday 8 am to 5 pm, Saturday 8 am to 12 pm Pacific time. Specializing in 1947-1987 Chevy and GMC trucks, restoration parts and custom accessories. Web site: www.brotherstrucks.com

Jim Carter's Antique Truck Parts   truck parts
1508 E Alton
Independence, MO 64055
800-336-1913; FAX: 800-262-3749
E-mail: jimcartertruckparts@worldnet.att.net

See full listing in **Section One** under **Chevrolet**

Chevy Duty Pickup Parts   pickup parts
1 Chevy Duty Dr
Kansas City, MO 64150
816-741-8029; FAX: 816-741-5255
E-mail: orders@chevyduty.com

See full listing in **Section One** under **Chevrolet**

Cobbaton Combat Collection   museum
Chittlehampton
Umberleigh
N Devon EX37 9RZ England
01769-540740; FAX: 01769-540141
E-mail: info@cobbatoncombat.co.uk

See full listing in **Section Two** under **military vehicles**

Desert Valley Auto Parts   salvage yard
2227 W Happy Valley Rd
Phoenix, AZ 85027
800-905-8024
623-780-8024; FAX: 623-582-9141
E-mail: sales@dvap.com

See full listing in **Section Five** under **Arizona**

Dixie Truck Works   parts
10495 Hwy 73 E
Mount Pleasant, NC 28124
704-436-2407

See full listing in **Section One** under **Chevrolet**

Dodge City Vintage Dodge Vehicles & Parts
18584 Hwy 108, PO Box 1687
Jamestown, CA 95327
209-984-5858; FAX: 209-984-3285
E-mail: mike@dodgecityvintage.com
| parts
restoration
research
vehicles

See full listing in **Section One** under **Dodge**

Dennis DuPont
77 Island Pond Rd
Derry, NH 03038
603-434-9290
| automobilia
literature
parts

See full listing in **Section One** under **Studebaker**

Dusty Memories and Faded Glory
118 Oxford Hts Rd
Somerset, PA 15501-1134
814-443-2393; FAX: 814-443-9452
| rentals

See full listing in **Section Two** under **military vehicles**

Finders Service
454-458 W Lincoln Hwy
Chicago Heights, IL 60411-2463
708-481-9685; FAX: 708-481-5837
E-mail: finderssvc@aol.com
| parts finders

See full listing in **Section Two** under **car & parts locators**

Flashback F-100s
2519 Wagon Wheel Rd
Reidsville, NC 27320
336-421-3979; FAX: 336-421-5901
| parts
parts locators

See full listing in **Section One** under **Ford 1954-up**

Ford Truck Enthusiasts Inc
PO Box 422
Lilburn, GA 30048
770-806-1955
E-mail: kpayne@ford-trucks.com
| literature

Mail order only. Web community services and literature for all years of Ford trucks, vans and SUVs. Web site: www.ford-trucks.com

Fort Wayne Clutch & Driveline
2424 Goshen Rd
Fort Wayne, IN 46808
219-484-8505; FAX: 219-484-8605
E-mail: clutches@skyenet.net
| axles
axleshafts
clutches
driveshafts

See full listing in **Section Two** under **clutches**

Fred's Truck Parts
4811 S Palant
Tucson, AZ 85735
520-883-7151
E-mail: fredstruckparts@aol.com
| parts

See full listing in **Section One** under **Chevrolet**

Fuller's Restoration Inc
Old Airport Rd
Manchester Center, VT 05255
802-362-3643; FAX: 802-362-3360
E-mail: chevy@vermontel.net
| repairs
restoration

See full listing in **Section Two** under **restoration shops**

Great Lakes Auto "N" Truck Restoration
PO Box 251
Mayville, MI 48744
989-683-2614
| parts

See full listing in **Section One** under **Chevrolet**

Green-Stuff Metal Polish
PO Box 7071
Knoxville, TN 37921
865-382-1286
E-mail: greenstuffpolish@aol.com
| metal polish

See full listing in **Section Two** under **plating & polishing**

Half Ton Fun
Bob Selzam
166 Toms River Rd
Jackson, NJ 08527
732-928-9421
| NOS parts

See full listing in **Section One** under **Ford 1932-1953**

Hank's Custom Stepside Beds
12693 Clay Station Rd
Herald, CA 95638
209-748-2193; FAX: 209-748-2976
E-mail: truckbeds@softcom.net
| pickup beds

Mail order and open shop. Monday-Friday 8 am to 5 pm. Manufactures custom Stepside pickup/truck beds and bed wood. We also build custom tube frames. We, at Hank's, take pride in manufacturing to assure you a quality product at an affordable price. If you are contemplating a serious show truck or an outstanding driver, don't settle for anything less.

Heavy Chevy Truck Parts
17445 Heavy Chevy Rd, PO Box 650
Siloam Springs, AR 72761
501-524-9575
FAX: 501-524-4873 or 800-317-2277
E-mail: heavychevy@heavychevy.com
| parts

See full listing in **Section One** under **Chevrolet**

Highway Products Inc
7905 Agate Rd
White City, OR 97503
800-TOOLBOX; FAX: 800-465-9545
E-mail: toolbox@cdsnet.net
| toolboxes

See full listing in **Section Two** under **storage**

Hodges Custom Haulers
9076 Scale Rd
Benton, KY 42025
800-851-7229; FAX: 270-898-2356
| truck beds

See full listing in **Section Two** under **trailers**

Bruce Horkey's Wood & Parts
46284 440th St
Windom, MN 56101
507-831-5625; FAX: 507-831-0280
E-mail: woodandparts@yahoo.com
| pickup parts

Mail order and open shop. Monday-Friday 8 am to 5 pm, Saturday by appointment. Replacement wood, metal and fiberglass pickup parts for 1928-2001 Ford, 1934-2001 Chevy/GMC, and 1939-2001 Dodge pickups.

John's F-Fun Hundreds
1575 W Broadway, Unit B
Anaheim, CA 92802
714-563-3100; FAX: 714-563-1592
E-mail: jfun100@aol.com
| parts

See full listing in **Section One** under **Ford 1954-up**

K C Obsolete Parts   parts
3343 N 61
Kansas City, KS 66104
913-334-9479; FAX: 913-788-2795

See full listing in **Section One** under **Ford 1954-up**

Bruce Litton Trailer Sales   car haulers
PO Box 34174
Indianapolis, IN 46234
317-293-7007; FAX: 317-293-7009
E-mail: info@brucelitton.com

See full listing in **Section Two** under **trailers**

Long Road Productions   documentaries
PO Box 1309
Sheffield, MA 01257
413-229-0474; FAX: 413-229-5903
E-mail: lindsey@longroadpro.com

See full listing in **Section Two** under **videos**

MAR-K Quality Parts   bed parts
6625 W Wilshire Blvd   customizing parts
Oklahoma City, OK 73132   trim parts
405-721-7945; FAX: 405-721-8906
E-mail: info@mar-k.com

MAR-K makes restoration and custom parts for your Chevy,
Ford or Dodge pickup. Includes bed parts, GM moldings, rear
pans, tailgate covers, billet accessories and more. Get MAR-K
Quality. Catalog is $3 or free with order. Shop online anytime at
our web site: www.mar-k.com

See our ad on this page

Michael's Classics Inc   Unimogs
954 Montauk Hwy
Bayport, NY 11705
631-363-4200; FAX: 631-363-9226
E-mail: michaelsmogs@aol.com

See full listing in **Section One** under **Mercedes-Benz**

N-News Magazine   magazine
PO Box 275
East Corinth, VT 05040

Quarterly publication, *N-News*, the magazine for the Ford tractor
enthusiast, covering the 9N (1939) to 6000 (1965). Subscription:
$16/year US, $19/year Canada. Web site: www.n-news.com

National Parts Locator Service   parts locator
636 East 6th St #81
Ogden, UT 84404-2415
877-672-7875, 801-627-7210

See full listing in **Section Two** under **car & parts locators**

North Yorkshire Motor Museum   museum
D T Mathewson
Roxby Garage, Pickering Rd
Thornton-le-Dale, North Yorkshire
England
01751 474455; FAX: 01944 758188

See full listing in **Section Six** under **England**

Nostalgia Productions Inc   shows
268 Hillcrest Blvd   swap meets
St Ignace, MI 49781
906-643-8087; FAX: 906-643-9784
E-mail: edreavie@nostalgia-prod.com

See full listing in **Section Two** under **auctions & shows**

Olson's Gaskets — gaskets
3059 Opdal Rd E
Port Orchard, WA 98366
PH/FAX: 360-871-1207
E-mail: info@olsonsgaskets.com

See full listing in **Section Two** under **gaskets**

On Mark International Inc — replicas
8923 S 43rd W Ave
Tulsa, OK 74132
888-373-2092, 918-446-7906
FAX: 918-445-1532
E-mail: onmark@igeotec.net

See full listing in **Section Two** under **models & toys**

**Paul's Select Cars & Parts
for Porsche®** — cars / parts
2280 Gail Dr
Riverside, CA 92509
909-685-9340; FAX: 909-685-9342
E-mail: pauls356-s90@webtv.net

See full listing in **Section One** under **Porsche**

Pick-ups Northwest — parts / trim
9911 Airport Way
Snohomish, WA 98296
360-568-9166; FAX: 360-568-1233

See full listing in **Section One** under **Chevrolet**

Power Effects® — exhaust systems
1800H Industrial Park Dr
Grand Haven, MI 49417
877-3POWRFX (376-9739) toll free
616-847-4200; FAX: 616-847-4210

See full listing in **Section Two** under **exhaust systems**

Power Steering Services Inc — pumps / rack & pinion / steering gearboxes
2347 E Kearney St
Springfield, MO 65803
417-864-6676; FAX: 417-864-7103
E-mail: chip@powersteering.com

See full listing in **Section Two** under **suspension parts**

Recks & Relics Ford Trucks — truck parts
2675 Hamilton Mason Rd
Hamilton, OH 45011
513-868-3489; FAX: 513-868-3461
E-mail: truck@choice.net

See full listing in **Section One** under **Ford 1932-1953**

Reynolds Museum Ltd — museum
4110-57th St
Wetaskiwin, AB Canada T9A 2B6
780-352-6201; FAX: 780-352-4666
E-mail: srsl@incentre.net

See full listing in **Section Two** under **car dealers**

Richardson Restorations — custom work / repairs / restoration
352 S I St
Tulare, CA 93274
559-688-5002
E-mail: cal5002@aol.com

See full listing in **Section Two** under **restoration shops**

Simons Balancing & Machine Inc — machine work
1987 Ashley River Rd
Charleston, SC 29407
843-766-3911; FAX: 843-766-9003

See full listing in **Section Two** under **machine work**

Slim's Garage — garden tractors
PO Box 49
Seminary, MS 39479-0049
PH/FAX: 601-722-9861

Mail order and open shop. Weekdays 9 am to 5 pm. Specializing in garden tractors.

Superior Pump Exchange Co — water pumps
12901 Crenshaw Blvd
Hawthorne, CA 90250-5511
310-676-4995; FAX: 310-676-9430
E-mail: autoh20@aol.com

See full listing in **Section Two** under **engine parts**

This Old Truck Magazine — magazine
PO Box 500
Missouri City, TX 77459
888-760-8108 subscriptions
937-767-1433 publishing office
FAX: 937-767-2726
E-mail: antique@antiquepower.com

See full listing in **Section Four** under **periodicals**

The Truck Shop — parts
104 W Marion Ave, PO Box 5035
Nashville, GA 31639
800-245-0556 orders
info: 229-686-3833, 229-686-3396
FAX: 229-686-3531

See full listing in **Section One** under **Chevrolet**

Valley Motor Supply — accessories / parts
1402 E Second St
Roswell, NM 88201
505-622-7450

See full listing in **Section One** under **Ford 1954-up**

Vintage Power Wagons Inc — parts / trucks
302 S 7th St
Fairfield, IA 52556
515-472-4665; FAX: 515-472-4824

See full listing in **Section One** under **Dodge**

Wallace W Wade Specialty Tires — tires
530 Regal Row, PO Box 560906
Dallas, TX 75356
800-666-TYRE, 214-688-0091
FAX: 214-634-8465
E-mail: wwwadest@earthlink.net

See full listing in **Section Two** under **tires**

Wales Antique Chevy Truck Parts — parts
143 Center
Carleton, MI 48117
734-654-8836

See full listing in **Section One** under **Chevrolet**

Harold Warp Pioneer Village Foundation
PO Box 68
Minden, NE 68959-0068
308-832-1181; FAX: 308-832-2750
800-445-4447 (out of state)
E-mail: pioneervllge@nebi.com

| museum |

See full listing in **Section Six** under **Nebraska**

Wheels O' Time Museum
PO Box 9636
Peoria, IL 61612-9636
309-243-9020
E-mail: wotmuseum@aol.com

| museum |

See full listing in **Section Six** under **Illinois**

Widmann's Garage
346 Bunting Ave
Hamilton, NJ 08611
609-392-1553; FAX: 609-392-1709
E-mail: widsgarage@aol.com

| repairs restorations |

See full listing in **Section Two** under **restoration shops**

trunks

Hampton Coach
6 Chestnut St, PO Box 6
Amesbury, MA 01913
888-388-8726, 978-388-8047
FAX: 978-388-1113
E-mail: lbb-hc@greenet.net

| fabrics interior kits top kits |

See full listing in **Section One** under **Chevrolet**

LeBaron Bonney Co
6 Chestnut St, PO Box 6
Amesbury, MA 01913
800-221-5408, 978-388-3811
FAX: 978-388-1113
E-mail: lbb-hc@greennet.net

| fabrics interior kits top kits |

See full listing in **Section One** under **Ford 1903-1931**

REM Automotive Inc
2610 N Brandt Rd
Annville, PA 17003
717-838-4242; FAX: 717-838-5091
E-mail: remautoinc@aol.com

| interior parts molded hood insulation trunk lining |

See full listing in **Section Two** under **interiors & interior parts**

Rust Busters
PO Box 341
Clackamas, OR 97015
503-223-3203
E-mail: info@rustbusters.com

| rust repair |

See full listing in **Section Two** under **restoration shops**

T-Bird Sanctuary
9997 SW Avery
Tualatin, OR 97062
503-692-9848; FAX: 503-692-9849

| parts |

See full listing in **Section One** under **Thunderbird**

Varco Inc
8200 S Anderson Rd
Oklahoma City, OK 73150
405-732-1637

| fitted luggage trunks |

See full listing in **Section One** under **Ford 1903-1931**

Vintage Trunks
5 Brownstone Rd
East Granby, CT 06026-9705
860-658-0353
E-mail: john.desousa@snet.net

| trunks |

Mail order only. Plans and hardware for authentic wood construction of luggage trunks for Model As and other vintage autos. Drawing package contains prints, hardware listing and prices, history, instructions and fabric samples. Send SASE for information and price list. Have full line of trunk hardware on hand for your trunk restoration.

upholstery

AAC Restorations
Rt 1 Box 409
Mount Clare, WV 26408
304-622-2849

| seat springs |

Accurate Auto Tops & Upholstery Inc
Miller Rd & W Chester Pike
Edgemont, PA 19028
610-356-1515; FAX: 610-353-8230

| tops upholstery |

Accurate Auto Tops is a full service top and upholstery shop specializing in classic and antique restorations and street rod interiors.

All Seams Fine
23 Union St
Waterbury, VT 05676
800-244-7326 (SEAM), 802-244-8843

| interior restorations |

In-house restorations only. Interior restorations, custom upholstery, carpet, headliner, panels, etc; convertible tops, antiques, late models, customs or street rods.

Andover Restraints Inc
PO Box 2651
Columbia, MD 21045
410-381-6700; FAX: 410-381-6703
E-mail: andoauto@clark.net

| seat belts |

See full listing in **Section Two** under **interiors & interior parts**

Arrow Fastener Co Inc
271 Mayhill St
Saddle Brook, NJ 07663

| nail guns rivet tools staple guns |

See full listing in **Section Two** under **tools**

Auto-Mat Co
69 Hazel St
Hicksville, NY 11801
800-645-7258 orders
516-938-7373; FAX: 516-931-8438
E-mail: browner5@ix.netcom.com

| accessories carpet sets interiors tops upholstery |

See full listing in **Section Two** under **interiors & interior parts**

Bassett Classic Restoration
2616 Sharon St, Ste D
Kenner, LA 70062-4934
PH/FAX: 504-469-2982

parts
restoration
service

See full listing in **Section One** under **Rolls-Royce/Bentley**

Bob's Rod & Custom
866 W 3200 S
Nibley, UT 84321
435-752-7467
E-mail: bobsrod@cache.net

car assembly
fabrication
interiors

See full listing in **Section Two** under **street rods**

Cerullo Performance Seating
2853 Metropolitan Pl
Pomona, CA 91767
909-392-5561; FAX: 909-392-8544
E-mail: cerullo@tstonramp.com

seating

See full listing in **Section Two** under **interiors & interior parts**

Clark's Corvair Parts Inc
Rt 2, #400 Mohawk Tr
Shelburne Falls, MA 01370
413-625-9776; FAX: 413-625-8498
E-mail: clarks@corvair.com

accessories
interiors
literature
parts
sheetmetal

See full listing in **Section One** under **Corvair**

Classic Chevrolet Parts Inc
8723 S I-35
Oklahoma City, OK 73149
405-631-4400; FAX: 405-631-5999
E-mail: info@classicchevroletparts.com

parts

See full listing in **Section One** under **Chevrolet**

Coachbuilt Motors
907 E Hudson St
Columbus, OH 43211
614-261-1541
E-mail: coachbuilt907@aol.com

repairs

See full listing in **Section One** under **Rolls-Royce/Bentley**

**Comfy/Inter-American
Sheepskins Inc**
1346 Centinela Ave
West Los Angeles, CA 90025-1901
800-521-4014; FAX: 310-442-6080
E-mail: sales@comfysheep.com

floor mats
seat covers

See full listing in **Section Two** under **interiors & interior parts**

Concours d'Elegance Upholstery
1607 Pine Ridge
Bushkill, PA 18324
888-ELEG-UPH
PH/FAX: 570-588-0969
E-mail: concoursuph@enter.net

upholstery

Shop open. Monday-Saturday 9 am to 4 pm. Deals in all classic and antique autos custom auto upholstery. Also upholstery training videos available. Most upholstery supplies available. Web site: www.concoursupholstery.com

**Custom Auto Interiors
by Ron Mangus**
18127 Marygold Ave
Bloomington, CA 92316
909-877-9342; FAX: 909-877-1741
E-mail: customautointeriors@
hotmail.com

accessories
carpet kits
die cast collectibles
seat frames

See full listing in **Section Two** under **interiors & interior parts**

Section Two – Generalists

Custom Interiors PO Box 51174 Indian Orchard, MA 01151 413-589-9176; FAX: 413-589-9178 E-mail: ci@customseatcovers.com	**carpets** **custom seat covers** **interior parts**

See full listing in **Section Two** under **interiors & interior parts**

Diamond Trim Gary Nolan 10 Furbacher Ln #7 Aurora, ON Canada L4G 6W1 905-726-3221; FAX: 905-726-3277 E-mail: garynolan@diamondtrim.com	**interiors**

See full listing in **Section Two** under **interiors & interior parts**

Doc's Jags 125 Baker Rd Lake Bluff, IL 60044 847-367-5247; FAX: 847-367-6363 E-mail: doc@docsjags.com	**appraisals** **interiors** **restoration**

See full listing in **Section One** under **Jaguar**

Firewall Insulators & Quiet Ride Solutions 6465 Pacific Ave, Ste 249 Stockton, CA 95207 209-477-4840; FAX: 209-477-0918 E-mail: timcox@quietride.com	**air plenums** **auto insulation** **firewall insulators** **gloveboxes** **sound deadening**

Mail order only. Manufacturer of firewall insulator upholstery panels just like OEMs did originally. Currently have patterns for nearly 600 cars and trucks, 1928-1986, including Bitchin', Poly-Form, Wescott and Direct Sheetmetal firewalls and street rods. If the pattern for your car is not available, send your old original for reproduction. Each insulator comes ready to install with insulation, all holes punched and detailed to look and fit just like the original. Standards are exacting and work is guaranteed. We specialize in automotive insulation and sound deadening materials and offer complete automotive insulation packages to reduce the noise, heat and vibration in older vehicles. Also make specialty items including gloveboxes, heater plenums, air/defroster ducts, etc. Web site: www.quietride.com or www.firewallinsulators.com
See our ad on page 290

Gliptone Manufacturing Inc 1595 A-6 Ocean Ave Bohemia, NY 11716 631-737-1130, FAX: 631-589-5487 E-mail: wmessina@gliptone.com or rcaporaco@gliptone.com	**car care products**

See full listing in **Section Two** under **car care products**

Hampton Coach 6 Chestnut St, PO Box 6 Amesbury, MA 01913 888-388-8726, 978-388-8047 FAX: 978-388-1113 E-mail: lbb-hc@greennet.net	**fabrics** **interior kits** **top kits**

See full listing in **Section One** under **Chevrolet**

Keleen Leathers Inc 10526 W Cermak Rd Westchester, IL 60154 708-409-9800; FAX: 708-409-9801	**leather hides**

See full listing in **Section Two** under **interiors & interior parts**

Dave Knittel Upholstery 850 E Teton #7 Tucson, AZ 85706 PH/FAX: 520-746-1588	**interiors** **tops** **upholstery**

Deal in upholstery, convertible tops, interiors, rebuild seat backs, rebuilds frames and springs, carpeting, custom interiors, vans, boats, aircraft, custom cars and trucks, etc.

Koala International PO Box 255 Uwchland, PA 19480 610-458-8395; FAX: 610-458-8735 E-mail: sales@koala-products.com	**convertible cleaners** **& protectants** **plastic coating** **plastic polish**

See full listing in **Section Two** under **car care products**

Land Cruiser Solutions Inc 20 Thornell Rd Newton, NH 03858 603-382-3555; FAX: 603-378-0431 E-mail: twbii@aol.com	**accessories** **restoration** **services**

See full listing in **Section One** under **Toyota**

LeBaron Bonney Co 6 Chestnut St, PO Box 6 Amesbury, MA 01913 800-221-5408, 978-388-3811 FAX: 978-388-1113 E-mail: lbb-hc@greennet.net	**fabrics** **interior kits** **top kits**

See full listing in **Section One** under **Ford 1903-1931**

Lyme Pond Restorations PO Box 202 Barnard, VT 05031 802-457-4657	**restoration**

See full listing in **Section Two** under **restoration shops**

Markel's Auto Upholstery 1163 S Robertson Blvd Los Angeles, CA 90035 310-274-1501	**upholstery**

All auto upholstery.

Memoryville USA Inc 2220 N Bishop Ave Rolla, MO 65401 573-364-1810; FAX: 573-364-6975 E-mail: memoryvl@fidnet.com	**restoration**

See full listing in **Section Two** under **restoration shops**

Midwest Hot Rods Inc 10 E Main St (Rt 126) Plainfield, IL 60544 815-254-7637; FAX: 815-254-7640 E-mail: mwhr@aol.com	**street rods** **service shops** **upholstery**

See full listing in **Section Two** under **street rods**

Original Auto Interiors 7869 Trumble Rd Columbus, MI 48063-3915 810-727-2486; FAX: 810-727-4344 E-mail: origauto@tir.com	**upholstery**

Mail order and open shop. Monday-Friday 9 am to 5 pm Eastern time. Upholstery materials for vehicles from the 1950s-1980s. All American made cars. Thunderbird seat covers 1961-1966, the most original available. NOS seat covers for selected Mopars 1957-1964 and Mopar reproductions 1963-1976. OEM carpet sets for most vehicles mid-1950s-present. Also available: headliners, floor mats, trunk mats, convertible tops and boots and windlace. Web site: www.originalauto.com

Paul's Jaguar | parts
4073 NE 5th Terr
Oakland Park
Fort Lauderdale, FL 33334
954-846-7976; FAX: 954-846-9450
E-mail: paulsjag@aol.com

See full listing in **Section One** under **Jaguar**

Performance Automotive Inc | accessories car care
1696 New London Tpke, PO Box 10
Glastonbury, CT 06033
860-633-7868; FAX: 860-657-9110
E-mail: pai@pcnet.com

See full listing in **Section Two** under **car care products**

Quality Sew | sewing machines upholstery
224 W 3rd St
Grand Island, NE 68801
800-431-0037, 308-382-7310
FAX: 308-382-7329
E-mail: 1@qualitysew.com

Mail order and open shop. Monday-Saturday 9 am to 5:30 pm
Central time. Deals in upholstery sewing machines and related
accessories. Web site: www.qualitysew.com

Rod Doors | door panels interior parts
PO Box 2160
Chico, CA 95927
530-896-1513; FAX: 530-896-1518
E-mail: sales@roddoors.com

See full listing in **Section Two** under **interiors & interior parts**

Sailorette's Nautical Nook | covers interiors
451 Davy Ln
Wilmington, IL 60481
815-476-1644; FAX: 815-476-2524

Monday-Friday 9 am to 5 pm, other times by appointment. Custom handcrafted vehicle interiors which includes seat reupholstering, door panels and carpets for old and new vehicles. Also
specializing in custom covers for cars, trucks, motorcycles,
marine covers, marine convertible tops.

Strange Motion Rod & Custom Construction Inc | customizing design fabrication
14696 N 350th Ave
Cambridge, IL 61238
309-927-3346
E-mail: strangemtn@cin.net

See full listing in **Section Two** under **street rods**

Tamraz's Parts Discount Warehouse | carpeting upholstery weatherstripping
10022 S Bode Rd
Plainfield, IL 60544
630-904-4500; FAX: 630-904-2329

See full listing in **Section One** under **Chevelle/Camaro**

Thermax Inc | interior detailing
5385 Alpha Ave
Reno, NV 89506
888-THERMAX (843-7629)
FAX: 775-972-3478

See full listing in **Section Two** under **car care products**

Xtreme Class CC | interior work stereo installation
Philip Patrick
25607 McDonald
Dearborn Heights, MI 48125
313-477-6799; FAX: 313-291-5744
E-mail: xtremeclass@aol.com

See full listing in **Section Two** under **accessories**

videos

Classic Auto Literature | manuals/models parts catalogs posters/videos sales brochures
1592 Seacrest Rd
Nanoose Bay BC Canada V9P 9B5
250-468-9522

See full listing in **Section Two** under **literature dealers**

Collector Car Restorations Inc | videos
611 Buckner St
Elsmere, KY 41018
800-899-1020; FAX: 859-727-4760
E-mail: fvagedes@home.com

Mail order only. Car restoration video tapes (6 tapes): #1 Getting
Started/Back on Track, #2 Chassis & Running Gear, #3 Patch-
work and Metal Finishing, #4 Leadwork and Plastic Filler, #5
Paintwork and Woodgraining, #6 Metal Trim Repair. Web site:
www.carestoration.com

Concours d'Elegance Upholstery | upholstery
1607 Pine Ridge
Bushkill, PA 18324
888-ELEG-UPH
PH/FAX: 570-588-0969
E-mail: concoursuph@enter.net

See full listing in **Section Two** under **upholstery**

Hot Rod Memories | videos
PO Box 280040
Northridge, CA 91328-0040
818-886-7637; FAX: 818-349-1403
E-mail: sales@hotrodmemories.com

See full listing in **Section Four** under **information sources**

Long Road Productions | documentaries
PO Box 1309
Sheffield, MA 01257
413-229-0474; FAX: 413-229-5903
E-mail: lindsey@longroadpro.com

Mail order only. Specializing in video documentaries of antique
heavy trucks, light trucks and muscle cars. Owner profiles and
action footage. Web site: www.longroadpro.com

MotorCam Media | automotive videos
138 N Alling Rd
Tallmadge, OH 44278
800-240-1777; FAX: 330-633-3249
E-mail: carvideo@motorcam.com

Most comprehensive source of automotive video available any-
where. From histories to do-it-yourself, movies to motorsports.
There's something for every auto buff. Call for free catalog.
Web site: www.motorcam.com

MotorWeek	TV program
11767 Owings Mills Blvd	
Owings Mills, MD 21117	
410-356-5600; FAX: 410-581-4113	
E-mail: motorweek@mpt.org	

See full listing in **Section Four** under **information sources**

Ocean Video Movies	videotapes
Box 321	
Oceangate, NJ 08740	
732-269-1206; FAX: 732-269-4263	
E-mail: doebel@adelphia.net	

Mail order only. Videotapes of vintage promotional films and car commercials. Web site: www.oceanvideomovies.net

Old GMC Trucks.Com	literature
Robert English	parts
PO Box 675	
Franklin, MA 02038-0675	
508-520-3900; FAX: 508-520-7861	
E-mail: oldcarkook@aol.com	

See full listing in **Section One** under **GMC**

Practical Images	int'l VHS video
PO Box 245	conversions
Haddam, CT 06438-0245	photo scanning
860-704-0525	photography
E-mail: services@practimages.com	

See full listing in **Section Two** under **photography**

Transport Books at DRB Motors Inc	books
16 Elrose Ave	manuals
Toronto, ON Canada M9M 2H6	periodicals
800-665-2665, 416-744-7675	videos
FAX: 416-744-7696	
E-mail: info@transportbooks.com	

See full listing in **Section Four** under **books & publications**

Video Resources NY Inc	videos
220 W 71 St	
New York, NY 10023	
212-724-7055; FAX: 212-595-0189	

Mail order only. We have a rare collection of automobile videos and TV shows, commercials from the 1950s and 1960s. Each tape is 60 minutes, SP speed. Send for free newsletter or $6 for our complete catalog. Web site: www.askira.com

water pumps

Automotive Friction	brakes
4621 SE 27th Ave	clutches
Portland, OR 97202	water pumps
800-545-9088; FAX: 503-234-1026	

See full listing in **Section Two** under **clutches**

East Coast Jaguar	parts
802B Naaman's Rd	service
Wilmington, DE 19810	
302-475-7200; FAX: 302-475-9258	
E-mail: ecjaguar@aol.com	

See full listing in **Section One** under **Jaguar**

Flowkooler	water pumps
289 Prado Rd	
San Luis Obispo, CA 93401	
805-544-8841; FAX: 805-544-5615	
E-mail: brassworks@thegrid.net	

Mail order and open shop. Monday-Friday 8 am to 5 pm. High-flow rate patent pending water pumps for domestic engines, 1955-1998. Lifetime warranty. Drops operating temperature as much as 30 degrees when cruising at low speeds. Doubles the water flow at idle. Web site: www.flowkooler.com

Skip's Auto Parts	chassis parts
Skip Bollinger	ignition parts
1500 Northaven Dr	water pumps
Gladstone, MO 64118	
816-455-2337; FAX: 816-459-7547	
E-mail: carpartman@aol.com	

Offer parts from 1938-present for various marques. Parts such as water pumps, reground camshafts, chassis parts, fuel pumps rebuilt for today's fuel with methanol, ignition parts and wiper motors, blades, arms. Fax and e-mail are the best as we are difficult to contact. Dealing globally, we are here at odd hours. Please leave your name including country and country code or state, area code and phone number, we will call you back on our nickel. Thank you for your consideration.

wheels & wheelcovers

AKH Wheels	Rallye wheels
200 Broadview Rd	styled steel wheels
Ellensburg, WA 98926-2522	vintage aluminum
509-962-3390	
E-mail: akhwheel@eburg.com	

Mail order. Sale of vintage wheels, 1950s-1985. American Racing Torque Thrusts, 200S (Coke bottles), slots, etc. Aluminum wheels by Ansen, Mickey Thompson, Parnelli Jones, Appliance, Superior, Forsythe, ET, Fenton, Halibrand and Radar Corp. Also have most factory styled steel and Rallye wheels from Ford, GM, Mercury, Dodge, Buick, Olds, Plymouth, Pontiac and AMC. Thousands of wheels available. For one rare wheel or a set. Reproduction vintage style wheels also available. Call!

American Arrow Corp	chroming
105 Kinross	mascots
Clawson, MI 48017	wire wheel
248-435-6115; FAX: 248-435-4670	rebuilding
E-mail: dsommer@greatid.com	

See full listing in **Section Two** under **novelties**

Antique Wheels	respoking
1805 SW Pattulo Way	
West Linn, OR 97068	
503-638-5275	

Respoking of wood and steel felloed wheels of all shapes and sizes of spokes. Only straight grain, FAS hickory wood used. Tracer lathing for uniformity and machine sandings for smoothness. Shipped with wood ready for paint or varnish.

Appleton Garage	car dealer
PO Box B	parts
West Rockport, ME 04865	wheelcovers
207-594-2062	

Mail order and open shop. Monday-Friday 9 am to 4 pm. Have over 10,000 used/new wheelcovers and hubcaps for sale from 1960-2000. Also sell GM cars, trucks and parts from 1960-1987. Specializing in 1962-1966 full-size Chevrolets, 1969-1972 Chevy/GMC pickups. Sorry, no catalog.

Section Two – Generalists

Arelli Alloy Wheels 164 W Jefferson Blvd Buena Park, CA 90620 323-733-0403; FAX: 323-733-0423 E-mail: sales@arelli.com	custom wheels

Featuring chrome exotic wheels in sizes from 16" through 22" for all foreign and domestic vehicles. Web site: www.arelli.com

BDI Automotive Design/Brandon 13985 Madison Pk Morningview, KY 41063 859-363-0086; FAX: 859-363-0081 E-mail: bdi@fuse.net	lettering painting pinstriping

See full listing in **Section Two** under **striping**

Calimer's Wheel Shop 30 E North St Waynesboro, PA 17268 717-762-5056; FAX: 717-762-5021	wooden wheels

Mail order and open shop. Monday-Friday 8 am to 5 pm. Rebuilding of wooden wheels using the customer's metal parts. Wheels made of hickory for years late 1890s-1930. Web site: www.calimerswheelshop.com

Sam Clark 10960 Christenson Rd, PO Box 1817 Lucerne Valley, CA 92356 PH/FAX: 760-248-9025 E-mail: sclark@lucernevalley.net	wheel rims

Producing ultra-quality wheel rims for Alco, Chadwick, Delauney-Belleville, Hispano-Suiza, Isotta-Fraschini, Locomobile, Lozier, Mercedes, Oldsmobile, Packard, Pope-Hartford, Thomas Flyer and other fine brass era autos. Since 1981.

Classic Chevrolet Parts Inc 8723 S I-35 Oklahoma City, OK 73149 405-631-4400; FAX: 405-631-5999 E-mail: info@classicchevroletparts.com	parts

See full listing in **Section One** under **Chevrolet**

Coker Tire 1317 Chestnut St Chattanooga, TN 37402 800-251-6336 toll free 423-265-6368 local & international FAX: 423-756-5607	tires

See full listing in **Section Two** under **tires**

Dayton Wheel Products 115 Compark Rd Dayton, OH 45459 800-862-6000, 937-438-0100 FAX: 937-438-9742 E-mail: sales@dwpco.com	parts restoration service

Office open Monday-Friday 8 am to 5 pm. Wire wheel restoration for Dayton, Borrani, Kelsey-Hayes, Motor Wheel, Dunlop, etc. Also, manufacturer of replacement spline-drive wire wheels and quality knock-off and bolt-on wire wheels. Web site: www.daytonwirewheel.com

Edelbrock Wheels 6300 Valley View Ave Buena Park, CA 90620 714-994-1444; FAX: 714-994-0723 E-mail: jay@mail.ultrawheel.com	aluminum wheels

A new line of cast one-piece aluminum wheels designed specifically for the hot rod and muscle car markets. Web site: www.edelbrockwheels.com

Green-Stuff Metal Polish PO Box 7071 Knoxville, TN 37921 865-382-1286 E-mail: greenstuffpolish@aol.com	metal polish

See full listing in **Section Two** under **plating & polishing**

Greg's Wheel & Tire 11032 S Trudie Ave Whittier, CA 90604 562-947-2346 E-mail: valvestems@aol.com	tools valve stems

We specialize in providing the largest selection of tire valve stems, tools and modification kits for original equipment, aftermarket, race and custom applications.

Hubcap Mike 2465 N Batavia Orange, CA 92865 714-685-8801; FAX: 714-685-8804	hubcaps wheelcovers

See full listing in **Section Two** under **hubcaps**

Roger Kraus Racing 2896 Grove Way Castro Valley, CA 94546 510-582-5031; FAX: 510-886-5605	shocks tires wheels

See full listing in **Section Two** under **tires**

LMARR Disk Ltd PO Box 910 Glen Ellen, CA 95442-0910 707-938-9347; FAX: 707-938-3020 E-mail: lmarr@attglobal.net	wheel discs

See full listing in **Section One** under **Rolls-Royce/Bentley**

Obsolete Ford Parts Inc 8701 S I-35 Oklahoma City, OK 73149 405-631-3933; FAX: 405-634-6815 E-mail: info@obsoletefordparts.com	parts

See full listing in **Section One** under **Ford 1954-up**

OJ Rallye Automotive N 6808 Hwy OJ, PO Box 540 Plymouth, WI 53073 920-893-2531; FAX: 920-893-6800 E-mail: ojrallye@excel.net	accessories car care products lighting parts

See full listing in **Section Two** under **lighting equipment**

Operations Plus PO Box 26347 Santa Ana, CA 92799 PH/FAX: 714-962-2776 E-mail: aquacel@earthlink.net	accessories parts

See full listing in **Section One** under **Cobra**

Performance Designed 11032 S Trudie Ave Whittier, CA 90604 562-947-2346 E-mail: valvestems@aol.com	valve stems

See full listing in **Section Two** under **tires**

Section Two – Generalists

Specialty Wheels Ltd	**wheels**
19310 NE San Rafael St	
Portland, OR 97230	
503-491-8848; FAX: 503-491-8828	
E-mail: wheelzrus@msn.com	

Mail order and open shop. Monday-Friday 8 am to 5 pm. Reproduction wheels for your classic and muscle cars from 1964-1976. Custom sizes and offsets, along with wheel restoration services are our specialty. Web site: www.wheelzrus.com

See our ad on this page

Stockton Wheel Service	**wheel repair**
648 W Fremont St	
Stockton, CA 95203	
800-395-9433, 209-464-7771	
FAX: 209-464-4725	
E-mail: sales@stocktonwheel.com	

Mail order and open shop. Monday-Friday 8 am to 5 pm. Specializing in wheel straightening and fabrication of GM and Mopar Rallye wheels in various offsets and widths. Straighten and repair all steel and aluminum wheels. Polishing and chroming. Since 1883. Web site: www.stocktonwheel.com

Tire & Wheel Emporium	**tires**
6416-C Franklin Blvd	
Sacramento, CA 95823	
916-424-4700; FAX: 916-424-1012	
E-mail: wheelbrokers@earthlink.net	

See full listing in **Section Two** under **tires**

Al Trommers-Rare Auto Literature	**automobilia/lit**
614 Vanburenville Rd	**hubcaps**
Middletown, NY 10940-7242	**wheelcovers**

See full listing in **Section Two** under **literature dealers**

Ultra Wheel Co	**aluminum wheels**
6300 Valley View Ave	
Buena Park, CA 90620	
714-994-1444; FAX: 714-994-0723	
E-mail: comments@mail.ultrawheel.com	

Manufacturer of cast one-piece aluminum wheels. All manufacturing done in-house, using CAD/CAMs, CPCs, robotic cells. ISO 9001 certified.

Valley Wire Wheel Service	**wheel restoration**
14731 Lull St	**wheels**
Van Nuys, CA 91405	
818-785-7237; FAX: 818-994-2042	
E-mail: valleywirewheel@aol.com	

Mail order and open shop. Monday-Friday 8:30 am to 5:30 pm. Restoration of all styles of wire, steel, aluminum and mag. Straightening, truing, polishing, painting, powdercoating, chrome. Since 1969, we have been restoring wheels from daily drivers to concours. References upon request. Sell new and used wheels and tires, custom jobs are no problem. Some antique wheels in stock, also buy old wheels. Helping to keep them on the road, call us, we're here to help.

Wheel Repair Service of New England	**new wire wheels**
317 Southbridge St, Rt 12	**wire wheel**
Auburn, MA 01501	**restoration**
508-832-4949; FAX: 508-832-3969	
E-mail: wheelrepairserv	

Mail order and open shop. Wire wheel restoration specialists since 1962. Replacement spokes available in bare, chrome or polished stainless finishes. New Dayton wire wheels available to fit most cars. Save up to 35% off factory prices.

The Wheel Shoppe Inc	**parts**
13635 SE Division St	**steering wheels**
Portland, OR 97236	
503-761-5119; FAX: 503-761-5190	
E-mail: rogeradams@	
thewheelshoppe.com	

See full listing in **Section Two** under **steering wheels**

windshield wipers

Bill's Speedometer Shop	**repairs**
109 Twinbrook Pl	**restoration**
Sidney, OH 45365	
937-492-7800	
E-mail: wheidemann@woh.rr.com	

See full listing in **Section Two** under **instruments**

C & G Early Ford Parts	**accessories/chrome**
1941 Commercial St, Dept AH	**emblems**
Escondido, CA 92029-1233	**literature**
760-740-2400; FAX: 760-740-8700	**mechanical**
E-mail: cgford@cgfordparts.com	**weatherstripping**

See full listing in **Section One** under **Ford 1932-1953**

Classic Chevrolet Parts Inc	**parts**
8723 S I-35	
Oklahoma City, OK 73149	
405-631-4400; FAX: 405-631-5999	
E-mail: info@classicchevroletparts.com	

See full listing in **Section One** under **Chevrolet**

Clean Sweep-Vacuum Windshield Wiper Motor Rebuilding	motors
760 Knight Hill Rd	repairs
Zillah, WA 98953	wiper parts
509-865-2481; FAX: 509-865-2189	
E-mail: dkjaquith@prodigy.net	

Rebuilding vacuum windshield wiper motors of all makes. Also rebuild hydro-wipe, hydraulically operated wiper motors on 1960s T-Birds and Lincolns.

East Coast Jaguar	parts
802B Naaman's Rd	service
Wilmington, DE 19810	
302-475-7200; FAX: 302-475-9258	
E-mail: ecjaguar@aol.com	

See full listing in **Section One** under **Jaguar**

Ficken Wiper Service	ignition parts
132 Calvert Ave	wiper parts
West Babylon, NY 11704	
631-587-3332; FAX: 631-661-9125	
E-mail: wiperman@aol.com	

Mail order only. Phone hours: Monday-Friday 9 am to 5 pm. Trico windshield wiper motors (vacuum), NOS or can also rebuild your vacuum motor. Arms, blades, linkages and repair kits. Ignition tune-up parts. In business for 30 years. Money back guarantee. Have booth at Hershey and Carlisle auto shows. Hershey space YL230, Carlisle (Fall and Spring) I-105.

Grossmueller's Classic Corvette	NOS parts
55 Sitgreaves St	used parts
Phillipsburg, NJ 08865	
908-213-8832; FAX: 908-213-7088	
E-mail: wfg@gccorvettes.com	

See full listing in **Section One** under **Corvette**

Hi-Tech Aluminum & Automotive Products Inc	accessories
100 Industrial Ave, PO Box 1609	windshield wipers
Cedartown, GA 30125	
800-541-4946	
E-mail: htechaluminum@aol.com	

Mail order and open shop. Monday-Friday 8:30 am to 4 pm Eastern time. Aluminum windshield wipers for most all makes and models of cars and trucks, all USA made aluminum accessories. Bolt covers, U-joint covers, alternator fans, dash knobs, hole plug covers and grease fitting covers. Web site: www.hitechautoparts.com

Obsolete Ford Parts Inc	parts
8701 S I-35	
Oklahoma City, OK 73149	
405-631-3933; FAX: 405-634-6815	
E-mail: info@obsoletefordparts.com	

See full listing in **Section One** under **Ford 1954-up**

J Pinto	electric motors
2306 Memphis St	relay repair
Philadelphia, PA 19125	solenoid repair
215-739-1132	switch repair
E-mail: lectri@yahoo.com	

See full listing in **Section Two** under **electrical systems**

Specialty Power Window	power window kits
2087 Collier Rd	windshield wiper
Forsyth, GA 31029	kit
800-634-9801; FAX: 912-994-3124	

See full listing in **Section Two** under **street rods**

Star Classics Inc	parts
7745 E Redfield #300	
Scottsdale, AZ 85260	
800-644-7827, 480-991-7495	
FAX: 480-951-4096	
E-mail: info@starclassics.com	

See full listing in **Section One** under **Mercedes-Benz**

Tanson Enterprises	performance parts
2508 J St, Dept HVA	restoration parts
Sacramento, CA 95816-4815	
916-448-2950	
FAX: 916-443-3269 *88	
E-mail: tanson@pipeline.com	

See full listing in **Section One** under **Oldsmobile**

Windshield Wiper Service	parts
9109 (Rear) E Garvey Ave	service
Rosemead, CA 91770	
626-280-4546	

Mail order and open shop. Monday-Friday 9 am to 5 pm. Arms, blades and miscellaneous parts. Repair and rebuilding of vacuum and electric windshield wiper motors. Five day service.

wiring harnesses

Ace Antique Auto Restoration	air conditioning
65 S Service Rd	body rebuilding
Plainview, NY 11803	restoration
516-752-6065; FAX: 516-752-1484	wiring harnesses

See full listing in **Section Two** under **restoration shops**

British Wiring Inc	wiring accessories
20449 Ithaca Rd	wiring harnesses
Olympia Fields, IL 60461	
PH/FAX: 708-481-9050	
E-mail: britishwiring@ameritech.net	

Specializing in wiring harnesses and wiring accessories for British classic cars and motorcycles. The US representative for the largest British harness manufacturer. Stock a large selection of harnesses, terminals, grommets, connectors, etc, along with bulk wire. Harnesses for pre-war models are available. Harness price lists (specify marque) and accessory catalog are available free of charge. Web site: www.britishwiring.com

C & G Early Ford Parts	accessories/chrome
1941 Commercial St, Dept AH	emblems
Escondido, CA 92029-1233	literature
760-740-2400; FAX: 760-740-8700	mechanical
E-mail: cgford@cgfordparts.com	weatherstripping

See full listing in **Section One** under **Ford 1932-1953**

C & P Chevy Parts	parts
50 Schoolhouse Rd, PO Box 348VA	restoration supplies
Kulpsville, PA 19443	
215-721-4300, 800-235-2475	
FAX: 215-721-4539	

See full listing in **Section One** under **Chevrolet**

The Car Shop	parts
10449 Rt 39	service
Springville, NY 14141	
716-592-2060; FAX: 716-592-5766	
E-mail: carshop77@aol.com	

See full listing in **Section Two** under **street rods**

Classic Chevrolet Parts Inc | parts
8723 S I-35
Oklahoma City, OK 73149
405-631-4400; FAX: 405-631-5999
E-mail: info@classicchevroletparts.com

See full listing in **Section One** under **Chevrolet**

Crutchfield Corp | car stereos
1 Crutchfield Park
Charlottesville, VA 22911
800-955-9009; FAX: 804-817-1010
E-mail: sales@crutchfield.com

See full listing in **Section Two** under **radios**

Danchuk Mfg | accessories / parts / restoration
3201 S Standard Ave
Santa Ana, CA 92705
714-751-1957; FAX: 714-850-1957
E-mail: info@danchuk.com

See full listing in **Section One** under **Chevrolet**

Ron Francis' Wire Works | fuel injection / harnesses / wiring accessories / wiring kits
167 Keystone Rd
Chester, PA 19013
800-292-1940 orders, 610-485-1937
E-mail: rfwwx@aol.com

Mail order only. Custom wiring kits for cars, trucks and kit cars. Fuel injection harnesses, wiring accessories. 72-page catalog filled with trick wiring and switches, $2. Web site: wire-works.com
See our ad on this page

Long Island Mustang Restoration Parts | convertible specialist / rebuilding services / reconditioned consoles 1965-1970 / repro parts
168 Silverleaf Ln
Islandia, NY 11722
516-232-2388; FAX: 516-272-5201
E-mail: tom@l-i-mustang.com

See full listing in **Section One** under **Mustang**

Obsolete Ford Parts Inc | parts
8701 S I-35
Oklahoma City, OK 73149
405-631-3933; FAX: 405-634-6815
E-mail: info@obsoletefordparts.com

See full listing in **Section One** under **Ford 1954-up**

Potomac Packard | wiring harnesses
PO Box 117
Tiger, GA 30576
800-859-9532 orders
706-782-2345 shop
FAX: 706-782-2344

See full listing in **Section One** under **Packard**

S&M Electro-Tech Inc | electrical parts
8836 Xylite St NE
Blaine, MN 55449
763-780-2861
E-mail: turnswitch@turnswitch.com

See full listing in **Section Two** under **electrical systems**

Studebakers West | mechanical / rebuilding / transmission parts / wiring harnesses
335A Convention Way
Redwood City, CA 94063
650-366-8787

See full listing in **Section One** under **Studebaker**

Visibolts From Classic Safety Products | accessories
7131 Hickory Run
Waunakee, WI 53597
888-212-2163; FAX: 608-824-9200
E-mail: clovis@www.visibolts.com

See full listing in **Section Two** under **lighting equipment**

woodgraining

Adams Custom Engines Inc | restorations
806 Glendale Ave
Sparks, NV 89431-5720
775-358-8070; FAX: 775-358-8040

See full listing in **Section Two** under **restoration shops**

Automotive Specialties | restoration
11240 E Sligh Ave
Seffner, FL 33584
800-676-1928

See full listing in **Section Two** under **steering wheels**

Dash Graining by Mel Erikson | dashboard / restoration
31 Meadow Rd
Kings Park, NY 11754
631-544-1102; FAX: 631-544-1107

Mail order and open shop. 5 days a week 9 am to 6 pm. Active service in dashboard restoration for 15 years. Most business conducted by phone and UPS delivery. Phone estimates given. A hand process, matching original patterns as close to original as possible. Also restoration of some clock and speedometer faces. Can also restore exterior simulated wood for station wagons. Restoration of simulated wood finish on metal dashboards and interior trim for autos 1920s-1950s.

Walter A Finner 11131 Etiwanda Ave Northridge, CA 91326 818-363-6076	woodgraining

Mail order and open shop. Many years' experience. Many show car winners. Send SASE for information.

Gary's Steering Wheel Restoration 2677 Ritner Hwy Carlisle, PA 17013 717-243-5646; FAX: 717-243-5072 E-mail: wheelrest@aol.com	repairs

See full listing in **Section Two** under **steering wheels**

Bill Gratkowski 515 N Petroleum St Titusville, PA 16354 814-827-1782 days or eves E-mail: billgrains@csonline.net	woodgraining

Mail order and open shop. Have been doing woodgraining for 20 years. National show winning quality, low prices, quick turn-around, with references.

C D Hall 1351 Locust Ave Long Beach, CA 90813 PH/FAX: 562-494-5048 E-mail: cdhallwoodgrain@webtv.net	woodgraining

Mail order and professional open workshop. 9 am to 6 pm Pacific time. Serving the West Coast and nationwide. Specializing in old time woodgraining faux finishes. Quality craftsmanship for your classics, woodys, hot rods, sports, antique interiors and exteriors. All work is done by hand with only fine artwork in mind. Most work completed in 3 to 4 weeks or less.

Bob Kennedy Woodgraining Service 8609 Ocean View Whittier, CA 90605 562-693-8739	woodgraining

Mail order and open shop. Monday-Friday 8 am to 5 pm. Duplication of original grain.

Mar-Ke Woodgraining 1102 Hilltop Dr Loveland, CO 80537 970-663-7803; FAX: 970-663-1138	woodgraining

Woodgraining dashes and moldings for autos, trucks. Metal or plastic trim pieces, original and custom. Specializing in burling.

Pilgrim's Auto Restorations 3888 Hill Rd Lakeport, CA 95453 707-262-1062; FAX: 707-263-6956 E-mail: pilgrims@pacific.net	bodywork metal fabrication paint restoration

See full listing in **Section Two** under **restoration shops**

Wooddash.com 438 Calle San Pablo, Unit B Camarillo, CA 93012 805-987-2086; FAX: 805-389-5375 E-mail: mrchrome@west.net	dashes steering wheels

Mail order and open shop. Monday-Friday 8 am to 5 pm. Wood dashes, steering wheels, shift knobs, exhaust tips, grilles, sunroof deflectors and license frames. Web site: www.wooddash.com

Woodgrain Restoration by Grain-It Tech Inc 528 Ave C SE Winter Haven, FL 33880 863-299-4494; FAX: 863-291-3094	woodgrain restoration

Mail order and open shop. Monday-Friday 10 am to 5 pm. Woodgrain restoration using factory original process. Web site: www.woodgraining.com

woodwork

Arrow Fastener Co Inc 271 Mayhill St Saddle Brook, NJ 07663	nail guns rivet tools staple guns

See full listing in **Section Two** under **tools**

Bassett Classic Restoration 2616 Sharon St, Ste D Kenner, LA 70062-4934 PH/FAX: 504-469-2982	parts restoration service

See full listing in **Section One** under **Rolls-Royce/Bentley**

Calimer's Wheel Shop 30 E North St Waynesboro, PA 17268 717-762-5056; FAX: 717-762-5021	wooden wheels

See full listing in **Section Two** under **wheels & wheelcovers**

Classic Wood Mfg 1006 N Raleigh St Greensboro, NC 27405 336-691-1344; FAX: 336-273-3074	wood kits wood replacement

Mail order and open shop. Monday-Friday 7:30 am to 5 pm Eastern time, appointment advised. Ford Model T and A, Chevrolet 1927-1936, MG T Series and MGA wood kits from stock. Dealer program available to qualifying full-line new parts dealers. Custom made wood for other cars from your old pattern.

County Auto Restoration 6 Gavin Rd Mt Vernon, NH 03057 603-673-4840 E-mail: CountyAutoRest@aol.com	bodywork brakes restoration woodwork

See full listing in **Section Two** under **restoration shops**

Chuck & Judy Cubel PO Box 278 Superior, AZ 85273 520-689-2734 FAX: 520-689-5815, 24 hours E-mail: cubel@theriver.com	wood parts

See full listing in **Section One** under **Ford 1903-1931**

JB Donaldson Co 2533 W Cypress Phoenix, AZ 85009 602-278-4505; FAX: 602-278-1112	castings steering wheels wood parts

See full listing in **Section Two** under **steering wheels**

David R Edgerton, Coachworks 9215 St Rt 13 Camden, NY 13316-4933 315-245-3113 E-mail: derods@excite.com	restoration woodworking

See full listing in **Section Two** under **restoration shops**

Section Two – Generalists

Enfield Auto Restoration Inc 4 Print Shop Rd Enfield, CT 06082 860-749-7917; FAX: 860-749-2836	**panel beating** **restorations** **Rolls-Royce parts** **woodworking**

See full listing in **Section Two** under **restoration shops**

David J Entler Restorations 10903 N Main St Ext Glen Rock, PA 17327-8373 717-235-2112	**woodwork**

Monday-Friday 8 am to 5 pm. Structural woodwork restoration for 1933-1936 General Motors bodies. Complete kits or individual pieces, coupes, sedans, trucks, roadsters, sedan deliveries. Rewooding of all bodies. Antique truck body fabrication. 18 years in business.

Glazier Pattern & Coachworks 3720 Loramie-Washington Rd Houston, OH 45333 937-492-7355; FAX: 937-492-9987 E-mail: s.glazier.fam@juno.com	**coachwork** **interior woodwork** **restoration of wood** **bodied cars**

See full listing in **Section One** under **Chrysler**

Grizzly Industrial Inc 2406 Reach Rd Williamsport, PA 17701 800-523-4777; FAX: 800-438-5901 E-mail: csr@grizzly.com	**tools**

See full listing in **Section Two** under **tools**

Hatfield Restorations PO Box 846 Canton, TX 75103 903-567-6742; FAX: 903-567-0645 E-mail: pathat@vzinet.com	**restoration**

See full listing in **Section Two** under **restoration shops**

KC Wood Manufacturing 470 Rock Church Rd SW Willis, VA 24380 540-789-8300 E-mail: info@chevywood.com	**structural wood** **parts**

Mail order and open shop. Monday-Friday 8 am to 4:30 pm. Specializing in structural wood parts for Chrvrolet cars and trucks 1926-1936. Web site: www.chevywood.com

M & T Manufacturing Co 30 Hopkins Ln Peace Dale, RI 02883 401-789-0472; FAX: 401-789-5650 E-mail: sales@mtmfg.com	**convertible** **hold-down cables** **wooden top bows**

Mail order only. Monday-Friday 9 am to 5 pm. Manufacturer of wooden top bows for classic convertible cars including VW, Jaguar, Mercedes, Rolls-Royce, old Fords and others. Also manufacturer of convertible hold-down cables. Distributor of domestic and foreign convertible tops and top cables.

Martin Carriage House 350 N Park Ave Warren, OH 44481 330-395-8442	**wood bodies**

New all wood bodies for most pre-1912 automobiles. Repair work to save a good original body.

Memoryville USA Inc 2220 N Bishop Ave Rolla, MO 65401 573-364-1810; FAX: 573-364-6975 E-mail: memoryvl@fidnet.com	**restoration**

See full listing in **Section Two** under **restoration shops**

New Era Motors 11611 NE 50th Ave, Unit 6 Vancouver, WA 98686 360-573-8788; FAX: 360-573-7461	**restoration**

Mail order and open shop. Monday-Friday 8 am to 5 pm. Offer complete or partial restoration of any wood framed composite antique or classic automobile body, complete frame-off restorations also available.

Oak Bows 122 Ramsey Ave Chambersburg, PA 17201 717-264-2602	**top bows**

Steam bent top bows duplicating your original bow. All bows steam bent like the original, not glued. No danger of separation. Send patterns, sockets or old bows for duplication. All SASEs will be answered.

Older Car Restoration Martin Lum, Owner 304 S Main St, Box 428 Mont Alto, PA 17237 717-749-3383, 717-352-7701 E-mail: marty@oldercar.com	**repro parts** **restoration**

See full listing in **Section Two** under **restoration shops**

Al Prueitt & Sons Inc 8 Winter Ave, PO Box 158 Glen Rock, PA 17327 800-766-0035, 717-428-1305 FAX: 717-235-4428	**restoration** **upholstery** **woodworking**

See full listing in **Section Two** under **restoration shops**

RAU Restoration 2027 Pontius Ave Los Angeles, CA 90025 310-445-1128; FAX: 310-575-9715 E-mail: wcrau@rau-autowood.com	**woodwork**

Mail order and open shop. Monday-Friday 8 am to 6 pm, Saturday and Sunday by appointment. We specialize in classic wood restoration and we have done well, with cars winning at numerous shows including a First in Class at last year's National Rolls-Royce meet and Best of Show at the Pebble Beach Concours. For new cars we design and produce show quality accessories including steering wheels, shift knobs, picnic tables and consoles. Web site: www.rau-autowood.com
See our ad on page 423

See our ad on page 423

Robert's Custom Metal 24 Lark Industrial Pkwy #D Smithfield, RI 02828 401-949-2361	**metal fabrication** **welding** **woodwork**

See full listing in **Section Two** under **sheetmetal**

Rod Jolley Coachbuilding Ltd 37 Gordleton Industrial Pk Sway Rd Lymington SO41 8JD England ++44 1590 683702 FAX: ++44 1590 683634 E-mail: enquiries@rodjolley.com	**ash frames** **panels**

Mail order and open shop. Monday-Friday 8 am to 6 pm. Manufactures and repairs of ash frames and panels for antique autos Web site: www.rodjolley.com

RX Autoworks
983 W 1st St
North Vancouver, BC Canada V7P 1A4
604-986-0102, 877-986-0102 toll free
FAX: 604-986-0175

restoration

See full listing in **Section Two** under **restoration shops**

Vintage Woodworks
PO Box 49
Iola, WI 54945
715-445-3791

upholstery
woodwork

Shop address: Depot St, Iola, WI. All automotive woodworking specializing in Chrysler Town & Country cars. Reproduction parts for Town & Country cars. Custom upholstery work.

Willys Wood
35336 Chaucer Dr
North Ridgeville, OH 44039
440-327-2916

wood parts

See full listing in **Section One** under **Willys**

Wood Excel Ltd
1545 Green Hill Rd
Collegeville, PA 19426
610-584-1725

woodwork

Mail order and open shop. Monday-Friday 10 am to 6 pm. Repair veneer and refinish wood in automobiles including Rolls-Royce, Jaguar, Mercedes-Benz, Packard, Cadillac, Lincoln, etc. If possible, one piece is given free before any business is done.

The Wood N'Carr
3231 E 19th St
Signal Hill, CA 90804
562-498-8730; FAX: 562-985-3360
E-mail: suzyq22222@aol.com

automotive wood

Mail order and open shop. Monday-Friday 8 am to 4:30 pm. Specializing in woody station wagons of all types, original or hot rod. We also do any and all automotive wood for cars other than woodys. If it's auto wood, we do it all, and have for 26 years. Web site: www.woodncarr.net

Wooddash.com
438 Calle San Pablo, Unit B
Camarillo, CA 93012
805-987-2086; FAX: 805-389-5375
E-mail: mrchrome@west.net

dashes
steering wheels

See full listing in **Section Two** under **woodgraining**

The Woodie Works
245 VT Rt 7A
Arlington, VT 05250
PH/FAX: 802-375-9305
E-mail: dkwoodie@vermontel.net

woodworking

Mail order and open shop. Monday-Saturday 9 am to 6 pm. Complete woodworking shop dedicated to the preservation of the wooden vehicle. Provide a complete range of services including research and design, repair, reproduction, replacement and refinishing. New work or custom work is welcome, as are unusual marques, trucks and commercial vehicles. Complete patterns for 1933-1936 Ford wagons, 1949-1951 Ford wagons and 1941-1954 Chevrolet Cantrells in house. If your vehicle has wooden parts, you should be talking to us.

Section Two – Generalists

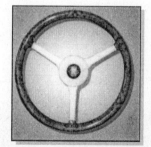

Tourguide:
Generalists

Planning a trip? Or perhaps you would just like to know what old-car resources are in your home territory. In either case, the tourguide to Section Two will help.

This tourguide offers you an alphabetical listing of old car generalists with open shops by state and foreign country. Simply turn to the page number indicated for complete information on the object of your visit, including hours of operation, complete address, and phone number.

Alabama
348 DBM Classic Auto, Andalusia
270 Replica Plastics, Dothan

Arizona
404 A AAdvantage Auto Transport Inc, Tempe
402 American Transmissions, Scottsdale
183 ARS Automotive Research Services, Phoenix
345 British Car Service, Tucson
264 Engines Direct, Scottsdale
233 Leo Gephart Inc, Scottsdale
403 Mid Valley Engineering, Phoenix
268 Pace Setter Performance Products, Phoenix
386 The Rod Factory, Phoenix

California
325 ACPlating, Bakersfield
209 Allied Bearing Sales, Los Angeles
380 American Street Rod, Rancho Cordova
304 Angeli Machine Co, Burbank
325 Ano-Brite Inc, North Hollywood
255 Antique Auto Electric, Rosemead
276 Antique Auto Fasteners, Huntington Beach
264 Atlas Engine Rebuilding Co Inc, Harbor City
182 Bell Motorsports/Pyrotect, Oakland
273 Best Gasket Inc, Whittier
336 Bob's Radio & TV Service, Pismo Beach
345 Bonnet to Boot, Reseda
182 Bonneville Speed & Supply, Tustin
305 BPE Racing Heads, Placentia
333 The Brassworks, San Luis Obispo
408 Brothers Truck Parts, Corona
334 Cal West Auto Air & Radiators Inc, Valencia
397 California Convertible Co, San Marcos
229 Car Cover Company, Monrovia
236 The Carburetor Refactory, Richmond
264 Carobu Engineering, Costa Mesa
286 Cerullo Performance Seating, Pomona
185 Classic Auto Appraiser, Laguna Niguel
229 Classic Motoring Accessories, Monrovia
347 Classic Motors, San Mateo
287 Comfy/Inter-American Sheepskins Inc, West Los Angeles
287 Custom Auto Interiors by Ron Mangus, Bloomington
175 Custom Autosound Mfg, Anaheim
382 Dagel's Street Rods, Orange
264 Damper Doctor, Redding

245 Don's Antique Auto Parts, Fremont
233 European Collectibles Inc, Costa Mesa
298 Faxon Auto Literature, Riverside
421 Walter A Finner, Northridge
389 Five Points Classic Auto Shocks, Santa Ana
416 Flowkooler, San Luis Obispo
326 Foss Plating Co Inc, Santa Fe Springs
349 Grand Touring, Anaheim
233 Grumpy's Old Cars, San Luis Obispo
421 C D Hall, Long Beach
409 Hank's Custom Stepside Beds, Herald
330 Gary Hill Auto Service, Arcadia
406 Interstate Towing Service, San Francisco
290 Just Dashes Inc, Van Nuys
421 Bob Kennedy Woodgraining Service, Whittier
277 King Bolt Co, Covina
377 Koch's, Canyon Country
283 David Lindquist, Automobile Clock Repair, Whittier
257 M & H Electric Fabricators Inc, Santa Fe Springs
334 Mac's Radiator Service & Gas Tank Renu LA, Bellflower
257 Jack Marcheski, Hollister
353 Alan Mest Early Model Auto Repair, Gardena
400 Mullins & Teardrop Reproductions, Auburn
390 National Spring Co., Inc, El Cajon
364 Painting & Stripping Corp, Santa Fe Springs
262 Performance Automotive Warehouse, Chatsworth
354 Pilgrim's Auto Restorations, Lakeport
268 Porcelain Patch & Glaze Co Inc, Oakland
220 Power Brake Systems, San Bernadino
400 R-D-T Plans and Parts, Merced
335 Rad Cap Products, Pacheco
391 Rare Parts Inc, Stockton
422 RAU Restoration, Los Angeles
193 Red Lion Racing, Cucamonga
262 Ross Racing Pistons, El Segundo
362 Rubber Age LM Mfg Inc, Gardena
313 Showcase Express, Huntington Beach
386 Specialized Street Rods, Huntington Beach
386 Specialty Cars Inc, Artesia
283 Speed-o-Tac, Thousand Oaks
418 Stockton Wheel Service, Stockton
263 Superior Pump Exchange Co, Hawthorne
248 Taylor Auto Parts, Esparato
393 Tire & Wheel Emporium, Sacramento
267 Valley Head Service Inc, Northridge
418 Valley Wire Wheel Service, Van Nuys
230 Van Raalte & Co LLC, Garden Valley
392 Vehicle Spring Service, Stanton
180 VPA International, Corona
304 WD-40 Company, San Diego
363 Wefco Rubber Manufacturing Company Inc, Canoga Park
283 Westberg Manufacturing Inc, Sonoma
397 Williams Lowbuck Tools Inc, Norco
419 Windshield Wiper Service, Rosemead
423 The Wood N'Carr, Signal Hill
421 Wooddash.com, Camarillo

Colorado
380 A-1 Street Rods, Colorado Springs
183 AMC Classic Appraisers, Arvada
279 CBS Performance Automotive, Colorado Springs
387 The Street Rod Place, Aurora
393 The Tire Source Inc, Boulder
306 Vintage Motor and Machine, Fort Collins

Connecticut
325 ANC Restoration, Waterbury
210 Auto Body Specialties Inc, Middlefield
236 Battery Ignition Co Inc, Hartford
321 Color-Ite Refinishing Co, Bethany
229 Cover-It , West Haven
402 Dynamic Racing Transmissions LLC, North Branford
232 Draggone Classic Motorcars, Bridgeport

349 Enfield Auto Restoration Inc, Enfield
219 Engineered Components Inc, Vernon
246 Manchester Motor Car Co, Manchester
273 Marren Motor Sports Inc, Derby
316 Moores Cycle Supply, West Hartford
313 Lloyd Ralston Gallery, Stratford
368 RB's Prototype Model & Machine Co, Stamford
292 Ridgefield Auto Upholstery, Ridgefield
195 Peter Tytla Artist, East Lyme
278 Vintage Glass USA, Tolland
371 Webber Engineering LLC, Pawcatuck

Delaware

400 Performance Shop, Newark

Florida

335 Antique Automobile Radio Inc, Palm Harbor
231 Berliner Classic Motorcars Inc, Dania Beach
226 Bill & Brad's Tropical Formula, Clearwater
344 BMC Classics Inc, New Smyrna Beach
223 Car Critic, Naples
347 Classics and Customs, Largo
347 Coach Builders Limited Inc, High Springs
202 Jerry Goldsmith Promos, Lakeland
350 Harbor Auto Restoration, Pompano Beach
212 Hoffman Automotive Distributor, Hilliard
245 IMCADO Manufacturing Co, Umatilla
384 KC's Rods & Customs, Winter Park
331 Moroso Motorsports Park, Palm Beach Gardens
328 Pot Metal Restorations, Tallahassee
234 Rader's Relics, Winter Park
283 Reynolds Speedometer Repair, Naples
328 Samson Technology Corporation, Davie
357 Chris Smith's Creative Workshop Motorcar Restoration, Dania
375 Ed Strain Inc, Pinellas Park
421 Woodgrain Restoration by Grain-It Tech Inc, Winter Haven

Georgia

184 Auto Appraisal Service, Augusta
199 Auto Motif Inc, Smyrna
231 Auto Quest Investment Cars Inc, Tifton
184 Automobile Classics Appraisal Services, College Park
346 Classic Car Works Ltd, Jasper
373 The Generation Gap, Byron
370 Goodmark Industries Inc, Lawrenceville
419 Hi-Tech Aluminum & Automotive Products Inc, Cedartown
254 Jim Osborn Reproductions Inc, Lawrenceville
386 Specialty Power Window, Forsyth
401 Trailersource, Marietta

Illinois

372 300 Below Inc, Decatur
401 4-Speeds by Darrell, Vermilion
394 A & I Supply, N Pekin
363 Bel Air Restorations, Pocahontas
231 Chicago Car Exchange, Libertyville
211 Desert Dog Auto Parts Inc, Woodstock
367 House of Powder Inc, Standard
395 HTP America Inc, Arlington Heights
283 Instrument Services Inc, Roscoe
315 Luback & Co, Chicago Heights
336 Marquette Radio, Orland Park
197 Dana Mecum Auctions Inc, Marengo
234 Memory Lane Motors Inc, Lake Bluff
385 Midwest Hot Rods Inc, Plainfield
265 Moline Engine Service Inc, Moline
354 Old Coach Works Restoration Inc, Yorkville
262 Partwerks of Chicago, New Lenox
364 Redi-Strip Company, Roselle
356 Restorations Unlimited II Inc, Cary
415 Sailorette's Nautical Nook, Wilmington
357 Sanders Antique Auto Restoration, Rockford
221 Speed Bleeder Products Co, Lemont

281 Speed Service Inc, Chicago
328 Star Chrome, Chicago
357 Sterling Restorations Inc, Sterling
359 Wilson's Classic Auto, Congerville

Indiana

296 Collins Metal Spinning, New Palestine
394 Custom Bandsaw Blades, Muncie
282 Electronic Safety Products Inc, Indianapolis
242 Fort Wayne Clutch & Driveline, Fort Wayne
311 Grandpa's Attic , Goshen
352 LaVine Restorations Inc, Nappanee
399 Bruce Litton Trailer Sales, Indianapolis
205 Natmus Roadside Market, Auburn
364 Pro-Strip, Fort Wayne
401 Wells Cargo Inc, Elkhart

Iowa

343 Anderson Restoration, Kanawha
232 Duffy's Collectible Cars, Cedar Rapids
192 Guenther Graphics, LeClaire
323 Time Passages Ltd, West Des Moines
303 Uhlenhopp Lock, Clarksville

Kansas

199 Automobilia, Wichita
256 Fifth Avenue Antique Auto Parts, Clay Center
336 Fred's Classic Auto Radio & Clocks, Lenexa
245 Gowen Auto Parts, Coffeyville
397 Superior Equipment, Valley Center

Kentucky

218 The Antique Auto Shop, Elsmere
399 Hodges Custom Haulers, Benton
385 Pro's Pick Rod & Custom, Erlanger
400 Trailer World Inc, Bowling Green

Maine

416 Appleton Garage, West Rockport
311 Karl's Collectibles, Lewiston
353 McCann Auto, Houlton
197 McIntyre Auctions, East Dixfield
371 Thompson Hill Metalcraft, Berwick

Maryland

285 Andover Restraints Inc, Columbia
270 Class Glass & Performance Inc, Cumberland

Massachusetts

402 AAdvanced Transmissions, Worcester
263 Aldrich Auto Supply Inc, Hatfield
243 Antique Auto Parts Cellar, South Weymouth
195 Auctioneer Phil Jacquier Inc, Southwick
380 Belmont's Rod & Custom Shop, Dedham
271 JJ Best & Co, Chatham
287 Dom Corey Upholstery & Antique Auto , Fairhaven
295 Norman D'Amico, Clarksburg
186 Dearborn Automobile Co, Topsfield
296 Richard Hurlburt, Greenfield
405 Intercity Lines Inc, Warren
273 JF Sullivan Company, Auburn
351 Keilen's Auto Restoring, North Attleboro
352 Libbey's Classic Car Restoration Center, Shrewsbury
209 South Shore Bearing Dist, Quincy
190 Steele's Appraisal, Maynard
400 Trailers of New England Inc, Palmer
363 Pat Walsh Restorations, Wakefield
418 Wheel Repair Service of New England, Auburn

Michigan

217 Allied Power Brake Co, Detroit
191 Antique Car Paintings, Dearborn Heights

310	Auto Zone, Birmingham
281	Bob's Speedometer Service, Farmington
200	C&N Reproductions Inc, Bloomfield Hills
286	CARS Inc, Berkley
307	Clark & Clark Specialty Products Inc, Holland
381	Classic Coachworks Rod & Custom, Grand Rapids
186	Russ Dentico's Sales & Auto Appraisal Consulting, Trenton
348	Deters Restorations, Temperance
295	Duane's License Plate Restoration, Lansing
389	Eaton Detroit Spring Service Co, Detroit
182	Horseplayactionwear.com, Bay City
350	Hyde Auto Body, Auburn Hills
376	ididit inc, Tecumseh
219	Inline Tube, Fraser
219	Muskegon Brake & Dist Co, Muskegon
261	Northwestern Auto Supply Inc, Grand Rapids
414	Original Auto Interiors, Columbus
214	Sherman & Associates Inc, Washington
181	Tubes-n-Hoses by TKM, Byron Center
269	Waldron's Antique Exhaust Inc, Nottawa

Minnesota

319	CJ Spray Inc, South St Paul
395	Goodson Shop Supplies, Winona
268	Headers by "Ed" Inc, Minneapolis
409	Bruce Horkey's Wood & Parts, Windom
326	Iverson Automotive, Minnetonka
260	Jackson's Oldtime Parts, Duluth
396	Northern Tool & Equipment, Burnsville
354	Odyssey Restorations Inc, Spring Lake Park
257	S&M Electro-Tech Inc, Blaine
235	Yesterday's Auto Sales, Minneapolis

Mississippi

411	Slim's Garage, Seminary

Missouri

325	A & A Plating Inc, Independence
381	The Chopper Rod Shop, Elmer
377	Fiesta's Classic Car Center, St Louis
339	Independence Porcelain Enamel, Independence
353	Memoryville USA Inc, Rolla
316	Moto Guzzi, Harper's, Greenwood
208	Paul's Rod & Bearing Ltd, Parkville
206	Scott Signal Co, Willard

Montana

222	Cam-Pro, Great Falls

Nebraska

184	Auto World Sales, Lincoln
200	Blast From the Past, Gretna
415	Quality Sew, Grand Island

Nevada

343	Adams Custom Engines Inc, Sparks
288	Dashtop by Palco Ind Inc, Reno
240	Innovative Rod Products, Moundhouse
396	Steelman/JS Products, Las Vegas

New Hampshire

347	County Auto Restoration, Mt Vernon
233	McLean's Brit Bits, Rye
266	R & L Engines Inc, Dover
356	Redding Corp, George's Mills
356	Rick's Relics, Pittsburg

New Jersey

254	Addison Generator Inc, Freehold
333	American Honeycomb Radiator Mfg Co, Holmdel
274	American Restorations Unlimited TA, Rochelle Park
236	Arch Carburetor, Newark
229	Auto Chic/Liquid Glass, Dover

344	Automotive Restorations Inc, Bernardsville
365	The Autoworks Ltd, Westwood
184	AVM Automotive Consulting, Montvale
344	Back-In-Time Automotive Restorations, Pompton Lakes
255	Robert D Bliss, Monroe
305	Bob's Automotive Machine, Harrison
346	Classic Garage, Red Bank
399	D & D Trailers Inc, Trenton
311	EWA & Miniature Cars USA Inc, Green Brook
402	Fatsco Transmission Parts, Pinebrook
350	Hibernia Auto Restorations Inc, Hibernia
321	Bill Hirsch Auto Parts, Newark
390	Kenask Spring Co, Jersey City
193	Thomas Montanari Automotive Artist, Hopewell
205	NJ Nostalgia Hobby, Scotch Plains
178	NMW Products, Raritan
257	M Parker Autoworks Inc, Bellmawr
189	CT Peters Inc Appraisers , Red Bank
386	Rod-1 Shop, Pitman
357	Schaeffer & Long, Magnolia
254	Street-Wise Performance, Tranquility
266	Thul Auto Parts Inc, Plainfield
359	Widmann's Garage, Hamilton

New York

343	Ace Antique Auto Restoration, Plainview
343	Adler's Antique Autos Inc, Stephentown
388	Apple Hydraulics Inc, Calverton
286	Auto-Mat Co, Hicksville
208	The Babbitt Pot, Fort Edward
314	Backwoods Auto, Esperance
381	The Car Shop, Springville
232	Classic Cars & Parts, Lindenhurst
244	Joe Curto Inc, College Point
420	Dash Graining by Mel Erikson, Kings Park
254	Denny's Driveshafts, Kenmore
349	David R Edgerton Coachworks, Camden
403	FB Performance Transmissions, Bay Shore
405	Five Star Transport, Valley Stream
202	Get It On Paper, Islip
334	Highland Radiator Inc, Highland
275	Hometown Auto Glass, Burnt Hills
219	Integrity Machine, Mount Sinai
384	Jackson & Wardick Hot Rods, Bedford Corners
228	KozaK® Auto Drywash® Inc, Batavia
204	l'art et l'automobile, East Hampton
331	Marcovicci-Wenz Engineering Inc, Ronkonkoma
234	Mountain Fuel, Gilboa
400	Nyles Haulmark Trailer Sales, Fairport
234	John T Poulin , North Troy
235	Retrospect Automotive, Huntington Station
220	Rochester Clutch & Brake Co, Rochester
257	Rockland Auto Electric, Pearl River
190	RL Smith Sales Inc, Rensselaer
207	Spirit Enterprises, Lockport

North Carolina

329	600 Racing, Inc. Harrisburg
309	Asheville DieCast, Asheville
320	Automotive Paints Unlimited, Roxboro
360	Clester's Auto Rubber Seals Inc, Salisbury
362	Steele Rubbber Products, Denver

Ohio

344	Bastian Automotive Restoration, Fairfield
231	Jerry Bensinger, Hubbard
231	Bill's Collector Cars, South Point
306	Brookville Roadster Inc, Brookville
345	Cars of the Past Restorations Inc, Newbury
256	Certified Auto Electric Inc, Bedford
326	CustomChrome Plating Inc, Grafton
288	Dave's Auto Restoration, Jefferson
417	Dayton Wheel Products, Dayton

233 George's Auto & Tractor Sales Inc, North Jackson
330 George's Speed Shop, Dayton
303 Jesser's Classic Keys, Akron
384 Kenny's Rod & Kustom, Newton Falls
265 Koffel's Place II, Huron
399 Lazy B Trailer Sales Inc, Bristolville
312 Little Old Cars, Canton
318 Ohio Jukebox Co, Cumberland
275 Pilkington Glass Search, Columbus
334 Powell Radiator Service, Wilmington
354 Prestige Automotive Inc, Tippecanoe
396 Production Tool Supply of Ohio, Cleveland
364 Riverbend Abrasive Blasting, Coshocton
266 Ross' Automotive Machine Co Inc, Niles
335 Skills Unlimited Inc, Tiffin
396 Steck Manufacturing Co Inc, Dayton
181 Stevens Car Care Products Inc, East Lake
342 TP Tools & Equipment, Canfield
401 Trailex Inc, Canfield

Oklahoma

372 Circle N Stainless, Lawton
395 Kwiklift Inc, Broken Arrow
357 Special Interest Autos, Ardmore
323 Vic's Place Inc, Guthrie

Oregon

242 Automotive Friction, Portland
244 Baxter Auto Parts , Portland
372 Brooks Performance Coatings, Sherwood
286 Cascade Audio Engineering, Bend
347 Concours Quality Auto Restoration, Gresham
378 Highway Products Inc, White City
220 Power Brake Booster Exchange Inc, Portland
357 Rust Busters, Clackamas
418 Specialty Wheels Ltd, Portland
209 SS Specialties, Milwaukie
357 Steve's Auto Restorations, Portland
377 The Wheel Shoppe Inc, Portland

Pennsylvania

255 American-Foreign Auto Electric Inc, Souderton
343 Auto Restoration by William R Hahn, Allison Park
344 Avanti Auto Service, Glen Mills
174 Blue Ridge Mountain Cookery Inc, Waynesboro
323 Boop Photography, Harrisburg
399 C & C Manufacturing Co, Hazleton
417 Calimer's Wheel Shop, Waynesboro
347 Classics 'n More Inc, Lancaster
413 Concours d'Elegance Upholstery, Bushkill
298 Crank'en Hope Publications, Blairsville
376 D&D Automobilia, South Fork
232 Driven By Desire, Kane
422 David J Entler Restorations, Glen Rock
319 Extreme Motorsports Painting Ltd, Stowe
202 Fill Er Up, Bird In Hand
399 Tommy Gale Trailer Sales & Service, Elizabeth
376 Gary's Steering Wheel Restoration, Carlisle
421 Bill Gratkowski, Titusville
383 Hillcrest Hot Rods, Greenville
311 Hobby Express Inc, Mars
351 Krem Engineering, Meadville
384 Lee's Street Rods, Rome
275 N/C Industries Antique Auto Parts, Sayre
354 Older Car Restoration, Mont Alto
354 Bob Ore Restorations, Erie
328 Paul's Chrome Plating Inc, Evans City
364 Pennsylvania Metal Cleaning, Monaca
220 Power Brake X-Change Inc, Pittsburgh

356 Al Prueitt & Sons Inc, Glen Rock
328 Qual Krom-Great Lakes Plant, Erie
356 Ray's Upholstering, Scranton
214 Raybuck Autobody Parts, Punxsutawney
356 Reinholds Restorations, Reinholds
247 Restoration Specialties and Supply Inc, Windber
356 Richard's Auto Restoration, Wyoming
385 R/T Street Rods, Coopersburg
357 Sports Car Haven, Danville
229 Stoner Inc, Quarryville
237 Sugarbush Products Inc, Chalfont
364 Tri-State Metal Cleaning, Erie
394 Universal Vintage Tire Co, Hershey
182 Viking Worldwise Inc, Manheim
293 Willow Grove Auto Top, Willow Grove
423 Wood Excel Ltd, Collegeville
365 Ziebart/Tidy Car, Pittsburgh

Rhode Island

258 B & B Cylinder Head Inc, West Warwick
388 The Pinstriper, Narragansett
257 Rhode Island Wiring Services Inc, W Kingston
371 Robert's Custom Metal, Smithfield

South Carolina

239 Atlantic Enterprises, Little River
304 FHS Supply Inc, Clover
334 GRIFFIN Radiator, Piedmont

South Dakota

265 Harkin Machine Shop, Watertown

Tennessee

394 Accessible Systems Inc, Jonesborough
325 Advanced Plating & Powder Coating, Nashville
346 Classic Carriages, Athens
282 Corvette Clocks by Roger, Jackson
367 Jack P Gross Assoc/Scott Manufacturing Inc, Helenwood
187 John H Heldreth & Associates, Hendersonville
177 Hunters Custom Automotive, Nashville

Texas

343 Auto Craftsmen Restoration Inc, San Antonio
369 Car-Line Manufacturing & Distribution Inc, Beaumont
231 Cars of the Times, Duncanville
381 Classic Auto Works, Travis Peak
402 Coffey Classic Transmissions, Fort Worth
275 Custom Cut Auto Glass/Southern Glass Inc, Pasadena
350 Hand's Elderly Auto Care, Grand Prairie
350 Hatfield Restorations, Canton
351 K & K Vintage Motorcars LC, Houston
395 Lake Buchanan Industries Inc, Buchanan Dam
233 Larson Motor Co, Amarillo
243 Mastercraft Body Works Inc, Ovilla
246 Parts House, Fort Worth
403 Phoenix Transmission Products, Weatherford
285 Pete Reinthaler Insurance, Bellaire
356 Roadrunner Tire & Auto, Fort Worth
328 Speed & Sport Chrome Plating, Houston
254 un-du Products Inc, Dallas
394 Wallace W Wade Specialty Tires, Dallas
319 Weber's Nostalgia Supermarket, Fort Worth

Utah

347 Customs & Classics Inc, Murray
268 High Performance Coatings, Bluffdale

Vermont

349 Fuller's Restoration Inc, Manchester Center

352 Last Chance Repair & Restoration, Shaftsbury
352 Lyme Pond Restorations, Barnard
354 Northern Motorsport Ltd, Wilder
237 Rick's Carburetor Repair, Hydeville
423 The Woodie Works, Arlington

Virginia

281 12 Volt Stuff, Radio & Speedometer Repair Co, Richmond
335 12 Volt Stuff, Radio & Speedometer Repair Co, Richmond
238 Casting Salvage Technologies, Fredricksburg
382 Flatlander's Hot Rods, Norfolk
422 KC Wood Manufacturing, Willis
385 P&J Automotive Inc, Danville
296 Skimino Enterprises, Williamsburg
375 Sports Car Rentals & Sales, Batesville
269 Thermal Tech Coatings Inc, Hopewell
229 Ultimate Appearance Ltd, Smithfield
359 WTH Service and Restorations Inc, Warrenton
359 WW Motor Cars & Parts Inc, Broadway

Washington

185 Blair Collectors & Consultants, Seattle
240 Greer Enterprises, Richland
422 New Era Motors, Vancouver
324 Nostalgic Reflections, Veradale
247 RB's Obsolete Automotive, Edmonds
398 The Bill Stevenson Company, Kent
253 The V8 Store, Vancouver
248 Vintage Auto Parts Inc, Woodinville
302 Vintage Books, Vancouver
303 Voss Motors Inc, Seattle

West Virginia

243 Antique Auto Parts, Elkview

Wisconsin

311 International House of Toys, Muskego
351 Ken's Klassics Inc, Muscoda
297 OJ Rallye Automotive, Plymouth
335 Glen Ray Radiators Inc, Wausau
313 Town & Country Toys, Marshall
235 Valenti Classics Inc, Caledonia

Australia

246 Obsolete Auto Parts Co P/L, Kurrajong, NSW 2758
362 Spectrum Rubber & Panels, Dunheved, Sydney

Belgium

284 Classic Car Lobby, 4800 Verviers

Canada

309 Auto Nostalgia Enr, Mont St Gregoire, QC
293 EVA Sports Cars, Vankleek Hill, ON
256 Ferris Auto Electric Ltd, North Bay, ON
187 Hawthorne's Happy Motoring, Coaldale AB
383 Horton, Breslau, ON
353 Memory Lane Motors, Fenelon Falls, ON
247 Pre-Sixties Cars and Parts Ltd, South Guelph, ON
357 RX Autoworks, North Vancouver, BC
248 Special Interest Cars, Oakville, ON
285 Zehr Insurance Brokers Ltd, New Hamburg, ON

Denmark

300 Kosters Motorboghandel, 8900 Randers
302 Samlerborsen, DK 1806 Frederiksberg C

Germany

299 International Automobile Archives, 85757 Karlsfeld

Netherlands

333 Blaak Radiateurenbedryf, Heinenoord

New Zealand

358 Te Puke Vintage Auto Barn, Te Puke

United Kingdom

395 Frost Auto Restoration Techniques Ltd, Rochdale
232 Malcolm C Elder & Son, Oxfordshire
268 London Stainless Steel Exhaust Centre, London
422 Rod Jolley Coachbuilding Ltd, Lymington
248 Speed & Spares America , Weymouth, Dorset
293 Woolies (I&C Woolstenholmes Ltd), Nr Peterborough

Section Two – Generalists

Section Three
Clubs & Organizations

3,372 listings

Since it began, the *Hemmings' Vintage Auto Almanac* has sought to present the most comprehensive list of old car hobby clubs and related organizations ever published. Here, with expanded listings and entries, the hobbyist will find six main categories:

Multi-marque clubs. Generally, these organizations welcome anyone with a sincere interest in the old car hobby. They are listed alphabetically by club name.

Marque clubs. These clubs specialize in serving enthusiasts of certain car makes. Some require ownership of the particular marque for membership. They are listed alphabetically by marque.

Registries. These are associations primarily interested in maintaining rosters of owners of particular marques, although some are also structured as actual clubs with activities, dues, events, etc. They are listed alphabetically by marque.

Specialty clubs. These are clubs with a specialized focus such as license plates, racing and other unique car subjects. They are listed alphabetically by club name.

Statewide and local clubs. These are organizations serving hobbyists within specific geographical area. They are listed alphabetically by state.

Legislative watch organizations. This is a listing of groups devoted to promoting and protecting the collector car hobby's interests in legislative matters. National organizations are listed first, followed by state/local groups. National and state/local groups are each listed alphabetically by organization name.

Multi-Marque Clubs

Aberdeen Antique and Classic Car Club Inc
10470 Hwy 382
Aberdeen, MS 39730
662-369-8245
E-mail: wandafduncan@yahoo.com

Founded 1987. 10 families. Non-profit organization with the purpose of promoting the restoration and preservation of vehicles through car shows. Have an annual car show the 1st or 2nd Saturday of April each year and proceeds go to local charities at Christmas. Dues: $10/year.

Advance Design Truck Association
PO Box 691867
Tulsa, OK 74169-1867
918-234-6035
E-mail: adta4755@hotmail.com

Founded 2000. 350+ members. We are based on 1947-1955 AD Truck Group. Truck show once a year. Discounts from some vendors. Nationwide. Newsletters, contest in all newsletters, family fun for all. Dues: $15/year US, foreign: inquire. Web site: www.clubs.hemmings.com/adta/

Alberta Association Antique Auto Clubs
14621 103rd Ave
Edmonton, AB Canada T5N 0T6
780-454-5589
E-mail: clements@oanet.com

Founded 1974. Members: 40 clubs, 2,000 individuals. Restricted to clubs involved with antique, modified, customized or off-road vehicles. Newsletter for clubs that are members only. Dues: $2 per individual member per club.

American Roadhouse Car Club
PO Box 1680
St Charles, MO 63302-1680
636-946-4389; FAX: 636-946-8602
E-mail: gtocharlie@aol.com

Founded 1994. 100 members. We accept all makes and models. Monthly meeting and monthly newsletter, family activities each month plus cruises April through September, active in community parades, charity functions. Presently holding 1 major car show per year. Web site: www.classicar.com/clubs/arcc/

American Station Wagon Owners Association
8922 Butternut Ct
Indianapolis, IN 46260
317-872-0004
E-mail: aswoa@aol.com

Founded 1996. 450+ members. The American Station Wagon Owners Association is dedicated to the enjoyment and preservation of this great vehicle. Open to all makes and models. Quarterly, full color magazine, *The Wagon Roundup*. Free classified ads for members. 2002 Sixth National Convention, Princeton, NJ, June 27-30. Dues: $25/year.

American Truck Historical Society
300 Office Park Dr
Birmingham, AL 35223
205-870-0566; FAX: 205-870-3069
E-mail: aths@mindspring.com

For membership information, contact at the above address: Larry L Scheef, General Manager. Founded 1971. 22,000+ members. Maintains library and archives containing history, photos and films of the truck industry. Bi-monthly magazine: *Wheels of Time*. Annual *ATHS Show Time* color album, $20. Dues: $25/year US, $35/year Canada (US funds). Web site: www.aths.org
chapters:

Alabama   *Heart of Dixie Chapter*, William Spain, 1213 Elm Dr, Alabaster, AL 35007-8302
205-621-8608

Arizona   *Arizona Chapter*, Jim Schwemm, 5562 N Warren Rd, Maricopa, AZ 85239-6119
520-568-2906

American Truck Historical Society chapters (continued)

Northern Arizona Chapter, Monte J Colucci, PO Box 316, Paulden, AZ 86334 520-636-7555

California *Central California Chapter*, Archie Crippen, 495 N Marks Ave, Fresno, CA 93706 559-442-1607

Central Coast Chapter of California, Stan Alles, 1755 N Jameson Ave, Fresno, CA 93722 559-275-6744

Redwood Chapter, David Anderson, 795 Richardson Ln, Cotati, CA 94931 707-792-0436

San Diego Chapter, Greg Long, 8510 Lemon Ave, LaMesa, CA 91941 619-460-3119

Southern California Chapter, Ken Lund, PO Box 10583, San Bernardino, CA 92423 909-794-2616

Westside San Joaquin Valley, Joseph A Leonard, 2620 N Lander Ave, Stevinson, CA 95374-9611 209-632-8988

Colorado *Intermountain West Chapter*, Gary Bramwell, 26135 Amy Cir, Conifer, CO 80433-6102 303-838-0180

Florida *Central Florida Chapter*, John E Gormican, 980 W McCormick Rd, Apopka, FL 32703-8957 407-889-9252

South Florida Chapter, Cliff Gibson, 9725 SW 146th St, Miami, FL 33176-7828 305-251-5839

Georgia *North Georgia Chapter*, Hillard Garrett, 1135 Antioch Church Rd, Mount Airy, GA 30563 706-754-9277

Idaho *Snake River Chapter*, Tim Smedley, 365 Clabby Rd, Weiser, ID 83672 208-549-3162

Illinois *Gateway Chapter*, John S Berquette, PO Box 243, Hamel, IL 62046 618-459-7419

Lincoln Trail Chapter, Charles R Flexter, PO Box 264, Dawson, IL 62520 217-364-4162

Mark Twain Chapter, Charles B Kendall, 1010 Greene St, Barry, IL 62312 217-335-2417

North West Illinois Chapter, Dale H Olson, 2250 Wessman Pkwy, Cherry Valley, IL 61016-9442 815-332-4496

Windy City Chapter, William Schutt, 4106 Gilbert Ave, Western Springs, IL 60558-1236 708-246-2406

Indiana *Auburn Heritage Truck Chapter*, John M Smith, PO Box 686, Auburn, IN 46706 219-925-5714

Northwest Indiana Chapter, Curt Zehner, 1166 N Salt Creek Rd, Chesterton, IN 46304-9706 219-787-9227

Iowa *Central Iowa Chapter*, Lee Snyder, 1627 230th St, Minburn, IA 50167-8021 515-465-2015

Heartland Chapter, Mike Pagel, 1809 Mulberry Ave, Muscatine, IA 52761-3554 319-263-8586

Midwest Plains Chapter, Gordon Watson, 610 E Hammond St, Red Oak, IA 51566-1955 712-623-2268

Kansas *Three Trails Chapter*, Eugene Wentz, 20260 Parellel Rd, Tonganoxie, KS 66086-5346 913-369-3600

Kentucky *Blue Grass Chapter*, Carl R Johnson Jr, Rt 1 Box 371A, Jacobs Ln, Cynthiana, KY 41031-9807 859-234-1588

Derby City Chapter, Ken Rabeneck, 4411 Rudy Ln, Louisville, KY 40207 502-897-5449

Louisiana *Bayou State Chapter*, Jerry L Dodson, PO Box 534, Haughton, LA 71037 318-949-3935

Maine *Pine Tree Chapter*, George Sprowl Sr, PO Box 220, Searsmont, ME 04973 207-342-5621

Maryland *Baltimore-Washington Chapter*, Henry Fowler Jr, 38777 Blossom Dr, Mechanicsville, MD 20659-3451 301-884-3390

Delmarva Chapter, Matt Twilley, 8321 West Rd, Salisbury, MD 21801 410-749-3569

Massachusetts *Antique Truck Club of New England*, Dave Mauro, 130 Cook Ln, Marlborough, MA 01752 508-481-0011

Nutmeg Chapter, Al Newhouse, 74 Dunn Rd, Longmeadow, MA 01106-1808 413-567-1451

Michigan *Michigan Chapter*, Warren Cooley, 505 W Ash St, Mason, MI 48854-1553 517-676-5910

Southeast Michigan Chapter, Robert J Ludwig, 5090 Timberview Ct, Saline, MI 48176 734-429-0619

West Michigan Chapter, Robert Roelofs, 10333 Eastern Ave SE, Wayland, MI 49348-9602 616-698-2912

Minnesota *Hiawathaland Chapter*, Joe Becker, 2401 Becker Dr, Albert Lea, MN 56007-6301 507-373-8598

Minnesota Metro Chapter, John Bradshaw, 14878 Furman St NE, Forest Lake, MN 55025-8896 651-982-9922

Missouri *Ozarks 4-State Chapter*, Douglas W Millam, 1712 S Oak Grove Ave, Springfield, MO 65804 417-886-5648

Nevada *Sierra Nevada Chapter*, Arch Libby, 220 Hercules Dr, Sparks, NV 89436-9213 775-425-0644

New Hampshire *Granite State Chapter*, Donald M Smith, PO Box 113, Barrington, NH 03825-0113 603-664-9761

Section Three – Clubs & Organizations

Green Mountain Chapter, David Durling, 31 Mountain View Rd, North Walpole, NH 03609-1115 603-445-5070

New Jersey *Metro Jersey Chapter*, Scott Baker, 10 South St, Mahwah, NJ 07430-1159 201-512-0056

South Jersey Shore Chapter, Gene Stoms, PO Box 142, Deerfield Street, NJ 08313 856-455-7645

New Mexico *New Mexico Chapter*, Paul G McLaughlin, 2720 Tennessee St NE, Albuquerque, NM 87110 505-296-2554

New York *Central New York Chapter*, Ollie Farstler, 6564 Minoa-Bridgeport Rd, East Syracuse, NY 13057-9423 315-656-7813

Hudson Mohawk Chapter, John A Wojtowicz, 14 Plant Rd, Clifton Park, NY 12065-4313 518-371-6907

Long Island Chapter, Denis Ryan, 16 Wainscott Dr, Sound Beach, NY 11789-2339 631-821-4845

Twin Tiers Chapter, Walter A Carmon, 2248 Dutchtown Rd, Endicott, NY 13760-6810 607-785-3244

Western New York Chapter, George Pursel Jr, 9673 Linwood Rd, LeRoy, NY 14482 716-768-6765

North Carolina *Piedmont Carolina Chapter*, Nollie W Neill Jr, PO Box 38, Ennice, NC 28623-0038 336-657-8083

Ohio *Black Swamp Chapter*, Bill Monaghan, 3113 Pickle Rd, Oregon, OH 43616-4024 419-663-5942

Buckeye Vintage Haulers Chapter, John Berger, 3491 Farley Dr, Hilliard, OH 43026-1742 614-876-4149

Greater Cincinnati Chapter, John T Wilcox, 3057 Southfork Dr, Cincinnati, OH 45248-5035 513-922-3760

Northeast Ohio Chapter, Bruce Pearson, 5631 S Ridge Rd, Madison, OH 44057-4615 440-428-4615

Oklahoma *Heartland Sooner Chapter*, Rob Butts, 1726 N Tulsa Ave, Oklahoma City, OK 73107 405-943-0935

Oregon *Oregon Trail Chapter*, Ken Goudy Jr, 15140 S Burkstrom Rd, Oregon City, OR 97045 503-657-8359

State of Jefferson Chapter, Nick R Sauer, 172 Brett Way, Grants Pass, OR 97526 541-479-0745

Pennsylvania *Philadelphia Chapter*, George W Kaiser, 1137 Walnut St, Collingdale, PA 19023-4122 610-586-4759

Steel Valleys Chapter, Mark Woods, 257 Mohican Ave, Pittsburgh, PA 15237-4767 412-358-8506

Susquehanna Valley Chapter, Lester W Sharar, 1422 State Rd, Duncannon, PA 17020 717-957-2482

Rhode Island *Ocean State Vintage Haulers Chapter*, James Izzi Sr, 174 Bracken St, Cranston, RI 02920 401-942-8290

South Carolina *Palmetto Central Chapter*, Frank McLane, 8106 Monticello Rd, Columbia, SC 29203 803-754-7230

Tennessee *Music City Chapter*, James Waller, 330 Hargrove Cir, Cunningham, TN 37052-4835 931-387-3375

Texas *Hi-Plains Chapter*, John Plank, 5115 Pico Blvd, Amarillo, TX 79110 806-355-4394

Yellow Rose Chapter, Lloyd Holden, 741 W Zipp Rd, New Braunfels, TX 78130-9048 830-608-1114

Virginia *Shenandoah Valley Chapter*, Don H Snodgrass, 3027 Cross Keys Rd, Harrisonburg, VA 22801 540-434-3239

Virginia Tidewater Chapter, HC Shackelford, PO Box 96, Gloucester Point, VA 23062 804-642-2380

Washington *Blue Mountain Chapter*, Nick Plucker, 803 Touchet N Rd, Touchet, WA 99360-9774 509-394-2413

Section Three – Clubs & Organizations

American Truck Historical Society chapters (continued)

> *Inland Empire Chapter*, Ric Hall, 1020 W Knox Ave, Spokane, WA 99205-4403 509-328-3942
>
> *Northwest Chapter*, Roy E Friis, 6518 32nd Ave NW, Olympia, WA 98502-9519 360-866-7716
>
> *Yakima Valley Chapter*, Ted Clemmens, 1407 S 18th St, Yakima, WA 98901-3652 509-248-4475

West Virginia   *Mason Dixon Chapter*, Allen Bond III, PO Box 62, Shepherdstown, WV 25443-0062 304-876-6790

Wisconsin   *Beer City Chapter*, Gene Buchanan, N 1544 Six Corners Rd, Walworth, WI 53184-5526 262-275-2882

> *Southern Wisconsin Chapter*, Larry Caves, N 5758 St Hwy 22, Wild Rose, WI 54984-9135 920-622-3484

Wyoming   *Wyoming Cowboy Chapter*, Robert Campbell, 4 Riggs Rd, Shoshoni, WY 82649-8601 307-856-4725

Australia   *Australian Chapter*, Laurie Kirby, PO Box 286, Wandin, Victoria 3139, 03-9-739-7092

Canada   *Alberta Chapter*, George P Kirkham Jr, 4310 9th Ave N, Lethbridge, AB, T1H 6N1 403-381-1617

> *British Columbia Interior Chapter*, Roger O Dillon, 430-1260 Raymer Ave, Kelowna, BC, V1W 3S5 250-862-8840
>
> *British Columbia Pioneers Chapter*, Richard Stevenson, 3940 254th St, Aldergrove, BC, V4W 2R3 604-856-7432
>
> *Saskatchewan Chapter*, Charles Loewen, PO Box 112, Mankota, SK, S0H 2W0 306-478-2643
>
> *SW Ontario Old Trucks Chapter*, Loraine Berge, 2895 Kressler Rd, Box 201, Heidelberg, ON, N0B 1Y0 519-699-5701
>
> *Vancouver Island Chapter*, Ed Petillion, PO Box 333, Shawnigan Lake, BC, V0R 2W0 250-743-7818

Antique Automobile Club of America
501 W Governor Rd, PO Box 417
Hershey, PA 17033
717-534-1910 AACA, 717-534-2082 library
FAX: 717-534-9101

Founded 1935. 60,000 members. Dedicated to the preservation, restoration and maintenance of automobiles and automotive history. Bi-monthly publication: *Antique Automobile*. Prospective membership sponsor not mandatory. Library and research center services available. AACA Museum Inc project well under way. Dues: $26/year (includes spouse).

regions:

Alabama   *Boll Weevil Region*, Allen F Kahl, 6 Palomino Rd, Phenix City, AL 36869

> *Catahoula Junque Collectors Assoc Region*, Paula Gould, 97 Model T Cir, Monroeville, AL 36460

> *Central Alabama Region*, John P Gieske, 1016 N Burbank Dr, Montgomery, AL 36117
>
> *Deep South Region*, Leah Musgrove, 10032 Airport Blvd, Mobile, AL 36608
>
> *Dixie Region*, David H Boyd, 15041 Hwy 69 N, Northport, AL 35475-3111
>
> *Muscle Shoals Region*, Thomas H Seale, 555 Malone Cir, Florence, AL 35630
>
> *North Alabama Region*, George Snellen, 1807 Buddy Williamson Rd, New Market, AL 35761
>
> *Northeast Alabama Region*, Kitta Michaels, 108 Tabor Ct, Gadsden, AL 35901
>
> *South Alabama Region*, Sue Jerkins, 114 Lottie Ln, East Brewton, AL 36426
>
> *Tennessee Valley Region*, Lloyd W Culp, 1819 Corrine Ave SW, Decatur, AL 35601

Alaska   *Antique Auto Mushers of Alaska Region*, Peg Stout, 6208 E 34th Ave, Anchorage, AK 99504

> *Vernon L Nash AAC of Fairbanks Region*, Loran W Benham, 1391 Ithaca Rd, Fairbanks, AK 99709

Arizona   *AACME Region*, Karen Rodgers, PO Box 48477, Phoenix, AZ 85075

> *Metro Phoenix Region*, Mike McQueen, 4210 E Grovers Ave, Phoenix, AZ 85032
>
> *Sedona Car Club Region*, Joseph A Tulley Jr, 2320 Buckboard Rd, Sedona, AZ 86336
>
> *Tucson Region*, John D McVay, 8350 E Albion Pl, Tucson, AZ 85715

California   *Antelope Valley Region*, Jill A Miller, 2059 Top Cir, Lancaster, CA 93536

> *Cabrillo Region*, Jack Passey Jr, 425 Hecker Pass Rd, Watsonville, CA 95076
>
> *California Region*, Donald Azevedo, 3802 Briarcliff Dr, Pittsburg, CA 94565
>
> *El Camino Region*, Robert B Tinkey, 2108 Sandpoint Dr, Modesto, CA 95358
>
> *Foothills Region*, Frank T Snyder III, 830 Shary Ave, Mountain View, CA 94041-2141
>
> *Golden Gate Region*, William G Black, 517 Pineo Ave, Mill Valley, CA 94941
>
> *Kern County Region*, John Bakich, 10806 Enger St, Bakersfield, CA 93312
>
> *Korean Antique Automobile Region*, Jchoo S Kimm, 3807 Wilshire Blvd #520, Los Angeles, CA 90010
>
> *Monterey Bay Classic European Motorcycle Club Region*, Timothy D Riley, PO Box 7411, Spreckels, CA 93962

Mother Lode Region, Duane C Bennett, PO Box 424, Sonora, CA 95370

Northern CA Antique Motorcycle Region, Lloyd Riggs, 880 Hawthorne Dr, Walnut Creek, CA 94546

Palm Springs Region, Richard McKelvey, 10961 Desert Lawn Dr, Calimesa, CA 92320

Redwood Empire Region, Mark Childers, 1117 Monroe Ct, Santa Rosa, CA 95404

Salinas Valley Region, Wayne Earnest, 1113 San Ysidro Way, Salinas, CA 93901

San Diego Region, Fallbrook Vintage Car Chapter, Norman R Kear, PO Box 714, Fallbrook, CA 92088

San Diego Region, Larry Larkin, 8490 Pueblo Rd, Lakeside, CA 92040-5405

San Luis Obispo Region, John Osborne, 4240 Rancho Rd, Templeton, CA 93465

Santa Barbara Region, J Thomas Deering, 1330 Camino Meleno, Santa Barbara, CA 93111

Santa Clarita Valley Region, Linda Pursell, 23324 8th St, Newhall, CA 91321

Southern California Region, Joe Pirrone, 2454 232nd St, Torrance, CA 90501

Southern California Region, Valley Chapter, John H Avans, 23614 Neargate Dr, Newhall, CA 91321

Southwestern Two-Wheelers Region, Harry A McGill, 1261 Emory St, Imperial Beach, CA 91932

Sun and Sand Region, Joan O Petitclair, 73601 Heatherwood Dr, Palm Desert, CA 92211

Valle Del Sur Region, Raymond Fairfield, 16481 Jackson Oaks Dr, Morgan Hill, CA 95037

Valley of the Flowers Region, Dott Brackin, PO Box 1952, Lompoc, CA 93438

Colorado   *Poudre Valley Region*, Charles R Phagan, 5114 Ute Dr, Greeley, CO 80634

Rocky Mountain Region, Denver Chapter, James T Preston, 955 Urban St, Golden, CO 80401

Rocky Mountain Region, JD Bernard, 14706 E 134th Pl, Brighton, CO 80601

Rocky Mountain Region, Ye Olde Auto Club Chapter, Harold L Buschman, 15785 Havana St, Brighton, CO 80601

Connecticut   *Central Connecticut Region*, John H Eicholtzer, 49 Webster Hill Blvd, West Hartford, CT 06107

Fairfield County Connecticut Region, Richard S King, 9 Admiral Ln, Norwalk, CT 06851

Gateway Antique Auto Club Region, Peter A Cavanna, 636 Hope St, Stamford, CT 06907

Housatonic Valley Region, Peter J Lucsky, 47 Liberty Ave, Danbury, CT 06810

Shoreline Antique Auto Club Region, Larry Burridge, 45 Essex Rd, Westbrook, CT 06498

Westerly-Pawcatuck Region, James Varas, 10 Marlin Dr, Pawcatuck, CT 06379

Delaware   *Brandywine Region*, George Barczewski, 2467 Pulaski Hwy, Newark, DE 19702

Florida   *Ancient City Region*, Ron Leone, 100 SE Woods Dr, St Augustine, FL 32084

Azalea Region, Molly Lloyd, PO Box 750, Hawthorne, FL 32640

Cape Canaveral Region, WR Underwood, 3600 Deerwood Tr, Melbourne, FL 32934

Edison Region, Merna Stein, 624 SE 23rd Terr, Cape Coral, FL 33990

Florida Region, Lee Dunkin, 1504 Overlake Ave, Orlando, FL 32806

Florida West Coast Region, Lois Blackard, 14968 Imperial Point Dr N, Largo, FL 33774

Fort Lauderdale Region, Fred Hunter, 3581 SW 116th Ave, Fort Lauderdale, FL 33330

Highland Lakes Region, Barbara Bazley, 2103 N Lake Sebring Dr, Sebring, FL 33870

Hillsborough Region, Angelo Rumore Jr, 5612 Paddock Trail Dr, Tampa, FL 33624

Indian River Region, AC Bowser, 49 Cache Cay Dr, Vero Beach, FL 32963

Kingdom of the Sun Region, Lee Mahoney, 5790 SW 89th Pl, Ocala, FL 34476

Kissimmee-St Cloud Region, Ralph Brueggeman, 145 Garman Ave, Davenport, FL 33837

Kumquat Region, Thomas M Brookover Jr, 32348 Caroline's Path, Dade City, FL 33525

Lemon Bay Region, Royal Palm Chapter, Richard F Ellsworth, PO Box 381151, Murdock, FL 33938

Lemon Bay Region, Sandy Heim, 10349 Sandrift Ave, Englewood, FL 34224

Lemon Bay Region, Venice Chapter, Peter Second, i3474 Papaya Rd, Venice, FL 34293

Miracle Strip Region, Robert B Porter, 306 Greenwood Cir, Panama City, FL 32407

Antique Automobile Club of America regions (continued)

Naples-Marco Island Region, John E Aibel, 300 Park Shore Dr #6D, Naples, FL 34103

Northeast Florida Region, Michael J Chalut, 6401 Jack Wright Island Rd, St Augustine, FL 32092

Peace River Region, Jim Kantor, PO Box 510508, Punta Gorda, FL 33951

Richey Region, James A Cook, 8811 Cessna Dr, New Port Richey, FL 34654

South Florida Region, Bob B Mayer, 10285 SW 135th St, Miami, FL 33176

Space Coast Region, James A LaCoy, 102 S Singleton Ave, Titusville, FL 32796

Sunshine Region, Eugene Cohen, 5273 Turtle Creek Ln, Sarasota, FL 34232

Sunshine Region, Rare Birds of Florida Chapter, William P Palmer, 1135 Larchmont Dr, Englewood, FL 34223

Suwannee River Region, Tony D Richards, Rt 20 Box 472, Lake City, FL 32055

Tallahassee Region, John R Schanbacher, 517 Collinsford Rd, Tallahassee, FL 32301

Treasure Coast Region, David A Brown, 1005 Ibis Ave, Fort Pierce, FL 34982

Vintage Auto Club Palm Beach Region, John E Hiscock, 13721 Edith Rd, Loxahatchee, FL 33470

Vintage Wheels of Manatee County Region, Bob Nolan, 1109 Harvard Ave, Bradenton, FL 34207

Volusia Region, Richard E Morgart, 100 Hay Bale Terr, Ormond Beach, FL 32174

West Florida Region, Ken Gunderson, 2594 Cove Dr, Navarre, FL 32566

Wheels in Motion Flagler County Region, Alfred J Wanser, PO Box 1656, Flagler Beach, FL 32136

Georgia   *Apple Country of North Georgia Region*, Melanie Cantrell, 312 Chauncey Rd, Cherrylog, GA 30522

Artesian City Region, Lillian Law, Box 143205 Sylvester Rd, Albany, GA 31705

Athens, Georgia Region, George C Bugg, 285 North Ave, Athens, GA 30601

Brunswick-Golden Isles Region, William Phillips, 106 Cayman Ct, Brunswick, GA 31525

Cherokee Region, Roger J Papp, 88 Wilderness Camp Rd, White, GA 30184

Clocktower Region, Joe N Kemp, 3 Emerson Dr SW, Rome, GA 30165

Coastal Georgia of Savannah Region, William Sullivan Sr, 4409 Ogeechee Rd, Savannah, GA 31405

Georgia-Alabama Region, Jack Wilson, 238 Linda Ln, LaGrange, GA 30240

Griffin Piedmont Region, Roy F Grant, 440 Hickory Ln, Griffin, GA 30223

Middle Georgia Region, Timothy A Edgar, 337 Sleepy Ln, Warner Robins, GA 31088

Northeast Georgia Antique Auto Region, Cleve A McAfee, PO Box 1777, Cleveland, GA 30528

Northwest Georgia Region, Cred W Trimble, 725 Tee Top Dr, Cohutta, GA 30710

Pecan Region, Bainbridge Cruisers Chapter, Lee West, 116 Flint River Heights Rd, Bainbridge, GA 31717

Pecan Region, Darrell T Lightfoot, 118 Bent Oak Cir, Thomasville, GA 31757

Southeastern Region, Byron W Hall, 3941 Brittan Glade Tr, Snellville, GA 30039

Sowega Region, Lee West, 116 Flint River Heights Rd, Bainbridge, GA 31717

Tiftarea Region, Frank E Branch, 1215 N Wilson Ave, Tifton, GA 31794

West Georgia Region, Bobby J Webb, 1560 Sand Hill-Hulett Rd, Carrolton, GA 30116

Hawaii   *Aloha Region*, Frederick Weisberger, 90 Aikahi Loop, Kailua, HI 96734

Idaho   *North Idaho-Phans Region*, Larry Cooke, 326 S Florence Ave, Sandpoint, ID 83864

Illinois   *Alden Ponds Region*, Gordon Williams, 25610 Graf Rd, Harvard, IL 60033

Blackhawk Region, Leland E Morrison, 10827 N Tower Rd, Byron, IL 61010

Gateway City Region, Mark D Linder, 42 Woodlawn Cir, Belleville, IL 62226

Illinois Region, Des Plaines Valley Chapter, Lee E Nelson, 522 S Washington St, Lockport, IL 60441

Illinois Region, Fox Valley Chapter, Daniel Sobczyk, 822 Bannock Rd, East Dundee, IL 60118

Illinois Region, Laura McDonald, 3633 Vernon Ave, Brookfield, IL 60513

Illinois Region, Momence Chapter, Ted Griffin, 2256 W Wolpers Rd, Park Forest, IL 60466

Illinois Region, North Shore Chapter, Wendell K Stevenson, 13041 W Pickford Ave, Waukegan, IL 60087

Illinois Valley Region, Ronald Verda, 112 E SilverspoonPO Box 463, Granville, IL 61326

Illinois Region, Silver Springs Chapter, Allen W Matison, 802 Grove St, Earlville, IL 60518

Mississippi Valley Region, Scott J Lohman, 5214 37th Ave Ct, Moline, IL 61265

Muddy T Region, Anthony J Verschoore, 3922 W Brummel, Skokie, IL 60076

Southern Illinois Region, James M Walters Jr, 2410 North Ave, Metropolis, IL 62960

Southern Illinois Region, Ohio Valley Chapter, Michael Hausman, 1001 Metropolis St, Metropolis, IL 62960

Indiana   *Lower Ohio Valley Region*, Jerry D Smith, 855 Mt Gilead Rd, Boonville, IN 47601

White River Valley Region, James B Nelson, 820 Millerwood Dr, Lebanon, IN 46052

Iowa   *Cedar Rapids Region*, Donald E Miller, 4151 Blairs Ferry Rd NE, Cedar Rapids, IA 52411

Cedar Valley Region, Ronald Adams, 2777 Larrabee Ave, Denver, IA 50622-1067

Des Moines Region, Dave Holzinger, 605 54th St, Des Moines, IA 50312

Iowa Great Lakes Region, Everett Amis, 2190 435th St, Greenville, IA 51343

Iowa Valley Region, Donald H Saxton, PO Box 122, Oxford, IA 52322

Marshalltown Area Restorers Region, James C Willey, 1107 S 4th St, Marshalltown, IA 50158

Niapra Region, Thomas Flagge, 1202 26th Ave N, Fort Dodge, IA 50501

Niva Region, Richard A Olson Sr, 672 7th NE, Mason City, IA 50401

Siouxland Region, Martin F Burke, 1618 Summit St, Sioux City, IA 51103

Tall Corn Region, Vernon Moorman, 1050 L Ave, Boone, IA 50036

Kansas   *Cherokee Strip Region*, Randall McMains, 211 N 3rd St, Arkansas City, KS 67005

Lawrence Region, Jack R Todd, 724 Elm St, Lawrence, KS 66044

Topeka Region, Herbert G Whitlow, 5035 SE 3rd St Terr, Tecumseh, KS 66542

Kentucky   *Blue Grass Region*, Carolyn Simpson, 972 Woodglen Ct, Lexington, KY 40515

Kyana Region, Chester Robertson, 10013 Northridge Dr, Louisville, KY 40272

Lincoln Trail Region, Jerry T Mills, 6495 Bardstown Rd, Elizabethtown, KY 42701

Southern Kentucky Region, Lynn A Goodman, 394 Martsinville Rd, Oakland, KY 42159

Twin Lakes Region, Howard Brandon, 1401 S 12th St, Murray, KY 42071

Louisiana   *Louisiana Region*, Baton Rouge Chapter, Wade Giles, 13318 Acres Ct, Baker, LA 70714

Louisiana Region, Central Louisiana Chapter, Cliff Fuselier, 1302 Plantation Dr, Alexandria, LA 71301

Louisiana Region, Charlie Matthews, 901 Sharp Rd, Baton Rouge, LA 70815

Louisiana Region, Contraband Chapter, Wallace H Baker, 2420 Dietz St, Lake Charles, LA 70601

Louisiana Region, Crescent City Chapter, John J Shaughnessy, PO Box 23503, New Orleans, LA 70183

Louisiana Region, Evangeline Chapter, Robert J Hoey Jr, 100 Jimmie St, Lafayette, LA 70506

Louisiana Region, Lagniappe Chapter, Louis Morrell III, 955 Martinez Rd, Thibodaus, LA 70301

Louisiana Region, Slidell Antique Car Chapter, Curtis A Wells, 576 Waverly Dr, Slidell, LA 70461

Louisiana Region, St Bernard Chapter, Curtis A Ducote, 1210 Hwy 39, Braithwaite, LA 70040

Maine   *Maine Region*, David G Merrill, 100 Woodville Rd, Falmouth, ME 04105

Maryland   *Bay Country Region*, Andrew R Wilhelm, 325 Dulin Clark Rd, Centreville, MD 21617

Chesapeake Region, Robert A Amos, 1116 Sleepy Dell Ct, Towson, MD 21286

Eastern Shore Region, Robert Kambarn, 3911 Five Friars Rd, Salisbury, MD 21804

Harford Region, O Evelyn Blevins, 202 W Jarrettsville Rd, Forest Hill, MD 21050

Mason-Dixon Region, T Lester Adelsberger, 10923 Roessner Ave, Hagerstown, MD 21740

Model A Ford Foundation Region, Howard A Minners, 4700 Locust Hill Ct, Bethesda, MD 20814

Queen City Region, Donald R Reid, 14805 Hill StPO Box 5157, Cresaptown, MD 21505

Sugarloaf Mountain Region, Louis D Harrington, 209 Harrison St, Rockville, MD 20850-1823

Massachusetts   *Connecticut Valley Region*, Keith A Korbut, 16 Saffron Cir, Springfield, MA 01129

Section Three – Clubs & Organizations

Antique Automobile Club of America regions (continued)

Massachusetts Region, Riley Randolph, 258 King St, Raynham, MA 02767

Michigan   *Blue Water Region*, Gary L Minnie, 7700 State Rd, Burtchville, MI 48059

Boyne Country Region, Arnold Hudson, PO Box 250, Walloon Lake, MI 49796

Flint Region, Kay Amman, 240 Raleigh Pl, Lennon, MI 48449

Illinois Brass Touring Region, David G Weishaar, 6204 140th Ave, Holland, MI 49423

Inland Lakes Region, Russell Lockwood, 178 Michelson Rd, Houghton Lake, MI 48629

Kalamazoo Valley Region, David Lyon, 27405 Shaw Rd, Lawton, MI 49065

Northwestern Michigan Region, Clarence V Smith, 1086 Rasho Rd, Traverse City, MI 49686

Saginaw Valley Region, Joan Kauer, 6271 Trinklein Rd, Saginaw, MI 48609

Snapper's Brass and Gas Touring Region, David G Weishaar, 6204 140th Ave, Holland, MI 49423

St Joe Valley Region, Richard W Chandler, 68244 Cassopolis Rd, Cassopolis, MI 49031

West Michigan Region, Robert L Dinger, 0-841 Parsons St, Grandville, MI 49418

Wolverine State Region, Robert Scheffler, 19963 Sumpter Rd, Belleville, MI 48111

Minnesota   *Minnesota Region*, 412 Lakes Chapter, Howard Fredine, 21488 Coaley Bay Dr, Detroit Lakes, MN 56501

Minnesota Region, Arrowhead Chapter, Stephen W Blaede, 1896 W Chub Lake Rd, Carlton, MN 55718

Minnesota Region, Capitol City Chapter, Richard Wolens, 6726 137th Ave NW, Anoka, MN 55303

Minnesota Region, Central Chapter, Ollie Moen, 4620 Westwood Ln, Eagan, MN 55122

North Dakota Region, David K Strong, 2013 Nelson Dr, Thief River Falls, MN 56701

Minnesota Region, Hiawatha Chapter, Kenneth K Stiles, 714 21st St NE, Rochester, MN 55906

Minnesota Region, Nancy M Garwick, 7214 Columbus Ave S, Richfield, MN 55423

Minnesota Region, Pioneer Chapter, Paul L Dudek, 6021 Vernon Ave S, Minneapolis, MN 55436

Minnesota Region, Prairieland Chapter, Richard D Carlson, Rt 2 Box 148, St James, MN 56081

Minnesota Region, River Bend Chapter, Lee Felmlee, 261 S Elmwood, Lesueur, MN 56056

Minnesota Region, Viking Chapter, Sydney A Smith, 953 W 5th, Winona, MN 55987

Mississippi   *Mid-South Region*, Thomas O Kuntz, PO Box 825, Olive Branch, MS 38654

Missouri   *KC Metro Region*, Robert M Hohimer, 1430 S Dodgion, Independence, MO 64055

Show Me Region, Gary Wallace, 600 Susan Rd, St Louis, MO 63129

Nevada   *Northern Nevada Region*, Ernest H Heying, PO Box 548, Fallon, NV 89407

New Jersey   *Ankokas Region*, Robert J Gundersen, 13 Dorado Rd, Laurel Springs, NJ 08021

Curved Dash Olds Owners Club Region, Robert Giuliani, 72 Northwood Ave, Demarest, NJ 07627

Garden State Half Century Region, David Evans, 4 Maple Leaf Dr, Park Ridge, NJ 07656

Garden State Model A Region, David W Mellor, 109 Erie Ave, Barrington, NJ 08007

Jersey Cape Region, Gerard A Desiderio, 6400 Landis Ave, Sea Isle City, NJ 08243

Lehigh Valley Region, Sam Mirenda, 165 Prospect St, Phillipsburg, NJ 08865

Mid-Jersey Region, Ron Dunster, 88 S Main St, Allentown, NJ 08501

New Jersey Region, Branda J Zimmerman, 6 Tainter St, PO Box 213, Peapack, NJ 07977

New Jersey Region, Depression Vehicles Chapter, Doris M Werndly, 164 Bowden Rd, Cedar Grove, NJ 07009

New Jersey Region, Watchung Mountain Chapter, John Bedner, 82 Ravine Dr, Colonia, NJ 07067

Ontelaunee Region, Judith Fischer, 56 Smith Rd, Somerset, NJ 08873-2726

South Jersey Region, Ronald W Scott, 1714 Herbert Blvd, Williamstown, NJ 08094

New Mexico   *Eastern New Mexico Region*, Paul Blair, 1918 Diamond Way, Portales, NM 88130

Southeastern New Mexico Region, Kenneth Cook, 306 W Castle, Hobbs, NM 88240

Valley Vintage Motor Car Region, Gene Peterson, 10 Everglade Ct, Roswell, NM 88201

New York   *Algonquin Region*, Peter P Ferrante, 2402 Co Rd 35, Bainbridge, NY 13733

Batavia Region, Joyce S Ladd, 9062 Chestnut Ridge Rd, Middleport, NY 14105

Black River Valley Region, William W Hulbert Jr, PO Box 151, Adanms Center, NY 13606

Catskill Region, John DeCastro, 29 Pinehurst Dr, Liberty, NY 12754

Chautauqua Lake Region, John R Watkins, 2381 S Hill Dr, Jamestown, NY 14701

Cooper's Cave Auto Enthusiasts Club Region, Martin Lemmo, 1 Southwoods Rd, Fort Edward, NY 12828

Fingerlakes Region, James Vitale, 7174 Beach Tree Rd, Auburn, NY 13021

FoMoCo Collectors Club of America Region, James Fink, PO Box 59, Masslon, OH 44648

FR Porter Region, Steven Kelman, 79 Katherine St, Port Jefferson Station, NY 11776

Genesee Valley Antique Car Soc Region, Richard H Walther, 141 Shale Dr, Rochester, NY 14615

Greater New York Region, Marie Dalia, 86-08 218th St, Queens Village, NY 11427

Greenwood Lake Region, John F Kerwan Jr, 3 Kalvin Terr, Monroe, NY 10950

Iroquois Region, Thomas W Martin, 829 Zeggert Rd, Endicott, NY 13760

Lake Erie Region, Raymond Noonan, 328 Grayton Rd, Tonawanda, NY 14150

Livingston Region, Mark A Fisher, 5985 Co Rd 37, Springwater, NY 14560

Mid-Hudson Region, Michael Baisley, 374 Wheeler Hill Rd, Wappingers Falls, NY 12590

Onaquaga Region, Douglas Tucker, 3 Dodd Rd, Windsor, NY 13865

Oneida Lake Region, H Eugene Satterfield, 115 Meadow Ln, North Syracuse, NY 13212

Peconic Bay Region, Robert J Barauskas, 1373 W Main StPO Box 1615, Riverhead, NY 11901

Ramapo Valley Region, Dr Stephen Lazar, 7 Arcadian Dr, Spring Valley, NY 10977

Rolling Antiquers OCC Norwich Region, Raymond C Hart, PO Box 168, Norwich, NY 13815

Schoharie Valley Region, David R Cross, RD 2 Box 286, Sharon Springs, NY 13459

St Lawrence-Adirondack Region, Raymond A Stiles, 2024 St Hwy 345, Madrid, NY 13660

Staten Island Region, Paul Arena, 98 Kennington St, Staten Island, NY 10308

Tioga Antique Auto Club Region, Howard M Seymour, 25 Stratton Rd, Newark Valley, NY 13811

Vanderbilt Cup Region, Spiro Cosmides, 36 Livingston Ave, Babylon, NY 11702

Wayne Drumlins Antique Auto Region, Martin Maslyn, 1267 Ridley Rd, Spelps, NY 14532

Westchester New York Region, Harold P Meschi, 133 Hutchinson Blvd, Scarsdale, NY 10583

Whiteface Mountain Region, Edward D Rielly, RD 1 Box 1053, Westport, NY 12993

Wyoming Valley Region, Richard Brooks, 4019 Silver Springs Rd, Silver Springs, NY 14550

North Carolina *Foothills Region*, Daniel B Bixby, 2356 Plainfield Dr, Conover, NC 28613

Great Smoky Mountains Region, Carroll L Rhodes, Rt 2 Box 323A, Flat Rock, NC 28731

Mid-Carolinas Antique Drivers Region, Eric C Marsh, 575 Paulownia Dr, China Grove, NC 28023

Mountaineer Region, Alvin J Brown, 35 Crystal Ln, Waynesville, NC 28786

North Carolina Region, Alamance Chapter, George F Milne, 5919 Oak Grove Church Rd, Mebane, NC 27302

North Carolina Region, Brass-Nickel Touring Chapter, G Barker Edwards Jr, 116 E Front St, Clayton, NC 27520

North Carolina Region, Cape Fear Chapter, Matthew C Hinson, 718 Woodlawn Ave, Wilmington, NC 28401

North Carolina Region, Coastal Plains Chapter, Frank Garrod, 101 York Ct, Chocowinity, NC 27817

North Carolina Region, Denise Breton, 153 Hickory Tree Ln, Angier, NC 27501

North Carolina Region, East Carolina Chapter, Mary Mashburn, 4896 McArthur Rd, Broadway, NC 27505

North Carolina Region, First Capital Antique Car Club Chapter, Michael G Kutkuhn, 498 King Neck Rd, New Bern, NC 28560

North Carolina Region, Freshwater Chapter, Ed Noble, 1093 Acorn Hill Rd, Hobbsville, NC 27946

North Carolina Region, Furnitureland Chapter, Arnold Gallimore, PO Box 482, Denton, NC 27239

North Carolina Region, General Greene Chapter, Don Ellis Jr, 4741 Kanora Dr, Julian, NC 27283

Antique Automobile Club of America regions (continued)

North Carolina Region, Hillbilly Chapter, Don Lewis Sprinkle, 9 Eller Ford Rd, Weaverville, NC 28787

North Carolina Region, Morehead City Chapter, Carl L Tilghman, 269 Copeland Rd, Beaufort, NC 28516

North Carolina Region, New River Chapter, Jim Cross, 105 Barbour Rd, Hubert, NC 28539

North Carolina Region, Ol' Lightnin' Rods Chapter, Dean Brown, 4842 S NC 41, Wallace, NC 28466

North Carolina Region, Old Salem Chapter, Matthew Eastling, 113 Bradford Lake Ct, Lewisville, NC 27023

North Carolina Region, San-Lee Chapter, Larry Wright, 1003 Post Office Rd, Sanford, NC 27330

North Carolina Region, Sandhills Chapter, C Frank Riggs, PO Box 1282, Pinehurst, NC 28370

North Carolina Region, Three Rivers Chapter, Paul Gover, 1071 Grogan Rd, Stoneville, NC 27048

North Carolina Region, Triangle Chapter, Marvin Gage, 209 Trotters Ridge Dr, Raleigh, NC 27614

North Carolina Region, Uwharrie Chapter, Marvin L Menius, 700 Holshouser Rd, Rockwell, NC 28138

Transylvania Region, Jerry M Arnold, PO Box 268, Brevard, NC 28712

Zooland Region, Jerry Rook, 5081 Burton Rd, Thomasville, NC 27360

North Dakota *Magic City Region*, Edward Bolte, 1601 University Ave W, Minot, ND 58703

North Dakota Region, Devils Lake Chapter, Glenn Lannoye, 910 Lake View Dr, Devils Lake, ND 58301-8731

Ohio *Irish Hills Region*, Martin O Zimmerman, 11518 Co Rd M, Wauseon, OH 43567

Lakelands Region, Teresa Ellway, 3325 Youngstown-Kingsville Rd, Cortland, OH 44410

Northern Kentucky Region, Joseph C Suwel, 7128 Gracely Dr, Cincinnati, OH 45233

Ohio Region, Canton Chapter, Roy C Hunkins, 17619 Cambier Rd, Mt Vernon, OH 43050

Ohio Region, Central Chapter, Shirley Young, 4915 Lithopolis-Winchester Rd, Canal Winchester, OH 43110

Ohio Region, Commodore Perry Chapter, Alex C Heyd, 838 Poplar St, Elyria, OH 44035

Ohio Region, Meander Chapter, William Stoneburner, 772 Gary Dr, Hubbard, OH 44425

Ohio Region, Northern Chapter, Regina Jandrey, 4373 Broadview Rd, Richfield, OH 44286

Ohio Region, Robert F Kayle, 3725 Amherst Ave, Lorain, OH 44052

Ohio Region, Southern Chapter, Ronald L Taylor, 6793 Bellefontaine Rd, Huber Heights, OH 45424

Ohio Region, Western Reserve Chapter, Walter Elliott, 6490 Taylor Rd, Painesville, OH 44077

Oklahoma *Enid Oklahoma Region*, Gordon C Smith Jr, 1210 Indian Dr, Enid, OK 73703

Okie Region, Roger Saxon, PO Box 271, Chickasha, OK 73018

Tulsa Region, Phil Judkins, 5820 E 76th St, Tulsa, OK 74136

Pennsylvania *Allegheny Mountain Region*, Governors' Chapter, Joseph A Horvath, 2018 Fairwood Ln, State College, PA 16803

Allegheny Mountain Region, Scott Deno, 1723 Houserville Rd, State College, PA 16801

Anthracite Region, Joseph S Forish, 607 E Blaine St, McAdoo, PA 18237

Bus Transportation Region, Richard J Maguire, PO Box 4214, Harrisburg, PA 17111

Butler-Old Stone House Region, Robert P Lane, 259 Lutz Rd, Zelienpole, PA 16063

Central Mountains Region, Carolyn A Gallaher, 622 Arnold Ave, Clearfield, PA 16830

Chemung Valley Region, Orman L Surina, RD 1 Box 1580, Osceola, PA 16942

Coke Center Region, Dale R Sleasman, 123 E End Rd, Connellsville, PA 15425

Covered Bridge Region, Donald Kobaly Sr, 559 Old Hickory Ridge Rd, Washington, PA 15301

Delaware Valley Region, Michael J Jones Sr, 1361 Patrick Henry Dr, Phoenixville, PA 19460

Endless Mountains Region, Alton E Homan, RR 5 Box 5630, Towanda, PA 18848

Flood City Region, James O Page, 191 Adams Ave, Mineral Point, PA 15942

Fort Bedford Region, Patricia Hensel, 164 Sunny Brook Ln, Bedford, PA 15522

Gettysburg Region, Harry P Sherwood, 801 Alison Ave, Mechanicsburg, PA 17055

Golden Triangle Region, Robert L Stauffer, 2414 Clearview Dr, Glenshaw, PA 15116

Hershey Region, Thomas E Oliver, 513 Gale Rd, Camp Hill, PA 17011

Keystone Region, Robert Burke, 350 S Old Middletown Rd, Media, PA 19063

Kinzua Valley Region, Philip L Vance, RD 1 Box 1517, Russell, PA 16345

Kiski Valley Region, Austin C Walker, RD 1 Box 3616 Oak Rd, Leechburg, PA 15656

Kit-Han-NE Region, Blaine E Fair, RD 7 Box 249, Kittanning, PA 16201

Lanchester Region, Albert E Storrs Jr, 4 Main-Lin Dr, Coatesville, PA 19320

Laurel Highlands Region, William O Holtzer, RD 6 Box 88-E, Greensburg, PA 15601

Lower Bucks Region, Anthony S Gray, 1312 Fulton Cir, Bensalem, PA 19020

Mon Valley Region, Leonard M Sapko, RD 1 Box 13, Smithton, PA 15479

New York State Allegheny Valley Region, Matthew Benson, 115 E 7th St, Coudersport, PA 16915

Northeastern Pennsylvania Region, George Albright, 216 Kirby Ave, Mountain Top, PA 18707

Pennsylvania Dutch Region, Marie Lesher, 3630 Kings Dr, Lebanon, PA 17046

Pennsylvania Oil Region, William F Gratkowski, 515 N Petroleum St, Titusville, PA 16354

Pocono Region, Michael Smeraldo, RR 4 Box 4102 Mills Rd, Saylorsburg, PA 18353

Pottstown Region, Pierre G DeMauriac, 26 Elaine Dr, Boyertown, PA 19512

Presque Isle Region, French Creek Valley Chapter, Jack O Wright 14069 W Townline Rd, Linesville, PA 16424

Presque Isle Region, Robert S Page, 1224 Idaho Ave, Erie, PA 16505

Punxsutawney Region, Shannock Valley Car Club Chapter, Randy Duncan, 833 Rt 156 Hwy, Shelocta, PA 15774

Punxsutawney Region, Theodore O Dunmire, 2229 Fulton Run Rd, Indiana, PA 15701

Scranton Region, Frank C Gardner, 2001 Amelia Ave, Scranton, PA 18509

Shenango Valley Region, Edward P Bailey Jr, 1343 Glenwood Dr, Sharon, PA 16146

Section Three – Clubs & Organizations

S27128

Antique Automobile Club of America regions (continued)

Shikellamy Region, George O Campbell, 36 Effie Ave, Hughesville, PA 17737

Sugar Bush Region, Edward F Reed, 703 Orchard St, Berlin, PA 15530

Susquehannock Region, Ferd D Page Jr, 1016 Cherry St, Williamsport, PA 17701

Susquehanna Valley Region, Frank J Rash, 915 E Front St, Berwick, PA 18603

Valley Forge Region, William C Mason, 125 Oaklyn Ave, Eagleville, PA 19403

Wayne-Pike Region, Carol Birdsall, PO Box 90, Sterling, PA 18463

Western Pennsylvania Region, Mark A DeFloria, 123 Fosterville Rd, Greensburg, PA 15601

Wolf Creek Region, Robert Buchanan, 46 Irishtown Rd, Grove City, PA 16127

South Carolina *Charleston-Lowcountry Region*, Jack F Eckhardt, 1704 Trout St, Moncks Corner, SC 29461

Chicora Region, Gus H Hardee, 106 W Coker Ln, Conway, SC 29526

Coastal Carolina Region, Jim Clees, 20 Forde Row, Charleston, SC 29412

Emerald City Region, Charles W Hatch, 1250 Jones St, Newberry, SC 29108

Gascar Region, James R Cobb, 11 Dogwood Glen Ct, North Augusta, SC 29841

Hornets Nest Region, James T Pinkston Sr, 1122 Tom Sadler Rd, Charlotte, SC 28214

Peach Blossom Region, Frank B Good, 180 Cromer St, Roebuck, SC 29376

Piedmont Carolina Region, Ricky Thompson, 515 White's Rd, Gaffney, SC 29340

Sandlapper Region, Ed Murphy, 1423 Corley Mill Rd, Lexington, SC 29072

Single Cylinder Cadillac Registry Region, Paul Ianuario, 541 W Lakeview Dr, Duncan, SC 29334

Sparkle City Region, CC Wheeler, 2004 Pine View Dr, Spartanburg, SC 29307

South Carolina Region, Donald Doria, 600 S Parker Rd, Greenville, SC 29609

Swamp Fox Region, Paul A Tuttle Jr, 837 Wedgefield Rd, Florence, SC 29501

South Dakota *South Dakota Region*, Cliff Glembin, 807 Hidden Valley Dr, Watertown, SD 57201

Tennessee *Appalachian Region*, Kyle A Reedy, 229 Edgefield Rd, Bristol, TN 37620

Battlefield Region, Jim Heidenway, 9320 Crockett Rd, Brentwood, TN 37027

Celebration City Region, James C Taylor, PO Box 502, Shelbyville, TN 37160

Cherokee Valley Region, Harold Miller, 151 Vermont Dr NW, Cleveland, TN 37312

Chickamauga Region, Ernie C Antes, 7525 Twisting Creek Ln, Ooltewah, TN 37363

Clinton Region, Benny S Houser, 19 Raintree Pl, Oak Ridge, TN 37830

Dan'l Boone Region, Mikel Smith, 253 Clearwater Dr, Kingsport, TN 37664

Davy Crockett Region, John Lingo, 50 Venice Ln, Greeneville, TN 37745

East Tennessee Region, Rick Lay, PO Box 461, Athens, TN 37371

Honk, Rattle & Roll Touring Region, Mark D Qualls, PO Box 298, Tullahoma, TN 37388

Middle Tennessee Region, Bruce Hickerson, 3722 Lascassas Rd, Murfreesboro, TN 37130

Stones River Region, Carolyn Hickerson, 3722 Lascassas Rd, Murfreesboro, TN 37130

Sumner County, Tennessee Region, Lonney R Young, 6 McMurtry Rd, Goodlettsville, TN 37072

Tims Ford Region, Robert Simms, 101 Hermitage Dr, Tullahoma, TN 37388

Tobacco Belt Region, J Gordon Botts, 3410 Greer Rd, Goodlettsville, TN 37072

Walden Ridge Region, Bill Vermillion, 505 W Ridgecrest Dr, Kingston, TN 37763

Texas *Amarillo Region*, Arthur Haley, 5103 Westway Tr, Amarillo, TX 79109

Big Spring Region, EL Hendon, 405 Westwood Ct, Lamesa, TX 79331

Central Texas Region, Victor L Donnell, 1801 Woods Loop, Driftwood, TX 78619

Deep East Texas Region, Wendall N Spreadbury, RR 13 Box 8600, Nacogdoches, TX 75961

Golden Crescent Region, Kristi Dieringer, 1407 W Grand, Yoakum, TX 77995

Gulf Coast Region, Golden Triangle Chapter, Edward M Wros, 1805 Grandview Dr, Nederland, TX 77627

Gulf Coast Region, JT Gorrell, 5615 Delange Ln, Houston, TX 77092

Hill Country Region, Phillip Koch, 709 Bluebonnet Dr, Kerrville, TX 78028

Northeast Texas Region, Leon Koze, Rt 1 Box 115G, Greenville, TX 75401

Red River Valley Honkers Region, John W Scharfe, PO Box 144, Paris, TX 75460

Rio Grande Valley Region, Tom Pipkin, PO Box 388, Mission, TX 78573

Snyder Wheels Region, Charlie Wilson, PO Box 795, Snyder, TX 79550

South Texas Region, Gene Watson, 12807 Provision, San Antonio, TX 78233

Texas Region, Kip F Lankenau, 2546 Cattail Ln, Carrollton, TX 75006

West Texas Region, Al Walvoord, 2805 Cockheed Dr, Midland, TX 79701

Wichita Falls Region, James D Edwards, 1606 Johnson Rd, Iowa Park, TX 76367

Wildflower Region, Mac E Smith, 2803 Slough Dr, Temple, TX 76502

Wool Capital Region, Harry G Carr, 1602 Kansas Ave, San Angelo, TX 76904

Virginia   *Accomack-Northhampton Region*, Bill Hoff, PO Box 95, Locustville, VA 23404

Bull Run Region, Betty P Waterfield, 13052 Hyla Dr, Manassas, VA 20112

Crater Antique Auto Club Region, Joseph H Newsome, 12330 Walkers Quarter Rd, Chesterfield, VA 23838

Historic Fredericksburg Region, Don Mohr, 41 Gold Cup Dr, Fredericksburg, VA 22406

Historic Virginia Peninsula Region, Melody Diamontopulos, 220 Sir John Way, Seaford, VA 23696

Lynchburg Region, Jean Mills, RR 2 Box 64, Concord, VA 24538

Martinsville-Danville Region, Bobby G Bolden, 3383 Daniels Creek Rd, Collinsville, VA 24078

Mountain Empire Region, Elmer D Mottesheard, 4843 Blackhollow Heights Ln, Dublin, VA 24084

National Capital Region, Anne Marie Zerega, 416 S Adams St, Arlington, VA 22204

North Carolina Region, North Central Chapter, Jimmy C Lawson, 127 Martindale Dr, Danville, VA 24541

Northern Neck Region, Earl D Beauchamp Jr, PO Box 999, Montross, VA 22520

Piedmont Region, Randall L Smith, PO Box 6585, Charlottesville, VA 22906

Richmond Region, Dayton G Leadbetter, 10508 Telegraph Rd, Ashland, VA 23005

Roanoke Valley Region, Jerry A Aker, 418 Cedar Ave, Vinton, VA 24179

Tidewater Region, Robert L Parrish, 1221 Smokey Mountain Tr, Chesapeake, VA 23320

Tri-County Region, Henry L Lilly, 2214 Mt Clinton Pike, Harrisonburg, VA 22802

Twin County Region, Charles Rudy, 212 Fish Pond Dr, Galax, VA 24333

Waynesboro-Staunton Region, Kenneth B Bahrs, 224 St James Rd, Fishersville, VA 22939

Washington   *Evergreen Region*, Steven C Schoos, E 210 Mason Lake Dr E, Grapeview, WA 98546

Tacoma Region, Sam D Burks, 10864 113th Ave SW, Tacoma, WA 98498

West Virginia   *Bluestone Region*, Benny R Buckner, 1807 Honaker Ave, Princeton, WV 24740

Greenbrier Valley Region, Raleigh L Sanford, HC 83 Box 697, Rainelle, WV 25962

Huntington Region, W Carroll Browning, 1269 Walker Branch Rd, Huntington, WV 25704

Kanawha Valley Region, Doy Maston, 417 18th St, Dunbar, WV 25064

Mid-Ohio Valley Region, Guy Estep, 217 S 1st Ave, Paden City, WV 26159

Northern Panhandle Region, James E Bowery, 260 Park Addition, Wellsburg, WV 26070

Shenandoah Region, Boyd E Kilmer, 411 Warm Springs Ave, Martinsburg, WV 25401

West Virginia Region, Russell D Davis, Rt 8 Box 326, Fairmont, WV 26554

Wisconsin   *Illinois Region*, Waukegan Chapter, Shirley Davidson, PO Box 4, Bristol, WI 53104

Minnesota Region, Dairyland Chapter, Henry Selle, 1426 US Hwy 63, Turtle Lake, WI 54889

Northern Lakes Region, C James Reinke, PO Box 981, Wausau, WI 54402-0981

Wisconsin Region, Sharan Weickelt, 14530 W Park Ave, New Berlin, WI 53151

Wyoming   *Big Horn Mountain Region*, HO Thobaben II, 60 Cato Dr, Sheridan, WY 82801

Buzzard's Breath Touring Region, Daniel Binger, 3578 Essex Rd, Cheyenne, WY 82001

High Plains Region, Laramie Hi Wheelers Chapter, Rick Knight, 1710 Sanders Dr, Laramie, WY 82070

High Plains Region, Oak Spokes Chapter, William F Karl, 4414 Charles St, Cheyenne, WY 82001

Section Three – Clubs & Organizations

Antique Automobile Club of America regions (continued)

High Plains Region, Peter M Lindahl, 5415 Meadow Ln, Laramie, WY 82070

Canada   *Maple Leaf Region*, David J Gurney, PO Box 809, Richmond, ON, K0A 2Z0

Lord Selkirk Region, S Jerry McCreery, 709-595 River Ave, Winnipeg, MB, R3L 0E6

Ontario Region, Gerald G Byers, RR 4, Port Hope, ON, L1A 3V8

Central America   *Club de Autos Antiquos de Costa Rica Region*, Gaspar Ortuno Sr, PO Box 3641-1000, San Jose, Costa Rica,

South America   *Colombia South America Region*, Arturo Vayda, PO Box 49477, Medellin, Colombia,

Antique Motorcycle Club of America Inc
Box 310
Sweetser, IN 46987
800-782-AMCA(2622); FAX: 765-384-5700
E-mail: amc@comteck.com

For membership information, contact at the above address: Dick Winger, 765-384-5421. Founded 1954. Over 9,500 members. A non-profit organization devoted to the hobby of seeking out, preserving, restoring and exhibiting antique motorcycles, and to the exchange of fellowship and information. For owners and those interested in old motorcycles. Considered antique: 35 years old. Quarterly publication: *The Antique Motorcycle*. Dues: $20/year US, $28/year Canada, $40/year foreign. Web site: www.antiquemotorcycle.org

chapters:

Arkansas Louisiana Mississippi Oklahoma Texas   *Cherokee*, Marian Guerin, 1144 Sycamore, San Marcos, TX 78666-7026

California   *Fort Sutter*, Richard Ostrander, 3132 T St, Sacramento, CA 95816-7032

Los Angeles, Todd Bertrang, 26767 Sand Canyon Rd, Canyon Country, CA 91351

Orcas, Peter Gagan, 14332 Magdalen, White Rock, BC, V4B 2X2

Southern California, Tim Graber, 2058 Aliso Ave, Costa Mesa, CA 92627-2109

Colorado   *Rocky Mountain*, Todd Vinzant, 16601 W 15th Ave, Golden, CO 80401-2809

Delaware Maryland Virginia   *Del Mar VA*, William Hoover, 24973 Harrington Rd, Greensboro, MD 21639-1553

East Pennsylvania   *Perkiomen*, Kathy Daya, 7 Pine Ln, Douglasville, PA 19518-1313

Florida   *Sunshine*, Greg Manders, 1864 Juneberry Ln, Inverness, FL 34453-3383

Georgia   *Dixie*, Louie Hale, 1708 Indian Hills Ct, Augusta, GA 30906-9312

Illinois Indiana Wisconsin   *Prairie*, Andy Anderson, PO Box 1028, Lake Zurich, IL 60047

Illinois Iowa Wisconsin   *Chief Blackhawk*, Del Schumacher, 2219 W Central Pk, Davenport, IA 52804

Illinois Missouri   *St Louis*, Steve Tettaton, 3067 Adayah Ln, Arnold, MO 63010-3802

Indiana Kentucky/Ohio   *Ohio Valley*, Kim Gadd, 3621 N Brownsville Rd, Brownsville, IN 47325

Indiana Michigan/Ohio   *Maumee Valley*, Randy Valko, 1265 W Wattles Rd, Troy, MI 48098-6302

Iowa/Nebraska   *Omaha*, Connie Schlemmer, 1218 Wedgewood Dr, Council Bluffs, IA 51503

Kansas Oklahoma   *Sunflower*, Terry Sawyer, 1238 N Doris, Wichita, KS 67212-1947

Maryland Virginia   *Chesapeake*, Tom Finn, 37 Glenwood Ave, Catonsville, MD 21228-3429

Michigan/Ohio   *Lake Erie*, Terry Austin, 407 Keltner Ave, Akron, OH 44319-3831

Minnesota   *Viking*, Ralph Overholt, 6321 Rolf Ave, Edina, MN 55439-1434

New England   *Yankee*, Charlie & Sandy Gallo, 31 Atwoodville Ln, Mansfield Center, CT 06250

New Jersey   *Seaboard*, John Scholz, 30 Summit Pass, Medford, NJ 08055

New York   *Empire*, Dick White, 182 Hartford Rd, Brooktondale, NY 14817

North Carolina   *Blue Ridge*, Chris Wolf, PO Box 708, Indian Trails, NC 28079-0708

North New Jersey   *Colonial*, "Gentleman" Ray Dhue, 33 Colonial Way, New Providence, NJ 07974-1104

NW Indiana SW Michigan   *River Valley*, Tom Rickey, 52092 Cheryl Dr, Granger, IN 46530-9112

Oregon   *Oregon Trail*, Thomas Krise, 1615 Court St NE, Salem, OR 97301

Oregon Washington   *Evergreen*, Mike Brown, PO Box 723, Tenino, WA 98589

Pennsylvania   *Neshaminy Valley*, Charles Grafenstine, 1009 Honeysuckle Ave, Parkland, PA 19047-3842

South Dakota   *Great Plains*, Walter Stearns, RR 3 Box 23, Luverne, MN 56156

Southern Colorado   *High Plains*, Zeke Rhodes, 1763 Mineola St, Colorado Springs, CO 80915

Southwest Virginia   *Highlands*, Barry Wuergler, 1071 Merriman Way Rd, Moneta, VA 24121

Tennessee   *Confederate*, Tina Schmalshof, 620 S Bellevue Blvd, Memphis, TN 38104-4533

Texas   *Tejas*, James Freeman II, 924 Gaye Ln, Arlington, TX 76012

Wisconsin   *Badger Heritage*, Roger Klopfenstein, N88 W17143 Main St, Menomonee Falls, WI 53051

Canada   *Buffalo*, Ross Metcalfe, 8729 Robin Blvd, Headingley, MB, R4J 1B7

Antique Truck Club of America Inc
PO Box 291
Hershey, PA 17033
717-533-9032

Founded 1971. 2,400 members. Open to owners of commercial vehicles or those who have an interest in the history, preservation, restoration and operation of antique commercial vehicles. *Double Clutch* magazine to members 6 times a year, free initial want and for sale ads to members. Dues: $25/year US, $30/year Canada, $35/year foreign. Web site: www.atca-inc.net

chapters:

Delaware	*Delaware Chapter*, Jack Smith, 35 Lynn Dr, Newark, DE 19711 302-731-5217
Michigan	*Blue Water Chapter*, Richard Vanderworp, 2728 N Belle River, East China, MI 48054 810-765-3473
New Jersey	*North Jersey Chapter*, Jack Moran, 284 Mt Hope Ave, Dover, NJ 07801
	South Jersey Shore Chapter, Douglas A Rodgers, 405 Cedar Ave, PO Box 306, Richland, NJ 08350 856-697-1225
	State Line Chapter, Robert J Abbott, 186 Rockland Ave, Norwood, NJ 07648 201-768-4018
New York	*Finger Lakes Area Chapter*, Ray Hildreth, 2097 Rt 14 N, Lyons, NY 14489 315-946-5006
	Long Island Chapter, Kevin Duffy, 50-42 195th St, Flushing, NY 11365 718-357-7382
	Sound Shore Chapter, Angelo J Sposta, 52 Park Ave, Port Chester, NY 10573 914-939-7910
North Carolina	*Smokey Mountain Chapter*, Dean Jenkins, 756 Old Fort Rd, Fairview, NC 28730
Pennsylvania	*Central Pennsylvania Chapter*, Tom Oehme, 7 Starlite Dr, Lititz, PA 17543 717-626-1204
	Greater Lehigh Valley Chapter, Frank Kline, 64 S 14th St, Catasauqua, PA 18032
	Greater Pittsburgh Area Chapter, Jeffrey Tenerovich, RD 3 Box 537, New Alexandria, PA 15670 724-668-7450
	Keystone Chapter, Jack Servello, 1604 22nd Ave, Altoona, PA 16601
	Northeast Pennsylvania Chapter, George F Marushock, 715 Kossuth St, Throop, PA 18512-1024 570-383-1593
	Southeastern Pennsylvania Chapter, Allison Whitcomb, 309 Euclid Ave, Ambler, PA 19002-4619 215-643-3517
Vermont	*Green Mountain Bulldawg Chapter*, Dave Zsido, 3 Haywood Ave, Rutland, VT 05701 802-775-6576
Canada	*Upper Canada Chapter*, David Muir, RR #3, Perth ON, K7H 3C5 613-264-0750

Appalachian British Car Society
c/o Al Bradley
143 Stonewall Hts
Abingdon, VA 24210
540-628-4763
E-mail: bradal@naxs.com

Founded 1992. 45 members. Interest in any British car required. Southwest VA/northeast TN areas, also KY & NC. Dues: $15/year. Web site: www.britcars.net

Ark-LA-Tex Antique & Classic Car Association
PO Box 3353
Shreveport, LA 71133
903-766-3958
E-mail: hcjc@shreve.net

Founded 1957. 125 members. Monthly newsletter, *The Piston Chatter*, monthly meeting, annual swap meet, partipcates in fundraiser car shows for local Burn Foundation and charity fun run to support local charities. Restoring a 1922 Bour Davis automobile, originally produced locally, the only one known to exist. Dues: $20/year.

Asphalt Angels Car Club Inc
PO Box 1450
Priest River, ID 83856
208-448-0318; FAX: 208-448-0414
E-mail: bates@pcez.net

Founded 1960. 100 members. No restrictions, monthly meeting second Thursday of each month. Annual show and shine last weekend in July, weekly social, provide scholarships, support seniors and needy familys. Monthly newsletter, frequent cruises. Dues: $20/year. Web site: www.expage.com/asphaltangels

Belltown Antique Car Club
PO Box 211
East Hampton, CT 06424

Founded 1968. 95 members. Open to anyone who enjoys old cars. Meetings 1st Wednesday of each month. Antique engine meet 4th Sunday in April, car show 1st Sunday in August. Dues: $10/year.

Borgward Owners' Club
77 New Hampshire Ave
Bay Shore, Long Island, NY 11706
PH/FAX: 516-BR-3-0458
E-mail: leftyny@aol.com

Founded 1974. 100 members. Open to owners of Borgward products: Borgward, Lloyd, Goliath, and to enthusiasts. Offers newsletter and an extensive stock of spares, some of which are made by special order. Get-togethers are arranged locally. Dues: $25/year. Web site: http://clubs.hemmings.com/borgward/

British Automobile Touring Association of Nova Scotia
PO Box 202
Waverley, NS Canada B0N 2S0
902-861-3277; FAX: 902-861-1361
E-mail: hamilton@batans.ca

Founded 1995. 195 members. British automobile ownership or interest, tours of the Canadian Maritime Provinces monthly (mostly Nova Scotia). Quarterly newsletter, *Small Torque*. Have a local list service for members. Dues: $30/year Canadian. Web site: www.batans.ca

British Boots and Bonnets Car Club
7060 Horizon Dr
Rockford, IL 61109-5128
815-963-2054; FAX: 815-963-0278
E-mail: mgnut@bigfoot.com

Founded 1995. 93 members. All British marques welcome, monthly newsletter, *The Chronicle,* annual event: All British Car & Motorcycle Show, held in July at Poplar Grove Airport, Popler Grove, IL. Dues: $20/year. Web site: www.britishbootsbonnets.com

British Car Club ASBL
Rue du College, BP 153
B-4800 Verviers Belgium
3287335507; FAX: 3287335122

Founded 1988. 2,500 members. Open to all British car lovers. Monthly magazine, *Gentleman Driver,* all you must know about British cars. Insurance scheme, spare parts and technical service, club shop, clubhouse for members. Dues: $30/year US.

British Motor Cars of New England
PO Box 368
Wyoming, RI 02898
401-539-2879
E-mail: frankk@intap.net

Founded 1984. 250-300 members. Multi-marque British car club, dues include *British Marque* subscription, event notices mailed to members. We host an annual BMCNE festival, a 3 day event. Dues: $15/year. Web site: www.bmcne.com

British Sports Car Club
PO Box 43923
Louisville, KY 40253
812-923-7349, IN; FAX: 502-499-7491
E-mail: jim@budgetprint.win.net

Founded 1983. 100 members. Monthly newsletter, annual car show, monthly club and driving activities. $20/year. Web site: http://members.aol.com/lucaselec/cars.html

Brown County Cruisers Car Club
PO Box 113
Georgetown, OH 45121-0113
937-378-3945; FAX: 513-248-4300
E-mail: dfetters@comcomach.com

Founded 1986. 20 members. No restrictions to join. Clubs annual car show benefits the American Heart Association. Dues: $20 one time fee.

CAdeAA-Club Amigos de Automoviles Antiguos
Sanchez de Loria 1666
Lomas de Zamora
Buenos Aires 1832 Argentina
PH/FAX: 54-11-4282-8292
E-mail: cadeaa@canopus.com.ar

Founded 1978. 250 members. Newsletter published quarterly, *La Luneta.* Many weekend outings during the year, one annual rally and one Autojumble. Every Friday night, between 80 and 100 members, family and friends meet to chat and dine at the club. Must own a more than 30 year old car to be a full member. Dues: $180/year. Web site: www.canopus.com.ar/cadeaa

Cape Cod British Car Club
210 Lakeview Ave
Falmouth, MA 02540
508-457-9199; FAX: 508-457-1778
E-mail: brian@comfacs.com

Founded 2000. 70 members. Membership open to people with an interest in classic and antique British cars. Benefits include participation in monthly meetings, tech sessions and weekly summer activities. Newsletter published in *British Marque.* Dues: $20/year. Web site: http://clubs.hemmings.com/capecodbritish

Cape Fear Classics Car and Truck Club
PO Box 997
Hope Mills, NC 28348
910-426-3314
E-mail: jpsmith6262@cs.com

Founded 1997. 350 members. Open to all classic car enthusiasts. Discounts from major restoration suppliers, monthly cruise-ins, multiple events sponsored year round. Dues: $20/year.

Cars of Yesteryear Inc
493 Citizens Rd
Newport, VT 05855
802-334-6079

Founded 1983. 100 members. Need only to have an interest in the promotion, appreciation and restoration of antique vehicles, classic cars, street rods or any vehicle 15 years old of special interest. Annual car show always held on first Sunday of August. Profits to support local charities and scholarship fund. Dues: $10/year.

Champlain Valley Classic Cruisers Inc
1796 Military Tpke
Plattsburgh, NY 12901
PH/FAX: 518-563-6657
E-mail: seymourd@westelcom.com

Founded 1998. 200 members. The purpose of CVCC is to have fun and promote preservation and restoration of all classic vehicles. Anyone is welcome to join if you live in the Champlain Valley. We have cruises, a major car show and fundraisers. Our monthly newsletter, *The Lug-Nut,* is published monthly. Dues: $10/year. Web site: http://clubs.hemmings/com/cvcc

Chandler-Cleveland Motor Club
43 Wide Beach Rd
Irving, NY 14081
716-549-0729
E-mail: hansen_chandler@mindspring.com

Founded 1994. 110 members. Open to all with interest in the Chandler-Cleveland automobiles. Dues: $15/year, $20 roster fee. Web site: http://clubs.hemmings.com/chandler/

Chicago Street Cruisers
2500 N Adams Rd
Jonesville, MI 49250
517-849-2718
E-mail: dauster@mail.rcskiz.org

Founded 1982. 60 members. No restrictions, everyone welcome. The cars of our members range from concours restorations to exotic street rods. Dues: $12/year.

The Chrysler Cordoba Club & Registry
1402 N Adams, Apt 3
Fredericksburg, TX 78624
830-997-0714 after 8 pm CST
E-mail: 440cuda@concentric.net

Founded 1997. 420 members. Club and registry for 1975-1983 Chrysler Cordoba, 1979 Chrysler 300, 1975-1978 Dodge Charger, 1978-1979 Dodge Magnum, 1980-1983 Dodge Mirada and 1981-1983 Imperial. Send SASE for information and newsletter subscription fee. Dues: none. Web site: www.concentric.net/~440cuda/ccr.htm

Class Cruisers Car Club of Lapeer, MI
305 Angle Rd
Lapeer, MI 48446
810-664-7417
E-mail: john2@tir.com

Founded 1990. 40 members. Classic Cruisers Car Club of Lapeer cruise night, Calvelli's Eatery, 44 W Park St, 6 pm to 9 pm. Call for more information. Dues: $25/year.

Classic Car Club of America
1645 Des Plaines River Rd, Ste 7
Des Plaines, IL 60018
847-390-0443; FAX: 847-390-7118
E-mail: classiccarclub@aol.com

Founded 1952. 5,500 members. Open to select makes and models of cars dating from 1925-1948. Dedicated to the collection, preservation and enjoyment of fine cars. Dues: $40/year. Web site: www.classiccarclub.org

regions:

Alabama   *Dixie*, Robert Bentley, 744 Grimwood Rd, Toney, AL 35773   256-828-4226

Arizona   *Arizona*, Barbara Klusman, 10040 E Ranch Gate Rd, Scottsdale, AZ 85255-2306   480-585-5599; FAX: 480-585-5598; E-mail: klusman@email.msn.com; Web site: http://clubs.hemmings.com/arizonaccca/

California   *Northern California*, Joe Kohlbecher, 730 Twinview Pl, Pleasant Hill, CA 94523   925-256-9400; E-mail: joebuickman@yahoo.com; Web site: http://norcalccca.tripod.com

       San Diego/Palm Springs, Ed McCormick, 1521 Randall Ct, Los Angeles, CA 90065   323-226-0250

       Southern California, Greg Vanley, 276 Bentley Cir, Los Angeles, CA 90065   310-476-9100

Colorado   *Colorado*, Tony Ficco, 12425 W 38th Ave, Wheat Ridge, CO 80033   303-431-6492

Florida   *Florida*, Edna Wieler, 420 Coconut Palm Rd, Vero Beach, FL 32963   561-234-4111; Web site: http://clubs.hemmings.com/flrccca/

       Gold Coast, William Raithel, 8 Torchwood Ln, Key Largo, FL 33037-5122   305-367-3170; E-mail: nrainthel@aol.com

Illinois   *Greater Illinois*, Bob Fleck, 360 Prospect Ave, Elmhurst, IL 60126   630-833-5768 home, 847-298-8400 business

Indiana   *Indiana*, George H Maley, 4531 N Meridian St, Indianapolis, IN 46208   Web site: www.4stargallery.com/incccca

Kansas   *Oil Belt*, John Holden, 2402 W 69th Terr, Mission Hills, KS 66208   913-677-2402

Maryland   *Chesapeake Bay*, Gene Sauter, 8431 Old Frederick Rd, Ellicott City, MD 21043-1915   410-461-1354 home; FAX: 410-750-1484; E-mail: genebetty5@aol.com

Michigan   *Michigan*, Lee Barthel, 21095 Halsted Rd, Northville, MI 48167   248-476-0702 home; FAX: 248-476-5120; Web site: www.classiccarsofmichigan.com/

Minnesota   *Upper Midwest*, Tom Brace, 1433 Idaho Ave W, St Paul, MN 55108   612-644-1716 home

Missouri   *Spirit of St Louis*, Allan Franz, 31 Sunfish Dr, Defiance, MO 63341   636-398-5599; E-mail: alaf@primary.net; Web site: http://members.primary.net/~alaf

New Jersey   *Metropolitan*, Michael Paone, 38 Orchard Ln, Berkeley Heights, NJ 07922   908-322-6486

New Mexico   *Rio Grande*, Michelle Ann Franowsky, PO Box 279, Corrales, NM 87048   505-890-4461

Ohio   *Ohio*, Margus Sweigard, 427 Lowell Dr, Highland Heights, OH 44143   440-461-6646; E-mail: buickman32@aol.com

Oregon   *Oregon*, Howard Freedman, PO Box 42127, Portland, OR 97242   503-234-8617

Pennsylvania   *Delaware Valley*, Wilson Borden, 207 S Waterloo Rd, Devon, PA 19333-1634   610-989-0259

       Western Pennsylvania, Doug Dudjak, 408F James St, New Wilmington, PA 16142-9521   724-946-3606 home, 800-525-7702 business

Rhode Island   *New England*, Ernest E Cormier, 21 Fairview Ave, Hope Valley, RI 02832-2112   401-539-2547

Texas   *Lone Star*, Jay McClure III, 314 Beverly Dr, San Antonio, TX 78228   210-735-8450

       North Texas, John Haynes, 4651 Beverly Dr, Dallas, TX 75209   214-526-8007

Washington   *Pacific Northwest*, Gary Johnson,   425-746-1098 home; PH/FAX: 425-649-8634 work; E-mail: garyjohnson@juno.com

Wisconsin   *Wisconsin*, John B Haydon, 317 E Acacia Rd, Fox Point, WI 53217   414-352-1669; Web site: http://clubs.hemmings.com/wirccca/

Classic Dream Car Club
1116 Chelsea St
Bakersfield, CA 93306
661-366-2515
E-mail: 47style@msn.com

Founded 1980. 40 members. Classic Dreams is a pre-1959 all make and model car club. We do community fundraising for the Boys' & Girls' Club of Bakersfield and Crippled Children's Society. Dues: $60/year.

Classic Nights Car Club
1136 Capitol Ave
Bridgeport, CT 06606
203-385-4610
E-mail: photogs189@aol.com

Founded 1984. 20 members. Family oriented car club. Own a classic car or will acquire one a year after membership into the club. Cruise nights every Friday mid May to mid October. Also car show each year to benefit a charitable organization. Dues: $30/year. Web site: www.classicnights.com

---

Club Jacq Japonaises Antiques et Classiques du Quebec
386 Chemin du Nvage
St-Antoine-Sur-Richelieu, QC Canada J0L 1R0
450-787-2058
E-mail: lucco@total.net

Founded 2000. 25 members. Car club specializing in 1985 or earlier Japanese classic and antique cars. Based in Montreal and servicing all Quebec Province mostly. Dues: none.

Section Three – Clubs & Organizations

Club MCC
8401 N Kentucky Ave, Ste M
Evansville, IN 47725
812-425-4454; FAX: 812-425-5169
E-mail: services@myclassiccar.com

Founded 1997. Open to all automotive enthusiasts. Club MCC is a spin-off of the television show "My Classic Car" on TNN. The club offers a membership kit and benefits including special online privileges at its web site and discounts at the annual Autofest each year in Evansville, Indiana, featuring an open car show and other events. Dues: $24.95/year US. Web site: www.myclassiccar.com

Collectors Car Club of Saskatchewan
PO Box 3562
Regina, SK Canada S4P 3L7
306-525-5117
E-mail: d.g.bobinski@sk.sympatico.ca or
k.kulach@sk.sympatico.ca

Founded 1984. Members: 30+ families. Open to all with an interest in collecting and showing vehicles. Meetings two Tuesdays per month in winter and spring. Car show end of May and cruise 2nd weekend in June. Many other club fuctions. Dues: $24/year. Web site: www.collectors.20m.com

Columbia Car Club
c/o Jake Coons
5 Maple View Ave
Nassau, NY 12123
518-766-3116

Founded 1974. 82 members. Prospective members should have an active interest in automobiles and club activities. Ownership of an antique or collectible vehicle is not necessary. Meetings are held at the Ghent, NY VFW at 7:30 pm on the 2nd Monday of the month. Prospective members are welcome. Monthly publication, *Rattles & Squeaks*. Newsletter brings members who are unable to attend a meeting up-to-date with meeting discussions and upcoming activities. Dues: $10/year.

Contemporary Historical Vehicle Assoc Inc
PO Box 493398
Redding, CA 96049

Founded 1967. 2,000 members. Recognizes all vehicles built since 1928 to 1978. Activities are open to all cars, commercial vehicles and military land vehicles. Annual week long tour for members. Dues: $25/year domestic, $29/year foreign, $300/life membership.

Cruzin Few Unique Vehicle Club
#54 Mansell Trailer Pk
New Brighton, PA 15066
724-846-7270
E-mail: wrlii@home.com

Founded 1993. 150 members. New members every March, limit 150. Monthly newsletter, monthly meetings, charity sponsors. Dues: $25/year.

Cyclone Car Club
PO Box 37
Revere, MA 02151-0001
781-286-4822
E-mail: two1tim1@aol.com

Founded 1998. 84 members. Open to all regardless of vehicle. Fuddruckers Restaurant, Rt 1, Saugus, MA, every Thursday night, 5 to 9 pm, April through September. Monthly newsletter: *Cyclone Cruiser*. Dues: none.

Dakota BOP Chapter
408 N Main
Hartford, SD 57033
605-528-3764
E-mail: danderso@dtgnet.com

Founded 1995. 35 members. Formed to serve all Buick, Olds and Pontiac enthusiasts and owners. Do not require membership in any national organizations but offer a monthly technical newsletter, monthly meetings. Annual all GM car show and a technical library. Dues: $15/year. Web site: www.dakotabop.homestead.com

Daytona-Super Bird Auto Club
13717 W Green Meadow Dr
New Berlin, WI 53151
262-786-8413
E-mail: dsac@execpc.com

Founded 1975. 500+ members. No restrictions, owners and admirers welcome to join. *Hightailer*, monthly newsletter featuring historical articles, members cars, events and free advertising to club members; national and local events. Specializing in information exchange and registry for 1969 Dodge Charger Daytona, 1970 Plymouth Superbird, 1969 Dodge Charger 500, 1969 Ford Torino Talladega, 1969 Mercury Cyclone Spoiler. Dues: $20/year, $22 Canada/rest of world.

Deutscher Automobil Veteranen Club
Dachsstr 52
Wiesbaden D-65207 Germany
06122-12180; FAX: 06150-52243

Founded 1965. 1,500 members. 15 sections all over Germany. Monthly meetings, quarterly club news, open to all marques. Dues: 120 DM/year.

Durant Motors Automobile Club
9331 NC Hwy 210
Four Oaks, NC 27524
919-989-9603
E-mail: oldcarnutz@cs.com

Founded 1998. 300+ members. No restrictions to join. Newsletter 4 times a year. Cars include Durant, Star, Flint, DeVaux, Frontenac and Locomobile. Dues: $25/year. Web site: http://clubs.hemmings.com/durant

Eastern Townships Vintage Automobile Club
PO Box 325
Lennoxville, QC Canada J1M 1Z5
819-563-6535, leave message

Founded 1977. 45 members. No restrictions to join. Friendship newsletter 2 weeks before meetings. One event per year, a car show plus a Christmas party. Dues: $10/year.

Frenchtown Auto Club
35279 TV Ln
Prairie du Chien, WI 53821
608-326-4544
E-mail: pdcvet@mhtc.net

Founded 1982. 20 members. Interest in cars needed to join. Monthly newsletter. Sponsors annual car show. Community service, roadside clean-up. Monthly meetings. Dues: $10/year.

Gateway Auto & Truck Club
2 Siesta Dr
West Wareham, MA 02576
508-295-0619

Founded 1991. 12+ members. Must have a love for the automobile and/or trucks. Dues: $20/year.

Gig Harbor Cruisers Automotive Club
PO Box 2642
Gig Harbor, WA 98335
253-265-3648; FAX: 253-851-1669
E-mail: ghcruisers@aol.com

Founded 1997. 120 members. All makes, models, years welcome, monthly newsletter (*Cruizletter*), host annual Cruise the Narrows Car Show, 4th Saturday in July. Dues: $25/year. Web site: www.gigharborcruisers.org

Good Times Car Club
4741 Pawnee Dr
Greeley, CO 80634
970-330-4033

Founded 1980. 29 members. Open to any person interested in auto or truck rebuilding and preservation, 14 years old, any make or model. We hold an annual Father's Day Rod Run, also sponsors a car show in the fall, we help fund charitable organizations. Build them to drive and show. Dues: $36/year.

Goodguys Rod & Custom Association
PO Box 424
Alamo, CA 94507
925-838-9876; FAX: 925-820-8241

Founded 1980. 45,000+ members. 20 events throughout the USA. Publisher of the giant sized *Goodtimes Gazette*. Dues: $25/year. Web site: www.good-guys.com

Great Autos of Yesteryear
PO Box 10856
Santa Ana, CA 92711-0856
714-838-0993
E-mail: webmaster@greatautos.org

Founded 1983. 960+ members. Classic and special interest club welcoming all makes and models. Large contingent of Classic American Luxury Cars. Monthly newsletter, monthly events. Annual north/south meet, annual Concours for charity. Chapters in Los Angeles and San Diego. Mostly gay and lesbian membership. Dues: $30/year. Web site: www.greatautos.org

Great Lakers Auto Club
PO Box 8719
Michigan City, IN 46361
PH/FAX: 219-874-4077
E-mail: greatlakers@csinet.net

Founded 1960. 75 members. Open interest car club, any make of car accepted, garage/work area for active members. Annual auto show, swap meet, monster truck display, indoor arts and crafts, model car shows, kids' activities. Dues: Assoc $25/year; Active $5/week.

Happy Days Car Club
1323 8th Ave
Beaver Falls, PA 15010
724-843-6911 days, 724-843-4476 eves

Founded 1991. 25 members. No restrictions, must be an active participant. Our club promotes interest in antique, classic and old cars in general. Dues: none.
Web site: http://clubs.hemmings.com/happydayscc/

Hart City Street Rods
506 Crystal Valley Dr
Middlebury, IN 46540
219-825-9212
E-mail: delrayman1@aol.com

Founded 1984. 10 members. Member cars to be 25 years or older, any make. We publish a monthly newsletter, have monthly business meetings and many outings centered on the season and common interest. We particularly enjoy driving our cars and we host the blind date dual poker run and car show at Bashor Childrens' Home in Goshen, Indiana on or around the 2nd weekend in October. Dues: $60/year.

Hendersonville Antique Car Club
PO Box 1190
Mountain Home, NC 28758
828-697-7876

Founded 1990. 75 members. No restrictions, monthly meeting 1st Tuesday of every month, monthly newsletters, 14 events in the year 2001 including cruises, shows, poker runs, etc. Dues: $12/year.

Historical Vintage Car Club of Delaware
PO Box 43
Dover, DE 19903
302-422-7437; FAX: 302-422-3516

Founded 1969. 300 members. Purpose of club is to preserve and restore the antique vehicles. Sponsors shows, tours and trips for enjoyment of membership. Publishes *Stovebolt* bi-monthly (six issues a year), free with membership, has calendar of club events and other antique car activities of interest to club. Dues: $10/year.

Hoosier Cruisers of Vincennes Inc
PO Box 1328
Vincennes, IN 47591
812-886-6556

Founded 1990. Members: 50 families. Annual cruise-in for June, annual cruise and dance and car show August, proceeds from car show buys clothes for needy children. Meetings held monthly. Newsletter sent monthly and the club does a cruise & eat monthly unless there is a cruise-in somewhere. Dues: $10/year.

Horseless Carriage Club of America
49239 Golden Oak Loop
Oakhurst, CA 93644
888-832-2374, 559-658-8800
E-mail: office@hcca.org

Founded 1937. 10,000 members. Membership offered to collectors, historians, anyone interested in early cars. Pioneer motor vehicles are the major interest of the HCCA and its members. Basically a touring club. Annual national tours are limited to vehicles of 1915 or older vintage. Membership includes 6 yearly issues of the *Gazette*. Dues: $35/year per family. Web site: www.hcca.org

Illiana Antique Auto Club
PO Box 245
Danville, IL 61832
217-765-4781

Founded in 1963. 60 families. Requires an interest in antique cars, parts, or literature. Monthly meetings and tours. Dues: $15/year.

Illini Collector Car Club
1911 N Duncan Rd
Champaign, IL 61822
217-355-1704; FAX: 217-355-9413
E-mail: mbalogh@balogh.com

Founded 1961. 100 members. Open to antique, special interest and classic car enthusiasts. Monthly newsletter, *The Roadmap*. Many annual events including a show in August. Dues: $15/year.

Iron Range Car Buffs
PO Box 210
Hoyt Lakes, MN 55750
218-225-2206
E-mail: rogsand@rangenet.com

Founded 1980. 30 members. Club is open to all car enthusiasts. Club hosts a car show every year in July on Sunday following the Iola Car Show. Provides a scholarship to a local tech school to a student in automotive curriculum. Dues: $10/year.

Section Three – Clubs & Organizations

Israel Classic Car & Motorcycle Club
PO Box 1193 Giv'at
Tel Aviv 53111 Israel
+972-3-7318818; FAX: +972-3-7319059
E-mail: 5club@5club.org.il

Founded 1985. 1,400 members. Israel's only classic and collectors vehicle club. Classic and vintage motor vehicles of all kinds. Weekly and monthly meetings and events. 3 annual shows. Monthly newsletter and quarterly publications, both in Hebrew. Old cars museum and transportation archives. As from the year 2001-member of FIVA, with the position "FIVA ANF". Dues: $50/year. Web site: www.5club.org.il

Jus'n Ol' Truck Club
723 9th Ave
DeWitt, IA 52742
563-659-2012
E-mail: whiskey@jdv.net

Founded 2000. 56 members. Open to enthusiasts of pre-1973 trucks, panels, Broncos, El Caminos, etc. All makes of trucks. Members receive a club T-shirt and a comprehensive monthly newsletter. Monthly meetings all year and outings April-October. Technical sessions held periodically. Dues: $25/year. Web site: www.jusnoltruck.com

Keene Area Klassics
PO Box 375
Keene, NH 03431
603-352-6571

Founded 1986. 40 members. There are no restrictions to join. All that is required is an interest in automobiles and the desire to associate with others of like interest. Meetings are held monthly at various locations in the area. Dues: $15/year.

Kent Island Cruisers Car Club
509 Victoria Dr
Stevensville, MD 21666-2625
410-643-4582

Founded 1994. 120+ members. No restrictions although the club is primarily made up of classic, street rods and antiques. Benefits include monthly newsletter and event information, discounts at some local stores, monthly membership meetings and summer cruise nights. Monthly newsletter with 12 pages of local events, classified ads, tech tips and other related information free with membership. Dues: $15/year. Web site: http://clubs.hemmings.com/kentcruis/

King Kruisers Car Club
491 Allendale Rd #106
King of Prussia, PA 19406
610-265-2611; FAX: 610-962-0872

Founded 1995. Everyone welcome. Cruise nights 3rd Saturday of month, April-September. Local runs. Monthly newsletter. Dues: $20/year. Web site: http://clubs.hemmings.com/kingkruiserscc/

Kingsport Antique & Rod Club
PO Box 775
Kingsport, TN 37662
423-224-2153
E-mail: carsmith@chartertn.net

Founded 1974. 51 members. Monthly meeting, monthly newsletter, annual car show and annual fundraiser for Ronald McDonald House. Open to all automobile enthusiasts. Dues: $20/year.

Klassy Kruzers Car Club
1 Kruzers Alley
Dunbar, WV 25064
FAX: 304-744-5192
E-mail: klassykruzers@excite.com

Founded 1989. 100 members. No restrictions to join. One meeting a month, two club cruise-ins, one car show, one cruise-in June 8, one cruise-in and show August 24, monthly newsletter. To conduct club functions and activities in a manner befitting members of the automobile sport and to encourage a better understanding of an open car club, constructive sport among members of the public, press and law enforcement agencies. To promote safety in driving, automobile maintenance and overall vehicle operation. Dues: $12/year. Web site: www.homestead.com/klassykruzerscarclub/klassykruzers.html

Kustom Kemps of America
Bill Hailey Dr, Rt 1 Box 1714
Cassville, MO 65625-9724
417-847-2940; FAX: 417-847-3647
E-mail: kustomkemps@mo-net.com

Founded 1980. 10,000 members. 1935-1964 (Lead Sled Division) and 1965-present (Late Model Division). Publication, *Trendsetter Magazine*. Dues: $28/year.

LA Roadsters Car Club
PO Box 11357
Burbank, CA 91510-1357
805-375-3170; FAX: 805-375-1394
E-mail: laroadsters@aol.com

Founded 1957. 30 members. Any person of good character owning an American type 1936 or older roadster in fine condition and finished. Must equal or better than existing club cars. The club sponsors the LA Roadster Show on Father's Day weekend held each year at the LA County Fairplex in Pomona, California. This year, 2001, makes 37 years. Dues: $50/year. Web site: www.laroadsters.com

Lake Granbury Vintage Car Club
PO Box 661
Granbury, TX 76048
817-279-0975; FAX: 817-279-6238
E-mail: rgrogers5@juno.com

Founded 1990. 65 members. Need to have an auto 20 years old or older. Club rallies and runs. Monthly newsletter. Club meets first Tuesday of month at Bodacious Bar-B-Q, Hwy 377 Business and the Bypass, Granbury, Texas. Dues: $24/year.

Lake Region Car Club
PO Box 2
Revillo, SD 57259
605-623-4538; FAX: 605-623-4215

Founded 1970. 25 members. Publish a bi-monthly newsletter, sponsor one car show a year, meet monthly (April-December) and take at least two driving tours each year. Dues: $10/year.

LeBarons Car Club
3195 5th Ave N
Lethbridge, AB Canada T1H 0P2
403-327-8525; FAX: 403-327-5671

Founded 1961. 35 members. No restrictions to join, fellowship and information. Annual Rod Run Reunion. Dues: $25/year.

Les Amis de Panhard & Deutsch-Bonnet
444 W Desoto St
Clermont, FL 34711
PH/FAX: 352-394-7797

Founded 1963. 86 members. Specializing in Panhard and Deutsch-Bonnet automobiles. Newsletter, meets. A non-profit organization run on volunteer labor devoted to those interested in the preservation, restoration or competition of all Panhard and Deutsch-Bonnet automobiles. Ownership of a vehicle is not required. All contributions are welcomed and appreciated. Dues: $15/year, make check/money order payable to: Les Amis de Panhard.

Liberty Cruisers Car Club
1212 Windover Ct
Fort Wayne, IN 46845
219-637-4338
E-mail: cruiserclub@aol.com

Founded 2001. 30 members. No restrictions to join. Open club. Monthly cruise-ins at Liberty Diner. Yearly benefit car show, yearly Christmas party and other club parties. Dues: $15/year includes whole family.

Long Island Moose Classic Car Club
Michael Silverman
15 Manorage Rd
Manorville, NY 11949
631-325-2004

Founded 2000. 16 members. Must be a member of the Moose Lodge, all benefits of the Moose Lodge, dinners, dances, bingo, car show, meetings third Wednesday of the month at Riverhead Lodge. Dues: $25/year.

Los Coyotes The Club
2 Impasse Josephine de Beauharnais
Noisy Le Grand 93160 France
33-6-10-83-79-08
E-mail: loscoyotesclub@aol.com

Founded 1996. 20 members maximum. Only American classic and muscle cars welcomed. An association of French collectors and amateurs. Monthly newsletter, monthly meeting, no humor means no member. All makes and models appreciated. Keeping America's vintage and memory on the road. H-A-N-D→F-S. Dues: $40/year.

Lovefords
2484 W Genesee Tpke
Camillus, NY 13031
315-672-5548
E-mail: info@lovefords.org

Founded 2000. 200 members. Lovefords is a club for owners and admirers of the Ford family of fine cars and trucks! Web site: www.lovefords.org

The Mid-America Old Time Automobile Association
8 Jones Ln
Morrilton, AR 72110
501-727-5427; FAX: 501-727-6482
E-mail: motaa@ipa.net

Founded 1959. 1,000 members in 29 affiliated clubs. The club recognizes automobiles built through 1972. *Antique Car Times* is published six times/year. Annual auto show and swap meet held the third weekend in June at the Museum of Automobiles on Petit Jean Mountain, Morrilton, Arkansas. Dues: $15/year. Web site: www.motaa.com

Mid Shore Cruisers
PO Box 1114
Cambridge, MD 21613
410-901-9788; FAX: 410-901-8999
E-mail: plymouth@fastol.com

Founded 1996. 55 members. Open to all types of cars, monthly newsletter, cruise-ins every 4th Saturday from April to October except in June. Dues: $10/year. Web site in progress: http://clubs.hemmings.com/midshorecruisers/

Midsouth Regional Old Car Club
3520 Lake DeSiard Dr
Monroe, LA 71201
318-361-9645; FAX: 318-387-4828
E-mail: charlesr@rsh.com

Founded 1972. 50 members. Meet 2nd Tuesday each month, spring and fall driving tours, car show 2nd Saturday of September. Monthly newsletter, *Recap*. Dues: $30/year.

Midwest Drag Racers Association
PO Box 290353
Brooklyn Center, MN 55429
651-213-6121; FAX: 612-623-8840
E-mail: mdrachair@aol.com

Founded 1974. 450 members. Monthly newsletter, *Eliminator;* car show last Sunday in April, bench racing Sunday, trade/car/swap show 1st Sunday in March, 8 race schedule with over $10,000 in contingencies, year end banquet. Dues: $20-$45/year. Web site: www.mdra.com

Midwestern Council of Sports Car Clubs
3618 E 1769th Rd
Ottawa, IL 61350
815-434-9999; FAX: 815-434-9882
E-mail: rossf@interaccess.com

Founded 1958. 980 members. Sports car racing for vintage and current era cars. On-track driver schools (3/yr). Open track autocross/time trials. Wheel to wheel racing. Free introductory series in Rolling Meadows, IL and Madison, WI. SASE for free info packet. Publications: *Klaxon* monthly newsletter, picture annual, annual rule book. Dues: $40/year. Web site: www.execpc.com/~mcscc

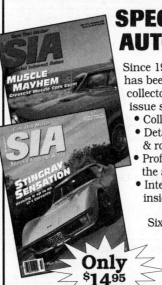

The Milestone Car Society
National Headquarters, Indianapolis
3743 E 71st St
Indianapolis, IN 46220
317-259-0959; FAX: 317-576-8027

Founded 1945. 650 members. No restrictions to join. Interest in cars in those years. *Milpost* publication, *Milestone Car* publication, Grand National meet and tour cars. Dues: $30/year.

Muhlenberg County Hot Rod Club
PO Box 366
Powderly, KY 42367
270-338-2940

Founded 1999. 35-40 members. We are a family oriented club that attends shows and cruise-ins as a group. We host yearly the Wayne Daniel Memorial car show and various events such as cruise-ins and cookouts. We meet twice a month. There are no restrictions to join. Dues: $12.50/year single, $25/year family. Web site: http://clubs.hemmings.com/mchrc

National Woodie Club
PO Box 6134
Lincoln, NE 68506
402-488-0990
E-mail: webmaster@nationalwoodieclub.com

Founded 1974. 3,000 members. The NWC is open to anyone interested in wood-bodied vehicles, original or modified. Ownership not required. Monthly magazine, *The Woodie Times*, with free ads to members 8 times per year, annual membership roster, regional chapters, tech advisors. Several Regional and National events each year, in all parts of the country. Dues: $25/year. Web site: www.classicar.com

New Old Stock Toronto Chapter
19 Falaise Rd
Scarborough, ON Canada M1E 3B6
416-724-1059; FAX: 416-393-8827
E-mail: newoldstk@home.com

Founded 1998. Approximately 20 members. Attend monthly meetings and events. Dues: monthly.

Newark Rodders
240 Thomas St
Newark, OH 43055
740-323-0780
E-mail: dougwilson@msmisp.com

22 members. No restrictions, monthly newsletter, Ye Olde Mill Rod Run & Picnic, Tri-County Chrysler/Plymouth Show, Lite the Nite Car Show. Dues: $25/one time.

Newfoundland Antique and Classic Car Club
Avalon Mall,PO Box 28147,
St John's, NF Canada A1B 4J8
709-754-3944; FAX: 709-737-1829
E-mail: chilliard66@hotmail.com

Founded 1980. 112 members. Open to anyone. Registered vehicles must be antiques, 25 years old or older, vehicles 20-25 accepted by vote. Meet 2nd Wednesday, evening, St John's Curling Club. Cruises every Thursday, A&W, weather permitting. Dues: $30/year. Web site: www.naccc.nfol.ca

Nor-Cal Galaxies/Mercurys
PO Box 3305
Livermore, CA 94551
925-455-9809; FAX: 925-292-8834
E-mail: rsheats@home.com

Founded 1987. 100 memberships, 200 cars. Dedicated to the preservation, restoration and enjoyment of 1959-1970 Ford Galaxies and Mercurys, by expanding interest, exchanging information and assisting others in obtaining and restoring these cars. Also share the responsibility of fighting detrimental legisla-tion aimed at removing classic cars from our roadways. Ownership is not a requirement. Club activities include outings, car shows, "Shop Days", holiday parties, monthly meetings. Newsletter is published monthly to inform members of meetings, activities and to share member car histories and technical information. Dues: $24/year.

North Valley Unique Car Club
PO Box 992
Chico, CA 95927-0992
530-345-0846
E-mail: woodbobjan@netzero.net

Founded 1961. 43 members. Have an interest in driving and preserving any unique make or model of automobile from 1900 to present, foreign or domestic. Monthly newsletter, yearly swap meet in September for the last 30+ years, picnics, tours and monthly meetings. Call, e-mail or write if you want more info. Dues: $10/year.

Northeast Hemi Owners Assoc
98 Cypress Ave
Tiverton, RI 02878
E-mail: rstp440@aol.com

Founded 1976. 380 members. Open to all Mopars and AMC products. Two meets a year, Memorial Day and Labor Day weekends. Newsletter, 6 issues a year. Dues: $25/year single, $30/year joint. Web site: www.nehoa.org

Northern Lights Car Club
55 NW 4th Ave
Forest Lake, MN 55025
651-464-4052
E-mail: rjford46@aol.com

Founded 1984. 90 members. Open club, monthly newsletter, monthly meetings and events. Dues: $20/year.

Nostalgia Knights Classic Car Club
PO Box 2672
Vineland, NJ 08362
856-794-9368
E-mail: fastback1@aol.com

Founded 1994. 70 members. Restricted to owners of cars 24 years of age or older, special interest, race cars, customs, modified, Limited Edition vehicles may be permitted at club's discretion. Monthly newsletter to all members. We do 4 shows and 7 cruises a year. Dues: $20/year.

Nostalgic Automobile Society of Montclair
92 Willowdale Ave
Montclair, NJ 07042
201-783-4732
E-mail: paparado@aol.com

Founded 1990. 16 members. Membership requires presence at two meetings plus one event and initiation fee. Activities include tours, parades, annual show, impromptu drives. Dues: $25/year. Web site: http://clubhemmings.com/nostalgicautomontclair/

Old Car Club Inc
PO Box 462
Shrewsbury, MA 01545
508-842-8628

Founded 1947. 90 members. No restrictions to join. Dues: $15/year. Web site: http://clubs.hemmings.com/oldcarclub/

Old Cars Unlimited of Washington, DC
112 Rhode Island Ave NW
Washington, DC 20001
202-638-1771

Founded 1990. 30 members. Vehicles must be fifteen years old or older and must be in stock condition. Meetings 1st Monday each month. Dues: $25/year.

The Olde Tyme Auto Club
Station A Box 4534
Evansville, IN 47724-4534
812-474-1716
E-mail: deager1998@aol.com

Founded 1953. 130 members. Car ownership is not a prerequisite to membership. We welcome any type of old car, members own everything from full classics to street rods, trucks and military jeeps. Dues: $15/year family.
Web site: http://clubs.hemmings.com/oldetymeauto/

Orange County Antique Auto Club Inc
PO Box 4649
Middletown, NY 10941

Founded 1973. 90 members. Our membership is open to stock, modified or to anyone even without a vehicle. Along with helping to organize the Rhinebeck meet, we also have a picnic, a holiday party, cruises and a monthly newsletter. We generally meet the first Friday of every month so come and have some fun. Dues: $10/year single or associate, $15/year family.

Past Pleasures Car Club
PO Box 663
Yucaipa, CA 92399
909-849-4282; FAX: 909-849-2245
E-mail: pstpleazurscarcl@aol.com

Founded early 1960s. Members: 50 families. Family oriented. All makes and models pre-1980s welcome. Monthly newsletter of activities, museum outings, shows, cruises, picnics, parades and BBQs. Monthly car show and shine. Annual charity fundraising show. Good fun for the whole family. Dues: $20/year. Web site: http://hometown.aol.com/pstpleazurescarcl/index.html

Police Car Owners of America
15677 Hwy 62 W
Eureka Springs, AR 72632
501-253-4948; FAX: 501-253-4949

Founded 1991. 700 members worldwide. Open to all makes of police vehicles. Also to model builders. Members receive shoulder patch, decal, key ring, ID card and subscription to quarterly newsletter which features free advertising to members. State and regional chapters. Dues: $25/year US, $30/year Canada, $35/year overseas. Web site: www.policecarowners.com
chapters:

Arizona David Gittner, 4701 N 68th St #107, Scottsdale, AZ 85251 602-946-9570

California *Northern California*, Darryl Lindsay, PO Box 412, San Carlos, CA 94070 650-592-7662; E-mail: dmlindsay@menlopark.org

Southern California, John Bellah, PO Box 156, LaHabra, CA 90633-0156 562-690-9637; E-mail: jbellah@csulb.edu

Colorado Larry Andriunas, 7219 S Marshall St, Littleton, CO 80123 303-429-6784

Connecticut Thomas Weglarz Jr, 1354 Saybrook Rd, Haddam, CT 06438 860-345-1088

Illinois Greg Reynolds, 7112 W Summerdale, Chicago, IL 60656 773-775-8031; E-mail: cpdgreg@aol.com

Indiana Edwin Sanow, 801 W 500 S, Boswell, IN 47921 765-869-5815; E-mail: sanow@localline.com

Iowa Jason A Bryan, 4763 Waterford Dr, West Des Moines, IA 50265 515-222-0944

Kansas Jack Attig, 12990 V4 Rd, Hoyt, KS 66440-9064 913-986-6426; E-mail: attig@holtonks.net

Maryland Victor E Colangelo, 1010 James St, Bel Air, MD 21014-2312 410-638-6309

Michigan Bob Johnson , 3726 Kane Rd, Carleton, MI 48117 734-654-9327; E-mail: rsj215@tdi.net

Missouri *Eastern Missouri*, Dennis Sanchez, 1205 W Main St, Festus, MO 63028 314-931-3644; E-mail: densanchez@jcn1.com

Jim Cordell, 300 16th Ave S, Greenwood, MO 64034 816-537-6248

Western Missouri, Joe Hayes, 15711 Terry Ave, Belton, MO 64012 816-331-6502; E-mail: pjh908@aol.com

Nebraska Monty McCord, PO Box 302, Juniata, NE 68955 402-751-2224

New Hampshire Bill Robarge, 38 Peter Ct, Belmont, NH 03220 603-527-1775; E-mail: jerdmrwlr@aol.com

New York New Jersey *New York/New Jersey*, Frank Goderre, 1561 Park St, Peekskille, NY 10566 914-739-7943

North Carolina South Carolina *North/South Carolina*, Phil Leonard, 2808 E Ridge Rd, Salisbury, NC 28144-1275 704-637-2172; E-mail: leonard@webkorner.com

Ohio Michael Berkemeier, 7834 Astra Cir, Reynoldsburg, OH 43068 614-759-7618

Oklahoma Charles Primeaux, 4813 Newport Dr, Del City, OK 73115 405-677-4952

Oregon Chris Watson, 2466 Applegate Ave, Grants Pass, OR 97527 541-479-3858

Pennsylvania John M O'Shea, 412 Jefferson St, Evans City, PA 16033-1107 724-537-8558; E-mail: oshea@blueknights.org

South Dakota Ron Rysavy, 2805 S Cinnabar Cir, Sioux Falls, SD 57103-6514 605-371-1195; E-mail: ronj24@hotmail.com

Texas Ken T DeFoor, RR 5 Box 272, Dayton, TX 77535-9412 409-258-0008; E-mail: kd1007@star11.net

Virginia West Virginia *Virginia/West Virginia*, Mark Hopkins, PO Box 404, Saluda, VA 23149 804-758-9883; E-mail: markhopkins@aol.com

Wisconsin Kurt Schlieter, W224S5734 Guthrie Rd, Waukesha, WI 53186 414-548-9487

Canada *Eastern Canada*, Robert McIlmoyle, 7 Lamantia Ave, Strathroy, ON, N7G 3Z5 519-245-1953; E-mail: biff@golden.net

Western Canada, Sid Gough, Box 25, Irricana, AB, T0M 1B0 403-935-4216

Germany Rudiger Lotz, Johannesstrabe 1, 53225 Bonn, 01149-228-473765

Section Three – Clubs & Organizations

Section Three – Clubs & Organizations

Portland Beater Car Club
aka International Beater Appreciation Society (IBAS)
c/o Beaterville Cafe, 2201 N Killingsworth
Portland, OR 97217
503-240-2837
E-mail: beaterville@aol.com

Founded 1981. 250 members. Beater attitude a must.
Definition: must be street legal and driveable. Everything "rusty
'n trusty 'n beat for everything there is that moves". Dues: none.
Web site: http://clubs.hemmings.com/portlandbeater/

Rest Stop Rodders Club
Run to the Pines Show
2413 Pine Cir
Lakeside, AZ 85929
520-524-6407 days, 520-368-5325 eves; FAX: 520-524-6824
E-mail: navfair@cybertrails.com

Founded 1984. 60+ members. No restrictions, just an interest in
the classic, old, custom, street rod vehicles. Various runs and
tours during year, annual Run to the Pines car show since 1984,
largest open pre-1973 show in Southwest. Newsletter, *The Stop
Sign,* almost monthly. Dues: donations.

Rideau Lakes ACCCC
c/o J Paul, Box 46
Manotick, ON Canada K4M 1A2
613-692-3293
E-mail: rlaac@visto.com

Founded 1965. 72 members. Meets 2nd Tuesday of each month.
Newsletter, *Passing Glance,* several tours each year. Rideau Lakes
is a region of Antique & Classic Car Club of Canada and a touring
club. Dues: $40/year. Web site: http://clubs.hemmings.com/rlaac

River Bend Auto Club
7001 Granada Ave S
Cottage Grove, MN 55016
651-459-5773; FAX: 651-483-0622
E-mail: fkirchner@knowlans.com

Founded 1978. 50 members. Car show, swap meet annually,
monthly newsletter. All cars accepted. Dues: $10/year.

River City Street Rods
509 Beaumont St
St Paul, MN 55101
651-776-7904
E-mail: terpetersn@aol.com

Founded 1974. 100 members. Membership meetings in busy months
(approx 9 meetings), yearly runs include bud run, mystery run, fall
run (approx 4 annual runs for members), big yearly show is
Indianhead Show & Swap in Chippewa Falls, WI. Dues: $15/year.
Web site: http://clubs.hemmings.com/rivercitystreetrods/

Road Knights Auto Club Inc
PO Box 837
Peekskill, NY 10566
914-788-6543, 845-562-5006
E-mail: wls@advinc.com

Founded 1955. 30 members. Non-profit organization dedicated to
the enjoyment and preservation of all types of vintage automobiles. The club supports and participates in a variety of auto related events encouraging safe driving and proper automotive maintenance. The organization produces its own judged car show each
September which benefits local community organizations.
Members share auto restoration projects and a wealth of technical
knowledge. Membership is open to anyone over sixteen with an
interest in any kind of automobile. Meetings are held Wednesdays,
7:30 pm, at the Columbian House Co #1 Fire Dept, Peekskill, NY
(1st & 3rd Wednesday, November-March). Call for further information. Dues: $25/year. Web site: www.roadknights.org

Roaring 20's Antique & Classic Car Club Inc
PO Box 956
Cheshire, CT 06410
860-628-2309

Contact: Mary Gura. Founded 1969. 147 members. No restrictions to join. Dues: $21/year.

Rods & Relics Car Club
PO Box 521
West Branch, MI 48661-0521

Founded 1981. Members: 83 families. Cruises, car show, meets
the third Thursday every month for meeting. We are family oriented and have potluck meal before meetings in warmer weather
and meet at a restaurant in colder weather. Our newsletter is
published monthly with minutes and information on upcoming
events. Dues: $15/year. Web site:
http://clubs.hemmings.com/rodsrelics/

Rods and Rides of Polk County
1056 Winifred Way
Lakeland, FL 33809-2365
PH/FAX: 863-859-2180
E-mail: tckcmc@rodsandrides.net

Founded 1999. 45 members. To join, must work one event and
come to 2 club meetings. Benefits Senior Orphans of Polk
County. Host club for Central Florida Auto Festival and Toy
Expo, host club for Good Guys Orlando show. Dues: $10/year.
Web site: www.rodsandrides.net

Route 26 Cruiser's
PO Box 488
Sandy, OR 97055
503-658-6473; FAX: 503-658-6622
E-mail: Barbso124@aol.com

Founded in 1995. 84 members. Open to all. Join a club that's
having fun. We do a great newsletter. Dues: $20/year.

San Antonio Antique/Classic Car Association
PO Box 17543
San Antonio, TX 78217-0543
210-828-6080 recorder; FAX: 830-276-3294
E-mail: carcruisenites@hotmail.com

Founded 1992. 200+ members. Must own/drive a pre-1975 vehicle to the weekly meetings. At meeting, discussion on repair,
parts, paint or body ideas are exchanged, with info on car shows
passed around. Dues: none.

Saskatchewan British Car Club
266 JJ Thiessen Cres
Saskatoon, SK Canada S7K 6A3
306-242-7710
E-mail: wilsona@abyss.usask.ca

Founded 1998. 75 members. A group of enthusiasts dedicated to
the enjoyment, preservation, restoration and use of British automobiles. Tours, workshops, shows, newsletter, web site, monthly
meetings. Dues: $25/year Canadian. Web site: www.sbcc.ca

Schoharie Valley Performance Street Machine
Schoharie, NY 12157
518-295-8919, 518-875-6538
E-mail: svpsm@yahoo.com

Founded 1998. 18 members. Join with member approval. Our
big show is at Howe Caverns on the first Sunday in June. Event
list on our web site: http://clubs.hemmings.com/svpsm

Sentimental Cruisers Car Club
PO Box 174
Barnegat, NJ 08005
609-693-1985

76 members. We meet every Friday night from April to

September, 6 to 9 pm. Car must be 25 years old to join. The benefit of joining our club is to have fun and cruise. Dues: $15/year.

Show & Go Car Club Inc
PO Box 248
Madisonville, KY 42431-0248
270-821-3522
E-mail: kcope@spis.net

Founded 1982. 40+ members. We are a group of car enthusiasts that formed a club. The only restriction to join is you must be 16 and have a valid driver's license. Summer cruise-ins, bowling parties and car shows are for fun, donating our time and money to charities is what we like to do. Dues: $15/year.

Siouxland Car Council
PO Box 119
Sioux Falls, SD 57101
605-528-3764
E-mail: ganderso@dtgnet.com

Founded 1986. 30 members. The Siouxland Car Council is a non-profit organization whose members belong to car clubs. We offer a monthly newsletter, two car shows a year and weekly cruises. All money raised is donated to children under 18 or organizations that cater to children. Dues: $25/year.

Sterling British Motoring Society
213 Springs Ct
Mt Sterling, KY 40353
859-498-8615; FAX: 859-498-7531
E-mail: mrazor@mis.net

Founded 1996. 40 members. We are a multi-British marque group. Anyone who owns, has owned or has an interest in British cars may join. Each member receives a copy of the *British Marque News*, in which we have a monthly column, as well as periodic newsletters and events calendars of local and Regional activities. Our monthly meeting is held the first Tuesday of each month with additional outings planned by group members throughout the spring and summer months. Our feature event is the Bluegrass Bash held the first weekend in May (Kentucky Derby weekend) at the Springs Motel in Lexington, Kentucky. Contact us for further information. Dues: $20/year. Web site: http://206.28.56.243/sbms/index.htm

Suomen Automobili-Historiallinen Klubi
PL 422
Helsinki 00101 Finland
358 9 728 95150; FAX: 358 9 728 95151
E-mail: timo.ohmero@sahk.fi

Founded 1959. 4,000 members. No restrictions to join. Benefits: magazine to members, there is the national meeting of the historical vehicles once a year. Publication: *Automobiili*, published 6 times a year, articles from historical vehicles, personalities, old photos, etc. Subscription rate: 170 FIM. Dues: depend on our local clubs. Notice that old advertisement of car in Finland 100 year exhibition. Web site: www.sahk.fi

Tellico Village Vintage Vehicles
124 Daksi Way
Loudon, TN 37774
865-458-1251
E-mail: gwworld@aol.com

Founded 1995. 50 members. Resident or property owner in Tellico Village, TN. Monthly cruise-in on the third Friday of each month in downtown Loudon, TN. Annual road rally and annual July 4th parade. Dues: $5/year.

Topeka British Car Club
3021 SW Tutbury Town Rd
Topeka, KS 66614
785-478-3799
E-mail: choch@networksplus.net

Founded 1992. 75 members. No membership restrictions. Monthly meetings and rallies. All British car enthusiasts welcomed. Web site: http://clubs.hemmings.com/topeka/

Tri-Town Cruzers Inc
87 Shenipsit St
Ellington, CT 06029
860-875-8004
E-mail: dave@tritowncruzers.com

Founded 1998. 30 members. Must have a cruise car and be willing to help out at our 2 weekly cruise nights and work at our many charities we help out. Dues: $25/year. Web site: www.tritowncruzers.com

Twin Bay British Car Club
410 N Elmwood Ave
Traverse City, MI 49684
231-947-2737
E-mail: tcphoto@aol.com

Founded 1996. 60 members. All owners or lovers of British automobiles are encouraged to join our club for tours, rallys, shows and monthly meetings and tech sessions. We also have a monthly newsletter. Dues: $15/year.

UP Antique Car Club
537 W Breitung Ave
Kingsford, MI 49802
906-774-0167; FAX: 906-774-2955
E-mail: ndcook@chartermi.net

Founded 1974. 65 members. Dues: $5/year. Web site: http://clubs.hemmings.com/upantiquecc/index.html

Veteran Motor Car Club of America
4441 W Altadena Ave
Glendale, AZ 85304-3526
800-428-7327, 602-978-5622
FAX: 602-978-1106

For information, contact at the above address: Richard Rigby. Founded 1938. 5,700 members. Dues $35/year.
regions:

Arizona   *NARHS Region*, Baja Arizona Chapter, Tedd deLong, President, PO Box 34, Valley Farms, AZ 85291 520-723-5290

Southwest Region, Central Arizona Chapter, Bob Davis, President, PO Box 2306, Camp Verde, AZ 86322-2306 520-567-0024

Southwest Region, Coyote Chapter, Tom Verrier, President, 10036 E Karen Pl, Tucson, AZ 85748 520-885-3521

Southwest Region, Hummingbird Chapter, Rob Shernick, President, 1640 N San Marcos DeNiza, Sierra Vista, AZ 85635 520-458-6790

Southwest Region, Phoenix Chapter, Frank Steinmetz, President, 4222 W Ironwood Dr, Phoenix, AZ 85051 623-937-3504

Southwest Region, Valley Roadrunners Chapter, Ron Lenocker, President, 4930 W Park View Ln, Glendale, AZ 85310 623-581-3229

Southwest Region, Vintage Motor Car Club of Arizona, Jack Dunigan, President, PO Box 745, Rimrock, AZ 86335 520-567-5864

Veteran Motor Car Club of America regions (continued)

California   *California Region*, Los Angeles Chapter, Charles White, President, 2684 Turnbull Canyon Rd, Hacienda Heights, CA 91745 310-693-5641

California Region, Nickel Age Touring Club, John Bertolotti, President, 150 Brooke Acres Dr, Los Gatos, CA 95032-6454 408-358-6740

California Region, Ray Williams, Regional Director, 12201 Gaston Rd, Madera, CA 93638 209-645-5737

Colorado   *Mountain and Plains Region*, Colorado West Chapter, Mike Kanocz, President, 393 Valley View Way, Grand Junction, CO 81503 970-256-0683

Mountain and Plains Region, Denver Mile High Chapter, Jerry Dale, President, 5192 S Cody Ct, Littleton, CO 80123 303-979-6471

Mountain and Plains Region, Estes Park Car Club, Dick Brown, President, PO Box 3728, Estes Park, CO 80517 970-586-3301

Mountain and Plains Region, Loveland Chapter, Mike Cwik, President, 753 Milner Ct, Loveland, CO 80537 970-663-2179

Mountain and Plains Region, Montrose Chapter, Ralph Merwin, President, 9009 60-75 Rd, Montrose, CO 81401 970-323-6641

Mountain and Plains Region, Pikes Peak Chapter, Elsie Ann Collins, President, 2502 Logan Cir, Colorado Springs, CO 80907 719-634-2047

Mountain and Plains Region, Pueblo-Arkansas Valley Chapter, Vince Chifalo, President, 1189 W Calle Antigua, Pueblo West, CO 81007 719-547-9072

Mountain and Plains Region, Royal Gorge Chapter, Harold Hunker, President, 827 Beech Ave, Canon City, CO 81212 719-275-3552

Florida   *Florida Region*, Citrus Capital Chapter, Richard T Gabrich, President, 8320 75th Ct, Vero Beach, FL 32967 561-589-0242

Florida Region, Gold Coast Chapter, Joel E Aronson, President, 6740 NW 74 Ct, Parkland, FL 33067-3945 954-341-4864

Florida Region, Palm Beach County Chapter, Buddy Pearce, President, 919 Helena Dr, Lake Worth, FL 33461 561-964-4567

Florida Region, Roadrunners Chapter, Cheryl Farnell, President, 4006 San Juan St, Tampa, FL 33629 813-837-1603

Florida Region, Southwest Florida Chapter, Donald Royston, President, 4062 San Massimo Dr, Punta Gorda, FL 33950 941-575-0202

Florida Region, Steve Wolf, Regional Director, 6720 SW 104 St, Pinecrest, FL 33156 305-665-9131

Florida Region, Sun Coast Chapter, Richard Bezzola, President, 6036 SW 62 Terr, Miami, FL 33173 305-274-0373

Georgia   *Southeast Region*, Christopher Padgett, Regional Director, PO Box 172, Jasper, GA 30143 706-692-2768

Idaho   *Bonneville Region*, Eastern Idaho Chapter, Chuck McGuffey, President, 5623 N 55th E, Idaho Falls, ID 83401 208-524-5155

Bonneville Region, Magic Valley Chapter, Clarence Dudley, President, 1062 Bluelakes, Twin Falls, ID 83303 208-733-7110

Bonneville Region, Ray Born, Regional Director, 3980 Georgia Ln, Idaho Falls, ID 83406 208-529-9188

Bonneville Region, Tri-City Chapter, Sam Otero, President, 4656 Navajo St, Pocatello, ID 83204 208-234-2917

Kansas   *Midwest Region*, Missouri Valley Chapter, Robert Jones, President, 9110 W 104th Terr, Overland Park, KS 66212 913-381-5391

Mountain and Plains Region, Bob Bethell, Regional Director, PO Box 186, Alden, KS 67512 316-534-3085

Mountain and Plains Region, Kanza Chapter, Dean Davison, President, 309 W Truesdell, Lyons, KS 67554 316-257-2914

Kentucky   *Kentucky Region*, Bluegrass Chapter, Jane Johnson, President, 3456 Belvoir Dr, Lexington, KY 40502 859-227-0327

Kentucky Region, James E Poe, Regional Director, 3204 Georgetown Rd, Paris, KY 40361 859-987-3708

Kentucky Region, Louisville Chapter, John H Caperton, President, 3112 Boxhill Ct, Louisville, KY 40222 502-895-4127

Maryland   *Mid-Atlantic Region*, Roy Lambden, Regional Director, 107 Jones Rd, Chester, MD 21619 410-643-6371

Massachusetts   *Connecticut Valley Region*, Keith A Korbet, Regional Director, 16 Saffron Cir, Springfield, MA 01129 413-783-5624

Michigan   *Great Lakes Region*, Battle Creek Chapter, Chris A Craft, President, 616 Linn Ave, Battle Creek, MI 49015 616-964-4634

Great Lakes Region, Blue Water Chapter, Bart Dickey, President, 2528 Riverwood Dr, Port Huron, MI 48060 810-982-9512

Great Lakes Region, Brass and Gas Chapter, William Achterhof, President, 56 Country Club Rd, Holland, MI 49423 616-396-7579

Great Lakes Region, Brighton Chapter, Richard Cardeccia, President, 12669 I Owe Dr, Brighton, MI 48114 248-685-2766

Great Lakes Region, Detroit Chapter, Gerard Van Ooteghen, President, 1850 Hunt Club, Grosse Pointe Woods, MI 48236 313-881-2813

Great Lakes Region, Huron Valley Chapter, George Schaffer, President, 9317 Mapletree Dr, Plymouth, MI 48170 734-453-7505

Great Lakes Region, Jackson Cascades Chapter, Leo E Warren, President, 3500 Hoyer Rd, Jackson, MI 49201 517-764-3731

Great Lakes Region, James Muldoon, Regional Director, 5367 Frago Rd, Avoca, MI 48006 810-324-2598

Great Lakes Region, Lakeshore Chapter, Ron Harris, President, 21916 Birchwood, East Pointe, MI 48021 810-779-4279

Great Lakes Region, Lansing Chapter, James R Neal, President, 1069 Applegate, East Lansing, MI 48823 517-332-7366

Missouri   *Midwest Region*, Heartland Chapter, Eldon Lacey, President, PO Box 323, Adrian, MO 64720 816-297-2345

Midwest Region, Kansas City Chapter, Don Oberholtz, President, 23903 Poindexter Dr, Lee's Summit, MO 64086 816-537-6256

Midwest Region, Michael Welsh, Regional Director, 7501 Manchester Ave, Kansas City, MO 64138 816-353-7890

Nevada   *Western Region*, Art Foote, Regional Director, 3535 Freedom Ave, Las Vegas, NV 89121 702-451-0026

Western Region, High Rollers Chapter, Gene Donley, President, 6349 Elmira Dr, Las Vegas, NV 89118 702-876-5593

Western Region, Pahrump Classics, Hoyt F Shaw Jr, President, 2351 W Machada St, Pahrump, NV 89048 702-751-1475

New Jersey   *New York Region*, Garden State Chapter, Robert Giuliani, President, 72 Northwood Ave, Demarest, NJ 07627 201-768-7973

New Mexico   *Southwest Region*, Albuquerque Chapter, Bill Sullivan, President, 324 Hermosa SE, Albuquerque, NM 87108 505-265-8113

New York   *New York Region*, Niagara Frontier Chapter, Paul H Will Jr, President, 11965 Liberia Rd, East Aurora, NY 14052 716-627-7857

New York Region, The Long Island Old Car Club, Chester Kelsey, President, 2379 Elk Ct, North Bellmore, NY 11710 516-221-1965

Ohio   *Buckeye-Keystone Region*, Emerald Necklace Chapter, Robert Ebert, President, 3300 Thomson Cir, Rocky River, OH 44116 440-333-8861

Buckeye-Keystone Region, Hall of Fame Chapter, Ron Leopold, President, 2635 Daffodil St NE, Canton, OH 44705 330-492-1654

Buckeye-Keystone Region, Walter Stockert, Regional Director, 985 Weber Ave SW, Strasburg, OH 44680 330-878-5008

Great Lakes Region, Black Swamp Chapter, John Zimmerman, President, 6127 Texas St, Whitehouse, OH 43571 419-877-0885

Great Lakes Region, Defiance Chapter, Robert Freytag, President, 1166 Kenilworth Ave, Napoleon, OH 43545 419-592-5796

Great Lakes Region, Toledo Chapter, Larry J Erd, President, 3905 Hillandale Rd, Toledo, OH 43606 419-535-5550

Kentucky Region, Nickel Age Touring Chapter, John Tarleton, President, 449 W 5th St, Salem, OH 44460-2107 330-332-0116

NARHS Region, Thomas F Saal, Regional Director, 1488 W Clifton, Lakewood, OH 44107 216-521-3588

Ohio Valley Region, Rick Donahue, Regional Director, 3552 Neiheisel Ave, Cincinnati, OH 45248-3124 513-574-5078

Tri-State Region, Albert Pavlik Jr, Regional Director, 1803 Norton Pl, Stuebenville, OH 43952 740-282-7197

Tri-State Region, Steel Valley Chapter, Robert H Kaine, President, 159 Gumps Ln, Wintersville, OH 43953 740-264-7219

Rhode Island   *New England Region*, Viking Chapter, Roger & Susan Paul, President, 43 Heritage Rd, North Kingston, RI 02852 401-885-1190

South Dakota   *Mountain and Plains Region*, Gold Dust Chapter, Joan S Lemer, President, HC 89 Box 169CD, Hermosa, SD 57744-9801 605-255-4659

Texas   *Texoma Region*, Bexar Touring Club, George Dickerson, President, 6631 Grist Mill, San Antonio, TX 78238 210-681-1439

Texoma Region, Cathy Womack, Regional Director, 6309 Mecca, Odessa, TX 79762 915-366-2388

Texoma Region, Cowtown Touring Club, Mike Jones, President, PO Box 100397, Fort Worth, TX 76185 817-738-4699

Texoma Region, Fredericksburg Vintage Car Club, Norman Canfield, President, 1146 Southwoods, Fredericksburg, TX 78624-8209 830-997-6134

Texoma Region, Key to the Hills Chapter, James E George, President, 25615 Dull Knife Tr, San Antonio, TX 78255 210-755-4633

Section Three – Clubs & Organizations

Veteran Motor Car Club of America regions (continued)

Texoma Region, Permian Basin Oil Burners, Bonnie Chambers, President, 4742 Cypress Rd, Odessa, TX 79764 915-381-2343

Texoma Region, Trans Pecos Triangle Chapter, Mitch Van Horn, President, PO Box 266, Van Horn, TX 79555 915-283-2342

Utah   Bonneville Region, Cache Valley Chapter, Winston Reese, President, 2895 N 920 E, North Logan, UT 84341 435-753-7823

Bonneville Region, Copper Classics Chapter, Phil Taylor, President, 2875 N 1200 E, Provo, UT 84604 801-374-2524

Bonneville Region, Utah Chapter, James D Fuchs, President, 2087 N Kingston Rd, Farmington, UT 84025 801-451-2608

Washington   Northwest Region, Capital City Chapter, John Ellingson, President, 18140 Milane, Rochester, WA 98579 360-273-5929

Northwest Region, Mari Andrus, Regional Director, 70 Shadow Tr, Sequim, WA 98382 360-681-0413

Northwest Region, Sequim Valley Chapter, Marc Richard, President, 182 Starry Rd, Sequim, WA 98382 360-683-9394

Wyoming   Mountain and Plains Region, Oil Country Chapter, Steve Johnson, President, 721 W 57 St, Casper, WY 82601 307-235-1051

Vintage Auto Club of Ocean County NJ
PO Box 1135
Toms River, NJ 08754
732-240-3275; FAX: 732-914-0280
E-mail: nbrab1@aol.com

Founded 1969. 165 members. Ownership not required. Non-profit organization, monthly meetings, newsletter, annual banquet, participation in parades, cruises, car shows and charitable events, annual car show in September. Dues: $20/year. Web site: www.vintageautoclub-nj.org

The Vintage Car Club of New Zealand Inc
PO Box 2546
Christchurch New Zealand
03-366-4461; FAX: 03-366-0273
E-mail: admin@vcc.co.nz or e-mail: beadedwheels@vcc.co.nz

Founded 1946. 6,700 members. Dedicated to the preservation of historic vehicles and New Zealand's motoring history. Members benefit from access to research material, parts, etc. Approximately 150 events and meets annually, 35 plus 1 international branches throughout the country and a national magazine, Beaded Wheels, New Zealand's only veteran and vintage motoring magazine containing restoration and rally articles, technical tips and swap meet information. Subscription rate: $27.00 (o/s rates on application), 6 times/year. Dues: $50-$70/year, varies by region.

Vintage Wheels Antique Car Club
Rt 4, Box 165
Great Bend, KS 67530
316-793-7162

Founded 1975. 50 members. Dedicated to the preservation of and interest in antique and special interest vehicles. Dues: $20/year.

Wenatchee Valley Antique Auto Club
211 River St
Cushmere, WA 98815
509-782-2612
E-mail: dryden@csiconnect.com

Founded 1959. Members: 50+ families. Must appreciate antique cars and the hobby of collecting and restoring them. Ownership is not required. Members generally enjoy sharing their cars in community events and at museums, convalescent centers, etc. Dues: $15/year family.

West Central Missouri Vintage Auto Club
PO Box 41
Sedalia, MO 65302-0041
660-826-2033 nights & weekends, 660-826-7456 days
E-mail: fourdoor@iland-net

Founded 1968. 36 members. Open to anyone interested in the use and preservation of antique and classic cars, no matter if original, modified or customized. We co-sponsor a cruise night at Eddie's Drive-In the 3rd Saturday of each month and an annual poker run event, as well as participation in numerous area events and parades and car shows. Dues: $20/year.

White Owners Register
1624 Perkins Dr
Arcadia, CA 91006
626-355-7679 evenings

Founded 1970. 300 members. Caters to owners of White, Indiana, Cletrac, Rollin, Templar, Rubay vehicles. Technical data shared. We cooperate with VWTA. Dues: none.

White Squirrel Cruisers
PO Box 14
Olney, IL 62450
618-393-7738; FAX: 618-395-4711
E-mail: gorace@omegabbs.com

Founded 1987. 20 members. Interest in automobiles, young or old. Newsletter, web page, 1 show, 3 cruises per year. Dues: $15/year. Web site: www.omegabbs.com/users.wsc

Willys-Overland-Knight Registry Inc
1440 Woodacre Dr
McLean, VA 22101-2535
703-533-0396; FAX: 630-879-7010
E-mail: elp90@aol.com

For membership information, contact at the above address: Duane Perrin. Founded 1960. 1,300 members. An organization of people interested in the Willys-Overland family of cars to 1942 and all Knight-engined vehicles and Stearns cars. Dues: $24/year US, $26/year Canada, $30/year all other countries. Web site: www.classicar.com/clubs/wokr/wokr.htm

Winamac Old Auto Club
1849 Chippewa Dr
Schererville, IN 46375
219-865-8019
E-mail: catbil@netnitco.net

Founded 1950. 125 members. Original restorations, monthly meetings, social activities, drive-outs, annual car show and swap meet, monthly newsletter on club activities. Dues: $12/year.

Woodland Wheels
9103 N Old 27
Hayward, WI 54843
715-634-3498
E-mail: cleaneau@jrec.net

Founded 1999. 31 members. Open to all. Meets 3rd Wednesday of month all year. Annual rendevous and picnic in October, cruises and road trip in summer months. Monthly newsletter. Dues: $10/year.

Ye Olde Car Club of Tri-Cities
3600 S Garfield St
Kennewick, WA 99336-0601
509-586-4933
E-mail: yaletc@bossig.com

Founded 1963. 170 members. No restrictions, just interest in old cars, enjoyment of association with others of similar interests. Monthly newsletter *The Gas Gauge*, included in annual dues. Information available: *Hemmings Motor News*, *Old Car Weekly* magazine, *Old Car Value Guides*. Swap meet and car tours. Dues: $10/year.

Marque Clubs

Abarth Owners International
Box 1917
Thousand Oaks, CA 91360
818-707-2301

Founded 1963. 800 members. Publications, meets and events. AOI books available are 001 through 008, hardcover and color. Dues: $28/year. Web site:
http://clubs.hemmings.com/abarthownersinternational/

The Abarth Register USA Inc
54 School St, Ste 102
Westbury, NY 11590-4469
516-876-8754; FAX: 516-538-7118

For membership information, contact at the above address: Gerald Rothman, Director. Founded 1973. 200 members. Vintage car club for Abarth and Cisitalia owners and enthusiasts. Do not have to own one to belong. Organized for the restoration, preservation and enjoyment of the Abarth and Cisitalia marques. Affiliated with Abarth Club of United Kingdom, Abarth Corsa Deutschland of Germany, Club Abarth, France, Club Abarth, Japan, Svenska Abarth Registret, Sweden, RIA, Registro Italiano Abarth, Italy. Quarterly newsletter. Club maintains excellent data base network of Abarth information and parts sources. Dues: $35/year US, $40/year foreign.

AC Owner's Club Ltd
11955 SW Faircrest St
Portland, OR 97225-4615
503-643-3225; FAX: 503-646-4009

For US registrar, contact at the above address: Jim Feldman. The world's largest organization of AC owners and enthusiasts. AC ownership not required. Monthly magazine.

ALFA Romeo Association (Nor Cal)
PO Box 1458
Alameda, CA 94501
510-521-8156; FAX: 510-865-2185
E-mail: neilajim@aol.com

Founded 1957. 650 members. No restrictions. Tech help hotline, many driving events, tours, autocrosses, race track driving tours, parts swaps, discount parts, monthly newsletter, monthly meetings, tech sessions, with ads for parts and services, tech tips in our newsletter. Dues: $25/year. Web site:
www.speedquest.com-ara

Texas Hill Country Alfa Romeo Owners Club
PO Box 523
Alpine, TX 79831-0523
915-837-1717; FAX: 801-838-5733, UT
E-mail: dividedbyzero@usaonline.net

Founded 1982. 50 members. Club events and benefits include Hill Country tours, local and national monthly newsletters, tech-

nical info, AROC tech hotlines, tech sessions. Meetings in Austin or San Antonio. Dues: $45/year. Web site: http://clubs.hemmings.com/texashillcountryaroc/

The Allard Register
8 Paget Close
Horsham
West Sussex, RH13 6HD   England
PH: Horsham 261372

For membership information contact at the above address: R W May. Phone: Horsham 61372. Founded 1966. 148 members. Free bulletins with technical and spare parts information. Membership meets in both the US and the UK.

Alvis Owner Club of North America
140 Race St, PO Box 46
Bainbridge, PA 17502
PH: 717-426-3842; FAX: 717-426-0104
E-mail: waynealvis@aol.com

150 members. Dues: $10/year.

Alamo AMC
30115 Hwy 281 N, Ste 126
Bulverde, TX 78163
830-980-3165
E-mail: akjamc@juno.com

Founded 1995. 60 members. No restrictions to join. You will receive 12 issues of *Alamo AMC News* filled with AMC info, parts, meets and events, membership card and/or your car photo on web page. Dues: $12/year. Web site:
http://ccwf.cc.utexas.edu/~cbrodsky/alamoamc

AMC World Clubs
7963 Depew St
Arvada, CO 80003-2527
303-428-8760; FAX: 303-428-1070

Founded 1974. 1,500 members. Comprised of the union of the Classic AMX Club International and American Motorsport Int. AMC World Clubs is for those interested in AMC/AMX/Rambler/AMC-Jeep vehicles, 1954-1987. Telephone technical and restoration assistance six days a week. Large 28-32 page bi-monthly magazine. Dues: $30/year US, $35/year Canada and overseas.

American Motors Cruisers Car Club
1340 Nickle Plate Rd
Ionia, MI 48846-9619
616-527-0477
E-mail: damier@pathwaynet.com

Founded 1994. 137 members. Requirements to join: a true interest in AMC autos, their restoration and preservation. Benefits: help with projects, nationwide updated news and family type group. Monthly meetings, annual car show and bi-monthly newsletter. Dues: $12/year. Web site:
www.amcruisers.freeservers.com

American Motorsport International
7963 Depew St
Arvada, CO 80003-2527
303-428-8760; FAX: 303-428-1070

Founded 1987. International club for owners and enthusiasts of American Motors cars, 1955-1988. Large bi-monthly club publication. Parent organization is AMC World Clubs Inc. Telephone-tech and restoration help six days a week for members. Dues: $30/year US, $35/year Canada and overseas. Web site: www.amcwc.com

chapters:

Arizona   *Arizona AMC Club*, Mark Fletcher, 7257 W Paradise Dr, Peoria , AZ 85345

American Motorsport International chapters (continued)

California   *American Motorsport of San Diego*, Tony Zamisch, 977 Florida St, Imperial Beach, CA 91932

South Bay AMC Club, Pat Whiteside, 2348 Richland Ave, San Jose, CA 95125

Colorado   *Rocky Mountain AMC Club*, Werner Fruhwirth, 210 S Alcott St, Denver, CO 80219 E-mail: bkenwor425

Indiana   *Hoosier Classic AMX/AMC Club*, Harold Lehman, 3420 S 700 W, Pierceton, IN 46562

New York   *Hudson Valley American Motors Club*, Joe Marsh, PO Box 165, Worcester, NY 12197

Metropolitan NY & NJ Chapter, Peter Stathes, 51 Twin Lawns Ave, Hicksville, NY 11801

Oregon   *American Motorsport of Portland*, Max Frye, 14950 S Bradley Rd, Oregon City, OR 97045

Pennsylvania   *Central Penn AMX/AMC Club*, Bruce Rambler, Rd 3 Box 75, Palmrya, PA 17078

Washington   *American Motors Club Northwest*, Al Barrie, PO Box 66672, Burien, WA 98166

Olympic Peninsula AMC Club, Robert Bale, 5851 NE Lincoln Rd E, Poulsbo, WA 98370

Team OPAMC Racing Homepage, Robert Bale, 5851 NE Lincoln Rd E, Poulsbo, WA 98370

Wisconsin   *Wisconsin AMX/AMC Club*, Jeff Sorenson, 2368 N 114th St, Milwaukee, WI 53226

Australia   *Javelin Register of Australia*, Craig Norling, 5 Two Bays Dr, Somerville Victoria, 3912

Dakota AMC Club
c/o Nancy Bott
25512 475th Ave
Renner, SD 57055-5909
605-543-5928
E-mail: snbott@gateway.net

Founded 1999. 33 members. Not restricted to the Dakotas, but have members in Iowa, Minnesota, Nebraska, Wyoming. A chapter of AMO. Three to four meets a year. Shows, parades, swap meets, newsletter: *Prairie Ramblings,* four to five issues a year. Dues: $20/year.

First Coast AMC
5618 Shorewood Rd
Jacksonville, FL 32210
904-783-9257
E-mail: fcamc@juno.com

Founded 1999. 60 members. Open to all AMC, Nash, Rambler and Jeep enthusiasts. Several events each year, newsletter every other month. Dues: $10/year. Web site: http://clubs.hemmings.com/firstcoastamc

The Javelin AMX Registry
5618 Shorewood Rd
Jacksonville, FL 32210
904-783-9257
E-mail: fcamc@juno.com

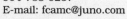

Founded 1997. 46 members. Dedicated to the preservation of the 1971-1974 American Motors Javelin AMX. Ownership required to join. Newsletter twice yearly. Dues: none.

Marlin Auto Club
902 Ellington Cir
Greenwood, IN 46143-8460
317-881-5357, 6 am-9:30 pm EST
E-mail: macwmac@in-motion.net

Founded 2000. 80 members and growing. For the restoration and preservation of the 1965 thru 1967 Marlin. Quarterly publication, membership roster, club stores, National meets, club web site. Anyone interested can join, ownership not required. A non-profit organization. Dues: $20/year US. Web site: http://clubs.hemmings.com/marlin

National American Motors Drivers & Racers Association
PO Box 987
Twin Lakes, WI 53181
PH/FAX: 262-396-9552
E-mail: namdra@juno.com

Founded 1978. 1,617 members. Open to all AMC and AMC/Jeep enthusiasts. Monthly newsletter. National and Regional meets which include drag racing, car shows and swap meets. Dues: $24/year. Web site: www.namdra.org

Pacific Gold Rush Ramblers
John Wiggins
199 Harrier
Vallejo, CA 94590
707-645-8487
E-mail: mmmmudd@aol.com

Founded 1996. Pacific Gold Rush Ramblers is a chapter of the American Motors Corporation Rambler Club. Our purpose is to encourage the use, restoration and preservation of automobiles built by Amerian Motors Corporation from 1957 through 1969. Although our focus is the cars made during these years, our club is open to anyone with an interest in the cars and trucks built by American Motors Corporation. We publish *The Gold Standard* bi-monthly. It is one of the many benefits that our members receive. Holds bi-monthly meetings. We meet at various sites in and around the area between San Francisco Bay and the Gold Country in the Sierra Nevada Foothills. Dues: $20/year, $18/year members.

Windy City Rambler/AMC Club
313 N Locust St
Sycamore, IL 60178
815-895-6518
E-mail: mwoodstrup@tbcnet.com

Founded 1990. 76 members. Interest in AMC cars, Jeeps or other American Motors vehicles. 6 newsletters. Meetings and picnic. Chapter of AMO (American Motors Owners Association). Newsletter, *Windy City Rambler,* and club covers the northern Illinois area for American Motors hobbyist. Many members in the Chicago area. Newsletter has listing of AMC events and classifieds. Dues: $20/year.

American Austin-Bantam Club
Marilyn Sanson
724 Maple Dr
Kirkville, NY 13082
315-656-7568

Founded 1962. 700 members. Annual meet with judging. Club newsletters 6 times a year. Roster updates, technical assistance, leads of parts and vehicles for sale. Dues: $20/year per family, $25/year Canada and foreign, US funds.

Pacific Bantam Austin Club
1589 N Grand Oaks Ave
Pasadena, CA 91104
626-791-2617
E-mail: njbooth@earthlink.net

For membership information, contact at the above address: Norm Booth. Founded 1969. 300 members. Club is open to

American Austin, American Bantam and all pre-World War II British Austin Seven enthusiasts. 2001 dues: $20/year US, $25/year other countries.

Amphicar Car Club
Rue du College, BP-153
B-4800 Verviers Belgium
3287335507; FAX: 3287335122

Founded 1988. 20 members. No restriction to join. The club is open to all Amphicar lovers. Free newsletter. Dues: none.

International Amphicar Club
PO Box 760
Burlington, KY 41005
E-mail: info@amphicar.com

Founded 1993. 250 members. Everybody welcome. World's largest club to the love of the Amphicar! Dues: $20/year USA, $25/year Canada, $30/year foreign. Web site: www.amphicar.com

Classic AMX Club International
7963 Depew St
Arvada, CO 80003
303-428-8760; FAX: 303-428-1070

Founded 1973. 1,235 members. Open to owners and enthusiasts of the 1968, 1969, 1970 two passenger sport coupe. Large 28 page all AMC bi-monthly magazine. Telephone assistance on restoration, questions of originality, etc. Largest collection of AMX historical artifacts in the world. Dues: $30/year US, $35/year Canada and overseas. Web site: www.amcwc.com

chapters:

Arizona	*Arizona AMC Club*, Mark Fletcher, 7257 W Paradise Dr, Peoria, AZ 85345
California	*South Bay AMC Club*, Pat Whiteside, 2348 Richland Ave, San Jose, CA 95125
Indiana	*Hoosier Classic AMX/AMC Club*, Harold Lehman, 3420 S 700 W, Pierceton, IN 46562
New Jersey	*The Mid-Atlantic Classic AMX Club*, George Watts, 18 Berlin Cross Keys Rd, Williamstown, NJ 08094
New York	*Metropolitan NY & NJ Chapter*, Peter Stathes, 51 Twin Lawns Ave, Hicksville, NY 11801
Oregon	*The Classic AMX Club of Portland*, Larry Lotter, 13575 SE 119th Dr, Clackamas, OR 97015
Pennsylvania	*Central Penn AMX/AMC Club*, Bruce Rambler, Rd 3 Box 75, Palmrya, PA 17078
Washington	*American Motors Club Northwest*, Al Barrie, PO Box 66672, Burien, WA 98166
	Olympic Peninsula AMC Club, Robert Bale, 5851 NE Lincoln Rd E, Poulsbo, WA 98370
	Team OPAMC Racing Homepage, Robert Bale, 5851 NE Lincoln Rd E, Poulsbo, WA 98370
Wisconsin	*Wisconsin AMX/AMC Club*, Jeff Sorenson, 2368 N 114th St, Milwaukee, WI 53226
Australia	*The Classic AMX Club of Australia*, Ray Sprague, 187 Adderly St, West Melbourne, Victoria 3003
Sweden	*The Classic AMX Club of Sweden*, Peter Carell, Lammholmsbacken 189, 14300 Warby

Austin-Healey Club of America Inc
PO Box 3220
Monroe, NC 28111-3220
877-5HEALEY toll free
FAX: 704-283-7765

For membership information, contact at the above address: Edie Anderson. Founded 1961. Over 3,500 members. Club offers services for all Austin-Healeys and Austin-Healey Sprites. Monthly newsletter, *Healey Marque*. Dues: $40/January-July, $25/August-December, plus local club dues. International dues: $56 service, $76 air. Web site: www.healeyclub.org

regions:

Alabama	85 Rifle Range Ridge, Wetumpka, AL 36092
California	*Golden Gate/Central Valley*, 1160 LaRochelle Terr #B, Sunnyvale, CA 94089-1754
	San Diego, 808 Seabright Ln, Solana Beach, CA 92075-1273
Colorado	*Rocky Mountain*, 8334 W Nevada Pl, Lakewood, CO 80226
DC (MD) (VA)	*Capital*, 9012 Sudbury Rd, Silver Spring, MD 20901
Florida	*Pensacola*, 9183 S Ponderosa, Mobile, AL 36575-7251
	Orlando, 33549 Linda Dr, Leesburg, FL 34788
	St John's, 14409 Mandarin Rd, Jacksonville, FL 32223
	Tampa Bay, 2696 66th Terr S, St Petersburg, FL 33712
Georgia	*Central Georgia*, 2140 Mountain Ln, Stone Mountain, GA 30087-1034
Illinois	*Illini*, 5624 S Washington, Hinsdale, IL 60521
	Midwest, 404 Peach Tree Cir, Loves Park, IL 61111
Indiana	*Indianapolis*, 10392 Connaught Dr, Carmel, IN 46032-9643
	Northern Indiana, 8792 N 500 E, Ossian, IN 46777
Iowa	*Heartland Healey*, 20167 E 200 St, Coal Valley, IL 61240
Kansas	13016 Cardiff, Olathe, KS 66062
Kentucky	*Bluegrass*, 110 N Rastetter, Louisville, KY 40206
Michigan	*Southeast Michigan*, 4618 Mandalay, Royal Oak, MI 48073-1624
Minnesota	729 Paul Birch Dr, Hudson, WI 54016-7034
Missouri	*Gateway*, 170 Doorack, Kirkwood, MO 63122
Nebraska	*Flatwater*, 3728 Schuemann Dr, Omaha, NE 68123
New England Eastern New York	*Northeast*, 117 Patricia Ave, Dalton, MA 01226-2046

Austin-Healey Club of America Inc regions (continued)

New Mexico   *Roadrunner*, PO Box 937, Cedar Crest, NM 87008

New York   *Niagara Frontier*, 210 W Hazeltine Ave, Kenmore, NY 14217

North Carolina   *Carolinas*, 7 Pickett Ave, Spencer, NC 28159

Triad, 9 Chestnut St, Lexington, NC 27292

Ohio   *Miami Valley*, 2058 S Belleview Dr, Bellbrook, OH 45305

Mid-Ohio, 945 Carpico Dr NE, Lancaster, OH 43130-1022

Northeast Ohio, 12535 Woodberry Ln, Strongsville, OH 44136

Ohio Valley, 1370 Karahill Dr, Cincinnati, OH 45240

Oklahoma   *Oklahoma A-H Owners*, 305 NW 22nd, Oklahoma City, OK 73103

Pennsylvania   *Three Rivers*, 218 Hoodridge Dr, Pittsburgh, PA 15234

Tennessee   *Middle Tennessee*, 212 Chapel Ave, Nashville, TN 37206

Smoky Mountain, 417 Shawnee Pl, Loudon, TN 37774

Texas   *Gulf Coast*, 11203 Crayford Ct, Houston, TX 77065

Northern Texas, Rt 2 Box 131, Boyd, TX 76023

Southern Texas, 2618 Old Gate, San Antonio, TX 78230

Utah   *Bonneville*, 1752 Paulista Way, Sandy, UT 84093

Virginia   *Tidewater*, 25 Museum Dr, Newport News, VA 23601

Washington   7015 Olympic View Dr, Edmonds, WA 98026

Wisconsin   PO Box 131, Laona, WI 54541-0131

Canada   *Bluewater*, Box 6, Sunset Acres, RR 5, Forest, ON N0N 1J0

Manitoba, 327 Ravelston Ave W, Winnipeg, MB R2C 1W3

Quebec, 317 Julie, St Eustache, QC J7P 3R8

Southern Ontario, 511 Guelph Line, Ste 702, Burlington, ON L7R 3M3

Austin-Healey Sports and Touring Club
PO Box 3539
York, PA 17402
215-536-5912
E-mail: info@austin-healey-stc.org

Founded 1976. 400+ members. Most members are affiliated with one of six regions: Harrisburg, Lehigh Valley, Philadelphia, Brandywine, North Jersey and Long Island. Generally, regional activities are held monthly. A monthly magazine, *The Flash*, provides club and regional information. An all region event, Encounter, is usually held in August and is hosted by one of these regions. The club is dedicated to helping members enjoy the marque. Dues: $30/year. Web site: www.austin-healey-stc.org

Mini Owners of New Jersey Car Club
24 Arrighi Dr
Warren, NJ 07059-5801
PH/FAX: 908-769-MINI
E-mail: miniac1@aol.com

Founded 1986. 150 members. A club for the Mini enthusiast. Also help people find Minis (1000s, Cooper S, etc) and parts for their Minis. A Mini is a small British auto created by Sir Alec Issigonis in 1959. Dues: $15/year. Web site: http://clubs.hemmings.com/miniownersofnj

Minis of Windsor Owner's Group
5040 Colbourne Dr
Windsor, ON Canada N8T 1T8
519-948-8383, 519-948-2265
E-mail: faucets@mnsi.net

Founded 1989. 60 members. Contact person: Karen Morneau, President, at the above address. Membership is limited to persons 18 years of age and older who own or have interest in the Mini. We hold a club sponsored event each month along with a monthly meeting which is held on the third Monday of each month. We have a monthly newsletter that is part of the membership fee. A family oriented club with children always welcome. The membership age group varies from 18 to 72. Dues: $25/year.

DKW Club of America
1141 Woodland Ave
Menlo Park, CA 94025
650-321-6640; FAX: 650-329-0129
E-mail: jowett@best.com

See full listing in **Section Three** under **DKW**

Avanti Owners Association Int'l
PO Box 28788
Dallas, TX 75228
800-527-3452 US
214-709-6185 foreign

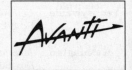

Founded 1963. 1,600 members. Open to all Avanti owners. Supports the Avanti marque from the 1963 Studebaker Avanti to the 1989 Avanti produced today. Ownership of an Avanti is not necessary to be a member. Publish *Avanti Quarterly* magazine. Contains information on meets, member experiences, repairs, parts and cars for sale. Dues: $25/year.

Berkeley Newsletter
PO Box 162282
Austin, TX 78716-2282
512-327-6231
E-mail: gerronsh@aol.com

Founded 1990. 50 members. The only newsletter in North America devoted exclusively to Berkeley automobiles. Free ads to subscribers. Dues: $12/year.

Bitter Owners Club
Medina Garden Centre, Staplers Rd
Wootton IOW PO33 4RW England
PH/FAX: 0044-1983-883430
E-mail: mgc.bw@virgin.net

Founded 1988. 47 members. Publishes *Best Bitter*, a bi-monthly magazine with 32-36 pages. Annual UK rally, representation at classic events, Bittermobilia range, sales/maintenance advice. Dues: £30/year (for US members), can be paid by credit card. Web site: www.bittercars.com

BMW Car Club of America
2809 E 35th St
Tulsa, OK 74105

Founded 1969. 50,000 members. Open to BMW enthusiasts and owners. Benefits include monthly *Roundel*, our colorful, informative 130-plus page magazine featuring maintenance tips, test results of new products and exciting articles with tips on enhancing your BMW and ensuring its lasting value. Many of 60+ local chapters offer driving schools, tech sessions, rallies, autocrosses, social events and more. Dues: $35/year. Web site: www.bmwcca.org

The BMW CS Registry
c/o Art & Marilyn Wegweiser
5341 Gibson Hill Rd
Edinboro, PA 16412
814-734-5107
E-mail: art@bmwcsregistry.org

Founded 1981. 350 members. No restrictions, for enthusiasts of the E9 Model and the E121 Model BMW CS coupe. Quarterly publication for $25 (included w/membership), $35 overseas. Web site: www.bmwcsregistry.org

The BMW tii Register
Bob Murphy
6790 Monarda Ct
Houston, TX 77069
PH/FAX: 281-583-2676
E-mail: tiireg@aol.com

Founded 1981. 200 members. A special interest group for the BMW 2002tii. Newsletter, technical data and assistance. Past newsletters and manuals available. Group is dedicated to keeping the tii enjoyable and available. Dues: $15/2 years.

BMW Z Series Register
PO Box 81807
Conyers, GA 30013
PH/FAX: 770-929-1358
E-mail: bmwcsreg@earthlink.net

Founded 1997. 900 members. Must be BMW Z3 owner. Quarterly magazine, supplements on the off months, which include events, classified and modification news. National Z3 Owners Homecoming September 2-5 at the BMW Z3 plant, Spartanburg, SC. Dues: $25/year. Web site: www.bmwregisters.com

Rocky Mountain Isetta Club
6516 Constellation Dr
Fort Collins, CO 80525
970-226-3544
E-mail: isettadr@aol.com

Founded 1983. 178 members. No restrictions. Quarterly newsletter published, free want ads for members, tech support, parts, cars, etc. Dues: $20/year US, $30/year foreign and Canada.

Vintage BMW Motorcycle Owners Ltd
PO Box 67
Exeter, NH 03833
603-772-9799
E-mail: vintagebmw@mediaone.net

For information, contact at the above address: Roland M Slabon, Editor. Founded 1972. 6,500 members. Devoted solely to the preservation, restoration, enjoyment and use of vintage, antique and classic BMW motorcycles 25 years old or older. Extensive worldwide parts and publication service. Quarterly illustrated publication, *Vintage BMW Bulletin*. Dues $12/year, $17 foreign. Web site: www.vintagebmw.org

Brough Superior Club
Box 393
Cos Cob, CT 06807
203-661-0526; FAX: 203-622-6093

Founded 1955. 270 members. Monthly newsletter. Brough ownership not necessary. Dues: $45/year.

American Bugatti Club
142 Berkeley St
Boston, MA 02116-5166
617-266-1217

Founded 1960. 300 members. Club encourages interest in Bugattis and provides network for members whereby they can learn more about each other and their cars. Open to Bugatti owners and genuine Bugatti enthusiasts. Publish a register of all known Bugattis in North America, as well as the quarterly magazine *Pur Sang*. Inquiries regarding the Register or *Pur Sang* should be sent to: ABC, 142 Berkeley St, Boston, MA 02116-5166. Dues: $60/year US and Canada, $60/year overseas, with a $10 initiation fee.

1929 Silver Anniversary Buick Club
75 Oriole Pkwy
Toronto, ON Canada M4V 2E3
416-487-9522; FAX: 416-322-7475
E-mail: rolltop@compuserve.com

Founded 1987. 300 members. Ownership or interest in 1929 Buick preferred. *1929 Silver Anniversary Buick Newsletter*, published 4 times a year, 18 pages each issue with restoration information and want ads for parts. Dues: $15/year. Web site: www.29buick.ca

1937-38 Buick Club
1005 Rilma Ln
Los Altos, CA 94022
PH/FAX: 650-941-4587
E-mail: harrylogan@earthlink.net

Founded 1980. Over 600 members. International club devoted to restoration, preservation and enjoyment of 1937 and 1938 Buick automobiles. Open to those interested in 1937-1938 Buicks, not necessary to own one. Magazine published 6 times a year, *The Torque Tube*. Dues: $34/year US, $35/year Canada and Mexico, $40/year all others.

Buick Club of America
Box 401927
Hesperia, CA 92340-1927
PH/FAX: 760-947-2485
E-mail: natbuickclubval@juno.com

Founded 1996. 10,000 members. For the preservation and restoration of those vehicles built by the Buick Motor Division of General Motors Corporation. Dues: $30/year US, $48/year foreign. Web site: www.buickclub.org

Buick GS Club of America
625 Pine Point Cir
Valdosta, GA 31602
912-244-0577

Founded 1982. 5,000 members. Dedicated to Buick owners who enjoy the performance of their cars. Emphasis is on racing as well as showing. Open to all Buick performance enthusiasts. Members receive the *GS X-tra* magazine containing performance build-ups, feature stories, tech tips, free classifieds and much more. Dues: $35/year.

Island Pacific Buick Club
3749 Shelbourne St, PO Box 32024
Victoria, BC Canada V8P 5S2
250-479-0088
E-mail: bmorin@pacificcoast.net

Founded 1991. 70 members. Bi-monthly newsletter, annual September show-n-shine and banquets, spring and summer cruises. Dues: $20/year Canadian. Web site: http://members.home.net/rubylit/buick

Manitoba Grand National Association
573 Lodge Ave
Winnipeg, MB Canada R3J 0S7
204-889-0503
E-mail: jobe@escape.ca

Founded 1998. 37 members. Catering to Turbo Buicks. 5 newsletters a year, monthly meetings, various discounts. Goal is to promote automotive hobby and give back to the comunity by donating to charity. Dues: $15/year.

New Zealand Buick Enthusiasts Club
26 Dunraven Pl
Torbay
North Shore City 1310 New Zealand
PH/FAX: 64-9-473-6856
E-mail: stock@extra.co.nz

Founded 1988. 130-160 members. Open to all Buick owners. Four magazines per year with stories, technical tips, dates of swap meets in New Zealand and United States plus member list every August. We also list member recommended suppliers of spare parts. Dues: $10/year local, $15/year overseas.

Riviera Owners Association
PO Box 26344
Lakewood, CO 80226
303-987-3712; FAX: 303-232-4368
E-mail: roa@rivowners.org

Founded 1984. 3,300 members. International membership open to owners and enthusiasts of the Riviera by Buick (1963-1999). Dues: $25/year US, $30/year foreign. Web site: www.rivowners.org

1958 Cadillac Owners Association
PO Box 850029
Braintree, MA 02185
781-843-4485
E-mail: sdn58@aol.com

Founded March 1991. 516 members. An international single year Cadillac club organized for the common good, mutual benefit and cooperative assistance of the 1958 Cadillac owner. Must own or be interested in 1958 Cadillacs. Send a large, self-addressed 75¢ stamped envelope to club address for membership application, brochure and sample newsletter. Publishes bi-monthly newsletter of *Motordom's Masterpiece*. Annual foreign postage for those who are not online; Canada and Mexico, $2; all other countries, $7 US funds, payable in advance. Lifetime membership fee $22. Web site: www.1958cadillac.com

Allante Appreciation Group
PO Box 225
Edgewood, IL 62426
PH/FAX: 800-664-5224
E-mail: allante@pointers.com

Founded 1994. 1,550+ members. Eight newsletters per year. Internet homepage. Fax back service. Member library, National and local group meets and shows. Dues: $40/year. Web site: www.allante.org

Allante Owners' Association
140 Vintage Way #456
Novato, CA 94945
888-ALLANTE toll-free
415-382-1973; FAX: 415-883-0203
E-mail: allantefan@aol.com

Founded 1991. 2,500+ members. *Allante Avenues* is a high quality, award winning quarterly magazine with many photos, technical information, regional events, accessory information and sales and resale Allantes and parts exchange. Visa, MasterCard and American Express. Dues: $40/year. Web site: www.allante.com

Cadillac Club of North Jersey
105 Brookview Dr
Woodcliff Lake, NJ 07677
PH/FAX: 201-930-1900

Founded 1991. 275 members. An active, local club dedicated to the preservation, restoration and enjoyment of Cadillacs over 15 years old. Parades, shows, monthly newsletter, weekly outdoor meetings during warm weather months. Dues: $25/year. Web site: www.tappedin.com/ccnj

Cadillac Drivers Club
5825 Vista Ave
Sacramento, CA 95824-1428
916-421-3193

Founded 1971. 113 members. No restrictions. Newsletter with free ads. 4 meets per year. Club library for research on your car, 1941-1980. Service information, buyer/seller price information. Production numbers 1902-1980. Dues: $18/year.

Cadillac LaSalle Club Inc
PO Box 1916
Lenoir, NC 28645-1916
828-757-9919; FAX: 828-757-0367
E-mail: cadlasal@twave.net

For membership information, contact at the above address: Jay Ann Edmunds. Founded 1958. 6,200 members. Illustrated monthly magazine, *The Self Starter* club directory. Director of Technical Service to help with members' problems. Local regions in most parts of the country. National and Regional events, gift and life memberships, jewelry, memorabilia. Dues: $30/year US 2nd class mail, $40/year US 1st class mail, $40/year Mexico and Canada, $45/year foreign. Web site: www.cadillaclasalleclub.org

Chicagoland Region-Allante Appreciation Group
3115 Deerfield Rd
Riverwoods, IL 60015-3768
PH/FAX: 847-940-7777

Founded 1996. 127 members. We are a very active club with lunch meetings, car shows, tech sessions, overnight trips, newsletters filled with info six times a year. A group that really appreciates their Allante with lots of enthusiasm and love for the car. Dues: $20/year.

Classic Cadillac Club Deutschland eV
Windmuehlenstr 49
50129 Bergheim Germany
FAX: +49-2238-945407
E-mail: cccd@classiccars.de

Founded 1991. 180 members. Open to all Cadillac owners or owners to be. Bi-monthly newsletter, *The Standard*, some regional meetings and a national meeting every May. Dues: 120 DM/year Europe, 150 DM/year worldwide. Web site: http://classiccars.de/cccd

South West Alliance
c/o Bud Morgan
16420 N 49th St
Scottsdale, AZ 85254
602-788-0609; FAX: 602-971-0655
E-mail: morganbud@aol.com

Founded 2001. 15 members. 1987-1993 Cadillac Allante owners' appreciation group of the Southwest. Meets quarterly, events throughout the winter months. Dues: none.

Tampa Bay Allante Group
4327 Sawgrass Dr
Palm Harbor, FL 34685
727-771-0011; FAX: 727-530-3610
E-mail: tlmackes@aol.com

Founded 1998. Approximately 20 members. Group meet get-togethers once a month with our Cadillac Allantes. We have events scheduled each month to enhance friendship and the Cadillac Allante marque (parties, parades, etc). Dues: none. Web site: www.allante.org

Checker Car Club of America Inc
10530 W Alabama
Sun City, AZ 85351-3544
PH/FAX: 623-974-4987
E-mail: carclub@gte.net

For membership information, contact at the above address: Roy Dickinson. Founded 1982. Over 900 members. Open to anyone interested in Checkers. Publishes quarterly newsletter, *Checkerboard News*, now includes members from all chapters, members contribute articles. Send for application. Dues: $20/year North America, $25/year foreign.

The 1965-66 Full-Size Chevrolet Club
15615 State Rd 23
Granger, IN 46530
219-272-6964; FAX: 219-272-1348
E-mail: hfoos@aol.com

Founded 1983. 2,181 members. Dedicated to the preservation, restoration and recognition of 1965 and 1966 full-size Chevrolets. This is a social organization with the whole family in mind. Dues: $18/year.
Web site: www.fullsizechevroletclub6566.com

Alamo Classic Chevy Club
14319 Ridge Falls Dr
San Antonio, TX 78233
210-771-7429
E-mail: twofewclassics@aol.com

Founded 1978. 45 members. No restrictions. Meeting last Wednesday of each month, 7 pm at Bun-n-Barrel on Austin Hwy. Newsletter, *Cruisin' News*, every month to all members. Dues: $20/year.

Blue Ribbon Classic Chevy Club
11926 W Hafeman Rd
Orfordville, WI 53576
608-879-3019
E-mail: toadnels@aol.com

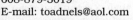

Founded 1977. 25 members. Those interested in or owners of

55-57 Chevys. Monthly newsletter to members. Dues: $24/year. Web site: http://clubs.hemmings.com/blueribbonchevys/

California Nomads
PO Box 340
5842 E Parapet St
Long Beach, CA 90808-2726
562-421-5862

Founded 1969. 40 members. Single and family club. 1955-1957 Nomads and Safaris. Dues: $25/year.

Capital District Chevrolet Club Inc
20 Dussault Dr
Latham, NY 12110
518-783-8728 (publicity)
518-465-1649 (membership)
E-mail: barnerr@yahoo.com

Founded 1977. 85 members. Holiday parties, technical meetings, picnics, annual show, cruises, monthly meetings, family functions, guest speakers at monthly meetings. Need not own a vehicle currently. Vehicle years 1900 to 1999, cars, trucks and street rods welcome. Dues: $18/year single, $24/year family. Web site: http://clubs.hemmings.com/cdcc/

Chevrolet Classics Club
PO Box 385
Omaha, NE 68101
402-733-4170

Founded 1971. 45 members. Owners of 1955 thru 1957 Chevrolet vehicles. Associated with Classic Chevy Intern and Bow Tie Chevrolet. Dues: $20/year.

Chevrolet Nomad Association
8653 W Hwy 2
Cairo, NE 68824
308-384-2622; FAX: 308-385-2970
E-mail: chevymad@gionline.net

Founded 1988. 1,200 members. Preservation of 1955, 1956 and 1957 Chevy Nomads. Vehicle ownership not required. 10 mailings a year, free ads to members, tech assistance, one annual convention and show. 13th annual convention in Spokane, WA; for information contact: Jan Duncan, 308-384-2622. Dues: $30/year US, $35/year Canada, $40/year foreign, US funds. Web site: www.chevynomadclub.com

Chevy Times
2166 S Orange Blossom Tr
Apopka, FL 32703
407-886-1963; FAX: 407-886-7571
E-mail: info@lategreatchevy.com

Founded 1980. 10,500 members. Open to those interested in 1958-1972 Chevys. Monthly publication: *Late Great Chevys*. Restoration parts, free advertising. Selling new and used parts worldly for 1955-1972 Chevys. Subscription: $35/year 2nd class, $45/year 1st class. Call for member information. Web site: www.lategreatchevy.com

Classic Chevy Cameo & GMC Suburban Pickup Club
4356 Riverview Dr
Port Allen, LA 70767-3808
225-383-8864
E-mail: cameo56@yahoo.com

Founded 1988. 100 members. Open to anyone interested in Cameos, owners or not. To unite owners, share ideas and technical tips. Promote reproduction of needed specialized parts and to edit a regular newsletter to aid owners in above areas. Dues: $25/year. Web site: http://clubs.hemmings.com/cameo/

Classic Chevy International
PO Box 607188
Orlando, FL 32860-7188
800-456-1957, 407-299-1957
FAX: 407-299-3341
E-mail: info@classicchevy.com

A national voice uniting car clubs and enthusiasts worldwide.
World's largest member-driven club devoted to 1955-1972 full
size Chevrolet cars and trucks. Huge in stock inventory including reproduction, modified, high performance and used parts.
Members receive monthly *Classic Chevy World* magazine, tech
help, 4 national conventions per year, special pricing and much
more. Dues: $39/year. Call for more info or visit us online. Web
site: www.classicchevy.com

Columbia Classic Chevy Club
PO Box 3122
West Columbia, SC 29171
803-536-6022

Founded 1983. 25 members. Open to all Chevy enthusiasts.
Benefit from fellowship with other Chevy enthusiasts. Meet 1st
Sunday every month, 5 pm. One car show, 2 old car drop-ins
and seven monthly cruise-ins. Newsletter *The Classic News* published monthly. Yearly donations to Children's Homes. Dues:
$20/year.

Cosworth Vega Owners Association
PO Box 5864
Pittsburgh, PA 15209
E-mail: cvoainc@aol.com

For information, contact at the above address: Michael Rupert,
Membership VP. Founded 1979. Dedicated to promote and preserve the 75-76 Chevy Cosworth Vega as a collector car. 16
regional chapters. Annual national roundup in varing cities.
Quarterly magazine, *Cosworth Vega Magazine*. Dues: $30/year,
$75/three years.

Fifty 5 6 7 Club
2021 Wiggins Ave
Saskatoon, SK Canada S7J 1W2
306-343-0567; FAX: 306-343-5670

For membership information, contact at the above address:
National Club Office. Founded 1974. 1,000 members. An organization for the support, promotion, restoration and preservation
of the 1955-1956-1957 Chevrolets, including Chevrolet and GM
trucks, Corvettes and Pontiacs. Owner or enthusiast. Dues:
$45/year (G/S tax included).

Houston Classic Chevy Club
127 Bellaire Ct
Bellaire, TX 77401
713-667-4085
E-mail: amcclosk@aol.com

Founded 1989. 100 members. Dedicated to the preservation,
restoration and enjoyment of 1955, 1956 and 1957 Chevrolet
automobiles and trucks. Monthly newsletter and meeting.
Cruises, picnics, shows and swap meets. Dues: $25/year.

Just Old Trucks of Austin, Texas
5209 Fort Mason Dr
Austin, TX 78745-2314
512-447-1446

Founded May 1991. 20 members and growing. Interest in Chevy
or GMC trucks to join. Affiliated with National Chevy/GMC
Truck Assoc. Meetings are held once a month. 1918-1972
Chevy/GMC trucks of all sizes including sedan delivery.

Michiana Classic Chevy Club
PO Box 713
Elkhart, IN 46515
219-674-9198

Founded 1976. 42 members. Must have an interest in 1955,
1956 or 1957 Chevy. Family club. Meet once every third Sunday.
Do a lot of things for charities in or around the area. Monthly
newsletter. Summer swap meet and a car show and winter swap
meet. Have lots of fun as a group. Dues: $12/year.

Mid-Atlantic Nomad Association
337 Springdale Ave
York, PA 17403

Founded 1970. 200 members. Dedicated to the preservation,
restoration and enjoyment of 1955-57 Chevy Nomad wagons and
Pontiac Safaris. Dues: $10/year.

National Impala Association
2928 4th Ave, PO Box 968
Spearfish, SD 57783
605-642-5864; FAX: 605-642-5868
E-mail: impala@blackhills.com

Founded 1980. 2,600 members worldwide. Bi-monthly publication. 1958-1970 full-size Chevrolets. Dues: $35/year second
class, $45/year first class, $65/year overseas. Web site:
www.impala.blackhills.com

**National Monte Carlo Owner's
Association**
38 S Blue Angel Pkwy, PMB 214
Pensacola, FL 32506
850-457-2957
E-mail: nmcoa@aol.com

Founded 1984. We are a national car club for Monte Carlo owners. Dedicated to the preservation and restoration of the Monte
Carlo. Bi-monthly magazine, *Class of Monte Carlo*. Free advertising in magazine to members. Annual convention. Dues:
$30/year.

National Nostalgic Nova
PO Box 2344
York, PA 17405
717-252-4192; FAX: 717-252-1666

Founded 1982. 6,000 members. Members receive 48-page *Nova Times* magazine. Free classified advertising. 3 shows each year. Carry a complete line of parts for original and hot rod Novas. Dues: $30/year, $40/year Canada. Web site: www.nnnova.com

Obsolete Fleet Chevys
PO Box 13944
Salem, OR 97309
503-585-5578

Founded 1974. 60 members. Interest in the preservation and restoration of 1955-1957 Chevrolet cars, Corvettes and pickups. Meet once per month, 2nd Friday. *Fleet Sheet* is the monthly publication. Club activities include monthly events, caravaning to events, social events. Dues: $20/year.

Oklahoma Chevelle & El Camino Owners Assoc
5553 S Peoria Ave
Tulsa, OK 74105
918-451-1657

Founded 1994. 100+ members. Dedicated to promoting interest in and preservation of 1964-1987 Chevelles and El Caminos. Dues: $20/year. Web site: www.okchevelle.com

Pikes Peak Super Chevys
PO Box 6764
Colorado Springs, CO 80934-6764
719-473-2364
E-mail: proto72@aol.com

Founded 1985. 50 members. A Colorado Non-Profit Corporation. Organized to promote the healthy existence of 1955-1972 Chevrolets through shared information, meeting people and having fun. A newsletter is published monthly to members. Dues: $12/year.

Steel City Classics
701 Prestley Ave
Carnegie, PA 15106
412-276-0384

Founded 1976. 150 members. Monthly newsletter. 2 swap meets, spring and fall; 2 bus trips to Spring and Fall Carlisle; 2 membership parties/meetings, spring and fall; picnic, family oriented club, try to include everyone (kids' model show at car show, kids judge cars at picnic). Began as 1955-1957 Chevy club, but in recent years expanded to include all Chevys. Dues: $18/year.

Vintage Chevrolet Club of America
PO Box 5387
Orange, CA 92613-5387
818-963-0205
E-mail: finkj@earthlink.net

Founded 1961. 8,000 members. Regions hold tours and meetings all over the US and the National holds an anniversary meet every 5 years. You must be a member of the National before you can join a region. The *Generator & Distributor* is issued monthly and included in membership. Dues: $25/year US, $30/year foreign.

American Camaro Association
5786 Buckeye Rd
Macungie, PA 18062
PH/FAX: 610-966-2492
E-mail: karlz28@earthlink.net

Founded 1998. 170 members. Free to all Camaro clubs. Event: Camaros at Carlisle. Dues: $20/year. Web site: http://clubs.hemmings.com/americancamaro

Camaro Club of San Diego
PO Box 421164
San Diego, CA 91942-1164
760-789-5151
E-mail: louheyn@aol.com

Founded 1993. 250 members. The Camaro Club of San Diego was established in August of 1993 to generate fellowship, provide information, technical assistance, and share the interest of the Chevrolet Camaro. Our main goal is to preserve, restore, and maintain the Camaro and its history. This includes all styles: stock, restored, original or modified. Dues: $25/year single. Web site: www.caam.com/ccsd

Connecticut Chevelle Connection
PO Box 6094
Wolcott, CT 06716-0094
203-879-4016
E-mail: ctchevel@portone.com

Founded 1991. Over 200 members and growing. Our purpose is to encourage restoration and/or preservation and promote general interest in the 1964-1987 Chevrolet Chevelle, Malibu and El Camino. Monthly meetings, tech talks by guest speakers, parts swaps, newsletter, cruises, car shows, picnic and Christmas party. Host of the largest all Chevy show in area, the Bow-Tie Classic, over 400 show cars and growing. Dues: $20/year. Web site: www.portone.com/ctchevel

Eastern Michigan Camaro Club
34113 Tonquish
Westland, MI 48185
734-728-2841
E-mail: superfest7@aol.com

Founded 1991. 50+ members. Fellowship, fun and information. No restrictions. Annual big event: Camaro Superfest at Domino's Farms in Ann Arbor, MI. All Camaros and owners welcome. Dues: $12/year. Web site: www.superfest7.com

Gateway Area Chevelle Club
1136 Washington Ave #750
St Louis, MO 63101
314-621-3666; FAX: 314-621-8080
E-mail: info@gatewaychevelles.com

Founded 2000. 70 members. GACC is for St Louis area Chevelle enthusiasts. We promote family oriented enjoyment of classic Chevelles. We publish a monthly, full color newsletter. We host cruises and shows and attend Regional events together. Dues: $25/year. Web site: www.gatewaychevelles.com

International Camaro Club Inc
National Headquarters
2001 Pittston Ave
Scranton, PA 18505
570-585-4082

3,500 plus members. No new members at this time, registry only. Dedicated to serving the needs of the Camaro owner and enthusiast. Helps fellow members locate parts and supply ID, body tag info, etc. Open to owners and enthusiasts of 1967-present Camaros.

Lehigh Valley Camaro Club
5786 Buckeye Rd
Macungie, PA 18062
PH/FAX: 610-966-2492
E-mail: karlz28@earthlink.net

Founded 1990. 90 members. No restrictions, monthly newsletter, events, local cruises, picnics, family outings. Dues: $15/year. Web site: http://clubs.hemmings.com/lehighvalleycamaro

Section Three – Clubs & Organizations

Maryland Chevelle Club
6030 Hunt Club Rd
Elkridge, MD 21075-5516
410-796-7725
E-mail: showcar402@aol.com

Founded 1985. 200+ members. Club is open to all who enjoy 1964-1972 Chevelles and El Caminos. Monthly meetings, cruises, picnics. Monthly newsletter. We also put on the largest Chevelle only show and swap meet on the East Coast. MCC is a associate chapter of ACES and NCOA. Dues: $25/year. Web site: www.clark/pub/chevelle/mcc.htm

National Chevelle Owners Association
7343-J W Friendly Ave
Greensboro, NC 27410
336-854-8935

Founded 1982. 7,000 members. Monthly color magazine, *The Chevelle Report*, features member's cars, tech tips, production data, factory photos and parts sources on 1964-1987 Chevelles and El Caminos. Dues: $30/year US, $40/year Canada, $55/year all other countries, US funds only. Web site: www.chevellereport.com

New England Chevelle & El Camino Association
Jim Goodwin
4 State St
Shrewsbury, MA 01545
PH/FAX: 508-845-9752

Founded 1990. 85 members. Open to those who own or have an interest in the real Heartbeat of America/Chevelles/El Caminos. Monthly newsletter. Friendly exchange of ideas, club meets and get togethers. Member discounts from parts suppliers. Dues: $20/yr. Look us up at www.erols.com/wlavigne (click on the bow-tie).

Northwest Jersey Camaro Club Inc
Rt 26, PO Box 36
Flanders, NJ 07836
973-584-1542

Founded 1993. 45 members. To join, we ask that the Camaro be in your best interest. A newsletter, the *Jersey Camaro*, is sent out monthly to notify members of local and National events. You have the opportunity to meet other Camaro enthusiasts and see their Camaros. We are a chapter of the worldwide Camaro Association of Orlando, FL. A magazine, *The Camaro World*, is printed bi-monthly. Dues: $15/year.

South Jersey Camaro Group Productions
1120 Fairmount Ave
Vineland, NJ 08360
856-692-8930; FAX: 856-205-1409

Founded 1996. 12 members. No club representation. Hosts the East Coast Camaro Gathering. Largest all Camaro show on the East Coast. Event open to all years of Camaros, Camaro/automotive vendors. Partial proceeds to benefit South Jersey Camaro Scholarship Fund at Cumberland County College in Vineland, NJ. Dues: none. Web site: http://clubs.hemmings.com/sjerseycamaro/

Twin Tiers Camaro Firebird Club
PO Box 3125
Binghamton, NY 13902
570-623-2217
E-mail: coyle@pronetisp.net

Founded 1988. 30 members. Regular membership open to Camaro/Firebird owners. Bi-monthly newsletter, bi-monthly meetings. Dues: $15/year. Web site: http://clubs.hemmings.com/camarofirebirdtwintiers

Western Michigan Camaro Club
1724 34th St SW
Wyoming, MI 49509-3311
E-mail: our96ss@aol.com

Founded 1975. 60 members. Serving Camaro enthusiasts from the western half of Michigan. Monthly meetings, monthly newsletter, co-host Camaro Superfest. Club sponsor: Berger Chevrolet in Grand Rapids, MI. Dues: $30/year. Web site: www.westernmichigancamaroclub.com or www.superfest.com

Worldwide Camaro Association
PO Box 607188
Orlando, FL 32860-7188
800-456-1957, 407-299-1957
FAX: 407-299-3341
E-mail: info@worldwidecamaro.com

A National Voice uniting car clubs and enthusiasts worldwide. World's largest member-driven club devoted to all generations of Camaro. Huge in stock inventory including reproduction, modified, high performance and used parts. Members receive monthly *Camaro World* magazine, tech help, four national conventions per year, special pricing and much more. Call for more info or visit us online. Dues: $39/year. Web site: www.worldwidecamaro.com

Central Pennsylvania Corvair Club
1751 Chesley Rd
York, PA 17403-4001
717-845-9347

Founded 1975. 90 members. Monthly meetings, tours, parades, shows and annual Mini-Convention. Monthly newsletter, *Action*. Dues: $10/year.

Circle City Corvairs
PO Box 17325
Indianapolis, IN 46217-0325
E-mail: valveclatter@aol.com

40 Members. Monthly newsletter; monthly meetings, tours, car show each September. Dues: $12/year. Web site: http://circlecitycorvairs.tripod.com/circlecitycorvairs

City Car Club (Corvairs) Inc
30 Camel St
Fairhaven, MA 02719-2102
508-993-2861

Founded in 1956 as a custom and hot rod club, became Corvair club in 1980. 27 members. Group of Corvair enthusiasts meeting every month to work on club members' cars and further Corvair interest. Monthly publication, *Vairgram*, free to members. Dues: $8/year.

Colonial Corvair Club
44 Columbia Rd
Arlington, MA 02174
781-648-1662
E-mail: cir@wjh.harvard.edu

Founded 1980. 25-30 members. Monthly business meetings, tech sessions, car shows, picnics and tours. A chapter of CORSA. Club area covers north of Boston, parts of southern New Hampshire, and Maine. Monthly publication, *Vair Waves*. Dues: $15/year. Web site: www.geocities.com/motorcity/downs/4450

Corvair Society of America (CORSA)
PO Box 607
Lemont, IL 60439-0607
630-257-6530; FAX: 630-257-5540
E-mail: corsa@corvair.org

Founded 1969. 5,500 members. Dedicated to the operation, preservation, restoration and enjoyment of the Corvair automobile and its derivatives. Monthly publication, *CORSA Communique*. Dues: $35/year US, $38/year Canadian, $48/year overseas, US funds please. Web site: www.corvair.org

chapters:

Alabama   *Alabama Corvair Club*, 3112 Clayborne Rd, Dothan, AL 36303

Vulcan Corvair Enthusiasts, PO Box 59071, Birmingham, AL 35259-9071

Arizona   *Cactus Corvair Club*, PO Box 11701, Phoenix, AZ 85061

Northern Arizona Corvair Club, 340 E David, Flagstaff, AZ 86001

Tucson Corvair Association, 2044 W Shalimar Way, Tucson, AZ 85704

Arkansas   *Arkansas Corvair Club*, PO Box 627, Little Rock, AR 72203

California   *Bakersfield Corvairs*, 10817 Sunset Canyon Dr, Bakersfield, CA 93311-2749

Central Coast CORSA, 8350 Santa Rosa Rd, Atascadero, CA 93422

Central Valley Corvairs, 3001 Lancelot Ln, Modesto, CA 95350-1408

Classic Corvairs of River City, 9801 Beechwood Dr, Orangevale, CA 95662

CORSA West of Los Angeles, PO Box 950023, Mission Hills, CA 91395

Corvanatics, 5000 Cascabel Rd, Atascadero, CA 93422-2302

Coyote Corvair Club, PO Box 2204, Vista, CA 92085-2204

Inland Empire Corvair Club, PO Box 52714, Riverside, CA 92517

Sacramento Corvair Tour Group, 9590 Appalachian Dr, Sacramento, CA 95827

San Diego Corvair Club, PO Box 23172, San Diego, CA 92193

San Francisco Bay Area CORSA, PO Box 422, Orinda, CA 94563

San Joaquin Corvair Club, PO Box 4693, Fresno, CA 93744

Shasta Corvairs, 2922 Quartz Hill Rd, Redding, CA 96003

South Coast CORSA, PO Box 213, Redondo Beach, CA 90277-0213

Valley CORSA, PO Box 2792, Santa Clara, CA 95055

Ventura County Corvairs, 1364 Cottonwood Ln, Fillmore, CA 93015

Vintage CORSA, PO Box 1180, Placentia, CA 92871-1180

Colorado   *Pikes Peak Corvair Club*, PO Box 15034, Colorado Springs, CO 80935

Rocky Mountain CORSA, PO Box 27058, Denver, CO 80227

Connecticut   *Connecticut CORSA*, PO Box 341, Georgetown, CT 06829-0341

Delaware   *First State Corvair Club*, 113 Linden Ave, Wilmington, DE 19805

Florida   *Central Florida Corvair*, 605 N Clayton, Mount Dora, FL 32757

First Coast Corvairs, PO Box 668, Yulee, FL 32041

Gulfcoast Corvairs, 2630 Webber St, Sarasota, FL 34239

Nature Coast Corvairs, 6735 W Rainhill Ct, Crystal River, FL 34429

South Florida Corvairs, PO Box 936652, Margate, FL 33093

Suncoast Corvairs, PO Box 788, Crystal Beach, FL 34681

West Florida Corvair Club, 2907 San Miguel, Milton, FL 32583

Georgia   *Corvair Atlanta*, 1147 Reading Dr, Acworth, GA 30102

Heart of Georgia Corvairs, 123 Hillsdale Rd, Forsyth, GA 31029

Idaho   *Boise Basin Corvairs*, PO Box 16734, Boise, ID 83715

Illinois   *Chicagoland Corvair Enthusiasts*, PO Box 704, Matteson, IL 60443-0704

Mad Anthony Corvair Club, 5401 Lower Huntington Rd, Fort Wayne, IN 46809

Prairie Capital Corvair Association, PO Box 954, Springfield, IL 62705

Indiana   *Circle City Corvairs*, PO Box 17325, Indianapolis, IN 46217-0325

Michiana Corvair Club, 2054 Carrbridge Ct, South Bend, IN 46614

Iowa   *Iowa Corvair Enthusiasts*, 23 Gleason Dr, Iowa City, IA 52240-5854

Kentucky   *Central Kentucky Corvair*, 300 Albany Rd, Lexington, KY 40503

Corvair Society of America (CORSA) chapters (continued)

Derby City Corvair, 7400 Greenwood Rd, Louisville, KY 40258

Louisiana   *New Orleans Corvair Enthusiasts*, PO Box 427, Denham Springs, LA 70727-0427

Maryland   *Chesapeake Corvair*, PO Box 554, Forest Hill, MD 21050-0554

CORSA of Baltimore, 619 Round Oak Rd, Towson, MD 21204-3867

Group Corvair, 12710 Lode St, Bowie, MD 20720

Mid-Maryland Corvair Club, 20620 Guard Ct, Rohrersville, MD 21779

Massachusetts   *Bay State Corvairs*, 344 Summer St, Rehoboth, MA 02769-1112

City Car Club Corvairs, 30 Camel St, Fairhaven, MA 02719-2102

Colonial Corvair Club, 44 Columbia Rd, Arlington, MA 02174

Michigan   *Detroit Area Corvair Club*, 5498 Duffield Rd, Swartz Creek, MI 48473-8587

West Michigan Corvair Club, 1411 Pickett St SE, Kentwood, MI 49508

Minnesota   *Corvair Minnesota*, 3370 Library Ln, St Louis Park, MN 55426-4224

Missouri   *Heart of America Corvair Owners' Assn*, 9802 Booth, Kansas City, MO 64134

Ozarks Classic Corvair Club, 4026 W Wayland, Springfield, MO 65807

Show-Me Corvair Club, 4067 Waterfall Dr, St Louis, MO 63034-0187

Nebraska   *Corvair Midwest*, 10100 Holdrege, Lincoln, NE 68527-9462

Nevada   *Vegas Vairs*, 4607 E Imperial Ave, Las Vegas, NV 89104-5816

New Hampshire   *Central New Hampshire Corvair Assn*, PO Box 334, Contoocook, NH 03229

New Jersey   *Bayshore Corvair Association*, PO Box 815, Jackson, NJ 08527

Delaware Valley Corvair Club, 1301 Union Landing Rd, Cinnaminson, NJ 08077

Lakewood-Monza Group, 14 Ashwood Dr, Brick, NJ 08723-3402

New Jersey Association of Corvair Enth, PO Box 631, Ridgewood, NJ 07451

New Mexico   *Corvairs of New Mexico*, 2226 Inez Dr NE, Albuquerque, NM 87110-4732

Group UltraVan, 1418 Apple Ave, Tularosa, NM 88352-2006

New York   *Association of Corvair Nuts*, 180 Prospect St, Spencerport, NY 14559

Capital District Corvair Club, PO Box 192, Rexford, NY 12148

Central New York Corvair Club Inc, PO Box 616, Jamesville, NY 13078

Long Island Corvair Association, PO Box 1675, West Babylon, NY 11704

Niagara Frontier Corvair Club, PO Box 45, Buffalo, NY 14224

Resurrection Corvairs of Yonkers, 522 Saw Mill River Rd, Yonkers, NY 10701

North Carolina   *CORSA/NC*, 6715 Branson Mill Rd, Pleasant Garden, NC 27313

Ohio   *Corvair Club of Cincinnati*, PO Box 40153, Cincinnati, Oh 45240

Dayton Corvair Club, PO Box 3514, Dayton, OH 45401

Friends of Corvair, 7354 Middlebranch Ave NE, North Canton, OH 44721

Mid-Ohio Vair Force, 4673 NW Pkwy, Hilliard, OH 43026

North Coast Corvair Enthusiasts, PO Box 902, Painesville, OH 44077

Tri-State Corvairs, PO Box 581, Bryan, OH 43506

V8 Registry, 4361 St Dominic Dr, Cincinnati, OH 45238

Vacationland Corvairs, 560 Lindberg Blvd, Berea, OH 44017-1418

Oklahoma   *Green Country Corvair Group*, 4250 S Oswego, Tulsa, OK 74135

Indian Nations Corvair Association, 3320 SE 24th St, Del City, OK 73115-1614

Oregon   *Beaver State Corvair Club*, PO Box 148, Crabtree, OR 97335-0148

CORSA Oregon, PO Box 1445, Portland, OR 97207-1445

Southern Oregon Corvair Owners, 512 Fairmount St, Medford, OR 97501-2426

Pennsylvania   *Blue Mountain Corvair Club*, HC 1 Box 2086, Tannersville, PA 18372

Central Pennsylvania Corvair Club, PO Box 142, Windsor, PA 17366

Lehigh Valley Corvair Club, 137 American St, Whitehall, PA 18052

Philadelphia Corvair Association, 2545 Broder St 1st Fl, Allentown, PA 18103

Western Pennsylvania Corvair Club, 458 Whitestown Rd, Butler, PA 16001

South Carolina   *Central Carolina CORSA*, RR 3 Box 1195, Manning, SC 29102

CORSA South Carolina, PO Box 5559, Greenville, SC 29606

Lowcountry Corvair Association, PO Box 505, Ladson, SC 29456

Tennessee   *East Tennessee Corvair Club*, PO Box 928, Kingsport, TN 37660

Knoxville Area Corvair Club, PO Box 5942, Knoxville, TN 37928-0942

Music City Corvair Club, 2416 Ravine Dr, Nashville, TN 37217

Upper Cumberland Corvair Club, 1360 E Broad St, Cookeville, TN 38501-3061

Texas   *Alamo City Corvair Association*, PO Box 2125, Seguin, TX 78155

Corvair Houston, PO Box 2331, Houston, TX 77252-2331

Desert Corvair Club, PO Box 220108, El Paso, TX 79913-2108

Lone Star Corvair Club, RR 1 Box 15A, McDade, TX 78650

North Texas Corvair Association, 2701 W 15th St, Box 153, Plano, TX 75075

Utah   *Bonneville Corvair Club*, 6114 W Contadora Dr, West Valley City, UT 84128

Vermont   *Vermont Independent Corvair Enth*, PO Box 235, East Arlington, VT 05252

Virginia   *Central Virginia Corvair Club*, 8015 Driftwood Dr, Prince George, VA 23875

Northern Virginia Corvair Club, 6839 Brimstone Ln, Fairfax Station, VA 22039-1850

Roanoke Valley Corvair Club, 202 Lemon Dr, Lynchburg, VA 24501

Tidewater Corvair Club, 2901 Cardo Pl, Virginia Beach, VA 23456

Washington   *Columbia Basin Corvairs*, PO Box 1022, Richland, WA 99352-1022

CORSA Northwest, PO Box 88, Renton, WA 98057-0088

Inland Northwest Corvair Club, PO Box 132, Four Lakes, WA 99014-0132

West Virginia   *Wild Wonderful Corvair Club*, 140 Scott Acres, Scott Depot, WV 25560

Wisconsin   *Capital City Corvair Club*, 2795 Allegheny Dr, Madison, WI 53719

Milwaukee Corvair Club, 6931 N Belmont Ln, Fox Point, WI 53217

North East Wisconsin Corvair Club, 1274 E Shady Ln, Neenah, WI 54956-1128

Canada   *CORSA Ontario*, 401 Beechwood Crescent, Burlington, ON L7L 3P7

Western Canada CORSA, 212-894 Vernon Ave, Victoria, BC V8X 2W6

France   *Chevrolet Corvair Club of Paris*, 93 rue d'AngervilleLes Granges le Roi, 91410 Dourdan

Netherlands   *Corvair Club Nederland*, Darwin Plantsoen 1, 1097 EX Amsterdam

Switzerland   *Swiss Corvair Club*, Bachtelenstrasse 39, CH-2540 Grenchen

First State Corvair Club Inc
1306 Friar Rd
Newark, DE 19713
302-737-3577

Founded 1982. 48 members. Annual show and banquet, monthly meetings and newsletters, various activities throughout the year. Dues: $12/year.

40th Anniversary Corvette Registry
PO Box 1094
Middleburg, VA 20118
E-mail: zqqmin@tidalwave.net

Founded 1994. Approximately 2,500 members. The purpose of the 40th Anniversary Corvette Registry is to document the 6,749 RPO Z25 ruby red Corvettes built in 1993. The Registry also promotes safe driving fellowship among Corvettes owners and gatherings of rubies at most of the major events in the US. The Registry is also committed in providing *Fun In Our Rubies*. Dues: none. Web site: www.40thregistry.com

Adirondack Corvettes Inc
PO Box 821
Glens Falls, NY 12801
518-793-8085; FAX: 518-761-6034
E-mail: c5vette@adelphia.net

Founded 1990. 30 members. Corvette owners, member NCCC. Monthly social activities, annual Corvette event in June, monthly newsletter. Dues: $35/year. Web site: www.adirondackcorvettes.com

Aquia Creek Corvette Club
PO Box 986
Stafford, VA 22555
540-659-5234
E-mail: optimumproducts@msn.com

Founded 1987. 70 members. Must be a member of National Council of Corvette Clubs. Participate in local parades, homecoming, rallies and car shows. Dues: $25/year, $15/year renewal, $10/year spouses. Web site: http://members.aol.com/accclub/index.htm

Blue Ridge Corvette Club Inc
PO Box 1
Stuarts Draft, VA 24477
540-886-2433 after 6 pm

Founded 1977. 106 members. Must attend 2 club events and must be elected into club. Benefits, club car shows, club picnic, cruise-ins and road tours in the Blue Ridge Mountains (money raised goes to Blue Ridge area food bank). Monthly newsletter. Dues: $20/year. Web site: www.citymotors/net/brcc.htm

Boardwalk Corvettes of Atlantic City
PO Box 546
Brigantine Beach, NJ 08203-0546
PH: 609-965-7817

Founded 1983. 45 members. Meetings 1st Thursday of each month, Oyster Creek Inn, Leeds Point, NJ. Club activities include weekend trips to Watkins Glen, Martha's Vineyard and various southern NJ locations. Three shows each year, an all Chevy show in June, a Corvette show on the Ocean City, NJ Boardwalk in September and a show in October at the historic town of Smithville. Club is open to all Corvette owners and enthusiasts. Dues: $40/year.

Boone Trail Corvette Club
300 St Theodore Ct
Wentzville, MO 63385
314-798-2671
E-mail: ghellyer@westfordcom.com

Founded 1972. 120 members. Must be 18 years of age and own a Corvette. Sharing knowledge of Corvettes, monthly meetings, many events yearly and a monthly newsletter. Dues: $15/year individual, $25/year couple. Web site: www.boonetrailcc.com

Candlewood Valley Corvettes Inc
PO Box 2205
Danbury, CT 06813-2205
203-438-7286; FAX: 203-796-6792

Founded 1978. 120 members. Anyone who owns or is the primary driver of a Corvette is welcome to join our club. Members' benefits include local trade discounts, reduced cost on club sponsored events and numerous social activities. Social activities include brunches, dinners, rallies, car shows and cruises. Annual August car show. Dues: $20/year single, $25/year family. Web site: http://clubs.hemmings.com/candlewoodvettes/

Cascade Corvette Club
PO Box 363
Eugene, OR 97440
541-683-2538; FAX: 541-484-0882
E-mail: duckvett@sprynet.com

Open to all Corvette owners. Our activities include tours, auto crosses, car shows, rallies, picnics, technical sessions and many social events throughout the year. Meets on the second Friday of every month at Romania Chevrolet, located at 2020 Franklin Blvd, Eugene, Oregon. Guests are always welcome!

Central Indiana Corvette Club
608 Pioneer Dr
Indianapolis, IN 46217-3650
317-783-7955

Founded 1989. 25 members. Have to be a member of the National Council of Corvette Club Inc. Dues: $20/year.

Circle City Corvettes Inc
3574 Lake Oakridge Dr
Enterprise, AL 36330
334-347-5908; FAX: 334-393-4864
E-mail: jhickman@ala.net

Founded 1978. 40 members. Members must have an interest in the Corvette. Main event: beach caravan each April from Dothan, AL to Panama City Beach. All proceeds to Dothan Girls' Home and National Corvette Museum. Newsletter published monthly. Dues: $40/year.

Classic Corvettes of Minnesota
PO Box 32123
Fridley, MN 55432
763-754-9987
E-mail: cruisin@classiccorvettesmn.com

Founded 1981. 346 members. Open to owners of Corvettes for 1953-present. Classic Corvettes of Minnesota is a Corvette club in the Minneapolis/St Paul and surrounding area. Various Corvette shows, Corvette cruises, picnics, dinners and assorted events each year. Visit our web site at: www.classiccorvettesmn.com or call our hot line, 763-754-9987. Dues: $35/year.

Classic Glass Corvette Club
PO Box 4936
Marietta, GA 30061
770-591-3578
E-mail: ronfloyd@mindspring.com

Founded 1958. 100 members. Must attend 3 meetings prior to joining. Primarily a social club, some car shows, Corvette restorations. Dues: $35/member. Web site: http://members.aol.com/cgvettec/

Clipper City Corvette Club
643B Broadway, US Rt 1 S
Saugus, MA 01906
781-231-0478; FAX: 781-938-8833
E-mail: paulferraro@mediaone.net

Paul Ferraro, President. Founded 1980. 44 members. Weekly summer cruises, Corvette weekends. Dues: $50/year per couple. Web site: http://people.ne.mediaone.net/cwarren/clippercitycorvettes.html

Club Corvette of Connecticut
PO Box 68
Monroe, CT 06468
203-795-9823 home
203-387-9038 office
FAX: 203-389-0680
E-mail: rongoldbe@aol.com

Founded 1993. 410 members. No restrictions to join (but nice if you have a Corvette). Receive a newsletter (12 pages) once a month. Go to Corvette shows and have 3 cruise nights this year. Support other Corvette car shows in the Northeast whenever possible. Dues: $35/year per family. Web site: www.clubcorvettect.com

Club Proteam
1410 N Scott St
Napoleon, OH 43545
419-592-5086; FAX: 419-592-4242
E-mail: proteam@proteam-corvette.com

Founded 1995. 200+ members. Receive monthly newsletter and catalog, T-shirt, hat and video (a $57 value). Dues: $29.95/year. Web site: www.proteam-corvette.com

Corvette Club Norway
Boks 55 Bryn
0611 Oslo Norway
47-227-61170; FAX: 47-227-61176

Founded 1992. 288 members. Club for Corvette owners, meeting 10 times a year, quarterly publication. Dues: 350 NOK/year.

Corvette Club of America
PO Box 9879
Bowling Green, KY 42102
PH/FAX: 270-737-6022
E-mail: ccabg@ekx.infi.net

Founded 1988. 5,800+ members. No restrictions to membership Publish quarterly newsletter, *Corvette Capers*, free with membership, 32 pages with info from Corvette plant, National Corvette Museum, tech advice by Gordon Killebrew, free members' swap shop, discounts from over 100 vendors, updates on shows. Dues: $35/year. Web site: www.corvetteclubofamerica.com

Corvette Club of Delaware Valley
PO Box 397
Willow Grove, PA 19090
215-938-7722; FAX: 215-698-5888
E-mail: ccdv@ccdv.com

Founded 1958. 370+members. Can be a member first year without a Corvette. Benefits include club discounts at various venders, technical seminars and problem solving assistance, newsletter *Gas Cap*, annual judged show since 1970 (1995 was 25th consecutive year) called The Cavalcade of Corvettes, other activities include charitable fund raising and shows, rallies, picnics, etc. Dues: $30/year. Web site: www.ccdv.com

Corvette Club of Manitoba
PO Box 42032, RPO Ferry Rd
Winnipeg, MB Canada R3J 3X7
204-792-VETTE (8388)
FAX: 204-231-1854

Founded 1971. 75 members. A non-profit organization raising money for local children's charities. Open to Corvette owners and enthusiasts and family members. General meetings held last Tuesday of every month, consultant hotline. Other activities, show and shine, driving tours and cruises. Dues: $55/year. Web site: www.airwire.com/~gilesj/corvette_club.html

Corvette Club of Michigan
PO Box 510330
Livonia, MI 48151
248-685-7145

Founded 1958. 300 members. Must be Corvette owner, 18 yrs of age or over and possessing a valid driver's license. Publication, *Slipstream*, is distributed 11 times a year and free to members; also a Corvette calendar, events, updates, articles, etc.

Corvette Club of Nova Scotia
12828 Hwy RR2
Wentworth, NS Canada B0M 1Z0
902-548-2068

Founded 1974. 48 members. Interest in Corvettes required. Get to meet and go on drives with fellow enthusiasts. Club puts out a newsletter monthly from April-December. Dues: $35/year. Web site: www.geocities.com/motorcity/track/1629

Corvette Marque Club of Seattle
PO Box 534
Kirkland, WA 98083-0534
206-527-3074
E-mail: crjsvette@aol.com

Founded 1963. 240+ members. Must own a Corvette. Dues: $30/year. Web site: www.corvettemarqueclub.com

Corvettes For Kids Inc
PO Box 23
Sassamansville, PA 19472
610-754-9149; FAX: 610-754-6476

Founded 1986. PA non-profit organization. Annual Corvette show second Sunday of August. Proceeds of which benefit local families of children with life threatening illnesses and disabling conditions.

Corvettes of Enid
PO Box 1285
Enid, OK 73702
580-233-6555

Founded 1992. 50 members. Interest in preserving, maintenance, restoration and having fun with America's only two-seater sports car. Monthly meets, monthly events, monthly newsletter. Dues: $25/year.

The Corvettes of Lancaster
2275 Blue Valley Rd
Lancaster, OH 43130
740-746-8570, 614-833-ANGL

Founded 1972. 80 members. Must own a Corvette and enjoy driving on rallies, hosting cruises, helping to organize and work shows and help with the 13th annual Earth Angel Super Cruise and Car Show. Non-profit and charity event. Monthly newsletter. Dues: $25/year. Web site: http://clubs.hemmings.com/corvettes/

Corvettes of Sonoma County Inc
Gary Michaud
PO Box 1318
Rohnert Park, CA 94927
707-829-7173; FAX: 707-829-8955

Founded 1979. 100 members. Must be an owner of a Corvette. Fun runs, socials, monthly meeting, overnighters, monthly newsletter. Club does swap meets yearly, money raised for charities. Dues: $40/year.

Corvettes of Southern California
PO Box 3603
Anaheim, CA 92803
714-776-6416
E-mail: vettedoc@aol.com

Founded 1956. 225 members. Must be registered owner of Corvette and 21 years old. Dues: $30/year.

Corvettes of the North
3403 Pelot Ln
Milladore, WI 54454
715-435-3707

Founded 1972. Over 80 cars. Must own a Corvette and be over 18 years of age. Our club has many rallies, tours and other events throughout the year. We also host the Wisconsin Rapids Car Show weekend. Dues: $25/year.

Corvettes of the Ozarks
PO Box 191
Mountain Home, AR 72654
870-431-8546
E-mail: rcyoung@superiorinter.net

Founded 1990. 60 members. Membership requires Corvette ownership, associate member does not require Corvette ownership. 4 or 5 cruises per year, caravan to car shows, host a major car (Vette) show, annual banquet, newsletter, monthly meetings, share the Corvette hobby. Dues: $35/year.

Corvettes of Western Australia Inc
PO Box 88
Innaloo City WA 6918 Australia
08 9446 6243; FAX: 08 9445 7738

Founded 1982. 140 members. The purpose is to encourage the preservation, restoration and enjoyment of all Corvettes. Membership is available to all Corvette owners and enthusiasts. A non-profit organization, meets and events advised in our newsletter, *West Coast Vette Torque*. Dues: $40/year.

Corvettes Unlimited
PO Box 33433
Granada Hills, CA 91394-0059
818-368-9059

Founded 1966. 28 members. Must own a Corvette. Members compete in car shows, races, rallies and attend various Corvette functions. NCCC membership is included with insurance coverage for events.

Corvettes Unlimited Corvette Club Inc
1120 Fairmount Ave
Vineland, NJ 08360
856-692-8930; FAX: 856-205-1409
E-mail: red63vette@icdc.com

Benjamin F Notaro Jr, President. Founded 1977. 250 members. Must own a Corvette. South Jersey's largest Corvette club. Meetings are second Wednesday of each month. Membership includes monthly newsletter, *Fiberglass Flyer* and club's magazine (3 times), *Cruisin' News*. Dues: $25/year couple. Web site: www.corvettesunlimitednj.com

Corvettes West (Car Club)
Lou Winget, PR
PO Box 945
Colton, CA 92324
909-389-9323, FAX: 909-389-9363
E-mail: coup84@aol.com

Founded 1972. 200 members. Restricted to owners of Corvette automobiles. Newsletter published monthly. Club outings and events monthly, annual sponsor of Big Bear Bash premier Corvette gathering, member discounts, charitable supporter of National Kidney Foundation, Ronald McDonald House, etc. Dues: $60/year. Web site: www.corvetteswest.com

Cyclone Corvettes Inc
3028 Northridge Pkwy
Ames, IA 50014-4581
515-292-0017

Founded 1978. 100 members. Only need interest in Corvettes. Monthly club newsletter *'Vette Lines*. Meetings, social events and parties, road trips and cruises, car shows and competitive events, Funkhanas, road rallies. Receive membership packet, jacket patch, club parts discounts, camaraderie. Sponsor of annual All Iowa Corvette Fest. Dues: $20/year active; $10/year associate. Web site: www.members.home.com/cyclonevette/

Essex County Corvette Club
177 Cameron Ave
Windsor, ON Canada N9B 1Y5
519-258-2071; FAX: 519-258-2036
E-mail: eccc@wincom.net

Founded 1995. 30 members. Monthly newsletter with free buy and sell section. Yearly Corvette and all car show. We currently mail to Canada, USA and Spain. Dues: $50/year. Web site: www.thewing.com/eccc

GMC Corvette Set
4721 Ardmore
Sterling Hgts, MI 48310
810-939-9146

Founded 1976. 135 members. Group of Corvette owners and enthusiasts with varying interest in restoring, showing and promoting Corvettes. Meetings are held the first Tuesday of each month. Membership is restricted to owners and enthusiasts of Corvettes, members must be at least 21 years of age and attend two of three consecutive meetings. Membership requires mandatory participation in the annual club car show and swap meet. Benefits: monthly club newsletter, free club shirt, free swap meet space in the club area during a club sponsored event, participation with other Corvette enthusiasts, advice or help in locating parts and service, Bill Fox Chevrolet special disounts on vehicles and parts. Dues: $40/year new; $30/year renewal.

Interior Corvetters' Associaton
2021 Tomat Ave
Kelowna, BC Canada V1Z 3L1
250-769-4003
E-mail: akregier@silk.net

Founded 2000. 6 members. Own a Corvette, all events on web site, no meetings. Dues: none. Web site: www.intca.virtualave.net

International Society Corvette Owners
PO Box 740614
Orange City, FL 32774
904-775-1203; FAX: 904-775-3042

Founded 1993. 3,000+/- members. Open to all Corvette enthusiasts. Bi-monthly newsletter, super Corvette insurance, two annual events, conventions, St Ignace, MI, in September, Fort Pierce, FL in January. Certification, logo merchandise. Dues: $27/year.

Liberty Region Corvette Club
PO Box 753
Fort Washington, PA 19034
215-757-6270; FAX: 215-281-9618
E-mail: mgarozzo@bciu.k12.pa.us

Founded 1997. 100 members. Must be a Corvette owner. Fall Corvette show. Caravans to dinner, shows, racing and other activities. Monthly general membership meetings 3rd Thursday of each month. Dues: $35/year, $55/year. Check web site for calendar. Web site: http://clubs.hemmings.com/liberty/

Majestic Glass Corvette Club
1103-23rd St
Anacortes, WA 98221
360-675-6251
E-mail: doublej@whidbey.net

Founded 1974. 120 members. Must own a Corvette, have valid driver's license and insurance, receive monthly newsletter, have average of 2 scheduled runs a month, 4 car shows a year, several weekend getaways. Dues: $25/year. Web site: www.geocities.com/~mgcc

Mid Maine Vettes
PO Box 265
Auburn, ME 04212-0265
207-782-8952

Founded 1979. 24 members. Must own Corvette. Publishes monthly newletter, schedules various Corvette related activities during the year. Dues: $20/year.

Midwest Early Corvette Club
1606 N 85th St
Omaha, NE 68114
402-391-5270

Founded 1972. 100+ members. Open to anyone who owns or has an interest in Corvettes. Monthly meetings, socialize and share information, monthly newsletter. Annual swap meet and car show 1st Sunday in June, annual Halloween rally and party, All Corvette Show and other shows at malls, World of Wheels, etc. Dues: $9/year single, $12/year couple.

Mohawk Valley Corvette Club
c/o 150 Forrest St
Deerfield, NY 13502
315-732-6629
E-mail: rogermac@borg.com

Founded 1977. 42 members. Must own a Corvette and be 18 years of age or older. Monthly newsletter, annual car show, various cruises, dinner meetings, Christmas party and club picnics. Dues: $40/year. Web site: http://clubs.hemmings.com/mohawkvalleycc

National Corvette Owners Association
900 S Washington St G13
Falls Church, VA 22046
703-533-7222; FAX: 703-533-1153
E-mail: ncoassoc@aol.com

Founded 1975. 20,000 members. For Corvette owners. Discounts on interior products, Chevy dealers, automotive outlets, Corvette auto insurance and more. Monthly publication, *For Vettes Only*. Dues: $39/year. Web site: www.ncoa-vettes.com

National Corvette Restorers Society
6291 Day Rd
Cincinnati, OH 45252-1334
513-385-8526, 513-385-6367
FAX: 513-385-8554
E-mail: info@ncrs.org

Founded 1974. 14,000 members. Membership is open to persons interested in the restoration, preservation and history of 1953-1982 Corvettes. 36 chapters in the US and foreign. Dues: $30/year US; $35/year Canada; $45/year foreign. Web site: www.ncrs.org

chapters

Alabama   *Southeast Chapter*, Jimmy McCutcheon, 205-967-8567; Web site: www.ncrssoutheastchapter.com

Tennessee Valley Chapter, Gary Wylie, 256-837-2886; E-mail: edwardmccomas@hsv.bna.boeing.com

Arizona   *Southwest Chapter*, Abe Feder, 480-839-5320

California   *Northern California Chapter*, Bob Grauer, 925-672-2523; Web site: www.netwiz.net/~steveb/index.htm

Southern California Chapter, Joyce Vario, 310-672-0330; Web site: www.ocnow.com/community/groups/sccncrs

Colorado   *Rocky Mountain Chapter*, Dennis Kazmierzak, 303-697-8428; Web site: www.ncrsrmc.org

Connecticut   *Northeast Chapter*, Jerry Cribbs, 203-272-4651

Florida   *Florida Chapter*, Ed Augustine, 352-394-6547; Web site: www.ncrsfl.com

Illinois   *Illinois Chapter*, Jay Stahl, 815-623-7562

Indiana   *Indiana Chapter*, Donna Hanner, 812-579-9152; Web site: members.iquest.net/~ncrs

Iowa   *Heartland Chapter*, Dick Bennett, 515-987-1410

Louisiana   *Louisiana Chapter*, James Youens, 337-334-9037; E-mail: j.youens@cox-internet.com

Maryland   *Mason-Dixon Chapter*, Dennis Moore, 410-879-2542; Web site: members.tripod.com/~masdix/masdix1.htm

Massachusetts   *New England Chapter*, Steve Cataldo, 978-774-7405

Michigan   *Michigan Chapter*, John Davin, 248-650-8363; Web site: www.michigan_ncrs.homestead.com

Minnesota   *North Central Chapter*, Ron Hendrickson, 651-484-6306

Missouri   *Kansas City Chapter*, Dana Forrester, 816-478-0427

Saint Louis Chapter, Jim Augustus, 636-462-4231

New Jersey   *Central New Jersey Chapter*, Edward DiNapoli, 732-297-4280

Delaware Valley Chapter, Charlie Busnack, 908-236-2524

New Mexico   *New Mexico Chapter*, Bilie Pyzel, 505-883-0291; E-mail: fallen@unm.edu

New York   *Adirondack Chapter*, Wayne Hammill, 518-587-3269

Metro-Long Island Chapter, Sergio Fernandez, 718-762-2606

Western New York Chapter, Jim Miller, 716-377-5214

North Carolina   *Carolinas Chapter*, Jimmy Gregg, 704-847-5408

Ohio   *Lake Erie Chapter (Northern Ohio)*, Steve Steffensen, 614-899-0643; E-mail: steves@eastman.com

Queen City Chapter (Southern Ohio), Tim Mickey, 513-984-8604; E-mail: ncrscincy@aol.com

Oklahoma   *Oklahoma Chapter*, Neal Kennedy, 918-749-8084

Pennsylvania   *Pittsburgh Tri-State Chapter*, Tom Barr, 724-853-0306; Web site: members.xoom.com/ncrs_pitt

Texas   *Texas Chapter*, Tom O'Grady, 281-292-6522; Web site: www.ncrstexas.org

Utah   *Bonneville Chapter*, Sergay Liston, 801-270-0272

Virginia   *Mid-Atlantic Chapter*, Bill Sangrey, 703-759-2160; Web site: www.ncrsmac.org

Washington   *Northwest Chapter*, Carl Davidson, 206-524-9312; E-mail: davcarl@aol.com

Wisconsin   *Wisconsin Chapter*, Jeff Zarth, 608-873-0703; E-mail: trailer@zarthtrailer.com

Canada   *Ontario Chapter*, Chris Kayser, 416-237-1264; Web site: www.homestead.com/ontari-oncrs

Quebec Chapter, Robert Cracower, 514-337-8220; Web site: www.ncrsquebec.com

United Kingdom   *United Kingdom Chapter*, Trevor Rogers, 01144(0) 20 1732 462 281 (+5 hours from the West Coast); Web site: www.ncrs.co.uk

National Council of Corvette Clubs (NCCC)
3701 S 92nd St
Milwaukee, WI 53228-1611
800-245-VETT
E-mail: sezmajeb@execpc.com

Founded 1960. 13,000 members. A non-profit club dedicated to the enhancement, promotion and enjoyment of the Corvette. A service organization that provides communication and exchange of ideas between members and promotes activities on a national scale. Must own a Corvette to join. Dues: $30/new membership, $20/renewal. Web site: www.corvettesnccc.org

Natural Glass Corvette Association
219 S New Jersey Ave
Lake Hopatcong, NJ 07849
973-663-5476
E-mail: ngca@bigfoot.com

Founded 1972. 100 members. *Glass Flash* newsletter, parts discounts, annual open car show, social events, technical help and driving events. Dues: $30/year. Web site: www.geocities.com/ngca_99

New England Corvette Club
PO Box 5909
New Bedford, MA 02742
508-984-7291
E-mail: corvette@ici.net

Founded 1997. 38 members. Must own a Corvette. Club meets every month on second to the last Tuesday of the month. We publish a monthly/weekly club newsletter, host Corvette and all-car shows and cruise nights. Dues: $35/year.

North Central Corvette Club of PA
43 S 3rd St
Hughesville, PA 17737
PH/FAX: 570-584-3644
E-mail: frcvette@yahoo.com

Founded 1992. 84 members. Dues: $10/year. Visit us on the web at: http://clubs.hemmings.com/ncccpa

North Shore Corvettes of Mass
18 Heather Dr
Wilmington, MA 01887
978-658-9701
E-mail: bjansen@mediaone.net

Founded 1965. 150 members. Meetings are 3rd Thursday of month at Wakefield Elks, Wakefield, MA; Tuesday night cruise night at Uno's, starts May until September. Call for information. Dues: $25/year. Web site: www.northshorecorvettes.com

Oceanside Vettes
23 Page Ave
Wiscasset, ME 04578
207-882-9617; FAX: 207-882-9086
E-mail: labaree@ibm.net

Founded 1997. Oceanside Vettes serves the state of Maine. Named for the famous Corvette weekend that was hosted in Maine for 17 years, the club is dedicated to fun, fellowship and sharing a common interest in Corvettes. Corvette ownership not required. The club hosts monthly meetings, social events and activities year round as well as an annual weekend event open to all Corvette clubs and enthusiasts. Dues: $20/year.

The Original Circle City Corvette Club Inc
9320 E Prospect St
Indianapolis, IN 46239
317-898-2222; FAX: 317-89-VETTE
E-mail: philsvette@aol.com

Founded 1977. 46 members. Must own Corvette. Meetings 1st Thursday at Blossom Chevrolet, 1800 N Shadeland Ave at 7 pm and the 3rd Wednesday of the month at the Moose, 7200 E 16th St. Rallies, parades, homecomings and car shows. Club and national dues: $65/year.

Ozaukee Corvette Club
PO Box 371
Cedarburg, WI 53012
414-284-0773

Founded 1979. For enthusiasts to get together and participate in activities with America's only true sports car, the Chevrolet Corvette. A social organization rather than a strict competitive group with activities that are geared toward individual and family enjoyment. Dues: $15/year individual, $20/year family.

Presque Isle Corvette Club
PO Box 604
Erie, PA 16512
814-838-6546; FAX: 814-899-6090
E-mail: apzz3vette@cs.com

Founded 1972. 20 members. Must own a Corvette. 6 month probation period, monthly newsletter and meeting, annual car show, charity cruise in and various other activities. Dues: $36/year.

Rebel Corvette Club of the Bluegrass
857 Glen Abbey Cir
Lexington, KY 40509
859-263-3478; FAX: 859-264-7306
E-mail: eddadams@home.com

Founded 1981. 85 members. Must own a Corvette. Dues: $20/year per person.

Regina Corvette Club
PO Box 496
Regina, SK Canada S4P 3A8
E-mail: sparent@sk.sympatico.ca

Founded 1981. 45 members. Must own a Corvette and conduct oneself accordingly. Celebrating 20th anniversary in 2001, hosting convention of Canadian Council of Corvette Clubs, Western Region, September 1-3, 2001. Dues: $25/year Canadian. Web site: www.geocities.com/shayneandlee/reginacorvet.html

Richmond County Corvette Club Inc
Jack Pally, President
PO Box 60456
Staten Island, NY 10306
718-979-7231
E-mail: rccorvette@aol.com

Founded 1995. 60 members. You must own a Corvette or buy one within a year of joining. Local businesses offer members' discounts on new and used cars, auto repairs, auto parts and related merchandise. We participate in a club picnic, local parades, car shows, cruise nights, club drives and member to member information and help. Dues: $50/year. Web site: www.sistuff.com/rccorvette

River Cities Corvette Club
9113 Stonecrest Dr
Louisville, KY 40272
502-935-2598; FAX: 502-935-2074

Founded 1986. 75 members. Must own Corvette. Publish local monthly newsletter. Volunteer car club for National Corvette Museum events. Dues: $30/year.

River City Corvette Club
6106 Turtle Pointe Dr
Hixson, TN 37343
423-847-8030
E-mail: gtalley99_99@juno.com

Founded 1983. We now have 102 members. Do not have to own a Corvette, just be an enthusiast. We currently have members that own from a 1957-2001 year model. Dues: $25/year. Web site: www.rivercitycorvetteclub.com

Santa Clara Corvettes
PO Box 2634
Santa Clara, CA 95055
510-744-0700

96 members. Must own a Corvette. Discounts from club sponsors and friendship, *First Class Glass* newsletter, meeting 1st Wednesday of the month, social events every month and Corvette Spectacular car show in September. Dues: $36/year. Web site: www.geocities.com/motorcity/7333/

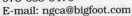

Silver City Corvette Club
2 Golen Dr
North Dartmouth, MA 02747
PH/FAX: 508-991-4630
E-mail: bamvette88@aol.com

Founded 1983. 25 members. Attend most southeastern New England Corvette events. Monthly newsletter, *Silver Streak*. Dues: $30/year.

Skyline Drive Corvettes Inc
PO Box 14231
Reading, PA 19612
E-mail: info@skylinedrivecorvettes.org

Founded 1964. 250 members. Monthly newsletter, Corvette shows, cruises, parades, rallies, mystery tours. Dues: $20/year. Web site: www.skylinedrivecorvettes.org

**Solid Axle Corvette Club,
Illinois Chapter**
1942 Concord Arenzville Rd
Chapin, IL 62628-9740
217-457-2555
E-mail: saccmb@hotmail.com

Founded 1987. 30 members. Must have an interest in 1953-1962 Corvettes. Host regional in conjunction with Bloomington Gold show. Dues: $24/year. Web site: www.solidaxle.org

Solid Axle Corvette Club (SACC)
Box 2288
North Highlands, CA 95660-8288
916-991-7040
E-mail: sacc@bigfoot.com

Founded 1986. 800 members. SACC is a national club dedicated to enjoying the 1953-1962 Corvettes. Founder: Noland Adams. Membership is a family membership. Ownership is not required and dues include a subscription to quarterly magazine. Provides technical panel assistance with annual national convention and regional meets. Show locations are selected to provide activities for the whole family and suitable facilities for the Corvette. Dues: $24/year US, $30/year Canada, $40/year foreign. Web site: www.solidaxle.org

**Southeastern Wisconsin
Corvette Club**
1467 32 Ave
Kenosha, WI 53144
262-552-9672

Founded in 1973. 70 members. Monthly meeting and newsletter. Must support club organizations. Annual Chevy car show in Bristol, WI, 80 awards given away. Dues: $25/year. Web site: www.sewcc.com

Spokane Corvette Club
PO Box 3032 TA
Spokane, WA 99220
509-922-8142; FAX: 509-495-8054

Founded 1966. 70 families. Corvette owners, monthly meetings, web site, newsletter, cruises. Dues: $40/year. Web site: www.corvette-club.spokane.wa.us

Steeltown Corvette Club
1707 Jancey St
Pittsburgh, PA 15206
412-361-3750

Founded 1972. 260 members. Open to all Corvette enthusiasts. Monthly meetings and newsletter. Annual car show, Christmas party and picnic. Other events include cruises, drag racing, auto cross and road rallies. Numerous parties and fun driving events including weekend road trips. Dues: $20/year.

Stuart Corvette Club
PO Box 1083
Port Salerno, FL 34992
561-466-5366

Founded 1988. 104 members. Own or lease a Corvette. Dues: $40/year. Web site: www.stuartcorvetteclub.com

Three Rivers Corvette Club
PO Box 85
South Park, PA 15129
412-343-7639
E-mail: 3riversvette@homestead.com

Founded 1980. 328 members. Anyone liking Corvettes is welcome, you don't have to own one to belong. Meetings second Wednesday of January, March, May, June, July, August, September and November. Cruising after the summer meetings. Dues: $25/year couple, $20/year single. Web site: www.3riversscorvetteclub.homestead.com/3rivers.html

Thunder Vette Set
PO Box 483
Sierra Vista, AZ 85636
520-378-6498
E-mail: woodst@c2i2.com

Founded 1986. 48 members. Meets 1st Thursday every month at the VFW. Publishes 6 issues a year club newsletter. Member NCCC and has 7 sanctioned events a year plus local club events. Dues: $12/year.

Treasure State Corvette Club
PO Box 6051
Helena, MT 59601
406-442-0650
E-mail: hamillmt@initco.net

Founded 1979. 37 members. Corvette interest only restriction. Newsletter once a month to members and other car clubs. Dues: $25/year single, $35/year couple.

Vettes in Perfection Ltd
1000 Waterford Rd
Mechanicville, NY 12118
518-664-7344; FAX: 518-664-2908
E-mail: auto@midtel.net

Founded 1983. 65 members. Open to all Corvette owners over the age of 21. Corvette only car show and road rallies, social events and Corvette related activities. Non-profit organization for charity. Dues: $50/year. Web site: http://club.hemmings.com/viperfection and www.marcelscorvette.com

Wasaga Beach Corvette Club
PO Box 305
Wasaga Beach, ON Canada L0L 2P0
866-VETCLUB
PH/FAX: 705-735-4051
E-mail:
wasagabeachcorvetteclub@on.aibn.com

Founded 1991. 50 members. Own a Vette, newsletter, holds largest Corvette event in Canada, meets 1st Tuesday of month in Wasaga Beach, ON, Canada. Dues: $60/year Canadian. Web site: www.wasaga.com/corvetteclub

Windy City Corvettes Inc
PO Box 353
Orland Park, IL 60462-0353
708-403-0129; FAX: 708-873-9519
E-mail: shadowlp@worldnet.att.net

Founded 1990. 175 members. Must own a Corvette (any year). Benefits: includes National Council of Corvettes membership, monthly club newsletter, quarterly NCCC magazine, events scheduled every weekend, liability insurance provided for all events and club activities. Dues: $40/year, $55/year couple. Web site: www.windycitycorvettes.com

Yakima Valley Vettes
PO Box 2373
Yakima, WA 98907
509-966-4462; FAX: 509-965-9681
E-mail: stngray@wolfenet.com

Founded 1973. 65 members. Must have Corvette to join. Have runs, events and monthly newsletter. Dues: $45/year.

Airflow Club of America
796 Santree Cir
Las Vegas, NV 89110-3939
702-438-4362; FAX: 702-438-8450
E-mail: gdayluv@earthlink.net

For membership information, contact at the above address: Bill Gordon, 702-468-4362. Founded 1962. 600 members. Should be Chrysler or DeSoto Airflow owner or enthusiast. Monthly newsletters including membership roster. National meets annually. Dues $25/year US, $32/year outside North America (US funds).

California Chrysler Products Club
PO Box 2660
Castro Valley, CA 94546
510-886-0931
E-mail: ccpc1967@home.com

Founded 1967. 450 members. Dedicated to the preservation, restoration and enjoyment of Chrysler product cars and literature. Open to all years and models of Chrysler products. Publication, *Silver Dome Gazette*. Dues: $15/year. Web site: http://clubs.hemmings.com/ccpc/index.html

Chrysler 300 Club Inc
PO Box 570309
Miami, FL 33257-0309
800-416-3443; FAX: 305-253-5978
E-mail: chrysler300@juno.com

Founded 1969. 900 members. No restrictions to join. Recognizes all letter and non-letter 300 automobiles. Bi-monthly newsletter, *Brute Force*, technical advice, buy and sell ads for Chrysler parts and cars, articles submitted by members, historical articles on 300 cars. Reporting of National 300 meets and show calendar. Visa/MasterCard accepted. Dues: $25/year USA, $30/year Canada (US funds only), $35/year foreign.

Chrysler 300 Club International Inc
4900 Jonesville Rd
Jonesville, MI 49250
517-849-2783; FAX: 517-849-7445
E-mail: crossram@optonline.net

For membership information, contact at the above address: Eleanor Riehl. Founded 1969. 950 members. Ownership of a 1955-1965 letter series 300 or a 1970 Hurst 300 preferred, but any interested person may join. Eight publications per year offering technical assistance, cars and parts locating assistance, classifieds as well as announcements of national and international meets. Dues: $20/year US and foreign. Web site: www.classicar.com/clubs/chrysler/300club.htm

Chrysler Town and Country Owners Registry
John Slusar, Membership Chairman
10240 W National Ave, PMB #121
West Allis, WI 53227
414-384-1843
E-mail: tandcregistry@cs.com

Founded 1973. 400 members. Quarterly magazine, *Timber Tales*, annual registry, meets held in conjunction with WPC Club and National Woodie Club. Specializing in 1941-1950 Chrysler Town and Country cars, 1949-1950 Chrysler Royal wagons, 1983-1986 LeBaron Town and Country convertibles only. Dues: $35/year 1st class, $40/year foreign.

Slant 6 Club of America
PO Box 4414
Salem, OR 97302
503-581-2230

Founded 1980. 2,000 members. Open to all slant 6 Chrysler products, especially Darts and Valiants. Ownership not required for membership. 20 regional chapters with meets and other events. Dues: $25/year. Web site: http://clubs.hemmings.com/slant6clubofamerica/

Citroen Quarterly USA
PO Box 130030
Boston, MA 02113-0001
617-742-6604
E-mail: citq@aol.com

Founded 1976. Members nationwide. Provides source of Citroen information, camaraderie, national rendezvous. Will host 12th International Citroen Car club Rally August 9-11th, 2002 in Amherst, MA. Membership includes a subscription to *Citroen Quarterly*, the journal of the Citroeniste. Sample issue $5. Dues: $20/year, $25/year overseas airmail. Web site: www.icccr.org

Cooper Car Club Ltd
17 Waterlaide Rd
Hartlebury, Worcestershire DY117TP
United Kingdom
+44(0)1299250227
FAX: +44(0)1215574177
E-mail: woody@coopercars.org

Founded 1987. 185 members. Worldwide organization to promote the use and restoration of Cooper cars. Also to recognize a place in motor racing history for Charles and John Cooper. Quarterly newsletter. Dues: £15 ($22)/year. Web site: www.coopercars.org

Crosley Automobile Club
217 N Gilbert
Iowa City, IA 52245-2125
319-338-9132
E-mail: cac@crosley.net

Founded 1969. 1,300 members. Quarterly magazine; hot sheet with want ads 4 times per year; annual meet, Wauseon, OH in July, several regional clubs. Dues: $15/year. Web site: www.ggw.org/cac

North Star Crosley
4716 Stinson Blvd NE
Columbia Heights, MN 55421
763-574-1743
E-mail: crosley@minn.net

Founded 1978. 50 members. Must be a member of the Crosley Automobile Club Inc, quarterly newsletter, *North Star Notes*. Dues: $2/year. Web site: http://clubs.hemmings.com/northstarcrosley

Cushman Club of America
PO Box 661
Union Springs, AL 36089
334-738-3874; FAX: 334-738-2711
E-mail: ccoa@ustconline.net

Founded 1980. 5,000 members. Bi-monthly member magazine, national meet. Dedicated to the restoration and preservation of Cushman motor scooters. Dues: $25/year. Web site: http://clubs.hemmings.com/cushmanclubofamerica/

Daewoo Car Club of America©
PO Box 3783
Riverside, CA 92519-3783
877-4-DAEWOO

Founded 1999. 12 members. The DCCA is the very first Daewoo car club in the USA and in North America. A prospective member must be an owner or leasee of a Daewoo auto. Currently, only members of the club receive the *Daewoo Driver Newsletter©*. Dues: $25/year. Web site: www.daewoocarclub.com

DAF Club-America
275 Hudson St
Hackensack, NJ 07601
201-343-1252, 201-342-3684
FAX: 201-342-3568

Founded 1980. 25 members. West Coast address: 706 Monroe St, Santa Rosa, CA 95405. Club consists of owners of DAF cars and others with an interest in DAFs. Dedicated to the preservation of DAFs and promotion of the CVT transmission pioneered by DAF. Publication: *DAF Bulletin*. Dues: $10/year.

Drone Datsun Roadsters of New England
16 Elizabeth St
Littleton, MA 01460
978-486-4075
E-mail: ale@ultranet.com

Founded 1996. 15 members. Open to anyone who likes vintage Datsuns. We have 4 meets a year with a road trip to Watkins Glen for Vintage Weekend in September. Dues: none.

Gateway Z Club
PO Box 3694
Ballwin, MO 63022
314-909-7410
E-mail: brianlzx@netscape.net

Founded 1976. 40 members. The Gateway Z Club is a not for profit organization comprised of owners of Datsun/Nissan sports cars. We share a driving interest in the care, preservation and maintenance of the Z cars. members receive discounts, a membership card and decal, as well as a monthly newsletter. Dues: $30/year. Web site: www.gatewayzclub.com

Group Z Sports Car Club of Southern California
PO Box 10497
Santa Ana, CA 92711
714-544-3308
E-mail: president@groupz.com

Founded 1970. 100 members. We meet the 2nd Thursday of each month at Fuddrucker's in Buena Park, CA, Beach Blvd and Orangethorpe Ave. All Z and ZX lovers welcome. Dues: $30/year. Web site: www.groupz.com

Nissan Patrol Club America
204 Hermosa NE
Albuquerque, NM 87108
505-321-6664; FAX: 505-262-1733
E-mail: nissanpatrol@att.net

Founded 1999. 275 members. The NPCA collects and distributes information via its web site for Patrol owners in the USA and Canada. This club is for owners of Patrols imported between 1962 and 1969. Dues: none. Web site: http://communities.msn.com/nissanpatrolclubalbuquerque

Z Club of Georgia
333 England Pl
Marietta, GA 30066
770-926-2390; FAX: 770-428-2780
E-mail: hcostanzo@gowebway.com

Founded 1992. 300 members. Must own a Z or ZX. Discounts, rallies, autocross, road racing, monthly newsletter. Monthly meeting 1st Tuesday at Hooter's, Jimmy Carter Blvd, Norcross, GA. Dues: $25/single, $30/family. Web site: www.georgiazclub.com

The Davis Automobile Club
527 Backus Rd
Webster, NY 14580
716-787-2880
E-mail: thedavisman@hotmail.com

Founded 2000. 3 members. No restrictions. This is a club for the 4-wheel Davis automobile. Purpose: to help source cars and parts. Dues: none.

Club Delahaye
B P 15
59640 Dunkerque
France
3 28 29 68 68; FAX: 3 28 61 07 32
E-mail: plooyen@looyen.fr

Two road meets in different towns in France each year as well as club sponsored dinners in Paris. Bulletin published four times a year. Dues: 500 francs/year. Web site: www.clubdelaye.com

DeLorean Midatlantic
1125 W Washington St
Allentown, PA 18102
610-434-9117
E-mail: dmc4414@aol.com

Founded 1985. 125 members. All DeLorean enthusiasts welcome. Annual regional meet. Monthly tech-socials, including free door adjustment social. Parts interchange list. Technical advisories. Dues: $15/year. Web site: http://clubs.hemmings.com/deloreanmidatlantic/

DeLorean Owners Association
879 Randolph Rd
Santa Barbara, CA 93111
PH/FAX: 805-964-5296
E-mail: delorean@impulse.net

Founded 1983. 2,000 members. Conducts national and regional events. Non-profit. Dues: $60/year US, $75/year foreign. Web site: www.delorean.com

De Soto Club of America
403 S Thornton St
Richmond, MO 64085
816-470-3048
E-mail: desotoclub@aol.com

For membership information, contact at the above address: Walter O'Kelly. Founded 1972. Dedicated to preserving and restoring the De Soto automobile. Publishes newsletter: *De Soto Days*, bimonthly. Dues: $15/year.

De Soto Owners Club of MD Inc
Ferd Driver, President
3301 Clipper Mill Rd
Millers, MD 21102
410-329-6509

Founded 1976. 175 members. Newsletter published every 2 months, lots of activities involving antique cars. Open to all. Dues: $10/year.

National De Soto Club Inc
PO Box 50652
Mendota, MN 55150
E-mail: desotodriver@cs.com

Founded 1986. 1,600 members. The purpose of the club is to promote the restoration, preservation and enjoyment of the De Soto automobile. Ownership of a De Soto is not required for membership. Club services include advisors for yearly models of De Sotos, a salvage yard directory, national conventions, a club store and a bi-monthly publication. Dues: $18/year. Web site: www.desoto.org

Pantera International
18586 Main St, Suite 100
Huntington Beach, CA 92648
714-848-6674; FAX: 714-843-5851

Founded 1973. Members worldwide. DeTomaso factory authorized. Ownership not required. Publishing quarterly color magazine and authoritative book. Your leading source for technical, collecting, restoration, vintage racing, historical, personality and feature car information. Many cars for sale. Annual convention in Monterey each August where we are the sole sponsoring club for the DeTomaso marque at the Concours Italiano. Club store has many DeTomaso theme items. Dues: $55/year US, $70/year foreign. Web site: www.panteracars.com

Pantera Owner's Club of America (POCA)
Forest Majors
PO Box 459
Hadlyme, CT 06439
860-526-5901; FAX: 860-526-4446
E-mail: membership@panteraclub.com

Founded 1973. 950 members. The Pantera Owner's Club of America, a not-for-profit organization, is the official factory recognized DeTomaso club in the United States. Through 15 regional chapters, POCA offers speed, social and technical events plus an annual fun rally in Las Vegas. Members receive an informative 32-page monthly newsletter and Profiles, the beautiful color quarterly magazine. Car ownership is not required for membership. Visa, MasterCard are accepted. Dues: $60/year domestic, $75/year foreign. Web site: www.panteraclub.com

Diamond T Register
PO Box 1657
St Cloud, MN 56302
320-632-8664

Founded 1978. 325+ members. Membership includes *Salmagundi*, a semi-annual publication. Magazine format with historical data, member vehicles featured, restoration tips, classified ads, etc. Dues: $16/year US, $21/year Canada, $26/year foreign, all US funds.

Divco Club of America
PO Box 1142
Kingston, WA 98346-1142
360-598-3938
E-mail: editor@divco.org

Founded 1991. Over 1,000 members. Dedicated to the history and preservation of multi-stop delivery trucks, particularly those made by Divco. Newsletter provides information, parts sources, history, help and encouragement, free classifieds for members. Dues: $24/year for individuals, other classes available. Web site: www.divco.org

DKW Club of America
1141 Woodland Ave
Menlo Park, CA 94025
650-321-6640; FAX: 650-329-0129
E-mail: jowett@best.com

For information, contact at the above address: Byron Brill. Serving Auto Union and DKW owners and enthusiasts world-wide. Fun, informative newsletter, parts and information sources and healthy doses of encouragement. Membership: $17/year North America, $23/year elsewhere. Web site: www.dkwclub.org.

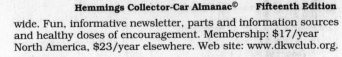

D.A.R.T.S.
PO Box 9
Wethersfield, CT 06129-0009
860-257-8434 evenings 8-10 pm
E-mail: dartsclub@snet.net

Founded 1986. 375 members. A service club for high performance 1967-1972 Dodge Darts and Demons. Quarterly newsletters provide events, technical information and restoration information. Free ads to buy and sell are encouraged to be used. Dues: $10/year. Web site at HMN Car Club Central.

Dodge Brothers Club
PO Box 292
Eastpointe, MI 48021-0292
E-mail: bcogan@ameritech.net

Founded 1983. 1,100 members. Membership inquiries to Barry Cogan at above address. Open to anyone interested in Dodge Brothers or Graham Brothers vehicles 1914-1938. Ownership of vehicle is not required for membership. Membership includes annual meets at locations across the US and Canada. Worldwide membership. Dues: $20/year US and Canadian, $26/year (US funds) foreign. Web site: http://home.wkpowerlink.com/~dodgebrothers/

Hampton Roads Lil' Red Express & Warlock Owners Club
971 Colleen Dr
Newport News, VA 23608
757-875-5270
E-mail: theadventurer@worldnett.att.net

Founded 1994. 195 members. A non-profit, member supported organization dedicated to the restoration and historical preservation of the Dodge Warlock and Lil' Red Express. Membership is open to all 1972-1980 Dodge Stepside pickup owners. Newsletter and annual truck show. Registry. Dues: $10/year. Web site: http://home.att.net/~theadventurer

Shelby Dodge Automobile Club
PO Box 182072
Shelby Township, MI 48318-2072
810-759-6160
E-mail: sdac@sdac.org

The Shelby Dodge Automobile Club (SDAC) is an automotive enthusiast club whose aim is to preserve the spirit of power by Dodge, unleashed by Shelby. The SDAC newsletter, *Up Front*, features articles and information on Shelby Dodge and Dodge Shelby vehicles (Omni GLH, Shelby Charger, GLHS, CSX, Lancer and Shelby Dakota, Daytonas, Shadow, Spirit R/T, Shelby Can Am and Viper and more). Annual national convention. Many local chapters and events. Web site: www.sdac.org

Ghia Enthusiasts Club
(Dual Ghia & Ghia Bodied 50s Cars)
Paul Sable, 29 Forgedale Rd
Fleetwood, PA 19522
610-987-6923; FAX: 610-282-2254
E-mail: docsable@fast.net

Founded 1990. Expanded in 1999 to include Ghia bodied cars of the 1950s. A forum for exchange of information. Open to enthusiasts, owners of Dual Ghias. Owner's registry and parts availability. Annual newsletter. Dues: none.

International Edsel Club
238 Fairview St
Paris, TN 38242
731-642-5356; FAX: 731-642-3399
E-mail: ebarrow@wk.net

Founded 1969. 1,000 members. A family club dedicated to restoring and owning Edsels. Annual meeting 4th weekend in July. Monthly newsletter: *Edseletter*. Dues: $20/year US and Canada, $30/year overseas.

chapters:

Arizona *Roadrunners Edsel Club*, Ty Triplett, 10835 N 45th Pl, Phoenix, AZ 85028 602-996-5844

California *Cal-Neva Chapter*, Steve Johnson, 3890 Gold Ridge Tr, Pollock Pines, CA 95726 530-647-9035

Redwood Empire Edsels Chapter, Michael Cowles, 6090 Valley View Rd, Oakland, CA 94611 510-339-9569

Southern California Chapter, Phil Skinner, PO Box 6784, Fullerton, CA 92834 714-738-1958

Florida *Florida Sunshine Chapter*, Robert Mayer, 1435 Larkspur Dr, Fort Myers, FL 33901 941-278-3251

Georgia *Peach State Edsel Club*, Conrad Kerwath, PO Box 967, Oakwood, GA 30566 770-945-0978

Illinois *Illinois Chapter*, Larry Turner, 6617 W Jones Rd, Peoria, IL 61604 309-676-6617

Indiana *Indiana Chapter*, John Craig, 3970 Hannah Ln, Clayton, IN 46118 317-539-7074

Iowa *Iowa Edsel Club*, Marty Scott, 509 Morton Ave, Des Moines, IA 50313 515-282-6163

Michigan *Michigan Chapter*, Bruce Raymond, 30715 Nine Mile Rd, Farmington Hills, MI 48336 248-471-6852

Minnesota *North Star Chapter*, Fred Aherns, 38033 Lincoln Tr, North Branch, MN 55056 651-674-5554

Missouri *Gateway Edsel Club*, Art Muser, 827 Reed Ave, St Louis, MO 63125 314-631-4590

New Jersey *New Jersey Chapter*, Richard Jump, 3 Hillside Ave, Clayton, NJ 08312 609-881-8956

New York *New York Chapter*, Mike Ternullo, 230 Ferndale Ave, Kenmore, NY 14217 716-876-0264

Ohio *Ohio Chapter*, John Hardy, 118 Hamilton St, Elyria, OH 44035 440-323-8338

Pennsylvania *Keystone Chapter*, Doug Harley, 2155 Wayne Ave, Abingdon, PA 19001 215-886-6665

South Carolina *Blue Ridge Chapter*, Greg Pack, 209 Bryson Dr, Boiling Springs, SC 29316 864-578-2952

Tennessee *Southeastern Chapter*, Lois Barrow, 238 Fairview St, Paris, TN 38242 931-642-5356

Virginia *Virginia-Maryland Chapter*, Jason Gilmore, Box 177, Vinton, VA 24179 540-890-3353

Wisconsin *Wisconsin Chapter*, Bernard Gentz, N 3766 Hwy K Rt 2, Jefferson, WI 53549 920-674-3278

Canada *Canada Chapter*, Merlin Jarmain, 44 Ford Crescent, London, ON N6G 1H9 519-438-8698

Sweden *Europe Chapter*, Lars Salmonson, Box 103, 17522 Jarfalla 468-580-2700

Elgin Motorcar Owners Registry
Attn Jay Wolf
2226 E Apache Ln
Vincennes, IN 47591
812-888-4172; FAX: 812-888-5471
E-mail: jwolf@indian.vinu.edu

Founded 1995. 6 members. A registry trying to track down and keep track of cars made by the Elgin Motorcar Company. Dues: none. Web site: http://beaver.vinu.edu/eowners.htm

North American English & European Ford Registry
PO Box 11415
Olympia, WA 98508
360-754-9585
E-mail: ifhp@aol.com

Founded 1992. 220 members. Now open to all English and European Ford built vehicles. Bi-monthly newsletter, best classifieds for English Ford cars and parts in this hemisphere. Also publish an *Annual Roster and Survival Count*. Call or write for a brochure and membership application. Web site: http://clubs.hemmings.com/naefr

Eshelman Owners Club
PO Box 007
La Jolla, CA 92038-0007
858-454-2628 evenings 6-8 PST
E-mail: singer@wans.net

Excalibur Car Club
1122 S LaJolla Ave
Los Angeles, CA 90035
310-278-0801; FAX: 310-278-0807
E-mail: suite-a@juno.com

Founded 1990. 35 members. Club open to all owners of Excalibur automobiles. Publishes *Circle & Sword*, 5 times yearly. Club newsletter announces club events and contains tech tips. Dues: $35/year.

Ferrari Club Argentino
3 de Febrero 312
Rosario Sta Fe 2000 Argentina
+54 341 425-0040
FAX: +54 341 421-9629
E-mail: romolo@ferrariclub.com.ar

Founded 1998. 40 members. Members: Ferrari owners, events, driving courses, meetings and shows. Dues: $600/year. Web site: www.ferrariclub.com.ar

Ferrari Club of America
PO Box 720597
Atlanta, GA 30358
800-328-0444; FAX: 770-936-9392

Founded 1962. 5,000 members. Open to all Ferrari enthusiasts. Quarterly magazine, monthly news bulletin, annual meet with concours and track event. Club has 15 active regions in the US and Canada each hosting different events. Many regions have their own newsletter. The Ferrari Club of America is a great place to meet other people with Ferrari interests. Ferrari ownership is not mandatory. Dues: $85-$120/year. Web site: www.ferrariclubofamerica.org

Section Three – Clubs & Organizations

Ferraristi Vermont
19 Marble Ave Box 3
Burlington, VT 05401
802-658-1270 ext 201
FAX: 802-658-3873
E-mail: ferrarisvt@aol.com

Founded 1996. 100+ members. A social club for Ferrari owners and enthusiasts. Monthly touring events May-October. Dues: $50/year.

Fiat 500 Club Canada
5289 Hwy 7, Unit 7, PO Box 56600
Woodbridge, ON Canada L4L 8V3
416-837-9376
E-mail: fiat500@home.com

Founded 1998. 120 members. Open to anybody with interest in Fiat 500. 1 international meet every year, show car, obstacle race, newsletter, cruise, spare parts, cars for sale, participates in many community events and fundraising, etc. Dues: none. Web site: http://clubs.hemmings.com/fiat500canada/

Fiat-Lancia Unlimited (FLU)
PO Box 193, Dept HVA
Shillington, PA 19607

Founded 1986. 600 members. Must have interest in Fiat group cars. Ownership not required. Enthusiast group dedicated to keeping the Fiat marque alive in North America. Many activities including annual meet. Bi-monthly newsletter: *Fiat Ricambi*. Ties with other American and foreign clubs. Not just Spyders and X1/9s. Strong Lancia Beta membership. Dues: $20/year US; $26/year Canada; $36/year international.

Fiat Twin Cam Register
1103 E Cartagena St
Long Beach, CA 90807
PH/FAX: 562-427-5358
E-mail: italianfrk@aol.com

Founded 1997. 40 members. No restrictions. Dedicated to the preservation of Fiat twin cam derivatives. Parts exchange and restoration advice. Dues: $20/year.

Rear Engine Fiat Club
PO Box 682
Sun Valley, CA 91353-0682
818-768-3552; FAX: 626-798-7784

Founded 1988 by Jonathan Thompson of *Road & Track* for lovers of rear engine Fiats and derivative cars. Our purpose is to promote the preservation and use of rear engine Fiats and related derivative cars: Fiat 500, 600, 850, X1/9; Lancia Scorpion; Abarth 750, 1000; NSU; Jagst; Autobianchi; Morette; etc. Yearly swap meet, car show, rally, canyon tour, barbecue in southern California. Dues: $15/year US, $30/year international.

Toronto Fiat Club FLU Ontario
c/o Scott McCraw
95 Snowdon Ave
Toronto, ON Canada M4N 2A8
416-487-7169

Founded 1998. 106 members. Canada's only chapter of Fiat Lancia Unlimited, North America's largest Fiat and Lancia club. *Ricambi* published 6-8 times a year, monthly meetings and events. All Italian marques welcome. Dues: $26/year US. Web site: http://clubs.hemmings.com/torontofiatclub

The 54 Ford Club of America
1517 N Wilmot #144
Tucson, AZ 85712
PH/FAX: 520-886-1184
E-mail: jstrobec@ix.netcom.com

Founded 1986. 520 members. Open to 54 Ford owners and those interested in 54 Fords. Quarterly newsletter. Dues: $15/year.

Club Ford Republica Argentina
Lavalle 1454 P5 to OF3
Capital Federal 1048 Argentina
PH/FAX: 4371 8046
E-mail: info@clubfordv8.com.ar

Contact: Gustavo Lafont, 4717 2814. Founded 1989. 170 members. V8 1932-1948. Meet every month. Main event is October 12. Club edits one magazine a year. Dues: $60/year. Web site: www.clubfordv8.com.ar

Country Road As
PO Box 1302
Morganton, NC 28680-1302
828-437-8411
E-mail: piercy42@bigfoot.com

Founded 2000. 15 members. Must also be a member of Model A Restorers Club. Monthly meetings, parades, shows, monthly newsletter. Dues: $20/year. Web site: http://clubs.hemmings.com/countryroads

Cowtown T's Inc
4424 Ideldell Dr
Fort Worth, TX 76116-7611
817-244-2340
E-mail: rggrunewald@juno.com

Founded 1982. 44 members. Monthly newsletter and meetings. Open membership to anyone interested in the Ford Model T. Dues: $15/year.

Crown Victoria Association
PO Box 6
Bryan, OH 43506-0006
419-636-2475; FAX: 419-636-8449
E-mail: fordpart@bright.net

Founded 1977. 1,650 members. Club recognizes all 1954-1956 Fords. Ownership of a car is not essential. Dues: $29/year US and Canada, $45/year foreign, US funds please. Web site: www.classicar.com/clubs/crownvictoria/index.htm

Early Bronco Registry
PO Box 1525
Poway, CA 92074-1525
619-530-2470; FAX: 619-530-2471
E-mail: ssampso11@san.rr.com

Founded 1985. 1,000 members. International association, not-for-profit. Open to anyone interested in the 1966-1977 Ford Bronco. Publish *Horsing Around* monthly, includes tips, trips and classifieds. Dues: $25/year. Web site: www.earlybronco.com

The Early Ford V8 Club of America
PO Box 2122
San Leandro, CA 94577
PH/FAX: 925-606-1925
E-mail: fordv8club@aol.com

Founded 1963. 9,000+ members. 150 regions worldwide. Must be interested in Ford, Mercury or Lincoln products, 1932-1953. A national historical society dedicated to the restoration and preservation of Ford Motor Company vehicles from 1932-1953. Bi-monthly publication, *V8 Times*, is included with membership. Dues: $30/year single, $32/year joint. Web site: www.earlyfordv8.org
regions:

Arizona	Jim LaDuc, PO Box 26243, Tucson, AZ 85726 520-546-4543
	Phil Pittman, 1834 W Navarro Ave, Mesa, AZ 85202 602-246-9531
California	Bruce Blackwell, PO Box 4600, Saticoy, CA 93007 661-268-0040
	Carol Rasmussen, PO Box 3302, Santa Rosa, CA 95404 707-226-5256

Charles Dildine, PO Box 2294, Costa Mesa, CA 92628 714-846-9677

Claude Henry, PO Box 11364, Fresno, CA 93773 559-299-0668

Dan Prager, PO Box 881107, San Diego, CA 92168 619-282-0645

Dan Schwartz, PO Box 60878, Sacramento, CA 95860 916-962-3521

Darrell LaFond, 42139 Camino Santa Barbara, Hayward, CA 94539 510-656-5726

Darrell Radford, PO Box 1911, Atascadero, CA 93423-1911 805-238-2509

Dick Chapman, PO Box 637, Rough & Ready, CA 95959 530-265-3025

Don Stout, 11076 Wicks St, Sun Valley, CA 91352 818-998-7054

Eric Hinrichs, PO Box 3181, Stockton, CA 95269 209-599-5460

Frank Tamayo, PO Box 2364, Castro Valley, CA 94546 510-794-8658

Jay Harris, 4265 Via El Dorado, Fallbrook, CA 92028 760-728-0311

Jim Teves, 350 Fitzpatrick Ct, Dixon, CA 95620 707-746-1012

Joe Immler, PO Box 456, Upland, CA 91786-0456 909-984-1051

Ken Check, PO Box 6864, San Jose, CA 95150 408-923-5661

Leonard Brewer, PO Box 1821, Placerville, CA 95667 530-333-2347

Marvin Nichols, 1119 S Speed St, Santa Maria, CA 93454 805-349-3449

Terry Pooler, 3 Brittany Ln, Chico, CA 95926 530-882-4211

Tom Jenkins, PO Box 354, Danville, CA 94526 925-449-3589

Connecticut Don Yeomans, Fairlane Farm, Broad Brook, CT 06016 860-623-4151

Florida Cecil Goff, PO Box 855, Geneva, FL 32732 407-349-9763

Charles White, PO Box 106, Sanibel Island, FL 33957 941-472-9172

Dan Clevenger, PO Box 12101, Lake Park, FL 33403 561-586-3586

Don Fales, 15250 NW Terrace, Trenton, FL 32693 352-493-0354

John Jackson, 801 E Gatepark Dr, Daytona Beach, FL 32114 904-322-9753

Paul Munyon, 101 Jettie Terrace, Port St Lucie, FL 34983 407-871-1934

Skip Sampson, 8040 SW 135th St, Miami, FL 33156 305-235-1544

Georgia Mitch Gwinn, 2622 Arlene Way, Atlanta , GA 30305 770-971-5329

Idaho Wallace Croghan Jr, 508 Colfax, Boise, ID 83709 208-325-8598

Illinois Don Tessendorf, 310 Kenmore Ave, Bloomington, IL 61704 309-827-2300

Frank Walker, PO Box 67, Knoxville, IL 61448 309-289-2425

John Davidson, 224 E 4th St, Byron, IL 61010 815-874-0136

Ken Bounds, PO Box 4076, Arlington Heights, IL 60006 630-858-9474

Louis Taylor, PO Box 471, Pekin, IL 61554-0471 309-699-1796

Indiana Debbie Sharp, PO Box 1381, Indianapolis, IN 46206 317-243-3172

Jim Brown, PO Box 1914, Highland, IL 46322 219-942-4232

Iowa Chuck Stanley, 3050 Meadow Rd, Adel, IL 50003 515-343-0925

Donald Shafer, 1435 Huntington Rd, Waterloo, IL 50701 319-235-0451

Kansas Warren Brandes, PO Box 1155, Wichita, KS 67201 316-721-5393

Kentucky James Rogers, 926 Hanley Ln, Frankfort, KY 40601 502-695-7080

Robert Ledford, 8610 Michael Ray Dr, Louisville , KY 40219 812-949-6021

Louisiana Gerald Hensen, 70 Belle Haven Dr, Destrehan, LA 70047 504-867-4866

Maine Oscar Blue, 48 Trunk Rd, Steuben, ME 04680 207-422-3987

Maryland Peggy Garrish, 27131 Ridge Rd, Damascusk, MD 20872-1047 410-266-6964

Massachusetts John Caron, PO Box 974, Acton, MA 01720 978-692-6063

Michigan Jack Beggs, 2586 Cheswick, Troy, MI 48084 248-646-5082

John Seeley, 4900 Churchill Rd, Leslie, MI 49251 517-750-3405

Minnesota Jerry Felton, PO Box 20236, Minneapolis, MN 55420 612-873-6754

Missouri David Crawford, PO Box 411844, Kansas City, MO 64141 913-491-4758

The Early Ford V8 Club of America regions (continued)

Doug Williams, PO Box 623, Chesterfield, MO 63006 636-671-0433

Montana Al Jenkins, 4729 Lewis Ave, Billings, MT 59106 406-652-6213

Nebraska James Snyder, 14620 Eastbourne St, Waverly, NE 68462 402-786-2427

Robert McKelvie, PO Box 6155, Omaha, NE 68106 402-333-2253

Nevada Les Cash, PO Box 98, Carson City , NV 89702-0098 775-246-0648

Joseph Hopfer, 2586 Boise St, Las Vegas, NV 89121 702-457-4270

New Jersey John Hunter, 11 Catalpa Rd, Morristown, NJ 07960 201-263-5060

New Mexico Joe Abbin, PO Box 21538, Albuquerque, NM 87154 505-296-7678

New York David Miller, 8855 Haven Circle, Brewerton, NY 13029 315-699-5363

Gene Giuliano, PO Box 51, East Schodack, NY 12063 518-477-6813

Mark Moriarty, PO Box 13514, Rochester, NY 14613 716-786-2876

Ray Beebe, 1551 Hillsboro Rd, Camden, NY 13316 315-245-0728

Tony Cotroneo, 20 Miller Dr, Hopewell Junction, NY 12533 914-226-4181

Wayne Duprez, PO Box 1204, Smithtown, NY 11787 631-265-2597

North Carolina James A Cashman, 246 Lakewood Dr, Wilkesboro, NC 28697 336-921-3729

Jay Temple, PO Box 628, Lexington, NC 27293-0628 336-956-4438

Ted Wilburn, 2508 Carriage Crossing Dr, Matthews, NC 28105 704-847-8756

Ohio Dave Dickey, 4444 Lefevre, Troy , OH 45373 937-339-4250

Ron Wertz, PO Box 1074, Cuyahoga Falls, OH 44223 330-533-4381

Oklahoma Ed Brummett, PO Box 4109, Tulsa, OK 74159 918-371-0744
Howard Shryock, 11200 Glendover Ct, Oklahoma City, OK 73162 405-721-5821

Oregon Dwain Davis, PO Box 3851, Central Point, OR 97502 541-779-5543

Dwain McPherson, PO Box 2291, Eugene, OR 97402 541-688-7653

Jack Zink, PO Box 1635, Roseburg, OR 97970 541-672-1071

Joel Anderson, PO Box 8311, Portland, OR 97202 503-472-0803

Ron Hill, PO Box 9123, Brooks, OR 97305 503-393-1426

Sid Campbell, 1815 Hill St SE, Albany, OR 97321 503-928-8751

Pennsylvania Ed Moran, PO Box 721, Bensalem, PA 19020 215-745-4929

Ed Urbansky, PO Box 12852, Pittsburgh, PA 15241 412-655-4095

Frank Vicente, PO Box 5301, Pleasant Gap, PA 16823 814-867-5517

Rick Slegel, PO Box 162, Blandon, PA 19510 610-926-3061

Rhode Island Paul Sheehan, PO Box 3263, Newport, RI 02840 401-846-2522

Tennessee Charlie Fleenor, 1836 Weaver Pike , Bristol, TN 37620 615-323-3122

Lorne Nedvidek, PO Box 111311, Nashville, TN 37222-1311 615-361-6614

Texas Bill Smith, PO Box 3093, Abilene, TX 79604 915-692-7967

Cpt Alan Bentz, PO Box 202085, San Antonio, TX 78220 830-276-3294

Jack Smith, 18022 Moss Point Dr, Spring, TX 77379 281-427-2575

Joyce Parsons, PO Box 151032, Austin, TX 78515-1032 512-515-5413

Kaye Sinkule, PO Box 460668, Garland, TX 75046-0668 972-475-3487

Murphy Stockton, 1453 FM 17, Grand Saline, TX 75140 214-341-1816

Ronald Allen, PO Box 1782, Amarillo, TX 79105 806-355-3708

Tom Walton, PO Box 592, Arlington, TX 76004 972-262-0324

Weldon Parker, PO Box 125, Hewitt, TX 76643 254-666-2002

Utah Gene M Miller, 2926 Banbury Rd, Salt Lake City, UT 84121 801-943-5893

Vermont John C Woodruff, RR1, Box 32, East Randolph, VT 05041 802-276-3058

Virginia David Westrate, PO Box 1195, Vienna, VA 22183 703-620-9597

Riley W Furrow, PO Box 241, Rocky Mount, VA 24151 540-334-5972

Thomas Anderson Jr, 1806 W Broad St, Richmond, VA 23220 804-272-8432

Washington	Alice Dailey, PO Box 12613, Seattle, WA 98111-4613 425-485-9050
	Don Orvis, PO Box 176, Veradale, WA 99037-0176 509-926-1295
	Gary Sybouts, PO Box 5, Buena Vista, WA 98021 509-452-4485
	Mike Dermond, PO Box 12413, Mill Creek, WA 98082-0413 206-745-8877
	Robby Hall, PO Box 3811, Federal Way, WA 98003 206-764-5788
Wisconsin	Jerry Bergdorf, PO Box 302, Waterford, WI 53185-0302 262-629-5622
Australia	Bryan Stephens, PO Box 546, Mulgrave BC 3170, 61.3.9889.1312
	Danny McCann, PO Box 13, Panania, NS Wales 2213, (02) 9679-1156
	Graham Tonkin, PO Box 332, North Adelaide, South Australia 5006, 82586547
Canada	Ken McKinnon, PO Box 8433, Victoria Central PO, Victoria, BC, V8W 3S1 250-656-2493
	Vernon Kipp, PO Box 21023290 Harwood Ave S, Ajax, ON, L1H 7H2 416-266-1628
	Yvette Decker, PO Box 602, Port Coquitlam, BC, V3B 6H9 604-576-2626
Colorado	Harry Lindsay, PO Box 3137, Littleton, CO 80122 303-703-3073
Denmark	PO Box 1932-534500 Nykoping Birger Blako, SJ Denmark
England	Chris Sanders, RG 12 Fairholm Gardens, Cranham, Upminister Essex, RM141HJ 01708-222729
New Zealand	Doug Tutill, PO Box 97288So Auckland Mail Ctr, Auckland 64-09-410-7113
	PO Box 16-396, Hornby, Christchurch 4
Norway	Harald Marthinsen, PO Box 2353, Bjoelsen, Oslo N-0406 47-66911424
Sweden	Jan Ryden, J. Alkmvist, Folkungagatan 94, SE-11622 Stockholm 08-6407013

Fabulous Fords Forever Inc
PO Box 855
Manchester, TN 37349
931-728-3238

Founded 1992. 23 members. The Fabulous Fords Forever club meets at 7 pm CST the 2nd Monday of each month at Al White Ford Motors. The organization is family oriented and the only restriction is to have an appreciation for Fords and Ford powered vehicles. As a meeting reminder, a brief newsletter is provided just prior to the next meeting. An annual All Ford Show is hosted by FFF on the Town Square, the 2nd Saturday in August. Dues: $12/year.

FoMoCo Owners Club
PO Box 19665
Denver, CO 80219
303-628-5330; FAX: 303-690-4305
E-mail: crown55@juno.com

A national, family oriented, social club devoted to the acquisition, restoration, maintenance and exhibition of all Ford Motor Co 4-wheeled vehicles from 1903 thru 15 years old.

Ford-Freak Club of Finland
PO Box 351
00531 Helsinki Finland
+358-40-5254114
E-mail: ffcf@nic.fi

Founded 1987. 200 members. For all US Ford fans. Keep up good Ford humor, *Ford-Freak* magazine 4 times year. Meets: Nestori snow race, Freak's Peak, swap and meet. Dues: 100 FIM/year. Web site: www.nic.fi/~ffcf

Ford Galaxie Club of America
4583 Wilburn Dr
Everton, AR 72633
870-429-8264; FAX: 870-429-8265
E-mail: galaxieclub@collector.org

Founded 1983. 2,100 members. FGCOA is an association dedicated to the restoration, preservation and enjoyment of the Galaxie passenger automobiles built by the Ford Motor Company from 1959-1974. The main goal of this club is to unite Galaxie owners the world over, and to preserve the name 'Galaxie' and its association as one of the first muscle cars of the 1960s in perpetuity. Dues: $30/year US, $35/year Canada and Mexico, $50/year others. Web site: www.galaxieclub.com

Ford Motorsports Enthusiasts
PO Box 1331
Dearborn, MI 48120-1331
313-438-2001
E-mail: teamfme@teamfme.com

Founded 1995. 1,500+ members. Track days and FME discounts plus special annual events and discount race tickets and auto parts, in addition to monthly meetings with guest speakers. *First On Race Day* is published 4-6 times per year and is included in membership dues. Also *FME Business Directory* is published annually in April. Dues: $12/year. Web site: www.teamfme.com

Forties Limited of Orange County
17163 Roundhill Dr
Huntington Beach, CA 92649-4216
E-mail: oldfordman@aol.com

Founded 1968. 100 members. The Forties Limited are dedicated to the preservation and maintenance of Ford motor cars of the years 1940, 1939 (Deluxe model) and 1941 (commercial models). They meet once a month, usually on the first Sunday. The *Script,*a monthly newsletter is sent to each member. There are events and cruises throughout the year. The club sponsors Forty Ford Day in June in southern California. You don't have to own a 1940 Ford to join, you just need a love of old cars. Dues: $50/year. Web site: www.classicar.com/clubs/forties/40shmepg.htm

The Great Lakes Roadster Club
PO Box 302
Bath, OH 44210

For membership information, contact at the above address: Jerry A Barker.

Greater Cleveland Model T Club
29249 Bolingbrook Rd
Pepper Pike, OH 44124
PH/FAX: 216-464-2159

Founded 1962. 32 members. This is for Model T owners and other makes of cars. It is a social & touring club for northeast Ohio. Monthly meetings & dinners in winter, touring in summer. Dues: $10/year.

**Hawk MTV-8 Ford Club of
Reading, PA**
145 S Blainsport Rd
Reinholds, PA 17569
717-336-2735

Contact: Rick Slegel, President, Blandon, PA. Founded 1974. 75
members. Annual July 4th Fleetwood, PA, car show and flea
market. Join club and belong to national club.

International Ford Retractable Club
PO Box 289
Brockport, NY 14420
716-395-0609

Founded 1971. 1,200 members. Promotes the restoration,
preservation and further interest in the 1957, 1958, 1959
Skyliner retractable hardtop produced by Ford Motor Co. Car
ownership not required. Dues: $32/year US, $34/year
Canadian, $43/year foreign. Web site: www.skyliner.org
chapters:

Connecticut	*New England Chapter*, Joel Pear, 1764 Bartholomew Rd, Middletown, CT 06475
Florida	*Sunshine Skyliners*, Clay Elliott, 4642 Hall Rd, Orlando, FL 32817
Illinois	*Gateway Chapter*, Bill Zimmerman, 916 W Hicks Hollow Rd, Edelstein, IL 61526
	Great Lakes Chapter, Donna Walters, 800 Navajo Dr, Carpentersville, IL 60110-1213
Indiana	*Hoosier Chapter*, Dan Shelton, 5890 Glen Haven Blvd, Plainfield, IN 46168
Michigan	*Michigan-Ontario Chapter*, Howard Voigt, 631 Golf Crest Dr, Dearborn, MI 48124
Minnesota	*Northland Chapter*, Judy Hofer, 22600 Pinto Ln, Lakeville, MN 55044
Nebraska	*Pathfinder Chapter*, Kiel Eliste, 1525 N Garfield, Fremont, NE 68025
Ohio	*Buckeye Chapter*, Donna Simpson, 24769 Stein Rd, Creola, OH 45622-8809
Pennsylvania	*East Coast Chapter*, Dick Trythall, 653 Homestead Dr, Elverson, PA 19520
	Penn-Allegheny Chapter, Don Hubsch, 307 Linden Rd, Box 66E, Cannonsburg, PA 15317
South Carolina	*Southeastern Chapter*, Jerreld Price, Hwy 221, PO Box 251, Mayo, SC 29368
Virginia	*Virginia-Carolina Chapter*, Nathan Jackson, 4736 Morgan Ford Rd, Ridgeway, VA 24148-4142

Model A Ford Cabriolet Club
PO Box 515
Porter, TX 77365
281-429-2505

Founded 1980. 400 members. The club is a special interest group of
the Model A Ford Club of America (MAFCA) and the Model A
Restorers Club (MARC). Club formed to provide a way to exchange
information and parts among owners and enthusiasts of the cabriolet, a rare body style of the Model A Ford made from 1929-1931.
Dues: $12/year US, Canada and Mexico; $14/year overseas.

Model A Ford Club of America
250 S Cypress
La Habra, CA 90631
888-2MODELA; FAX: 562-690-7452
E-mail: mafcahq@aol.com

Founded 1957. 16,000 members. Interest in the Model A Ford.
National meets on the even year. Dedicated to the restoration
and preservation of the Model A Ford. Over 300 chapters, 22
international chapters, 16 special interest and body style
groups. The club is the largest car club in the world devoted to a
single model. Dues: $30/year, $34/year foreign, $36/year for-
eign 1st class. Web site: www.mafca.com
chapters:

Alabama	*Central Alabama Model A Ford Club*, Terry Longest, 2732 W Aberdeen Dr, Montgomery, AL 36116
	Gulf Coast Model A Club, Carl L Bailey, PO Box 1113, Robertsdale, AL 36567 334-947-5262
	Heart of Dixie A's, Gene Taylor, 26561 Martin Branch Rd, Madison, AL 35756 256-232-9000
Alaska	*Alaskan A's*, 3612 Delores Dr, Eagle River, AK 99577
Arizona	*Ah-ooo-gah A's of Arizona*, PO Box 3502, Carefree, AZ 85377
	Arizona Traveling A's, 1212 E Alameda Dr, Tempe, AZ 85282
	Hi-Country A's, PO Box 12211, Prescott, AZ 86304
	Model A Restorer's Club of Arizona, PO Box 5255, Mesa, AZ 85201
	Patagonia T & A, PO Box 2175, Nogales, AZ 85628
	Phoenix Model A Club, Gary Jones, PO Box 35702, Phoenix, AZ 85702-5702
Arkansas	*50th Anniv. A's*, 16921 Crystal Valley Rd, Little Rock, AR 72210
	Natural State A's, 17644 Fox Hollow, Garfield, AR 72732
	Texarkana A's, 213 Wood, Texarkana, AR 71854
California	*A-400 Group*, 2912 McCray Rd, Lake Isabella, CA 93240
	Acorn A's, Gail Baxley, Box 2321, Castro Valley, CA 94546
	Adobe A's, 1250 Orange St, Red Bluff, CA 96080
	Amador A's, PO Box 967, Pine Grove, CA 95665
	Angel City, 4528 2nd Ave, Los Angeles, CA 90043
	Auburn A's, Marjorie Taylor, Box 4345, Auburn, CA 95604

Bakersfield, Edwina, Box 1616, Bakersfield, CA 93302 661-399-1429

Bay Area, 181 Alpine Way, San Bruno, CA 94066

Blossom Trail A's, PO Box 26, Reedley, CA 93654

Brake Away A's, 5121 Vernon Ave, Fremont, CA 94536

Butte-View A's, PO Box 3591, Yuba City, CA 95992

Capistrano Valley A's, Box 614, Capistrano, CA 92693

Capitol A's, Jim Marshall, Box 1416, Carmichael, CA 95609-1416 916-972-9439

Central California Regional Group, 4326 E Lane Ave, Fresno, CA 93702

Charter Oak A's, Box 3696, Visalia, CA 93278-3696

Chico A's, 2674 Ceres Ave, Chico, CA 95926

Conejo Valley, PO Box 332, Newbury Park, CA 91319

Cruisin' A's, 42221 Harmony Dr, Hemet, CA 92544

Cuesta Crankers, Box 714, San Luis Obispo, CA 93406

Delta A's, Box 7328, Stockton, CA 95267

Diablo A's, Steve Mick, Box 6125, Concord, CA 94524 925-838-7570

Diamond Tread, Bud Bartlett, Box 4563, Downey, CA 90241

Eastern Sierra Model A Ford Club, 2772 Sunset Rd, Bishop, CA 93514

Eel River Valley A's, Box 688, Fortuna, CA 95540

El Camino A's, Carl Pileri, PO Box 1754, San Mateo, CA 94401

FAST (Ford A Speed Technology), Jim Brierly, 39480 Coleen Way, Temecula, CA 92390 909-695-3713

Feather River A's, PO Box 1833, Quincy, CA 95971

Flying Quail, Steve Santillan, Box 151, Salinas, CA 93907 831-449-5346

Four Ever Four Cylinder A's, Jim Brierly, 39480 Colleen Way, Temecula, CA 92592-8438 909-695-3713

Gateway A's, Austin Drake, Box 1429, Merced, CA 95340

Golden Feather, 2016 W Lincoln St, Oroville, CA 95965

GRAMPA, Box 2201, Monterey, CA 93940

Gra-Neva, Bruce Davis, Box 2415, Grass Valley, CA 95945 530-477-2846

Hangtown A's, Box 2296, Placerville, CA 95667

Happy Honker A's, Seldon Kempton, PO Box 1912, Porterville, CA 93258-1912 209-592-2959

Harbor Area MAFCA/MARC, Carla Hibbard, 5153 Willow Wood Rd, Rolling Hills, CA 90274 310-371-3008

Heartland A's, Priscilla Redmond, PO Box 3665, Ontario, CA 91761

Henry's A's, Box 46, Livermore, CA 94550

Henry's Originals, 8821 La Entrada, Whittier, CA 90605

Humboldt Bay A's, Jon B Reed, PO Box 6664, Eureka, CA 95501 707-822-1847

Jewel City, Walt Thompson, Box 1833, Glendale, CA 91209

Johnies Broiler Flying A's, Bob Trousil, 7447 Firestone Blvd, Downey, CA 90241

Lake County A's, Ron Oliver, PO Box 634, Clear Lake, CA 95422

Linden A's, PO Box 572, Linden, CA 95236

Los Amigos A's, 13720 Oak Crest Dr, Cerritos, CA 90703

Main Bearings, 2870 Brandt, La Verne, CA 91750

Marin A's, Box 2864, San Rafael, CA 94901

Modesto Area A's, Box 6073, Modesto, CA 95355

Mother Lode A's, Box 1500, Murphys, CA 95247

Mountain Quail, Box 539, Loyalton, CA 96118

Mountain Road Rattlers, PO Box 3416, Oakhurst, CA 93644-3416

Napa Valley A's, Box 2656, Napa, CA 94558

Northern California Regional Group (NCRG), Dick McManus, PO Box 131, Inverness, CA 94937

Oakdale A's, PO Box 60, Oakdale, CA 95361

Orange Blossom A's, James Treadwell, PO Box 51824, Riverside, CA 92517

Orange County, John Riggs, PO Box 10595, Santa Ana, CA 92711 562-431-8783

Section Three – Clubs & Organizations

Model A Ford Club of America chapters (continued)

Palomar A's, John Pickrell, Box 821, Carlsbad, CA 92018   760-631-5720

Paradise Valley, Mark Sandefur or Pat Holley, PO Box 1120, Rialto, CA 92377   909-849-8930

Paso Robles A's, PO Box 2778, San Luis Obispo, CA 93403

Phaeton Club (35-A, B), 1049 Don Pablo Dr, Arcadia, CA 91006

Pomona Valley, Box 2302, Pomona, CA 91769

Queen Mary, Martha Trousil or Carla Maricle, 8820 Mulberry Dr, Sunland, CA 91040   818-352-3670

Redding Rambling A's, Gayle Wright, Box 3872, Redding, CA 96049

Reliable A's, Box 160322, Sacramento, CA 95816

San Diego, PO Box 19805, San Diego, CA 92159

San Fernando Valley, Box 2713, Van Nuys, CA 91404

Santa Anita A's, Bob Moore, PO Box 660904, Arcadia, CA 91066-0904

Santa Barbara, Steve Bartlett, PO Box 60358, Santa Barbara, CA 93160   805-964-3638

Santa Clara Valley, John Guzzetta, PO Box 6072, San Jose, CA 95150

Santa Ynez Valley A's, Floyd Keinath, 715 Kolding Ave, Solvang, CA 93463   805-686-9234

Sierra, Floyd Dupras, Box 2065, Fresno, CA 93718-2065

Sis-Q-A's, Dick Mace, 523 N Oregon St, Yreka, CA 96097

Solano A's, Ron Tribbett, PO Box 426, Elmira, CA 95625   707-678-4270

Sonoma A's, Joe Gensley, Box 4052, Santa Rosa, CA 95402   530-268-9539

Sonora A's, Bill Harrison, Box 382, Sonora, CA 95370-0382   209-586-2929

South Bay Touring 'A's, Richard Valot, 2018 W 178th St, Torrance, CA 90504   310-532-9142

Southern California Region, Bob Trousil, 8535 Lubec St, Downey, CA 90240

Sparkin A's, Don Kunkel, 6394 Perrin Way, Carmichael, CA 95608   916-967-1343

Tokay A's, Noel Stetson, Box 861, Lodi, CA 95241

Touring A's, Will Lancaster, 1777 Rosswood Dr, San Jose, CA 95124

U.S.A's, Bruce Davis, PO Box 805, Cedar Ridge, CA 95924   530-477-2846

Ventura, PO Box 5584, Ventura, CA 93005

Whittier, Box 1908, Whittier, CA 90609

Colorado   *Animas A's*, 6842 Cty Rd 203, Durango, CO 81301

Ford Model AA Truck Club, Neil Wilson, 1365 Cherryvale Rd, Boulder, CO 80303   303-443-1464

Mile-Hi, Box 5554Terminal Annex, Denver, CO 80217

Pike's Peak, Fred Lewis, PO Box 1929, Colorado Springs, CO 80901

Southern Colorado A's, Box 5221, Pueblo, CO 81002

Connecticut   *Connecticut*, John de Sousa, 5 Brownstone Rd, East Granby, CT 06026

Fairfield County A's, Al Wood, 5 Ridge Dr, Westport, CT 06880

Northwestern Connecticut A's, 65 Woodbridge Ln, Thomaston, CT 06787

Florida   *First Coast*, Henry Coleman, 744 Arran Ct, Orange Park, FL 32073   904-272-3174

Model A's of Greater Orlando, Dick Hardman, 5029 Water Vista, Orlando, FL 32821   407-354-3875

Moonport, PO Box 1611, Cocoa, FL 32922

Northwest Florida, 728 Rodney Ave, Ft Walton Beach, FL 32548

Palm Beach, Larry Langer, 17737 122nd Dr North, Jupiter, FL 33478   561-746-6641

Panhandle A's, PO Box 411, Panama City, FL 32402

Georgia   *River Cities Model A Ford Club*, Dr Alberto Lugo, PO Box 342, Columbus, GA 31902

Shade Tree A's, J McPherson, 4424 Reynolds St, Hephzibah, GA 30815

Georgia, PO Box 5, Lilburn, GA 30247

Idaho   *Magic Valley A's*, Gary Crawforth, PO Box 592, Albion, ID 83311   208-673-5326

Treasure Valley, Ron Carr, 4114 Hill Rd, Boise, ID 83703

Illinois   *A's-R-Us*, Ken Chamis, PO Box 1108, Peotone, IL 60468   708-598-2777

Chain O'Lakes, Box 420, Antioch, IL 60002

Chicagoland A's, 1201 W Glenn Ln, Mount Prospect, IL 60056

Forever Fours, Kay Lee, PO Box 6407, Peoria, IL 61601   309-444-9840

Naper A's, Bob Reynolds, Box 245, Naperville, IL 60566

North Shore Model A's, 1764 Bowling Green, Lake Forest, IL 60045

Prairie A's, 309 Carrie Ave, Urbana, IL 61801

Rock-Ford A's, PO Box 4001, Rockford, IL 61110

Salt Creek A's, 611 E Harding Ave, La Grange Park, IL 60525

Sangamon Valley, PO Box 4462, Springfield, IL 62708

Indiana   *Sycamore A's*, RR 22, Box 410, Terre Haute, IN 47802

Iowa   *Central Iowa MAFC*, PO Box 259, Des Moines, IA 50301

Humboldt, Jon Reed, 909 S Taft, Humboldt, IN 50548

Kansas   *Henry Leavenworth*, 3909 Shrine Park, Leavenworth, KS 66048

Plain Ol' A's, 24250 W 83rd, Lenexa, KS 66227

Wichita A's, PO Box 25, Wichita, KS 67201-0025

Kentucky   *Falls City*, 6495 Bardstown Rd, Elizabethtown, KY 42701

Louisiana   *Acadiana*, Box 12401, New Iberia, LA 70562

New Orleans, PO Box 1674, Metairie, LA 70001

Red Stick, Jim Boles, 9837 Great Smokey Ave, Baton Rouge, LA 70814

Maryland   *MAFC of Greater Baltimore*, 5930 Old Washington Rd, Sykesville, MD 21784

Model A Ad Collectors, Howard Minners, 4700 Locust Hill Ct, Bethesda, MD 20814

Massachusetts   *Cape Cod*, 115 Windjammer Ln, Eastham, MA 02642

Connecticut Valley Working A's, 15 Sycamore Terrace, Agawam, MA 01001

Massachusetts Bay, Lou Zadra, PO Box S, Norton, MA 02766

Minutemen, Marlies Plaggenborg, PO Box 545, Sudbury, MA 01776   508-881-8751

Model A Ford Foundation Inc - MAFFI, Art Callan, PO Box 95151, Nonantum, MA 02495

Postal A's, Aldie Johnson Jr, 22 Burlington Rd, Bedford, MA 01730

Town Car Society, 197 Amity St, Amherst, MA 01002

Western MA Model A Ford Restorers, Denis Lessard, PO Box 784, Agawam, MA 01001-0784

Worcester County, Frank E Miller, PO Box 36, North Oxford, MA 01537   702-673-6868

Worcester County Model "A" Club, Mary Sheridan, 718 Oxford St, Auburn, MA 01501   508-757-1478

Minnesota   *Twin Cities*, Neal Anderson, 3326 Larchmore Ave, Wayzata, MN 55391   612-473-5269

Lady Slipper A's, 110 6th St NE, Stewartville, MN` 55976

Town Sedan Club, 9325 31st Ave N, New Hope, MN 55427

Missouri   *Heart of America*, Bob Frentrop, 2100 Walnut St, Kansas City, MO 64108   816-453-6484

Mid-Missouri Model A Restorers' Club, 1407 Colonial Dr, Fulton, MO 65251

Show Me Model A Club, R#3 Box 292D, Cole Camp, MO 65325

Southwest Missouri, PO Box 9735, Springfield, MO 65801

Montana   *The Big Sky A's*, Darrell Beckstrom, 601 Pattee Canyon Rd, Missoula, MT 59803-1618

Nebraska   *Cornhusker*, 7801 E Avon Ln, Lincoln, NE 68505

Golden Rod, 1605 Ave C, Cozad, NE 69130

Meadowlark, Box 6011, Omaha, NE 68106

Nevada   *Battleborn Model A Club*, Laura McAuliffe, 1380 Watt St, Reno, NV 89509   702-322-8316

Las Vegas Valley, Jim Hildreth, 5425 N Durango Dr, Las Vegas, NV 89129

Sagebrush, Box 1034, Carson City, NV 89702

Silver State A's, 829 Hillside, Elko, NV 89801

New Hampshire   *White Mountain*, 16 Martin Rd, Weare, NH 03281

New Jersey   *Cohanzick Region*, PO Box 1446, Millville, NJ 08332

MAFC New Jersey, Berlene Horne, 649 Canistear Rd, Highland Lakes, NJ 07009

Watchung Valley, 116 Ashland Rd, Summit, NJ 07901

Model A Ford Club of America chapters (continued)

New Mexico   *Poco Quatros*, PO Box 21058, Albuquerque, NM 87154-1058

New York   *Adirondack A's*, PO Box 1246, Clifton Park, NY 12065

Lakeshore, Art Drummond, 2789 Chili Ave, Rochester, NY 14624 716-247-0072

Long Island, PO Box 1204, Smithtown, NY 11787-0959

Model A Ford Club of Westchester, 23 Main St, Mt Kisco, NY 10549

Mohican, Nick Montalbano, Rte 1, Mason Rd, Mohawk, NY 13407

NY-PA Twin Tiers, PO Box 100, Big Flats, NY 14814-0100

Southern Tier, RR #1, Box 53A, Mannsville, NY 13661

North Carolina   *Eastern Carolina*, 107 Portside Ln, New Bern, NC 28562

Queen City, Bruce Hyland, 8711 McCartney Way, Charlotte, NC 28216

Thermal Belt, Rte #1, Box 220-B, Ellenboro, NC 28040

Ohio   *Dayton-Buckeye*, PO Box 271, Englewood, OH 45322

Northern Ohio, Louis F Tull, 410 North St, Chardon, OH 44024

Ohio Valley Region, PO Box 62303, Sharonville, OH 45241

Oklahoma   *Okie A's*, 401 S Owen Dr, Mustang, OK 73064

Sooner, CA Coffman, PO Box 83192, Oklahoma City, OK 73148

Tulsa, Box 580581, Tulsa, OK 74158

Oregon   *Azalea A's*, Art Peary, 2350 Quines Creek Rd, Azalea, OR 97410

Beaver, Lloyd Dilbeck, 14655 NW Bonneville Loop, Beaverton, OR 97006

Blue Mountain A's, Box 1724, Pendleton, OR 97801

Deluxe Tudor Sedan Owners Group, Rick Black, 5595 Pioneer Rd, Medford, OR 97501 541-770-9481

Enduring A's, Mark Bullock, PO Box 1428, Albany, OR 97321

Henry's Lady, Rick Black, Box 1442, Grants Pass, OR 97528-1442 541-770-9481

High Desert A's, PO Box 5602, Bend, OR 97708

McKenzie A's, Box 7271, Eugene, OR 97401

Myrtlewood A's, Box 996, Coos Bay, OR 97420

Northwest Region, 17470 SE Tickle Creek Rd, Boring, OR 97009

Snake River A's, 2349 9th Ave, Vale, OR 97918

Willamette Valley, PO Box 3031, Salem, OR 97302

Puerto Rico   *San Juan A's*, Escarlata 84, UrbMunoz Rivera, Guaynabo, PR 00969

Pennsylvania   *Beaver Valley*, 3763 37th St, Beaver Falls, PA 15010

Delaware Valley, Michael Etling, Box 39047, Philadelphia, PA 19136

Lehigh Valley, Jim Upton, Box 9031, Bethlehem, PA 18018-9031

Mercer A's, PO Box 580, Revere, PA 18953

North Penn A's, Dick Lawn, 1651 N Wales Rd, Norristown, PA 19403

Steamtown A's, 1251 Gravel Pond Rd, Clarks Summit, PA 18411

Rhode Island   *Little Rhody*, Dawne Strickland, 860 Fletcher Rd, North Kingstown, PA 02852

South Carolina   *Low Country Chapter*, 1675 Wappoo Rd, Charleston, SC 29407

Palmetto, Bill Prince, 2413 Robin Crest Dr, West Columbia, SC 29169 803-791-3759

Western Carolina Model A Ford Club, 6 Crestline Dr, Greenville, SC 29609

Tennessee   *Lookout A's*, 5410 Sky Valley Dr, Hixson, TN 37343

Memphis, 691 Stratford Rd, Memphis, TN 38122

Smoky Mountain, PO Box 3816, Knoxville, TN 37917

Texas   *1931 Fordor Slant Windshield Group*, 6919 Cornelia Ln, Dallas, TX 75214

Abilene, Donna Carlsen, PO Box 2962, Abilene, TX 79604

Alabama, 7708 Briaridge Rd, Dallas, TX 75248

Alamo A's, Rick Melendez, Box 700156, San Antonio, TX 78270 210-698-8710

Autumn Trails, John Icenhower, Rte 5, Box 52635, Winnsboro, TX 75494

Blackland A's, 6711 Finch Dr, Greenville, TX 75402

Bluebonnet, Clarence Milligan, PO Box 1, Copperas, TX 76522 254-547-6645

Brazos Valley A's (Bryan College Station), Jim Corry, RR 3, Box 612, Franklin, TX 77856

Cabriolet Club (68-A,B,C), PO Box 515, Porter, TX 77365

Capitol City A's, Paul Koncak, CCAS, 8002 Baywood Dr, Austin, TX 78759

Cross Timbers Model A Ford Club, PO Box 407, Hico, TX 76457

Dallas, Box 1028, Addison, TX 75001-1028

Fort Worth, 6611 Anglin Dr, Fort Worth, TX 76119

Four States A's, 11 Azalea, Texarkana, TX 75503

Golden Triangle A's, Curtis Linderman, PO Box 21185, Beaumont, TX 77707

Greater Houston Model A Restorers Club, Tom Torget, 11318 Brandy Ln, Houston, TX 77044

International Victoria Association, John Icenhower, 11084 Windjammer, Frisco, TX 75034

Lone Star Model A Ford Club, Max Phillips, PO Box 1049, Georgetown, TX 78627

Oil City A's, PO Box 567, Luling, TX 78648

Piney Wood A's, Box 7855, The Woodlands, TX 77387

Texas Panhandle, PO Box 9602, Amarillo, TX 79105

Texas Road A O's, PO Box 449, Montgomery, TX 77356

Texoma A's, PO Box 1055, Wichita Falls, TX 76307-1055 903-566-2609

Vag-A-bons, Lyle Meek, 1725 Isaac Creek, New Braunfels, TX 78132

Victori-A's, Allen Maeker, Box 441, Victoria, TX 77902

Woody Wagons, PO Box 341, McAllen, TX 78505

Utah   *Beehive A's*, George Hawkins, 3310 Taylor Ave, Ogden, UT 84403

Vermont   *Green Mountain*, John Gaudette or Peter Crosby, 4295 States Prison Hollow Rd, Monkton, VT 05443-9350

Virginia   *Colonial Virginia*, Bill Lee, PO Box 2044, Williamsburg, VA 23187-2044

George Washington, 3903 Old Lee Hwy, Rte 237, Fairfax, VA 22030

Old Dominion, 7207 Hermitage Rd, Richmond, VA 23228

Skyline, N Flora, Rte 1, Box 162, Gottoes, VA 24441

Washington   *Apple Valley*, Box 1205, Yakima, WA 98907

Columbia Basin, Rick Budzeck, Box 6904, Kennewick, WA 99336 509-943-2522

Cowlitz Valley A's, 1006 N 7th Ave, Kelso, WA 98626

Evergreen, Frank Rosin, Box 15133, Wedgewood Sta, Seattle, WA 98115

Gallopin' Gertie, Ed Crosby, Box 14, Tacoma, WA 98401 253-566-4374

Inland Empire A's, Steve Schmauch, PO Box 614, Veradale, WA 99037-0614 509-747-2496

Moon on A's, Barbara Friske, 2214 8th St, Everett, WA 98201 425-252-5322

Olympia Model A Club, Derry Suther, 13821 Logez Ct SW, Olympia, WA 98512 360-273-4200

Volcano A's (Western WA), Dick Bay, PO Box 87633, Vancouver, WA 98684 360-835-2209

Walla Walla Sweet A's, 1406 Shelton Rd, Walla Walla, WA 99362

Wisconsin   *Central Wisconsin*, Box 492, Wisconsin Rapids, WI 54494

Nickle A's, W799 County Rd 2, Kaukauna, WI 54130

Wisconsin, 11728 North Ave, Wauwatosa, WI 53226

Australia   *Model A Ford Club of Queensland, Inc*, 1376 Old Cleavand RdCarindale 4152 Brisbane, Queensland 07-32061028

Model A Ford Club of Victoria Australia, 38 Hoddle St, Essendon, Victoria 3040,

Model A Restorers of Australia, PO Box 320, Dickson ACT 2602

New South Wales & Down Under, PO Box 162, Panania NSW

Model A Restorers Club of Western Australia, David Bussard, 39 Sovereign Dr, Thornlie, Western Australia 6108

Canada   *Abby's A's*, 3565 Horn St, Abbotsford, AB, V2S 3B7

Canada Capitol A's, 54 Perrin Ave, Nepean, ON, K2J 2X5

Golden Boy A's, 1158 Redwood, Winnipeg, MB, R2X 0Y6

Model A Ford Club of America chapters (continued)

MAOC-Trillium Chapter, Roy Bebee, RR #4-S1985, Sunderland, ON, L0C 1H0 705-357-1599

Model A Owners of Canada, Box 31 Sta A, Scarborough, ON, M1K 5B9

Model A Owners of Canada (So ON Chapter), Paul Wilson, 63 Charlotte Cres, Kitchener, ON, N2B 2K2 519-745-6554

Pacific Model A Club, Richard Gaska, 19759 28th Ave, Langley, BC, V3A 4P5

Scotia A's, S Ohio RR #2, Yarmouth, NS, B0W 3E0

Stampede City Model A Club, Box 22, Site 3, RR 12, Calgary, AB, T3E 6W3

Totem A & T, PO Box 18563, 4857 Elliot St, Delta, BC, V4K 4V7

Van Isle A&B Ford Club, Robert Braaten, PO Box 48031, Victoria, BC, V8Z 3L0

Europe   Ancient Ford Club of Belgium, 350 Micksebaan, B2930 Brasschaat, Belgium

Eiker A Ford Club Norway, c/o Leif RustSamsmoveien 135, 3300 Hokksund, Norway

Sweden Svenska A-Fordarna, Hogabergsgatan 43, 331 41 Varnamo, Sweden

New Zealand   Canterbury, Box 4212, Christchurch

Foveaux Ford A's, 116 George St, Invercargill

Hawkes Bay Model A Club, Peter & Suzanne McCool, 42 Gemini Ave, Palmerston North

North Island Model A Ford Club, Box 57017, Owairaka, Auckland

Rebel A's, Justin Bicknell, 492 Main Rd Hope RR 1, Richmond Nelson

Top of the South A's, PO Box 3260, Richmond Nelson

Other International   Model A Club of Japan, 2-15-13 Taira-Cho, Meguro-Ku, Tokyo, Japan

South Africa, 84 Provident S, Parow 7500, Cape Province, So Africa

South America   Clube do Fordinho, Rua Almirante Mariath144-CEP-0418, Sao Paulo, Brazil

United Kingdom   Model A Ford Club of Great Britain, 10/14 Newland StColeford Royal Forest of Dean, Glouchestershire GL168AN

Model A Restorer's Club
24800 Michigan Ave
Dearborn, MI 48124-1713
313-278-1455; FAX: 313-278-2624
E-mail: info@modelaford.org

Founded 1952. 10,000 members. No restrictions to join. The club was formed in 1952 and encourages its members to acquire, preserve, restore, exhibit and make use of the Ford Model A vehicle, model years 1928-1931, and all things pertaining to the Model A Ford and to promote the introduction of ideas and fellowship among MARC members. Dues: $26/year (subscription included). Web site: www.modelaford.org

regions:

Alabama   Alabama Region, Richard Evens, 4640 Woodfield Ln, Trussville, AL 35173 205-655-7680

Heart of Dixie A's, Harold Taylor, 26561 Martin Branch Rd, Madison, AL 35756 256-232-9000

Rambling A's Region, David Black, 892 Co Rd 107, Breman, AL 35033-3322 256-287-0317

Arizona   The Four Cylinder Gang of Phoenix, Bill Chester, 3621 W El Camino, Phoenix, AZ 85051 602-973-5266

Arkansas   Natural State A's Region, Dick Knapp, 17644 Fox Hollow Rd, Garfield, AR 72732 Doug, 501-756-3576

California   Harbor Area Region, Drain Marshall, 5153 Willowwood Rd, Rolling Hills, CA 90274

MARC of San Diego Region, PO Box 19805, San Diego, CA 92159-0805 858-278-6317

San Gabriel Valley Region, PO Box 29, San Gabriel, CA 91776 626-282-2936

Touring A's of California Region, Diane Dove, 1777 Rosswood Dr, San Jose, CA 95124-5224 408-739-1444

Colorado   Mile High Region, Brett Plu, Terminal Annex PO Box 5554, Denver, CO 80217 303-765-0090

Connecticut   Blue Script Region, PO Box 165, Stafford, CT 06075 860-684-6532

Connecticut 'A' Region, Frederic Galabau, 20 Misty Mountain Rd, Kensington, CT 06037 860-828-9328

Delaware   Active A's Region, Frank Pollack, 3324 Cross Country Dr, Wilmington, DE 19810

Florida   Citrus A Region, Eugene Harvey, 20828 SW 93 Ln, Dunnellon, FL 34431

Crankin A's Region, Eric Evans, 16 Foxhunter Flat, Ormond Beach, FL 32174 904-672-4807

First Coast Region, Nancy Ulrich, 11863 Mandarin Forest Dr, Jacksonville, FL 32223 904-262-5698

Gold Coast Region, Clark Ballard, 22371 Martella Ave, Boca Raton, FL 33433

Lakeland Region, Steve Sopko, 419 E Belmar St, Lakeland, FL 33803 941-683-1129

Model A's of Greater Orlando, Richard Hardman, 5029 Water Vista, Orlando, FL 32821 407-354-3875

New Florida Region, Louis Valdez, 7617 Horse Pond Rd, Odessa, FL 33556 813-792-2947

Palm Beach Region, Bob Carpenter, 1340 Scottsdale Rd E, West Palm Beach, FL 33417

Sara-Mana Region, Ed Greer, 1836 Rivera Circle, Sarasota, FL 34232

Georgia   *Georgia Region*, Jim Guy, 1067 Atherton Ln, Woodstock, GA 30189

Griffin Georgia Region, E Marshall Pape, 790 Turner Rd, Williamson, GA 30292 770-228-7677

Shade Tree "A's" Region, Jack Horner, 4167 Quil Springs Cir, Martinez, GA 30907 706-855-0695

Illinois   *Arling-Meadows A's Region*, Roy Bertola, 5406 Chateau Dr Unit 4, Rolling Meadows, IL 60008 847-818-0728

Calumet Region, Art Lemere, 26451 S Woodlawn Ave, Crete, IL 60417 815-476-4153

Chicagoland A's Region, David Shadduck, 1201 W Glenn, Mt Prospect, IL 60056 847-806-1931

Fox Valley Region, Jack Anderson, PO Box 4, Geneva, IL 60134 630-584-2380

Illinois Region, James Antoni, 828 Hahsen Pl, Park Ridge, IL 60068 847-698-2637

Joliet Region, 29635 N Readman Ln, Wilmington, IL 60481 815-476-4153

My First A Region, James Chiappetta, 2213 Northgate, N Riverside, IL 60546 708-447-3085

North Shore A's Region, Don Schreiber, 3550 Glen Flora, Gurnee, IL 60031

Rock-Ford "A" Region, Don Benthal, PO Box 4001, Rockford, IL 61110 815-282-3443

Rock River Restorers Region, Hearold Montgomery, 14966 Norrish Rd, Morrison, IL 61270 815-772-3755

Sangamon Valley Region, William Tarr, PO Box 4462, Springfield, IL 62708-4462

Starved Rock Region, John Timmons, 506 Arch St, Ottawa, IL 61350 815-434-0316

Windy City A Region, Jerry Lyons, 19714 S 114th Ave, Mokena, IL 60448 708-479-1336

Indiana   *Columbus Region*, Wayne Arnholt, 12609 E Hwy 50, Seymour, IN 47274 812-522-1007

Fountain City Region, Roger Adams, 719 Lee St, Connersville, IN 47331 765-825-8863

Highland Indiana Region, Richard Moore, 9040 Grace St, Highland, IN 46322 219-838-4116

Hoosier "A" Ford Region, Gene Pullin, PO Box 1931, South Bend, IN 46624

Indiana Madison Region, Fred Wilkerson, 8108 West SR 56, Lexington, IN 47138 812-866-2825

Indiana-Ohio Region, Ervin Jackman, 201 N 11th St, Elwood, IN 46036 765-552-6900

Mid-Hoosier "A's" Region, Bill Johnson, PO Box 764, Greenwood, IN 46142 765-643-5169

Old Fort Model "A'" Club, Bill Heidenreich, PO Box 13586, Ft Wayne, IN 46869

Sycamore "A's", Robert Murphy, 6625 West St Rd 246, Lewis, IN 47858 812-495-6216

Tri State Model A Region, John Tanner, 724 Cypress St, Newburgh, IN 47630 812-490-0664

Iowa   *Central Iowa Region*, Jon Christensen, PO Box 259, Des Moines, IA 50301

Hawk A Region, Mardell Kohl, 1912 WM Blvd SW, Cedar Rapids, IA 52404 319-842-2571

Kansas   *Wichita A Region*, Eric Weninger, PO Box 25, Wichita, KS 67201 316-685-2553

Kentucky   *Bluegrass Valley Region*, Doug Wilson, 1125 Duncan Rd, Frankfort, KY 40601

Central Kentucky Region, E H Swicher, 1801 Catnip Hill Pike, Nicolasville, KY 40356

Falls City A Region, Jerry T Mills, 6495 Bardstown Rd, Elizabethtown, KY 42701

Maine   *Back Forty Region*, Alan Foster, PO Box 22, Standish, ME 04084

Maryland   *Greater Baltimore Region*, Tom Kortisses, 2750 Belhaven Rd, Westminster, MD 21157-7620 301-262-4792

Hub City Model A Club, John Lloyd, 816 The Terrace, Hagerstown, MD 21742 301-790-0556

Southern Maryland Region, Bill Bushey, PO Box 1553, California, MD 20619-9739

Massachusetts   *Cape Cod A's*, Larry Kingsbury, PO Box 1395, Orleans, MA 02653 508-255-6352

MARCOM, Marion Brown, 141 Country Way, Scituate, MA 02766 781-545-2120

Minuteman Region, Jo Johnson, PO Box 545, Sudbury, MA 01776

Section Three – Clubs & Organizations

Model A Restorer's Club regions (continued)

Model A Ford Foundation Region, Howard Minners, PO Box 95151, Nonantum, MA 02495

Out of the Barn A's, Wally Franklin, 19 Upper Church St, West Springfield, MA 01089 413-733-9558

Western Massachusetts Region, Peter Strzempek, PO Box 784, Agawam, MA 01001 413-532-5759

Michigan   *Au Sable Valley Region*, Robert Tamplin, 288 Lakeview Dr, Hale, MI 48739 517-473-2137

Cherry Capitol Region, Bob Fitzgerald, 4903 Hoxie E, c/o Fitzgerald, Cedar, MI 49621 616-228-5476, 616-946-6238

Crank and Throttle Region, Keith Ball, 6687 H Dr S, Battle Creek, MI 49014 616-979-2171

East Side A Region, Don, PO Box 775, Royal Oak, MI 48068 810-656-1928

Floral City "A's", Roger Van Houte, 1876 E Hurd Rd, Monroe, MI 48162 734-289-3661

Grand "A's" Region, PO Box 2831, Grand Rapids, MI 49501-2831 616-361-8896

Grape Country Region, David Lyon, 27405 Shaw Rd, Lawton, MI 49065 616-624-6757

Livingston "A's" Region, Ed Thibodeau, 8740 Chambers, Pinckney, MI 48169 734-878-6290

Oakleaf Region, Herbert von Rust, 6620 Pineway Dr, Troy, MI 48098 248-878-8728

Mid-Michigan Region, Charles "Dan" Crane, 3447 W Stoll Rd, Lansing, MI 48906 517-321-0905

Motor Cities Region, Nick Markes, 16028 Brentwood, Livonia, MI 48154 248-332-0233

Muskegon Portside "A's" Region, Richard Mullall, 1839 Auble Rd, Muskegon, MI 49445

Script "A" Region, Nate Rupprecht, 9990 Marilyn, Reece, MI 48757 517-868-4356

Sparton Horn Region, Leroy Duke, 5305 Bull Run Rd, Gregory, MI 48137 517-223-9751

Sunrise Side Model "A" Ford Club, Larry Cornell, 4803 Kirshoff Rd, Alpena, MI 49707 517-595-5021

Minnesota   *Twin City Region*, Dale Pomerleau, 11109 Gettsburg Ave N, Champlin, MN 55316 763-421-4681

Missouri   *Heart of America Region*, Robet Frentrop, 2100 Walnut St, Kansas City, MO 64108 816-279-0489

Mid-Missouri Region, Phil Shocklee, 1423 W

Georgetown Loop, Columbia, MO 65203 Phil or Alice, 573-445-3958

Missouri Valley Region, Terry Oberer, 3609 Traci Ln, Byrnes Mill, MO 63051-1047

Southwest Missouri Model A Club, Jessie Cooper, PO Box 9735, Springfield, MO 65801-9735 800-468-1929

Nebraska   *Meadowlark Region*, Rich Molden, PO Box 6011, Omaha, NE 68106 402-291-8233

Nevada   *Las Vegas Aces Model "A's"*, Eugene Tendvahl, 6727 W El Campo Grande, Las Vegas Valley, NV 89130 702-658-8226

New Hampshire   *North Country Region*, George Hibbard, RR 3 Box 448, Claremont, NH 03743 603-542-6269

New Jersey   *Keystone Region*, David Baldwin, 1235 Lower Ferry Rd, Trenton, NJ 08618-1405

Mid-Jersey Region, David Baldwin, 1235 Lower Ferry Rd, Trenton, NJ 08618

Model A Ford Club of New Jersey, Bruce Acheson, 649 Canistear Rd, Highland Lakes, NJ 07422 201-764-4910

North Jersey Regional "A's", James B Ewings, 16 Brook Ave, Montvale, NJ 07645-2164 201-391-7269

Watchung Valley Region, Louis Della Veccia, 64 Washington Ave, Chatham, NJ 07928 973-635-6239

New York   *Adirondack A Region*, Jim Wolcot, 9 A Mes Pl, Queensbury, NY 12804 518-792-9252

Hudson Valley Region, John Monforte Sr, Box 589 RD 1, Rock Cut Rd, Walden, NY 12586 914-564-2366

Lakeshore Region, Arthur Drummo, 2786 Chili Ave, Rochester, NY 14624 716-247-0072

Long Island Region, Janice Slott, 75 Magnolia Dr, Kings Park, NY 11754 516-798-6991

Mohican Model "A" Ford Club Inc, Sondra Roberts, 390 Mason Rd, Mohawk, NY 13407 Sondra, 315-866-6876; Laverne, 315-337-2138

Niagra Frontier Region, Lee Wass, 6518 Aiken Rd, Lockport, NY 14094 716-625-9396

Southern Tier Model "A" Region, Fred Blyler, 7 Crescent Dr, Apalachin, NY 13732

Twin Tiers Vintage Ford Region, James Dix, PO Box 100, Big Flats, NY 14814 607-562-3501

North Carolina   *Country Road "A's"*, David Piercy, PO Box 1302, Morganton, NC 28680 828-437-8411

Eastern Carolina Region, Dr Sid Christian, PO Box 608, Battleboro, NC 27809

Fayetteville A Region, Phillip Musselwhite, 823 E Great Marsh Church Rd, St Pauls, NC 28384 910-865-4011

Old Timers Region, Richard Wilson, 15 Elk Mont Place, Asheville, NC 28804 828-645-7864

Piedmont Region, Murray Linker, 814 Reynolds Rd, Lewisville, NC 27023 336-731-8673

Queen City Region, Danny Enos, 3430 Fawnhill Rd, Matthews, NC 28105 704-321-2389

Tar Wheel A Region, Edward Cook, 5824 Roxboro Rd, Durham, NC 27712

Ohio   *Central Ohio Region*, Willie Haffler, 134 Oak Hill Ave, Delaware, OH 43015

Dayton-Buckeye Model "A" Club, Roger Kauffman, PO Box 322, Englewood, OH 45322

Northern Ohio Region, Dave Di Francesco, 34520 Appleview Way, Solon, OH 44139 440-248-1365

Ohio Valley Region, Dave Cradler, PO Box 62303, Sharonville, OH 45241 513-769-4061

Scattered "A" Region, Bruce Palmer, 10635 Lithopous Rd, Canal Winchester, OH 43110 614-837-9747

Southern A's Region, Gene Myer, 2171 Vanco Rd, Gallipolis, OH 45631 740-245-9296

Western Lake Erie Region, Janice Barker, 10662 Longnecker St, Whitehouse, OH 43571 419-877-0513

Oklahoma   *NE Oklahoma Region*, Merv Snowden, 8128 E 63rd St S, Tulsa, OK 74133 918-835-7341

Okie A Region, George Chapman, 2405 Rambling Rd, Edmond, OK 73003 405-340-1277

Oregon   *Oregon Trail Model "A" Club*, Karl Hering, PO Box 5163, Aloha, OR 97006-5163

Willamette Valley Region, Tom Morrison, 5222 Cobb Lane S, Salem, OR 97302 503-364-3090

Pennsylvania   *Delaware Valley Region*, Edwin White, 501 S Warminister Rd, Hatboro, PA 19040-4102 215-672-8633

Lehigh Valley Region, James Upton, PO Box 90344, Allentown, PA 18018-9034 610-868-3424

Mercer A's, Bob Adams, PO Box 425, Pipersville, PA 18947-0425 Vern, 215-453-2141

North Penn Region, 1025 Pross Rd, Lansdale, PA 19446 215-855-3214

Running Board "A's", Roger de Socarras, PO Box 580, Revere, PA 18953

Susquehanna Valley Region, Randall Sierk, 121 Germantown Ave, Christianna, PA 17509 610-593-2128

Three Rivers Region, Ceasare Garron, 213 Clubside Dr, Coraopolis, PA 15108 412-264-3489

Rhode Island   *Little Rhody Model A Ford Club*, Pat Howard, 622 Hatchery Rd, N Kingstown, RI 02852 401-294-2268

South Carolina   *Foothills Region*, Darrell Mercer, 6 Crestline Ln, Greenville, SC 28726

Low Country Model A Club, George W Miller, 2625 Elissa Dr, Charleston, SC 29414 843-556-9213

Palmetto A's, Mark Temple, 228 Continental Dr, West Columbia, SC 29170 803-794-6106

South Dakota   *South Dakota Territories Region*, Gary Haugan, 2428 Kenwood Manor #9, Sioux Falls, SD 57104 605-334-1212

Tennessee   *East Tennessee Region*, Ken Miller, 40 Oakmont Ln, Greeneville, TN 37743

Ken-Tenn Region, Billy Collins, 902 High St, Union City, TN 38261

Mid Tennessee Region, Bill Dobson, PO Box 626, Ridgetop, TN 37152

Smokey Mountain Region, Bill Gray, PO Box 3816, Knoxville, TN 37917

Texas   *Alamo A's*, Eddie Morris, PO Box 700156, San Antonio, TX 78270-0156 210-349-7655

Capital City "A's", Larry Hanvey, 7505 Stepdown Cove, Austin, TX 78731 512-261-3972

Dallas Region, Don Park, PO Box 1028, Addison, TX 75001-1028

Fort Worth Region, Randy Mayfield, 4401 Starlight, Fort Worth, TX 76117

Greater Houston Region, Bill Coleman, 11318 Brandy Ln, Houston, TX 77044 281-456-9248

Piney Wood Region, 16030 Algrave Ln, Spring, TX 77379 281-376-0346

Victori A Region, Richard Tumlins, PO Box 441, Victoria, TX 77902

Vermont   *The Green Mountain Region*, 4295 States Prison Hollow Rd, Monkton, VT 05443-9350 802-453-2038

Virginia   *Blue Ridge Model "A's" Region*, James Gordon, 4222 Amber Rd, Redford, VA 24141

Model A Restorer's Club regions (continued)

Cape Henry Region, Bill Goff III, 1113 W Revere Pt Rd, Virginia Beach, VA 23455 757-491-7215

Colonial Virginia Regional, Bill Lee, PO Box 2044, Williamsburg, VA 23187-2044 757-898-9460

Mount Vernon Region, William Worsham, 3903 Old Lee Hwy, Fairfax, VA 22030 703-273-1800

Southwestern Virginia Region, Andrew Buchana, 20069 Cleveland Rd, Abington, VA 24211

Washington   *Emerald City Region*, Jim Barbee, 25050 SE 200 St, Maple Valley, WA 98038 256-776-2602

Fun Timers Region, William Smart/Stan Shafer, 1804 Roosevelt, Yakima, WA 98902 509-453-6246

Gallopin' Gerties Region, Ed Crosby, PO Box 14, Tacoma, WA 98401 253-566-4374

South Puget Sound Region, Mark Callender, 1136 E Eastside St, Olympia, WA 98506-1850

West Virginia   *Mountain Region*, Joe Davis, PO Box 3175, Clarksburg, WV 26302 304-622-2333

Wisconsin   *Chippewa Valley A Region*, Charles Veicht, 22698 Cty Z, Cornell, WI 54732 715-239-6710

Cream City A Region, Don Egner, 1807 Minnesota Ave S, S Milwaukee, WI 53172 414-764-1667

Nickel A Region, Gene Hegner, N 1872 Manley Rd, Hortonville, WI 54944 920-779-4415

Up North Model A Club, 5605 Hwy 51, Hazelhurst, WI 54531 715-358-7817

Wisconsin Region, Ethel Wold, 4610 Tonyawatha Tr, Monona, WI 53716 608-222-9496

Canada   *Capital A's Region*, Colin Lawson, 54 Perrin Ave, Nepean, ON, K2J 2X5 613-825-9136

Kingston Region, Terry Foley, 209 E St, Napanee, ON, K7R 1S9 Henning Jensen, 613-3879-1650

Model A Owners of Canada, Ross Milne, PO Box 31, Postal Station A, Scarborough, ON, M1K 5B9 705-844-8250

Pacific Region, Mike Breed, 19759 28th Ave, Langley, BC, V2Z 1Y1

Stampede City Region, Kathy, Box 22, Ste 3, RR 1E, Calgary, AB, T3E 6W3 403-242-9341

New Zealand   *Top of the South "A's"*, Gae Galway, PO Box 3260 Richmond, Nelson,

Norway   *Norsk "A" Modell Klubb*, Terje Kalstad, Postboks 1930 Vika 0125, Oslo 1,

The Model T Ford Club International Inc
PO Box 276236
Boca Raton, FL 33427-6236
PH/FAX: 561-750-7170
E-mail: hgustav@aol.com

Founded 1952. 4,000 members. Model T Fords 1909-1927 (cars and trucks). Publishes *Model T Times*, 6 issues per year, included with membership. Dues: $25/year US, $30/year elsewhere (all in US funds payable on a US bank). Web site: www.modelt.org

chapters:

Alabama   *Heart of Dixie Ts*, Vic Zannis, 2924 Ave W, Birmingham, AL 35208

Alaska   *Frigid Ford Ts*, Bruce Campbell, 14104 Hancock Dr, Anchorage, AK 99515

Colorado   *Colorado High Peaks Ts*, Benjy Kuehling, PO Box 541, Ouray, CO 81427

Connecticut   *Informal Ts*, Ronald St Amand, 69 Garfield Ave #2, East Hampton, MA 01027

Delaware   *Delaware Ts*, James Riggleman, PO Box 122, Montchanin, DE 19710

District of Columbia   *Nation's Capital*, Frank Gable, 6416 Summerfield Ln, Warrenton, VA 20186

Florida   *Flywheeler Park Flivvers*, Bill Portier, 700 Avon Park Cut-off Rd, Ft Meade, FL 33841

Fun Ts of Central Florida, Donald Lewis, 14830 Boland Ave, Spring Hill, FL 34610

Model T Ford Club of Central Florida, Tom Henry, 2830 Ambergate Rd, Winter Park, FL 32792

Sunny Ts of South Florida, Michael Madden, 320 Lake Dr, Coconut Creek, FL 33066

Treasure Coast Ts, Bill Poffenberger, 3020 Bucking Hammock Trl, Vero Beach, FL 32960

Wel-Ler Ts of Miami, John Weller Jr, 5200 N Kendall Dr, Miami, FL 33156

Georgia   *North Georgia Ts*, Calvin Watts, PO Box 132, Fairmount, GA 30139

Illinois   *Bismarck Tunklin Ts*, Russell Potter, 206 South St Box 79, Bismarck, IL 61814

Crawling Ts, Dewey Asher, 1402 Pine Tree Dr, Washington, IL 61571

Dupage Touring, Herbert Pasch, 8751 B High Point Rd E, Yorkville, IL 60560

Franklin County Garage Ts, Herbert S Tedrow, 11880 Bluebell Rd, Benton, IL 62812

Fox Valley, Maury Dyer, 117 Pecos Cir, Carpentersville, IL 60110

Gem City Ts, Elkvin Townsend, 2911 S 48th St, Quincy, IL 62301

Midwest Chapter, Nick Markese, 3047 N Rutherford, Chicago, IL 60634

Rockford Chapter, Ron Niday, 2115 Sauber Ave, Rockford, IL 61103

Speedster Chapter, Frank Woodin, 1N914 Killaney, Elburn, IL 60119

Indiana   *Circle City Model T Ford Club*, Rallie Murphy, 8441 New London Ct, Indianapolis, IN 46256-9783

Indiana Travelin' Ts, Joe M Batthauer, RR 1 Rd 700 W, Yorktown, IN 47396

Old Fort Ts, Robert Summers, 12330 S Anthony Blvd, Fort Wayne, IN 46819

Temperamental Ts of Indiana, John W Dennis, 212 Iwo St, Auburn, IN 46706

Tippawa Chapter, Ed Ferringer, 700 Avondale St, West Lafayette, IN 47906

Iowa   *Great River Flivver's*, Fred Classon, 4405 Regency Pl, Davenport, IA 52806

Nift's North Iowa Ford Ts, Gary Ludwig, 20306 340th St, Forrest City, IA 50436

Kansas   *Kansas City Chuggers*, Dick Padula, 6600 Wenonga Terr, Mission Hills, KS 66208

Kentucky   *Blue Grass Ts of Kentucky*, F M Saulton, 104 Erskine Ln, Scott Depot, WV 25560

Noken Ts, Ginny Scudder, RR 3, Box 99, Alexandria, KY 41007

Ohio Valley of Kentucky, Owen "Jeep" Whitehouse Jr, 2419 S Hwy 53, La Grange, KY 40031

Louisana   *New Orleans Chapter*, Allen Aucoin, 147 Moss Ln, River Ridge, LA 70123

Maine   *Nubble Light Chapter*, David Currier, 211 Clay Hill Rd, Cape Neddick, ME 03902

Maryland   *Chesapeake Bay Ts*, Cathy Prouse, 105 S Main St, Federalsburg, MD 21632

Heart of Maryland Ts, Frank Easterday, 3401 Kemptown Church Rd, Monrovia, MD 21770

Maryland Chapter, Evaline Miller, 3345 Florence Rd, Woodbine, MD 21797

Massachusetts   *Pioneer Valley Ts*, Joseph F Bergamini, 107 Fairway Village, Leeds, MA 01053

Michigan   *Boilin Ts Chapter*, Tom Taylor, 22115 Brunswick, Charlotte, MI 48813

Borderline Ts of St Clair County, Jack Zimmer, 1660 S Allen Rd, St Clair, MI 48078

Casual Ts, Ray Miras, 21801 Garfield Rd, Northville, MI 48167

Central Michigan Ts, Jim Neal, 1069 Applegate Ln, East Lansing, MI 48823

Crankun Ts Chapter, Bob Fitzgerald, 3357 S McGee Rd, Lake City, MI 49652

Huron Valley Cranks, Mike Christiaens, 326 Hollywood Dr, Saline, MI 48176

Maumee Valley Ts, Jeff Versteeg, 7970 Sumerfield, Petersburg, MI 49270

Model T Flivver's, Joseph Van Evera, N 6079 Shore Dr, Wallace, MI 49893

Tin Lizzie Travelers, Faye Oldenburg, 11840 Barker, White Pigeon, MI 49099

Tinkerin Ts, Leon Rader, Rt 3, Box 1072, Baldwin, MI 49304

Vehicle City Ts, Bill Barth, 11285 E Coldwater Rd, Davison, MI 48423

Washtenaw Nau Ties, Max Marken, 5124 Church Rd, Ann Arbor, MI 48105

Western Michigan Chapter, Stan Windermuller, A-1164 Graafschap Rd, Holland, MI 49423

Minnesota   *T Totalers Chapter*, Art Moran, 4490 W 41st St, Webster, MN 55088

Missouri   *Greater St Louis*, Marlet Ort, 7123 S Rock Hill Rd, Afton, MO 63123

Kansas City Chuggers, Hathon Fields, 3804 S Pleasant St, Independence, MO 64055

Nebraska   *Cornhusker Model T Ford Club*, Robert McKelvie, 15731 Weschester Cir, Omaha, NE 68118

Nebraskaland Chapter, Ken Cheney, 2221 S 37th St, Lincoln, NE 68506

New Hampshire   *New Hampshire Granite T'ers*, Karen Simmering, 121 South Rd, Hopkinton, NH 03229

New Jersey   *B & W T's Chapter*, John Jonas, 301 Whitaker St, Riverside, NJ 08075

New York   *Classic T & Antique*, Robert L Hark, 61 Pickford Ave, Kenmore, NY 14223

Niagara Frontier, Francis Licata, 6746 Akron Rd, Lockport, NY 14094

Twin Tiers Chapter, Bruce Bruckner, 5065 Co Rd 14, Odessa, NY 14869-9730

North Carolina   *Blue Ridge Riders*, William Guiney, 213 Deerpath Ln, Hendersonville, NC 28739

Carolina T's Chapter, Edward Kendall, 4829 Currituck Dr, Charlotte, NC 28210

East Carolina Ts, William A Eads, 923 Bonham Ave, Wilmington, NC 28403

Ohio   *Akron Chapter*, Todd Ranney, 280 Merriman Rd E, Akron, OH 44303

The Model T Ford Club chapters (continued)

Greater Cleveland, Larry Hengenius, 18633 Ridge Rd, North Royalton, OH 44131

Southwest Ohio Model T, Tony Gebhart, 2217 Johnsville-Brookville Rd, Brookville, OH 45309

Stark County Chapter, Thomas Michalek, 2021 Barnard Rd, Wooster, OH 44691

Tickin' Ts of Central Ohio, Jerry Banks, 609 Stinson Dr, Columbus, OH 43214

Youngstown Chapter, Robert Stewart, 312 E Friend St, Columbiana, OH 44408

Oklahoma   Oklahoma Special Ts, David Baker, 10005 SE 44th St, Oklahoma City, OK 73150

Oregon   Rose City of Oregon, PO Box 3901, Portland, OR 97208

Pennsylvania   Keystone Cops, Mark Golding, Star Rt, Box 67, Pleasant Mount, PA 18453-9612

Tired Ts Chapter, Arthur Evans, 32 Richmond-Belvidere Rd, Bangor, PA 18013

South Carolina   South Carolina Model T Ford Club, Ed Meloan, Secretary, 1110 Terrace Circle Dr, North Augusta, SC 29841-4349

South Dakota   Black Hills Model T, Les Schuchardt, 427 E Meier, Spearfish, SD 57783

Tennessee   The Tennessee Ts, Larry Williams, 235 Mariah Church Ln, Waverly, TN 37185

Texas   Cowtown Ts Chapter, Bruce Wesson, 4424 Idledell Dr, Fort Worth, TX 76116

T Fords of Texas, James Deatherage, 606 River Springs Dr, Seguin, TX 78155

Texas Hill County Chapter, Julius Neuhoffer, 2505 Lower Turtle Creek Rd, Kerrville, TX 78028

Texas Tin Lizzies, Ralph Reeder, PO Box 669, Dickinson, TX 77539

Virginia   Central Virginia Model T Chapter, Paul Carreras, 2206 Oakwood Ln, Richmond, VA 23228

Cranky T Chapter of the Blue Ridge, John Harris, 2404 Windsor Ave, Roanoke, VA 24015

Hampton Roads Model T Ford Club, Mark Williams, 2205 Carolina Rd, Chesapeake, VA 23322

Shenandoah Valley Racket T-ers, Bill Price, 1631 Stonyman Rd, Luray, VA 22835

Washington   Carbon Canyon Model T Ford Club, Larry Fairchild, PO Box 275, Carbonado, WA 98323

Graham Model A & Model T Club, Jerome "Sonny" Anseth, 19416 90th Ave E, Graham, WA 98338

Tacoma Chapter, Mike Rebsamen, 9014 67 Ave, Ct E, Puyallup, WA 98371

West Virginia   Charles Ulrich, RD #3, Box 577, Wellsburg, WV 26070

Mountain State Ts/WV, John Harper, PO Box 304-9381, Jacksontown, OH 43030

Wisconsin   Central Wisconsin Ts, Gary Allworden, 541 Market St, Port Edwards, WI 54469

Greater Milwaukee, Kevin A Esser, 4241 N 69th St, Milwaukee, WI 53216

Ocooch Mt Chapter, Steve Stevenson, 18798 Deere Path Ln, Richland Center, WI 53581-5866

"T"riffic Ts of Wisconsin, William Glass, 716 Miles St, Chippewa Falls, WI 54729

Australia   Model T Ford Club of Australia, PO Box 2658, North Parramatta NSW 2151,

Model T Ford Club of Victoria, Roger Wotherspoon, PO Box 383Chadstone Centre, Victoria 3148,

Canada   Ontario Region, Charlie Muli, PO Box 848, Minden ON, K0M 2K0

Europe   Halsinge Model T, Sven-Olov Hansson, Alvagen 14Kvissleby, 862 33,

The Irish Model T Club, John Boland, Waterford Rd, New Ross, Co Wexford,

The Irish Model T Club, John Boland, Waterford Rd, New Ross, Co Wexford,

South America   The First Model T Club of Argentina, c/o Jorge Eduardo Baez, Romulo Carbia 2897B Poetal Lugones, Cordoba 5008,

---

The Model T Ford Club of America
PO Box 126
Centerville, IN 47330-0126
765-855-5248; FAX: 765-855-3428
E-mail: admin@mtfca.com

Founded 1965. Over 20,000 members. Dues: $22/year US, $27/year Canada, $28/year foreign (US funds please). Web site: www.mtfca.com
chapters:

Arizona   Canyon Country Model T Club, c/o Russ Furstnow, 4030 N Lugano Way, Flagstaff, AZ 86004

Model T Ford Club of Southern Arizona, c/o Frank Hoiles, 2121 N Nightshade Dr, Tucson, AZ 85715

Sun Country Model T Club, Terry Loftus, Box 56634, Phoenix, AZ 85079

Tucson Touring T's, c/o Tom Russell, 2947 E 20th St, Tucson, AZ 85716

California   *Antelope Valley Chapter*, c/o T V Gorden, PO Box 2058, California City, CA 93504

Bay Area T's, c/o Rick Silvera, 2949 Los Altos Way, Antioch, CA 94509

Central Coast Model T Club, PO Box 1117, Templeton, CA 93465

Don Pedro Model T Club, c/o John Skaggs, 26978 S Banta Rd, Tracy, CA 95376

Long Beach Model T Club, PO Box 15841, Long Beach, CA 90815

Model T Ford Club of Kern County, Box 885, Bakersfield, CA 93302-0885

Model T Ford Club of San Diego, PO Box 23324, San Diego, CA 92193

Mother Lode Model T Ford Club, Box 4901, Auburn, CA 95603-0901

Northern California Model T Club, PO Box 1696, Martinez, CA 94553

Orange County Model T Ford Club, PO Box 1071, Westminster, CA 92684

Redwood Empire Model T Club, PO Box 1058, Forestville, CA 95436

Riverside-Corona Chapter, PO Box 51177, Riverside, CA 92517

Sacramento Valley Model T Club, Box 492, Carmichael, CA 95608-0492

Salinas Valley 4 Bangers, c/o Genelle Azevedo, 2105 Jeanie Ln, Gilroy, CA 95020

San Fernando Valley Chapter, c/o Clara Jo Ostergren, 8656 Balcom Ave, Northridge, CA 91325

Santa Clara Valley Model T Ford Club, PO Box 2081, Saratoga, CA 95070

South Bay Model T Ford Club, PO Box 797, Manhattan Beach, CA 90267-0797

Vintage Rally Group, c/o Morris Kindig, 255 S Rengstorff Ave, Apt 138, Mountain View, CA 94040

Colorado   *Centennial Model T Club of Northern Colorado*, c/o Dave Hudson, 311 Hubble St, Berthoud, CO 80513

High Plains Model T Club, Box 366, Akron, CO 80720

Mile High Chapter, c/o Mel VanBuren, 7450 W 35th Ave, Wheat Ridge, CO 80003

Northeast Colorado Model T Club, c/o Don Hagstrom, 11753 County Rd 27, Sterling, CO 80751

Southern Colorado Model T Club, Box 3356, Pueblo, CO 81002-3356

Connecticut   *Connecticut Crankin' Yanks*, c/o Will Revaz, 13 Scott Rd, Oxford, CT 06478-1553

Four Seasons Model T Association, c/o Grant Bombria, 11 Cards Mills Rd, Columbia, CT 06237

Model N-R-S Chapter, c/o Bruce Hartel, 173 Birdseye Rd, Shelton, CT 06484

Delaware   *Heart of Delaware Ts*, c/o Pete Ratledge, 307 Ratledge Rd, Townsend, DE 19834

Florida   *Model T Ford Club of Central Florida*, c/o Tom Henry, 7449 Citrus Ave, Winter Park, FL 32792

Northeast Florida Chapter, 844 River Rd, Orange Park, FL 32073

Idaho   *Western Idaho Model T Ford Club*, c/o Don Borchers, 3590 Jullion St, Boise, ID 83704

Illinois   *ILL-IA-MO Chapter*, c/o Darla Eden, 1278 Hwy 2, Farmington, IA 52626

Indy 500 Chapter, c/o Mary Potter, PO Box 79, Bismarck, IL 61814

Prairie State Model T Ford Club, 46-1300 Ave, Mt Pulaski, IL 62548

Indiana   *Circle City Model T Ford Club*, c/o Rallie Murphy, 8441 New London Ct, Indianapolis, IN 46256-9783

Iowa   *Early Chariots of Council Bluffs*, c/o Jerry Bogatz, 16 Lakewood Villa St, Council Bluffs, IA 51501

Heart of Iowa T's, c/o Thomas Gray, 3923 52nd St, Des Moines, IA 50310

Upper Iowa Vintage Ford Club, c/o Dave Dunlavy, 2895 Bluffton Rd, Decorah, IA 52101-7802

Kansas   *East Central Kansas T's*, c/o Mrs Bud Redding, 1938 Reaper Rd NE, Waverly, KS 66871

Flatland T's Model T Club, c/o Marion Shirk, 1529 N Charles, Wichita, KS 67203

Sunflower State Crankers, c/o Frank C Banta, 302 E Iowa, Greensburg, KS 67054

Kentucky   *Burley Belt Chapter*, c/o Jack Lemley, 340 Savannah Dr, Nicholasville, KY 40356

Golden Crossroads Chapter, c/o Ted Aschman, 214 Morningside Dr, Elizabethtown, KY 42701

Northern Kentucky Model T Club, c/o Bud Scudder, RR 3 Box 99, California, KY 41007

River City Chapter, c/o Jim Hicks, 112 W Flaget St, Bardstown, KY 40004

Somerset Chapter, c/o Andy Mounce, PO Box 1, Somerset, KY 42502

Section Three – Clubs & Organizations

The Model T Ford Club of America chapters (continued)

Maine *Down East Chapter*, c/o John Anderson, 120 Intervale Rd, Temple, ME 04984

Maryland *Blue and Gray Chapter*, c/o Connie Grimm, 21216 Chewsville Rd, Smithsburg, MD 21783

Massachusetts *Central Mass Model T Club*, c/o George Shepard, PO Box 371, Upton, MA 01568

Model T Snowobile Club, c/o Sean O'Brien, PO Box 1, Forestport, NY 13338

Old Colony Model T Club, 130 Old Oaken Bucket Rd, Scituate, MA 02066

Western Massachusetts Model T Club, c/o Curtis Girard, 25 Green St, Chicopee, MA 01020

Yankee Ingenui T's, c/o George Livermore, 92 Miller St PO Box 158, Lancaster, MA 01561

Minnesota *Model T Club of Lake Minnetonka*, c/o Gary Blesi, 2615 Park Ave, Apt 610, Minneapolis, MN 55458

North Star State Chapter, c/o Ken Schult, 649 19th Ave N, South St Paul, MN 55075

Missouri *Greater St Louis Chapter*, c/o Don Hoelscher, 52 Waynesboro Ct, St Charles, MO 63304

Heart of the Ozarks Chapter, c/o Frank Radtke, 3891 Bell Spring Rd, Marshfield, MO 65706

Kingdom of Callaway Chapter, c/o Vicki McDaniel, 5 Bartley Ln, Fulton, MO 65251

Show-Me Ts, c/o Karol Spencer, 1124 W Swan, Springfield, MO 65807

Montana *Rocky Mountain Model T Club*, c/o Ralph Starr, 2108 Rattlesnake Rd, Missoula, MT 59802

Nebraska *Centennial T Club of Omaha*, c/o Lee Matson, 903 E 9th St, Schuyler, NE 68661

Nebraskaland Model T Club, c/o Steve Hughes, 8705 W Branched Oak Rd, Raymond, NE 68428

Nevada *Silver State Model T Ford Club*, c/o Jack Middleton, 620 Highland, Carson City, NV 89703

Southern Nevada Model T Club, c/o Harold Mann, 5617 Alfred Dr, Las Vegas, NV 89108

New Hampshire *Central New Hampshire Model T Club*, c/o David Simmering, 121 South Rd, Hopkinton, NH 03229

New Jersey *North Jersey Tinker Ts*, c/o Gary Paulsen, 790 Franklin Tpke, Allendale, NJ 07401

T-Bones Chapter, c/o Jim Dowgin, PO Box 257, Dayton, NJ 08810

Tri-State Tin Lizzie Tourists, c/o Chris Paulsen, 790 Franklin Tpke, Allendale, NJ 07401

New Mexico *Tin Lizzies of Albuquerque*, PO Box 30473, Albuquerque, NM 87190-0473

New York *Adirondack Foothills Chapter*, c/o Les Trainor, 135 Ford St, Booneville, NY 13309

Capital District Chapter, c/o William Clough, PO Box 27, Knox, NY 12107-0027

Central New York Chapter, c/o Curtis Ackerman, PO Box 158, West Burlington, NY 13482

Flivver Drivers Inc, c/o Douglas H Lockwood, 347 S Clinton St, Albion, NY 14411

NY-PA Twin T'ers Vintage Ford Club, c/o Bruce Bruckner, 5065 Co Rd 14, Odessa, NY 14869-9730

North Carolina *Blue Ridge Model T Club*, c/o William C Guiney, 213 Deerpath Ln, Hendersonville, NC 28379

North Dakota *Viking Country Chapter*, c/o Reginald Urness, 3510 Belmont Rd, Grand Forks, ND 58201

Ohio *Model T Ford Club of Northwest Ohio*, c/o Dave Benny, 3081 N Eastown Rd, Elida, OH 45807

North Coast Bumps and Grinds Chapter, c/o Charles F Bayorek, 439 Whitman, Elyria, OH 44035

Ohio River Valley T's, c/o Lola Wells, 7359 Millers Run Fallen Timber Rd, Lucasville, OH 45648-8353

Southwest Ohio Model T Club, c/o Tony Gebhart, 2217 Johnsville-Brookville Rd, Brookville, OH 45809

Oklahoma *Heartland Ts of OKC*, c/o Ed Lamport, PO Box 21387, Oklahoma City, OK 73156

Model T Ford Club of Tulsa, PO Box 691874, Tulsa, OK 74169-1874

Oregon *Northwest Vintage Speedsters*, c/o Tom Elliott, 12185 SW Parkway, Portland, OR 97225

Rose City Model T Ford Club, Box 3901, Portland, OR 97208

Willamette Valley Chapter, Box 13313, Salem, OR 97309

Pennsylvania *Valley Forge Chapter*, c/o Robert Caramanico, 4114 Naamans Creek Rd, Boothwyn, PA 19061-2421

Rhode Island *Model T Ford Owners of Southern New England*, c/o George Taber, 34 W Warick Ave, West Warren, RI 02893

South Carolina *SC Model T Ford Club*, c/o Ed Meloan, 1110 Terrace Cir Dr, North Augusta, SC 29841

South Dakota *Black Hills Model T Club*, c/o Les Schuchardt, Box 136, Spearfish, SD 57783

Dakota Hills Climbers Chapter, c/o David Grow, 13120 Mountain Park Rd, Rapid City, SD 57702

Tennessee   *Tennessee Ts*, 235 Mariah Church Ln, Waverly, TN 37185

Texas   *Brazos Valley Ts*, c/o Ben Hardeman, 1820 Gray Stone Dr, Bryan, TX 77807

Cen-Tex Tin Lizzies, PO Box 70, Manchaca, TX 78652

Cowtown Model T Ford Club, 4424 Idledell Dr, Fort Worth, TX 76116-7611

Lone Star Ts, c/o Bill King, President, 13005 Audelia, Apt 3132, Dallas, TX 75243

Paso Del Norte Model T Ford Club, c/o Vaughn Rodgers, 407 Lombardy, El Paso, TX 79922

Space City T's Chapter, c/o Dan McDonald, 6430 Neff St, Houston, TX 77074

Texas Model T Speedster Club, c/o Royce Peterson, 6471 Stichter, Dallas, TX 75230

Washington   *Inland Empire Chapter*, PO Box 11708, Spokane, WA 99211-1708

Montana Cross Country Model T Association, c/o Tom Carnegie, 7516 E Mission, Spokane, WA 99212

Puget Sound Chapter, c/o Ray Steele, 17408 17th Pl NE, Shoreline, WA 98155

Three Rivers Chapter, PO Box 7083, Kennewick, WA 99336-7083

Wisconsin   *Dairyland Tin Lizzies*, c/o Jim Rodell Jr, 5585 Butternut Dr, Kewaskum, WI 53040

Kettle Moraine Model T Ford Club, c/o Burdella Miller, W211 N6876 Pheasant St, Menomonee Falls, WI 53051

Marshfield Model T Ford Club, c/o Dennis Rose, W5351 Co Rd N, Owen, WI 54460

Wisconsin Capital Model T Ford Club, c/o Glenn Spaay, 9227 Cty S, Mt Horeb, WI 53572

Argentina   *Primer Club del Ford T de Argentina*, c/o Jorge E Baez, Romulo Carbia 2897 Bo Poeta Lugones, 5008 Cordoba

Australia   *Ford T Register of Australia*, PO Box 380, Hindmarsh SA 5007

Model T Ford Club of Australia, PO Box 2658, No Parramatta NSW 1750

Model T Ford Club of Victoria, PO Box 383, Chadstone Centre, Victoria 3128

Austria   *Model T Ford Club of Austria*, c/o Alfred Slamena, Kirchengasse 1, A 7210 Mattersburg

Belgium   *Ancient Ford Club of Belgium*, c/o Roger de Decker, 350 Micksebaan, B-2930 Brasschaat

Canada   *Calgary Foothills Model T Ford Club*, c/o Reg Kober, 6119 Norfolk Dr NW, Calgary AB T2K 5J8

Running Board Bandits, c/o Ralph Anderson, Rt 5 Box 11 Site 15, Prince Albert SK S6V 5R3

Sasketchewan Dus't Spokes Chapter, c/o Allan Clow, 16 Acadia Bay, Regina SK S4S 4T6

The 24-Ts Club, c/o Warren Johnstone, 3187 Stevenson Pl, Victoria, BC V8X 1C4

Totem Model A and T Club, PO Box 18563, Delta, BC V4K 4V7

Vintage Car Club of Canada, Box 441942947 Tillicum Rd, Victoria, BC V9A 7K1

Great Britain   *Model T Ford Register of Great Britain*, c/o Martin Riley, Addistone, Woodland, Broughton in Furness LA20 6AQ

Holland   *Ford T Register of Holland*, c/o A Martini, Meander 15, 1180 Wn Amstelveen

New Zealand   *Model T Ford Club of New Zealand*, c/o Rod McKenzie, 39 Francis Drake St, Waipukurau 4176

Nifty Fifties Ford Club of Northern Ohio
PO Box 142
Macedonia, OH 44056

Founded 1976. 100 members. Limited to northeast Ohio. Publication: *Nifty Fifties News*. Club events, local car shows, general club news. Dues: $20/year.

Nor-Cal Fiestas
2135 Via Roma
Campbell, CA 95008
408-866-1390

Founded 1998. 2 members. Open to all northern California Ford Fiesta enthusiasts. There is no newsletter due to lack of members. I hope to stay in contact by phone, mail and in person to organize social events, parts swap meets, auto crosses and general sharing of Fiesta knowledge. Member input is very valuable.

Nor-Cal Ford Car Club Council
PO Box 6682
Concord, CA 94524-1682
925-684-3505; FAX: 925-684-2044
E-mail: mechamrs@pacbell.net

Founded 1996. 15 clubs. Council is made up of 15 Ford car/truck clubs. Dues: $25/year.

Northeast Chapter Falcon Club of America
73 Francis Rd
Glocester, RI 02857
401-934-2105; FAX: 401-934-2105
E-mail: raysfalcon@msn.com

Founded 1983. The Northeast Chapter has over 150 members in the southern New England, eastern New York and upper New Jersey area. Members must belong to the parent club, Falcon Club of America. Newsletters published 6 times a year, annual regional meets. We specialize in activities and services for 1960-1970 1/2 Ford Falcon automobiles. Dues: $8/year. Web site: www.bestweb.net/~heuy/nefalcon.html

Northern Ohio Model A Club
31870 Hiram Tr
Moreland Hills, OH 44022
216-292-6445
E-mail: hmbell@voyager.net

Founded 1972. 97 members. The Northern Ohio Model A Club is open to anyone with an interest in the Model A Ford. The club provides technical assistance and information on the construction and operation of the Model A Ford. The club offers monthly technical seminars, annual tours and semi-annual driving events. The newsletter is published monthly. Dues: $15/year. Web site: http://clubs.hemmings.com/nomac

Penn-Ohio Model A Ford Club
1542 Gotthard St
Sugarcreek, OH 44681-9323
330-852-4700; FAX: 330-852-2100
E-mail: bhudec@aol.com

Founded 1956. 550 members. Penn-Ohio is a social and driving club. It is open to anyone with the interest of owning, preserving and driving the Model A Ford. The club is comprised of 14 chapters across northern Ohio and western Pennsylvania. Each chapter meets once a month throughout the year. The club holds monthly driving events during the driving season, an annual tour, and a swap meet/car show annually. Communications are provided by the clubs newsletter, *The Quail Call*. The newsletter is published 9 times a year. Dues: $20/year.

Queen City Model A Club
4511 Twin Oaks Pl
Charlotte, NC 28212
704-536-0551; FAX: 704-399-6025
E-mail: dwoodp@aol.com

Founded 1958. Members: 50 families. Membership meetings 3rd Monday each month. Newsletter is *The Distributor* published monthly. Model A owners. Spring/fall tours. Dues: $20/year.

Secrets of Speed Society (SOSS)
Charlie Yapp, Executive Director
PO Box 957436
Hoffman Estates, IL 60195-7436
312-558-9338; FAX: 312-558-9337
E-mail: cy4fn@aol.com

Founded 1989. Over 2,600 members worldwide. Model T, A & B Ford four-cylinder high performance society. Primarily a publishing society. Racing, touring, hill climbs, dirt track racing, cross country touring. Dues: $35/year. Web site: www.secretsof-speed.com

Shelby American Automobile Club
PO Box 788
Sharon, CT 06069
860-364-0449; FAX: 860-364-0769
E-mail: saac@discovernet.net

For information contact at the above address: Rick Kopec. Founded 1975. 6,200 members. Ownership not essential. Open to all enthusiasts of high performance Fords, Bosses, Panteras, Griffiths, Mustangs, etc. Club magazine is the *The Shelby American*. Dues: $47/year. Web site: www.saac.com

Tri-State F-100s
2510 Minton Rd
Hamilton, OH 45013
513-863-6629

Founded 1984. 45 members. 1953-1956 Ford pickups and panels. Socialize at shows and cruise-ins, family activities, monthly newsletter, F-100 Super Nationals in Pigeon Forge, TN. Annual car show and two cruise-ins. Dues: $30/year.

Washington Ford Retractable Club
8524 S 125th
Renton, WA 98055
206-772-5418

Founded 1978. 50 members. 6 newsletters, meetings and local car shows a year. Benefits: meet friends with same interest and exchange of parts. Chapter of Skyliners of America. Dues: $10/year.

1970 Mustang Mach I Registry
200 Thomas Pepin
Boucherville, QC Canada J4B 1N8
450-449-4587
E-mail: raytags@hotmail.com

Founded 2000. 550 members. Open to all owners of 1970 Mustang Mach I in any condition. Please send your serial number, all original data and clear copy of your original invoice, include a couple of pictures of your Mach I. Dues: none. Web site: www.homestead.com/1970mach1/home.html

Alberta Mustangs Auto Club
PO Box 36092
Lakeview PO
Calgary, AB Canada T3E 7C6

Founded 1979. 80 members. A non-profit organization made up of individuals and families who share a common interest in Mustangs, Cougars and special interest Fords. Membership entitles holder to bi-monthly newsletter, membership roster and discount at various retailers and on admission to club events. Major event is the Presidential Show and Shine held in June. Dues: $30/year, $25/year renewal. Web site: www.abmustang.com

Big Horn Basin Mustang Assoc
Jim Popescu
107 South 1st St E
Cowley, WY 82420
PH/FAX: 307-548-6836
E-mail: jimpascu@tctwest.net

Founded 1989. 25 members. Mustang & specialty Ford autos. Dues: $15/year. Web site: www.dtmn.com/cody20/

Club Mustang Quebec
180 St Antoine
Levis QC Canada G6V 5Y8
418-837-5709

Founded 1989. 150+ members. Open to everyone, owner or not. Many activities, monthly meeting. Dues: $40/year Canadian.

Early Mustang Club
PO Box 21706
Denver, CO 80221
303-430-0433; FAX: 303-430-4070
E-mail: bob@protsys.com

Founded 1973. 150 members. No restrictions to joining club. Newsletter and club event each month. Monthly meeting 1st Friday of the month, otherwise noted in newsletter. Qualifications: Mustang enthusiasts. Dues: $25/year. Web site: www.earlymustang.com

Green Mountain Mustang Club
20 Maplewood Dr
South Burlington, VT 05403
802-865-7656
E-mail: rjb2vt@yahoo.com

30 members. No restrictions. Monthly meetings, annual Ford show, benefit organization is MADD. Dues: $15/year. Web site: http://clubs.hemmings.com/gmmc/

Mustang Club of America
3588 Hwy 138 PMB 365
Stockbridge, GA 30281
PH/FAX: 770-477-1965, 10 am to 5 pm

For membership information, contact at the above address: National Headquarters. Founded 1976. Over 8,500 members and 110 regional groups. Should be an enthusiast of Ford Mustangs, Bosses and Shelbys. Largest Mustang club in the world. Dues: $30/year US, $40/year Canadian, $65/year foreign. Visa/MasterCard accepted.

regions:

Alabama
Heart of Dixie Mustang Club, Shawn Lowry, President, 4348 Ray Dr, Montgomery, AL 36117 334-273-9992

Mobile Bay Mustang Club, John Kaeser, President, 7688 Cornwallis St, Saraland, AL 36571 334-675-7391

Model City Mustang Club, Mike Osburn, President, PO Box 324, Anniston, AL 36202 256-831-8985

Southern Stallions Mustang Club, Andy Davis, President, 402 Carr Cir, Headland, AL 36345 334-693-0069

Arizona
Copperstate Mustang Club, Vinny Tuccillo, President, 435 W Buena Vista Dr, Tempe, AZ 85284 480-753-0110

Old Pueblo Mustang Club, David Hoverstock, President, PO Box 1776, Tucson, AZ 85731 520-298-5442

Arkansas
Arkansas Valley Mustang Club, Bill Whitman, President, PO Box 6715, Fort Smith, AR 72906 918-626-4986

Central Arkansas Mustangers, Joe Mitchell, President, 1200 Southridge, Little Rock, AR 72212 501-233-4055

Ozarks Regional Mustang Club, Kathy Dees, President, 401 N Cherry, Harrison, AR 72601 870-741-1589

NW Arkansas Mustang Club, Steve McCarney, President, PO Box 254, Springdale, AR 72764 501-362-2232

California
Beach Cities Mustang Club, Jon Schultz, President, PO Box 1982, Redondo Beach, CA 90278 310-370-3368

Diablo Valley Mustang Club, John Neary, President, PO Box 21674, Concord, CA 94521

Golden Hills Mustang Club, Chris Barkman, President, PO Box 524, Rio Vista, CA 94571 707-374-6055

Mustang Owners Club of California, Marlon Mitchell, President, 11035 White Oak Ave, Granada Hills, CA 91344 626-795-2901

Sacramento Area Mustang Club, Mike Hess, President, PO Box 188455, Sacramento, CA 95818 916-973-1854

Vintage Mustang Owners Association, Esteban Chabolla, President, PO Box 5772, San Jose, CA 95150 408-997-6089

Colorado
Front Range Mustang Club, Jennifer Opila, President, 463 Melody Dr, North Glenn, CO 80260 303-451-7357

Delaware
Lower Delaware Mustang Club, Gary Trader, President, PO Box 400, Felton, DE 19943 410-749-8351

Florida
Bay Mustang Club, Jeffrey Duggins, President, 6105 Boatrace, Callaway, FL 32404 850-874-0386

Classic Mustang of Tampa, Kevin Riley, President, PO Box 290493, Tampa, FL 33617

Emerald Coast Mustang Club, Eric Brawner, President, 17 Bens Ln, Eglin AFB, FL 32542 850-651-8916

Fort Lauderdale Mustang Club, Ted Parkhurst, President, 8100 NW 185th St, Miami, FL 33015 305-821-2869

Gold Coast Mustang Club, Larry Bedford, President, PO Box 771091, Coral Springs, FL 33077 954-752-5047

Gulf Coast Region Mustang Club, Charles Hayes, President, PO Box 7634, Pensacola, FL 32534 850-457-1223

Gulf Shore Mustang Club, Richard Hayman, President, 15551 Doveland Ln, Fort Myers, FL 33912 941-489-1996

Hernando County Mustang Assoc, Tony Lagone, President, 25266 Plum St, Brooksville, FL 34601 352-796-0854

Imperial Mustangs of Polk County, Dave LaRocco, President, 2106 Groveglen Ln N, Lakeland, FL 33813 941-644-4514

Magic City Mustangs Inc, George Barber, President, 10981 SW 44th St, Miami, FL 33165 305-221-6777

Mid Florida Mustang Club, Larry Goebel, President, 31 Oak Hollow Dr, Apopka, FL 32712 407-889-0799

Mustang Club of America regions (continued)

Mustang Club of West Central Florida, Raymond Baker, President, 3215 48th St, Sarasota, FL 34235 941-351-3789

Southwest Florida Mustang Club, Steve Keppen, President, 1722 SE 2nd St, Cape Coral, FL 33904 813-939-7245

Space Coast Mustang Club, Steve Kinnaird, President, 1002 Slocum St NW, Palm Bay, FL 32907 321-725-7791

Suncoast Mustang Club, John T Moody, President, 1802 Willow Oak Dr S, Palm Harbor, FL 34683 727-786-3048

Surf Mustang of South Florida, Marc Schultz, President, 124 SE 5th St N, Belle Glade, FL 33430 407-996-5520

Georgia *Central Savannah River Area Mustang Club,* Keith Hazelrigs, President, 1602 Hinton Wilson Rd, Harlem, GA 30814 706-556-3755

Cherokee Regional Mustang Club, Jeff Kirkland, President, 948 Russell Hill Rd NW, Sugar Valley, GA 31591 706-625-8411

Flag City Mustang Club, Lynn Watson, President, 2336 Canwood Dr, Macon, GA 31220 478-474-9430

Georgia Regional Mustang Club, Joe Krumpelman, President, 1466 Wood Thrush Way, Marietta, GA 30062 770-578-1354

Mustang Powerhouse of Atlanta, Kenneth Washington, President, PO Box 475, Red Oak, GA 30272 404-899-6905

Northeast Georgia Mustang Club, John Garrett, President, 4449 Benfield Rd, Braselton, GA 30517 770-967-2809

Savannah Mustang Club, Ed Daly, President, 1410 E Hwy 80, Bloomingdale, GA 31302 912-748-8102

Tara Mustang Club, Nathaniel Key, President, 4602 High Gate Ln, Lithonia, GA 30038 770-981-2208

Tri-City Mustang Club of Columbus, Ken Baskerville, President, 2550 Wedgefield Ct, Apt #34, Columbus, GA 31903 706-682-6957

Illinois *Central Illinois Mustangers,* Bill Walter, President, 4424 Palmer Ct, Decatur, IL 62526 217-245-4848

Northern Mustang Corral, Terry Hebert, President, 1200 King Arthur Ln, Bourbonnais, IL 60914 815-932-5282

Rock Valley Mustang Club, Scott Fleming, President, 6079 Wild Rose Ln, Roscoe, IL 61073 815-623-9161

Shiloh Valley Mustang Association, Mike Chace, President, 125 Bobbie Dr, Swansea, IL 62226 618-277-5934

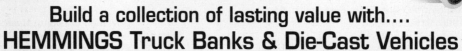

Southern Illinois Mustang Association, Ron Reid, President, 9945 Farley Ln, Gillespie, IL 62033 618-362-6210

Indiana   Falls City Mustang Club, Charlie Smith, President, 2005 Poppy Pl, Jeffersonville, IN 47130 812-283-6543

Michiana Mustangs, Bob Goeller, President, 312 N Pine St, Mishawaka, IN 46545 219-256-5787

Mustang Club of Indianapolis, Jerry Sullivan, President, 2442 S Lockburn, Indianapolis, IN 46241 317-244-2935

Old Fort Mustangers Club, Eric Symonds, President, 9034 Stoneridge Ct, Fort Wayne, IN 46825 219-490-7700

Pony Express Mustang Club, Joe Willett, President, 2015 N Heidelbach Ave, Evansville, IN 47711 812-424-1523

Wabash Valley Mustang Club, Matthew Michaels, President, 422 Trailwood Dr, Terre Haute, IN 47802 812-298-9000

Iowa   Central Iowa Mustang Club, Curt McKim, President,   515-685-3397

Kansas   S C Kansas Mustang Club, Richard Mann, President, 1653 S Wichita St, Wichita, KS 67214 316-263-1644

Vintage Mustang Club of Kansas City, Randy Francis, President, PO Box 40082, Overland Park, KS 66204 816-587-5869

Kentucky   Bluegrass Mustang Club, Todd Glenn, President, 1001 Rain Ct, Lexington, KY 40031 606-273-8866

Derby City Mustang Club, Gene Smith, President, 2510 Regal Rd, LaGrange, KY 40031 502-241-8170

Louisiana   Baton Rouge Mustangers, Kathy Pourciau, President, 17034 Hunters Trace W, Prairieville, LA 70769 225-677-5490

Cajun Mustangers, Rodney Breaux, President, 1216 Post Oak Rd #9, Sulphur, LA 70663 337-625-2650

Classic Mustang Association of New Orleans, David Rouse, President, #3 Santa Anna, Jefferson, LA 71217

Michigan   Mustang Club of Mid-Michigan, Brian Sutherland, President, 976 W Saginaw Rd, Vassar, MI 48768 517-823-8802

Mustang Owners Club of Southeastern Michigan, Ronald Movinski, President, 42695 Saltz, Canton, MI 48187 734-981-2836

West Michigan Mustang Club, Richard May, President, 540 Hull Rd, Sparta, MI 49345 616-887-2673

Minnesota   Twin Ports Mustang Club, Scott Twinnings, President, 4640 Schultz Rd, Duluth, MN 55803 218-721-3166

Mississippi   Gumtree Mustang Club, Kenneth Hanks, President, 213 Joanne St, Tupelo, MS 38801 662-842-2276

Mid Mississippi Mustangs, Ricky Sullivan, President, 811 Sherman Ave, Vicksburg, MS 39180 601-634-0001

Mississippi Coast Mustang Club, Paul Loetz, President, 440 Carmague Ln, Biloxi, MS 39531 228-385-1217

Missouri   Greater Ozarks Mustang Club, Robert Snook, President, 269 Kansas Dr, Ozark, MO 65721 417-581-8988

Mid America Mustangers, Wayne Blair, President, PO Box 2185, Independence, MO 64055 816-741-5372

Show-Me Mustang Club, Dave Reed, President, 1186 Rue La Chelle, Creve Coeur, MO 63141 314-439-0843

Nevada   Mustang Club of Las Vegas, Bill Neely, President, PO Box 28705, Las Vegas, NV 89126 702-434-3250

New Jersey   First State Mustangs, Dave Birchmire, President, 5 Bogart Dr, Pennsville, NJ 08070 856-678-6584

Garden State Region Mustang Club, Mike DeLiberto, President, PO Box 289, Wood Ridge, NJ 07075 201-933-6915

South Jersey Mustang Club, Herb Sharp, President, 1013 Cheateau Ct, Atco, NJ 08004 856-768-8428

New Mexico   Rio Grande Mustang Club, Wally Short, President, 12825 Cedarbrook Ave NE, Albuquerque, NM 87111 505-299-4573

New York   Adirondack Shelby-Mustang Club, John Waters, President, PO Box 4424, Halfmoon, NY 12065 518-644-5390

Classic Mustang Long Island, Trudy Kent, President, PO Box 1011, North Massapequa, NY 11758 516-798-6223

Twin Tiers Regional Group, Bill Griffith, President, 336 Castleman Rd, Vestal, NY 13850 607-748-2168

North Carolina   Carolina Regional Mustang Club, Norm Demers, President, 3306 Rillet Ct, Charlotte, NC 28269 704-599-0324

Chrome Pony Mustang Club, Gerald Williams, President, 44429 NC 32N, Sunbury, NC 27979 252-465-8661

Eastern North Carolina Regional Mustang Club, Leslie Joyner, President, 301 S Caswell St, LaGrange, NC 25551 252-566-3826

Section Three – Clubs & Organizations

Mustang Club of America regions (continued)

Gate City Triad Mustang Club, Richard Mullis, President, 138 Dove Meadow Dr, Archdale, NC 27263 336-861-5546

Heart of Carolina Mustang Club, Al Dulaney, President, PO Box 523, Cary, NC 27512 919-387-4585

Mustangers of Western North Carolina, James Jackson, President, Pace Creek Rd, Hendersonville, NC 28792 828-685-9567

Sandhills Regional Mustang Club, Laurin Cooper, President, 349 Rock Hill Rd, Fayetteville, NC 28301 910-483-3854

Southeastern North Carolina Regional Mustang Club, Danny Barnhill, President, 20999 E Hwy 210, Ivanhoe, NC 28447 910-669-2926

Tarheel Mustang Club, Bill Weaver, President, 304 Fosterri Dr, Rocky Mount, NC 27801 919-446-6639

Ohio   Classic Mustang Club of Ohio, Mark Morley, President, 1233 Colston Dr, Westerville, OH 43081 614-895-7059

Mahoning Valley Mustangs, Ken Beadnell, President, 726 N 18th St, Sebring, OH 44672 330-938-6529

Northeastern Ohio Mustang Club, Becky Bose, President, 73 Charlotte St, Akron, OH 44303 330-376-0915

Tri-State Mustang Club, Bob Masraum, President, 330 Miami Valley Rd, Loveland, OH 45140 513-831-2117

Oklahoma   Green Country Classic Mustangs, Randy Voyles, President, PO Box 471361, Tulsa, OK 74147-1361 918-622-1348

Oklahoma Mustang Club, Bob Mollohan, President, PO Box 244, Mustang, OK 73064 405-262-6650

Pennsylvania   Centre Region Mustang Club, Edward Johnstonbaugh, President, 112 Ridge Ave, Centre Hall, PA 16828

First Pennsylvania Mustang Club, Blair Rittenhouse, President, 2600 Northwood Ave, Easton, PA 18045 610-923-6255

Greater Pittsburgh Mustang Club, Duane Lashua, President, 214 Westminster Dr, Moon Township, PA 15108 412-299-7942

Lake Erie Mustang Owners Club, Jerry Seamens, President, 1206 E Gore Rd, Erie, PA 16504 814-825-5421

Mustang Club of Central Pennsylvania, Bobby McNew, President, 20 W York St, Dillsburg, PA 17019 717-432-9503

North Central Mustang Club, Tom Shreiner, President, PO Box 439 Boston Cove, Picture Rocks, PA 17762 570-546-5941

Valley Forge Mustang Club, Jim Aberts, President, 1407 Whitford Rd, West Chester, PA 19380 610-962-4815

Wyoming Valley Mustang & Ford, John Stefanick, President, 121 Lincoln Ave, West Wyoming, PA 18644 717-387-3925

Puerto Rico   Puerto Rico Mustang Club, Luis F Lugo, President, GPO Box 3397, Aguadilla, PR 00605 787-891-3266

Rhode Island   Mustang Club of New England, Jim Silverman, President, 72 Westhaven Dr, Brockton, RI 02301 508-584-8848

South Carolina   Central South Carolina Regional Group, David Phillips, President, PO Box 232, Springfield, SC 29146 803-258-3839

Eastern South Carolina Mustang Club, Gene Turner, President, 780 St Andrews Rd, Florence, SC 29501 843-669-0385

Foothills Regional Group, Brad Center, President, 3324 Oneal Church Rd, Greer, SC 29651

South Carolina Coastal (Low Country) Region Mustang Club, Mike Smith, President, 1836 Belgrade Ave, Charleston, SC 29407 843-571-4536

South Dakota   Rapid Mustang Club, Scott Nixon, President, 103 Starling Ct, Box Elder, SD 57719 605-923-2610

Tennessee   First Tennessee Regional Mustang Club, Mark Marcus, President, 116 Rose Trace Ct, Blountville, TN 37617 423-323-8345

Golden Circle Mustang Club, Tom Cunningham, President, 10 Scenic Hill Dr, Paris, TN 38242 901-642-3369

Lakeway Mustang Club, Carl D Dunn, President, Rt #1 Box 40-1A, Rutledge, TN 37861 423-828-4095

Music City Regional Group, Jim Chism, President, PO Box 780, Fairview, TN 37062 615-446-0520

Mustangs of Memphis, Rick Duncan, President, 582 Dunwick Ct, Collierville, TN 38017 901-854-9896

Rocket City Mustang Club, Michele Wilson, President, 237 Howell Hill Rd, Fayetteville, TN 37334 931-937-6819

Tennessee Valley Mustang Club, Jim McFarland, President, 7030 Whitestone Rd, Knoxville, TN 37938 423-925-3334

Thunder Valley Mustang Club, Randy Dickey, President, 8914 Brow Lake Rd, Soddy-Daisy, TN 27379 423-332-4474

Section Three – Clubs & Organizations

Texas   *Coastal Bend Mustang Club*, Charlie Wright, President, PO Box 72044, Corpus Christi, TX 78472 316-814-0473

Mustang Club of Houston, Les Blankenship, President, 15034 Margison, Houston, TX 77084 281-463-4245

Mustang Owners Club of Austin, Bryan Doty, President, 1422 Deer Ledge Pk, Cedar Park, TX 78613 512-257-7585

Mustangs of East Texas, J Lindsey Bradley, President, PO Box 8970, Tyler, TX 75711 903-561-2568

North Texas Mustang Club, Steve Gaul, President, PO Box 531374, Grand Prairie, TX 75053 972-469-9055

San Antonio Mustang Club, Alan Hibler, President, 2107 Town Oak Dr, San Antonio, TX 78232 210-494-6154

South Texas Mustang Club, Jim Lofino, President, 2700 S Cynthia #2, McAllen, TX 78503 956-971-0133

Southeast Texas Mustang Club, Chris Cormier, President, 8496 Mitchell Rd, Lumberton, TX 77657 409-755-4081

Texas Panhandle Mustang Club, Cathy Pruiett, President, PO Box 2574, Amarillo, TX 79105 806-359-3608

Texoma Mustang Club, Bob Brown, President, 1908 Laurel Rd, Gainesville, TX 76240 817-665-9295

Utah   *Northern Utah Mustang Owners*, Brian Blater, President, 13254 S Forest Meadow Dr, Riverton, UT 84065 801-298-8482

Vermont   *Green Mountain Mustang Club*, Frank Montani, President, 452 Rt 2, South Hero, VT 05486 802-372-8288

Virginia   *Central Virginia Mustang Club*, George Cosier, President, 4915 Leconbury Rd, Richmond, VA 23234 804-271-2139

Lynchburg Area Mustang Club, Robert Guthrie, President, Rt 4, Box 394, Nathalie, VA 24577 804-349-6247

Mustang Club of Tidewater, Doug Sample, President, 132 Cynthia Dr, Hampton, VA 23666 757-399-6334

National Capital Region Mustang Club, Richard Porter, President, 4886 Tobacco Way, Woodbridge, VA 22193 703-590-4512

Roanoke Valley Mustang Club, David Schultz, President, 6043 Old Manor Ct, Roanoke, VA 24019 540-563-4660

Shenandoah Valley Mustang Club, Bob Snyder, President, PO Box 2015, Winchester, VA 22601 304-876-6830

Southeastern Virginia Mustang Club, Jason Stout, President, 8662 Morwin St, Norfolk, VA 23503 757-468-6660

Styling Stangs of Hampton Roads, Omer Gowin, President, 698 Carywood Ln, Newport News, VA 23602 757-874-8202

Valley Mustangs Unlimited, Steven Roadcap, President, 26 Surry Ln, Fisherville, VA 22939 540-943-0712

Washington   *Island Classic Mustang Club*, David Clem, President, PO Box 2628, Oak Harbor, WA 98277

Mustangs Northwest, Jeanie McCain, President, 18514 Marine View Dr SW, Seattle, WA 98166 206-242-4980

Mustangs West Car Club, Al Schaffler, President, 3722 Long Lake Dr SE, Olympia, WA 98503 360-493-1035

Pierce County Mustang Club, Dwight Crumpacker, President, PO Box 1784, Sumner, WA 98390 253-862-6730

West Virginia   *Mid-Ohio Valley Mustang Club*, Russ Alton, President, 2306 Prunty St, Parkersburg, WV 26101 304-428-4851

Wisconsin   *Badgerland Mustang Club*, Dennis Fields, President, PO Box 133, South Wayne, WI 53587 608-439-4648

Western Wisconsin Regional, Herb Long, President, 755 W US Hwy 16, West Salem, WI 54669 608-786-1142

Wisconsin Early Mustangers, Scott Moen, President, 2511 W Carrington Ave, Oak Creek, WI 53154 414-567-2622

Wyoming   *Hoof Beats Mustang Club*, Michele Scott, President, 611 S Oregon Ave, Gillette, WY 82716 307-682-7887

Australia   *Mustang Owners Club of Australia*, Kevin Musgrave, President, 72 Eisemans Rd, Yarrambat, Victoria, 3091

Canada   *Golden Horseshoe Mustang Association*, Bob Swent, President, 519 Limerick Rd, Burlington, ON, L7L 2K5

Mustang Club of Maryland
2317 Bulls Sawmill Rd
Freeland, MD 21053
410-357-5615
E-mail: lhdodsonjr@yahoo.com

Founded 1990. 100 members. Dedicated to keeping the legend of the Mustang alive. Open to all Mustangs and Fords. Five shows yearly, spring and fall cruise, monthly cruise nights, parade participation, summer picnic, Christmas party, monthly newsletter and meetings. Dues: $15/year.

Mustang Owners Club International
Paul McLaughlin
2720 Tennessee NE
Albuquerque, NM 87110
505-296-2554

Founded 1975. 500 members. Open to all Mustangs and Mustang enthusiasts from the earliest to the latest. Stock, restored, modified, race, etc., all welcomed. Large reference library available to answer questions pertaining to Mustangs. Newsletter: *The Pony Express*. Dues: $15/year US, $18/year foreign.

Mustang SVO Owners Association Inc
4234 I-75 Business Spur, PMB 429
Sault Ste Marie, MI 49783-3620
705-525-7861 (SVO1)
FAX: 705-525-5178
E-mail:
svooa.nationaloffice@sympatico.ca

Founded 1989. 350 members. Dedicated to locating and documenting the SVO Mustang and serving the needs of SVO Mustang owners. Collectible insurance appraisal service. National convention, technical support and modification support. Dues: $20/year. Web site: www.corral.net/svo/html

Sierra Mustang Club
PO Box 1793
Fair Oaks, CA 95628
916-967-6659; FAX: 916-967-6044

Founded 1981. 150 members. Need only be interested in the classic Mustang. Primary purpose is to promote the enjoyment and preservation of the 1964-1/2 to 1973 classic Mustang. Meetings held fourth Wednesday of each month at the Smud Building, 6201 S St, Sacremento, CA at 7 pm. Benefits include discounts at various Ford dealerships and participating vendors. Dues: $25/year. Web site: www.geocities.com/motorcity/factory/3629

Sonoma County Mustang Club
PO Box 8716
Santa Rosa, CA 95407
707-544-5852

Founded 1990. 50 members. Interest in Ford Mustangs (all years) and/or other Ford products. Meet 3rd Thursday of each month (except December) at 7:30 pm at Round Table Pizza Parlor, Occidental Rd (one block west of Stony Point), Santa Rosa, CA. Dues: $25/year family. Web site: http://clubs.hemmings.com/sonomamustang/

Southeast Texas Mustang Club
6142 Pine Hill Dr
Kountze, TX 77625
409-246-4081
E-mail: semustclub@aol.com

Founded 1986. 65 members. No restrictions to join, just love Mustangs. We meet every month for monthly meetings. We attend car shows, parades, swap meets, Ford events, etc. Our club has a monthly newsletter and annual car show. Dues: $20/year. Web site: www.setexasmustangclub.org

Stallions Gate Mustang & Ford Club Inc
4736 W Berenice Ave
Chicago, IL 60641
773-685-4748

Founded 1993. 75 members. Club newsletter, parts and service discount with local vendors, club decal, free classified ads, annual club car show, weekly cruises, monthly meetings, social events and wearing apparel. Open to all Mustang and Ford owners. Dues: $25/year. Web site: www.stallionsgate.com

Tri County Thoroughbred Corral
8014 Woodcreek Dr
Bridgeville, PA 15017
412-220-0336; FAX: 412-833-8916
E-mail: mark@mbelectronics.com

Founded 1998. 32 members. We welcome all years of Mustangs. Monthly meetings, car cruises, car shows, restorations, annual oldies benefit dance. Family oriented club. Dues: $25/year. Web site: http://clubs.hemmings.com/tctc

Tri-State Mustang & Ford Club
10423 Lochcrest Dr
Cincinnati, OH 45231
513-771-4558
E-mail: afriedel@cinci.rr.com

Founded 1979. 146 members. Monthly meetings (3rd Wednesday) at Ford Training Center. Annual show, usually 240-260 cars. Monthly newsletter, picnic, fall tour, Christmas party. No restrictions to join. Dues: $25/year. Web site: www.tristatemustang.com

The West Michigan Mustang Club
3736 Parkland Ave SW
Wyoming, MI 49509
616-538-5579
E-mail: mj302boss@aol.com

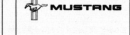

Founded 1981. 200+ members. Our purpose is to preserve, restore and enjoy 1964-1/2 to current Mustangs. Monthly meetings and/or events, newsletter. We have technical advisors and sponsor an all Ford show in June. Ownership not necessary to join, only enthusiasm for Mustangs. Dues: $20/year. Web site: www.wmmc.stangnet.com

Classic Thunderbird Club International
1308 E 29th St, Dept HV
Signal Hill, CA 90806
562-426-2709
E-mail: office@ctci.org

Founded 1961. 8,000 members. Dedicated to the 1955, 1956 and 1957 Thunderbirds. Sells manuals, posters, brochures to members only. We have 6 regional conventions and one international convention. Works with Ford Motor Co for continuance of parts. Everyone welcome to join. Dues: $25/year plus $15 initiation fee. Web site: www.tbird.org/ctci/

Early Birds of Hoosierland
711 S Center St
Flora, IN 46929
219-967-3640
E-mail: marchand@netusa1.net

Founded 1972. 90 members. A club dedicated to the preservation of the 1955, 1956 and 1957 Thunderbirds. Membership is open to anyone with an interest in the classic Thunderbird. Dues: $15/year.

Edmonton Thunderbird 55-66 Club
c/o Marie Knipelberg
1041 Blackburn Close SW
Edmonton, AB Canada T6W 1C7
780-988-5506; FAX: 780-436-5201
E-mail: thunderbirdcalls@excite.com

Founded 2000. 70+ members. You do not have to own a Thunderbird to belong to our club. Show quality is not essential either, but Thunderbird enthusiasm is essential. We accept Thunderbirds from 1955-1966. Monthly publication, *Thunderbird Tweeter*. Our newsletter is available to our members and advertisers only. It contains interesting articles about Thunderbirds, news of club events and activities and illustrations with photos. Material submitted is subject to editing and in no way will infringe on the rights of others. Dues: $15/year Canadian.

**Heartland Vintage Thunderbird
Club of America**
2861 Comanche Dr
Kettering, OH 45420
PH/FAX: 937-235-9343
E-mail: tbirdclub@aol.com

Founded 1985. 2,600 members worldwide. National club dedicated to the preservation of all Thunderbirds 1958-1969. We have regional and national shows and monthly newletter. Club store has jackets, patches, windshield decals and Concours rule books. Dues: $20/year, US funds only. Web site: www.tbirdclub.com

International Thunderbird Club
1 Laurel Mountain Way
Califon, NJ 07830
908-439-3432; FAX: 908-439-3122
E-mail: meg2424@csnet.net

Founded 1993. 1,050 members. Must be Thunderbird owners and/or lovers. Script magazine, international and district shows yearly, technical information and helps locate parts and cars. Dues: $24/year. Web site: www.intl-tbirdclub.com

Long Island Thunderbird Club
100 Van Bomel Blvd
Oakdale, NY 11769-2025
516-963-6828

Founded 1994. 90 members. Meeting once a month, open to all people with interest in Thunderbirds. Social club with various activities such as cruisers, weekend trips, scavenger hunts, picnic, rock and roll shows. Monthly award winning newsletter, *Bird Talk*. Strongly supports the preservation of T-Birds. Dues: $25/year. Web site: http://clubs.hemmings.com/lithunderbird/

**New England's Vintage
Thunderbird Club Inc**
c/o Don Seymour, President
5 Ridgewood Ln, Box 102, RR 3
Farmington, NH 03835
603-859-3491 days, 603-859-7818 eves
FAX: 603-859-3499
E-mail: dseymour@worldpath.net

Membership director: Tom Beggan, 170 Pheasant Ln, Manchester, NH 03109, PH: 603-647-7869. Founded 1991. 300+ members. NEVT is a non-profit club dedicated to the enjoyment and advancement of the motoring sport, with a special emphasis on the Ford Thunderbird. Club membership is open to all owners and enthusiasts interested in the restoration and preservation of Thunderbirds. Membership includes annual subscription to club newsletter, *The Bird's Nest*. Dues: $25/year. Web site: www.nevtclub.com

Rocky Mountain Thunderbird Club
PO Box 620284
Littleton, CO 80162-0284
303-429-6230

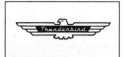

Founded 1980. 150 members. Accept all Thunderbirds. Monthly meetings, tours and special events. Ownership not required, but enthusiasm is. Dues: $21/year. Web site: http://clubs.hemmings.com/rockymttbird/

**TOWNE Thunderbirds of Western
New England**
55 Cherry Ln
Amherst, MA 01002
413-549-0568
E-mail: calswift@mediaone.net

Tucson Thunderbird Club
8945 N Hickory
Tucson, AZ 85737
602-429-4309 work,
520-297-8697 home

Founded 1976. 50 members. Chapter of CTCI, #103. Membership in CTCI is not required. Ownership is not required. Dues: $10/yr. Web site: http://clubs.hemmings.com/tucsonthunderbird/

**Upstate New York Thunderbird
Club Inc**
7 Burton Rd
Greenwich, NY 12834
518-692-7815

Founded 1981. 57 members. A member would benefit by meeting people across the state who are dedicated to preserving, restoring, driving and enjoying T-Birds, a monthly newsletter, meet once a month, annual general membership meeting, Syracuse, first Sunday in November. Dues: $20/year.

**Vintage Thunderbird Club
International**
PO Box 2250
Dearborn, MI 48123-2250
913-390-0439; FAX: 913-390-5215
E-mail: tast@earthlink.net

Founded 1968. 3,000 members worldwide. Enjoying and preserving the "personal luxury experience". Embracing all Thunderbirds, from 1955-today. Serving Thunderbird enthusiasts since 1968. Five regional/one international convention yearly. Chapters across the US and abroad. Award winning bi-monthly *Thunderbird Scoop* magazine. Send for information/application or mail dues to above address. Dues: $30/year US and Canada, $50/year foreign. Web site: www.tbirdclub.net or www.classicar.com/clubs/vintbird/vintbird.htm
chapters:

Arizona	*Central Arizona Chapter*, Mark Gullett, 10542 E Desert Cove Ave, Scottsdale, AZ 85259 480-614-9540; E-mail: amwma@aol.com
California	*Funbirds of Southern California*, John Peters, 9649 Cloverwood St, Bellflower, CA 90706 562-925-6585; E-mail: funbirdsclub@aol.com
	South West Region, Ralph Nunez, Director, 854 N Glenhaven, Fullerton, CA 92832 714-992-1658; E-mail: gotbird@mindspring.com
	Sunbirds of Palm Springs, Herb Rothman, 2822 Alondra Way, Palm Springs, CA 92264 760-323-2482; E-mail: herbted@aol.com
	Wunderbirds of San Diego, Dave Lindquist, 12427 E Penn St, Whittier, CA 92602 E-mail: david@autoclock.com
Colorado	*Rocky Mountain Thunderbird Club*, Cliff Rullman, PO Box 620284, Littleton, CO 80162-0284 303-429-6230; E-mail: funfunfun63x2@aol.com
Florida	*South East Region*, Chuck Volz, Director, 8 Avalon Terr, Palm Coast, FL 32137-2506 904-445-9430; E-mail: jump33@gateway.net
	Space Coast Thunderbirds, Irv Skov, 937 Buford St NW, Palm Bay, FL 32907 407-728-1823; E-mail: clells@aol.com (not person listed)
	Sunshine State Vintage T-Bird Club, Nora Roberts, 155 23rd Ave SE, St Petersburg, FL 33705 813-823-6656

Vintage Thunderbird Club chapters (continued)

Vintage Thunderbirds of Florida, Edward Weigand, 7701 Hatteras Dr, Hudson, FL 34667 727-868-4074

Georgia   *North Georgia Vintage T-Bird Club*, Roger Lindros, 104 Paddock Tr, Peachtree City, GA 30269 404-487-5096; E-mail: rwlndy@aol.com

Illinois   *Chicagoland Thunderbirds*, Wayne Warner, 170A S Highland Ave, Apt A, Lombard, IL 60148 630-627-2866; E-mail: 428@ameritech.net

Land of Lincoln Thunderbirds, Terry Fletcher, 1020 W Walnut, Jacksonville, IL 62650 217-245-5468

North Central Region, Madonna Bednarz, Director, 112 E Dorset Ln, Schaumburg, IL 60193-2912 847-352-0832; E-mail: steve-madonna@juno.com

Indiana   *Vintage Thunderbird Club of Indiana*, Mike Sercer, 8575 N Co Rd 650 E, Brownsburg, IN 46112 317-852-7669; E-mail: serc1mp@iquest.net

Iowa   *Mid America T-Birds of Iowa*, Gene Adkins, PO Box 4511, Brooklyn, IA 52211 515-522-9467

Kansas   *Classic Thunderbird Club of Omaha*, Alan H Tast (interim), 17547 W 158th Pl, Olathe, KS 66062 913-390-0439; E-mail: tast@earth-link.net

Kentucky   *Tri-State Thunderbirds*, Larry Sands, 1531 KY Hwy 144, Owensboro, KY 42303 270-281-5817; E-mail: lstbird@bellsouth.net

Louisiana   *Acadian Thunderbirds*, JV Gale Jr, 1605 Nie Pkwy, New Orleans, LA 70131-1907 504-368-1209; E-mail: ostergale1@aol.com or tbird2@gs.verio.net (not person listed)

Michigan   *Water Wonderland Thunderbirds*, Paul Nichols, 144 Elmwood, Dearborn, MI 48124 313-561-8895; E-mail: tbirdpaul@aol.com

Western Michigan Thunderbird Club, Ed Elzinga, 17040 Ransom St, Holland, MI 49424 616-399-6568; E-mail: sqtbird@macatawa.com

Minnesota   *Thunderbird Midwest*, Barry Blazevic, 8136 Narcissus Ln, Maple Grove, MN 55311 612-494-8477; E-mail: mattcin@uswest.net (not person listed)

Missouri   *Gateway Thunderbirds*, Wayne Evans, 6244 N Lakeshore Dr, Hillsboro, MO 63050 636-274-8844; E-mail: wwayneevans@netscape.net

Vintage Thunderbirds of Kansas City, Timothy E Pundt, 609 E 72nd St, Kansas City, MO 64131-1613 630-627-2866; E-mail: tpundt@aol.com

Nevada   *Sierra Nevada Thunderbird Club*, Chuck MacLeod, 240 Bonnie Briar Pl, Reno, NV 89509 775-826-7848; E-mail: chuckmac@nvbell.net

New Jersey   *Garden State Latebirds Inc*, Al Perilli, 2411 Columbia Ave, Ewing, NJ 08638-3021 609-882-3013; E-mail: urvz92a@prodigy.net (not person listed)

North East Region, Jim Cappuzzo Jr, Director, 10 Amagansett Dr, Morganville, NJ 07751 732-970-0299; E-mail: mseries63tbird@aol.com

New York   *Buffalo Thunderbird Club*, Rich DeMarco, 12023 Brunning Rd, Akron, NY 14001 716-542-4913; E-mail: classicarz@aol.com (not person listed)

Long Island Thunderbirds, Joe Apicella, 100 Van Bomel Blvd, Oakdale, NY 11769-2075 516-589-4620

North Carolina   *Carolinas*, Jim Cockerham, 710 Barney Ave, Winston-Salem, NC 27107 919-788-8780

Ohio   *Buckeye Vintage Thunderbird Club of Ohio*, Kevin Wallenhorst, 15044 Highland Dr, North Royalton, OH 44133 440-582-3589; E-mail: birds2nv@aol.com (not person listed)

Oregon   *Northwest Vintage T-Bird Club of Oregon*, Ted Cooper, 5147 NW 167th Pl, Portland, OR 97229 503-645-7903; E-mail: tpcoop@home.com

Texas   *Capital City Thunderbird Club*, Harold Clark, 8200 Pitter Pat Ln, Austin, TX 78736 512-288-4524; E-mail: bgclark@swbell.net

South Central Region, Lou Paliani, Director, 1304 Greenwood, Schertz, TX 78154 210-566-2118; E-mail: lpaliani@satx.rr.com

South Texas Vintage Thunderbird Club, Kevin M Bois, 12918 Hunters Moon, San Antonio, TX 78214 210-690-3580; E-mail: dbois@satx.rr.com

Vintage Thunderbirds of Houston, Bill Pastor, 615 E 10-1/2 St, Houston, TX 77008 713-862-3556; E-mail: billypastor@pdq.net

Virginia   *Mid-Atlantic Chapter (MA, VA, PA)*, Jim Fratarcangelo, 14079 Winding Ridge Ln, Centerville, VA 20121 703-818-3874

Washington   *Inland Northwest Thunderbird Club*, Leonard Shore, 3710 E 36th, Spokane, WA 99213 509-448-1098

North West Region, Ron Bates, Director, PO Box 135, Southworth, WA 98386 360-871-4100

VTCI-Pacific Northwest (WA, OR), Gary Nevius, 1724 214th St NE, Bothell, WA 98021-7632 206-487-2228; E-mail: ianwall@ix.netcom.com (not person listed)

Wisconsin   *Classic Thunderbird Club of Wisconsin*, James Rugg, W239 S5860 Hwy 164, Waukesha, WI 53186-9302 414-544-0571; E-mail: wibirds@execpc.com (not person listed)

Australia   *Pacific Rim Region*, Pamela Wright, Director, 12 Banstead St, Birkdale QLD 4159, 011-61-7-3822-2067

Thunderbird Owners Club of Australia, Barry Wright, 125 Lyons Rd, Drummone NSW 2047, 029-819-6786; E-mail: tonybren@chariot.net.au (not person listed)

Thunderbirds of Queensland, Mark O'Neill, 5 Vautin Way, Eagleby QLD 4207, 07-3807-4207; E-mail: spica@ecn.net.au (not person listed)

Canada *Club Thunderbird Renaissance du Quebec*, Pierre Blais, 93 Brodeur St, Vaudreuil-Dorion, QC, J7V 1R4 450-455-9961; E-mail: piebla@total.net

Edmonton Thunderbird Club, Marie Knipelberg, 1041 Blackburn Close SW, Edmonton, AB, T6W 1C7 780-988-5506

Okanagon Classic Thunderbird Club, Laurence Wilson, 1660 Simpson Ave, Kelowna, BC, V1X 5Z4 604-762-0602

Southern Ontario Thunderbird Club, Steve Town, 10012 Urlin CresPO Box 92, Port Franks, ON, N0H 2L0 519-243-1193; E-mail: tbirdcan@htl.net

Thunderbird Club of Manitoba, Reid Dewbury, 5706 Roblin Blvd, Winnipeg, MB, R3R 0H2 204-888-1398

Totem Classic Thunderbird Club, Al Wright, 1995 Parkway Blvd, Coquitlam, BC, V3E 3J8 604-464-1061; E-mail: cricket@lightspeed.bc.ca

England *Thunderbirds of England*, Graham Hurley, 11 Wheatley RdCorringham, Essex SS17 9EQ, 011-44-1375-679177; E-mail: hurleybird@talk21.com

France *Thunderbirds of France*, Jean Pierre Champagnol, 46 Av Edouard Branly, 92370 Chaville, 33-1-47-50-52-1221

New Zealand *New Zealand Sulfur City T-Birds*, Fred Rice, PO Box 820, Rotorua, 07-348-9389

Sweden *Squarebird Thunderbird Club of Sweden*, Ulf Gustafsson, Laxvagen 7, 17539 Jarfalla, 46-8-580-19678; E-mail: ulf.gustafsson@mbox322.swipnet.se

Chevy Club
PO Box 11238
Chicago, IL 60611
773-769-6262; FAX: 773-769-3240
E-mail: info@chevyclub.com

Founded 1992. 1,000 members. For enthusiasts of Tracker, Blazer, Storm, Metro, Prizm, Cavalier, Silverado, Suburban and Tahoe. Quarterly publication, *The Chevy & Geo World*. Annual convention. Dues: $25/year. Web site: www.chevyclub.com

Bill Hoover
227 Providence Rd
Annapolis, MD 21401
410-757-0530
E-mail: whhoover@toad.net

Founded 1994. A club for the Glasspar G2 sports roadster owner and enthusiast. The club's object is to provide a registry for all

Glasspars, to be a history and knowledge source for members and a place for member resource exchange. A club newsletter is published. Dues: none.

Dakota Truckin' Chapter
408 N Main
Hartford, SD 57033
605-528-3764
E-mail: daren@willinet.net

Founded 1996. 20 members. Formed to serve all GMC/Chevy pickup, truck, sport utility vehicle owners and enthusiasts. Monthly meetings, quarterly newsletter, technical library, technical support staff, monthly cruises and an annual car show. Dues: $10/year.

National Chevy/GMC Truck Association
PO Box 607458
Orlando, FL 32860
407-889-5549; FAX: 407-889-4110
E-mail: chevnut283@aol.com

Founded 1989. Association dedicated to the preservation and restoration of all 1911-1987 Chevy/GMC trucks. In our official publication, *Pickups 'n Panels In Print* magazine, subscribers have access to classified ads, event notices and it also features subscribers' trucks in this quality four color publication. Free classified ads, tech advice. Dues: $35/year. Web site: www.chevygmctrucks.com

chapters:

California *Central California Chevy/GMC Truck Association*, Mike Percy, 1631 W Magill, Fresno, CA 93711 559-673-7963

Northern California Chevy/GMC Truck Club, Rich Barbaria, 5837 Soltero Dr, San Jose, CA 95123 408-238-3869; E-mail: truckjim@aol.com

Florida *Classic GM Trucks of Central Florida*, Dennis Oakley, 11309 Porto Ct, Orlando, FL 32837 407-438-3655

Illinois *Early Haulers Truck Club*, Vic Lombardo, 8918 Menard, Morton Grove, IL 60053 847-966-0741

Louisiana *Classic Chevy Cameo & GMC Suburban Pickup Club*, Dale Mayeaux, 4356 Riverview Dr, Port Allen, LA 70767-3808 225-383-8864; E-mail: cameo56@yahoo.com

Massachusets *North-East Chevy/GMC Truck Club*, Bryant Stewart, PO Box 155, Millers Falls, MA 01349 978-544-3856

Michigan *Just Truckn' In Michigan*, Jerry Emmendorfer, 21815 Gratiot Rd, Merrill, MI 48637 517-643-5885

Minnesota *Classic Chevy/GMC Truck Club of MN*, Mark Berger, 11231 Norway St NW, Coon Rapids, MN 55448 612-784-0783

Missouri *Genuine Chevy/GMC Truck Club of Kansas City*, Galleen Jackson, 10606 N Main, Kansas City, MO 64155-1630 816-734-5444

Midwest Classic Chevy/GMC Truck Club, Mike Kelley, 1158 Airglades Dr, Arnold, MO 63010-3111 314-464-7256; E-mail: mckelley@lolstl.com

Section Three – Clubs & Organizations

National Chevy/GMC Truck Association chapters (continued)

Nebraska   *The Classic GM Truck Club*, John Ritchey, 3100 N 60th St, Lincoln, NE 68507-2221 402-464-7949; E-mail: jritc65610@aol.com

New Jersey   *Jersey Classic Pickups 'n Panels*, Gary Mulford, 201 N Maple Ave, Tuckerton, NJ 08087-3463 609-294-9459; E-mail: gmulf@worldnet.att.net

Ohio   *Buckeye Chevy/GMC Truck Club*, Don Berringer, 1303 US 42 Rt 1, Ashland, OH 44805 419-289-0591; E-mail: ninjia@bright.net

Oregon   *GM Haulers*, Doug Fyfe, 581 Lancaster Dr SE, PMB 111, Salem, OR 97301 503-399-9670; E-mail: dfyfe36for@aol.com

Texas   *Just Old Trucks, Austin, Texas*, Terry M Stepan, 5209 Ft Mason Dr, Austin, TX 78745-2314 512-447-1446

Pickups 'n Panels of North Texas, Billie Stockton, 1501 Sunnyslope, Carrollton, TX 75007 972-243-5393; E-mail: nei@airmail.net

Utah   *Great Mountain Chevy/GMC Truck Association*, Ken Fisk, PO Box 57344, Murray, UT 84157 801-228-9990 evenings

Washington   *Cameos Northwest*, Carl Hanson, 16740 Meridian Ave N, Shoreline, WA 98133 253-538-1106; E-mail: cameolane@aol.com

Canada   *Maple Leaf Chevy/GMC Truck Club*, Dale Billington, 7168 45th Line, Milton, ON L9T 2X8 905-702-7500

New Zealand   *Kiwi Classic Chevrolet Club*, Doreen Van Ness, PO Box 15-539, New Lynn, Aukland 09-627-1493

Gotfredson Group
15 Davis Dr
Alton, ON Canada L0N 1A0
519-942-0436

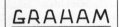

For information, contact at above address: Ed Thornton. Founded 1988. 52 members. International membership. Interest of complete historical information on the Gotfredson truck (1920-1948) and the American Auto Trimming Co (1909-1948). We offer assistance in restoration, preservation, parts location, technical and historical material. Ownership of a Gotfredson is not necessary. Newsletters published.

Graham Brothers Truck & Bus Club
9894 Fairtree Dr
Strongsville, OH 44149
440-238-4956

For membership information, contact at the above address: Edwin L Brinkman. Founded 1975. 215 members. 20 page owners's roster list available for $4 postpaid. Dues: none.

Graham Owners Club International
Terry Graham
401 Center St
Huron, OH 44839-1609
419-433-5609
E-mail: grampaige@aol.com

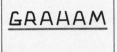

Founded 1971. 600 members. Open to all the world for those dedicated to the preservation and restoration of all Graham built

vehicles. The club provides great information through its quarterly publication, *The Supercharger*, and the many regional meets, as well as the annual international meet. Dues: $20/year US, $24/year other (US funds). Web site: www.members.home.com/rjsill

Competition Network for Harley Racers
PO Box 44
Chagrin Falls, OH 44022
PH/FAX: 440-247-6021

Founded 1990. 1,000+ members. We are a group of enthusiasts that cover the complete racing history for Harley-Davidson racing bikes including XR, XRTT, XR 1000, XLCR, VR, KR, KRTT, WR, MX, RR, XLR, XLRTT, CR, CRTT, CRS, ERS, Baja and all others. Newsletter containing articles, racing news, business cards section. Want and for sale ads, all free with subscription. Also all back issues available and interviews with racers, collectors, dealers and jumpers. Dues: $25/year US, $50/year overseas. Web site: www.hi-speedmotorcycles.com

Heinkel Trojan Club Ltd
c/o John Bennett
11 Cranmer Close
Lewes East Sussex BN7 2JN
United Kingdom
E-mail: heinkeljb@tesco.net

Founded 1980. Approximately 250 members. We cater for the Heinkel/Trojan 3-wheel microcars produced between 1955 and 1964. Also Heinkel scooters. Can supply parts, technical information, advice. Dues vary.

Hillman, Commer & Karrier Club
Capri House
Walton-On-Thomas
Surrey KT12 2LY England
(UK) 01932-269109

Founded 1991. 1,000 members. Club for Hillman, Commer and Karrier vehicles and all derivatives sold under Dodge, Plymouth, etc, plus Chrysler or Talbot badged Hunters, Avengers, Sunbeams and Sunbeam Lotus. Bi-monthly publication: *HCKC News*, free to members. Dues: £15/year.

Hispano-Suiza Society
175 St Germain Ave
San Francisco, CA 94114
415-664-4378

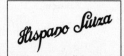

For membership information, contact at the above address: Mr. Jules M Heumann. President. Founded 1975. 150 members. Membership for enthusiasts of Hispano-Suiza cars. Quarterly newsletter, repro owner's manuals, parts books, blazer patches, membership pins, etc. Dues: $50/year US; $60/year overseas.

Hudson-Essex-Terraplane Club
PO Box 8412
Wichita, KS 67208-0412

Founded 1959. 3,500 members. Bi-monthly magazine with free classifieds, clug library, club store, four regional meets, one national meet, over 40 local chapter, parts locator, car registries, technical advisors. Also recognize the British built Railton and Brough-Superior. Ownership not required. Write for current dues. Web site: www.classicar.com/clubs/hudson/hethome.htm chapters:

Alabama   *Midsouth*, Virgil Adcock, 2335 Cherokee Co Rd 24, Piedmont, AL 36272 256-927-5217

Arizona   *Grand Canyon Chapter*, Phil Garrett, 7753 E Alyssum Ln, Mesa, AZ 85208 480-986-4311

California   *California Inland*, Craig Kistler, 1011 Cypress, La Habra, CA 90631

Northern California, Alan Pryor, 1009 Santa Clara Ave, Alameda, CA 94501 510-521-5052; E-mail: hudnut@jps.net

Sacramento Valley, Larry Slocum, 7555 Circle Pkwy, Sacramento, CA 95823-3454 916-421-6080

Southern California, Ken Perkins Jr, 20543 Soledad St, Canyon Country, CA 91351 805-298-9266; E-mail: doctorp99@earthlink.net

Southwestern Borders, Pete Laughton, 10711 Prince Ln, La Mesa, CA 91941 619-442-4811

Colorado *Rocky Mountain*, Linden Welle, 421 Cheyenne St, Fort Morgan, CO 80701 303-867-6589

Florida *Orange Blossom Chapter*, Edward Lathrop, 405 Ridge Rd, Fern Park, FL 32730-2231 407-837-9771; E-mail: elhornet@aol.com

Georgia *Dixie Chapter*, John Upchurch, 107 Granite Bluff, Dahonega, GA 30533 706-864-0164

Idaho *Gem State*, Judy Browning, 1322 Birch Ave, Lewiston, ID 83501 208-746-0679; E-mail: ebrowning6@home.com

Illinois *Central Mississippi Valley*, Bob Hoyle, 2076 IL Pt 26, Dixon, IL 61021 815-288-6140

Gateway Chapter, Terry Meier, RR 7 Box 418, Decatur, IL 62521 217-877-3717; E-mail: tplane@fgi.net

Indiana *South Central*, Ross Woodbury, RR 3 Box 58-1, Elizabeth, IN 47117 812-969-2612

Southern Indiana, Douglass Wildrick, 9225 Indian Creek Rd S, Indianapolis, IN 46259 317-862-4171; E-mail: drdoug@indy.net

Iowa *Central Iowa*, Jay DeJong, 2404 Hwy 163, Pella, IA 50219 515-682-3375

Kansas *Hudsonite Family Chapter*, Jerry Alcorn, 817 W Lincoln, Wellington, KS 67152 316-488-2705

Mo-Kan Hudson Family Chapter, James Durand, 4236 74th St, Meriden, KS 66512 785-484-2756; E-mail: durand@inlandnet.net

Louisiana *Red River Chapter*, Gil Weimer, 279 Bertran St, Lafayette, LA 70503 318-233-0672

Maryland *Chesapeake Bay*, Lewis Mendenhall, 3513 Oxwed Ct, Westminster, MD 21157 410-795-4992; E-mail: essexadv@aol.com

Massachusetts *New England*, Tom Brintnall, 80 Jewell St, Mansfield, MA 02048-1729 E-mail: super6esx@aol.com

Yankee, Jerre Hoffman, 27 Howard St, Chicopee, MA 01013 413-594-2368

Michigan *Hudson Motor Car Co Home Chapter*, Bob Elton, 860 Edwards, Ann Arbor, MI 48103 313-663-1020

Minnesota *North Central*, Mary I Hestness, 5201-34th Ave S, Minneapolis, MN 55417 612-724-9268

Montana *Big Sky*, Dave Amsk, 120 N G St, Livingston, MT 59047 406-222-3817; E-mail: mamsk@mcn.net

Nebraska *Iowa-Nebraska*, Bob Dittrich, 112 N 2nd, PO Box 126, Ceresco, NE 68017 402-665-2132; E-mail: userrkd@aol.com

New Jersey *Garden State Chapter*, Charlie Becht, 32 Starlight Dr, Morristown, NJ 07960 973-539-3144

New Mexico *Southwest*, Leonard Murray, 1805 New Mexico Ave, Las Cruces, NM 88001 505-523-2960

Zia/New Mexico Chapter, Pat Sheeley, 2904 Arno NE, Albuquerque, NM 87107 505-344-6783; E-mail: hudsonwasp@aol.com

New York *Hudson Mohawk*, Ted Wilming, PO Box 324, Corinth, NY 12822 518-654-7108

Long Island, John Salemmo, 145 Sempton Blvd, Franklin Square, NY 11010 516-481-1506

Western New York/Ontario, Dick DeTaeye, 322 Stony Point Rd, Rochester, NY 14624 716-594-2008

North Carolina *Dogwood Chapter*, Darwin White, 752 North Dr, Rocky Point, NC 28457 910-259-9858

Ohio *North Indiana/Ohio*, Noel Renner, 116 Hill, Box 363, Pleasant Hill, OH 45359 513-676-5111

Western Reserve, Fred Lorenz, 6251 Taylor Rd, Leroy Twp, OH 44077 440-254-4781; E-mail: fclorenz@yahoo.com

Oklahoma *Dust Bowl*, Wanda Shelton, 117 S Stevens, Ponca City, OK 74601 580-765-5839

Pennsylvania *Pennsylvania Dutch*, Burl J Gingerich, 45 E Maple St, Dallastown, PA 17313 717-244-9082

Tennessee *Smoky Mountain Heartland*, Harry J (Jerry) Hobbs, 1221 Ownby Cir, Sevierville, TN 37862 865-428-3123; E-mail: cohobbs@aol.com

Texas *North Texas*, Mike Harrel, 5603 Hudson St, Dallas, TX 75206 214-821-4546; E-mail: obidos@cyberramp.net

South Texas, Steve Brookins, 6401 Rusty Ridge Rd, Austin, TX 78731 512-323-6212; E-mail: flcb8844@aol.com

Utah *Deseret*, Gert Kristiansen, 1731 S 500 E, Salt Lake City, UT 84105 801-486-1635

Washington *Northwest*, Doug Henschel, 708 NW 87th Ave, Vancouver, WA 98665 360-574-0301; E-mail: critter20@juno.com

Wisconsin *Chicago-Milwaukee*, Jack Stewart, 2025 Aubutus St, Janesville, WI 53546 608-756-3273

Section Three – Clubs & Organizations

Hudson-Essex-Terraplane Club chapters (continued)

Wyoming *High Plains Chapter*, Bill Marcus, PO Box 404, Shoshoni, WY 82649 307-876-2789

Australia *Australia Chapter*, Phil Haxby, 216 Ryans RdEltham North, 3095 Victoria, E-mail: phaxby@melbpc.org.au

Australia/New South Wales, Les Pendlebury, Hudson AMC Group19 Kay St, Carlingford 2118 NSW, E-mail: huddy@zip.com.au

New Zealand *New Zealand Rep*, Geoffrey Clark, 72 Scotia St, Nelson, E-mail: geoffclark@xtra.co.nz

South Africa *South African Rep*, Mike Davidson, PO Box 19805 Fishers Hill, 1408

Hupmobile Club Inc
158 Pond Rd
North Franklin, CT 06254
860-642-6697
E-mail: hupmobile@99main.com

Founded 1970. 600 members worldwide. Dedicated to the restoration, preservation and enjoyment of Hupmobiles, Hupp-Yeats and RCH automobiles. Publish *Hupp Herald* magazine, 3 times a year; *Hupmobile Parts Locator Bulletin*, bi-monthly. Dues: $22.50/year US, $25/year Canada, $30/year overseas (US funds). Web site: http://clubs.hmn.com/hupmobile/

The 101 Association
PO Box 296
Brookfield, MA 01506
508-867-8097
E-mail: rwmc101@aol.com

Founded 1983. 420 members. Interest in Indian 101 Scout, 1928-1931. Quarterly publication, *The Wow!*. Annual meets with awards, fun run and mini meets. Dues: $20/year US. Web site: www.101scout.com

---

Scout & International Motor Truck Association
PO Box 313
New Palestine, IN 46163
PH/FAX: 765-763-8736
E-mail: ihsimta@aol.com

Founded 1990. 1,100+ members. International Harvester trucks, pickups, Scouts. *International Happenings* magazine is published 6 times per year, features articles, member rigs, best buys, tech tips, member exchange. Dues: $30/year.

Iso & Bizzarrini Owners Club
2025 Drake Dr
Oakland, CA 94611
PH/FAX: 510-339-8347

Founded 1980. 200 members. Founded to promote the preservation and awareness of the marques. Membership includes quarterly magazine *Griffon* and bi-monthly newsletter *Bresso Express*. No restrictions to join. Club sponsors meets and social gatherings, with an annual international meet at the Annual Monterey Historic Races. Dues: $35/year USA, $45/year overseas.

Classic Jaguar Association
2860 N Victoria Dr
Alpine, CA 91901
619-445-3152
E-mail: ottersrest@home.com

Founded 1952. 1,000 members. Dedicated to the restoration, preservation, and enjoyment of SS cars and older Jaguars. Publishes news and technical bulletins. Dues: $25/year.

Classic Oldtimer Veteranen Club of Austria
Mittersteig 11/1/6
Vienna 1040 Austria
++43 (664) 1821965; FAX: ++43 1 5052663
E-mail: millersclassic@compuserve.com

Founded 1998. 63 members. Publishes *Oldtimer Gazette* quarterly, includes news around Austria, Switzerland and Germany. Dues: $30/year Euro. Web site: www.leather.at

---

Jaguar Club of Connecticut
219 Greenwich Ave
New Haven, CT 06519
203-776-8148

Founded 1981. 135 members. No restrictions to join. Newsletter each month, *Purrings*. Events monthly. Dues: $20/year. Web site: http://welcome.to/thejaguarclubofct.com

---

The Jaguar Club of Montreal
c/o Daniel Thompson
2075 Melba St
St Bruno, QC Canada J3V 3R9
450-441-0197
E-mail: dthompson@gbc.ca

Founded 1956. 100 members. Informal, no-cost club comprising of 100 members/owners who exchange ideas, technical expertise, parts and repair sources and information on British car events of interest. Dues: none.

Jaguar Club of Tulsa Inc
Rt 1, Box 650
Talala, OK 74080-9724
918-371-6445; FAX: 918-371-0610
E-mail: willjag@ionet.net

Founded 1970. 200 members. Membership applications are accepted from anyone with a love of automobiles, especially Jaguars. Members receive our monthly newsletter and a national magazine. Members from a 5-state area enjoy over 24 activities per year including our Concours d'Elegance that is one of the largest in this region. Dues: $36/year. Web site: www.ionet.net/~willjag

---

Jaguar Clubs of North America Inc
Membership Dept
9685 McLeod Rd, RR 2
Chilliwack, BC Canada V2P 6H4
FAX: 604-794-3654
E-mail: parkhill@uniserve.com

Founded 1954. 5,500 members who belong to 51 local clubs in the US, Canada and Mexico which are affiliated with JCNA. JCNA sponsors championships in Concours d'Elegance, rally and slalom competition. The local clubs offer their own social, technical and other programs. Dues, vary according to location. Web site: www.jcna.com

---

Jewett Owners Club
24005 Clawiter Rd
Hayward, CA 94545
510-785-1948

For membership information, contact at the above address: Terrell Shelley. Founded 1982. 30 members. Open to Jewett

owners. Register of Jewett cars and clubs, parts, location and literature for all Jewett models. Information on request.

Kaiser Frazer Owner's Club International
PO Box 1014
Stroudsburg, PA 18360

Founded 1959. 1,800 members. Monthly news bulletin, quarterly magazine, various regional meets, annual national meet. Dues: $25/year USA and Canada; $30/year foreign. Web site: http://members.tripod.com/~ben1937/kfoci.htm

King Motor Car Club of America
PO Box 99155
Seattle, WA 98199
206-285-3490; FAX: 206-727-7928
E-mail: kingmotorcars@ix.netcom.com

Founded 1996. 12 members. Membership is open to all who have an interest in the life, times and contributions of Charles Brady King 1869-1957, the state of the art design of Mr King's cars and restoration knowledge to enjoy the active hobby. Dues: $5/year. Web site: http://clubs.hemmings.com/kingmotorcar

The International King Midget Car Club
9409 W St Rt 571
Laura, OH 45337
PH/FAX: 937-698-5144
E-mail: kmidgetcar@aol.com

Founded 1992. Now over 250 members. No restrictions to join. Benefits are meeting other King Midget owners and to preserve the history of the King Midget car. There is an International King Midget Car Club Jamboree in August every year. Also, mini events such as parades or tours starting spring through fall. Dues: $15/year.

Kissel Kar Klub
147 N Rural St
Hartford, WI 53027
414-673-7999

For membership information, write to the above address. 197 members. Membership limited to owners of cars produced by the Kissel Motor Car Company, Hartford, WI (1906-1931), also to owners of their commercial vehicles including funeral cars, taxi cabs and fire trucks, and to personnel of the old company and family members who signify interest. Dues: none. Donations accepted.

Knox Motor Car Club of America
6 Concord Dr
East Longmeadow, MA 01028
413-525-6782

Founded 1986. 25 members. Monthly newsletter. No restrictions. Car owners or interested people. Dues: $25/year.

Lamborghini Owners' Club
Jim Kaminski
PO Box 7214
St Petersburg, FL 33734
FAX: 727-392-3474

Founded 1978. 1,100+ members. Oldest Lamborghini club in the world. Quarterly newsletter with technical tips, parts sources, meeting information, marque items for sale. Send for application form.

Dansk Lancia Register
Boserupvej 510
DK-3050 Humlebaek Denmark
PH/FAX: +45-49191129
E-mail: aurelia@teliamail.dk

Founded 1989. 120 members. Club for owners of Lancia cars. Technical aid and information. Rallies, meetings. Dues: 200 DKK/year.

Lancia Motor Club
David Baker
PO Box 51
Wrexham, LL11 5ZE England
PH/FAX: 01270 620072

Founded 1947. 2,500 members worldwide. For owners and lovers of the marque. "We cater to all models from 1911 Eta to current production models." Web site: www.lanciamotorclub.co.uk

Colorado Continental Convertible Club
385 S Olive Way
Denver, CO 80224-1354
PH/FAX: 303-322-2674
E-mail: wr77@com

Founded 1973. 60-75 members. Devoted to 1961-1967 Lincoln Continental 4-door convertibles. Anyone owning or interested in the 4-door convertibles is welcome. Trips, shows, parades, social functions, dealership displays and technical sessions. Publishes bi-monthly *CCCC Comments*, included in membership. Information on club trips, shows, parades, social functions, members activities, technical tips, advertisement for persons or services for the cars, pictures of events and members and their cars. Dues: $25/year.

Continental Mark II Association
5225 Canyon Crest Dr, Ste 71-217CMA
Riverside, CA 92507
909-686-2752; FAX: 909-686-7245
E-mail: markiient@earthlink.net

Founded 1965 as Continental Mark II Owners Association. 700 members. A fellowship of owners and enthusiasts with the goal of maintaining, restoring and enjoying 1956-1957 Continental Mark II automobiles. Membership includes four quarterly issues of *The Continental* newsletter. Dues: $20/year US & foreign.

Lincoln and Continental Owners Club
PO Box 570709
Dallas, TX 75357-0709
800-527-3452, 972-617-8876
FAX: 972-617-8371

Founded 1953. Over 4,000 members. Dedicated to the enjoyment, preservation and restoration of all Lincolns and Continentals. Membership includes *Continental Comments* magazine, published bi-monthly. Three national meets annually. National dues: $30/year US, Canada and Mexico; $40/year other countries (US funds). Web site: www.lcoc.org

Lincoln Owners Club
PO Box 660
Lake Orion, MI 48361
248-693-4636; FAX: 810-274-1010

Organized in 1956. 500 members. Primarily interested in Lincolns built between 1921 and 1939. Specifically models L, K, KA and KB. However, ownership of such a Lincoln is not necessary for membership. Anyone interested in Lincolns is welcome. Dues: $25/year. Web site: http://clubs.hemmings.com/lincolnowners/

Lincoln Zephyr Owners Club
PO Box 422-H
Hazel Green, AL 35750-0422
931-433-0065; FAX: 931-438-4742
E-mail: mead@vallnet.com

Founded 1968. 1,200 members. Bi-monthly issues of the award winning publication, *The Way of the Zephyr*. Western, central US and eastern meets each year, sites vary. Central and western chapters host regional events. Specializing in V12 engined Lincolns consisting of 1936-1948 Lincoln Zephyrs, 1941-1942 Lincoln Customs, 1940-1948 Lincoln Continentals. Dues: $35/year US, $43 Canada/Mexico, $53 overseas. Web site: www.lzoc.org

Road Race Lincoln Register (RRLR)
726 E Ind Pk Dr, #13
Manchester, NH 03109
603-666-4995

Founded 1972. 340 members. Must be interested in 1949 through 1957 Lincoln Premieres, Capris, Customs or Cosmopolitans and 1949 through 1951 "Baby" Lincolns on Mercury body shell, ownership not required. We have several annual regional meets and have about 35 Canadian and overseas members. Dues: $19/year.

Club Elite (Lotus Type 14)
6238 Ralston Ave
Richmond, CA 94805-1519
PH/FAX: 510-232-7764

Founded 1971. 210 members. Open to any Lotus enthusiast. Annual register. Newsletters as available. Parts sources. Dues: $20/year US and Canada, $25/year foreign.

Lotus Ltd
PO Box L
College Park, MD 20741
PH/FAX: 301-982-4054
E-mail: lotusltd@lotuscarclub.org

Founded 1973. 1,500 members. Lotus Ltd is the largest club for Lotus car enthusiasts in the US. The club is an entirely non-profit volunteer organization with 15 affiliated local groups. Technical assistance. Monthly publication: *Lotus ReMarque*. Dues: $35/year new members, $25/year renewals in US; outside US add $5. Web site: www.lotuscarclub.org

Marmon Club
3044 Gainsborough Dr
Pasadena, CA 91107
626-449-2325

For membership information on Marmon and/or Roosevelt, contact at the above address: Duke Marston, Secretary. Founded 1970. 250 members. Annual directory of members and their Marmon and/or Roosevelt cars. Ownership not required for membership. Worldwide membership, bimonthly publication. Dues: $20/year US, $25/year foreign (US funds, US bank).

The Maserati Club
PO Box 5300
Somerset, NJ 08875-5300
732-249-2177; FAX: 732-246-7570
E-mail: email@themaseraticlub.com

Founded 1986. 5,000 members. A multi-national club with 4+ US chapters and 3+ international chapters (Canada, Japan, Australia). Open to all Maserati enthusiasts. We publish *Il Tridente* magazine and hold over 50 events per year worldwide. Dues: contact your local chapter. Web site: www.themaseraticlub.com

Mazda Club
PO Box 11238
Chicago, IL 60611
773-769-6262; FAX: 773-769-3240
E-mail: info@mazdaclub.com

For information, contact at the above address: Ernest Feliciano, President. Open to all Mazda owners including the RX-7, Miata, MX-6, 626, MX-3, trucks and SUVs. Technical advice, parts discounts and newsletters. Publication, *The Only Way*. Dues: $25/year. Web site: www.mazdaclub.com

Mazda RX-7 Club
1774 S Alvira St
Los Angeles, CA 90035
323-933-6993, 1 pm to 6 pm

Founded 1978. 1,400 members. A technical service club aimed at the enthusiast who does some of his own maintenance and would like to improve his RX-7 with performance and cosmetic accessories. Sample *Rotary Review*, $5. Dues: $30/year; $40/year foreign.

Miata Club of America
6850 Shiloh Rd E, Ste D
Alpharetta, GA 30023
770-205-8832; FAX: 770-205-8837
E-mail: Diane@Miataclub.org

Founded 1988. 25,000 members. No restrictions to join. The club has over 100 chapters thoroughout the US and 15 foreign affiliates. Dues: $29/year US, $39/year Canada, $50/year foreign. Web site: www.miataclub.org

Northstar RX-7 Club
8510 Nicollet Ave S
Bloomington, MN 55420
E-mail: president@nrx7club.com

Founded 1999. 43 members. Must own a Mazda RX-7 or acquire one within 1 year of joining. Multiple monthly events in summer and some during the winter. Monthly newsletter, discounts at local Mazda dealers and select web sites. Serves MN, IA, ND, SD and WI. Dues: $25/year. Web site: www.nrx7club.com

International 190SL Group Inc
3895 Bailey Ridge Dr
Woodbury, MN 55125
PH/FAX: 612-714-1211
E-mail: 190slgroup@mmm.pcc.org

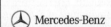

Founded 1983. 450 members. Bi-monthly newsletter, regional and national meets, technical support, camaraderie of other Mercedes 190SL enthusiasts. Dues: $30/year.

Mercedes-Benz 190SL Club e.V.
Wilfried Steer
Wittinger Strasse 154
29223 Celle Germany
05141-930190; FAX: 05141-381787

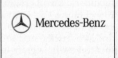

Founded 1989. 700 members. The club is specialized in the Mercedes-Benz 190SL type. We are accepted by the factory with worldwide memberships. At the moment we are organizing meetings, parts services (used and reproduction ones) and we do our own coloured magazine. Dues: DM120/year.

Mercedes-Benz 300SL Gullwing Group International
776 Cessna Ave
Chico, CA 95928
530-345-6701
E-mail: gestep3457@aol.com

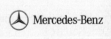

Founded 1961. 600 members. Open to owners of 300SL gull-wings and roadsters and those interested in them. Monthly publication *300 Star Letter*, tech tips, parts, projects, annual convention in different parts of USA. Dues: $75/year USA, $95/year Canada and foreign.

Mercedes-Benz Club of America
1907 Lelaray St
Colorado Springs, CO 80909
800-637-2360; FAX: 719-633-9283
E-mail: info@mbca.org

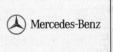

Founded 1956. 27,000 members. Bi-monthly magazine, section newsletter, National events, local events. Dues: $45/year. Web site: www.mbca.org

Mercedes-Benz Club of America-Toronto Section
35 Birchcroft Rd
Etobicoke, ON Canada M9A 2L5
PH/FAX: 416-233-6599
E-mail: dees_frohlich@sympatico.ca

Founded 1990. 250 members. Must be an owner or have an interest in Mercedes-Benz and be a resident of Province of Ontario, Canada. Sections in Toronto and Ottawa, Ontario. Dues: $40/year US. Web site: www.mbca-toronto.org

Mercedes-Benz IG Germany
PO Box 444
Kreuztal 57211 Germany
+49 2737 25300; FAX: +49 2737 1325
E-mail: info@mbig.de

Founded 1988. 2,000 members. Cars from 1953 to 1982, all types including trucks. Technical literature. Club magazine: *Ponton-Kurier*, free to members, quarterly, 2,500 subscribers. Dues: EUR 50/year. Web site: www.mbig.de

Brewtown Cruisers Mercury Car Club
N21 W22139 Glenwood Ln
Waukesha, WI 53186
414-549-5646
E-mail: mercrews@aol.com

Founded 1980. 50 plus members. Open to all owners of 1949, 1950, 1951 Mercurys and Lincolns. Monthly meetings; annual show in May at The Nite Owl Drive-In; monthly newsletter, *Mercrews News*. Dues: $20/year.

Capri Club of Chicago
7158 W Armitage
Chicago, IL 60707
773-889-5197; FAX: 630-971-2875

For membership information, contact at the above address: Wayne H Tofel. Founded 1974. 45 members. Club functions include events, information and discounts for Capri owners. Monthly newsletter. Dues: $20/year. Web site: www.niagara.com/~bevc/ccc.htm

Carolina Cougar Club
5970 Fairview Rd, Ste 106
Charlotte, NC 28210
704-643-6430; FAX: 704-643-6425
E-mail: panther@webserve.net

Founded 1998. 60 members. Any family with an appreciation for and the preservation of the Mercury Cougar automobile. Memberships are for family members. You do not have to own one to be a member. Quarterly publication, *Scratching Post* is included in the membership. Publication has club meeting news, calendar of shows in the Carolina region, tech tips, letters from members. Dues: $15/year.

Cougar Club of America
Ron Crouch
1637 Skyline Dr
Norfolk, VA 23518
757-587-5498
E-mail: membership@cougarclub.org

Founded 1980. 1,200 members. For enthusiasts of Mercury Cougars. Quarterly publication. Dues: $25/year US, $30/year Canadian and foreign. Web site: www.cougarclub.org

CT Cougar Club
Richard Clark
75 Thayer Rd
Manchester, CT 06040
860-649-8520

Founded 1989. 40 members. Interest in or ownership of Mercury Cougars. Dedicated to the preservation of the 1967-73 Mercury Cougar. Bi-monthly newsletters, cruises, meetings, picnics, rallies, car shows, swap meets and technical sessions. Dues: $12/year. Web site: http://clubs.hemmings.com/ctcougar/

International Mercury Owners Association
6445 W Grand Ave
Chicago, IL 60707-3410
773-622-6445; FAX: 773-622-3602

Founded 1991. 1,250 members. Open to all Mercury enthusi-

asts. Quarterly publication, *Quicksilver*. Ads listed free to members (non-commercial). Dues: $35/year US and Canada, $40/year international.

Mercury Cyclone/Montego/Torino Registry
19 Glyn Dr
Newark, DE 19713-4016
302-737-4252 5-9:30 EST
E-mail: robscyclone@juno.com

Founded 1992. 175 members. This low key club registers all known 1964-1972 Cyclones, 1968-1979 Montegos and Torinos & Rancheros as well as 1970-1/2 Falcons. It doesn't matter if they are on the road or in a junkyard. Restoration help, classifieds, feature cars, history and info all put out in the *Registry Update*, 3 times per year. Specializing in 1970-1972 cars. There is no charge to add a car to the list or ask questions! Dues: $5/year, $6/Canada, $8/foreign (in US funds). Web site: http://clubs.hemmings.com/cyclonemontegotorinoregistry/

Mid-Century Mercury Car Club
1816 E Elmwood Dr
Lindenhurst, IL 60046
847-356-2255
E-mail: cruzinmerc@aol.com or cwalter@kusd.kusd.edu

For more information, contact at the above address: Rusty Bethley. Founded 1977. 400 members. Ownership not required. Dedicated to the preservation of 1949-1951 Mercurys, custom or stock. Dues: $15/year US and Canada, $21/year foreign.

Southwest Mercury Club
1336 E Rock Wren Rd
Phoenix, AZ 85048
480-460-7692; FAX: 480-460-7693
E-mail: geclor@prodigy.net

Founded 1995. 48 members. Must be a member of IMOA (International Mercury Owners Association). Dues are paid to IMOA, region dues included. Web site: www.southwestmercuryclub.com

Metz Chain Gang
25 Middle Valley Rd
Long Valley, NJ 07853
908-832-2186

Founded 1952. 85 members. We are a very low-key but highly enthusiastic group. Our forte is in history of vehicle, Metz family and preservation of Metz cars.

American MGB Association
PO Box 11401
Chicago, IL 60611-0401
800-723-MGMG, 773-878-5055
FAX: 773-769-3240
E-mail: info@mgclub.org

For membership information, contact at the above address: Frank Ochal, President. Founded 1975. 3,000 members. Open to MG owners and enthusiasts. North America's official registry for MGBs, MG Midgets, MGB/GT V8s and MG 1100/1300s. Publication: *AMGBA Octagon*. Dues: $30/year. Web site: www.mgclub.org

Big Bend MGs
638 E College Ave
Tallahassee, FL 32301
850-222-9317; FAX: 850-561-0021
E-mail: pkaiser@nettally.com

Founded 1998. 68 members. Members receive monthly newsletter, *Tally-Ho*, as well as a subscription to *British Marque*. Club meets 2nd Tuesday of each month. Host of Rendezous 2001 in Tallahassee, FL. Dues: $24/year. Web site: www.bigbendmgs.com

Central Ohio MG Owners
10260 Covan Dr
Westerville, OH 43082-9295
614-882-6191

Founded 1983. 185 members. A group of MG enthusiasts who welcome participation of all MG owners. The club encourages the preservation and driving of MGs and the opportunity to enjoy the friendship of other families involved in the hobby. Several events are held each year including tours, car shows, picnics and an annual Christmas party. A newsletter is published 5 times a year to keep members informed. Initiation fee, $2.50. Dues: $7.50/year.

Chicagoland MG Club
PO Box 455
Addison, IL 60101

Founded 1976. 350 members. Enjoy MGs, any year. Publishes *Driveline* monthly. Dues: $20/year. Web site: www.chicagolandmgclub.com

Connecticut MG Club
240 New Harwinton Rd
Torrington, CT 06790
860-482-MGMG
E-mail: woofmg@snet.net

Founded 1988. 350 members. Welcomes all MG drivers. Holds informal but regular meetings, travels to MG events throughout New England, holds joint events with other clubs. Provides technical information and advice. Dues: $20/year. Web site: www.homestead.com/mgclub

Eastern New York MGA Club
Jon Rubel, President
3010 Avenue T
Brooklyn, NY 11229-4008
718-891-5776; FAX: call first
E-mail: eemgee@aol.com

Founded 1990. 100+ members. Club serves the entire MG community including MGTs, MGAs, MGBs, MGCs and MG Midgets in the New York, Long Island, New Jersey, Pennsylvania and Connecticut area. Award winning 30-page newsletter with full color pages is printed bi-monthly. Club hosts all British marque car shows, an annual gymkhana, superb tech sessions all through the winter months, picnics, an annual Winterfest dinner and more. Dues: $20/year.

Emerald Necklace MG Register
PO Box 81152
Cleveland, OH 44181
216-228-1063
E-mail: info@mgcleveland.com

Founded 1980. 230 members. Serving the northern Ohio area and open to all MG enthusiasts. Monthly newsletter, tech sessions, rallies, special events and support for those who are octagonally inclined. Dues: $20/year. Web site: www.mgcleveland.com

Florida Suncoast MG Car Club
PO Box 0251
Tampa, FL 33601-0251

Founded 1980. 200 members. A social club organized to promote the knowledge, understanding and preservation of the MG. The club has monthly meetings, organizes a full calendar of car related activities, charitable endeavors, inter-club events, and publishes a monthly newsletter. Membership is open to all MG car owners and individuals interested in the MG motor car. Dues: $20/year. Web site: http://members.aol.com/fsmgcc

Kansas City MG Car Club
1113 NE Franklin Dr
Lees Summit, MO 64064
816-795-9628
E-mail: mgcarclub@kansascity.com

Founded 1982. 200 members. Open to all enthusiasts that enjoy sharing good times. Monthly newsletter, socials and events. Dues: $22/year. Web site: www.kcmgcc.com

MG Car Club Central Jersey Centre
PO Box 435
Convent Station, NJ 07961
973-267-3630; FAX: 973-731-0370
E-mail: swag11@worldnet.att.net

Founded 1963. 150 members. Call phone number listed for further information regarding time and place of monthly meetings, scheduled activities, etc. Dues include monthly newsletter, *Meshing Gears*. Dues: $20/year. Web site: www.geocities.com/~mgcarclub/

MG Car Club-Long Island Centre
177 Truburg Ave
N Patchogue, NY 11772
PH/FAX: 631-475-2889
E-mail: mgblackwell@webtv.net

Founded 1956. 200 members. *Skidmarks* newsletter. Events: The British Are Coming, the Vanderbilt Invitation Concours. We also do tours, rallies, swap meets and a lot of fun and information. Dues: $25/year.

MG Car Club Ltd, Washington DC Centre
PO Box 6321
Arlington, VA 22206
703-207-9048
E-mail: schooler@erols.com

Founded 1951. 220 members. One of the oldest US centres of the MG Car Club Ltd, UK. Membership open to all MG enthusiasts (MG ownership not a prerequisite). Host 35 events annually, they include: tech sessions, rallies, gymkhanas, caravans, membership meetings, car shows, etc. All events are free to members. Dues: $25/year. Web site: http://members.aol.com/mgccwdcc

MG Classics of Jacksonville
227 Hollywood Forest Dr
Orange Park, FL 32073
904-264-3676; FAX: 904-264-7023
E-mail: nwnel@bellsouth.net

Founded 1971. 100+ members. Full membership restricted to owners of MG automobiles. Monthly meetings, monthly newsletter, car shows, tours, driving events. We sponsor the "Gathering of the Faithful South" every third year in Florida. Dues: $25/year. Web site: www.mgclassics.org

MG Drivers Club of North America
18 George's Place
Clinton, NJ 08809-1334
PH/FAX: 908-713-6251
E-mail: marfmil@hotmail.com

Founded 1997. First US/Canada wide club open to all types of MGs. Open to anyone interested in the MG marque. Supporting existing registers and associations. Strong voice for car hobbyist rights. Discounts from major British car parts suppliers. Annual gathering, "The Drive-In". Expert technical advice. Our quarterly publication, *The Log Book*, covers all aspects of the MG marque, past, present and future as well as club news. Dues: $20/year. Web site: www.mgclub.com

MG Octagon Car Club
Unit 1/2, Parchfields Enterprise Pk
Colton Rd, Trent Valley
Rugeley, Staffs WS15 3HB England
01889 574666; FAX: 01889 574555
E-mail: harry@mgoctagoncarclub.com

For membership information, contact at the above address:
Harry Crutchley. Founded 1969. 2,500 members. Open to all,
but full membership is given only to owners of pre-1956 MGs, so
that we can give more personal service to our members. Dues:
$50/year. Web site: www.mgoctagoncarclub.com

MG Vintage Racers Newsletter
Mark Palmer, Editor
253 Bridlepath Rd
Bethlehem, PA 18017
FAX: 610-954-9489
E-mail: mgvmark@hotmail.com

Founded 1981. 200 members. Must actively race a vintage MG
(up to 1967) to join. Newletter for people who actively race a vintage MG. Includes race reports, tech articles, historic articles
and news. Joining fee: $10. Web site: www.mgvr.org

Minnesota MG T Register
16780 St Mary's Dr
St Mary't Point, MN 55043
E-mail: mnmgtr@mn.mediaone.net

Founded 1975. 85 members. Open to all enthusiasts of the T
Series MG and earlier. Monthly publication, *The Tattler,* monthly
or more frequent events including tours, tech sessions, rallys,
picnics, etc. Weekly lunches and natter. Dues: $20/year plus $5
initiation. Web site: http://people.mn.mediaone.net/mnmgtr

New England MG T Register Ltd
PO Drawer 220
Oneonta, NY 13820-0220
607-432-6835; FAX: 607-432-3342
E-mail: knudsonr@norwich.net

For membership information, contact at the above address:
Richard L Knudson. Founded 1963. 4,000 members. Regular
membership is open only to owners of 1955 or older MGs powered by original type engine; all others may become associate
members. Our bimonthly journal, *The Sacred Octagon,* is regard-
ed as the best source of MG historical material in the world.
Dues: $35/year, plus $15 initiation fee. Web site:
www.nemgt.org

**North American MGA Register
(NAMGAR)**
PO Box 11746
Albuquerque, NM 87192-0746
505-293-9085; FAX: 505-332-3116

Founded 1975. Over 2,000 members. A volunteer, non-profit,
national register. Serving the MGAs, Magnettes and period variants 1954-1963. Annual event "Get Together". Local chapters in
many areas. A register of MGCC, England. Dues: $25/year US,
$40/year foreign.
Web site: http://members.aol.com/namgarusa/mg.htm

North American MGC Register
Tom Boscarino, Chairman
3 Horseshoe Rd
Barnardsville, NC 28709-7700
704-274-2269

Founded 1980. 500 members. A volunteer, non-profit, national
register. Serving the MGC and MGC/GT 1968-1969. Annual
event, Challenge of Brute Aggressives. A register of the MGCC,
England. Annual membership: $20.

The Philadelphia MG Club
1913-D Darby Rd
Havertown, PA 19083-2407
610-446-2073
E-mail: mgbgt1@hotmail.com

Founded 1980. 100 members. No restrictions. We participate in car
shows, road rallies (spring and fall MG vs Triumph rallies), tech
sessions and car museum trips. We sponsor the MGs at Mercer
British car show in October and have an annual Octagonal Holiday
dinner in December. Monthly 'GT' get-together at a local restaurant.
Publishes a monthly newsletter, *The Nuffield News.* Dues:
$20/year. Web site: www.clubs.hemmings.com/phillymgclub

Texas MG Register
1243 Chandler Cir
Prosper, TX 75078
972-346-2551
E-mail: gary@sandusky.cc

Founded 1975. 200 members. The Texas MG Register is a long
time Texas organization dedicated to the preservation and enjoyment of any model of MG. The club is open to everyone and it
publishes a monthly newsletter. Dues: $30/year. Web site:
www.tmgr.org

Capital Area Mopars
415 9th St
Watervliet, NY 12189
518-274-5840
E-mail: aarmaniac@yahoo.com

Founded 1996. 95 members. Open to all Mopar enthusiasts.
Benefits include member only discounts at local dealers and discounts at shows. Put on two shows each year. Have cruises to
local dealerships. Phone hotline to pass information. Dues:
$10/year. Web site: www.capitalareamopars.com

Section Three – Clubs & Organizations

Capital City Mopars Car Club of California Inc
PO Box 340426
Sacramento, CA 95834-0426
916-925-0336
E-mail: editor@capitalcitymopars.com

Founded 1992. 150 members. Restrictions: must be 18+ years old, registered owner of a Chrysler Corp (Daimler-Chrysler) any vintage vehicle, valid driver's license and must be active member. Monthly newsletter, monthly meeting, annual car show, various club member events (poker runs, picnics, parades, dinners, cruises, etc), club member only T-shirt, member discounts at various businesses (Year One, Summit, Kragen, etc). This club is a member of the Association of California Car Clubs and the Towe Auto Museum (free admission for members). Publishes *Capital City Chronicle* monthly, $15/year (non-member). Sale/want ads, legislative updates pertaining to car collectors, how-to articles, upcoming events listings, other Mopar related info, club info and event, car show flyers. Dues: $30/year. Web site: www.capitalcitymopars.com

Central New York Mopar Association
PO Box 3451
Syracuse, NY 13220-3451
315-452-1255; FAX: 315-699-9780
E-mail: nwaracing@msn.com

Founded 1988. 180 members. Monthly newsletter, annual car show to benefit The Clark Burn Center, University Hospital, Syracuse, New York, spring and fall picnic, monthly meetings, cruises, drag races, etc. Mopars and AMC welcome. Dues: $20/year. Web site: www.homestead.com/centralnewyorkmopar/main.html

The Coastal Empire Mopar Club
1432 Fort Argyle Rd
Savannah, GA 31419
912-748-2986
E-mail: mikeF17767@aol.com

Founded 1989. 15 members. Must own a Mopar product, annual car show for benefits, monthly newsletter, cruise-ins, monthly meetings, shows and events. Attend other shows and Mopar related events as a club within our region. Dues: $15/year.

Edmonton Mopar Club
4308 73rd St
Edmonton, AB Canada T6K 0V7
780-461-7612
E-mail: mpoholko@telusplanet.net

Founded 1998. 109 members. No restrictions to join, quarterly newsletter, 15% off for parts purchased at participating Chrysler dealerships, weekly meets in summertime, monthly meets in winter, annual car show. Dues: $20/year.

Florida Mopar Association Inc
PO Box 486
Eagle Lake, FL 33839-0486
321-729-6236
E-mail: charger6@earthlink.net

Founded 1991. Members: 12 clubs. Association of Mopar only clubs in state of Florida. Annual car show 1st weekend in November. Dues: $25/year.

Freddie Beach Mopars
1834 Woodstock Rd
Fredericton, NB Canada E3C 1L4
506-450-9074; FAX: 506-459-0708
E-mail: vallise@city.fredericton.nb.ca

Founded 1988. Prospective members must own or have an interest in any Mopar or AMC. General meetings every second month. The newsletter is also bi-monthly. It includes general club information as well as a buy and sell section. The club operates the following events: Capital City Show and Shine at Norrad's Chrysler Thunder on Freddie Beach annually on Labor Day at Wandlyn Inn. We also operate the weekly cruise to the Regent Mall every Wednesday from June to September. Dues: $20/year Canadian.

The Hoosier Mopar Association
PO Box 1892
Valparaiso, IN 46384
219-988-2493

Founded 1993. 136 members. Must own or have interest in classic Mopars (Chrysler, Dodge, Plymouth, Jeeps and AMCs). Monthly newsletter of club activities. Monthly meetings 3rd Tuesday of each month, 7 pm, Denny's US 30 (in front of Walmart), Valparaiso, IN. Mopar car show (swap and crafts), 2nd Saturday in September, 49er Drive-In. Dues: $24/year.

Lake Erie Tri-State Mopar
PO Box 35
Westfield, NY 14787
814-899-6732
E-mail: letsmopar@hotmail.com

Founded 1986. 90 members. Restrictions: own or have interest in Chrysler (Mopars) 1924-1993. Big car show and swap meet annually, monthly meeting or event, except winter. Bi-monthly newsletter. Dues: $20/year.

Michiana Mopar Association
PO Box 1256
Mishawaka, IN 46546

Founded 1994. 30 members. No restrictions. Receive club shirt with membership, monthly club meetings, attend car shows and cruise-ins through the season, monthly newsletter. Dues: $25/year. Web site: www.michianamopar.homestead.com

Mid-America E-Body Mopar Club
PO Box 418
Onawa, IA 51040
712-423-2134; FAX: 712-423-2411
E-mail: ebodies@willinet.net

Founded 1998. 30 members. Open to owners and enthusiasts of 1970-1974 Plymouth Barracuda, Gran Coupe, Cuda, AAR and Dodge Challenger, SE, R/T, T/A models. Hope to have regional E-Body meets in the future. Offer technical and restoration assistance. Publish *Broadcast Sheet* bi-monthly, includes member's features, detailing, restoration, technical tips, event coverage, production facts, historical information, etc. Dues: $25/year. Web site: http://homepages.go.com/~ebodymoparclub/index70.html

Midwest Mopars Inc
1548 Mike Ct
Shakopee, MN 55379
612-445-3835

Founded 1985. 465 members. Monthly newsletter, *Mopar Muscle* magazine subscription, annual Mopars in the Park show, monthly meetings, lots of activities. Dues: $25/year. Web site: www.midwestmopars.com

Mighty Mopars of Orlando
8956 Cherrystone Ln
Orlando, FL 32825-6427-46
407-282-1632
E-mail: gbarg@mpinet.net

Founded 1991. 150+ members. Must be a Mopar enthusiast. Multiple discounts; monthly newsletter; monthly cruise-in; spring parts extravaganza; fall Mopar car show; monthly family events. Dues: $15/year. Web site: www.geocities.com/motorcity/flats/456

Mopar Alley
2409 Villanueva Way
Mountain View, CA 94040
408-296-8186; FAX: 650-565-7931
E-mail: admin@moparalley.org

Founded 1990. 180 members. Monthly meetings and newsletter. Member discounts at select businesses. Yearly show and swap meet. Cruises and other events throughout the year. Dues: $25/year. Web site: www.moparalley.org

Mopar Scat Pack Club
PO Box 2303
Dearborn, MI 48123
313-278-2240
E-mail: moparnats@aol.com

Founded 1981. 500+ members. Should be a Chrysler owner. Dedicated to the restoration and preservation of Chrysler high performance vehicles. Parts discount program and member super offers throughout the year. Bi-monthly publication: *Mighty Mopars*. Dues: $25/year.

Mr Norm's Sport Club
15774 S LaGrange Rd, Ste 256
Orland Park, IL 60462-4766
905-508-0772; FAX: 905-508-0773
E-mail: sportclub@mrnorms.com

Founded 1963. Own, have owned or love Mopars? Here is your opportunity to return to the excitement of the muscle car era. Be a founding member of Mr Norm's Sport Club. When you join you receive a member exclusive shirt, sticker, card and a quarterly magazine filled with tech and how-to topics as well as nostalgic facts and photos. Members receive discounts on many parts, accessories, services and apparel from all the best Mopar related resources in North America. Dues: $29.95/year US. Web site: www.mrnorms.com

Northeast Mighty Mopar Club
19 Treasure Island Rd
Plainville, MA 02762
508-695-1583
E-mail: plymthpaul@aol.com

Founded 1984. 680 members. Must own or be a fan of Mopar, any year Mopars welcome. The club puts on at least one Mopar only show in each of the Northeast states we cover. The club puts on a two day Mopar show, swap, banquet at a hotel in CT in August. Membership includes 6 newsletters (8 pages each) and a T-shirt. Dues: $25/year, $15/year renewal. Web site: www.mightymoparclub.com/nemightymoparc

Northern Mopars Auto Club
4416 16A St SW
Calgary, AB Canada T2T 4L5
403-287-0765; FAX: 403-287-6787
E-mail: llgammon@telusplanet.net

Founded 1986. 300 members. For all Mopar enthusiasts (AMC, Dodge, Plymouth, Chrysler, DeSoto, etc). A Calgary, Alberta, Canada based club with members from across Canada and the US. Some overseas members. Dues: $30/year Canadian. Web site: www.mopars.org

Power & Speed Racing Promotions
3612 W 50th
Fairway, KS 66205
913-831-9754; FAX: 913-831-0291
E-mail: mardi33@hotmail.com

Founded 1985. 400+ members. Open to Mopar enthusiasts. 2 shows a year, monthly cruise, 15th annual car show, June 12th and 13th; 13th annual show, race, swap and road course racing, September 25th and 26th at Heartland Park, Topeka. Over 600 cars and 150 swap in 1998. Bi-monthly newsletter. Dues: $15/year. Web site: www.powerandspeed.com

Southwest Mopar Club
10870 Pellicano Dr, Ste 274
El Paso, TX 79935
915-592-9179; FAX: 915-592-9970
E-mail: hpdart@aol.com

Founded 1994. Approximately 70 members. The club's purpose is to create enthusiasm for Mopars, to promote public awareness of Mopars, to showcase Mopars, to stimulate pride in Mopars and to provide and promote communications and camaraderie between Mopar owners and enthusiasts. Activities include cruises, rallies, car shows and picnics. Family oriented club. Monthly newsletter. Dues: $20/year.

Space Coast Mopars
John Warner
PO Box 307
Melbourne, FL 32902-0307
PH/FAX: 321-635-8581
E-mail: 104527.110@compuserve.com

Founded 1988. 50 members. Non-profit club for Mopars only. Annual car show, cruises, family oriented. Monthly meeting with monthly newsletter. Dues: $18/year. Web site: http://clubs.hemmings.com/spacecoastmopars/

Winged Warriors/National B-body Owner's Association (NBOA)
216 12th St
Boone, IA 50036
515-432-3001, IA; 703-893-9370, VA
E-mail: hemi@willinet.net

Founded 1975. 500 members. Open to all 1962-1974 B-body performance Mopars, specializing in Daytonas, Superbirds and 1969 Charger 500s. Ownership is not required for membership. Knowledgeable staff of advisors to provide technical and restoration information to members. Monthly newsletter. Free classified ad section for members. Dues: $25/year US, $30/year outside US. Web site: www.wwnboa.org

Wisconsin Mopar Muscle Club
Jerry Hegler
S103 W 20913 Heather Ln
Muskego, WI 53150
262-679-2952
E-mail: info@wmmc.net

Founded 1983. 125+ members. Open to all Chrysler, Dodge, Plymouth, DeSoto, Jeep & AMC vehicle interest. All Mopar vehicles invited to 3 shows and 2 swap meets annually. Dues: $25/year. Web site: www.wmmc.net

WPC Club Inc
PO Box 3504
Kalamazoo, MI 49003-3504
FAX: 616-375-5535
E-mail: wpc@pacificcoast.net

The WPC Club Inc is a non-profit corporation dedicated to the preservation and enjoyment of Plymouth, Dodge, Chrysler, DeSoto, Imperials and related cars. *WPC News* is a monthly publication with feature articles and want/sale ads, plus other features. Subscription rate: $28/year US, $30/year Canada and Mexico, $32/year foreign. Web site: www.pacificcoast.net/~wpc/

See our ad on page 522

chapters:

Arizona	*Grand Canyon Region*, Gary Kuhstoss, President, PO Box 5537, Glendale, AZ 85312-5537
California	*Inland Empire Region*, Ed Powley, President, 11917 Cactus Ave, Bloomington, CA 92316-3802
	Orange County Region, Ed Cook, President, 8110 Carnation, Buena Park, CA 90620

Section Three – Clubs & Organizations

WPC Club Inc chapters (continued)

San Diego Region, Jim Jensen, President, PO Box 420, El Cajon, CA 92022-0420

San Fernando Valley Region, Aaron Kahlenberg, President, PO Box 57564, Sherman Oaks, CA 91412-2564

Colorado Rocky Mountain Region, Jay Thomas, President, PO Box 315, Niwot, CO 80554-0315

Florida Florida West Coast Region, Ralph Brueggeman, President, 145 Garman Ave, Davenport, FL 33837-9595

Sunshine State Region, Paul Fell, President, PO Box 291, Bunnell, FL 32110-0291

Illinois Northern Illinois Region, Guy Morice, President, 22 Eagle View Ln, Oswego, IL 60543

Iowa Iowa Region, Bill German, President, 2814 35th St, Des Moines, IA 50310-4001

Michigan Great Lakes Region, Pete Williams, President, 15561 Sherwood Ln, Fraser, MI 48026

West Michigan Region, Bob Howard, President, 6086 Taggers Tr, Richland, MI 49083-9773

Minnesota 10,000 Lakes Region, Bruce Knapp, President, 3212 Kentucky Ave S, St Louis Park, MN 55426-3419

Nebraska Greater Omaha Region, Gail Hunt, President, 7701 Pacific St #215, Omaha, NE 68114

Nevada Silver State Region, William Borton, President, PO Box 98019, Las Vegas, NV 89193-8019

New Jersey Garden State Region, Don Piscitelli, President, 265 Hillcrest Rd, Boonton, NJ 07005

New Mexico New Mexico Region, William B Fisher, President, 1521 Van Cleave Rd NW, Albuquerque, NM 87107

North Carolina Carolina Chrysler Club, R David Lahr, President, 11410 April Day Ln, Charlotte, NC 28226

Ohio North Coast Region, Eric Poti, President, 8626 Avery Rd, Broadview Heights, OH 44147

Oregon Columbia River Region, Jeffrey Locke, President, 9308 SE Pardee, Portland, OR 97266

Pacific Wonderland Region, Tom Fox, President, 19305 SW Madeline St, Aloha, OR 97007-2912

Pennsylvania Liberty Bell Region, Bruce Foelker, President, 918 N Broad St, Allentown, PA 18102

Tennessee Tennessee Valley Region, Mike Bennett, President, PO Box 345, Hixson, TN 37343-0345

Texas Houston Region, Gary P Hamel, President, 6914 Dillon St, Houston, TX 77061-3826
North Texas Region, Ken Angyal, President, 2905 Natches, Arlington, TX 76014

Texas Region, Bill Robertson, President, 225 N Santa Clara Rd, Marion, TX 78124-9747

Utah Great Salt Lake Region, Richard E Stephens, President, 1042 E Cambridge, Kaysville, UT 84037

Washington Puget Sound Region, Rob Baker, President, 18126 191st St SW, Woodinville, WA 98072

Wisconsin Wisconsin Region, Dave Lonscar, President, #2, 1943 S 89th St, West Allis, WI 53214

Canada Vancouver Island Region, Mike Davies, President, 1151 Heald Ave, Victoria, BC V9A 5J7

Great Britain Chrysler Corp Club of UK, Peter Grist, President, 30 Purbrook CloseLordswood, Southampton, Hampshire, SO16 5NZ

Norway Norway Region, Tor Eigil Danielson, President, Postboks 57Bekkelaget, 0137 Oslo 1

Sweden Sweden Region, Bo Bengtsson, President, c/o Stefan FarkasSagdalsvandan 15, S-136 72 Haninge

Morgan Car Club, Washington DC
616 Gist Ave
Silver Spring, MD 20910
301-585-0121

Founded 1959. 325 members. No restrictions to join. Gathering of Morgan enthusiasts with frequent meetings, events, competitions, worldwide communications and historical files. Monthly publication: *The Rough Rider*. Dues: $25/year. Web site: www.morgandc.org

Morgan Motor Car Club
PO Box 50392
Dallas, TX 75250-0392
214-321-1648
E-mail: wmj3@airmail.net

Founded 1975. 50+/- members. No membership restrictions. Club activities center around interest in the Morgan automobile. Publishes a monthly newsletter called the *Mog Log*. Participates in approximately 11 meetings and 7 social events annually. Dues: $20/year.

Morgan Sports Car Club of Canada
1532 King St W
Toronto, ON Canada M6K 1J6
416-530-4599
E-mail: vern_dj@msn.com

Founded 1967. 125 members. An international club of Morgan car and British sports car enthusiasts. Members receive 6 editions of our newsletter, *The Blurb*, per year. We stage several events each year, including our annual fall weekend and British Car Toy Run for charity. Affiliates of: The Morgan Sports Car Club (UK), The British Car Council (Canada) and Specialty Vehicle Association of Ontario. Dues: $25/year Canada & US. Web site: http://clubs.hemmings.com/msccc/

Morgan Three-Wheeler Club
W C Towner
56 Brick Hill Rd
Orleans, MA 02653
508-255-6432 eves
FAX: 508-255-9393

For membership information, contact: Chris Towner at above address. Founded 1947. 700+ members worldwide. Membership offers monthly bulletin, tech information, spares and other assistance. Web site: www.mtwc.co.uk

Morgan Three-Wheeler Racing
1240 Taylor Ave
Vallejo, CA 94591-7509
707-554-1787; FAX: 415-954-4003
E-mail:
RedMorganRacing@earthlink.net

Founded 1997. Information provided to other owners of Morgan Trikes to encourage racing in pre-war classes at tracks in the US. Dues: none.

Morgans on the Gulf
3304 Sunset Blvd
Houston, TX 77005
713-661-7405
E-mail:
rchamber@mail.mdanderson.org

Founded 1986. 50 members. Interest and enthusiasm for Morgan sports cars. Newsletter, social and driving events. Dues: $40/year. Web site: www.mogmog.org

Metropolitan Owners Club of North America
2308 Co Hwy V
Sun Prairie, WI 53590
608-825-1903; FAX: 608-825-3363
E-mail: mbjaco@fastbytes.com

Founded 1975. 2,300 members. Open to all Metropolitan enthusiasts and owners. National, regional and chapter meets. Monthly newsletter: *The Met Gazette*. Dues: $20/year, $36/2 years, $52/3 years, $266 lifetime; international rates in US dollars only: $29/year, $53/2 years, $80/3 years, $366 lifetime.

chapters:

Arizona   *Arizona*, Nancy Gnepper, 2520 W Chiricuaha, New River, AZ 85087

Arkansas   *Arkansas Razorbacks*, Alan Fortney, 970 Crosspoint Rd, Conway, AR 72032

California   *Greater Bay Area Mets*, Wayne Metz, 1500 A St, Antioch, CA 94509

                  Greater San Diego Metropolitan Club, Karen Hughes, 4321 Maryland St, San Diego, CA 92103

Colorado   *Rocky Mountain Mets*, Char & Fred Frederick, 724 Berkely Ave, Alamosa, CO 81101

Georgia   *Georgia Peach Met Club*, Arlan Zimmerman, 182 Jackson Rd SE, Milledgeville, GA 31061

Illinois   *Illini Mets*, Gary Bosselman, 6812 E Rockton Rd, Roscoe, IL 61073-7662

Indiana   *Hoosier Mets*, Bill Wood, 1200 W 300 N, Anderson, IN 46011

Kansas   *Central Kansas Metropolitan Club*, Ben Love, 4144 W 11th St, Wichita, KS 67212

                  Nash Met Club of Northeast Oklahoma, Frank Brewster, 219 S Penn, Independence, KS 67301

Kentucky   *Derby City Metropolitan Car Club (KY)*, Ralph Coultas, 3523 Huon Dr, Louisville, KY 40218

Maryland   *Maryland Metropolitan Club*, Tom Thompson, 2121 Cox Rd, Jarretsville, MD 21084

Massachusetts *Yankee Mets (CT, ME, MA, NH, RI, VT)*, Howie Green, 11 Trescott St #3, Boston, MA 02125

Michigan   *Mitten Mets*, Diana Hawkinson, 20650 Breezewood Ct, Birmingham, MI 48025

Minnesota   *Mets From Minnesota Inc*, Richard Osmundson, 2810 Beam Ln, Eagan, MN 55121

Missouri   *Unforgettable MO-Mets*, Wayne B Chapin, PO Box 466, Mt Vernon, MO 65712

Nebraska   *Midwest Mets*, John M Christ, 2341 S 35th St, Omaha, NE 68105

New Jersey   *The Metropolitan Mets (NY, NJ, CT)*, Chris Custin, 54 Chestnut Dr, Wayne, NJ 07470

New York   *Upstate New York Mets*, Leonard Hass Jr, 6366 Co Rt 4, Central Square, NY 13036

Metropolitan Owners Club of North America chapters (continued)

Ohio   *Buckeye Mets (Northern Ohio)*, Rose Kerekes, 1444 Parkhaven Row, Lakewood, OH 44107

Pennsylvania   *Glad We Met (Northwestern PA)*, Kent Mowery, 245 Beachgrove Dr, Erie, PA 16505

Metropolitan Motoring Club (PA), Les Keller, 225 W Main St, Annville, PA 17003

Tri-State Chapter (PA, DE, NJ), John Bokeeno, 509 W Germantown Pike, Norristown, PA 19403

Texas   *Tex-Mets*, Kip Lankenau, 2127 Crown Rd, Dallas, TX 75229

Virginia   *Old Dominion Metropolitan Club*, Bill Green, 295 Queens Lace Rd, Mechanicsville, VA 23111

Washington   *Columbia-Willamette*, Bobbie Woodruff, 2615 Delameter Rd, Castle Rock, WA 98611

Pacific Northwest (WA, ID, AK, BC), Mark Mayhall, 414 145th Ave NE, Bellevue, WA 98007

Wisconsin   *Met Set (WI)*, Sid Mead, N 3140 US Hwy 12 & 16, Mauston, WI 53948

Canada   *BC Mets*, Eric Leha, 2343 Hamphue Pl, Abbotsford, BC, V2S 6N4

Manitoba Metropolitan Car Club of Canada, Gerald A Henry, 288 Wallasey St, Winnipeg, MB, R3J 3C1

Nash Car Club of America
1-N-274 Prairie
Glen Ellyn, IL 60137
630-469-5848
E-mail: bracewell@nashcarclub.org

Founded 1970. 1,850 members. Should have an interest in Nashes, related automobiles and their history. Family oriented activities. Advisor service and travel assistance offered. Publishes six magazines and six ad flyers. Dues: $23/year US and $24/year Canada, $41/year foreign air. Web site: www.nashcarclub.org

The NSU Club of America
717 N 68th St
Seattle, WA 98103
206-784-5084

For membership information contact at the above address: Jim Sykes. Quarterly 20+ page booklet. Dues: $15/year.

NSU Enthusiasts USA
c/o Terry Stuchlik
2909 Utah Pl
Alton, IL 62002
618-462-9195
E-mail: stuchlik2@aol.com

Founded 1971. 100 members. Quarterly newsletter containing 24-28 pages. Annual meeting and occasional regional meetings. Dues: $15/year.

Henry Nyberg Society
17822 Chicago Ave
Lansing, IL 60438
PH/FAX: 708-474-3416 collect
E-mail: nyberg1soc@aol.com

Founded 1988. Nearly 40 members. Promotes and encourages

the educational, research and scientific purposes or activities associated with the design, production and preservation of the Nyberg vehicles manufactured in the USA between the years 1903-1913. The name Nyberg is trademarked and we are a 501(c)3 not for profit organization with nearly 500 pieces of literature and still searching. Periodic publications. Dues: $20/year.

Oakland Owners Club International inc
767 McCoy Rd
Franklin Lakes, NJ 07417
201-337-1996; FAX: 201-847-4857
E-mail: norman_j_hutton@bd.com

Founded 1998. Incorporated 2001. 46 members. The Oakland Owners Club International Inc is dedicated to the preservation, restoration and exhibition of all Oakland motor cars built by GM between 1907-1931, as well as the Oakland highwheeler manufactured by the Oakland Ironworks of California. *The Oaklander* publication is sent quarterly. The only prerequisite for membership is the love of Oakland motor cars. Dues: $20/year US, $25/year international.

4-4-2 Club of Oregon
2239 NE 18th Ave
Portland, OR 97148
503-287-8878
E-mail: dbertrand@worldnet.att.net

Founded 1977. 45-60 members. All Oldsmobile enthusiasts are invited to join (Cutlass, 4-4-2 or any year and style). A monthly newsletter is published for members announcing meetings and events. Dues: $20/year single, $25/year family.

Hurst/Olds Club of America, HMN
8710 W Winegar Rd
Laingsburg, MI 48848
517-651-6221; FAX: 517-651-5746
E-mail: hursobdman@msn.com

Founded 1983. 600 members worldwide. Dedicated to the preservation and enjoyment of the Hurst/Olds automobile. National meet held annually. Members also have access to tech advisors, newsletter, free ads, research library and more. Dues: $25/year. Web site: www.hurstolds.com

National Antique Oldsmobile Club
13903 Roanoke St
Woodbridge, VA 22191-2416
703-491-7060
E-mail: paulthomas@iname.com

Founded 1981. 2,000 members. Anyone interested in the model year Oldsmobile from 1897-1964. Club membership is open to all. Publication is *Runabouts to Rockets*, published monthly. Advertising is free for members. The high point of each year is our annual National meet and show restricted to 1897-1964 Oldsmobiles. We also have technical advisors on each model year to assist members with answers about their cars. Dues: $25/year US, $40/year Canada and Mexico, $50/year other countries. Web site: www.antiqueolds.org

Oldsmobile Club of America
PO Box 80318
Lansing, MI 48908-0318
517-663-1811; FAX: 517-663-1820

Founded 1971. 6,400 members. No restrictions. All years, no car necessary, just interest. Monthly publication, *Journey With Olds*. National meet annually, over 45 chapters. Chapter and regional meets all over the country. Dues: $30/year 3rd class, $40/year 1st class. Web site: www.oldsclub.com

chapters:

Arizona   *Oldsmobile Club of Arizona*, 7711 E Tardes Dr, Scottsdale, AZ 85255 FAX: 602-636-7284

California   *1957 Chapter*, PO Box 661224, Arcadia, CA 91066

Northern California Chapter, PO Box 5474, Walnut Creek, CA 94596

Oldsmobile Club of Southern California, PO Box 661224, Arcadia, CA 91066

Colorado   *Rocky Mountain Olds Club*, PO Box 54, Arvada, CO 80001   FAX: 303-423-6020

Florida   *Oldsmobile Club of Florida*, c/o Handren, 5818 Princess Caroline Pl, Leesburg, FL 34748

Georgia   *Dixie Olds Chapter*, 2570 Hwy 29, Lawrenceville, GA 30044   770-925-9501

Illinois   *Illinois Valley Olds Chapter*, 20232 Blackstone, Matteson, IL 60443   708-481-7973

Indiana   *Indiana Olds Chapter*, 11730 Mann Rd, Mooresville, IN 46158

Iowa   *Oldsmobile Club of Iowa*, 14693 Fame Ave, Colfax, IA 50054   E-mail: oldsclubofia@hotmail.com

Kansas   *Toronado Chapter*, PO Box 211, Council Grove, KS 66846

Kentucky   *Derby City Olds Club*, 136 Harding St, Mt Washington, KY 40047   E-mail: olds442nut@aol.com

Maryland   *Oldsmobile Centennial Club*, PO Box 483, Severn, MD 21144

Massachusetts   *New England Olds Club*, Box 603, Southampton, MA 01073-0603

Michigan   *RE Olds Chapter*, PO Box 80101, Lansing, MI 48909-0101

Minnesota   *Minnesota Olds Club*, 9319 Nantwick Ln, Brooklyn Park, MN 55443

Missouri   *Heart of America Chapter*, 3511 S Crane St, Independence, MO 64055

Nebraska   *Great Plains Olds Club*, PO Box 19256, Omaha, NE 68119

New Jersey   *Oldsmobile Club of New Jersey*, 382 Thurman Ave, West Berlin, NJ 08091

Rallye 350 Chapter, Joane LaTorre, Secretary, 37 Georgia St, Cranford, NJ 07016   PH/FAX: 908-276-4395; E-mail: jojo442@aol.com

New Mexico   *Oldsmobile Club of New Mexico*, 1715 Geraldine Pl, Rio Rancho, NM 87124

New York   *Long Island/New York City Olds Club*, 527 S Pecan St, Lindenhurst, NY 11757

Western New York Olds Club, 50 Cramer St, North Tonawanda, NY 14120-4502   716-692-1564; E-mail: tigerpaw65@aol.com

North Carolina   *Mid-Atlantic Chapter*, 1310 Victory St, Greensboro, NC 27407

Ohio   *Gem City Rockets*, 155 Sesame St, Springboro, OH 45066   513-748-3540

Greater Cincinnati/Northern Kentucky Chapter OCA, Jeff Brockman, 6738 Springdale Rd, Cincinnati, OH 45247   E-mail: ho442nut@aol.com

Northern Ohio Chapter of OCA, 3887 Cumberland Dr, Austintown, OH 44515

Oklahoma   *Oklahoma Oldsmobile Club*, 1008 W 69th St, Oklahoma City, OK 73139

Pennsylvania   *Blue-Gray Chapter*, 6 Arwin Dr, Hummelstown, PA 17036

Tennessee   *Music City Rockets*, 645 Atlanta Dr, Hermitage, TN 37076

Smokey Mountain Olds Club, PO Box 1543, Powell, TN 37849-1543

Texas   *North Texas Oldsmobile Club*, PO Box 38524, Dallas, TX 75238

South Texas Oldsmobile Club, 9826 Balanced Rock, Converse, TX 78109

Texas Gulf Coast Chapter, 21034 Settlers Valley Dr, Katy, TX 77449-4211

Utah   *Oldsmobile Performance Chapter*, Attn: Owen Griesemer, 953 E Atkin Ave, Salt Lake City, UT 84106

Rendezvous Rockets, 615 E Mutton Hollow Rd, Kaysville, UT 84037

Virginia   *Capitol City Rockets*, PO Box 331, McLean, VA 22101-0331

Eastern Virginia Oldsmobile Club, PO Box 34935, Richmond, VA 23234-0935

Washington   *Puget Sound Chapter*, PO Box 82042, Kenmore, WA 98028-0042

Wisconsin   *Olds Club of Wisconsin*, PO Box 435, Sturtevant, WI 53177

Oldsmobile Cutlass Coupes (73-77), N 24 W 26339 Wilderness Way, Pewaukee, WI 53072-4568

The Opel Association of North America
394 Mystic Ln
Wirtz, VA 23113
E-mail: oana@opel-na.com

⊖ OPEL

For membership information: Gary Farias, President, 508-679-2740. Founded 1985. 250 members. Online newsletter. Annual events: Carlisle Imports, first of May, Carlisle, PA; Opels on the Lawn, late June, Boston, MA; mid-July, Tacoma, WA; MOA picnic, late September, Richmond, VA; multiple events throughout the year, Colorado Springs area, CO. Six chapters: The Mid-Atlantic Opel Association, New England Opel Club, Rocky Mountain Opels, Pacific Northwest Opel Association, Great Lakes/Mid-West Opel Association, Central OK Opel Club. Dues: None. Web site: www.opel-na.com
chapter:

Massachusetts   *New England Opel Club*, Gary Farias President, 24 Columbia Rd, Swansea, MA 02777   508-679-2740; E-mail: gary@opelgt.com; Web site: www.opelgt.com

Section Three – Clubs & Organizations

Opel Motorsport Club
5161 Gelding Cir
Huntington Beach, CA 92649
E-mail: president@opelclub.com

Founded 1981. 265 members. Subscription to the monthly newsletter, *The Blitz*, including technical tips, parts suppliers, annual member roster, classified ads, calendar of activities, meeting minutes and financial statement. Annual list of parts suppliers, free ads in the newsletter, access to club promotional items, invitation to the annual picnic and show. Dues: $45/year US. Web site: www.opelclub.com

The Packard Club
Packard Automobile Classics, Inc.
420 S Ludlow St
Dayton, OH 45402
800-527-3452; FAX 972-296-7920

Founded 1953. 4,500 members. Annual nationwide membership meet. Monthly: *Cormorant News Bulletin*. Quarterly: *Packard Cormorant Magazine*. Dues: $35/year US, $45/year Canada, $55/year Mexico, $95/year overseas. US funds

regions:

Alabama	*Alabama Packards*, PO Box 660652, Birmingham, AL 35266
Arizona	*Grand Canyon Packards*, 2827 N Comanche Dr, Chandler, AZ 85224
California	*Delta Sierra Packards*, PO Box 413, Carmichael, CA 95609
	Northern California Packards, PO Box 7763, Fremont, CA 94537-7763
	Packard Motor Car Club, Earle C Anthony, PO Box 24973, Los Angeles, CA 90024
Colorado	*Rocky Mountain Packards*, PO Box 343, Wheatridge, CO 80033
Florida	*The Florida Packard Club*, 2805 Sarasota Golf Club Blvd, Sarasota, FL 34240-9097
Georgia	*Peachstate Packards*, PO Box 720622, Atlanta, GA 30358
Illinois	*Land of Lincoln Packards*, 736 Wonderview Dr, Dunlap, IL 61525
	Packards of Chicagoland, PO Box 1031, Elmhurst, IL 60126-9998
Indiana	*Wabash Valley Packards*, PO Box 5774, Lafayette, IN 47903-5774
Iowa	*Hawkeye Packards*, 11987 Co Hwy D-25, Alden, IA 50006-9164
Kansas	*Great Plains Packards*, PO Box 75, Maize, KS 67101
	Indian Territory Packards, 935 Sunnyslope St, Emporia, KS 66801
Kentucky	*Blue Ribbon Packards*, 4210 St Thomas Ave, Louisville, KY 40218
Louisiana	*Pelican State Packards*, PO Box 4888, Shreveport, LA 71134-0888

Maryland	*Mid-Atlantic Packards*, PO Box 123, Fulton, MD 20759
Michigan	*Motor City Packards*, 65 Southbound Gratiot Ave, Mount Clements, MI 48043
Minnesota	*Minnesota Packards*, PO Box 19119Diamond Lake Station, Minneapolis, MN 55419
Missouri	*Mid-America Packards*, 15214 NE 188th St, Holt, MO 64048
	Mississippi Valley Packards, PO Box 451, Farmington, MO 63640
Nevada	*Silver Circle Packards*, 2225 Watt St, Reno, NV 89509
New Hampshire	*North Atlantic Packards*, 117 Hampton Meadows, Hampton, NH 03842
New Jersey	*Packards East*, 84 Hoy Ave, Fords, NJ 08863-1938
New Mexico	*Southwest Packards*, 2211 Alhambra SW, Albuquerque, NM 87104
New York	*East Grand Packards*, 724 Shanlee Dr, Webster, NY 14580
Ohio	*Buckeye Packards*, PO Box 1162, Worthington, OH 43085
	Wright Brothers Packards, 420 S Ludlow St, Dayton, OH 45402
Pennsylvania	*Allegheny Packards*, 2386 Shevlin Rd, Sewickley, PA 15143
	Keystone Packards, 979 Sheffield Ln, Huntingdon Valley, PA 19006
South Carolina	*Blue Ridge Packards*, 2037 Gap Creek Rd, Greer, SC 29651
Texas	*Arklatex Packards*, RR 13 Box 8600, Nacodoches, TX 75961-9599
	Heart of Texas Packards, 735 Ware St, San Antonio, TX 78221
	Lone Star Packards, 16014 Mill Point Dr, Houston, TX 77059
	Packards North Texas, 4009 Tamworth Rd, Fort Worth, TX 76116-7337
Utah	*Intermountain Packards*, 3362 S 1100 E, Salt Lake City, UT 84106
Virginia	*Packards Virginia*, PO Box 4012, Falls Church, VA 22044-0012
Washington	*Pacific Northwest Packards*, PO Box 475, Maple Falls, WA 98266
Wisconsin	*Wisconsin Packard Club*, 1170 Woodview Dr, Hubertus, WI 53033
Argentina	*Packard Club Argentina*, Moreno 1249, 1838 Luis Guillon BA

Australia	*Packard Automobile Club of Australia*, PO Box 14, Turramurra NSW 2074
Austria	*Packard Austria Club*, Hotel Goldener HirschGetreidegasse #37, A-5020 Salsburg
Belgium	*Packard Chauffers Club of Belgium*, Rue de L'Aurore 1A, BE-1000 Bruxelles
Brazil	*Brazil Packards*, Ave Bandeirantes 1975 Apto 1901, 30210-420 Belo Horizonte MG
Canada	*Niagara Packards*, 855 Brant St, Burlington, ON, L7R 2J6
England	*Packard Automobile Club of Great Britain*, 16 Ruskin DrWorcester Park, Surrey KT4 8LG
Germany	*Packard Club of Germany*, Vier Grenzen 1, DE-30177 Hannover
Netherlands	*Packard Automobiel Club Nederland*, Van der Hooplaan 30, 1185 GE Amstelveen
New Zealand	*South Pacific Packards*, c/o D & E Mitchell, 56 Hetley Crescent, Taradale Napier 4001
Spain	*Packard Club España*, Sanlucar de BarramedaN° 5 - 1 Piso - 3° B, ES-28033 Madrid
Switzerland	*Packard Club Switzerland*, Scheurenstrasse 15, CH-3293 Dotzigen

Packard Truck Organization
1196 Mountain Rd
York Springs, PA 17372
717-528-4920

Founded 1981. 50 members. For membership information, contact at the above address: David B Lockard. Open to Packard truck owners. Interested in all materials relating to 1905-23 Packard trucks. Quarterly publication. Annual meet in York Springs, PA (October). Technical assistance.

Packards International Motor Car Club
302 French St
Santa Ana, CA 92701
714-541-8431

Founded 1963. 2,500 members. Dedicated to the preservation and driving enjoyment of the Packard automobile. Publications as well as reproduction parts and literature. Publications: *Packards International* magazine and *News Counselor*, both quarterly. Dues: $35/year US, $40/year Canada and Mexico, $55/year overseas.
regions:

Arizona	*Arizona Region*, Packards of Arizona, 3008 E Cheery Lynn Rd, Phoenix, AZ 85016
California	*Northern California Region*, 5717 Moddison Ave, Sacramento, CA 95819
	San Diego Region, PO Box 503605, San Diego, CA 92150-3605
	Southern California Region, PO Box 11192, Santa Ana, CA 92711
Ohio	*Midwest Region*, 365 St Leger Ave, Akron, OH 44305
Oregon	*Oregon Region*, PO Box 42127, Portland, OR 97242

Washington	*Northwest Region*, PO Box 88881, Seattle, WA 98188
Australia	*Australia Region*, c/o Packard Auto Club, 152 Bannockburn Rd, Turramurra 2074 NSW
Canada	*Alberta Region*, Box 40343 Highfield PO, Calgary AB T2G 5G7

Patriot Truck Registry
8600 Buckboard
Lincoln, NE 68532
402-438-5839

PATRIOT

Founded 1988. 17 members. Members share information and parts for Patriot trucks manufactured in Lincoln, NE, during the years 1918-1925. Dues: none.

Peerless Motor Car Club Inc
5001 Femrite Dr
Madison, WI 53716
608-222-4528; FAX: 608-222-4693
E-mail: peerless19@aol.com

Peerless

Founded 1998. 120 members. Dedicated to the history, preservation and restoration of Peerless Motor cars. Peerless restoration pictures and stories, factory history, executive personnel profiles, want list and for sale list, repro literature, repro casting of parts, repro ads for all years Peerless. Repros of original Peerless Co-Operator. Publish bi-monthly newsletter, *Peerless Co-Operator*. Dues: $30/year US, $37/year overseas.

Pierce-Arrow Society Inc
135 Edgerton St
Rochester, NY 14607

PIERCE-ARROW

Founded 1957. 1,000 members. Technical and historical information provided for all Pierce vehicles including bicycles, cars, trucks, buses, trailers and motorcycles. Members receive four magazines, six service bulletins, a membership roster, a technical index and free advertising privileges each year. Several regions offer local activities. Dues: $25/year US. Web site: www.pierce-arrow.org

Golden Fin Society
13765 S 1300 W
Riverton, UT 84065
801-254-6817
E-mail: reatawhippets@worldnet.att.net

PLYMOUTH

Founded 1997. 83 members. 1956, 1957, 1958 Plymouth Fury Registry, 6 issues of newsletter per year, annual National meet. Dedicated to the preservation, maintenance and restoration of the 1956-1958 Plymouth Fury. Dues: $15/year. Web site: http://clubs.hemmings.com/goldenfin

Plymouth Barracuda Owners Club
16 Brentwood Dr
Peabody, MA 01960

PLYMOUTH

Founded 1978. 800 members. Devoted to preservation/restoration of 1964-1974 Barracuda/Cuda automobiles. Annual meets. Bi-monthly publication. Dues: $16/year US, $20/year foreign (US funds).

Plymouth Owners Club Inc
(formerly Plymouth 4 & 6-Cylinder
Owners Club)
PO Box 416
Cavalier, ND 58220-0416
701-549-3746; FAX: 701-549-3744
E-mail: benji@utma.com

For membership information, contact at the above address: Jim Benjaminson. Founded 1957. 3,800 members. Open to 1928-1976 Plymouth passenger and Plymouth and Fargo commercial vehicles. Recognized by Chrysler Corporation. Publishes bi-monthly magazine, sample issue $2. Dues: $24/year (Canada and foreign must remit US funds).

regions:

Colorado   *Rocky Mountain Region*, Bill Sullivan, 1015 Redwood Dr, Loveland, CO 80538

Illinois   *Dairyland Region*, Ed & Julie Hovorka, 598 Banbury Rd, Mundelein, IL 60060 E-mail: flory@sdb.k12.wi.us; http://silverstone.fortunecity.com/gordon/449

Lincoln Land Region, Bob Kerico, 3204 West Blvd, Belleville, IL 62221

Indiana   *Hoosier Region*, Stan W Peel, 5128 E Rowney, Indianapolis, IN 46203

Iowa   *Mid-Iowa Region*, Dave Jones, 123 Paine St SE, Bondudrant, IA 50035

Kansas   *Heart of America Region*, Don Wood, 1402 N 64th Terr, Kansas City, KS 66102

Maryland   *Mid-Atlantic Region*, Paul Gibbs, 309 N Elwood Ave, Baltimore, MD 21224

Massachusetts   *Colonial Region*, Betty Kibbe, 456 Holyoke St, Ludlow, MA 01056

Michigan   *Detroit Region*, Joseph B Lewis, 9145 Hazelton, Redford, MI 48239

Minnesota   *Tall Pines Region*, Carl Wegner, 19600 Cardinal Dr, Grand Rapids, MN 55744

Missouri   *Missouri "Show Me" Region*, Tommy G Pike, 1602 E Dale, Springfield, MO 65803

Nebraska   *Prairie Region*, Shawn & Crystal Dewey, 2145 Main St, Crete, NE 68333

New Jersey   *Delaware Valley Region*, Dave Geise, 417 Tennessee Tr, Brown Mills, NJ 08015

North Carolina   *Carolina Region*, Thomas E Carroll, 181 Charles St, Forest City, NC 28043

Ohio   *Ohio Region*, Larry Schroeder, 9721 Shaw Rd, Spencer, OH 44275

Oregon   *Cascade Pacific Region*, Bill Call, 12076 SE Deerfield Dr, Portland, OR 97236 E-mail: billsplymouths@aol.com

Texas   *High Plains Region*, Roland Keenan, 1305 LaPaloma, Amarillo, TX 79106

Lone Star Region, Thomas Heidorf, 19506 Oak Briar Dr, Humble, TX 77346

Virginia   *Old Dominion Region*, Bob Klinker, 1614 Mill Oak Dr, Virginia Beach, VA 23464

Canada   *Western Canada Region*, Trevor Landage, 75 Strathaven Ci SW, Calgary, AB T3J 2G2

Buckeye GTO Club
1500 Lourdes Dr
Cleveland, OH 44134
440-888-0416

Founded 1980. 30 members. Must own a GTO or have an interest in one. Monthly newsletter, 4 or 5 events per year with an estimated attendance of 100 per event, attend numerous cruises in and around the Cleveland area. Dues: $20/year.

Cactus GTOs Inc
17662 N 45th Ave
Glendale, AZ 85308
602-938-6802, 602-482-1620
E-mail: azautohobe@aol.com

Founded 1986. 80+ members. Club focuses on the preservation and fun of driving the Pontiac GTO (1964-1974). We also welcome LeMans and Tempest lovers too. Dues include a monthly newsletter. Activities throughout the year (car shows, breakfast cruises, club drag racing, etc). Dues: $12/year. Web site: http://members.aol.com/cactusgto

Canadian Pontiac Registry
9424 Abbott Pl SE
Calgary, AB Canada T2J 0Z8
403-252-4076

Founded 1995. The Canadian Pontiac Registry promotes the preservation, restoration, racing and customizing of the proud Pontiac automobile. All Pontiacs owned by Canadians and all Canadian built Pontiacs owned outside of Canada (worldwide) are eligible for membership. Dues: none.

Fiero Owner's Club of America
1598 S Anaheim Blvd Unit B
Anaheim, CA 92805
714-635-0898; FAX: 714-912-2007

Founded 1983. 7,000 members. Magazine: *Fiero Owners*, four times a year, guide to upgrades, parts, resource information, subscription rate: $34. National convention. Dues: $34/year US; $45/year other. Web site: www.fieroowners.com

GTO Association of America
5829 Stroebel Rd
Saginaw, MI 48609
800-GTO-1964

Founded 1979. 3,000 members. Monthly magazine, *The Legend*. International convention each year hosted by local chapters, travels to different cities across US. Approximately 50 local chapters. Also, regional meets throughout summer. Dues: inquire.

Jet City Fieros
12530 182nd Ave SE
Snohomish, WA 98290
PH/FAX: 360-794-7436
E-mail: benjamatic@aol.com

Founded 1992. 37 members. Monthly newsletter, E-group, lots of driving events. We put on the Northwest Fiero Fest every year (2nd weekend August) in the tri-cities area of Washington state. Dues: $20/year. Web site: www.jetcityfiero.com

The Judge GTO International Club
114 Prince George Dr
Hampton, VA 23669
757-838-2059

Founded 1982. 329 members. Open to owners and enthusiasts of 1969-71 Pontiac GTO Judge. Quarterly publication: *The Judge's Chambers*. Yearly convention at Virginia Beach, VA. Dues $20/year.

Section Three – Clubs & Organizations

Land of Lakes GTO Club Inc
13210 35th Ave N
Plymouth, MN 55441-2227
763-559-1797; FAX: 763-694-0017
E-mail: leekatmn@aol.com

Founded 1984. 200 members. Interest in promotion and preservation of Pontiac GTOs. Ownership of a GTO, however, is not a membership requirement. The club sponsors cruises, technical sessions, swap meets, a charity fundraiser for the Shriner's Hospital for Children, the annual Muscle Car Classic Show, Muscle Car Shoot-Out and World of Wheels. In addition, the chapter acts as a source of information and assistance to the local GTO owner and restorer. Dues: $24/year/family. Web site: http://members.xoom.com/old68goat/home.htm

Michigan Fiero Club
PO Box 1437
Dearborn, MI 48121-1437
313-274-8188
E-mail: sjb@tir.com

Founded 1993. 400 members. No restrictions. Interest in America's only small two-seater. In addition to our annual Fiero festival, we participate in cruises, shows, picnics, monthly meetings, conventions and Christmas dinner. Dues: $25/year US, $35/year foreign. Web site: www.tir.com/jaski/mi-fiero.htm

National Firebird & T/A Club
PO Box 11238
Chicago, IL 60611-0238
773-769-6262; FAX: 773-769-3240
E-mail: info@firebirdtaclub.com

North America's largest club for all year Firebirds and Trans Ams including the Formula, GTA and Firehawk. Established 1984. Offers magazines, e-magazines, free classified ads, tech advice and much more. Web site: www.firebirdtaclub.com

Northern Illinois Fiero Enthusiasts Inc
6226 Trinity Dr
Lisle, IL 60532
630-305-9806
E-mail: jjh93@juno.com

Founded 1991. 350 members. Bi-monthly, award winning newsletter, *Fiero Focus*. Monthly events, our own car show called Fierorama, free to members, we are expecting over 125 Fieros this year, September 9. Parts discounts, mechanic referrals and much more. Dues: $20/year. Web site: www.fierofocus.com

Oakland-Pontiac Enthusiast Org
3520 Warringham Dr
Waterford, MI 48329-1380
248-623-7573; FAX: 248-623-6180
E-mail: 72602,344@compuserve.com

Founded 1971. 200 members. Interest in Oaklands and Pontiacs. Publishes *Warrior*. Specializing in information for 1926-current Oaklands and Pontiacs. Dues: $10/year.

Pacific Northwest Pontiac Club
47525 SE Coalman Rd
Sandy, OR 97055
503-668-5416; FAX: 503-826-9019
E-mail: ohc6@pnnw.net

Founded 1978. 50-60 members. Monthly newsletter, *Wide Trackin News*, annual all Pontiac car show held last Sunday in August, annual club BBQ, Christmas dinner, tours, many other events. Dues: $20/year.

Pontiac Commercial & Professional Vehicles
1165 Co Rd 83
Independence, MN 55359
763-479-2248
E-mail: pontiacranch1@aol.com

Founded 1998. 50 members. Publishes bi-monthly, *PCPV News*. Chapter of POCI. Dedicated to Pontiac station wagons, hearses, ambulances, limos, sedan deliveries, police and fire cars. Dues: $20/year US, $25/yr international.

Pontiac-Oakland Club International Inc
PO Box 9569
Bradenton, FL 34206
941-750-9234; FAX: 941-747-1341
E-mail: smokecen@gte.net

Founded 1972. 10,000+ members. One of the largest marque specific clubs in the country. An active and extensive local chapter network brings the club close to home for most of its members, something the club actively encourages and supports. *Smoke Signals*, POCI's monthly magazine, is one of the hobby's best, with lots of useful articles and a large classified ad section (free to members) with hundreds of Pontiac cars and parts for sale. Dues: $25/year US; $27/year Canada; $36/year foreign (US funds). Web site: www.poci.org

chapters:

Alabama   *Alabama Chapter*, 4367 Alabama Hwy 9, Anniston, AL 36207

Arizona   *Arizona Chapter*, c/o Ross Whitehead, 5460 Calle Cayeus, Tucson, AZ 85741

Desert Renegades of Arizona, c/o George Dehavilland, 1307 W Mesquite, Chandler, AZ 85224

Arkansas   *Arkansas River Chapter*, c/o Louie Reed, 675 S 28th, Rogers, AR 72758

California   *Channel Islands Chapter*, c/o David McGarry, 5690 Aurora St, Ventura, CA 93003 805-654-0401

Pontiacs of Central CA, c/o Joel Garret, 3155 Sylmar, Clovis, CA 93612 559-292-9130

Sacramento Chapter, c/o Rick Kauer, 9964 Stone Oak Way, Elk Grove, CA 95624 916-685-1283

San Diego Chapter, c/o Dave Keetch, 154 El Camino Pequena, El Cajon, CA 92019

Southern California Chapter, c/o Gregg Miller, 1811 W Panoramic Dr, Corona, CA 91720

Colorado   *Colorado Chapter*, c/o PO Box 56, Arvada, CO 80001

Connecticut   *Nutmeg Chapter (ct)*, c/o Starr F Evans, Churchhill Rd, Washington Depot, CT 06794

Florida   *Dixie Chapter (FL)*, c/o Ken Wales, 3201 Bliss Rd, Orange Park, FL 32065

Florida Chapter, c/o Joan Webb, 1104 39th St W, Bradenton, FL 34205

Hurricane Chapter (FL), c/o Marvin Diaz, PO Box 14-0342, Coral Gables, FL 33114-0342

Pontiac-Oakland Club International Inc chapters (continued)

North Florida Ponchos, c/o Gary Bunch, 1106 N Hwy 22A, Panama City, FL 32404

Illinois   *Blackhawk Chapter (IL/IA)*, c/o Dean Fait, 2526 5th Ave, Moline, IL 61265-1534

Early Times Chapter, c/o Les Schwerdtner, 457 S Glencoe Ave, Decatur, IL 62522

Grand Prix Chapter, c/o Fred Engers, 8 N 597 Lisa Ln, Elgin, IL 60123 847-697-0712

Illinois Chapter, c/o Carla Knotek, 15456 Scott Ct, Lockport, IL 60441

Pontiacs of Central Illinois Chapter, c/o Gary Mruz, 4511 Butler Dr, Decatur, IL 62526

Indiana   *Hoosier Chapter (IN)*, c/o Nina Belk, 616 College Ave, Culver, IN 46511

Tri State Arrowhead Cruisers Chapter, c/o Kelly Knaebel, 7121 North St, Newburgh, IN 47630

Kansas   *KC Arrowhead Chapter*, c/o Vicky Cochran, 3535 SE Tecumseh Rd, Tecumseh, KS 66542

Maine   *All American Oakland Chapter*, c/o Arthur Archie, 22 Washington St, Millinocket, ME 04462 207-723-8759

Massachusetts   *Yankee Chapter (MA/ME)*, c/o Tom Dubois, 197 Brimbal, Beverly, MA 01915-1840

Michigan   *Michigan Widetrackers*, c/o Gary Pitts, 5525 Floria Dr, Swartz Creek, MI 48473

West Michigan Chapter, c/o Wendell Miller, 8830 Taylor St, Zeeland, MI 49464

Minnesota   *Pontiac Commercial & Professional Vehicle Chapter*, Paul Bergstrom, 1165 Co Rd 83, Independence, MN 55359

Tomahawk Chapter (MN), Dave Bennett, 109 Crystal View Cir, Burnsville, MN 55306

Missouri   *Arch Chapter (MO)*, c/o Richard Locavich, 808 Carman Woods Dr, Manchester, MO 63011

Greater Ozarks Chapter (MO), c/o Arthur Barrett, 211 W Alice, Mt Vernon, MO 65712

Nebraska   *Nebraskaland Chapter*, c/o Chuck Merica, Newsletter Editor, 4232 Harrison, Omaha, NE 68147

Overhead Cammer's Chapter, c/o Jim Black, 307 Summerset Dr, Papillion, NE 68133

Nevada   *Silver State Chapter*, c/o Russel Horning, 2265 Pennswood, Reno, NV 89509

New Hampshire   *NOR-Eastern Chapter*, c/o Matt Turner, 28 Robin Hood Dr, Nottingham, NH 02190

New Jersey   *Garden State Chapter (NJ)*, c/o Stephen Kiellar, 118 Starr Pl, Wyckoff, NJ 07481

South Jersey Pontiac Chapter (NJ), c/o Chuck Catalano, 112 Park Ct, Medford, NJ 08055 856-596-0937

New York   *Custom Safari Chapter*, c/o Rich Pye, 436 LaDue Rd, Brockport, NY 14420 716-637-2720

Finger Lakes Chapter (NY), c/o Debby Arend, 14 Judd Ln, Hilton, NY 14468

Long Island Chapter (NY), c/o Dave Worthington, PO Box 226, Aqueboque, NY 11931

Six Nations Chapter (ny), c/o Bob Klaisle, PO Box 2145, Syracuse, NY 13220

Western New York Chapter, c/o Barb Fuller, 20 Circle Ct, East Aurora, NY 14052

North Carolina   *Cape Fear Chapter*, c/o Dick Hiller, 418 Mohigan Tr, Wilmington, NC 28409 910-799-7336

Piedmont Chapter, c/o Bill Sykes, 1202 Elmwood Ave, High Point, NC 27265 336-883-2260

Ohio   *North Coast Ohio Chapter*, c/o Marilyn Nicholas, 13896 Aquilla Rd, Burton, OH 44021 440-834-1220

Northwest Ohio Chapter, c/o Ann Tasch, 16221 Martin Moline Rd, Grayton, OH 43422

Oklahoma   *Indian Nations Chapter*, c/o Larry Crider, 12510 W 67th St, Sapulpa, OK 74066

Oregon   *Emerald Valley Chapter*, c/o Rosie Henderson, 2084 Lemuria, Eugene, OR 97402

Pennsylvania   *Keystone State Chapter (PA)*, c/o Frank Kemp, 448 S Main St, Bechtelsville, PA 19505

Western Pennsylvania Chapter, c/o Walter "Pete" Rust, 11 Ellendell St, Pittsburgh, PA 15210-3534

Rhode Island   *Little Rhody Pontiac Chapter (RI)*, c/o John Pagliarini, 46 Chatsworth Ave, Warwick, RI 02886

South Carolina   *Palmetto Chapter*, c/o Erik Nagel, PO Box 65, Taylors, SC 29687

South Dakota   *Empire Chapter*, c/o Kirk Lee, 3809 S Holbrook Ave, Sioux Falls, SD 57106

Tennessee   *Little Indians Chapter*, c/o Greg Walters, 1706 Winding Ridge Tr, Knoxville, TN 37922

Pontiacs of Tennessee, c/o Bob Woodside, 2230 Oakleaf Dr, Franklin, TN 37064

Smokey Mountain Pontiacs of East Tennessee, c/o Jeffrey M Widner, 815 Smoke Creek Rd, Knoxville, TN 37992

Texas   *Lone Star Chapter (TX)*, c/o Joe Rakoczy, 7208 Tumbleweed Ct, Colleyville, TX 76034

South Central Texas Chapter, c/o Jay Lord, PO Box 34654, San Antonio, TX 78265

Utah   Great Salt Lake Chapter, c/o Kenny Gregrich, 59 N Broadway, Tooele, UT 84074

Virginia   National Capital Area, c/o George Richardson, 1509 Baltimore Rd, Alexandria, VA 22308

Old Dominion Chapter (VA), c/o Michael L Abernathy, 1400 Fortingale Cir, Sandston, VA 23150

Star City Chapter, c/o Randy Hurt, PO Box 20652, Roanoke, VA 24018

Washington   Puget Sound Chapter, c/o Karen E Housley, 21210 124th Ave SE, Kent, WA 98031

Wisconsin   Badger State Chapter (WI), c/o David Keach, 820 N 49th St, Milwaukee, WI 53208-3014

Street Rod/Modified Chapter, c/o Ginny Simmons, 5209 84th St, Kenosha, WI 53142-2215 414-694-2500

Pontiac Owners Association
1202 Cork Ave
Papillion, NE 68046
402-593-1737
E-mail: pontiac@mitec.net

Founded 1982. 75 members. We are a midwest (Nebraska) based club who is devoted to the preservation of all Pontiac, GMC, Oakland vehicles. Our club is family based and partake in various family oriented activities. Call or visit our web site for more information. Monthly publication, *Pontiac Owner's Manual*. Dues: $15/year. Web site: www.geocities.com/poay2k/poa.html

---

Royal Pontiac Club of America
PO Box 593
Keego Harbor, MI 48320
248-855-6291; FAX: 248-855-6299

Founded 1994. 185 members. Must be a Pontiac enthusiast. The club is dedicated to performance Pontiacs of all years. Club discounts at several retail auto suppliers. Tech information. Monthly newsletter. A seven event club drag racing series with awards dinner at end of season. Family fun. Participate in Woodward Dream Cruise. Ability to meet people that made these muscle cars the icon they are today. Dues: $25/year. Web site: www.royalpontiac.org

---

356 Registry Inc
Barbara Skirmants
27244 Ryan Rd
Warren, MI 48092
810-558-3692; FAX: 810-558-3616
E-mail: skirmants@home.com

Founded 1974. 7,000 members. No restrictions to join, ownership is not required. Local and national events and a complete listing of local clubs, free classified ads to members. The most complete source of parts and suppliers for the Porsche 356 model car. Bimonthly publication (on every odd numbered month), *356 Registry*, 50 page color cover magazine with 5-8 full feature color articles every year. Technical, mechanical and restoration articles. Historical information and book reviews. Literature and model collecting, vintage racing coverage. Visa/MasterCard. Dues: $30/year US, $40/year Canada/Mexico, $50/year international. Web site: www.356registry.org
regions:

Arizona   Arizona Outlaws Porsche 356 Club, Mike Wroughton, 19870 N 86th Ave, Peoria, AZ 85382 623-362-8356; E-mail: mwroughton@aol.com

California   356 CAR Club, Jim Hardie, 1920 Shelfield Dr, Carmichael, CA 95608 916-972-7232

Central Coast, Wes & Diane Morrill, 25209 Caslano, Salinas, CA 93908 831-643-0356

Porsche 356 Club, Bob Fitzpatrick, 23738 Barona Mesa Rd, Ramona, CA 92065 760-788-9354; E-mail: 356bob@home.com

Colorado   Rocky Mountain Porsche 356 Club, Al Gordon, 12773 Grizzly, Littleton, CO 80127 303-979-1072

Connecticut   356 Southern Connecticut Register Ltd, PO Box 35, Riverside, CT 06878 http://w3.nai.net/~edwardh/ed4yhtm

Florida   Florida Owners Group, Rich Williams, 4570 47th St, Sarasota, FL 34235 941-355-4856; E-mail: rich356fog@earthlink.net

Georgia   Southern Owners Group, Ray Ringler, 3755 Creek Stone Way, Marietta, GA 30068 three56@aol.com

Hawaii   Hawaii 356 Owners Group, Terry Felts, 161 Hanohano Pl, Honolulu, HI 96825-3515 808-396-6017; E-mail: wtfelts@aol.com

Illinois   Windige Stadt 356 Klub, Dale Moody, 19532 Governor's Hwy, Homewood, IL 60430 708-798-2637

Massachusetts   Typ 356 Northeast, Fran DeLeo, 18 Corning St, Beverly, MA 01905 E-mail: info@Typ356NE.org; Web site: www.Typ356NE.org

Michigan   356 Motor Cities Gruppe, Barbara Skirmants, 27244 Ryan Rd, Warren, MI 48092 810-558-3692

Minnesota   Fahr North, Phil Saari, 3374 Owasso St, Shoreview, MN 55126 651-464-0303; E-mail: p&k@aol.com

Missouri   Groupe 356 St Louis Region, Ted Melsheimer Sr, 10517 E Watson Rd, St Louis, MO 63127 314-966-2131

Nevada   Sierra 356 Porsche Club, Glenn Lewis, 2000 Royal Dr, Reno, NV 89503

New Mexico   Zia 356, David J Berardinelli, PO Box 1944, Santa Fe, NM 87504-1944 505-989-9566; E-mail: djblaw@ni.net

Ohio   OhioTub Fanatics, Richard King, OH 330-678-6259; E-mail: tubfanatic@aol.com

Pennsylvania   356 Mid Altantic, Dan Haden, 13 W Carpenter Ln, Philadelphia, PA 19119

Texas   Tub Club, Bob Morris, 397 Creekwood Dr, Lancaster, TX 75146 972-227-8357; E-mail: bob.morris@haliburton.com

Lone Star 356 Club, Mark Roth, 4915 S Main, Ste 114, Stafford, TX 77477 281-277-9595; E-mail: mroth356@aol.com

Utah   Mountainland Porsche 356 Club, Edward Radford, 1568 Connecticut Dr, Salt Lake City, UT 84103 801-521-7330

356 Registry Inc regions (continued)

Washington	*356 Group Northwest*, Bruce Rockwell, 4309 Reid Dr NW, Gig Harbor, WA 98335 253-858-2788; E-mail: bnmrock@msn.com
West Virginia	*Potomac 356 Owner's Group*, Dan Rowzie, 900 S Samuel St, Charles Town, WV 25414-1416
Australia	*Australian Porsche 356 Register*, PO Box 7356St Kilda Rd, Melbourne Victoria, 3004
Canada	*Maple Leaf 356 Club of Canada*, Dave Hinze, 2304 Weston Rd #1407, Weston, ON M9N 1Z3 416-244-4759
New Zealand	*356 Down Under*, PO Box 47-677, Ponsonby, Auckland

Porsche 914 Owners Association and 914-6 Club USA
100 S Sunrise Way, PMB 116H
Palm Springs, CA 92262
PH/FAX: 760-325-6583
E-mail: deeds@earthlink.net

Founded 1978. 2,000 members. An international organization with members in 20 countries. Members receive informative quarterly magazine, *Mid-Engined Views*. Contains articles about 914 maintenance, restoration and history. Now combined with the 914-6 Club USA. Dues: $25/year US, $32/year overseas. Web site: http://home.earthlink.net/~deeds/

Renault Owner's Club of North America
13839 Old Highway 80
El Cajon, CA 92021
619-561-6687; FAX: 619-561-1656
E-mail: renaultj@pacbell.net

Founded 1991. 200 members. This is the only Renault club in the US. Join the North American network for Renault owners. Receive 1 year of the *Renault News*, published quarterly; monthly marketplace ads; yearly registry/directory; technical support, parts and documentation from other experienced Renault enthusiasts. Owners of Renault derivatives, such as Alpine, Eagle, Lotus, Matra, etc, are encouraged to join. Dues: $20/year. Web site: www.renaultownersclub.org

Reo Club of America Inc
115 Cherry Rd
Chesnee, SC 29323
864-461-2894
E-mail: reoclub@yahoo.com

Founded 1974. 750 members. Reo owners and enthusiasts. Send SASE when writing to club. Worldwide group dedicated to the preservation of the works of Ransom E Olds. Dues: $18/year US, $23/foreign. Web site: http://clubs.hemmings.com/reo/

Svenska Rileyregistret
c/o Erik Hamberg
Salagatan 41 A
SE-753 26 Uppsala Sweden
+46 18 12 82 83
E-mail: erik.hamberg@posten.se

Founded 1977. 130 members. Newsletter 4 times a year, at least 1 rally each year. Open to everyone interested in Riley cars. Dues: SEK 100/year Sweden, SEK 125/year abroad.

Rolls-Royce Owner's Club Inc
191 Hempt Rd
Mechanicsburg, PA 17055
717-697-4671; FAX: 717-697-7820
E-mail: rroc.hq@rroc.org

Founded 1951. 6,700 members. Dedicated to the preservation,

restoration and enjoyment of Rolls-Royce and Bentley motorcars. Dues: $50/year. Web site: www.rroc.org

Rolls-Royce Owners' Club
191 Hempt Rd
Mechanicsburg, PA 17050
717-697-4671; FAX: 717-697-7820
E-mail: rrochq@rroc.org

Founded 1951. 8,500 members. Publishes *The Flying Lady* bi-monthly. Dues: $50/year.

Silver Ghost Association
1115 Western Blvd
Arlington, TX 76013-3838
817-861-6605; FAX: 817-861-1029
E-mail: sga@silveghost.org

Founded 1986. 475+ members worldwide. Newsletter, *The Tourer*, published quarterly, technical assistance by telephone or fax included with membership. Tech bible with 1,600+ pages of articles published about Silver Ghosts, club store, annual Wholly Ghost tour for Silver Ghosts only. Do not need to own a Silver Ghost to join. Dues: $40/year. Web site: www.rroc.org/regions/sga/

The Rover Car Club of Canada
2671 Sechelt Dr
North Vancouver, BC Canada V7H 1N9
PH/FAX: 604-929-7500
E-mail: erussellrv@yahoo.com

Founded 1988. 76 members. Members in Canada, US and UK. Bi-monthly magazine, discount Rover parts, monthly meetings or roves. Dues: $35/year Canadian. Web site: www.roverclub.ca

Rover Saloon Touring Club of America
733 S Providence Rd
Wallingford, PA 19086
610-872-2109

Primary contact: Glen Wilson. Founded 1998. 75 members. Open to anyone interested in Rover automobiles. Nearly all Rover models are already represented in our club including pre-war, P4, P5, P6, SD1 and Sterling models. RSTCA members will receive eleven issues of the British marque multi-club newspaper that will include a monthly column dedicated to the RSTCA. Dues: $15/year plus a one-time joining fee of $3 to partially offset the cost of the initial membership package. Web site: http://clubs.hemmings.com/rstca/

New England Sonett Club
PO Box 4362
Manchester, NH 03108
914-778-2469
E-mail: sonett@frontiernet.net

Founded 1980. 150 members US. Objectives include maintenance and preservation of Sonetts and vintage Saabs. Historical data, tech tips, quarterly newsletter. Dues: $18/year.

The Sabra Connection
7040 N Navajo Ave
Milwaukee, WI 53217
414-352-8408

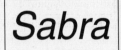

An organization to share interest and information about the Sabra Sport automobile produced by Autocars of Haifa, Israel and Reliant of England between 1961 and 1963. Publication: *The Sabra Connection*.

Saxon Times
c/o Walter Prichard
5250 NW Highland Dr
Corvallis, OR 97330
541-752-6231
E-mail: prichard@proaxis.com

Founded 1983. Approximately 90 members. Saxon automobiles, all years. Publication is *Saxon Times*, which includes roster of owners, for sale and wanted cars and parts, factory literature.

Shay Owners Club International (SOCI)
4845 Dixie Garden Dr
Shreveport, LA 71105
318-673-1237
E-mail: bwatson@kpmg.com

Founded 1999. 85 members. The Shay Owners Club International (SOCI) is open to everyone. We celebrate the 1929 Ford replicas produced by Harry Shay for Ford Motor Company. These cars were sold and warranteed through Ford dealers, beginning in 1976. Dues: none. Web site: www.bobbyjwatson.com

SIMCA Car Club of America
644 Lincoln St
Amherst, OH 44001
440-988-9104 evenings (no return calls)
E-mail: us.simca.carclub@centurytel.net

Founded 1985. Approx 100 members in 15 countries. Dedicated to the restoration and preservation of SIMCA, Chrysler-SIMCA, and special-bodied SIMCA exotics from 1936-1982. Parts inventory, information sources and European connections. Monthly newsletter: *Vitesse*. Dues: $20/year. Web site: www.centurytel.net/SIMCA/

Squire SS-100 Registry
c/o Arthur Stahl
11826 S 51st St
Phoenix, AZ 85044-2313
602-893-9451; FAX: 602-705-6649
E-mail: squirepal@aol.com

Founded 1989. 43 members at present. Membership is restricted to ownership or intended ownership of the Squire SS-100 manufactured in Torino, Italy, by Intermeccanica in 1968-1972. Intended to find and list the owners of the fifty-odd Squire SS-100s that were produced in Italy in 1968-1972 by Intermeccanica. Bi-monthly newsletter. Dues: $40/first year; $10/year thereafter. Web site: www.team.net/www//ktud/squir.html

Stevens-Duryea Associates
3565 Newhaven Rd
Pasadena, CA 91107
626-351-8237

For membership information, contact at the above address: Warwick Eastwood. Founded 1960. 100 members. Open only to owners of Stevens-Duryea automobiles. Affiliated with Horseless Carriage Club. Dues: none.

1956 Studebaker Golden Hawk Owners Register
31700 Wekiva River Rd
Sorrento, FL 32776-9233
E-mail: 56sghor@prodigy.net

See full listing in **Section One** under **Studebaker**

The Antique Studebaker Club Inc
PO Box 28845
Dallas, TX 75228-0845
800-527-3452, 972-709-6185
E-mail: dochemp@c-zone.net

Founded 1971. 1,300 members. Has yearly national meet and zone meets. Dues: $23/year.

Orange Empire Chapter, SDC
7812 Vicksburg Ave
Westchester, CA 90045
310-645-3438

Founded 1969. 147 members. A chapter of the Studebaker Drivers Club. Monthly meetings and newsletter, *Wheels & Deals*. Purpose is sharing information on parts, tips, activities and cars. Must be a member of the Studebaker Drivers Club to join chapter. Annual LaPalma show. Dues: $15/year.

Wisconsin Region Studebaker Drivers Club
PO Box 296
Allenton, WI 53002-0296
414-629-9969; FAX: 414-629-4171
E-mail: leighm@pmihwy.com

Founded 1968. 320 members. Dedicated to the preservation and operation of Studebaker vehicles, the exchange of technical information and the publication of information pertaining to Studebaker and affiliated companies. Dues: $15/year. Web site: http://studebaker.madison2000.org

The Stutz Club Inc
7400 Lantern Rd
Indianapolis, IN 46256
812-988-9325

For membership information, contact at the above number: John Kirkman, Membership VP. Founded 1988. 350 members. Membership open to all who have an interest in Stutz vehicles (Stutz and Blackhawk autos and fire engines, HCS autos and taxicabs, Stutz Pak-Age-Car and aircraft engine) or in history of the companies producing these marques and the man responsible, Harry Clayton Stutz. Annual meeting held with Grand Stutz car meet. Provides technical information, full current directory of members and vehicles. Dues: $25/year worldwide.

Subaru 360 Drivers' Club
1421 N Grady Ave
Tucson, AZ 85715
520-290-6492

Founded 1980. 350 members. Members help each other keep their Subaru 360s on the road and running on both cylinders. Quarterly newsletter. Dues: $6/year.

California Association of Tiger Owners
18771 Paseo Picasso
Irvine, CA 92612-3328
949-854-2561; FAX: 818-541-1784
E-mail: catmbr@best.com

Founded 1968. 1,000 members. Alpines welcome. Worldwide membership devoted to advancing the Sunbeam marque. Extensive parts supply. Dues: $25/year US, $27/year Canada, $35/year foreign. Web site: http://clubs.hemmings.com/cat/

Tigers East/Alpines East
PO Box 1260
Kulpsville, PA 19443
E-mail: teae@aol.com

Founded 1975. Approximately 800 members. Annual meet, local meets, newsletter. Publishes *Rootes Review* monthly. Dues: $33/year US, $36/year outside. Web site: www.teae.org/

534 Section Three — Marque Clubs   Tatra - Triumph

Hemmings Collector-Car Almanac©   Fifteenth Edition

Tatra Enthusiasts
PO Box 93
Littlestown, PA 17340
E-mail: tatrabill@aol.com

Tatra: the only cars to have a rear-engined air-cooled ohc V8. The club specializes in information, parts, service and anything pertaining to Tatra cars and trucks 1922 to present. Also includes earlier Nesseldorfer vehicles.

Toyota MR2 Mk I Club
35 Alma St
Luton, Bedfordshire LU1 2PL England
01582-454971; FAX: 01582-415368
E-mail: rmorgan.park301@nrlworld.com

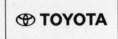

Founded 1995. 450 members. 20 national meetings a year, quarterly magazine, club insurance scheme, technical help. Dues: £15/year. Web site: www.welcome.ro/mr2mk1register

Detroit Triumph Sportscar Club
39148 Boston
Sterling Heights, MI 48313
PH/FAX: 810-979-4875
E-mail: snydley@home.com

Founded 1959. 180 members. Open to all British car enthusiasts. Our goal is to provide events, assistance and comraderie to all fans of British cars, especially the Triumph. Monthly newsletter. Meetings are the 2nd Tuesday of each month. Dues: $30/year. Web site: www.detroittriumph.org

Georgia Triumph Association Inc
PO Box 1138
Tucker, GA 30085-1138

Founded 1984. 100 members. Open to Triumph car owners and non-owners. Monthly newsletter, monthly business meetings & monthly drives or tech sessions. Dues: $24/year. Web site: www.gatriumph.com

New England Triumphs
6 Island Cove Rd
Eliot, ME 03903-1508
PH/FAX: 207-439-3038
E-mail: grove@acornworld.net

Founded 1978. 220 members. Official chapter of the Vintage Triumph Register and the Triumph Register of America. Activities include monthly meeting, many tours/rallies and annual Day of Triumph. Dues: $18/year.

TR8 Car Club of America
266 Linden St
Rochester, NY 14620
716-244-9693
E-mail: bsweeting@aol.com

Founded 1983. 350 members. Quarterly newsletter with technical data, news items, etc. Regalia and back issues of newsletters available. Dues: $15/year.

Triumph Roadster Club
59 Cowdray Pk Rd
Little Common, Bexhill on Sea
East Sussex TN39 4EZ England
(UK) 01424-844608
E-mail: john@cattaway.freeserve.co.uk

Founded 1960. 500 members. Restricted to Triumph 1800 and 2000 roadster models 18TR and 20TR, manufactured between 1946 and 1949. Ten magazines or newsletters annually. Technical publications available to members. Dues: UK/EEC GBP20/Euro 33; elsewhere: GBP25 paid in GBP; USA paid to US chapter, $40 US. Web site: www.triumphroadsterclub.fsnet.co.uk

**Triumph Sports Car Club
of San Diego**
PO Box 84342
San Diego, CA 92138-0633
619-484-6114

Founded 1963. 120 members, 1997 year. Owning a Triumph not necessary to join. Non-profit organization to promote the enthusiasm of the Triumph marque by rallies, slaloms, trips, Concours, restorations, technical, and, of course, social events. Dues: $22/year. Web site: http://clubs.hemmings.com/sandiegotriumph/

Triumph Stag Register
210 Bass Cir
Lafayette, CO 80026-1811
303-665-6040; FAX: 303-665-7820
E-mail: tristagreg@aol.com

Founded 1997. 1,400+ members. Get it together with the Triumph Stag Register, the Stag club dedicated to providing technical support to Stag owners and enthusiasts worldwide. Bi-monthly newsletter in full color delivered by e-mail, TSR logo window sticker and button, technical sessions, annual meets, brochure available. Dues: $20/year plus $5 1 time fee to join. Web site: www.triumphstagregister.org

Vintage Triumph Register
PO Box 655
Howell, MI 48844-0655
847-940-9347
E-mail: vtr-www@www.vtr.org

Founded 1974. 2,900 members. For owners and enthusiasts of all Triumph automobiles. Membership includes quarterly magazine, free classified ads, technical information consultants and more. Dues: $30/year, $35/year Canada, $40/year all other countries, US funds. Web site: www.vtr.org

chapters:

Arizona   *Desert Centre Triumph Register*, John Lindly, Editor, 6434 E Corrine Dr, Scottsdale, AZ 85254

Tucson Area, Jeff Durant, PO Box 5156, Tucson, AZ 85703-0156

Arkansas   *British Motoring Club of Arkansas*, Bob Ross, VTR Liaison, PO Box 22865, Little Rock, AR 72221 501-888-3396; E-mail: bross3396@aol.com

California   *Central Coast British Car Club*, C Darryl Struth, President, PO Box 503, Ventura, CA 93002

Southern California Triumph Owners Assoc, Bill Burroughs, VTR Liaison, 7250 McCool Ave, Westchester, CA 90045 E-mail: trbilbo@aol.com

Triumph Register of Southern California, Sue Davis, VTR Liaison, 20929 Lassen St, #112, Chatsworth, CA 91311 E-mail: wottatr@aol.com

Triumph Sports Car Club of San Diego, Leslie Harpenau, Editor, PO Box 84342, San Diego, CA 92138-0633

Triumph Travelers Sports Car Club, Jim Sudduth, VTR Liaison, PO Box 60314, Sunnyvale, CA 94088-0314 510-528-1441; E-mail: jsudduth@eshaman.com

Section Three – Clubs & Organizations

Colorado   *Rocky Mountain Triumph Club*, Glenn Sorensen, VTR Liaison, 6821 S Forest St, Littleton, CO 80122   330-220-9742; E-mail: tsorensen1@earthlink.net

Connecticut   *Connecticut Triumph Register*, Joe Barile, Membership Director, PO Box 521, Southington, CT 06489 E-mail: trspitty1500@aol.com

Florida   *Central Florida Triumph Register*, Harry Connor, President, 102 Garfield Rd, Deltona, FL 32725

Gold Coast Triumph Club, Larry Miceli, President, PO Box 10451, Pompano Beach, FL 33060   E-mail: lgmiceli@mediaone.net

Temple of Triumph, Joe Carter, President, Rt 4, Box 155, Westville, FL 32464   850-574-8823

Triumph Club of North Florida, Walt Lanz, 1900 Kusaie Dr, Jacksonville, FL 32246   904-646-0616; E-mail: wlsserv@aol.com

Triumph Standard Motor Club, Bob Menzies, Newsletter Editor, 2518 Lk Ellen Cir, Tampa, FL 33618   813-968-3731; E-mail: gt64ev4@aol.com

Georgia   *Georgia Triumph Association*, Don Burns, VTR Liaison, 1824 Vermillion Bay Cir, Duluth, GA 30097   770-623-9311; E-mail: daburns@mindspring.com

Idaho   *Northwest British Classics*, Donnel Schmidt, VTR Liaison, 1924 Lakeside Ave, Coeur D Alene, ID 83814   208-664-5062; E-mail: donneltr6@aol.com

Illinois   *Central Illinois Triumph Owners Assoc*, Mark Joslyn, VTR Coordinator, 1406 Winding Ln, Champaign, IL 61820   E-mail: mbjosyln@prairienet.org

Illinois Sports Owners Association, Jack Billimack, VTR Liaison, 23 Elmhurst Ave, Crystal Lake, IL 60014   815-459-4721; E-mail: jbillimack@aol.com

Quad Cities British Auto Club, Naomi Swanson, VTR Liaison, 4828 47th Ave, Moline, IL 61265

Indiana   *Indiana Triumph Cars*, Tom Beaver, Secretary, 7510 Allisonville Rd, Indianapolis, IN 46250 E-mail: tbe749@aol.com

Iowa   *Hawkeye Triumphs*, Brian Fanton, President, PO Box 81, Hiawatha, IA 52233-0081

Kentucky   *British Sports Car Club Louisville*, Gordon & Becky Carnes, 208 E Morrison St, Wilmore, KY 40390

Louisiana   *British Motoring Club-New Orleans*, Harold O'Reilly, VTR Liaison, PO Box 13803, New Orleans, LA 70185   haroldor@bellsouth.net

Maine   *New England Triumphs*, Bob Lang, Newsletter Editor, 6 Island Cove Dr, Eliot, ME 03903-1508   lang@isis.mit.edu

Maryland   *Triumphs Around the Chesapeake (TRAC)*, Gary Klein, 8153 Quarterfield Farms Dr, Severn, MD 21144   410-551-2055; E-mail: gklein@toad.net

Massachusetts   *British Motorcars, FTR, LTD of New England*, Roger Jusseaume, Club Contact, 404 Spring St, PO Box 666, N Dighton, MA 02764-0666

Western Massachusetts Triumph Association, Bob O'Donnel, President, 5 Louise Ave, Easthampton, MA 01027

Michigan   *Detroit Triumph Sportscar Club*, Terry Walters, Newsletter Editor, 8972 Deborah Ct E, Livonia, MI 48150   E-mail: twalters@ameritech.net

Michigan Triumph Association, Joseph Germay, 9349 South Westnedge, Kalamazoo, MI 49002

Minnesota   *Minnesota Triumphs*, Bob Lee, VTR Liaison, PO Box 201054, Bloomington, MN 55420   E-mail: triumph@pressenter.com

Mississippi   *English Motoring Club-A Central Mississippi Chapter VTR*, Terry Trovato, President, PO Box 5263, Jackson, MS 39216   E-mail: terryt@callon.com

Missouri   *Kansas City Triumphs*, Jay Smith, Director, 8404 NE 74th Ct, Kansas City, MO 64158   E-mail: jsmith@mjharden.com

St Louis Triumph Owners Association, David Massey, President, 321 Peeke, Kirkwood, MO 63122   E-mail: 105671.471@compuserve.com

Nebraska   *Nebraska Triumph Drivers*, Bill Redinger, Director, 1014 N 127 Ave, Omaha, NE 68154 E-mail: aredinger@juno.com

Nevada   *British Auto Club of Las Vegas*, Ken Korotkin, Editor, 16 Barton Spring Cir, Henderson, NV 89121

New Jersey   *British Motor Club of Southern New Jersey*, Ed Gaubert, Director, 13 Fox Hollow Dr, Cherry Hill, NJ 08003   609-751-7773

New Jersey Triumph Association, Jerry Havel, PO Box 6, Gillette, NJ 07933   E-mail: jhavel@eagle.org

New York   *Adirondack Triumph Association*, Rik Schlierer, VTR Liaison, PO Box 13481, Albany, NY 12212-3481   E-mail: rgs03@juno.com

Finger Lakes Triumph Club, Russ Moore, President, 49 Caroline Depot Rd, Brooktondale, NY 14817

Long Island Triumph Association, Geoffrey Levy, Director, 14 Churchill Dr, Brentwood, NY 11717   631-968-9772

Syracuse Area, Vincent Paul Heuber, 101 Vieau Dr, Syracuse, NY 13207-1121

North Carolina   *Triumph Club of the Carolinas*, Jamie Palmer, President, 100 Chinaberry Ln, Angier, NC 27501   E-mail: jamiep@cris.com

Vintage Triumph Register chapters (continued)

Ohio   *Buckeye Triumphs*, Robert Mains, President, PO Box 584, Lithopolis, OH 43136-0584 E-mail: buckeyetriumphs@ameritech.net

Miami Valley Triumphs, Frank Ciboch, President, 1045 S Sr 73, Springboro, OH 45066 513-748-4185

North Coast Triumph Association, Eric Langreder, Membership Chairman, 226 Aultman Ave NW, Canton, OH 44708-5525 E-mail: elangtr4@aol.com

Oklahoma   *Central Oklahoma Vintage Triumph Register*, Barney Emberton, President, PO Box 12272, Oklahoma City, OK 73157-2272 E-mail: barneye

Green Country Triumphs, Norman Price, President, 13415 S 127th E Ave, Broken Arrow, OK 74011 E-mail: noddyp@aol.com

Oregon   *Portland Triumph Owners Association*, Ray Marty, VTR Liaison, PO Box 33140, Portland, OR 97292-3140 E-mail: baw@teleport.com

Pennsylvania   *Central Pennsylvania Triumph Club*, Joe Laurito, VTR Liaison, PO Box 7001, Mechanicsburg, PA 17055 E-mail: trglory@msn.com

Delaware Valley Triumphs, Ltd, Frank Markowitz, VTR Liaison, 1430 Old West Chester Pike, West Chester, PA 19382 E-mail: slqs21a@prodigy.com

Keystone Triumphs, Ltd, Bruce Strock, President, PO Box 4903175 Center & Church Sts, Springtown, PA 18081-0490

Western Pennsylvania Triumph Association, Ed Woods, Membership, 105 Hawk Dr, Glenshaw, PA 15116 E-mail: fogbros@nb.net

South Carolina   *Southeastern British Motorcar Owners Club*, Rick Morrison, President, PO Box 1274, Gramling, SC 29348

Texas   *El Paso Triumph Club*, Charles Beck, 1641 Bert Green Dr, El Paso, TX 79936-5301

Hill Country Triumph Club, Bob Kramer, Membership, 8006 Bernard St, Volente, TX 78641 E-mail: rgk@flash.net

Red River Triumph Club, Duncan Wood, President, 2915 Lakeside Cir, Grapevine, TX 76051 E-mail: sheiladuncan@msn.com

South Texas Triumph Association, Kathie Hulka, Membership, 5306 La Cieniga, San Antonio, TX 78233 512-650-4660; E-mail: hulka@ibm.net

Texas Triumph Register, Mike Hado, Membership, PO Box 40847, Houston, TX 77240-0847 713-937-9042; E-mail: mhado@hal-pc.org

Utah   *British Motor Club of Utah*, Jim Pivirotto, 1419 S 900 E, Salt Lake City, UT 84105 801-486-0547

Vermont   *Vermont Centre of British Motorcars*, Dave & Joyce Silveira, 4 Farmstead Dr, Shelburne, VT 05482 802-985-2860

Virginia   *Blue Ridge Triumphs*, Bill Brooks, President, 3960 Bower Rd SW, Roanoke, VA 24018-2933 540-989-3030

Capital Triumph Register, Keith Dunklee, 3008 South 2nd St, Arlington, VA 22204 703-521-2245; E-mail: kdunklee@egginc.com

Richmond Triumph Register, Glenn Larson, Newsletter Editor, 10204 Warren Rd, Glen Allen, VA 23060 804-755-6037; E-mail: glarson182@aol.com

Tidewater Triumph Register, Martin Pachey, Membership, 3437 Petunia Crescent, Virginia Beach, VA 23456 757-468-9903; E-mail: martintr3-7@erols.com

Washington   *Tyee Triumph Club*, Jack Adams, VTR Liaison, PO Box 27668, Seattle, WA 98125-2668 206-338-3366; E-mail: jackdian@juno.com

Wisconsin   *Vintage Triumphs of Wisconsin, Ltd*, Mary Jo Ploetz, President, W330 S3435 Bryn Mawr Rd, Dousman, WI 53118-9719 262-392-2559; E-mail: mjbrian@execpc.com

Canada   *British Columbia Triumph Registry*, Paul Barlow, VTR Liaison, 4455 Peterson Dr, Richmond, BC V7E 4X6 604-272-4328; E-mail: paulbarlow@translink.bc.ca

Triumph Drivers Club, Dave Terrick, 476 Borebank St, Winnipeg, MB R3N 1E7 204-487-7755; E-mail: dterrick@home.com

Ontario Triumph Club, Doug Bell, President, 166 Church St, Thamesford, ON N0M 2M0

Toronto Triumph Club, Don Mills, PO Box 39, Toronto, ON M3C 2R6

Tucker Automobile Club of America Inc
9509 Hinton Dr
Santee, CA 92071-2760
619-596-3028; FAX: 815-346-6398
E-mail: tuckerclub@home.com

Tucker

450+ members. Monthly publication, *Tucker Topics*, is included in membership. Annual convention, mini-meets. Tucker Historical Collection and Library located at the GIlmore Museum. Dues: $25/year US, $40/year foreign. Web site: www.tuckerclub.org

---

TVR Car Club North America
1116 Hamilton Ave SW
Roanoke, VA 24015
540-344-6530
E-mail: tasmin@rev.net

Founded 1980. 500 members. Newsletter, the *TVR Times*, 9 regions, parts location, web site, regalia, discussion list. All available from the web site. Dues: $25/year. Web site: http://clubs.hemmings.com/tvr/

Vanden Plas Princess Register
16643 Rt 144
Mt Airy, MD 21771
301-854-5956, 410-442-3637
FAX: 301-854-5957

Vanden Plas

Club for Princess limousines, sedans, hearses and ambulances from 1947-1968. Clearinghouse for information, parts, workshop and owner's manuals, repair help, Whitworth tools. Please provide chassis number in any correspondence. Large supply of original and reproduction parts including rubber seals, brake, suspension and body parts. 12 Princess parts cars on hand. Web site: http://clubs.hemmings.com/vandenplasprincess/

Common Gear Antique Volkswagen Society
PO Box 3353
Stony Creek, CT 06405
E-mail: commongear@aol.com

Founded 1998. Common Gear is a loosely based community of antique VW enthusiasts with focus at the web site. Although we have a discussion group, there is no membership per se. Drop by the web site to find out more about us! Web site: http://members.aol.com/commongear/

Houston Volkswagen Club
PO Box 841784
Houston, TX 77284-1784
713-595-2103 ext 5801
E-mail: info@hvwc.net

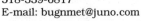

Founded 1982. 109 members. Oldest Volkswagen Club in Texas with largest web site and E-mail list covering TX, LA, AR, OK, NM and Mexico. Dues: $20/year. Web site: www.hvwc.net

Hudson & Mohawk Society of Volkswagen Owners
784 Sacandaga Rd
Scotia, NY 12302
518-339-6817
E-mail: bugnmet@juno.com

Founded 1994. 50 members. Membership is open to any owner, former owner, admirer of Volkswagens. The club consists of members from the Hudson and Mohawk Valley regions of New York State (eastern New York), but also includes western MA, VT and CT. Membership is open to anyone. Dues: $15/year.

Long Island VW Club
PO Box 184
Levittown, NY 11756
E-mail: nuts4vws@erols.com

Contact: Eddie Hoffmann. Welcome all to attend our monthly meetings and you don't need to own a car, even enthusiasts are welcome. Deal with VWs ranging from the 40s thru the 70s. Publish a monthly newsletter, have window decals and club jackets. Web site: www.howlingdogstudios.com/livc

Northern Wisconsin Volkswagen Club
516 Bruce St
New London, WI 54961
920-982-0171
E-mail: nwvc@nwvc.itgo.com

Founded 2000. 70 members. A love for Volkswagens, especially Beetles and buses. Our group consists mainly of air-cooled VW owners but we do have a few water-cooled VW owners as well. We are a non-profit club located in northern Wisconsin. We get together in various locations throughout the year for cruises, car shows, camp outs, picnics, etc. Our club is also a chapter of Vintage Volkswagen Club of America. Dues: none. Web site: www.nwvc.itgo.com

Omaha Volkswagen Club
4974 Corby St
Omaha, NE 68104
402-558-1300
E-mail: captoaster@home.com

Founded 1985. 75 members. No restrictions. We have a yearly show and shine, monthly meetings, bi-monthly newsletters, monthly get-togethers (picnics, camping, tech sessions, etc). Dues: $20/year. Web site: www.omahavwclub.com

South Eastern Volkswagen Club
257 Oak Trace Rd
Hahira, GA 31632
229-896-4957
E-mail: sevwc@sevwc.com

Founded in 1994 to serve the southeast USA. We provide a bi-monthly newsletter, web site, classified,and host our own car shows just for Volkswagens. We are currently 300 members strong and still growing. Web site: www.sevwc.com

Volvo Club of America
PO Box 16
Afton, NY 13730
607-639-2279; FAX: 607-639-2279

VOLVO

For information, write, phone or fax to the above address. Founded 1983. 3,500 members. National club of owners and enthusiasts of all Volvo automobiles. Membership benefits include: subscription to *Rolling* magazine, parts discounts, technical assistance, local chapters and regional and national meets. Dues: $25/year. Web site: www.vcoa.org

chapters:

Arizona   *Cactus*, Randall Pace, 14414 North 51st St, Scottsdale, AZ 85254   602-953-0650; E-mail: randallp@sprintmail.com

California   *Golden Gate (California)*, Lee Cordner, 313 Pt San Pedro Rd, San Rafael, CA 94901   415-455-9192; E-mail: mrlee@ix.netcom.com

     San Francisco/Northern California, David Spieler, 1908 California #7, Berkeley, CA 94703   510-849-0961; E-mail: dspiel@aol.com

Florida   *Florida*, Dave Montgomery, 4424 Ortega Farms Cir, Jacksonville, FL 32210   904-771-1154; E-mail: d.w.montgomery@worldnet.att.net

     Florida/Southwest, Bill or Pat Rose, 124 Trinidad St, Isles of Capri, FL 34113   941-263-4505

Georgia   *Bertone Register*, Pat and Jon Evans, 1303 Swann Dr, Dalton, GA 30720   706-226-0488

Maine   *Maine*, Tom Roane, RR1, Box 1433, Limerick, ME 04048   207-793-2418

Massachusetts   *Boston/Merrimack Valley*, Duncan LaBay, 4 Ferry Rd, Newburyport, MA 01950   978-462-1607; E-mail: dlabay@seacoast.com

Missouri   *Missouri/Southern Illinois*, Jim Jeske, 4734 Sunnyview Dr, St Louis, MO 63128   314-894-3575

New Jersey   *240 Classic Register*, Carl Bauske, 298 Pennington-Titusville Rd, Pennington, NJ 08534   609-730-8124; E-mail: cabauske@us.ibm.com

Section Three – Clubs & Organizations

Volvo Club of America chapters (continued)

Garden State, Tom Lamb, 6 Pergola St, Jamesburg, NJ 08831 732-521-0253; E-mail: tlamb@gateway.net

New York   New York Metro, Howie Silverman, 207 Bayview Ave, Massapequa, NY 11758 516-798-3618; E-mail: jojokev@worldnet.att.net

Volvo Amazon Register, Mark Heyburn, PO Box 733, Vails Gate, NY 12584 914-569-1390; E-mail: pvpickup@frontiernet.net

Volvo PV Register, Mark Heyburn, PO Box 733, Vails Gate, NY 12584 914-569-1390; E-mail: pvpickup@frontiernet.net

North Carolina   Blue Ridge, Del Lance, 1008 Winwood Dr, Cary, NC 27511-4349 919-380-0428

Ohio   Southwestern Ohio, Chris Ward, PO Box 42, Willard, OH 44890 E-mail: vcoaohio@hotmail.com

Oregon   Pacific NW/SW Washington, Mike Harding, 4114 SW Lee St, Portland, OR 97214 503-245-2971

Pennsylvania   Philadelphia, Michael Leslie, 29 Thomas Ave, Bryn Mawr, PA 19010 610-525-4872; E-mail: mikelesli@aol.com

South Carolina   South Carolina, John Crabtree, 135 Ridge Glen, Simpsonville, SC 29680 864-862-6737; E-mail: crabtree@prodigy.com

Tennessee   Appalachian, Bill Holt, 974 Hamilton Cir, Cleveland, TN 37312 423-476-9076; E-mail: billhholt@mindspring.com

Texas   Texas, Al Ringle, 3417 Forrester Ln, Waco, TX 76708 254-753-1115; E-mail: texaschaptervcoa@angelfire.com

Virginia   240 Limited Edition Register, Ray Parsons, 1248 Bond St, Herndon, VA 22070 703-742-8274; E-mail: rdp10@juno.com

Washington   Washington/Puget Sound, Wes Urbanec, 128 Fifth Ave NW, Puyallup, WA 98371 253-848-8958; E-mail: wesu@mckinney-sea.com

Volvo Owners' Club
34 Lyonsgate Dr
Downsview, ON Canada M3H 1C8
416-633-6801

Founded 1976. 250 members from US, Canada, Europe, Brazil and Australia. Covers all Volvo models, old and new. Dues: none.

Volvo Sports America 1800
1203 W Cheltenham Ave
Elkins Park, PA 19027
215-635-0117; FAX: 215-635-4070
or 718-863-0964, NY
E-mail: bobfv1800@aol.com

Founded 1976. 2,000 members. International club devoted to the milestone/classic 1800 and other vintage Volvos. Technical service. Bimonthly magazine, parts/service discounts, national meets, concours, touring schools, rallies. Local chapters. Dues: $30/year US, $32/year Canada and $40/year foreign. Web site: www.vsa.org

Wills Sainte Claire Club
3546 Conger St
Port Huron, MI 48060
810-987-2854
E-mail: ternest@tir.com

Founded 1959. 100+ members. Anyone may join who has an interest in Wills Sainte Claire automobiles produced in Marysville, Michigan from 1921-1927. Dues: $15/year.

Mid-America Willys Club
18222 N 661 Ave
Glendale, AZ 85308
PH/FAX: 602-439-2502
E-mail: kmcintyre1@prodigy.net

Founded 1988. 1,650 members. We are a nostalgia drag raced based group that love the 1933-1942 Willys. No restrictions to join. We have members worldwide. Dues: $35/year US, $38/year Canada, $40/year international. Web site: www.gasserclub.com

Midstates Jeepster Association
5905 N 300 W
Michigan City, IN 46360
219-326-5589; FAX: 219-324-9096
E-mail: wrightd1@csinet.net

Founded 1966. 360 families. Must have an interest in Jeepsters, 1948-1951. We encourage you to join. You will receive: information for the restoration and preservation of Jeepsters; access to classified advertising for items for sale and things wanted; notices of future meets where you can meet other Jeepster lovers; articles sent in by our members showing "what worked for me"; a roster of our 360+ family memberships. Publish monthly newsletter. Have two main meets each year, one in spring and one in fall. Encourage mini-meets in areas throughout the year for those that can't make our two main meets or just want to get together more often. Dues: $25/year, $3 one time application fee. Web site: http://members.tripod.com/~dan_wright/index-2.html

Willys-Overland-Knight Registry
1341 Orion Rd
Batavia, IL 60510
PH/FAX: 630-879-7010
E-mail: elp90@aol.com

Founded 1960. 1,500 members. 12 newsletters, quarterly magazine, annual meets, tours, library research center. International club with local chapters in regional parts of the US and foreign countries. Publishes quarterly Knight-Overland Starter, historical, educational, tech tips, human interest stories and rally news. Dues: $24/year. Web site: www.wokr.org

Zimmer Motor Car Club
1415 W Genesee St
Syracuse, NY 13204
315-422-7011 ext 125
FAX: 315-422-1721
E-mail: azimmer@syracusenewtimes.com

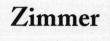

Founded 1995. 538 members. For all Zimmer motor car owners. Newsletters and information on Zimmers. Specializing in Zimmer Golden Spirits, 1980-2001. Free publication, Zimmer Times, published quarterly, information about Zimmer motor cars. Dues: none. Web site: www.zimmermotorcars.com

Registries

The Super Stock AMX Registry
30115 Hwy 281 N, Ste 126
Bulverde, TX 78163
830-980-3165
E-mail: akjamc@juno.com

Founded 1986. 32 members. Must own one of the 53 1969 Hurst SS/AMXs, vintage clone (1968-1970 AMX converted to SS racing) or current AMX run in Super Stock racing. Dues: none. Web site: www.southtexasamc.bigstep.com

North American Mini Moke Registry
1779 Kickapoo St, PO Box 9110
South Lake Tahoe, CA 96150
530-577-7895
E-mail: minimoke@mindspring.com

Founded 1982. 99 members. Need not own a Moke to join. No meetings, newsletter provides contact between owners. In contact with Mini Moke Club of England, Moke Club of Australia and exchange letters with Mini Clubs worldwide. Dues: $15/year. Web site: http://clubs.hemmings.com/mokeregistry

Brabham Register
1611 Alvina Ave
Sacramento, CA 95822
916-454-1115

Brabham

Founded 1979. Formed to provide information to Brabham owners for use in the authentic restoration of the cars. Must own Brabham race car to join. Initiation fee: $40.

Bristol Register of New Zealand
61 Rothesay Bay Road
Rothesay Bay
Auckland, 10 New Zealand
PH/FAX: 64-9-478-7426

Maintain a register of all Bristol and Bristol engined cars in New Zealand. Limited spares for Bristol 400-406 cars and 85-100-110-BS engines.

1932 Buick Registry
3000 Warren Rd
Indiana, PA 15701
724-463-3372; FAX: 724-463-8604
E-mail: buick32@adelphia.net

Founded 1974. 400 members. Open only to 1932 Buicks. Manufacture and sell reproduction parts for Buicks 1925-1935. Disseminate information on 1932 model Buicks, including sales of literature. Free *1932 Buick Registry* newsletter. Printed parts list available for 1925-1935 Buicks, send SASE. Dues: none.

Marquette Owners Registry for Enthusiasts
Don Holton
803 Cedar St
Elmira, NY 14904-2643
607-734-5340
E-mail: topsdown@stny.rr.com

Founded 1996. Approximately 100 members. There are no restrictions to join. This is an international registry for anyone interested in the Buick built Marquette. Dues: $10/year US and Canada, $14/year international (US money order). Web site: http://homepage.mac.com/topsdown/marquette.html

Chalmers Automobile Registry
c/o Dave Hammond
110 Sourwood Dr
Hatboro, PA 19040-1922
215-672-0764
E-mail: dchamm@worldnet.att.net

Chalmers

Founded 1995. 58 active members. 104 owners (120 cars) listed in US, Canada and England. Dedicated to the restoration, preservation and enjoyment of Chalmers automobiles. Provides a means for information exchange between owners and access to historical and technical database. Registration is free and newsletter (3-4 per year) is $5.

Clenet Registry
Donald C Royston
11311 Woodland Dr
Lutherville, MD 21093
410-825-2010

Clenet

A registry of this limited production luxury car listing present owners, previous owners (many custom built for celebrities), year built, color combinations, production number, maintenance tips, parts sources, etc.

The Delage Section of the VSCC
c/o Peter Jacobs (Hon secretary)
Cloud's Reach, The Scop
Almondsbury, Bristol, BS32 4DU
England
PH/FAX: +44 1454-612434
E-mail: peter@delage-world.co.uk

Founded 1956. 170 members and growing. Catering to owners of all models of Delage 1905 to 1954. Provides quarterly newsletters, annual journal, register of surviving cars worldwide, technical/historical advice, motoring events and free advertising for Delage sales and wants. Dues: £10 Sterling/year.

Section Three – Clubs & Organizations

De Vaux Registry
647 Ridgeview Dr
Corunna, MI 48817
517-743-5390

Registry of existing 1931-32 De Vaux automobiles.

1939-1947 Dodge Truck Registry
c/o Dave Fenner
1625 Jason St
San Diego, CA 92154
619-575-1543; FAX: 619-571-3457
E-mail: dfenn@sdcoe.k12.ca.us

Founded 1998. 125+ members. Periodic newsletter is planned, annual truck show is planned during fall months. Dues: none. Web site: http://clubs.hemmings.com/dodgetrucks39-47/

1970 Dart Swinger 340's Registry
PO Box 9
Wethersfield, CT 06129-0009
860-257-8434 evenings
E-mail: dartsclub@snet.net

Founded 1986. 500+ members. Must own a 1970 Dodge Dart Swinger 340. Verifies and locates all 13,785 1970 Dodge Dart Swinger 340s. Free information to help restore and preserve these cars. Newsletter subscription, $10/year for 4 quarterly issues. Dues: none. Web site at HMN Car Club Central.

Dodge Charger Registry
PO Box 184
Green Bay, VA 23942
804-223-1305
E-mail: chargerreg@hovac.com

Founded 1986. 487 members. No restrictions to join. Founded in 1986 to help owners restore their cars, to build a database for comparisons against factory info and to promote preservation and friendship. To encourage manufacturers to produce Charger related items. 5 once-a-year regional meets. Meets involve cruise, picnic, parts swap plus many other activities. Dues: $25/year initial, $20/year renewal. Web site: http://clubs.hemmings.com/chargerregistry/

International Viper Registry
PO Box 914
Arkadelphia, AR 71923-0914
501-246-0015; FAX: 501-246-0762
E-mail: viperjay@iocc.com

Founded 1992. 750 members. Dedicated to the care, preservation and history of the Dodge Viper. Registration certificate, $15. Web site: www.viperclub.org/ivr

North American English & European Ford Registry
PO Box 11415
Olympia, WA 98508
360-754-9585
E-mail: ifhp@aol.com

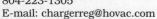

See full listing in **Section Three** under **Marque Clubs**

Erskine Register
441 E St Clair, Box 431
Almont, MI 48003
810-798-8600

For membership information, contact at the above address: Norman Hamilton. For information please send SASE.

Topolino Register of North America
3301 Shetland Rd
Beavercreek, OH 45434
937-426-0098
E-mail: mike7353@aol.com

For information, contact at the above address: Mike Self.

Founded 1969. 72 members. This is a register of Fiat 500 A/B/C, Simca 5, NSU-Fiat 500 owners and owners of Topolino-based vehicles, 1936-1955. Serves as a restoration, information and parts source exchange for owners. Register published periodically. Dues: none.

1938 Ford Street Rod Registry
68 Delaware Ave
Lambertville, NJ 08530
609-397-1571
E-mail: marvess@hotmail.com

Founded 1999. 135 members so far. Street rods and customs only. 1938 Standard and Deluxes and 1939 Standards only. Not a club, just a list. Newsletter every so often. Dues: none. Web site: http://clubs.hemmings.com/1938fordstreetrod

SHO Club
902 S Main St
Washington, IL 61571
309-444-2540; FAX: 309-444-8570
E-mail: comments@shoclub.com

Founded 1990. Formed to enhance the ownership of the Taurus SHO. Perhaps the finest high-performance sedan of this generation. Only enthusiasm is required. Publishes a quarterly magazine and annual convention. Dues: $35/year. Web site: www.shoclub.com

Mustang Special Order Paint Registry
c/o Tony Popish
6113 S Cherry Ct
Littleton, CO 80121
720-489-1504
E-mail: tpopish@aol.com

Founded 1994. 300 members. Interest in first generation Mustang history, especially dealing with special order paint Mustangs. Publish *Horse of a Different Color* for $9/4 issues. Dedicated to the special order paint Mustang, featuring color information, interviews with former FoMoCo employees, etc, for 1964-1/2 to 1973 Mustangs. Dues: none. Web site: http://members.aol.com/dsomustang/

Honda 600 Roster of Owners
c/o Bill Colford
7518 Westbrook Ave
San Diego, CA 92139
619-267-0485
E-mail: aahonda600@juno.com

No rules or regulations. A source of: reliable technical information, location of mechanics that "know" the Honda 600, restoration information and assistance, location of hard to find parts, information on the next gathering of the Honda 600 Group. No dues. No membership fee. Web site: www.freeyellow.com/members2/zcoupe/index/html

Inter-State Motor Car Registry 1909-1919
Jay Arendt, Registrar
13883 Tesson Ferry Rd
St Louis, MO 63128
314-849-3391; FAX: 636-326-0520
E-mail: jaygayla@321.net

Inter-State

Founded 1994. 13 members. Open anytime day/night, weekends, etc, 8 am to 10 pm CST. Inter-State Motor Cars 1909-1919 registry for the free exchange of information, parts, services and publications. No restrictions to join, just an interest in the 1909-1919 Inter-State automobile, period publications upon request. Meets and events to be announced. Copies of *Inter-State Motor Car* publications available to all registry members.

The Jordan Register
2099 Pheasant Dr
Yuba City, CA 95993
530-673-7382
E-mail: worledge@succeed.net

Founded 1983. 110 members. Celebrating Jordan Motor Car Company automobile collecting and restoring. Historical archives, tours and appreciation for this company's wonderful advertising. Quarterly magazine. Dues: $20/year.

Kaiser Darrin Owners Roster
734 Antram Rd
Somerset, PA 15501-8856
814-443-6468; FAX: 814-443-9452

Approximately 300 members. Club caters to owners of Kaiser Darrins. Publishes *Darrin Roster* yearly. Roster includes information on car history, parts, restoration help, etc. The Kaiser Darrin Owners Roster operates with the Kaiser Frazer Owners Club International. Dues: none (donations).

Kellison & Astra Registry and Club eV
c/o Michael Dziedzic
Emdener Str 19
10551 Berlin Germany
0049 30 390 39944
FAX: 0049 30 390 39949
E-mail: kellisonre@aol.com

The US contact: Hager Hedfield, 3402 Valley Creek Cir, Middleton, WI 53562. Founded 1996. The registry is for all actual and former owners. The club is looking for enthusiasts of Kellison and Astra too.

Manx Dune Buggy Club
PO Box 1491
Valley Center, CA 92082
760-749-6321; FAX: 760-751-0610
E-mail: manxclub@cts.com

See full listing in **Section Three** under **Specialty Clubs**

70 Mercury Marauder X-100 Registry
18376 228th St
Tonganoxie, KS 66086
913-845-3458

Founded 1991. Dedicated to the preservation of 1970 X-100s. Source of help and encouragement. Registry progress reports. Web site: www.marauder.netfirms.com

72/73 Mercury Montego GT Registry
11715 Winterpock Rd
Chesterfield, VA 23838
804-639-7289
E-mail: joe@mercurymontegogt.com

Founded 1998. 100+ members. Promotes the preservation of these rare vehicles by being a link between various owners. Mails out a newsletter three times yearly. Dues: none. Web site: www.mercurymontegogt.com

Big M Mercury Registry
5 Robinson Rd
West Woburn, MA 01801
781-932-8495
E-mail: n1elc@hotmail.com

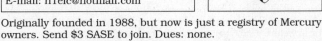

Originally founded in 1988, but now is just a registry of Mercury owners. Send $3 SASE to join. Dues: none.

Monteverdi Registry and Club eV
c/o Michael Dziedzic
Emdener Str 19
10551 Berlin Germany
0049 30 390 39944
FAX: 0049 30 390 39949
E-mail: montereg@aol.com

Founded 1983. The registry is for all actual and former owners. The club is looking for enthusiasts of Monteverdi GT-Cats, like the 375 high speed or the Safari, Sahara Jeep too.

Morris Register
20 Chestnut Ave
Gosfield, Near Halstead
Essex, CO9 1TD England
01787-473220

For membership information, contact: A Peeling, 171 Levita House, Chalton Street, London, NW1 1HR England. Founded 1959. 2,000 members. Open to all, but full membership is given only to owners of Morris vehicles designed before 1940. Dues: £14.50/first year plus £2 entry fee.

Morris Minor Registry of North America
Tony Burgess
318 Hampton Park
Westerville, OH 43081-5723
614-899-2394; FAX: 614-899-2493
E-mail: minornews@aol.com

750 members nationwide and 34 regional representatives. Dedicated to the preservation, restoration and use of the postwar Morris Minor automobile. Bi-monthly newsletter, *Minor News*, contains technical tips, feature stories on cars and related topics, meet reports, calendar of events, club and car regalia, classified ads and much more. Car registration is free. Dues: $20/year US and Canada, $30/year overseas via airmail.

Muntz Registry
21303 NE 151st
Woodinville, WA 98072
425-788-6587; FAX: 425-844-2331
E-mail: bvmunsen@aol.com

Historical information and registration for Muntz Jet automobiles 1950-1954. *Muntz Registry* is published as requested and includes production history and owner's listing for Muntz Jet automobiles produced 1950-1954.

1948-1950 Packard Convertible Roster
84 Hoy Ave
Fords, NJ 08863
732-738-7859; FAX: 732-738-7625
E-mail: stellacapp@earthlink.net

Founded 1989. Seeking information on all 1948-1950 Packard Super Eight and Custom Eight convertibles. Send an SASE for roster form.

The Packard V-8 Roster, 1955-1956
84 Hoy Ave
Fords, NJ 08863
732-738-7859; FAX: 732-738-7625
E-mail: stuartrblond@earthlink.net

For more information, contact at the above address: Stuart R Blond. Founded 1982. Roster for all 1955-1956 Packards and Clippers. Send an SASE for roster form.

Jolyon Hofsted
PO Box 66
Shady, NY 12409

Paige Registry for Paige and Jewett cars and trucks.

1969-1971 Pontiac GTO The Judge Convertible Registry
c/o Classic Pontiac Ranch
1165 County Rd 83
Independence, MN 55359
763-479-2248
E-mail: pontiacranch1@aol.com

Founded 1993. 50 members. Providing a list of owners and enthusiasts of the Pontiac GTO "The Judge" convertibles (manufactured from 1969-1971).

Firehawk Association of America
c/o W Thomas
PO Box 96
Uniontown, PA 15401
724-437-6736
E-mail: wayne@waynethomas.com

Founded 1994. 700+ members. Registry, quarterly newsletter, includes new products, improvements, recalls, problems and members' articles and a sell and want section. Two shows a year: Firehawk Rally in Norwalk, Ohio and Firehawk Fest in Northern California. Dues: $12/year. Web site: www.firehawk.org

Pontiac Sedan Delivery Registry
1165 Co Rd 83
Independence, MN 55359
763-479-2248
E-mail: pontiacranch1@aol.com

Founded 1993. 50 members. Registry for American made and Canadian made Pontiac sedan deliveries. Dues: none.

The Association of Rootes Vehicle Owners
Capri House
Walton-On-Thames
Surrey, KT12 2LY England

An association of the owners of vehicles built and sold by the Rootes Group and their various subsidiary companies. Objective is to provide a means of communication and cooperation between these owners and maintain a watching brief on UK and European legislation affecting members' vehicles. Membership is open to owners and enthusiasts of Rootes vehicles. Publication, *ARVO News*. Dues: £18=00/year US.

Scripps-Booth Register
735 W Lemon Ave
Monrovia, CA 91016-2507
626-358-7327
E-mail: scrippsbooth@earthlink.net

Founded 1982. 50 members. Free annual newsletter and register updates. Free copies of factory literature with car and engine serial number. Dues: free to owners. Web site: http://home.earthlink.net/~scrippsbooth/

Stephens Registry
Dick Farnsworth
1034 Henderson
Freeport, IL 61032
815-232-3825

Sunbeam Rapier Registry of North America
3212 Orchard Cir
West Des Moines, IA 50266-2140
515-226-9475
E-mail: jmazour@aol.com

Founded 1992. A registry and club for the identification and preservation of Sunbeam Rapiers (Series I-V, 1955-1967). Publications: *Sunbeam Rapier Registry of North America* (1999) and quarterly club newsletter, *Rapier News*. A free registry publication to each Rapier owner who participates in this registry. Dues: $16/year US, $19/year Canada.

Velie Register
1811 E Stella Ln
Phoenix, AZ 85016
602-274-6049
E-mail: velie@goodnet.com

Founded 1993. 200 members. Open to anyone. *Velie Vehicles and Their Vitals*, 55-page book, is the official register of Velie cars and trucks, 1909-1928. Publishes 6-8 Velie newsletters per year. Have now found Velies in 12 countries: Australia, Canada, Denmark, Ecuador, Finland, Germany, New Zealand, Norway, Poland, South Africa, Sweden and the USA. Dues: $10/year. Web site: www.goodnet.com/~velie

Vespa 400 Registry
100 Prince St
Fairfield, CT 06432
203-336-1505

Founded 1996. 125 members. Only interest in the Vespa 400 necessary. We keep a registry of cars and extra parts listings. Dues: none.

Victoria Registry
100 Prince St
Fairfield, CT 06432
203-336-1505

Founded 1996. 13 members. Only interest in the Victoria necessary. We keep a list of owners and spare parts. Dues: none.

Willys Aero Survival Count
952 Ashbury Heights Ct
Decatur, GA 30030-4177
404-288-8222
E-mail: aeroman@aol.com

Founded 1981. 600 members. This is a registry for 1952-1955 Willys Aero and 1960-1972 Brazilian built Aeros. Web site: http://clubs.hemmings.com/willyaero/index.html

Zimmerman Registry
2081 Madelaine Ct
Los Altos, CA 94024
PH/FAX: 650-967-2908
E-mail: zmrmn@macconnect.com

Founded 1989. 42 members. Dedicated to the preservation and restoration of Zimmerman automobiles manufactured in Auburn, Indiana, from 1908-1915. Information exchanged between members by letter and fax. No meetings, publications or dues.

Specialty Clubs

95 Pace Car Registry
T Noel Osborn
12000 Network Blvd, Ste 100
San Antonio, TX 78249-3353
210-641-7733; FAX: 210-641-9654
E-mail: thewave@texas.net

Founded 1995. 180 members. Quarterly newsletter, *Pace Setter*. Information, networking between owners of 1995 Indy pace car (Corvette) replicas. Dues: none.

The American Built Classic Car Club Inc
837 Woodbine Blvd
Jackson, MI 49203
517-787-1000; FAX: 517-783-3503
E-mail: acme@acd.net

Founded 1999. 140+ members. Auto must be an American built product manufactured between 1929 and 1979. We recognize the classic car (second generation) and those grand old classics built before 1929 as Grand classics. Dues: $10/year.

Antique Auto Racing Association Inc
Dale Mathews, President
PO Box 46579
Oakwood Village, OH 44146

Founded 1973. 300 members. Open to vintage race car owners and enthusiasts. Holds five meets each year. Provides the opportunity for vintage 1948 and earlier open wheel speedsters, midgets and big car owners to participate in actual dirt track racing exhibitions. Spectactors welcome. Dues: $25/year.

Asphalt Draggins' Racing Assn
63 Fenton Ave
St Paul, MN 55117
612-489-7417

Founded 1992. 25 members. No membership restrictions. Annual car show at Perfect 10 Car Wash, Spring Lake Park, MN, always 1st Saturday night in June. Monthly publication, *Draggins' Tale*, included with membership. Dues: $20/year

Association for Preservation of Historic Ambulances
3922 W Watersville Rd
Mt Airy, MD 21771
301-607-8068
E-mail: stevel200@worldnet.att.net

Founded 1995. 100 members. Newsletter *Omaha Orange*. Open to anyone with an interest in ambulances (car or truck chassis) and the history of ambulance service. Dues: $10/year. Web site: www.historicambulances.org

Atlantic Coast Old Timers Auto Racing Club
55 Hilliard Rd
Old Bridge, NJ 08857
732-251-4148
E-mail: gewhite@crosslink.net

Newsletter address: c/o Gordon White, Box 129, Hardyville, VA 23070. Membership: c/o Bradley Gray, 55 Hilliard Rd, Old Bridge, NJ 08857. Founded 1983. 550 members, 250 cars. Dedicated to restoring and running antique American oval-track race cars. Also has an active program of searching out and preserving records of racing history. Bimonthly newsletter: *Pit Chatter*. Dues: $14/year. Web site: www.crosslink.net/~gewhite/

BAD Burlington Area Drivers
4 Riverside Dr
Milton, VT 05468
802-893-7495
E-mail: mrmopar1@msn.com

Founded 1998. 35 members. We have been putting on one car show per year and just get-togethers and go to shows. Monthly newsletter, Dues: $10/year.

Bent Axles
4522 Boardwalk Ln
Santa Maria, CA 93455
805-937-0555

Founded 1978. 80 families. Social club for the enjoyment of pre-1949 street rods, the only requirement needed for joining, with monthly cruises and get-togethers. *Bent Action* is the monthly newsletter. The annual cruise and Santa Maria style bar-b-que is held on the third weekend of July with about 200 street rods in attendance. Dues: $26/year.

Bow Tie Chevy Association
PO Box 608108
Orlando, FL 32860
407-880-1956; FAX: 407-886-7571
E-mail: chevy55-72@ao.net

Founded 1992. 3,000 members. Monthly magazine *Bow Times* (24-page full color magazine). Put on conventions around the US and Canada. Dues: $30/year. Web site: www.ao.net/chevy55-72/

Bridge Hampton Historical Society
PO Box 977
Bridgehampton, NY 11932
516-537-1088; FAX: 516-537-4225

Founded 1950. 350 members. Recreates annual in the street automobile races. Races open to all pre-1954 cars, membership to all. Dues: $10/year. Web site: www.hamptons.com/bhhs

British Car Club of Charleston
Jack Lambert, President
1382 Woodlock Rd
Mt Pleasant, SC 29464
843-849-9707 (home); FAX: 843-577-2061
E-mail: dlambert@bennetthofford.com

Founded 1983. Approximately 85 members. Open to all British marques. Holds annual British Car Day in October at Patriots Point in Mt Pleasant, SC. Publishes *The Windscreen*, a monthly publication. Dues: $20/year. Web site: www.geocities.com/britishcars

British Motoring Club Inc
4200 Wares Ferry Rd
Montgomery, AL 36109
334-279-0971
E-mail: fishdoctor@aol.com

Founded 1992. 84 members. Must be a British car lover. Meet 2nd Monday each month. One driving event each month and one car show a year. Monthly newsletter. Dues: $20/year. Web site: www.bmcmontgomery.com

Central Ohio Antique Fire Apparatus Assn
293 Lyncroft Dr
Gahanna, OH 43230
614-471-2120

Founded 1986. 100 members. Meeting monthly, 1st Monday. Hosts annual antique fire engine muster. Dues: $12.50/year.

Chris-Craft Antique Boat Club
217 S Adams St
Tallahassee, FL 32301-7708
850-224-BOAT; FAX: 850-224-1033
E-mail: wwright@nettally.com

2,700 members. Monday-Friday 9 am to 5 pm. Open to anyone interested in antique or classic Chris Crafts, 1920-1972. Benefits include subscription to quarterly magazine, group insurance, online discussion group, archival information, library access. Quarterly publication, *Brass Bell*, includes calendar of events, member profiles, boat reviews,helpful hints, reports on current events, free classified ads for members. Dues: $25/year. Web site: www.chris-craft.org

"Classics" Car Club Inc
720 Iowa Ave
Onawa, IA 51040
712-423-3837; FAX: 712-423-2411
E-mail: classics@willinet.net

Founded 1976. 83 members. Open to classic, custom, special interest auto enthusiasts. Annual Graffiti Nights, June 23, July 21 and August 18; annual swap meet, 3rd Sunday in August; various cruise nights, parties, get-togethers throughout the year. Bi-monthly publication, *Cruisin' News*, includes club and area event coverage, member's features, meeting reports/club business, technical and how-to articles, new products, etc. Dues: $15/year. Web site: www.alistauto.com/classiccars/

Classtiques Rod & Custom Club
PO Box 459
Bismarck, ND 58502
701-222-2069; FAX: 701-222-0736

Founded 1980. 30 members. Monthly newsletter, yearly rod run, weekly cruises. Maximum 30 members. Dues: $10/year. Web site: www.geocities.com/classtiques

Cole Motor Car Club of America
Box 183
Goodrich, MI 48438
810-636-7221
E-mail: leroycole2@aol.com

Leroy D Cole, President. Founded 1990. 72 members. Open membership. *Cole Bulletin* is published 2 times per year and gives news on members and their cars, club meets and historical articles. Dues: $12/year.

Country Cruisers Car Club
1624 155th St
Manchester, IA 52057
319-927-4676
E-mail: johnymack@n-connect.net

Founded 1992. 38 members. Must have specialty car or classic car. Annual car cruise, August 11, 2001, 300+ cars. Annual car show at Dele Co fairgrounds, August 12, 2001. Our main charity is Special Olympics. Other donations go to Operation Santa Claus, food pantry, March of Dimes. Dues: $20/year.

Cumberland Valley Rod & Custom Club Inc
PO Box 781
Waynesboro, PA 17288
717-762-9624
E-mail: rocki@supernet.com or scottb@pa.net

Founded 1989. 30 members. Everyone is welcome. All meets and events are listed on the web site. Dues: $15/year single person, $20/year family. Web site: http://clubs.hemmings.com/cvrcc

Dells Area Cruisers
S 3051 Fox Hill Rd
Baraboo, WI 53913
608-356-2494; FAX: 608-355-0965
E-mail: cruisers@jvlnet.com

40 members. Must work the car show in the spring called Automotion. Discount at Napa Auto Parts Store, Baraboo, 10% discount on $100 or more at Year One. Monthly newsletter. Christmas party, bowling party, go to car show, put on the show, Cold Wisconsin Dells Automotion, the 3rd weekend in May, 750+ cars. Dues: $20/single one time fee, $25/double one time fee.

The DeRidder Car/Truck Show (DCTS)
321 Tanglewood Lp
DeRidder, LA 70634
337-463-7336

Founded 1988. 50 members. Host annual car/truck show plus arts and crafts, swap meet and car corral. Dues: $15/year.

The Dominators
445 Shawsheen Ave
Wilmington, MA 01887
978-658-6082; FAX: 978-988-3769
E-mail: cabrio33@prodigy.net

Founded 1957. 18 members. Pre-1949 cars. Quarterly newsletter, yearly runs and invitational picnic/rod run. Dues: $60/year. Web site: www.members.aol.com/thedominators

The Early Valiant and Barracuda Club
34A School St
Mystic, CT 06355
860-572-1706
E-mail: llkizer@snet.net

Founded 2000. 90 members. A club catering to Valiants from 1960 to 1966 and Barracudas from 1964 to 1966. Membership includes club window decal, bi-monthly newsletter, *The Early Connection*, access to lots of info, specs, tech articles and issues, photos and magazine ads and much more. We also have internet chat on Fridays at 10 pm EST. Dues: $20/year. Web site: http://pages.cthome.net/earlycuda

East Coast Car Association Toys for Tots
PO Box 790366
Middle Village, NY 11379
718-417-8052
E-mail: toys4tots.8k.com

Founded 1999. 45 members. We run a number of car shows a year to raise funds for St Mary's Hospital for Children. If you're interested, contact us at our web site or address. Web site: www.toys4tots.8k.com

Electric Car Owner's Society
167 Concord St
Brooklyn Heights, NY 11201
718-797-4311 ext 3262; FAX: 718-596-4852
E-mail: mail@didik.com

Founded 1982. 520 members. BBS, special electric car database CD-ROM, electric car library and registry. $25 donation requested. Web site: www.didik.com

Firewalker Four Wheel Drive Club
242 Pilgrims Path
Gurnee, IL 60031
E-mail: firewalkerfwdc@aol.com

Founded 1999. 35 members. Jeep vehicles only. Quarterly newsletter. Several trips. Dues: $10/year. Web site: www.homestead.com/firewalker

Foothills Street Rod Association
PO Box 30294, Chinook Post Office
Calgary, AB Canada T2V 1W9
403-259-4764; FAX: 403-253-1412
E-mail: webmaster@fsra.org

Founded 1968. 100+ members. Interest in pre-1954 rods and customs. Dues: $20/year. Web site: www.fsra.org

Fordnutz Cougar Club
Airport RPO, PO Box 24015
Richmond, BC Canada V7B 1Y2
604-786-3673
E-mail: fordnutz@bigfoot.com

Founded 1997. 100+ members. Dedicated to the preservation of all Mercury Cougars and other Ford and Mercury vehicles. Benefits: discount program with parts and service vendors, *Nutz Letter* newsletter published in color and available by e-mail and regular mail, many social events and car shows. Dues: $30/year. Web site: www.bigfoot.com/~fordnutz/

Fredericksburg Street Rods
College Station, PO Box 1021
Fredericksburg, VA 22402-1021
202-314-3456, DC
E-mail: hkjenk@erols.com

Founded 1989. 12 members. Must own a vehicle made prior to 1948. Must be a member of NSRA (National Street Rod Association). Meets monthly, first Wednesday. Has web site, color on-line photo album, color monthly newsletter, annual Mother's Day show benefits special eduction for Walker Grant Middle School. Dues: $20/year. Web site: www.geocities.com/hkjenk/fsr.html

Friends of the Crawford Auto-Aviation Museum
10825 E Blvd
Cleveland, OH 44106
216-721-5722; FAX: 216-721-0645

Founded 1972. 380 members. The Friends of the Crawford Auto-Aviation Museum (CAAM) promotes and supports the museum through social activities, volunteerism and fundraising. In addition to sharing the company of other enthusiasts, Friends have the opportunity to work with the collection artifacts and to participate in museum program development. Friends' raffle proceeds have purchased five vehicles for the museum and funded restoration projects. Membership in the Friends of the CAAM is open to members of the Western Reserve Historical Society. Dues: $40/year.

Gibson Road Antique Fire Association
1545 Gibson Rd
Bensalem, PA 19020
215-245-1545
E-mail: alf@grafa.org

Founded 1992. 148 members. Ownership of apparatus not a requirement. A family oriented club. We publish a quarterly newsletter, have a fire muster and fire related flea market every September and annual picnic and Christmas party. Active in community events. Dues: $25/1st year, $10/additional years. Web site: www.grafa.org

Heartland Vintage Truck Club
425 E North St
DuQuoin, IL 62832
618-542-6554
E-mail: phoenix@cybalink.com

Founded 1997. 15 members. Classic trucks 1972 or older, any make or model. The club is a family club that holds picnics and Fall get togethers at the local state park. Dues: $10/year. Web site: www.geocities.com/motorcity/7622/oletruck.club.html

Historic Vehicle Society of Ontario
6155 Arner Town Line, RR 2
Kingsville, ON Canada N9Y 2E5
519-776-6909; FAX: 519-776-8321
E-mail: swoheritagevillage@on.aibn.com

Chartered 1959. 98 members. Monthly publication *Through the Windshield*. Benefits include free admission to 12 annual events, April-October. Must attend three meetings, must be recommended and sponsored by a current member in good standing. Dues: $25/year. Web site: www.cnls.com/swo.heritage.village

Hoosier Model Car Association
1019 N Tuxedo St
Indianapolis, IN 46201
317-264-9387

Founded 1979. 20 members. For builders and collectors, any marque, scale or building style. Serving central Indiana area. Annual swap meet and involvement in local shows. Monthly newsletter. Dues: $12/year.

Inliners International
R Linnell
14408 SE 169th St
Renton, WA 98058
425-228-2028
E-mail: chevysix@home.com

Founded 1981. 1,500 members. Devoted to all makes inline engines. Bi-monthly newsletter, *12 Port News*. Regional chapters, annual convention. Dues: $24/year. Web site: www.inliners.com

Intermountain's Finest Truck Club
276 N Harrison Blvd
Ogden, UT 84404-4153
801-399-5941

Founded 1987. 25 members. Restricted to show quality trucks, 4x4 and two-wheel drive. Anyone can join with truck. Meeting held every month. We put on 2 different car and truck shows every year and participate in most shows throughout the Intermountain West. Dues: $120/year.

International Society for Vehicle Preservation
PO Box 50046
Tucson, AZ 85703-1046
520-622-2201; FAX: 520-792-8501
E-mail: isvp@aztexcorp.com

Founded 1983. A non-profit organization dedicated to gathering and disseminating information for the restorer, preservationist and auto historian. Actively encourages preservation and restoration of vehicles and artifacts and acts as "government watchdog," alerting of governmental actions, which may infringe our right to continued enjoyment of such vehicles. Sponsor and organizing body of the International Automotive Awards, Banquet & Conference held each December. Dues: $15/year. Web site: www.aztexcorp.com

Jackson Street Cruisers
837 Woodbine Blvd
Jackson, MI 49203-2657
517-787-1000; FAX: 517-784-3503
E-mail: acme@acd.net

Founded 1992. 462 members. Car must be 20 years or older. We have one rule, no rules, no meetings. Entitlements: a membership card, certificate, copy of Michigan auto shows/swap meets calendar, summer picnic, Christmas dinner, newsletters, fellowship in an association with many others of similar interests. Dues: $10/year.

Gary Keating
CT Military Vehicle Collectors
98 Schuyler Ave
Middletown, CT 06457
860-347-7881
E-mail: keats@gateway.net

Founded 20+ years. 70 members. Open to anyone with an interest in historic military vehicles. Ownership not necessary. Family oriented. Club holds annual vehicle rally each year and is involved in various community activities such as parades, car shows, veteran activities, etc. Dues: $15/year.

Lincoln Highway Association
136 N Elm St, PO Box 308
Franklin Grove, IL 61031-0308
815-456-3030
E-mail: lnchwyhq@essex1.com

Founded 1992. 1,000 members. 501(c)3 not for profit organization. Promoting and preserving the Lincoln Hwy. Annual conference. Quarterly publication, *The Lincoln Highway Forum*. Dues: $25/year individual, $30/year family. Web site: www.lincolnhighwayassoc.org

Local Cruisers Car Club
19 Circle Dr
Rockaway, NJ 07866
973-625-8408; FAX: 973-625-4683
E-mail: smokey225@aol.com

Founded 1994. 40+ members. You must have an antique or rare vintage car or working on one. Free breakfast meeting each month, get-togethers to make a club presence at certain shows or cruise nights. Monthly newsletter, T-shirts, jackets, sweatshirts available. Sponsoring our own car show (annual). Dues: $60/year per person, $120/year per couple.

Long Island Street Rod Association
263 Laurel Rd
East Northport, NY 11731
631-261-2488

Founded 1965. 150+ members. Must own a street rod. Monthly newsletter, *LISRA Newsletter*, included in membership. 3 annual car shows/swap meets. Dues: $24/year. Web site: http://clubs.hemmings.com/listreetrod/

Lost Highways
The Classic Trailer & Motorhome Club
PO Box 43737
Philadelphia, PA 19106
215-925-2568; FAX: 215-925-5646
E-mail: tincanners@aol.com

Founded 1993. 1,500 members and growing. A club and archive. Teens and twenties through the seventies. You do not have to own a classic trailer or motorhome to join. Regional meets and rallies. Vintage station wagon, step van, VW bus and any other type of auto campers also very welcome. Extensive archive for research, always seeking related materials. Dues: $24/year.

Mac's Pack
429 Co Rd 332
Bertram, TX 78605
512-355-3618
E-mail: camac@bigfoot.com

Founded 1987. To become a member, you must help put on an event or showing in two events, we put on several events. A benefit for the Burnet Co Sheriff's Teddy Bear Program in March, also 2 driving events and poker run and a Gimmick Rally in the spring and fall.

Mad Dogs & Englishmen
630 E Cork St
Kalamazoo, MI 49001
616-344-5555; FAX: 616-344-8431

Founded 1991. 40 members. No restrictions, all makes of cars welcome to belong to club. Major event: Mad Dogs & Englishmen British car fair. Car show in July, all British marques welcome at show, 1998 was eighth year. Dues: $10/year.

Manx Dune Buggy Club
PO Box 1491
Valley Center, CA 92082
760-749-6321; FAX: 760-751-0610
E-mail: manxclub@cts.com

Founded 1994. 1,575 members internationally. Open to all owners of street-legal dune buggies and a registry for any Meyers kit car. There is a quarterly newsletter, *Manx Mania*, with announcements about future meets and events. Dues: $25/year. Registry: $5/year. Web site: www.manxclub.com

Marauders Hot Rod Club
821 Valley Crest St
LaCanada, CA 91011-2433
818-790-5772

Founded 1999. 2 members. Early Ford hot rods only, 1934 and earlier. No fiberglass or reproduction steel bodies. Events: roadsters and coupes at the Rose Bowl (monthly), early Ford hot rod swap meet (4 times a year), Saturday night car show at Fuddruckers.

Massachusetts Antique Fire Apparatus Association Inc
Robert Noseworthy, Secretary
PO Box 3332
Peabody, MA 01960
978-664-4533
E-mail: paulromano@pipeline.com

Paul Romano, President, 781-334-3132 days; 781-334-3573 evenings. Founded 1976. 200 members. Open to persons interested in the development and history of motorized fire apparatus. Monthly publication: *The Box Alarm*. Dues: $15/year. Web site: www.home.att.net/~MAFAA/index.html

Massena Olde Car Club Inc
PO Box 465
Massena, NY 13662
315-769-6739
E-mail: mocc@mail.com

Founded 1997. 138 members. The club is open to all. Meet every Thursday night (May-October) at the Massena Dairy Queen. The club helps to raise money for charity and other organizations. Dues: $10/year. Web site: http://clubs.hemmings.com/mocc

The Microcar and Minicar Club
PO Box 43137
Upper Montclair, NJ 07043
973-366-1410

Founded 1991. 900+ members. Successor to the Heinkel-Messerschmitt-Isetta Club. Dedicated to the enjoyment and preservation of all small and unusual cars. Our quarterly magazine, *Minutia*, features news, technical information, parts sources and classified advertisements. Nationwide events and club representatives. Monthly meetings in Hackensack, NJ. Dues: $20/year US/Canada, $30/year overseas. Web site: www.microcar.org

Mid-Atlantic Nostalgia Drag Racers Assn
123 Franklin Ave
Palmerton, PA 18071
610-826-5907; FAX: 610-824-5375
E-mail: bitsnpieces58@yahoo.com

Founded 1999. 80 members. 1972 or older drag car. Newsletter. 12 to 15 races per year in PA, NJ, MD and DE. Dues: $50/year.

Mid-Michigan Antique Fire Apparatus Association
2910 Meister Ln
Lansing, MI 48906-9010
517-676-5910

Founded 1983. 40 members. No membership restrictions other than having an interest in fire apparatus history and preservation. Fire apparatus ownership is not required. Members participate in a number of parades and musters throughout the year. We also tour area fire depts and hold meetings at different fire stations. Dues: $10/year.

Midwest Mopar Club-Sioux Empire Chapter
26471 467th Ave
Sioux Falls, SD 57107
605-334-9161; FAX: 605-331-6065
E-mail: 79volare@gateway.net

Founded 1986. 50 members. Open to all Mopar and Mopar powered vehicles. Monthly newsletter and subscription to *Chrysler Power* magazine included in membership. Host the annual Moparama at Tufty Dodge in Sioux Falls in September each year. Dues: $25/year.

Midwest Street Rod Association of Illinois
620 Fairfield Ln
Algonquin, IL 60102
847-854-2054

Founded 1969. 115 members. Members must own a modified pre-1949 vehicle. MSRA hosts one of Illinois' largest car shows, Gears & Ears. Attended many local and National shows. Meetings are held twice a month, members receive bi-monthly newsletters. Members are treated to annual Christmas party, breakfast, pig roast and dinner dance. Dues: $50/year. Web site: www.midweststreetrodsofil.com

Midwest Vintage Snowmobile Shows Inc
1669 Howard Ave
Maple Plain, MN 55359
764-479-2907

Founded 1999. 26 members. Dedication to preserving vintage and antique era snowmobiles by offering events to participate and promote the hobby. Promoting vintage and antique snowmobile shows for 1950s-1970s era snowmobiles. Dues: none.

Military Transport Association of North Jersey
12 Indian Head Rd
Morristown, NJ 07960
973-285-0716

John Sobotka, President. Founded 1973. Approximately 150 members. Dedicated to restoring historic military vehicles. Members participate in more than 30 parades, trail rides, and shows every year. Monthly newsletter. Meetings second Monday of the month, 8 pm at Godfather's Pizza, Rt 10W, East Hanover, NJ 07936. New members get a free hat, t-shirt, and embroidered patch. Dues: $10/year.

Military Vehicle Preservation Assoc
PO Box 520378
Independence, MO 64052
816-737-5111; FAX: 816-737-5423
E-mail: mvpa-hq@mvpa.org

Founded 1976. 8,500 members. MVPA is a not-for-profit organization dedicated to the restoration and preservation of military transport. Host to the largest annual swap meet and military vehicle display in the United States. Dues: $30/year US, $43/year overseas. Web site: www.mvpa.org

Motor Bus Society Inc
PO Box 251
Paramus, NJ 07653-0251
201-967-0410; FAX: 201-967-0712
E-mail: mct@shore.net

Founded 1948. 1,100 members. Collect and publish the colorful and fascinating history of the bus industry. Two quarterly publications (8 per year both publications), *Motor Coach Age* and *Motor Coach Today.* Dues: $30/year US, $35/year Canada, $40/year overseas. Web site: www.motorbussociety@yahoo.com

National Historic Route 66 Federation
PO Box 423
Tujunga, CA 91043-0423
PH/FAX: 818-352-7232
E-mail: national66@national66.com

Founded 1994. Over 1,600 members around the world. Dedicated to preserving America's most famous highway. Members receive access to Route 66 maps, guides, books, videos, etc. Dues: $30/year. Web site: www.national66.com

Northern Illinois Street Rod Association
PO Box 565
Elgin, IL 60121
E-mail: jeff@hotrodranch

Founded 1970. 27 members. Vehicles 25 years or older, modified from stock. Monthly meetings on first Monday of each month, monthly newsletter, web site, annual Fiesta Days car show and other events. Dues: $25/year. Web site: http://webgo.net/nilsra

NZMVCC Inc
c/o President Kevin Longshaw
455 Lower Duthie Rd, RD 15
Hawera New Zealand
PH/FAX: 00646-7646229

Founded 1979. 160 family members. Open to anyone interested in the collection and restoration of military vehicles. Monthly magazine. Local monthly meetings and April national meet. 11 branches throughout New Zealand. We participate in off-road events, displays, air shows, camp outs and swapping of ideas and information. Dues: NZ $40/year.

Ocala Jeep Club of FL
PO Box 5781
Ocala, FL 34478
E-mail: bethbluejeep@aol.com

Founded 1995. 100+ members. Family club, active with the community. 4x4 Jeep only (any model Jeep). Meet 2nd and 4th Saturday each month, annual show-n-shine, monthly event/trail ride, trips out of state for off-road events, monthly newsletter, how-to clinics, Christmas parades, trail maintenance. Dues: $40/year per family. Web site: www.ocalajeepclub.com

Old Town Cruisers
PO Box 1104
Van Buren, AR 72957
501-474-9207
E-mail: marfo57@aol.com

Founded 1992. 24 members. Annual car show to be held September 8 and 9, 2001. Entry fee: $20. Contact: Donna Bredrick, secretary, at the above phone number. Pre-registration until September 1st. Our show is held in historical downtown Van Buren, AR. Lots of antique shopping for the ladies. Dues: $40/year.

The Over the Hill Gang of Pennsylvania
4848 Jasper Rd
Emmaus, PA 18049
610-965-9977
E-mail: www.wwweld@enter.net

Founded 1990. 20 members. Limited membership by invitation only. Street rods only. Dues: $55/entrance fee only.

Pedal Pumpers Club of America PPCA
Box 430
Needham, MA 02494

Founded 1989. 400+ members. Club dedicated to hard to start cars and pedal pumping. Share an interest in the old time hard to start cars long before fuel injection. Dues: none.

Phantoms Motor/Model Club
2328 Goodhue St, Box 195
Red Wing, MN 55066
651-388-1800
E-mail: avollan@hager.net or rwred@redwing.net

For information see the Phantoms at hemmings.com under clubs.

Pittsburgh Vintage Grand Prix Association
PO Box 2243
Pittsburgh, PA 15230
412-734-5853; FAX: 412-221-1923
E-mail: pvgpa@trfn.clpgh.org

Founded 1983. 1,600 members. All volunteer organization holds annual vintage races and largest collector car show in western Pennsylvania every 3rd weekend in July. All proceeds benefit Autism Society of Pittsburgh and Allegheny Valley School. Web site: http://trfn.clpgh.org/pvgpa

Professional Car Society
PO Box 9636
Columbus, OH 43209-9636
614-237-2350
E-mail: b1ruff@freenet.columbus.oh.us

Founded 1976. 1,300 members. The Professional Car Society is dedicated exclusively to the preservation, maintenance and restoration of "professional" vehicles of passenger car styling, without regard to age or origin. Ownership of a professional car is not required for membership. Dues: $20/year. Web site: www.professionalcar.org

P-Town Street Rods Car Club
4180 Jensen St
Pleasanton, CA 94566
925-846-5550; FAX: 925-846-4480
E-mail: gewithers@aol.com

Founded 1997. 65 members. While we have no restrictions, our primary focus is on hot rods, street rods and custom cars. We meet on the 2nd Tuesday and 4th Thursday of each month. Please visit our web site. Dues: $15/year. Web site: www.streetrodder.net/ptown

Puget Sound British Automotive Society
17610 NE 8th Pl
Bellevue, WA 98008
425-644-7874; FAX: 425-747-0205
E-mail: ataub@worldnet.att.net

Founded 1989. 450 members. Club's purpose is the sponsorship of the Western Washington All British Field Meet. A car show and swap meet for all British marques with over 500 entrants, held annually, fourth Saturday of July in Bellevue, WA. Web site: www.abfm.com

Relics & Rods Car Club
PO Box 1516
Lake Havasu City, AZ 86405
PH/FAX: 520-855-0933

Founded 1978. 170 members. Must be 1959 or earlier car or truck. We are the hosts of Run to the Sun car show, approximately 1,000 cars enter. Call for fax number. Dues: $30/year. Web site: www.relicsandrods.com

Rhein-Main-Cruiser/Goodguys Member Germany
Limesst 28
63128 Dietzenbach Germany
01149-172-6224394; FAX: 01149-6074-26637
E-mail: rhein-main-cruiser@gmx.de

Founded 1978. 120 members. US hot rod, custom and classic cars. Visit of US car meetings in Europe, no rules or dues. Please check web site, doing a hot rod special at Europe's biggest drag race events (Nitro Olympics). Dues: none. Web site: www.rmc-goodguys.de

Riverside Park Machines (RPM)
1729 N 8th St
Independence, KS 67301
316-331-0233

Founded 1981. 15 members. Annual Riverside Fun Run Car Show first Sunday in June every year. Local area cruises. Meet twice a month. Dues: $20/year.

Rod Warriors
PO Box 42
Canal Winchester, OH 43130
614-837-4235; FAX: 614-837-7016
E-mail: rodwarriors@ohiocarclubs.com

Founded 1996. 6 members. You must love to cruise your pride and joy. We are a bunch of friendly car enthusiasts that promote the collector car hobby, help charities and support our community organizations. Car clubs, car shows, cruise-ins, swap meets in Ohio and the USA. Check the show pages to plan a weekend or your entire cruisin' season. Brought to you free by the Rod Warriors. Dues: $35/year. Web site: www.ohiocarclubs.com

Rodmasters Car Club
PO Box 191
Mount Hope, ON Canada L0R 1W0
905-692-5353
E-mail: classic@rodmasters.com

Founded 1971. 25 members. 1948 and older or classics. Fully equipped garage with year round usage of bays to build up to 20 cars. We hold an indoor/outdoor swap meet on the last Sundays of March and October. Dues: $540/year. Web site: www.rodmasters.com

Rogue Valley Street Rods
PO Box 3185
Central Point, OR 97502
541-857-9394; FAX: 541-773-6257
E-mail: clstalions@aol.com

Founded 1970. 65 members. Must have 1954 or older car to join. Members receive monthly newsletter. Members put on annual West Coast Charity Benefit Rod & Custom Show (Eagle One Award of Merit Club). Dues: $20/year. Web site: www.roguevalleystreetrods.com

Saddleback Rods-Southern California
PO Box 4284
Mission Viejo, CA 92690

Founded 1984. 38 members. Pre-1949 street rods only.

Sandhills Classic Street Rod Assocation
1312 Doubs Chapel Rd
West End, NC 27376
910-947-2875
E-mail: fordlafe@utinet.net

Founded 3 years ago. 19 members. 1972-back American made cars or trucks. Meetings first Monday of every month. One car show a year for charity. Non-profit organization. Monthly cruises to different places. Dues: $10/month.

Skyline Street Rod Assoc Inc
PO Box 481
Edinburg, VA 22824
540-984-9312

Founded 1975. 26 members. Annual rod run, 3rd Sunday in June; cruise-in every third Saturday April thru October at Rite Aid in Woodstock, VA. Dues: $20/year.

Society of Automotive Historians Inc
1102 Long Cove Rd
Gales Ferry, CT 06335-1812
860-464-6466; FAX: 860-464-2614
E-mail: foster@netbox.com

Founded 1969. 1,000 members. Welcomes all persons interested in automotive history worldwide. Bi-monthly newsletter, periodic magazine, biennial history conference, annual meeting at Hershey in October, winter meeting in Paris in February. Dues: $25/year. Web site: www.autohistory.org

Solid Rock Cruisers Christian Car Club
5302 Bridget Ave SE
Auburn, WA 98092
253-939-0980
E-mail: sldrckpres@aol.com

Founded 1996. 50+ members. Like classic cars (need not own one to join), discounts at local businesses, monthly newsletter, meets 3rd Friday or each month, yearly car show put on by club, various club activities each month. Dues: $25/year. Web site: www.solidrockcruisers.com

South Jersey Street Rod Association
PO Box 63
Williamstown, NJ 08094
609-629-9754

Founded 1974. 30 members. Must own pre-1948 modified vehicle, attend 3 meetings and help and participate in our annual street rod event every September. Dues: $24/year.

Southern Mopar Association
c/o Larry Jordan
5781 Aljon Dr
Theodore, AL 36582
334-653-5154

Founded 1988. 30 members. Established for the preservation and restoration of Chrysler products. You do not have to own a car or truck to join, Meets monthly and has an annual Mopar show in Mobile, AL. Proceeds of show are given to charity. Dues: $15/year.

Sportscar Vintage Racing Association
1 Maple St
Hanover, NH 03755
603-640-6161; FAX: 603-640-6130
E-mail: pbench@valley.net

Founded 1976. 1,900 members. SVRA is one of the largest organizations presenting vintage race events for historically significant race cars in North America. SVRA organized its first event in 1976, and has grown into an international organization with 1,900 members in 43 states, Canada and several foreign countries. SVRA offers regular spouse and competition memberships which include entry into spectacular events. Dues: $75/year and $100/year.

St Joe Valley Street Rods
PO Box 137
Mishawaka, IN 46544

Founded 1971. 25 members. Dues: $60/year.

Steam Automobile Club of America Inc
1227 W Voorhees St
Danville, IL 61832
217-442-0268; FAX: 217-442-3299
E-mail: jreynol@aol.com

Founded 1958. 850 members. Open to all steam automobile enthusiasts. A non-profit organization dedicated to the preservation of steam auto history and to the development of modern steam automobiles. Quarterly publication, *Steam Automobile Bulletin*. Dues: $15/year US funds. Web site: http://members.aol.com/jreynol/sacaarc.htm

Street Machines of Rochester
409 Bennington Dr
Rochester, NY 14616
716-663-0393
E-mail: streetmachines64@aol.com

Founded 1974. 127 members. No restrictions for our club. Discount on parts and accessories. Not-for-profit organization, meets monthly and sponsors 1 or more monthly events, usually free or at reduced rates and a monthly newsletter is mailed out. Dues: $42/year. Web site: www.streetmachinesofrochester.com

Street Machines of Table Rock Lake
HC 3 Box 4250
Reed's Spring, MO 65737
417-338-5233; FAX: 417-338-2179
E-mail: billbob42@aol.com

Founded 1996. 60 members. Car show April 27, 2002, Kim Berling City, MO. Dues: $25/year. Web site: www.geocities.com/tr_street_machines/

Street Magic of Portland Car Club
15777 SE Ruby Dr
Milwaukie, OR 97267
503-250-0498; FAX: 503-654-8868

Founded 1978. 25 members. American made production cars, trucks, 1949 and newer. Car shows, beach trips, movie nights, monthly newsletter. Dues: $15/year.

Sweet Dreamz Auto Club
342-89 Quaker Church Rd
Randolph, NJ 07869
973-366-3357
E-mail: sweetdreamzac@aol.com

Founded 1998. 11 members. Must have three noticeable modifications, dedication and positive attitude. We attend most local and National shows. We are looking for imports, custom domestics and low riders. Dues: $180/year. Web site: www.sweetdreamzautoclub.com

Tarrant County Street Rod Association
5801 Graham
Fort Worth, TX 76114
817-626-2708

Founded 1971. 25 members. You must own a 1948 or earlier model vehicle with some modifications. We meet the first Sunday of each month at members' homes. Dues: $5/monthly.

Texas Joy Ride
2622 Micliff
Houston, TX 77068
281-444-8680; FAX: 281-444-0687

Founded 1988. Joy Williams, founder. Rod run.

Tobacco Road Street Rodders Inc
c/o 194 Geary Rd
Valley Falls, NY 12185
518-753-6074 after 6 pm
E-mail: sandyasprion@att.net

Founded 1982. 18 members. Must have a pre-1958 car or truck. Have meetings once a month during winter months and every other week during good weather. Have get-togethers, cruises, put on a rod run every August (1st weekend). Dues: $5/month.

Toy Car Collectors Club
33290 W 14 Mile, #454
West Bloomfield, MI 48322
248-682-0272; FAX: 248-682-5782
E-mail: fossoh1@aol.com

Founded 1993. 164 members. A club for collectors of all miniature vehicles, all manufactures, materials, scales, types, eras, etc. Services: monthly meetings (Detroit area), annual convention. Dues: $15/year. Web site: www.unicycling.com/toycar

Tri-Chevy Association
24862 Ridge Rd
Elwood, IL 60421
815-478-3633

Founded 1972. 160 members. Open to all 1955-57 Chevy owners and enthusiasts. Annual swap meet and car show (largest 1-day show & swap in the midwest) held on second Sunday in June. Dues: $15/year. Web site: www.tca567.homestead.com

Tri County Cruisers Inc
PO Box 3671
Wayne, NJ 07470
973-628-0026; FAX: 973-628-7576

Tucson Miniature Auto Club
Lou Pariseau, President
1111 E Limberlost Dr 164
Tucson, AZ 85719-1062
PH/FAX: 520-293-3178

Founded 1976. 92 members. Toy wheeled vehicles. Meetings once a month. Toy show once a year. Dues: $10/year.

The Tuna Club Inc
c/o CAR Products Inc
120 Bosworth St
West Springfield, MA 01089
413-733-0599

Founded 1985. 10 members. Must be a car enthusiast and willing to donate time to the annual Tuned by Tuna car show and swap meet, held 3rd Sunday of every August, benefiting the Shriners Hospital for Children. Over 500 show cars and 20,000 people attend. It is held at Smith and Wesson, 2100 Roosevelt Ave, Springfield, Massachusetts. Dues: none.

Ultra Van Motor Coach Club
73 Sargent St
Haines City, FL 33844
863-422-4535
E-mail: corvair@fan.net

Founded 1996. 150 members. Promotion and restoration of
Corvair powered Ultra vans. Open to anyone with an interest.
Regional rallies and annual National convention. 6 newsletters a
year, *Ultrasounder*. Due: $15/year.

United Detroit Car Modelers
13856 Roxanne Rd
Sterling Heights, MI 48312-5673
810-268-3479
E-mail: paully@home.com

Founded 1991. 17 members. Membership open to all. For
builders and collectors. Semi-monthly publication, *Model Car
Breeze*. Monthly club meetings at Great Lakes Hobby Shop,
Shelby Township, second Thursday of month, 7 pm to 9 pm,
that include model building how-to. Club located in NE Detroit
suburb. New members wanted. Dues: voluntary pay.

Valley Cruisers Car Club
PO Box 1184
Gardnerville, NV 89410
702-265-7119; PH/FAX: 702-265-2256
E-mail: rls@aol.com

Founded 1989. 147 members. No restrictions other than a love
of cars/vehicles 1969 and older. Family oriented non-profit
group going on cruises, tours and outings throughout the year.
We host our Main Street Event Show and Shine yearly as a
money maker and donate the profits back to the community. The
2001 Main Street Event was August 17-19. Dues: $15/year.

Villa Capri Cruisers
RR 7, Box 7355
Moscow, PA 18444
717-842-2736
E-mail: caprimail@aol.com

Founded 1994. 127 members. No restrictions to join, benefits
include friendship. We meet every Monday. We have 2 main
shows. Cruise once a month and over $33,000 to charities in 5
years. Web site:
www.geocities.com/Motorcity/pit/8003/index/html

West Coast Kustoms
PO Box 8028
Moreno Valley, CA 92552
909-488-0413, 909-488-9383

Founded 1982. 1,800+ members. Open to those who remember
how it was in the 1950s to early 1960s when Kustoms, rods and
classics cruised to the local drive-ins and diners as well as to
Kustoms, classics and rod owners and admirers. Dues:
$20/year.

Winchester Speedway Old Timers' Club Inc
PO Box 291
Urbana, OH 43078
937-652-2145; FAX: 937-652-2147

Founded 1972. 500 members. Held annual Winchester
Speedway Old Timers' convention/exhibition at Winchester
Speedway, Winchester, IN, May 5-6, 2001. Vintage race car own-
ers, drivers, mechanics and fans are encouraged to join.
Membership includes newsletter 4 times/year. Dues: $10/year
includes spouse.

Wisconsin Convertible Classic
PO Box 44781
Madison, WI 53744
608-271-1335 tour line
608-231-3884 administration
FAX: 608-236-9999
E-mail: openair@aol.com

Founded 1993. 150 members. Open to any driving enthusiast.
Annual tour is 3rd full weekend in August, four day tour open to
any convertible of any make or vintage. Tour limited to first 200
registrations received. We host the Wisconsin Sports Car Classic
tour each June. Dues: $25/year. Web site: www.wiautotours.com

Women's Committee of the Crawford Auto-Aviation Museum
10825 E Blvd
Cleveland, OH 44106
216-721-5722; FAX: 216-721-0645

Founded 1964. 35 members. The Women's Committee of the
Crawford Auto-Aviation Museum (CAAM) endeavors to promote
the Museum, assists the Museum's educational programs and,
through fundraising, augment its collection. Activities include
the Millionaire's Run, Concours d'Ordinaire, holiday staff lun-
cheon and seasonal decorating. The Women's Committee purchased the CAAM's 1948 Chrysler Town and funded restoration
of the Museum's 1932 Peerless V16 prototype. Women's
Committee membership is open to all members of the Western
Reserve Historical Society. Dues: $55/year.

State Clubs

Arizona Bus Club	Arizona
3121 E Yucca	
Phoenix, AZ 85028-2616	
PH/FAX: 602-867-7672	
E-mail: vwstuff@uswest.net	

200+ members. Monthly meetings, car shows, swap meets.
Largest VW club in Arizona. All VWs and family welcome. Web
site: www.mindspring.com/~deasterw/jess/jess.html

Good Times Rods & Customs	Arizona
PO Box 86413	
Tucson, AZ 85754	
520-743-7899, 520-883-9173	

Founded 1975. 25 members. Must own a rod or custom.
Modified autos, 1964 and earlier. Family oriented. Meet 4th
Friday each month at Archer Community Center, La Cholla Blvd.
Dues: $25/year.

Prescott Antique Auto Club	Arizona
PO Box 2654	
Prescott, AZ 86302	
520-778-5386	
E-mail: ware@cableone.net	

Founded 1970. 250 members. Oldest and largest car club in
northern Arizona. Monthly newsletter, annual swap meet and
car show the first weekend in August. Dues: $20/year.

North Central Arkansas Cruisers	Arkansas
200 Stacy Springs Rd	
Heber Springs, AR 72543	
501-362-7408; FAX: 501-362-1781	
E-mail: jde@arkansas.net	

Founded 1995. 21 members. Christian car club, no drinking or
bad language. We love to drive our vehicles everywhere, meetings
1st Friday of each month. Monthly newsletter. Fun, fun, fun.
Dues: $25/year. Web site: http://clubs.hemmings.com/ncac/

Northwest Arkansas Corvette Club | **Arkansas**
PO Box 124
Fayetteville, AR 72702
501-271-0210
E-mail: jmbell@specent.com

Founded 1996. 100 members. Open to all Corvette owners.
Dues: $30/year. Web site: www2.arkansas.net/~jyount/

Cal-Rods Car Club | **California**
745 N Frijo Ave
West Covina, CA 91790
626-962-1112
E-mail: calrods@hotmail.com

Founded 1954. Two current member referral. Bi-monthly
newsletter, web site w/members' names, events, newsletter, photos, sponsors, annual picnic and car show. Dues: $20/year. Web
site: www.calrods.com

Early Iron of Ukiah Inc | **California**
PO Box 107
Ukiah, CA 95482
707-463-2483; FAX: 707-263-3223
E-mail: moorehotwheels@pacific.net

146 members. Pre-1959, monthly newsletter, monthly outings,
annual Fabulous Flashback Car Show and Poker Run held in
late September. Dues: $24/year.
Web site: http://clubs.hemmings.com/ukiahearlyiron/

The Mid Peninsula Old Time Auto Club Inc | **California**
751 Laurel St #350
San Carlos, CA 94070
650-344-8216
E-mail: ba.dfg@rlg.org

Founded 1960. 400 members. The club is a general classic,
antique, or vintage auto club for people interested in the preservation and enjoyment of these older vehicles. We hold monthly
meetings on the 4th Friday of every month (except December) at
8 pm in the SAM-TRANS building, 2nd floor auditorium, San
Carlos Ave & Laurel St, San Carlos, CA. Dues: $30/year.

Litchfield Hills Historical Automobile Club | **Connecticut**
16 Calhoun St
Torrington, CT 06790
860-482-4500

Contact: Glenn Royals at the above address or telephone.
Founded 1956. 55 members. Annual auto show and swap meet
is held at the Goshen fairgrounds, Rt 63 North, Goshen, CT, 3rd
Sunday in August, rain or shine. Dues: $10/year.

All British Car Club of Vol Co FL | **Florida**
1122 E Wisconsin Ave
Orange City, FL 32763
904-917-0235
E-mail: rstorke@cfl.rr.com

Founded 1993. 122 members. Our club is open to all British
cars and to those who have an interest in the restoration and
preservation of the British car and the enjoyment of the car. Our
club is a chapter of NAMGAR (North American MGA Registry).
Monthly publication, *British Connection*, which gives a list of
activities, wanteds and classifieds, general club information and
tech tips. Dues: $10/year (single), $16/year (married). Web site:
http://geocities.com/motorcity/downs4777

Avanti Club of Florida | **Florida**
John Ebstein, Chapter AOAI
319 Toledo St
Sebastian, FL 32958
561-388-5379
E-mail: rdoty32958@aol.com

Founded 1994. 120 members. Must be a member of National

organization, Avanti Owners Association International (AOAI).
Hobby for owners of Avanti automobiles for 1963 and 1964,
Studebaker Avantis through 1990, Avanti IIs or for people interested in their history. Publish *Florida Avanti News* 6 times a
year, included with membership. Newsletter lists local and
national events, items for sale, history of owners' cars. Dues:
$12/year.

Central Florida Ford Club | **Florida**
619 Durango Loop St
Davenport, FL 33837
941-424-4224

Founded 1997. 10 members. Open to all Ford cars and trucks,
any year. Dues: none.

Florida Keys Corvette Club | **Florida**
PO Box 420807
Summerland Key, FL 33042-0807
305-872-9641; FAX: 305-872-4093
E-mail: racinvet@aol.com

Founded 1992. 30 members. Meets 2nd Tuesday of every month
in alternating locations, also southernmost Corvette club in continental US, specialties, cruising the Islands, cruise-ins and
annual Corvettes in Paradise show in November. Publication,
Keyvette Redliner, available thru membership, published bi-
monthly, includes car care information, calendar of events,
social happenings within the club, person profiles, web sites.
Member: National Council Corvette Clubs (NCCC). Dues:
$25/year. Web site: www.members.aol.com/racinvet/fkcc.html

Rods 'N Classics | **Florida**
610 Manatee Dr SW
Ruskin, FL 33570
813-645-9101

Founded 1997. 11 members. No restrictions. All classics, customs and rods welcome. Informal get-togethers for information
and magazine swapping, no newsletter, one cumulative bulletin
of accumulated tech, custom, engine information to new members. Dues: $6/year.

Suncoast British Car Club | **Florida**
1355 W Way Dr
Sarasota, FL 34236-1122
941-388-1600
E-mail: judyalex1@aol.com

Founded 1990. 80+ members. No restrictions to join, just an
interest in British cars. Annual rally, monthly meeting 2nd
Wednesday of the month. Dues $30/year. Web site:
http://clubs.hemmings.com/suncoastbritish/

Good Neighbors Auto Club | **Georgia**
2221 Blue Ridge Hwy
Blairsville, GA 30512
706-745-2596
E-mail: aberharp@grove.net

Founded 1983. 103 members. Fun run, 1st Saturday in May;
car show, 3rd Saturday in October; cruise night, 3rd Saturday,
May-September. Dues: $12/year, $15/year couple.

Peach State Nova Club | **Georgia**
PO Box 1393
Lilburn, GA 30048-1393
770-921-5422

Founded 1988. 75 members. Monthly meeting 2nd Sunday of
each month. Also monthly newsletter. Dues: $15/year individ-
ual, $18/year husband and spouse.

Classic Cruisers	Idaho
PO Box 232	
Filer, ID 83328	
208-326-4561; FAX: 208-543-8162	

Founded 1992. 536 members. No restrictions to join. Three club shows a year, open to everyone. We promote restoration to young enthusiasts through a mentor program. Dues: none.

Idaho Vintage Motorcycle Club	Idaho
10346 Foxbrush Ct	
Boise, ID 83709-7407	
208-362-0319	
E-mail: norton99@micron.net	

Founded 1977. 110 members. Open to all interested. Newsletter 5-6 times per year. Want ads are free to members. Largest vintage bike show in the Northwest in late March. Dues: $10/year.

Blood Sweat & Gears Illinois Valley Car Club	Illinois
PO Box 1421	
LaSalle, IL 61301	
815-224-2064; FAX: 815-223-3501	

Founded 1995. 60 members. Monthly meetings 2nd Tuesday of month, monthly newsletters, many club social events, cruises, shows, non-profit with money going to charity and scholarships. Dues: $25/year. Web site: www.bloodsweatandgears.com

Centerville Antique Auto Touring Society	Illinois
PO Box 33	
Woodstock, IL 60098-0033	
815-338-2204	

Founded 1981. 60 members. Must have an interest in old vehicles to join. Monthly newsletter, picnics, tours and overnighters. Dues: $20/year.

Collector Car Club of Greater Belleville Area	Illinois
30 Troy-O'Fallon Rd	
Troy, IL 62294	
618-667-3958	

Founded 1980. 105 members. No restrictions. Entertainment at all monthly meetings. Monthly publication, *The Spotlight*. 6 shows and numerous annual events. Dues: $12/year.

Dekalb-Sycamore Vintage Auto Club	Illinois
15623 Derbyline Rd	
Genoa, IL 60135	
815-784-5623	

Founded 1973. 58 members. No restrictions to join. Club newsletter once a month; meet first Sunday of the month; annual car show in August. Dues: $10/year.

North Shore Rods, Southside	Illinois
318 Charlestown Dr	
Bolingbrook, IL 60440	
630-739-3324; FAX: 708-788-7038	
E-mail: dave46@freewwweb.com	

Founded 1975. 36 members. No restrictions. Must enjoy working with others, involvement with our charity car show and other events, we work to earn money for our selected charities. Meet 1st Saturday of every month.

Rustic Auto Club of Pontiac Inc	Illinois
PO Box 482	
Pontiac, IL 61764	
815-844-5783 days	
FAX: 815-844-6179 days	

Founded 1968. 33 members. Anyone with interest in old vehicles

can join. The club has sponsored the Hang Loose 50s and 60s weekend for 13 years. The event is the biggest in the area and includes a car show, craft booths, food and a cruise-in. The club has restored a 20s gas station and has built an old fashioned root beer stand. Both are used throughout the summer for numerous activities. Dues: $10/year new, $5/year renew.

4 Wheels to Freedom	Indiana
PO Box 342	
Shelbyville, IN 46176	
317-729-5752; FAX: 317-729-5930	
E-mail: info@4wtf.org	

Founded 1976. 50+ families. Ownership of a four-wheel drive vehicle is required. Organized as a non-profit organization for the purpose of providing social, educational and recreational activities, events including trail rides, swap meets and parades. Monthly publication, *Winchline*, and meet on the first Sunday of the month at 6 pm in Shelbyville, IN. Dues: $30/year. Web site: www.4wtf.org

Central Indiana Vintage Vehicles	Indiana
PO Box 635	
Noblesville, IN 46060	
317-773-5480; FAX: 317-773-0551	
E-mail: slpyhollow@aol.com	

Founded 1988. 73 members. No restrictions to join. Monthly newsletter, activities, yearly car show. Dues: $15/year.

Cruisin Classics Inc	Indiana
401 E Grimes	
Bloomington, IN 47401	
812-824-7924	

Founded 1993. 100 members. No alcoholic beverages. Newsletter, 2 car shows per year. Dues: $20/year.

Hoosier Volks Club	Indiana
8694 Bell St	
Crown Point, IN 46307	
219-365-6973; FAX: 219-365-4925	
E-mail: pspi@jorsm.com	

Founded 1996. 80+ members. All Volkswagens welcome, air and watercooled. Dues include membership to the Volkswagen Club of America. Monthly meetings and events. The Hoosier Volks newsletter is called *Fahrverg"news"en*. The Volkswagen Club of America newsletter is called *The Autoist*. Car shows, fix-it days, car cruises, fund raisers for charities. Dues: $31/year. Web site: http://clubs.hemmings.com/hoosiervolks/

Michiana Antique Auto Club Inc	Indiana
910 State St	
La Porte, IN 46350	
PH/FAX: 219-362-6316	

Founded 1967. 75 members. No restrictions other than the desire to preserve and enjoy antique and special interest automobiles. Annual swap meet and car show on the Sunday of Memorial weekend, 200 plus cars shown and attendance of 2,000 plus. We publish a newsletter monthly and have outings every month to drive our cars. Dues: $20/year.

Northern Indiana Cruisers-R-Rides	Indiana
357 W Division Rd	
Valparaiso, IN 46383	
219-462-5818; FAX: 219-962-4502	
E-mail: ebjca@netnitco.net	

Founded 2000. 40 members. Open to all cars, trucks and bikes. Non-profit organization for enjoyment of car restoration and preservation. Our meetings are held the second Saturday of each month, open to all. Dues: $25/year. Web site: www.geocities.com/rridesnic/

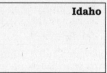
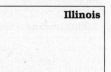

Pioneer Automobile Association   **Indiana**
PO Box 1971
South Bend, IN 46634
219-266-4257
E-mail: laurie.a.wenger.1@nd.edu

Founded 1952. 60 members. Family oriented all makes car club. Monthly car tours and fall color tour. Sponsor a large swap meet/car show on the last Sunday in April of every year at the St Joseph county fairgrounds. Dues: $15/year.

Hawkeye Area Classic Chevy Club   **Iowa**
PO Box 8755
Cedar Rapids, IA 52408
319-622-3293
E-mail: dnsjanda@webtv.net

Founded 1977. 21 members. Monthly newsletter, annual car show, spring and fall cruises, tech sessions, specializing in preservation, restoration and enjoyment of 1955, 1956 and 1957 Chevrolets, Corvettes and trucks. Need not own one to join. Dues: $10/year.

Mid-Iowa Shows Inc   **Iowa**
c/o Warren Harper
211 S G St
Indianola, IA 50125
515-961-8926

Founded 1997. 11 members. Non-profit organization that has the best of all makes, having car and truck show in central Iowa annually. 1998 was 10th annual. Also support other local shows and cruise nights. Meetings are held February-August. Call for more information.

Ottawa Antique Car Club   **Kansas**
2451 Oregon Rd
Ottawa, KS 66067
785-242-2036

Founded 1969. 20 members. Dues: $10/year.

Southern Knights of Central Kentucky Car Club   **Kentucky**
2214 Leestown Rd
Frankfurt, KY 40601
502-695-0831
E-mail: tingle@dcr.net

Founded 1989. 40 families. Open to old and young car enthusiasts. Two car shows yearly. Meet 1st Sunday of every month. Monthly newsletter. Non-profit organization. Dues: $12/year.

Florida Parishes Vintage Car Club   **Louisiana**
PO Box 38
Ponchatoula, LA 70454
504-386-3714

Founded 1977. 47 member families. Applicants must be voted in by members. Affiliated with Mid-America Old Time Automobile Association (MOTAA). Dues: $10/year.

Antique Motor Club of Greater Baltimore Inc   **Maryland**
10909 Falls Rd
Lutherville, MD 21093-1895
410-296-3387
E-mail: big.bill@home.com

For membership information, contact at the above address: Bill Long. Founded 1968. 650 members. Offers activities which every member of the family can participate in and enjoy. No judging. Activities are open to the general public. Publication, *Olde Jalopy News*. Dues: $17/year.

Classy Chassis Car Club   **Maryland**
15720 Brice Hollow Rd SE
Cumberland, MD 21502
301-759-4767

Founded 1991. 80 members. We are a great club. We are involved in helping others and having a great time. Dues: $10/year. Web site: www.bandtfords.com

Convertible Owners Club of Greater Baltimore   **Maryland**
208 Brightside Ave
Pikesville, MD 21208-4806
410-484-1715, 410-825-2010

Founded 1985. 100 members. Convertible owners (both antique and modern) enjoying their cars by participating in parades, exhibits, promotions, movies, etc. Dues: $12 application fee, $6/year thereafter.

Mid-Maryland Ford Club Inc   **Maryland**
PO Box 3171
Frederick, MD 21705-3171
301-663-6903; FAX: 301-694-7624
E-mail: mmfc@xecu.net

Founded 1993. 169 members (Maryland, Pennsylvania, Virginia, West Virginia, DC). National award-winning newsletter, *The Ford Express*, 12 issues, contains full page of calendar of event listings of local and regional shows and 26 Ford flyers, etc. The club unites Ford enthusiasts from the five-state area of Ford, Mercury and Lincoln cars and trucks, from antique to modified or any Ford powered vehicles. Dues: $15/year double, $10/year single. Web site: www.xecu.net/mmfc

Street Cars of Desire Car Club   **Maryland**
David C Cohen, President
PO Box 831
Cockeysville, MD 21030
410-628-6262
E-mail: info@streetcarsofdesire.com

Founded 1990. 166 families. Open membership, American made cars. Fun car club that has donated over $350,000 to charity since 1990. Monthly meetings and newsletter. Holds largest indoor car show for charity in December of each year at Timonium fairgrounds. Dues: $20/year. Web site: www.streetcarsofdesire.com

Bay State Antique Auto Club   **Massachusetts**
PO Box 486
Dedham, MA 02027-0486
781-326-2008

Founded 1968. 200 members. Open to all. Friendly monthly meetings at Endicott Estate, East St, Dedham, second Thursday. Annual antique car show, Sunday after July 4th, Endicott Estate. Over 1,000 cars. Additional mid-October show for pre-1940. Tours, parades, socials. Newsletter. Dues: $15/year.

Maynard Area Auto Club   **Massachusetts**
PO Box 633
Maynard, MA 01754
978-897-3445; FAX: 978-897-3175
E-mail: jmalcolm@juno.com

Founded 1988. 200 members (closed). No restrictions, 1 show each year, monthly newsletter. Dues: $20/year. Web site: http://clubs.hemmings.com/maynardaac/

Plymouth County Auto Club   **Massachusetts**
PO Box 88
Carver, MA 02330
Chuck: 508-866-2709
E-mail: chevy55@adelphia.net

Founded 1980. 46 members. Monthly meetings. All makes and models. Monthly meetings, cruises, bowling nights, annual picnic and Christmas party. Dues: $20/year.

Section Three – Clubs & Organizations

Section Three – Clubs & Organizations

Silver Lake Auto Club
PO Box 1437
Pembroke, MA 02359

Massachusetts

Founded 1978. 50 members. All monies made at shows, dances, cruise nights goes to charities. Dues: $60/year.

Spindles Auto Club
c/o 17 Sycamore Rd
Squantum, MA 02171-1336
617-472-3572
E-mail: deskjet894@worldnet.att.net

Massachusetts

Founded 1957. 50 members. Currently have a building with 25 cars inside. Yearly car show (over 500 vehicles) with a portion of the proceeds to benefit local charities on the Sunday of Labor Day weekend, Marshfield fairgrounds, Marshfield, MA. Dues: (start at) $25/year. Web site: http://members.tripod.com/spindlescarclub

Wachusett Old Car Club
PO Box 414
Holden, MA 01520
508-829-3168

Massachusetts

Founded 1952. 70 members. You should have an interest in old cars, their history and preservation. Meet monthly and sponsor one of the best classic car shows in New England on the first Sunday of August each year. Dues: $15/year.

Capitol City Old Car Club
PO Box 16075
Lansing, MI 48910
517-663-1785 after 5 pm

Michigan

Founded 1962. 200 members. No restrictions. Monthly newsletter, annual spectacular Memorial Day weekend car show, swap meet. Monthly meetings (3rd Thursday), great club house, Father's Day nursing home tour, overnighter, mystery run, awards banquet, cruise-ins, much fun for all. Dues: $14.50/year single, $16.50/year family. Web site: http://clubs.hemmings.com/ccocc/

Michigan Great Lakes Antique Car Club
25555 Cherry Hill Rd
Dearborn Heights, MI 48125-1017
313-274-0272

Michigan

Founded 1993. 110 families. No restrictions, only an interest in automotive preservation is required. All marques. Slogan: automotive reminiscense in a modern world. Once a month meetings and outings, flea market to benefit children's hospital. Incorporated and insured to protect members. Dues: $12/year.

Michigan Monte Carlo Cruizers
1102 W 13 Mile Rd
Royal Oak, MI 48073-2413
248-435-0265
E-mail: rtcouture@yahoo.com

Michigan

Founded 2000. 20 members. We are owners of the Chevrolet Monte Carlo residing in Michigan. Our annual event is the Monte Carlo Cruiz on Woodward in August. Dues: none. Visit our web page for details at: http://communities.msn.com/michiganmontecarlocruizers

Central Lakes Cruzers
Box 212
Osakis, MN 56360
320-859-2887

Minnesota

Founded 1991. 45 members. Open to all classes of cars. Meeting every 2nd Thursday at Lake Osakis Pub & Grill, monthly newsletter. Event: Roddin Round the Lake Car Show every 2nd weekend in July. Dues: $10/year.

Gopher State Timing Association
1533 89th Ave N
Brooklyn Park, MN 55444-1222
763-425-5124

Minnesota

Founded 1954. 150 members. GSTA is an association of member clubs, sponsor of the annual rod and custom spectacular car show and a 1964 nostalgia dragster. Monthly newsletter is *The Timer*. Dues: $25/year. Web site: www.gstarod-custom.com

Granite City Street Machines
Gary Hartgers
210 S 3rd St #111
St Cloud, MN 56301
320-255-5352

Minnesota

Founded 1996. 20 members. Group of people interested in cars. Car show each May. Members MSMA, Minnesota Street Machine Assoc. Newsletter, *White Line Flyer*. State club has approximately 200+ members.

Jaguar Club of Minnesota
5610 Woodcrest Dr
Minneapolis, MN 55424
612-927-8126

Minnesota

Founded 1977. 100+ members. Open to owners or enthusiasts of Jaguar cars. Dues: $35/year.

Minnesota Street Machine Association
PO Box 491032
Blaine, MN 55449
E-mail: gamer@prodigy.net

Minnesota

Founded in 1976. 200 members. Newsletter: *White Line Flyer*. Monthly meetings 3rd Wednesday of every month. Anyone with an interest in cars and/or trucks is welcome to join. Dues: $25/year.

Phantoms of Red Wing
PO Box 195
Red Wing, MN 55066
651-388-1800; FAX: 651-267-0809

Minnesota

Founded 1998. 90 members. Quarterly newsletter, sponsor organizations receive advertising. Members receive discounts at local businesses. Dues: $25/year.

St Cloud Antique Auto Club
PO Box 704
St Cloud, MN 56302-0704
320-253-5895
E-mail: dwest8804@aol.com

Minnesota

Founded 1971. 263 members. For membership information, contact at the above address: Pantowners, attn: Secretary. Our club nickname of "Pantowners" is named after the Pan automobile made in St Cloud from 1917-1919. Family centered club. Monthly meetings and newsletter, summer tours, car show and swap meet each August, always the third Sunday. Over 500 cars and 400 swappers. Smaller shows and tours throughout the year. Welcomes all antique, pioneer or collector car enthusiasts. Dues: $10/year.

Sundowners
PO Box 93
Northfield, MN 55057

Minnesota

Founded 1992. 95 members. Must have interest in automobiles. Monthly newsletter, sponsor and organize the Defeat of Jesse James Day car show in September, over 350 cars in 1997. Dues: $20/year.

Twin Cities Roadsters   Minnesota
9811 Hamilton Rd
Eden Prairie, MN 55344
952-941-2918; FAX: 952-941-8315
E-mail: v8ford@juno.com

Founded 1969. 25 members. Must have pre-1949 roadster or
other open car, be invited, sponsored and voted upon. Dues:
none.

Willmar Car Club   Minnesota
PO Box 428
Willmar, MN 56201

Founded 1979. 65 members. No restrictions, monthly newsletters, annual banquet, monthly meetings, sponsor monthly car
buffs' breakfasts at area restaurants, annual car show and swap
meet. Publication: *The Polishing Rag*, included in membership,
published monthly. Includes calendar of events, classified ads,
features on club members or vehicles, theme features and general information for club members. Dues: $10/year single;
$15/year family. Web site: www.willmarcarclub.com

Wright County Car Club   Minnesota
PO Box 662
Buffalo, MN 55313
612-682-3772

Founded 1986. 112 families. No restrictions. Annual picnic and
banquet with membership, car show in June each year. Old Car
Run lunch stop, several cruises each summer, breakfast first
Saturday and meeting third Tuesday of each month. Dues:
$15/year.

Treasure State Classics   Montana
817 Edith
Missoula, MT 59801
406-549-5798

Founded 1974. Must be a supporter of 1955-1956-1957
Chevrolet cars or trucks. More fun if you own one as we use
them. Chapter of Bow Tie Chevys and Classic Chevy
International. Meetings in spring, summer and fall. Members live
all across Montana. Dues: $15/year.

Platte'rs Car Club   Nebraska
347 Highland Dr
Gretna, NE 68028
402-332-4423
E-mail: stadiumcon@aol.com

Founded 1991. Members: 20 couples. Members need interest in
classic and antique vehicles, couple oriented, monthly meetings.
Spring and Fall Poker Runs, fundraisers, sponsor July car show,
average 200+/- vehicles. Non-profit, proceeds to a variety of
charities. Member of Eastern NE-Western IA Car Council. Open
to all makes and models. Dues: $25/year per couple.

Amoskeag Reserve Engine Co   New Hampshire
PO Box 307
Lebanon, NH 03766
603-632-4998

Founded 1984. 110 members. Chapter of the Society for the
Preservation and Appreciation of Antique Motorized Fire
Apparatus in America. Bi-monthly meetings held on the second
Friday of the month at various locations around the state.
Annual meet and show. Bi-monthly newsletter. Dues: $15/year.

Mt Washington Valley Old Car Club   New Hampshire
PO Box 872
Conway, NH 03818
603-356-3451

150 members. Annual car show, cruise nights, mystery rides,
news magazine, scholarship to automotive students. Dues:
$10/year.

New Hampshire Mustang Club   New Hampshire
c/o Rick Lacourse
5 Jenkins Ave
Portsmouth, NH 03801
PH/FAX: 603-529-0844
E-mail: gtamustang@aol.com

Founded 1988. 182 members. Ownership not required. Non-
profit organization devoted to Ford Mustangs, past and present.
Monthly meets, newsletter, shows, rallies, etc. Dues: $25/year.
Web site: http://clubs.hemmings.com/nhmustangclub/

Now & Then Vehicles Club Inc of   New Hampshire
Southern Vermont
19 Mountain Rd
Hinsdale, NH 03451
802-257-3053
E-mail: cranney@sover.net

Founded 1978. 70 members. Interest in history or preservation of
autos. Family oriented club endeavoring to inform and enrich our
understanding of the history and kinds of motor vehicles from the
early flivvers through the modern performance cars. The club sponsors a car show and other events to enhance the enjoyment of members of "special interest" cars and trucks. Dues: $10/year. Web site:
http://clubs.hemmings.com/nowandthen/

Be-Bop Cruisers Inc   New Jersey
PO Box 233
Spotswood, NJ 08884
732-303-7187; FAX: 732-303-1349
E-mail: bebopcruisers@aol.com

Founded 1993. 150 members. Vehicles must be 15 years old (or
older) with the exception of special interest vehicles. These must
be voted on by charter members. Dues: $20/year. Web site:
www.bebopcruisers.com

Jersey Late Greats Inc   New Jersey
PO Box 1294
Hightstown, NJ 08520
609-448-0526

See full listing in **Section One** under **Chevrolet**

Summer Knights Cruisin' Classics   New Jersey
200 N 9th Ave
Manville, NJ 08835
908-722-0859
E-mail: KEYS1352@aol.com

Founded 1992. 10 members. All makes, models of antique, classic and muscle cars. Dues: $15/year. Web site:
http://clubs.hemmings.com/summerknightscc/

Unforgettable Autos of Mid-Jersey   New Jersey
PO Box 423
Dunellen, NJ 08812
732-752-1551
E-mail: unforgettable@att.net

Founded 1986. 60+ members. Attend 2 meetings and join.
Receive technical assistance, receive monthly newsletter. We run
2 shows and a banquet each year. Dues: $25/year. Web site:
http://clubs.hemmings.com/unforgettablemj

Section Three – Clubs & Organizations

The Automobilists of the Upper Hudson | New York
125 Woodlawn Ave
Albany, NY 12208
518-435-0334
E-mail: silver_fox@msn.com

Founded 1950. 295 members. Newsletter once a month. Winter meetings January thru April at the Desmond, Albany, NY. Summer meets and events begin May. Touring to places of interest, picnics, parades, showing cars, annual car show, Nov election of officers and awards banquet. Dues: $20/year. Web site: http://clubs.hemmings.com/automobilistsuhv/

British Car Club of Western New York | New York
c/o Sally Genco
11560 Genesee St
Alden, NY 14004
716-937-6986; FAX: call first
E-mail: sscraps@aol.com

Founded 1990. 200+ members. Open to all who have interest in any of the British marques. A very social organization, our membership is as diverse as our cars. Meet monthly at the Rose Garden Restaurant on Wehrle Dr in Williamsville, adding many other events in season (runs, dinners, tech sessions, picnics). EuroCar Day is held on the second Sunday in June. Unique to western New York, draws 150 fabulous European cars from as far away as Toronto, the Finger Lakes, Ohio and Pennsylvania. Dues: $15/year single, $20/year family. Web site: http://clubs.hemmings.com/bccwny/

Long Island Corvette Owners Assoc | New York
PO Box 191
East Meadow, NY 11554
631-874-4229
E-mail: licoa@aol.com

Founded 1959. 250 members. Must own, lease or have access to Corvette. Monthly publication of club news, our own *Corvette Courier*. Car shows, caravans, rallies, socials, weekend trips, displays, etc. Dues: $45/year. Web site: www.licoa.net

Long Island Motor Touring Club Inc | New York
415 Outlook Ave
West Babylon, NY 11704-4309
PH/FAX: 631-422-1353
E-mail: saldorie@cs.com

Founded 1957. 83 families are members. Pre-WW II, 1942 and older, multi-marque, annual picnic, Christmas/holiday party. Monthly 10-page newsletter, monthly meeting 2nd Thursday except December. Annual flea market and show, monthly tour or event and youth events. Club located on Long Island, New York. Dues: $20/year family or single.

Malone Auto Club | New York
PO Box 732
Malone, NY 12953
518-483-4904
E-mail: maloneautoclub@yahoo.com

Founded 1979. 185 members. All you need is a love of old cars. *The Generator* is the club's monthly newsletter publication. 22nd annual show dates are July 20-22, 2001. Auto show dates are always 3rd weekend in July. Dues: $10/year USA, $13/year Canada.

Saugerties Antique Auto Club | New York
PO Box 111
Saugerties, NY 12477
914-679-6810; FAX: 914-679-8517

Founded 1957. 60 members. Club open to individuals 16 years or older that have an interest in the preservation and restoration of antique, classic interest vehicles, accessories and their history and to further enjoyable and safe motoring on the highways. Dues: $7.50/year single, $10/year family.

Thunder Road Cruisers | New York
22 Mesier Ave S
Wappingers Falls, NY 12590
914-297-2446

Founded 1995. 100 members. 1980 & older vehicles. Meet the 2nd Monday of each month. Host our own cruise once a month during summer. Members own stock, chopped, custom and unique vehicles.

Central Carolina Vintage Car Club | North Carolina
PO Box 2162
Chapel Hill, NC 27515
919-929-9039

Founded 1970. 50 members. Must have genuine interest in restoration and preservation of antique autos. Annual car show and tours. Dues: $15/year.

Colonial Capital Rods and Classics | North Carolina
505 Crump Farm Rd
New Bern, NC 28562
252-633-5860
E-mail: jwoods@coastalnet.com

Founded 1985. 12 members. Open to all makes of cars and trucks, old or new, stock or custom. Annual car show for charity. Participate in local Christmas parades. Support Toys for Tots. Monthly dinner meetings. Dues: $50/year. Web site: www2.coastalnet.com/~i7f6m5nb\

North Carolina Studebaker Drivers Club | North Carolina
770 Pine Ridge Rd
China Grove, NC 28023
704-857-2562
E-mail: hmwalter@prodigy.net

Founded 1971. 200 active members. Member of National Studebaker Drivers Club is a local club requirement. Six newsletters per year. Tickets to Spring Autofare in Charlotte. Monthly meetings across state. Dues: $10/year. Web site: www.dailytrader.com/stude1/

Dakota Western Auto Club | North Dakota
Ken Praus
976 Elm Ave
Dickinson, ND 58601
701-225-8097

Founded 1977. 55 members. Open to anyone with an interest and love of the automobile. Car show held in June at Medora, North Dakota. Also hosts Wendy's Big Classic auto show held the 4th Sunday in July at Wal-Mart parking lot in Dickinson, ND, no fee. Dues: $10/year.

North Dakota Street Rod Association | North Dakota
PO Box 459
Bismarck, ND 58502
701-255-6382, 701-222-2069
FAX: 701-222-0736
E-mail: ndsra@btigate.com

Founded 1985. 500 members. Six newsletters per year, annual Christmas party, co-sponsor rodding events in North Dakota. Dues: $10/year.

Buckeye Ramblin' Rods | Ohio
958 E Milltown Rd
Wooster, OH 44691
330-345-6971

Founded 1979. 30 members. Must have an interest in antique cars and attend 3 meetings. Host Runt Roast 3rd weekend

August; also downtown cruises, June, July, Aug. Dues: $12/year. Web site: http://clubs.hemmings.com/buckeye/

Car Coddlers Club of Ohio Inc — Ohio
PO Box 2094
Sandusky, OH 44871-2094
419-935-0635; FAX: 419-935-0161
E-mail: swingert@hmcltd.net

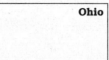

Founded 1963. 500 members. Monthly newsletter. Sponsors several car shows, 2 trophy meets. Primarily antique, collectible and classic cars. Tours, picnics. Dues: $10/year. Web site: http://clubs.hemmings.com/carcoddlers/

Clinton County Antique and Classic Car Club — Ohio
662 W Locust
Wilmington, OH 45177
513-382-3980

For membership information, contact at the above address: Willard Skidmore. Founded 1960. Annual car show in September. Dues: $5/year.

Delphos Area Car Club — Ohio
PO Box 234
Delphos, OH 45833
419-692-4821

Founded 1982. 15 members. No restrictions. Annual car show in July, monthly newsletter, helps charitable organizations. Dues: $20/year.

Mahoning Valley Old Car Club — Ohio
1498 Brantford Blvd
Youngstown, OH 44509
330-792-6807

Founded 1977. 120 members. Must have an interest in old cars. We take part in parades, car shows, nursing home shows. Our club has a monthly newsletter membership book; also an annual car show that we use the money to help the needy. Dues: $15/year (single), $20/year (couple). Web site: www.mvocc.com

Massillon Area Car Club — Ohio
7981 Windward Trace Cir NW
Massillon, OH 44646
330-837-5069

Founded 1974. 100 members. Monthly meetings, yearly car shows. Monthly newsletter, *Gas Line*. Dues: $10/year.

Mid-Ohio Ford Club — Ohio
5262 Broadview Rd
Columbus, OH 43230
614-475-3585; FAX: 614-475-3589

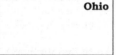

Founded 1985. 160 members. Do a lot of charity work. Take trips, rent drag strip for 1/2 day (4 times a year), monthly newsletter. All Ford show in June, all Ford swap meet first weekend of April. No restrictions at all to join. Just like old cars and trucks, do favor Ford, Lincoln and Mercury. Dues: $20/year. Web site: www.springswap.com

Tulsa Vette Set — Oklahoma
PO Box 470381
Tulsa, OK 74147
918-493-4235

Founded 1971. 300 members. We hold social gatherings, racing events, road rallies and caravan trips. Our meetings are the first Tuesday of every month at the Martin East Library at 7:30 pm. *The Vette Gazette* keeps our members informed. Dues: $70/year. Visit our web site: www.tulsavetteset.com

Historical Automobile Club of Oregon — Oregon
5724 SW Vermont St
Portland, OR 97219
503-245-5444

Founded 1947. 200+/- members. Monthly newsletter, tours, swap meet sponsors. Dues: $25/year. Web site: http://clubs.hemmings.com/haco/

Central Pennsylvania Street Machines — Pennsylvania
310 Wright St
Flemington, PA 17745-3829
717-748-7070

Founded 1991. 50 members. Ownership of a vehicle is not a requirement. Family oriented organization and exist solely for the people of this club so that they can share their interests with others in the area. Our club is run for and by the people. It serves through an elected board of directors and officers. Informative newsletter, technical advice, enjoyable monthly meetings, and an annual auto and truck show with proceeds to benefit local charity. Dues: $10/year.

Chester County Antique Car Club — Pennsylvania
445 Concord Ave
Exton, PA 19341-1801
610-363-9272

Founded 1951. 200+ members. Approval by board of directors needed to join. Monthly membership meetings. Club activities throughout the year. Monthly newsletter. Oldest non-National club in Pennsylvania. Dues: $20/year. Web site: http://clubs.hemmings.com/chestercountypa/

Historical Car Club of Pennsylvania — Pennsylvania
PO Box 688
Havertown, PA 19083
610-325-4264; FAX: 610-325-2022
E-mail: mail@spokenwheel.com

Founded 1949. 600 members. *Spokenwheel* is a publication of HCCP. Fall meet at the Delaware County Community College, October 17, 1999. Dues: $10/year. Web site: www.spokenwheel.com

Pittsburgh CARS — Pennsylvania
1008 Wren Dr
Kennedy Twp, PA 15136
412-331-7153

Founded 1991. 150 members. To have an interest in classics, antiques, rods and specialty CARS. Monthly newsletter, numerous cruises or car show, picnic, Christmas party, etc. Dues: $20/year.

The Rodfathers of Butler — Pennsylvania
4125 Loring St
Butler, PA 16001
724-482-4387 after 6 pm

Founded 1991. 31 members. The club that promotes motorsports fun of all types. We have cruises, car shows, 50s dances, swap meets, etc. We also help all local charities with their fund raising. Dues: $15/year.

The Wanderers Car Club — Pennsylvania
2620 Old Elizabeth Rd
West Mifflin, PA 15122
412-466-8626

Founded 1991. 100+ members. Must be a car lover. Newsletter, event schedules, car cruises, club picnics and parties. Anti-litter campaign, car shows, rod runs. Dues: $20 to join, $10/year. Web site: http://clubs.hemmings.com/thewandererswpa/

Section Three – Clubs & Organizations

Rhode Island Chevy Owners Association — Rhode Island

PO Box 804
Woonsocket, RI 02895
401-647-7823
E-mail: chevyprez@aol.com

Founded 1990. 78 members. Must be 18 years old. Sponsors of the All Chevy Show held the last Sunday of every June. Monthly newsletter, various year round family activities. Open to car and truck owners. Dues: $20/year.

Pulaski Area Car Enthusiasts — Tennessee

PO Box 126
Pulaski, TN 38478
931-363-5673

Founded 1982. 80 members. 18th Annual Pulaski Area Car Enthusiasts Antique Car Show, Saturday, September 22, 2001, located at Pulaski, Tennessee at Martin Methodist College Campus, 29 classes thru 1975. Call for more information and ask for Brenda Edwards, 931-363-5673 nights, 931-363-2585 days. Dues: $10/year.

West Tennessee Antique Car Club — Tennessee

595 Liberty Claybrook Rd
Beech Bluff, TN 38313-9335
901-427-6633
E-mail: wtacc@bellsouth.net

Founded 1964. 50 members. Open to any individual or family with an interest in original and restored antique cars. Monthly meetings, tours, annual car show second Saturday in May. Dues: $10/year.

Alamo City Historical Car Club — Texas

Jack Faulkenberry, President
416 Dallas St
San Antonio, TX 78215
210-224-9419

Founded 1954. 58 members. Open to all owners of any 20 year or older vehicles. Participates in tours, cruises, parades. Monthly newsletter. Fun and friendship. Dues: $15/year.

Bondo Buddies Car Club — Texas

516 Cottonwood
Coleman, TX 76834
915-625-3052

Founded 1982. 12 members. Land of the Lakes Fun Run, third weekend in June. Fiesta DaLopaloma Fair, car show, second weekend in October. Dues: none.

Caprock Classic Car Club Inc — Texas

PO Box 53352
Lubbock, TX 79453
806-744-0317; FAX: 806-744-7855
E-mail: mr58chvy@nts-online.net

Founded 1992. 160 members. Monthly newsletter, charity car show and also Rock and Roll Nostalgia car cruise and car show, both in the summer. All car enthusiasts are encouraged to join. Meet on the 2nd Thursday at Garden and Arts Center, 4215 S University Ave. Call or write for dates on above shows. Dues: $25/year. Web site: www.ccccinc.org

Texas Fords Alamo Chapter — Texas

PO Box 17543
San Antonio, TX 78217-0543
210-828-6080 recorder
FAX: 830-276-3294
E-mail: carcruisenites@hotmail.com

Founded 1996. 9 members. Own a Ford powered/Ford bodied Ford, Lincoln or Mercury vehicle. Monthly newsletter, one all Ford car show a year, members are from other Ford clubs, so at our meetings we speak Model A to current models. Dues: $15/year. Web site: http://clubs.hemmings.com/alamochaptertexasfords/

West Texas Cruisers — Texas

PO Box 9716
Midland, TX 79708-9716
915-620-0536; FAX: 915-520-7886
E-mail: fandango@nwol.net

Founded 1991. 150 members. All car nuts welcome. You don't even have to own a car to join, but you must love cars. Dues: $24/year. Web site: www.westtexascruisers.com

Associated Wheels of Utah — Utah

c/o The Arc of Utah
455 E 400 S, Ste 202
Salt Lake City, UT 84111
801-364-5060 ext 12
FAX: 801-364-6030
E-mail: marilyn-w@mindspring.com

Founded 1982. 36 members. AWU was formed solely to plan and implement the Annual Charity Car Show benefitting the Arc of Utah. 100% of the funds go to the mini-grant fund to help children and adults with mental retardation and their families with things they need. All club members totally volunteer their time and talents. Many are also members of other clubs. Dues: none. Web site: www.arcutah.org

Virginia Classic Cruisers — Virginia

9721 Raven Wing Dr
Chesterfield, VA 23832
804-739-1614
E-mail: fstreetrodlady@aol.com

For information, contact at the above phone number: Linda Foster, secretary. Founded 1995. 50 family members. To promote family involvement in the sport, become an effective influence in the classic car community by supporting a variety of charitable community needs, being directly involved in maintaining the sport of classic cars, educating other hobbyists of the legislative concerns that evolve around classic car ownership. Annual show. Dues: $20/year. Web site: www.envy.nu/vcc

Bremerton Auto Club — Washington

3230 View Crest Dr NE
Bremerton, WA 98310-9785
360-373-5358

Founded 1976. 30 members. Anyone interested in pre-1970 vehicles can join. Do not need to own a collectible vehicle. Dues: $10/year. Web site: http://clubs.hemmings.com/bremerton/index.htm

The Friendly OK Car Club — Washington

48 Wagon Trail Rd
Tonasket, WA 98855
509-826-4631, 509-826-3154
E-mail: schukar@bossig.com

Founded 1994. 120 members. Car show and swap meet 2nd weekend in May. Dues: $10/year. Web site: http://clubs.hemmings.com/friendlyok/

Northwoods Cruisers — Wisconsin

408 W Leather Ave
Tomahawk, WI 54487
715-453-1955
E-mail: 55chevy@bfm.org

Founded 1994. 45 members. Sponsors Main Street Memories, an annual car show and craft fair conducted on Sunday of Memorial Day weekend. Also have cruises, poker runs, picnics, etc. All activities revolve around vintage automobiles and trucks. All types, years and makes available. Dues: $10/year single, $15/year couple, $20/year family.

Nostalgic Car Club John Gruetzmacher, President 2137 W College Ave #620 Oak Creek, WI 53154 PH/FAX: 414-304-1080 E-mail: bigjohngross@cs.com	**Wisconsin**

Founded 1978. Members: 44 families. Nostalgic Car Club of Milwaukee and surrounding area annually hosts a 1950s style dance, car show event and publishes a newsletter monthly. We often help charity events with car displays and member participation. We welcome anyone with a 1960 or older vehicle as new members. We are a fun-loving club. Dues: $50/1st year, $20/year thereafter (includes metal club plaque). Web site: www.hemmings.com/carclubs/nostalgic

RACE Car Club c/o Lee Soda PO Box 598 Ripon, WI 54971 920-748-5800	**Wisconsin**

Founded 1989. 80 members. Monthly newsletter, meet 2nd Wednesday of each month, car and truck show 3rd weekend of May. Club is open to all makes with various activities, cruises, etc throughout the year. Dues: $15/year.

Rods-N-Relics Car Club Ltd PO Box 737 Cedarburg, WI 53012 262-376-1060; FAX: 262-376-0623	**Wisconsin**

Meetings are the first Thursday evening of each month in Cedarburg, WI. Events: annual 1950s sock hop each January, annual car show (Grafton, WI) each July, annual holiday party each December, plus road rallies, parades, cruises and custard stand outings. No restrictions. If you own a rod, a relic, a classic or even an ordinary car, truck or motorcycle, or if you crave to some day own one, you are welcome to join Rods-N-Relics Car Club Ltd. Charities: Ozaukee County (WI) schools, Ozaukee County Humane Society and Southeast Wisconsin Health Education Center. Dues: $25/year.

Southwest Wisconsin Auto Club 425 Sowden St Platteville, WI 53818 608-348-8297	**Wisconsin**

Founded 1980. 153 members. The club is for all interested in restoring, maintaining or admiring collector cars and trucks. Monthly newsletter, monthly meeting and almost monthly cruise. Annual show and swap early in September and a toy model show each February. Most noted for good cars, good hospitality and good eats. Dues: $6/year.

Dusty Wheels Auto Club Box 1813 Rosetown SK Canada S0L 2V0 306-882-4007, 306-882-3197	**Canada**

Founded 1986. 30 members. General interest car club for any car enthusiast. Holds an annual car show on the fourth weekend in September. Also holds a "Cruise Night" the 3rd Saturday of June every year. Meetings are held the second Wednesday of each month. Dues: $15/year.

Southern Alberta Antique & **Classic Auto Club** Box 1723 Lethbridge AB Canada T1J 4K4 403-327-9188	**Canada**

Founded 1964. Francis Wright, President. We are a multi-marque club interested in the preservation of the automobile as well as a club that just enjoys getting out with our cars and having fun. Numerous outings throughout the year such as a swap meet, picnics, parades, tours, etc. Ownership of antique or classic car is not required. Dues: $25/year Canadian.

Voitures Anciennes Du Quebec Inc 230 Brebeuf St #202 Beloeil, QC Canada H4R 2S6 514-990-9111; FAX: 514-446-3806 E-mail: voituresanciennes@videotron.net	**Canada**

Founded 1974. Almost 2,000 members. Association regrouping owners and amateurs of antiques and classic cars. Our mission is to preserve the authenticity and origin of an antique in its most condition. Publisher of a French 32-page monthly magazine (largest in North America). Organizer of many events and shows throughout the Province of Quebec. For car owners (20 years and up). Dues: $45/year Canada, $67/year US/Europe.

Legislative Watch Organizations

National

Automotive Restoration Market Organization (ARMO) PO Box 4910 Diamond Bar, CA 91765-0910 909-396-0289; FAX: 909-860-0184 E-mail: sema@sema.org

For information, contact at the above address: membership. ARMO, a council of the Specialty Equipment Market Association (SEMA), was created for the purpose of meeting the legislative, educational and communications needs of the automotive restoration industry. Through cooperative action, ARMO works to address those legislative and/or regulatory issues which may impact on the restoration industry and strives to ensure the viability of the industry/hobby. Any business or club serving the automotive restoration industry or the collector-car hobby is invited to join. Web site: www.sema.org

Clean Air Performance Professionals (CAPP) 84 Hoy Ave Fords, NJ 08863 732-738-7859; FAX: 732-738-7625 E-mail: stellacapp@earthlink.net

Founded 1991. Over 1,200 subscribers. CAPP is an award-winning international coalition interested in personal property and the environment. CAPP was created to promote common sense in vehicle inspection and maintenance programs.

Council of Vehicle Associations/Classic Vehicle **Advocate Group Inc** aka COVA/CVAG Inc PO Box 2136 West Paterson, NJ 07424-3311 800-CARS-166, 973-881-8838; FAX: 973-279-3779 E-mail: info@covacvag.org

Carmen "Butch" DeZuzio, President and winner of the Hemmings Motor News 2000 Hobby Hero Award. Founded 1992. Representing over 85,000 hobbyists. COVA/CVAG Inc is a not-for-profit organization devoted to the interests of all individuals, clubs, organizations and companies involved in the automotive, truck, motorcycle hobby/industry. All members receive the fact and information filled monthly newsletter. Founder of the "Wheels Across America," a national rally to be held every year. When fighting for your rights, remember: "If not you, who? If not now, when?" Dues: $25/year or more. Web site: www.covacvag.org

chapters:

Arizona *Southwestern America Vehicle Enthusiasts*, PO Box 18353, Tucson, AZ 85731-8353

California *COVA/CVAG Inc*, Los Angeles Area Rep, Brandon Brooks, 4550 Longridge Ave, Sherman Oaks, CA 91423 PH/FAX: 818-784-9690

Council of Vehicle Associations/Classic Vehicle Advocate Group Inc chapters (continued)

Legislative Watch, Denver Kissinger, 5050 E Garford St #110, Long Beach, CA 90815-2857

The Oldsmobile Club of America, PO Box 5474, Walnut Creek, CA 94596

Connecticut   *COVA/CVAG Inc*, Connecticut State Rep, Jim Gay, 22-17 Rose Ln, Danbury, CT 06811 203-744-3210

Florida   *Antique Automobile Club of Cape Canaveral*, PO Box 1611, Cocoa, FL 32922 407-724-6015

COVA/CVAG Inc, Florida State Rep, Irene Katcher, 9350 Sunrise Lakes BlvdApt #108, Sunrise, FL 33322

Pontiac-Oakland Club International, PO Box 9569, Bradenton, FL 34206

Illinois   *Centerville Antique Auto Touring Society*, c/o Jim Kaven, 4621 Billings Gate Ln, Woodstock, IL 60098-3059

Fox Valley Model A Ford Club, c/o Jack Anderson, PO Box 4, Geneva, IL 60134

Illinois Valley Olds Chapter, 20232 Blackstone, Matteson, IL 60443 PH/FAX: 708-481-7973

Kane County Car CLub, w/o Walter Hoffman, 1015 W State St, Geneva, IL 60134

Salt Creek Chapter Model A Ford Club of America, 6155 Pershing Ave, Downers Grove, IL 60516-1724

Windy City Chapter American Truck Historical Society, Bill Schutt, President, 4106 Gildert Ave, Western Springs, IL 60558

Iowa   *Southeast Iowa Antique Car Club*, c/o Robert Carleton, 17841 50th St, Morning Sun, IA 52640-9427

Kentucky   *Iron City Antique Auto Club*, c/o Carl E Virgin, 1308 Sparks St, Flatwoods, KY 41139-1760

Indiana   *Southwind COVA/CVAG Inc*, Indiana State Chapter, 3106 N 12th Ave, Evansville, IN 47720 812-423-2142

United Four Wheel Drive Assoc, PO Box 3553, Evansville, IN 47734

Maine   *COVA/CVAG Inc*, Maine State Reps, Linda & Norman Noble, 1118 Lewiston Rd, Topsham, ME 04086

Michigan   *Citizens Against Repressive Zoning*, c/o Jack Down, PO Box 536, Haslett, MI 48840-0536 517-351-6751; PH/FAX: 519-339-4926

COVA/CVAG Inc, Michigan State Rep, J Steven Kiraly, 7844 Enzian Rd, Delton, MI 49046-9716

Floral City A's Region Model A Restorers Club, c/o Roger Van Houten, 1876 E Hurd Rd, Monroe, MI 48162-9308

Metro Detroit Chapter of National Nostalgic Nova, c/o Jan Marie Hoenle, 3462 Michael Ave, Warren, MI 48091-3482

Mississippi   *Antique Vehicle Club of Mississippi*, c/o Bob Jackman, 2206 Scenic Dr, Brandon, MS 39047

Missouri   *Heart of America 364 Corvair Owners Assoc*, 9802 Booth, Kansas City, MO 64134 816-763-9025

Hudson Essex Terraplane Club Inc, Dick Sheridan, 650 Breeze Park Dr, St Charles, MO 63304 636-939-9231

New Jersey   *ACT - NJ Chapter*, c/o Betty Schroeck, PO Box 5792, Clark, NJ 07066-5792

AIMC, c/o Ed Natale, Box 222, Wyckoff, NJ 07481-0222

Cadillac Club of North Jersey Inc, c/o Gerald S Meisel, President, 105 Brookview Dr, Woodcliff Lake, NJ 07677

COVA/CVAG Inc & Legislative Watch, Rachel D Thiemann, Trustee, 8 Fritz St, Bloomfield, NJ 07003-4044 E-mail: axlnova@aol.com

COVA/CVAG Inc, Automotive Industry Liason, John Dydo,, NJ mrmuffler@earthlink.net

COVA/CVAG Inc, Carmen "Butch" DeZuzio, President, PO Box 2136, West Paterson, NJ 07424 973-881-8838, FAX: 973-279-3779

COVA/CVAG Inc, Central New Jersey Area Rep, Ben Deutschman, Building 11, Apt A-1Redfield Village, Metuchen, NJ 08840-3033 732-549-0188; FAX: 732-549-2478

COVA/CVAG Inc, Harold Duryea Jr, Trustee, 44 Barbara St, Bloomfield, NJ 07003

COVA/CVAG Inc, North Jersey Area Rep, Steven Falker, 53 West Gouverneur Ave, Rutherford, NJ 07070-2627 201-460-4592

COVA/CVAG Inc, Truck Division, Peter Boeck, President, 6 Cypress Ave, Verona, NJ 07044 973-239-3539

COVA/CVAG Inc, Trustee, Charles J Osborn, 200 W Sherman Ave, Edison, NJ 08820

COVA/CVAG Inc, William J Brennan, Trustee, 82 Devonshire Rd, Cedar Grove, NJ 07009

Dayton's Raiders Car Club, 319 Grand St, Paterson, NJ 07505 973-279-3770

Jaguar Touring Club,, NJ jagman@webspan.net

Motorcycle Division, Alan D Price, President,, NJ flyinace@erols.com

NJ Open Road Thunderbird Club, c/o Richard Martin, PO Box 565, Hewitt, NJ 07421

NJ VORC, c/o JJ Duffett, 17 Larsen Park Dr, Medford, NJ 08055-8169

North Jersey Thunderbird Association, Ezra Hinkle, 7 Carol Pl, Wayne, NJ 07470 973-694-9597

Trans-AM Formulas - Firebirds of America, 2486 Vauxhall Rd, Union, NJ 07083-5024 908-686-1886 days, 908-851-2063 eves

Tri-County Cruisers, c/o Mike Steinberg, President, PO Box 3671, Wayne, NJ 07470-3671

United Group Harmony Association, c/o Ronnie Italiano, PO Box 185, Clifton, NJ 07011 973-470-UGHA (8442)

New York   *AACA Livingston Region*, c/o WR Laidlaw, 3475 North Rd, Geneseo, NY 14454

COVA/CVAG Inc, New York City Area Rep, Nicholas DeCresce, 332 Bleecker St, #F6, New York City, NY 10014 E-mail: ndcnyc@mindspring.com

COVA/CVAG Inc, New York State Rep, Richard Golanec, 6 Rockland Ave, Port Chester, NY 10573 914-937-6486

Westchester Street Rod Association, c/o Bob Duncan, POBox 466, White Plains, NY 10603-0466

Ohio   *Coalition Against Testing*, c/o Bill McNeil, 2514 Montclair Ave, Cleveland, OH 44109

COVA of Ohio, c/o Glenn Miller, 17190 US Route 20A, West Unity, OH 43570

Penn-Ohio A Ford Club, c/o Jeffrey L Johnson, 2432 Bethlehem Rd, Prospect, OH 43342-9556

Oregon   *COVA/CVAG Inc*, Oregon State Rep, Dick Larrowe, PO Box 1239, Sandy, OR 97055 503-668-8213 days, 503-688-4096 eves

Emerald Valley Chapter, POCI, c/o Rosie Henderson, 2084 Lemuria St, Eugene, OR 97402-1098

Rose City Model T club, PO Box 3901, Portland, OR 97208-3901

Pennsylvania   *National Nostalgic Nova Inc*, c/o Wayne Bushey, PO Box 2344, York, PA 17405 717-252-4192, FAX: 717-252-1666

OH-Penn Region Nash Club of America, c/o George R Vollmer, 2335 Dutch Ridge Rd, Beaver, PA 15009

Rhode Island   *Little Rhody Pontiac Club*, c/o Bob Desrocmers, 570 Iron Mill Hill Rd, North Smithfield, RI 02896

South Carolina   *Carolina Mopar Clubs*, c/o WS "Dan" Larrabee, 742 E Butternut Rd, Summerville, SC 29483

Virginia   *Coalition for Auto Repair Equality*, 119 Oronoco St, Ste 300, Alexandria, VA 22314-2015 800-229-5380, 703-519-7555, FAX: 703-519-7747

George Washington Chapter Inc, Model A Ford Club of America, 3903 Old Lee Highway, Fairfax, VA 22030

Washington   *COVA/CVAG Inc*, Washington State Rep, T Alexander Swavely, 6910 Roosevelt Way NEApt #302, Seattle, WA 98115

Wisconsin   *COVA/CVAG Inc*, Wisconsin State Rep, Richard H Dorsey, 5114 State Rd 44, Oshkosh, WI 54904-6851 920-589-4652

COVA/CVAG Inc, Wisconsin State Rep, Vincent Ruffolo, 2104 Washington Rd, Kenosha, WI 53140-5335 262-658-2600, 262-658-9245

Wisconsin Auto Clubs in Association Inc (1972), c/o Richard Dorsey, 5114 State Rd 44, Oshkosh, WI 54904-6851

Motorsports Parts Manufacturers Council (MPMC)
PO Box 4910
Diamond Bar, CA 91765-0910
909-396-0289; FAX: 909-860-0184
E-mail: sema@sema.org

For more information, contact at the above address: membership. MPMC is a council of the Specialty Equipment Market Association (SEMA) established specially for companies engaged in manufacturing performance parts used in sanctioned racing applications. Dedicated to addressing industry-specific issues and to promoting and preserving the motorsports parts industry. All companies that meet at least two of these criteria are eligible and encouraged to become involved. Membership is open to all companies that manufacture, assemble and/or design performance products. Web site: www.sema.org

---

National Motorists Assn
402 W 2nd St
Waunakee, WI 53597-1342
608-849-6000
800-882-2785 membership information
FAX: 608-849-8697
E-mail: nma@motorists.org

Founded 1982. 7,000 members. Represents the interests of American drivers. Promotes rational traffic regulation, motorist courtesy and works to eliminate abusive insurance company practices, speed traps and other infringements of motorists' rights. Strong grass roots organization. State chapter coordinators. State and national lobbying. Political campaign involvement. Editorials and news releases. Bi-monthly national newsletter. Quarterly statewide newsletters. Dues: $29/year individual, $39/year family, $65/year business. Web site: www.motorists.org

---

Professional Restylers Organization (PRO)
PO Box 4910
Diamond Bar, CA 91765
909-396-0289; FAX: 909-860-0184
E-mail: sema@sema.org

For information, contact at the above address: membership. The Professional Restylers Organization (PRO), a section of the Specialty Equipment Market Association (SEMA), is dedicated to addressing the challenges facing the restyling segment of the automotive aftermarket and to developing effective strategies for dealing with industry-specific issues. All companies involved in aftermarket accessorizing, be they manufacturers, distributors or restylers/installers, should be members of PRO. In fact, it is critical that as many companies as possible become involved. Once in PRO, members work through subcommittees to focus on specific aspects of the restyling industry: OE/dealer-awareness programs; membership retention and recruitment; promotional and project-vehicle activities; and installer educational services. Web site: www.sema.org

Specialty Equipment Marketing Association (SEMA)
PO Box 4910
Diamond Bar, CA 91765
909-396-0289 ext 113; FAX: 909-860-0184
E-mail: sema@sema.org

Founded 1963. 3,400 members including manufacturers, distributors, retailers, installers, restylers, jobbers, restorers, car dealers, race facilities, and others. SEMA is a trade association that represents the producers and marketers of specialty equipment products and services for the automotive aftermarket. SEMA's mission is to help members' businesses succeed and prosper. Web site: www.sema.org

Street Rod Marketing Alliance (SRMA)
PO Box 4910
Diamond Bar, CA 91765
909-396-0289; FAX: 909-860-0184
E-mail: sema@sema.org

SRMA is a council of the Specialty Equipment Market Association (SEMA). Dedicated to addressing the challenges facing this segment of the automotive aftermarket and to preserving and promoting the street rod industry. SRMA members are the manufacturers, builders/fabricators, dealers, car clubs and enthusiast publications that make up the street rod industry. SRMA focuses on industry-specific issues, developing effective strategies and programs that will assist members in improving their businesses. Special attention is given to addressing those legislative and/or regulatory matters which affect the rodding industry. Web site: www.sema.org

Vehicle Preservation Society
PO Box 9800
San Diego, CA 92169
619-449-1010; FAX: 619-449-6388
E-mail: vehicles@vps.cc

See full listing in **Section Two** under **appraisals**

Wheel Industry Council (WIC)
PO Box 4910
Diamond Bar, CA 91765
909-396-0289; FAX: 909-860-0184
E-mail: sema@sema.org

For information, contact at the above address: membership. The Wheel Industry Council (WIC) is a council of the Specialty Equipment Market Association (SEMA). Dedicated to addressing the challenges facing the custom wheel industry, the Wheel Industry Council focuses its efforts on preserving and promoting this vital segment of the specialty equipment market.
Membership in the WIC is open to all companies that manufacture, import or are the sole, exclusive distributors of custom wheels or which serve as subcontractors to the wheel industry. Companies that meet these criteria are encouraged to become actively involved. Once in the Wheel Industry Council, members work through subcommittees to address the council's educational, technical, and communications needs. Web site: www.sema.org

State and Local

Car Club Council of Central Virginia
15628 Rowlett Rd
Chesterfield, VA 23838
804-590-9583; FAX: 804-590-0718
E-mail: fredfann@hotmail.com

Founded 1995. Members: 31 clubs. Members are car club and car hobbyist organizations. Council offers communications between clubs, monitors legislation. Meets last Monday of even numbered months. Newsletter is called *The Relay*. Dues: $10/year. Web site: www.angelfire.com/va2/ccccva

Citizens Against Repressive Zoning
PO Box 536
Haslett, MI 48840
517-351-6751; FAX: 517-339-4926
E-mail: malzoning@earthlink.net

Founded 1988. 100 members. Incorporated foundation. We are concerned with zoning zealots who abuse property and civil rights of individual collectors, salvage yards, rechrome shops and paint shops. Dues: donations only. Web site: http://clubs.hemmings.com/fightcityhall/

DC Council of Car Clubs
6629 32nd St NW
Washington, DC 20015
202-966-2737
E-mail: lackie@erols.com

Founded 1977. Legislative watchdog group for District of Columbia auto hobbyists. Drafted existing DC Historic Motor Vehicle License Law in 1978 and 1998. Dues: none, contributions welcome.

Tri-River Car Club Council
116 Wayne Dr
Cranberry Twp, PA 16066
724-776-1707; FAX: 724-776-1780

Founded 1993. 20 clubs and 15 individual members. No restrictions. Benefits: benefactor of new collectible license plate we had approved, eliminated CET from PA. Dues: $40/year club, $15/year individual.

United Street Rods of Idaho
2165 Bruneau Dr
Boise, ID 83709
208-336-0223; FAX: 208-377-0344
E-mail: paulshere@micron.net

Founded 1979. 1,400 members. No restrictions to join. Automotive hobby organization for legislative watch and lobbying to improve laws that encourage street rod, classic and vintage car continued use. Yearly events calendar. Dues: $5/year. Web site: www.usri.org

Wisconsin Automobile Clubs in Association Inc
PO Box 3135
Oshkosh, WI 54903-3135

Founded 1970. We are the oldest state car council in the US. The Association meets once each year to frame the legislation/action agenda. Members and non-members and member and non-member clubs are sent a notice of the annual meeting inviting their attendance. Dues: $8/year individuals, $24/year clubs.

Wisconsin Car Clubs Alliance (WCCA)
PO Box 562
Menomonee Falls, WI 53052-0562
414-255-5385

Founded 1989. 60 clubs. We are an alliance of car clubs. Each club has one vote, no matter how large or small. We are a watchdog group for legislation for and against our hobby. Also offer an individual membership, they can come to any meeting (4 a year), get our newsletter but have no vote. *WCCA Newsletter* comes with membership once a month. It contains any information we can get on things that affect our hobby. Dues: $20/year club, $15/year individual.

Section Four
Publications & Information Sources

181 listings

This section contains publications for car collectors as well as sources of information, photos, technical data, restoration information, and historical data. It does not include literature dealers, which are found both in Section One under marque specialists and Section Two under literature generalists. There are five categories.

Information Sources. These are businesses or individuals offering specific or general information which may be purchased.

Books & Publications. In this category are publishers and other suppliers of books, single pamphlets, and magazine back issues.

Periodicals. Included here are magazines and other publications to which the hobbyists may subscribe. Many are also available in the form of back issues. Subscription prices were current when the publishers submitted listings, but may have increased by the time the *Almanac* reaches you.

Newsletters ordinarily deal with investment/ market condition aspects of car collecting and related fields.

Research & Reference Libraries. Includes private and public archives, libraries, specialized collections and reference sources. Many are not open to the general public and may require special arrangements to visit. Most libraries and other organizations will charge for finding and sending research material. When writing to them, be as specific as possible. Don't for instance, ask them to "send everything you have on 1951 XYZ's." The more precise you are in your request the better the response will be.

Information Sources

1958 Thunderbird Convertible Registry
Bill Van Ess
6780 Kitson NE
Rockford, MI 49341
616-874-1004; FAX: 616-363-2870
E-mail: billvaness@juno.com

book

See full listing in **Section One** under **Thunderbird**

AACA Library & Research Center
501 W Governor Rd
PO Box 417
Hershey, PA 17033
717-534-2082; FAX: 717-534-9101
E-mail: libraryaaca@aol.com

research library

See full listing in **Section Four** under **research & reference libraries**

ARS Automotive Research Services
Division of Auto Search International
1702 W Camelback #301
Phoenix, AZ 85015
602-230-7111; FAX: 602-230-7282

appraisals research

See full listing in **Section Two** under **appraisals**

Auto Nostalgia Enr
332 St Joseph
Mont St Gregoire, QC
Canada J0J 1K0
PH/FAX: 450-346-3644
E-mail: autonostalgia@vif.com

literature manuals models tractor decals

See full listing in **Section Two** under **models & toys**

AutoGuide.net
150 Consumers Rd, Ste 403
Toronto, ON Canada M2J 1P9
416-499-8351
E-mail: info@autoguide.net

automotive directory

We are the Internet's largest automotive directory, find anything you need on cars, trucks and motorcycles on the web. Web Site: www.autoguide.net

Automotive Information Clearinghouse
PO Box 1746,
La Mesa, CA 91944
619-447-7200
FAX: 619-447-8080, include address
E-mail:
service@automotiveinformation.com

information source

America's largest stocking warehouse for original manufacturer's publications. Shop, owner's, parts manuals, sales brochures and more. Totally computerized. 10 second quotes. 34 years' experience. Web site: www.automotiveinformation.com

AutoWire.Net
PO Box 1011
San Mateo, CA 94403
650-340-8669; FAX: 650-340-9473
E-mail: autowire@pacbell.net

web site

Automotive Article Communication Network, a web site about cars, trucks, sport utility vehicles, classic car auctions, events and automotive information. Web site: www.autowire.net

Bavarian Quality Parts
A Silvermine Classics Inc Company
2205 Rt 82
LaGrangeville, NY 12540
800-782-7199; FAX: 845-223-5394
E-mail: sales@bavarianquality.com

parts

See full listing in **Section One** under **BMW**

Bimmer Magazine   magazine
42 Digital Dr #5
Novato, CA 94949
415-382-0580; FAX: 415-382-0587

See full listing in **Section Four** under **periodicals**

Bill Boudway   restoration info
105 Deerfield Dr
Canandaigua, NY 14424-2409
716-394-6172
E-mail: gnbboudway@msn.com

See full listing in **Section One** under **Packard**

Car Critic   appraisals
202 Woodshire Ln   inspections
Naples, FL 34105
941-435-1157; FAX: 941-261-4864
E-mail: carcritic@earthlink.net

See full listing in **Section Two** under **car & parts locators**

"Check The Oil!" Magazine   magazine
PO Box 937
Powell, OH 43065-0937
614-848-5038; FAX: 614-436-4760
E-mail: ctomagazine@aol.com

See full listing in **Section Two** under **petroliana**

Classic Motorbooks   books
PO Box 1/HMN   videos
729 Prospect Ave
Osceola, WI 54020
800-826-6600; FAX: 715-294-4448

See full listing in **Section Four** under **books & publications**

Clean Air Performance   legislative watch
Professionals (CAPP)   organization
84 Hoy Ave
Fords, NJ 08863
732-738-7859; FAX: 732-738-7625
E-mail: stellacapp@earthlink.net

See full listing in **Section Three** under **legislative watch organizations**

Collector Car & Truck   price guide
Market Guide
41 N Main St
North Grafton, MA 01536
508-839-6707; FAX: 508-839-6266
E-mail: vmr@vmrintl.com

See full listing in **Section Four** under **periodicals**

Custom Solutions & Services   badges
2218 Pleasant View Ct   keychains
Deer Creek, IL 61733-9672   software
309-447-6320
E-mail: jscharfcss@juno.com

Computer software which contains vintage car specifications and
includes: model designations, original prices and shipping
weights, engine specifications, overhaul data, tune-up, carburetor, distributor, starter, generator/alternator, brake, rear axle
and alignment specifications. I also produce custom prepared
badges and key chains. In addition I have an extensive database
containing feature articles and reports on vintage cars which I
can search to provide a source for articles on specific year, make
and model of car. Web site: http://sites.netscape.net/csscardata

DeTomaso Registry   book
Bill Van Ess
6780 Kitson NE
Rockford, MI 49341
616-874-1004; FAX: 616-363-2870
E-mail: billvaness@juno.com

See full listing in **Section One** under **DeTomaso/Pantera**

Dusty Memories and Faded Glory   rentals
118 Oxford Hts Rd
Somerset, PA 15501-1134
814-443-2393; FAX: 814-443-9452

See full listing in **Section Two** under **military vehicles**

Excellence Magazine   magazine
42 Digital Dr #5
Novato, CA 94949
415-382-0580; FAX: 415-382-0587

See full listing in **Section Four** under **periodicals**

Forza Magazine   magazine
42 Digital Dr #5
Novato, CA 94949
415-382-0580; FAX: 415-382-0587

See full listing in **Section Four** under **periodicals**

Bob Francis Auto Writer &   history research
Historian   trivia
1503 W Bristow Dr
Tupelo, MS 38801
662-844-6070
E-mail: bigbob@ebicom.net

Mail order only. Will attempt to report on history of any make or
model car. No technical questions, no questions about repair,
etc. Usually give the "whole nine yards" when answering questions. Pictures available, reasonable rates, satisfaction.
Automotive history books available; two with chronolgesical
dates: one by days *"Who What When Where"* and another by
years *"Wheeling Through The Years"*. A third book is on automotive trivia and mini stories about the automobile industry, its
people, products, etc. It's called *"Big Bad Bob's Wonderful World
of (Little Known) Automotive History."* All books are soft bound
and range from about 200-250 pages. Each book is $20 postpaid
in the US. A fourth book, similar to *"Big Bob's Trivia"* will be
available soon at the same price.

Arthur Freakes   researcher
Capri House   writer
Walton-On-Thames
Surrey KT12 2LY England
PH/FAX: (UK) 01932 269109

Motoring writer, historian, researcher. Editor of *HCKC News*,
Rootes Group Vehicles, and *The Mitchamian*. Research and information on Rootes Group, Hillman, Commer and Karrier for
motor vehicle publications.

The Garden of Speedin   books
4645 Q Ruffner St
San Diego, CA 92111
800-MOTORHEAD
FAX: 858-467-0777
E-mail: cars@gardenofspeed.com

Mail order only. *Vintage Part Sources* is updated annually.
Publishing highly organized books on where to find parts for specific old cars. 14 different editions for different cars (full-size
Chevy, Mustang, Mopar, Pontiac). Separate sections for dealers
specializing in parts for body, interior, trim, engine, rubber, suspension, as well as literature. The book also contains parts
restoration specialists and a nationwide listing of salvage yards
specializing in old cars. Guaranteed to find any part or your
money back. $24.95 plus shipping per book. Web site:
www.gardenofspeedin.com

Golden Mile Sales Inc   NORS parts
J DeAngelo   NOS parts
2439 S Bradford St   sheetmetal
Allentown, PA 18103-5821
PH/FAX: 610-791-4497, 24 hours
E-mail: abguy@enter.net

See full listing in **Section One** under **American Austin/Bantam**

Greater Manchester Fire Service Museum
Maclure Rd
Rochdale Lancashire OL11 1DN
England
01706 900155

museum

See full listing in **Section Six** under **England**

Leon Henry Inc
455 Central Ave, Dept HVA
Scarsdale, NY 10583
914-723-3176; FAX: 914-723-0205
E-mail: lh@leonhenryinc.com

list brokers
package inserts

Full service package insert/mailing list broker/manager. In our 45th year. Our brokers can place your inserts into merchandise packages, statements, co-ops, ride-alongs, card decks, sample kits, etc, to target your prospective customer. We are managers for package insert programs including *Cars and Parts* magazine, *Ecklers Corvette Parts*, *Performance Products & Summit Racing Equipment*. Let us put inserts into your packages. Web site: www.leonhenryinc.com

James Hill
935 Sunnyslope St
Emporia, KS 66801
620-342-4826 evenings/weekends
E-mail: jwhill@osprey.net

ignition parts
source list

See full listing in **Section One** under **Packard**

Hot Rod Memories
PO Box 280040
Northridge, CA 91328-0040
818-886-7637; FAX: 818-349-1403
E-mail: sales@hotrodmemories.com

videos

We have hundreds of classic 1950s hot rod, sci-fi, rock n' roll and juvenile delinquent films. Have beach movies from the 1960s, drag racing and other movies from the 1950s, 1960s and 1970s. Web site: www.hotrodmemories.com

Jaguar Cars Archives
555 MacArthur Blvd
Mahwah, NJ 07430
201-818-8144; FAX: 201-818-0281

research

Mail order only. On-site research by appointment only. Provides individual vehicle research from Jaguar/Daimler build records for owners only. Fee includes JDHT certificate. Other holdings include Jaguar parts, service and owner's manuals, technical/service bulletins, paint/trim information, marketing, advertising and photographic collection. Send SASE to receive a form for vehicle or other technical research or for a list of items for sale (please specify).

Eliot James Enterprises Inc
PO Box 3986
Dana Point, CA 92629-8986
949-661-0889; FAX: 949-661-1901

development info

See full listing in **Section Four** under **books & publications**

Jersey Late Greats Inc
PO Box 1294
Hightstown, NJ 08520
609-448-0526

documentation
service
restoration details

See full listing in **Section One** under **Chevrolet**

M & L Automobile Appraisal
2662 Palm Terr
Deland, FL 32720
904-734-1761,
386-734-1761 (effective 11/01)

appraisals

See full listing in **Section Two** under **appraisals**

McLellan's Automotive History
Robert and Sharon McLellan
9111 Longstaff Dr
Houston, TX 77031-2711
713-772-3285; FAX: 713-772-3287
E-mail: mclellans@mclellansautomotive.com

books
factory literature
magazines
memorabilia
press kits/
programs
sales literature

See full listing in **Section Two** under **literature dealers**

Mopar Collector's Guide Magazine
PO Box 15489
Baton Rouge, LA 70895-5489
225-274-0609; FAX: 225-274-9033
E-mail: mopar@intersurf.com

magazine

See full listing in **Section One** under **Mopar**

MotorWeek
11767 Owings Mills Blvd
Owings Mills, MD 21117
410-356-5600; FAX: 410-581-4113
E-mail: motorweek@mpt.org

TV program

Mail order only. Weekly TV program, *MotorWeek*. Television's original automotive magazine can be seen on more than 250 public television stations. It also appears weekly on Speedvision. Check local listings for the time and date in your area. Web sites: www.pbs.org or www.mpt.org/motorweek

MPH Interactive Designs
7766 W 450 S
Williamsport, IN 47993
765-491-9604; FAX: 765-893-4017
E-mail: park@mphinteractive.net

photography
research
web site design
writing

Freelance journalist specializing in automotive historical research, writing, photography and web design. Published in *Autoweek*, *Automobile*, *Special Interest Autos*, *Classic Auto Restorer*, *Car Collector* and others. See web site for services and online samples, plus the "Beater du Jour" feature. Web site: www.mphinteractive.net/

Museum of British Road Transport
St Agnes Ln
Hales St
Coventry CV1 1PN England
44-01203-832425
FAX: 44-01203-832465
E-mail: museum@mbrt.w.uk

museum

See full listing in **Section Six** under **England**

Northeast Classic Car Museum
NYS Rt 23
24 Rexford St
Norwich, NY 13815
607-334-AUTO (2886)
FAX: 607-336-6745
E-mail: info@classiccarmuseum.org

museum

See full listing in **Section Six** under **New York**

CT Peters Inc Appraisers
2A W Front St
Red Bank, NJ 07701
732-747-9450 Red Bank
732-528-9451 Brielle
E-mail: ctp2120@aol.com

appraisals

See full listing in **Section Two** under **appraisals**

Petroleum Collectibles Monthly
PO Box 556
LaGrange, OH 44050
440-355-6608; FAX: 440-355-4955

periodical

See full listing in **Section Four** under **periodicals**

Section Four – Publications

PTE Publishing
1975 Ripplerock Rd
Fort Mill, SC 29715
PH/FAX: 803-547-4585
E-mail: starpieces@rmtc.net

magazine

Magazine geared toward Chrysler PT Cruiser enthusiasts, how-to tips, exclusive calendar of events, classifieds and more. *PTE Cruisin'* quarterly magazine, $19.95; PT Custom Cruiser calendar, $10.95. We also operate a fan web site: http://ptenthusiasts.org

Rolls-Royce Foundation
505 Fishing Creek Rd
Lewisberry, PA 17339
717-932-9900; FAX: 717-932-9925
E-mail: rds@flightsystems.com

library
literature
museum

See full listing in **Section One** under **Rolls-Royce/Bentley**

Ed Rouze
746 N Memorial
Prattville, AL 36067
334-365-2381

painting guide book

See full listing in **Section Two** under **painting**

S&P Creations
971 Colleen Dr
Newport News, VA 23608
757-875-5270
E-mail:
theadventurer@worldnett.att.net

books
data analysis
information

See full listing in **Section One** under **Dodge**

Shoreline Antique Auto Connection
PO Box 3353
Stony Creek, CT 06405
E-mail: commongear@aol.com

web site

News source for antique auto hobby related activities on the Connecticut shoreline. Publishes *Shoreline Antique Auto Connection*. Web site: http://members.aol.com/saacregion/

Silvermine Classics Inc
24 East Ave
PO Box 222
New Canaan, CT 06840
800-782-7199; FAX: 845-223-5394
E-mail: parts@silvermineclassics.com

accessories
catalogs
parts

SCI knows what you need: easy-to-find new and used parts and accessories for your classic automobiles; an expert knowledge-base to support your projects and reliable, friendly service. SCI's on-line catalogs and toll free call center cover a wide range of marques. Order by fax, phone or on-line. Credit cards accepted. Web site: www.silvermineclassics.com

Richard Spiegelman Productions Inc
19 Guild Hall Dr
Scarborough, ON Canada M1R 3Z7
416-759-1644
E-mail: carphoto@sympatico.com
or carphoto@yahoo.com

photography
slides

Photography, large slide file on old cars, color slide, 4x5 transparencies, slide shows, film productions.

Sports Car International
42 Digital Dr #5
Novato, CA 94949
415-382-0580; FAX: 415-382-0587

magazine

See full listing in **Section Four** under **periodicals**

Star Quality Parts
A Silvermine Classics Inc Company
1 Alley Rd
LaGrangeville, NY 12520
800-STAR199 (782-7199)
FAX: 845-223-5394
E-mail: sales@starqualityparts.com

accessories
parts

See full listing in **Section One** under **Mercedes-Benz**

Sunburst Technology
PO Box 598
Lithia Springs, GA 30122
FAX: 770-942-6091
E-mail: sunburst2000@juno.com

electronic
technical
consultant

Sunburst Technology can customize your electrical, electronic and micro processor controls for: auto, home and shop. A Sunburst multi parameter controller can be designed to monitor, control or adapt your machine to operate the way you want. As a technical consultant, manufacturer, Sunburst can write custom software programs to control almost any electro mechanical powered options. Let Sunburst design your next application for engine, electrical options, alarms/monitoring and power drives. Call, we can help.

This Old Truck Magazine
PO Box 500
Missouri City, TX 77459
888-760-8108 subscriptions
937-767-1433 publishing office
FAX: 937-767-2726
E-mail: antique@antiquepower.com

magazine

See full listing in **Section Four** under **periodicals**

Thunderbird Information eXchange
8421 E Cortez St
Scottscale, AZ 85260
480-948-3996

newsletter

See full listing in **Section One** under **Thunderbird**

University Motors Ltd
6490 E Fulton
Ada, MI 49301
616-682-0800; FAX: 616-682-0801

events
line/bench service
restoration

See full listing in **Section One** under **MG**

Vintage Jag Works
1390 W Hwy 26
Blackfoot, ID 83221
877-251-5183 toll free order line
208-684-4767; FAX: 208-684-3386
E-mail: walt@vintagejag.com

consulting
how-to articles

See full listing in **Section One** under **Jaguar**

Wolverine Video
300 Stonecliffe Aisle
Irvine, CA 92612-5728
949-854-5171; FAX: 949-854-2154

videos

Wolverine Video takes you to the center of the great American car culture. Crank up the volume and the noise of whining blowers, gear driven cams and throbbing open headers fills the air. The colors are vibrant and true as Bitchin' hot rods, dusty dry lakes racers, way cool customs, outlaw's bikes, gnarly woodys, illustrated low riders appear for hours to your delight and amusement. This is the magic of Wolverine Video. Free catalog upon request, call or write.

Books & Publications

1956 Studebaker Golden Hawk Owners Register
31700 Wekiva River Rd
Sorrento, FL 32776-9233
E-mail: 56sghor@prodigy.net

information exchange

See full listing in **Section One** under **Studebaker**

1958 Thunderbird Convertible Registry
Bill Van Ess
6780 Kitson NE
Rockford, MI 49341
616-874-1004; FAX: 616-363-2870
E-mail: billvaness@juno.com

book

See full listing in **Section One** under **Thunderbird**

ADP Hollander
14800 28th Ave N #190
Plymouth, MN 55447
800-761-9266; FAX: 800-825-1124
E-mail:
info@hollander-auto-parts.com

interchange info manuals

See full listing in **Section Two** under **car & parts locators**

Archway Press Inc
19 W 44th St
New York, NY 10036
800-374-4766; FAX: 212-869-5215
E-mail: archway@mindspring.com

garage blueprints

Protect Your Vintage Beauty (and gain affordable loft/living space). Fully illustrated brochure describes 20 garage/loft plans for two to five cars. Professional building blueprints available for every plan. Call or write to order. Web site: www.archwaypress.com

Auto Interchange Systems/ Automotive Business Forms
Sue Johnson
PO Box 27498
Golden Valley, MN 55427-0498
763-587-0666; FAX: 763-587-0667

books

Mail order. Interchange parts manuals covering 1950-1965 Ford, GM, Chrysler and 1963-1974 Ford products. 15 day money back guarantee. Web site: www.autocars.com

Auto Review Publishing
5 Rowan Oak Ln
Columbia, IL 62236
618-281-3311
E-mail: autrev@aol.com

publications

Publisher of automotive restoration and historical books. Recent titles include: *AA Truck* Supplement to *Restorer's Model A* Shop Manual; *Fleetwood, The Company and the Coachcraft*. Price list and information available upon request. The Auto Review was established in 1906. Web site: http://users.aol.com/fordmoval/schild.html

Auto Zone
33202 Woodward Ave
Birmingham, MI 48009
800-647-7288; FAX: 248-646-5381
E-mail: info@azautozone.com

books
magazines
models
videos

See full listing in **Section Two** under **models & toys**

Automotive Information Clearinghouse
PO Box 1746
La Mesa, CA 91944
619-447-7200
FAX: 619-447-8080, include address
E-mail:
service@automotiveinformation.com

information source

See full listing in **Section Four** under **Information Sources**

Autophile Car Books
850 Eglinton Ave E
Toronto, ON Canada M4G 2L1
PH/FAX: 416-425-1555
E-mail: info@autophile.ca

books
models

Retail store specializing in new and used car books and 1/43 scale models and kits of cars. Web site: www.autophile.ca

Bentley Publishers
1734 Massachusetts Ave
Cambridge, MA 02138-1804
800-423-4595; FAX: 617-876-9235
E-mail: sales@rb.com

books
manuals

Bentley Publishers is the authoritative source for official factory service information and enthusiasts books on a multitude of automotive topics including parts identification, high-performance tuning, fuel injection, aerodynamics, engineering, vintage racing and competition driving. Bentley has books and service manuals for Volkswagen, Audi, BMW, Bosch, Saab, Volvo, Alfa Romeo, MG, Austin-Healey, Jaguar, Land Rover, Range Rover, MG, Triumph, Morris Minor, Jeep, Ford, Chevrolet and Toyota. Web site: www.rb.com

BritBooks
PO Box 321
Otego, NY 13825
PH/FAX: 607-988-7956
E-mail: britbooks@britbooks.com

books

BritBooks catalog, free. Published annually. 32-page catalog of books on British sports cars. We have a large selection of new and out of print books. Our prices are always competitive. Please write or call for our catalog. Web site: www.britbooks.com

British Car Magazine
343 Second St, Ste H
Los Altos, CA 94022-3639
650-949-9680; FAX: 650-949-9685
E-mail: editor@britishcar.com

magazine

See full listing in **Section Four** under **periodicals**

Michael Bruce Associates Inc
PO Box 396
Powell, OH 43065
740-965-4859

publication

Corvette and Camaro publications: *Corvette Black Book*, *Camaro White Book*.

Cadillac Motor Books
PO Box 7
Temple City, CA 91780
626-445-1618
E-mail: cadbooks@pacbell.net

books

See full listing in **Section One** under **Cadillac/LaSalle**

"Check The Oil!" Magazine
PO Box 937
Powell, OH 43065-0937
614-848-5038; FAX: 614-436-4760
E-mail: ctomagazine@aol.com

magazine

See full listing in **Section Two** under **petroliana**

Classic Auto Literature 1592 Seacrest Rd Nanoose Bay BC Canada V9P 9B5 250-468-9522	manuals/models parts catalogs posters/videos sales brochures

See full listing in **Section Two** under **literature dealers**

Classic Motorbooks PO Box 1/HMN 729 Prospect Ave Osceola, WI 54020 800-826-6600; FAX: 715-294-4448	books videos

Monday-Friday 8 am to 4:30 pm. The world's largest selection of automotive literature. Motorbooks is a long established publisher and mail order company offering thousands of books on repair, restoration, racing, buying, driving and general marque studies and histories. We also offer a wide selection of videos and auto related items. Call or visit our web site for a free 120 page catalog. Web site: www.motorbooks.com

The Classic Motorist PO Box 363 Rotterdam Junction, NY 12150-0363	automobilia books & publications

See full listing in **Section One** under **Packard**

Alfred Cosentino Solo Books Box 1917 Thousand Oaks, CA 91360 818-707-2301	books publication

Mail order only. Federal Express, air cargo, truck, sea freight. *Abarth Owners International*, published semi-annually, about Abarth, Abarth Fiat auto activities, plus books on Abarth, Ferrari and Fiat group. These books are only available through the author and publisher, no longer through the trade.

DeTomaso Registry Bill Van Ess 6780 Kitson NE Rockford, MI 49341 616-874-1004; FAX: 616-363-2870 E-mail: billvaness@juno.com	book

See full listing in **Section One** under **DeTomaso/Pantera**

Dobbs Publishing Group Inc 3816 Industry Blvd Lakeland, FL 33811 863-644-0449; FAX: 863-648-1187	periodicals

Publishers of automotive magazines: *Mustang Monthly*, *Musclecar Review*, *Super Ford*, *Corvette Fever*, *Mopar Muscle*, *Chevy Truck*, and *Jp Magazine*.

The Evergreen Press 30430 Point Marina Canyon Lake, CA 92587 909-244-1114; FAX: 909-244-5771 E-mail: evpress@aol.com	books

Publisher and distributor of well illustrated hardcover books. Each is a photographic record of a specific marque. Each contains approximately 1,000 clear, sharp photos (b/w and color) illustrating model changes on a year-by-year basis.

Finest In Fords Larry Blodget Box 753 Ranchero Mirage, CA 92270 E-mail: info@finestinfords.com	books Ford 1954-up model cars restoration services

Mail order only. We publish soft-bound books on promotional car models, plus newsletters for same. SASE required. Online museum of Ford promotional and sales incentives. Worlds smallest Ford dealer. Web site: www.finestinfords.com

Bob Francis Auto Writer & Historian 1503 W Bristow Dr Tupelo, MS 38801 662-844-6070 E-mail: bigbob@ebicom.net	history research trivia

See full listing in **Section Four** under **information sources**

The Garden of Speedin 4645 Q Ruffner St San Diego, CA 92111 800-MOTORHEAD FAX: 858-467-0777 E-mail: cars@gardenofspeed.com	books

See full listing in **Section Four** under **information sources**

Greater New York Automobile Dealers Association 18-10 Whitestone Expressway Whitestone, NY 11357 718-746-5300; FAX: 718-746-9333 E-mail: darlene@autoshowny.com	book

Mail order only. Publishes *A History of the NY International Auto Show*. Covers the history of the New York International Automobile Show 1900-2000. Book price: $30.

Hemmings Motor News Sunoco Filling Station 216 Main St Bennington, VT 05201 HMN Customer Service: 1-800-CAR-HERE ext 550 HMN Sunoco Filling Station: 802-447-9652	books, videos HMN caps, t-shirts HMN sweatshirts HMN tote bags HMN truck banks Free Vintage Vehicle Display

"Old-tyme" Filling Station and Gift Shop offers a variety of automobilia and gifts including porcelain & tin signs, old license plates, die-cast models and kits, automotive books, Vermont products and more. Located at Hemmings Motor News Sunoco Filling Station and Gift Shop in downtown Bennington. Open 7 am to 10 pm every day but Christmas. Call or write for Free Mail Order Catalog of *HMN* products or visit our web site: www.hemmings.com

Hot Rod Nostalgia™ PO Box 249 West Point, CA 95255-0249 209-293-2114; FAX: 209-293-2120 E-mail: hvaa@hotrodnostalgia.com	"magalog"

Hot Rod Nostalgia is published annually. Dave Wallace's fifth nostalgia "magalog" is expanded to 68 pages of gearhead gifts, editorials, artist profiles and humor. Pro and sportsman racers of the 1950s, 1960s and 1970s are featured in books, videos, prints, posters and 200 action photos. Send $5 or charge by phone. Web site: www.hotrodnostalgia.com

Jacques Rear Engine Renault Parts 13839 Hwy 8 Business El Cajon, CA 92021 619-561-6687; FAX: 619-561-1656 E-mail: renaultj@pacbell.net	parts

See full listing in **Section One** under **Renault**

Eliot James Enterprises Inc PO Box 3986 Dana Point, CA 92629-8986 949-661-0889; FAX: 949-661-1901	development info

EJE offers products and services to help hobbyists profit from their hobby as well as create and protect new ideas for their hobby and profit from them through licensing or starting a business. Web site: www.bugstik.com

Jack Juratovic 819 Absequami Trail Lake Orion, MI 48362 PH/FAX: 248-814-0627	**artwork** **magazine**

See full listing in **Section Two** under **artwork**

David M King, Automotive Books 5 Brouwer Ln Rockville Centre, NY 11570 516-766-1561; FAX: 516-766-7502 E-mail: rollskingusa@yahoo.com	**literature**

See full listing in **Section One** under **Rolls-Royce/Bentley**

The Klemantaski Collection 65 High Ridge Rd, Ste 219 Stamford, CT 06905 PH/FAX: 203-968-2970 E-mail: klemcoll@aol.com	**books** **photography**

See full listing in **Section Two** under **photography**

LaCarrera-The Mexican Road Race PO Box 1605 Studio City, CA 91614 323-464-5720; FAX: 323-656-7111 E-mail: lacarrera@earthlink.net	**road race**

See full listing in **Section Two** under **racing**

Lamm Morada Publishing Co Inc Box 7607 Stockton, CA 95267 209-931-1056; FAX: 209-931-5777 E-mail: lammmorada@aol.com	**books**

Publish books for auto enthusiasts. Latest: *Thunderbird 2002*, $39.95; also *A Century of Automotive Style*, $59.95; and

Fabulous Firebird, $39.95. Please add $5.50 per book for postage and handling. Web site: www.lammmorada.com

McFarland & Company Inc **Publishers** Box 611 Jefferson, NC 28640 336-246-4460; FAX: 336-246-5018 E-mail: info@mcfarlandpub.com	**books**

Books on classic cars and automotive history. Catalogs free on request and queries from prospective authors always welcome. Web site: www.mcfarlandpub.com

McLellan's Automotive History Robert and Sharon McLellan 9111 Longstaff Dr Houston, TX 77031-2711 713-772-3285; FAX: 713-772-3287 E-mail: mclellans@mclellansautomotive.com	**books** **factory literature** **magazines** **memorabilia** **press kits/** **programs** **sales literature**

See full listing in **Section Two** under **literature dealers**

Don Montgomery's Hot Rod Books 636 Morro Hills Rd Fallbrook, CA 92028 760-728-5557; FAX: 760-731-4835 E-mail: montysbooks@nethere.com	**books**

Hot rod and drag racing history books, hardcover books with hundreds of pictures covering the 1940s to 1960s.

Mopar Collector's Guide Magazine PO Box 15489 Baton Rouge, LA 70895-5489 225-274-0609; FAX: 225-274-9033 E-mail: mopar@intersurf.com	**magazine**

See full listing in **Section One** under **Mopar**

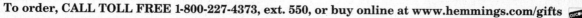

Section Four – Publications

Section Four – Publications

MotorCam Media | automotive videos
138 N Alling Rd
Tallmadge, OH 44278
800-240-1777; FAX: 330-633-3249
E-mail: carvideo@motorcam.com

See full listing in **Section Two** under **videos**

MPH Interactive Designs | photography research writing
7766 W 450 S
Williamsport, IN 47993
765-491-9604; FAX: 765-893-4017
E-mail: park@mphinteractive.net

See full listing in **Section Four** under **information sources**

NADA Appraisal Guides | appraisal guides
PO Box 7800
Costa Mesa, CA 92628
800-966-6232; FAX: 714-556-8715

NADA Classic, Collectible & Special Interest Car Appraisal Guide, 76 years of used values for all cars and trucks 1926-1981 including used values on exotic cars 1946-2001. The most comprehensive guide available today! Complete model listings, optional equipment, engine information, vehicle weight and three values (low-average-high) based on vehicle condition. Updated January-May-September. Subscription: $40/year. Web site: www.nadaguides.com

See our ad on page 8

Oil Company Collectibles Inc | books gasoline globes signs
PO Box 556
LaGrange, OH 44050
440-355-6608; FAX: 440-355-4955
E-mail: scottpcm@aol.com

See full listing in **Section Two** under **automobilia**

Petroleum Collectibles Monthly | periodical
PO Box 556
LaGrange, OH 44050
440-355-6608; FAX: 440-355-4955

See full listing in **Section Four** under **periodicals**

PM Research Inc | books models
4110 Niles Hill Rd
Wellsville, NY 14895
716-593-3169; FAX: 716-593-5637
E-mail: pmrgang@pmresearchinc.com

See full listing in **Section Two** under **models & toys**

Portrayal Press | books manuals
PO Box 1190
Andover, NJ 07821
PH/FAX: 973-579-5781
E-mail: info@portrayal.com

See full listing in **Section Two** under **military vehicles**

PTE Publishing | magazine
1975 Ripplerock Rd
Fort Mill, SC 29715
PH/FAX: 803-547-4585
E-mail: starpieces@rmtc.net

See full listing in **Section Four** under **information sources**

Ed Rouze | painting guide book
746 N Memorial
Prattville, AL 36067
334-365-2381

See full listing in **Section Two** under **painting**

S&P Creations | books data analysis information
971 Colleen Dr
Newport News, VA 23608
757-875-5270
E-mail: theadventurer@worldnett.att.net

See full listing in **Section One** under **Dodge**

Samlerborsen | books toys
Jacobys Alle 2-4
DK 1806 Frederiksberg C Denmark
+45-33254022; FAX: +45-33250622

See full listing in **Section Two** under **literature dealers**

Steve Smith Autosports Publications | books
PO Box 11631
Santa Ana, CA 92711
714-639-7681; FAX: 714-639-9741

Mail order only. Publisher of automotive technical books such as *Street Rod Building Skills*, *Practical Engine Swapping*, *How to Build a Repro Rod*, *Racing the Small Block Chevy*, etc. 245 titles available. Free catalog. Web site: www.ssapubl.com

TMC Publications | literature manuals
5817 Park Heights Ave
Baltimore, MD 21215-3931
410-367-4490; FAX: 410-466-3566
E-mail: carolyny@tmcpubl.com

Mail order automobile literature-factory original workshop manuals, owner's manuals, electrical troubleshooting manuals and miscellaneous literature (sales brochures, microfiche, parts manuals, etc). Mercedes-Benz, BMW, Jaguar, Porsche, Audi, Infiniti, Lexus, Mazda, Range Rover, Subaru, Suzuki, Mitsubishi, Daewoo, Hyundai, Saab, (Ford 1986-1998). TMC Publications also purchases literature.

Transport Books at DRB Motors Inc | books manuals periodicals videos
16 Elrose Ave
Toronto, ON Canada M9M 2H6
800-665-2665, 416-744-7675
FAX: 416-744-7696
E-mail: info@transportbooks.com

Mail, e-mail, phone order and retail store. Monday-Saturday 10 am to 5 pm, closed holidays. Cars, bikes, boats, planes, trucks, tractors, tanks, trains. Canada's largest selection of transportation books and videos. Choose from 10,000+ histories, biographies, gift books, repair manuals, racing and driving books, videos and art from Canada and around the world. Magazines include *Hemmings*, *Old Autos* and *Wheels & Tracks*. Visit our store, just off Highway 401. Visit our web site catalog and location map. Web site: www.transportbooks.com

Vintage Oval Racing | magazine
2460 Park Blvd #6
Palo Alto, CA 94306
650-321-1411; FAX: 650-321-4426
E-mail: victorymag@aol.com

Monthly publication. Keeping American track racing heritage alive. Event reports, tech articles, resource guide, event schedule, classifieds, nostalgia articles. Featuring Champ/Indy, coupes, sedans, hardtops, jalopies, midgets, modifieds, Sportsman, Sprints, stocks, super modifieds, track roadsters and much more. Subscription: $29.95/year. Web site: www.vintageovalracing.com

Jim Wangers | memorabilia
1309 Melrose Way
Vista, CA 92083
760-941-9303; FAX: 760-941-9305
E-mail: info@jimwangers.com

See full listing in **Section One** under **Pontiac**

T E Warth Esq Automotive Books   **books**
261 Parker St
Marine on St Croix, MN 55047
651-433-5744; FAX: 651-433-5012
E-mail: tew@bitstream.net

Office open by chance or appointment. Deal in pictorial, history and technical books relating to automobiles, trucks, motorcycles, tractors, models, racing, etc; out of print and rare. No manuals, handbooks or sales literature.

Vic Zannis   **book**
735 Montgomery Hwy Box 337H
Birmingham, AL 35216
205-788-7752
E-mail: viczannis@aol.com

Mail order only. *Rebuilding the Model T Ford Power Plant*, a guide designed to let the owner with average mechanical ability rebuild his own Model T Ford engine and transmission. Includes plans for pouring and line boring bearings and recharging magnets. Price: $23.50 ppd. Web site: http://members.aol.com/viczannis/pages/t-book.htm

Periodicals

America's Most Wanted Publishing   **periodical**
PO Box 17107
Little Rock, AR 72222
501-614-8017
E-mail: amwc1@aol.com

Publishes *America's Most Wanted to Buy* quarterly. Packed with wanted to buy ads from collectors in all areas. Subscription: $9.95/year. Web site: www.mostwantedtobuy.com

Automotive Fine Art Society Journal   **periodical**
PO Box 325
Dept HMN
Lake Orion, MI 48361-0325
PH/FAX: 810-814-0627

The definitive auto art journal. *AFAS Journal* includes trends, auctions, exhibitions and recent print releases. Browse original art by early artists including Helck, Crosby, Ham, Nockolds. Visit private museums, galleries. Profile *AFAS* artists each issue. Regular departments: galleries, where they are; hows and exhibitions, when and where; collectibles. Contributors include David Brownell, B S Levy, Keith Marvin and other great auto writers and experts. Subscription: $24/2 years US; $32/2 years Canada; $36/2 years overseas.

AutoWire.Net   **web site**
PO Box 1011
San Mateo, CA 94403
650-340-8669; FAX: 650-340-9473
E-mail: autowire@pacbell.net

See full listing in **Section Four** under **Information Sources**

Bimmer Magazine   **magazine**
42 Digital Dr #5
Novato, CA 94949
415-382-0580; FAX: 415-382-0587

Bimmer is a full-color magazine about BMWs. Critical reviews and drive reports put you in the driver's seat of these cars, from the latest models to the classics. Each bi-monthly issue brings you everything, good and bad, about BMW. Subscription (6 issues): $14.99/year; $21/year foreign USD.

British Car Magazine   **magazine**
343 Second St, Ste H
Los Altos, CA 94022-3639
650-949-9680; FAX: 650-949-9685
E-mail: editor@britishcar.com

Since 1985. Publish *British Car Magazine* bi-monthly. The only American magazine exclusively for British car enthusiasts, owners, restorers and industry devoted to the use and appreciation of classic and contemporary British cars, including marque profiles, photo essays, history, technical advice, humor, calendars and report on North American events and sources for parts and services. Subscription: $22.95/year US, $26/year Canada; $39.95/two years US, $46/two years Canada.

Cars & Parts Magazine   **periodical**
PO Box 482
Sidney, OH 45365
800-448-3611, 937-498-0803
FAX: 937-498-0808

Cars & Parts is a monthly magazine with full-color editorial features on collector cars, restoration, salvage yards, shows and swap meets, display advertising and large classified ad section with vintage cars, parts and related items for sale and wanted. Subscription: $26.95/year US, $41.95/year foreign; second class: $46.95/year US; first class: $66.95/year foreign, airmail. Web site: www.carsandparts.com

"Check The Oil!" Magazine   **magazine**
PO Box 937
Powell, OH 43065-0937
614-848-5038; FAX: 614-436-4760
E-mail: ctomagazine@aol.com

See full listing in **Section Two** under **petroliana**

Collector Car & Truck Market Guide   **price guide**
41 N Main St
North Grafton, MA 01536
508-839-6707; FAX: 508-839-6266
E-mail: vmr@vmrintl.com

The only complete market guide in the hobby. Editorial features include auction reports and commentary, market analysis and vehicle market profiles. Lists current pricing for over 12,000 1946-1979 domestic and import cars and trucks. Extensive engine, transmission and optional equipment listings for every vehicle. Used worldwide by appraisers, auction firms, insurance and finance firms, investors and enthusiasts. Subscription: $16.95/year. Web site: www.vmrintl.com

Corvette Fever   **periodical**
3816 Industry Blvd
Lakeland, FL 33811
863-644-0449; FAX: 863-648-1187

Magazine with full color feature spreads on Corvettes of every era, Corvette lifestyle, touring and racing coverage, technical data, club news coast-to-coast, parts and service information, Corvette investment values and price guides. Subscription: $24.97/year.

Cruisin' Style Magazine   **magazine**
324 8th Ave W #103
Palmetto, FL 34221
941-729-6669; FAX: 941-729-7773
E-mail: chop48@gte.net

Cruisin' Style is published monthly in Florida with the custom and classic car enthusiast in mind. We feature informative articles on everything related to our hobby, car owners and their toys. Plus we have a section covering all Florida races. Also in each issue: car shows, car clubs, new products, classifieds, business directory, race news and much more. *Cruisin' Style* magazine is the #1 magazine of its type in the southeastern and southwestern United States. Subscription: $14.95/year. Web site: www.cruisinstyle.com

Deals On Wheels
PO Box 205
Sioux Falls, SD 57101
605-338-7666, 800-334-1886 sales
FAX: 605-338-5337

periodical

Monthly publication, *Deals On Wheels*. Buy/sell/trade. Specializing in classics, muscle cars, performance cars, high line imports and exotic cars and sports cars. Ads with photos from across the US and Canada. Subscription: $21.95/year. Web site: www.dealsonwheels.com

EWA & Miniature Cars USA Inc
205 US Hwy 22
Green Brook, NJ 08812-1909
732-424-7811; FAX: 732-424-7814
E-mail: ewa@ewacars.com

books
models
subscriptions
videos

See full listing in **Section Two** under **models & toys**

Excellence Magazine
42 Digital Dr #5
Novato, CA 94949
415-382-0580; FAX: 415-382-0587

magazine

Excellence is a magazine about Porsches. Each full-color issue brings you the latest news and information about Porsche along with technical features. *Excellence* also includes an extensive classified section. Subscription (9 issues): $23/year; $36/year foreign USD.

Forza Magazine
42 Digital Dr #5
Novato, CA 94949
415-382-0580; FAX: 415-382-0587

magazine

Forza is a magazine about Ferraris, and is published eight times a year. Each full color issue is packed with the latest Ferrari news and information from around the world. Subscription (8 issues): $24.95/year; $35/year foreign USD.

Grassroots Motorsports
555 W Granada Blvd, Ste B-9
Ormond Beach, FL 32174
386-673-4148; FAX: 386-673-6040
E-mail: grmhq@aol.com

periodical

Glossy, colorful national publication *Grassroots Motorsports*, for amateur motor sports enthusiasts. Autocross rally vintage and road race news, events, personalities and car preparation tips. Published bi-monthly. Free sample copy. Subscription: $14.97/year. Web site: www.grmotorsports.com

Hemmings Motor News
PO Box 100
Bennington, VT 05201
1-800-CAR-HERE, ext 550
802-447-9550
E-mail: hmnmail@hemmings.com

The monthly "bible" of the collector-car hobby

"The bible" of the collector-car hobby, monthly trading place, 98% paid hobby advertising with world's largest paid circulation to old car hobbyists (nearly 246,000) and publishing world's largest number of hobby advertisements and special-interest collector cars, trucks, motorcycles, custom cars, &c, plus parts, literature, services, automobile, etc, without limitations. One year subscriptions: Fourth class mail: $28.95 USA; $58 Canada. First class mail: $72 USA; $90 Canada; $96 Mexico. US funds only. Airmail to other countries (inquire for current rates). Wholesale terms available. Visitors welcome at HMN Sunoco Filling Station/Book Store/Gift Shop, 7 am to 10 pm everyday but Christmas. Web site: www.hemmings.com

Hemmings Rods & Performance
PO Box 2000
Bennington, VT 05201
1-800-CAR-HERE, ext 550
802-447-9550; FAX: 802-447-1561
E-mail: hmnmail@hemmings.com

periodical

A bi-monthly magazine with a unique one-stop marketplace for

street rod, racing, and performance enthusiasts. Each issue is jam-packed with extensive cars and parts classified ads, display advertising, latest aftermarket performance products, informative tech articles and how-to's, products, services, and web directories. One year (6 issues) subscription: $17.95 USA, $23.95 Canada, $48.00 Mexico. US funds only. Web site: www.rodsandperformance.com

La Vie de l'Auto Elvea
BP 424
77309 Fontainebleau Cedex France
01-331-60-715555
FAX: 01-331-60-72-22-37
E-mail: lva@elvea.fr

magazine

The leader of the French classic car magazines. Every week it contains everything you have to know when you own a classic car: events, news and a lot of ads to buy or sell anything about cars; about 50 pages. Subscription: 560 francs/year.

Late Great Chevrolet Association
Robert Snowden
PO Box 607824
Orlando, FL 32860
407-886-1963; FAX: 407-886-7571
E-mail: info@lategreatchevy.com

magazine

Mail order and open shop. Monday-Friday 8 am to 5 pm. Dedicated to the restoration and preservation of all 1955-1972 Chevrolets. Specializing in 1955-1972 Chevrolet parts and monthly magazine publication, *Chevy Times*, approx 40-pg, color/b-w. The magazine displays our members' automobiles along with their story. Also provides restoration help, club events, general information on events around the US. Subscription: $40/year second class, $50/year first class, $64/year airmail. Web site: www.lategreatchevy.com

The Latest Scoop-Auto Enthusiast Magazine
PO Box 7477
Loveland, CO 80537-0477
970-686-6155
E-mail: scoopautoevents@aol.com

periodical

Handy guide for automotive enthusiasts and businesses providing you with the most up-to-date information on car-related events taking place in the Rocky Mountain Region of CO, WY, NE, KS, OK, TX, NM, AZ and UT. Published 9 times a year. Send for free sample issue. Visa, MasterCard and American Express accepted. Subscription: $12/year, $23/2 years, outside US add $8 per year.

Mopar Collector's Guide Magazine
PO Box 15489
Baton Rouge, LA 70895-5489
225-274-0609; FAX: 225-274-9033
E-mail: mopar@intersurf.com

magazine

See full listing in **Section One** under **Mopar**

Mopar Muscle
3816 Industry Blvd
Lakeland, FL 33811
863-644-0449; FAX: 863-648-1187

periodical

Magazine features articles and photos on the mighty Mopars of lore and legend. From Hemi, six-pack, Roadrunner and Super Bee to Darts, Demons and Dusters, plus how-to help, technical info, parts and service sources, restoration and repair data, buying tips, news on Mopar events nationwide and more. Subscription: $24.97/year, 12 issues.

Musclecar Review
3816 Industry Blvd
Lakeland, FL 33811
863-644-0449; FAX: 863-648-1187

periodical

Puts the latest Detroit iron against the earth-shaking muscle cars of the past, or takes readers' favorite cars to the track for "shootouts and showdowns". Plus loads of restoration, repair and maintenance information, parts and service sources, news on national muscle car events and more. Subscription: $24.97/year.

Mustang Monthly
3816 Industry Blvd
Lakeland, FL 33811
863-644-0449; FAX: 863-648-1187

magazine

America's first, and only, monthly Mustang magazine brings you coast-to-coast coverage on the best original and restored Mustangs in the country, with exciting full color feature articles and photos, technical and how-to help, news on all the major Mustang clubs and car shows, plus parts and service sources, classifieds and more. Monthly magazine, $24.97/year.

N-News Magazine
PO Box 275
East Corinth, VT 05040

magazine

See full listing in **Section Two** under **trucks & tractors**

Old Cars Weekly & Old Cars Price Guide
700 E State St
Iola, WI 54481
715-445-2214; FAX: 715-445-4087

periodical
price guide

Publishes *Old Cars Weekly News & Marketplace* weekly, $39.98 per year. Covers the entire field of collectible autos. Includes historical perspectives, reports on attractions and shows, technical information and hobby news. Also publishes *Old Cars Price Guide* bi-monthly, $19.98 per year. The nation's most respected authority for valuing antique and collectible automobiles. Includes years from 1901-1994. Web site: www.oldcarsweekly.com

Petroleum Collectibles Monthly
PO Box 556
LaGrange, OH 44050
440-355-6608; FAX: 440-355-4955

periodical

Publication: *Petroleum Collectibles Monthly*. Most comprehensive magazine covering all aspects of collecting gas pumps, globes, signs, cans, etc. Auctions, ads, historical, discoveries, color photos, Q&A and more. Subscription: $29.95/year US, $38.50/year Canada, $65.95/year international. Web site: www.pcmpublishing.com

PTE Publishing
1975 Ripplerock Rd
Fort Mill, SC 29715
PH/FAX: 803-547-4585
E-mail: starpieces@rmtc.net

magazine

See full listing in **Section Four** under **information sources**

Recycler Classifieds
2898 Rowena Ave
Los Angeles, CA 90039
323-668-1220; FAX: 323-665-3157

classified
publications

Published weekly, on sale at over 7,000 locations in southern California. *Auto Buys*, photo classified publication featuring thousands of autos, parts and accessories; subscription rate: $1.75. *Truck Buys*, photo classified publication featuring thousands of trucks, parts and accessories; subscription rate: $1.75. *RV Buys*, leading photo publication featuring RVs, parts and accessories; subscription rate: $1. *Cycle Buys*, leading photo classified publication featuring thousands of motorcycles, parts and accessories categorized by year, make and model; subscrip-

tion rate: $1.50. *Boat Buys*, leading photo classified publication featuring thousands of boats, parts and accessories; subscription rate: $1. Web site: www.recycler.com

Retroviseur
Chateau de la Magdeleine
77920 Samois s/Seine France
(01) 331-60-71-55-55
FAX: (01) 331-60-72-22-37
E-mail: retrovis@elvea.fr

periodical

Retroviseur is a monthly publication specializing in classic cars; four-color, about 150 pages, news, various features, ads. Subscription: 455 francs/year.

Rollin' Review Magazine
PO Box 910
Alcoa, TN 37701
800-434-4132; FAX: 865-681-0174
E-mail: editorrrm@aol.com

magazine

Publishes *Rollin' Review* magazine monthly, $23.75 per year. Best list of car and truck show schedules east of Kansas. Rides for sale and show coverage of two to three shows in each publication. Street rods, customs, classic cars and trucks for sale at web site: www.rollinreview.com

Skinned Knuckles
175 May Ave
Monrovia, CA 91016
626-358-6255
E-mail: skpubs@earthlink.net

periodical

A monthly publication devoted to the restoration, operation and maintenance of all authentic collector vehicles. Subscription: $22/year domestic, $25/year foreign.

Southern Wheels Magazine
6739 Ringgold Rd #B
Chattanooga, TN 37412
423-899-4300
FAX: 706-375-7711, GA
E-mail: sowheels@aol.com

magazine

Southern Wheels Magazine is a monthly magazine for restorers and car builders. Your source for parts and services, plus restoration articles and tech tips. Monthly car quiz. Published by restoration specialist Bill Johnson. Subscription: $9.99/year. Web site: www.southernwheels.com

Special Interest Autos
PO Box 196
Bennington, VT 05201
1-800-CAR-HERE, ext 550
802-447-9550; FAX: 802-447-1561
E-mail: hmnmail@hemmings.com

periodical

A bi-monthly magazine featuring collector cars and trucks from 1900-1990. In-depth, thoroughly researched articles and road tests. Over 100 photos in each issue. Authoritative information throughout. Most back issues available. One year (6 issues) subscription, $19.95 US, $21.95 foreign. Ask about our retail dealer program. Wholesale terms available. To view sample articles, visit our web site: www.hemmings.com

Specialty Car Marketplace
PO Box 205
Sioux Falls, SD 57101
605-338-7666, 800-334-1886 sales;
FAX: 605-338-5337

periodical

Monthly publication, *Specialty Car Marketplace*. Buy/sell/trade. Ads with photos featuring hot rods, street rods, customs, pro street, race cars and more. Ads in black and white and four color from across the US and Canada. Subscription: $12.95/year. Web site: www.dealsonwheels.com

Sports Car International
42 Digital Dr #5
Novato, CA 94949
415-382-0580; FAX: 415-382-0587

magazine

Sports Car International is a full color magazine featuring performance and sports cars from around the world. The critical reviews give you a unique perspective on each car. News reports keep you abreast of the latest information on the cars you want to hear about, not minivans. Subscription (6 issues): $14.99/year; $21/year foreign USD.

TheAlternate
PO Box 239-393
Grantville, PA 17028-0239
717-469-0777; FAX: 717-469-1388
E-mail: thealternate@racepaper.com

periodical

A chronicle of 20th century motor racing history. Subscriptions: $21/12 monthly issues or $41/24 monthly issues.

This Old Truck Magazine
PO Box 500
Missouri City, TX 77459
888-760-8108 subscriptions
937-767-1433 publishing office
FAX: 937-767-2726
E-mail: antique@antiquepower.com

magazine

Devoted to the preservation of all makes and vintages of antique trucks, station wagons, pickups and commercial vehicles. Includes color photos, restoration tips, truck company history, plus free classified ads for subscribers. Publishes *This Old Truck* bi-monthly. Subscription: $26.95/year US and Canada, $41.95/year foreign. Web site: www.thisoldtruck.com

**Transport Books
at DRB Motors Inc**
16 Elrose Ave
Toronto, ON Canada M9M 2H6
800-665-2665, 416-744-7675
FAX: 416-744-7696
E-mail: info@transportbooks.com

books
manuals
periodicals
videos

See full listing in **Section Four** under **books & publications**

Truck, Race, Cycle and Rec
PO Box 205
Sioux Falls, SD 57101
605-338-7666, 800-334-1886
FAX: 605-338-5337

periodical

Monthly publication, *Truck, Race, Cycle & Rec*. Buy/sell/trade. Specializing in trucks, 4x4s, SUVs, motorcycles, ATVs, boats, recreational vehicles and repairable trucks and cars. Ads with photos from across the US and Canada. Subscription: $15.95/year. Web site: www.dealsonwheels.com

Vette Vues Magazine
PO Box 741596
Orange City, FL 32774
386-775-8454; FAX: 386-775-3042
E-mail: comments@vettevues.com

magazine

Publishes *Vette Vues* magazine monthly, Corvette related magazine. Subscription: $21.95/year. Web site: www.vette-vues.com

Victory Lane
2460 Park Blvd #4
Palo Alto, CA 94306
650-321-1411; FAX: 650-321-4426
E-mail: victory@best.com

periodical

Monthly news magazine covering vintage auto racing in US and international. Features include race reports with results, columns by insiders, technical articles, event schedules, vintage race car classifieds, marque histories, collector car stories and more. Subscription: $39.95/year. Web site: www.victorylane.com

Newsletters

**1956 Studebaker Golden Hawk
Owners Register**
31700 Wekiva River Rd
Sorrento, FL 32776-9233
E-mail: 56sghor@prodigy.net

information
exchange

See full listing in **Section One** under **Studebaker**

The 60 Oldsmobile Club
Dick Major
10895 E Hibma Rd
Tustin, MI 49688
616-825-2891; FAX: 616-825-8324
E-mail: dmajor@netonecom.net

newsletter

See full listing in **Section One** under **Oldsmobile**

AutoWire.Net
PO Box 1011
San Mateo, CA 94403
650-340-8669; FAX: 650-340-9473
E-mail: autowire@pacbell.net

web site

See full listing in **Section Four** under **Information Sources**

**Eastern New York MGA Club
Newsletter**
Jon Rubel, President
3010 Avenue T
Brooklyn, NY 11229-4008
718-891-5776; FAX: call first
E-mail: eemgee@aol.com

publication

Catering to owners of all MGs in the NY, NJ, PA and CT area. Bi-monthly award winning 30-page newsletter is really a magazine. It includes four pages in full color, superb technical and restoration articles, human interest stories, editorials, letters to the editor, coverage of local car events and tech sessions, complete calendar of events covering the Northeast and more. Subscription included with annual club membership of $20.

International Ford History Project
PO Box 11415
Olympia, WA 98508
360-754-9585
E-mail: ifhp@aol.com

newsletter

The International Ford History Project was founded in 1997 and publishes *The Universal Car* on an occasional basis. The purpose of the IFHP and its newsletter is to promote fellowship and the international free flow of information among those interested in the development of the Ford Motor Company and its products worldwide. Subscription: $10/year for 4 issues, $14/year outside US and Canada.

Mercedes-Benz Market Letter aka SL Market Letter 2020 Girard Ave S Minneapolis, MN 55405 612-377-0155; FAX: 612-377-0157 E-mail: slmarket@aol.com	**newsletter**

Specializes in Mercedes-Benz special models only. Especially SL Models 1954-1996 and SLC, SEC. All convertibles, coupes and 6.3, 6.9 and 600. Subscription based collation of price trends, restoration and parts sources and rare Mercedes-Benz models offered for sale. Now in 19th year. Subscription: $89 for 18 issues; $49/trial subscription of 9 issues. Web site: www.slmarket.com

Research & Reference Libraries

AACA Library & Research Center 501 W Governor Rd PO Box 417 Hershey, PA 17033 717-534-2082; FAX: 717-534-9101 E-mail: libraryaaca@aol.com	**research library**

Open Monday-Friday 8:30 am to 3:45 pm. Library located adjacent to AACA National Headquarters. Collection contains books, periodicals, sales literature, manuals, wiring diagrams, paint chips, etc, 1895-present. Web site: www.aaca.org

ARS Automotive Research Services Division of Auto Search International 1702 W Camelback #301 Phoenix, AZ 85015 602-230-7111; FAX: 602-230-7282	**appraisals research**

See full listing in **Section Two** under **appraisals**

Automobile Reference Collection Free Library of Philadelphia 1901 Vine St Philadelphia, PA 19103-1189 215-686-5404; FAX: 215-686-5426 E-mail: refarc@library.phila.gov	**information source**

Open year round. Monday-Friday 9 am to 5 pm . Major collection of automotive literature located in one of the country's major public libraries. Web site: www.library.phila.gov

AutoWire.Net PO Box 1011 San Mateo, CA 94403 650-340-8669; FAX: 650-340-9473 E-mail: autowire@pacbell.net	**web site**

See full listing in **Section Four** under **Information Sources**

Beamish, The North of England Open Air Museum Beamish County Durham DH9 0RG England E-mail: museum@beamish.org.uk	**0191 370 4000 FAX: 0191 370 4001**

See full listing in **Section Six** under **England**

Car Critic 202 Woodshire Ln Naples, FL 34105 941-435-1157; FAX: 941-261-4864 E-mail: carcritic@earthlink.net	**appraisals inspections**

See full listing in **Section Two** under **car & parts locators**

Clean Air Performance Professionals (CAPP) 84 Hoy Ave Fords, NJ 08863 732-738-7859; FAX: 732-738-7625 E-mail: stellacapp@earthlink.net	**legislative watch organization**

See full listing in **Section Three** under **legislative watch organizations**

Collector Car & Truck Market Guide 41 N Main St North Grafton, MA 01536 508-839-6707; FAX: 508-839-6266 E-mail: vmr@vmrintl.com	**price guide**

See full listing in **Section Four** under **periodicals**

Robert DeMars Ltd Auto Appraisers/Historians 222 Lakeview Ave, Ste 160/256 West Palm Beach, FL 33401 561-832-0171; FAX: 561-738-5284 E-mail: carapraisr@aol.com	**appraisals auto historians auto locating research library resto consultants**

See full listing in **Section Two** under **appraisals**

Dodge City Vintage Dodge Vehicles & Parts PO Box 1687 18584 Hwy 108 Jamestown, CA 95327 209-984-5858; FAX: 209-984-3285 E-mail: mike@dodgecityvintage.com	**parts restoration research vehicles**

See full listing in **Section One** under **Dodge**

Section Four – Publications

Ralph Dunwoodie Research and Information 5935 Calico Dr Sun Valley, NV 89433-6910 775-673-3811	research information

Car and truck histories researched. Extensive library from 1895-present. Research of all phases of automobile and truck information for writers, restorers, historians and enthusiasts.

Duncan F Holmes 493 King Philip St Fall River, MA 02724 508-672-0071	research library

Automotive research library. GM, Ford, Chrysler, all independent manufacturers of 1949-1967 model years, earlier years on some cars. Over 8,000 original magazine and newspaper ads on file. Over 500 original owner's manuals, over 500 original dealer's sales catalogs. New items constantly being added. Duplicate items offered for sale. Can Xerox most items at nominal cost.

Horseless Carriage Foundation Inc 8186 Center St, Ste F La Mesa, CA 91942 619-464-0301; FAX: 619-464-0361 E-mail: hcfi@aol.com	research library

Automotive research library. We are an independent 501(c)(3) organization serving auto hobbyists worldwide. Our specialty is the 1895-1942 period. We have factory sales catalogues, owner's manuals, parts catalogues and promotional material. We feature a computerized index to information in early auto trade periodicals. America's most user friendly source. Web site: www.hcfi.org

International Motor Racing Research Center at Watkins Glen 610 S Decatur St Watkins Glen, NY 14891 607-535-9044; FAX: 607-535-9039 E-mail: research@racingarchives.org	research

A research facility dedicated to the collection and preservaton of material documenting the rich heritage of amateur and professional motor racing. Quarterly publication, *From the Racing Archives*. Subscription: $25 donation. Museum is open all year Monday-Saturday 9 am to 5 pm. Closed Christmas and New Year's Day. Web site: www.racingarchives.org

Jersey Late Greats Inc PO Box 1294 Hightstown, NJ 08520 609-448-0526	documentation service restoration details

See full listing in **Section One** under **Chevrolet**

MPH Interactive Designs 7766 W 450 S Williamsport, IN 47993 765-491-9604; FAX: 765-893-4017 E-mail: park@mphinteractive.net	photography research writing

See full listing in **Section Four** under **information sources**

Reynolds-Alberta Museum Box 6360 (1km West on Hwy 13) Wetaskiwin, AB Canada T9A 2G1 800-661-4726, 403-361-1351 FAX: 403-361-1239 E-mail: ram@gov.ab.ca (museum general) sean.moir@gov.ab.ca (library)	museum

See full listing in **Section Six** under **Canada**

Rolls-Royce Foundation 505 Fishing Creek Rd Lewisberry, PA 17339 717-932-9900; FAX: 717-932-9925 E-mail: rds@flightsystems.com	library literature museum

See full listing in **Section One** under **Rolls-Royce/Bentley**

Alfred P Sloan Museum 1221 E Kearsley St Flint, MI 48503 810-237-3450; FAX: 810-237-3451	museum

See full listing in **Section Six** under **Michigan**

Chris Smith's Creative Workshop Motorcar Restoration 118 NW Park St Dania, FL 33004 954-920-3303; FAX: 954-920-9950 E-mail: restor1st@aol.com	parts restoration service

See full listing in **Section Two** under **restoration shops**

Topper Luback Historical Library 458 W 14th St 2A Chicago Heights, IL 60411 708-481-9685; FAX: 708-481-5837 E-mail: partsneed@aol.com	library

Mail order only. Replacement OEM genuine parts, specializing 1959-1965. Research publications for a nominal charge, retail sales only. Scooter literature including service manual, parts catalog, owners manual, keys cut from code or from original lock.

Section Five
Salvage Yards

67 listings

Sometimes the search is just as interesting as the item sought, and for those who'd like to track down a car or a needed part where it was once laid to rest, the *Almanac* presents this state-by-state listing of salvage yards. Check the individual listings for era or marque specialties. Many of the yards will not ship parts and require a personal visit. Be sure to phone ahead or check business hours carefully before making a long drive, as some of the yards operate on irregular schedules.

Alabama

Vintage Automobiles 1261 Old Hackleburg Rd Hackleburg, AL 35564	205-935-3649

Mail order and open by appointment only. 1930-1948 Ford parts. 1933-1952 Dodge parts, mainly original running gear parts. Some body parts, mechanical parts, wheels, transmissions, etc.

Alaska

Binder's Auto Restoration & Salvage 1 Mile Maud Rd, PO Box 1144 Palmer, AK 99645	907-745-4670 FAX: 907-745-5510

Mail order, SASE required. Salvage yard open by appointment only. Specializing in 1960-present Cadillac cars only. Complete line of used parts and some NOS. No part too small. Shipping worldwide. MasterCard and Visa accepted. Complete and partial restorations. Car transporting local and long distance. Please call between 6-9 pm local time for free advice.

Arizona

Desert Valley Auto Parts 22500 N 21st Ave Phoenix, AZ 85027 E-mail: rust-free-parts@worldnet.att.net	800-905-8024 602-780-8024 FAX: 602-582-9141

Mail order and open shop. Monday-Friday 8 am to 5:30 pm, Saturday 8 am to 2 pm. Rust-free Arizona parts. 80 full acres of classic and hard to find parts or cars for restoration projects, from the 1950s to the 1980s. Quality parts, dependable service and competitive prices guaranteed. New classics arrive daily to our existing inventory of thousands. Daily shipping worldwide via UPS and freight. No part too large or too small. Visa/MasterCard accepted. Web site: www.dvap.com

See our ad on page 578

Hoctor's Hidden Valley Auto Parts 21046 N Rio Bravo Rd Maricopa, AZ 85239	520-568-2945 602-252-2122 602-252-6137 FAX: 602-258-0951

Mail order and open shop. Monday-Friday 8 am to 5 pm, Saturday 9 am to 3 pm. 80 acres of rust-free foreign and American autos and trucks. Just over 8,000 cars for parts. From 1920s-1980s, mostly 1950s, 1960s. Also 2 other Phoenix stores for convenience. Shipping worldwide. Send specific list of needs w/SASE or call.

Revolvstore The Volvo Place 5275 E Drexel Rd Tucson, AZ 85706 E-mail: revolvstore@revolvstore.com	800-288-6586 FAX: 520-574-3629

All Volvos, all the time. Specializing in new, used and rebuilt Volvo parts, sales and service. All of our used parts backed by a 6 month/6,000 mile warranty. Web site: www.revolvstore.com

Wiseman's Auto Salvage 900 W Cottonwood Ln Casa Grande, AZ 85222	PH/FAX: 520-836-7960

Mail order and open shop. Monday-Friday 8 am to 5:30 pm, Saturday 9 am to 1 pm. Arizona desert salvage yard. 2,500 cars and trucks for parts. All types of auto and truck parts. Good, used, guaranteed. 1920s-1970s. Browsers welcome. Sale of used auto and truck parts. SASE please. MasterCard, Visa, Discover card. Web site: www.wisemansalvage.com

California

A&A Auto Parts & Sales PO Box 72 Brentwood, CA 94513-0072 e-mail:gar@1800caddys1.com	925-634-1188 FAX: 925-634-1949

Mail order and open shop. Monday-Friday 7:30 am to 5 pm, Saturday 8 am to 2 pm. Specializing in parts, sales and service for Cadillac all years from 1940 to the present. Web site: www.1800caddys1.com

American Auto & Truck Dismantlers 12172 Truman St San Fernando, CA 91340	818-365-3908

Mail order and open shop. Monday-Friday 8:30 am to 5 pm, Saturday 9 am to 4 pm. Salvage yard specializing in 1955-1957 Chev cars; 1958-1989 all GM cars and trucks; 1967-1989 Camaros; 1964-1972 Chevelles.

Buick Bonery 6970 Stamper Way Sacramento, CA 95828	916-381-5271 FAX: 916-381-0702

See full listing in **Section One** under **Buick/McLaughlin**

Pearson's Auto Dismantling & **Used Cars** 2343 Hwy 49 Mariposa, CA 95338	209-742-7442

Open Friday-Saturday only 8:30 am to 5:30 pm. A G Pearson, owner. Specializing in all cars 1959 and older. Also has some 1959 and newer used cars and parts in stock. Enclose an SASE.

Colorado

Steering Systems Disivion of A-1 Shock Absorber Co 365 Warren Ave, PO Box 2028 Silverthorne, CO 80498	800-344-1966 Cell 970-389-3193 FAX: 970-513-8283

See our ad on the last page

Connecticut

Mostly Mustangs Inc 55 Alling St Hamden, CT 06517	**203-562-8804** **FAX: 203-562-4891**

See full listing in **Section One** under **Mustang**

Royals' Garage 16-24 Calhoun St Torrington, CT 06790	**860-489-4500**

See full listing in **Section One** under **Corvette**

Leo Winakor and Sons Inc 470 Forsyth Rd Salem, CT 06420	**860-859-0471**

Open Saturday-Sunday 10 am to 2 pm. Specializing in old car parts 1926-1987.

Florida

Anderson Automotive 1604 E Busch Blvd Tampa, FL 33612	**813-932-4611** **FAX: 813-932-5025**

See full listing in **Section One** under **Oldsmobile**

Collectors Choice Antique Auto Parts PO Box 7605 Sarasota, FL 34278 E-mail: choiceparts@home.com	**941-923-4514**

Located in Sarasota, Florida. All makes and models of American cars, 1930s-up.

Mustang Village 8833 Fowler Ave Pensacola, FL 32534 E-mail: rmcneal@aol.com	**850-477-8056** **FAX: 850-484-4244**

Specializing in Mustangs 1964-1/2 and up.

Georgia

Bayless Inc 1111 Via Bayless Marietta, GA 30066-2770 E-mail: baylessfiat@mindspring.com	**770-928-1446** **FAX: 770-928-1342** **800-241-1446** **order line US & Canada**

See full listing in **Section One** under **Fiat**

Old Car City USA 3098 Hwy 411 NE White, GA 30184	**770-382-6141** **FAX: 770-387-2122**

Est 1931. Call for time. Selling all restorable cars, pickups. Pre-1972 all American cars. Also parts cars. Videos of OCC USA, $19.95 plus $3 s&h.

Illinois

Gus Miller Box 604 Heyworth, IL 61745	**PH/FAX:** **309-473-2979**

Open by appointment only. 10 acres of cars and parts from the forties, fifties and sixties for sale. All FOB. No mail orders.

Indiana

Webb's Classic Auto Parts 5084 W State Rd 114 Huntington, IN 46750	**219-344-1714** **FAX: 219-344-1754**

See full listing in **Section One** under **AMC**

Section Five – Salvage Yards

Iowa

Van Horn Auto Parts Inc
Rt 4 20966 Monroe St
Mason City, IA 50401
E-mail: vanhornautoparts@hotmail.com

641-423-0655
FAX: 641-423-2570

Open Monday-Saturday. Over 2,000 1975 and newer cars and light trucks in stock. Web site: www.vanhornautoparts.com

Kansas

**Easy Jack & Sons Antique
Auto Parts Store**
2725 S Milford Lake Rd
Junction City, KS 66441-8446

785-238-7541
785-238-7161
FAX: 785-238-8714

Open Monday-Friday 8 am to 5:30 pm, Saturday 8 am to 2 pm CST. Specializing in 1912-1985 parts and vehicles. Over 80 different makes and brands available. Store and yard covers over twenty acres. Hundreds of restorable vehicles. Millions of parts. Buying and selling antique and collector type vehicles and parts since 1963. Located six miles west of Junction City on Interstate #70, at Milford Lake Road exit #290. We accept MasterCard/Visa/Discover. SASE for more information.

Bob Lint Motor Shop
101 Main St, PO Box 87
Danville, KS 67036

316-962-5247

Mail order and open shop. Monday-Friday 8 am to 5 pm, Saturday 8 am to 12 pm. Thousands of parts, mostly Ford and Chevrolet, Plymouth, Buick, Studebaker, A and T Fords, lots of truck parts. Many 1920s and 1930s wire wheels, old car parts, also tires. Many old car radiators & hubcaps. Also have complete old cars and trucks, NOS tires, used transmissions, rear ends, motors, brake shoes, generators & starters, etc. In business for 45 years same location.

Louisiana

Fannaly's Auto Exchange
41403 S Range Rd, PO Box 23
Ponchatoula, LA 70454

504-386-3714

Mail order and shop open by appointment. Approximately 400 parts cars. Cadillacs, Buicks 1939-1970, Mopar, NOS parts, obsolete marques, Blue Crown spark plugs. Antique and contemporary cars and trucks. Antique parts, both used and NOS.

Maine

Classic Ford Sales
PO Box 60
East Dixfield, ME 04227
E-mail: classicford@quickconnect.com

207-562-4443
FAX: 207-562-4576

Mail order and open shop. Monday-Friday 9 am to 5 pm, closed Saturday. Ford products only, 1949-1972 full size, Thunderbird, Lincoln, Mercury, Falcon, Fairlane, Comet, F100, quality used parts with some NOS. Web site: www.classicford.com

Maryland

Driving Passion Ltd USA
Marc Tuwiner
7132 Chilton Ct
Clarksville, MD 21029
E-mail: mt.tees@erols.com

PH/FAX:
301-596-9078

See full listing in **Section One** under **Cadillac/LaSalle**

Massachusetts

R E Pierce
47 Stone Rd
Wendell Depot, MA 01380
E-mail: robin@billsgate.com

978-544-7442
FAX: 978-544-2978

See full listing in **Section One** under **Volvo**

Michigan

Michigan Corvette Recyclers
11995 US 223
Riga, MI 49276

800-533-4650
FAX: 517-486-4124

See full listing in **Section One** under **Corvette**

Minnesota

Bill's Auto Parts
310 7th Ave
Newport, MN 55055

612-459-9733

Mail order and open shop. Monday-Friday 8 am to 5:30 pm, Saturday 8 am to 12 pm. Auto parts dismantling and recycling. Used parts only, all years, makes and models 1930-1980s.

Doug's Auto Parts
900 North Hwy 59, PO Box 811
Marshall, MN 56258

507-537-1488
FAX: 507-537-0519

Doug's Auto Parts, Douglas J Mosch, owner. Celebrating 25 years in business, 1973-1998. Specializing in 1949-1953 Mercurys, 1928-1959 Fords, 1937-1969 Chevys. Many good complete restorable cars including coupes and convertibles. Buick, Olds, Pontiac and others included. We like solid and rust-free cars like everyone else does. Also gas pumps, both visible and electric, old signs, other collectibles.

Missouri

J & M Vintage Auto
2 Mi W Goodman on B Hwy
Goodman, MO 64843

417-364-7203

Open Tuesday-Friday 8 am to 5 pm, Saturday 8 am to 3 pm, closed Sunday-Monday. 1,600 cars, 1930-1972. Customers may browse unassisted.

Montana

Freman's Auto
138 Kountz Rd
Whitehall, MT 59759

406-287-5436
FAX: 406-287-9103

See full listing in **Section Two** under **car dealers**

Medicine Bow Motors Inc
343 One Horse Creek Rd
Florence, MT 59833

406-273-0002

See full listing in **Section Two** under **car dealers**

New Hampshire

Parts of the Past
Rt 2, Box 118A
Canaan, NH 03741

603-523-4524
FAX:
603-523-4524 *49

Mail order and open shop. Monday-Friday, weekends by appointment. 1924-72 General Motors, Ford, Mopar, Hudson, Kaiser-Fraser, Edsel, Graham, Mercury, Nash, Packard, Studebaker, Lincoln, LaSalle parts. "If I don't have it, I will try to find it." Sale of parts, pieces and whole cars and restorable antiques.

New Jersey

Unique Auto & Truck LLC
470 Chandler Rd
Jackson, NJ 08527
E-mail: uniqueauto@hotmail.com

732-363-0677
Cell: 973-332-5130

Mail order and open shop. Monday-Saturday dawn to dusk. Vintage, collector and special interest cars and trucks, parts or whole. Over 250 Cadillacs plus 13 acres of Lincolns, muscle, Mopar, Jeep, Ford, GM and orphan cars. Foreign includes but not limited to: Mercedes-Benz, BMW and VW. Supporting member of 20 clubs and organizations, national and local.

Section Five – Salvage Yards

New Mexico

Discount Auto Parts 4703 Broadway SE Albuquerque, NM 87105	505-877-6782

Mail order and open shop. Monday-Friday 8 am to 5:30 pm. Salvage yard. Specialist in Volkswagen and Audi.

Route 66 Reutilization 1357 Historic Rt 66 E Tijeras, NM 87059	505-286-2222 FAX: 505-281-6555

Storage yard. Sell vintage autos and trucks, parts and Route 66 memorabilia.

New York

Adler's Antique Autos Inc 801 NY Rt 43 Stephentown, NY 12168 E-mail: advdesign1@aol.com	518-733-5749

Over 600 1935-1980 Chevrolets. Specializing in 1947-55 Chevrolet Advance Design trucks. Parts vehicles and restoration projects, shipping service available. Browsers welcome to the outdoor museum. Complete restoration facility. All work and parts guaranteed. Towing available. In business over 27 years.

Elmer's Auto Parts Inc 137 Donovan St Webster, NY 14580	716-872-4402 FAX: 716-872-2519

See full listing in **Section One** under **Corvette**.

Halpin Used Auto & Truck Parts 1093 Rt 123 Mayfield, NY 12117 E-mail: junkyard2064@webtv.net	518-863-4906

Mail order and open shop. Monday-Saturday 8 am to 4 pm. We deal in used and NOS auto and truck parts, 1930-present. We ship UPS and deliver. If we don't have it, we will try to locate it for you. No part too small, we sell anything you need. Large selection of taillights, all years. In business since 1972.

Reardon Enterprises Box 1633, Rt 28 Mohawk, NY 13407	315-866-3072

Mail order and open shop. Weekends and evenings open 24 hours. Large selection of 1928-1960 GM parts cars, plus oddballs. Trucks too. Antique motorcycles, gas pumps, oil filters, fan belts, memorabilia. Cars bought and traded as well as antique snowmobiles.

Tucker's Auto Salvage Raymond A Tucker 5121 St Rt 11 Burke, NY 12917	518-483-5478

Open Monday-Friday 8 am to 5 pm, Saturday 8 am to 12 pm. Cars and parts, sandblasting, body and mechanical restoration.

Ohio

Alotta Auto Parts 8426 Upper Miamisburg Rd Miamisburg, OH 45342 E-mail: unc8426joe@aol.com	937-866-1849 FAX: 937-866-6431

Mail order and open shop. Monday-Friday 8:30 am to 5 pm, Saturday 8:30 am to 2 pm. Six acre salvage yard with cars and parts. Specializing in 1950s and 1960s autos and light trucks. NOS and used parts. COD shipping available.

Oklahoma

Aabar's Cadillac & Lincoln Salvage & Parts 9700 NE 23rd St Oklahoma City, OK 73141 E-mail: aabar@ilinkusa.net	405-769-3318 FAX: 405-769-9542

See full listing in **Section One** under **Cadillac/LaSalle**

East West Auto Parts Inc 4605 Dawson Rd Tulsa, OK 74115	800-447-2886 FAX: 918-832-7900

Mail order only. All General Motors parts: Pontiac, Chevrolet, Oldsmobile, Buick, Cadillac and GMC. Have a 17 acre facility with over 950 cars and trucks ranging in years from 1946-1988. Also have parts for European imports: Saab, Volvo, Volkswagen and Opel. Oklahoma based mail order business with over 50 years of combined experience. Ship parts anywhere. Sorry, no catalogs. Credit cards accepted. Web site: www.eastwestautoparts.com

Hauf Antique & Classic Cars & Pickups PO Box 547 Stillwater, OK 74076	405-372-1585 FAX: 405-372-1586

Open Tuesday-Friday 8 am to 5 pm, weekends by appointment. Specialize in classic, antique cars and pickups.

North Yale Auto Parts Rt 1, Box 707 Sperry, OK 74073	918-288-7218 800-256-6927 (NYAP) FAX: 918-288-7223

Mail order and open shop. Monday-Friday 8 am to 5 pm. Specializes in 1950-1980s Chevys, Chryslers, Fords, Cadillac. New and used body fillers for most GM cars. Nationwide parts locating of new, used, aftermarket parts, ask for Bobby.

Oregon

Rapido Group 80093 Dodson Rd Tygh Valley, OR 97063	541-544-3333 FAX: 541-544-3100

See full listing in **Section One** under **Merkur**

Pennsylvania

Barton Auto Wrecking 175 School Dr Waynesburg, PA 15370 E-mail: bartons@greenepa.net	724-627-3351

Open Monday-Friday 8 am to 5 pm EST, Saturday 8 am to 2 pm, closed Sundays. Our salvage yard specializes in foreign and domestic automobiles from the 1970s, 1980s and 1990s. We are located 50 miles south of Pittsburgh and have been a family owned business since 1937. As 3rd generation salvage yard operators, we are well known for our fast, friendly and courteous customer service. At Barton Auto Wrecking no part is too big or too small. Feel free to take advantage of our new e-mail and web page. Web site: www.bartonautowrecking.com

Corvair Ranch Inc 1079 Bon-Ox Rd Gettysburg, PA 17325	717-624-2805 FAX: 717-624-1196

See full listing in **Section One** under **Corvair**

Ed Lucke's Auto Parts RR 2, Box 2883 Glenville, PA 17329	717-235-2866

Open Monday-Friday 9 am to 5 pm, Saturday 9 am to 12 noon. 1,200 to 1,500 vehicles, many parts already removed. Parts for 1939-56 Packards, 1939-present Chryslers and 1949-present Fords and GMs.

South Dakota

Dakota Studebaker Parts RR 1, Box 103A Armour, SD 57313	605-724-2527

See full listing in **Section One** under **Studebaker**

Wayne's Auto Salvage RR 3, Box 41 Winner, SD 57580-9204	605-842-2054

Mail order and open shop. Monday-Saturday 9 am to 6 pm. Twenty acres of cars from the forties, fifties and sixties. A few from the thirties. Cars and pickups. Sell complete vehicles or parts. Mechanics shop.

Tennessee

Kelley's Korner 22 14th St Bristol, TN 37620	423-968-5583

See full listing in **Section One** under **Studebaker**

Volunteer State Chevy Parts Hwy 41 S, PO Box 10 Greenbrier, TN 37073	615-643-4583 FAX: 615-643-5100

See full listing in **Section One** under **Chevrolet**

Texas

South Side Salvage Rt 2, Box 8 Wellington, TX 79095	806-447-2391

Open Monday-Friday 8 am to 5 pm, Saturday 8 am to 12 noon. Specializing in old and rebuildable vehicles and parts. Over 40 years at same location. Owner: Marshall Peters, 806-447-2490 home. Ready to retire, will sell entire business.

Virginia

Philbates Auto Wrecking Inc PO Box 28 Hwy 249 New Kent, VA 23124	804-843-9787 804-843-2884

Open Monday-Friday 9 am to 5 pm, Saturday 9 am to 2 pm. Parts for 1940-1982 cars. Mail order sales. Over 6,000 autos in stock at all times. Old, odd, collector autos our specialty. Browsers welcome.

Bill Thomsen 1118 Wooded Acres Ln Moneta, VA 24121	540-297-1200

Mail order and open shop by appointment only, phone hours vary, call up to 9:30 pm EST. Small private salvage yard specializing in 1953-1973 full-size Chevrolet cars. Primarily mail out shipping worldwide. Hundreds of used hard to find parts. Consistently adding to inventory.

Washington

Vintage Auto Parts Inc 24300 Hwy 9 Woodinville, WA 98072 E-mail: erics@vapinc.com	800-426-5911 425-486-0777 FAX: 425-486-0778

See full listing in **Section Two** under **comprehensive parts**

West Virginia

Antique Auto Parts 60 View Dr, PO Box 64 Elkview, WV 25071	304-965-1821

See full listing in **Section Two** under **comprehensive parts**

Wisconsin

Zeb's Salvage N3181 Bernitt Rd Tigerton, WI 54486	715-754-5885

Open Monday-Friday 8 am to 5 pm, Saturday 8 am to 3 pm. Have about 1,000 parts cars, mid-20s to late 80s. Ship small parts only.

Australia

Aussieutes/Old Tin PO Box 26 Wendouree Victoria 3355 Australia E-mail: dave@aussieutes.com	03 5339 FORD FAX: 03 5339 9900

Exporting Aussie Utes to America. Fords, Chevrolets, 1928-1953. Web site: www.aussieutes.com

Canada

British Luxury Automotive Parts 257 Niagara St Toronto ON Canada M6J 2L7	416-693-8400 FAX: 416-694-3202 Cell: 416-820-4323

See full listing in **Section One** under **Jaguar**

Scotts Super Trucks 1972 Hwy 592 W Penhold AB Canada T0M 1R0	403-886-5572 FAX: 403-886-5577

See full listing in **Section One** under **Chevrolet**

Section Five – Salvage Yards

Section Six
Museums

315 listings

Auto museums are like scotch whiskey. Some are better than others, but there really are no bad ones. For the hobbyist seeking a car or auto-related exhibit close to home or on a vacation trip, museums are listed under state categories.

When planning a visit to a museum, be sure you've checked its exhibition hours as well as the months of the year when it is open. Some operate all year, but others are only open seasonally, generally in the spring, summer, and early fall. Some listed here are private museums and are open only by appointment.

Most every museum charges admission. Some, however, will offer group rates for clubs wishing to tour their collections. Many of the entries list the person in charge of the museum, and he or she should be contacted, in advance, to arrange a group visit. Some of the museums operate in conjunction with other exhibition attractions, while a few also serve as the showrooms for vintage car dealers. The latter group may be stretching the definition of a museum a bit far, but the hobbyist may find such displays interesting in their own right.

Alabama

International Motorsports Hall of Fame 3198 Speedway Blvd, PO Box 1018 Talladega, AL 35161 E-mail: imhof@coosavalley.net	**256-362-5002** **FAX: 256-362-5684**

Open year round. Daily 8:30 am to 5 pm. Located 45 miles east of Birmingham and 95 miles west of Atlanta, International Motorsports Hall of Fame contains vehicles and memorabilia from all forms of racing. In addition to historic race cars, there are muscle cars, classics and prototypes. There is also memorabilia such as helmets, uniforms, trophies, photos, paintings and programs. There is a full gift shop, a 55-seat theater, video racing simulators and a comprehensive motorsports research library. Exhibit includes stock cars, Indy cars, drag racers, motorcycles, power boats, karts, sprint cars. Web site: historyonwheels.com

Mercedes-Benz Visitor Center PO Box 100 Tuscaloosa, AL 35403-0100	**888-2TOUR-MB** **205-507-2253** **FAX: 205-507-2255**

See full listing in **Section One** under **Mercedes-Benz**

Arizona

Franklin Museum 3420 N Vine Ave Tucson, AZ 85719 E-mail: hhff2@aol.com	**520-326-8038**

See full listing in **Section One** under **Franklin**

Hall of Flame Museum of Firefighting 6101 E Van Buren St Phoenix, AZ 85008 E-mail: webmaster@hallofflame.org	**602-275-3473** **FAX: 602-275-0896**

Open year round. Monday-Saturday 9 am to 5 pm, Sunday 12 noon to 4 pm. Nation's largest firefighting museum, with almost 90 restored pieces of fire apparatus in 33,000 square feet of air conditioned galleries. Hand, horse drawn and motorized pieces from the US, England, Germany and France. Membership. Web site: www.hallofflame.org

Jerome State Historic Park Douglas Mansion Rd. Jerome, AZ 86331 502-634-5381	**502-634-5381**

Early 1900's buggys, fire wagon, and freight wagon.

Riordan Mansion State Historic Park 409 Riordan Rd Flagstaff, AZ 86001	**520-779-4395**

Early 1900s logging vehicles.

Sharlot Hall Museums 415 West Gurley St Prescott, AZ 86301 E-mail: sharlot@lib.az.us	**520-445-3122** **FAX: 520-776-9053**

Open Monday-Friday 10 am to 5 pm, Sunday 1 pm to 5 pm. The museum is the public face of the Arizona State agency Prescott Historical Society. Its mission is the human and natural history of the central Highland of Arizona. Sharlot Hall Museum events are: Folk Arts Fair - 1st Weekend in June. Includes antique car show and stationary engine fire up. Prescott Indian Art Market - 2nd weekend in July. Cowboy Poets - 3rd Weekend in August. Folk Music Festival - 1st Weekend in October. Each of these is attended by artists and/or crafts people from all over the southwest, and is a major regional event.

Yuma Crossing State Historic Park 201 N 4th Ave Yuma, AZ 85364 E-mail: gemert@pr.state.az.us	**520-329-0471** **FAX: 520-782-7124**

Open 7 days a week November-April 9 am to 5pm, May-October closed Tuesday and Wednesday. Closed Christmas Day. Site of the Yuma Qtr. Master Depot (1864-1883). Was used by the army to store and distribute supplies for all military posts in Arizona territory. Supplies were brought from California by ocean vessels and put on river streamers to Yuma. The storehouse is now our history transport museum.

Arkansas

Good Old Days Vintage Motorcar Museum Main St, PO Box 311 Hardy, AR 72542	**870-856-4884** **FAX: 870-856-4885**

Open year round. Monday-Saturday 9 am to 5 pm, Sunday 12:30 pm to 5 pm. Over 50 cars on display plus automobilia dating back to early 1900s. Gift shop with memorabilia, souvenirs and models of all kinds. Cars from the teens, 1920s, 1930s, 1940s and 1950s. A wide variety of vehicles.

The Last Precinct Police Museum 15677 Hwy 62 W Eureka Springs, AR 72632	**501-253-4948** **FAX: 501-253-4949**

Open year round. Tuesday-Saturday 10 am to 6 pm, Sunday by appointment. A police museum featuring 150 years of law enforcement history including: 5 decades of police cars and motorcycles, uniforms, badges, equipment from around the world. Largest private collection of police cars on display in the US. Movie memorabilia, old west displays. Also, large gift shop. Exhibit includes: last one of 12 Z-28 Camaros (1979) built for CHP, Bluesmobile, Dick Tracy squad car, propane powered police car. Web site: www.policeguide.com/policemuseum.htm

The Museum of Automobiles 8 Jones Ln Morrilton, AR 72110 E-mail: moa@ipa.net	501-727-5427 FAX: 501-727-6482

Open daily 10 am to 5 pm. Buddy Hoelzeman, Director. Exhibits include antique and classic cars on loan from private collectors. An auto fair and swap meet is held the third weekend in June with auto judging, style shows and driving events. In addition, a fall swap meet is held the fourth week of September. The museum serves as National headquarters for the Mid-America Old Time Auto Assoc (MOTAA). Web site: www.museumofautos.com

California

Antique Gas & Steam Engine Museum 2040 N Sante Fe Avenue Vista, CA 92083 E-mail: tomwalt@pacbell.net	760-941-1791 FAX: 760-941-0690

Open daily 9 am to 4 pm. We have all kinds of trucks, cars, and tractors along with a multitude of stationary engines - gas, diesel, and steam.

Blackhawk Automotive Museum 3700 Blackhawk Plaza Cir Danville, CA 94506 E-mail: museum@blackhawkauto.org	925-736-2277 925-736-2280 FAX: 925-736-4818

Open Wednesday-Sunday 10 am to 5 pm PST. Admission is charged and group tours are available. Located 45 miles southeast of San Francisco in Danville, CA, the Blackhawk Automotive Museum presents and displays historically significant and artistically inspired automobiles, automotive art and related artifacts from the very earliest to the contemporary for public enjoyment and educational enrichment. The 100,000 square foot multi-level glass and granite architectural masterpiece showcases an ever-changing exhibition of over 120 of the world's greatest autos dating from the 1890s. The Automotive Art wing features *Moving Inspiration*, a rotating exhibition of nearly 1,000 artifacts in an amazing variety of media from the automobile's first 110 years. The museum's shop and bookstore is open during museum hours and has a large selection of automotive books, posters, models and kits. The museum and its facilities are totally wheelchair accessible. Web site: www.blackhawkauto.org

Ed Cholakian Enterprises Inc dba All Cadillacs of the 40s and 50s 12811 Foothill Blvd Sylmar, CA 91342	818-361-1147 800-808-1147 FAX: 818-361-9738

See full listing in **Section One** under **Cadillac/LaSalle**

JA Cooley Museum 4233 Park Blvd San Diego, CA 92103	619-296-3112

Open year round. Monday-Saturday 10 am to 5 pm. 21 antique vehicles. 1886 Benz, 1895 Benz, 1899 Mobile, 1903 Olds, 1904-1905-1913 Cadillacs, 1907 International, 1907 Brush, plus much more. Old phonographs, toys, trains, tools, clocks, cameras, and much more. Exhibit includes: Stevens Duryea used by President Wilson and XP2000 concept Buick.

Fiero Owner's Club of America 1598 S Anaheim Blvd, Unit B Anaheim, CA 92805	714-635-0898 FAX: 714-912-2007

Open January-December, Monday-Friday, 10 am-6 pm. Special Fiero display cars, memorabilia, historical archives, etc. Exhibition cars: convertible, signed Formula, pace car with 0 miles, 3800, V8s. Web site: www.fieroowners.com

Firehouse Museum 1572 Columbia St San Diego, CA 92101	619-232-3473

Open all year Thursday and Friday 10-2, Saturday and Sunday 10-4. Multiple fire engines, steamer, horse drawn 1920s-1960s, fire memorabilia and gift shop on display. Hall rentals for all occasions. Aerial ladders, vintage 1910 also.

Hays Antique Truck Museum 1962 Hays Ln, PO Box 2347 Woodland, CA 95776-2347 E-mail: hatm@wheel.dcn.davis.ca.us	530-666-1044 FAX: 530-666-5777

Open year round. Daily 10 am to 5 pm. Founded 1982. Non-profit public benefit corporation formed for the preservation and display of antique trucks. Over a hundred antique trucks representing a large number of makes dating from 1903 to mid-1950s are on display. The history of the trucking industry is shown through a variety of displays. A quarterly newsletter, *Old Truck Town News*, is published and mailed to the museum's members. There are various classes of membership in addition to a subscription only support. Web site: www.dcn.davis.ca.us/~hatm/

Justice Brothers Inc 2734 E Huntington Dr Duarte, CA 91010	818-359-9174 FAX: 818-357-2550

Open all year Monday-Friday 9 am to 5 pm. A broad collection of Midget race cars with classic street cars, a GT-40 and other unique vehicles.

Muffler Museum Box 1917 Thousand Oaks, CA 91360	818-707-2301

Open by appointment. The only muffler museum. 10,000 on view. Maximum guarantee 10 years (not warranty).

The Nethercutt Museum 15151 Bledsoe St Sylmar, CA 91342 E-mail: scuderiam@aol.com	818-364-6464 FAX: 818-364-6420

Open Tuesday-Saturday 9 am to 4:30 pm. A great collection of many of the worlds finest automobiles.

NHRA Motorsports Museum Fairplex Gate 1 1101 W McKinley Ave Pomona, CA 91768	909-622-2133 FAX: 909-622-1206

The museum, which is open year round Wednesday-Sunday 10 am to 5 pm (except Thanksgiving and Christmas), features an impressive array of vintage and historical racing vehicles, along with photographs, trophies, helmets and driving uniforms, artifacts, paintings, and other memorabilia chronicling more than 50 years of American motorsports. A gift shop offers a wide variety of souvenir items.

Petersen Automotive Museum 6060 Wilshire Blvd Los Angeles, CA 90036	323-930-CARS (2277) FAX: 323-930-6642

Open all year. Tuesday-Sunday 10 am to 6 pm. Largest, most definitive automotive museum in North America. Dedicated to the interpretive study of the automobile and its influence on American life and culture. Three levels of exhibits, secure parking and large gift shop. Venue for car shows, auctions and 3rd party social events. Features include Hollywood star cars, motorcycles, petroliana, automotive themed art and our hands-on interactive children's discovery center. Web site: www.petersen.org

Route 66 Territory Visitors Center Foothill Marketplace 12759 Foothill Blvd, Stes E5 & E6 Rancho Cucamonga, CA 91730 E-mail: rte66@citivu.com	800-JOG-RT66 909-592-2090 FAX: 909-599-5308

A dozen show windows decorated with such nostalgic exhibits as gas pumps, a pegasus, road signs, automobilia, telephone pole insulators, water bags, oil bottles, oil pumps, road maps, sheet music and records of Route 66, paintings and photos of historic places along Route 66. Web site: www.citivu.com/rc/rte66/rte66

San Diego Automotive Museum 2080 Pan American Plaza Balboa Park San Diego, CA 92101	**619-231-2886** **FAX: 619-231-9869**

Open year round. Daily 10 am to 4:30 pm (last admission 4 pm); summer hours, 10 am to 5:30 pm (last admission 5 pm). A breath taking array of rare and exotic automobiles and a world class motorcycle display with feature shows changing 2-3 times a year. Also special interest shows during the year including the annual "Motorcycles in the Park Show". Call for current show information. Full service gift shop. Museum membership available ($25 a year) providing many car enthusiast benefits, including free entry to museum and guest passes, updates on museum activities and invitations to special events.

San Jose Historical Museum 16 Senter Rd San Jose, CA 95112-2599	**408-287-2290**

Carriages, wagons, sleighs, farm machinery, large collection of harnesses and saddles.

Santa Ynez Valley Historical Museum - Parks-Janewa 3596 Sagunto St, PO Box 181 Santa Ynez, CA 93460	**805-688-7889**

35 carriages, wagons, carts, and stagecoaches harness and other equipment also featured as well as a blacksmith shop.

Seeley Stables Calhoun and Twiggs St San Diego, CA 92110	**619-220-5422**

Collection of wagons, carriages and other western memorabilia.

Towe Auto Museum 2200 Front St Sacramento, CA 95818 E-mail: khartley@toweautomuseum.org	**916-442-6802** **FAX: 916-442-2646**

Open daily 10 am to 6 pm (closed Thanksgiving, Christmas and New Year's Day). Be dazzled by chrome headlights and two-toned glistening paint as you hit the high road to the new Towe Auto Museum. Come see the history of the automobile in America; our motoring heritage which is brought to life by the dreams of hope, desire and fantasy stimulated by our passion for automobiles. The Museum now shows its collector cars in a series of exhibits built around these dream themes. Free parking, gift shop, group rates, special evening functions, located south of Old Sacramento, a block off Broadway. Web site: www.toweautomuseum.org

Colorado

Buffalo Bill Wax Museum 404 W Manitou Avenue Manitou Springs, CO 80829	

Stagecoach exhibit.

Forney Transportation Museum 1416 Platte St Denver, CO 80202	**303-433-3643**

Summer hours: May 1st-Sept 30, 9 to 5 Mon-Sat, 11 to 5 Sundays; winter hours: Oct 1st-April 30, 10 to 5 Mon-Sat, 11 to 5 Sundays. Motor into the past with 150 antique and classic cars from the 1890s through the early 1960s. Other exhibits include motorcycles, bicycles, carriages and three steam locomotives (including Big Boy #4005), plus several railroad cars and other railroad equipment, all housed in and around the almost 100 year old historic huge former Denver Tramway powerhouse building.

Gunnison Pioneer Museum 696 County Rd 16 Gunnison, CO 81230	**970-641-4530** **970-641-0740**

Open Memorial Day to Labor Day, Monday thru Saturday 9 am to 5 pm. Collection represents the cultural history and heritage of the people of Gunnison County. The museum has 8 buildings that house antique cars, wagons, arrowhead and mineral collections, etc. AD & RG narrow gauge train is a special feature.

Pikes Peak Auto Hill Climb Educational Museum 135 Manitou Ave Manitou Springs, CO 80829 E-mail: ppihc@ppihc.com	**719-685-4400** **FAX: 719-685-5885**

Open year round. Daily 9 am to 5 pm, Sunday 12 pm to 5 pm. The museum contains cars and motorcycles from the Pikes Peak International Hill Climb, the "Race to the Clouds" that started in 1916. The race held on July 4 is the highest and most spectacular motorsports event in the world. The museum includes actual cars that have competed and won, including a 1918 Pierce-Arrow, a 1920 Lexington and Bobby Unser's open wheel race car, as well as photographs, memorabilia, videos and a gift shop. Web site: www.ppihc.com

Rocky Mtn Motorcycle Museum & Hall of Fame 308 E Arvada St Colorado Springs, CO 80906	**PH/FAX:** **719-633-6329**

Open year round Monday-Saturday from 10 am-7 pm, free admission. Established in 1992, the museum is now home to over 75 classic and antique motorcycles from around the world. The authentic period memorabilia, photographs, banners, pins, patches and apparel, coupled with names and faces of pioneers in motorcycling insure visitors experience and enjoy the history of 2-wheeled ingenuity.

Connecticut

Barnum Museum 820 Main St Bridgeport, CT 06604	**203-331-1104** **FAX: 203-339-4341**

Open Tuesday-Saturday 10 am 4:30 pm. 3 carriages, 1 wagon. All items used by Tom Thumb and other small people in Barnum's shows. We have an annual month-long celebration promoted by the Barnum Festival which offers assorted family activities.

Connecticut Fire Museum PO Box 297 Warehouse Point, CT 06088	**860-623-4732**

Open April to Memorial Day. Saturday 10 am to 5 pm and Sunday 12 pm to 5 pm. Memorial Day to Labor Day Wednesday to Saturday 10 am to 5 pm, Sunday 12 pm to 5 pm. Labor Day to November, Saturday 10 am to 5 pm and Sunday 12 pm to 5 pm. Dedicated to the preservation and appreciation of antique fire apparatus and associated equipment. A non-profit and historical association organized in 1968, incorporated in 1971 and opened in 1975. The collection equipment ranges from a fire sleigh circa 1894 to a 1967 Walter airport crash truck. In addition, fire truck models and fire alarm equipment are displayed. Membership: $10/year. Send SASE for a copy of museum brochure and application. Web site: www.ctfiremuseum.org

Delaware

Hagley Museum and Library Rt 141, PO Box 3630 Wilmington, DE 19807-3630 E-mail: danmuir@udel.edu	**302-658-2400** **FAX: 302-658-0568**

Open daily 9:30 am to 4:30 pm; special winter hours January-mid March. Hagley Museum is where the Dupont story begins in the Brandywine Valley and features the original Dupont Mills estate and gardens. The museum has an antique automobile exhibit that higlights the Dupont Motor Cars Manufactory.

Florida

Elliott Museum
825 NE Ocean Blvd
Stuart, FL 34996
E-mail: elliottmusuem@cwix.com
561-225-1961
FAX: 561-225-2333

Open year around 10-4, except major holidays. Americana 1900-1950 featuring 24 antique cars (1902-1950), spotlighting automotive inventions of Sterling and Harmon Elliott. Exhibits include antique and classic automobiles, motorcycles, bicycles. Web site: www.goodnature.org/elliottmuseum

Ft Lauderdale Antique Car Museum
1527 SW 1st Ave
Ft Lauderdale, FL 33315
E-mail: packcarmsm@hotmail.com
954-779-7300
FAX: 954-779-2501

Open daily 9 am to 4 pm. Our mission is to preserve a piece of America and education of our youth by taking them back to an era where the automotive industry involved craftsmanship and progress.

Don Garlits Attractions
13700 SW 16th Ave
Ocala, FL 34473
Toll free:
877-271-3278
352-245-8661
FAX: 352-245-6895

Open daily 9 am to 5 pm, closed Christmas. Garlits Auto Attractions offers a unique variety of vehicles from 1908 to the 1970s in the antique collection. Our drag racing exhibit traces the sport from the 1940s to the present day record breakers. Call for more information. Web site: www.garlits.com

Historical Society of Martin County
825 NE Ocean Blvd
Stuart, FL 34996
561-225-1961
FAX: 561-225-2333

Open every day except major holidays, 10 am to 4 pm. Exhibits include antique and classic automobiles, motorcycles, bicycles.

Sarasota Classic Car Museum
5500 North Tamiami Trail
Sarasota, FL 34243
E-mail: ClassicCarMuseum@aol.com
941-355-6228
FAX: 941-358-8065

Open daily 9 am to 5 pm (closed Christmas). Home to the nation's third oldest automotive museum. World-class collection of more than 95 vehicles. The museum operates as a non-profit organization, funded primarily through visitor admissions and membership donations. The Iso Rivolta Automobile & Motorcycle Collection is on extended loan to the museum along with the John & Mable Ringling Automobile Collection. Guided tours begin every 30 minutes. Additional exhibits include an antique music exhibit, camera and bicycle collection, and an antique game arcade exhibit. The museum hosts an annual vintage and collector car auction on the first weekend of each December, Kruse/ebay.com are the event auctioneers. The museum will also be host to the 2002 Spring AACA regional automobile meet. Car club meetings, cruise-ins and swap meets also held at the museum facility. For information on how to become a member, make a donation or to become a volunteer contact us by e-mail.

Georgia

Auto Quest Investment Cars Inc
710 W 7th St, PO Box 22
Tifton, GA 31793
E-mail: info@auto-quest.com
912-382-4750
FAX: 912-382-4752

See full listing in **Section Two** under **car dealers**

Museo Abarth
1111 Via Bayless
Marietta, GA 30066-2770
770-928-1446

Open Monday-Friday 9 am to 5 pm, except holidays. Admission free. Display of original Abarth, Fiat and Lancia memorabilia.

Museum of Aviation
Robins Air Force Base
Warner Robins, GA 31099
912-926-6870

Open 7 days a week 9 am to 5 pm. Closed Thanksgiving, Christmas and New Year's. Visitors to Warner Robins will discover the "Crown Jewel" of Middle Georgia – the Museum of Aviation, now the second largest museum in the United States Air Force. Displaying 93 aircraft and hundreds of exhibits on a beautiful 43 acre site, the museum has grown into a significant exhibit, education and cultural center drawing more than 630,000 visitors a year. Rated the fourth largest aviation museum in the country, the Museum is comprised of four main buildings: Heritage Building, Hangar One, Eagle Building, Century of Flight Hangar.

Pebble Hill Foundation
319 South Tellahassee Rd, PO Box 830
Thomasville, GA 31799
912-226-2344

11 carriages, 6 wagons, 9 carts, farm machinery and assorted accessories.

Illinois

Blackberry Historical Farm/Village
RR 3, Box 591
Barnes Rd and Galena
Aurora, IL 60506
708-264-7405

Collection of 43 vehicles.

Hartung's Automotive Museum
3623 W Lake St
Glenview, IL 60025
847-724-4354

Auto museum, call for hours. License plate and auto museum with over 100 antique autos, trucks and motorcycles on exhibit. Vehicles on display include 75 antique bicycles, 28 motorcycles from 1901-1941; Whizzers, sidecars and scooters; Ford Model As, Ts, V8s, plus many other automobiles. License plate collection contains plates from 50 states and Canada. Also promotional model cars, auto hubcaps, radiator emblems, etc. Also police badge collection.

Illinois Railway Museum
PO Box 427
Union, IL 60180
800-BIG-RAIL
815-923-4000

Weekdays - adults $6, children $3.50. Weekends - adults $7, children $5. Steam/Diesel Weekends - adults $8, children $6. Museum is probably the ultimate railroad historian special interest group. Originally formed to preserve one important piece of rolling stock, it has evolved into an educational and historic preservation organization recreating possibly the largest operating demonstration railroad showcase on the North American continent.

Lena Area Historical Society
427 West Grove St
Lena, IL 61048
815-369-2215

Hearse, John Adams buggy, fire fighting equipment.

Volo Antique Auto Museum
27582 Volo Village Rd
Volo, IL 60073
815-385-3644
FAX: 815-385-0703

Open daily 10 am to 5 pm. Located 13 miles west of I-94 on Volo Village Rd, one traffic light north of Rt 120. Exhibits include approximately 200 restored collector cars, automobilia gift shop. Exquisite homemade food and 3 giant antique malls to browse. We buy, sell Hemmings appraise collector cars. Admission: adults, $4.50; seniors and children ages 6-12, $2.50; under 6, free. Group rates by advance reservation. Web site: www.volocars.com

Wheels O' Time Museum PO Box 9636 Peoria, IL 61612-9636 E-mail: wotmuseum@aol.com	309-243-9020

Open Wednesday-Sunday (May-October), 12 noon to 5 pm. Also summer holidays. A hands-on museum housed in three buildings. Among displays are vintage automobiles, Austin-Healey, L-29 Cord, Glide, Packards, Pierce-Arrow, Rolls-Royce (Bentley), airplanes, bicycles, steam engines, tools, musical instruments, clocks, model trains, toys, old-fashioned barbershop with life-size singing quartet, a miniature animated circus, tractors, gasoline engines, grain-handling machines. A replica of an early 20th century firehouse contains fire engines, more automobiles and other displays. On a track rests a 130 ton steam engine of early 1900 vintage, Combo car, caboose, handcar and switch engine. Located 9 miles north of downtown Peoria, IL on Route 40. Web site: www.wheelsotime.org

Wheels Through Time Museum Rt 1 Waltonville Rd Mt Vernon, IL 62864 E-mail: daleshd@dales-hd.com	PH/FAX: 618-244-5470

Open year round. Monday-Friday 9 am to 5 pm, Saturday 9 am to 4 pm. One of the very few places in the country where such a volume of privately owned motorcycles can be viewed by the public at no charge and where such a wealth of information on the early days of motorcycling can be gained. Web site: www.dales-hd.com

Indiana

Auburn Cord Duesenberg Museum 1600 S Wayne St Auburn, IN 46706	219-925-1444 FAX: 219-925-6266

Open year round. Daily 9 am to 5 pm. Robert Sbarge, Executive Director. More than 100 automobiles on exhibit, featuring Auburns, Cords and Duesenbergs. The Museum is housed in the 1930 art deco factory showrooms of the Auburn Automobile Company. Autos on exhibit include the earliest Auburn known to exist and a cross section of all types of collector cars. Discount admission for any old car club member. Museum store, banquet facilities. Auburn Cord Duesenberg festival, Labor Day weekend. Web site: http://acdmuseum.org
See our ad on this page

Automotive Heritage Museum 1500 N Reed Rd (US 31 N) Kokomo, IN 46901	765-454-9999 FAX: 765-454-9956

Open daily 10 am to 5 pm, closed Christmas & New Year's Day. Museum introduces visitors to automotive heritage in Kokomo, IN and its resident, Elwood Haynes, the first inventor of the horseless carriage.

Hall of Fame Museum 4790 West 16th St Indianapolis, IN 46222	317-484-6747 FAX: 317-484-6449

Open daily 9 am to 6 pm, closed Christmas Day. The Hall of Fame Museum on the grounds of the famed Indianapolis Motor Speedway, a National Historic Landmark since 1987, appeals to more than just the racing enthusiast. Displayed are more than 75 racing cars, including Indianapolis winners as well as race cars from internationally renowned motorsports events world wide. Also displayed are several examples of early antique and classic passenger cars, such as Stutz, Cole, Marmon, National and Duesenberg. The Tony Hulman Theatre shows a 30 minute highlights film with no additional admission fee required.

Elwood Haynes Museum 1915 S Webster Kokomo, IN 46902-2040	765-456-7500

Open year round. Tuesday-Saturday 1 pm to 4 pm, Sunday 1 pm to 5 pm. The museum is located in the home of inventor Elwood Haynes. 1st floor Haynes history, 2nd floor industrial history,

basement movie "On The Road" (documentary). There are 4 Haynes cars on the premises, 1905-1924: 1905 Haynes Model L, 1923 Haynes roadster, 1924 Haynes touring car, 1916 Haynes.

Historical Military Armor Museum 2330 Crystal St Anderson, IN 46012	765-649-TANK FAX: 765-642-0262

Open year round. Tuesday, Thursday, Saturday 1 pm to 4 pm, other times by appointment. History of Armor from WW I to current issue (light tanks, jeeps, trucks). 35 pieces of armor, etc, on display. Vintage military vehicle rally held each July (call for details).

Kokomo Automotive Heritage Museum 1500 N Reed Rd Kokomo, IN 46901 E-mail: aldridge@kokomo.org	765-454-9999 FAX: 765-454-9956

Open daily 10 am to 5 pm. Museum houses over 80 antique automobiles ranging from 1895-1960. Also includes numerous automotive industry antiques and displays. Web site: www.kokomo.org

Miller Auto Museum Inc 2130 Middlebury St Elkhart, IN 46516 E-mail: millermuseum@earthlink.net	219-522-0539 FAX: 219-522-0358

Open year round. Monday-Friday 10 am to 4 pm, last weekend of each month 12 pm to 4 pm. Forty uniquely displayed antique and award winning classic autos along with miscellaneous auto memorabilia, collectibles, vintage clothing and antiques. Many National winners on display. Web site: www.millerautomuseum.org

National Automotive & Truck Museum of the United States 1000 Gordon M Buehrig Pl Auburn, IN 46706	219-925-9100 FAX: 219-925-4563

Open year round Monday-Sunday 9 amto 5 pm EST. NATMUS is located in the former factory buildings of the Auburn Automobile

Section Six – Museums

Co and is adjacent to the Auburn, Cord, Duesenberg museum. Focus is on postwar cars and trucks from all eras. There are periodical special exhibits. Over 100 cars and trucks on exhibit at any time. A large collection of toys and models is always on display.

NATMUS Roadside Market 1000 Gordon M Buehrig Pl Auburn, IN 46706 E-mail: natmus@ctlnet.com	PH/FAX: 219-925-9100

See full listing in **Section Two** under **automobilia**

RV/MH Hall of Fame 801 Benham Ave Elkhart, IN 46516	800-378-8694 FAX: 219-293-3466

Open January-December, Mon-Fri 9 am-5 pm. The History of the Recreational Vehicle and Manufactured Housing Industry displayed in museum and library. An Exhibition of 1913 Earl travel trailer, 1934 covered wagon house trailer. Web site: rv/mhhalloffame.org

Studebaker National Museum 525 S Main St South Bend, IN 46601 E-mail: stumuseum@skyenet.net	219-235-9714 888-391-5600 FAX: 219-235-5522

Open Monday-Saturday 9 am to 5 pm; Sunday 12 pm to 5 pm. Admission fee. Depicts 112 years of Studebaker transportation history. Collection includes wagons, carriages, automobiles and trucks produced by Studebaker, and industrial treasures of northern Indiana. See President Abe Lincoln's carriage and the last car made in South Bend. Great museum shop. Web site: www.studebakermuseum.org

Wayne County Historical Museum 1150 North A St Richmond, IN 47374	765-962-5756 FAX: 765-939-0909

Open February-mid December Tuesday-Friday 9 am to 4 pm, Saturday-Sunday 1 pm to 4 pm. Features curiosities from around the world. Authentic Egyptian mummy, Davis airplane, Wooten desk, pioneer life exhibits, Gaar-Scott steam engine, early automobile collection that includes six Richmond made cars. 1908 Wescott, 1909 Richmond, 1920 Pilot, 1918 Davis, 1925 Davis, 1939 Crosley. Plus: 1912 Baker Electric, 1921 Detroit Electric, 1906 Detroit, 1909 Maxwell, 1914 Model T Ford, 1926 Dodge, 1926 Model T Ford fire engine, 1929 Ahrens Fox fire engine.

Iowa

Mid West Old Threshers Museum Rt 1 Threshers Rd, Dept B Mt Pleasant, IA 52641	319-385-8937

Open daily Memorial Day-Labor Day and April-October.

National Sprint Car Hall of Fame & Museum PO Box 542 Knoxville, IA 50138 E-mail: sprintcarhof@sprintcarhof.com	641-842-6176 FAX: 641-842-6177

Open year round. Monday-Friday 10 am to 6 pm, Saturdays 10 am to 5 pm, Sundays 12 pm to 5 pm. The world's only museum dedicated to preserving the history of the sport of big car, super modified and sprint car racing. Handicapped accessible. Gift shop. Group tours available. All cars on loan and rotated yearly. Web site: www.sprintcarhof.com

Olson-Linn Museum 323 East 4th Villisca, IA 50864	PH/FAX: 712-826-2756

Open year round. Daily 9 am to 4 pm. Specializing in antique cars, trucks and tractors, pre-1930s. Also many other primitives. Exhibition of 1917 Cole 8 (Cloverleaf), 1909 2-cylinder Maxwell, several other makes 1909-1930.

Van Horn's Antique Truck Museum 15272 North St Mason City, IA 50401	515-423-0550 museum 515-423-9066 off season

Open daily May 22-September 22 (admission charged). This unique private museum displays 65 makes of nation's oldest restored motor trucks with many displayed in settings of the era in which they were manufactured. Trucks on display date from 1930 back to 1908. Plus hundreds of other early automotive items on display. Also featured is a large scale model circus that one man created over his lifetime.

Kansas

Frontier Army Museum 100 Reynolds Ave (Bldg 801) Fort Leavenworth, KS 66027-2334	913-684-3767

Carriages, wagons, sleighs and others.

Kansas State Historical Society 6425 SW 6th Ave Topeka, KS 66615-1099 E-mail: btarr@kshs.org	785-272-8681 FAX: 785-272-8682

Open year round. Monday-Saturday 9 am to 4:30 pm, Sunday 12:30 pm to 4:30 pm. General history museum for the State of Kansas. Featuring 1910 Thomas, 1908 Great Smith and 1955 Ford F600 farm truck (off-exhibit). Web site: www.kshs.org

Wheels & Spokes Inc 383 Mopar Dr, HC 39 Box 360 Hays, KS 67601	913-628-6477

Open year round Monday-Friday 8 am to 6 pm, Saturday 10 am to 5 pm CST. Museum contains mainly all performance Mopar. Displays include factory Duster I protype, factory 1970 Daytona, Hemis & six-packs.

Kentucky

International Museum of the Horse Kentucky Horse Park 4089 Iron Works Rd Lexington, KY 40511	606-233-4303

37 carriages, carts and sleighs, and also many models. Also, a 2,000 volume research library.

The National Corvette Museum 350 Corvette Dr Bowling Green, KY 42101-9134 E-mail: bobbiejo@corvettemuseum.com	800-53-VETTE FAX: 270-781-5286

Open 7 days a week. Features changing displays/exhibits of over 60 Corvettes to celebrate the invention of the Corvette, preserve its past, present and future and serve as an educational model for all. Web site: www.corvettemuseum.com

Rineyville Sandblasting Model A Ford Museum 179 Arvel Wise Ln Elizabethtown, KY 42701	270-862-4671

Open year round by phone or by chance. Ernest J Pyzocha, curator and proprietor. Located off Hwy 1538 between Fort Knox and Elizabethtown, KY. 6,000 sq ft warehouse packed with nearly 40 unrestored Model A Ford cars and trucks of various body styles. Also license plate collection, porcelain signs, tools, new, used and NOS parts, accessories and much, much more. Admission $2. Call first.

Swope's Cars of Yesteryear Museum 1100 North Dixie Ave, PO Box 606 Elizabethtown, KY 42701 E-mail: bills13@juno.com	270-765-2181 FAX: 270-763-6187

Open Monday-Saturday 9 am to 5 pm. 26 original or beautifully restored cars from the 1920s, 1930s, 1940s and a few from the 1950s. Packards, Lincolns, LaSalle, Cadillac, Pierce Arrow, Fords, Dodges and others. Some are classics...all are museum quality. A brand new facility, handicapped accessible and temperature controlled. Tour buses and car clubs welcome. Admission: free. Open Monday through Saturday 9 am to 5 pm, closed Sundays and holidays.

Louisiana

Ark-La-Tex Antique & Classic Vehicle Museum 601 Spring St Shreveport, LA 71101	318-222-0227 FAX: 318-222-5042

Open Monday-Friday 9am to 5pm, Saturday 9am to 5pm, Sunday 1pm to 5pm. Established in 1921, the George T Bishop Building, one of this area's oldest car dealerships, has been restored and made the museum's home. The museum represents vehicles of the United States and those specific to Louisiana, Texas, and Arkansas. 48,000 square feet. The Street Floor of the museum was the actual showroom and assembly area of the Graham Truck Brothers and Dodge Brothers Car Companies. The displays feature an array of automotive history with both antique and classic vehicles, which include vintage automobiles, motorcycles and antique fire trucks. Memorabilia exhibits consist of period costumes, tools, toys, historic photos and related items displayed in nostalgic settings. The exhibits are changed twice a year.

Maine

Belfast Fire Department Museum 281 Main St 131 Church St (mailing) Belfast, ME 04915	207-338-3362

Open daily, closed winter months. Exhibit includes: 1880s horse drawn Amos Keag Pumper, 1922 La France Pumper, 1927 McCann Ladder and 1940 Mack Pumper. Contact is Jim Richards.

Boothbay Railway Village Rt 27, PO Box 123 Boothbay, ME 04537	207-633-4727

Open daily mid-June to mid-October, 9:30 am to 5 pm. Turn of century village containing historical exhibits including Thorndike and Freeport railroad stations, Boothbay Town Hall, general store, blacksmith shop, filling station. Ride on a coal-fired, narrow gauge steam train to an exceptional antique vehicle display housing more than 50 vehicles from 1907-1949. Web site: www.railwayvillage.org

Cole Land Transportation Museum 405 Perry Rd Bangor, ME 04401 E-mail: mail@colemuseum.com	207-990-3600 FAX: 207-990-2653

Open May 1-November 11, daily 9 am to 5 pm. Home of Maine State World War II Memorial. 200 Maine land transportation vehicles; 2,000 photos of life in early Maine communities; military artifacts from Civil War to Desert Storm, including vehicles, weapons, uniforms, etc. If it moved over land in this century or last, it is probably represented here, from roller skates to a locomotive. Covered bridge, 72'x15', 1840s design; trucks and cars include 1912 Reo, 1913 Stanley Steamer to 1964 Tank-Van; 1923 Packard, 1931 Reo Royale coupe, 1928 Buick, 1941 Pontiac, etc. Web site: www.colemuseum.org

Owls Head Transportation Museum PO Box 277, Rt 73 Owls Head, ME 04854 E-mail: ohtm@midcoast.com	207-594-4418 FAX: 207-594-4410

Open daily except Thanksgiving, Christmas and New Years. 10 am-5 pm April-October, 10 am-4 pm November-March. Web site: www.ohtm.org

Stanley Museum Sue Davis Exec Director PO Box 280 Kingfield, ME 04947 E-mail: stanleym@somtel.com	207-265-2729 FAX: 207-265-4700

Open year round. May 1-October 31, Tuesday-Sunday 1 pm to 4 pm; November 1-April 30, Monday-Friday 8 am to 12 pm and 1 pm to 5 pm; other times by appointment. Stanley Museum keeps and shares the traditions of Yankee ingenuity and creativity as exemplified by the Stanley family in order to inspire those values in children and adults. Membership levels from $25/individual through $2,500/lifetime. Members receive quarterly newsletter with historical and technical articles, free museum admission, 10% off gift shop items and advance event notification. On exhibit: 1910 Stanley Model 70, 1916 Stanley Model 725, 1905 Stanley Model CX. Web site: www.stanleymuseum.org

Wells Auto Museum Rt 1, PO Box 496 Wells, ME 04090	207-646-9064

Open weekends from Memorial weekend-Columbus weekend 10 am to 5 pm. Open daily mid-June-September 10 am to 5 pm. Non-profit museum displaying automotive history from 1900-1964. Gas, electric and steam cars on display along with motorcycles and a few horse-drawn vehicles. A fine selection of nickelodeons, mutoscopes, and arcade games from the twenties and thirties. Toys, photos and paintings, and other automobilia.

Maryland

B & O Railroad Museum 901 W Pratt St Baltimore, MD 21223	410-752-2490

Conestoga wagon, fire engine, hose reel carts, horse cars, express wagon and one carriage.

Fire Museum of Maryland 1301 York Rd Lutherville, MD 21093 E-mail: firemuseumofmaryland@ erols.com	410-321-7500 FAX: 410-769-8433

Open Saturdays May-November, 11 am to 4 pm; open Tuesday-Friday June-August, 11 am to 4 pm. The Fire Museum of Maryland is America's premier collection of firefighting apparatus dating from 1806. More than 40 hand-pulled, horse-drawn and motorized vehicles are on display. Web site: www.firemuseummd.org

Thrasher Carriage Museum 19 Depot St Frostburg, MD 21532	301-689-3380 301-777-5905

Over 100 horse-drawn vehicles. Open May thru October, Tuesday-Sunday; November/December on weekends only. Other times by appointment. Carriage collection of the late James R. Thrasher.

Massachusetts

Bartlett Museum 270 Main St, PO Box 692 Amesbury, MA 01913	508-388-4528

Two carriages, one sleigh, farm machinery. Also, a number of historical documents and brochures.

Section Six – Museums

Chesterwood Museum
4 Williamsville Rd
Stockbridge, MA 01262
E-mail: chesterwood@nthp.org

413-298-3579
FAX: 413-298-3973

Open May through October, daily 10 to 4. Home of sculpter Daniel Chester French. Host annual show every Memorial Day weekend. Part of the National Historical Trust for Historic Preservation. Web site: www.nthp.org

Duryea Transportation Society & Museum
25 Mill St, Ste 5
Springfield, MA 01108-1098

413-525-6782

Open Wednesdays & Sundays, 11 am to 3 pm or by appointment. Specializing in all the transportation in Springfield and surrounding areas. Cars, trucks, buses, trolley and affiliated company, Bosch Moore Drop Forge, 2nd floor of the Old Mill St Fire House, Tavern Restaurant on first floor.

Heritage Plantation of Sandwich
JK Lilly III Automobile Museum
67 Grove St
Sandwich, MA 02563-2147
E-mail: museumcc@aol.com

508-888-3300
info: 508-888-1222
FAX: 508-888-9535

Open May to mid-October daily 10 am to 5 pm. Museum of Americana and Gardens on 76 acres. Antique Automobile Museum with 39 vintage and classic cars. Shown in a replica of a Shaker round barn. Stars of the collection are 1930 Duesenberg originally owned by Gary Cooper, 1932 Auburn boattail speedster and 1915 Stutz Bearcat. Military museum and art museum. Picnic area. Admission. Web site: www.heritageplantation.org

Museum of Transportation
Larz Anderson Park
15 Newton St
Brookline, MA 02445

617-522-6547
FAX: 617-524-0170

Open year round. Tuesday-Sunday. New England's premier auto museum with a changing exhibits program, monthly lecture series and a full calendar, May through October lawn events. Check our web site for current information. Web site: www.mot.org

Waltham Museum
17 Noonan St
Waltham, MA 02453
E-mail: aaarena@hotmail.com

781-893-8017

Open March-December. Sunday 1 pm to 4:30 pm. A museum on the history of Waltham, Massachusetts. Bi-monthly newsletter to members. Special focus on the Metz automobile, Orient Buckboard and Waltham Watch Co. Exhibit includes 1903 Orient Buckboard, 1913, 1915 and 1916 Metz. Web site: www.geocities.com/walthammuseum

Yankee Candle Car Museum
Yankee Candle Co Rt 5
South Deerfield, MA 01373

413-665-2020
FAX: 413-665-2399

Open year round. Daily 9:30 am to 6 pm, closed Thanksgiving and Christmas. Car museum is a world class collection of more than 80 American and European automobiles. Our 20,000 sq ft museum features an array of automobiles from the hottest sports cars to the coolest and most regal automobiles. Museum store is stocked with hats, T-shirts, model cars, books, videotapes and much more. Call for admission prices.

Michigan

Walter P Chrysler Museum
Auburn Hills, MI 48326

888-456-1924

Opened on October 5, 1999, the museum is located at the southeast corner of Daimler Chrysler's headquarters in Auburn Hills, MI and showcases about 75 vehicles. The Walter P Chrysler Museum is an interactive, multi-dimensional tribute to a great company, its people and products, and to the visionary Kansas farm boy and self-made mechanic who founded the Chrysler Corporation in 1925. Open Tuesday-Saturday 10 am to 6 pm, Sunday 12 pm to 6 pm, closed Mondays; closed New Years Day, Easter, Fourth of July, day before Thanksgiving, Thanksgiving Day, Dec 24 and Christmas.

Henry Ford Museum & Greenfield Village
20900 Oakwood Blvd
Dearborn, MI 48121-1970

313-271-1620
FAX: 313-982-6247

Open year round. Daily 9 am to 5 pm, closed Thanksgiving and Christmas. Henry Ford Museum and Greenfield Village provides unique educational experiences based on authentic objects, stories and lives from America's traditions of integrity, resourcefulness and innovation. 10th Motor Muster, June 16-17, 2001, vehicles 1933-1969; 51st annual Old Car Festival (the longest, continuous running car show in North America), September 8-9, 2001, vehicles 1932 and earlier. Exhibit includes: 1896 Duryea motor wagon, 1st American production car; "Old 16" 1906 Locomobile, 1st American car to win an international auto race, 1908 Vanderbilt cup; 1961 Lincoln limousine JFK was assassinated in. Automobile in American Life exhibit, 100 car display, from its earliest beginnings to modern day. Web site: www.hfmgv.org

Gilmore-Classic Car Club of America Museum
6865 Hickory Rd
Hickory Corners, MI 49060
E-mail: gcccam@gilmorecarmuseum.org

616-671-5089
FAX: 616-671-5843

Open daily 10 am to 5 pm, early May-late October. A transportation museum run in cooperation with the Classic Car Club of America Museum, dedicated to preserving and displaying the historical significance of the automobile industry. 130 cars displayed in several exquisite barns situated on ninety manicured acres. Cars featured include Packard, Cadillac, Tucker, Duesenberg, Corvette and cars made in Kalamazoo. Web site: www.gilmorecarmuseum.org/

RE Olds Transportation Museum
240 Museum Dr
Lansing, MI 48933
E-mail: eolds@voyager.net

517-372-0529
FAX: 517-372-2901

Open Monday-Saturday 10 am to 5 pm, Sunday 12 pm to 5 pm, closed most major holidays. The R E Olds Transportation Museum was developed as an exhibition of Lansing's contribution to the transportation industry. Today the Museum displays the world's largest collection of "museum quality" Oldsmobiles. Not only do we have the oldest Oldsmobile, but the fastest, and everything in between. Come take an exciting tour back in time through transportation history. See buggies, bicycles, trucks, engines, automobiles, and airplanes.

Poll's Museum of Transportation
1715 104th Ave
Zeeland, MI 49464-1403

616-399-1955

Open May 1-October 1 Monday-Saturday. Located 5 miles north of Holland on US 31. Exhibits include over 30 vehicles, such as a 1921 Pierce-Arrow roadster, a 1929 Marmon roadster, 1931 Packard touring, 1931 Amplicar, fire trucks and 300 antique and new model trucks. Other exhibits include displays of bicycles, trains, model steam traction engine, toys and many other antiques and military exhibits. Donation: adults $2, children 10 through 12 50¢, under 10 free.

Alfred P Sloan Museum
1221 E Kearsley St
Flint, MI 48503

810-237-3450
FAX: 810-237-3451

Open Monday-Friday 10 am to 5 pm, Saturday-Sunday 12 pm to 5 pm. Major exhibition, "Flint and the American Dream", traces the dramatic history of Flint, MI, in the 20th century, from the birth of General Motors to the present. Changing automotive gallery. Automotive archives available to researchers by appointment. Visit our Annual Summer Auto Fair, the fourth weekend in June, over 1,000 vehicles displayed on the grounds of the Flint Cultural Center. Web site: www.sloanmuseum.com

Yesterday's Collection 5899 Jackson Rd Ann Arbor, MI 48103	734-668-6304 FAX: 734-662-0342

Open year round. Monday-Saturday 10 am to 9 pm, Sunday 12 noon to 9 pm. Restored gasoline pumps, signs, oil dispensers, some cars. Gift shop, ice cream parlor. Large selection of automotive books and Franklin Mint precision models.

Minnesota

Ellingson Car Museum 20950 Rogers Dr Rogers, MN 55374 E-mail: ellingsoncarmuseum.com	763-428-7337 FAX: 763-428-4370

Open 7 days a week 10 am to 5 pm. Start in the 1900s on a nostalgic trip through the automotive past by viewing a 1917 Buick Touring, and "Tin Lizzies," in the 1930s display you will find Packards, Fords, Dodges, Chevrolets and others. The Museum's 1940s display includes cars of the period plus several authentic military vehicles. In the 1960s, Factory Muscle Cars fed the public's hunger for more powerful automobiles. The Museum's rendition of a 60s dragstrip includes Roadrunners, GTOs, Impalas, Mustangs, Vettes and race cars.

Glensheen Historic Estate 3300 London Rd Duluth, MN 55804	218-724-8864

Carriage House and family carriages by Brewster and Studebaker.

Minnesota Historical Society 345 Kellogg Blvd W St Paul, MN 55102-1906	612-296-0148

The following items are in inventory but not on regular display: four carriages, 10 sleighs, 10 wagons, ox cart, fire cart, hearse, caison and miscellaneous farm machinery.

Mississippi

Classique Cars Unlimited 7005 Turkey Bayou Rd, PO Box 249 Lakeshore, MS 39558 E-mail: parts@datasync.com	800-543-8691 228-467-9633 FAX: 228-467-9207

See full listing in **Section One** under **Lincoln**

Missouri

Auto World Car Museum by Backer Business 54 N, PO Box 135 Fulton, MO 65251 E-mail: webacker@kiis.net	573-642-2080 573-642-5344 FAX: 573-642-0685

Open daily 10 am to 4 pm April-November, closed Easter. 100 rare vehicles including Wills St Claire, Scripps-Booth, Stanley Steamer, DeLorean and a 1986 Pulse (only 60 were made). Vintage fire trucks and tractors. Unique gift shop. Mini flea market.

Bigfoot 4X4 6311 N Lindbergh Blvd St Louis, MO 63042-2876 E-mail: bigfoot@bigfoot4x4.com	314-731-2822 FAX: 314-731-8114

Open daily 9 am to 6 pm.

Museum of Transportation St Louis County Parks & Recreation 3015 Barrett Station Rd St Louis, MO 63122	314-965-7998 FAX: 314-965-0242

Open daily 9 am to 5 pm, closed New Year's, Thanksgiving and Christmas. Exhibits include 1901 St Louis automobile, 1906

Ford Model N, 1963 Chrysler Turbine car (operational), 1960 Dia Dia/Darrin dream car as well as locomotives, rail cars, busses, trucks, street cars and horse drawn vehicles. Admission: adults $4, children 5-12, $1.50, children under 5, free and senior citizens, $1.50.

Patee House Museum 12th & Penn, Box 1022 St Joseph, MO 64502	PH/FAX: 816-232-8206

Open weekends only November-March, Monday-Saturday 10 am to 4 pm, Sunday 1 pm to 5 pm April-October. Served as the Pony Express headquarters in 1860. Focus is on transportation and communications. Newsletter published 10 times yearly and sent to members. Also, operate the Jesse James home where the outlaw was gunned down in 1882, just two blocks away. Exhibits include: 1983 Fiat Bertone X1/9, Franklin, Flint, Model T, Federal truck, fire trucks and Sprinter. Web site: www.stjoseph.net/ponyexpress

St Louis Car Museum & Sales 1575 Woodson Rd St Louis, MO 63114	314-993-1330 FAX: 314-993-1540

Open year round. Monday-Saturday 9 am to 5 pm, Sunday 11 am to 5 pm. Largest car museum in the midwest with over 150 cars displayed in a showroom covering 65,000 sq ft. Wide variety of cars from nearly every era including some that are one of a kind. Many of our cars are on consignment for sale. We also offer storage of classic cars. We also have a large automobile memorabilia shop, including T-shirts, hats, signs, books, videos, and the largest selection of die cast cars in the midwest. Exhibition cars include: 26th Anniversary Lamborghini Countach, 1969 Corvair w/12 miles, last one built off assembly line and Steed Stealth motorcycle. Web site: http://stlouiscarmuseum

Montana

Miracle of America Museum 58176 Hwy 93 Polson, MT 59860 E-mail: museum@cyberport.net	406-883-6804 406-883-6264

Open year round. Daily 8 am to 8 pm summer, 8 am to 5 pm winter. Focus stresses America's progress from the walking plow to walking on the moon. Memorial displays include Veterans' tribute, DUI victims' memorial, Mt Fiddlers Hall of Fame. Between 20 to 30 vehicles in each section, motorcycles, autos, military trucks, etc. Web site: cyberport.net/museum

Old Prison Museums Montana Auto Museum 1106 Main St Deer Lodge, MT 59727	406-846-3111 406-846-3114 FAX: 406-846-3156

Open daily 8 am to 8 pm, Memorial Day through Labor Day; shorter hours after Labor Day. Features 100-plus cars on rotating exhibit. In 1999, the museum will feature muscle cars and Mustangs in addition to the museum's always changing collection.

Oscar's Dreamland Rt 9 Billings, MT 59102	406-245-4598

Started by the late Oscar Cooke, a pilot in WWI. A jewel of a museum if you like old steam engines. Also has a vast collection of old farm equipment.

Nebraska

Arbor Lodge State Historical Park 2300 W Second Ave Nebraska City, NE 68410	402-873-7222

10 carriages including a stagecoach, surrey, brake, brougham and phaeton. One sleigh.

| Chevyland USA Auto Museum
Rt 2 Box 11
Elm Creek, NE 68836 | 308-856-4208 |

"World's largest display of vintage and classic Chevys from 1914 to 1975." All sport models including roadsters, convertibles, hardtops, coupes, Nomads, pickups and vintage motorcycles. "This beautiful collection of over 100 vehicles is open daily for your enjoyment."

| Sandhills Museum
440 Valentine St
Valentine, NE 69201 | 402-376-3293 |

Open by appointment. Located on West Highway 20. Exhibits include: 16 antique cars from 1900-1928, in running order; bar room piano; band box and other musical items; 2-headed calf; band saw; firearms; Indian artifacts; broom making machine; moonshine still; barb wire collection; glassware; all types of lamps.

| Stuhr Museum of the Prairie Pioneer
3133 W Hwy 34
Grand Island, NE 68801 | 308-385-5316
FAX: 308-385-5028 |

Open daily May-October 9 am to 6 pm. Exhibits included: 1916 Pullman, 1903 American, Ford Model As and Ts, Dodge, Chevrolet, Velie and Overland. Museum also has a 200-piece collection of antique farm machinery including an 1880 threshing machine, steam engines of the 1890s, early kerosene, distillate and gasoline tractors and numerous examples of horse and tractor drawn farm implements.

| Harold Warp Pioneer Village
Foundation
PO Box 68
Minden, NE 68959-0068
E-mail: pioneervllge@nebi.com | 308-832-1181
800-445-4447
(out of state)
FAX: 308-832-2750 |

Open year round. Daily 8 am. 50,000 historic items from every field of human endeavor. 26 buildings. Authentic originals arranged in their order of development to show visually the history of our country. 350 antique autos on display. Restaurant, motel, camping, all within walking distance. Stay overnight, come back next day, 2nd day free admission. Write for more information. Pioneer Village® is a registered trademark of the Harold Warp Pioneer Village Foundation. Web site: www.pioneervvillage.org

Nevada

| The Auto Collections at the
Imperial Palace
3535 Las Vegas Blvd S
Las Vegas, NV 89109
E-mail: info@autocollections.com | 702-794-3174
FAX: 702-369-7430 |

Open year round. Daily 9:30 am to 9:30 pm. The world's largest classic car showroom. Over 300 world class automobiles available for sale. Web site: www.autocollections.com

| Grand Prix Museum
712 Breezy Ridge Dr
Henderson, NV 89015 | 702-558-3862 |

Open by appointment only. Pontiac Grand Prix and Pontiac related memorabilia, miscellaneous automotive displays. Free admission.

| Imperial Palace Auto Collection
Imperial Palace Hotel & Casino
3535 Las Vegas Blvd S
Las Vegas, NV 89109 | 702-794-3174
FAX: 702-369-7430 |

Open daily 9:30 am to 11:30 pm. Features over 200 antique, classic and special interest autos on display in a plush, gallery-like setting. Cited by *Car & Driver* magazine as one of the ten best auto collections in the world.

| National Automobile Museum
The Harrah Collection
10 Lake St S
Reno, NV 89501-1558 | 775-333-9300
FAX: 775-333-9309 |

Open Monday-Saturday 9:30 am to 5:30 pm, Sunday 10 am to 4 pm, closed Thanksgiving and Christmas. The museum exhibits over 220 antique, classic, vintage and special interest automobiles in 4 galleries and on 4 authentic street scenes representing each quarter of the 20th Century. Features include a unique multi-media theatre presentation; multi-media time lines chronicling the automobile; museum store; and riverside cafe. World-famous automotive library offers research by mail. Museum is available in the evenings for group and convention activities. Web site: www.automuseum.org

New Hampshire

| Crossroads of America
6 Trudeau Rd
Bethlehem, NH 03574
E-mail: cofa@together.net | 603-869-3919 |

Open June 1st-mid October. Tuesday-Sunday 12-5. Many models of transportation on display, cars, trains, truck, ships and planes, operating model railroads. Scale, toy and model trains. Lots of miniature classic and sports cars on display.

| Museum of New Hampshire History
6 Eagle Sq
Concord, NH 03301 | 603-226-3189
FAX: 603-226-3198 |

Open July 1-December 15 Tuesday-Saturday 9:30 am to 5 pm, Sunday 12 pm to 5 pm, Thursday evenings 8:30 pm. One carriage, two sleighs, two wagons, one buggy.

New Jersey

| Fosterfield Living History Farm
73 Kahdena Rd
Morristown, NJ 07960 | 973-829-8419 |

Restored carriage house. Five to seven carriages on display with several more in storage.

| Frelinghuysen Arboretum
53 East Hanover Ave
Morristown, NJ 07962-1295 | museum |

Display area of original stalls, and carriage storage. 8-10 vehicles including some Brewster carriages that belonged to the Frelinghuysen family. Lovely gardens as well.

| Space Farms Zoo & Museum
218 Rt 519
Sussex, NJ 07461
E-mail: fpspace@warwick.net | 973-875-3223
FAX: 973-875-9397 |

Open May 1st-October 31st daily 9 am to 6 pm. 100 acre complex. Over 500 animals, 50 antique cars, old wagons, sleds, 2,500 old firearms, Indian museum, tools, children's toys and much more. Special cars: Kaiser Darrin, Premiere, Reo, Chevy, Ford, Dodge, Willys and motorcycles. Web site: http://spacefarms

| Waterloo
525 Waterloo Rd
Stanhope, NJ 07874
E-mail: info@waterloovillage.org | 973-347-0900
FAX: 973-347-3573 |

Open April-November Wednesday-Friday 10 am to 4 pm, Saturday and Sunday 11 am to 5 pm. Waterloo is a historic site featuring a fully restored village along the Morris Canal as well as a farmsite, trades and crafts exhibit, and recreated Lenape Indian Village. Waterloo's calendar of events includes classic car shows, festivals, and concerts.

New York

Adirondack Center Museum
Colonial Garden and Brewster Library
Route 9
Elizabethtown, NY 12932

518-873-6466

Features pioneer life, 1887 Concord Coach.

The Adirondack Museum
Route 28N & 30, PO Box 99
Blue Mountain Lake, NY 12812-0099
E-mail: acarroll@adkmuseum.org

518-352-7311
FAX: 518-352-7653

Open Memorial day -Columbus day, 7 days a week 9:30 am to 5:30 pm. 1921 Model T Ford Touring Car, 75 horse-drawn vehicles including buggies, carts, stagecoaches, wagons, hearse, fire pumper, snow roller, sprinkler wagon and cutters.

Agricultural Memories Museum
1110 Townline Rd
Penn Yan, NY 14527-9002
E-mail: jrjensen@linkny.com

315-536-1206

Open by appointment. Over forty, horse-drawn carriages, over eighty gasoline engines; over fifty John Deere tractors; many toys and miscellaneous items. Lots to see.

**The Buffalo Transportation/
Pierce-Arrow Museum**
263 Michigan at 201 Seneca
Buffalo, NY 14203
E-mail: msandoro@aol.com

716-853-0084

Open May-October. Call for days and hours. Newly opened. Featuring Pierce-Arrow, Thomas Flyer and made in western New York automobiles, bicycles, motorcycles, trucks and memorabilia. The non-profit museum houses items donated and loaned from the James T Sandoro and other collections. Web site: www.pierce-arrow.com

Glenn Curtiss Museum
8419 St Rt 54
Hammondsport, NY 14840

607-569-2160
FAX: 607-569-2040

Open January-March, Wednesday-Sunday; April-December, daily 10 am to 4 pm. Focus on aviation/motorcycling pioneer Glenn Curtiss and on turn-of-the-century life. Early aircraft, early motorcycles, early engines, exhibits on daily life, open workshop, annual classic motorcycle weekend. Exhibition cars of special note include: 1918 Buick opera coupe, 1904 Orient Buckboard, 1937 Curtiss Aerocar travel trailer, Curtiss motorcycles.

Erie Canal Village
5789 New London Rd
Rome, NY 13440

315-337-3999

Small outdoor museum with 12 wagons and carriages used in upstate New York.

Farmer's Museum
Cooperstown, NY 13326

607-547-2533

Library of 70,000 volumes on early American life.

Genesee Country Village
Flint Hill Rd, PO Box 310
Mumford, NY 14511

716-538-6822

Authentic 19th Century village and Carriage Museum. 60 horse-drawn vehicles.

**Granger Homestead
and Carriage Museum**
295 N Main St
Canandaigua, NY 14424

716-394-1472

Historic 1816 home, over 50 carriages.

**Hall of Fame & Classic Car
Museum, DIRT**
1 Speedway Dr, PO Box 240
Weedsport, NY 13166

315-834-6606
FAX: 315-834-9734

Open April-Labor Day Monday-Saturday 10 am to 5 pm, Sunday 12 pm to 7 pm; September-December Monday-Friday 10 am to 5 pm, Saturday-Sunday 11 am to 4 pm; closed January-March. Dozens of classic cars on display throughout the showroom. Our classic car finder's network assists in selling, buying and locating classic cars. A classic car corral located outdoors adds to the rare and continuously changing models already shown. Rarity can easily be found. Web site: www.dirtmotorsports.com

**The Himes Museum of Motor
Racing Nostalgia**
15 O'Neil Ave
Bay Shore, NY 11706

516-666-4912

Open 7 days a week 9 am to 9 pm. Motor racing museum. Autos, boats, motorcycles. Exhibits also include Midgets, Sprints, stock cars.

**International Motor Racing
Research Center at Watkins Glen**
610 S Decatur St
Watkins Glen, NY 14891
E-mail: research@racingarchives.org

607-535-9044
FAX: 607-535-9039

See full listing in **Section Four** under **research & reference libraries**

**Lake George Antique Boat
& Auto Museum**
19 Sagamore Rd, Box 760
Bolton Landing, NY 12814
E-mail: ric@berkshiretv.com

518-644-2868

Open May-October. The museum's purpose is to preserve, interpret, teach and interactively exhibit the history of life on Lake George through the vessels and vehicles used there, and their significant impact on the economic, social and cultural heritage of the Adirondack region and the nation.

Museum of Automobile History
321 N Clinton St
Syracuse, NY 13202

315-478-CARS
FAX: 315-432-8256

Open year round. Wednesday-Sunday 10 am to 5 pm. The largest museum of its kind in the world. Over 10,000 objects on display devoted to the history of automobiles, trucks and motorcycles from the 19th century to the present. Web site: www.autolit.com

Museum Village in Orange County
130 Museum Village Rd
Monroe, NY 10950

914-782-8247

50+ carriages, 20+ sleighs, farm machinery, fullly outfitted wagon makers shop, fully outfitted harness makers shop.

The Museums at Stony Brook
Carriage Museum
1208 Route 25A
Stony Brook, NY 11790
E-mail: merriferrell@yahoo.com

631-751-0066 x222
FAX: 516-751-0353

Open Wednesday-Saturday 12 pm to 5 pm, Sunday 12 pm to 5 pm. 100+ carriages on display, total of 500+ in collection, reference library. Likely the most significant carriage collection in America.

Nassau County
Division of Museum Services
Eisenhower Park
East Meadows, NY 11554

516-571-7901

Historic pre-1870 vehicles. 20 carriages, 20 wagons, 15 sleighs, farm machinery and accessories.

Northeast Classic Car Museum
NYS Rt 23, 24 Rexford St
Norwich, NY 13815
E-mail: info@classiccarmuseum.org

607-334-AUTO (2886)
FAX: 607-336-6745

Open daily 10 am to 5 pm. Featuring over 100 rare and classic automobiles from days gone by. Cars like Auburns, Cords, Duesenbergs, Chalmers-Detroit, Chandler, Crestmobile, Firestone Columbus, Holmes, Pierce Arrow, Hupmobile, Stutz Roadster, Peerless, Stanley Steamer, and the largest collection of Franklin luxury automobiles in the world. Admission: adult $8, seniors $7, students $4, children under 6-Free. Call for group rates of visit us on the web: www.classiccarmuseum.org

Old Bethpage Village Restoration
1303 Round Swamp Rd
Old Bethpage, NY 11804

516-572-8401
FAX: 516-572-8413

Old Bethpage Village Restoration is a living history museum depicting farm and town life on Long Island in the mid. 19th century with over 55 historic structures staffed by costumed guides and craftspersons.

Old Rhinebeck Aerodrome
Stone Church & Norton Rd
Rhinebeck, NY 12572

845-752-3200
FAX: 845-758-6481

Open May 15-October 31, 10 am to 5 pm. Living museum of vintage airplanes featuring WW I and earlier aircraft in weekend air shows, air museums and airplane rides. Features 1909 Renault, 1916 Packard moving van, 1918 GMC WW I ambulance, 1911 Baker Electric, 1911 International Auto Buggy, 1911 Hupmobile, 1910 Maxwell Runabout, 1913 Brewster Town Car, 1916 Studebaker, 1914, 1919, 1927 Ford Model Ts, 1920 Buick, 1916 Royal Enfield motorcycle, 1917 Indian motorcycle, 1936 Indian motorcycle used in conjunction with weekend air shows. New air show schedule: every Saturday and Sunday mid-June through mid-October, at 2 pm. Great meeting place for an outing, especially for vintage car clubs. Web site: www.oldrhinebeck.org

Saratoga Antique Auto & Carriage Museum
PO Box 1240
Saratoga Springs, NY 12866
E-mail: cfcook@global2000.net

518-583-4955
FAX: 518-583-4955

Museum founded to preserve and interpret automobile and carriage heritage and related artifacts. Goal is education about role of automobile and carriages as reflections of technical advancement and impact on society, economics, and art.

Wilson Historical Society – Car Museum
645 Lake St
Wilson, NY 14172

716-751-9886

Open April-November. Sundays 2 pm to 4 pm. Exhibits include 14 classic and collector cars.

North Carolina

Backing Up Classics Motor Car Museum
4545 Hwy 29 (Concord Pkwy)
Concord, NC 28075
E-mail: buc@vnet.net

704-788-9494
FAX: 704-788-9495

Open daily year round 9 am to 5:30 pm, closed Christmas and Thanksgiving. 50 motor vehicles on display with special focus on 1950s, classic and race cars. Web site: www.backingupclassics.com

Gaston County Museum of Art and History
131 W Main St, PO Box 429
Dallas, NC 28034-0429

704-922-7681

Carriages, sleighs, wagons, miscellaneous farm machinery.

Greensboro Historical Museum
130 Summit Ave
Greensboro, NC 27401

910-373-2043
FAX: 336-373-2204

Open Tuesday-Saturday 10 am to 5 pm; Sunday 2 pm to 5 pm. 1760 covered wagon.

Memory Lane Motorsports & Historical Automotive Museum
769 River Hwy
Mooresville, NC 28117
E-mail: info@
memorylaneautomuseum.com

704-662-3673 (FORD)
FAX: 704-660-0137

Open year round except holidays. Monday-Saturday 9 am to 5 pm, Sunday 1 am to 5 pm. New opening June 2001, 40,000 sq ft, over 100 displays, antique cars, toys, motorcycles, tractors, specializing in race cars with over 50 on display. Gift shop selling unusual items such as NASCAR sheetmetal. On exhibit: Richard Petty's original 1969 Ford, also world's largest collection of racing go-karts. Web site: www.memorylaneautomuseum.com

North Carolina Transportation Museum at Spencer
411 S Salisbury Ave, PO Box 165
Spencer, NC 28159

704-636-2889

Open April 1-October 31, Monday-Saturday 9 to 5, Sunday 1 to 5; November 1-March 31, Tuesday-Saturday 10 to 4, Sunday 1 to 4. Museum is housed in Southern Railway's former repair facility. Visitor center, gift shop, movies, rail cars, transportation displays, steam/ diesel train rides with roundhouse tour, and "bumper to bumper" antique auto exhibit. Special events include train excursions, railroad equipment show, AACA show and lectures.

North Dakota

Cass County Historical Society
1351 W Main Ave, PO Box 719
West Fargo, ND 58078
E-mail: info@bonanzaville.com

701-282-2822
FAX: 701-282-7606

Open Memorial Day weekend through September daily 9 am to 5 pm. Located within the historic village of Bonanzaville, this vintage auto museum contains more than 80 cars including a 1902 Oldsmobile, Model Ts through 1927, to a 1964-1/2 Mustang convertible. Also featured at Bonanzaville are main street businesses, log cabins, Bonanza farm homes, country school and church. Web site: www.bonanzaville.com

Ohio

British Museum of Transportation
2304 Wrenside Ln
Kettering, OH 45440-2324
E-mail: BritCarMuseum@aol.com

937-434-1750

The Museum, through it's operating board and members, has worked actively in support of the Dayton Boonshoft Museum of Discovery Concours D'Elegance as well as providing support and People's Choice award trophy for the Dayton British Car Days, sponsored by the MG Car Club, Southwestern Ohio Centre and the Miami Valley Triumphs.

Canton Classic Car Museum	**330-455-3603**
Market Ave S at 6th St SW	**FAX: 330-455-0363**
Canton, OH 44702	

Open year round. Daily 10 am to 5 pm. 40 cars focusing on pre-war classics. Cars range from 1911 Model T to 1981 DeLorean. Many memorabilia items, gift shop and more. Exhibition cars include: 1914 Benham, 1922 Holmes, 1937 Packard 1508 V12 carved side hearse. Web site: www.cantonclassiccar.org

Carillon Historical Park	**937-293-2841**
1000 Carillon Blvd	**FAX: 937-293-5798**
Dayton, OH 45409	
E-mail: chpdayton@main-net.com	

Open April 1-October 31, Tuesday-Saturday 9:30 am to 5 pm, Sunday 12 pm to 5 pm. 23 buildings and structures on a 65-acre site. Auto related exhibits include a 1908 Stoddard-Dayton, 1910 Speedwell, 1923 Maxwell, 1910 Courier, 1914 Davis and 1918 Cleveland motorcycles located in the Dayton sales building; a 1912 Cadillac, Charles Kettering and Delco exhibits inside Deeds Barn, and a 1924 Sun Oil Company Station. Web site: www.carillonpark.org

The Citizens Motorcar Company	**937-226-1917**
America's Packard Museum	
420 S Ludlow St	
Dayton, OH 45420	

Open Monday-Friday 12 pm to 5 pm, Saturday-Sunday 1 pm to 5 pm. America's only Packard dealership operating as a museum. *Car Collector* magazine says it's one of the ten best small museums in the United States. Elegant Packards in an art deco showroom. World's largest collection of Packard only automobiles, artwork and artifacts. Don't miss America's Packard Museum.

Crawford Auto-Aviation Museum	**216-721-5722**
10825 East Blvd	**FAX: 216-721-0645**
Cleveland, OH 44106	

Open 12 months, Monday-Saturday 10 am to 5 pm, Sunday 12 pm to 5 pm. Over 150 automobiles, airplanes, bicycles, specializing in Cleveland built automobiles. 1st Cleveland car (1898 Winton) to last Cleveland car (1932 Peerless). Special exhibition. White Motors, Crawfords' Cleveland, Cleveland air races. Web site: www.wrhs.org

Motorcycle Hall of Fame Museum	**614-882-2782 info**
13515 Yarmouth Dr	**614-856-1900**
Pickerington, OH 43147	**office**
E-mail: afitch@ama-cycle.org	**FAX: 614-856-1920**

Open year round. Monday-Friday 9 am to 5 pm, Saturday-Sunday 9 am to 5 pm March-October, special summer holiday hours, closed weekends November-February. Exhibits depict the development of motorcycling in America with rotating themes. The 26,000 sq ft facility usually has 100 motorcycles on display. The museum also maintains archives pertaining to the history of motorcycling and a Hall of Fame honoring the heroes of the sport. The museum features a gift shop, refreshment vending area and covered motorcycle parking, all on a beautiful 23 acre wooded site. Web site: www.ama-cycle.org

National Packard Museum	**330-394-1899**
1899 Mahoning Ave NW	
Warren, OH 44483	
E-mail: national@packardmuseum.org	

Closed Mondays and holidays, Tuesday-Saturday 12 pm to 5 pm, Sunday 1 pm to 5 pm. Packard's birthplace, family, Packard Electric, Packard Motor Car Company archives. 15 to 20 Packard cars, 1900-1958. Large gift shop, quarterly newsletter. Membership to the Association: $25/year. Web site: www.packardmuseum.org

National Road-Zane Grey Museum	**800-752-2602**
8850 East Pike	**FAX: 740-872-3510**
Norwich, OH 43767	

Open March-November, Wednesday-Sunday 9:30 am to 5 pm. The museum features three subject areas. Featured are the National Road, America's First Highway, Western novel writer Zane Grey and Zanesville, Ohio, art pottery. Exhibition cars of special note: 1899 Locomobile, 1914 Chevrolet Royal Mail and 1915 Ford depot hack. Web site: www.ohiohistory.org/places/nat/road

Charlie Sens Antique Auto Museum	**614-389-4686**
Pole Lane Rd	**614-386-2521**
Marion, OH 43302	

Open Monday-Saturday 10 am to 5 pm, Sunday 12 pm to 5 pm. With more than 100 of the most beautiful cars ever made, the museum offers a taste of history for the young and old alike of America's automotives beginnings. From a 1903 Ford, one of only 20 such cars remaining in the world today, to a 1969 Corvair sporting only 11 actual miles, each and every car of the Sens collection is in perfect running order and could be driven from the museum floor for a Sunday joy ride.

Welsh Classic Car Museum	**800-875-5247**
223 N 50 St, PO Box 4130	**FAX: 740-282-1913**
Steubenville, OH 43952	
E-mail: contact@welshent.com	

Open year round. Summer Wednesday-Sunday 12 pm to 6 pm; Winter Thursday-Sunday 12 pm to 6 pm. Displays a number of XK and XKE Jaguars along with other antique and classic cars of interest. We also feature new displays of Steubenville china and pottery. Web site: www.welshent.com

Oklahoma

Fort Sill Museum	**580-442-5123**
437 Quanah Rd	**FAX: 580-442-8120**
Fort Sill, OK 73503-5100	
E-mail: spivet@sill.army.mil	

Open Sunday-Saturday 8:30 am to 4:30 pm. Closed December 25 and 26, January 1 and 2. 26 Buildings in the Fort Complex - 6 buildings open to the public for interpretation - Cannon Walk, Missle Park, Desert Storm Park (outdoor displays). Fort Sill was founded by General Philip H. Sheridan on January 8, 1869, during a winter campaign agains the South Plains tribes. The Post was constructed by the black troopers of the 10th US Calvary, the famed "Buffalo Soldiers." Since 1911 Fort Sill has been the home of the U.S. Army Field Artillery Center and School. On the broad firing ranges of its 94,000-acre military reservation, generations of Field Artillerymen have learned the art of tube, missle, and aerial gunnery as defenders of the free world.

Mac's Antique Car Museum	**918-583-7400**
1319 E 4th St	**FAX: 918-583-3108**
Tulsa, OK 74120	
E-mail: macs@ionet.net	

Open Saturday-Sunday 12 pm to 5 pm. An impressive collection of over 60 fully restored classic automobiles. The collection includes Packards (Twin Six, Super Eight and V12s), LaSalles, Cadillacs, Rolls-Royces, Fords, Chevrolets, Dodges and Chryslers and others dating primarily from the 1920s and 1930s. The 19,200 square foot facility is climate controlled, handicapped accessible and conveniently located near downtown Tulsa. Group tours welcome. Banquet facilities available.

Muscle Car Ranch	**405-222-4910**
3609 S 16th	
Chickasha, OK 73018	

Open year round. Monday-Friday sunup to sundown. Many barns and fields, pond area and amphitheater decorated with towering vintage signs, functional 40s, restored diner (the Woodstock of swap meets). Exhibition cars: 1969 Camaro RS Z-28 to 1969 Indy pace car (pair). 1960s Camaros, Mustangs, late 1960 Olds 442, extensive collection of 1966-1969 Toronados (1968 specialty), rare Mopars, 1976 GTX to convertible Coronets. Extensive Japanese 1960s-1970s cycles, British bikes, etc. Huge sign collection in the air, large 1950s, 1960s B-61 Mack trucks, extensive unique big truck, milk trucks. Web site: www.musclecarranch.com

Section Six – Museums

Museum of the Great Plains 601 Ferris Ave, PO Box 68 Lawton, OK 73502	405-581-3460

Two carriages, wagons, farm machinery, harness, wheels. Research library with carriage material.

Townsend Motors LLC Harrison & I40 Hwy 4901 N Harrison, PO Box 456 Shawnee, OK 74801	405-273-0330 FAX: 405-273-0761

Open year round by appointment. 268 vehicles. Exhibit includes Mae West's V16 Cadillac, Sammy Davis' Stutz Black Hawk and Elvis Presley's Lincoln Mark 2.

Oregon

Eastern Oregon Museum 3rd St Haines, OR 97833	503-856-3233

Impressive collection of relics and implements used in development of the West, including horse-drawn equipment.

Oregon Historical Society 1230 SW Park Ave Portland, OR 97205-2483	503-222-1741

Ivan Collins collection of model carriages. Reproductions of detailed vehicle plans avalible through the Research Library.

Tillamook County Pioneer Museum 2106 2nd St Tillamook, OR 97141	PH/FAX: 503-842-4553

Open Monday-Saturday 8 am to 5 pm, Sunday 12 noon to 5 pm. Open all holidays except Thanksgiving and Christmas. History museum and large natural history collection. Exhibits include 1902 Holsman, 1909 Buick.

Pennsylvania

Auto Literature Shoppe Box 238, HC 75 Fort Littleton, PA 17223	800-526-7099 717-987-3702 FAX: 717-987-4284

Free admission museum.

Boyertown Museum of Historic Vehicles 28 Warwick St Boyertown, PA 19512 E-mail: mail@boyertownmuseum.org	610-367-2090 FAX: 610-367-9712

Open year round. Our museum participates in public events, our own events, including Duryea Day Antique and Classic Car Show and Flea Market annually since 1965.

The Car and Carriage Museum The Frick Art and Historical Center 7227 Reynolds St Pittsburgh, PA 15208 E-mail: wsheerer@frickart.org	412-371-0600 FAX: 412-241-5393

Open Tuesday-Saturday, 10 am to 5 pm; Sunday 12 pm to 6 pm. Free admission. We have cars dating from the 1880's and made in Pittsburgh. We have 19 automobiles 1898 to 1940 and

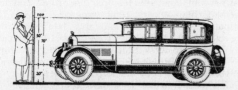

12 carriages 1888 to 1903. All carriages were owned by the Frick family as well as two autos.

Carriage Museum of America-Library PO Box 417 Bird-in-Hand, PA 17505	717-656-7019

The CMA is an information center for horse-drawn vehicle scholars. The CMA makes more information on horse-drawn vehicles available through its publications of books than any other library. The CMA has a full-time librarian to answer mail order requests, so that patrons don't have the expense of traveling long distances.

Drake Well Museum RD #3, Box 7 Titusville, PA 16354 E-mail: drakewell@usachoice.net	814-827-2797 FAX: 814-827-4888

Open Monday-Saturday 9 am to 5 pm, Sunday 10 am to 5 pm. Site of world's first oil well, Amoskeag Steam Pumper #283, and Nitro Wagon.

Dusty Memories and Faded Glory 118 Oxford Hts Rd Somerset, PA 15501-1134	814-443-2393 FAX: 814-443-9452

See full listing in **Section Two** under **military vehicles**

Eastern Museum of Motor Racing Williams Grove Old Timers 100 Baltimore Rd York Springs, PA 17372	717-528-8279

Open April-October, Saturday and Sunday 10 am to 4 pm. Founded 1975, 1,700 members. Dedicated to the preservation of motor racing history. Dues: $10/year or $15/year first class mail. Call for museum tours and rates. Donation. Restored fairgrounds, vintage car exhibition racing during the summer months.

Frick Art and Historical Center 7227 Reynolds St Pittsburgh, PA 15208-2923	412-371-0600

Museum is restored home of Henry Clay Frick and includes an art museum, a car and carriage museum, all depicting the early part of the twentieth century.

Gast Classic Motorcars Rt 896, 421 Hartman Bridge Rd Strasburg, PA 17579-9601	717-687-9500

Open year round 7 days a week. Closed Thanksgiving, Christmas, New Years Day and Easter Sunday. You'll enjoy seeing over 50 outstanding antique, classic, sports, and hi-performance cars at the ever changing Gast Classic Motorcars Exhibit.

Gruber Wagon Works Park and Recreation Department of Berks County RD 5, Box 272 Sinking Spring, PA 19608	610-372-8939

Restored wagon factory and wagons. 24 horse-drawn vehicles.

Historical Society of Berks County & Museum 940 Centre Ave Reading, PA 19601 E-mail: larebee@epix.net	610-375-4375 FAX: 610-375-4376

Open Tuesday-Saturday 9 am to 4 pm. Exhibits representing all aspects of county history including transportation, fine arts, penna. German arts and crafts. Handson history room for children. Changing special exhibits through out the year.

J.E.M. Classic Car Museum
Rt 443 RD #1, Box 120 C
Andreas, PA 18211

570-386-3554
FAX: 570-386-2767

Open May-October 10 am to 5 pm. Located on Route 443 just north of Lehighton, PA. Approximately 50 classic cars on site at all times, snack bar, gift shop. Hours are 10 am to 5 pm beginning in May thru October. Reservations accepted for group tours and luncheons/meetings.

Landis Valley Museum
2451 Kissel Hill Rd
Lancaster, PA 17601
E-mail: smiller@phmc.state.pa.us

717-569-0401
FAX: 717-560-2147

Open every day 9 am to 5 pm, Sunday 12 pm to 5pm. Landis Valley Museum is a nationally significant museum of 19th century PA German rural culture. It consist of two farmsteads, a Victorian house, Country Store, crossroads village, transportation exhibit. You will be escorted by costumed guides through each building. There is a unique museum shop and ample parking lot.

Meadowcroft Village
RD 2
Avella, PA 15312

412-587-3412

Conestoga Wagon, Concord Mail Coach, Hearse, and more.

Mifflinburg Buggy Museum
598 Green St, PO Box 86
Mifflinburg, PA 17844
E-mail: buggymus@csrlink.net

570-966-1355
FAX: 570-966-9231

Open May-October Thursday-Saturday 10 am to 5 pm, Sunday 1 pm to 5 pm. Guided tours of an original family owned and operated carriage factory, the carriage maker's home and repository (showroom). Over 20 horse-drawn vehicles on display, including a Conestoga Wagon and other work vehicles, surreys, piano box buggies and sleighs. The museum is thought to be the only museum in the United States housed in an orginal carriage factory with original contents. The visitors' center features an introductory video and exhibit, museum store and auditorium.

Rolls-Royce Foundation
505 Fishing Creek Rd
Lewisberry, PA 17339
E-mail: rds@flightsystems.com

717-932-9900
FAX: 717-932-9925

See full listing in **Section One** under **Rolls-Royce/Bentley**

Spruance Library
84 S Pine St
Doylestown, PA 18901

215-345-0210

Located on 3rd floor of Mercer Museum. Books on carriages.

State Museum of Pennsylvania
Pennsylvania Historical and
Museum Commission
PO Box 1026
Harrisburg, PA 17108-1026

717-772-6997

John Zwierzyna, Senior Curator. 30 carriages (six on display) 20 sleighs (one on display) 15 wagons (three on display).

Strasburg Rail Road
PO Box 96
Strasburg, PA 17579-0096

717-687-7522

1855 town coach made by Rodgers, Philadelphia.

Swigart Museum
Museum Park, Box 214
Huntingdon, PA 16652
E-mail: cars@swigartmuseum.com

814-643-0885
FAX: 814-643-2857

Open Memorial Day-October. Admission: adults, $4; children 6-12, $2; senior citizen and group rates available. Located three miles east of Huntingdon, PA, on US Rt 22. One of the foremost collections of antique cars including 3 Duesenbergs, Dupont, Scripps-Booth, Carroll, Herbie-The Love Bug and two Tuckers-The Tin Goose and #13. Plus a memorable collection of toys, lights, clothing and a large collection of license plates and emblems. Web site: www.swigartmuseum.com

West Overton Museum
West Overton Village
Scottsdale, PA 15683

Carts, Sleigh and other items for the Pony/Donkey carts used in the mining/coke industry.

Wheatland Historic Mansion
1120 Marietta Ave, Rt 23
Lancaster, PA 17603
E-mail: wheatland@wheatland.org

717-392-8721
FAX: 717-295-8825

Open April-mid December seven days a week 10 am to 4 pm. Victorian mansion home of President James Buchanan. Tours led by costumed guides.

Zippo Manufacturing Company
33 Barbour St
Bradford, PA 16701

814-368-2700
FAX: 814-368-2874

Historic Zippo lighters and Case knives, interactive exhibits, unique audio/kinetic sculpture and the Zippo repair clinic at work. Shop the Zippo Case Store for the world's most complete selection of Zippo and Case products. Catch the famous Zippo car, a 1947 Chrysler Saratoga-New Yorker, when it's not on tour. Visit our web site and see if the Zippo car is lighting up a town near you. Web site: www.zippo.com

Rhode Island

Breakers Stable and Carriage House
Coggeshall and Bateman Aves
Newport, RI 02840

401-847-1000

Carriage House and Stable of Cornelius Vanderbilt. Numerous carriages and harness on display including The Venture, a road coach.

Pronyne
PO Box 1492
Pawtucket, RI 02862-1492

401-725-1118

Founded 1970. 100 members. Open all year, 9-5. Restoration and display of historic NASCAR modifieds events, Feb thru Oct. Ole Blue (37 Chevy coupe) and the Woodchopper coupe (37 Chevrolet) on display. Dues: $15/year.

South Carolina

Middleton Place
Ashley River Rd
Charleston, SC 29414

803-556-6020

Small carriage collection.

South Dakota

Days of 76 Museum
Chamber of Commerce
17 Crescent St, PO Box 391
Deadwood, SD 57732

605-578-2872

Open May 1st to September 30th. Collection of 50 original vehicles ranging from buggies to stages. Plus artifacts dating back 4,000-25,000 years and Indian artifacts dating back over 100 years.

Motion Unlimited Museum and Antique Car Lot
Hwy 79
Rapid City, SD 57702-8467
E-mail: mjanssen@GWTC.NET

605-348-7373

Open May-October Monday-Friday 9 am to 6 pm, Saturday 9 am to 4 pm, Sunday by appointment. Antique car lot open year round. Admission: $4 adults, children 12 and under free. Admission good for the season, you only pay once a year. Make: Ford, Chevy, Dodge, Studebaker, Buick, Mitchell. Model: 1925 Studebaker Motor Home, 1934 Studebaker Dual Sidemount Commander Coupe, Airplane Car, 38 Lincoln Zypher 3-window coupe, 1920 Mitchell Touring, 55-57-58-59-60 Chevys, plus 90 motorcycles, Harleys, Indians, Triumphs, Webly Vickers, Japanese race bike, and much more.

Museum of Pioneer Life 1311 S Duff St, PO Box 1071 Mitchell, SD 57301	**605-996-2122**

Three carriages, a hearse, three wagons including a sheep wagon, and the Stage Coach used between Deadwood and Piedmont, South Dakota.

National Motorcycle Museum and Hall of Fame 2438 Junction Ave, PO Box 602 Sturgis, SD 57785	**museum**

Open year round 7 days a week, 9 am to 6 pm. Featuring 90 plus antique motorcycles including a part of Steve McQueen's world renowned collection, his 1915 Cyclone. The museum gift shop is filled with items that will please any motorcycle enthusiast. Web site: www.museum.sturgis-hall.com

Performance Car Museum 3505 S Phillips Ave Sioux Falls, SD 57105	**museum**

Open year round Monday-Friday 9 am to 5 pm, Saturday 7 am, Sunday 10 am to 5 pm. Specializing in performance cars, celebrity cars and exotics. Attractions include every year Shelby, low mileage muscle cars, 289 Cobra, 1955/56 Corvette prototype formerly owned by Zora Duntov, 1973 Trans Am formerly owned by Clint Eastwood, and many, many more.

Pioneer Auto Museum and Antique Town I-90 Exit 192, PO Box 76 Murdo, SD 57559 E-mail: pas@pioneerautoshow.com	**605-669-2691** **FAX: 605-669-3217**

Open June-August 7 am to 10 pm; March-May and September-October 9 am to 6 pm. Dave Geisler, manager. Located at I-90, Exit 192 and US Highways 16 and 83 in Murdo. Exhibits include over 250 antique and classic cars from a 1902 Oldsmobile to a 1970 Superbird. Also several other exhibits of different modes of transportation from covered wagons to trains. Motorcycles on display include Elvis Presley's motorcycle. We have added muscle cars and a 1950s display. Joined with Pioneer Hallmark, Food Court and Super 8. Web site: www.pioneerautoshow.com

Sturgis Motorcycle Museum and Hall of Fame PO Box 602 Sturgis, SD 57785 E-mail: sturgismotorcyclemuseum@ yahoo.com	**605-347-0849** **FAX: 605-423-5225**

Open year round. Displaying 100s of antique motorcycles and memorabilia on a rotation basis. A museum that shows the history of the great sport of motorcycling. The museum gift shop will meet your needs for that special gift. We would love to have your antique or special interest motorcycle in our museum.

Telstar Mustang-Shelby-Cobra Museum 1300-1400 S Kimball St Mitchell, SD 57301	**605-996-6550**

Open year round upon request. Exhibits every year, model and body style of Shelbys, Boss 302s and Boss 429s, AC Cobras, fastbacks, GTs, convertibles.

Tennessee

Belle Meade Plantation 5025 Harding Rd Nashville, TN 37205 E-mail: bellemeade@home.com	**615-356-0501** **FAX: 615-356-2336**

Queen of Tennessee Plantations - 19th century world famous thoroughbred horse farm. Once 5,400 acres, tours of 1853 mansion by guides in period costume. Explore 1790 log cabin and 9 other remaining buildings. Home of Iroquois until 1954, the only American-bred winner of the English Derby (1881).

Dixie Gun Works Old Car Museum 1412 Reelfoot Ave Union City, TN 38261 E-mail: dixiegun@iswt.com	**901-885-0700** **FAX: 901-885-0440**

Open Monday-Friday 8 to 5. Admission $2. Exhibits include 36 fully restored antique automobiles dating from before 1947. All are in running condition. Also thousands of automobile accessories are on display. Web site: www.dixiegun.com

International Towing & Recovery Museum 401 Broad St Chattanooga, TN 37402	**PH/FAX:** **423-267-3132**

Open year round. Weekdays 10 am to 4:30 pm, weekends 11 am to 5 pm. The museum displays antique vehicles with a variety of antique wreckers and tow trucks. The Hall of Fame honors individuals from around the world who have made contributions to the towing and recovery industry. Other memorabilia and artifacts are on display from the earliest inventions. Exhibitions of special interest include 1913 Locomobile w/Holmes 485 wrecker and 1929 Chrysler w/Weaver 3 ton auto crane.

Old Car Museum Hwy 51 S Union City, TN 38261	**901-885-0700** **FAX: 901-885-0440**

Open Monday-Friday 8 am to 5 pm. Admission $2. Exhibits include 36 fully restored antique automobiles dating from before 1947. All are in running condition. Also thousands of automobile accessories are on display.

Texas

Central Texas Museum of Automotive History Hwy 304, PO Box 160 Rosanky, TX 78953	**512-237-2635**

Open April 1-September 30, Wednesday-Saturday 10 am to 5 pm, Sunday 1:30 pm to 5 pm; October 1-March 31, Friday-Saturday 10 am to 5 pm, Sunday 1:30 pm to 5 pm. Central Texas Museum of Automotive History is dedicated to the collection, restoration and preservation of historic automobiles, accessories and related items. There are usually 120-125 vehicles on display. Also included are European estate cars, town cars, limousines and sports cars. Other displays include a large number of gasoline and oil pumps, automobile and oil company signs, accessories, automobile models and automotive toys. Web site: www.tourtexas/rosanky

John E Conner Museum Texas A&M University Campus Box 134 821 W Santa Gertrudis Kingsville, TX 78363	**512-593-2810**

Two carriages, one wagon, one goat cart and farm machinery.

Corpus Christi Museum of Science and History 1900 N Chaparral Corpus Christi, TX 78401	**512-883-2862**

Two carriages, a stage coach and various harness items.

GAF Auto Museum 340 W Tyler St Longview, TX 75601	903-758-0002 800-234-0124 FAX: 903-758-0133

Open Monday-Friday 8 am to 5 pm. No admission charge. 55 autos from 1916-1976. Auto memorabilia. Original drawings by Herb Newport, automobile designer. Old car parts, 1920s-1960s.

Great Race Automotive Hall of Fame 114 N Crockett Granbury, TX 76048	817-573-5200 FAX: 817-573-4994

Our mission is to provide a journey wrapped in nostalgia and patriotism throughout automobile history.

Panhandle Plains Historical Museum US Hwy 87 on 4th Ave PO Box 967 WT Sta Canyon, TX 79016	806 656-2244

Open daily Monday-Saturday 9 am to 5 pm, Sundays 2 pm to 6 pm.

Pate Museum of Transportation 1227 W Magnolia Ave, Ste 420 Fort Worth, TX 76104	817-922-9504 FAX: 817-922-9536

Open daily except Monday and holidays. Located on Highway 377 between Fort Worth and Cresson. Exhibits include antique and special interest automobiles, aircraft and a 1,500-volume library.

The Sterquell Collection 5501 Everett Amarillo, TX 78294	806-372-7522

59 horse drawn vehicles, carriages, sleighs and related objects.

David Taylor Classic Car Museum 918 Mechanic Galveston Island, TX 77550	409-765-6590

Open year round daily 10 am to 5 pm. Closed Thanksgiving and Christmas. The museum features 55 vintage American automobiles housed in the historic CJ Marschner Bldg. It has the atmosphere typical of a car dealership of the 1930s, with every car in immaculate running condition. The cars range from 1919 to 1970. The museum is the home of a 1940 Mercury convertible which belonged to Carole Lombard from her husband Clark Gable. Other favorites include a 1935 Cadillac, V12 Fleetwood convertible, 1934 Ford roadster, 1927 Buick roadster and a 1937 Cord phaeton 812.

Witte Museum 3801 Broadway San Antonio, TX 78209 E-mail: wittemuseum.org	210-357-1900

14 carriages, one sulky, two hearses, and a mud wagon.

Utah

Bonneville Speedway Museum 1000 E Wendover Blvd Wendover, UT 84083	801-665-7721

Open daily May-November, 10 am to 6 pm. Displays Bonneville race cars, general antique cars, special interest cars and a line of general antiques. On exhibition are Bonneville World race car films.

Classic Cars International Museum **Displays & Sales** 335 W 7th St S Salt Lake City, UT 84101	PH/FAX: 801-322-5509 801-322-5186

Open year round. Monday-Friday 9 am to 4 pm. Special hours available by phone appointment. Over 200 antique and classic cars on display. Select units for sale to rotate cars. Classics

range from Rolls-Royces to Rickenbackers, Cords, Hupmobiles, Essex, LaSalles, Packards, Pierce-Arrows, V16s, V12s, 1903-1960 classics. Approximately 50 classics on sale year round to rotate displays. Web site: www.classiccarmuseumsales.com

Vermont

American Precision Museum 196 Main St Windsor, VT 05089	museum

Open Memorial day-November 1, Monday-Friday 9 am to 5 pm. This museum has the largest collection of historic precision machine tools in the nation.

Billings Farm & Museum River Rd and Rt 12, PO Box 489 Woodstock, VT 05091	802-457-2355

Working dairy farm and farm life museum with several c. 1890 wgons including a lumber wagon, hay wagon, freight wagon, and Democrat wagon.

Hildene Historic Rt 7A, PO Box 377 Manchester, VT 05254 E-mail: info@hildene.org	802-362-1788 FAX: 802-362-1564

Open May-October, daily 9:30 am to 4 pm. Former 412 acre estate of Robert Todd Lincoln. A 1928 Franklin once owned by Jesse Lincoln Randolph is on display. Annual antique and classic car show second weekend in June. Web site: www.hildene.org

Park-McCullough House Corner of Park and West Sts PO Box 388 N Bennington, VT 05257 E-mail: thehouse@sover.net	802-442-5441 FAX: 802-442-5442

Open May-October, 10 am to 4 pm, last tour at 3 pm. The Second Empire style "summer cottage" of Trenor and Laura Hall Park. Designed by prominent NY architects Diaper and Dudley, it was completed in 1865. It is one of the finest, most significant, and best preserved Victorian mansions in New England.

Shelburne Museum US Route 7, PO Box 10 Shelburne, VT 05482	802-985-3346 FAX: 802-985-2331

Open late May-late October Monday-Sunday 10 am to 5pm. The museum is home to vast collections of fine and decorative arts, paintings, folk sculpture, weathervanes, decoys, quilts, toys, dolls, circus memorabilia and more.

Westminster MG Car Museum Kimber Close Westminster, VT 05158	603-756-4121 FAX: 603-756-9614

Open weekends only June, July and August; and on Memorial Day, Labor Day and on Columbus Day weekend, 10 am to 5 pm. Museum houses 29 MG models, including a 1927 14/28 Flatnose Tourer, one of six known to exist, and a 1955 EX 182 Prototype, the lone survivor of four made.

Virginia

Car & Carriage Caravan Museum Luray Caverns Corp PO Box 748 Luray, VA 22835	540-743-6551

One of the oldest motor transportation museums on the East Coast. Located at the world famous Luray Caverns, our mission is to educate visitors to the history of transportation in this country. We have 51 cars on display, plus 17 carriages, 13 engines, and lots of memorabilia.

Glade Mountain Museum 703-783-5678
Rt 1 Box 360
Atkins, VA 24311

Open May-August, Sundays 1 pm to 8 pm. Glade Mountain Museum, take exit #54 off I-81, west 1 mile on US 11, south 1 mile on VA 708, east 1/2 mile on VA 615 to museum. Features old cars, 1803 blacksmith shop, 1850 bear trap, 1900 washing machine, 1907 1-cyclinder engine. Many more items from late 1800's. Cars are mostly Fords, 1926 and later. Salvage yard operating undr Jack's Garage at above address. Has over 200 vehicles from 1935 to 1970 and a few older parts.

Maymont Carriage Collection 804-358-7166
1700 Hampton St
Richmond, VA 23220

Excellent carriage house. 20 carriages including whitechapel cart, 1870 wicker phaeton.

Morven Park 703-777-2414
Westmoreland Davis Foundation
PO Box 6228
Leesburg, VA 20178

Carriage collection with over 125 vehicles.

Mount Vernon Ladies Association of the Union 703-799-8662
End of George Washington Pkwy S
Mount Vernon, VA 22121

Carriages, wagons, sleighs, harnesses.

National Sporting Library 703-687-6542
301 W Washington St, PO Box 1335
Middleburg, VA 22117

Extremely high quality library of sporting books including some rare pieces on coaching and driving.

Roaring Twenties Antique Car Museum 540-948-6290 FAX: 540-948-3744
Rt 1, Box 576
Hood, VA 22723-9802
E-mail: info@roaring-twenties.com

Open Sunday 1 pm to 6 pm from June-October, other times by appointment. Located in Madison County on State Route 230 between Route 29 and 33. John Dudley, owner. Exhibits include cars from the 1920s and 1930s, trucks, stationary engines, horse-drawn equipment, farm tools, household goods and other Americana. Examples of Carter, Stephens, Cleveland, Star, Hupmobile, Paige, Essex and Nash cars are on display. Cars and parts for sale. Web site: www.roaring-twenties.com

Virginia Museum of Transportation Inc 540-342-5670 FAX: 540-342-6898
303 Norfolk Ave
Roanoke, VA 24016
E-mail: info@vmt.org

Open year round. Monday-Saturday 10 am to 5 pm, Sunday 12 pm to 5 pm, closed on certain holidays as well as on Mondays in January and February. Auto Gallery opening in 2001. Currently exhibiting vintage cars, carriages, trucks, avaiation equipment, locomotives and rail cars. Also exhibiting model layouts, models, historic and interactive exhibits. Library and archives for research by appointment. Special events including annual Cool Wheels Festival in August. Memberships available at various levels. Special exhibits showcase VWs, Studebakers, Porsches, Harley-Davidsons, Packards, customized creations, street rods, stock cars, antique automobiles and more. Web site: www.vmt.org

Washington

Carr's One of a Kind in the World Museum 509-489-8859 800-350-6469 FAX: 509-489-8859
5225 N Freya St
Spokane, WA 99207

Open year round. Saturday-Sunday 1 pm to 4 pm. Showcasing under chandeliers such wondrous cars as JFK and Jackie's private 62 Lincoln, Jackie Gleason's personal limo, Elvis' 1973 Mark IV and hundreds of beautiful Asian treasurers. $1,000,000 entertainment for only $5. This is a hands-on museum. All may sit in the precise seats that were occupied by JFK, Jackie, Marilyn, Elvis, Jackie Gleason and the June Taylor Dancers. A subsidiary of Trom Publications.

Lynden Pioneer Museum 360-354-3675
217 Front St
3rd and Front St
Lynden, WA 98264

Open Monday-Saturday 10 am to 4 pm, closed Sundays and Holidays. The Pioneer Home and barn begin the journey with artifacts similar to those used in the early settlement of Lynden. The Puget Sound Antique Tractor and Machinery Association always has a fine display of old tractors and farm machinery from the big steam engine to the one cyclinder antique gas engine. In addition to the buggies and tractors, the basement contains the vehicle collection. Unusual cars, trucks, and Lynden's first Rural Fire Truck, and a 1929 Reo share space with bicycles and other related collections.

Yakima Valley Museum and Historical Association 509-248-0747 FAX: 509-453-4890
2105 Tieton Dr
Yakima, WA 98902
E-mail: info@yakimavalleymuseum.org

Open weekdays 10 am to 5 pm, weekends 12 pm to 5 pm. A variety of different interests for anyone. There is a Children's Underground Hands-on Learning Center, historic Yakima, pioneer life, American Indian culture and history, wagons, carriages, and coaches. The museum also has a natural history exhibit, special exhibitions, a research library, and a gift and book shop. For those who love sweets, there is a working soda fountain from the 1930s in the museum.

Wisconsin

Alfa Heaven Inc 715-449-2141
2698 Nolan Rd
Aniwa, WI 54408-9667

See full listing in **Section One** under **Alfa Romeo**

Brooks Stevens Auto Collection Inc 414-241-4185
10325 N Port Washington Rd
Mequon, WI 53092

Open year round Monday-Friday 9 am to 5 pm. The Brooks Stevens Auto Collection is a museum with 65 to 70 autos. A repair and service facility and a restoration shop for autos of all years, makes and models. On exhibit: one of a kinds and Excaliburs along with many other autos.

Circus World Museum 608-356-8341
426 Water St
Baraboo, WI 53913

Open May-Labor Day 9 am to 6 pm, 10 am to 4 pm remainder of the year. Over 100 circus wagons.

Dells Auto Museum 920-648-2151 608-254-2008
Richard W Tarnutzer
591 Wisconsin Dells Pkwy
Wisconsin Dells, WI 53965

Open daily 9 am to 9 am from May 15-Labor Day. An exhibition of convertibles built from 1901 to 1982 featuring Indianapolis pace cars. Also on display are 400 antique dolls and toys along with period clothing from the turn of the century through the fifties. Also license plate collection. Cars and antiques bought and sold.

Hartford Auto Museum 147 N Rural St Hartford, WI 53027 E-mail: automu@netwurx.net	**414-673-7999**

Open year round except holidays. Features Kissel automobiles, Nash, along with Pierce-Arrow, Locomobiles, Terraplanes and various pieces of fire fighting equipment. Also displays gasoline pumps and gasoline and steam engines. Museum houses 90 vehicles of all kinds in its 60,000 square feet of display area. Admissions: $6 adults, $5 seniors and students, $2.50 children 8 to 15, free to children under 8.

Madline Island PO Box 9 LaPointe, WI 54850	**715-747-2415**

Sleighs, logging-sleds, sleds.

Old Wade House and Wisconsin Carriage Museum PO Box 34 Greenbush, WI 53026	**414-526-3271**

80 horse-drawn vehicles built 1870-1915.

Old World Wisconsin S103 W37890, Hwy 67 Eagle, WI 53119	**414-594-6300**

Doctor's buggy, sleigh, spring wagon, butter and egg wagon, four farm wagons and miscellaneous farm machinery.

Rock County Historical Society 10 S High St, PO Box 8096 Janesville, WI 53545	**608-756-4509**

Four carriages, six sleighs, one wagon and farm machinery. Janesville Carriage Company catalogs and papers. Also, miscellaneous robes, whips, jacks, bells, and harnesses.

Wisconsin Automotive Museum 147 N Rural St Hartford, WI 53027	**262-673-7999** **FAX: 262-673-7999**

Open year round except holidays. Features Kissel automobiles, Nash, Pierce-Arrow, Locomobiles, Terraplanes and various pieces of fire fighting equipment. Also displays gasoline pumps and gasoline and steam engines. Museum houses 90 vehicles of all kinds in its 40,000 square feet of display area. Admission: $5 adult, $4 seniors and students, $2 children 8 to 15, free to children under 8.

Wyoming

Cheyenne Frontier Days **Old West Museum** 4610 N Carey Ave in Frontier Park PO Box 2720 Cheyenne, WY 82003 E-mail: lcouture1@juno.com	**307-778-7290** **FAX: 307-778-7288**

The Old West Museum features a carriage and wagon collection - 147 to date. History exhiibits on Cheyenne Frontier Days - The city of Cheyenne - Wyoming Native American - Western Art - rodeo.

Trail Town Museum of the Old West PO Box 696 Cody, WY 82414-0696	**museum**

Sleighs, caissons, spring wagons, ice wagons.

Australia

Illawarra Motoring Museum 634 Northcliffe Dr Kembla Grange Wollongong NSW 2506 Australia	**61-2-4228-7048** **FAX: 61-2-4272-7246**

Open Wednesday-Sunday year round, 10 am to 4 pm. Small, quality museum, monthly newsletter, membership open $35PA, focus on automobilia includes 1920 Paige racer.

National Motor Museum Main St Birdwood STH 5234 Australia E-mail: motor@history.sa.gov.au	**(08) 85685 006** **FAX: (08) 85685 195**

Daily 9 am to 5 pm. Home to Australia's largest and most important collection of motor vehicles. The collection comprises over 300 cars, motorcycles and commercial vehicles and is considered to be one of the best in the world. Web site: www.history.gov.sa.au

Raverty's Motor Museum 23-33 Ogilvie Ave Echuca Victoria 3564 Australia	**03 54 822730**

Open most days 10 am to 4 pm. Display of over 100 veteran, vintage, classic and historic vehicles, cars and trucks. Pierce-Arrow, Gardner, Yellow Cab, Fords, Chevrolets.

Bavaria

BMW Group Petuelring 130 Munchen 80788 Bavaria Germany E-mail: bmw.tradition@bmw.de	**089-382-23307** **FAX: 089-382-27500**

Open daily 9 am to 5 pm, last entry 4 pm. Special focus on BMW. The museum shows this century's technical development and social history, plus predictions into the new millennium, illustrated by aircraft engines from 1916-onward, motorcycles from 1923-onward, motorcars from 1928-onward, as well as videos, slide shows and films.

Belgium

Automuseum Oldtimer Tempelare 12 (Road Ypres-Furnes) Reninge 8647 Belgium	**32 57 40 04 32** **FAX: 32 57 40 11 64**

Open Monday 1:30 pm to 6:15 pm, Tuesday-Friday 1 pm to 6:15 pm, Saturday 10:30 am to 5:15 pm, closed Sunday and bank holidays. On the N8 road between Ypres and Furnes (Leper and Veurne) 130 km west of Brussels, towards the French border (40 km east of Lille, France). Collection of 95 cars from 1899-1970 and 25 motorcycles. Cars: 1898 Decauville, 1906 Werner, 1912 Unic, 1930 Minerva, 1924 FN, 1931 Pierce-Arrow, 1936 NSU-Fiat, 1938 BMW 327, 1953 Hotchkiss Tour de France, 1953 Peugeot 203 Tour de France, 1986 Range Rover Paris-Dakar. Motorbikes: 1938 Ariel, 1974 Suzuki Wankel. Cafeteria with snacks.

Mahymobiles Rue Erna 3 Leuze-Hainaut-B7900 Belgium E-mail: mahymobiles@online.be	**32-69-35-45-45** **FAX: 32-69-35-44-83**

Meet a century of automobile history: about 120 vehicles (original condition or restored) between 1898 and 1990, didactical hall, miniatures exhibition, children's mini-circuit, shop, cafeteria, library (25 tons of paper). More than 600 cars will also be shown in the same building from April 2002. Restoration workshop and test track planned for the end of 2002. Web site: www.mahymobiles.be

Musee du Circuit de Spa-Francorchamps Abbaye de Stavelot BP 52 4970 Stavelot Belgium E-mail: etc@abbayedestavelot.be	+32 80 88 08 78 FAX: +32 80 88 08 77

Open year round. 10 am to 6 pm, last admission at 5 pm. Closed on Mondays. Closed on January 1, Laetare Sunday (fourth Sunday in Lent, March 10, 2002 and March 30, 2003). Discover the history of car and motorbike racing on one of the finest race tracks in the world in the outstanding setting of the vaulted cellars of Stavelot Abbey, just a stone's throw from the Spa-Francochamps race track. A large number of collector's cars, information panels, videos, virtual animation, etc, will guide you throughout your visit. Web site: www.abbayedestavelot.be

Canada

Nova Scotia Museum of Industry 147 N Foord St, PO Box 2590 Stellarton, NS Canada B0K 1S0 E-mail: industry@gov.ns.ca	902-755-5425 FAX: 902-755-7045

Open year round. Allows the visitor to experience the fascinating human story of industry in Nova Scotia. Each visitor receives a time card so they may punch in and travel back through the working lives of our Nova Scotian ancestors. Visitors can work a steam engine, feel waterpower, hook a rag mat, build a model car on an assembly line. Samson, Canada's oldest steam locomotive, 1899 "Victorian" horseless carriage, 1912 McKay car, 1963 Volvo. Web site: www.industry.museum.gov.ns.ca

Reynolds Museum Ltd 4110-57th St Wetaskiwin, AB Canada T9A 2B6 E-mail: srsl@incentre.net	780-352-6201 FAX: 780-352-4666

See full listing in Section Two under car dealers

Reynolds-Alberta Museum Box 6360 (1km West on Hwy 13) Wetaskiwin, AB Canada T9A 2G1 E-mail: ram@gov.ab.ca (museum general) sean.moir@gov.ab.ca (library)	800-661-4726 403-361-1351 FAX: 403-361-1239

Open Tuesday-Sunday 9 am to 5 pm winter, 9 am to 7 pm summer. The Reynolds-Alberta Museum interprets the history of ground and air transportation, agriculture and industry from the 1890s-1950s. Collection of over 1,400 vintage automobiles, trucks, aircraft and agricultural machinery. 60,000 sq ft exhibit hall with over 100 major artifacts on display. Vehicles in collection include: 1929 Duesenberg phaeton Royale Model J214, 1927 LaSalle convertible coupe, 1913 Locomobile sport phaeton, 1918 National V12 sport phaeton, 1912 Hupp-Yeats electric coach. Museum is also home to Canada's Aviation Hall of Fame. Web site: www.gov.ab.ca/mcd/mhs/ram/ram.htm

Saskatchewan Western Development Museum 2935 Melville St Saskatoon, SK Canada S7J 5A6	306-934-1400 FAX: 306-934-4467

Open daily 9 am to 5 pm; Yorkton Museum closed in winter. Head office at above address, branches at North Battleford, Saskatoon, Moose Jaw and Yorkton. Moose Jaw Museum features exhibits on transportation theme. All museums display vintage automobiles.

Southwestern Ontario Heritage Village 6155 Arner Town Line, RR 2 Kingsville, ON Canada N9Y 2E5 E-mail: swoheritagevillage@on.aibn.com	519-776-6909 FAX: 519-776-8321

Open April-June and September-mid November, Wednesday-Sunday 10 am to 5 pm, July and August daily 10 am to 5 pm. Large collection of vintage automobiles and early transportation devices. Expanded transportation museum will open June 24,

2001, with exhibit Canadians on the Move. Web site: www.cnls.com/swo.heritage.village

Western Development Museum History of Transporation 50 Diefenbaker Dr, Box 185 Moose Jaw, SK Canada S6H 4B8 E-mail: wdm.mj@sk.sympatico.ca	306-693-5989 FAX: 306-693-0511

Open year round. Daily 9 am to 6 pm (closed Mondays January-March). History of Transportation, an extensive collection of automobiles, buggies, planes and locomotives as well as related artifacts. Classy cars on exhibit. Located at the junction of Highways 1 and 2. Web site: www.wdmuseum.sk.ca

Channel Islands

Jersey Motor Museum St Peter's Village Jersey JE3 7AG Channel Islands	01534-482966

Open March-late October daily 10 am to 5 pm. Veteran and vintage cars, motorcycles, Allied and German military vehicles of WW II, aero engines, models, memorabilia and accessory displays. Cars on display: Rolls-Royce Phantom III used by General Montgomery, also Sir Winston Churchill's car.

Czech Republic

Skoda Auto Museum Vaclava Klementa 294 29360 Mlada Boleslav Czech Republic E-mail: museum@skoda-auto.cz	00420-326-831138 FAX: 00420-326-832028

Open daily 9 am to 5 pm, except January 1, December 24, December 25 and December 31 open 9 am to 2 pm. Exposition: 100 years of Skoda, Motor gallery, How a car is produced. Conference halls: Laurin and Klement for 600 people; Hieronimus I and II for 20-80 people; Kolowrat for 16 people. Factory tours for visitors under the age of 15. Restoration workshop a part of the museum. Admission: 36 Kc adults, 18 Kc children. Rallye bar open from 9 am till 6 pm. Visitors service: Petra Fadrhonsova, PH: 00420-326-831134, FAX: 00420-326-832039, e-mail: petra.fadrhonsova@skoda-auto.cz Web site: www.skoda-auto.cz/history

Technical Museum Zahumenni 369 Koprivnice 742 21 Czech Republic E-mail: technika@tatramuseum.cz	PH/FAX: +420-656-821415

Open Tuesday-Sunday. Winter hours: 9 am to 4 pm; summer hours: 9 am to 5 pm. Tatra cars, trucks, railroad carriages, aircraft, chassis, engines, etc. Seven audio/video boxes with the Tatra history from 1850 till this time. Replica of the first car Prasident (1897) and the first truck (1898) manufactured in former Austrian-Hungary monarchy. Web site: www.tatramuseum.cz

Denmark

Jysk Automobilmuseum 8883 Gjern Denmark	86-87-50-50

Open April 1-May 15 Saturday-Sunday and holidays 10 am to 5 pm, May 16-September 15 daily 10 am to 5 pm, September 16-October 31 Saturday-Sunday 10 am to 5 pm. 140 vehicles, 68 different makes from the period 1900-1948, primarily cars and motorcycles, but also trucks and fire engines.

England

Atwell-Wilson Motor Museum Downside Stockley Ln Calne Wiltshire SN110NF England	PH/FAX: 01249-813119

Open year round Sunday-Thursday 11 am to 5 pm (4 pm winter). Collection of 100 vintage, post vintage and classic motor vehicles from the UK, Europe and the USA. This collection started in 1962 with the 1957 Albemarle Buick, which has a Canadian chassis and an English body, and has grown from this. Daimlers, Jaguars, Mercury, Lincoln, Buick, Ford Model A, Model Y and Model T. Collection also includes classic motorcycles, Vincent Rapide, Rolls-Royce Silver Wraith, Ford Model T, Alvis Speed 20, Allard Palm Beach, Brough Superior SS80, Daimler EL24, Rolls-Royce Silver Shadow. Web site: www.atwell-wilson.org

Beamish, The North of England Open Air Museum Beamish Co Durham DH9 0RG England E-mail: museum@beamish.org.uk	0191 370 4000 FAX: 0191 370 4001

Open year round. Summer hours: 10 am to 5 pm; winter hours: closed Mondays and Fridays, times vary according to season. Open Air Museum illustrating life in the North of England in the early 1800s and 1900s in The Town, Colliery Village, Home Farm, 1825 Railway and Pockerley Manor, including period "Motor and Cycle Works" with showroom, spares department and workshop. Exhibit includes: 1906 Armstrong Whitworth, 1914 Model T Ford, several restored motorcycles. Web site: www.beamish.org.uk

Betws-Y-Coed Motor Museum Betws-Y-Coed Conwy Valley Gwynedd LL24 0AH England	01690710760

Open Easter to October, daily 10:30 to 6. Created from the private collection of the Houghton family and housed in the Mellow Stones buildings of the old Betws farm which overlooks the beautiful river Llugwy in the heart of the village. Normally over 30 motor vehicles on display including Aston Martin, Bugatti, Bentley, Riley MPH, MGs, Morgan, motorcycles, child's cars, LSR jet engine and motoring memorabilia. Exhibits include Bugatti Type 57 1934, racing Bentley 1924 (unrestored), Riley MPH, rare and beautiful.

The CM Booth Collection of Historic Vehicles Falstaff Antiques 63-67 High St Rolvenden Kent TN17 4LP England	01580-241234

Open year round. Monday-Saturday 10 am to 6 pm. Specializing in Morgan 3-wheel cars, 11 normally on display, other interesting cars, motorcycles, cycles, 1936 Bampton Caravan, much automobilia, toy and model cars. Books, restoration, information and museum for 1910-1952 Morgan 3-wheelers.

British Cycling Museum The Old Station Camelford Cornwall PL32 9TZ England	PH/FAX: 01840-212811

Open year round. Sunday-Thursday 10 am to 5 pm. The nation's foremost museum of cycling history. Showing over 300 various cycles and cycling memorabilia from 1818-present day. Web site: www.chycor.co.uk

Canterbury Motor Museum 11 Cogans Terr Canterbury Kent CT1 3SJ England	01227-451718

Open April-October. Please telephone to view. Privately owned collection of veteran and vintage cars, stationary engines and automobilia.

Cars of the Stars Motor Museum Standish St Keswick Cumbria CA12 5LS England E-mail: cotsmm@aol.com	017687 73757 FAX: 017687 72090

Open Feb-Dec (phone), daily 10 am-5 pm. Cars of the Stars features vehicles from TV and films including the Batmobiles, KITT, Herbie, Chitty Chitty Bang Bang, James Bond collection, Flintstones, Munsters, Koach, Back to the Future DeLorean.

Most of the most famous TV and film cars in the world. Web site: www.carsofthestars.com

Cobbaton Combat Collection Chittlehampton Umberleigh N Devon EX37 9RZ England E-mail: info@cobbatoncombat.co.uk	01769-540740 FAX: 01769-540141

See full listing in **Section Two** under **military vehicles**

Donington Grand Prix Collection Donington Park Castle Donington, Derby Derbyshire DE74 2RP England E-mail: enquiries@ doningtoncollection.co.uk	01332-811027 FAX: 01332-812829

Open year round. Daily 10 am to 5 pm, closed Christmas and New Years. The world's largest collection of single seater racing cars. See Senna's car which won the 1993 European Grand Prix at Donington, plus many more. Ascari's Ferrari, Mansell's Red 5, the only complete collection of Vanwalls in the world. Web site: www.doningtoncollection.com

Geeson Bros Motorcycle Museum & Workshop 2-6 Water Ln South Witham Grantham Lincs NG33 5PH England	01572 767280 01572 768195

Open April 15, May 13, August 26, October 7, November 11, December 27, December 29, 10:30 am to 5 pm. 85 British motorcycles dating back to 1913. All restored to new condition, workshop open to show work in progress and serve refreshments.

Greater Manchester Fire Service Museum Maclure Rd Rochdale Lancashire OL11 1DN England	01706 900155

Open year round by prior arrangement. The official museum of the Greater Manchester County Fire Service. Portrays the history of firefighting in UK, generally and particularly Manchester area. 17 fire appliances from 1741-1957 plus uniforms, equipment, models, photos. Archives. Exhibit includes Newsham manual 1741, Dennis-Metz 125 ft turntable ladder/aerial truck.

Heritage Motor Centre Banbury Rd Gaydon Warwickshire CV35 0BJ England E-mail: enquiries@ heritagemotorcentre.org.uk	0044 1926 641188 FAX: 0044 1926 641555

Open year round. 10 am to 5 pm. Closed December 24, 25, 26, 2001. Home of the largest collection of historic British cars in the world. Houses 200 vehicles charting the development of the British motor industry from the 1890s-present day. The collection includes the world famous marques of Rover, Austin, Morris, Wolseley, Riley, Standard, Triumph, MG and Austin-Healey. Attractions also include 4-wheel drive demonstration circuit, quad bike, children's roadway, cafe and gift shop. Many special events held throughout the year, please call for further details. Admission: adults, £6; seniors, £5; children (up to 16 years), £4; under age 5 free; group rates available (20 people and over); family ticket (2 adults and 3 children), £17. Web site: www.heritage.org.uk

Keighley Bus Museum Trust Limited 47 Brantfell Dr Burnley Lancashire BB12 8AW England	PH/FAX: 01282-413179

Open year round. Tuesday and Thursday evenings, Sunday 10 am to 5 pm. A collection of fifty buses and coaches from 1931-1970s, many under active restoration. Free bus services run on open days and other special occasions. Web site: www.kbmt.freeuk.com

Lakeland Motor Museum
Holker Hall Cark-in-Cartmel
Grange-over-Lands
Cumbria LA11 7PL England

PH/FAX: **015395 58509**

Open April-October Sunday-Friday 10:30 am to 4:45 pm, closed Saturday. Over 150 classic and vintage cars, motorcycles, tractors, cycles and engines plus rare automobilia and the Campbell Legend. Bluebird exhibition. The best small visitor attraction in England, English Tourism Council, England for Excellence Awards 2000.

Llangollen Motor Museum
Pentrefelin
Llangollen
Denbighshire LL20 8EE England

01987860324

Open February-November Tuesday-Sunday 10 am to 5 pm. A collection of cars, motorbikes, toys and memorabilia dating from 1920s-1960s plus an exhibition depicting the history of Canals in Britain. Vauxhall 30/98 and 1919 Model T Ford on display.

Sammy Miller Motorcycle Museum
Bashley Cross Rd
New Milton
Hampshire BH25 5SZ England

01425 620777
FAX: **01425 619696**

Open year round. 10 am to 4:30 pm. Sammy Miller is a legend in his own lifetime. He is still winning competitions, 47 years after his first victory. The Museum houses the finest collection of fully restored motorcycles in Europe including factory racers and exotic prototypes. The tea rooms, craft shops and animals are open all year. Web site: www.sammymiller.co.uk

Mouldsworth Motor Museum
Smithy Lane
Mouldsworth
NR Chester Cheshire CH3 8AR England

01928 731781

Open February through end of November, Sundays & bank holiday weekends 12 pm to 5 pm. Housed in an amazing 1930s Art Deco building in its own grounds and safe for children. Close to Delamere Forest and 6 miles east of Chester Roman city. A unique collection of over 60 motor cars, motor bicycles and early bicycles. Quiz for children, famous collection of automobilia. Exhibit includes MG 12/12 1930, MG J2 1933, McEvoy Special 1932, Alfa Romeo 8C Zagato bodied. Specializing in MGs, early cars, vintage period. Parts and particularly automobilia for mascots, badges, enamel signs. Motoring art. Web site: www.fia.com

Museum of British Road Transport
St Agnes Ln
Hales St
Coventry CV1 1PN England
E-mail: museum@mbrt.w.uk

44-01203-832425
FAX: **44-01203-832465**

Open year round daily 10 am to 5 pm. The largest display of British road transport covering many of the marques which made this city of Coventry the home of the British road transport industry. Thrust 2 (holder of World Land Speed Record 1983-1997) and Royal Daimlers on display.

The Museum of Science & Industry in Manchester
Liverpool Rd
Castlefield
Manchester M34FP England
E-mail: info@msim.org.uk

+44 (0) 161-832-2244
FAX: **+44 (0) 161-606-0186**

Open daily 10 am to 5 pm. The museum is based in the world's first passenger railway station dating from 1830. Exhibits include working stationary steam engines, land and air transport, industrial and scientific collections, all related to Manchester's industrial past. Manchester made vehicles including early Rolls-Royce and Crossleys. Web site: www.msim.org.uk

National Motor Museum
John Montagu Building
Beaulieu, Brockenhurst
Hampshire SO42 7ZN England
E-mail: beaulieu@tcp.co.uk

01590-612345
FAX: **01590-612624**

Open daily (except Christmas Day) 10 am to 6 pm Easter-September, 10 am to 5 pm October-Easter. The National Motor Museum is one of the finest in the world and tells the story of motoring on the roads of Great Britain from 1895-present day. There are over 250 vehicles on show including four land speed record breaking cars. Excellent reference, photographic and film libraries. Web site: www.beaulieu.co.uk

The National Tramway Museum
Crich, Matlock
Derbyshire DE4 5DP England
E-mail: info@tramway.co.uk

01773 852565
FAX: **01773 852326**

Open January-March Sunday-Monday 10:30 am to 4 pm, also half term week February 20-24; March 31-October 31 daily 10 am to 5:30 pm (Starlight Special event until 7:30 pm); November-December 23 Saturday-Monday 10:30 am to 4 pm. Fully operational vintage tramway, indoor and outdoor attractions. Drivers of classic vehicles built and registered before January 1, 1968, admitted free if vehicle is parked in the Museum Street for a minimum of 3 hours. Web site: www.tramway.co.uk

North Yorkshire Motor Museum
D T Mathewson
Roxby Garage, Pickering Rd
Thornton-le-Dale, North Yorkshire England

01751 474455
FAX: **01944 758188**

Open year round. Daily 10 am to 4 pm, closed Christmas Day. Classic and vintage cars, motorbikes, commercials and memorabilia. Owned and run by a family of enthusiasts.

REME Museum of Technology
Isaac Newton Rd
Arborfield, Reading
Berkshire RG2 9NJ England
E-mail: reme-museum@gtnet.gov.uk

PH/FAX: **0118-976-3375**

Open year round. Telephone for opening times. History of British Army's Corps of Royal Electrical and Mechanical Engineers and its role repairing military equipment. Displays include part of a total collection of over 100 military vehicles. Web site: www.rememuseum.org.uk

Sandringham House Museum & Grounds
Sandringham
Nr King's Lynn
Norfolk PE35 6EN England

01553-772675
FAX: **01485-541571**

Open daily 11 am to 5 pm Easter-mid July and early August-October. Converted stables and coach houses in the grounds of her Majesty Queen Elizabeth IIs country home containing collections of vintage Royal vehicles and carriages, limousines and miniature cars. 1900 Daimler phaeton, the first car owned by the British Royal family on display. Web site: www.sandringhamestate.co.uk

Skopos Motor Museum
Alexandra Hills, Alexandra Rd
Batley
West Yorkshire WA7 6JA England

01924-444423

Open year round. Wednesday to Sunday 10:30 am to 4:30 pm. Over 60 cars on display ranging from 1894 Benz Velo to a 180 mph Lamborghini. Also on display are 2 Doble steam cars and a Mercedes-Benz 300SL gullwing which was owned by Roger Whitaker, the folk singer.

West of England Transport Collection
15, Land Park
Chulmleigh
Devon EX18 7BH England

01769 580811

Annual opening day in Winkleigh, Devon, Sunday, October 6, 2002, otherwise by prior appointment, 10 am to 4 pm. Large collection of mainly west country buses, coaches and commercial vehicles, 1920s to 1970s. Quantities of early engines, transmissions, etc, held. Bus exhibit includes: Leyland, AEC, Guy, Bristol, Austin. Also much archive material of passenger transport operation in the area. Annual open day at Winkleigh, Devon, is always first Sunday in October.

Whitewebbs Museum of Transport Whitewebbs Rd Enfield Middlesex EN2 9HW England	208-367-1898 FAX: 208-363-1904

Open year round. 4th Sunday of the month, 10 am to 5 pm, and every Tuesday 12 pm to 4 pm. Museum run and funded by Enfield and District Veteran Vehicle Trust (local old car club). Can be open by appointment at other times. Call before visiting. Cars and motorcycles, unique 1912 Belsize Motor fire engine on exhibit.

France

The Presidential Cars Museum Chateau de Montjalin Sauvigny le Bois 89200 France E-mail: odelafon@aol.com	(333) 863-44642 FAX: (333) 863-16683

Open year round, every day 9 am to 7 pm. The Presidential Cars Museum exhibits big convertible cars of the 60s used to transport in parades the Head of States, JFK, Eisenhower, de Gaulle, Kruschev, Popemobiles, etc.

Germany

Deutsches Museum Museumsinsel 1 D-80538 Munchen Germany E-mail: deutsches-museum@ deutsches-museum.de	089 2179-1 089 2179-260 089 2179-255 FAX: 089 2179-324

Open daily from 9 am to 5 pm, closed January 1, Shrove Tuesday, Good Friday, May 1, Corpus Christi, November 1, December 24, 25, 31. The Deutsches Museum covers the development of science and technology from its origins to the present day. It shows 55 automobiles, 25 sectioned cars and 40 motorcycles. On exhibit is the first motor vehicle, Karl Benz' three-wheeler 1886. Web site: www.deutsches-museum.de

Deutsches Technikmuseum v Berlin Trebbiner Str 9 10963 Berlin Germany E-mail: info@dtmb.de	++49-30-254840 FAX: ++49-30-25484-175

Open year round Tuesday-Friday 9 am to 5:30 pm, Saturday-Sunday 10 am to 6 pm. Holidays: January 1-2, April 13, 15, 16, May 24, June 3-4, 10 am to 6 pm. Closed Monday. Museum of transport and technology (50 locomotives on display), cars and motorcycles and bicycles, printing, photography, navigation, shipping, aviation. Rumpler Tropfen wagon (streamline car 1921).

Motorcycle Museum (Motorrad Museum) Lengericher Str 49479 Ibbenburen Germany	05451-6454

Open April-October Saturday 2 pm to 6 pm, Sunday 10 am to 6 pm, other days by special request. More than 150 motorcycles are waiting for you in an old school. They cover a wide range reaching from the ordinary from 1882 to the heaviest motorcycle ever produced in Germany, the Munch Mammut. Experts will enjoy rarities like the watercooled Diel from 1927.

Rosso Bianco Sportscar Museum Obernauer Str 125 D-63743 Aschaffenburg Germany	06021 21358 FAX: 06021 20636

Open April-October daily, except on Monday, 10 am to 6 pm; November-March, Sunday 10 am to 6 pm. The world's greatest sportscar collection and art & auto forum, one of the most significant automobile art collections in the world. 220 sportscars and old-timers, 50 motorbikes, approximately 600 art objects. Large collections of Ferraris, Maseratis, Alfa Romeos, Can Am cars, Imsa cars. New: collection of 150 scooters. Web site: www.rosso-bianco.de

Stiftung AutoMuseum Volkswagen Dieselstr 35 Wolfsburg 38446 Germany E-mail: ext1.automuse@vwmail.de	05361 52071 FAX: 05361 52010

Open year round. 7 days a week. Specializing in Volkswagen cars for all models of the Volkswagen AG. Jazz concerts, cabaret events. Publication: Ein Wolfsburger Erlebnis. Sales brochure, gift shop.

Hungary

Auto Muzeuma Haris (Bross) Testverek 1117 Budapest XI, Moricz Zsigmond Korter 12 Hungary	01 (1) 3656893

Private collection. Antique cars and motorcycles, 1875-1900. On exhibit are Hungarian history cars and Hungarien-Marklin cars toy series. Experimental cars 45 pieces: fire cars series, police, lorries, Vandenlence and racing cars 1/20. MSM-Haris Marc! MCA.BUDAPEST. Forma-1. Club. Alfa Romeo Journal (club).

Ireland

Museum of Irish Transport Scotts Hotel Gardens, Killarney Co Kerry Ireland E-mail: kevin@kygems.iol.ie	353-64-34677 FAX: 353-64-31582

Open April-October daily 10 am to 6 pm. Exhibition of veteran, vintage and classic cars, cycles, motorcycles, carriages and automobilia. Fire fighting equipment. Special exhibits include 1902 Oldsmobile, 1904 Germain, 1907 Silver Stream and 1900 Argyll. Fascinating collection of American number plates.

National Transport Museum Howth Demesne Howth Co Dublin Ireland	00-353-1-8320427 00-353-1-8480831

Open weekends 2 pm to 5 pm (including bank holidays), June-August daily 10 am to 5 pm. Ireland's only comprehensive collection of public service and commercial road transport. Approximately 150 vehicles at present. Members are drawn from all walks of life, people interested in commercial vehicles. Our major publication is The Winged Wheel, a history of CIE (the National transport company).

Japan

HRC Inc Kawaguchiko Motor Museum 2-33-19 Minami Kugahara Ohta-Ku Toyko Japan E-mail: racing@big.or.jp	03-3757-5496 FAX: 03-3757-8598

Open March to December, 9 am to 5 pm, closed Thursdays. Focuses on 100 years of an automobile and the car starts from 1886 Benz Patent-Motowagen to a very recent Ferrari F40. Total of 70 to 80 cars are always displayed (both domestic and world automobiles). Two Model T Fords, Maxwell, Mercedes-Benz 540K, Bugatti T57s, VW, Rolls-Royce, 1930s and 1960s Japanese early 8 cars, etc. Web site: www.big.or.jp/~atmuseum

HRC Inc Racing Palace 2-33-19 Minami Kugahara Ohta-Ku Toyko Japan E-mail: racing@big.or.jp	03-3757-5496 FAX: 03-3757-8598

Open year round 6 days 9-5, closed Tuesday. Very first pure racing car museum in Japan. The museum consists of world racing cars such as F1, Indy, F3000, F2, F3, FF, Kart, Rally, prototypes, touring cars, GTs, Moto, etc. Total of 80 cars are displayed for both domestic and international. 1991 McLaren and 1994 Williams which late Ayrton Senna drove are on display. Web site: www.big.or.jp/~atmuseum

| Transportation Museum
25 Kanda=Sudacho
1-Chome Chiyoda-ku
Tokyo 101-0041 Japan
E-mail: gakugei@kouhaku.or.jp | 03-3251-8481
FAX: 03-3251-8489 |

Open year round. Tuesday-Sunday 9:30 am to 5 pm (admission until 4:30 pm). In the Transportation Museum original vehicles and models of all sorts of means of transportation on land, on the seas and in the air are collected and exhibited. On exhibit: first JNR (Japanese National Railways) bus, type TGE-MP, 1930. Web site: www.kouhaku.or.jp

Netherlands

| Internationaal Museum 1939-1945
Dingeweg 1
9981 NC Uithuizen Netherlands
E-mail: mus39-45@tref.nl | *31 595-434100
FAX:
*31 595-431837 |

Open April 1-October 31 daily 9 am to 6 pm. Soft skin and armoured military vehicles from parabike up to and including Sherman tank, restored to full running order, documents, photographs, models, uniforms, equipment, guns, utilities and telecommunication sets. Maybach German WW II staff car on display. Web site: www.museum1939-1945.nl

| Oldtimermuseum De Rijke
De Pinnepot 23
Ind area De Pinnepot
Oostvoorne 3233 LP Netherlands
E-mail: oldtimermuseum@derijke.com | +31(0)181-483876
FAX:
+31(0)181-486143 |

Open April 1-October 29 Saturday-Sunday 12 pm to 5 pm, July 1-October 29, also open every Wednesday 12 pm to 5 pm. Approximately 200 cars, all kinds of makes and models, the oldest ones date from 1904. Web site: www.derijke.com/museum

| Portanje's Vespa Scooter &
Nostalgia Collection
Stationsweg 41
3981AB Bunnik Netherlands
E-mail: portanje@worldmail.ul | PH/FAX:
+31-30-6563838 |

Private collection open by appointment. The collection contains pre-war, military and mainly Vespa motor scooters plus posters, photos and Vespa Club memorabilia of the 1950s/1960s. 6 days Vespa (1951), Paris Dakar Vespa (1980), early Vespa (1947), etc on display. Web site: www.portanje.com

Scotland

| Albion Archive
The Biggar Albion Foundation Ltd
9 Edinburgh Rd
Biggar ML12 6AX Scotland | PH/FAX:
01899-221497 |

Open Easter-October 31st daily 10 am to 5 pm, other times by appointment. Archive of the Albion Company (cars 1899-1913, trucks 1899-1972), Albion Owners Club (branch in Australia), rally each August. 1902 Dog Cart car, 1922 hotel bus, 1936 traveling home on display.

| Moray Motor Museum
Bridge St
Elgin Moray 1V30 2DE Scotland | 01343 544933
FAX: 01343 546315 |

Open April-October daily 11 am to 5 pm. Veteran, vintage and classic cars and motorbikes. Exhibit includes: Jaguars, Astons, Maserati, Bentley.

Sweden

| Smalands Cars, Toys & Music
Museum
Hjortsjo
330 17 Rydaholm Sweden
E-mail: info@motorima.com | PH/FAX:
0472-200 05 |

Open June-September daily 10 am to 6 pm, May-October Sundays 11 am to 5 pm. Automobiles, motorcycles, mopeds, toys, Meccanical Music instrument, old museum church, antik and coffee shop. On exhibit: Roll-Royce, Bentley Speed Six, cars from 1901-1969.

| Svedino's Automobile and
Aviation Museum
Ugglarp
SE-31050 Sloinge Sweden
E-mail: info@svedinos.se | +46 346 43187
FAX:
+46-31-144848 |

Open daily June, July and August 10 am to 4 pm. 140 vintage cars, mainly 1900-1950. 30 aircrafts. Web site: www.svedinos.se

| Tidaholms Museum
S-52283
Tidaholm Sweden | 00946-502-16192
FAX:
00946-502-14329 |

Open May-August, Tuesday-Sunday 1 pm to 5 pm; September-April, Tuesday-Thursday, Sunday 2 pm to 5 pm; December-February, closed Sundays. A company called Tidaholms Bruk in Sweden produced some 1,000 motor vehicles between 1903 and 1934. Some of these vehicles have been saved and are shown at Tidaholms Museum. On exhibit: a truck from 1927, a bus from 1925 and 6 firefighting vehicles.

Uruguay

| Automovil Club Del Uruguay's
Museum
Colonia Y Y1
Montevideo Uruguay | 5982 9024792
FAX: 5982 9021406 |

Open February-December Tuesday-Sunday 5 pm to 7 pm. Always 40 or more cars being exhibited from an 1899 Delin to a 1967 Rago. Entrance is free.

Wales

| National Cycle Collection
The Automobile Palace Temple St
Llandrindod Wells Powys
Mid Wales LD1 5DL Wales | PH/FAX:
01597-825531 |

Open year round. Daily 10 am to 4 pm. Large displays of bicycles from 1818-1999. An amazing exhibition that will fascinate and entertain you. Walk through the lanes of bicycle history.

Section Seven:
Useful Lists and Compilations

Classic Cars 1925-1948 Classic Car Club of America

The term "classic car" is one that has been so distorted and abused over the past twenty years or so that it might be handy to those seeking a single authoritative list of Classic Cars to include this in the *Almanac*. This group of cars and no others can truly be called "Classic," as defined and chosen through the years by the Classic Car Club of America.

<u>FC</u>: Full Classic <u>NC</u>: Non-Classic
<u>Please</u> <u>apply</u> <u>to</u> <u>CCCA</u>: Call or write with specifics on the vehicle. Note: 1925-48 Custom-bodied cars not listed should apply to CCCA.

Our thanks to the Classic Car Club of America, Suite 7, 1645 Des Plaines River Rd., Des Plaines, IL 60018. PH: 847-390-0443. See their free listing, including regional chapters, on page 447.

A

AC...FC
Adler...............................please apply to CCCA
Alfa Romeo...FC
Alvis, Speed 20, Speed 25 and 4.3 Litre ....FC
   Others............................please apply to CCCA
Amilcar ....please apply to CCCA
Armstrong Siddeley...................please apply to CCCA
Aston-Martin, all 1927-39....................................FC
   Others............................please apply to CCCA
Auburn, all 8 and 12-cyl......................................FC
Austro-Daimler ....FC

B

Ballot..............................please apply to CCCA
Bentley ....FC
Benz ....please apply to CCCA
Blackhawk..FC
BMW, 327, 328, 327/318 and 335 ....FC
Brewster, all Heart Front Fords............................FC
   Others............................please apply to CCCA
Brough Superior ....please apply to CCCA
Bucciali, TAV 8, TAV 30, TAV 12 and Double Huit..FC
   Others............................please apply to CCCA

Bugatti, all except type 52....................................FC
Buick, 1931-42 90 Series......................................FC
   All others..NC
   Custom-bodied ....please apply to CCCA

C

Cadillac, all 1925-35..FC
   All 12s and 16s ....FC
   1936-48, all 63, 65, 67, 70, 72, 75, 80, 85, 90 Series
   ....FC
   1938-47 60 Special...FC
   1940-47 all 62 series ....FC
   All others..NC
Chenard-Walcker.......................please apply to CCCA
Chrysler, 1926-30 Imperial 80, 1929 Imperial L, 1931-
   37 Imperial series CG, CH, CL and CW................FC
   Newports and Thunderbolts...............................FC
   1934 CX ....FC
   1935 C-3...FC
   1936 C-11..FC
   1937-48 Custom Imperial, Crown Imperial Series
   C-15, C-20, C-24, C-27, C-33, C-37, C-40 ....FC
   All others..NC
Cord...FC
Cunningham, Series V6, V7, V8, V9 ....FC

D

Dagmar, 6-80 ....FC
Daimler, all 8-cyl and 12-cyl ....FC
   Others ....please apply to CCCA
Darracq, 8-cyl and 4-litre 6-cyl ....FC
   Others ....NC
Delage, Model D-8...FC
   4-Cylinder cars ....NC
   Others ....please apply to CCCA
Delahaye, Series 135, 145, 165.............................FC
   4-Cylinder cars ....NC
   Others ....please apply to CCCA
Delaunay Belleville, 6-cyl ....FC
   Others ....NC
Doble ....FC
Dorris ....FC
Duesenberg...FC
duPont..FC

E

Excelsior ....please apply to CCCA

Section Seven – Lists

F

Farman......................................please apply to CCCA
Fiat..please apply to CCCA
FN...please apply to CCCA
Franklin, all models except 1933-34 Olympic ....FC
Frazer Nash ....please apply to CCCA

G

Graham, 1930-31 Series 137 ....FC
Graham-Paige, 1929-30 Series 837 ....NC
  Custom-bodied ....please apply to CCCA

H

Hispano-Suiza, all French models, Spanish models
  T56, T56BIS, T64 ....FC
Horch...FC
Hotchkiss.................................please apply to CCCA
Hudson, 1929 Series L.......................................FC
  Custom-bodied ....please apply to CCCA
Humber ....please apply to CCCA

I

Invicta...FC
Isotta Fraschini...FC
Itala ....FC

J

Jaguar, 1946-48 2-1/2 Litre, 3-1/2 Litre (Mark IV)..FC
  4-Cylinder cars...NC
Jensen ....please apply to CCCA
Jordan, Speedway Series 'Z'...............................FC
  All others ....NC
Julian ....FC

K

Kissel, 1925-26, 1927 8-75, 1928 8-90 and
  8-90 White Eagle, 1929-31 8-126 ....FC
  All others ....NC

L

Lagonda, all models except 1933-40 Rapier ....FC
Lanchester.................................please apply to CCCA
Lancia......................................please apply to CCCA
LaSalle, 1927-33..FC

Lincoln, all L, KA, KB and K, 1941 168 H,
  1942 268 H..FC
Lincoln Continental ....FC
Locomobile, all Models 48 and 90, 1927-29 Model 8-
80, 1929 8-88 ....FC
  All others ....NC

M

Marmon, all 16-cyl, 1925-26 74, 1927 75, 1928 E75,
  1930 Big 8, 1931 88 and Big 8 ....FC
  Others ....NC
Maserati...................................please apply to CCCA
Maybach..FC
McFarlan TV6 and 8 ....FC
Mercedes...FC
Mercedes-Benz, all 230 and up, K, S, SS, SSK,
  SSKL, Grosser and Mannheim ....FC
Mercer ....FC
MG, 1935-39 SA, 1938-39 WA................................FC
Minerva, all except 4-cyl ....FC

N

NAG...please apply to CCCA
Nash, 1931 Series 8-90, 1932 series 9-90, Advanced
  8 and Ambassador 8, 1933-34 Ambassador 8 .....FC
  All others ....NC

P

Packard, all Sixes and Eights, 1925-34...................FC
  All 12-cylinder models.....................................FC
  1935 Models 1200 thru 1205, 1207 and 1208......FC
  1936 Models 1400 thru 1405, 1407 and 1408......FC
  1937 Models 1500 thru 1502 and 1506 thru 1508 FC
  1938 Models 1603 thru 1605, 1607 and 1608.....FC
  1939 Models 1703, 1705, 1707 and 1708............FC
  1940 Models 1803, 1804, 1805, 1806, 1807 and
    1808 ....FC
  1941 Models 1903, 1904, 1905, 1906, 1907 and
    1908 ....FC
  1942 Models 2023, 2003, 2004, 2005, 2055, 2006,
    2007 and 2008 ....FC
1946-47 Models 2103, 2106 and 2126 ....FC
  All Darrin-bodied ....FC
  All other models..NC
  Custom-bodied ....please apply to CCCA
Peerless, 1925 Series 67, 1926-28 Series 69, 1930-31
  Custom 8, 1932 Deluxe Custom 8 ....FC
  Others ....NC

Peugeot.....................................please apply to CCCA
Pierce-Arrow ....FC

R

Railton ....please apply to CCCA
Raymond Mays ....please apply to CCCA
Renault, 45 hp...FC
Reo, 1931-33 8-31, 8-35, 8-52, Royale Custom 8,
    1934 N1, N2, and 8-52 ....FC
Revere...FC
Riley.......................................please apply to CCCA
Roamer, 1925 8-88, 6-54e, 4-75, 4-85e; 1926 4-75e,
    4-85e and 8-88; 1927-29 8-88; 1929 and
    1930 8-120 ....FC
Rochet Schneider......................please apply to CCCA
Rohr ....please apply to CCCA
Rolls-Royce ....FC
Ruxton...FC

S

Squire ....FC
SS and SS Jaguar, 1932-40 SS 1, SS 90, SS
    Jaguar and SS Jaguar 100 ....FC
Stearns-Knight ....FC
Stevens-Duryea ....FC
Steyr...please apply to CCCA
Studebaker, 1929-33 President, except Model 82 ....FC
    All others..NC
Stutz..FC
Sunbeam, 8-cyl and 3 Litre twin cam ....FC

T

Talbot, 105C and 110C..FC
Talbot Lago, 150C..FC
Tatra...please apply to CCCA
Triumph, Dolomite 8 and Gloria 6 ....FC

V

Vauxhall, 25-70 and 30-98 ....FC
Voisin ....FC

W

Wills Sainte Claire...FC
Willys-Knight, Series 66, 66A, 66B custom bodied only
    ....please apply to CCCA

FC: Full Classic
NC: Non-Classic
Please apply to CCCA: Call or write with specifics on
the vehicle.

None of the above Classic Marques are acceptable in race car configuration.

Statement of Policy
"Race Car Configuration,"
March 10, 1993

As of March 10, 1993, the Classic Car Club of America will no longer accept any automobile which is in a "race car configuration." The race car configuration is a vehicle which is missing some or all of the following: fenders, lights, windshield, windshield wipers, bumpers, top. It may be without doors, or reverse gear or starting motor. It may not have an exhaust system other than a straight pipe, nor have proper instrumentation or upholstery. In short, it would not be considered a legal, road worthy vehicle which is licensable in a majority of the states.

Certified Milestone Cars, 1945-1972

There's also continual debate over the meaning of "Milestone" cars. Like Classics, they do have a precise meaning. Basically, they're post-WWII Classic Cars — cars of superior design or engineering or performance or innovation or craftsmanship — or a combination of these characteristics. Following is the list of Milestones, courtesy of the Milestone Car Society of California Inc, National Headquarters, 3743 E. 71st St., Indianapolis, IN 46220, PH: 317-259-0959. See their full listing on page 452.

A

AC Ace 1954-61
AC Aceca 1955-61
AC Buckland Open Tourer 1949
AC (Shelby) Cobra 1962-67
Alfa Romeo Giulietta Spider 1956-64
Alfa Romeo Giulietta-Giulia Sprint Speciale ...1959-61
Alfa Romeo 6C 2500 Super Sport 1949
Allard Series J2, K2, K3 1946-56
AMX, 2-seater 1968-70
Apollo 1963-66
Arnolt Bristol...................................1952-62
Aston Martin 1948-63
Aston Martin DB4, DB5, DB6 (all)..........1964-67
Austin-Healey 100/100M......................1953-56
Austin-Healey 100-6...........................1956-59
Austin-Healey 3000............................1959-67
Austin/Morris Mini 1959-70

B

Bentley (all) 1946-67
BMW 507 1957-59
BMW 2800 CS....................................1969-71
Bugatti Type 101 1951
Buick Riviera....................1949; 1963-70
Buick Skylark 1953-54

C

Cadillac Eldorado 1953-58
Cadillac Eldorado 1967-70
Cadillac Eldorado Brougham 1957-58
Cadillac 60 Special.............................1948-49
Cadillac 61 Coupe (Fastback)................1948-49
Cadillac 62 Sedanet/Convertible/deVille........1948-49
Cadillac 75 Sedan/Limo.......................1946-70

Chevrolet Bel Air, V8, Hardtop and Convertible...........
....1955-57
Chevrolet Camaro SS/RS, V8 and Z-28 1967-69
Chevrolet Corvette...............................1953-70
Chevrolet Impala Sport Coupe/Convertible 1958
Chevrolet Nomad................................1955-57
Chrysler 300 Letter Series.....................1955-65
Chrysler 300 Hurst..............................1970
Chrysler Town & Country 1946-50
Cisitalia GT (Pininfarina).......................1946-49
Citroen Chapron 1960-70
Citroen DS and ID 19...........................1955-64
Citroen SM......................................1970
Continental Convertible 1958-60
Continental Mark II..............................1956-57
Continental Mark III.............................1969-70
Corvair Monza...................................1960-64
Corvair Monza Spyder 1962-64
Corvair Monza & Corsa 1965-69
Crosley Hotshot/SS 1950-52
Cunningham.....................................1951-55

D

Daimler DE-36 (Custom built)...................1949-53
Daimler 2.5 Special Sport Convertible............1949-53
Delage D-6 Sedan................................1946-49
Delahaye Type 135, 175, 180....................1946-51
DeSoto Adventurer..............................1956-58
Deutsch-Bonnet GT 1950-61
Devin SS...1958-62
Dodge Charger R/T and Daytona................1968-70
Dodge Coronet R/T 1967-70
Dual Ghia 1956-58

E

Excalibur II Series I...............................1965-69

F

Facel Vega, V8 1954-64
Ferrari, V12 (all front engined) 1947-70
Ford Crestline Skyliner..........................1954
Ford Crown Victoria Skyliner 1955-56
Ford Mustang Boss 302/Mach I.................1969-70
Ford Mustang GT/GTA, V8 1965-67
Ford Skyliner (Retractable)......................1957-59
Ford Sportsman 1946-48
Ford Thunderbird................................1955-60
Frazer Manhattan 1947-50

G

Gaylord 1955-57

H

Healey Silverstone 1949-50
Hudson (all) 1948-49
Hudson Hornet 1951-54

I

Imperial 1955-56

J

Jaguar XK 120 1945-54
Jaguar Mark V Drophead 1951
Jaguar Mark VII and 1954 Mark VII M 1951-54
Jaguar XK 140 1954-57
Jaguar Mark VIII 1956-57
Jaguar Mark IX 1958-61
Jaguar Mark X 1962-64
Jaguar XK 150 1958-61
Jaguar 3.4/3.8 Sedans 1957-64
Jaguar E-Type 1961-67

K

Kaiser Darrin 161 1954
Kaiser Deluxe/Deluxe Virginian 1951-52
Kaiser Dragon 1951-53
Kaiser Manhattan 1954-55
Kaiser Vagabond 1949-50
Kaiser Virginian (Hardtop) 1949-50
Kurtis 500S & 500KK 1953-55
Kurtis 500M & 500X 1953-55

L

Lagonda, V12 1948-49
Lagonda, 2.5 Liter Drophead Coupe 1949-53
Lancia Aurelia B.20 and B.20 Coupe 1951-59
Lancia Aurelia B.24 Spyder and Convertible ..1953-59
Lancia Flaminia GT 2-Passenger Coupe or Convertible
....1961-63
Lancia Flaminia Zagato 1959-64
Lancia Flavia Coupe 1962-66
Lea Francis 2.5 Liter Eighteen Sports 1950-54
Lincoln Capri 1952-54
Lincoln Continental 1946-48
Lincoln Continental 1961-67
Lincoln Continental Custom Limos (Lehmann-
Peterson) 1963-67
Lotus Elite 1958-63

M

Maserati A6/1500, A6G/2000/A6GCS Berlinetta ....
....1946-57
Maserati 3500/3700 GT 1957-64
Maserati Ghibli, Mexico, Indy, 5000 GT 1959-70
Maserati Quattroporte 1963-69
Maserati Sebring, Mistral 1965-70
MG Series TC 1946-49
MG Series TD 1950-53
MG Series TF 1954-55
MGA Twin Cam 1958-62
Mercedes-Benz 190 SL 1955-62
Mercedes-Benz 220A Coupe and Convertible ....
....1951-54
Mercedes-Benz 220S/220 SE Coupe and Convertible ..
....1956-65
Mercedes-Benz 230 SL Coupe and Convertible ....
....1963-67
Mercedes-Benz 250 SE/SL Coupe and Convertible ......
....1965-67
Mercedes-Benz 280 SL 1969-70
Mercedes-Benz 300S/SE/SL Coupe and Convertible ...
....1952-64
Mercedes-Benz 300 SE Coupe and Convertible ....
....1965-67
Mercedes-Benz 300 SEL 6.3 1969-70
Mercedes-Benz 600 1964
Mercedes-Benz 600, SWB/LWB 1965-70
Mercury Cougar XR-7 1967-68
Mercury Sportsman 1946
Mercury Sun Valley 1954-55
Morgan 4/4 1955-70
Morgan Plus Four 1950-67
Muntz Jet 1950-54

N

Nash Healey 1951-54
NSU Wankel Spyder 1964

O

Oldsmobile 88 (Coupe, Convertible, Holiday) ..1949-50
Oldsmobile 98 Holiday Hardtop 1949
Oldsmobile 442 1964-70
Oldsmobile Fiesta 1953
Oldsmobile Toronado 1966-67
OSCA MT-4 1948-56

P

Packard Caribbean 1953-56
Packard Custom (Clipper and Custom Eight) ....
....1946-50
Packard Pacific/Convertible 1954

Packard Panther Daytona 1954
Packard Patrician/400 1951-56
Panhard Dyna 1946-67
Pegaso (all) 1951-58
Plymouth Barracuda Formula S 1965-69
Plymouth Fury 1956-58
Plymouth Roadrunner & Superbird 1968-70
Plymouth Satellite SS & GTX 1965-70
Pontiac GTO 1964-69
Pontiac Safari 1955-57
Porsche Series 356 1949-65

R

Riley 2.5 (RMA, RME) 1945-55
Rolls-Royce (all) 1947-67
Rover 2000/2000 TC 1964-70

S

Shelby 350GT & 500GT 1965-67
Studebaker Avanti 1963-64
Studebaker Convertible (all) 1947-49
Studebaker Gran Turismo Hawk 1962-64
Studebaker President Speedster 1955
Studebaker Starlight Coupe (all) 1947-49
Studebaker Starlight Coupe (Six and V8) 1953-54
Studebaker Starliner Hardtop (Six and V8) 1953-54
Sunbeam Tiger 1965-67

T

Talbot Lago 4.5 (all) 1946-54
Triumph TR2/TR3 1953-63
Tucker 1948

V

Volkswagen Karmann Ghia 1956-70
Volvo P.1800S, E, & ES Series 1961-70

W

Willys Overland Jeepster 1948-51
Woodill Wildfire 1952-58

US Vehicle Makes Past to Present

One of the most fascinating lists, and one which is changing even today, is the long, long list of makes of cars built in the US during the past century. There are literally thousands of them from every corner of the nation, distilled and diminished by competition and changing markets into the small handful of volume manufacturers of motorcars left today. This list, large as it is, is not totally complete as more and more tinkerers and backyard geniuses who built cars through the decades are discovered and documented by automotive historians. But it's a hefty list nonetheless and one which we think you'll enjoy browsing through.

A

A.B.C.	1908 and 1922
Abenaque	1900
Abendroth and Root	1907
Abbott	1909-1916
Abbott-Cleveland	1917
Abbott-Detroit	1909
Abbott-Downing	1919
A.C.	1938
Acadia	1904
Acason	1915
Ace	1920-1922
A.C.F.	1926
Acme	1902-1911
Acorn	1925
Adams	1911 and 1924
Adams-Farwell	1904-1913
Adelphia	1921
Adette	1947
Adria	1921-1922
Advance	1909
A.E.C.	1914-1916
Aero	1921
Aerocar	1905-1906 and 1948
Aerotype	1921
Ahrens-Fox	1927
Airphibian	1946-1952
Air Scout	1947
Airway	1949
Ajax Electric	1901-1903
Ajax	1914 and 1923-1925
Akron	1901
Alamobile	1902
Aland	1917
Albany	1907
Alco	1909-1912
Aldo	1910
Alden-Sampson	1904-1909

All American	1919
Allegheny	1908
Allen	1914-1922
Allen and Clark	1908
Allen Cyclecar	1914
Alith	1908
Allen-Kingston	1907-1909
Allis-Chalmers	1914-1917
All Steel	1915-1916
Alma	1908
Alpena	1910-1914
Alsace	1920-1921
Alter	1916-1917
Altha	1905
Altham	1897 and 1898
Amalgamated	1905
Ambassador	1921-1922
AMC (American Motors Corporation)	1958-1988
Amco	1920
American	1901, 1905-1914, 1916-1918, 1922-1925 and 1937
American Austin	1930
American-Bantam	1937
American Beauty	1916
American Benham	1917
American Berliet	1906
American Chocolate	1903
American Coulthard	1907
American Electric	1899-1900
American Fiat	1912
American Gas	1902-1903
American-LaFrance	1910
American Mercedes	1903
American Mors	1903
American Napier	1904
American Populaire	1904
American Power Carriage	1900
American Simplex	1908
American Steam Car	1935
American Steamer	1922-1923
American Southern	1921
American Tri-Car	1912
American Underslung	1908
American Voiturette	1900
Americar	1941
Ames	1895, 1898 and 1912-1915
Amesbury	1898
Amex	1895
Amplex	1908-1915
Ams-Sterling	1917
Anchor	1909
Anderson	1908 and 1916-1926
Anger	1913
Angus	1908
Anheuser-Busch	1905
Anhut	1909
Anthony	1897
Apex	1920
Apell	1911
Appel	1915
Appelo	1973
Apperson	1902-1926

Apple 1917
Appleton 1922
Apollo 1906
Arbenz 1911-1919
Arcadia 1911
Ardsley 1905
Argo-Borland 1914
Argo-Case 1916
Argo Electric 1912-1917
Argo-Gas 1914
Argonne 1920
Ariel 1906
Aristos 1913
Armlader 1914
Arnold Electric 1895
Arrow..1914
Arrow Cyclecar 1914
Artzberger Steamer 1864
Astor...1925
Astra...1920
Atlantic...1915
Atlas 1907-1913
Auburn 1903-1936
Auglaize 1911
Aultman 1901
Aurora 1907
Austin 1903-1922
Auto-Acetylene....................................1899
Autobain...1900
Auto-Bug..1910
Autobuggy 1907
Autocar 1899-1911
Auto Cycle 1913
Auto Dynamic......................................1901
Auto Fore Carriage 1900-1901
Auto-Go 1900
Automatic ....1908 and 1921
Automobile Voiturette...................1900-1902
Automote 1900
Automotor 1901-1904
Autoplane 1947
Auto-Tricar 1914
Auto Two 1900
Auto Vehicle 1903
Avanti..1963-present
Avery 1921

B

Babcock 1909-1913
Babcock Electric 1906-1911
Bachelles 1901
Backhus 1925
Bacon 1925
Badger...1911-1912
Bailey 1907-1916
Baker-Electric 1899-1917
Baker Steam...................................1917-1924
Balboa 1924
Baldner 1902-1903
Baldwin 1900

Ball...1902
Ball Steam..1900
Balzer 1900
Banker...1905
Banker Electric....................................1905
Bantam 1914
Barbarino...1923
Barley 1922-1924
Barlow 1922
Barnes 1907-1912
Barnhart...1905
Barrett & Perret 1895
Barrow..1896
Barrows Motor Vehicle........................1897
Bartholomew 1901-1903
Barver...1925
Bateman..1917
Bates 1903
Bauer...1914
Bauroth 1899
Bayard...1903
Bay State ....1906-1907 and 1922-1924
Beacon...1933
Beacon Flyer...1908
Beardsley.....................1901 and 1914-1917
Beau-Chamberlain 1905
Beaver 1920
Beck 1947
Beebe...1907
Beggs...1918-1922
B.E.L. 1921-1923
Belden 1907-1911
Belfontains 1907
Bell.............................1907 and 1915-1922
Bellmay 1904
Belmont ....1904, 1908, 1910 and 1912-1916
Bemmel & Burham...............................1898
Bendix...1907
Bendix-Ames 1911
Benham..1914
Ben-Hur 1908-1917
Benner...1908-1909
Benson 1913
Bentley 1907
Benton Harbor Motor...........................1896
Berg...1902-1903
Bergdoll..1908-1911
Berkshire......................................1904-1911
Berwick Electric...................................1926
Bessemer 1904
Bertolet..1908-1912
Best 1900
Bethlehem 1904-1908
Betz 1919
Beverly..1904
Bewis 1915
Bewman 1912
Beyster 1910-1911
Beyster By-Autogo 1904
B.F.S. 1908
Biddle 1916-1922
Biddle-Murray 1906

Bierderman	1915
Bimel	1917
Binney-Burnham	1888-1902
Birch	1916-1923
Bird	1911
Birmingham	1921-1922
Birnel	1911
Black	1899 and 1908
Black Crow	1905 and 1909-1910
Black Diamond	1904
Blackhawk	1902-1905 and 1928-1929
Blair	1915
Blaisdell	1903
Blakeslee	1906
Blemline	1898
Bliss	1906
B.L.M.	1907-1909
Block	1905
Block Bros.	1905
Blomstrom	1904-1908
Blood	1903 and 1914
Bluebird	1910
Blumberg	1918
Bob Cat	1923
Bobbi-Car	1945
Boggs	1903
Boisselot	1901-1906
Bolte	1901
Borbein	1905
Borland	1913-1914
Boss	1903
Boston	1900 and 1903
Boston and Amesbury	1902
Boston High Wheel	1908
Bour-Davis	1916-1922
Bournonville	1914
Bouton and Bateman	1899
Bowman	1921-1922
Boynton	1922
Bradfield	1929
Bradley	1920
Bramwell	1900-1902
Bramwell-Robinson	1899
Brasie	1915
Brecht	1902-1903
Breer	1900
Breeze and Lawrence	1905
Breman	1908
Brennan	1908
Brew and Hatcher	1904-1905
Brewster	1915-1937
Bridgeport	1922
Briggs	1914
Briggs and Stratton	1920-1923
Briggs-Detroiter	1912
Brighton	1896 and 1914
Brightwood	1912
Brintel	1912
Briscoe	1914-1921
Bristol	1903 and 1908
Broc	1909-1917
Brock	1920

Brockville-Atlas	1911
Brockway	1912
Brodesser	1909
Brogan	1948
Brook	1920-1921
Brooks	1908 and 1925
Brower	1890
Brown	1898, 1914 and 1916
Brown-Burtt	1904
Brownell	1910
Brownie	1915-1916
Browniekar	1908-1910
Brunn	1906
Brunner	1910
Brunswick	1916
Brush	1907-1911
Bruss	1907
Buck	1925
Buckeye	1901 and 1906-1912
Buckeye Gas Buggy	1895
Buckles	1914
Buckmobile	1903-1907
Buffalo	1900-1907
Buffalo Electric	1901-1907
Buffington	1900
Buffman	1900
Buffum	1901-1909
Buford	11915
Buggyaut	1895 and 1908
Buggycar	1908-1909
Bugmobile	1907
Buick	1903-present
Bundy	1895
Burdick	1909-1910
Burg	1910
Burns	1910
Burroughs	1914-1916
Bus	1917-1924
Bush	1909 and 1917
Busser	1915
Buzmobile	1917
Byrider	1908-1909

C

Cadillac	1903-present
California	1902 and 1912-1914
California Cyclecar	1914
Californian	1916
Calvert	1927
Cameron	1905-1907 and 1909-1921
Campbell	1916-1921
Canda	1901
Cannon	1904
Canton	1906
Capital	1902
Capps	1908
Car Deluxe	1907
Car Nation	1913
Carbon	1902
Cardway	1923

Carhart	1871
Carhartt	1911
Carlisle	1900
Carlson	1904-1911
Carovan	1948
Carpenter	1895
Carqueville-MacDonald	1930
Carrison	1908
Carroll	1908, 1912-1918 and 1920-1922
Cartecar	1907-1911
Carter	1901 and 1903
Cartermobile	1924
Carter Twin Engine	1909
Carthage	1924
Cartone	1905
Casco	1926
Case	1909-1927
Caseler	1901
Casward-Dard	1924
Cato	1907
Cavac-Plymouth	1910
Cavalier	1927
C.B.	1917
Ceco	1914
Celt	1927
Centaur	1902
Central	1905
Century	1901, 1903 and 1911-1912
Century Tourist	1901
C.F.	1908
C.G. Gay	1915
C.G.V.	1902
Chadwick	1905-1912
Chalmers	1908-1923
Chalmers Detroit	1907
Champion	1902, 1909-1910 and 1919-1926
Champion Electric	1899-1901
Chandler	1913-1929
Chapman	1899 and 1901
Charter Car	1904
Charter Oak	1917
Chase	1910
Chatham	1906
Checker Cabs	1923-1958
Checker Motors	1958-1982
Chelfant	1906-1912
Chelsea	1901-1904
Chevrolet	1911-present
Chicago	1898, 1906 and 1914-1916
Chicago Commercial	1905
Chicago Electric	1914-1917
Chicago Motor Buggy	1908
Chicago Steam	1906
Chief	1908 and 1947
Christie	1904-1906
Christman	1901-1902
Christopher	1908
Chrysler	1924-present
Church	1903 and 1913
Churchfield	1911-1913
Cincinnati	1903
Cino	1909-1913
Cinov	1909-1912
Cistalia	1948
Clapps Motor	1898
Clark	1901-1902
Clark Electric	1906-1910
Clark Hatfield	1908-1909
Clark Steamer	1900-1909
Clarke Carter	1900-1906
Clarkmobile	1903-1906
Clarkspeed	1928
Classie	1917-1920
Clear and Durham	1905
Cleburne	1912
Clegg	1885
Clement	1903
Clendon	1908
Clermont	1903 and 1922
Cleveland	1902-1906, 1909 and 1919-1926
Climber	1919-1923
Clinton	1923
Cloughley	1902-1903
Club Car	1911
Clyde	1919
Clymer	1908
Coates	1921-1922
Coates-Goshen	1908-1910
Coey	1911
Coffon	1898
Cogswell	1912
Colburn	1906-1911
Colby	1911-1914
Cole	1910-1925
Collins	1901 and 1920
Colly	1900
Colonial	1907 and 1921-1922
Colonial Electric	1912
Colt	1908 and 1971
Columbia	1892-1913 and 1916-1925
Columbia Dauman	1900
Columbia Electric	1898-1906
Columbia Knight	1916
Columbian Electric	1915
Columbus	1903-1905 and 1906-1909
Comet	1907, 1914 and 1917-1923
Comet 3 Wheel	1947
Comet Cyclecar	1914
Commander	1921 and 1923
Commerce	1916
Commercial	1903
Commodore	1921
Commonwealth	1917-1922
Compound	1904-1906
Concord	1916
Conklin Electric	1895
Connersville	1914
Conover	1907
Conrad Steam	1900
Consolidated	1904
Continental	1907, 1909-1912, 1914 and 1933-1934
Cook	1908
Cooley	1900
Copley Minor	1917

Coppock 1907
Corbin 1903-1912
Corbitt 1907-1916
Cord ....1929-1932 and 1936-1937
Corinthian 1922
Corl 1911
Corliss 1917
Cornelian..1913-1915
Cornish 1917-1919
Correja 1911-1914
Cort 1914
Cortez...1947
Corweg...1905
Coscob...1900
Cosmopolitan.........................1907-1910 and 1951
Cotay 1921
Cotta 1901
Couch 1899-1900
Couch Steamer 1900
County Club 1903
Couple-Gear 1905
Courier ....1904-1912 and 1919-1924
Covert 1902-1907
Covert Motorette 1902
Coyote 1909
C.P..1908
Craig Toledo 1906-1907
Crane 1912-1914
Crane and Breed 1912-1917
Crane-Simplex 1923-1924
Crawford...1902-1924
Crescent ....1905-1908 and 1914-1915
Crest...1902
Crestmobile 1901-1904
Cricket....................1913-1915 and 1971-1973
Criterion 1912
Crock 1909
Croesus Jr. 1906
Crompton 1903-1905
Crosley ....1939-1941 and 1947-1952
Cross Steam Carriage 1895
Crother-Duryea 1915
Crow...1915
Crowdus 1901-1903
Crow-Elkhart..1914-1925
Crown ....1907 and 1915
Crown High Wheel 1897
Crown Magnetic...1907
Crowther-Duryea.....................................1915-1917
Croxton 1911-1914
Croxton Keeton......................................1909-1912
Cruiser 1918
Crusader...1923
Cucmobile 1907
Cull...1901
Culver 1905
Cunningham 1911
Cunningham Steamer 1900-1907
Curtis 1921
Custer ....1920-1946 and 1953-1960
Cutting 1910-1912
C.V.I. 1907

Cyclecar..1901
Cyclemobile 1920
Cycleplane...1914-1915

D

D.A.C. 1923
Dagmar 1922-1927
Daley 1893
Dalton...1911
Dan Patch 1911
Daniels 1916-1924
Darby 1909
Darling ....1901-1902 and 1917
Darrow 1903
Dart 1922
Dartmobile...1922
Davenport...1902-1903
Davids 1902
Da Vinci..1925
Davis.............1914, 1919-1928 and 1947-1950
Dawson..1904
Day..1911-1914
Day Utility 1911
Dayton.......................1904 and 1909-1911
Dayton Electric 1911
Dayton Steam......................................1900
Deal...1911
Decker 1902-1903
De Cross..1914
De Dion Bouton.....................................1888-1904
Deemaster 1923
Deemotor..1923
Deere...1906-1909
Deere Clark...1906
Deering..1915
Deering Magnetic...................................1917-1919
Defiance..1919
Dekalb...1919
De La Vergne Motor Drag................................1896
Delcar...1947-1949
Delling Steamer....................................1924-1927
Delmore...1923
Deltal...1914
De Mar...1949
De Mars Electric 1905
De Mot.......................1905 and 1909-1911
De Motte 1904
Denby 1922
Deneen 1916
De Rair 1911
Desberon Steamer.................................1901-1902
De Shaum 1908
Deshaw...1906
De Soto...1928-1961
De Tamble 1909-1912
Detroit...............1900, 1905, 1916 and 1922
Detroit Air Cooled 1923
Detroit Dearborn...................................1909-1910
Detroit Electric 1907-1938
Detroit Steamer 1922

Detroiter 1912
De Vaux 1931-1932
Dewabout 1899
Dey Electric 1894
Dial 1923
Diamond 1907
Diamond Arrow 1909
Diamond T. 1905-1911
Diana 1924-1928
Diebel 1900-1901
Diehl 1923
Differential 1921
Dile 1914-1916
Direct Drive 1907
Disbrow 1917-1918
Dispatch 1912-1922
Divco Twin 1946
Dixie ....1912 and 1917
Dixie Flyer 1915-1924
Dixie Tourist 1908-1909
Dixon 1922
Doble 1914-1931
Dodge 1914-present
Dodgeson 1926
Dodo 1909
Dolson 1904-1907
Dorris 1906-1926
Dort 1915-1925
Douglas 1918-1922
Dover 1929
Dowagiac 1908
Downing 1914
Downing Detroit 1913
Dragon 1921
Dragon Steam 1906-1908
Drake 1921-1922
Drexel 1916-1917
Driggs 1915-1916
Drummond 1915-1916
Duck 1913
Dudgeon Steam 1866
Dudley 1914
Duer ....1907-1909 and 1925
Duesenberg 1921-1937
Dumont 1909-1912
Dunn 1914-1917
Duplex 1909
Dupont 1915-1923
Duquesne 1913-1916
Durable 1902
Durant 1921-1932
Durocar 1908-1910
Duryea 1895-1913
Duryea Gem 1916
Dusseau 1912
Dyke 1903
Dymaxion 1933

E

Eagle ....1905-1906, 1908-1909, 1914 and 1924
Eagle Cyclecar 1914-1915
Eagle Electric 1915-1917
Eagle Macaober 1917
Eagle Rotary 1917
Earl 1907-1909, 1916-1924
Eastman 1897
Eastman Steam 1900
Easton 1907
Easton Electric 1898
Eaton 1910
Eaton Electric 1898
ECK 1903-1909
Eclipse 1901-1902
Economy ....1906 and 1917-1919
Economy Car 1914
Eddy Electric 1902
Edsel 1958-1960
Edwards Knight 1912-1914
E.H.V. 1903
Eichstaedt 1902
E.I.M. 1916
Eisenhuth 1896
Elberon Steam 1903
Elbert 1915
Elcar 1908-1930
Elco 1915-1916
Eldridge 1906
Electra 1913
Electric Vehicle 1897
Electric Wagon 1895
Electrobat 1895
Electrocar 1922
Electronomic 1901
Elgin 1914-1924
Elinor 1903
Elite 1909-1919
Elite Steamer 1901
Elk 1912
Elkhart 1908-1922
Elliott 1899-1902
Ellis Electric 1901
Ellsworth 1917
Elmore 1900-1911
Elrick 1896
Elston 1895
Elwell-Parker 1909
Elysee 1926
Emancipator 1909
Emerson 1907
Emerson and Fisher 1896
E.M.F. 1909-1912
Empire ....1898-1901 and 1910-1919
Empire State 1901
Empress 1906
Endurance Steamer 1922-1923
Engelhardt 1901
Enger 1909-1917

Enterprise...1901
Entyre..1911
Entz...1914
Erie...1897 and 1916-1921
Erskine...1926-1930
Ernst..1896
Erving...1911-1913
Essex...1918-1932
Euclid..1907
Eureka..................................1908 and 1909-1914
Evans...1904
Evans Steam...1887
Evansville..1907-1909
Everitt..1909-1911
Everybodys.......................................1908-1909
Ewing...1908-1910
Excalibur..........................1952 and 1965-1990

F

Facto...1920
Fageol..1916-1917
Fairbanks-Morse 1909
Fairmont.....................................1906 and 1978
F.A.L...1909
Falcar.......................................1908, 1910 and 1922
Falcon......................................1909-1911 and 1922
Falcon Knight...................................1927-1928
Famose..1909
Fanning Electric.................................1902-1904
Farmack..1916
Farmobile...1906-1907
Farner...1922-1924
Fauber......................................1900 and 1914
Fay..1912
Fedelia..1903
Federal...1907-1909
Federal Steam..1905
Fee..1908
Felton..1914
Fergus..1915-1922
Ferris..1920-1923
Findley..1910-1912
Firestone Columbus 1906-1911
Fischer.............................1902-1904 and 1914
Fish...1908
Fisher..1914
Fitzjohn...1946
Flagler...1914
Flanders...1911-1912
Flanders Electric.......................................1914
Flexbi..1904
Flexibel...1935
Flint.........................1902-1904 and 1922-1927
Flyer...1913-1914
Foos..1913
Ford...1903-present
Forest..1908
Forest City...1906
Forster Six...1920
Fort Pitt..1908-1909

Foster Steam 1898-1905
Fostoria ....1906-1907 and 1916
Four Traction...1907
Fox...1921-1925
Frankford...1922
Franklin..1901-1934
Frayer..1905
Frayer Miller......................................1905-1909
Frazer...1945-1951
Fredonia..1902-1904
Fredrickson..1914
Freeman..1900-1903
Fremont...1922-1923
French..1903
Friedberd...1908
Friedman...1900-1903
Friend..1921-1923
Fritchie Electric..................................1907-1917
Frontenac ....1909-1911, 1917 and 1922
Frontmobile..1917
F.R.P...1915-1917
F.S...1908
Fuller...1907-1911
Fulton......................................1908 and 1948
F.W.D..1911

G

Gabriel...1912
Gadabout 1914-1915
Gaeth...1902-1906
Gaethmobile...1902
Gale..1906
Galt...1914
Gardner...1919-1931
Garford..1907-1913
Garvin..1900
Gas Au Lac..1905-1906
Gas Engine...1905
Gasmobile..1900
Gasoline Motor 1897
Gawley..1895
Gaylord..1910-1913
Gearless...1908 and 1920
Geer Steam...1900
Gem..1917
General..1903
General Cab..1929
General Electric...1899
General Vehicle...1906
Genesee..1911-1912
Geneva ....1901-1909 and 1917
German American.......................................1902
Geronimo...1917-1921
Gersix..1921
Ghent..1918
Gibbs Electric 1903
Gibson...1899
Gifford Pettitt...1907
Gillette...1916
G.J.C...1909-1915

Gleason ....1910-1912 and 1914
Glide 1902-1919
Globe 1921-1922
Glover 1921
Golden State 1928
Goldeneagle 1906
Goodspeed 1922
Gorson...1907
Graham 1903
Graham-Paige.............................1927-1941
Grant...................................1914-1923
Gray ....1916 and 1922-1925
Gray-Dort 1917
Great Eagle...........................1911-1914
Great Smith 1911
Great Southern.......................1910-1914
Great Western 1909-1916
Greeley 1903
Gregory 1948
Gregory Front Drive 1922
Greyhound 1914
Griffith.............................1962-1966
Grinnel Electric 1910-1915
Griswold 1907
Grout Steam..........................1899-1912
Guilder 1922
Gurley...1901
Guy Vaughn 1912
Gyroscope 1914

H

Hackett..................................1916-1919
H.A.L. 1918
Hale 1917
Hall 1903
Hall Gasoline 1895
Halladay ....1908-1912 and 1919-1921
Halsey...1901
Hamilton...1909
Hamilton Holmes.........................1920-1921
Hammer 1905
Hammer Sommer....................................1905
Handley 1921-1923
Handley-Knight 1921-1922
Hanger...1916
Hanover..................................1922-1924
Hansen 1902
Hanson...................................1917-1923
Harding 1916
Hardy 1904
Hare 1918
Harper 1907
Harrie 1925
Harrigan 1922
Harris Six 1923
Harrisburg.......................................1922
Harrison.................................1904-1907
Harroun..................................1917-1922
Hart Kraft 1908
Hartman..1898

Harvard 1916
Harvey 1914
Hasbrouck 1900
Haseltine 1916
Hassler 1917
Hatfield................................1906-1908
Hathaway 1924
Haupt 1909
Havers 1912-1914
Haviland 1895
Havoc 1914
Hawkeye 1923
Hawley 1907
Hay Berg................................1907-1908
Haydock 1907
Haynes 1904-1925
Haynes-Apperson 1898-1904
Hayward 1913
Hazard 1914-1915
H. Brothers 1908
H.C.S. 1920-1925
Healy 1912-1916
Heine-Velox ....1906-1909 and 1921
Henderson 1912-1915
Henley Steam.....................................1899
Henney 1921-1931
Henrietta 1901
Henry..1911
Henry J. 1950-1954
Hercules 1914
Hercules Electric................................1902
Herff Brooks 1915
Hermes 1915
Herreshoff...............................1909-1914
Herschell-Spillman 1904-1907
Herschmann 1906
Hertel 1895-1900
Hertz..1925
Hess Steam.......................................1902
Hewitt...................................1905-1910
Hewitt Linstrom 1900
Heymann..................................1898-1899
Hicks 1900
Highlander.......................................1922
Hill 1907-1908
Hill Locomotor 1895
Hillsdale..1908
Hilton 1908
Hines 1908
Hobbie 1909
Hoffman 1902-1904
Hoffman Steam....................................1902
Hol Tan 1908
Holden 1915
Holland Steam 1905
Holley 1900-1903
Hollier..1915
Holly ....1900 and 1916-1917
Holmes ....1908 and 1918-1923
Holsman 1903-1911
Holyoke Steam....................................1901-1903
Homer Laughlin 1916

Hemmings Collector-Car Almanac©   Fifteenth Edition   U.S. Vehicle Makes, Past to Present   H-L   621

Hopkins 1902
Hoppenstand 1948
Houpt-Rockwell 1910-1912
Howard ....1901, 1903-1905 and 1914
Howard Gasoline Wagon 1895
Howey 1903
Hudson 1909-1957
Hupmobile 1908-1940
Hupp-Yeats 1911-1919
Hydro Carbon 1901
Hydromotor 1917
Hylander 1922

I

Ideal 1902, 1903, 1909-1914
Ideal Electric 1909
I.H.C. 1911
Illinois 1910-1914
Imp ....1914-1915 and 1955
Imperial ....1903-1904, 1907-1916 and 1928
Ingram Hatch 1917-1918
Innes 1921-1922
International 1900
International Harvester ......1907-1911 and 1961-1984
Interstate 1909-1918
Iroquois 1904-1908
Izzer 1910

J

Jackson 1903-1923
Jacquet Flyer 1921
James 1909
Janney 1906
Jarvis Huntington 1912
Jeannin 1908-1909
Jeep 1963-present
Jeffery 1914-1917
Jenkins 1907-1912
Jewel 1906-1909
Jewett 1923-1926
Johnson 1905-1912
Jones 1915-1920
Jones Corbin 1902-1907
Jonz 1908-1911
Jordan 1916-1931
J.P.L. 1913-1914
Julian ....1922 and 1925

K

Kaiser 1945-1955
Kalamazoo 1922
Kankakee 1919
Kansas City 1909
Karbach 1908
Kato 1907

Kauffman 1909-1912
Kavin 1905
K.D. 1914
Kearns 1908-1916
Keasler 1916
Keating 1899
Keene Electric 1900-1901
Keene Steam 1948
Keeton 1908-1914
Keller Chief 1947
Keller Kar ....1914 and 1927
Kenmore 1909-1912
Kennedy ....1898-1903 and 1915-1918
Kensington 1899-1904
Kent 1916-1917
Kenworthy 1920-1922
Kermath 1907-1908
Kermet 1900
Kessler 1921-1922
Keystone ....1909-1910 and 1915
Kiblinger 1907-1909
Kidder 1901
Kimball 1910-1912
King ....1896 and 1910-1924
King Midget 1946-1969
King Remick 1910
Kissell 1906-1931
Kline Kar 1910-1923
Kling 1907
Klink 1907-1909
Knickerbocker 1901-1903
Knox 1900-1915
Koppin 1914
Kreuger 1904-1905
K.R.I.T. 1909-1916
Kunz 1902-1906
Kurtis 1948-1955
Kurtz 1921-1923

L

L and E 1922-1931
Laconia 1914
Lads Car 1912-1914
Lafayette ....1920-1924 and 1934-1939
Lambert 1904-1917
Lane Steamer 1899
Lanpher 1909-1912
Lansden Electric 1906-1908
La Petite 1905
La Salle 1927-1940
Lauth Jergens 1907-1910
Law 1905
Leach ....1899-1901 and 1920-1923
Leader 1905-1912
Lehigh 1912
Lende 1908-1909
Lenox 1911-1918
Lenox Electric 1908-1909
Lescina 1916
Lewis ....1899-1902, 1914-1916 and 1937

Section Seven – Lists

Lewis Six 1913
Lexington 1909-1928
Liberty 1916-1924
Lima 1915
Limited 1911
Lincoln ....1908, 1914 and 1920-present
Lion 1909-1912
Little 1912-1915
Littlemac 1930-1931
Locomobile 1899-1929
Logan 1903-1908
London 1921-1924
Lone Star 1920-1922
Loomis 1896-1904
Lorraine ....1907-1908 and 1920-1922
Los Angeles 1913-1915
Lowell 1908
Lozier 1905-1917
Lutz Steam 1917
Luverne 1903-1918
Luxor Cab 1920
Lyman 1903-1904
Lyman and Burnham 1903-1904
Lyon Atlas 1912-1913
Lyon Knight 1914-1915

M

MacDonald 1923
Mackle-Thompson 1903
MacNaughton 1907
Macomber 1917
Macon 1915-1917
Madison 1915-1918
Magnolia 1902
Mahoning 1904-1905
Maibohm 1916-1922
Mais 1911
Majestic 1917
Malcolm 1915
Maltby 1900-1902
Manexall 1921
Manhattan 1905
Manistee 1912
Mann 1895
Maplebay 1908
Marathon 1908-1915
Marble Swift 1902-1905
Marion 1904-1915
Marion Handley 1916-1919
Maritime 1913-1914
Mark Electric 1897
Marlboro Steam 1899-1902
Marmon 1902-1933
Marquette ....1912 and 1929-1931
Marr 1903-1904
Marsh ....1898-1899, 1905 and 1920-1921
Marshall 1919-1921
Martin ....1920, 1926-1928 and 1931
Marvel 1907
Maryland 1900-1901

Mason 1906-1910
Mason Steamer 1898-1899
Massachusetts 1901
Massilon 1909
Master 1918
Mather 1901
Matheson 1903-1912
Maxwell Briscoe 1904-1925
Maytag 1910-1911
McCue 1909-1911
McCullough 1899
McFarlan 1910-1928
McGill 1922
McIntyre 1909-1915
McKay Steam 1900-1902
McLaughlin 1908-1922
McLean 1910
Mecca 1914-1916
Melbourne 1922
Menard 1908-1910
Menges 1908
Mercer ....1910-1925 and 1931
Merchant 1914
Mercury ....1904, 1914, 1918 and 1938-present
Merit 1920-1923
Merkel 1905-1906
Merz 1914-1915
Meteor ....1898, 1902-1903, 1904-1908 and 1914-1921
Metropol 1913-1914
Metropolitan ....1922 and 1954-1961
Metz 1909-1922
Michigan 1908-1914
Middleby 1908-1913
Midland 1908-1913
Mier 1908-1909
Milburn Electric 1914-1922
Militaire 1916-1922
Miller ....1912-1913 and 1915-1932
Miller Steam 1896
Milwaukee Steam 1900-1902
Minneapolis 1915
Mino 1914
Mitchell 1903-1923
Mobile Steam 1899-1903
Model 1903-1909
Modoc 1913
Moehn 1895
Mogul 1912
Mohawk ....1903-1904 and 1914-1915
Mohler 1901
Moline 1904-1913
Moline Knight 1914-1920
Moller 1920-1921
Monarch ....1908 and 1914-1917
Moncrieff 1901-1902
Monitor 1916
Monroe 1914-1924
Moody 1900-1903
Mooers 1900
Moon 1905-1930
Moore ....1906-1907 and 1916-1921
Mora 1906-1911

Morlock 1903
Morris Salom 1895-1897
Morrison Electric 1891
Morse ....1904-1909 and 1909-1916
Motorette 1910-1912
Moyea 1902-1904
Moyer 1909-1915
M.P.M. 1914-1915
Mueller 1895-1900
Multiplex 1912-1913
Munson 1899-1902
Murdaugh 1901
Murray ....1902-1903 and 1916-1918
Murray Mac 1921-1928
Mustang 1948-1949

N

Napoleon 1916-1917
Nash 1917-1957
National 1900-1924
Navajo 1953-1955
Navarre 1921
Nelson 1917-1921
Neuman Electric 1922
Neustadt Perry...........................1902-1907
Nevada...1908
Neville 1910
Newcomb 1921
New Departure Cab 1904
New England 1898-1900
New England Electric...................1899-1901
New Haven...1904
New York 1928-1929
Niagara...................1903-1907 and 1915-1916
Nichols...1908
Noble 1902
Noma 1919-1923
Northern.......................................1902-1909
Northway 1921
Norwalk 1910-1922
Novara 1917
Nyberg..1912-1914

O

Oakland...1907-1931
Oakman...1898
Oakman Hertel 1902
Obertine 1915
O'Connor 1916
Odelot..1916
Ofeldt 1899-1902
Ogren 1915-1923
Ohio 1909-1913
Ohio Electric 1910-1918
Okey...1907-1908
Oldfield..1917-1922
Oldsmobile.............................1897-present

Oliver..1905
Olympian.....................................1917-1921
Omaha...1912-1913
Only 1909-1915
Orient 1901-1905
Ormond 1904-1905
Orson 1908-1909
Otto 1909-1912
Overholt...1912
Overland ....1903-1929 and 1939
Overman Steam 1899-1900
O We Go 1914-1915
Owen 1910-1914
Owen Magnetic 1914-1922
Owen Schoeneck 1915-1916
Owen Thomas.....................................1909
Oxford 1913-1915

P

Pacific...1914
Pacific Special 1914
Packard 1899-1958
Packet 1916-1917
Page.......................1907 and 1923-1924
Paige..1908-1927
Pak Age Car...............................1935-1938
Palmer 1906
Palmer Singer 1907-1914
Pan..1918-1922
Pan American ....1902 and 1917-1922
Panda 1955-1956
Panoz.....................................1989-present
Panther..1962-1963
Paragon ....1905-1907 and 1922
Parenti..1920-1922
Parker...1921-1923
Parkin..1908
Parry 1910-1912
Parsons Electric...........................1905-1906
Partin Palmer...............................1913-1917
Paterson 1908-1923
Pathfinder....................................1911-1918
Patriot..1922
Patterson Greenfield 1916-1918
Patton Electric 1890
Patton Gas...1890
Pawtucket Steam 1900-1901
Payne Modern..............................1906-1909
Peabody...1907
Peck...1897
Peerless 1900-1931
Peninsular 1915
Penn 1911-1913
Pennington...................................1894-1902
Pennsy..1916-1919
Pennsylvania 1907-1911
People's...1901
Perfection 1906-1908
P.E.T. 1914
Peter Pan 1914-1915

Peters 1921-1922
Petrel 1908-1912
Phelps 1903-1905
Phianna 1916-1922
Philadelphia 1924
Phipps 1901-1912
Pickard 1908-1912
Piedmont 1917-1922
Pierce-Arrow 1901-1938
Pierce Racine 1904-1909
Piggins 1909
Pilgrim 1914-1918
Pilliod 1915-1918
Pilot 1909-1924
Pioneer 1909-1911
Pitcher 1920
Pittsburgh 1909-1911
Plass Motor 1895
Playboy 1946-1951
Plymouth ....1910 and 1928-present
P.M.C. 1908
Pomeroy 1902
Ponder 1923
Pontiac.....................1902-1908 and 1926-present
Pope Hartford 1904-1914
Pope Robinson 1903-1904
Pope Toledo 1904-1909
Pope Tribune 1904-1906
Pope Waverly Electric 1904-1907
Poppy Car..1917
Porter 1919-1922
Porter Steam.....................................1900-1901
Port Huron...1922
Portland..1914
Postal 1907-1908
Powercar..1909-1912
Prado...1920-1922
Pratt 1907
Pratt Elkhart 1911-1917
Preferred...1920
Premier..1903-1925
Premocar..1921-1923
Prescott Steam 1901-1905
Pridemore 1914-1915
Primo...1910-1912
Prince 1902
Princess...1914-1918
Princeton 1923-1924
Publix 1947-1948
Pullman..1903-1917
Pungs Finch 1904-1910
Pup..1947
Puritan Steam 1902-1903

Q

Queen..1904-1906
Quick 1899-1900
Quinlan 1904

R

R and L Electric................................1922-1928
R and V Knight..................................1920-1924
R.A.C..1910-1911
Racine...1909-1911
Radford ....1895 and 1903
Rae ....1898 and 1902
Railsbach..1914
Rainier...1905-1911
Raleigh 1921-1922
Rambler..1902-1913
Randall Steam 1902-1903
Rand Harvey Steam 1899
Randolph Steam 1910
Ranger.........................1907 and 1920-1922
Ranlet 1900
Rapid 1903
Ras Electric 1898
Rauch & Lang.....................................1905-1928
Rayfield..1911-1915
R.C.H..1912-1916
Read..1912-1915
Reading..1913-1914
Reading Steamer 1901-1902
Real...1914-1915
Reber...1902-1903
Red Bug...1924-1930
Red Jacket..1904
Red Wing...1909
Reed...1909
Rees...1921
Reese..1887
Reeves ....1896-1898 and 1905-1912
Regal...1907-1918
Regas...1903-1905
Reinertsen..1901
Relay 1903-1904
Reliable Dayton 1906-1909
Reliance..1904-1906
Remal Steam 1923
Remington...1914-1916
Reo..1905-1936
Republic 1910-1916
Re Vere..1918-1926
Rex..1914-1915
Reya...1917
Reynolds...1899-1901
Richard..1914-1919
Richards..1896-1903
Richelieu 1922-1923
Richmond..1904-1917
Rickenbacker.....................................1922-1927
Ricketts 1909-1911
Riddle...1916-1926
Rider Lewis 1908-1911
Riess Royal 1921
Riker Electric......................................1897-1902
Riley and Cowley......................................1902
Ripper...1903

Ritz	1914-1915
R.O.	1911
Roadable	1946
Roader	1911-1912
Road Cart	1896
Roamer	1916-1929
Robe	1923
Roberts	1904 and 1915
Robie	1914
Robinson	1900-1902
Robson	1909
Roche	1924-1925
Rochester Steam	1901-1902
Rock Falls	1919-1925
Rockaway	1902-1903
Rocket	1903
Rockne	1932-1933
Rockwell	1910-1911
Rodgers	1921
Roebling	1909
Rogers	1895 and 1911-1912
Rogers and Hanford	1902
Rogers Steam	1903
Rollin	1924-1925
Rolls-Royce	1921-1935
Roman	1909
Romer	1921
Roosevelt	1929-1930
Roper Steamer	1860-1896
Ross	1915-1918
Ross Steam	1906-1909
Rotary	1904-1905 and 1922
Rowe	1908 and 1910
Rowena Front Drive	1926
Royal Electric	1904-1905
Royal Tourist	1904-1911
Ruggmobile	1922
Ruler	1917
Rumley	1920
Rushmobile	1901-1903
Russell	1903-1904 and 1921
Russell-Knight	1914
Rutenber	1902
Ruxton	1929-1930
Ryder	1900

S

S and M	1913
S and S Hearse	1924-1929
Saf T Cab	1926-1928
Saginaw	1916
Salisbury	1895
Salter	1909-1913
Salvador	1914
Sampson	1911
Samuels Electric	1899
Sandusky	1913
Santos	1902-1904
Saturn	1991-present
Savage	1914

Saxon	1914-1922
Sayers	1917-1924
Scarab	1935
Schacht	1904-1913
Schaum	1900-1903
Schebler	1908
Schleicher	1895
Schlosser	1912
Schnader	1907
Schoening	1895
Schwarz	1899-1900
Scootmobile	1947
Scott	1901
Scott Newcomb	1921
Scout	1914
Scripps-Booth	1912-1922
Seabury	1904-1905
Seagrave	1914
Searchmont	1900-1903
Sears Motor Buggy	1908-1912
Sebring	1910-1912
Seely Steam	1905
Sekine	1923
Selden	1907-1914
Sellers	1908-1912
Senator	1906-1910
Seneca	1917-1924
Serpentina	1915
Serrifile	1921
Servitor	1907
Seven Little Buffaloes	1909
Severin	1920-1921
S.G.V.	1911-1915
Shad Wyck	1917-1918
Shain	1902-1903
Sharon	1915
Sharp Arrow	1908-1910
Sharp Steam	1901
Shatwells Steam	1901-1903
Shavers Steam	1895
Shaw	1920-1921
Shaw Wick	1917-1919
Shawmut	1906-1908
Shelby	1903
Sheridan	1921
Shoemaker	1906-1907
Sibley	1911
Sibley Curtiss	1911-1912
Sigma	1914
Signel	1915
Silent	1912
Silent Knight	1905-1907
Silver Knight	1914-1919
Simmons Stream	1895
Simms Light Four	1920
Simplex	1907-1919
Simplex Crane	1915-1919
Simplicity	1907-1911
Simplo	1908-1909
Sinclair Scott	1908
Singer	1914-1920
Single Center	1906-1908

Sintz...1902-1904
S.J.R. 1915-1916
Skelton 1920-1922
Skene 1900-1901
Slater 1909
Smisor 1899
Smith...1905
Smith and Mabley Simplex 1904-1907
Smith Motor Buggy 1896
Smith Motor Wheel 1916-1919
Smith Spring Motor 1896
S.N. 1921
Snyder..1906-1908
Sommer...1904-1905
South Bend 1913-1914
Southern 1906-1908
Southern Six..1921
Sovereign..1906-1907
Spacke...1919
Spartan 1910
Spaulding...................1902-1903 and 1910-1916
Special 1904
Speedway 1905-1906
Speedwell 1907-1914
Spencer 1921-1922
Spencer Steam ....1862 and 1901
Sperling 1921-1923
Sperry...1899-1901
Sphinx..1914-1916
Spicer 1902
Spiller 1900
Spoerer 1908-1914
Sprague 1896
Springer...1903-1905
Springfield Electric..1908
Springfield Steam 1900-1901
Sprite..1914
Spurr 1901
Squires Steamer 1899
S.S.E. 1917
Stafford..1908-1914
Stammobile Steam..1900-1901
Standard...1900, 1902,
     1904-1905, 1909-1910, 1915, 1916-1922 and 1948
Standard Electric O 1911
Standard Steamer.....................1900 and 1911-1915
Stanley Steamer 1897-1927
Stanley Whitney...1899
Stanton Steam 1901
Stanwood 1920-1922
Staples...1900
Star ....
     ...1902-1904, 1907-1908, 1909-1911 and 1922-1928
Starin 1903-1904
States 1914-1915
Staver 1907-1914
Steam Vehicle 1900
Steamobile..1901-1902
Stearns 1901-1929
Stearns Steam Car...1898
Steco...1914
Steel Swallow...1907-1908

Stageman 1915
Stein Koenig 1926
Steinhart Jensen 1908
Steinmetz 1922-1923
Stephens 1917-1924
Sterling ....1909-1911 and 1914-1916
Sterling Knight 1920-1922
Sterling Steam 1901-1902
Stetson 1916
Stevens 1899
Stevens-Duryea 1901-1927
Stewart ....1895 and 1915-1916
Stewart Coates Steam.......................................1922
Stickney..1914
Stilson 1907-1909
St. Joe 1909
St. John 1903
St. Louis ....1899-1901, 1903-1907 and 1922
Stoddard Dayton 1904-1913
Storck Steam 1902
Storms Electric 1915
Stout 1946
Stout Scarab..1932-1936
Stranahan 1906
Strathmore 1899-1901
Strattan Premier 1923
Streator 1902
Stringer Steary 1899-1902
Strong and Rogers 1900
Strouse Steam 1915
Strouss 1897
Studebaker 1902-1966
Sturgis 1897
Sturtevant 1905-1907
Stutz...................................1911-1935 and 1970-1975
Stuyvesant 1911-1912
Suburban 1911-1912
Success 1906-1909
Sultan 1908-1912
Summit 1907-1909
Sun 1916-1917
Sunset 1900-1913
Super Cooled 1923
Super Kar 1947
Superior..1914
Supreme 1917-1922
Sweany Steam 1895
Synnestvedt...1904-1905
Syracuse Electric..1899-1903

T

Tait Electric 1923
Tally Ho 1914
Tarkington..1922-1923
Tasco 1947
Taunton 1901-1903
Taylor 1895
Templar 1917-1924
Temple 1899
Templeton 1910

Terraplane 1932-1938
Terwilliger Steam 1904
Tex...1915
Texan 1920-1922
Texmobile 1920-1921
Thomas 1903-1918
Thomas Detroit...1906-1908
Thompson 1901-1907
Thomson Electric 1901
Thorobred 1901
Thresher Electric 1900
Tiffany 1913-1914
Tiger 1914-1915
Tiley 1904-1913
Tincher 1903-1909
Tinkham 1899
Tjaarda 1935
Toledo Steamer..1901-1903
Tonawanda 1900
Toquet 1905
Torbensen 1902-1906
Touraine 1912-1916
Tourist 1902-1910
Tower...1899
Trabold ....1898 and 1905
Tractobile Steam...1900-1902
Trask Detroit 1922-1923
Traveler ...1907, 1910-1911, 1913-1914 and 1924-1925
Trebert...1907-1908
Triangle 1918
Tribune 1913
Tri Moto...1900-1901
Trinity Steam..1900-1901
Triumph 1907-1912
Trumbull 1914-1915
Tucker 1948
Tulsa 1917-1922
Turner 1900
Twin City 1914
Twombly...1913-1915
Twyford ....1899-1902 and 1904-1907

U

Ultimate...1914
Union.................................1902-1909 and 1912
United...1914
United Power 1901
Unito 1909
Universal ....1910 and 1914
University 1907
Unwin 1921-1922
Upton ....1902-1903 and 1905-1907
U.S. 1908
U.S. Electric 1899-1903
U.S. Long Distance 1900-1904
U.S. Motor Vehicle 1899-1900

V

Valley..1908
Van..1911-1912
Van Wagoner 1899
Vandergrift...1907
Van Dyke 1912
Vanell Steam 1895
Vanette 1946
Vaughan........................1910-1914 and 1921-1923
V.E. Electric..1903-1904
Vector 1979-1999
Veerac...1905
Velie 1909-1929
Vernon...1918-1921
Verrett 1895
Vestal 1914
Victor..1913-1917
Victor Steam..1899-1903
Victoria..1900
Victory...1920-1921
Viking................................1907-1908 and 1929-1930
Vim Cyclecar..1914
Virginian..1911-1912
Vixen...1914-1916
Vogel...1909
Vogue 1921-1922
Vulcan...1913-1915

W

Waco 1915-1917
Wagenhals..1910-1915
Wagner 1900-1901
Wahl..1913-1914
Waldron..1908-1911
Walker ....1895 and 1905
Wall...1900-1903
Walter..1902-1906
Waltham ....1898, 1905-1908 and 1922
Walther..1903
Walworth..1904-1905
Ward Electric..1914-1916
Ward Leonard 1903
Ware 1861
Warren 1909-1914
Warren Detroit..1910-1913
Warwick 1901-1905
Washburn 1896-1902
Washington ....1908-1909, 1911-1923 and 1925
Wasp 1919-1924
Waterloo 1903-1905
Waterman 1900
Waters 1900-1903
Watrous..1905
Watt Steam...1910
Waukeshaw 1906-1910
Waverley Electric 1898-1916
Wayne 1904-1908

Webb Jay Steam 1908
Weeks 1908
Welch 1903-1911
Welch and Lawson 1895
Welch Detroit 1910-1911
West Gasoline 1895
Westcott 1909-1925
Western 1901
Westfield Steam 1901-1903
Westinghouse 1905-1907
Weston 1899-1903
W.F.S. 1912
Whaley Henriette 1900
Wharton 1922-1923
Wheeler 1900-1902
Whippet 1927-1931
White 1900-1918
White Star 1909-1911
Whiting 1910-1912
Whitney 1896-1899
Wichita 1920-1921
Wick 1902-1903
Wilcox 1910-1913
Wildman 1902
Willard 1903-1905
Williams 1905
Wills St. Claire 1921-1927
Willys 1916-1955
Willys-Knight 1914-1933
Wilson 1906
Windsor 1929-1930
Wing ....1896 and 1922
Winkler 1911
Winner 1907-1909
Winther 1921-1923
Winton 1896-1924

Wisconsin 1899
Witt 1912
Wizard 1914
Wolfe 1907-1909
Wolverine ....1904-1906, 1917-1919 and 1927-1928
Wonder 1907-1909
Woodruff 1902-1903
Woods 1899-1918
Woods Electric 1901
Woods Mobilette 1913-1916
Worth 1906-1910
Worthington 1904-1905
Wright ....1904 and 1910-1911

X

Xenia 1914

Y

Yale ....1902-1905 and 1916-1918
Yates 1914
Yellow Cab 1915-1930
York 1905

Z

Zeitler 1917
Zent 1900-1906
Zentmobile 1903
Zimmer ....1908-1988 and 1997-present
Zimmerman 1908-1915
Zip 1913-1914

Section Seven – Lists

Index to this Almanac

This index is a complete roster of all listings appearing in the *Almanac*. The page number in-dicated will direct you to the main listing for that supplier or organization.

Please note that numerical names (e.g. 1932 Buick Registry) and symbols (& for example) come before alphabetical names.

Also, vendors who use their own names are alphabetized by their last names. However, to make reading the index easier, we have printed the vendor's full name in its proper order. In addition, vendors who use a nickname or title as part of their business name are listed under that nickname or title — so that you find Mopar Jack Dyson under "M" rather than "D".

Numerical Listings

1 CAAT Limited Co 342
12 Volt Stuff, Radio & Speedometer Repair Co ... 281
12 Volt Stuff, Radio & Speedometer Repair Co ... 335
The 101 Association 514
1866 Estimate 183
1929 Silver Anniversary Buick Club 463
1932 Buick Registry 539
1937-38 Buick Club 463
1938 Ford Street Rod Registry 540
1939-1947 Dodge Truck Registry 540
1948-1950 Packard Convertible Roster 541
1956 Studebaker Golden Hawk Owners Register ... 160
1958 Cadillac Owners Association 464
1958 Thunderbird Convertible Registry 100
The 1965-66 Full-Size Chevrolet Club 465
1969-1971 Pontiac GTO The Judge Convertible
    Registry 542
1970 Dart Swinger 340's Registry 540
1970 Mustang Mach I Registry 502
2002 AD 21
3-D Imagery Inc 323
300 Below Inc 372
356 Enterprises 152
356 Registry Inc 531
4-CV Service 154
4 ever 4 165
4-Speeds by Darrell 401
4 Wheels to Freedom 552
40th Anniversary Corvette Registry 471
442 Club of Oregon 524
The 54 Ford Club of America 482
60 Chev Sam 33
The 60 Oldsmobile Club 141
600 Headquarters 108
600 Racing Inc 329
70 Mercury Marauder X-100 Registry 541
72/73 Mercury Montego GT Registry 541
95 Pace Car Registry 542

A

A&A Auto Parts & Sales 577
A&A Mustang Parts & Mfg Co 95

A & A Plating Inc 325
A & I Supply 394
A & M SoffSeal Inc 360
A-1 Shock Absorber Co 388
A-1 Street Rods 380
A AAAdvantage Auto Transport Inc 404
A/Altered Hot Rod Parts 75
A Bygone Era Motorcars 155
AAAC-Antique Automobile Appraisal &
    Consulting 27
Aabar's Cadillac & Lincoln Salvage & Parts 27
AAC Restorations 412
AACA Library & Research Center 575
AAdvanced Transmissions 402
AAG-Auto Appraisal Group Inc 183
Randal Aagaard 109
Aardvark International 173
Abarth, Museo 586
Abarth Owners International 459
The Abarth Register USA Inc 459
ABC Auto Upholstery & Top Company 86
Aberdeen Antique and Classic Car Club Inc 432
Abingdon Spares Ltd 130
AC Enterprises 173
AC Owner's Club Ltd 459
Accent Models Inc 309
Accessible Systems Inc 394
Accessoryland Truckin' Supplies 33
Accurate Auto Appraisers 183
Accurate Auto Tops & Upholstery Inc 412
Accurate Ltd 134
Accurate Machine Products 388
Ace Antique Auto Restoration 343
Ace Automotive Cleaning Equipment Co 363
ACPlating 325
Adams Custom Engines Inc 343
Addison Generator Inc 254
Adirondack Center Museum 593
Adirondack Corvettes Inc 471
The Adirondack Museum 593
Adler's Antique Autos Inc 343
Adler's Antique Autos Inc 580
ADP Hollander 223
Advance Design Truck Association 431
Advanced Plating & Powder Coating 325
Advanced Racing Technologies Inc 329
Agricultural Memories Museum 593
Air Cooled Motors 105

Air Flow Research.................................34
Airflow Club of America 478
Airplane Plastics..............................274
The Airplane Shop................................309
AIS Gator Exports Inc...............................372
Dennis Akerman................................27
AKH Wheels....................................416
Alamo AMC.......................................459
Alamo City Historical Car Club.....................558
Alamo Classic Chevy Club..........................465
Albers Rolls-Royce.................................155
Alberta Association Antique Auto Clubs..............431
Alberta Mustangs Auto Club 502
Albion Archive...................................606
Wm Albright's Vintage Coach......................108
Aldrich Auto Supply Inc............................263
Alfa Heaven Inc 13
ALFA Romeo Association (Nor Cal)...............459
Alfa Romeo Owners Club, Texas Hill Country 459
Alfas Unlimited Inc.................................14
Algar 73
All American Rambler.............................15
All British Car Club of Vol Co FL 551
All British Car Parts Inc........................255
All Chevy/Canadian Impala............................34
All Ford Parts 79
All Seams Fine 412
Allante Appreciation Group 464
Allante Group, Tampa Bay.........................465
Allante Owner's Association......................464
Allante Store, Tom Rohner's.......................32
The Allard Register.............................459
David Allen, Citroen Specialist.....................65
Allied Bearing Sales..............................209
Allied Power Brake Co 217
Alloy-Fab.....................................80
Alotta Auto Parts 580
Alt Auto Sales....................................230
Alum-Line Inc..................................399
Alvis Owner Club of North America...............459
AMC, Blaser's Auto, Nash, Rambler, ...15
AMC Classic Appraisers...........................183
AMC Club, Dakota..............................460
AMC Club, Windy City Rambler/ 460
AMC, First Coast 460
AMC, South Texas...............................16
AMC World Clubs................................459
AMC, Wymer Classic 16
American Arrow Corp 317
American Austin-Bantam Club.....................460
American Auto & Truck Dismantlers 577
American Autowire/Factory Fit.....................380
American Bugatti Club 463
The American Built Classic Car Club Inc 542
American Camaro Association 467
American Classic Truck Parts........................34
American Classics Unlimited Inc 309
American Collectors Insurance Inc 284
American Dream Machines............................62
American-Foreign Auto Electric Inc 255
American Honeycomb Radiator Mfg Co 333
American MGB Association..........................517

American Motors Cruisers Car Club 459
American Motorsport International....................459
American Performance Products..........................15
American Plastic Chrome..............................324
American Precision Museum 599
American Restoration Services.........................62
American Restorations Unlimited TA 274
American Roadhouse Car Club 431
American Stamping Corp..............................80
American Station Wagon Owners Association 431
American Street Rod...............................380
American Transmissions 402
American Truck Historical Society 431
America's Most Wanted Publishing 571
Dick Ames Stainless Steel Exhaust.................109
Amherst Antique Auto Show..........................195
AMK Products Inc..................................86
Amoskeag Reserve Engine Co 555
Amphicar Car Club.................................461
Amphicar Club, International 461
AMX Club International, Classic....................461
AMX, Eddie Stakes' Planet Houston.................16
AMX Enterprises Ltd 15
AMX Registry, The Javelin 460
AMX Registry, The Super Stock 539
John Analla's Auto Appraisal Service...............183
ANC Restoration..................................325
Anderson Automotive 141
Anderson Racing Inc 263
Anderson Restoration 343
Anderson's Car Door Monograms..................173
Andover Restraints Inc 285
Andy's Classic Mustangs 95
Angeli Machine Co................................304
Anglia Obsolete 17
Ano-Brite Inc...................................325
Antique & Classic Auto Appraisal 183
Antique & Classic Automobiles 230
Antique & Classic Car Restoration 130
Antique Auto Battery...............................208
Antique Auto Electric..............................255
Antique Auto Fasteners 276
Antique Auto Keys.................................303
Antique Auto Parts 243
Antique Auto Parts Cellar 243
Antique Auto Parts et al............................76
Antique Auto Parts Sales 210
Antique Auto Racing Association Inc................543
Antique Auto Restoration...........................343
The Antique Auto Shop.............................218
The Antique Auto Shop.............................343
Antique Automobile Club of America 434
Antique Automobile Radio Inc......................335
Antique Automotive Engineering Inc................76
Antique Car Paintings..............................191
Antique Cars, Parts & Trains 55
Antique DeSoto-Plymouth..........................134
Antique Ford V8 Parts 80
Antique Gas & Steam Engine Museum 584
Antique Motor Club of Greater Baltimore Inc 553
Antique Motorcycle Club of America Inc...........444
Antique Motorcycle Restoration 107

Antique Radio Doctor 335
Antique Radio Service.............................335
Antique Refinishing Service 321
The Antique Studebaker Club Inc 533
Antique Truck Club of America Inc 445
Antique Wheels 416
A-One Auto Appraisals 183
Appalachian British Car Society 445
Apple Hydraulics Inc 388
Applegate and Applegate........................55
Appleton Garage....................................416
Appraisals R Us ET..................................183
Aquia Creek Corvette Club 471
ARASCO...80
Arbor Lodge State Historical Park 591
Arch Carburetor 236
Archer & Associates................................195
Archive Replacement Parts.......................27
Archway Press Inc 567
Arelli Alloy Wheels 417
Aremco Products Inc 173
Arizona Bus Club 550
Arizona Parts..134
Ark-La-Tex Antique & Classic Car Association ...445
Ark-La-Tex Antique & Classic Vehicle Museum..589
Armstrong's Classic Auto Appraisals.......183
Arrow Fastener Co Inc 394
ARS Automotive Research Services 183
Art's Antique & Classic Auto Services 24
ASC&P International 270
Arthur W Aseltine 160
Asheville DieCast....................................309
Ashton Keynes Vintage Restorations Ltd..........155
Asom Electric 255
Asphalt Angels Car Club Inc...................445
Asphalt Draggins' Racing Assn 543
Associated Wheels of Utah......................558
Association for Preservation of Historic Ambulances
543
The Association of Rootes Vehicle Owners..........542
Astra Registry and Club eV, Kellison & 541
Astro Models 309
Atlantic British Ltd..................................158
Atlantic Coast Old Timers Auto Racing Club 543
Atlantic Enterprises.................................239
Atlas Engine Rebuilding Co Inc................264
Atlas Obsolete Chrysler Parts 135
ATVM..122
Atwell-Wilson Motor Museum 602
Auburn Cord Duesenberg Museum..........587
"The Auction"-Las Vegas.........................195
Auctioneer Phil Jacquier Inc 195
Aussieutes/Old Tin 581
Austin-Bantam Club, American...............460
Austin Club, Pacific Bantam....................460
Austin-Healey Club of America Inc 461
Austin-Healey Restorations, Von's 21
Austin-Healey Sports and Touring Club...........462
Authentic Automotive..............................35
Auto Advisors 184
Auto Appraisal Service............................184
Auto Art by Paul G McLaughlin 191

Auto Body Specialties Inc 210
The Auto Buff, Books & Collectibles.................297
Auto Chic/Liquid Glass...........................229
The Auto Collections at the Imperial Palace 592
Auto Consultants & Appraisal Service 184
Auto Craftsmen Restoration Inc..............343
Auto Custom Carpet Inc 237
The Auto Doctor Inc 22
Auto Etc Neon 55
Auto Hardware Specialties........................35
Auto Interchange Systems/Automotive Business
 Forms...567
Auto Italia 75
Auto Krafters Inc 87
Auto-Line Enterprises Inc........................184
Auto Literature Shoppe 596
Auto-Mat Co...286
Auto Motif Inc 199
Auto Muzeuma Haris (Bross) Testverek..............605
Auto Nostalgia Enr 309
Auto Quest Investment Cars Inc 231
Auto Restoration by William R Hahn.......343
Auto Restorations.....................................76
Auto Review Publishing 567
Auto Transport Services 404
Auto Upholstery Unlimited 286
Auto-West Advertising 297
Auto World Books....................................297
Auto World Car Museum by Backer..................591
Auto World Sales.....................................184
Auto Zone...310
Autobahn Transportation Services Inc 404
AutoFashions Restoration & Parts 210
AutoGuide.net...563
Autohobbies 199
Autolifters 394
Autolux Inc 122
AutoMatch Cars (Computer Aided Referral Service)..
231
Automobile Appraisal Service & Special Interest
 Autos..184
Automobile Classics Appraisal Services 184
Automobile Reference Collection 575
Automobilia...199
Automobilia...310
Automobilia Auctions Inc........................195
Automobilia International 200
The Automobilists of the Upper Hudson...........556
Automotion Classics Inc 343
Automotive Art Specialties 191
Automotive Artistry 162
Automotive Design Center Inc 55
Automotive Fine Art................................191
Automotive Fine Art Society Journal.................571
Automotive Friction 242
Automotive Heritage Museum.................587
Automotive Information Clearinghouse.............563
Automotive Interiors 286
Automotive Legal Service Inc 184
Automotive Paints Unlimited 320
Automotive Restoration Market Organization
 (ARMO)..559

Automotive Restorations Inc 344
Automotive Specialties..376
Automovil Club Del Uruguay's Museum...........606
Automuseum Oldtimer 601
Autophile Car Books..567
Autosport Inc 130
AUTOTEC...303
Autowire Division 87
AutoWire.Net..563
The Autoworks Ltd 365
Avanti Auto Service 344
Avanti Club of Florida..551
Avanti Owners Association Int'l 462
Avanti Sales & Service, Southwest.....................21
AVM Automotive Consulting..............................184

B

B & B Cylinder Head Inc.....................................258
B&C Fiberglass Co 80
B & L Body Shop..344
B & O Railroad Museum 589
B & W Antique Auto Parts Inc.............................80
The Babbitt Pot 208
C E Babcock..28
Back-In-Time Automotive Restorations 344
Backing Up Classics Motor Car Museum 594
Backwoods Auto..314
Backyard Buddy Corp 174
BAD Burlington Area Drivers..............................543
Baer Brake Systems 218
Bud Bagdasarian Studios 182
Baker's Auto 118
Baldwin/Chevy 35
Bantam Austin Club, Pacific...............................460
Banzai Motorworks...67
Skip Barber Racing School 329
Barnett & Small Inc..255
Barnett Design Inc 310
Barnum Museum 585
Barrett-Jackson Auction Co LLC 195
Bartlett Museum 589
Barton Auto Wrecking 580
BAS Ltd Jaguar Trim Specialist 110
Basic Inc 122
Bassett Classic Restoration 155
Bassett's Jaguar..110
Bastian Automotive Restoration........................344
Bathurst Company 255
Battery Ignition Co Inc 236
Battlefield Antique...76
Bavarian Autosport 22
Bavarian Quality Parts 22
Baxter Auto Parts 244
Bay State Antique Auto Club 553
Bayless Inc...75
Bayliss Automobile Restorations.......................344
Dave Bayowski 184
BCP Sport & Classic Co 130
BDI Automotive Design/Brandon 387
Be-Bop Cruisers Inc 555
Be Happy Automatic Transmission Parts...........402

The Beachwood Canvas Works 308
Beam Distributors Trailer Sales........................399
Beamish, The North of England Open Air Museum ..
....603
Dave Bean Engineering 120
Becker of North America Inc 122
Bel Air Restorations 363
Bel-Kirk Mustang 95
Belfast Fire Department Museum 589
Bell Motorsports/Pyrotect 182
Belle Meade Plantation 598
Belltown Antique Car Club 445
Belmont's Rod & Custom Shop 380
Dwight H Bennett..276
Jerry Bensinger 231
Bent Axles 543
Bentley Publishers..567
Berkeley Newsletter 462
Berkshire Auto's Time Was 344
Berliner Classic Motorcars Inc 231
Andy Bernbaum Auto Parts 135
JJ Best & Co 271
Best Deal...152
Best Gasket Inc 273
Best of Britain 110
Betws-Y-Coed Motor Museum.............................603
Bicknell Engine Company.....................................24
Big Bend MGs 517
Big Boys Toys 174
Big Boys' Toys Inc 200
Big Flats Rivet Co 276
Bigfoot 4X4 591
Big Horn Basin Mustang Assoc..........................502
Big M Mercury Registry 541
Bill & Brad's Tropical Formula 226
Billie Inc..226
Billings Farm & Museum....................................599
Bill's Auto Parts..579
Bill's Birds 149
Bill's Collector Cars 231
Bill's Model Acres Ford Farm 76
Bill's Speed Shop 35
Bill's Speedometer Shop 281
Bimmer Magazine...571
Binder's Auto Restoration and Salvage 577
Bird Nest...101
Birkin America 120
Irv Bishko Literature 297
Bitter Owners Club...463
Bizzarrini Owners Club, Iso & 514
Blaak Radiateurenbedryf 333
Blackberry Historical Farm/Village....................586
Blackhawk Automotive Museum........................584
Blackhawk Collection...72
Blackhawk Collection...231
Blackhawk Editions 191
Blackheart Enterprises Ltd..................................33
Leon Blackledge Sales Co 226
Blair Collectors & Consultants 185
Blaser's Auto, Nash, Rambler, AMC.....................15
Blast From the Past 200
EJ Blend 144

Index

Blint Equipment Inc 87
Robert D Bliss 255
Blood Sweat & Gears Illinois Valley Car Club.....552
Bloomington Gold® Corvettes USA 56
Blue Ribbon Classic Chevy Club........................465
Blue Ribbon Motoring...174
Blue Ribbon Products..56
Blue Ridge Corvette Club Inc 471
Blue Ridge Mountain Cookery Inc......................174
BMC Classics Inc 344
BMW Car Club of America 463
The BMW CS Registry...463
BMW Group 601
BMW Motorcycle Owners Ltd, Vintage 463
The BMW tii Register 463
BMW Z Series Register 463
Boardwalk Corvettes of Atlantic City 472
M K Boatright 298
Bob's 36-48 Continental & Zephyr Parts...........118
Bob's Antique Auto Parts Inc 76
Bob's Automobilia 25
Bob's Automotive Machine..................................305
Bob's Bird House 101
Bob's Brickyard Inc 23
Bob's Classic Auto Glass 274
Bob's Radio & TV Service...................................336
Bob's Rod & Custom 380
Bob's Speedometer Service 281
John E Boehm 191
Bondo Buddies Car Club 558
Boneyard Stan's 149
Bonk's Automotive Inc...394
Bonnet to Boot 345
Bonneville Speed & Supply 182
Bonneville Speedway Museum 599
Bonneville Sports Inc..182
Boone Trail Corvette Club...................................472
Boop Photography 323
Gideon Booth 139
The CM Booth Collection of Historic Vehicles 603
Boothbay Railway Village....................................589
Borgward Owners' Club.......................................445
Borla East 155
Bill Boudway 144
Bow Tie Chevy Association 35
Bow Tie Chevy Association 543
Bow Tie Reproductions..35
Boyer's Restorations 25
Boyertown Museum of Historic Vehicles 596
BPE Racing Heads 305
Brabham Register..539
Brakelock USA 181
Tony D Branda Performance 95
Brandeberry Antique Auto Appraisal 185
Brass Script 332
The Brassworks...333
Breakers Stable and Carriage House...................597
Bremerton Auto Club 558
Brewer's Performance Inc 135
Brewtown Cruisers Mercury Car Club 517
Brian's 4wd Parts LLC 167
Bricklin Literature 23

Bridge Hampton Historical Society.....................543
Brinton's Antique Auto Parts 144
Bristol Register of New Zealand 539
BritBooks..567
British Auto Parts Ltd..140
British Auto Shoppe 131
British Auto/USA 110
British Automobile Touring Association of Nova
    Scotia 445
British Boots and Bonnets Car Club....................446
British Car Club ASBL...446
British Car Club of Charleston 543
British Car Club of Western New York 556
British Car Keys 19
British Car Magazine 571
British Car Service 345
British Car Specialists...19
British Cycling Museum 603
British Invasion Inc 196
British Luxury Automotive Parts..........................110
British Miles 131
British Motor Cars of New England 446
British Motor Co 110
British Motoring Club Inc 543
British Museum of Transportation 594
British Only Motorcycles and Parts Inc 314
British Pacific Ltd..158
British Parts International 110
British Parts NW 163
British Racing Green 131
British Restorations...111
British Sports Car Club 446
British Sportscars & Classics 111
British Triumph & Metropolitan 129
British Wire Wheel 19
British Wiring Inc 419
Brit-Tek Ltd...130
Bronco Registry, Early...482
Bronx Automotive...279
Brooklyn Motoren Werke Inc 123
Brooks Performance Coatings..............................372
Brooks Stevens Auto Collection Inc.....................600
Brookville Roadster Inc..306
Brothers Truck Parts 408
Brough Superior Club 463
Brown County Cruisers Car Club 446
Michael Bruce Associates Inc..............................567
Francois Bruere..191
Bryant's Antique Auto Parts 76
Bryn Dana International.......................................321
Buckeye GTO Club...528
Buckeye Ramblin' Rods 556
The Buckle Man 276
Bud's Auto Carpets 237
Bud's Chevrolets, Corvettes, ZR1s 56
Bud's Parts for Classic Mercedes-Benz 123
Buenger Enterprises/GoldenRod Dehumidifier ..226
Buffalo Bill Wax Museum 585
Buffalo Milke Automotive Polishing Products Inc..226
The Buffalo Transportation/Pierce-Arrow Museum ..
   593
Bugatti Club, American 463

Index

Buick Bonery 25
Buick Club, 1929 Silver Anniversary 463
Buick Club, 1937-38 463
Buick Club, Island Pacific................................464
Buick Club of America.....................................463
Buick Enthusiasts Club, New Zealand..............464
Buick GS Club of America 464
The Buick Nut-Joe Krepps...............................25
Buick Registry, 1932 539
Buick Specialists...25
Buicks Inc, Classic...25
The Bumper Boyz...35
Bob Burgess 1955-56 Ford Parts.....................87
Burrell's Service Inc 35
Butch's Trim 35

C

C & C Manufacturing Co 399
C & G Early Ford Parts....................................80
C&N Reproductions Inc 200
C & P Chevy Parts 35
C&V Classic Restorations 345
Cactus GTOs Inc 528
Caddy Central..28
Caddy Corner, Honest John's 31
Caddytown™/Pawl Engineering Co...................28
CAdeAA-Club Amigos de Automoviles Antiguos..446
Cadillac & Lincoln Salvage & Parts, Aabar's........27
Cadillac Club Deutschlan eV, Classic 465
Cadillac Club of North Jersey 464
Cadillac Corner Inc, Frank Corrente's................29
Cadillac Drivers Club 464
Cadillac International.......................................28
Cadillac King..28
Cadillac LaSalle Club Inc.................................464
Cadillac Motor Books 28
Cadillac Owners Association, 1958 464
Cadillac Parts & Cars Limited...........................28
Cadillac Parts, Holcombe 31
Cadillac Parts, Sam Quinn 32
Cal-Rods Car Club 551
Cal West Auto Air & Radiators Inc 334
California Association of Tiger Owners...............533
California Car Cover Co 229
California Chrysler Products Club 478
California Collectors' Classics (CCC) 28
California Convertible Co..................................397
California Jaguar...405
California Nomads...465
California Pony Cars..95
California Thunderbirds 101
Calimer's Wheel Shop.....................................417
Cam2 Oil Products Company...........................304
Cam-Pro...222
Camaro Association, American 467
Camaro Association, Worldwide.......................54
Camaro Club, Eastern Michigan.......................467
Camaro Club Inc, International.........................467
Camaro Club Inc, Northwest Jersey..................468
Camaro Club, Lehigh Valley 467
Camaro Club of San Diego..............................467

Camaro Club, Western Michigan 468
Camaro Group Productions, South Jersey 468
Camaro, Old Dominion Mustang/.....................99
Camaro Parts & Accessories, Rick's First
    Generation 53
Camaro Specialties...51
Camaros, Steve's..53
Cameo & GMC Suburban Pickup Club, Classic
    Chevy 465
The Can Corner...200
Canadian Mustang...96
Canadian Pontiac Registry...............................528
Candlewood Valley Corvettes Inc 472
Cantab Motors Ltd 139
Canterbury Motor Museum 603
Canton Classic Car Museum 595
Cape Cod British Car Club 446
Cape Fear Classics Car and Truck Club............446
Capital Area Mopars..519
Capital City Mopars Car Club of California Inc ..520
Capital District Chevrolet Club Inc 465
Capitol City Old Car Club 554
Capri Club of Chicago......................................517
Caprock Classic Car Club Inc 558
Car & Carriage Caravan Museum 599
The Car and Carriage Museum 596
Car Club Council of Central Virginia..................562
Car Coddlers Club of Ohio Inc 557
Car Collectables 191
Car Controls Div...81
Car Cover Company 229
Car Critic 223
Car-Line Manufacturing & Distribution Inc 369
The Car Shop 381
Car Values Plus...185
The Carburetor Refactory 236
The Carburetor Shop.......................................236
Cardmakers..200
Caribou Imports Inc 75
Carillon Historical Park 595
Carlisle Productions 196
Carl's Ford Parts...96
Carobu Engineering...264
Carolina Classics...87
Carolina Cougar Club.......................................517
Dennis Carpenter Cushman Reproductions........67
Dennis Carpenter Ford Reproductions...............87
Carriage Museum of America-Library 596
Carr's One of a Kind in the World Museum........600
Cars & Parts Magazine 571
Cars II..28
CARS Inc..286
Cars of the Past Restorations Inc....................345
Cars of the Stars Motor Museum 603
Cars of the Times 231
Cars of Yesteryear Inc.....................................446
Carson's Antique Auto Parts............................259
Jim Carter's Antique Truck Parts......................36
Cascade Audio Engineering 286
Cascade Corvette Club 472
Ken Case 298
John Cashman...118

David Casimir Philpa-Augustyn 54
Cass County Historical Society 594
Casting Salvage Technologies 238
Castle Display Case Co 310
Caswell Electroplating in Miniature 326
CBS Performance Automotive 279
Centerline Products 14
Centerville Antique Auto Touring Society 552
Central Alabama Restorations LLC 345
Central Carolina Vintage Car Club 556
Central Florida Auto Festival & Toy Expo 196
Central Florida Ford Club 551
Central Indiana Corvette Club 472
Central Indiana Vintage Vehicles 552
Central Lakes Cruzers 554
Central New York Mopar Association 520
Central Ohio Antique Fire Apparatus Assn 543
Central Ohio MG Owners 518
Central Pennsylvania Corvair Club 468
Central Pennsylvania Street Machines 557
Central Texas Museum of Automotive History 598
Ceramicar 192
Certified Auto Electric Inc 256
Cerullo Performance Seating 286
Chalmers Automobile Registry 539
Charles Chambers Parts 140
John Chambers Vintage Chevrolet 36
Champion Luggage Trailers 399
Champlain Valley Classic Cruisers Inc 446
Chandler Classic Cars 88
Chandler-Cleveland Motor Club 446
Michael Chapman 201
Charger Registry, Dodge 540
Charleston Custom Cycle 107
Chassis Engineering Inc 239
"Check The Oil!" Magazine 322
Checker Car Club of America Inc 465
Checker Motors 224
Checker Parts 33
Checker, Turnpike 33
Chernock Enterprises 399
Stan Chernoff 67
Chester County Antique Car Club 557
Chesterwood Museum 590
Chev Sam, 60 33
Chevelle & El Camino Association, New England ... 468
Chevelle & El Camino Owner's Assoc, Oklahoma .. 467
Chevelle Club, Gateway Area 467
Chevelle Club, Maryland 468
Chevelle Connection, Connecticut 467
Chevelle Owners Association, National 468
Chevelle World Inc 51
Chevi Shop Custom Casting 36
Chevrolet Association, Late Great 572
Chevrolet Classics Club 465
Chevrolet Club Inc, Capital District 465
Chevrolet Club of America, Vintage 467
Chevrolet Club, The 1965-66 Full-Size 465
Chevrolet, John Chambers Vintage 36
Chevrolet Nomad Association 465
Chevrolet Parts Co, Cliff's Classic 38
Chevrolet Parts Co, Obsolete 45

Chevrolet Parts Inc, Classic 38
Chevrolet Parts Obsolete 36
Chevrolet Parts of Arizona Inc, Vintage Ford & 95
Chevrolets, Corvettes, ZR1s, Bud's 56
Chev's of the 40's 36
Chevy Association, Bow Tie 35
Chevy Association, Bow Tie 543
Chevy Association, Tri- 549
Chevy Cameo & GMC Suburban Pickup Club,
    Classic 465
Chevy, Baldwin/ 35
Chevy/Canadian Impala, All 34
Chevy Club 511
Chevy Club, Alamo Classic 465
Chevy Club, Blue Ribbon Classic 465
Chevy Club, Columbia Classic 466
Chevy Club, Hawkeye Area Classic 553
Chevy Club, Houston Classic 466
Chevy Club, Michiana Classic 466
Chevy Duty Pickup Parts 36
Chevy/GMC Truck Association, National 511
Chevy Inc, East Coast 40
Chevy International, Classic 38
Chevy Owners Association, Rhode Island 558
Chevy Parts, C & P 35
Chevy Parts, JR's 43
Chevy Parts, Merv's Classic 44
Chevy Parts, Mike Drago 40
Chevy Parts, Mike's 45
Chevy Parts Store, Old 46
Chevy Parts, Tom's Obsolete 49
Chevy Parts, Volunteer State 50
Chevy, Performance 59
Chevy Pickup Parts, Gilbert's Early 41
Chevy Sales, Lee's Classic 43
Chevy Stuff, J & K Old 43
Chevy Times 465
Chevy Truck Parts, Heavy 42
Chevy Truck Parts, Wales Antique 50
Chevy Warehouse, Lutty's 44
Chevyland Parts & Accessories 51
Chevyland USA Auto Museum 592
Chevy's Obsolete Fleet 467
Chevys, Pikes Peak Super 467
Chewning's Auto Literature 298
Cheyenne Frontier Days Old West Museum 601
Cheyenne Pickup Parts 38
Chicago Car Exchange 231
Chicago Corvette Supply 56
Chicago Street Cruisers 446
Chicagoland MG Club 518
Chicagoland Region-Allante Appreciation Group .. 464
Chief Service 346
Chief Studios 192
Ed Cholakian Enterprises Inc 29
The Chopper Rod Shop 381
Chris-Craft Antique Boat Club 543
Chris' Parts Cars 244
Christian Motorsports Illustrated 135
Chrysler 300 Club Inc 478
Chrysler 300 Club International Inc 478
The Chrysler Cordoba Club & Registry 446

Index

Chrysler, DeSoto Parts, Plymouth, Dodge 68
Walter P Chrysler Museum 590
Chrysler NOS Parts, Obsolete 64
Chrysler Parts, Atlas Obsolete 135
Chrysler Products Club, California 478
Chrysler Town and Country Owners Registry.....478
Circle City Corvairs 468
Circle City Corvettes Inc 472
Circle N Stainless 372
Circus World Museum 600
Citizens Against Repressive Zoning..................562
The Citizens Motorcar Company, America's Packard
    Museum 595
Citroen Quarterly USA...................................478
Citroen Specialist, David Allen........................65
City Car Club (Corvairs) Inc............................468
City Imports Ltd 111
CJ Pony Parts Inc...96
CJ Spray Inc 319
Clark & Clark Specialty Products Inc.................307
Sam Clark 417
Charles W Clarke Automotive Consultants 249
Clark's Corvair Parts Inc................................54
Class Cruisers Car Club of Lapeer, MI 446
Class Glass & Performance Inc 270
Class-Tech Corp 256
Classic American Parts Inc 130
Classic AMX Club International........................461
Classic Auto 346
Classic Auto Air Mfg Co 96
Classic Auto Appraisals 185
Classic Auto Appraiser 185
Classic Auto Brokers 222
Classic Auto Literature 298
Classic Auto Rebuilders/CAR 346
Classic Auto Restoration.................................156
Classic Auto Restoration.................................346
Classic Auto Restoration Service Inc..................38
Classic Auto Supply Company Inc 101
Classic Auto Works 381
Classic Autopart Repro Service 221
Classic Buicks Inc...25
Classic Cadillac Club Deutschland eV 465
Classic Car Appraisal Service 185
Classic Car Appraisals 185
Classic Car Club of America 447
Classic Car Lobby...284
Classic Car Publications 192
Classic Car Radio Service® 336
Classic Car Research.....................................185
Classic Car Works Ltd 346
Classic Carriage House 346
Classic Carriages 346
Classic Cars & Parts......................................232
Classic Cars Inc 144
Classic Cars International Museum Displays &
    Sales 599
Classic Chevrolet Parts Inc 38
Classic Chevy Cameo & GMC Suburban Pickup
    Club 465
Classic Chevy International 38
Classic Chevy International 466

Classic Coachworks.......................................346
Classic Coachworks Rod & Custom 381
Classic Corvettes of Minnesota 472
Classic Creations of Central Florida..................96
Classic Cruisers 552
Classic Dream Car Club 447
Classic Enterprises..160
Classic Ford Sales 579
Classic Garage 346
Classic Glass Corvette Club............................472
Classic Impressions Inc 175
Classic Industries Inc....................................38
Classic Industries Inc....................................51
Classic Industries Inc....................................149
Classic Jaguar...111
Classic Jaguar Association 514
Classic Mercury Parts....................................127
Classic Motor Works 165
Classic Motorbooks 568
Classic Motoring Accessories 229
The Classic Motorist 144
Classic Motors 232
Classic Motors 347
Classic Mustang Inc 96
Classic Mustang Parts of Oklahoma 96
Classic Nights Car Club..................................447
Classic Oldtimer Veteranen Club of Austria 514
Classic Performance Products...........................38
Classic Sheetmetal Inc 101
Classic Showcase 347
Classic Sunbeam Auto Parts Inc.......................161
Classic Thunderbird Club International..............508
Classic Trailers 399
Classic Tube...219
Classic Wood Mfg 421
Classics and Customs 347
"Classics" Car Club Inc..................................543
Classics 'n More Inc......................................347
Classique Cars Unlimited 118
Classtique Upholstery & Top Co 76
Classtique Upholstery Supply 287
Classtiques Rod & Custom Club 543
Classy Chassis Car Club 553
Clean Air Performance Professionals (CAPP).......559
Clean Seal Inc...274
Clean Sweep-Vacuum Windshield Wiper Motor
    Rebuilding 419
Clenet Registry 539
Clester's Auto Rubber Seals Inc.......................360
Cliff's Classic Chevrolet Parts Co 38
Clinton County Antique and Classic Car Club ...557
Clipper City Corvette Club 472
The Clockworks..282
Club Corvette of Connecticut 472
Club Delahaye...479
Club Elite (Lotus Type 14) 516
Club Ford Republica Argentina........................482
Club Jacq Japonaises Antiques et Classiques du
    Quebec..447
Club MCC 448
Club Mustang Quebec...................................502
Club Proteam 472

C'NC Sheetmetal ... 338
Coach Builders Limited Inc ... 347
Coach Builders Muscle Car Parts & Services ... 40
Coachbuilt Motors ... 156
The Coastal Empire Mopar Club ... 520
Cobbaton Combat Collection ... 308
Cobra Museum, Telstar Mustang-Shelby- ... 598
Cobra Restorers Ltd ... 65
Coffey's Classic Transmissions ... 402
Coil Spring Specialties ... 389
Coker Tire ... 392
Cole Land Transportation Museum ... 589
Cole Motor Car Club of America ... 544
Cole's Ign & Mfg ... 279
Collectibles For You ... 201
Collector Car & Truck Market Guide ... 571
Collector Car Club of Greater Belleville Area ... 552
Collector Car Insurance Inc ... 284
Collector Car Restorations Inc ... 415
Collector's Auto Supply ... 244
Collectors Car Club of Saskatchewan ... 448
Collector's Carousel ... 232
Collectors Choice Antique Auto Parts ... 578
Collectors Choice LTD ... 68
Collins Metal Spinning ... 296
Colonial Capitol Rods and Classics ... 556
Colonial Corvair Club ... 468
Color-Ite Refinishing Co ... 321
Color-Plus Leather Restoration System ... 295
Colorado Continental Convertible Club ... 515
Columbia Car Club ... 448
Columbia Classic Chevy Club ... 466
Comet Connections, Thunderbird, Falcon, Fairlane & ... 104
Comet Products ... 276
Comet, Ranchero, Fairlane Interiors, Original Falcon, ... 93
Comfy/Inter-American Sheepskins Inc ... 287
Common Gear Antique Volkswagen Society ... 537
Commonwealth Automotive Restorations ... 168
Competition Chemicals Inc ... 326
Competition Network for Harley Racers ... 512
Competitive Automotive Inc ... 51
Concours Cars of Colorado Ltd ... 22
Concours d'Elegance Upholstery ... 413
Concours Quality Auto Restoration ... 347
Connecticut Chevelle Connection ... 467
Connecticut Fire Museum ... 585
Connecticut MG Club ... 518
John E Conner Museum ... 598
Robert Connole ... 144
Conte's Corvettes & Classics ... 56
Contemporary and Investment Automobiles ... 381
Contemporary Historical Vehicle Assoc Inc ... 448
Continental & Zephyr Parts, Bob's 36-48 ... 118
Continental Convertible Club, Colorado ... 515
Continental Mark II Association ... 515
Continental Owners Club, Lincoln and ... 515
Convertible Owners Club of Greater Baltimore ... 553
Convertible Service ... 397
Bob Cook Classic Auto Parts Inc ... 88
Robert W Cook Corvette Art ... 192

JA Cooley Museum ... 584
Cooper Car Club Ltd ... 478
Coopers Vintage Auto Parts ... 29
The Copper Cooling Works ... 334
Corbeau USA ... 287
Cord Duesenberg Museum, Auburn ... 587
Lance S Coren, CAA, CMA ... 186
Dom Corey Upholstery & Antique Auto ... 287
Corpus Christi Museum of Science and History ... 598
Frank Corrente's Cadillac Corner Inc ... 29
Corvair Club, Central Pennsylvania ... 468
Corvair Club, Colonial ... 468
Corvair Club Inc, First State ... 471
Corvair Parts Inc, Clark's ... 54
Corvair Parts, Larry's ... 54
Corvair Ranch Inc ... 54
Corvair Society of America (CORSA) ... 469
Corvair Underground ... 54
Corvairs, Circle City ... 468
(Corvairs) Inc, City Car Club ... 468
Corvette & High-Performance ... 56
Corvette & Hi-Performance Center Inc, Wild Bill's ... 61
Corvette America ... 56
Corvette Art Prints, Hugo Prado Limited Edition ... 60
Corvette Art, Robert W Cook ... 192
Corvette Association, Natural Glass ... 476
Corvette Center, Rogers ... 60
Corvette Central ... 56
Corvette Clocks by Roger ... 282
Corvette Club, Aquia Creek ... 471
Corvette Club, Boone Trail ... 472
Corvette Club, Cascade ... 472
Corvette Club, Central Indiana ... 472
Corvette Club, Classic Glass ... 472
Corvette Club, Clipper City ... 472
Corvette Club, Essex County ... 474
Corvette Club, Florida Keys ... 551
Corvette Club, Illinois Chapter, Solid Axle ... 477
Corvette Club Inc, Blue Ridge ... 471
Corvette Club Inc, Richmond County ... 476
Corvette Club Inc, The Original Circle City ... 476
Corvette Club, Liberty Region ... 474
Corvette Club, Majestic Glass ... 474
Corvette Club, Midwest Early ... 474
Corvette Club, Mohawk Valley ... 474
Corvette Club, New England ... 476
Corvette Club, Northwest Arkansas ... 551
Corvette Club Norway ... 472
Corvette Club of America ... 472
Corvette Club of Delaware Valley ... 473
Corvette Club of Manitoba ... 473
Corvette Club of Michigan ... 473
Corvette Club of Nova Scotia ... 473
Corvette Club of PA, North Central ... 476
Corvette Club of the Bluegrass, Rebel ... 476
Corvette Club, Ozaukee ... 476
Corvette Club, Presque Isle ... 476
Corvette Club, Regina ... 476
Corvette Club, River Cities ... 476
Corvette Club, River City ... 476
Corvette Club (SACC), Solid Axle ... 477
Corvette Club, Silver City ... 477

Corvette Club, Southeastern Wisconsin 477
Corvette Club, Spokane 477
Corvette Club, Steeltown 477
Corvette Club, Stuart 477
Corvette Club, Three Rivers 477
Corvette Club, Treasure State............................477
Corvette Club, Wasaga Beach 477
Corvette Clubs (NCCC), National Council of 475
Corvette Cosmetics..57
Corvette, County 57
Corvette, Davies 57
Corvette Enterprise Brokerage 57
Corvette Fever 571
Corvette, Grossmueller's Classic........................58
Corvette, Gulf Coast 58
Corvette Marque Club of Seattle 473
Corvette Museum, The National.........................588
Corvette of Connecticut, Club............................472
Corvette Owners Assoc, Long Island 556
Corvette Owner's Association, National..............474
Corvette Owners, International Society 474
Corvette Pacifica...57
Corvette Parts Inc, RC 60
Corvette Parts & Car Trailers, Myers Model A Ford,
    Mustang & 78
Corvette Parts, Mary Jo Rohner's 1953-1962.......60
Corvette Parts, Rik's Unlimited 60
Corvette Recyclers, Michigan 59
Corvette Restorers Society, National 475
Corvette Rubber Company.................................57
Corvette Sales Inc, Proteam..............................60
Corvette Service..57
Corvette Set, GMC..474
Corvette Shop Inc, Marcel's 59
Corvette Specialists Ltd, D&M 57
Corvette Specialties of MD Inc 57
Corvette Supply, Chicago...................................56
Corvette Supply Inc, Long Island 59
Corvette Wiper Transmission Service, Dean's.......57
Corvette World 57
Corvettes & Classics, Conte's............................56
Corvettes, Eckler's Quality Parts & Accessories for ..58
Corvettes For Kids Inc 473
Corvettes Inc, Adirondack 471
Corvettes Inc, Candlewood Valley 472
Corvettes Inc, Circle City 472
Corvettes Inc, Cyclone 474
Corvettes Inc, Skyline Drive 477
Corvettes Inc, Windy City 477
Corvettes of Atlantic City, Boardwalk.................472
Corvettes of Enid..473
The Corvettes of Lancaster 473
Corvettes of Mass, North Shore.........................476
Corvettes of Minnesota, Classic 472
Corvettes of Sonoma County Inc.......................473
Corvettes of Southern California........................473
Corvettes of the North.......................................473
Corvettes of the Ozarks 473
Corvettes, RARE..60
Corvettes of Western Australia Inc.....................473
Corvettes, Santa Clara.......................................476
Corvettes, Still Cruisin'......................................61

Corvettes Unlimited..473
Corvettes Unlimited Corvette Club Inc 474
Corvettes USA, Bloomington Gold® 56
Corvettes West (Car Club)..................................474
Corvettes, ZR1s, Bud's Chevrolets, ...56
Alfred Cosentino Solo Books 568
Cosworth Vega Owners Association 466
Bill Cotrofeld Automotive Inc 54
Cougar Club, Carolina..517
Cougar Club, CT...517
Cougar Club, Fordnutz.......................................544
Cougar Club of America......................................517
Cougars, John's Classic......................................128
Cougars, Ken's 128
Council of Vehicle Associations/Classic Vehicle
    Advocate Group Inc 559
Country Cruisers Car Club..................................544
Country Road As 482
County Auto Restoration 347
County Corvette 57
Cover-It 229
Cowtown T's Inc 482
Coys of Kensington 196
CPR..149
CPX-RTS Auto Parts 40
CR Plastics Inc 29
Charles S Crail Automobiles 156
Crank'en Hope Publications................................298
Crawford Auto-Aviation Museum 595
CRC Industries...304
Creative Automotive Consultants........................250
Creative Connections Inc....................................76
Creative Products of Minnesota Inc....................201
Tom Crook Classic Cars 232
Crosley Automobile Club 478
Crosley, North Star..478
Crosley Parts, Edwards 66
George Cross & Sons Inc 196
Crossroads of America..592
Crown Victoria Association 482
Cruisin Classics Inc...552
Cruisin for MDA...196
Cruisin' Style Magazine 571
Cruising International Inc 295
Crutchfield Corp...336
Cruzin Few Unique Vehicle Club 448
CSi...22
CT Cougar Club..517
Chuck & Judy Cubel 76
Cumberland Valley Rod & Custom Club Inc 544
Glen Curtiss Museum...593
Joe Curto Inc 244
Cushman Club of America..................................478
Cushman Reproductions, Dennis Carpenter........67
Custom Auto Interiors by Ron Mangus 287
Custom Autocraft Inc 101
Custom Autosound Mfg......................................175
Custom Bandsaw Blades 394
Custom Cut Auto Glass/Southern Glass Inc....275
Custom Exhaust Specialties Inc 267
Custom Interiors 287
Custom Plating..326

Index

Custom Solutions & Services.............................564
CustomChrome Plating Inc...............................326
Customs & Classics...186
Customs & Classics Inc...................................347
Cyclo Industries LLC......................................226
Cyclone Car Club..448
Cyclone Corvettes Inc.....................................474

D

D&D Automobilia...376
D&D Instruments Inc......................................282
D & D Plastic Chrome Plating..........................287
D & D Trailers Inc..399
D&J GTO Parts..149
D&M Corvette Specialists Ltd............................57
Daewoo Car Club of America©.........................479
DAF Club-America..479
Dagel's Street Rods...382
Dakota AMC Club...460
Dakota BOP Chapter..448
Dakota Studebaker Parts..................................160
Dakota Truckin' Chapter...................................511
Dakota Western Auto Club................................556
Dalmar...326
Norman D'Amico..295
Damper Doctor...264
Danchuk Mfg...40
Dan's Volvo Service...166
Dansk Lancia Register......................................515
Danspeed..282
Dare Classics...175
Alan Darr Early Ford Parts..................................81
Darryl's...295
Dart Swinger 340's Registry, 1970.....................540
D.A.R.T.S...480
Dash Graining by Mel Erikson...........................420
Dash Specialists...29
DashCovers of Florida......................................175
Dashhugger..288
Dashtop by Palco Ind Inc..................................288
Datsun Roadsters of New England, Drone..........479
Dave's Auto Machine & Parts..............................40
Dave's Auto Restoration...................................288
Davies Corvette..57
Chris Davis...192
The Davis Automobile Club...............................479
The Davis Registry..67
Len Dawson..135
Days of 76 Museum...597
Dayton Wheel Products....................................417
Daytona Cams..223
Daytona MIG..394
Daytona-Super Bird Auto Club..........................448
Daytona Turbo Action Camshafts.......................209
DBM Classic Auto...348
DC Council of Car Clubs..................................562
Deals On Wheels..572
Dean's Corvette Wiper Transmission Service........57
Dearborn Automobile Co..................................186
Dearborn Classics..88
Dekalb-Sycamore Vintage Auto Club..................552

The Delage Section of the VSCC........................539
Delahaye, Club...479
Dells Area Cruisers...544
Dells Auto Museum...600
DeLorean Literature..68
DeLorean Midatlantic.......................................479
DeLorean One..68
DeLorean Owners Association...........................479
Delphos Area Car Club.....................................557
Del's Decals...253
Robert DeMars Ltd Auto Appraisers/Historians..186
Demon Carburetion...236
Mike Dennis, Nebraska Mail Order......................81
S D Dennis..77
Denny's Driveshafts..254
Russ Dentico's Sales & Auto Appraisal Consulting..
....186
The DeRidder Car/Truck Show (DCTS).............544
Desert Dog Auto Parts Inc................................211
Desert Muscle Cars...51
Desert Valley Auto Parts..................................577
Design Engineering Inc....................................284
DeSoto Club Inc, National................................480
DeSoto Club of America...................................479
DeSoto Owners Club of MD Inc.........................479
DeSoto Parts, Plymouth, Dodge, Chrysler,..........68
DeSoto-Plymouth, Antique...............................134
DETAILS License Plate Restoration...................295
Deters Restorations...348
DeTomaso Registry...69
Detroit Triumph Sportscar Club.........................534
Deutscher Automobil Veteranen Club.................448
Deutsches Museum..605
Deutsches Technikmuseum v Berlin...................605
De Vaux Registry..540
Development Associates...................................256
DeWitts Reproductions......................................57
Dials For Cars/Scott Young...............................282
Diamond Back Classics....................................392
Diamond T Register...480
Diamond Trim...288
Diecast & More...311
Richard Diehl...295
Daniel N Dietrich..135
DiSchiavi Enterprises Inc.................................348
Discount Auto Parts..580
Distinctive Metal Polishing...............................107
Divco Club of America.....................................480
Dixie Gun Works Old Car Museum....................598
Dixie Truck Works..40
DKW Club of America......................................480
Dobbins Restoration Publishing..........................58
Dobbs Publishing Group Inc.............................568
Doc's Jags...111
Doctor Jaguar Inc...111
Dodge Automobile Club, Shelby........................480
Dodge Brothers Club.......................................480
Dodge Charger Registry...................................540
Dodge, Chrysler, DeSoto Parts, Plymouth,..........68
Dodge City Vintage Dodge Vehicles & Parts........70
Dodge Truck Registry, 1939-1947.....................540
The Dominators...544

Dominion Models 311
Greg Donahue Collector Car Restorations Inc 88
JB Donaldson Co 376
Done Right Engine & Machine Inc 264
Donington Grand Prix Collection 603
Donovan Motorcar Service Inc 111
Don's Antique Auto Parts.................................245
Don's Hot Rod Shop Inc....................................382
Double Park Lifts...377
Doug's Auto Parts..579
Doug's British Car Parts...................................111
Doug's British Car Parts...................................163
Douglass Interior Products 288
Downton 18
Dr Vette 58
Mike Drago Chevy Parts 40
Dragone Classic Motorcars 232
Drake Well Museum 596
Bob Drake Reproductions Inc.............................81
Driven By Design..153
Driven By Desire 232
Driving Passion Ltd USA.....................................29
Dri-Wash 'n Guard 227
Drone Datsun Roadsters of New England 479
Drummond Coach and Paint 73
DTE Motorsports 123
Duane's License Plate Restoration 295
Duesenberg Museum, Auburn Cord...................587
Duffy's Collectible Cars....................................232
Ralph Dunwoodie Research and Information 576
Dennis DuPont...160
Durabuilt Automotive Hydraulics 398
Durant Motors Automobile Club 448
Duryea Transportation Society & Museum.........590
Dusty Memories and Faded Glory.....................308
Dusty Wheels Auto Club....................................559
DW Electrochemicals Ltd..................................256
Dynamic Racing Transmissions LLC..................402
Dynatech Engineering 260

E

Early Birds of Hoosierland................................508
Early Bronco Registry.......................................482
Early Ford Engines...82
Early Ford Parts...82
The Early Ford V8 Club of America....................482
Early Ford V8 Sales Inc......................................82
Early Iron of Ukiah Inc......................................551
Early Mustang Club 502
The Early Valiant and Barracuda Club 544
East Coast Car Association Toys for Tots 544
East Coast Chevy Inc 40
East Coast Jaguar..112
East West Auto Parts Inc..................................580
Eastern Michigan Camaro Club.........................467
Eastern Museum of Motor Racing.....................596
Eastern New York MGA Club 518
Eastern New York MGA Club Newsletter 574
Eastern Oregon Museum...................................596
Eastern Townships Vintage Automobile Club.....448
The Eastwood Company......................................394

Easy Jack & Sons Antique Auto Parts Store.......579
Eaton Detroit Spring Service Co.........................389
EC Parts..41
EC Products Design Inc......................................58
Eckler's Quality Parts & Accessories for Corvettes..58
Economy Racing Components Inc.......................373
Eddie's Restorations 112
Edelbrock Wheels...417
David R Edgerton Coachworks...........................349
Edmonton Mopar Club 520
Edmonton Thunderbird 55-66 Club...................508
Edsel Associates..72
Edsel Club, International...................................481
Edwards Crosley Parts.......................................66
David Edwards-Transmission Parts 402
Egge Machine Company Inc...............................260
Eightparts 163
EIS Engines Inc..123
El Camino Owners Assoc, Oklahoma Chevelle &...467
The El Camino Store 52
Malcolm C Elder & Son 232
Electric Car Owner's Society 544
Electronic Safety Products Inc 282
Elgin Motorcar Owners Registry........................481
Ellingson Car Museum 591
David Elliott 405
Elliott Museum...586
Elliott's Car Radio 336
Elmer's Auto Parts Inc.......................................58
Emblemagic Co 276
Emerald Necklace MG Register 518
Emgee/Clean Tools 227
Energy Suspension...389
Enfield Auto Restoration Inc.............................349
Engine Master Conversions Ltd 382
Engineered Components Inc..............................219
Engineering & Manufacturing Services 82
Engines Direct..264
English & European Ford Registry, North American
....481
English Auto 20
The Enthusiasts Shop 156
Enthusiast's Specialties....................................202
David J Entler Restorations 422
Environmentally Safe Products Inc 382
Erie Canal Village...593
Erskine Register 540
Eshelman Owners Club 481
ESPO Springs 'n Things.....................................389
Essex County Corvette Club 474
ETC/Every Thing Cars 135
European Collectibles Inc 233
European Connection 123
Eurosign Metalwerke Inc...................................296
Eurosport Daytona Inc......................................296
EuroTech Services International 123
EVA Sports Cars..293
Daniel A Evans 89
The Evergreen Press 568
EWA & Miniature Cars USA Inc.........................311
Excalibur Car Club..481
Excellence Magazine...572

Excitement Inc 317
Exhaust Tech 267
Exotic Car Transport Inc 405
Exoticars USA 73
Explicit Concepts Customs & Minis 252
Extreme Motorsports Painting Ltd 319

F

F100 Connection 89
Fabulous Fords Forever Inc 485
Fairlane Automotive Specialties 82
Fairlane & Comet Connections, Thunderbird, Falcon, ...104
Fairlane Interiors, Original Falcon, Comet, Ranchero, ...93
Falcon, Fairlane & Comet Connections, Thunderbird, ...104
Falcon Club of America, Northeast Chapter 501
Falcon, Comet, Ranchero, Fairlane Interiors, Original 93
Falcon's Forever 89
Falcons Inc, Northwest Classic 93
Family Sports Storage Inc 377
Fannaly's Auto Exchange 579
Farmer's Museum 593
Fast Lane Products 227
Bob Fatone's Mercedes Used Parts 123
Fatsco Transmission Parts 402
Faxon Auto Literature 298
FB Performance Transmissions 403
Richard H Feibusch 186
FEN Enterprises of New York Inc 30
Feno's T-Bird 55-57 102
Ferrari Club Argentino 481
Ferrari Club of America 481
Ferraristi Vermont 482
Ferris Auto Electric Ltd 256
FHS Supply Inc 304
Fiat 500 Club Canada 482
Fiat Auto Service 75
Fiat Club FLU Ontario, Toronto 482
Fiat Club, Rear Engine 482
Fiat-Lancia Unlimited (FLU) 482
Fiat Twin Cam Register 482
Ficken Wiper Service 419
Steve Fields' Automobilia 298
Fiero Club, Michigan 529
Fiero Enthusiasts Inc, Northern Illinois 529
Fiero Owner's Club of America 528
Fiero Owner's Club of America 584
Fieros, Jet City 528
Fiesta's Classic Car Center 377
Fifth Avenue Antique Auto Parts 256
Fifties Forever 41
Fifty 5 6 7 Club 466
John Filiss 187
Fill Er Up 202
The Filling Station 41
Finders Service 224
The Fine Car Store 73
Finest In Fords 568

Fini-Finish Metal Finishing 326
Finish Line 65
The Finished Look 365
Walter A Finner 421
Fire Museum of Maryland 589
Firebird & T/A Club, National 529
Firehawk Association of America 542
Firehouse Museum 584
Firewalker Four Wheel Drive Club 544
Firewall Insulators & Quiet Ride Solutions 414
First Coast AMC 460
First National Bank of Sumner 271
First State Corvair Club Inc 471
Jay M Fisher 176
Five Points Classic Auto Shocks 389
Five Star Transport 405
Flashback F-100s 89
Flatlander's Hot Rods 382
Flex-a-lite 270
Florida Inspection Associates 187
Florida Keys Corvette Club 551
Florida Mopar Association Inc 520
Florida Parishes Vintage Car Club 553
Florida Suncoast MG Car Club 518
Flotamex Automotive Inc 272
Flowkooler 416
Don Flye 20
FoMoCo Owners Club 485
Foothills Street Rod Association 544
For Ramblers Only 15
Ford & Chevrolet Parts of Arizona Inc, Vintage 95
Ford & Hot Rod Parts, Joe Smith 85
Ford Cabriolet Club, Model A 486
Ford Car Club Council, Nor-Cal 501
Ford Center Inc, Vintage 79
Ford Club, Central Florida 551
Ford Club Inc, Mid-Maryland 553
Ford Club Inc, Stallions Gate Mustang & 508
Ford Club International Inc, The Model T 496
Ford Club, Mid-Ohio 557
Ford Club of America, Model A 486
Ford Club of America, The 54 482
Ford Club of America, The Model T 498
Ford Club of Northern Ohio, Nifty Fifties 501
Ford Club of Reading, PA, Hawk MTV-8 486
Ford Club, Penn-Ohio Model A 502
Ford Club, Tri-State Mustang & 508
Ford Engines, Early 82
Ford Farm, Bill's Model Acres 76
Ford-Freak Club of Finland 485
Ford Galaxie Club of America 485
Ford History Project, International 574
Ford Mercury Inc, Loyal 98
Ford Molded Rubber, Mercury & 128
Ford Motor Co Literature, Original 84
Ford Motorsports Enthusiasts 485
Henry Ford Museum & Greenfield Village 590
Ford Museum, Rineyville Sandblasting Model A ..588
Ford, Mustang & Corvette Parts & Car Trailers, Myers Model A 78
Ford, Northeast 92
Ford Obsolete 77

Ford Parts, Alan Darr Early 81
Ford Parts, All 79
Ford Parts, Bob Burgess 1955-56.................87
Ford Parts, C & G Early 80
Ford Parts, Carl's 96
Ford Parts Co, Obsolete................................93
Ford Parts, Early 82
Ford Parts Inc, Melvin's Classic 91
Ford Parts Inc, Obsolete 93
Ford Parts, Mark's 1941-1948 83
Ford Parts, New Old Stock 84
Ford Parts, Old 84
Ford Parts, Rocky Mountain V8 85
Ford Parts, Sam's Vintage 94
Ford Parts, Sixties 94
Ford Parts Specialists....................................77
Ford Parts, Specialty 85
Ford Parts Store 89
Ford Powertrain Applications.......................89
Ford, PV Antique & Classic..........................78
Ford Registry, North American English & European
....481
Ford Reproductions, Dennis Carpenter.........87
Ford Republica Argentina, Club....................482
Ford Retractable Club, International..............486
Ford Retractable Club, Washington 502
Ford Sales, Classic 579
Ford, Sanderson..94
Ford Speed Equipment, Red's Headers & Early....85
Ford Street Rod Registry, 1938 540
Ford Truck Enthusiasts Inc 409
Ford Trucks, Recks & Relics 85
Ford V8 Club of America, The Early..............482
Ford V8 Parts, Antique 80
Ford V8 Sales Inc, Early 82
Fordnutz Cougar Club...................................544
Fords Alamo Chapter, Texas..........................558
Fords Forever Inc, Fabulous 485
Foreign Autotech 166
Foreign Motors West.....................................156
Forney Transportation Museum.....................585
Fort Sill Museum...595
Fort Wayne Clutch & Driveline 242
Forties Limited of Orange County 485
Jim Fortin 267
Forza Magazine 572
Foss Plating Co Inc.......................................326
Fosterfield Living History Farm.....................592
Fourintune Garage Inc 20
Fowlkes Realty & Auction Co 197
AT Francis/Blue Thunder..............................260
Bob Francis Auto Writer & Historian 564
Ron Francis' Wire Works 420
Franklin Museum...105
Arthur Freakes 564
George Frechette 219
Freddie Beach Mopars 520
Fredericksburg Street Rods 544
Fred's Classic Auto Radio & Clocks 336
Fred's Truck Parts..41
Freedom Street Rods 382
Freeman's Garage...77

Frelinghuysen Arboretum 592
Freman's Auto 233
French Stuff 154
Frenchtown Auto Club 448
Frick Art and Historical Center 596
The Friendly OK Car Club 558
Friends of the Crawford Auto-Aviation Museum ..544
From Rust To Riches 245
Frontier Army Museum 588
Frost Auto Restoration Techniques Ltd 395
Ft Lauderdale Antique Car Museum 586
Fuller's Restoration Inc.................................349
Fun Projects Inc 256
Fusick Automotive Products 142

G

GAF Auto Museum 599
Galaxie Club of America, Ford 485
Galaxies/Mercurys, Nor-Cal 452
Tommy Gale Trailer Sales & Service................399
Irving Galis...159
Galvin's Rambler Parts 15
Gano Filter 334
The Garden of Speedin 564
Eugene Gardner 296
Gardner Exhaust Systems 267
Don Garlits Attractions...................................586
Garton's Auto 82
Gary's Steering Wheel Restoration 376
Gas Tank and Radiator Rebuilders 272
Gas Tank Renu USA..272
Gaslight Auto Parts Inc 77
Gasoline Alley LLC...176
Gast Classic Motorcars...................................596
Gaston County Museum of Art and History 594
Gateway Area Chevelle Club 467
Gateway Auto & Truck Club 448
Gateway Z Club..479
Gaylord Sales 333
Gear Vendors Inc..403
Gearhead Auction.com 197
Gearheads Cruiser Products & Services............90
Geeson Bros Motorcycle Museum & Workshop ..603
The Generation Gap 373
Genesee Country Village 593
Jim Gensch 336
Gent-l-Kleen Products Inc..............................242
Georgia Triumph Association Inc 534
George's Auto & Tractor Sales Inc...................233
George's Speed Shop 330
Leo Gephart Inc..233
Germany Direct 123
Mike Gerner, The Lincoln Factory 119
Get It On Paper 202
Ghia Enthusiasts Club 480
Gibson Road Antique Fire Association 545
Gig Harbor Cruisers Automotive Club 449
Gilbert's Early Chevy Pickup Parts 41
J Giles Automotive 224
Mark Gillett 233
Gilmore-Classic Car Club of America Museum...590

Glade Mountain Museum 600
The Glass House 275
Glazier Pattern & Coachworks 63
Glazier's Mustang Barn Inc 97
Glensheen Historic Estate 591
Gliptone Manufacturing Inc.....................227
GM Obsolete...25
GMC Corvette Set..................................474
GMC Suburban Pickup Club, Classic Chevy
    Cameo &...465
GMC Truck Association, National Chevy/.....54
GMP (Georgia Marketing & Promotions).....311
Gold Eagle Classics 52
Golden Fin Society 527
Golden Mile Sales Inc 16
Golden Rods...317
Golden State Parts 42
Jerry Goldsmith Promos 202
Good Neighbors Auto Club 551
Good Old Days Garage Inc.......................77
Good Old Days Vintage Motorcar Museum....583
Good Times Car Club 449
Good Times Rods & Customs....................550
Goodguys Rod & Custom Association 449
Randy Goodling 128
Goodmark Industries Inc.........................370
Goodson Shop Supplies...........................395
Gopher State Timing Association 554
Gordon Imports Inc 16
Gotfredson Group...................................512
Gowen Auto Parts..................................245
Graf International...................................365
Graham Brothers Truck & Bus Club 512
Graham Owners Club International.............512
Gran Turismo Jaguar..............................112
Grand Prix Association, Pittsburgh Vintage ...547
Grand Prix Classics Inc 330
Grand Prix Museum 592
Grand Touring..349
Grandpa's Attic 311
Grandpa's Radio Shop 90
Granger Homestead and Carriage Museum....593
Granite City Street Machines....................554
Grant Products Inc 377
Grassroots Motorsports 572
Bill Gratkowski......................................421
Great American Insurance 284
Great Autos of Yesteryear 449
Great Lakers Auto Club 449
Great Lakes Auto "N" Truck Restoration 42
The Great Lakes Roadster Club 485
Great Race Automotive Hall of Fame...........599
Greater Cleveland Model T Club 485
Greater Manchester Fire Service Museum.....603
Greater New York Automobile Dealers Association...
   568
Green Mountain Mustang Club 503
Green Mountain Vintage Auto 187
Green Oak Enterprises Inc 395
Green-Stuff Metal Polish©.......................326
Green Valentine Inc................................233
Greensboro Historical Museum.................594

Greer Enterprises 240
Greg's Automotive 42
Greg's Wheel & Tire 417
Grey Hills Auto Restoration 349
GRIFFIN Radiator..................................334
Griot's Garage 395
Grizzly Industrial Inc..............................395
Jack P Gross Assoc/Scott Manufacturing Inc 367
Grossmueller's Classic Corvette................58
Group Z Sports Car Club of Southern California ..479
Alan Grove Components Inc 383
Gruber Wagon Works 596
Grundy Worldwide..................................284
Grumpy's Old Cars.................................233
GTO Association of America......................528
GTO Club, Buckeye 528
GTO Club, Land of Lakes.........................529
GTO International Club, The Judge 528
GTOs Inc, Cactus 528
Guenther Graphics 192
Guild of Automotive Restorers 350
Guldstrand Engineering Inc......................58
Gulf Coast Corvette 58
The Gullwing Garage Ltd 23
Gunnison Pioneer Museum 585
Guyson Corp of USA...............................363

H

Hagerty Classic Insurance 284
Hagley Museum and Library......................585
Hale's Products 296
Half Ton Fun 82
C D Hall 421
Hall of Fame & Classic Car Museum, DIRT........593
Hall of Fame Museum..............................587
Hall of Flame Museum of Firefighting 583
Hall Pantera 69
Halpin Used Auto & Truck Parts.................580
Hamel's Automotive Inc 350
Richard Hamilton 299
Hampton Coach 42
Hampton Roads Lil' Red Express & Warlock Owners
    Club 480
Hancock's Engine Rebuilders and Balancing
    Service..77
Tony Handler Inc....................................156
Hand's Elderly Auto Care 350
Haneline Products Co..............................176
Hank's Custom Stepside Beds 409
Happy Days Car Club..............................449
Happy Daze Classic Cars.........................233
Harbor Auto Restoration..........................350
Harbort Automotive Art 192
Harkin Machine Shop..............................265
Harley Rendezvous Classic 315
Harmon's Incorporated 42
Harnesses Unlimited 256
Jim Harris 136
W F Harris Lighting 297
Hart City Street Rods..............................449
Harter Industries Inc..............................245

Hartford Auto Museum....................................601
Justin Hartley 30
Hartung's Automotive Museum.......................586
Hasslen Co...105
Hastings Enterprises 256
Hatch & Sons Automotive Inc.........................123
Hatfield Restorations 350
Hauf Antique & Classic Cars & Pickups.............580
Haulmark Industries Inc 399
Hawk MTV-8 Ford Club of Reading, PA............486
Hawkeye Area Classic Chevy Club 553
Hawthorne's Happy Motoring...........................187
Elwood Haynes Museum 587
Hays Antique Truck Museum 584
H D Garage 315
Headers by "Ed" Inc...268
Headlight Headquarters....................................297
Healey Lane..20
Healey Surgeons Inc 20
Heartland Vintage Thunderbird Club of America..509
Heartland Vintage Truck Club 545
Heavy Chevy Truck Parts...................................42
Bill Heeley...90
Heinkel Trojan Club Ltd 512
Heinze Enterprise...16
John H Heldreth & Associates 187
Hemmings Motor News.....................................572
Hemmings Motor News Sunoco Filling Station...568
Hemmings Rods & Performance........................572
Henault's Enterprises..90
Hendersonville Antique Car Club......................449
Leon Henry Inc...565
Henry's Model T & A Parts.................................77
Heritage Motor Centre 603
Heritage Plantation of Sandwich.....................590
Heritage Upholstery and Trim...........................20
Bill Herndon's Pony Warehouse.........................97
Mike Hershenfeld 136
Hibernia Auto Restorations Inc........................350
Hidden Valley Auto Parts...................................42
High Performance Coatings 268
Highland Radiator Inc 334
Highway One Classic Automobiles and
    Highwayone.com..13
Highway Products Inc.......................................378
Hildene...599
James Hill...145
Gary Hill Auto Service 330
Hillcrest Hot Rods...383
Hillman, Commer & Karrier Club......................512
Hill's Classic Car Restoration...........................102
Hillsboro Trailers..399
The Himes Museum of Motor Racing Nostalgia..593
Howard Hinz...296
Bill Hirsch Auto Parts.......................................321
Hi-Speed 107
Hispano-Suiza Society 512
Historic Vehicle Society of Ontario..................545
Historic Video Archives....................................203
Historical Automobile Club of Oregon 557
Historical Car Club of Pennsylvania.................557
Historical Military Armor Museum....................587

Historical Society of Berks County & Museum...596
Historical Society of Martin County 586
Historical Vintage Car Club of Delaware...........449
Hi-Tech Aluminum & Automotive Products Inc..419
Hi-Tech Software...58
Hi-Town Automotive...383
Hjeltness Restoration Inc..................................350
Hobby Express Inc..311
Hoctor's Hidden Valley Auto Parts 577
Hodges Custom Haulers 399
Don Hoelscher, Auto Appraiser........................187
Hoffman Automotive Distributor.......................212
Holcombe Cadillac Parts....................................31
Hollywood Classic Motorcars Inc 102
Duncan F Holmes...576
Hometown Auto Glass 275
R O Hommel...119
Honda 600 Roster of Owners 540
Honest John's Caddy Corner 31
Wayne Hood...70
Hoosier Cruisers of Vincennes Inc 449
Hoosier Model Car Association.........................545
The Hoosier Mopar Association........................520
Hoosier Volks Club...552
Bill Hoover 511
Bruce Horkey's Wood & Parts 409
The Horn Shop 350
Horseless Carriage Club of America 449
Horseless Carriage Foundation Inc 576
Horseplayactionwear.com.................................182
Horton...383
Horst's Car Care...123
Bill Horton 128
Hosking Cycle Works..315
Hot August Nights 197
Hot Heads Research & Racing Inc......................63
Hot Rod & Custom Supply.................................83
Hot Rod Art 192
Hot Rod Coffee..176
Hot Rod Memories...565
Hot Rod Nostalgia™...568
The Hot Rod Shop 383
Hot Rod Things 203
Hotchkiss Mfg/Clear Case................................311
Hotchkiss Vacuum Tank Service.......................272
House Of Imports Inc.......................................123
House of Powder Inc..367
Art Houser's Rear End Service.........................254
Houston Classic Chevy Club............................466
Houston Volkswagen Club................................537
J K Howell..66
Howell's Sheetmetal Co 77
HRC Inc, Kawaguchiko Motor Museum.............605
HRC Inc, Racing Palace 605
HTP America Inc...395
Hubbard and Associates....................................187
Hubbard Classic Car Appraisals 187
Hubcap Mike...279
Hudson & Mohawk Society of Volkswagen Owners
   537
Hudson-Essex-Terraplane Club.........................512
Hudson Motor Car Co Memorabilia..................108

David Hueppchen..............................166
Wayne Huffaker, Automobilia Artist..................192
William Hulbert Jr..............................336
Hunters Custom Automotive 177
Hupmobile Club Inc..............................514
Richard Hurlburt..............................296
Hurst/Olds Club of America, HMN 524
Hurst Racing Tires/Traction By Hurst 392
Hyde Auto Body..............................350
Hyde Products Inc 42
Hydro-E-Lectric 398

I

Idaho Vintage Motorcycle Club 552
Ideal Signs 192
ididit inc..............................376
Ignition Distributor Service..............................280
Illawarra Motoring Museum..............................601
Illiana Antique Auto Club 449
Illini Collector Car Club 449
Illinois Railway Museum..............................586
Imaginographx..............................193
IMCADO Manufacturing Co 245
Impala, All Chevy/Canadian..............................34
Impala Association, National 466
Impala Bob's Inc..............................43
Imperial Motors..............................63
Imperial Palace Auto Collection 592
Imperial Restorations POR-15 Products 365
Imtek Environmental Corporation..............................307
Independence Porcelain Enamel 339
Indian Adventures Inc 245
Indian Parts, Kiwi..............................109
Inline Tube..............................219
Inliners International..............................545
Innovative Rod Products 240
Instrument Services Inc..............................283
Integrity Machine 219
Intercity Lines Inc..............................405
Interesting Parts Inc 245
Interior Corvetters' Association 474
Intermountain's Finest Truck Club 545
Internationaal Museum 1939-1945 606
International 190SL Group Inc 516
International Amphicar Club 461
International Automobile Archives..............................299
International Automotive Appraisers Assoc........187
International Camaro Club Inc 467
International Classic Auctions 197
International Edsel Club..............................481
International Ford History Project..............................574
International Ford Retractable Club..............................486
International House of Toys 311
The International King Midget Car Club..............515
International Mercantile 153
International Mercury Owners Association........517
International Motor Racing Research Center at
     Watkins Glen..............................576
International Motor Truck Association, Scout &..514
International Motorsports Hall of Fame..............583
International Museum of the Horse 588
International Restoration Specialist Inc 350
International Society Corvette Owners 474
International Society for Vehicle Preservation 545
International Thunderbird Club..............................509
International Towing & Recovery Museum........598
International Viper Registry..............................540
Inter-State Motor Car Registry 1909-1919 540
Interstate Towing Service..............................406
Iowa Gas Swap Meet..............................197
Iron Range Car Buffs..............................449
Isis Imports Ltd 139
Island Pacific Buick Club..............................464
Iso & Bizzarini Owners Club..............................514
Israel Classic Car & Motorcycle Club 450
Italy's Famous Exhaust 268
Itsashoka Innovations 307
Iverson Automotive 326

J

J & C's Parts 26
J & G Auto Parts 339
J & K Old Chevy Stuff 43
J & L Industries 326
J&M Auto Parts 43
J & M Vintage Auto 579
Jacks Wholesale Division..............................119
Jackson & Wardick Hot Rods 384
Jackson Street Cruisers 545
Jackson's Oldtime Parts 260
Jacobs Electronics Inc..............................280
Jacques Rear Engine Renault Parts 155
JAE..............................120
Jag Works, Vintage..............................115
Jags, Doc's 111
Jaguar Association, Classic 514
Jaguar, Bassett's 110
Jaguar, California..............................405
Jaguar Car Keys..............................113
Jaguar Cars Archives 565
Jaguar, Classic..............................111
Jaguar Club of Connecticut..............................514
Jaguar Club of Minnesota 554
The Jaguar Club of Montreal..............................514
Jaguar Club of Tulsa Inc 514
Jaguar Clubs of North America Inc..................514
Jaguar, East Coast..............................112
Jaguar, Gran Turismo..............................112
Jaguar Heaven..............................113
Jaguar Hoses, John A Meering 113
Jaguar Inc, Doctor..............................111
Jaguar of Puerto Rico Inc 113
Jaguar Parts Inc, Terry's 115
Jaguar, Paul's 114
Jaguar Spares, Vintage..............................115
Jaguar, Straight Six 115
Jaguar Trim Specialist, BAS Ltd 110
Jaguar, Vicarage 115
The Jaguar Warehouse..............................113
Jaguar, Western..............................115
JAM Engineering Corp..............................236
Eliot James Enterprises Inc..............................568

Jarvis Old Car Locks & Keys..........................303
The Javelin AMX Registry 460
JCM Industries..227
JECC Inc..26
Jeeps® & Willys® Parts, Obsolete.................168
Jeepsamerica 63
Jeepster Association, Midstates 538
The Jeepster Man 168
Jefferis Autobody..275
J.E.M. Classic Car Museum 597
Jensen Cars Ltd 116
Jerome State Historic Park 583
Jerry's Classic Cars & Parts Inc......................90
Jersey Late Greats Inc....................................43
Jersey Motor Museum 602
Melissa & Jerry Jess......................................165
Jesser's Auto Clinic 187
Jesser's Classic Keys 303
Jet City Fieros 528
Jet-Hot Coatings/MCCI 268
Jewett Owners Club 514
JLM..275
Joblot Automotive Inc......................................83
Joe's Auto Sales 90
John's Auto Classics 187
John's Car Corner 165
John's Cars Inc 113
John's Classic Cougars...................................128
John's F-Fun Hundreds 90
Kenneth L Johnson 280
Jeff Johnson Motorsports 136
Bob Johnson's Auto Literature 300
Jolyon Hofsted 541
The Jordan Register 541
Joyce's Model A & T Parts................................77
JR's Antique Auto...43
JR's Chevy Parts 43
The Judge GTO International Club 528
The Judge's Chambers 150
Jukebox Friday Night 336
Jack Juratovic 193
Jus'n Ol' Truck Club 450
Just Dashes Inc 290
Just Old Trucks of Austin, Texas....................466
Justice Brothers Inc 584
JWF Restorations Inc 13
Jysk Automobilmuseum 602

K

K&D Enterprises 116
K & K Vintage Motorcars LC 351
K&S Industries...311
Kaddies Inc 378
Kaiser Darrin Owners Roster 541
Kaiser Frazer Owner's Club International 515
Kaiser Illustration..193
Kansas City MG Car Club...............................518
Kansas State Historical Society......................588
Kanter Auto Products 245
Karl's Collectibles 311
Karmann Ghia Parts & Restoration..................165

Karr Rubber Manufacturing 361
Katen and Associates Inc...............................374
KATO USA Inc...162
Dave Kauzlarich 300
K C Obsolete Parts 90
KC Wood Manufacturing 422
KC's Rods & Customs......................................384
Gary Keating 545
Keene Area Klassics 450
Keighley Bus Museum Trust Limited 603
Keilen's Auto Restoring...................................351
Keiser Motors 162
Keleen Leathers Inc 291
Kelley's Korner 160
Kellison & Astra Registry and Club eV 541
Kurt Kelsey 150
Kelsey Tire Inc 392
Kenask Spring Co 390
Kennedy American Inc......................................15
J A Kennedy Inc 188
Bob Kennedy Woodgraining Service 421
Kenny's Rod & Kustom 384
Ken's Carburetors 83
Ken's Cougars 128
Ken's Klassics 351
Kensington Motor Group Inc...........................124
Kent Island Cruisers Club 450
Kessler's Antique Cars & Body Shop.................43
K-F-D Services Inc...116
K-GAP 108
Kick-Start Motorcycle Parts Inc 107
Kimble Engineering Ltd 132
King Bolt Co..277
King Kruisers Car Club 450
Dale King Obsolete Parts 90
David M King, Automotive Books 157
King Midget Car Club, The International...........515
King Motor Car Club of America 515
Kingsbury Dolly Co Inc 395
Kingsport Antique & Rod Club........................450
Shepard Kinsman...300
Kip Motor Company Inc....................................18
Kissel Kar Klub 515
Kiwi Indian Parts 109
KJ Classic Metal Designs................................203
Klasse 356 153
Klassic Kolor Auctions....................................197
Klassy Kruzers Car Club.................................450
Mike Z Kleba 333
Dale Klee 193
The Klemantaski Collection 323
Knight Registry Inc, Willys-Overland- 458
Dave Knittel Upholstery..................................414
Knox Motor Car Club of America 515
Koala International..227
Koch's 377
Koffel's Place II 265
Kokomo Autmotive Heritage Museum 587
Chuck Konesky 113
Kosters Motorboghandel 300
KozaK® Auto Drywash® Inc...........................228
Kramer Automotive Specialties 136

Roger Kraus Racing.................................392
Kreimeyer Co/Auto Legends Inc 124
Krem Engineering.................................351
Kruse International 197
Kustom Kemps of America.........................450
Kwiklift Inc......................................395

L

L & L Antique Auto Trim..........................374
L & N Olde Car Co................................352
LA Ltd Design Graphics...........................204
LA Roadsters Car Club............................450
La Vie de l'Auto Elvea...........................572
LaCarrera-The Mexican Road Race 331
Joe Lagana...77
Laigle Motorsporte Ltd...........................188
Lake Buchanan Industries Inc.....................395
Lake Erie Tri-State Mopar........................520
Lake George Antique Boat & Auto Museum 593
Lake Granbury Vintage Car Club...................450
Lake Oswego Restorations 17
Lake Region Car Club.............................450
Lakeland Motor Museum............................604
Lamborghini Owners' Club.........................515
Lamm Morada Publishing Co Inc....................568
Lancia Motor Club................................515
Lancia Register, Dansk...........................515
Land Cruiser Solutions Inc.......................162
Land of Lakes GTO Club...........................529
Landis Valley Museum 597
Landry Classic MotorCars.........................188
Lares Manufacturing...............................91
Larry's Corvair Parts.............................54
Larry's Thunderbird and Mustang Parts Inc.......102
Col Glenn Larson 188
Larson Motor Co..................................233
l'art et l'automobile............................204
LaSalle Club Inc, Cadillac.......................464
Last Chance Repair & Restoration 352
The Last Precinct Police Museum..................583
Late Great Chevrolet Association 572
The Latest Scoop-Auto Enthusiast Magazine 572
LaVine Restorations Inc..........................352
Layson's Restorations Inc 136
Lazy B Trailer Sales Inc 399
L B Repair..90
Leatherique Professional Leather Restoration &
    Preservation Products 157
LeBaron Bonney Co.................................78
LeBarons Car Club................................450
Lectric Limited Inc...............................58
Lee's Classic Chevy Sales 43
Lee's Street Rods................................384
Legendary Auto Interiors Ltd......................63
Legendary Motorcars LLC..........................312
Lehigh Valley Camaro Club 467
Lena Area Historical Society 586
Lester Building Systems..........................378
Les Amis de Panhard & Deutsch-Bonnet 450
LES Auto Parts....................................43
Gerald J Lettieri 274

LEX-AIRE Nationwide Sales........................395
LHI Inc..177
Libbey's Classic Car Restoration Center..........352
Liberty Harley-Davidson..........................107
Liberty Cruisers Car Club........................451
Liberty Region Corvette Club.....................474
Bob Lichty Content & Consulting 188
Lilliput Motor Co, LLC...........................312
Jeff Lilly Restoration Inc.......................352
Dave Lincoln.....................................296
Lincoln and Continental Owners Club 515
The Lincoln Factory, Mike Gerner.................119
Lincoln Highway Association......................545
Lincoln Land Inc Showroom 119
Lincoln Owners Club..............................515
Lincoln Parts International 119
Lincoln Register (RRLR), Road Race 516
Lincoln-Rubber Reproductions 119
Lincoln Salvage & Parts, Aabar's Cadillac &.......27
Lincoln Services Ltd 119
Lincoln Zephyr Owners Club 515
Lindley Restorations Ltd.........................113
David Lindquist, Automobile Clock Repair 283
Leo R Lindquist 136
PK Lindsay Co Inc................................363
Lindskog Balancing 265
Linearossa International Inc......................75
Bob Lint Motor Shop 579
Liquid Glass Enterprises Inc.....................228
Litchfield Hills Historical Automobile Club........551
Little Old Cars..................................312
Bruce Litton Trailer Sales 399
Ed Liukkonen......................................91
Llangollen Motor Museum 604
Lloyd's Literature...............................300
LMARR Disk Ltd...................................157
LMC Truck...44
Local Cruisers Car Club..........................545
Loga Enterprises 161
London Stainless Steel Exhaust Centre 268
Lone Wolf..204
George & Denise Long 204
Long Island Corvette Supply Inc 59
Long Island Corvette Owners Assoc 556
Long Island Moose Classic Car Club 451
Long Island Motor Touring Club Inc 556
Long Island Mustang Restoration Parts 98
Long Island Street Rod Association 545
Long Island Thunderbird Club.....................509
Long Island VW Club..............................537
Long Road Productions............................415
Lonny's Fabrication..............................307
Lord Byron Inc 230
Los Coyotes The Club.............................451
Lost Highways 546
Lotus Ltd..516
(Lotus Type 14), Club Elite 516
Lovefords..451
Loyal Ford Mercury Inc...........................98
Luback & Co 315
Ed Lucke's Auto Parts 580
Lutty's Chevy Warehouse 44

Lyco Engineering Inc ...124
Lyme Pond Restorations ...352
Lynden Pioneer Museum ...600

M

M & G Vintage Auto ...132
M & H Electric Fabricators Inc ...257
M & L Automobile Appraisal ...188
M & M Automobile Appraisers Inc ...188
M & R Products ...177
M & S Enterprises ...197
M & T Manufacturing Co ...422
Larry Machacek ...204
Machina Locksmith ...303
Mack Products ...83
Mac's Antique Auto Parts ...78
Mac's Antique Car Museum ...595
Mac's Custom Tie-Downs ...400
Mac's Euro Motorcars & Transport ...14
Mac's Pack ...546
Mac's Radiator Service & Gas Tank Renu LA ...334
Mad Dogs & Englishmen ...546
Madline Island ...601
Magnet Paints ...321
Mahoning Auto ...31
Mahoning Valley Old Car Club ...557
Mahymobiles ...601
Maintenance Specialties Company ...365
Majestic Glass Corvette Club ...474
Majestic Truck Parts ...44
Jim Mallars ...70
Malone Auto Club ...556
Malm Chem Corp ...228
Manchester Motor Car Co ...246
Mancini Racing Enterprises ...136
Manitoba Grand National Association ...464
W L Wally Mansfield ...246
Manx Dune Buggy Club ...546
Maplewood Motors ...55
Marauders Hot Rod Club ...546
Marcel's Corvette Shop Inc ...59
Jack Marcheski ...257
Marcovicci-Wenz Engineering Inc ...331
Randall Marcus Vintage Automobiles ...222
Mark Auto Co Inc ...78
MAR-K Quality Parts ...410
Mar-Ke Woodgraining ...421
Mark II Enterprises ...177
Mark's 1941-1948 Ford Parts ...83
Markel's Auto Upholstery ...414
Marlin Auto Club ...460
Marmon Club ...516
Cathie Marples & The Marples Team ...250
Marquette Owners Registry for Enthusiasts ...539
Marquette Radio ...336
Marren Motor Sports Inc ...273
Gerry Martel's Classic Carriages ...188
Martin Carriage House ...422
Martin's of Philadelphia ...328
Maryland Chevelle Club ...468
Mascots Unlimited ...333

The Maserati Club ...516
Massachusetts Antique Fire Apparatus Association Inc ...546
Massena Olde Car Club Inc ...546
Massillon Area Car Club ...557
Master Plating ...328
Master Power Brakes ...52
Mastercraft Body Works Inc ...243
Mastermind Inc ...31
The Masters Company ...396
The Maverick Connection ...91
Max Neon Design Group ...204
Maximillian Importing Co ...23
Maximum Downforce ...324
Maximum Torque Specialties ...31
Maymont Carriage Collection ...600
Maynard Area Auto Club ...553
Mazda Club ...516
Mazda RX-7 Club ...516
Ben McAdam ...280
McCann Auto Restoration ...353
Bill McCoskey ...188
McCoy's Memorabilia ...300
McDonald Obsolete Parts Company ...91
McFarland & Company Inc Publishers ...569
Ken McGee Auto Literature ...301
McInnes Antique Auto ...78
McIntyre Auctions ...197
Donald McKinsey ...280
McLean's Brit Bits ...233
McLellan's Automotive History ...301
Meadowcroft Village ...597
Mean Mustang Supply Inc ...98
Mecham Design, Performance ...44
Dana Mecum Auctions Inc ...197
Medicine Bow Motors Inc ...234
John A Meering Jaguar Hoses ...113
Melvin's Classic Ford Parts Inc ...91
Memory Lane Motors ...353
Memory Lane Motors Inc ...234
Memory Lane Motorsports & Historical Automotive Museum ...594
Memoryville USA Inc ...353
Mercedes-Benz 190SL Club e.V. ...516
Mercedes-Benz 300SL Gullwing Group International ...516
Mercedes-Benz, Bud's Parts for Classic ...123
Mercedes-Benz Club of America ...516
Mercedes-Benz Club of America, Toronto Section ...516
Mercedes-Benz IG Germany ...517
Mercedes-Benz Market Letter ...575
Mercedes-Benz Service by Angela & George/ABS Exotic Repair Inc ...124
Mercedes-Benz Visitor Center ...124
Mercedes Used Parts, Bob Fatone's ...123
Mercer Automobile Company ...127
Mercury & Ford Molded Rubber ...128
Mercury Car Club, Brewtown Cruisers ...517
Mercury Car Club, Mid-Century ...517
Mercury Club, Southwest ...517
Mercury Cyclone/Montego/Torino Registry ...517

Mercury Inc, Loyal Ford...........................98
Mercury Marauder X-100 Registry, 70 541
Mercury Montego GT Registry, 72/73 541
Mercury Owners Association, International.......517
Mercury Parts, Classic...........................127
Mercury Registry, Big M 541
Mercury Research Co 128
Mercurys, Nor-Cal Galaxies/ 452
Charlie Merrill.................................222
Max Merritt Auto Parts 145
Merv's Classic Chevy Parts 44
Alan Mest Early Model Auto Repair..............353
Metro Motors....................................130
Metropolitan Owners Club of North America......523
Metropolitan Pit Stop...........................130
Metz Chain Gang.................................517
MG Car Club Central Jersey Centre...............518
MG Car Club, Florida Suncoast 518
MG Car Club, Kansas City........................518
MG Car Club-Long Island Centre..................518
MG Car Club Ltd, Washington DC Centre..........518
MG Classics of Jacksonville.....................518
MG Club, Chicagoland............................518
MG Club, Connecticut............................518
MG Club, The Philadelphia.......................519
MG Drivers Club of North America................518
MG Octagon Car Club 519
MG Owners, Central Ohio.........................518
MG Register, Emerald Necklace 518
MG Register, Texas..............................519
MG T Register Ltd, New England 519
MG T Register, Minnesota........................519
MG, The Proper 133
MG Vintage Racers Newsletter 519
MGA Club, Eastern New York 518
MGA Club Newsletter, Eastern New York 574
MGA Register (NAMGAR), North American 519
MGB Association, American.......................517
MGC Register, North American 519
MGs, Big Bend 517
Miata Club of America 516
Michael's Classics Inc..........................124
Michiana Antique Auto Club Inc 552
Michiana Classic Chevy Club.....................466
Michiana Mopar Association......................520
Michigan Antique & Collectible Festivals........198
Michigan Corvette Recyclers......................59
Michigan Fiero Club.............................529
Michigan Great Lakes Antique Car Club 554
Michigan Monte Carlo Cruizers...................554
The Microcar and Minicar Club 546
Mid-America Auctions 198
Mid America Direct...............................59
Mid-America E-body Mopar Club...................520
The Mid-America Old Time Automobile
    Association 451
Mid-America Willys Club 538
Mid-Atlantic Nomad Association..................466
Mid-Atlantic Nostalgia Drag Racers Assn 546
Mid-Century Mercury Car Club....................517
Mid-Iowa Shows Inc 553
Mid-Jersey Motorama Inc 31

Mid Maine Vettes................................474
Mid-Maryland Ford Club Inc......................553
Mid-Michigan Antique Fire Apparatus Association...
   546
Mid Ohio Ford Club.............................557
The Mid Peninsula Old Time Auto Club Inc........551
Mid Shore Cruisers..............................551
Mid Valley Engineering 403
Mid West Old Threshers Museum 588
Midbanc Financial Services 271
Middleton Place 597
Midsouth Regional Old Car Club 451
Midstates Jeepster Association 538
Midwest Drag Racers Association 451
Midwest Early Corvette Club 474
Midwest Hot Rods Inc 385
Midwest Mopar Club-Sioux Empire Chapter 546
Midwest Mopars Inc 520
Midwest Restoration Parts 45
Midwest Street Rod Association of Illinois 546
Midwest Vintage Snowmobile Shows Inc 546
Midwestern Council of Sports Car Clubs..........451
Midwestern KlipperKarts 312
MIE Corporation 121
Mifflinburg Buggy Museum 597
Mighty Mopars of Orlando 520
MikeCo Antique, Kustom & Obsolete Auto Parts..136
Mike's Auto Parts 63
Mike's Chevy Parts 45
Mild to Wild Classics 385
Miles Auto Parts & Machine......................265
Milestone Motorcars 312
The Milestone Car Society.......................452
Military Transport Association of North Jersey...547
Military Vehicle Preservation Assoc 547
Mill Supply Inc 370
Gus Miller 578
Walter Miller...................................301
Miller Auto Museum Inc 587
Miller Energy Inc 159
Sammy Miller Motorcycle Museum 604
Miller Obsolete Parts 92
Millers Incorporated 124
Miltronics Mfg Inc 181
Mini Moke Registry, North American..............539
Mini Motors Classic Coachworks 20
Mini Owners of New Jersey Car Club 462
Mini Store 18
Minis of Windsor Owner's Group 462
Minnesota Historical Society....................591
Minnesota MG T Register.........................519
Minnesota Street Machine Association............554
Miracle of America Museum 591
Miracle Steel Structures 378
MITCHCO 204
Dennis Mitosinka's Classic Cars and Appraisals
    Service 188
Mobile Structures Inc/MSI Trailers..............400
Model A Club, Northern Ohio.....................502
Model A Ford Cabriolet Club.....................486
Model A Ford Club of America 486
Model A Ford Club, Penn-Ohio 502

Index

Model A Ford Museum, Rineyville Sandblasting...588
Model A Restorer's Club 492
Model Engineering...239
The Model T Ford Club International Inc 496
The Model T Ford Club of America....................498
Mohawk Valley Corvette Club 474
Molina Gaskets 274
Moline Engine Service Inc.................................265
Monikers 318
James J Montague 124
Thomas Montanari Automotive Artist 193
Monte Carlo Cruizers, Michigan........................554
Monte Carlo Owner's Association Inc, National ..466
Monteverdi Registry and Club eV......................541
Don Montgomery's Hot Rod Books....................569
Moon Registry 134
Moores Cycle Supply 316
Mopar Alley 521
Mopar Association, Central New York 520
Mopar Association Inc, Florida 520
Mopar Association, Michiana.............................520
Mopar Association, Southern.............................548
Mopar Association, The Hoosier........................520
Mopar Club, Edmonton 520
Mopar Club, Mid-America E-body 520
Mopar Club, Northeast Mighty...........................521
Mopar Club, Southwest 521
Mopar Club, The Coastal Empire 520
Mopar Collector's Guide Magazine 137
Mopar, Lake Erie Tri-State...............................520
Mopar Muscle..572
Mopar Muscle Club, Wisconsin..........................521
Mopar Scat Pack Club 521
Mopars Auto Club, Northern.............................521
Mopars, Capital Area...519
Mopars Car Club of California Inc, Capital City ..520
Mopars, Freddie Beach 520
Mopars of Orlando, Mighty 520
Mopars, Space Coast 521
Mike Moran...45
Moray Motor Museum 606
Morgan Car Club, Washington, DC....................523
Morgan Motor Car Club.....................................523
Morgan Motor Company Ltd 139
Morgan Oasis Garage 139
Morgan Spares Ltd 139
Morgan Sports Car Club of Canada 523
Morgan Three-Wheeler Club 523
Morgan Three-Wheeler Racing 523
Morgans on the Gulf..523
Moroso Motorsports Park..................................331
Morris Minor Registry of North America 541
Morris Register 541
Morrison Motor Co Inc..59
Morven Park 600
Moss Motors Ltd..132
Mostly Mustangs Inc 98
Motion Unlimited Museum and Antique Car Lot..597
Moto Guzzi, Harper's...316
Moto Italia 107
MotoMedia 301
Motor Bus Society Inc.......................................547

MotorCam Media...415
Motorcar Gallery Inc...74
Motorcars International..74
Motorcars Ltd..114
Motorcycle Hall of Fame Museum 595
Motorcycle Museum (Motorrad Museum) 605
Motorhead Ltd..20
MotorLit.com...301
Motormetrics...164
Motorsport Auto..67
Motorsports Insurance Services.........................285
Motorsports Parts Manufacturers Council
    (MPMC)..561
MotorWeek..565
Mouldsworth Motor Museum.............................604
Mount Vernon Ladies Association of the Union ..600
Mountain Vintage Radio Repair 336
Mountain Fuel...234
MPH Interactive Designs....................................565
Mr G's Enterprises 137
Mr Moly..304
Mr Norm's Sport Club..521
Mr Sport Car Inc...114
MSC Fasteners..277
MSD Ignition...280
Mt Washington Valley Old Car Club...................555
Muffler Museum 584
Muhlenberg County Hot Rod Club 452
Mullins & Teardrop Reproductions 400
Muncie Imports & Classics................................114
Muntz Registry..541
Murphy's Motoring Accessories Inc....................230
Muscle Car Ranch 595
Muscle Express 52
Musclecar Review..573
Musee du Circuit de Spa-Francorchamps 602
Museo Abarth..586
Museum of Automobile History..........................593
The Museum of Automobiles..............................584
Museum of Aviation...586
Museum of British Road Transport....................604
Museum of Irish Transport................................605
Museum of New Hampshire History...................592
Museum of Pioneer Life....................................598
The Museum of Science & Industry in Manchester ..
   604
Museum of the Great Plains 596
Museum of Transportation 590
Museum of Transportation 591
Museum Village in Orange County.....................593
The Museums at Stony Brook............................593
Muskegon Brake & Dist Co................................219
Mustang & Corvette Parts & Car Trailers, Myers
    Model A Ford, ...78
Mustang & Ford Club Inc, Stallions Gate...........508
Mustang Assoc, Big Horn Basin.........................502
Mustang Barn Inc, Glazier's 97
Mustang/Camaro, Old Dominion.........................99
Mustang, Canadian...96
Mustang Classics...98
Mustang Club, Early 502
Mustang Club, Green Mountain 503

Mustang Club, New Hampshire 555
Mustang Club of America 503
Mustang Club of Maryland 507
Mustang Club, Sierra 508
Mustang Club, Sonoma County 508
Mustang Club, Southeast Texas 508
Mustang Club, The West Michigan 508
Mustang & Ford Club, Tri-State......................508
Mustang Inc, Classic 96
Mustang Inc, Virginia Classic 100
Mustang Mach I Registry, 1970 502
Mustang Monthly 573
Mustang of Chicago Inc 98
Mustang Owners Club International 508
Mustang Parts & Mfg Co, A&A 95
Mustang Parts Inc, Larry's Thunderbird and......102
Mustang Parts of Oklahoma, Classic 96
Mustang Quebec, Club....................................502
Mustang Parts, Texas 100
Mustang Restoration Parts, Long Island 98
Mustang Service Center....................................98
Mustang-Shelby-Cobra Museum,
    Telstar 598
Mustang Special Order Paint Registry................540
Mustang Supply Inc, Mean................................98
Mustang SVO Owners Association Inc 508
Mustang Village...578
Mustangs & More 99
Mustangs, Andy's Classic 95
Mustangs Auto Club, Alberta............................502
Mustangs Inc, Mostly 98
Mustangs Plus Inc 99
Mustangs Unlimited 99
Myers Model A Ford, Mustang & Corvette Parts &
    Car Trailers 78
Myk's Tools 396

N

NADA Appraisal Guides...................................570
JC Nadeau 234
Narragansett Reproductions 257
Nash Car Club of America 524
Nash, Rambler, AMC, Blaser's Auto 15
Nassau County...594
National American Motors Drivers & Racers
    Association 460
National Antique Oldsmobile Club 524
National Automobile Museum...........................592
National Automotive & Truck Museum of the United
    States 587
National Chevelle Owners Association................468
National Chevy/GMC Truck Association 511
The National Corvette Museum.........................588
National Corvette Owners Association................474
National Corvette Restorers Society 475
National Council of Corvette Clubs (NCCC) 475
National Cycle Collection 606
National DeSoto Club Inc 480
National Firebird & T/A Club 529
National Historic Route 66 Federation 547
National Impala Association 466

National Monte Carlo Owner's Association Inc ...466
National Motor Museum 601
National Motor Museum 604
National Motorcycle Museum and Hall of Fame ..598
National Motorists Assn...................................561
National Nostalgic Nova 467
National Packard Museum................................595
National Parts Depot 99
National Parts Locator Service 225
National Road-Zane Grey Museum 595
National Sporting Library 600
National Spring Co Inc 390
National Sprint Car Hall of Fame & Museum 588
The National Tramway Museum 604
National Transport Museum 605
National Woodie Club 452
NATMUS Roadside Market...............................205
Natural Glass Corvette Association 476
N/C Industries Antique Auto Parts 275
NCA Automotive 354
Neil's Wheels Inc 312
Clayton T Nelson 142
Nelson's Surplus Jeeps and Parts 309
Neonetics Inc..318
The Nethercutt Museum 584
Neumaclassic 393
Neuspeed 18
New England Chevelle & El Camino Association ..468
New England Corvette Club 476
New England MG T Register Ltd 519
New England Sonett Club................................532
New England Triumphs 534
New England's Vintage Thunderbird Club Inc....509
New Era Motors...422
New Hampshire Mustang Club 555
New Old Stock Ford Parts.................................84
New Old Stock Toronto Chapter.......................452
New Zealand Buick Enthusiasts Club 464
Newark Rodders 452
Dave Newell's Chevrobilia 45
Newfoundland Antique and Classic Car Club.....452
Next Generation Restoration and Performance by
    Year One 53
NHRA Motorsports Museum 584
Niagara CHT Productions Inc...........................198
Nifty Fifties Ford Club of Northern Ohio............501
Nissan Patrol Club America 479
N-News Magazine 410
NJ Nostalgia Hobby 205
NMW Products 178
No 1 Performance 261
Noble Racing Inc 261
Charles Noe...222
Nomad Association, Chevrolet 465
Nomad Association, Mid-Atlantic 466
Nomads, California 465
Nor-Cal Fiestas...501
Nor-Cal Ford Car Club Council........................501
Nor-Cal Galaxies/Mercurys 452
Norman's Classic Auto Radio..........................337
North American English & European Ford
    Registry 481

Index

North American MGA Register (NAMGAR) 519
North American MGC Register 519
North American Mini Moke Registry..................539
North Carolina Studebaker Drivers Club 556
North Carolina Transportation Museum at Spencer. 594
North Central Arkansas Cruisers.....................550
North Central Corvette Club of PA 476
North Dakota Street Rod Association 556
North GA Patterns 239
North Shore Corvettes of Mass.......................476
North Shore Rods, Southside..........................552
North Star Crosley......................................478
North Valley Unique Car Club 452
North Yale Auto Parts 580
North Yorkshire Motor Museum.......................604
Northeast Chapter Falcon Club of America 501
Northeast Classic Car Museum........................594
Northeast Ford 92
Northeast Hemi Owners Association 452
Northeast Mighty Mopar Club.........................521
Northern Auto Parts Warehouse Inc..................261
Northern Illinois Fiero Enthusiasts Inc 529
Northern Illinois Street Rod Association............547
Northern Indiana Cruisers-R-Rides...................552
Northern Lights Car Club 452
Northern Mopars Auto Club............................521
Northern Motorsport Ltd................................354
Northern Ohio Model A Club...........................502
Northern Tool & Equipment............................396
Northern Wisconsin Volkswagen Club 537
Northstar RX-7 Club 516
Northwest Arkansas Corvette Club 551
Northwest Classic Falcons Inc 93
Northwest Import Parts 133
Northwest Jersey Camaro Club Inc...................468
Northwest Transmission Parts 403
Northwestern Auto Supply Inc 261
Northwoods Cruisers....................................558
NOS Only 246
NOS Reproductions 137
Nostalgia Knights Classic Car Club...................452
Nostalgia Productions Inc 198
Nostalgic Automobile Society of Montclair..........452
Nostalgic Car Club 559
Nostalgic Images Inc (formerly NEO) 205
Nostalgic Motor Cars 21
Nostalgic Reflections....................................324
Nova Club, Peach State 551
Nova, National Nostalgic 467
Nova Parts...45
Nova Scotia Museum of Industry 602
Now & Then Vehicles Club Inc of Southern
    Vermont 555
The NSU Club of America 524
NSU Enthusiasts USA 524
NSU/USA Jim Sykes 141
Nu-Chrome Corp 374
NW Cruisers 198
Henry Nyberg Society 524
Nyles Haulmark Trailer Sales 400
NZMVCC Inc 547

O

Oak Bows..422
Oakland Club International Inc, Pontiac............529
Oakland Owners Club International Inc.............524
Oakland-Pontiac Enthusiast Org 529
C Obert & Co..75
O'Brien Truckers 324
Obsolete Auto Parts Co P/L 246
Obsolete Chevrolet Parts Co 45
Obsolete Chrysler NOS Parts 64
Obsolete Fleet Chevys..................................467
Obsolete Ford Parts Co 93
Obsolete Ford Parts Inc 93
Obsolete Jeep® & Willys® Parts....................168
Obsolete Parts of Iowa 137
Ocala Jeep Club of FL 547
Ocean Video Movies 416
Oceanside Vettes 476
O'Connor Classic Autos 133
Joe Odehnal 93
Odyssey Restorations Inc...............................354
OEM Glass Inc 275
OEM Paints Inc 321
Ohio Jukebox Co 318
Ohio Limo and Coach Sales 234
Oil Company Collectibles Inc 205
OJ Rallye Automotive 297
Oklahoma Chevelle & El Camino Owners Assoc..467
OlCar Bearing Co 209
Old Air Products..59
Old Bethpage Village Restoration.....................594
Old Bridge Township Raceway Park 198
Old Cabot Village...182
The Old Car Centre.......................................78
Old Car City USA...578
Old Car Club Inc 452
Old Car Co 189
Old Car Museum 598
Old Car Parts 46
The Old Carb Doctor.....................................237
Old Cars Unlimited of Washington, DC 452
Old Cars Weekly & Olds Cars Price Guide..........573
Old Chevy Parts Store 46
Old Coach Works Restoration Inc 354
Old Dominion Mustang/Camaro........................99
Old Ford Parts..84
Old GMC Trucks.com 106
Old Gold Retold Inc Florida Swap Meets 198
Old Prison Museums 591
Old Rhinebeck Aerodrome 594
Old Town Cruisers 547
Old Wade House and Wisconsin Carriage Museum.. 601
Old World Wisconsin 601
The Olde Tyme Auto Club..............................453
Olde World Restorations 139
Oldenbetter Restorations Inc 46
Older Car Restoration 354
Olds Club of America, HMN, Hurst/ 524
RE Olds Transportation Museum......................590
Oldsmobile Club, National Antique...................524

Oldsmobile Club of America..........................524
Oldsmobile Club, The 60 141
Oldtimermuseum De Rijke...........................606
Olson-Linn Museum..................................588
Olson's Gaskets.....................................274
Omaha Volkswagen Club.............................537
Omni Specialties 133
On Mark International Inc............................312
Only Yesterday Classic Autos Inc......................46
The Opel Association of North America 525
Opel GT Source 143
Opel Motorsport Club................................526
Opels Unlimited......................................143
Operations Plus.......................................66
Orange County Antique Auto Club Inc..............453
Orange Empire Chapter, SDC.......................533
Bob Ore Restorations 354
Oregon Crewe Cutters Inc...........................157
Oregon Historical Society............................596
ORF Corp 145
Original Auto Interiors..............................414
The Original Circle City Corvette Club Inc.........476
Original Falcon, Comet, Ranchero, Fairlane
    Interiors..93
Original Ford Motor Co Literature.....................84
Original Parts Group Inc.............................150
Orion Motors European Parts Inc 14
Orphan Motorsports 144
Jim Osborn Reproductions Inc 254
Oscar's Dreamland...................................591
OSJI...114
Ottawa Antique Car Club............................553
The Over the Hill Gang of Pennsylvania 547
Overland-Knight Registry Inc, Willys-...............458
Owls Head Transportation Museum...................589
Ozaukee Corvette Club 476

P

P&J Automotive Inc.................................385
P&J Products 178
P-Ayr Products.......................................46
Pace Setter Performance Products 268
Pacific Bantam Austin Club..........................460
Pacific Gold Rush Ramblers..........................460
Pacific International Auto 114
Pacific Northwest Pontiac Club 529
Packard Archives....................................145
Packard/Chirco Automotive, Tucson 146
The Packard Club....................................526
Packard Convertible Roster, 1948-1950............541
Packard Museum, National...........................595
Packard Museum, The Citizens Motorcar Company,
    America's......................................595
Packard, Potomac...................................145
Packard, Steve's Studebaker.........................145
Packard Truck Organization.........................527
The Packard V-8 Roster, 1955-1956 541
Packards International Motor Car Club 527
Packards, Sierra Grove..............................145
The Paddock® Inc 46
Painting & Stripping Corp...........................364

Paintwerks by Jeff Tischler..........................388
Palm Springs Exotic Car Auctions 198
Palo Alto Speedometer Inc 125
Panhandle Plains Historical Museum.................599
Pantera, Hall...69
Pantera International 480
Pantera Owner's Club of America (POCA)..........480
Pantera Parts Connection............................69
Pantera Performance Center 69
PAR Porsche Specialists.............................153
Paradise Classic Auto Appraisal......................189
Paragon Models & Art...............................206
Paragon Reproductions Inc...........................59
Park-McCullough House 599
M Parker Autoworks Inc.............................257
Parts House...246
Parts of the Past....................................302
Parts of the Past....................................579
The Parts Place......................................47
Parts Unlimited Inc 47
Partsource 74
Partwerks of Chicago...............................262
Passport Transport Ltd..............................407
Past Gas Company 206
Past Lane Auto 206
Past Pleasures Car Club 453
Pate Museum of Transportation.....................599
Pate Swap Meet 198
Patee House Museum 591
Patrician Industries Inc 145
Patriot Truck Registry...............................527
Patton Orphan Spares 155
Paul's Chrome Plating Inc...........................328
Paul's Jaguar 114
Paul's Rod & Bearing Ltd...........................208
Paul's Select Cars & Parts for Porsche 153
PE/Snappin Turtle Tie-Down Straps.................400
Peach State Nova Club 551
Lyle Pearson Company 125
Pearson's Auto Dismantling & Used Cars..........577
Pebble Hill Foundation 586
Pedal Pumpers Club of American PPCA 547
Pedal Toys..312
Peerless Motor Car Club Inc 527
Pelham Prints.......................................193
Peninsula Imports 23
Peninsula Restoration Parts 47
Penn Auto Sales Co 21
Penn-Ohio Model A Ford Club 502
Pennsylvania Metal Cleaning 364
People Kars 165
Perfect Panels of America...........................154
Performance Analysis Co 125
Performance Automotive Inc 228
Performance Automotive Warehouse.................262
Performance Car Museum 598
Performance Chevy...................................59
Performance Coatings...............................268
Performance Designed 393
Performance Shop 400
Performance Years Pontiac 151
Pertronix Inc 280

Bill Peters...377
CT Peters Inc Appraisers 189
Petersen Automotive Museum.................584
Garth B Peterson..................................247
Peterson Auto Transport.......................407
A Petrik 278
Petro Classics......................................322
Petroleum Collectibles Monthly.............573
Phantoms of Red Wing..........................554
Phantoms Motor/Model Club..................547
The Philadelphia MG Club 519
Philbates Auto Wrecking Inc 581
Phil's Studebaker 161
Phoenix Graphix Inc..............................254
Phoenix Transmission Products..............403
PI Motorsports Inc.................................69
Pick-ups Northwest 47
R E Pierce..167
Pierce-Arrow Museum, The Buffalo Transportation/
   593
Pierce-Arrow Society Inc 527
Pikes Peak Auto Hill Climb Educational Museum ....
   585
Pikes Peak Super Chevys.......................467
Pilgrim's Auto Restorations....................354
Pilkington Glass Search..........................275
Pine Ridge Ent......................................230
The Pinstriper......................................388
J Pinto 257
Pioneer Auto Museum and Antique Town 598
Pioneer Automobile Association 553
JT Piper's Auto Specialties Inc 59
John E Pirkle...59
Piru Cads 31
Pittsburgh CARS 557
Pittsburgh Vintage Grand Prix Association 547
Platte'rs Car Club 555
Plymouth, Antique DeSoto-....................134
Plymouth Barracuda Owners Club 527
Plymouth County Auto Club....................553
Plymouth, Dodge, Chrysler, DeSoto Parts 68
Plymouth Owners Club Inc.....................528
Plymouth Parts '46-'48..........................148
Plymouth, Riddle's/Mr...........................138
PM Research Inc....................................312
PMD Specialties....................................151
Jack Podell Fuel Injection Spec................60
Pole Position Racing Products.................241
Police Car Owners of America 453
Poll's Museum of Transportation 590
Poly All Fast Set International Inc............340
Ponti-Action Racing..............................151
Pontiac Club of America, Royal...............531
Pontiac Club, Pacific Northwest 529
Pontiac Commercial & Professional Vehicles 529
Pontiac Engines Custom Built 151
Pontiac Enthusiast Org, Oakland- 529
Pontiac GTO The Judge Convertible Registry,
    1969-1971.......................................542
Pontiac Inc, Rustic Auto Club of 552
Pontiac-Oakland Club International Inc............529
Pontiac Owners Association....................531

Pontiac, Performance Years 151
Pontiac, Precision..151
Pontiac Registry, Canadian..................................528
Pontiac Sedan Delivery Registry...........................542
Pony Enterprises..99
Pony Parts of America..99
Porcelain Patch & Glaze Co Inc...........................268
Porsche 914 Owners Association and 914-6 Club
    USA...532
Porsche®, Paul's Select Cars & Parts for 153
Porsche Specialists, PAR.....................................153
Portanje's Vespa Scooter & Nostalgia Collection .606
Dennis Portka 60
Portland Beater Car Club aka International Beater
    Appreciation Society (IBAS)...........................454
Portrayal Press 309
Pot Metal Restorations..328
Potomac Packard 145
John T Poulin Auto Sales/Star Service Center ...234
Powell Radiator Service 334
Power & Speed Racing Promotions.....................521
Power Brake Booster Exchange Inc.....................220
Power Brake Systems 220
Power Brake X-Change Inc 220
Power Effects® 269
Power Steering Services Inc 391
Powers Parts Co 274
Powers Parts Inc..157
Practical Images 324
Hugo Prado Limited Edition Corvette Art Prints ...60
Prairie Auto..234
Prairie Auto Porcelain...269
Pre-Sixties Cars and Parts Ltd 247
Precious Metal Automotive Restoration Co Inc ...125
Precision Autoworks 125
Precision Babbitt Service 208
Precision Coachworks..84
Precision Pontiac 151
Precision Rubber 362
Premier Designs Historic Costume.....................182
Prescott Antique Auto Club 550
The Presidential Cars Museum 605
Presque Isle Corvette Club.................................476
Prestige Automotive Inc 354
Prestige Motors..234
Prestige Thunderbird Inc....................................103
Prezerve Inc...228
Private Garage LC..74
PRO Antique Auto Parts 47
Production Tool Supply of Ohio 396
Professional Car Society 547
Professional Metal Refinishing Inc 364
Professional Restylers Organization (PRO)..........561
Pronyne...597
The Proper MG 133
Proper Motor Cars Inc 157
Pro's Pick Rod & Custom 385
Pro-Strip 364
Proteam Corvette Sales Inc 60
Protective Products Corp 341
Prototype Research & Dev Ltd 48
Bert Provisor 302

Index

Al Prueitt & Sons Inc 356
PTE Publishing..566
P-Town Street Rods Car Club 547
Puget Sound British Automotive Society 548
Pulaski Area Car Enthusiasts................................558
Pulfer & Williams..333
PV Antique & Classic Ford 78

Q

QA1 Precision Products Inc 391
Qual Krom-Great Lakes Plant.........................328
Quality Sew 415
Quality Tire Barn Inc..393
Queen City Model A Club 502
Quik-Shelter 230
Sam Quinn Cadillac Parts 32

R

R & L Engines Inc..266
R&L Model A 78
R & R Fiberglass & Specialties...........................270
RACE Car Club 559
Racing Consultants 332
Rad Cap Products...335
Rader's Relics 234
Radiator & Gas Tank Specialist 335
Ragtops & Roadsters 13
Lloyd Ralston Gallery 313
Rambler, All American..15
Rambler, AMC, Blaser's Auto, Nash, ...15
Rambler/AMC Club, Windy City 460
Rambler Parts, Galvin's 15
Ramblers Only, For 15
Ranchero, Fairlane Interiors, Original Falcon,
    Comet,..93
William H Randel..103
Rapido Group 129
The Rappa Group 189
RARE Corvettes 60
Rare Parts Inc 391
RAU Restoration 422
Raverty's Motor Museum 601
Glen Ray Radiators Inc......................................335
Raybuck Autobody Parts 214
Rayce Inc 14
Ray's Upholstering 356
RB's Obsolete Automotive 247
RB's Prototype Model & Machine Co 368
RC Corvette Parts Inc 60
RD Enterprises Ltd 121
R-D-T Plans and Parts..400
The Real Source 166
Realistic Auto Restorations Inc 356
Rear Engine Fiat Club 482
Reardon Enterprises 580
Rearend Specialties 254
Rebel Corvette Club of the Bluegrass 476
Recks & Relics Ford Trucks 85
Recycler Classifieds 573
Red Bird Racing 48

Red Lion Racing 193
Redden's Auto Glass Engraving 275
Redding Corp 356
Redi-Strip Company 364
Red's Headers & Early Ford Speed Equipment.....85
The Reflected Image...375
Re-Flex Border Marker 278
Regal International Motor Cars Inc 157
Regal Roadsters Ltd...103
Regent Trading Corp..94
Regina Corvette Club...476
Reinholds Restorations.......................................356
Pete Reinthaler Insurance..................................285
Reliable Carriers..407
Relics & Rods Car Club 548
REM Automotive Inc 292
REME Museum of Technology 604
Renault Owner's Club of North America............532
Renault Parts, Jacques Rear Engine 155
Reni Studio 193
Renner's Corner 85
REO Club of America Inc 532
Replica Plastics 270
Replicarz 332
Repro Parts Mfg...60
Reproduction Parts Marketing.............................48
Rest Stop Rodders Club 454
Restoration Specialties 48
Restoration Specialties and Supply Inc 247
Restoration Supply Company 341
Restorations By Julius 148
Restorations Unlimited II Inc 356
Retrospect Automotive.......................................235
Retroviseur..573
Revolvstore The Volvo Place 577
Reward Service Inc 114
Reynolds-Alberta Museum.................................602
Reynolds Museum Ltd 235
Reynolds Speedometer Repair............................283
Rhein-Main-Cruiser/Goodguys Member Germany ...
   548
Rhode Island Chevy Owners Association............558
Rhode Island Wiring Services Inc......................257
Richard's Auto Restoration 356
Richardson Restorations.....................................356
Richmond County Corvette Club Inc..................476
Rick's Carburetor Repair 237
Rick's First Generation Camaro Parts & Accessories
   53
Rick's Relics 356
Riddle's/Mr Plymouth 138
Rideable Antique Bicycle Replicas.....................316
Rideau Lakes ACCCC 454
Ridgefield Auto Upholstery 292
Rik's Unlimited Corvette Parts 60
Frank Riley Automotive Art 193
Rineyville Sandblasting Model A Ford Museum..588
Riordan Mansion State Historic Park 583
River Bend Auto Club 454
River Cities Corvette Club..................................476
River City Corvette Club 476
River City Street Rods..454

Index

Riverbend Abrasive Blasting 364
Riverside Park Machines (RPM) 548
Riviera Owners Association 464
RJ Tool & Supply 396
RM Classic Cars 198
Road Knights Auto Club Inc 454
Road Race Lincoln Register (RRLR) 516
Roadrunner Tire & Auto 356
The Roadster Factory 164
Roaring 20's Antique & Classic Car Club Inc 454
Roaring Twenties Antique Car Museum 600
Roaring Twenties Antiques 248
Douglas D Roark 189
Garry Roberts & Co 74
Robert's Custom Metal 371
Roberts Motor Parts 64
Leon J Rocco 53
Rochester Clutch & Brake Co 220
Rock County Historical Society 601
Rock Valley Antique Auto Parts 85
Rocker King 371
Rockland Auto Electric 257
Rocky Mountain Isetta Club 463
Rocky Mountain Motorworks Inc 166
Rocky Mountain Thunderbird Club 509
Rocky Mountain V8 Ford Parts 85
Rocky Mtn Motorcycle Museum & Hall of Fame ..585
Rod-1 Shop 386
Rod Doors 292
The Rod Factory 386
Rod Jolley Coachbuilding Ltd 422
Rod Shop Performance Center Inc 269
Rod Warriors 548
Rode's Restoration 99
The Rodfathers of Butler 557
Walter E Rodimon 78
Rodman's Auto Wood Restoration 48
Rodmasters Car Club 548
Rods & Relics Car Club 454
Rods and Rides of Polk County 454
Rods 'N Classics 551
Rods-N-Relics Car Club Ltd 559
Rodster Inc 386
Rogers Corvette Center 60
Roger's Motors 114
Rogue Valley Street Rods 548
Mary Jo Rohner's 1953-1962 Corvette Parts 60
Tom Rohner's Allante Store 32
Rollin' Review Magazine 573
Rolling Steel Body Parts 214
Rolls-Royce, Albers 155
Rolls-Royce Foundation 158
Rolls-Royce of Beverly Hills 158
Rolls-Royce Owner's Club 532
Ron's Restorations Inc 125
Don Rook 64
Rootes Vehicle Owners, The Association of 549
Rootlieb Inc 79
Ross' Automotive Machine Co Inc 266
Ross Racing Pistons 262
Rosso Bianco Sportscar Museum 605
Route 1 Scale Models 313

Route 26 Cruiser's 454
Route 66 Corvette Show 198
Route 66 Reutilization 580
Route 66 Territory Visitors Center 584
Ed Rouze 320
The Rover Car Club of Canada 532
Rover Saloon Touring Club of America 532
Rovers West 159
Royal Coach Works Ltd 189
Royal Pontiac Club of America 531
Royals' Garage 60
RPM Catalog 332
RT-Designs USA 195
R/T Street Rods 385
Rubber Age LM Mfg Inc 362
Rush Performance Fitters 271
Rust Busters 357
Rustic Auto Club of Pontiac Inc 552
RV/MH Hall of Fame 588
RX Autoworks 357
RX-7 Club, Mazda 516
Richard C Ryder 189

S

S&M Electro-Tech Inc 257
S&P Creations 71
S & S Antique Auto 85
The Sabra Connection 532
Saddleback Rods-Southern California 548
Sailorette's Nautical Nook 415
Salem Speed Shop 85
Samlerborsen 302
Sam's Vintage Ford Parts 94
Samson Technology Corporation 328
Harry Samuel 292
San Antonio Antique/Classic Car Association 454
San Diego Automotive Museum 585
San Jose Historical Museum 585
Sanders Antique Auto Restoration 357
Sanders Reproduction Glass 275
Sanderson Ford 94
Sandhills Classic Street Rod Assocation 548
Sandhills Museum 592
James T Sandoro 189
Sandringham House Museum & Grounds 604
Santa Clara Corvettes 476
Santa Ynez Valley Historical Museum - Parks-
    Janewa 585
Sarasota Classic Car Museum 586
Saratoga Antique Auto & Carriage Museum 594
Saskatchewan British Car Club 454
Saskatchewan Western Development Museum ..602
Saugerties Antique Auto Club Inc 556
Saxon Times 533
Schaeffer & Long 357
Chuck Scharf Enterprises 48
Doug Schellinger 75
Schiff European Automotive Literature Inc 302
T Schmidt 364
Jack Schmitt Studio 195

Donald E Schneider Marinette & Menominee Auto Club ...248
Schoharie Valley Performance Street Machine ...454
Ron Scobie Enterprises ...322
Scott Signal Co ...206
Scotts Manufacturing ...257
Scotts Super Trucks ...48
Scout & International Motor Truck Association ..514
Scripps-Booth Register ...542
Sea Expo Freight Services Inc ...408
Sea Yachts Inc ...32
Secrets of Speed Society (SOSS) ...502
Seeley Stables ...585
Charlie Sens Antique Auto Museum ...595
Sentimental Cruisers Car Club ...454
E J Serafin ...32
Service Motors ...66
Seven Enterprises Ltd ...19
Shadetree Motors Ltd ...133
Dick Shappy Classic Cars ...32
Sharlot Hall Museums ...583
Shay Owners Club International (SOCI) ...533
Shelburne Museum ...599
Shelby American Automobile Club ...502
Shelby-Cobra Museum, Telstar Mustang- ...598
Shelby Dodge Automobile Club ...480
Shepard's Automotive ...266
Sherco Auto Supply ...257
Sherman & Associates Inc ...214
Shiftworks ...53
SHO Club ...540
Shoreline Antique Auto Connection ...566
Show & Go Car Club Inc ...455
Showcase Express ...313
Showroom Auto Sales ...125
Sidecurtain Bags & Accessories ...164
Bernard A Siegal, ASA ...190
Sierra Grove Packards ...145
Sierra Mustang Club ...508
Sierra Specialty Auto ...220
SIGNPAST ...207
Silicone Wire Systems ...55
Silver City Corvette Club ...477
Silver Ghost Association ...532
Silver Lake Auto Club ...554
Silvermine Classics Inc ...566
Henri Simar J R ...302
SIMCA Car Club of America ...533
Simons Balancing & Machine Inc ...306
Sinclair's Mini-Auto ...313
Siouxland Car Council ...455
Sixties Ford Parts ...94
Skills Unlimited Inc ...335
Skimino Enterprises ...296
Skinned Knuckles ...573
Skip's Auto Parts ...416
Skoda Auto Museum ...602
Skopos Motor Museum ...604
Sky Signs Balloons Ltd ...318
Skyline Drive Corvettes Inc ...477
Skyline Street Rod Assoc Inc ...548
Slant 6 Club of America ...478
Paul Slater Auto Parts ...71
Slim's Garage ...411
Alfred P Sloan Museum ...590
Sloan's Kwik Load Inc ...400
SL-Tech 230 SL-250 SL-280SL ...125
Smalands Cars, Toys & Music Museum ...606
Smartire Systems Inc ...179
Smith & Jones Distributing Company Inc ...79
Joe Smith Ford & Hot Rod Parts ...85
RL Smith Sales Inc ...190
Steve Smith Autosports Publications ...570
Chris Smith's Creative Workshop Motorcar Restoration ...357
Smithy Company ...396
Smooth Line ...398
SMS Auto Restoration Services ...368
Robert H Snyder ...32
Snyder's Antique Auto Parts Inc ...79
So-Cal Speed Engineering ...269
Society of Automotive Historians Inc ...548
Solid Axle Corvette Club, Illinois Chapter ...477
Solid Axle Corvette Club (SACC) ...477
Solid Rock Cruisers Christian Car Club ...548
Solow Suspension ...49
Sonic Motors Inc ...151
Sonnett Club, New England ...532
Sonoma County Mustang Club ...508
Bob Sottile's Hobby Car Auto Sales Inc ...60
Sound Move Inc ...49
The Source Inc ...55
South Eastern Volkwagen Club ...537
South Jersey Camaro Group Productions ...468
South Jersey Street Rod Association ...548
South Shore Bearing Dist ...209
South Side Salvage ...581
South Texas AMC ...16
South West Alliance ...465
Southeast Texas Mustang Club ...508
Southeastern Wisconsin Corvette Club ...477
Southern Alberta Antique & Classic Auto Club ...559
Southern Knights of Central Kentucky Car Club ..553
Southern Mopar Association ...548
Southern Wheels Magazine ...573
Southwest Avanti Sales & Service ...21
Southwest Mercury Club ...517
Southwest Mopar Club ...521
Southwest Wisconsin Auto Club ...559
Southwestern Ontario Heritage Village ...602
Space Coast Mopars ...521
Space Farms Zoo & Museum ...592
Dick Spadaro ...85
Sparrow Auction Company ...198
Spec Cast ...313
Special Interest Autos ...357
Special Interest Autos ...573
Special Interest Cars ...248
Special T's Unlimited Inc ...138
Specialized Street Rods ...386
Specialty Car Marketplace ...574
Specialty Cars Inc ...386
Specialty Equipment Market Association (SEMA) ..562
Specialty Fasteners ...278

Specialty Ford Parts 85
Specialty Power Window 386
Specialty Wheels Ltd 418
Specter Off-Road Inc 162
Spectral Kinetics 159
Spectrum Rubber & Panels..................362
Speed & Spares America......................248
Speed & Sport Chrome Plating Inc........328
Speed Bleeder Products Co 221
Speed-o-Tac 283
Speed Service Inc 281
Speedzone..313
Richard Spiegelman Productions Inc 566
Spindles Auto Club.............................554
Spirit Enterprises 207
Spokane Corvette Club........................477
Sports Car Haven 164
Sports Car Haven 357
Sports Car International.......................574
Sports Car Rentals & Sales..................375
Sports Car Services 133
Sports Leicht Restorations...................126
Sportscar Vintage Racing Association.....548
Springfield Swap Meet & Car Show........199
Spruance Library...............................597
Spyder Enterprises Inc 207
Squire SS-100 Registry........................533
Rajam Srinivasan 158
SS Specialties...................................209
Ssnake-Oyl Products Inc 292
St Cloud Antique Auto Club 554
St Joe Valley Street Rods.....................549
St Louis Car Museum & Sales 591
Sta-Dri Pouches/Beach Filler Products Inc........379
Michael A Stahl..................................32
Stahl Headers Inc..............................269
Eddie Stakes' Planet Houston AMX........16
Stallions Gate Mustang & Ford Club Inc............508
Standard Abrasives Motorsports Division 341
Stanley Museum 589
Star Chrome.....................................328
Star Classics Inc 126
Star Motors 126
Star Quality Parts..............................126
Start/Finish Productions......................199
State Museum of Pennsylvania 597
Steam Automobile Club of America Inc...........549
Steck Manufacturing Co Inc 396
Steel City Classics 467
Steele Rubber Products Inc..................362
Steele's Appraisal 190
Steelman/JS Products..........................396
Steeltown Corvette Club 477
Steelwings.......................................18
Steering Systems...............................375
Stencils & Stripes Unlimited Inc 254
Stephens Registry..............................542
Sterling British Motoring Society 455
Sterling Restorations Inc 357
Sterling Specialties............................228
The Sterquell Collection......................599
Brooks Stevens Auto Collection Inc.......600

Stevens Car Care Products Inc 181
Stevens-Duryea Associates 533
The Bill Stevenson Company 398
Steve's Antiques/POR-15.....................365
Steve's Auto Restorations 357
Steve's Camaros.................................53
Steve's Studebaker-Packard 145
Stiftung AutoMuseum Volkswagen 605
Still Cruisin' Corvettes........................61
Stilwell's Obsolete Car Parts 99
Stinger by Axe 379
Stockton Wheel Service 418
Stoddard Imported Cars Inc 154
Stone Barn Inc..................................358
Stoner Inc..229
Stormin Norman's Bug Shop 166
Stoudt Auto Sales..............................61
Straight Six Jaguar 115
Ed Strain Inc....................................375
Strange Motion Rod & Custom Construction Inc..387
Strasburg Rail Road 597
Street Cars of Desire Car Club..............553
Street Machines of Rochester................549
Street Machines of Table Rock Lake........549
Street Magic of Portland Car Club.........549
Street Rod Engineering Inc 387
Street Rod Marketing Alliance (SRMA) 562
The Street Rod Place...........................387
Street-Wise Performance......................254
Street-Wise Performance......................403
Stuart Corvette Club 477
Studebaker Club Inc, The Antique.........533
Studebaker Drivers Club, North Carolina 556
Studebaker Drivers Club, Wisconsin Region 533
Studebaker Golden Hawk Owners Register, 1956 ....
....160
Studebaker International.......................161
Studebaker National Museum 588
Studebaker-Packard, Steve's 145
Studebaker Parts, Dakota.....................160
Studebaker, Phil's 161
Studebaker, Volunteer.........................161
Studebakers West 161
Sturgis Motorcycle Museum and Hall of Fame ...598
Stuhr Museum of the Prairie Pioneer 592
Stuttgart Automotive Inc 154
The Stutz Club Inc 533
Subaru 360 Drivers' Club.....................533
Suburban Pickup Club, Classic Chevy Cameo &
GMC...465
Norman Sudeck Restorations 103
Sugarbush Products Inc 237
JF Sullivan Company 273
Summer Knights Cruisin' Classics..........555
Sunbeam Auto Parts Inc, Classic...........161
Sunbeam Rapier Registry of North America 542
Sunbeam Specialties 161
Sunburst Technology...........................566
Sunchaser Tools.................................341
Suncoast British Car Club.....................551
Thomas C Sunday Inc 408
Sundowners......................................554

Sunyaks 103
Suomen Automobili-Historiallinen Klubi 455
The Super Stock AMX Registry 539
Supercars Unlimited 143
Superior Equipment 397
Superior Pump Exchange Co 263
Supreme Metal Polishing 328
Svedino's Automobile and Aviation Museum 606
Svenska Rileyregistret 532
Swedish Classics Inc 167
Sweeney's Auto & Marine Upholstery Inc 126
Sweet Dreamz Auto Club 549
Swigart Museum 597
Swope's Cars of Yesteryear Museum 589

T

TA Motor AB 32
Tags Backeast 375
Tampa Bay Allante Group 465
Tamraz's Parts Discount Warehouse 53
Tanson Enterprises 143
Tar Heel Parts Inc 328
Tarrant County Street Rod Association 549
Tatom Custom Engines 266
Tatra Enthusiasts 534
JC Taylor Antique Automobile Insurance Agency .....
.... 285
Taylor Auto Parts 248
David Taylor Classic Car Museum 599
T-Bird 55-57, Feno's 102
T-Bird Sanctuary 103
T-Birds By Nick 103
TCMB Models & Stuff 313
Te Puke Vintage Auto Barn 358
Team Simpson Racing 308
Technical Museum 602
Teddy's Garage 158
Tee-Bird Products Inc 94
Tellico Village Vintage Vehicles 455
Telstar Mustang-Shelby-Cobra Museum 598
Telstar Mustang-Shelby-Cobra Restorations 358
The Temperature Gauge Guy 283
Terry's Jaguar Parts Inc 115
Texas Fords Alamo Chapter 558
Texas Hill Country Alfa Romeo Owners Club 459
Texas Joy Ride 549
Texas MG Register 519
Texas Mustang Parts 100
Texas Viper Hotline 71
Jay Texter 324
TheAlternate 574
Thermal Tech Coatings Inc 269
Thermax Inc 229
This Old Truck Magazine 574
Thompson Hill Metalcraft 371
Bill Thomsen 581
Barry Thorne 67
Thoroughbred Motors 115
Thrasher Carriage Museum 589
Three Rivers Corvette Club 477
Thul Auto Parts Inc 266

Thunder Road Cruisers 556
Thunder Vette Set 477
Thunderbird 55-66 Club, Edmonton 508
Thunderbird and Mustang Parts Inc, Larry's 102
Thunderbird Center 104
Thunderbird Club Inc, New England's Vintage ... 509
Thunderbird Club Inc, Upstate New York 509
Thunderbird Club, International 509
Thunderbird Club International, Classic 508
Thunderbird Club International, Vintage 509
Thunderbird Club, Long Island 509
Thunderbird Club of America, Heartland Vintage ....
.... 509
Thunderbird Club, Rocky Mountain 509
Thunderbird Club, Tucson 509
Thunderbird Convertible Registry, 1958 100
Thunderbird, Falcon, Fairlane & Comet
 Connections 104
Thunderbird Headquarters 104
Thunderbird Inc, Prestige 103
Thunderbird Information eXchange 104
Thunderbird Parts 104
Thunderbird Parts, Pat Wilson's 104
Thunderbirds, California 101
Thunderbirds East 104
Thunderbirds of Western New England, TOWNE .. 509
Thunderbolt Traders Inc 72
Tidaholms Museum 606
Lars Tidblom Automobil 61
Tigers East/Alpines East 533
Tillack & Co Ltd 358
Tillamook County Pioneer Museum 596
Edward Tilley Automotive Collectibles 207
Timber Wolf Trailers Inc 400
Time Passages Ltd 323
Timeless Masterpieces 190
The Tire Source Inc 393
Tire & Wheel Emporium 393
TK Performance Inc 108
TMC Publications 570
Tobacco Road Street Rodders Inc 549
Sol W Toder 190
Tom's Cars 167
Tom's Classic Parts 49
Tom's Obsolete Chevy Parts 49
Top Hat John 190
Topeka British Car Club 455
Topolino Register of North America 540
Topper Luback Historical Library 576
Toronto Fiat Club FLU Ontario 482
Toronto Vintage Vehicles 376
Torque Tech Performance Exhaust 269
Totally Auto Inc 138
Totally Stainless 278
Towe Auto Museum 585
Tower Paint Co Inc 321
Town & Country Toys 313
TOWNE Thunderbirds of Western New England .. 509
Townsend Motors LLC 596
Toy Car Collectors Club 549
Toyota MR2 Mk I Club 534
Toys n' Such 316

TP Tools & Equipment 342
TR8 Car Club of America 534
Trail Town Museum of the Old West 601
Trailer World Inc 400
Trailers of New England Inc 400
Trailersource 401
Trailex Inc 401
Translog Motorsports..................................154
Transport Books at DRB Motors Inc 570
Transport Designs Inc 401
Transportation Museum 606
Treasure Chest Sales..................................140
Treasure State Classics 555
Treasure State Corvette Club........................477
Lou Trepanier, Appraiser #1 190
Triangle Automotive...................................143
Tri-Chevy Association 549
Tri-County Calabasas Insurance 285
Tri-County Cruisers Inc 549
Tri County Thoroughbred Corral.....................508
Tricks Custom Hot Rods...............................320
Tri-Five Classics 49
Trim Parts Inc 49
Triple C Motor Accessories 133
Tri-River Car Club Council 562
Tri-State F-100s 502
Tri-State Insurance 285
Tri-State Metal Cleaning..............................364
Tri-State Mustang & Ford Club......................508
Tri-Town Cruzers Inc 455
Triumph Association Inc, Georgia 534
Triumph Register, Vintage 534
Triumph Roadster Club 534
Triumph Sportscar Club, Detroit 534
Triumph Stag Register.................................534
Triumph Sports Car Club of San Diego 534
Triumph World Magazine..............................164
Triumphs, New England 534
Al Trommers-Rare Auto Literature 302
Tru-Cut Automotive....................................397
Truck, Race, Cycle and Rec 574
The Truck Shop...49
True Connections 53
Trunzo's Antique Cars 199
Tubes-n-Hoses by TKM................................181
Tucker Automobile Club of America Inc 536
Jim Tucker "The Heater Valve Guy" 248
Tucker's Auto Salvage 580
Tucson Miniature Auto Club..........................549
Tucson Packard/Chirco Automotive 146
Tucson Thunderbird Club 509
Tulsa Vette Set 557
The Tuna Club Inc.......................................549
Turnpike Checker...33
Tuxedo Turntables by Tuxedo Enterprises 180
TVR Car Club North America.........................536
Twin Bay British Car Club............................455
Twin Cities Roadsters.................................555
Twin Tiers Camaro Firebird Club....................468
Peter Tytla Artist 195

U

U S Oldies & Classics 235
Uhlenhopp Lock 303
John Ulrich 146
Ultimate Appearance Ltd 229
Ultra Shield Race Products 308
Ultra Van Motor Coach Club..........................550
Ultra Wheel Co 418
un-du Products Inc 254
Unforgettable Autos of Mid-Jersey 555
Unique Auto & Truck LLC 579
United Detroit Car Modelers 550
United Street Rods of Idaho 562
Universal Transmission Co 404
Universal Vintage Tire Co 394
University Motors Ltd 133
UP Antique Car Club 455
Upstate New York Thunderbird Club Inc............509
USA Auto Appraisers 190
USAopoly Inc..313
USAppraisal 190

V

The V8 Store 253
VACO Inc 304
Tom Vagnini..146
Valco Cincinnati Consumer Products Inc...........397
Valenti Classics Inc 235
Valiant and Barracuda Club, The Early 544
Valley Cruisers Car Club 550
Valley Head Service Inc 267
Valley Motor Supply 94
Valley Wire Wheel Service 418
Van Horn Auto Parts Inc...............................579
Van Horn's Antique Truck Museum 588
Van Nuys M-B 126
Van Raalte & Co LLC 230
Vanda Die Cast 313
Vanden Plas Princess Register 537
Vantage Motorworks Inc 158
Varco Inc..79
Glenn Vaughn Restoration Services Inc 358
V-Dub's 'R' Us 166
Vehicle Appraisers Inc 190
Vehicle Preservation Society 190
Vehicle Spring Service 392
Velie Register..542
Verdone's Custom Stainless Casting.................239
Vermont Visual Experts................................324
Verne's Chrome Plating Inc...........................328
Vespa 400 Registry.....................................542
Veteran Motor Car Club of America 455
Vette Dreams Inc..61
Vette Vues Magazine...................................574
Vettes in Perfection Ltd...............................477
Vibratech Inc (Fluidampr).............................263
Vicarage Jaguar 115
Vic's Place Inc 323
Victoria British Ltd 133
Victoria Registry 542

Victory Lane 574
Video Resources NY Inc 416
Viking Worldwise 182
Villa Capri Cruisers 550
Vintage Auto Club of Ocean County NJ 458
Vintage Auto Ent 191
Vintage Auto LLC 166
Vintage Auto Parts 23
Vintage Auto Parts Inc 248
Vintage Automobiles 577
Vintage Automotive Art 207
Vintage BMW Motorcycle Owners Ltd 463
Vintage Books 302
The Vintage Car Club of New Zealand Inc 458
Vintage Chevrolet Club of America 467
Vintage Ford & Chevrolet Parts of Arizona Inc......95
Vintage Ford Center Inc 79
Vintage Gas, Ltd 195
Vintage Glass USA 275
Vintage Jag Works 115
Vintage Jaguar Spares 115
Vintage Motor and Machine 306
Vintage Oval Racing 570
Vintage Power Wagons Inc 71
Vintage Radio Shop 337
Vintage Restorations 283
Vintage Sales 126
Vintage Shop Coats 183
Vintage Speed Parts 79
Vintage Steam Products 160
Vintage Thunderbird Club International 509
Vintage Triumph Register 534
Vintage Trunks 412
Vintage Wheels Antique Car Club 458
Vintage Woodworks 423
Viper Hotline, Texas 71
Viper Registry, International 540
Virginia Classic Cruisers 558
Virginia Classic Mustang Inc 100
Virginia Museum of Transporation Inc 600
Virginia Vettes Parts & Sales 61
Visibolts From Classic Safety Products 297
Voitures Anciennes Du Quebec Inc 559
Volks Club, Hoosier 552
Volkswagen Club, Houston 537
Volkswagen Club, Northern Wisconsin 537
Volkswagen Club, Omaha 537
Volkswagen Club, South Eastern 537
Volkswagen Collectors 166
Volkswagen Society, Common Gear Antique 537
Volkswagen Owners, Hudson & Mohawk Society of
....537
Volo Antique Auto Museum 586
Volunteer State Chevy Parts 50
Volunteer Studebaker 161
Voluparts Inc 167
Volvo Club of America 537
Volvo Owners' Club ..,.......................................538
Volvo Place, Revolvstore, The 577
Volvo Service, Dan's 166
Volvo Shop Inc 167

Volvo Sports America 1800 538
Von's Austin-Healey Restorations 21
Voss Motors Inc 303
VPA International 180

W

Wachusett Old Car Club 554
Wagon Works 79
Wallace W Wade Specialty Tires 394
Waldron's Antique Exhaust Inc 269
Wales Antique Chevy Truck Parts 50
Walker's Auto Pride Inc 117
Walneck's Inc 195
Pat Walsh Restorations 363
Waltham Museum 590
The Wanderers Car Club 557
Jim Wangers 152
Brady Ward-Scale Autoworks 314
F Todd Warner's Mahogany Bay 376
Harold Warp Pioneer Village Foundation 592
T E Warth Esq Automotive Books 571
Wasaga Beach Corvette Club 477
Washington Ford Retractable Club 502
Waterloo 592
Pete Watson Enterprises 359
Wayne County Historical Museum 588
Wayne's Auto Salvage 581
WD-40 Company 304
Paul Weaver's Garage 263
Webber Engineering LLC 371
Webb's Classic Auto Parts 16
Weber's Nostalgia Supermarket 319
Wefco Rubber Manufacturing Company Inc 363
Weimann's Literature & Collectables 148
Mary Weinheimer 208
WELD USA 397
C Wells Appraisals 191
Wells Auto Museum 589
Wells Cargo Inc 401
Welsh Classic Car Museum 595
Welsh Enterprises Inc 115
Wenatchee Valley Antique Auto Club 458
Wenner's 16
Wescott's Auto Restyling 86
West Central Missouri Vintage Auto Club 458
West Coast Classics Inc 359
West Coast Kustoms 550
West Coast Metric Inc 166
West Michigan Die-Cast Cars 314
The West Michigan Mustang Club 508
Bob West Muscle Cars 148
West of England Transport Collection 604
West Overton Museum 597
West Tennessee Antique Car Club 558
West Texas Cruisers 558
Westberg Manufacturing Inc 283
Westchester Vintage Coach Inc 235
Western Development Museum 602
Western Jaguar 115
Western Michigan Camaro Club 468

Westminster MG Car Museum..................599
Westwind Limousine Sales 120
Wheatland Historic Mansion..................597
Wheel Industry Council (WIC)..................562
Wheel Repair Service of New England 418
The Wheel Shoppe Inc 377
Wheel Vintiques Inc...................50
Wheeler's Classic Parts..................221
Wheels & Spokes Inc 588
Wheels O' Time Museum 587
Wheels Through Time Museum..................587
Whippet Resource Center 168
Colonel Bill White..................303
Kirk F White..................314
White Owners Register 458
White Post Restorations..................221
White Post Restorations..................359
White Squirrel Cruisers 458
Whitewebbs Museum of Transport..................605
Wholesale Express..................180
Widmann's Garage 359
Wild About Wheels 376
Wild Bill's Corvette & Hi-Performance Center Inc..61
Wilk-Bilt Cars..................86
Willhoit Auto Restoration..................154
Williams 387
Dan Williams Toploader Transmissions 95
Williams Lowbuck Tools Inc..................397
Willmar Car Club 555
Willow Automotive Service 359
Willow Grove Auto Top 293
Wills Sainte Claire Club..................538
Willys Aero Survival Count 542
Willys Club, Mid-America 538
Willys-Overland-Knight Registry..................538
Willys-Overland-Knight Registry Inc 458
The Willys Man..................168
Willys® Parts, Obsolete Jeep® &..................168
Willys Wood..................168
Willys Works Inc..................168
Wilson Historical Society-Car Museum 594
Wilson's Classic Auto 359
Pat Wilson's Thunderbird Parts 104
Leo Winakor and Sons Inc 578
Winamac Old Auto Club 458
Winchester Speedway Old Timers' Club Inc 550
Windshield Wiper Service 419
Windy City Corvettes Inc 477
Windy City Rambler/AMC Club 460
Gene Winfield's Rod & Custom 129
Winged Warriors/National B-body Owner's
    Association (NBOA)..................521
Winslow Mfg Co..................263
WiperWorks..................50
Wirth's Custom Automotive 180
Wisconsin Automobile Clubs in Association Inc .562
Wisconsin Automotive Museum..................601
Wisconsin Car Clubs Alliance (WCCA) 562
Wisconsin Convertible Classic 550
Wisconsin Mopar Muscle Club..................521
Wisconsin Region Studebaker Drivers Club 533

Wiseman Motor Co Inc 235
Wiseman's Auto Salvage 577
Witte Museum..................599
Wittenborn's Auto Service Inc..................139
Wolf Steel..................116
Wolfson Engineering..................376
Wolverine Video..................566
Women's Committee of the Crawford Auto-Aviation
    Museum 550
Wood Excel Ltd..................423
James Wood..................191
The Wood N'Carr 423
WoodArt..................86
Wooddash.com..................421
Woodgrain Restoration by Grain-It Tech Inc 421
The Woodie Works..................423
Woodland Wheels 458
Woolies (I&C Woolstenholmes Ltd)..................293
Worldwide Camaro Association..................54
Worldwide Camaro Association..................468
WPC Club Inc..................521
Wright County Car Club..................555
WTH Service and Restorations Inc 359
WTH-VMC (formerly Vintage Mercedes Cars Inc) ..126
WW Motor Cars & Parts Inc 359
www.albertsgifts.com..................296
Wymer Classic AMC 16

X

Xanders' Britbikes 316
XKs Unlimited 116
Xtreme Class CC 180

Y

Yakima Valley Museum and Historical Association ..
   600
Yakima Valley Vettes 478
Yankee Candle Car Museum..................590
Ye Olde Car Club of Tri-Cities 459
Year One Inc 248
Yesterday's Auto Sales..................235
Yesterday's Collection 591
Yesterday's Radio 146
YnZ's Yesterdays Parts 258
Clarence Young Autohobby..................314
Yuma Crossing State Historic Park 583

Z

Z Club of Georgia 479
George Zaha..................337
Vic Zannis 571
Zeb's Salvage..................581
Zehr Insurance Brokers Ltd..................285
Zephyr Owners Club, Lincoln 515
Zephyr Parts, Bob's 36-48 Continental &..................118
Zephyrhills Festivals and Auction Inc 199
Zeug's K-F Parts..................117

Ziebart/Tidy Car 365
Zippo Manufacturing Company 597
Zimmer Motor Car Club....................................538
Zimmer Neo-Classic Motor Car Co 168
Zimmerman Registry 542
Zim's Autotechnik 154

Index to Display Advertisers

This index is a complete roster of all display advertisers appearing in the *Almanac*. The page number indicated will direct you to the display ad for that supplier or organization.

Please note that symbols (& for example) come before alphabetical names.

Also, advertisers who use their own names are alphabetized by their last names. However, to make reading the index easier, we have printed the advertiser's full name in its proper order. In addition, advertisers who use a nickname or title as part of their business name are listed under that nickname or title — so that you find Mopar Jack Dyson under "M" rather than "D".

Numerical

3-D Imagery Inc 323

A

A-1 Shock Absorber Co 672
A AAAdvantage Auto Transport Inc 405
All Cadillacs of the 40s and 50s 29
American Classic Truck Parts 34
American Honeycomb Radiator Mfg Co 333
Antique Auto Fasteners 277
Antique Auto Parts Cellar 244
The Antique Auto Shop 218
Auburn Cord Duesenberg Museum 589
Autobahn Transportation Service Inc 405

B

Bathurst Company 255
Becker of North America Inc 122
Billie Inc 379
Bob's Speedometer Service 282
British Miles 131

C

Cadillac King 28
Carlisle Productions 196
Chev's of the 40's 36
Chevy Duty Pickup Parts 37
Clark's Corvair Parts® Inc. 54
Classic Jaguar 112
Classic Mustang Parts of Oklahoma 97
Classic Tube 219
Coil Spring Specialties 389
Coker Tire 392
Color-Plus Leather Restoration System 294
Custom Autosound Mfg 335

D

Danchuk Mfg. 39
Mike Dennis, Nebraska Mail Order 81
Desert Valley Auto Parts 578
Diamond Back Classics 393
Douglass Interior Products 289

E

Egge Machine Company Inc .... inside front cover

F

FEN Enterprises of New York Inc 30
Firewall Insulators & Quiet Ride Solutions 290
Ron Francis' Wire Works 420

H

Harbor Auto Restoration 350
Headers by "Ed" Inc 268
Hemmings Motor News-Subscriptions 575
Hemmings Motor News-Web Site 345
Hemmings Rods & Performance 576
Art Houser's Rear End Service 247
Hydro-E-Lectric 398

I

Instrument Services Inc 283

J

Jet-Hot Coatings/MCCI 327
Bob Johnson's Auto Literature 300

L

L & N Olde Car Co 352
Layson's Restorations 137
Lutty's Chevy Warehouse 44

M

MAR-K Quality Parts 410
Mr G's Enterprises 138
Melvin's Classic Ford Parts Inc 91

N

NADA Appraisal Guides 8
National Spring Co Inc 390
Northwest Classic Falcons Inc. 92
Nu-Chrome Corp 355

O

Obsolete Chevrolet Parts Co...................46

P

Passport Transport Ltd 406
Peterson Auto Transport 407
Power Brake Booster Exchange Inc 220

R

Rau Restoraion................423
Reliable Carriers 406

S

SMS Auto Restoration Services 368
Special Interest Autos....................351
Specialty Wheels Ltd....................418
Stahl Headers Inc 269
Star Classics Inc....................126
Steele Rubber Products....................362
Sunchaser Tools and Auto Restoration
....................inside back cover
Thomas C Sunday Inc....................407

T

Terry's Jaguar Parts Inc....................115
This Old Truck Magazine 342
Thompson Hill Metalcraft....................371

U

Universal Transmission Co 404

V

Victoria British Ltd 134
Vintage Gas Ltd 194

W

Wells Cargo Inc....................401
Welsh Enterprises Inc....................116
White Post Restorations....................359
Pat Wilson's Thunderbird Parts....................104
WPC Club Inc 522

Z

Zimmer Neo-Classic Motor Car Co 168

Index

Special Interest Autos

SIA

Cars That Matter

Selected Index, SIA #8-#185

Is your car here?
Or the car you used to own?
Or the car you wish you had?

Enjoy detailed specs, facts and photos of your favorite cars in *Special Interest Autos* back issues!

Past issues of *SIA* give you the complete stories on over 300 makes and models including specs, diagrams, unique features, histories, photographs, marketing strategies and sales.

Plus you can select entertaining and useful articles on other topics ranging from general automotive history to restoration "how-to's."

Most driveReports average 6 to 8 pages of text and photos, and each back issue includes driveReports on two to three other makes or models plus articles on the collector-car hobby.

Special Interest Autos (a publication of *Hemmings Motor News*), has been the leading authority on collector cars since 1970. Select your back issues today and enjoy big savings when you order more than one!

MAKES

This section includes all drive-Reports, historical articles and Spotter's Guides dealing with established makes of cars which have appeared in SIA.

AEROCAR
1956 dR ....#141, p 50

AHRENS-FOX
1926 piston pumper dR...........#57, p 34

AIRSTREAM
1964 Globe Trotter dR...........#163, p 28

ALFA-ROMEO
1967 Duetto dR.....................#151, p 8

ALLARD
1950 J2 dR ....#120, p 46

ALLSTATE
1953 dR ....#155, p 38

AMC
1968 Javelin SST dR ....#94, p 22
AMC Amitron ....#116, p 54
Metropolitan Show Cars ....#184, p 54

AMERICAN AUSTIN
1929 in Canadian cellar ....#86, p 58

AMERICAN BANTAM
1941 dR ....#142, p 52

AMPHICAR
1967 777 dR ....#66, p 26

AMX
1969 dR ....#139, p 26

AUBURN
1929 Cabin Speedster dR......#130, p 30
1932 8-100A coupe dR........#74, p 56
1932 Speedster dR ....#101, p 50
1933 Salon Twelve dR........#109, p 50
1934 convertible sedan dR......#20, p 10
1935 851 dR ....#124, p 36
Auburn Timeline ....#178, p 30

AUSTIN-HEALEY
1956 100M dR ....#67, p 52
1967 3000 Mk III dR ....#90, p 38

BENDIX
1934 SWC 4-door sedan dR........#8, p 40

BILL FRICK SPECIAL
1957 dR ....#143, p 24

BMW
1959 Michelotti-designed 507...#174, p 54
1963 700 dR ....#130, p 44
1968 convertible dR ....#104, p 14
Isetta 300 dR ....#70, p 10

BREWSTER
1934 dR ....#104, p 36

BRICKLIN
1975 SVI dR....................#68, p 40

BUGATTI
1932 Royale dR.....................#135, p 12

BUICK
1920 Model K-44 dR.............#175, p 40
1930 Marquette dR ....#16, p 44
1931 Buick Gläser cabriolet ...#166, p 38
1936 Century conv coupe dR......#46, p 12
1937 Century dR....................#151, p 24
1938 semi-automatic Special business
    coupe dR.....................#20, p 24
1938 Y-Job dR ....#157, p 32
1948 Roadmaster dR ....#136, p 12
1948 Roadmaster sedanet dR....#70, p 24
1949 Riviera dR ....#89, p 16
1950 Special Sedanet dR........#141, p 28
1952 Riviera Super.................#183, p 24
1954 Skylark dR ....#144, p 54
1955 CHP Buick dR ....#142, p 28
1955 Roadmaster dR ....#154, p 36
1957 Caballero dR ....#147, p 38
1957 Special dR ....#161, p 32
1959 Electra 225 dR ....#126, p 36
1962 Skylark dR ....#87, p 30
1962 Wildcat dR ....#144, p 22
1965 Riviera dR ....#148, p 14
1967 GS 400 dR ....#172, p 46
1970 GSX dR ....#146, p 20
Road Masters (Postwar Buicks) ..#183, p 12

CADILLAC
1932 V-8 dR........................#108, p 16
1935 V-12 dR......................#133, p 10
1936 60 dR.........................#69, p 10
1938 60 Special dR.................#62, p 10
1939 convertible sedan dR.......#107, p 50
1940 Bohman & Schwartz dR....#162, p 26
1941 Series 63 dR ....#159, p 8
1948 61 dR ....#171, p 18
1949 Coupe de Ville dR ....#132, p 34
1949 Woodie dR ....#143, p 40
1950 60 Special dR ....#86, p 50
1953 Eldorado dR ....#118, p 52
1953 LeMans dR ....#169, p 32
1953-89 Eldorado Timeline......#181, p 48
1954 Eldorado dR ....#151, p 34
1958 Sixty Special dR ....#182, p 32
1959-60 Broughams ....#46, p 34
1959 Eldorado Biarritz dR........#88, p 14
1967 Fleetwood Eldorado dR....#67, p 38

CHEVROLET
1923 copper cooled coupe dR...#30, p 44
1927 Imperial landau dR........#55, p 10
1930 sport roadster dR..........#138, p 12
1932 cabriolet dR.................#145, p 12
1935 Master dR....................#165, p 36
1935 Standard dR................#121, p 20
1937 sport sedan dR.............#39, p 12
1937-38 spotter's guide............#39, p 18
1938 Coupe-Pickup dR........#183, p 32
1939 coupe dR.....................#101, p 16
1940 Special DeLuxe dR..........#98, p 16
1941 coupe dR....................#45, p 12
1942 Fleetline Aerosedan dR.....#149, p 10
1947 convertible coupe dR .....#146, p 42
1950 Bel Air dR...................#108, p 46

1952 Half-ton pickup dR..........#99, p 38
1954 Bel Air dR.....................#131, p 46
1955 Corvette dR ....#160, p 10
1955 Gold Chevrolet ....#124, p 44
1955 V-8 dR.........................#123, p 28
1957 150 V-8 dR...................#150, p 24
1957 Corvette SS dR.............#107, p 16
1958 Corvette dR ....#169, p 10
1959 El Camino dR.................#82, p 20
1959 Impala dR....................#105, p 14
1960 Impala dR....................#120, p 12
1961 348 dR ....#147, p 12
1962 Corvette dR ....#116, p 12
1963 Chevy II Nova SS dR......#136, p 38
1963 Impala SS dR.................#170, p 36
1964 Bel Air Police Car dR .....#156, p 26
1964 Impala 409 dR...............#61, p 48
1965 Chevelle Malibu L-79 dR...#153, p 24
1967 Camaro dR ....#166, p 52
1967 Impala SS dR ....#178, p 24
1968 Corvette dR ....#112, p 12
1969 Camaro SS/RS dR..........#155, p 52
1970 LT-1 Corvette dR ....#173, p 14
1970 Monte Carlo dR ....#167, p 36
1970 Monte Carlo SS 454 dR ...#123, p 44
1972 Chevelle SS 454 dR.........#162, p 22
1975 Cosworth Vega dR ....#129, p 38
Corvair Ultra Van ....#151, p 40
Four Corvairs Compared ....#180, p 12

CHRYSLER
1924 touring car dR ....#45, p 46
1928 Imperial dR ....#149, p 40
1932 Imperial dR ....#105, p 46
1934 Airflow dR ....#16, p 12
1934-37 Royal conv sedan dR....#99, p 56
1935 Airstream dR...................#168, p 10
1938 Imperial dR ....#132, p 48
1940 Newport phaeton dR........#28, p 36
1941 New Yorker dR...............#119, p 12
1941 Saratoga ....#131, p 54
1942 Windsor dR ....#170, p 28
1948 Highlander dR ....#110, p 52
1949 Town & Country dR ....#116, p 46
1950 Traveler dR ....#104, p 50
1951 Imperial dR ....#135, p 26
1953 D'Elegance dR ....#136, p 26
1955 Falcon roadster dR ....#30, p 21
1955-99 Chrysler 300 Timeline ..#180, p 48
1957 300-C dR ....#107, p 42
1959 300-E dR ....#72, p 28
1964 Turbine dR ....#127, p 36
1965 300L convertible dR..........#93, p 26
1982 Imperial dR ....#169, p 42
Imperial by Waterhouse.........#116, p 28
Chrysler's Lost Norseman.......#155, p 18

CITROEN
The Selling of the Tin Snail.....#161, p 54

CONTINENTAL
1956 Mark II dR ....#134, p 48

CORD
1930 L-29 dR ....#103, p 48
1937 812-SC dR ....#110, p 28
The Real Lost Cord, Part I.......#119, p 30
    Part II ....#120, p 18

CROSLEY
1937-1952 Crosley Timeline...#182, p 48
1952 wagon dR ....#113, p 54
Big Bunch of Little Crosleys ...#160, p 50

CUNNINGHAM
1959 C-3 cabriolet dR ....#80, p 12

CUSHMAN
1957 Eagle dR......................#137, p 50

DAIMLER
1962 SP-250 dR ....#166, p 30

DATSUN
1972 240Z dR ....#124, p 52

DAVIS
Saga of the Davis, The.......#113, p 36

DELAHAYE
1948 convertible....................#98, p 52

DE LOREAN
1982 dR ....#147, p 24

DE SOTO
1942 Custom Club Coupe dR...#178, p 32
1948 Suburban dR.................#23, p 46
1949 wagon dR ....#122, p 42
1956 Pacesetter convertible dR....#20, p 30
1959 Adventurer dR ....#112, p 34
Adventurer II dR ....#137, p 38

DE TOMASO
1972 Pantera dR ....#119, p 46

DE VAUX
1931 sedan dR ....#88, p 48

DETROIT ELECTRIC
1918 Model 75 dR ....#181, p 24

DIANA
1926 phaeton dR....................#62, p 32

DINO
1974 246GTS dR ....#151, p 8

DODGE
1930s Straight Eights.............#48, p 30
1937 convertible sedan dR .....#127, p 50
1938 D-8 convertible dR........#175, p 24
1939 Airflow ....#104, p 46
1946 pickup dR....................#118, p 22
1947 Power Wagon dR...........#168, p 48
1949-76 Coronet Timeline......#184, p 38
1954 Royal 500 dR.................#8, p 10
1955 Custom Royal Lancer dR...#121, p 50
1956 C-3 Express pickup dR....#87, p 62
1957 Dart/Diablo dR ....#30, p 21
1959 D-500 dR ....#117, p 12
1960 Polara dR.....................#164, p 26
1961 Dart Phoenix dR.............#180, p 32
1962 Lancer dR.....................#163, p 44
1966 Charger dR...................#111, p 16
1967 Coronet R/T dR ....#156, p 46
1969 Charger 500 dR ....#140, p 16
1970 Challenger dR ....#134, p 40
1979 Li'l Red Truck dR...........#161, p 40

DUESENBERG
1929 J-101 dR ....#113, p 42

1935 SSJ dR ....#100, p 30

DU PONT
1929 Speedster dR ....#137, p 22

DURANT
1929 sport roadster dR ....#39, p 48

EDSEL
1958 Amblewagon dR ....#184, p 32
1958 Bermuda dR ....#103, p 14

ERSKINE
1929 Model 52E dR ....#70, p 36

ESSEX
1932 Terraplane dR ....#143, p 58

FAGEOL
1927 Safety Coach ....#185, p 24

FERRARI
1949 166 Inter dR ....#74, p 20

FIAT
1958 1200 TV convertible dR ....#176, p 48
1960 Fiat 500 and Bianchina...#166, p 18
1969 Spider dR ....#155, p 22
Fiat 500 and 600 Jolly ....#172, p 44

FITCH
1966 Phoenix dR ....#117, p 28

FORD
1911-48 European assembled....#12, p 22
1931 Ford AA postal truck .....#111, p 46
1931 Model A dR ....#181, p 16
1931 Model A Deluxe pickup ...#154, p 42
1932 Model B dR ....#130, p 12
1934 Ford convertible victoria ...#163, p 36
1935 Ford V-8 dR ....#114, p 36
1935 Ford Collection ....#114, p 44
1936 Station Wagon dR ....#163, p 12
1939 DeLuxe convertible dR....#178, p 40
1938 V-8/60 dR ....#55, p 34
1939 Woody dR ....#63, p 10
1941 V-8 dR ....#140, p 42
1947 Sportsman dR ....#10, p 24
1947 V-8 dR ....#133, p 50
1949 dR ....#139, p 50
1950 Crestliner dR ....#119, p 36
1952 Canadian Meteor dR ......#74, p 32
1953 F-100 ½-ton pickup dR .....#80, p 28
1954 Customline 4-door dR.....#99, p 18
1954 V-8 dR ....#145, p 24
1956 Sunliner dR ....#148, p 46
1957 Fairlane 500 dR ....#64, p 10
1957 Ranchero dR ....#89, p 52
1957 Skyliner dR ....#168, p 26
1958 Thunderbird dR ....#151, p 42
1959 Country Squire dR........#127, p 26
1960 Sunliner convertible dR ....#88, p 22
1961 Starliner dR ....#153, p 40
1962 Thunderbird dR ....#44, p 12
1963 Falcon Sprint V-8 dR .....#67, p 26
1963 Thunderbird Monaco .....#121, p 42
1963½ Galaxie 427 dR ....#81, p 60
1964 ¼-99 Mustang Timeline ..#185, p 30
1965 Galaxie dR ....#115, p 22
1965 Mustang dR.................#24, p 121
1965 Mustang GT 2+2 dR......#164, p 10
1966 7-Litre dR ....#154, p 44
1966 Ford Fairlane 427 dR.....#114, p 14

1966 Mustang Sprint 200 ....#98, p 58
1968 Mustang Cobra Jet dR...#180, p 40
1969 Mustang Grandé dR ......#160, p 42
1969 Shelby GT 350 dR.........#171, p 10
1970 Mustang Mach I Cobra Jet dR.......
....#122, p 50
1974 Maverick vs. Henry J dR ......#23, p 30
Ford X2000 Concept Car ....#171, p 26
Model A Milestones.................#181, p 12
Russian Fords ....#123, p 40
Thunderbird Timeline ....#177, p 30

FRANKLIN
1912 Model D dR ....#184, p 40
1932 Franklin Pursuit ....#123, p 52
1932 V-12 phaeton dR ....#93, p 18

GARDNER
1929 Eight dR ....#61, p 34

GAYLORD
1956 Gran Turismo dR............#61, p 12

GM
1956 Firebird II dR ....#159, p 20

GMC
1949 FC-152 pickup dR ....#179, p 24
1955 Suburban dR.................#95, p 44

GRAHAM
1936 Supercharger dR ....#176, p 40
1940 Hollywood dR ....#177, p 40
1940-41 Hollywood, Part II.......#66, p 18

GRIFFITH
1966 200 dR ....#126, p 24

HAYNES
1923 sport sedan ....#127, p 32

HENRY J
1951 coupe dR ....#23, p 30

HUDSON
1927 Super Six dR ....#99, p 48
1929 sport phaeton dR ....#127, p 32
1936 Terraplane sedan dR ....#12, p 30
1946 Super Six dR ....#72, p 38
1948 Commodore ....#89, p 36
1951 Hornet dR ....#134, p 10
1953 Hornet dR ....#177, p 12
1953-54 Jet dR ....#60, p 26
1954 Hornet dR ....#185, p 32
1955 Italia coupe dR ....#8, p 30
1956 Hornet Special dR ....#77, p 54

HUPMOBILE
1927 dR ....#124, p 28
1932 dR ....#120, p 22
1935 4-door sedan dR ....#10, p 30
1938-39 Senior Series ....#48, p 50
1940-41 Skylark, Part II..........#66, p 18

IMPERIAL
1955 Newport dR ....#129, p 50
1957 Crown Southampton dR...#138, p 38
1962 Crown convertible dR .....#120, p 36
1967 Crown coupe dR ....#146, p 24

JAGUAR
1948 drophead coupe dR........#63, p 26

1960 XK-150S dR ....#131, p 12
3.8 Mark 2 dR ....#168, p 40
Series III XK-E dR ....#150, p 38

JEEP
1954 Universal CJ-3B dR ....#170, p 20
1973 CJ-5 roadster ....#174, p 30

KAISER
1949 Traveler dR ....#87, p 40
1953 Manhattan dR ....#94, p 14

KELLER
1948 Super Chief dR ....#30, p 32

KING MIDGET
1950: Improbable Success......#144, p 18
1968 roadster dR ....#20, p 48

KISSEL
1926 Speedster dR ....#111, p 38

LANCHESTER
1925-40 touring ....#72, p 26

LA SALLE
1933 town sedan dR ....#87, p 22
1939 dR ....#167, p 10

LINCOLN
1928 L dR ....#155, p 10
1933 KB Victoria dR ....#180, p 24
1936 K dR ....#129, p 30
1941 Continental dR ....#122, p 10
1942 Zephyr dR ....#68, p 28
1950 sport sedan dR ....#130, p 54
1950 Cosmopolitan dR...........#16, p 36
1955 Capri dR ....#177, p 32
1956 Premiere dR ....#60, p 12
1957 Premiere/Futura dR ....#136, p 46
1958 Continental dR ....#157, p 24
1960 Continental dR ....#108, p 34
1967 Continental dR ....#117, p 38

LOCOMOBILE
1926 Junior 8 dR ....#88, p 40

LOTUS
1969 Cortina MK II dR ....#174, p 22

MC FARLAN
1926 TV series dR ....#115, p 36

MACK
1918 AC Bulldog truck dR.......#70, p 50
1936 Jr., dR.........................#131, p 38

MARMON
1919 Marmon 34 dR ....#132, p 22
1929 Roosevelt sedan dR.........#44, p 46

MARMON-HERRINGTON
1947 Ford truck conversion .....#46, p 24

MARTIN
1928: Plainly Aerodynamic .....#165, p 26

MERCEDES-BENZ
1952 220 Cabriolet A dR ....#170, p 10
1961 190SL dR ....#93, p 42
1971 280SL dR ....#162, p 10

MERCER
1931 convertible coupe dR ....#72, p 12

MERCURY
1939 99-A coupe dR................#23, p 14

1940 dR ....#171, p 42
1941 Eight convertible dR ......#134, p 24
1946 Sportsman dR ....#152, p 24
1947 Monarch dR.................#183, p 40
1949 station wagon dR ....#81, p 12
1950 convertible coupe dR ......#12, p 10
1950 Monterey dR ....#135, p 12
1954 Sun Valley dR ....#113, p 28
1956 Montclair dR ....#161, p 8
1959 Commuter dR ....#154, p 22
1964 Marauder dR ....#162, p 32
1967 Cougar XR-7 dR ....#77, p 40
1968 Yacht Panel convertible ...#117, p 36
James Dean Mercury ....#169, p 50

MG
1955 Magnette dR ....#109, p 28
1955 TF 1500 dR ....#122, p 26
1960 MGA Twin Cam dR ......#152, p 12
1956-62 MGA spotter's guide ....#69, p 30
1959 MGA 1500 dR ....#69, p 22
1961 Midget dR ....#171, p 30
1970 MGB GT dR ....#103, p 36

MOON
Recollections of a Moon Man ....#170, p 48

MORGAN
1939 Super Sports dR ....#48, p 20
One-off Morgan Plus 4 ....#177, p 50

NASH
1929 Special Six dR ....#147, p 52
1932 1060 Sedan dR ....#179, p 32
1932 convertible sedan dR .....#118, p 12
1932 Special 8 dR ....#66, p 42
1935 Lafayette dR ....#77, p 12
1940 Ambassador dR ....#131, p 28
1940 Lafayette cabriolet dR.....#12, p 44
1941 600 dR ....#60, p 46
1950 Rambler dR ....#24, p 30
1952 Ambassador dR ....#46, p 28
1956 Rambler dR ....#133, p 36
1957 dR ....#115, p 48
In Search of the Junior Nash ..#157, p 52

OLDSMOBILE
1931 F-31 cabriolet dR...........#82, p 26
1938 L-38 dR ....#117, p 52
1949 98 Holiday dR ....#121, p 34
1949 Rocket 88 dR ....#139, p 24
1954 98 Starfire dR ....#55, p 48
1956 Super 88 dR ....#145, p 42
1957 J-2 dR ....#114, p 54
1962 Jetfire dR ....#152, p 50
1964 442 Cutlass dR ....#69, p 50
1964 Jetstar I dR ....#86, p 22
1968 Hurst/Olds dR ....#164, p 46
1970 4-4-2 dR ....#109, p 16

OPEL
1970 GT dR ....#159, p 36

PACKARD
1928 526 (fifth series) dR ....#86, p 16
1930 734 Speedster dR ....#126, p 50
1933 Sport Phaeton dR ....#173, p 32
1935 Eight dR ....#166, p 10
1937 Six, Series 115C dR.......#67, p 10

1947 Custom Super Eight dR...#144, p 10
1950 Deluxe Eight dR..............#64, p 50
1958 4-door sedan dR............#142, p 40
Clipper Styling History ....#121, p 56
Vignale dR..............................#140, p 32

PEERLESS
1932 Eight dR..........................#80, p 36

PIERCE-ARROW
1936 Eight dR.........................#139, p 38
1937 Travelodge......................#145, p 20
Fatty Arbuckle's Fabulous Pierce-Arrow ....#115, p 44

PLYMOUTH
1933 six PD dR ....#57, p 10
1935 dR..................................#172, p 36
1949 Suburban dR...................#72, p 52
1950 P-19 Fastback dR ....#164, p 38
1954 Suburban dR...................#95, p 28
1955 Belvedere V-8 dR............#68, p 12
1956 Belvedere dR ....#160, p 32
1956 Fury dR...........................#10, p 10
1960 Valiant dR ....#144, p 38
1962 Sport Fury dR................#143, p 10
1963 Savoy dR ....#182, p 40
1964 Canadian Valiant dR .....#137, p 10
1965 Barracuda dR.................#82, p 12
1970 'Cuda 440 Six-Pack dR......#98, p 44
1971 Hemi 'Cuda ....#174, p 32

PONTIAC
1926 landau coupe dR ....#44, p 34
1929 Big Six sedan dR ....#182, p 24
1938 Pontiac ....#104, p 58
1949 Chieftain dR..................#111, p 50
1954 Laurentian dR ....#129, p 18
1955 Star Chief conv dR.........#101, p 22
1957 Bonneville dR ....#48, p 12
1958 Bonneville dR.................#90, p 18
1959 Bonneville dR ....#149, p 30
1960 Bonneville dR ....#172, p 28
1961 Tempest dR ....#48, p 36
1962 Super Duty dR ....#124, p 12
1963 Bonneville dR ....#135, p 54
1965 Tri-powered GTO dR......#175, p 32
1967 Firebird dR...................#150, p 48
1968 Firebird dR.....................#95, p 18
1970 GTO Judge dR...............#132, p 12
1971 SSJ dR ....#152 p 40
Firebird Timeline...................#179, p 30

PORSCHE
1954 speedster dR ....#89, p 28
1961 356 dR...........................#157, p 8
1966 911 coupe dR ....#100, p 14

RAILTON
1933-37 (Hudson with British accent).... ....#61, p 20
1934 (Hudson chassis) dR........#86, p 38

RAMBLER
1957 Rebel dR........................#159, p 44
1963 Ambassador wagon dR....#179, p 40
1965 Classic V-8 dR..................#63, p 44
1965 Marlin dR......................#148, p 34
1967 Rogue dR.......................#141, p 44
1969 Hurst SC/Rambler dR...#161, p 24

REO
1927 Wolverine Brougham dR..#74, p 44
1936 Flying Cloud dR...............#45, p 26

RICKENBACKER
1925 coach brougham dR ....#28, p 22

SAAB
1968 Sonett dR ....#145, p 54
1971 96 dR............................#173, p 40

SABRA
1962 dR.................................#183, p 48

SHELBY
1965 AC Cobra 289 dR...........#118, p 44

STEARNS-KNIGHT
1929 J8-90 dR..........................#81, p 36

STOUT
1936 Scarab dR ....#123, p 12

STUDEBAKER
1926 Taxi dR..........................#140, p 52
1930 President dR..................#119, p 22
1931 Indycar dR.....................#142, p 12
1932 St. Regis brougham dR.....#46, p 40
1940 Commander dR ....#157, p 40
1941 "Double Dater" ....#118, p 28
1941 President Land Cruiser dR ....#90, p 26
1947 M-5 Coupe Express dR..#173, p 24
1951 Commander dR ....#116, p 32
1953 Starliner dR....................#126, p 12
1956 Golden Hawk dR............#165, p 10
1958 Scotsman dR...................#81, p 22
1963 R2 Lark dR.....................#57, p 50
1963 Wagonaire dR................#176, p 24
1964 RB Avanti dR..................#96, p 30

STUTZ
1927 Vertical Eight dR ....#160, p 24
1929 Blackhawk dR ....#148, p 22

SUNBEAM
1964 Tiger dR ....#62, p 46
Alpine Roots..........................#185, p 48

TATRA
1947 dR................................#165, p 52
1951 ....#98, p 40

TEMPLAR
1920 dR.................................#172, p 16

TERRAPLANE
1934 Tourer dR......................#112, p 46
1937 Utility Coupe Pickup......#136, p 54

THOMAS
1909 Flyer dR ....#174, p 14

TOYOTA
1934-on history.........................#39, p 20

TRIUMPH
1949 2000 dR ....#169, p 18
1955 TR2 dR..........................#172, p 10
1966 Spitfire dR ....#184, p 48
1967 TR4A dR........................#105, p 28
1969 TR6 dR..........................#121, p 44
1972 TR6 dR..........................#178, p 12
1981 TR8 dR..........................#156, p 10
TR7/TR8 Spotter's Guide ....#156, p 18

TVR
1974 2500M dR ....#110, p 40

VESPA
1960 400 dR ....#181, p 40

VIKING
1929 V-8 conv. coupe dR ....#10, p 42

VOLKSWAGEN
1968 1500 dR ....#167, p 20

VOLVO
1972 1800E dR.........................#94, p 48
PV445 convertible ....#105, p 34

WHIPPET
1927 roadster dR ....#66, p 10
1930 dR.................................#146, p 20

WHITE
1942 Scout Car dR..................#138, p 24

WHIZZER
1951/52 Whizzer dR ....#133, p 24

WILLS SAINTE CLAIRE
1921-27 history ....#41, p 30

WILLYS
1937 Willys 37 dR..................#156, p 38
1938 Model 38 pickup dR.......#185, p 40
1943 Jeep dR.........................#150, p 12
1950 Jeep ....#57, p 26
1950 Jeepster dR ....#165, p 28
Chic Surrey: The Jaunty Jeep ....#161, p 38
Missing in Action: Jeep CJ-4 .#166, p 60

WILLYS-KNIGHT
1928 66-A dR.............................#8, p 25

WINDSOR
1929 White Prince dR..............#64, p 36

YUGO
1990 Cabrio dR.......................#175, p 48

ZIS and ZIL
Packards with Russian accent ....#55, p 18

AUTOMOTIVE HISTORY

This section contains diverse articles dealing with auto-related developments and events as well as certain industry personalities.

1958: It Was a Very Bad Year ...#138, p 48
'58 Hudson That Might Have Been, The .. ..#143, p 48
Ads Infinitum ....#20, p 20
All In and Out of the Family ...#148, p 30
"Almost" Hupp-Willys, The ....#44, p 18
Back in Nash Styling...................#177, p 24
Battle of the Overpass (Ford labor struggle) ....#39, p 39
Brief History of Productmobiles, A........... ....#147, p 46
Cute Utes ....#138, p 44
Did Pontiac Plan Its Own El Camino?...... ....#137, p 46
Dunbar Deception (David Buick) ....#60, p 43
Edward B. Jordan and the Last Jordans ....#127, p 44
Fluid drive, history ....#116, p 40
Ford's Whiz Kids ....#60, p 54
The Game of the Name ....#88, p 60
Gasoline 1900-1940 ....#70, p 32
GM's Golden Engineering Decade........... ....#132, p 42
Half-Hour History of Straight Eights ....#135, p 48
Home is Where You Park It (motor homes)...#77, p 32
Interview with Donald Healey.....#67, p 18
Interview with George Romney...#66, p 50
A Life in Cars: The Bob Estes Story ....#105, p 20
Mail-Order Mobility ....#136, p 58
The Man Who Put Quality in the Hudson (Howard Coffin) ....#55, p 56
Mr. Jaeger's Five Sixes ....#69, p 58
Mitchell's Corvair Super Monza.............. ....#143, p 32
Nuccio, Wacky and Me ....#132, p 30
Packard's Col. Vincent (Jesse G.) ....#45, p 35
Playboys Are Back in Town.....#120, p 44
Postwar Canadian Variants ......#61, p 56
Self-Parking New Yorker ....#71, p 44
Service Station Architecture .....#30, p 27
Service with a Smile ....#46, p 28
"Son of a Gun!" (Hotchkiss) ......#63, p 40
Spark-Plug History..................#112, p 54
Stutz's Grand Finale..................#82, p 52
"There's a Ford in Your Future".............. ....#110, p 36
The Tucker Story ....#107, p 24
Where Did All the V-16s Go?....#106, p 32
The Year the Future Arrived: Chrysler's Airflow ....#113, p 24

BLUEPRINTS

This section is short profiles of the history of a given car accompanied by original artwork illustrating the auto under discussion.

427 Cobra ....#113, p 66
1927 Stutz Blackhawk racer....#100, p 60
1928 Lincoln...........................#150, p 93
1932 Chevrolet.......................#138, p 62
1933 DeSoto ....#148, p 64
1933 Plymouth........................#122, p 68
1935 Pontiac ....#168, p 71
1937 Ford ....#93, p 60
1937 Lincoln Zephyr ....#124, p 66
1937 Plymouth........................#164, p 61
1938 Graham..........................#126, p 68
1941 Buick Century..................#99, p 64
1948 Ford ....#120, p 64
1949 Mercury...........................#98, p 62
1948 Nash ....#162, p 59
1950 MG TD ....#90, p 66
1953 Dodge............................#153, p 59
1953 Sunbeam Alpine ....#127, p 68
1954 Chrysler ....#109, p 66
1955 Packard...........................#95, p 64
1956 Dodge D-500 ....#130, p 68
1957 Chevrolet..........................#91, p 64
1957 Imperial.........................#133, p 68
1957 Pontiac...........................#149, p 68
1959 El Camino ....#170, p 61
1959 Mercury..........................#154, p 60
1960 Ford ....#163, p 69
1961 Cadillac...........................#118, p 68
1961 Dodge Lancer ....#135, p 70
1961 Ford ....#122, p 64
1961 Studebaker Lark Cruiser...#173, p 59
1961 Tempest ....#114, p 66
1964 Comet Cyclone ....#117, p 68
1966 Oldsmobile Toronado.......#89, p 62
1968 Dodge Charger...............#101, p 62
1969 Chevy Nova SS ....#151, p 61
1970 Ford Torino Cobra ....#105, p 66
1970 Hemicuda.........................#94, p 62
1971 Checker Marathon.........#165, p 69
1971 Hornet SC/360...............#167, p 69
1973 Pontiac Grand Am ....#140, p 72
1977 Chrysler New Yorker......#142, p 65
Aero-Willys.............................#103, p 66
Austin-Healey Sprite ....#146, p 76
Austin-Healeys, Four-Cylinder ....#166, p 68
Barney Oldfield ....#131, p 68
Bill Vukovich..........................#169, p 69
Buick GS 400..........................#145, p 76
Buick Riviera..........................#112, p 66
Corvair Monza Spyder ....#115, p 64
Crosley Hotshot......................#110, p 66
Cunningham C-4R ....#137, p 68
Early Rods ....#134, p 68
Ford F-100 ....#129, p 62
Henry J ....#121, p 68
Jaguar 2.4 to 3.8 Liter sedans...#139, p 68
Jeep Forward Control Trucks...#143, p 70
Jimmy Murphy.......................#144, p 65
Jowett Jupiter........................#171, p 61
Kurtis Sports Cars ....#116, p 66
Pegaso....................................#104, p 66
Pontiac Catalina 2+2 ....#123, p 68
Seville by Cadillac ....#136, p 68
Stout Scarab ....#119, p 68
Stutz Super Bearcat ....#107, p 60
Triumph TR2..........................#152, p 60
Whizzer Motor Bike ....#108, p 66
Wills Sainte Claire ....#111, p 66

COMPARISON REPORTS

These are articles which test and compare competitive makes of cars from the same year of manufacture.

1918 Mercer vs Stutz ....#121, p 12
1926 Chevrolet vs Ford............#151, p 16
1929 LaSalle vs Packard.........#117, p 20
1930 Duesenberg SJ vs '31 Rolls-Royce Phantom I..........................#141, p 36
1930 Marquette vs 1931 Buick .....#99, p 24
1931 Buick vs Chrysler...........#133, p 16
1931 Chevrolet, Ford, Plymouth............. ....#77, p 24
1932 DeSoto vs Essex ....#87, p 54
1933 Ford vs Chevrolet ....#88, p 34
1933 Ford V-8 vs Terraplane Eight......... ....#109, p 42
1933 Packard 12 vs Pierce-Arrow V-12.... ....#114, p 22
1934 Chevrolet vs Ford ....#174, p 40
1934 Chevrolet vs Plymouth...#152, p 32
1935 Chrysler Airflow vs 1937 Lincoln Zephyr ....#120, p 28
1935 Oldsmobile 6 vs 8 ....#111, p 24
1936 LaSalle vs Oldsmobile....#144, p 30
1937 LaSalle vs Packard 120....#135, p 34
1937 Railton vs 1938 Jensen ....#147, p 32
1938 Buick vs LaSalle ....#126, p 18
1938 Buick Century vs Packard Eight.... ....#107, p 30
1939 Cadillac V-16 vs 12........#138, p 30
1941 Cadillac 62 vs Packard 160 ....#80, p 44
1941 Chevrolet, Ford, Plymouth..#69, p 36
1941 GM phaetons ....#113, p 16
1941 Oldsmobile vs Pontiac....#108, p 22
1941 Packard 110 vs 120.......#136, p 20
1942 Lincoln-Zephyr vs Packard One-Sixty...........................#164, p 18
1946 Chrysler vs 1947 Lincoln...#101, p 42
1947 Cadillac vs 1948 Lincoln Continental ....#137, p 30
1947 Cadillac vs Packard ....#130, p 20
1948 Buick Roadmaster vs Chrysler New Yorker...............................#167, p 28
1948 Buick vs Packard...........#116, p 20
1948 and 1951 Chevrolet fastbacks ....#82, p 34
1948 Chrysler Imperial vs Packard Super 8...........................#112, p 20
1949 Cadillac vs Old 98 ....#149, p 18
1949 Cadillac vs Packard ....#157, p 16
1949 Chevrolet, Ford, Plymouth............. ....#104, p 28
1950 Mercury vs Oldsmobile...#124, p 20
1950 vs 1954 Mercury............#103, p 22
1952 Ford Six vs V-8..............#143, p 16

1952 vs 1953 Buick Roadmaster.............
....#150, p 30
1952 Pontiac Eight vs Six.......#155, p 30
1953 Cadillac Eldorado, Buick Skylark
  and Oldsmobile Fiesta........#134, p 32
1954 Corvette vs Kaiser Darrin...#81, p 44
1954 vs 1955 Chevrolet..........#100, p 46
1954 Rambler, Willys, and Hudson Jet ...
....#159, p 28
1955 Cadillac, Imperial, Lincoln,
  Packard..........................#74, p 10
1955 T-Bird vs Mustang.........#145, p 34
1956 Chevrolet vs Ford ....#98, p 22
1956 Chevrolet Nomad vs Pontiac
  Safari............................#115, p 10
1957 Cadillac, Imperial and Lincoln.......
....#118, p 30
1957 Chevy Black Widow vs
  supercharged '57 Ford ....#142, p 20
1957 Corvette Fuelie vs Two-Pot T-Bird
....#139, p 18
1957 Facel Vega vs Dual-Ghia ....
....#131, p 20
1957 Metropolitan vs VW ....#129, p 10
1957 Pontiac Bonneville vs Chrysler 300
....#166, p 44
1958 vs 1959 Chevrolet Impala...............
....#140, p 24
1958 Edsel vs Ford..............#123, p 20
1959 Chevrolet/Ford/Plymouth ....
....#153, p 30
1960 Buick LeSabre vs. Edsel Ranger ....
....#181, p 32
1960 Corvair/Falcon/Valiant ...#165, p 16
1960 Pontiac Tri-Power vs Chrysler 300
....#127, p 18
1961 Cadillac, Imperial, and Lincoln.......
....#105, p 38
1962 Chevrolet 409/409 vs Chevrolet
  409/340 ....#163, p 20
1963 Chevrolet SS 409 vs Ford XL 406 ...

....#95, p 34
1963 MGB vs TR4 ....#146, p 10
1963 Riviera vs T-Bird..........#94, p 34
1964 Ford Falcon Sprint vs 1965 Falcon
  Futura............................#169, p 24
1964 Pontiac Tempest GTO vs 1964
  Ferrari Series II GTO ....#161, p 16
1965 Ford Falcon vs Mustang...#110, p 18
1966 GTO vs 1967 4-4-2 ....#122, p 18
1966 Oldsmobile Toronado vs 1967
  Cadillac Eldorado.............#168, p 18
1976 vs 1996 Jaguar XJS ......#160, p 18
Automobile Air Conditioning in 1954 ......
....#156, p 20
Dodge Firearrow vs Dual-Ghia ....
....#154, p 14
MG-T Series ....#173, p 52
Plymouth Pride (5 prewar Plymouths ....
....#185, p 12
Studebaker Sampler.............#179, p 12

CAR COMPONENTS

This lists articles which have surveyed body and mechanical parts including explanations of how these components work as well as developmental histories of many components.

Boss Kettering and the Electric Starter
....#178, p 54
Cast and Forged Pistons........#184, p 54
Chrysler's FirePower Hemi V-8...............
....#177, p 54
Continental spares ....#70, p 58
Engine, hot roddable ....#12, p 36
Engines, V-8 history.............#24, p 36
Four speeds of early 30s........#10, p 28
Franklin's Air-cooled Engine ...#185, p 54

Front drive: Chrysler's A-227 .....#24, p 28
Gas Saving Gadgets and Gimmicks
  Part I ....#64, p 58
General Motors' High Energy Ignition ....
....#179, p 54
Half-hour history of the rotary engine ....
....#41, p 40
Hubcaps and Wheel Covers
  Part I ....#62, p 18
  Part II ....#63, p 20
Oldsmobile's Hydra-Matic........#180, p 54
Safety devices, vintage.............#41, p 52
Updraft carburetors................#182, p 54

COACHBUILDING

This includes histories on certain body styles as well as articles on custom coachwork and large-volume body building companies such as Briggs and Fisher.

Body by Fisher ....#45, p 18
Body by Murray ....#20, p 36
A Brood of Brewsters ....#104, p 44
The Coachbuilders, Part I: Brewster........
....#152, p 20
  Part II: LeBaron ....#153, p 48
  Part III: Dietrich, Inc. ....#155, p 46
  Part IV: Hibbard & Darrin ....#156, p 32
  Part V: Derham & Co. ....#157, p 48
  Part VI: J.B. Judkins Co. ...#158, p 18
  Part VII: Brunn & Co..........#159, p16
  Part VIII: Fleetwood Metal Body Co. ...
....#160, p 38
  Part IX: LaGrande ....#161, p 30
  Part X: Rollston/Rollson ....#163, p 42
  Part XI: Willoughby ....#164, p 44

Part XII: Biddle & Smart and The
  Amesbury Group.............#165, p 26
Part XIII: Earl Automobile Works and
  Don Lee Coach and Body Works ....
....#167, p 18
Part XIV: The Walter M. Murphy
  Co. ....#168, p 34
Part XV: Bohman & Schwartz ....
....#169, p 40
Part XVI: Coachcraft Ltd. .....#170, p 26
Coachbuilt Special-Interest Cars
  Part II: Foreign Bodies ....#8, p 46
Convix (convertible Victorias)....#12, p 40
Custom Bus Bodies ....#148, p 42
Derham Dodges ....#41, p 45
Found: One of the Survivors! 1934
  McQuay-Norris Streamliner...#167, p 52
Germany's Kustom King (Carosserbiau
  Spohn) ....#20, p 40
Keepin' on Truckin' (pickups) ...#16, p 30

DO IT YOURSELF

This section lists SIA's articles on care, restoration and replacement of various automotive components.

Casting small parts ....#8, p 36
Checking Out a Corvair...........#88, p 56
Giving Your GM A-Body a Brake...#87, p 38
How to Apply Body Lead...........#99, p 32
Making dashboard knobs ....#12, p 50
Making your own tail pipes.......#93, p 32
New Life for Old Fords ....#48, p 47
Re-arcing leaf springs...............#68, p 56
Repairing rust with lead ....#66, p 56
Respoking Wire Wheels ....#101, p 30

Restoring padded dashboards.....#62, p 40
Reupholstering bucket seats ....#90, p 54
Routing rust with repair panels..#61, p 42
Torch welding & shrinking steel ..#94, p 30
Welding aluminum...................#89, p 24

EXPERIMENTALS & PROTOTYPES

This section deals with these vehicles as produced by or for recognized auto manufacturers.

'63 plastic Studebaker proposal..#30, p 41
Ahead of Its Time (Brooks Stevens's Willys
  Truck Transformations) ....#48, p 18
Airflow Prototypes (Chrysler)......#16, p 18
Albatross 133.........................#67, p 34
Beechcraft Plainsman ....#12, p 28
Brooks Stevens's Latin Jeepster .#16, p 28
Cadillac's postwar multi-cylinders...........
  ....#64, p 24
Corvairs for the 70s.................#68, p 20
Exner's Ghia-Chrysler show cars ..#30, p 12
Ford Fiesta's Godfather project....#41, p 18
Ford's '50s Forays into Future ......#64, p 18
GM's X-Cars ....#8, p 16
Henry's Pushers ....#8, p 22
LeSabre & XP-300 (1957 Buick proto-
  types)..............................#16, p 22
L'Universelle: the first van ....#70, p 18
Mercer-Cobra ('64 prototype) dR ..#39, p 34
MoPar's Star Cars ....#10, p 16
On the Way to the '49 Mercury.....#12, p 16
Packard Balboa ....#74, p 28
Plainsman (MoPar show car) ......#55, p 40
Pontiac Banshee ....#109, p 58
Pontiac Show Cars ....#107, p 38
Some Almost 1938 Fords ....#10, p 21
Some Not Quite Continentals (1949-51
  Lincoln Continental prototypes) ....
  ....#16, p 42
Stainless Reputations ....#60, p 40
Stevens's Startling Scimitar....#129, p 26
Studebaker by Porsche, A (1954 Type
  542 prototype) ....#24, p 40
The Truth About Chevy's Cashiered
  Cadet (1945-47 prototype)......#20, p 16
Two Far-Out Farmans.............#44, p 40

Two for the Road ....#28, p 20
XP-500: GM's Free-Piston Dream Car......
  ....#105, p 36
Yesterday's Cars of the Future..#57, p 18

NOW AND THEN

This section contains compari-son reports between similar models of old and new ex-amples of a make of car.

1965 vs 1985 Volvo..................#90, p 46
1966 vs 1985 Ford Mustang.......#89, p 40
1976 vs 1996 Jaguar XJS ......#160, p 18

ONE-OF-A-KIND (or nearly so)

This section contains one-off or extremely low-volume experi-mental cars which never achieved production in any form.

1933 Texaco Doodlebug.........#149, p 38
1952 Maverick ....#115, p 18
1953 Buick Skylark hardtop ......#81, p 52
1954 Panther Daytona ....#131, p 36
1954 Zeder: The Second Z Car..#142, p 36
1971 Hurst Jeepster...............#140, p 40
The Arrowhead Teardrop Car....#107, p 56
Biautogo (car-motorcycle).........#62, p 24
Boattail Chevy for a Prince ......#24, p 20
Chevrolet's "Almost" (1963) 4-Place
  Vette..............................#60, p 20
The Colonel's Curious Conveyances ....
  ....#108, p 54
Convertible Chevy Never Built....#80, p 22
Diamond T in the Rough ....#95, p 52
Father Juliano's Fantastic Flop...........
  ....#135, p 60
Found! Darrin's Crosley Sportster...........
  ....#117, p 44
Hard-Luck Vlachos (Constantios H.,
  frustrated inventor).............#23, p 44
Harleigh Holmes' Homely-Honeys...........
  ....#45, p 32
Harris's Sensational FWD Streamliner ....

  ....#112, p 42
Hewson's Rotund Rocket ....#129, p 46
Hurst's Stillborn (Dodge) Street
  Fighters.........................#95, p 26
Kaiser's Jeeplet ....#120, p 42
The Kanters' Furry Patrician...#100, p 20
LaSalle-Looking Lincoln ....#16, p 21
Littlemac's Little Cars and Trucks...........
  ....#127, p 56
Misguided Missile (rocket-powered cars)
  ....#55, p 24
Mr. Bostwick's Indestructible Rolls ....
  ....#93, p 36
Mr. Morrison's Mellow Machine (1934
  dream car) ....#46, p 46
One and Only Brunn 120 ....#103, p 44
One-Off MK III Continental Sedan...........
  ....#110, p 60
Packard's Abarth...................#99, p 60
Parisienne: Pontiac's Three-in-One
  Dream Car ....#123, p 20
Rarest Rickenbacker ....#28, p 28
Remarkable Saga of Kerosene Kate
  ....#112, p 28
Reuben Allender's El Moroccos ..#119, p 54
Stretched and shortened cars ....#66, p 34
Supreme Whatzit (1935 Hoffman X-8 ex-
  perimental 4-door sedan dR)..#24, p 50
Transformed Ford by McNear ....#132, p 20
Wasp Comes Home...................#74, p 38
Whatever Happened to XJ001? ....
  ....#119, p 44

RACING AND COMPETITION

This includes record runs, oval track and road racing articles.

The Battlebird Flies Again ......#147, p 18
Great Racing from Anaheim to Beantown
  ....#108, p 42
Indy Incidents ....#28, p 44
Mightiest Stutz of All ....#82, p 46
MoPar's Winged Wonders ....#45, p 52
Odds Against The Brickyard....#28, p 31
Old Man's Last Fling (1941 Gulf-Miller

Special dR)............................#28, p 12
Racing's Back in the Bahamas...#86, p 46
Shakespeare Meets Super Bird ....
  ....#100, p 22
World's Oldest Active Racing Driver.......
  ....#109, p 64

SPECIAL FEATURES

Includes photo stories, articles on oddball events and products in the industry, automotive-related events, etc.

A Collector's Collector...Since 1928! ....
  ....#136, p 34
A Day at the Races..................#169, p 54
Afternoons Among the Ruins....#133, p 32
American Cars in Japan ....#152, p 48
America's Swedehearts...........#171, p 50
As Shot in Minneapolis (pix) .....#66, p 60
As Shot in Montana (pix) ....#20, p 29
As Shot in Montevideo (pix) ......#20, p 28
Auto Adventures in a Son of Moscow......
  ....#115, p 20
Back from the Dead................#101, p 56
Back Lot Bargains ....#142, p 48
Bakersfield Beaters (pix)...........#147, p 60
Big One-Make Collectors ....#46, p 18
Birds of the Same Feather? East Grand
  Blvd. Meets Gorky Park ....#162, p 50
Boston. . . 1941 (pix) ....#67, p 18
Bubbletoppers: The Future that Never
  Arrived............................#114, p 48
California Parts Yard Bites the Dust........
  ....#114, p 32
Camaro That Came Back.........#86, p 60
Caught at the Curb (pix)...........#82, p 42
Cleaning up the Streets (pix) ...#163, p 56
Clipped Clippers and Bashed Buicks.......
  ....#55, p 30
Clyde's Convertible Collection...#133, p 44
Collector Car Shopping at Wal Mart (pix)
  ....#165, p 60
Complex Simplex (Ed Roy's miniature
  cars) ....#60, p 22
Counterfeit Classics ....#39, p 22

SIA SPOTTER'S GUIDES

These Spotter's Guides from past issues of SIA come to you rolled in a cardboard tube so you can display them without creases. Each is printed on heavy, glossy paper suitable for framing. Just $2.00 per copy or $10.00 for all six. We pay the postage. See order form on last page.

MGA
Includes illustrations and hand-lettered text on important features and styling. Dark green & black, 23" x 29". Item #P-6F

Jaguar XK-120, 140 & 150
Includes illustrations and hand-lettered text on features and styling changes. Dark green & black, 23" x 29". Item #P-5F

MG-TC, TD, and TF
Includes illustrations and hand-lettered text of facts & features. Dark green & black, 23" x 29". Item #P-1F

Corvette Sting Ray
Includes illustrations and hand-lettered text on changes in hoods, tops, wheels, tail lights & louvers. Red & black, 23" x 29". Item #P-2F

Town & Country
Includes important features and styling developments for the 1941-50 Town & Country, along with fact-filled text. Brown & black, 25" x 38". Item #P-3F

Cadillac Eldorado
Includes important features and styling developments for the 1953-66 Eldorado, along with fact-filled text. Blue & black 25" x 38". Item #P-4F

Days at the Races (pix) ....#137, p 58
Disc wheels (album covers) ......#60, p 34
Discovered! The Motorama Chevy V-8
   Cutaway ....#139, p 34
Doozy of a Showroom ....#61, p 24
Duplicate Drophead ....#122, p 38
Ernie Adams's Dwarf 1939 Chevrolet
   ....#139, p 46
Exiled Americans ....#115, p 56
Family Affair: Normandin Chrysler-
   Plymouth ....#124, p 48
Foreign Intrigue: 1986 London to
   Brighton Run......................#98, p 30
Fort Wayne, Indiana, 1939 .....#163, p 52
Frozen in Time (Stude pix)........#94, p 42
Fuel Economy Part I.................#62, p 28
   Part II ....#63, p 52
Gas 'Em Up (airport refueling trucks) .....
   ....#173, p 48
GM's Parade of Progress ....#39, p 30
Going Nuts at Ford (beating assembly
   line impersonality) ....#44, p 54
Harrah Foundation's Future.......#88, p 28
Harrah's Last Hurrah..............#95, p 40
Heap O'Cars ....#119, p 18
Henry and the Buzz Bomb......#111, p 60
Here Come The Cops ....#172, p 24
Home-Made Haulers..............#141, p 58
Hooked on '41 Chevys ....#93, p 48
Hot Dog! Here Come the Wienermobiles!
   ....#133, p 56
How Rare It Is! (special interest car val-
   uations) ....#10, p 22
In the Garages of the Maharajas ....
   ....#113, p 50
Inside Pacific Auto Rental's Legendary
   Treasure Trove ....#171, p 36
Last Writes: Final Ads from the
   Independents ....#130, p 38
Madcap Midgets Menace Motown! ....
   ....#105, p 54
Made in USA (foreign cars assembled
   here) ....#70, p 44
Man Who Keeps His Cars Forever ....
   ....#77, p 62
Mexico: Happy Hunting Ground for Car
   Collectors ....#145, p 50
Mr. Hunt's Home-Grown House Cars
   ....#138, p 18
More Days at the Races (pix) ....#140, p 60
Motoring Minister ....#80, p 56
My Father's Cars......................#93, p 54
Myloe's Marvelous Mechanical
   Menagerie ....#117, p 50

Of Auburns in Fields and Duesies in
   Barns ....#140, p 50
Old Cars Meet Old Man Winter (pix) ....
   ....#145, p 62
Oldest Active Police Car............#99, p 44
On the Streets of Chicago 1951 (pix) ....
   Part I ....#77, p 20
Outside Inskip's (pix)................#69, p 32
Parked Near the Pentagon (pix)
   Part I ....#86, p 32
   Part II ....#87, p 50
Personal Luxury Cars................#77, p 48
Picking Up in Uruguay (pix)....#165, p 50
Picking Up Pups, 1900-1950...#167, p 48
Post CARds ....#24, p 23
Princes, Presidents, Potentates and
   Popes............................#150, p 46
Racing in the Streets, Midwest style ....
   ....#81, p 30
Radio Drama on the Road ....#64, p 44
Restoration vs Preservation ....#166, p 24
A Rolls in Mothballs, (1927 Phantom I
   coupe)............................#100, p 42
Route 66 Revisited ....#134, p 56
Saito-San's Cadillac House (pix) ....
   ....#90, p 62
See You in the Funny Papers (cars in
   comics) ....#23, p 22
Seen Close To Home—Today! (pix) ....
   ....#118, p 50
Seen in Eugene (pix)..............#111, p 34
Seen in Havana—Today! (pix) ..#124, p 58
Seen in North Dakota (pix) ....#108, p 52
Seen in San Rafael (pix)..........#122, p 34
Seen in the San Joaquin ....#170, p 44
Seen in the South...1965 (pix) ...#94, p 56
Seen on the Streets of Berkeley...Today!...
   (pix) ....#104, p 22
Show Me in Missouri ....#146, p 48
SIA Ten Best ....#100, p 38
Sleepers: The Top Ten Collector Cars
   For the Year 2000 ....#173, p 10
Splintered Wagons ....#63, p 18
Streets of San Diego (pix) ......#109, p 34
Styling Speculations:
   Chrysler Airflow ....#99, p 67
   Cord - 1939-59 ....#98, p 65
   Packard - 1948 ....#100, p 65
Suddenly It's 1958! ('58 Chevys for rent)...
   ....#48, p 28
Three Years in the Life of a Rickenbacker
   ....#57, p 58
Tin Treasures of Chloride ....#137, p 18
Treasures of Route 66 ....#141, p 62
Twenty Best Auto Ads of All Time..........

   ....#118, p 50
Uncle Mundy's Boneyard........#103, p 56
Uncovered in Uruguay............#151, p 40
Upstate Photo Bonanza From Long Ago
   ....#122, p 56
Used Car Smorgasbord (pix) ...#72, p 48
Vintage Cadillac Returns to a Vineyard ...
   ....#112, p 60
Watkins Glen Wonderland......#110, p 46
When Packards Went to War................
   ....#111, p 58
Who Bought Crosleys When They Were
   New?................................#89, p 60
Willys Californian Conundrum..............
   ....#131, p 44
World's Last Hudson Dealership ....
   ....#80, p 52

SPECIAL PURPOSE VEHICLES

Includes trucks, cars, modified to perform different tasks other than passenger transportation, oddball cars, etc.

All Fired Up (fire apparatus) .....#62, p 54
Bodies for Bottles and Brew ......#48, p 42
Byrd's Big Bertha (Antarctic explorer) .....
   ....#87, p 70
Cars That Fly ....#10, p 36
Cars That Swim .... #16, p 50
Carting Coal ....#45, p 40
Coachwork Trucks ....#44, p 30
Dollars at Your Doorstep (bank-on-
   wheels) ....#81, p 54
50 Years of Pontiac Commercials (deliv-
   ery trucks) ....#64, p 30
Have Oil Will Travel (mobile gas stations)
   ....#57, p 32
Hydrocar................................#68, p 38
Ice Trucks We've Known And Loved........
   ....#46, p 50
Moxie's Four-Legged Productmobile ....
   ....#68, p 52
1930s Trailer Boom, The (campers) ....
   ....#24, p 44
The Only Way to Go (hearse) ....#20, p 43
Self-Parkers ....#12, p 18
The Topper Buick's Many Meta-
   morphoses..........................#90, p 34

STYLING

Encompasses design histories of various makes and model years as well as stories on a number of auto stylists and their work.

After the Nash-Healey............#151, p 32
Alex Tremulis: Advocate of
   Aerodynamics ....#82, p 56
AMC's Ed Anderson ....#121, p 28
Autos by Architects ....#39, p 26
Bob Gregorie Biography..........#162, p 16
Body Politics (GM's interchangeability
   program)............................#39, p 42
Chrysler's Classy Coupes (1939 Hayes
   body)................................#69, p 44
Chrysler's Transatlantic Translations......
   ....#89, p 48
Design Disasters ....#103, p 30
The Designers, Part I: Amos Northup ......
   ....#153, p 18
The Designers, Part II: Elwood Engel.......
   ....#154, p 30
Designing the Future at AMC................
   Part I ....#134, p 20
   Part II ....#135, p 22
   Part III ....#161, p 46
Different as Chalk and Cheese ....
   ....#108, p 30
Early Days in GM Art & Colour (Thomas
   L. Hibbard recollects) ....#23, p 40
Fabulous Firebird....................#57, p 42
Family Album........................#156, p 54
Fisher Body Craftsman's Guild ...#61, p 26
Fishleigh Fords ....#39, p 54
From GT to Gremlin ....#130, p 52
GM's Far-Out '59s, Part II ......#126, p 30
Gregorie Biography, Bob........#162, p 16
I Remember My Father (John Tjaarda) ....
   ....#10, p 50
Jim Gaylord ....#74, p 52
Non-Classic Towncars ....#23, p 36
Rolling Greenhouses: 1959-60 GM 4-dr
   hardtops ....#67, p 46
Sidecars to Sports Cars (Jaguar)............
   ....#63, p 34
Virgil M. Exner ....#72, p 20